THE STEEL BAR

PITTSBURGH LAWYERS
AND THE MAKING OF AMERICA

The Steel Bar: Pittsburgh Lawyers and the Making of America
Copyright © 2019 by Ron Schuler. All Rights Reserved.

An early version of material from Parts One and Two of this book was previously published in University of Pittsburgh Law Journal, Vol. 73, No. 4 (2012).

No part of this publication may be reproduced, stored in a retrieval system or transmitted, in any form or by any means — electronic, mechanical, photocopying, recording or otherwise — without prior written permission from the publisher, except for the inclusion of brief quotations in a review.

For information about this title or to order other books and/or electronic media, contact the publisher:

Marquez Press
Pittsburgh, Pennsylvania
United States
info@marquezpress.com
www.marquezpress.com

ISBN: 978-1-73318-410-6 (hardcover)
ISBN: 978-1-73318-411-3 (paperback)

Library of Congress Control Number: 2019946227

Publisher's Cataloging-in-Publication Data

Names: Schuler, Ronald William, 1963- author.

Title: The Steel Bar : Pittsburgh lawyers and the making of America / Ron Schuler.

Description: Pittsburgh : Marquez Press, 2019. | Includes bibliographical references and index.

Identifiers:
LCCN 2019946227 (print)
ISBN 978-1-73318-410-6 (hardcover)
ISBN 978-1-73318-411-3 (paperback)

Subjects: LCSH: Law--Pennsylvania--History. | Law--United States--History. | Pittsburgh (Pa.)--History. | Pennsylvania--History. | BISAC: LAW / Legal History. | HISTORY / United States / State & Local / Middle Atlantic (DC, DE, MD, NJ, NY, PA)

Classification: LCC KF354.P4 S38 2019 (print) | LCC KF354.P4 (ebook) | DDC 974.8/86--dc23.

Cover and interior design by Melissa Neely, Neelyhouse Design.
Cover photo: Collection of the Allegheny County Bar Association

THE STEEL BAR

PITTSBURGH LAWYERS
AND THE MAKING OF AMERICA

By Ron Schuler

MarQUEZ

ADVANCE PRAISE FOR
THE STEEL BAR

"[A] thoroughly researched and easily readable account of an untold story. Schuler takes the microcosm of the Pittsburgh legal community ... to illustrate far broader social themes about the rule of law."

— **Harry Litman**, ex-U.S. Attorney, professor of constitutional law at UCLA and UC San Diego, *Washington Post* columnist, and the creator/executive producer of the podcast "Talking Feds"

"[T]he best and most engaging history of a city bar that I've read in many years. Far from being just another chronicle of a local profession, THE STEEL BAR shows how Pittsburgh lawyers played leading roles in the development of national politics, economic growth and social change. It's a great story written with verve, panache and wit that properly puts Pittsburgh at the center of the American narrative."

—**Bernard J. Hibbitts**, Publisher and editor of *JURIST*, professor at University of Pittsburgh Law School

"Ron Schuler has written a remarkable 232-year history of the practice of law in Pittsburgh that reminds us of a quote from Justice Holmes: 'The life of the law has not been logic: it has been experience. The felt necessities of the time ...' Schuler captures the historical context, those 'felt necessities' that were the burning social issues of the time, sometimes rivetingly—showing the experiences of Pittsburgh's lawyers not only as advocates but also as judges and elected officials, as they defined outcomes and charted a path forward for our democracy ... This is a must-read, not only about the Pittsburgh bar but about how the American style of the rule of law has evolved since our nation's founding."

—**Richard G. Jewell**, JD, President Emeritus, Grove City College

"THE STEEL BAR is more than a history of Pittsburgh's legal profession. Ron Schuler's scholarship and deft storytelling give readers a front row seat to the birthplace of the American Industrial Revolution. Find out about the 'Captains of Industry' who fueled the growth of the U.S. economy, and the attorneys who advised them. It is a must-read for anyone who wants to appreciate the unique role Pittsburgh has played in the history of American commerce."

—**Michael F. Walsh**, PhD, Chair and Associate Professor of Marketing, West Virginia University

CONTENTS

INTRODUCTION

PART I: THE EARLY BAR, 1788-1866 — 1

Whiskey, Guns and Lawyers — 3

On the frontier of the new Republic, Hugh Henry Brackenridge and Pittsburgh's first lawyers wrestle with the balance between freedom and order, helping to define the limits of dissent within a democracy during the Whiskey Rebellion, judicial impeachment proceedings, political duels and ultimately, on the U.S. Supreme Court, as Pittsburgh lawyer Henry Baldwin joins the Court and helps to initiate the tradition of the dissenting opinion.

Conflagration! — 33

The Great Fire of Pittsburgh destroys the city's only law school; Edwin Stanton arrives from Ohio and helps to transform the methods and habits of the Pittsburgh trial bar; Pittsburgh lawyers risk everything in the service of constitutional principles as abolitionists, on the Underground Railroad, and as soldiers in the Union Army; and in the aftermath of Abraham Lincoln's assassination, a controversy over constitutional rights pits Secretary of War Stanton, the former Pittsburgh trial attorney, against Judge Andrew Wylie, the former Pittsburgh city solicitor.

PART II: THE GILDED BAR, 1866-1901 — 61

Thomas Mellon: Lawyer as Capitalist — 71

Thomas Mellon, best known as the founder of a great American banking family who provided the capital that launched Pittsburgh's industrial revolution, began his career as a business-minded lawyer, inspiring the next generation of Pittsburgh business lawyers as they advised the entrepreneurs of the Gilded Age.

The Corporation Men — 79

A new group of Pittsburgh lawyers emerges after the Civil War who, as the social peers of tycoons such as Carnegie, Frick, Mellon and Westinghouse, helped to define the institution of the American corporation and set the laissez-faire regulatory tone of the age.

What a Strike Looks Like — 89

The 1877 national Railroad Strike erupts violently in Pittsburgh, and while corporate railroad lawyers attempt to maneuver state and local authorities into calling out their own officers to protect private property, another lawyer sits on a hillside and watches the gunfire erupt, and a former County prosecutor leads the state militia through the thick of the street battle.

A Genius Devises a Legal Engine — 97

George Westinghouse demonstrates vision in assembling a team of lawyers—outside advisors and in-house counsel, corporate and patent lawyers, Pittsburgh and New York, U.S. and foreign—to help him build his industrial conglomerate.

Absconding Attorneys — 107

Two Gilded Age examples of Pittsburgh lawyers who committed financial fraud—one who got away with it and was vilified, and another who served time in prison and yet was later mourned by the bar.

New Pioneers — 115

Josiah Cohen becomes the first Jewish lawyer in Pittsburgh; African American lawyer George Vashon is rebuffed as he attempts to enter the Pittsburgh bar; in the 1890s, two African American lawyers finally cross the Pittsburgh bar's color line; and Pittsburgh's first woman lawyer, Agnes Fraser Watson, marries and shuts down her practice.

Mighty Casey at the Bar — 127

The Pittsburgh Pirates ballcub gets its name following an arbitration proceeding, and Pittsburgh lawyers become involved in the "kidnapping" of the owner of the St. Louis ballclub.

Gilded Twilight, in Four Acts

I. Billy — 133

Barrel-chested Billy Brennen, a steel mill machinist who decides to study law, becomes the first attorney to take on the plight of workers as his cause.

II. Johnstown — 139

The tragedy of the Johnstown Flood teaches America a lesson about the liability of corporate owners, and sets the tone for an age of Bosses versus Workers.

III. Homestead — 147

Carnegie's partner, Henry Clay Frick, works with his lawyer, Philander Knox, on a plan to disrupt the strike of the Amalgamated Association of Iron and Steel Workers at the Homestead Steel Works, while Billy Brennen attempts to preserve the Union's bargaining power.

IV. The Greatest Lawsuit, and the Deal of the Century — 171

Andrew Carnegie and Henry Clay Frick take aim at each other in a lawsuit that threatens the social stability of Pittsburgh's upper classes; and out of the settlement of what had been billed as the "Greatest Lawsuit," comes the negotiation of the transactions that helped to create the world's largest corporation, U.S. Steel.

PART III: THE PROGRESSIVE ERA BAR, 1902-1942 — 193

Three Rivers, Running Dirty — 205

A reform-minded bank lawyer, George Guthrie, and his bulldog litigator friend, Leo Weil, battle urban machine politics—in the service of environmental issues as well as a new city charter—through dirty mayoral elections and an elaborate sting operation that sends dozens of city politicians to prison.

Big Work, Big War — 229

As Pittsburgh's downtown law firms begin to grow larger in order to handle the needs of increasingly large Pittsburgh businesses, World War I interrupts the growth trend, and impacts the careers of a number of young lawyers, as well as providing a new career opportunity for a down-and-out older lawyer.

Anarchy: Interrupting and Interrupted — 245

Billy Brennen's role as a union lawyer fades, while Jacob Margolis, a self-avowed anarchist, begins to take on the cause of the workers until he is disbarred for his political views.

Lawyer, Where Do You Stand? — 265

Two "ethnic" lawyers, an Austrian Jew (Henry Ellenbogen) and an Italian (Michael Musmanno), gain fame as civil rights lawyers and later emerge as popular politicians and judges as the politics of Depression-era Pittsburgh shifts from Anglo Republican dominance to the province of an ethnic Democratic coalition.

'The Plainest Facts of Our National Life' — 287

As the FDR administration attempts to level the playing field between management and labor, a seminal constitutional challenge of the National Labor Relations Board is argued by a Pittsburgh corporate lawyer, supported by a coalition of some of America's most powerful business leaders, and an obscure Pitt Law professor—setting the stage for later battles between true believers on both sides of the labor-management war, liberal government lawyers versus conservative corporate lawyers.

Out in the Open — 327

Women and African Americans struggle in their own ways to reach the top of the legal profession before World War II: Sara Soffel becomes a judge, Ella Graubart becomes a partner in a downtown law firm and Anne X. Alpern emerges as a formidable political lawyer and judge. Meanwhile, Robert Vann and Homer S. Brown battle tokenism and prejudice—Vann as publisher of the Pittsburgh Courier, *and Brown as an influential state legislator.*

Bad Company — 349

President Theodore Roosevelt and his Attorney General, former Pittsburgh corporate lawyer Philander Knox, launch the course of twentieth century antitrust enforcement with an attack on Northern Securities. Later, Pittsburgh lawyers do battle against the government in the Standard Oil *and* U.S. Steel *cases, and the twenty-year long prosecution of Alcoa.*

PART IV: THE WWII AND POST-WAR BAR, 1942-1988 — 371

Won't You Be My Neighbor? — 395

The general counsels of large Pittsburgh corporations, strongly motivated by community fiduciary values, play key leadership roles in the revitalization of Pittsburgh's physical and cultural landscape after World War II.

Red to the World — 417

Pittsburgh becomes a center of the anti-Communism movement during the late 1940s and 1950s, as several influential members of the bar, including Judge Michael Musmanno, launch crusades against lawyers with alleged Communist leanings—attempting to disbar one, trying to get another thrown out of the D.A.'s office, and trying to keep another from entering the bar altogether.

Continuity and Loss in the Golden Triangle — 437

With meditations on the "brand name" strength of old city law firms, two of Pittsburgh's largest firms experience defections that result in the establishment of two of the other largest Pittsburgh firms, and other downtown firms grow large and suddenly implode amid scandals or in-fighting.

Years for Inches — 455

Empowered by wartime experiences, Pittsburgh's African American lawyers take the lead in local civil rights causes; Neighborhood Legal Services, created by the bar association, begins to represent indigent plaintiffs in some far-reaching class actions while the Law Collective creates a "leftist" law firm; and by the end of the twentieth century, with the future still uncertain, African American lawyers begin to enter large downtown Pittsburgh law firms.

Self-Inflicted — 477

The federal versus the local: Robert Duggan is elected County District Attorney on a pledge to take down the numbers rackets that his Democrtaic predecessor, Easy-going Eddie Boyle, left unchecked; meanwhile, moderate Republicans secure the appointment of Dick Thornburgh as U.S. Attorney, and as questions are raised about Duggan's commitment to cleaning up the rackets, Thornburgh pursues an investigation into Duggan's finances, and Duggan decides to go muskrat hunting on his Ligonier estate...

Backwards and in High Heels — 499

Law schools were only too happy to admit more women during the WWII male talent drain, but their admission to large downtown firms was sporadic until the 1970s, amid embarrassing displays of male paternalism and gender comedy. Even after assuming firm leadership roles in the 1990s, Pittsburgh women lawyers are still wrestling with issues relating to equal pay and "work-life balance."

Beyond Renaissance — 517

During a period of drastic decline in steel and other heavy manufacturing, Pittsburgh rebuilds its skyline and become America's "most livable city." While some Pittsburgh lawyers turn their attention to saving the old-line industry, the city faces the proposect of losing its baseball team (twice), and other downtown lawyers turn their attention to helping to build the new technology economy that emerges in Pittsburgh in the 1990s.

LAW CITY: AN EPILOGUE — 541

An assessment of the Pittsburgh lawyer's experience of the changes in the legal profession during the late twentieth / early twenty-first century, including the rush of new technologies, the delocalization of major law firms, the phenomenon of the disappearing jury trial, and the increased influence of Washington, New York and Los Angeles on the practice; and a coda on the role of the lawyer—especially the local lawyer, such as in Pittsburgh—in perpetuating the institutions of American democracy.

ILLUSTRATIONS / CREDITS	**315**
ACKNOWLEDGMENTS	**557**
SELECTED BIBLIOGRAPHY	**559**
ENDNOTES	**567**
INDEX	**621**

INTRODUCTION

For anyone wondering why on Earth the world needs a book about the history of the legal profession in Pittsburgh, let me explain. I humbly believe the reasons transcend both the idea of a legal profession and the idea of Pittsburgh.

For some reason, historians sometimes do a poor job at portraying what lawyers do on a day-to-day basis—or more importantly, perhaps, how lawyers have left their imprint on significant moments in American history. Of course, we see them at work debating Independence in the Continental Congress, or negotiating the finer points of the U.S. Constitution in 1789—but after that, outside of political contexts and apart from some attention to Lincoln's early career as a lawyer in Illinois or the heroic exploits of some civil rights lawyers during the 1950s and 60s, the picture grows fuzzy. Lawyers are sometimes pasted inside historical narratives as players in the action, without much in the way of detail. Go and read a dozen books about the Homestead Steel Strike of 1892—considered to be one of the seminal events in U.S. labor history, which occurred about eight miles southeast of Pittsburgh—and you will barely understand that any lawyers had been involved in the course of the conflict. Go and read a dozen books about the tempestuous relationship between Andrew Carnegie and Henry Clay Frick—two Pittsburgh men who were among the wealthiest entrepreneurs the world had ever seen—and you will occasionally see someone referred to as someone's lawyer, a nameless stick figure who always seems to be departing from the action the minute he appears on the page, sent exiting stage right to write a contract or file a writ.

Yes, I am a lawyer—but this is more than a beef between rival professional guilds.

"Rule of Law" is a phrase that is bandied about frequently these days by Americans on cable news and on Twitter, but its meaning is frequently misunderstood by those who angrily invoke it. The phrase is often used as an indignant punctuation mark at the end of a bitter monologue about the law-and-order scandal of the day—from spurious anecdotes about undocumented immigrants or welfare recipients; to the failure to prosecute a policeman accused of shooting an unarmed black youth; to issues and arguments surrounding "executive privilege," the separation of powers between Congress and the Executive branch; or a fight between a president and the FBI. "If only we had 'Rule of Law'..." so the homily ends, with emphasis on the ellipses, apparently pointing to the conclusion that if we only had Rule of Law, then all that bad stuff would go away. One state governor even offered, during the 2016 presidential election, that he thought we needed someone "to show some authoritarian power in our country and bring back the Rule of Law."

What is missed in all the hand-wringing—and what all those, I would hope, who have a firm grounding in American civics know deep in their hearts—is that the Rule of Law is a system, not an outcome. It is not designed for the purpose of producing winners and losers, nor is it some kind of magic wand that produces instant "Justice" with a puff of smoke and a flourish. Rule of Law is, in fact, the justice that our ancestors imagined for us. It would be too meek for us to say that the Rule of Law exists only in "due process"—the sum total of constitutional rights and mundane procedures that we cling to when faced with a lawsuit or an indictment. Against the backdrop of laws, rules, regulations and the common law, however, the effect of justice that results from the Rule of Law is produced through argument, through dissent, through the free dialectic between opposing forces. Based on the notion that the old orthodoxy—an authoritarian Divine Right of Kings—was not the only orthodoxy, the activity of robust disagreement pits my orthodoxy versus your orthodoxy with the aim of producing a comfortable consensus of ethical continuity and commercial stability in the community that is consistent with core American values such as tolerance, personal liberty and egalitarianism.

Love lawyers or hate them—and we mostly seem to hate them in America, at least in the abstract, even if we sometimes accord them with a measure of begrudging respect—lawyers are essential actors in the dynamic system that is the American brand of the Rule of Law. Not only is it their role to take a side in the inevitable next conflict, but by virtue of the values ingrained in them by their education and their code of ethics, their instincts run to the preservation of order, and they are allergic to the arbitrary and the capricious. They are, in effect, the bees that pollinate this institution of the Rule of Law. We can argue that it would be more efficient for the plants to fertilize themselves, and that apart from the honey we should be able to do without the bees and their stingers. That's not how plants work, however, and that's not what perpetuates the Rule of Law in our society. And if you want to understand what makes pollination sustainable, it's not a bad idea to take a look inside the hive.

Inside the hives of lawyers in America, one may see the Rule of Law being perpetuated through the thousands of things that a lawyer does each day, most of which have nothing to do with arguing cases in court—like saying "no" to a client; like calculating the risks of taking one course of action versus another course of action; like considering the power and the meaning and the effects of the use of language; like policing the bad behavior of others within the guild, standing up for the rights of the disenfranchised, and managing that delicate balance between arguing for change where it is warranted, while keeping an eye on maintaining the social order. Sometimes they do it just by exercising leadership in their community, helping to give shape to civic projects as experts in civil order. These are some of the things that are sometimes missing from historians' accounts of the great moments and movements in American history, notwithstanding that attending to such things can often reveal something of the tactics, the drama, the intellectual chain-reactions and civic discourse impacting those events.

What, then, about this hive called Pittsburgh?

For the last couple of decades, there have been persistent rumors that somewhere in fly-over country, there is a rust-belt city where engineers build driverless cars and genius hackers go after bad guys on the Internet, where artificial hearts and lungs and esophagi are grown on scaffolds in laboratories, and where there is more natural gas underfoot than in some of the largest gas fields in the world; a city with glistening rivers and a glimmering skyline that is noted for its livability, and that also, after years of being known as a city of people who like to put fries and slaw *inside* their sandwiches, is suddenly ranked by Zagat as the "top food city" in the country in 2015, known for its "abundance of ... refined food glories." Every five years or so, someone shows up from *The New York Times* and writes another earnest piece about Pittsburgh's surprising "renaissance."

Little did I understand, when I first arrived in Pittsburgh as an LA exile in 1987, that I was walking right into the bitter aftermath of what has been called the worst peacetime economic decline of a region outside the Soviet Union. Nor could I have foreseen that I would witness some of the inner-workings of the revitalization of that region. Living inside an era of transition, however, means that the city's people have one foot aimed at the future, and one foot firmly planted in the past.

Pittsburghers are almost unique in the depth of their awareness of their city's heritage, in part because it has been such a rich and important subset of American history. During the early days of the young Republic, Pittsburgh was the frontier outlier, politically distinct and powerful as the voice of those who suffered both physical and civic privations at the edge of the North American wilderness. After the Civil War, Pittsburgh was at the center of the second American industrial revolution, the rise of the corporation, and the greatest engine of wealth creation that the country has ever seen. As progressive reforms gained traction throughout the early years of the twentieth century, Pittsburgh became an essential laboratory, or battleground if you prefer, for working out the parameters of federal power, as the federal government imposed new regulations on everything from hiring and firing to how big you were allowed to be as a corporation in America. And at the turn of the twenty-first century, Pittsburgh becomes one of the leading examples of how a great American city built on manufacturing can come back from its awesome decline and function and thrive in a post-manufacturing economy. All of that in fly-over country, no less—somewhere on the frontier of current media and pop consciousness.

Examining Pittsburgh's hive of lawyers, the Steel Bar, over the course of that history is an opportunity to look at some of the thousands of things they did each day, for better or for worse, including navigating the tightrope between civic order and civic chaos and wrestling with issues that are as familiar to us living in twenty-first century America as they are to American historians: ... the one percent vs. the ninety-nine percent ... federal surveillance of political targets ... skirmishes over the limits of political dissent ... fights over the right to collective bargaining ... enemy combatants on trial in military tribunals ... official and unofficial prejudices against immigrant communities ... confidence in the independent judiciary ... defiant tax protests ... the glass ceiling for women ... corporations as "persons" ... the private inurement of government officials ... an African American lawyer getting roughed up by the police ...

If you can't find the Rule of Law in the thousands of things that Pittsburgh lawyers did and said, about such things and during such times, then I'll challenge you to find it anywhere at all in America. If anyone sees the system of the Rule of Law as being imperiled, then there is a forest here to see, and not just a bunch of trees and bushes and shrubs; and the question is not so much "why on Earth?," but ultimately, "where on Earth?" It is a question that matters. If one were inquiring to see how this system has worked, in a practical setting—its pitfalls as well as some of its greatest achievements—this rumored location, somewhere in fly-over country, with its rich and essential role in the American narrative, may be among the better places to find that information. With all due respect to Manhattan and Wall Street, to K Street and Capitol Hill, to Silicon Valley, and to Hollywood and my old hometown of LA, some important part of what we experience today as America was made here, too.

—RWS

PART I

THE EARLY BAR
1788-1866

WHISKEY, GUNS AND LAWYERS

On a November day in 1794, Pittsburgh's first lawyer stood before Alexander Hamilton, the Secretary of the Treasury of the United States, at the center of a hastily convened federal inquest, suspected of attempting to overthrow the government, and fully expecting that he would soon be summarily arrested, convicted and executed.

"I was received by Mr. Hamilton," said the lawyer, Hugh Henry Brackenridge, "with that countenance which a man will have when he sees a person with regard to whom his humanity and his sense of justice struggle . . . [H]e would have him saved, but is afraid he must be hanged; was willing to treat me with civility, but was embarrassed with a sense that in a short time I must probably stand in the predicament of a culprit, and be put in irons."[1]

The occasion for Hamilton's inquest was the aftermath of an underappreciated episode in American history known as the Whiskey Rebellion. Often regarded simply as an uprising on the Western frontier of Pennsylvania in which a few drunken farmers fired some gunshots and tarred-and-feathered a few revenue agents before President George Washington personally led thirteen thousand federal troops westward to quell the riots, the shorthand version of the insurrection obscures its significance. The Whiskey Rebellion was actually the first large-scale resistance to a law enacted by Congress under the newly-ratified United States Constitution. It was, in fact, the first serious test of Constitutional power and authority, and its key protagonists were not merely a gang of drunken farmers. Rather, among them were some relatively sober lawyers who were pushing the limits of democratic discourse—the ongoing dialogue, in a free democracy, between the authorities and those who dissent from the authorities—and by doing so, helped to define the limits of dissent in the new Republic.

Hugh Henry Brackenridge was a self-conscious agent in this process of defining democratic discourse, although he could hardly have expected to find himself facing death for it. On the other hand, it was a violent age.

For Pittsburghers at the end of the eighteenth century, violence and brutality were still palpable possibilities in daily life on the frontier. Choosing a life in the West was a calculated risk—even for Pittsburgh's lawyers, who practiced a profession not generally known for its risk-taking. Infected with the contrarian spirit of the frontier, however, it should perhaps be no surprise that the mannerisms of Pittsburgh lawyers during this period—operating, it would seem, in the heat of the moment, aiming toward basic self-preservation in the face of the dramatic urgencies of the frontier—also displayed an element of risk-taking that would be uncharacteristic of the elite lawyers of Philadelphia and Boston, revealing behaviors ranging from aggressive declarations of dissent, to blistering personal attacks, to brawls, whippings, duels, and outright rebellion.

On the other hand, Brackenridge and other lawyers from the early days of the Republic were inspired to become lawyers, in part, by their patriotism, and by the roles they could be expected to play as lawyers within their communities, educating their neighbors about and protecting a new kind of democracy. Perhaps the greatest risks to their own reputations and livelihoods—greater, in some sense, than the brutal physical setting of the frontier itself—were the risks inherent in advocating for a line between the liberties that the new Republic provided, and the chaos that would ensue if the rules of the new Republic were not followed in the pursuit of liberty. Already contrarian in their political views, these frontier lawyers could find themselves caught between a hot-tempered, disaffected populace, on the one hand, and the executives of a young Republic, on the other, feeling out the limits of the Republic's newly-imagined authority. The outstanding Pittsburgh lawyers of the late eighteenth and early nineteenth centuries also frequently found themselves taking moderating positions that alienated them from the extremes of the central intellectual debate of the day—the running argument between those who supported a strong central government and those who favored greater autonomy at the local level. By seeking a more practical, politically-informed "middle course," they risked being continually misunderstood by their brethren in the East, the statesmen and intellectual lawyers who considered themselves members of the ruling class of the new nation.

For Pittsburgh lawyers in the earliest years of our nation's history, being professional moderates during an era of revolutionary spirit was a thankless task.

Forty-six years before he would find himself standing at the center of Hamilton's federal inquest, Hugh Henry Brackenridge was born to poor farmers in Kintyre, Scotland in 1748. He came to America with his parents, and by the age of sixteen, he was hired as a schoolmaster in Gunpowder Falls, Maryland, near Joppa Town on the Chesapeake.[2] A few years later, he attended the College of New Jersey at Princeton with fellow patriots-in-training James Madison, Philip Freneau—later, the editor of the *National Gazette*—and William Bradford—who later became the second Attorney General of the United States. Brackenridge had demonstrated his commitment to a free and independent United States of America well before the Continental Congress would vote on the issue, in a prophetic commencement poem, *The Rising Glory of America,* co-written with Freneau, and later in politically-tinged sermons he wrote while serving as a chaplain in the Continental Army during the Revolution.[3]

Brackenridge presumptuously thought of writing as his true calling at a time when American literature did not functionally exist; but in any event he needed a living after the Revolution, and law was a practical outlet for a literate man, one that could lead to a measure of personal prosperity. "I have loved Miss Theology," Brackenridge wrote in 1779, "yet we both saw the necessity of ceasing to indulge any fond thought of a union ... The present object of my soft attentions is a Miss Law, a grave and comely young lady, a little pitted with the small pox ... This young lady is of a prudent industrious turn, and though she does not possess at present any great fortune, yet what she has in expectancy is considerable."[4] He studied law with Samuel Chase, a member of the Continental Congress and a signer of the Declaration of Independence, in Annapolis, and moved to Philadelphia, where he briefly established a newspaper, the *United States Magazine*, and intended to open a law practice. Awed, however, by the presence of such imposing legal minds as Benjamin Chew, Pennsylvania's colonial chief justice, and other leading lights of the Continental Congress such as John Dickinson and James Wilson, Brackenridge quickly came to realize that he "had no chance of being anything in that city, there were such great men before me."[5] Thus, at the age of thirty-three, he moved to Western Pennsylvania in 1781—"to advance the country and thereby advance myself"[6]—and began practicing law in Pittsburgh, as a member of the Westmoreland County bar.

The Pittsburgh that Brackenridge encountered in 1781 was a mingling of steep hills, surrounded by dense clumps of trees, with a few unpromising wisps of stove smoke floating over the muddy confluence of three lazy rivers—not necessarily an auspicious spot for one who desired to start another newspaper and support his writing habit with a career in the law. Historian Thomas Slaughter described the region as "a place where poverty was the standard in 1780 and where living conditions declined over the next fifteen years."[7] While land would have appeared to be the region's most plentiful resource, it was largely controlled by absentee landowners from the East, with a few resident landowners. It was an area in which few new settlers had any opportunity to acquire property, at least through legal means. Slaughter concludes that "the richest citizens grew considerably wealthier, owned a greater percentage of the land, and monopolized the overwhelming number of public offices in the region."[8] One of the few alternatives available to the poor settler was to ignore the claims of absentee landowners, taking possession of land by squatting. Thus, one of the defining economic tactics of the place and time was one that denied the authority of both courts of law and written land deeds. Such was the economic climate within which a professional bar—a guild of lawyers—was born in Western Pennsylvania during the 1780s.

When William Penn founded the colony of Pennsylvania in 1682, he envisioned it as a "lawyerless" society in which county magistrates would appoint panels of three lay peacemakers every three months to settle controversies.[9] That visionary premise, inspired by Penn's harsh experiences with English law courts, proved to be impractical almost immediately, however, and although there were only four lawyers in all of Philadelphia County as late as 1709, formal courts were firmly established in Pennsylvania by the 1720s.[10] Nevertheless, courts were practical as forums for the settlement of disputes only to the extent one could physically get to them at the appointed times. They did not meet on a daily basis, but rather only on a few days a year, and the schedules of a circuit justice were at the mercy of weather and other travel conditions. In 1771, the entire population of Pitt Township—which comprised most of what would eventually become Allegheny County and portions of the future Beaver, Washington and Westmoreland Counties—consisted of fifty-two landowners, twenty tenants, and thirteen single "free men."[11] Thus, the administration of courts in southwestern Pennsylvania was not considered a high priority for the colonial leaders of Pennsylvania. For the pioneers who lived at the confluence of the Ohio, the Allegheny and the Monongahela Rivers, the only justice practically available, for long periods of time, was rough justice—exacted largely on a hand-to-hand basis, with trusted neighbors occasionally acting as mediators or enforcers.

Prior to 1771, Pittsburgh was considered a part of Cumberland County, whose current seat is at Carlisle, about 190 miles east of Pittsburgh. In that year, however, Pittsburgh became a part of "Bedford County," the first Pennsylvania county to be formed west of the Allegheny Mountains. Two years later, Pittsburgh became part of newly-formed "Westmoreland County," and while two of the trustees who were named to establish the county seat argued that it should be in Pittsburgh, the remaining three trustees preferred Hannastown, still about thirty-five miles east of Pittsburgh—almost a full day's journey. The fight for supremacy between Pittsburgh and Hannastown continued without any firm resolution throughout the Revolutionary War. Greensburg, then called Newtown, was ultimately selected as the county seat in 1785, after Seneca warriors burned Hannastown to the ground. In the meantime, however, a log house owned by Robert Hanna became the site of the first courts held near Pittsburgh, and Colonel William Crawford, a friend of George Washington, was the first presiding justice. The citizens soon built a log jail, a whipping post and a pillory nearby, revealing the early courts' emphasis on criminal prosecutions rather than civil matters.[12] Brackenridge had occasion to defend a Delaware tribesman named Mamachtaga in one of the two murder trials held in Hannastown during the period. Mamachtaga was found guilty and was hanged on a scaffold built in an area west of Hannastown known as Gallow Hills. Brackenridge was paid "forty weight of beaver" pelts for his services in the case.[13]

Pittsburgh's elder sister city three hundred miles to the east, Philadelphia, had been transformed into the center of a civilized society by its proximity to European import trade routes and by a hundred years' head start on the business of building and educating. In the 1780s and 1790s, Philadelphia's lawyers were, by and large, conservative by nature. The leading members of the bar had not supported American independence. They were men whose relatively small income from legal work was often generously supplemented by family wealth, and most of their lives were spent within the relative safety of an established urban environment.[14] By contrast, Pittsburgh in the 1780s and 1790s was still an outpost on the frontier of the United States, in which attacks by nearby indigenous peoples were still occurring—for example, the capture of Thomas and Jane Dick near the mouth of Deer Creek, north of Pittsburgh, in March 1791, and the massacre of the Russ family along the Allegheny River, four days later.[15] Tensions with Native Americans were, in fact, still on the rise, as under the Northwest Ordinance of 1787, the Northwest Territory was theoretically opened for settlement. President

Washington's new federal government saw expansion westward as one cure for its financial problems after an expensive war with the British. While refusing to engage Native Americans in diplomatic dialogues or in armed conflict, the federal government began to sell claims on land north and west of the Ohio River, leading inevitably to disputes between white settlers and indigenous tribes.[16]

Out of necessity, in this uncertain climate, the best of Pittsburgh's earliest lawyers were nimble and opportunistic, both physically and mentally. Fresh from one test of his skill, a Pittsburgh lawyer might jump on his horse and ride across the rolling hills like an armored knight, speeding toward another field of battle; and after a breakneck journey over bad roads—as Pittsburgh lawyer James Mountain famously would do in the course of defending one James Bell on a charge of murder in 1809—he might jump off his horse and grab the reins of a case just at the close of evidence, hastily learning the leading points and launching headlong into his closing address to the jury, electrifying them, and gaining a quick acquittal for his client.[17] Lawyering in Pittsburgh during the early years was, in part, an outdoor activity that required physical stamina and athleticism as well as quick-wittedness.

The successful Pittsburgh lawyer during this period would have been a master of the land; he would, quite literally, know the terrain, and often he would become skilled in land speculation. Collecting debts locally for his Eastern clients, he would develop a sharp insight into human character, and a nose for the next lucrative opportunity. Although, like his Eastern counterparts, he might have a healthy respect for erudition, he was unlikely to have an extensive library. Rather, he had to rely on his shrewdness and his practical, street-level common sense, both in providing advice and in persuading judges and juries. Sometimes, the Pittsburgh lawyer would be a rough and ready combatant outside the courtroom. Thomas Mercer Marshall, a well-known Pittsburgh trial lawyer, was once so angry about the deplorable state of the Perrysville Plank Toll Road, on which he traveled every day on his way into town, that he took an axe to the toll gate. Marshall correctly surmised that the toll road proprietor would never take him to court due to the proprietor's fear of being exposed for failing to maintain the road properly.[18] The best of Pittsburgh's early lawyers would have had the steadiest hands available when it came to preserving order for the sake of progress. "Law followed the ax[e]" in frontier America, as American legal historian Lawrence M. Friedman has appropriately observed[19]; but in Western Pennsylvania, the lawyers sometimes defined order by wielding the axe themselves. In this respect, the early bar of Pittsburgh became engaged in defining and perpetuating a uniquely American kind of lawyer, a different breed than the inns-bound British barrister, or his bookish near-cousin on the Eastern seaboard of North America.

Pittsburgh lawyers also naturally assumed political leadership in the community. Late in his career, while serving as a justice on the Pennsylvania Supreme Court, Brackenridge wrote, "The profession of the law under a Republican Government, not only leads to emolument, but qualifies for political eminence."[20] In his actions and written words he embodied the notion that lawyers—as educated, rational men, and agents of civilization—were specially equipped, if not obliged, to play a key role in defining the new Republic and its political institutions. They would help to create order out of the passions that transformed the colonies into independent states, especially in the unruly Western frontier. As Daniel Marder writes:

> *The problem ... how to be both free and orderly ... consumed the life of Hugh Henry Brackenridge at the beginning of the democratic experiment. He was totally committed and utterly involved ... He was committed completely to the requirement of an educated and sensitized population, and he was involved, therefore, in overcoming ignorance and licentiousness.*[21]

Brackenridge arrived in the village of Pittsburgh at the height of a secessionist boomlet. There on the Western frontier, some of the locals had been agitating for the creation of a new state or perhaps even a new nation in the region, largely because of the apparent indifference of the federal government in the East to the problems of the Westerner.[22] In 1786, now married and a father of one son—future lawyer Henry Marie Brackenridge—Brackenridge helped launch a newspaper, the *Pittsburgh Gazette*, and shortly thereafter was elected to the Pennsylvania Assembly. Brackenridge supported Western issues, such as rights to navigation on the Mississippi River, and he voiced his frustrations with Eastern nearsightedness and hypocrisy on many occasions. Criticizing the parochial urban legislators in Philadelphia, he noted that their approach to Native Americans, for example, was "like young women who have read romances, and have as improper an idea of the Indian character ... as the female mind has of real life."[23] Nonetheless, he was known to have represented Native Americans, such as the time he defended Mamachtaga, a Delaware, on a charge of murder. Although Brackenridge took the case because he believed that the rights of "Indians" should be protected under the law, his defense of Mamachtaga led to conflicts with his Western neighbors. When one of his neighbors, a Mr. Simpson, challenged him to a duel over the issue, Brackenridge responded that he neither dueled nor loved "Indians," and then proceeded to break a chair over Simpson's head and toss him into a fireplace.[24]

Although Brackenridge may have been operating on principle, he nevertheless began to earn a reputation for being unpredictable—or worse, mentally unstable—while he was in the Assembly. His tireless efforts on behalf of establishing "Allegheny County" and on procuring the charter and the state endowments for the academy that would eventually become known as the University of Pittsburgh unmistakably marked him as a leader who wanted local self-governance and home-grown educational opportunities for Western Pennsylvania. However, he was mercilessly criticized by voters back home when he opposed a measure that would permit settlers to pay for land in certificates of state indebtedness. While Western settlers saw the measure as an expansion of currency that would make it easier for them to acquire land, Brackenridge's position was that Eastern speculators had acquired a large number of such certificates, and that the measure would probably benefit Eastern creditors more than Western farmers.[25] Brackenridge, however, went out of his way to repudiate the notion that he, as an educated, rational lawyer serving in the legislature, should bend to the will of a poorly informed constituency. "From this oath [i.e., his oath of office] it must appear that a representative is not supposed to be a mere machine, like a clock wound up to run for many hours in the same way," he wrote; "he is sent to hear from others, and to think for himself, as well as to vote ... It is certain the people do not always know their own interest, nor do individuals know."[26]

Brackenridge tested that theory to its limits by supporting the proposed federal Constitution. Among legislators from the Western side of the state, he was the only one to support the initiative, again asking how his constituents could "oppose a government which must so greatly advance their own interest."[27] Despite the fact that many of his constituents already believed that their ills could be blamed on authority exercised from a distance by powerful Eastern interests, Brackenridge saw a galvanizing federal Constitution—much like James Madison and others with whom he spent his young adulthood—as a logical extension to independence, "which after all the pains taken was with great difficulty brought about."[28] Furthermore, he saw cooperation among the states as essential to fixing Western ills. "For without the energy of such a constitution," he asked, "how can we expect the opening of the Mississippi river, the surrender of the [British] posts on the lakes, the support of the troops on the frontier, and the protection of settlements ...?"[29] Advocating on behalf of federal authority in order to accomplish those objectives was precisely, in his view, what he meant when he wrote that he wished to "advance the country." Due to the Constitution's unpopularity in Pittsburgh, however, he failed to thereby advance himself.

He lashed out at his opponents with his pen. After several Western legislators, including William Findley—a clothmaker by trade whose political rise, despite failing to possess much in the way of intellectual gifts, became something of a nagging obsession for Brackenridge—left the Assembly chambers rather than permit a vote on the creation of a convention to consider the proposed federal Constitution, he satirized his fellow lawmakers in a comic poem, "On the Running Away of the Nineteen Members of the Assembly from the House, When it Was Proposed to Call a Convention to Consider the New System of Congressional Government; and on the Apology Made by Them in Their Address. A Hudibrastic."[30] Findley's views prevailed with Pittsburghers, however, even as Pennsylvania ultimately called its constitutional convention. Brackenridge returned home from the legislature in 1787, unsuccessful in his bid for re-election. "My character was totally gone with the populace," he wrote, "My practice lost."[31] In December 1787, Pennsylvania ratified the Constitution, the second of nine states required for its adoption, but Brackenridge had little cause for celebration as his wife had recently died. He withdrew from public life for a time.

On September 24, 1788, largely through Brackenridge's efforts in the Assembly, all Pennsylvania territory north of the Ohio River and west of the Allegheny River was designated as "Allegheny County," with Pittsburgh as its seat.[32] The first periodic "court of Quarter Sessions," held in a room on the corner of Second and Market streets, was convened by George Wallace, a non-lawyer, on December 16, 1788. On that day, eleven men were admitted as lawyers to practice in the courts of Allegheny County: Hugh Henry Brackenridge, John Woods, James Ross, George Thompson, Alexander Addison, Robert Galbraith, David Bradford, David Redick, James Carson, David St. Clair and Michael Huffnagle. All had previously been admitted in either the Westmoreland or Washington County courts.[33] The fact that a non-lawyer such as Wallace was permitted to serve as a judge was a point of controversy. In recognition of a need for more uniformity in the courts, the Pennsylvania Constitution of 1790 reorganized the existing state courts and all but required at least president judges, in most cases, to be "learned in the law." Following the terms of the state constitution, in 1791 the legislature created new judicial districts around the state, with Pittsburgh as the seat of the Fifth Judicial District, to be convened by a president judge to be appointed by the governor for life (or at least, "during good behavior"), and four associate judges.[34]

Alexander Addison, one of Pittsburgh's first eleven lawyers, was appointed by Governor Thomas Mifflin as the first president judge of the Court of Common Pleas of the Fifth Judicial District in Allegheny County. Addison was also born in Scotland, in 1758. After receiving a Master's degree from the University of Aberdeen, he became a Presbyterian minister in Aberlowe, Scotland in 1781. Four years later Addison accompanied Dr. Charles Nesbit to America, where Nesbit had accepted an appointment as president of Dickinson College in Carlisle. Addison moved on from Carlisle and settled in Pittsburgh, where he preached and studied law, entering the Washington County bar in 1787.[35] Judge Addison had taken his seat on the bench in time for the opening of Pittsburgh's first true courthouse—a square, two-story wood-and-brick building with a hip roofed cupola and bell, located on the public square at Market Street known as the "Diamond." There, Justice presided over a boisterous plaza of market stalls, wagons and horses rushing through. In this small but noisy metropolis, the new courthouse functioned as a multi-purpose venue, where public assemblies, religious services and dramatic performances were also held.[36]

By 1790, Brackenridge was coming out of his self-imposed period of social seclusion. When the ninth and last required state, New Hampshire, ratified the Constitution on June 21, 1789, approximately fifteen hundred Pittsburghers and nearby inhabitants strolled up Grant's Hill for a celebration. A vindicated Brackenridge addressed the crowd:

> *Oh my compatriots; I have great news to give you. A union of nine states has taken place, and you are now citizens of a new empire; an empire, not the effect of chance, nor hewn out by the sword; but formed by the skill of sages, and the design of wise men. Who is there who does not spring in height, and find himself taller by the circumstance? For you have acquired superior strength; you are become a great people.*[37]

"The crowd cheered three times and tossed hats wildly in the air," writes historian William F. Keller.[38] The "energy of such a constitution" seemed to give the forty-two year-old Brackenridge a buoyancy he had lacked for a couple of years, as not only did he emerge from his isolation, but he found himself a new wife. While riding back to Pittsburgh from Washington County, he stopped at the tavern of Jacob Wolfe, a Revolutionary War veteran, in order to feed his horse and escape the rain. Wolfe's beautiful, black-eyed, nineteen year-old daughter Sabina had waited on table that day. After spending the evening at Mr. Wolfe's, the next morning Brackenridge asked for his horse. He watched as the illiterate "Dutch" girl he met the day before ran barefoot across Wolfe's cow pasture and jumped over the rail fence to fetch his horse. Brackenridge rode ten miles, then impulsively returned and negotiated a ten dollar dowry to obtain Mr. Wolfe's daughter's hand in marriage, as Mr. Wolfe had then complained that it would cost him as much to find someone to replace Sabina for shrubbing his meadow. Brackenridge obtained Sabina's consent, and subsequently married her. Shortly thereafter Brackenridge sent Sabina to Philadelphia to obtain her education. She apparently read Latin decently by the time their third child was three years old.[39]

Four years later, however, Brackenridge now found himself facing Secretary Hamilton's interrogations and the potential of death by hanging—misunderstood by both his neighbors and by the federal government. "Had we listened to some people," Hamilton later concluded, "I do not know what we might have done."[40]

With the ratification of the Constitution in 1789, the new federal government was beset by a number of challenges—principal among them, the fact that the new nation was beginning its life under the weight of millions of dollars in debts left over from the Revolutionary War. In response to the cash concerns of the federal government, Alexander Hamilton—a former New York City lawyer and an aide-de-camp to General George Washington who was now serving as President Washington's, and the nation's, chief financial officer—pushed for a plan that he hoped would reduce the remaining debts from the Revolution, in addition to creating a steady stream of revenue that would begin the process of turning the United States government into a suitable vehicle for raising capital through the sale of bonds. In the summer of 1790, Hamilton called for an excise tax to be levied on the production of whiskey.

As enacted in March 1791, the regressive tax tended to weigh more heavily on country stills west of the Alleghenies than it did the larger commercial stills of the metropolitan East, with the result that smaller distillers often ended up having to pay more than twice per gallon what larger producers paid. The burden of this inequity was compounded by the fact that farmers in the West, as a matter of course, processed their rye into whiskey in order to preserve it for transportation over the Alleghenies to the nearest large markets. Whiskey was used as currency in places like Pittsburgh, where cash was scarce; every fifth Pittsburgher had a whiskey still, just to help make ends meet. Adding insult to injury, anyone who wished to protest the levy of the tax on their stills in Western Pennsylvania would be forced to leave their farming and other business unattended for a significant period of time to travel to Philadelphia and wait out a notoriously vague and imprecise court calendar. To be sitting outside the courthouse in Philadelphia while it was harvest time in Allegheny County could be financially devastating for a Pittsburgh-area farmer.[41]

In September 1791, several unidentified hoodlums ambushed a supposed revenue collector named Robert Johnson near Pigeon Creek, south of the Monongahela River in Washington County. They yanked Johnson from his horse, stripped him naked, and tarred and feathered him. They left no ambiguity as to how they felt about the new federal excise tax. Several similar events followed: another man set up a collections office in Washington County, but was forced out after his home was invaded and his family was threatened; a Fayette County tax collector was beaten and his documents were destroyed; a deputy tax collector in Washington County was tarred and feathered and his house was torn down; and a farmer who complied with the tax saw his whiskey still destroyed, and his grist and saw mills damaged, by angry mobs.[42]

Brackenridge propelled himself to the forefront of a petition movement to repeal the whiskey tax. While Brackenridge was opposed to the excise tax, he was also against the violent redress of grievances; he was, after all, a wounded veteran of the fight to ratify the Constitution, "formed by the skill of sages, and the design of wise men," and he urged his fellow Westerners to work through Congress to have the law changed. "A revolution did not suit me," Brackenridge recalled, "nor any man else who had anything to lose."[43] Nevertheless, as Brackenridge continued in his opposition to the tax, Secretary Hamilton and others within the federal government perceived Brackenridge, through his position of influence, as a dangerous radical, and they began to link Brackenridge with the violence in Western Pennsylvania.

Appearing at a protest meeting in Pittsburgh shortly after the incident at Pigeon Creek in 1791, Brackenridge delivered an opening address and proposed that concerned citizens should send a petition to the Pennsylvania Assembly and the U.S. Congress expressing opposition to the excise tax.[44] Shortly thereafter, Brackenridge took on the defense of twelve men who were allegedly involved in tarring and feathering another tax collector named Graham, and took part in a "great case" involving seventy distillers who failed to register their stills under the law. As his son Henry Marie observed, "A popularity of this kind no doubt led to some inconvenience as it in some measure identified him with opinions and movements which he did not always approve."[45] In February 1792, however, Brackenridge published "Thoughts on the Excise Law, so far as it respects the Western Country" in Freneau's *National Gazette*, cataloguing his reasons for opposing the tax, and warning that "in due time ... oppression will make the wise mad, and induce them to resist with intemperance what they ought to resist with reason." While Brackenridge was careful to state that "I am not one of those who have appeared in committees on this subject in the Western country," Freneau's notorious journal was one that Hamilton and the Federalists monitored closely, and Brackenridge's predictions about the "intemperance" of the populace were interpreted by Hamilton as a call to arms rather than a friendly warning.[46]

Brackenridge was also the likely author, perhaps with Freneau again, of a brief churlish note in the *National Gazette* in August 1792, in which the author, "H.B.," confesses that the excise tax reminds him of the plight of Negro slaves, arguing, "The yoemanry of the United States are reduced to the situation of slaves on West-India estates ... as they dare not make use of their own industry without being subject to heavy penalties upon the information of a pimping exciseman, placed in every quarter of the country to watch the private actions of the citizens—O tempora, O mores!"[47] Eastern suspicions about Brackenridge's stomach for rebellion seemed to be confirmed by Brackenridge's 1793 Independence Day address, in which he declared that "[t]he heart of America feels the cause of France," and questioned the federal government on its apparent diplomatic preference for monarchical England over revolutionary France. Brackenridge's address was published by a New York bookseller within the same pamphlet as an oration by Maximilien de Robespierre, one of the central figures of France's "reign of terror." The bookseller listed the authors as "Citizen Brackenridge" and "Citizen Robespierre," respectively, leaving no doubt about the intended comparison.[48]

David Bradford was another of the first eleven members of the Allegheny County bar. A slightly younger contemporary of Brackenridge, Bradford was first admitted to the Washington County bar upon Brackenridge's motion to the county court.[49] Bradford was virtually unknown outside of Western Pennsylvania, but he was popular locally, and in his quest for notoriety he would become considerably more radical in his aims. Although he served as Deputy Attorney General (or District Attorney) for Washington County and had family connections with powerful men (his sisters had married John McDowell and James Allison, two very prominent Western Pennsylvania lawyers), Bradford did not enjoy significant political influence before the enactment of the whiskey excise. Like Brackenridge, he served briefly in the Assembly, but he was considered to be an undistinguished legislator. Albert Gallatin, who also served with him there, called Bradford "an empty drum, as ignorant, [indolent] & insignificant as he is haughty & pompous," saying that "Tenth rate lawyers are the most unfit people to send there."[50] While initially Bradford alleged that he had come out "in the Strongest Terms" against the anti-tax violence, as the unrest continued to build in Western Pennsylvania, Bradford curried favor with an angry populace by refusing to prosecute anyone for the attacks on revenue agents.[51]

In July 1794, matters came to a head. On July 15, General John Neville, a wealthy landowner who had been appointed the federal inspector of revenue for Western Pennsylvania, attempted to serve a writ upon farmer William Miller, ordering him to set "aside all manner of business and excuses" and appear before the judge of the federal District Court in Philadelphia for failure to pay the whiskey tax. Miller refused to accept the summons; and while General Neville continued to press his case with Miller, he saw thirty or forty men coming down the lane with pitchforks and muskets. General Neville turned and left Miller's homestead on horseback, but as he did, a menacing gunshot rang out after him. Neville went home to Bower Hill, about eight miles southwest of Pittsburgh in present-day Scott Township. The next morning, he awoke to find about forty armed rebels outside his home. He ordered them to stand back. Then, he fired his gun, mortally wounding Oliver Miller, William's nephew. The rebels fired back, and a twenty-five-minute musket fight ensued between the rebels and Neville's slaves, in which several of the rebels were wounded. The rebel militia retreated to Fort Couch, about three miles away, and they were thirsty for revenge for the death of Oliver Miller. Under the command of James MacFarlane, approximately five hundred armed rebels marched back to General Neville's house at Bower Hill, demanding his surrender. Bolstered by a small federal army presence in the house, Neville refused. In the ensuing battle, Neville's home was burned to the ground; MacFarlane was shot dead by a federal officer; several rebels were severely wounded; and Neville barely escaped with his life.[52]

At a gathering of rebels sixteen miles south of Pittsburgh at Mingo Creek on July 23, after the incident at Bower Hill, David Bradford delivered what an eyewitness called a "violent and inflammatory oration" in support of amassing an army to oppose the federal government, talking of setting up guillotines and predicting that an army of Western Pennsylvania rebels would defeat any federal army that might come over the Alleghenies. By his own account, however, Bradford had encountered a crowd that was already "of the general opinion ... that they should support those who attacked the Neville house and not let them be persecuted by the law."[53]

Brackenridge was ostensibly invited to Mingo Creek to provide legal counsel to the gathering. "My situation was delicate," he recalled. "I was but a moment between treason on the one hand, and popular odium on the other." Having learned something about "popular odium" from his experience in the Assembly, Brackenridge led with some jokes "in order to put them in good humour, and at the same time lead to the point I had in view, the practicability of obtaining an amnesty ..." Once he had gotten them to laugh, doing a "bit" about old President Washington trying to negotiate with indigenous tribes, he broke his monologue and told the gathering that they were guilty of high treason. He concluded by observing that what had been done at Neville's farm may have been "morally right, but it was legally wrong" and that President Washington now had unequivocal grounds to bring a federal militia to Western Pennsylvania. The crowd went quiet. Fearing an unreceptive audience, Brackenridge quickly departed.[54]

David Bradford's activities, meanwhile, began to look a lot like a war of independence. According to a report by Judge Addison, Bradford allegedly directed the ambush of a postal rider carrying letters from Washington, Pennsylvania to Pittsburgh.[55] Supposedly after examining the letters, Bradford drew up a circular calling for the assembly of a militia at Braddock's Field, around nine miles southeast of Pittsburgh. Approximately seven thousand men showed up at Braddock's Field on August 1, and Bradford wasted no time in calling for the assembled militia to march into Pittsburgh—both as a show of force, and to take hold of the federal garrison there, with its stores of ammunition and other supplies.

Brackenridge observed that among those who were amassing at Braddock's Field there was the feeling that "the law was dissolved, and that the people themselves, in their collective capacity, were the only tribunal."[56] For many of the landless country boys who joined the rebel army, Pittsburgh ironically symbolized the greed and power of the big cities of the East, and they were motivated by more than military strategy to take hold of Pittsburgh and burn it to the ground. Brackenridge met with David Bradford, who had assumed the role of "general" of the insurgent army, and did his best behind the scenes to file down the edges of the conflict, advising him that an orderly and peaceful march through Pittsburgh would impress upon the government "that we are no mob."[57] Bradford, who remained defiant but did not want the blood of innocent Pittsburghers on his hands, also gave Pittsburgh an opportunity to escape destruction, demanding the expulsion of certain persons friendly to the federal cause in exchange for sparing the city. The rousing welcome disarmed the rebels as they entered Pittsburgh on August 2, and they soon dispersed peacefully, if somewhat aimlessly. A combination of whiskey and lawyers, judiciously applied, outmaneuvered the guns on the occasion. "It cost me four barrels of whiskey, that day, and I would rather spare that than a single quart of blood," Brackenridge recalled.[58]

Still, Brackenridge feared that the situation was volatile. He wrote a letter to Tench Coxe, an aide to Secretary Hamilton, stating that if an attempt were made to suppress the rebels, "I am afraid the question will not be whether you will march to Pittsburgh, but whether they will march to Philadelphia ..."[59] The letter would come back to haunt Brackenridge before Secretary Hamilton began his inquest in the aftermath of the Rebellion.

While Washington's Secretary of State, Edmund Randolph, recommended to President Washington that he pursue a plan for reconciliation with the rebels, the rest of the cabinet, including Secretary Hamilton, urged the president to put on a show of force. The president adopted both recommendations: while raising a militia, Washington sent a group of three peace commissioners—Senator James Ross, a Western Pennsylvania lawyer then serving in the U.S. Senate; Brackenridge's old friend William Bradford, the U.S. Attorney General; and Pennsylvania Supreme Court judge Jasper Yeates—to meet with leaders of the opposition.[60]

Washington's peace commission met with a group of negotiators elected by a gathering of over two hundred protesters at Parkinson's Ferry, now Monongahela, Pennsylvania, in August 1794. The peace commissioners were instructed by President Washington to offer amnesty to all who would swear not to obstruct the law, but could not commit that the U.S. government would repeal the tax. In effect, they offered only total submission—an outcome unacceptable to a rebel such as David Bradford, a member of the Parkinson's Ferry committee, and politically untenable for Hugh Henry Brackenridge, another member of the committee, who did not desire to obstruct the law but did hope to come away from peace talks with concessions from the federal government. During the August parley, no agreement emerged. Trying again in September, a faction of compromisers—which included Albert Gallatin—seemed to be gaining ground, but public anger was still running hot enough that members of the committee were uneasy about casting their vote for a compromise. Hearing the news, Hamilton apparently believed that the committee's refusal to accept the offer of amnesty was evidence enough of the guilt of its members, including Brackenridge.[61]

In early October, the conciliatory faction of protesters took matters into its own hands and met again at Parkinson's Ferry, appointing William Findley and Washington County lawyer David Redick, with Judge Alexander Addison as recording secretary, to deliver the message to the president that a military solution was not required, and that the Westerners would agree to submission and peace. It was too late, however. Marking the only time in American history that a sitting president ever personally led an army into potential battle, the sixty-two year-old President Washington—donning his buff-and-blue general's uniform, not worn since the end of the Revolution a decade before—rode upon his white steed as far west as Bedford, stiff and suffering from back pain, with thirteen thousand federal troops under his command. Findley, Redick and Judge Addison encountered the president at Carlisle, who, according to historian J.P. Taylor, told the committee that "the army was on its way and he could make no change but no violence would be used unless needed."[62]

Then President Washington, in preparation of the arrival of federal troops, asked Judge Alexander Addison to lead an investigation of the activities of the rebels. Judge Addison immediately departed for Washington County, where he made notes and secured key documents detailing rebel movements. As he left the town of Washington alone on horseback, with his valuable papers in his saddlebag, news of Addison's purpose reached the rebel leaders, and they sent a party to follow him. Before nightfall, Judge

Addison stopped at the home of his friend, Judge James Finley, in Westmoreland County. Addison's pursuers waited outside Finley's house as the lights were extinguished, with the intention of raiding the house just before dawn to get hold of Addison's evidence—and perhaps Addison himself. Judge Addison could not sleep, however; and around midnight, without wishing to awaken his hosts, he decided that he would get dressed and ride for the rest of the evening toward Bedford, where President Washington was awaiting his report. He slipped away undetected. As dawn approached, the rebels entered Finley's home, but found Addison's chamber empty. In their pique, they wrecked Finley's home, and only upon Judge Addison's return to Pittsburgh did he learn how close he was to being captured by the rebels.[63]

On October 24, 1794, Washington's army, now led by General Henry "Light-Horse Harry" Lee, whom Brackenridge had tutored while at Princeton, arrived in Washington County to subdue what was left of the rebellion, and rounded up a number of the protesters from Mingo Creek. Meanwhile, Brackenridge was aware of the fact that the soldiers in Lee's militia "were hewing me in imagination with their sabres as they came along and bayoneting every bush or other thing upon the road and calling what they bayoneted 'Brackenridge.'"[64] As he contemplated his impending arrest, he consoled himself by reading Plutarch's *Lives*, in particular about Solon's laws

> *making it death for a citizen, in a civil tumult, not to take a part; for by taking a part, on one side or the other, the moderate citizens will be divided, and mixing with the violent, will correct the fury, on both sides, until an accommodation can be brought about. It was on that principle I had acted in the insurrection; and by seeming to be of the insurgents, had contributed to soften all their measures, and finally prevent a civil war. But I saw that the law of Solon would apply chiefly to a small republic, where the moderate men were known to each other, and could explain themselves in the course of the negociation. I had been treading upon a precipice; making an experiment extremely dangerous. My intentions were laudable, but my conduct hazardous.*[65]

He turned himself in, acknowledging that "it would increase the ignominy, to be dragged hence under a guard," and encountered his old student, General Lee. He wrote that he "had never expected to see him the general of an army, arresting me for an attempt to overthrow the government."[66] No doubt embarrassed at the prospect of interrogating his former tutor, General Lee quickly handed the duty over to Secretary Hamilton. Brackenridge had prepared well for his arraignment, however. "Brackenridge had the foresight," Ellis observed, to populate the Mingo Creek meeting with friends who would testify as to his moderating influence, placing his predictions about mobs marching on Philadelphia in the proper context. William Bradford, Hamilton's fellow cabinet member, testified to Brackenridge's good character. "After one day of testimony," Ellis writes, "Hamilton changed his mind."[67] On the second day, Hamilton declared, "You are in no personal danger ... You will not be troubled even by a simple inquisition by the Judge." Brackenridge was not detained and was never charged.[68]

Brackenridge's release was, in hindsight, a key moment in the history of American political dissent. Not only was it a vindication of Brackenridge's Solonic duty to "take a part" in the "tumult" and to attempt to interject moderation between the extremes, walking a tight-rope walk between treason and reason (i.e., a fair disagreement over federal policy); but it was a tangible acknowledgement by the federal government that, in a time of political crisis, there would be no need for bloodshed. There would be no need for identifying a human scapegoat and extinguishing a life over a political disagreement. Dissent, if tolerable, would be tolerated. Out of some moments of uncertainty, during which Hamilton wrestled between his "humanity and sense of justice," Brackenridge and Hamilton had ultimately taken steps toward the creation of a template for the orderly exchange of political views within the most heated circumstances. It was, perhaps, a lesson that only two veterans of the violent Revolutionary era could have taught to an ensuing generation.

Nevertheless, Brackenridge was on the wrong side of popular sentiment in Western Pennsylvania after the Whiskey Rebellion. "Local settlers concluded he had to be guilty of something," Ellis writes. "[E]ither he had supported the rebellion and deserved punishment from the government or he had opposed it and should have suffered at the hands of the rebels."[69] The subtleties of Brackenridge's position were completely lost on his neighbors. His desire to hold the center, to moderate between political extremes, ironically led him to be seen by them as a subversive, not capable of being trusted by either side. His law practice diminishing, it would not be long before he decided to leave Pittsburgh for good, moving his family to Carlisle. In 1799, the Democratic-Republican governor of Pennsylvania Thomas McKean appointed him to the Pennsylvania Supreme Court, where he presided as a man who "seemed to have lost all social awareness," according to Marder, sitting with his "breast exposed, his beard unshaven, his hair uncombed, his 'cravat twisted like a rope' ... with his boots off and his feet propped on the desk."[70] He had become the picture of the madman that some had always claimed he truly was.

As a rational man with a belief in the "skill of sages" and in the duty of the lawyer to assume "political eminence," but nonetheless a man living in the brutal exigencies of the frontier, Brackenridge's vision was that local autonomy needed to be nurtured, but that a strong federal government was essential to solving the problems of the frontier. These sentiments were echoed in the desire for "a middle course" in the work that consumed much of his final years, a picaresque satirical novel—some would say, America's first novel—called *Modern Chivalry*. Appearing in serial form between 1792 and 1815, and ostensibly an account of the travels and travails of Captain John Farrago and his man Teague, American counterparts to Don Quixote and Sancho Panza, it was also, as Ellis writes, a depiction of "American culture as a bundle of polarities, a set of irreconcilable contradictions and tensions."[71] While ultimately acknowledging through the comic incidents of his characters that moderation does not work well in practice, Brackenridge continually refers to the "middle course"—as Ellis recounts, "'There is a medium in all things'; 'the best men are the most moderate'; the wise leader is one who recognizes when 'active and uninformed spirits are useful or perhaps absolutely necessary' and when 'deliberate reason, and prudent temperament are necessary.'"[72] The "middle course" was Brackenridge's practical frontier strategy for self-preservation and advancement within the new Republic, but ironically, it also served to be his undoing;

and in his later years, this paradox arguably became the object of his literary obsession, as he publicly assumed the character of the mad old iconoclast.

David Bradford, meanwhile, "was disgusted" that the compromisers had won the day, according to Taylor. "His star had set and his glory grown dim," Taylor observes, and he decided to leave the area.[73] He wrote to Governor Mifflin asking for a pardon on October 2, ahead of the arrival of the troops, but was refused. Shortly before the arrival of General Lee and his army, David Bradford fled the region with a price on his head, taking a coal barge from Pittsburgh down the Ohio River. He made his way down the Mississippi, eventually landing at Bayou Sara, above Baton Rouge in Spanish Louisiana, where he gave a statement to Spanish authorities about his involvement in the insurrection, picturing himself as a public figure riding along the top of a wave of anti-government sentiment rather than as a fomenter of rebellion.[74] Obtaining a land grant of 650 acres from the governor of the Spanish territory of Louisiana and West Florida, Bradford established a successful plantation at Bayou Sara, The Myrtles. In May 1795, a federal grand jury indicted David Bradford on a charge of high treason, and he was specifically excluded from a number of general pardons that were granted in the aftermath of the insurrection. Bradford then applied to Washington's successor, President John Adams, for a specific pardon in the fall of 1798. As tempers cooled, Bradford was finally pardoned in March 1799. Adams' successor, Thomas Jefferson, successfully called for the repeal of the whiskey tax in 1801.

In the winter of 1803-04, President Jefferson thought of David Bradford once again. Conferring with members of the Senate, Jefferson expressed the view that the Florida Territory rightfully belonged to the United States; and in aid of taking possession of it, Jefferson thought of David Bradford and whether he could be convinced to lead an insurrection of American squatters against the Spanish.[75] The possibility of bringing Bradford out of retirement was halted when Jefferson started negotiations for the purchase of Florida in 1805, but Adams' pardon and Jefferson's aborted plan do tend to show that at least some members of the American establishment saw Bradford's actions in Western Pennsylvania as forgivable under the circumstances. Significantly, there does not seem to have been any effort to have David Bradford disbarred.

In the months and years that immediately followed the Rebellion, Western Pennsylvanians started to enjoy the benefit of increased attention from the federal government: the Native American tribes would be pushed further west, the Mississippi would be opened for traffic by treaty, and eventually a new federal court would be located in Pittsburgh. In 1818, Congress created the United States District Court for the Western District sitting in Pittsburgh, providing a federal District Court to be shared by all of the Western counties of Pennsylvania. Congress authorized President James Monroe to appoint a judge for the new federal court at a salary of sixteen hundred dollars per year, and his choice, Cumberland County native Jonathan Hoge Walker, convened the new court for the first time on December 7, 1818, at the courthouse in the Diamond.[76]

Meanwhile, Judge Alexander Addison, who disagreed with the excise tax but advocated submission to federal authority at the height of the conflict, ultimately fared even worse than either Bradford or Brackenridge following the Whiskey Rebellion.

The tale of his heroism in the service of President Washington after their meeting at Bedford was enough alone to set Judge Addison at odds with the emerging political climate in Western Pennsylvania after the insurrection.

As a preacher and an attorney, Addison was known as something of an orator, with a booming voice and a broad Scottish brogue. Even when he became a judge, he continued to indulge his penchant for giving speeches, providing long sets of instructions to his juries in the form of political homilies. In the December session of the grand jury in 1798, for example, his discourse wandered to a justification of the constitutionality of the Alien and Sedition Acts, recently signed into law by President John Adams, and a condemnation of the Virginia and Kentucky Resolutions that protested the federal legislation.[77] With the onset of the "reign of terror" in the French Revolution, Judge Addison became increasingly concerned about French influence in the U.S. He worried about French immigrants bringing radical ideas to the U.S., and about the kinds of secret political societies that the Alien and Sedition Acts were designed to curb. During one famous jury charge in 1800, Judge Addison delivered an address on the "Rise and Progress of Revolution," observing that revolution occurs in phases, beginning with the destruction of the Christian religion, followed by the destruction of political and social institutions, and giving examples from the activities of the Jacobins in France and the Illuminati in Germany.[78]

Judge Addison's concerns about French influence turned out to be ill-timed in light of the change of administrations at both the state and federal level—with the election of Democratic-Republican Thomas McKean as governor of Pennsylvania in 1799 and the election of Democratic-Republican Thomas Jefferson as president in 1800—which tended to favor the French over the British. With Governor McKean's appointment of John C.B. Lucas as an associate judge on the Fifth District Common Pleas Court, Judge Addison now found himself serving alongside not only a Democratic-Republican, but a Frenchman. Lucas, a relatively recent immigrant from France, was said to have practiced law in his home country, but he never entered the local bar, and according to one historian he spoke only broken English.[79] Judge Lucas did his best to irritate Judge Addison, and Judge Addison returned the favor.

In his annual charge to the grand jury in June 1801, Judge Addison gave another variation of his speech on the French Jacobins, along with the observation that the election of Thomas McKean as governor was evidence of the growing influence of radicalism in Pennsylvania. This time, however, Judge Lucas began to address the jury with a prepared speech defending the Democratic-Republicans. Judge Addison and his fellow Federalist, Associate Judge John McDowell, constituting a majority, interrupted Judge Lucas' response, threatening to have Judge Lucas removed from the courtroom if he proceeded, and ordering the jury to disregard Judge Lucas' entire speech.[80]

In his anger over being embarrassed by Judge Addison in open court, Judge Lucas appealed to the Pennsylvania Supreme Court by filing an indictment against Judge Addison for a misdemeanor in office. The Court dismissed the indictment, stating that Judge Addison had shown no malice in stopping Judge Lucas from speaking; so Judge Lucas brought his cause to the Pennsylvania House of Representatives in January 1802, with petitions signed by almost seven hundred inhabitants of Allegheny and surrounding counties asking for the impeachment of Judge Addison. In compliance with the petitions, the House made out articles of impeachment and presented them to the State Senate.

Alexander J. Dallas, who later served as President Madison's Secretary of the Treasury, led the prosecution in the Senate. Judge Addison represented himself. The trial began on January 17, 1803. Dallas took testimony from Judge Lucas and a collection of Democratic-Republicans, including the young county prothonotary,[a] Tarleton Bates. Addison's only witness was Judge John McDowell, Addison's Federalist colleague and the third remaining member of the Fifth District Common Pleas bench. Addison tried to present affidavits from witnesses who were unable to make the trip from Pittsburgh to the Senate sitting in Lancaster, but was rebuffed. The parties all agreed that Judge Addison had restrained Judge Lucas from speaking and had threatened to find the means to stop him if he persisted. What remained in conflict from the testimony was whether or not Judge Addison did so angrily, which would be evidence of malice. It was difficult to tell; Judge Addison ordinarily spoke in a loud voice and was known to be imperious during the routine administration of court business.[81]

In his closing address, Judge Addison admitted the unpopularity of his Federalist bias, but did not veer from his belief that his exercise of judgment on the bench was for the good of the Republic:

> *No man can be less qualified than I for avoiding unpopularity. I have no taste for intrigue, no disposition for flattering the follies or passions of men; no propensity to false arts; no desire for revenge, to spur my invention of means to oppose my adversaries. ... In a republican government, it ought to be deemed the honour of an officer to discharge his duty with fidelity, regardless of favour or resentment; to be guided by the laws and interest of the country, not by popular prejudices, passions, or opinions; and to pursue the public good, whether public favour followed it or not. On such principles and conduct have I rested my official reputation; and not on trimming my sails to the gale of popularity, or shifting the course with the tide of the times.[82]*

The impeachment trial was a political trial, however, brought by Democratic-Republicans against a defiant Federalist, and Judge Addison went down in defeat by a vote of twenty to four. On January 27, 1803, the Senate pronounced its sentence, removing Judge Addison as president judge of the Fifth District Common Pleas Court, and declaring him forever disqualified from holding a judicial office in the state.[83]

Addison's impeachment occurred at the beginning of a brief American "reign of terror" in which some judges became targets of politically-motivated impeachment proceedings.[84] In 1804, the Pennsylvania House prepared articles of impeachment against all of the Federalist justices on the Pennsylvania Supreme Court—Chief Justice

---

a   Clerk of the courts, pronounced "pro-THON-uh-TAIR-ee." Historian Paul Beers reports that when President Harry S Truman met Dr. William McClelland, then serving as Allegheny County prothonotary, on a stop in Pittsburgh during the 1948 presidential campaign, he exclaimed, "What the hell is a prothonotary?" Pittsburghers often get this question. See, Paul Beers, *Pennsylvania Politics Today and Yesterday: The Tolerable Accommodation* (University Park, PA: Penn State University Press, 1980) 269.

Edward Shippen and associate justices Jasper Yeates and Thomas Smith—in response to a petition from a merchant, Thomas Passmore, who argued that their conviction of him for contempt of court was a violation of the Bill of Rights.[85] The remaining associate justice, Hugh Henry Brackenridge, may have been a Democratic-Republican sympathizer, but he was outraged by the use of impeachment for political means, and demanded to be impeached along with his Federalist brethren. In Book III of *Modern Chivalry*, Brackenridge wrote: "When people madly destroy confidence in the judiciary, they destroy all security for their own rights ... judges should be held accountable but ought to be placed in a position to be out of the way of demagogues and the shifting winds of popular prejudice."[86] Shocked at Brackenridge's lack of party loyalty, the House urged Governor McKean to remove Brackenridge, but the governor refused. Shippen, Yeates and Smith were eventually acquitted. Later that year, Brackenridge's old mentor, Justice Samuel Chase of the United States Supreme Court, an appointee of President Washington, was served with eight articles of impeachment by the Democratic-Republican controlled U.S. House of Representatives, but the Senate voted to acquit Chase of all charges on March 1, 1805.

Justice Chase's acquittal, under the glare of partisan floodlights, was the last ripple in this wave of early impeachments, and it is given by legal historians as evidence of the maturation of the young Republic. But the evolution would come too late for Judge Addison. After his impeachment trial, Addison returned half-heartedly to private practice, and died four years later, at the age of forty-eight.

Boisterous and savage political disagreement would continue to consume the Pittsburgh bar in the decade that followed. "We are just beginning our political violence," wrote the prothonotary, Tarleton Bates, to his brother Frederick in 1805. "God knows how it will end."[87]

With the incorporation of Pittsburgh as a city in March 1816, a Mayor's Court was established to adjudicate all criminal offenses and ordinance violations within the city. It was composed of the mayor; a recorder, who was considered to be the law judge of the court; and twelve aldermen, three of whom were required to be present for a quorum. The cases, nonetheless, were generally tried before juries.[88] Ephraim Pentland was a short, round-faced, heavy-set fellow from Philadelphia who came to Pittsburgh as a young man around 1801. He served as the prothonotary of Allegheny County from 1809 to 1821, after which he became a member of the Allegheny County bar and was almost immediately named as recorder, or principal judge, of the Pittsburgh Mayor's Court. During the eighteen years he served as recorder, he conducted the Mayor's Court as if it were a vaudeville stage, frequently breaking up the proceedings with jokes and other displays of low-brow humor. His behavior probably contributed to the Court's eventual demise, a few months after his death in 1839.[89]

There was a certain cruel irony concerning the fact that Pentland would serve as prothonotary of Allegheny County for so many years, because, in the heat of the political battles of the first decade of the nineteenth century, Ephraim Pentland played a central role in an episode that resulted in the death of one of his predecessors, Tarleton Bates.

Tarleton Bates was a handsome, wavy-haired Virginian, a somewhat romantic character who was known to write love poems to girls who caught his eye.[90] He was born in 1775, the second son of a wealthy plantation owner who had lost most of his fortune while supporting the Revolution. Bates and his brothers—Charles, James (who would serve in Congress representing the Arkansas Territory), Frederick (who would become the first governor of the Missouri Territory) and Edward (who would serve as Attorney General under President Lincoln)—managed to receive a decent education, despite the family's setbacks; all of them were trained for the law. Tarleton sought his fortune in the frontier, arriving in Pittsburgh just after the conclusion of the Whiskey Rebellion in 1795. Rather than entering the bar, however, he secured a position as a clerk in the U.S. Army Commissary Department under Major Isaac Craig, son-in-law to General John Neville, the government inspector who lost his home during the Whiskey Rebellion. Soon thereafter, Bates became the assistant to the prothonotary, James Gilkinson, and was promoted to prothonotary upon Gilkinson's death in 1800. As Bates took his position with the courts, the electoral tide was just beginning to turn in favor of the Democratic-Republicans, and as a passionate Democratic-Republican, still in his twenties, Bates became one of the most public supporters of the Party.[91]

In the same year, John Israel, aided by Hugh Henry Brackenridge, founded an anti-Federalist newspaper called the *Tree of Liberty*. Soon Bates was writing polemical pieces for the *Tree*, and he became involved with a pair of like-minded young men, Henry Baldwin and Walter Forward. Henry Baldwin had come from New Haven, Connecticut, by way of Yale and the Philadelphia bar, in 1801, and quickly established himself as one of the leading lawyers in Pittsburgh. Walter Forward, who was also from Connecticut, came to Pittsburgh in 1803 with nothing but a change of clothes and a dollar in his pocket. Along the way, he picked up a horseshoe, which he used as payment for the ferry ride across the river on his way into Pittsburgh. Upon his arrival, he headed straight for Henry Baldwin's office, on the strength of Baldwin's reputation back in Connecticut. M. Flavia Taylor writes:

> *As [Forward] was reading the signs along Market Street to find Baldwin's office, Baldwin himself, who was just mounting his horse to start for Kittanning to attend court, asked him if he could be of any service. When Baldwin heard that Forward had come to Pittsburgh to study law with him, he gave him the key to his office and told him to study Blackstone until his return. In this way, Forward became associated with Baldwin ...*[92]

During the earliest days of the bar, even in the absence of formalized training for lawyers, one could argue that "reading law" was less an educational requirement than an opportunity to gain the society of a lawyer who would eventually support his admission—and, despite Forward's later reputation as an erudite lawyer and judge, this may have been especially true of the acceptance by Baldwin (age twenty-three) of Forward (age seventeen) as his law student.

This is not to say, however, that the process of "reading law" was not taken seriously by some preceptors. In 1825, Thomas Williams, a nineteen year-old graduate of Dickinson College in Carlisle, paid his customary two hundred dollars for three years of study to lawyer Richard Coulter, who was subsequently elected to Congress and called to Washington, D.C. before Williams could complete his course. He resumed his study with John Kennedy of Uniontown, who was known to suggest that every citizen of Pennsylvania, not just the lawyers, should read the following books in order to conduct himself with the requisite appreciation of his status and duties within American society: "Rollins' *Ancient History*, Gibbons' *Rome*, Gillie's *Greece*, Caesar's *Commentaries*, Tacitus' *Livy*, Plutarch's *Lives*, Hume's *England*, Hallam's *Middle Ages*, Robertson's *Charles the 5th*, Puffendorf's *Law of Nature*, Grotius *de jure pacis ac belli*, Paley's *Moral Philosophy*, Vatel's *Law of Nations*, Blackstone's *Commentaries*, Kent's *Commentaries*, Coke's *Commentary on Littleton*, Reed's *Blackstone*, The Constitution of the United States, in connection with the works called *The Federalist*, and *Rawle on the Consitution*."[93] It is probably safe to assume that Kennedy would have required Thomas Williams to master these works and more before he was admitted to the bar in 1828. By contrast, as Thomas Mellon recalled, "Our preceptor, Judge [Charles] Shaler, had taken little trouble with our legal education. He excused himself on the ground of press of business and because, as he alleged, we were progressing very well without his assistance. The most he did was occasionally to offer a word of advice."[94]

During this era, a would-be lawyer applied for admission to a local court rather than to a state bar, as the latter did not exist. After a lawyer was admitted in one county within Pennsylvania—"even in the most slipshod local court," as historian Robert R. Bell observes[95]—he could then customarily seek admission to the bar of any other county as a matter of right, "on certificate" of his prior admission to the other county bar. It was not until 1803, with the admission of James E. Heron, that a novice would be admitted following an examination in Allegheny County without a prior admission in another county.[96] By rule of the Pennsylvania Supreme Court, however, a novice candidate for the practice of law was required to serve four years of clerkship and one year of practice in the Court of Common Pleas, or to register for and complete three years of study and two years of practice (which apparently could be concurrent), to be followed by an oral examination by a standing panel of the county's lawyers, acting as a local board of examiners.[97]

Thomas Mellon recalled his own 1838 examination in detail:

The examining board at the time were not very punctual or attentive to their duties, though frequently exacting and critical when once in session; and it was only after several efforts and abortive attempts that [fellow candidate Thomas] MacConnell and I procured a meeting of a majority of the members at Mr. [Walter] Lowrie's office ... Those of the board who attended were Mr. Lowrie, James Finley—son of ex-governor Finley, and then a prominent lawyer here, Thomas H. Baird, ex-judge of Fayette and Washington county courts, and James Dunlop, author of the 'Digest;' all able and critical lawyers and rather jealous of each other's pretensions ... [T]he first question [to me] was by Judge Baird: 'Whether the consignor or consignee should bring suit against a common carrier in case of non-delivery of the goods' ... Discretion had taught me to answer as I had heard the judge rule, to the effect that the suit should be brought by the consignee ... Baird at once pronounced my answer erroneous, but Finley as promptly pronounced it correct; and the two immediately went into an excited discussion ... This was soon joined in by the other members of the board and kept up till it was time to adjourn.[98]

Despite the brevity and apparent inconclusiveness of the inquiry, Mellon received a note the next morning that the board was satisfied with his examination. After a successful examination, a young lawyer-candidate of the early nineteenth century such as Mellon would slip a dollar gratuity to George Kinzer, the chief tipstaff to the courts, and then be sworn into the Allegheny County bar.[99]

Walter Forward entered the bar in 1806. In the meantime, the three young professionals—Bates, Baldwin and Forward—soon became known as the "Great Triumvirate" around town. Young, robust and handsome, they were all fervent Democratic-Republicans with terrific powers of expression. They were dashing men-about-town, attending all the best picnics, concerts, horse races and parties. They were also the leaders of what became known as the "Clapboard Row Junto," meeting most evenings at the "Sign of General Butler," a tavern in the Diamond where Steele Semple, a Falstaffian land lawyer known to enjoy his wine, held court. There one could find Baldwin, smoking one of his favored small, black Spanish cigars and lecturing his student, Walter Forward, about the finer points of some case on which he was working; and in the breaks, the Great Triumvirate talked about politics endlessly into the night.[100]

In 1805, Governor McKean's second term was drawing to a close, and although he was a Democratic-Republican, he had gone against many of the ideas proposed by the more radical wing of his own Party, causing a split. Governor McKean's partisans, calling themselves the "Constitutionalists," found themselves being opposed by a group calling themselves the "Friends of the People" or "True Republicans," who nominated Simon Snyder to oppose McKean in his re-election bid.[b] The members of the Great Triumvirate counted themselves among Governor McKean's supporters, the Constitutionalists. As the split among the Democratic-Republicans became more heated, a new newspaper was launched to represent the point of view of the "Friends": Ephraim Pentland, another ambitious man in his twenties, became the editor and publisher of the *Commonwealth*, which spared no words in its efforts to discredit both Governor McKean and the *Tree of Liberty*, with personal attacks as brutal and provocative as those that we may now see on Twitter.

Governor McKean won re-election that November, with support from his former foes among the Federalists, who were nearly finished as an organized political party. On Christmas Day, 1805, still sore from McKean's victory, Pentland ran a column in the *Commonwealth* attacking Bates and Baldwin as "two of the most abandoned political miscreants that ever disgraced the state—despicable sycophants," and accusing them of being political opportunists. "[L]ike spaniels they lick the foot and court the favor of" the conservatives in power, Pentland wrote.[101]

On the night of January 2, 1806, Tarleton Bates decided to take his revenge on Pentland. Seeing him outside the offices of the *Commonwealth*, Bates stormed across the Diamond and began to cowhide Pentland with his whip. Suffering two or three lashes from Bates, Pentland turned and ran to the authorities. Pentland's account was that he was ambushed in the dark, and that Bates brought along two of his friends,

---

b   During the campaign, the "Friends" disparaged the Constitutionalists by calling them "Quids," while the Constitutionalists did the same by referring to the "Friends" as "Clodhoppers."

Henry Baldwin and Steele Semple, in case he needed help. Pentland added, sarcastically, that Baldwin and Semple were both "limbs of the law," and that, as lawyers, they were also "students of morality."[102] Bates, however, wrote on January 4 in the *Tree of Liberty* that the moon was full that evening, and so there was plenty of light for a good fight, and that he was alone. Moreover, he wrote, Pentland acted like a complete coward. The same issue of the *Tree of Liberty* also carried a letter from Baldwin and Semple, confirming Bates' account of the event.[103]

Although he originally intended to file assault charges against Bates, Pentland made a tactical decision to challenge Bates to a duel instead.

Duels were not altogether uncommon among these men in this day. Not long before, Henry Baldwin had fought a duel against another lawyer, Isaac Meason, Jr., over a grievance that has been described as either political or romantic in nature—possibly both. During the first round of pistol-fire, Baldwin was hit in the chest and began spitting up blood, so witnesses feared he had been shot through; but apparently a Spanish silver dollar in Baldwin's waistcoat pocket deflected Meason's bullet. The parties were scared off by a posse sent by Judge James Riddle before they could lob a second volley.[104] At Meadville in 1800, Pittsburgh lawyer Alexander W. Foster dueled with Major Roger Alden over a love affair; and despite the fact that Major Alden was crippled by Foster's shot, history records that Major Alden won the escapade, having won the heart of the woman in question in the process of being wounded by Foster.[105] In *Modern Chivalry*, Brackenridge had written about one of his protagonists, Captain Farrago, being the recipient of a challenge, answering as follows:

> *I have two objections to this duel matter. The one is, lest I should hurt you; and the other is, lest you should hurt me. I do not see any good it would do me to put a bullet through any part of your body. I could make no use of you when dead for any culinary purpose, as I would a rabbit or a turkey. ... If you want to try your pistols, take some object, a tree or a barn door about my dimensions. If you hit that, send me word, and I shall acknowledge that if I had been in the same place, you might also have hit me.*[106]

When Pentland challenged Bates, it had been a year and a half since Alexander Hamilton had been shot and killed by Aaron Burr in the most notorious duel of the young Republic; but even before that dreadful case, Pennsylvania had outlawed dueling in 1794, punishable by suspending one's citizenship for seven years, as well as a fine and imprisonment.[107] Pentland's challenge posed a dilemma for Bates. Although accepting a duel would mean that Bates could lose his public position as prothonotary, not accepting it could have been viewed by the public as taking the coward's way out.

One of Pentland's associates, a dry goods merchant named Thomas Stewart, carried the challenge to Bates personally on January 6, and as Pentland expected, Bates declined. That night, Pentland placed printed placards around the town that declared that Bates was a "coward and a poltroon." Bates responded angrily in the next issue of the *Tree of Liberty*, saying that he was provoked, after receiving so much personal insult in the pages of the *Commonwealth*, "into correcting the licentiousness of the press with the liberty of the cudgel" quoting Benjamin Franklin's "maxim." As to the invitation to duel, however, he said he had no more respect for the man who delivered the challenge (Stewart) than for Pentland himself, and that therefore he might be tempted to lash at Stewart as well.[108]

To Pentland and his friends, Bates' insult of Stewart was an escalation. Another young member of the bar, William Wilkins, showed up at the *Tree of Liberty* office and demanded an apology and a retraction from Bates on behalf of Pentland and Stewart. Bates refused, sending a note back saying that he "did not especially intend an implication of Mr. Stewart, nor specifically mean to excuse him." Egged on by Pentland and Wilkins, Stewart immediately challenged Bates to a duel, and Bates felt he had no choice at that point but to accept. Wilkins acted as Stewart's second, and Bates had Morgan Neville, a law student who was the grandson of General John Neville. The seconds worked out the details: they were to fight the duel the next day on land near the old Chadwick Farm where Three Mile Run emptied into the Monongahela River a few miles east of the city. On the night of January 7, Tarleton Bates made his last will and testament, naming his friend Henry Baldwin as his executor and asking to be either cremated or buried with no marker.[109]

On the cold and damp morning of January 8, 1806, the parties and their seconds met at Three Mile Run. The seconds prepared the pistols, loading powder and ball in each, and Bates and Stewart took their stands ten paces apart. As Michael Franchioni writes: "Standing back to back, then marching 10 paces, turning and firing, was not typical—aiming these weapons was difficult enough from a stationary position. The short, smooth bore of the pistols, an imprecise measure of powder and an only approximately spherical ball made the weapons wildly inaccurate, even as close as 10 paces. Only about one duel in 14 proved fatal."[110] The two men stood in the traditional sidestance dueling pose—with one's right leg in front of the left, looking over one's right shoulder and extended arm. Wilkins called out to Bates that an apology could still be accepted, but Bates did not answer him. One of the attending party then gave the commands. "Ready? Fire!"

Stewart and Bates each fired twice; the first shots missed, but in the second round, Stewart struck Bates in the chest. Bates fell over, and before a physician could be reached, he died from his wound.

The *Pittsburgh Gazette* observed that "The behaviour of the principals on the ground was perfectly calm and undaunted, and this unfortunate transaction was conducted in conformity to the arrangements, which had been previously made, and to the strictest rules of honour."[111] In his own newspaper, however, Pentland still could not resist his worst editorial instincts, persisting in calling the late Tarleton Bates a "coward" and a "liar."[112]

The largest funeral crowd in the history of Pittsburgh up to that time gathered at Trinity Episcopal Church for the funeral of Tarleton Bates, who was buried in an unmarked grave on the church grounds in accordance with his wishes. In view of the public outrage over Bates' death, Thomas Stewart fled to Baltimore; his store in Pittsburgh closed within a month after the incident. William Wilkins, too, was forced to leave Pittsburgh for a time, fleeing to a brother's home in Kentucky. In 1808, Simon Snyder, the "True Republican," was finally elected governor, which assured the installment of Ephraim Pentland as prothonotary. And Tarleton Bates was immortalized by the naming of Bates Street, which plunges down old Three Mile Run toward the Parkway East and the Monongahela River, near the site of the fatal duel.[113]

Not only would the Bates-Stewart duel be the last duel in Pittsburgh; it would also mark the end of a rough-and-tumble era of Pittsburgh politics, after which even the lawyers of the Pittsburgh bar would settle down and mostly confine their combat to wars of words. Henry Baldwin, Walter Forward and even William Wilkins would all survive their connection as supporting players in the sordid story surrounding the death of Tarleton Bates. The fact that they would prosper—not only as leading members of the bar of Allegheny County but as actors on the national legal and political stage—was probably a testament both to the unquestioned talent and integrity of these young men, as well as the growing political and economic importance of Pittsburgh.

Both Forward and Wilkins went on to very successful political and diplomatic careers, as well as serving on the bench. Forward even served in the same presidential cabinet as Wilkins, whom he referred to as "accessory to the death of the best of citizens the world has ever witnessed" shortly after Bates' death.[114] After a turn in Congress, Forward served as first comptroller of the U.S. Treasury under President William Henry Harrison, and then served as the fifteenth Secretary of the Treasury, under President John Tyler. He later served as charges d'affaires (ambassador) to Denmark under President Zachary Taylor and ended his career as the president judge of the District Court of Allegheny County. Wilkins, after his return from exile, became a judge of the County District Court, federal District Court judge and U.S. senator before serving as Minister to Russia and Secretary of War under President Tyler.[115]

Henry Baldwin, meanwhile, was elected as an Independent Republican[c] to Congress in 1816 on the strength of his support for higher tariffs on European goods—a position near-and-dear to the awakening manufacturing interests of greater Pittsburgh following the opening of trade after the War of 1812, but one which put him at odds with his agrarian friends in the old Democratic-Republican Party and his Democratic brethren in the South. As chair of the Committee on Manufactures, his advocacy of higher tariffs was so strident and so effective that among contemporaries he shared the title of "father of the American System" with his House colleague, Henry Clay.[116] While in Congress, however, Baldwin did manage to gain the unfailing gratitude of one prominent Southern Democrat, General Andrew Jackson. In 1818, General Jackson invaded Spanish-controlled Florida, allegedly without obtaining permission from President Monroe, and he nearly sparked an international incident when he summarily ordered the execution of two British subjects whom he had accused of inciting rebellion among the Seminoles. While many of Baldwin's colleagues in the House were ready to censure Jackson for his actions, Baldwin rose in defense of the General, and—taking a point of view that

---

c   Pennsylvania's "Independent Republicans" were, during this period, a faction of the Jeffersonian Democratic-Republican party. While they appealed to partisans of what was left of the Federalist party, many Independent Republicans were, like Baldwin, former Constitutionalist supporters of the Democratic-Republican governor of Pennsylvania, Thomas McKean. See James A. Kehl, *Ill Feeling in the Era of Good Feeling: Western Pennsylvania Political Battles 1815-1825* (Pittsburgh: University of Pittsburgh Press, 1956) 90-99.

was no doubt inspired by the prevailing legal climate in Pittsburgh—said that Jackson understood American laws and principles better in the wilderness of Florida, without a library, than many men who had actual books at their disposal.[117]

Baldwin resigned from Congress in the spring of 1822, suffering from a bout of illness and failing personal finances at the age of forty-two, but he returned to Pittsburgh to be greeted with a hero's welcome and a public banquet. During his absence from Washington, Baldwin kept up his acquaintance with Jackson; and when Jackson began to be touted for the presidency, Baldwin signed on with Pittsburgh attorney James Ross, the ex-U.S. senator from Pennsylvania, as one of Jackson's chief boosters in Western Pennsylvania, kicking things off with a toast to General Jackson at the 1823 St. Patrick's Day Celebration of the Erin Benevolent Society in Pittsburgh. The fete was attended by other prominent lawyers such as Baldwin's long-time intimate Walter Forward, their former adversary William Wilkins, Sidney Mountain and Harmar Denny.[118]

By the fall of 1824, Baldwin had done such an excellent job of organizing in Pennsylvania that the state went "Jackson mad" in the general election, handing Jackson his northernmost state victory against his opponents—John Quincy Adams, William H. Crawford and Henry Clay. Although Jackson led the national popular vote with forty-one percent to Adams' thirty percent, no candidate had gained an electoral majority. The fate of the election was handed to the U.S. House of Representatives, where Henry Clay threw his support behind Adams, thus permitting Adams to win the House vote. Much like the aftermath of the Bush-Gore disputed election of 2000, Jackson supporters felt that the election had been stolen from them, and they immediately began to campaign to elect Jackson in 1828. In the rematch, Jackson was elected handily over Adams, 178 to eighty-three electoral votes.

President Jackson nominated his friend Henry Baldwin to serve as Secretary of the Treasury, but Baldwin's confirmation was blocked by Vice President John C. Calhoun, who resented Baldwin's successful support of higher tariffs while in Congress. Baldwin thought that he had heard the last from President Jackson; however, in November 1829, U.S. Supreme Court Justice Bushrod Washington, the nephew of George Washington, died while on circuit duty in Philadelphia, and Jackson nominated Baldwin for Washington's seat on the U.S. Supreme Court. Baldwin was easily confirmed over the protests of the vice president, forty to two, and Baldwin took his seat on the Supreme Court in January 1830.[119]

The Court at that time was led by Chief Justice John Marshall, an old-time Federalist whose opinions on the Court reflected an overall expansion of federal powers. Long before Baldwin arrived on the Court, Marshall had abolished the old habit of permitting seriatim opinions (a series of opinions by more than one justice on the Court), which resulted in the Marshall Court appearing to speak with a unified voice. Thus, there were few published dissents on the Marshall Court until Baldwin joined it; in his first three terms on the Court, Baldwin dissented twelve times.[120] Baldwin's perseverance on the matter of dissenting opinions was partially responsible for inspiring today's common practice of publishing them alongside the majority opinion in the official reports. When Richard Peters, Jr., the reporter of the decisions of the Supreme Court, failed to publish some of Baldwin's dissenting opinions as part of the official record of the Supreme Court, Baldwin argued violently with Peters. Baldwin and Peters reached a kind of stilted détente on the matter, reflected, for example, in the extant footnotes to *Ex Parte Bradstreet*: at the end of the opinion, Peters includes a note to Baldwin *("Sir—I take the liberty to inclose a copy of the clerk's entry of the case 'Ex parte Martha Bradstreet,' and to ask if you dissented from the order of the court in the case. I shall be obliged by the return of the paper.")*, followed by the text of Baldwin's written dissent in the case.[121]

Not content to wait for Peters to agree with the idea of publishing dissenting opinions as a matter of course, however, Baldwin published some of his opinions in his own pamphlet, *A General View of the Origin and Nature of the Constitution and Government of the United States* (1837) in which he explained his "peculiar view of the constitution."[122] Asserting that the Constitution "shows the creature and the creator; the power which has made and can unmake the machine it has set in motion, as the work of its own hands, moving within defined limits, operating only on specified subjects, by delegated authority, revocable at will,"[123] he analyzes the positions of the federal and states' rights factions, noting

> *Those of one class, fearful of the recurrence of the evils of the [Articles of] confederation, adopt the most liberal rules of construction, in order to enlarge the granted powers of the federal government, and extend the restrictions on the states, and state laws, beyond their natural and obvious import. Those of the other class, more fearful of the gradual absorption of the powers of the states, by the assumption of powers tending to turn "a federal government of states" into a consolidated government of the Union; adopt the most narrow construction which can be put upon words, to contract the granted powers of the one, and the restrictions on the others, by which the reserved powers will be proportionably enlarged.*

He asserts that he is a member of neither class.[124] Frustrated by the ideological posturing of the federalists versus the states-rightists, Baldwin attempts to occupy the middle ground, protesting against federal restraints on interstate commerce, although he was never inflexible about the supremacy of state or federal power.

It has been fashionable for many years to say that Baldwin was an erratic jurist—that not only was he subject to paranoia and mood swings in his later years, the kind of behavior that led Justice Joseph Story to describe Baldwin as "uncomfortable, conceited, willful and wrong-headed," not to mention "partially deranged"[125]—but that his jurisprudence was inconsistent.[126] In the final analysis, despite the obtuseness of his pamphlet, Baldwin's opinions demonstrate that he believed that both an extreme view of state sovereignty and a too-enthusiastic expansion of federal power were both bad for jurisprudence; and that by being aware of the political context of a dispute, the Court could play the role of mediator in disputes between the federal and state governments, achieving an acceptable middle ground in the debate over federalism. Like Brackenridge before him, it would seem, the rough-and-tumble training he received in Pittsburgh—still considered to be a part of the Western frontier, although rapidly growing into a civilized metropolis—inspired Baldwin to seek moderation, or a "middle course."

Despite their differences over federalism and the administration of the Court, Baldwin and Chief Justice Marshall ultimately became close friends, and when Marshall fell mortally ill in Philadelphia in 1835, Baldwin kept vigil at Marshall's bedside.[127]

There is no question that Baldwin suffered from the workload of the Court. Baldwin had tried to leave the Court at the end of the 1831 Term, both for health and financial reasons, but President Jackson persuaded him to stay. He suffered a seizure and missed most of the 1833 Term; and many people believed that his personality was forever altered by the episode, that it was perhaps responsible for the mercurial temper he exhibited in his later years. Justice Baldwin passed away in Philadelphia on April 21, 1844 at the age of sixty-four, and unfortunately, he was so deeply in debt at the time of his death that his friends had to take up a collection to pay for his burial.[128]

Baldwin was ultimately succeeded on the United States Supreme Court by Allegheny County District Court Judge Robert Cooper Grier. After the death of Henry Baldwin in 1844, President John Tyler made two attempts to appoint his successor, but neither candidate was acceptable to the Senate. The seat was still open when Democrat James K. Polk entered the White House in 1845, and he, too, made two unsuccessful attempts to fill the vacancy. President Polk finally settled on the obscure Judge Grier, and the Senate unanimously approved Grier's appointment in August 1846.

The collegiality of the small Pittsburgh bar is readily apparent from an episode depicted in the diary of Robert McKnight, who entered the bar in 1842. On August 9, 1846, the day that news of Judge Grier's appointment by the Democratic president reached Pittsburgh, McKnight, who was a staunch Whig, wrote:

> *After tea, in company with W.B. McClure and T.J. Bigham—[I] crossed the bridge & called at the residence of Hon. Robert C. Grier, just appointed one of the Associate Justices of the U.S. Supreme Court, a highly honourable post. He had a long table plentifully covered with viands and an abundant supply of wines & ice. Most of the members of the Bar were there, & other friends, & festivity was the order of the night. The appointment is a good one, and the chief regret here is that our own Bench will be deprived of his services.*[129]

Such impromptu gatherings, involving nearly the entire bar, would become rare as the bar continued to grow in size. As tensions between North and South grew toward crisis, the most significant meetings of members of the bar would not be celebrations, nor would they be intellectual colloquia; instead they became recruiting rallies for the units of the Pennsylvania Volunteers who would go to battle for the preservation of the Union, or memorial tributes to fallen comrades.

To live in the frontier, away from the civilized center, is to take a risk; it is to flirt with the potential violence and brutality of the unknown. It was, in and of itself, tantamount to dissenting from the norms of the establishment, which is perhaps an indication of why themes of dissent, rebellion, risk-taking and occasional violence are so prevalent in the tales of the early bar of the little frontier settlement of Pittsburgh. Brackenridge and Baldwin were the leading Pittsburgh lawyers of their respective turbulent times, and both had been called mentally unstable at some point during their careers. Both sought advancement as political leaders, with only passing success; and after their political careers were over, both had managed to save enough political capital to merit appointments as judges on high courts. Despite some rhetorical gifts, especially in Brackenridge's case, both were misunderstood as they attempted to express the nature of their dissent from the status quo—a dissent not only from the status quo itself, but also a dissent from the nature of the debates between ideologues at both ends of the political spectrum. In an environment of violence, brutality and unknown risks, ideology was seen as a luxury by these Pittsburgh lawyers.

Henry Baldwin's unlikely ascent to the Supreme Court and his role in institutionalizing dissent on the Court may be seen as a frontier influence on American jurisprudence, coming by way of the habits of the Pittsburgh bar. As that tradition was enacted, however, the maturation of Pittsburgh's frontier democratic discourse was also on display. As Pittsburgh was beginning to evolve from a frontier town into an industrial capital, Pittsburgh lawyers would put away their whips and dueling pistols—even if some of them would soon resort to rifles and cannons in order to help preserve the viability of a legal document, the Constitution, in the coming decade.

CONFLAGRATION!

April 10, 1845: Amid the hustle and bustle of the city, at the corner of Third and Cherry there stood the imposing Greek Revival three-story building that served as the home of the Western University of Pennsylvania, now known as the University of Pittsburgh. It was the school created by the state charter secured by Hugh Henry Brackenridge when he was a member of the Pennsylvania State Assembly. A little over a year before this date, in the Fall of 1843, Heman Dyer, the principal of the University, established a law school under the direction of a well-respected Pittsburgh attorney, Walter Hoge Lowrie, announcing classes in law for $37.50 per term, "payable in advance."[130]

In the 1840s, there were less than a dozen law schools in the country.[131] Throughout the United States, most lawyers were still trained through the apprentice system, although many attended college and obtained undergraduate degrees before "reading law" with a practicing attorney. The rolls of Pittsburgh lawyers from the period list many graduates from Dickinson, Washington College, Jefferson College and the Western University, but apparently only two members of the County bar from 1788 to 1843 had attended law schools. Andrew Wylie, who served as Pittsburgh city solicitor, studied law at Transylvania University in Lexington, Kentucky, and John A. Wills graduated from Harvard Law School which, as the nation's oldest law school, had been established in 1817.[132] Although students sometimes agitated for a formal education in the law because the drudgery of office training could leave them a bit restless, practicing lawyers had a stake in perpetuating the apprenticeship system. Taking on students was a source of both revenue and cheap labor for the practicing lawyer, in that students generally paid a fee to their preceptors and did routine work around the office. Moreover, the system allowed lawyers to maintain direct control over the membership of the bar. Lowrie's law school was, to say the least, an experiment that was viewed warily by his colleagues.[133]

On this particular morning, April 10, 1845, it was a clear, cloudless and blustery day. High winds were kicking up billows of dust in the streets. There was plenty of dust to go around. Pittsburgh had not seen any rain for several weeks, and the parched streets needed a good rinsing.[134]

That morning, Thomas Mellon, indefatigable in both law and capital projects, was running back and forth between a house he had under construction at the corner of Wylie and Fifth Avenue, and the courthouse, where he was checking his cases on the trial list.[135] Young Robert McKnight, just three years at the bar, was in the office he shared with his law partner, old Henry Magraw, writing letters.[136] Samuel Kingston, a lawyer who was described by the diarist Mrs. Ann Royall as "thin and fair, with a full lively grey eye … a perfect gentleman in his manners and countenance peculiarly interesting,"[137] was presumably working on conveyances in his office on the corner of Fourth and Smithfield. Now in his late fifties and a member of the bar for a little over thirty years, Kingston had in 1808 opened one of the city's earliest schools, teaching "reading, writing, arithmetic, book-keeping, English grammar, geography, measuration, trigonometry and navigation."[138]

Around noon, McKnight heard the firehouse bells. He rushed outside his office and "followed the crowd down Second Street, to the corner of Ferry, where an icehouse and shed were burning. A pretty strong wind was blowing from the West," McKnight recalled, "and some alarm existed to the spread of flames."[139]

Although the exact cause remains unproven to this day, legend holds that an "Irish washerwoman" had entered a vacant lot not far from her employer's establishment to do some laundry. She lit a fire to boil some water and stepped inside a shed on the lot. In a matter of moments, the wind kicked up some embers against the adjoining wooden building, Colonel Diehl's icehouse, and soon all the nearby wooden buildings along the south side of Second Street were burning. Pittsburgh's volunteer fire companies, such as the Allegheny, the Vigilant and the Neptune, responded to the call for help, but their violent pumping for water from the city wells yielded little more than a muddy trickle with which to douse the flames, and their hoses were too short to reach the river. They went at the growing conflagration with mere bucketfuls of water, to no avail.[140]

McKnight was, at the time, beginning a flirtation with Elizabeth O'Hara Denny, the daughter of one of Pittsburgh's wealthiest lawyers, Harmar Denny.[d] Grasping the seriousness of the situation, Robert McKnight first rushed to Mr. Denny's downtown home, where he found all the male members of the family absent. McKnight helped the women and servants rescue some of their belongings. After lending his aid there, he soon found himself fighting through "[d]rays, cars, furniture, horses … running in all directions" to get back to his law office, where he helped Magraw to pack their law books in bed ticking and take them out to the street, whisking them away from the fire as it came "hissing and leaping from house to house & square to square."[141]

At first, Thomas Mellon paid no attention to the sound of the firehouse bells, until he encountered several excited people running up the street declaring that the town was on fire. Getting a taste of the chaos that McKnight had encountered down in the

---

d   Robert McKnight married Elizabeth O'Hara Denny in 1847.

streets, Mellon went up to the roof of the courthouse, "from which the sight was grand and appalling. It was about four o'clock," he recalled,

> *and the fire had progressed from Ferry street consuming everything between Fourth street and the river, and was now in its utmost fury approaching Smithfield, surging like a vast flood, devouring dwellings, warehouses and churches ... In a few minutes it approached the Monongahela House; the flames soon shot into the sky from the entire area of the building, and directly the wooden covered Monongahela bridge was on fire, one span speedily falling into the river after another, like a straw rope on fire, until in about twenty minutes the fire reached the South Side and the structure disappeared.*[142]

Someone must have seen Samuel Kingston hurrying down Second Street towards his house, straight into the thick black smoke. Some said he had some of his private papers on his mind and that he meant to go in and save them; others said that the former schoolmaster was particularly interested in rescuing a treasured "painted piano."[143] Most of the city's inhabitants, however, simply turned and fled the encroaching flames. "It was as much as the occupants of stores and dwellings and factories could do," Mellon later wrote, "to escape with their lives."[144]

By five o'clock, the fire had done its worst. Approximately one thousand buildings, across twenty to twenty-six blocks or fifty-six acres of the city, were destroyed, and another one hundred and fifty buildings were heavily damaged. Estimates of the value of personal and property damage from the fire were reliably placed between ten to twenty million dollars—losses of such incomprehensible magnitude that most of Pittsburgh's insurance agencies were ultimately ruined.[145] On April 11, the day after the fire, McKnight took a walk through the burnt-out streets, lamenting "the sad spectacle of the fairest portion of the city 'a heap of ruins laid.'"[146]

Pittsburgh's local government encountered some difficulty in marshaling and reforming its parts and pieces under trying circumstances—especially in light of the fact that the mayor's office itself was destroyed. When the select and common councils of Pittsburgh finally did meet, however—although there was not a single lawyer among their members—they decided to send two of the city's most prominent lawyers to Harrisburg to plead the city's case for financial assistance. Cornelius Darragh, then serving in Congress, and Wilson McCandless were directed to proceed to the State Capitol at once to ask for relief while the legislature was still in session, and the legislature responded in kind by providing immediate emergency funds to be distributed to the fire's victims, and by remitting state and local taxes paid on real estate that had been destroyed in the fire.[147] In addition to state aid, within days Pittsburgh began to receive personal contributions from around the world. President James K. Polk and former president John Quincy Adams sent donations, as did future president James Buchanan; and a Steubenville lawyer named Edwin Stanton, soon to cut his own wide swath within the courtrooms of Pittsburgh, gave twenty-five dollars.[148]

In the aftermath, it became clear that Pittsburgh's lawyers suffered as much as anyone did. Harmar Denny's four-bedroom house on Market Street did indeed go up in flames, as did the homes of lawyers Edward Simpson and James Ross Jr.; many others lost their offices.[149] Poor Thomas James "T.J." Bigham, one of the up-and-coming leaders of the bar, lost everything—his "office, lodging, furnishings, library of law, scientific and general works, notes, papers, and memoranda."[150] He was lucky to get away with the suit of clothes on his back.

Sadly, there were also two mortal casualties among Pittsburgh's legal community. The body of Samuel Kingston was found nearly a month after the fire in a neighbor's house on Second Street. Apparently blinded by the smoke on his way home, he stumbled into his neighbor's cellar and became trapped. Miraculously, only one other person died in the fire—a Mrs. Maglone, who was last seen wearing a crossbarred flannel dress and a hood bonnet, walking near the Scotch Hill Market House on Second Street.[151]

The legal community's other "death" at the hands of the "Great Fire of Pittsburgh" came a little more gradually. The University building on Third and Cherry and all its contents were completely destroyed. Since the University's law students had, after all, paid in advance, Walter Lowrie kept the ill-fated law school together, eventually holding classes in a new University Building on Duquesne Way. Of the first four students who graduated with a "bachelor of laws" degree (in the Class of 1847), only two entered the Pittsburgh bar, and both of them left town shortly thereafter. In 1849, the Duquesne Way building was also destroyed in a fire, and Lowrie moved his classes to the basement of the Third Presbyterian Church. Heman Dyer, the principal who had founded the law program, left Pittsburgh for Philadelphia to work with the American Sunday School Union. Already disrupted by two fires, Pittsburgh's first experiment in establishing a law school closed its doors for good in 1851, when Lowrie was elevated to the Pennsylvania Supreme Court.[152]

Although the law school had folded, the Pittsburgh bar was supporting other institutions. In 1831, a cadre of elite lawyers formed the Pittsburgh Law Academy, an exclusive club that met weekly, holding debates on such topics as "Is an act of the Legislature granting authority to the Supreme Court to charter religious and charitable institutions constitutional?" or "Ought the United States Bank be rechartered?" The Academy continued to meet over the next few decades, though with declining frequency, until the 1880s.[153]

A "bar association" had not yet been formed, but by the 1850s, the Pittsburgh bar was large enough to support another adjunct institution, the *Pittsburgh Legal Journal*. Its founder, Thomas Johnston Keenan, attended Dickinson College before entering the bar in 1846. His uncle, Hugh Keenan, a former U.S. consul in Ireland, had established what must be considered Pittsburgh's first international law firm, the European and American Law Agency, and had crossed the Atlantic more than fifty times in support of it. Shortly after Thomas' entry to the bar, Uncle Hugh decided to curtail his travels and enlisted Thomas as his proxy abroad; by 1853, Thomas had crossed the Atlantic eighteen times, developing a particular expertise in the preparation of documents for use "in the British Dominion."[154]

Like his uncle before him, however, Thomas grew tired of transatlantic travel, and decided to enter the newspaper business. On Saturday, April 23, 1853, Keenan, assisted in the editing room by his Dickinson classmate and fellow lawyer Albert McCalmont, published the first weekly issue of the *Pittsburgh Legal Journal*. The price was five cents, or two dollars in advance for a year's subscription. Emblazoned across the first page were the lurid details of the local trial of Mary Jones, alias Mary Delaney, for the murder of Jacob Shaw. Colonel Samuel W. Black and Cornelius Darragh represented Miss Delaney, while District Attorney Francis Flanegin acted for the prosecution, aided by Thornton Shinn and John Henry Hampton.

Despite the sensationalist debut of the *Journal*, Keenan had high-minded objectives for the publication. In an editorial entitled "Our First Number," Keenan declared that he founded the *Journal* "because there is a necessity for the enterprise, and a reasonable hope of its ultimate success ... [rather than for] any expectation of immediate profit." Noting that "[i]n times of violence the history of a nation is the detailed events of its battles," he declared that in times of peace, it is in the courts of law that we come to know a nation. "We learn the state of society, the intelligence of the people, their degree of refinement—all in the proceedings of a single case." On a more practical level, Keenan explained that the bench and bar of Pittsburgh stood at the forefront of the legal profession in the "Western United States," and that

[t]he immense amount of cases disposed of in our different Courts, varied and interesting in character, the ability of the Judges who preside in them, and the well-earned reputation of the Pittsburgh Bar, warrant the presumption, that a paper which shall afford an accurate view of the course of judicial proceedings, and the state of legal sentiment in this city, will be a valuable acquisition to the legal profession in the West, and to our citizens generally.[155]

While continuing to edit the *Journal*, Keenan was named prothonotary of the Pennsylvania Supreme Court, Western District, in 1858, which gave him direct access to many opinions and proceedings that would not have otherwise been covered by the general press, and continued to put him in direct contact with the community of Pittsburgh lawyers who would regularly appear as "characters"—and advertisers[e] - in his weekly chronicle. Keenan's instincts about the formula for the *Journal's* success ultimately proved to be right. Still published today by the Allegheny County Bar Association, the *Journal* is known as the second oldest legal periodical in the United States and the third oldest in the world.

The *Journal's* success was also undoubtedly a reflection of the growth in legal activity in the city, a result of the growth in commerce in Pittsburgh after the Great Fire. As it was being rebuilt, Pittsburgh began to assume a new identity. From the ashes of the Great Fire grew a city of little factories, nestling by the riverfront, poised to take advantage of Pittsburgh's natural resources. Its proud and abundant labor force, rubbing up against the rapacity of the region's entrepreneurs, would provide the spark for other conflagrations during the era.

One case in point occurred on Monday morning, July 31, 1848. The Allegheny County high sheriff, his posse of Pittsburgh policemen, and a detachment of Allegheny City policemen proved to be no match for an army of several hundred potato-throwing, axe-wielding women and girls who broke down barricades and stormed the Penn Cotton Factory in Allegheny City. By the time the mob fought its way into the inner

---

e Typically, a name and an address, a business card printed on a page of the *Journal*—nothing like the full or half page advertisements for law firms that would become commonplace in the 1980s.

yard of the Factory—provoked, in part, by one of the Factory owners shooting hot steam at the picketers, scalding a young girl as she stood outside the Factory gates—the outnumbered peacekeepers had no choice but to run away or get beaten. Once inside, the rioters proceeded to smash equipment and machinery. They remained in control of the Factory until the late afternoon.[156]

The women and girls were all wage-earning textile workers, paid between two dollars and $6.50 per week to a man's $7.50 per week, who were protesting the Factory's unwillingness to submit to a new Pennsylvania law limiting a day's work in textile factories to ten hours. Up until the passage of the law in March 1848, the standard work-day in a Pittsburgh textile mill was twelve hours. The new law had a loophole, however, which had essentially defined a choice for all workers over fourteen years old—either submit to reduced wages for a ten-hour day, or enter a special contract with the mill waving one's statutory right to a ten-hour day and committing to a twelve-hour day for higher wages.[157]

Pittsburgh's textile trade ground to a halt while newspapers and speakers at public meetings debated the merits of the ten-hour work day and either called for justice against the rioters or justice against the mill owners. Once the mills returned to something resembling the old routine that October, however, public attention turned to the upcoming trial of sixteen alleged ringleaders of the Penn Cotton Factory riot—five of whom were young women.

There was no shortage of eminent lawyers who rushed forward to defend the rioters. Colonel Samuel W. Black and Cornelius Darragh, two of the finest orators of the bar, took the lead for the defense, assisted by Harry M. Kennedy and Edmund Snowden, a couple of young lawyers who had been active in public meetings supporting the workers, and Albert B. McCalmont, who opened the defense case. When Judge Benjamin Patton, president judge of the Common Pleas Court, asked who was appearing for the defense, Colonel Black shouted, "The whole of the Bar, and one or two from Mercer [County]," sending the courtroom into gales of laughter.[158]

Allegheny County, of course, had its own District Attorney, then called a "Deputy Attorney General" of the Commonwealth. It was customary, however, for the county to bring in private lawyers to take the lead in criminal prosecutions, and several of the mill owners contributed funds for the engagement of Charles Shaler and his new law partner, Edwin McMasters Stanton from Steubenville, to conduct the prosecution on behalf of the County, along with T.J. Bigham and James Callam. Shaler was a towering figure in Pittsburgh legal circles as the former president judge of the Allegheny County Court of Common Pleas and a former associate law judge of the Allegheny County District Court. Shaler was also, incidentally, a Democrat who was sympathetic to the rioters' cause. He had even given a speech in support of the ten-hour day to a crowd of cotton workers at a rally at the Allegheny Market House on July 18, thirteen days before the riot.[159]

That Steubenville lawyer, Edwin Stanton, was a bit of an unknown in Pittsburgh. Stanton had studied at Kenyon College for a year before financial hardship forced him to drop out and take on gainful employment to support his widowed mother and sisters. He was invited to read law with a friend of the family and entered the bar at St. Clairsville, Ohio in 1835. By the 1840s, Stanton had become one of the busiest lawyers in Ohio: he maintained separate law partnerships with George W. McCook in Steubenville, S.G. Peppard in Cadiz, and Theobald Umbstaetter and Jonathan H. Wallace in New Lisbon, and loose affiliations with lawyers Daniel Peck in St. Clairsville, E.R. Eckley in Carrollton, and Joseph Sharon in Harrison, Ohio.[160] Edwin McMasters Stanton was a one-man Ohio mega-firm when he took up residence in the newly-rebuilt Monongahela House Hotel in Pittsburgh, in search of more challenging cases, and entered a new partnership with Charles Shaler in October 1847.

Law partnerships were the exception rather than the norm during this period in Pittsburgh.[161] Many lawyers of the period preferred to practice alone, making associations with other lawyers only in particular cases. Thomas Mellon went so far as to say that "as a general rule there is no benefit in law partnerships. The confidential relation of attorney and client is of a personal character, and the attorney who has sufficient ability to attract clients can accomplish as much by competent clerks as by partners."[162] When partnerships did exist, the ties were often familial: the Fetterman brothers, Washington and Nathaniel, practiced criminal law and presented themselves to the city as a partnership beginning in the early 1820s;[163] Metcalf & Loomis, a partnership of two politically active cousins, Orlando Williams Metcalf and Andrew Williams Loomis, was a significant firm in Pittsburgh from 1831 until Orlando Metcalf's death from cholera in 1850;[164] and Moses Hampton practiced in partnership with his brother-in-law, Alexander H. Miller, until Hampton was elected to Congress in 1846. He later practiced with his son, John Henry Hampton, their firm styled as Hampton & Son.[165] By way of exception to the rule, Thomas M. Marshall recalled that during the 1840s, the firm of McCandless & McClure (consisting of unrelated lawyers Wilson McCandless and William B. McClure) "did half the business of the Bar" before both partners ultimately went on the bench.[166]

Stanton had developed his law partnerships in Ohio as a means for staying busy constantly. Historian Monte A. Calvert referred to him as a "veritable legal machine, driven by a kind of power lust" after the death of his first wife in 1844 left him in a state of depression, with little to live for but his work.[167] In Pittsburgh, the firm of Shaler, Stanton and Umbstaetter (Theobald Umbstaetter moved to Pittsburgh in 1850) became a successful early example of the division of labor among lawyers. Shaler was a well-known community figure and a former judge, undoubtedly an attractor of law business in downtown Pittsburgh. "As neither Shaler nor Stanton had an aptitude for keeping accounts," recalled Robert T. Hunt, Umbstaetter "was brought in to take care of the office business." With Stanton working at the reins of the firm's cases, the firm began to command large fees—ten thousand dollars for a single opinion, as Shaler's son recalled.[168]

Meanwhile, Stanton's brusqueness and impatience with colleagues and opponents alike seem to have been deep-seated personality traits; but, hurried along by the pressures of travel and a crowded docket, these qualities evidently contributed to the evolution of a courtroom style unlike that of most other lawyers of his time. Most Pittsburgh trial lawyers of the early nineteenth century were stage performers who played to the gallery and composed their arguments as though they were telling stories around a campfire: they let their narratives unfold chronologically, laden with elaborate detail and punctuated with witty asides to keep the crowd alert, drawing their audiences in and leading them to an inevitable punch-line—the moral of the story, the astonishing hidden fact, the capstone of the argument.

In the early nineteenth century, law was a public profession, practiced before a live audience, to a much greater extent than we can fathom today, even with the advent of cameras and cable television networks inhabiting courtrooms. In an era when leisure pursuits were scarce, especially for the working class, a trip to the courthouse to hear the latest courtroom speech by James Ross or Walter Forward, particularly in a scandalous criminal case, was an inexpensive dramatic entertainment, a free spectator sport. The blurring of the lines between trial advocacy and theater took a more obvious turn with the formation in 1823 of a Thespian Society, in which some of the more prominent younger members of the Pittsburgh bar were active. The Thespians—who included such lawyers and judges as Magnus Murray, William Wilkins, Richard Biddle, Charles Shaler, Duncan Walker, Alexander Brackenridge, Sidney Mountain, Benjamin Evans, Trevanion B. Dallas and James S. Craft—put on shows such as *Tom and Jerry, or High Life in London*, a stage adaptation of the popular serialized novel by Pierce Egan, at the Third Street Theatre, with the proceeds going to charity. The financial failure of the venture after less than two years had more to do with the acquisition of expensive stage scenery,[169] it seems, than to the quality of the performances. Eager audiences continued to flock to the courthouse on Market Street to see the actors on their own stage.

Edwin Stanton was generally dismissive of dramatic excesses and florid oratory. His cousin William recalled how Stanton had once shown his short-fuse over the humorous opening statement of his opposing counsel. Stanton sprang to his feet haughtily after his opponent finished and barked, "Now that this extraordinary flow of wit has ceased I will begin"—to which his opponent replied, "Wit always ceases when you begin," causing an uproar of laughter. Cousin William records, however, that Stanton nonetheless won the case with his sober, unerringly logical and deliberate presentation.[170]

Perhaps one key to the difference in Stanton's way of developing his trial speeches can be found in the assertion by at least one journalism historian that Edwin Stanton, through his relations with the press as President Lincoln's Secretary of War, was influential in the adoption of the "inverted pyramid" style of writing by American journalists—a system of ordering facts in descending order of importance, providing the "gist" of the news first and the details later, as opposed to leading the reader through the chronological details of the story, only to provide the "gist" in the last paragraph. Nowhere is Stanton's use of this style more evident than in his official dispatch concerning the assassination of President Lincoln, in which, as his biographer Benjamin P. Thomas notes, Stanton assembled a "logical narrative of the attacks on Lincoln and Seward from the incoherent accounts he had heard," a narrative that was published almost verbatim by the major newspapers of the day. It is for this reason that historian David T.Z. Mindich states that on or about April 15, 1865, the date of Lincoln's death, "the character of news writing changed" in the U.S.[171]

Stanton's approach was anomalous enough in 1848, however, that at the close of the case against the Allegheny Cotton rioters, it was decided that both Shaler and Stanton would make closing arguments for the prosecution. Shaler's closing was typical of the day. As Calvert writes, Shaler was "florid, eloquent, and occasionally witty or sarcastic in his remarks" to the jury, and the spectators were not disappointed by his performance. Stanton's address was more focused, constructing for his listeners a picture of the legal relations among the state, the employers and the laborers, and emphasizing that it was not the ten-hour day that was on trial in the case, but rather whether the state would tolerate mob rule. In a free government, Stanton explained, where people make the laws, there is no excuse for the violent redress of grievances. Finally, in an attempt to counteract the defense's attempts to draw sympathy from the jurors due to the fact that some of the defendants were young women, Stanton turned his sharp tongue on them: when females engage in mob violence, he declared, they forfeit "all title to consideration of pity." The defense's closing arguments, made by Kennedy and Colonel Black, were said to be masterful pieces of oratory but were, by contrast, fragmented and somewhat superficial. The jury was out for nine hours before returning with a verdict against thirteen of the fifteen defendants—including all of the women.[172] Within a few years, the ten-hour law as applied in textile factories began to be a moot issue, as factory owners moved their factories elsewhere; the riots were the beginning of the end of Pittsburgh's textile industry.[173]

Stanton was, in any event, "writing ... inverted pyramids at a time when chronological forms were still standard," according to Mindich,[174] suggesting a kind of stubbornly focused, "fact-intensive" method of organizing information that was not generally shared by other communicators of his day, but one that nonetheless proved to be quite effective. In this sense, Stanton has to be seen as a forerunner of the modern trial lawyer, who is advised during his or her training, for example, to provide an overview of the issues at trial first, followed by a list of what facts he or she intends to prove at trial, and finally a preview of how he or she will prove such facts—all in an orderly, disciplined and focused manner.

If the Allegheny Cotton riots case established Stanton's reputation as a formidable combatant within the Pittsburgh legal community, the *Wheeling Bridge* case made him something of a legend in the Pittsburgh bar for the lengths and depths of his case preparation, factual research, extraordinary tactical sense, and flawless execution.

Ever since 1816, the river men of Pittsburgh lived under the threat that a bridge might be built on the Ohio River at Wheeling, Virginia,[f] that might be too low to allow river traffic north to Pittsburgh, thus rendering Pittsburgh's importance as a gateway port to the West less significant. In 1816, the states of Ohio and Virginia tried to convince Congress to build such a bridge, but the outcry from the northern cities on the river shouted down the initiative. In 1847, however, a few private parties obtained a state charter from the Virginia legislature for the Wheeling & Belmont Bridge Company, and started to build the 1,010-foot long suspension bridge across the Ohio at Wheeling.[175]

---

f   Prior to the breakaway of Unionist counties of Northwest Virginia to form the state of West Virginia in 1863, Wheeling was a part of the Commonwealth of Virginia.

As a resident of the newly-rebuilt Monongahela House at the corner of Smithfield and Water (Fort Pitt) Streets, overlooking the steamboat docks on the Monongahela, Stanton became a familiar figure to the river men. In the spring of 1849, Stanton represented a steamboat bartender in a murder case, beating the indictment on an argument of self-defense.[176] He was also engaged in representing the interests of the Pittsburgh river men by trying to get the townships along the river to stop charging wharf fees, challenging them on the basis that the fees were a tax on interstate commerce in plain violation of the Constitution.[177] As the Wheeling & Belmont Bridge Company busied itself with building the bridge, the river men came to Stanton.

Stanton laid out a precise plan of action. He decided immediately that he could not bring suit in the Virginia courts because they were not likely to hear a case by out-of-staters against the state itself. He also ruled out bringing suit in federal District Court, because he anticipated that there would be delays and appeals over which federal venue was most appropriate. Stanton calculated that he had to get the suit into the U.S. Supreme Court as a case of original jurisdiction, arguing for an injunction to abate the bridge as a state versus state conflict, an issue worthy of the Supreme Court's attention. Stanton filed the lawsuit in July 1849, a few days after Pennsylvania attorney general Cornelius Darragh announced that Pennsylvania would take a direct interest in the controversy. John Cadwalader, the Philadelphia lawyer who was engaged by Wheeling & Belmont to oppose Stanton, had trouble finding the suit on the docket, until he had a chance meeting with Supreme Court Justice Robert Cooper Grier, the former Allegheny County judge, who told Cadwalader that he had recently received a telegram from Stanton asking if he would be available in August to hear an application for an injunction.[178]

At the injunction hearing, although Justice Grier was impressed by Stanton's argument on the Supreme Court's jurisdiction over the controversy, he failed to grant a preliminary injunction against the building of the bridge. Grier did, however, send the case to the full Supreme Court for a determination over whether Pennsylvania could show actual injury from the bridge.

Unrestricted by the courts, the bridge was completed and formally opened on November 15, 1849. A few days before the formal opening, however, there were a pair of clashes between the Pittsburgh river men and the Bridge Company. First, on November 10, the steamship *Messenger* traveled from Pittsburgh to the nearly-finished bridge, and could not clear it until it had seven and a half feet of chimney cut off. The next day, the steamer *Hibernia No. 2* attempted to navigate past the bridge. But again, its chimneys were too high. Rather than ram through the bridge or cut down the ship's chimneys, the captain of the *Hibernia No. 2* ordered that the ship's passengers and cargo should be transferred to other conveyances. The Wheeling press insisted that Stanton had himself suggested that the ships should test the bridge, after rains raised the level of the river,[179] and the Bridge Company complained that the *Hibernia No. 2* in particular had chimneys that were simply outlandish in their height. A few days later, Stanton amended Pennsylvania's complaint to include the "loss and injury" to the owners of the *Messenger* and the *Hibernia No. 2*, as well as to the trade and commerce of Pittsburgh and Pennsylvania.[180] Stanton meanwhile proceeded to build his argument around painstaking research proving that the current state of steamship art demanded certain ship dimensions. He commissioned scientific investigations on different fuel types and ships of different heights, and collected statistics up and down the river on the cost of transport by rail, wagon and boat to support the economic argument.

Extensive practical research was a hallmark of Stanton's approach to a case. After Stanton delivered his argument in a lawsuit against the Harmony Society, a religious community in Economy, Pennsylvania, for example, one of the Harmony elders crossed the aisle to compliment him on his speech and to ask Stanton where he had studied Divinity; Stanton had to admit that he had only studied it informally, as preparation for the case.[181] Such painstaking research did not come without a price for Stanton, however. While doing his research for the *Wheeling Bridge* case, Stanton slipped and fell down the companionway of the steamship *Isaac Newton,* and broke the kneecap of the leg he had already recently injured slipping on some ice in downtown Pittsburgh.[182]

After lying flat on his back recuperating for a few weeks, Stanton endured the pain from his injuries while traveling to Washington, D.C. for the first full Supreme Court argument on the case on February 25, 1850. In the interim, the parties had submitted their evidence to a special master appointed by the Court, but neither side was satisfied with the master's report. The final arguments on the case were heard in December 1851.

By all accounts, Stanton was brilliant at the final oral argument—so brilliant that three of the Supreme Court justices thanked Stanton for bringing the case before them. Walking painstakingly through the research he had collected, he gave them a barrage of facts and figures. Stanton argued that the Wheeling Bridge represented the only obstruction to large steamships on the Ohio-Mississippi river systems, which made it an unusual feature; that larger packets were best adapted to conducting Ohio river commerce, evidenced by the fact the seven large boats of the Pittsburgh and Cincinnati Packet Line represented three-fourths of the travels and one-half of the trade on the river; that the peculiar design of the Wheeling Bridge offered no level headway, so that even if a certain height were available at the center of the bridge, the slope of the bridge's form made it too low for a ship of any width to pass through; that tall chimneys "were essential to the end [of greater steam power]" based on observations of ocean and river operations and that modifications of steamships to shorten chimneys would be costly and potentially dangerous. He even offered evidence that the Wheeling Bridge was supposed to be profitable enough that to modify its span to permit tall steamships to pass through would not be a hardship to the Wheeling & Belmont Company.[183] Ultimately, the Court ordered a full judgment, with costs, in favor of the Commonwealth of Pennsylvania and the Pittsburgh river men.[g] [184]

After the *Wheeling Bridge* case, Stanton began receiving invitations from around the country to join lawyers in important cases as co-counsel, including the McCormick reaper patent case in Chicago and Cincinnati, beginning in 1854—during which Stanton famously snubbed his local co-counsel, a little-known Springfield lawyer named Abraham

---

g   In August 1851, Congress passed a law legalizing the existing conditions of the Bridge and requiring steamboats to regulate their chimneys in such a way as to pass under the Bridge. In 1854, however, a gale force wind knocked the Bridge down.

Lincoln, by refusing to dine with him or walk with him into the courthouse.[185] After permanently leaving Pittsburgh for Washington, D.C. in 1856, Stanton played a key role in the infamous Daniel Sickles murder trial in Washington, in which Stanton was part of the team that gained Sickles' acquittal for murdering the lover of his wife on the grounds that Sickles was temporarily insane, marking the first prominent use of the insanity defense in American jurisprudence.[186]

In 1860, Stanton—who was an anti-slavery Democrat—was appointed U.S. Attorney General by his fellow Democrat, President James Buchanan. After Abraham Lincoln, a Republican, succeeded Buchanan, Stanton remained in Washington, acting as an outside advisor to Lincoln's first Secretary of War, Simon Cameron, until Lincoln removed Cameron in 1862 for his mismanagement of War Department contracts. At the urging of his Secretaries of State and Treasury, William Seward and Salmon Chase, Lincoln appointed Stanton as his Secretary of War.

For nine years, Edwin Stanton was not only considered to be one of the most effective lawyers in Pittsburgh, with an approach to trial advocacy that was ahead of its time, but he also became one of the nation's leading lawyers. Undoubtedly, his national status reflected well on the Pittsburgh bar, and even helped elevate the status of members of the Pittsburgh bar when Stanton ultimately assumed his duties within the president's cabinet and, during a time of great crisis, provided indispensable leadership.

One of the issues that consumed the political passions of Americans in the years leading up to that crisis—the controversies surrounding slavery and African American citizenship—were ideas with which Pittsburgh lawyers, as well as other partisans around the country, had been wrestling for some time. The first stirrings of the abolitionist movement in Western Pennsylvania were recorded inside the Sign of General Butler tavern in the early 1800s, where Henry Baldwin, Tarleton Bates and Walter Forward held court with other members of the Jeffersonian "Clapboard Row Junto" such as Dr. William Gazzam and Dr. Andrew Richardson. Dr. Gazzam, for one, spoke for the Junto when he said that he "abhorred slavery and relied upon the constituted authorities to effect the very desirable object of the gradual abolition thereof."[187] Anti-slavery was a leitmotif for one of the honorary senior members of the Junto, Hugh Henry Brackenridge. Writing in his *United States Magazine* in December 1779, Brackenridge declared that "[i]t casts a shade upon the face of this country that some of those who cultivate her soil are slaves," and suggested that slaves be granted their freedom and given land in the wilderness beyond the Ohio River.[188] Brackenridge's anti-slavery activities went beyond mere pamphleteering: in 1793, he had successfully defended in court an African American woman who had been kidnapped from Pittsburgh and sold into slavery into Kentucky, securing her freedom.[189]

As early as the 1810s, anti-slavery sentiment in the U.S. found its expression in the "colonization movement." Supported by such leading lights as Thomas Jefferson, Henry Clay, Daniel Webster and Francis Scott Key, the aim of "colonization" was to resettle free African American men and women in Africa on a voluntary basis, specifically to the West coast of Africa in the area that eventually became the independent state of Liberia, and to encourage slaveowners to give up their claims to African American slaves on the condition that they agree to such resettlement. In September of 1826, following a meeting of concerned citizens at the First Presbyterian Church on Sixth Avenue, the Pittsburgh Colonization Society was formed as a chapter of the American Colonization Society; Henry Baldwin was named president of the Society, and lawyers Walter Forward, Neville Craig and Charles Israel were among its other leaders. Almost immediately, however, the Pittsburgh Colonization Society became crippled by the mixed motives of its supporters, some of whom saw "colonization" primarily as a way to rid Pittsburgh of what they perceived to be an undesirable element of its population. African American leaders such as John B. Vashon, an African American Pittsburgh barber shop owner who had served in the War of 1812, expressed their misgivings about such schemes to the leaders of the Society, and the Pittsburgh Colonization Society withered away into inactivity after several years.[190]

Having established himself as the wealthiest African American merchant in Pittsburgh, Vashon would later become Pittsburgh's leading African American advocate of abolishing slavery, as the founder of the Pittsburgh African Education Society and the Anti-Slavery Society of Pittsburgh, and as the Pittsburgh distributor of William Lloyd Garrison's abolitionist journal, *The Liberator*. Vashon's activities would keep issues of African American civil rights at the forefront of political discussions of the day.

At the Pennsylvania Constitutional Convention of 1837, Pittsburgh attorneys Walter Forward and Harmar Denny made impassioned pleas for the adoption of the principle of African American suffrage as part of the Pennsylvania Constitution. Forward, who was serving as a representative in the state assembly for Western Pennsylvania, spoke forcefully on the topic:

> *Why do you give a man the right of suffrage at all? Is it because he has or has not the right of protection? Has the black man of property, not an equal stake in the gov't. with you? And is protection not equally dear to him? Does your color give you a larger interest in the matter than it does him?*

> *If a black man be as intelligent, as virtuous, and as patriotic as you, no man can give a reason why he ought not to enjoy the right of suffrage on an equality with you. But, say gentleman, he is an inferior with regard to the offices and duties of life? There is no duty which you do not exact from them, and they are subject to all the obedience to rules and law, that the white man is subject to.[191]*

Likewise, on July 8, 1837, Denny presented to the Convention a "Memorial of the Free Citizens of Color in Pittsburgh and Its Vicinity, Relative to the Right of Suffrage," drafted by a committee led by Vashon, which became the subject of heated debate at the Convention.[192] As ratified, however, despite the good efforts of Forward and Denny, the Pennsylvania Constitution of 1837 ultimately denied the African Americans of Pennsylvania the right to vote.[193]

T.J. Bigham kept the issue of male African American suffrage alive in the Pennsylvania House during the 1840s. Bigham had managed to recover his footing after losing all of his worldly possessions in the Great Fire. He entered the Pennsylvania House of Representatives as a Whig in 1845, the year of the Fire, and served on and off for almost ten years, gaining a reputation as a "first class legislative encyclopedia" and "one of [the legislature's] most profound and logical debaters,"[194] with a booming voice, a seemingly inexhaustible reservoir of ready wit and humor, and a prodigious command of facts and figures. In December 1846, Bigham married Maria Louisa Lewis, a granddaughter of Major Abraham Kirkpatrick and the heir to a vast estate on Mount Washington, the hill overlooking Pittsburgh from the other side of the Monongahela River. By the end of the decade, Bigham had settled with his wife and family in a fourteen-room home known as "Woodlawn," with a view of the rebuilding of the city's downtown. Now Bigham was using his influence in vigorous support of various petitions from the citizens of Pittsburgh demanding African American voting rights, and as the founder of an anti-slavery newspaper, the *Pittsburgh Commercial Journal*.[195]

Even as Bigham continued to fight the battle for the right of African Americans to vote, however, the focus of the civil rights debate began to shift toward the issue of how runaway slaves were to be treated under the law. For a number of years, the rights of slaveowners to recover fugitive slaves as their property was protected under Article IV, Section 2 of the Constitution and the federal Fugitive Slave Act of 1793. In *Prigg v. Pennsylvania* (1842),[196] however, the opinion of the U.S. Supreme Court by Justice Joseph Story declared unconstitutional a Pennsylvania law criminalizing the capture of fugitive slaves, but left the door open for states to enact laws that might still limit the means by which slaveowners reclaimed fugitive slaves, under the auspices of the states' police power.

After Pennsylvania bolstered its kidnapping statute following the *Prigg* case,[197] Bigham served as prosecutor in a kidnapping trial in 1847. The case arose when an escaped slave named Daniel Lockhart was recaptured at Monongahela House by his former master, Lloyd Logan, and two of Logan's assistants from Winchester, Virginia. As Logan prepared to ship Lockhart down the Ohio River on a steamboat, word of Lockhart's capture reached African Americans living in the Hayti district of Pittsburgh (now known as the "Lower Hill"), and a crowd of them rushed to surround Logan and his assistants just in time to facilitate Lockhart's escape. Logan and his aides were arrested and charged with kidnapping, and Bigham won their convictions, although the men skipped bail and left town before they could be sentenced.[198]

The loophole for state action left by the *Prigg* case and the anti-slavery activities of Northern lawyers such as Bigham, although they were considered to be victories for abolitionists, ultimately prompted Congress to enact a more brutal law in support of slaveowners, the Fugitive Slave Act of 1850. This Act declared that alleged fugitive slaves would not be allowed trial by jury, would be forbidden from testifying on their own behalf, and would not be allowed to call witnesses on their behalf. Finally, the Act included a provision that criminalized aiding and abetting fugitive slaves, making it punishable with a one thousand dollar fine or six months' imprisonment.

The Fugitive Slave Act of 1850, in turn—despite the penalties for aiding and abetting—prompted the development of a secret network of pathways and safe houses through the Northern states leading, as historian Irene Williams put it, "from Southern bondage to Canadian liberty" for escaped slaves.[199] Pennsylvania, nestled against the Mason-Dixon line, was one of the most active Northern centers for what became known as the "Underground Railroad," a nickname apparently coined by slave trackers in York County,

Pennsylvania who, flummoxed by the ability of runaway slaves to disappear once they reached the Susquehanna River, surmised that "there must be an underground railroad somewhere."[200] There were pathways of the informal network of friendly enablers that led to Southeastern Pennsylvania, leading either north through New Jersey to New York, or further westward in Pennsylvania. At least three other pathways converged on Uniontown in the West, but two very well-traveled lines of the Underground Railroad led to Pittsburgh, where fugitives could receive aid and comfort from a rather large urban African American population, led by John B. Vashon, or from the Allegheny Institute and Mission Church on the North Side, whose white pastor, Rev. Charles Avery, led the first Pittsburgh anti-slavery rally in the Pittsburgh Diamond after the enactment of the 1850 Act. Both men, and many others like them, risked liberty and property in protecting fugitive slaves, smuggled to Pittsburgh in covered wagons or closed carriages, and sending them north to Erie or Buffalo. "After leaving Pittsburg," recalled businessman William Stewart, "they were scarcely ever captured."[201]

T.J. Bigham also threw himself into the Underground Railroad effort, and his home became known locally as a "station" on the Railroad. At Woodlawn, the Bigham family nurse was a free African American servant named Lucinda Bryant. With Bigham's approval, Bryant frequently sat in the top tower window of Woodlawn, keeping a steady watch for both runaway slaves and slave hunters on the rivers below. Bigham kept a lantern burning on his porch all night, signifying that the home was a safe haven for fugitive slaves; and Bryant and the rest of the household staff frequently hid fugitives in Bigham's home, either in the cellar crawl spaces, the attic, or the outbuildings.[202]

In a sense, T.J. Bigham risked more than most of the rest of the Underground Railroad leaders in Pittsburgh; as an "officer of the court," Bigham could not only have been subject to fines and imprisonment were he to be caught helping runaway slaves in violation of the law, but he could also be disbarred and lose his principal livelihood, a form of punishment not likely to be suffered by Vashon the barber or Avery the pastor. Yet Bigham's participation in the Underground Railroad movement was consistent with the character of both his legislative service and his reputation as a Pittsburgh trial lawyer—bold and unabashed, perhaps imprudently conspicuous at times, and rigidly principled.

After the election of Abraham Lincoln as president, and the firing on Fort Sumter in April 1861, the Pittsburgh bar witnessed an even greater measure of loyalty to principle—when so many of its members set down their quill pens and took up arms in the fight to preserve the Union, risking not only liberty and property, but life and limb as well. On April 15, 1861, President Lincoln called for seventy-five thousand volunteers to serve ninety days to help to quash what was hoped to be a very short Confederate rebellion, and the bar was quick to respond to President Lincoln's call.

The first two prominent lawyers to join the Union cause had served in the Mexican War a decade and a half before. Oliver H. Rippey, who had served as city solicitor of Pittsburgh and was a Private in the 2nd Regiment of the Pennsylvania Volunteers during the Mexican War, enlisted in one of the three-month regiments, the 7th, which was organized at Camp Curtin in Harrisburg on April 22, 1861. The 7th Regiment went on patrol and fought skirmishes with the Confederate cavalry in Maryland in June. Although the 7th

Regiment was mustered out in July when its commission expired, Lieutenant Colonel Rippey returned at end of the summer to organize the 61st Pennsylvania Volunteers.[203]

Meanwhile, the news of the firing on Fort Sumter reached Colonel Samuel W. Black in Nebraska City, Nebraska. Once known as one of the great orators of the Pittsburgh bar, remembered by Thomas Mellon as "impulsive and passionate,"[204] Black had briefly attended West Point as a young man and served as a Lieutenant Colonel in the same regiment as Rippey during the Mexican War. He ran for Congress as a Democrat in Pittsburgh and lost in 1852, and shortly thereafter he moved to Nebraska, where he became a justice on the Supreme Court of the Nebraska Territory. In 1859, President Buchanan appointed Black as governor of the Nebraska Territory. He had been serving in the statehouse for two years and was about to be replaced under the new Republican administration when the news of Fort Sumter reached him, and, like Rippey, he immediately left office and returned to Pittsburgh to enlist.[205] Upon his return to Pittsburgh, Colonel Black became chief of staff to General William Wilkins, the aging judge and ex-Secretary of War who had assumed command of the forty or fifty Allegheny County Home Guard companies that had begun to be assembled, strictly for "home defense," after Lincoln's call to arms.

On July 4, 1861, General Wilkins and his officers organized a rally and parade of the Home Guard companies through the Allegheny City parks. "General Wilkins' appearance on horseback, with imposing chapeau of Revolutionary style, and immense epaulettes, and accompanied by a brilliant staff of young officers in full uniform, led by Colonel Black," noted a regimental historian, "presented an imposing spectacle of a most impressive character, long to be remembered."[206] On their way back, Colonel Black received a dispatch from Lincoln's Secretary of War, Simon Cameron, giving him authority to raise his own regiment. As the regimental historian recounts:

> *On Penn avenue Colonel Black, on horseback, with his message in his pocket, overtook the Eighth ward Home Guards, commanded by Captain E.S. Wright. Out of respect to Colonel Black the company halted and divided its ranks so as to allow them to present arms as Colonel Black passed through on his way from the review. The Colonel stopped to thank Captain Wright for the honor of the salute, and announced to him the contents of the dispatch ... stating that, although he was authorized, he had not as yet secured a single recruit for his regiment. He ended by inviting Captain Wright to have his company of Home Guards to be the first to volunteer ...*

The company joined, unanimously. In less than a day, Colonel Black managed to recruit his entire regiment, which came to be known as the 62nd Regiment of the Pennsylvania Volunteer Infantry.[207]

Back in action, Colonel Rippey's 61st Pennsylvania Volunteers joined the defense of Washington until March 1862, when they were deployed within the Yorktown Peninsula. They saw action at the siege of Yorktown and the Battle of Williamsburg before being ambushed by General Joseph E. Johnston's Confederate Army at Fair Oaks, Virginia on May 31, 1862. Ninety-two men from the 61st suffered mortal wounds, including Colonel Rippey, who was killed in action.[208]

Colonel Black's 62nd Pennsylvania Volunteers were also deployed to the defense of Washington, camping at Fort Corcoran and near Falls Church, Virginia until March 1862, when the Regiment saw action against the Confederates at the siege of Yorktown, the Battles at Hanover Court House and Mechanicsville, and finally, the Battle at Gaines' Mill. In the early afternoon of June 27, 1862, after a morning of fierce fighting, the 62nd Pennsylvania and the 9th Massachusetts were ordered to push forward against General Robert E. Lee's Confederate Army. Colonel Black ordered a bayonet charge across a swampy ravine, but he was killed almost instantly by a Confederate sniper.

One of Colonel Black's colleagues from the Pittsburgh bar, Lieutenant Colonel J. Bowman Sweitzer—a former U.S. Attorney in Pittsburgh—immediately assumed command of the 62nd Pennsylvania and succeeded for a time in driving the Confederates back until he was caught short on supplies and effectively surrounded. The Confederates moved in and captured seventy-four soldiers of the 62nd Regiment, including Colonel Sweitzer, who by that time was badly wounded. The 62nd suffered more casualties at Gaines Mill than anywhere except Gettysburg.

The Confederates recognized the body of Colonel Black and buried him behind Confederate lines, although his remains were later removed to Allegheny Cemetery.[209] Colonel Sweitzer, meanwhile, was nursed back to health at Libby Prison in Richmond and released in a prisoner exchange, after which he assumed command of his old brigade, leading his troops with great discipline at Antietam in September 1862 and at Fredericksburg three months later—where General Ambrose Burnside observed, watching Sweitzer direct his men, that "[n]o troops ever behaved handsomer."[210] A few moments after Burnside's observation, however, Sweitzer's men encountered heavy Confederate fire, and Colonel Sweitzer was wounded and had his horse killed under him. Again recovering from his wounds, Sweitzer later saw action at Gettysburg, in the "Wheatfield." After being mustered out in July 1864, Sweitzer was promoted to brevet Brigadier General for gallantry and meritorious service during the War.[211]

The War tore on for weeks, months and years beyond anyone's expectations. Pittsburgh's repository of experienced soldiers was exhausted fairly rapidly in the early days of the conflict, and many younger men, including a number of fresh young attorneys of the Pittsburgh bar and numerous law students and college men who would eventually enter the bar, interrupted their careers and studies, and began to take their places within the ranks of the Pennsylvania Volunteers.

Thirty-six year-old Frederick H. Collier, another prominent member of the Pittsburgh bar who had beaten Oliver Rippey in the 1856 election for County District Attorney, organized the 139th Regiment of the Pennsylvania Volunteers with businessman William Semple in August 1862. Albert B. McCalmont, age thirty-seven, who had been Thomas Keenan's associate in the founding of the *Pittsburgh Legal Journal* and had more recently served as assistant U.S. Attorney General under Jeremiah Black, mustered in as a Lieutenant Colonel in the 142nd Regiment the following month. Cyrus O. Loomis, a forty-four year-old former Pittsburgh city solicitor and nephew of the esteemed Pittsburgh lawyer Andrew W. Loomis, joined a Michigan artillery unit in October. Each of them attained the rank of General for their service in the War.

Colonel Collier's contemporary John Harper observed:

Col. Collier went at once to work to study his new profession, and he soon became acquainted with its principles and details ... In the battle of Salem Heights Col. C particularly distinguished himself and received the commendation of Genl Sedgwick. Unfortunately on the field of Gettysburg he received a severe accidental wound which crippled him for a considerable time, and deprived the regiment of his services.[212]

Secretary of War Edwin Stanton had developed an appreciation for Collier's skill as a lawyer while he was in Pittsburgh, and appointed Collier as a member of the Military Court Martial in Washington. Collier was brevetted Brigadier General in March 1865 for gallant and meritorious service.[213] Lieutenant Colonel McCalmont also fought at Gettysburg in July 1863 with the First Army Corps, where the 142nd suffered heavy casualties, but his shining moment came when he commanded a brigade during the Union breakthrough at Petersburg in April 1865.[214] Colonel Loomis eventually took charge of the Artillery of the Army of the Cumberland, through which the name "Loomis' Battery" came to be recognized and feared by the Confederates at Perryville and Stones River. After an artillery duel at Murfreesboro, a *New York Herald* columnist called Loomis "the envy of all artillerists" while describing how Loomis and his men dismounted five enemy guns and drove a Confederate battery off the field. General William Rosencrans said of Loomis, who was brevetted Brigadier General in June 1865: "He was born for war."[215]

Joseph B. Kiddoo, age twenty-four, was serving as assistant principal of the Old Wilkinsburg Academy and contemplating a career in the law when he joined the 63rd Regiment of the Pennsylvania Volunteers in 1861, fighting with General McClellan in the Peninsular Campaign. He rose quickly through the ranks to win the command of the 137th Regiment in March 1863 shortly before being mustered out three months later. In May 1863, the War Department commenced the formation of African American volunteers into "colored units" commanded by white officers; and in the following October, Kiddoo re-enlisted as a Major with the Sixth United States Colored Regiment, a post that many assumed would mean his certain death in the event of capture. In January 1864, he nonetheless helped to form the 22nd Regiment of United States Colored Troops at Camp William Penn in Philadelphia. There he was joined by Lieutenant George H. Christy, who became adjutant to the 22nd—a young mathematics professor who would subsequently become one of Pittsburgh's leading patent lawyers. Kiddoo led a pair of daring charges against Confederate positions east of Richmond at the onset of the Richmond-Petersburg Campaign in June 1864. During a skirmish at Darbeytown Road in Fair Oaks, Virginia on October 27, 1864, Colonel Kiddoo led another, perhaps ill-considered, charge across an open field at enemy entrenchments, and was seriously wounded in the hip. Immediately afterwards, seven officers of the 22nd Regiment requested an investigation of Colonel Kiddoo's command at Darbeytown Road, charging him with "mismanagement" and drunkenness. The charges came to nothing, however, and Kiddoo was ultimately brevetted Brigadier General.[216]

Alfred L. Pearson, age twenty-four, was a young married man who had only just entered the bar in 1862 when he enlisted in the Union cause, joining the 155th Regiment. At the battle of Lewis Farm (Quaker Road) in February 1865, Colonel Pearson demonstrated extraordinary courage under fire. As historian Richard D. Sauers describes it:

Here, as the brigade was advancing, it received a withering fire from gray-clad soldiers sheltered behind breastworks. There was some temporary confusion in the Union ranks. Colonel Pearson saw the momentary wavering and decided to act quickly to keep the troops moving forward. He galloped to the color-guard and demanded the flag from Sergeant Marlin. The sergeant, having carried the flag for more than a year, "had become so attached to it that he would have carried it into the jaws of death rather than part with it." Marlin curtly refused Pearson's demand, telling his commander: "Tell where you wish the flag to be carried, Colonel, and I'll take it there." Pearson wrenched the flag from Marlin's grasp and shouted, "Follow me, men, or lose your colors." He rode ahead of the battleline and found some enemy soldiers concealed behind a sawdust pile. The 155th quickly sprang forward and seized the Rebel position.[217]

In the aftermath, Pearson was brevetted Brigadier General for his heroism. His command fired the last shot at Appomattox Court House before the surrender of the South, and in 1897 he received the Congressional Medal of Honor.

Approximately 115 Allegheny County lawyers saw active service with the Union Army during the Civil War,[218] although certainly not every able-bodied lawyer took the initiative to join. Attorney Noah Webster Shafer, who delighted in playing the heretic throughout his career which included a stint as Register in Bankruptcy, was apparently drafted for service; but under the Enrollment Act of 1863, a man who was drafted could legally avoid the order to report by paying a substitute to appear in his place. In later years, Shafer was proud to tell his friends that he "was not in military service except by proxy," and that he had heard but could not verify "that [his] representative was all shot to pieces."[219]

Although only Colonel Black, Colonel Rippey and a few other men who were members of the Allegheny County bar but practiced elsewhere lost their lives, many of Pittsburgh's lawyers were seriously injured during the War. General J. Bowman Sweitzer, having been wounded more than once during the War, returned to Pittsburgh and served as an Internal Revenue supervisor and as the Supreme Court prothonotary for the Western District. General Frederick H. Collier, despite the severity of his wounds, went on to serve as Common Pleas judge for over thirty years. Captain Samuel C. Schoyer was "badly wounded at the battle of Cold Harbor," as his grandson, attorney Edward Schoyer, recalled. "They threatened to cut off his leg [but] he told them not to do it."[220] Although Samuel Schoyer enjoyed a respectable career after the War as a Pittsburgh lawyer, his War wound caused him incessant pain and cut short his life at the age of forty-nine—twenty-six years after the battle of Cold Harbor.[221]

Many War veterans—from stalwarts such as William B. Negley and Jacob F. Slagle, to future leaders of the bar such as D.T. Watson, Edward A. Montooth, and George H. Christy—returned from the War to cultivate distinguished careers as Pittsburgh lawyers.

Among the other survivors, while some managed to rise above their experiences of the War, others never seemed to be able to rally to peace. General Cyrus O. Loomis developed "softening of the brain" following his service, which was most likely a non-medical characterization of a condition we might without further evidence wish to equate with what is now known as post-traumatic stress disorder, and was confined to the National Military Asylum in Washington, D.C. for the rest of his relatively short life.[222] General Alfred L. Pearson, too, probably suffered to a degree from the absence of armed combat in his life. While his War-time heroism succeeded in getting him elected as Pittsburgh's District Attorney on three occasions, he practiced law only sporadically. The judges of the Common Pleas Court secured for him an appointment as gas inspector for Allegheny County, a post at which he worked when he was not otherwise occupied as a Major General in the Pennsylvania National Guard, which kept him in the saddle for a good portion of the rest of his life.[223]

Elizabeth Bacon Custer, wife of the ill-fated General George Armstrong Custer, recalled, after the War, that Major General Kiddoo "had still the open wound from which endured daily pain and nightly torture, for he got only fragmentary sleep. To heal the wound was to end his life, the surgeons said."[224] Still in active service despite his wound, Kiddoo went to Galveston, Texas, where the Army appointed him as assistant commissioner of the U.S. Freedman's Bureau—a position which placed him immediately within the cauldron of Southern racial strife during the Reconstruction. Kiddoo suspended Texas' "Black Codes," legislation passed after the War to reaffirm the inferior citizenship of African Americans in Texas, and worked tirelessly to improve the education of African Americans in Texas. It has been estimated that as many as ten thousand African Americans learned to read and write under Kiddoo's programs. His tenure in Texas was controversial enough that his War wound was used against him as an excuse to have him relieved from the position after only a year. Shortly thereafter, Kiddoo returned to Pittsburgh, finished his law studies with John Henry Hampton and Edwin Stowe and was admitted to the bar. He died a little over a decade later, at the age of forty-three—another delayed victim of Civil War wounds—and was buried with honors in the United States Military Cemetery at West Point.[225]

For the first Pittsburgh lawyer to die in battle, Lieutenant Colonel Oliver H. Rippey, the reason why a lawyer would heed the call to take up arms was summed up simply with a rhetorical question. "What will advance the interests of the cause for which I fight?," he asked.[226] For lawyers who were born within, or just after, a brutal age of political strife, the idea of going to the battleground to fight for the principles laid out in the Constitution was not so extraordinary. During this era, Pittsburgh lawyers saw soldiering as an extension of their roles as preservers of order. However, as Bernard Hibbitts writes, the Civil War "was not a lawyers' triumph but rather a lawyers' failure—a failure of catastrophic proportion that revealed not lawyers' collective strength as defenders of the Republic but rather their weakness, and arguably their ultimate unsuitability and unfitness for that self-appointed role." Hibbitts reinforces his point with a contemporary quote from Walt Whitman: "Were you looking to be held together by lawyers?/ Or by an agreement on paper? or by arms?/ Nay, nor the world, nor any living thing, will so cohere."[227]

Alone among Pittsburgh lawyers, and perhaps among only a few American lawyers, Edwin Stanton, serving as Secretary of War, left his significant, lasting individual imprint on the defense of the Republic. Even after the Pittsburgh lawyer-soldiers all came home, catastrophic events catapulted Edwin Stanton into a position of leadership during the worst hours of the disorder and crisis that followed immediately after the end of the War.

Around ten o'clock in the evening on April 14, 1865—five days after the surrender of General Robert E. Lee at Appomattox Court House in Virginia—President Lincoln attended the comedy *Our American Cousin* at Ford's Theater in Washington with his wife, Mary Todd Lincoln. He was sitting in the state box with Clara Harris and her escort, Major Henry Rathbone, when a stranger leapt into the box, aimed his .44-caliber Derringer at Lincoln's head and pulled the trigger. After the assailant jumped to the stage below, shouting "Sic semper tyrannis!" (*"Thus always to tyrants!"*), many members of the audience observed that the attacker was a well-known stage actor, John Wilkes Booth. Although he suffered a broken leg in the jump, Booth fled the scene before he could be restrained.

Before midnight, Secretary of War Edwin Stanton effectively took charge of the U.S. government and ordered federal agents to track down and capture Booth, remaining "focused and uncowed, ruthlessly determined to mobilize the massive resources he commanded to hunt down the assassins and choke off the conspiracy," according to historian Anthony S. Pitch:

> *No one knew the scope or depth of the conspiracy, nor the brains behind it. Where would they strike next? What was the ultimate aim? ... Stanton's gruff and steely presence gave hope and reassurance in a time of doubt and despair. As Dr. Leale held [Lincoln's] hand in the hush of the adjoining room, the physician listened with awe to Stanton dictating orders to the military and giving directives for the manhunt. ... Stanton was commanding at his administrative best, exuding drive and authority, marshalling his forces, pulling the strings, devising strategy, and creating order in a time of turmoil.*[228]

Dr. Leale later recalled that on that horrible evening, Stanton was "in reality, acting President of the United States,"[229] approaching his job with the same relentless concentration and extraordinary tactical sharpness that he once exhibited in the courtrooms of Pittsburgh. It was Stanton who set his voice against the silence that ensued following the president's last breath, murmuring, as best as anyone could hear or recall, "Now he belongs to the ages."[230]

The news of the attack on the president reached Pittsburgh by telegram around two o'clock in the morning on Saturday, April 15. President Judge Moses Hampton of the District Court of Allegheny County had served two terms in Congress, one of them alongside Lincoln, a fellow Whig. The two maintained a sporadic correspondence for some years. At half past nine on Saturday morning, scarcely two hours after Lincoln's passing, Judge Hampton announced the death of his old friend and adjourned the Court. The Court of Common Pleas and the U.S. District Court followed suit shortly thereafter. At ten thirty in the morning, members of the Allegheny County bar assembled at the courthouse, where a committee was appointed to arrange for a fitting demonstration by the bar, scheduled for Monday morning. In a public meeting convened at eleven in the morning by Mayor James Lowry, Jr. in Wilkins Hall on Fourth Street, it was decided that all business in Pittsburgh should be suspended until the following Tuesday, that people should be asked to drape their homes and shops with black crepe in mourning, and that all citizens should attend their churches on Sunday and join in prayers for the safety of their country.[231]

Flags throughout the city were placed at half-mast; at the Fort Pitt Foundry, where so many cannons used by the Army of the Potomac were manufactured, a gun salute was fired; and all around town, firehouse and church bells tolled. Into Saturday evening, hundreds gathered along the lanes of Fifth Street, anxiously awaiting further news about the fate of the nation. Over the course of the next several days, Pittsburghers would gather to hear eulogies of the president delivered by several prominent members of the bar, including Thomas Williams; T.J. Bigham, the Underground Railroad conductor and sage of Mt. Washington; Andrew W. Loomis; Judge Wilson McCandless; and Thomas Mercer Marshall. At the synagogue on Eighth Street, a law student named Josiah Cohen delivered an address on Lincoln's character and achievements.[232]

By Wednesday, Edwin Stanton had publicly offered a one hundred thousand dollar reward for the arrest and capture of John Wilkes Booth, drawing public attention to the president's alleged assailant. In addition to being known as a stage actor, however, John Wilkes Booth was known to Western Pennsylvanians—including James H. Osmer, a Venango County trial lawyer who frequently appeared in the Allegheny County courts and later represented Booth's sister in a lawsuit—as a partner in the Dramatic Oil Company, which operated none-too-successfully in the oil country around Franklin, Pennsylvania during the better part of 1864. According to Osmer, Booth's company never managed to pump any oil out of the ground, and it is thought that Booth lost around five thousand dollars on a couple of bad oil wells before departing Western Pennsylvania for the South. Folks from the Pennsylvania oil patch seem to have uniformly remembered him as a hot-tempered fellow with Southern sympathies; yet none of them would later admit to imagining that he could be capable of murdering the president.[233]

With Booth still on the loose, on April 17, federal agents raided the boarding house of a forty-two year-old widow named Mrs. Mary Surratt, on 541 H Street in Washington. There they found and arrested Lewis Powell—a hulking Florida farm boy who had escaped detection after brutally attacking Secretary of State William Seward on the night of Lincoln's murder as part of Booth's overall plan to decapitate the Union government. When they searched Mrs. Surratt's house, they discovered a hidden photograph of John Wilkes Booth, and arrested Mrs. Surratt as well. On April 20, George Atzerodt, who had been assigned by Booth to kill Vice President Andrew Johnson, was found and arrested on a Germantown, Maryland farm. Booth, meanwhile, had escaped to a farm in Caroline County, Virginia, where he and co-conspirator David Herold were surrounded in a tobacco barn by a Union cavalry detachment. The soldiers set fire to the barn in hopes of smoking Booth and Herold into surrender; when they still refused, Booth was shot and killed by Sergeant Boston Corbett, despite Stanton's strict orders to the Army that Booth should be captured alive and brought to trial. David Herold was captured at the scene. Sergeant Corbett was immediately arrested by his commanding officer for insubordination, but Stanton ultimately dropped the charges, stating, "The rebel is dead. The patriot lives."[234]

While the nation was still in mourning, Stanton continued to move swiftly and ruthlessly in the investigation of the conspiracy, directing the arrest of scores of other suspected accomplices, observing that "The recent murders show such astounding wickedness that too much precaution cannot be taken."[235] By the end of April, however, Stanton had focused his prosecutorial zeal on a core set of surviving conspirators: Powell,

Atzerodt, Herold, Mrs. Surratt, two other men who were alleged to have been involved in the attacks, a stagehand at Ford's Theater who was thought to have helped Booth get away from the scene of the crime; and Dr. Samuel Mudd, who was accused of aiding and abetting in Booth's escape after setting Booth's broken leg. Stanton personally ordered that each of the prisoners—other than Mrs. Surratt, as a concession to her gender, and Dr. Mudd—should be brought to the military prison inside the Washington Arsenal wearing canvas hoods over their heads, in leg irons and handcuffs. All of them were placed in solitary confinement in accordance with Stanton's orders on "secure detention," so as to eliminate the possibility of interaction among the accused conspirators, and no one would be permitted to enter their cells without Stanton's written approval. Stanton was so determined to see them go to trial that he gave broad powers to General Winfield Scott Hancock to impose any other rules he saw fit "to prevent the escape of the prisoners alive, or their cheating the gallows by self-destruction."[236]

Stanton decided to bring the conspirators to trial before a military tribunal made up of senior Army officers, where the "rules of evidence would be less constricting and punishment was more likely to be stern and swift," according to Stanton biographers Thomas and Hyman—a move that provoked denunciations from newspaper editors as well as the likes of Edward Bates, brother of the ill-fated Pittsburgh duelist Tarleton Bates, and Lincoln's own one-time Attorney General. Bates privately castigated the then-current Attorney General, James Speed of Louisville, for yielding to Stanton's directive despite the mandate of the Fifth Amendment that "no person shall be held to answer for a capital ... crime," without an indictment by a grand jury. "If [Speed] be, in the lowest degree, qualified for his office," Bates wrote, "he must know better. Such a trial is not only unlawful, but it is a gross blunder in policy: It denies the great, fundamental principle, that ours is a government of law, and that the law is strong enough to rule the people wisely and well."[237]

On June 30, after a seven-week trial featuring the testimony of over three hundred and fifty witnesses, all of the defendants were found guilty by a majority vote of the nine senior Army officers selected for the tribunal. Powell, Herold, Atzerodt and Mrs. Surratt were sentenced to death by hanging, although five members of the tribunal separately issued a letter recommending clemency for Mrs. Surratt; and Dr. Mudd and the others received life sentences.

The hesitancy with which the tribunal delivered its sentence upon Mrs. Surratt gave hope to her supporters that she might avoid execution. Reverdy Johnson, a famed Maryland trial lawyer who had faced Stanton in the *Wheeling Bridge* case, a former Attorney General and U.S. senator who had been an honorary pall bearer at Lincoln's funeral, had been Mrs. Surratt's lead defense attorney, but had retreated from the trial after making an impassioned speech against the jurisdiction of the tribunal, leaving the case to his young associates Frederick Aiken and John Clampitt. President Andrew Johnson signed Mrs. Surratt's execution warrant on July 5, and Aiken and Clampitt rushed to the White House in hopes of delaying her execution, but President Johnson refused to see them. They telegraphed Reverdy Johnson, pleading with him to come to Washington, but the counsel declined, advising his associates to apply for a writ of habeas corpus which, if successful, would free Mrs. Surratt from military custody.

No one was more bereft by the loss of President Lincoln than Justice Andrew Wylie. Wylie, the former Transylvania law student and solicitor of the city of Pittsburgh who had moved to the Washington, D.C. area following his marriage to Miss Caroline Bryan of Alexandria, Virginia in 1848, was "fearlessly public" in his support for Lincoln in the election of 1860, according to Pitch. It is believed that he cast the lone vote in Lincoln's favor within the heavily Democratic precincts of Alexandria. Subsequently, Wylie survived an assassination attempt as Virginia seceded from the Union the following year. Lincoln rewarded Wylie for his loyalty by appointing him as an associate justice of the Supreme Court of the District of Columbia, the predecessor of today's U.S. District Court for the District of Columbia.[238]

Although the execution of convicted women was rare, it was not unheard of. Justice Wylie was probably aware of some high-profile hangings of Pittsburgh women during the previous decade. In 1852, Pamela Lee Worms was sentenced to death by hanging in Pittsburgh for poisoning her husband, and six years later, thirty-five year-old Charlotte Jones was hanged alongside her co-assailant Henry Fife for the murder of her aunt and uncle.[239] Up to this time, however, the federal government had never executed a woman.

It was two in the morning on July 7, the day upon which Mrs. Surratt and her co-defendants were set to be executed, when Aiken and Clampitt rang Justice Wylie's doorbell. Wylie opened a second-floor window and asked the men to identify themselves and their business; Aiken and Clampitt replied that they had business of "an important judicial character." Justice Wylie came to the door in his dressing gown and led them into his gaslit study, where he listened to their petition, which described Stanton's military tribunal as illegal and asking that General Hancock be ordered to bring Mrs. Surratt before Justice Wylie for indictment and trial by a jury of her peers. The young lawyers may or may not have been aware that Justice Wylie was a close friend of the Secretary of War. After the plea, Justice Wylie stood and left the study for a moment; and, as Pitch relates:

> *In a few moments, [Wylie] returned... "Gentlemen, my mind is made up," he said. "I have always endeavored to perform my duty fearlessly, as I understand it." He told them the points in the petition were well taken, but, conscious of the gravity of the moment and the risks to himself, he declared, "I am about to perform an act which, before tomorrow's sun goes down, may consign me to the Old Capitol Prison. I believe it to be my duty as a judge to order this writ to issue, and I shall so order it."[240]*

Aiken and Clampitt hurried to the clerk of the court, who made out the writ, and by eight-thirty in the morning, General Hancock was receiving service of the writ from the hands of a federal marshal at his suite in the Metropolitan Hotel in Washington.

Justice Wylie opened the Court's session at ten in the morning, but encountered neither General Hancock nor Mrs. Mary Surratt. General Hancock, he declared from the bench, "has neglected to obey the order of the court." Without inviting any discussion on the matter, however, he noted, with resignation, "If it is their determination to treat the authority of this court with contempt, they have the power and will to treat with equal contempt any other process this court might order ... The court must submit to the supreme physical force, which now holds custody of the petitioner."[241]

An hour and a half later, while Aiken and Clampitt were at the penitentiary attempting to see their client, General Hancock and Attorney General James Speed entered Justice Wylie's courtroom, and apologized for their tardiness. Then Attorney General Speed handed Justice Wylie the president's written order suspending the writ of habeas corpus and affirming the execution. After reading the president's order, Justice Wylie declared, "This court finds itself powerless to take any further action in the premises, and therefore declines to make orders, which would be vain for any practical purpose." Speed explained that war-time exigencies required that human life must be taken, at times, "without the judgment of the court, and without the process of the courts."[242] As Pitch relates:

> *Wylie acknowledged the limits of judicial enforcement, though he could not help but be rueful. "The writ was applied for, and I had no authority to refuse to grant it," he said. "It is a writ dear and sacred to every lover of liberty, indispensable to the protection of citizens, and can only be constitutionally set aside in times of war. I could not, I dared not, refuse to grant the writ." But he had no choice other than to submit to the might of the ruling authority, concluding, "the posse comitatus of the court is not able to overcome the armies of the United States under the command of the president."*[243]

Stanton's military tribunals were thus permitted to stand, and Mrs. Surratt, along with Herold, Powell and Atzerodt, was hanged shortly after one o'clock in the afternoon that same day.

Stanton stayed on as President Johnson's Secretary of War for a time, but eventually clashed with the president on Johnson's lenient implementation of Reconstruction in the South. In 1867, President Johnson suspended Stanton for his underground support for the Radical Republicans in Congress, and six months later he fired Stanton. However, Stanton barricaded himself inside the War Department, refusing to leave office by relying on the Tenure of Office Act, passed the previous year, which purported to prohibit the president from firing cabinet members without Senate approval. Johnson's defiance of that Act where Stanton was concerned precipitated the introduction of impeachment proceedings against Johnson in the House and Senate. Johnson was narrowly acquitted in the Senate, after which the exhausted Stanton retired to private life. The following year, Stanton was appointed to the U.S. Supreme Court by President Grant and confirmed by the Senate on the same day; but he died four days later, before he could be sworn in, on December 24, 1869.[244]

Robert Carnahan, the U.S. Attorney in Pittsburgh, announced Stanton's death in federal court, and moved for adjournment. "On the adjournment of the court," reported the *Pittsburgh Legal Journal*, "the United States Court Room was crowded with, perhaps, the largest meeting within the recollection of the oldest member of the bar" to pay tribute to Stanton as a fellow Pittsburgh lawyer and as a statesman.[245]

In his last will and testament, signed on July 19, 1869, Stanton named Justice Andrew Wylie as one of his executors.[246] Although they had been legal adversaries, after a fashion, over a fundamental Constitutional issue in the wake of the worst crisis ever faced by the U.S. government, they were able to forgive and forget, it would seem. The former Pittsburgh solicitor remained on the District of Columbia court until 1885, and died in Washington in 1905 at the age of ninety-one.

After President Lincoln's death, Pittsburgh eventually turned from mourning and fell back into step. In Washington, Johnson's impeachment trial and Stanton's War Department siege set the stage for a decade of bitter political battles, a fact that has left some tarnish on Stanton's historical reputation. In Pittsburgh, however, an engine had been ignited during the Civil War which was to transcend the politics of Reconstruction. On the very same day in April 1861 that Lincoln put out his first call for troops to fight the War, Stanton remarked in a letter to his brother-in-law: "I think it will result in a great activity in all mechanical & productive classes of business, and especially in whatever is connected with the supplies & transports required by a State of War ... This will create a demand for boats, provisions, arms, ammunition, & supplies generally. The manufacturing interests of Pittsburg will I think receive a strong impulse."[247]

Stanton had foreseen the future correctly. The loudest noises in Pittsburgh during the time of national political division following the Civil War were not the sounds of Democrats and Republicans disagreeing over the limits of government authority—the Republicans, at any rate, would have a lock on Pittsburgh politics during the last quarter of the nineteenth century under the thumbs of the Christopher Magee-William Flinn machine. Rather, commerce and trade made the largest noise in post-Civil War Pittsburgh, with the clank of iron against iron, the hissing of steam, and the roar of railroad engines and coal-furnaces. The ongoing lawyers' dialectic concerning the line between chaos and order would not now be so much concerned with the relationship between the individual and the state, as it had been from the Whiskey Rebellion through the Civil War; it would now focus on the relationship between capital and labor. Within that context, Pittsburgh's lawyers during the last half of the nineteenth century would conjure up the best of Stanton's methods and habits in the service of this new society—his aggressive pragmatism and focus, as well as his behind-the-scenes leadership and tactical acuity—in an effort to keep pace with and occasionally direct the course of Pittsburgh's industrial growth.

PART II

THE GILDED BAR, 1866-1901

THE GILDED BAR, 1866-1901

―――――――――――――

Even the filth and wondrous blackness of the place are picturesque when looked down upon from above. The tops of the churches are visible and some of the larger buildings may be partially traced through the thick brown settled smoke. But the city itself is buried in a dense cloud. I was never more in love with smoke and dirt than when I stood here and watched the darkness of night close in upon the floating soot which hovered over the house-tops of the city.

—Anthony Trollope, 1863[1]

The first thing one might have noticed, walking through the Diamond shortly after the Civil War, would have been the smoke. It had been there since the 1830s—even before, remarked upon by every visitor—but with the rapid expansion of the city's iron manufacturing capacity to meet the demand for armaments during the Civil War, the cloud over Pittsburgh darkened and grew as its fortunes rose. When the War began, Pittsburgh's future seemed uncertain—the secession of the South meant the loss of an important market for Pittsburgh's goods—but the forges and foundries that produced odd bits and bars before the War were expanded and replaced by giant blast furnaces and rolling mills that ultimately produced fifteen percent of the cannons and eighty percent of the heavy guns used by the Union Army.[2] After 1875, these furnaces and mills and their progeny became the world's leading center of mass produced steel. Colonel Drake's well, which he drilled sixty-nine-and-one-half feet into the ground north of Pittsburgh near Titusville in 1859, gave birth to another industry; and soon the Allegheny River was dotted with oil refineries from Venango County down to the

Point, in Pittsburgh, where the Allegheny River intersects the Ohio and Monongahela Rivers. With tons of coke and coal moving up and down the Monongahela on barges, by the 1890s, there were riverside factories turning out glass and railroad equipment and machine parts in staggering quantities. The smoke was so thick, the streetlamps remained lit all day.

By the end of the nineteenth century, two great icons stood tall near the corner of Grant and Fifth, pushing skyward through the smoke. The first, completed in 1888, was the new, massive Allegheny County Courthouse and Jail, designed by H.H. Richardson in the image of a Romanesque fortress, with borrowed notes and hints of the grandeur of the Piazza San Marco and the Palazzo Ducale in the city-state of Venice. The complex, built in rugged, pinkish-gray Milford granite, featured a nine-story campanile, topped with a pyramidal roof, and a "bridge of sighs" linking the halls of justice with the county prison over Ross Street. Seven years later, a block away from the courthouse door on Fifth Avenue, a steel-framed thirteen-story skyscraper bearing the surname of one of Pittsburgh's great industrialists opened its doors. The Carnegie Building, actually named in memory of Andrew Carnegie's late brother Thomas, was the headquarters of the Carnegie Steel Company and its many subsidiaries, but it was also a symbol of Pittsburgh's industrial power at the end of the nineteenth century, an instant example of the combination of the strength and dignity and ambition of steel, on the one hand, and the idea of a business living inside a legal construct, a "company," on the other. These two iconic buildings—dominating the Pittsburgh skyline as they did at that time, standing as solid evidence of both the independent institutional importance and the institutional symbiosis of law and commerce—would have been unthinkable projects before the Civil War. Pittsburgh's own industrial revolution had not only transformed the city's landscape, but it was changing the way law and commerce, eyeing each other warily from either side of Grant Street, would interact.

The last three and a half decades of the nineteenth century were a time of unprecedented growth in the Pittsburgh legal profession. Over 1,100 lawyers were admitted to the Allegheny County bar during the last thirty-three years of the nineteenth century, after the Civil War. That was more than double the number of new Allegheny County lawyers during the previous thirty-three years, from 1834 to 1866. Recalling that eleven lawyers were admitted to the Allegheny bar in 1788, it took until the dawn of the next century, 1800, for the County's forty-fifth lawyer to be admitted. By contrast, forty-five lawyers were admitted in 1888 alone, the bar's one-hundredth anniversary year. The rate of admission of new lawyers increased steadily during the period: 301 new lawyers were admitted in the 1870s; 335 during the 1880s; and four hundred during the 1890s.[3] As dramatic as the increase in lawyers was during the period from 1860 to 1900, the rate of population growth in Allegheny County outpaced the rate of growth in new Allegheny County lawyers by more than two hundred percent; during this period, the County grew from 179,000 residents in 1860 to 775,000 in 1900.[4]

In addition to growth in numbers, the legal profession was experiencing other fundamental changes. One tends to think of many lawyers' practices today as being characterized by ongoing relationships with clients, but in the early nineteenth century, a lawyer's career was more often than not charted by a series of cases, and not a portfolio of clients. The development of a lawyer's career, therefore, was more closely tied to his reputation as a trial advocate, where he could display his abilities in full public view. In the smaller world of antebellum Pittsburgh—whose outer reaches were almost literally within earshot of the Diamond—oratorical skill, the ability to hold and entertain a courtroom audience, was the most obvious measure of an attorney's talents, under the circumstances.

The industrialization of Pittsburgh changed the character of the Pittsburgh lawyer's practice because industrialization demanded capital, and the sources of capital demanded that entrepreneurs create a structure within which to receive capital and to share profits. Initially, the favored structure was the creation of a partnership—two or more persons contributing a combination of ideas, cash and sweat to a common enterprise. "It was the age of partnerships in business enterprises," as Pittsburgh attorney Francis R. Harbison observed,

> *and no device in business has been more fruitful of litigation. They are subject to varying moods of the individuals and just as good as the least scrupulous member of the firm. Individual mistakes of judgment, resulting in losses, if made independent of other members' approval, invariably induced friction. The death of a member brought dissolution; and if the survivors were unscrupulous, they tried to outwit the deceased member's heirs; if scrupulous, the deceased's heirs still thought they were being cheated in the settlement.*[5]

Some of the inherently unstable aspects of the partnership form led forward-thinking businessmen to favor an old form of organization that had been around for some time, but had rarely been used for purely private purposes: the corporation. "The corporate form," as Lawrence Friedman suggests, "was a more efficient way to structure and finance" industrial ventures, in part because of its ability to erect a shield against liabilities to the individuals who owned it, but also because the charter of a corporation could exist permanently and independently of any single human being.[6]

In Pennsylvania, beginning in the eighteenth century, corporate charters were granted solely by a special act of the legislature, and often only for a community activity, such as the building of a bridge. As Dean Edward Sell writes, such special legislation "was but a trickle in the legislative stream at the beginning of the nineteenth century," but "by the time of the Civil War reached full flood proportions," meaning that private parties were becoming increasingly active in soliciting corporate charters from the legislature. By 1872, the situation was out of hand: out of 1,193 acts passed by the Pennsylvania legislature that year, 1,145 of them were pieces of special legislation, the vast majority of which were for the creation of private corporations, and only forty-eight were pieces of general legislation. Reformers complained that corporate charters were held out as cherries by lobbyists, bought and paid for as favors from corrupt legislators, and they clamored for a new system. The Pennsylvania Constitutional Convention of 1873—spurred on by the excesses of government-subsidized railroad companies that had been granted private corporate charters—voted to ban all special legislation creating corporate charters, clearing the way for the enactment of the Corporation Act of 1874, which provided that for-profit corporations could be created by the simple act of filing a corporate charter with an agency of the State.[7] If there were reformers who were suspicious of corporations generally, however, the reforms of 1873 and 1874 succeeded only in multiplying the number of Pennsylvania corporations.

Whether an entrepreneur chose to act through partnerships or corporations, however, the emerging rules of governance under these forms of existence required that commercial decision-making was to be done in a collective manner, with the deliberation and assent of a group of stakeholders in the enterprise through a set of agreed-upon procedures, thus giving dimension to a fiction that has become a bedrock assumption of American legal ontology today: a partnership, and a corporation to a greater degree, is a person—with the ability to act, the right to pursue claims, and the capacity to have claims pursued against it. These chimerical forms of existence inevitably required their own legal counselors, skilled in the arcane application of the fiction to every-day commercial reality.

Corporations may have been immortal beings, yet they required constant care and feeding. Instead of merely being called upon, fresh from a horseback sprint across the Allegheny Valley, to argue a case before a judge and jury, with his voice raised high to the rafters of the courtroom, the new Pittsburgh lawyer of the latter half of the nineteenth century—especially an elite member of the Pittsburgh bar—inhabited the board room. He had clients now, not just cases; the immortality of the corporation required continuity in advice and long-term planning. He drew his clients closely in conference, observed the tensions and motives of the stakeholders, made analyses, devised strategies, supervised implementations, and authored detailed documentations of corporate activity. As the men who whispered into the ears of people like Carnegie, Westinghouse and the sons of Thomas Mellon, the new generation of elite Pittsburgh lawyers—men like Knox and Reed, Hampton and Dalzell, George Shiras and D.T. Watson— developed a mystique of power and wisdom about them, in emulation of the mystique that was building at the same time around the famous Wall Street lawyers of the day, such as William Nelson Cromwell and Paul Cravath. In essence, the Pittsburgh lawyer who emerged in the second half of the nineteenth century had evolved from functioning as Sir Galahad, knight-errant bold in battle, into something closer to Merlin, the King's cunning wizard.

None of this was to say that, in Pittsburgh, courtroom skill was no longer important for a lawyer to possess, or that litigators were not among the elite lawyers of the bar. In fact, some of the finest corporate advisors of the era were also great courtroom advocates; and to this day some of the finest trial lawyers, among the leaders of the Pittsburgh bar, have little to do with corporate board rooms. Times and circumstances called for a change in the decorum of courtroom advocacy, however, for a myriad of reasons. Literary tastes were changing, and the fulminations of a chest-thumper like Colonel Samuel W. Black were coming to be seen as quaint and dated. While litigation was popular entertainment at the beginning of the nineteenth century, it had taken a backseat to theater and, by the 1880s, vaudeville; playing to the gallery was no longer as rewarding or as effective as it had once been. And when men of business and finance, operating as fiduciaries for a group of stakeholders, found themselves in need of a good trial lawyer, they wanted anything but a circus performance, with its attendant high-wire risks; they wanted the courtroom versions of their board room wizards—strong, confident, no-nonsense men who approached trials with a level of tactical planning and preparation, emulating the habits of Edwin Stanton, that was designed to win a case even before the opening gavel.

To the extent this sounds like clients preferring to hire lawyers who reflected their own self-image, it should be noted that the rise of the entity as client during the latter half of the nineteenth century also tended to coincide with the rise of the law partnership. In the 1870 *Pittsburgh City Directory*, twenty-six law firms were identified among the listings for attorneys; in 1888, there were forty-three; and in the 1899 *City Directory*, there were sixty-eight law firms identified.[8] Clients who did business as associations or entities were increasingly being served by lawyers who practiced through entities of their own.

The impetus to form companies and partnerships, followed by entrepreneurs and lawyers alike, soon took root in the bar itself. During most of the nineteenth century, there were no organizations, either national or local, that purported to speak for the entire Pittsburgh bar, or for any other bar for that matter. The old Pittsburgh Law Academy, founded in 1831, was virtually moribund by the end of the Civil War, functioning weakly, if at all, as a social club.

There was, however, cause to be hopeful for the galvanization of Pittsburgh's lawyers with the activity surrounding the establishment of the Allegheny County Law Library. While a Pittsburgh Law Library Association had flourished briefly during the late 1830s, after the Civil War certain prominent members of the bar began to be concerned about the fact that there was no common collection of law reports or other law books for the general benefit of Pittsburgh's lawyers. John Henry Hampton, the son of Judge Moses Hampton and one of the post-Civil War bar's leading lights, drafted a bill in 1867 entitled, "An Act Relative to the Purchase of a Law Library in County of Allegheny," which was passed by the legislature and signed into law on April 15, 1867. Funded by the County, members of the bar opened the Law Library in two small rooms within Tilgman Hall on the corner of Grant and Diamond, with a collection of five hundred books, including the *Pennsylvania Reports*, *Purdon's*, and some leading textbooks.[9] While attorney Joseph A. Katarincic observed that the founding of the law library "did not reflect or generate a community type effort or spirit that might have motivated and accounted for the subsequent development" of a bar association,[10] it was at least a benchmark of collective action on the part of some members of the bar.

Roughly two years after the Law Library was founded, in December 1869, a group of lawyers met in the Supreme Court Room in Pittsburgh to discuss the possibility of forming a bar association. James W. Murray, a lawyer who was Thomas Keenan's successor as publisher of the *Pittsburgh Legal Journal*, introduced a motion to form a committee to look into the establishment of a bar association. The committee—consisting of Jacob F. Slagle, David Reed, William B. Negley and James E. McKelvy—recommended that an association should be established, and that a charter should be secured. Once again, John Henry Hampton was on hand to write the enabling charter legislation; and on February 28, 1870, an act of the Pennsylvania legislature was signed into law by Governor

John W. Geary establishing the "Pittsburgh Law Association." At its first meeting on March 19, 1870, twenty of the original forty-one charter members were present for the election of Adam Mercer Brown as the first president of the Bar Association, John H. Bailey as vice president, W.S. McCune as secretary and Marcus W. Acheson as treasurer. Within two months of its founding, 165 out of the approximately 350 lawyers who were members of the Pittsburgh bar had been accepted or applied for membership. They met monthly during that first year, on a Saturday afternoon, to discuss such topics as eliminating the minor judiciary, setting standards for admission to the bar, and establishing minimum fees.

From the outset, it seems, the new bar association identified itself as a Allegheny County-wide organization—making the Pittsburgh Law Association the first county-wide organization of lawyers founded in the United States.[11] Interestingly, however, a group of the elite members of the bar of New York City also met in December 1869 to discuss the formation of a bar association, and on February 15, 1870—thirteen days before the establishment of the Pittsburgh Law Association by statute—eighty-five members of the New York City bar signed their names to the charter of the "Association of the Bar of the City of New York." The surviving statements of the purpose of the New York lawyers in organizing a bar association give us some indication of what must have also been on the minds of the Pittsburgh lawyers who established their own association not two weeks later:

> *It seems like an abdication of its legitimate position, that the Bar of the City of New York, numbering its members by the thousands, should have absolutely no organization whatever; that its influence in all matters affecting either its own dignity and interests as a profession, or the general good as connected with the advance of jurisprudence or reforms in the administration of justice, should be only that divided and dispersed influence of its members, which from being divided and dispersed, goes for nothing ... Many say ... [the] glory and dignity [of the Bar] are gone, that it has ceased to be a noble profession and is merely a trade with the rest. We do not admit this charge. But we mean to come together as a body, to look the question fairly in the face, and if we find that we have been tainted by the influence of the times to undertake ourselves the work of purification, to revive a past renown, and give new life to traditions which we believe to be only dormant, not extinct.[12]*

In his outgoing address as the first president of the Pittsburgh Law Association in March 1871, Adam Mercer Brown had similar sentiments in mind:

> *Organization is the great industrial, commercial and professional lever of the age. Other professions, industries and trades have their local and general organizations. The medical profession has its local, State and National societies for the advancement of science and the general good. But the legal profession, the most important and the most influential of them all ... seem[s] to be careless of [its] traditional glory, careless of the advantages to be derived from organization, local, State and National. When earnest, honest and fearless associations shall be formed and work together for the same end, then the spirit*

of reform will be promoted, the character and morality of the profession elevated and improved, and the dignity of the American Bar advanced.[13]

Brown was succeeded as president in March 1871 by James W. Murray, the publisher of the *Pittsburgh Legal Journal*; but by the following March, the activities of the Law Association ground to a halt, and no election was held for a new slate of officers. It remained dormant until 1882. Although the reasons for the Law Association's temporary suspension of its activities are unknown, Katarincic offers two theories: first, when John Henry Hampton, author of the enabling legislation for the charter, failed to be elected president in 1870, he immediately withdrew from the activities of the Law Association, and its decline followed shortly thereafter; and second, while the rallying point for the establishment of the Association of the Bar of the City of New York may have been the corruption and imminent prosecution of Boss Tweed and his ring, Pittsburgh lacked a similar focal point for reform activities—at least in 1870. What is certainly true is that when the Law Association was revived in March 1882, John Henry Hampton was elected president. Shortly thereafter, during Hampton's tenure, the name of the Law Association was officially changed to "Allegheny County Bar Association."[14]

At the end of Hampton's term, it looked as though the Bar Association might again fall dormant; but with the election of William B. Negley in 1884, the Bar Association finally found its stride. During his inaugural address, Negley admonished his colleagues: "Since the grant of our charter, fourteen years ago, practically nothing has been done. If no more is to be accomplished, it would be far better for us to disperse at once and not longer attempt to maintain an empty form ..."[15] The members heard Negley's call, and under his leadership, the Bar Association established permanent standing committees on Legislation, Fee Bills and Biography and History, as well as a committee of Censors for the handling of disciplinary matters, and a special committee to investigate public distrust of the jury system. Negley also established the annual banquet of the Bar Association—the first being held at the Monongahela House in 1888, limited to members willing to pay three dollars per plate—and an annual summer outing to the picnic area at Rock Point, near Elwood City, to the north of Pittsburgh. Negley served for six consecutive one-year terms, more than any other president of the Bar Association.[16]

The Bar Association lacked a permanent physical home until 1888, meeting in various rooms around the city. When the work commenced on the new Allegheny County Courthouse in 1883, a committee of the Bar Association reported that the County commissioners had agreed to provide rooms within the courthouse for the Law Library and the Association; by 1888, however, when the building was completed and ready for its public dedication, the Bar Association had apparently quarreled with the commissioners. Not only was there no permanent room offered to the Bar Association, but the Bar Association was conspicuously absent from the dedication ceremonies. Upon the motion of Charles C. Dickey at a meeting on November 3, 1888, the Bar Association resolved to bring legal action against the commissioners. An accommodation was reached, however, and the Bar Association was given the exclusive use of a room on the second floor of the courthouse overlooking the corner of Ross Street and Fifth Avenue. The Bar Association wasted no time in installing telephones and hiring a permanent clerk.[17]

Telephones had arrived in Pittsburgh in 1877,[18] but their adoption by Pittsburgh's lawyers was gradual at best. George Shiras had one installed in his office in the 1880s, but it was used only by his office boy, Tommy Boyd, to take messages; Shiras himself disliked it, and "so abiding was Shiras' prejudice against the telephone that never, throughout his life, did he utter a single word into the instrument."[19] Like so many technologies that would ultimately transform the habits of the legal profession, lawyers initially tended to think of such machines as tools for the use of their staff, not for themselves.

The pre-Civil War practice of setting up one's office on the first floor in one's downtown living quarters had all but disappeared by the 1870s.[20] Indeed, the whole notion of a street-level storefront law office downtown was beginning to be considered quaint, as more and more lawyers began to situate themselves in office buildings. Most of these buildings were located on the Diamond or Grant Street, or on Fourth or Fifth Avenue during the 1880s, before the Carnegie and St. Nicholas Buildings offered fashionably appointed offices for lawyers in brand new Pittsburgh skyscrapers in the 1890s. In an attempt to avoid the smoke of the city, Pittsburgh's affluent professionals were moving their residences to nearby suburbs. As a result, many Pittsburgh lawyers were commuting to work during this period: George Shiras, Jr., in the early years of his practice, used to walk across the Allegheny River from the North Side to his two-room office suite on Grant Street—a three mile round trip[21]; Thomas Mercer Marshall made his home on Perrysville Road in McClure Township, present day Brighton Heights, and commuted to his office on Diamond Street each day by horse and buggy[22]; and John Dalzell, the railroad lawyer, lived in Hawkins Station on the main line of the Pennsylvania Railroad, and probably took the train to his office on Grant Street, or later, in the St. Nicholas Building.[23] John F. Sanderson, who lived on Hay Street in Highland Park and had an office at 118 Diamond Street, rode his horse Commodore to work each day and was, according to some of his descendants, one of the last Pittsburgh lawyers to ride a horse to work on a regular basis.[24]

With the expansion in the number of lawyers in Pittsburgh and the rapid increase in Pittsburgh's industry, the judiciary was overdue for some structural changes. The Pennsylvania Constitution of 1874 abolished what had been known as the District Court within the county, and transferred all of the judges to one of two Common Pleas Courts—No. 1 and No. 2. Under the Constitution, in Allegheny County, plaintiffs were empowered to choose between the two Common Pleas Courts in which to initiate a case, and the case would be subject to the exclusive jurisdiction of that court—a fact which made the Allegheny County Common Pleas Courts very different from their counterparts in Philadelphia, where a consolidated Common Pleas Court system enabled judges to apportion cases across the judges' panel according to workload. In addition, the Constitution of 1874 removed from the jurisdiction of the Allegheny County Common Pleas Courts all matters relating to decedents' estates, minors and incompetents and established the Orphans' Court of Allegheny County. William G. Hawkins was elected as the first Orphans' Court judge.[25]

One of the more colorful local judges during the era was John William Fletcher "J.W.F." White, who served as an Allegheny County Common Pleas judge from 1873 (he would be known as a "district judge" until the following year) until his death in 1900, the last three years as the president judge. He was known as a "no-nonsense" judge, which perhaps contributed to his election to the bench for three consecutive terms. He publicly vowed to conduct a "terrific cleaning out" of saloons in Allegheny County, especially those that existed in close proximity to the steel mills, which undoubtedly helped to attract more affluent voters. In conducting alcohol licensing hearings, he generally deferred to the wishes of the Law and Order League, an anti-saloon organization that began in the 1880s, and succeeded in reducing the number of licensed saloons in the County from 3,500 to 389 in just two years.[26] Impatient and opinionated, according to attorney and bar historian Archibald Blakeley he frequently "jumped acknowledged precedents to reach a result which head and heart told him was law and justice," and while on the criminal bench, would frequently accept pleas of guilty and render sentences without having cases first appear before a grand jury. As Blakeley observes, "Possibly no one could legally object, except the defendants, and perhaps they were estopped by their own action. In any event, no case of the kind was taken to a Superior Court, and the result was a vast saving of expense to the county and the parties."[27]

With regard to the U.S. District Court for the Western District of Pennsylvania, Judge Wilson McCandless served until his retirement in 1876, and was succeeded in turn by Winthrop W. Ketchum, a Luzerne County lawyer and congressman, who served until his death in 1879; Marcus W. Acheson, a respected Pittsburgh trial lawyer who served until his elevation to the Third Circuit in 1891; James Hay Reed, who served one year before returning to his practice with Knox & Reed (1891-92); and Joseph Buffington, an Armstrong County lawyer who would serve from 1892 to 1906. Prior to 1869 (excluding a brief period during 1801-2), federal District Court judges and Supreme Court justices sat for appeals to the federal circuit courts. In 1869, however, Congress created circuit judgeships for the nine existing federal circuit courts. William McKennan from Washington County served as the first Third Circuit judge from 1869 until his retirement in 1891, and was succeeded by Judge Acheson.[28]

George Shiras, Jr. was nominated in 1892 by President Benjamin Harrison to succeed the late Joseph P. Bradley as Pittsburgh's third United States Supreme Court associate justice (fourth, if one counts Edwin Stanton, who was appointed but did not live long enough to take office), over the objections of Pennsylvania's Senator J. Donald Cameron, who charged that the president defied senatorial courtesy. Although Cameron and Harrison were both Republicans, Harrison did not enjoy good relations with the last dying gasps of the Cameron-Quay political machine in Pennsylvania. Seeing the handwriting on the wall, however, Senator Matthew Quay broke ranks with Cameron and dropped his opposition to Shiras' nomination, and Shiras was confirmed on July 26, 1892, right in the midst of the aftermath of the Homestead strike. On the Court, he would be known primarily for supposedly being the swing vote on the majority in *Pollock v. Farmers' Loan & Trust Co.* (1895), in which the Court struck down as unconstitutional a private and corporate income tax. Despite the contemporary notoriety and drama surrounding Shiras' vote, recent scholarship suggests that Shiras had always intended to vote to strike down the tax, however, and that another justice may have been the surprise swing vote against the constitutionality of the tax. In general, however, despite his corporate law pedigree, Shiras was a moderate justice on questions of business regulation. He resigned after ten years, honoring a commitment he had made when he was nominated, and was the last of Pittsburgh's homegrown Supreme Court justices to date.[29] His background as a Pittsburgh corporate lawyer helped to place Pittsburgh, and its bar by extension, at the center of American discourse about law and business at the height of the Gilded Age.

THOMAS MELLON: LAWYER AS CAPITALIST

Thomas Mellon sat on the roof of the courthouse on the day of the Great Fire of Pittsburgh, April 10, 1845, and the capitalist in him could not be suppressed. As he wrote in his memoir, published forty years after the Great Fire, "I remember when on the Courthouse viewing the scene of disaster and contemplating the vast amount of wealth destroyed." He initially speculated that the event was likely to "produce a depression in business and hard times"; however, his instinctive attraction to commercial enterprises enabled him to recognize that the Great Fire also produced a great opportunity in Pittsburgh. As he subsequently reported, "Mechanics of all kinds flocked in from other places, and all obtained ready employment at better wages than formerly; and new life and increased value infused into real estate, and rents were higher for several years."[30]

Mellon wasted little time taking advantage of the great opportunity. Later that year, he completed his development of the dwellings and offices at the corner of Wylie Avenue and Fifth—the ones that had preoccupied him on the day of the Great Fire—and in the following year, he built "some eighteen small dwellings" elsewhere in Pittsburgh which brought him an income of about ten percent on his initial investment, until he sold them at a profit in 1860.[31]

Well before the Great Fire, in fact, the twenty-five year-old Mellon actively sought investment opportunities from the moment he entered the bar. While reading law, he was employed as a clerk in the prothonotary's office, and after his admission he decided to stay for another six months before opening his own practice. There he came into contact with numerous chances to "invest from time to time in little speculations in the purchase of small judgements, mechanic's liens and like securities wherever the holders were anxious to realize without the delay of awaiting their maturity."[32]

The "some seven hundred dollars" he made from such speculations helped to fund his first purchase of law books for his new law office, which he opened in June 1839. By the time of his 1843 marriage to Sarah Jane Negley, daughter of the founder of Pittsburgh's East Liberty neighborhood, Mellon's fortune had increased to twelve thousand dollars—not inconsiderable for a young man in his day.[33]

Up until the late nineteenth century—arguably, even later—the ideal of the American lawyer, especially among the bars of the larger metropolitan cities in the East, was that he was a member of a profession, not a trade, and that his principal interest was in justice, not commerce. Cotton Mather, the famed Puritan evangelist from Boston, defined the shape of the American lawyer for many years with what has been called "the First American Address to Lawyers" in 1710:

A Lawyer should be a Scholar, but, Sirs, when you are called upon to be wise, the main Intention is that you may be wise to do Good ... A Lawyer that is a Knave deserves Death, more than a Band of Robbers; for he profanes the Sanctuary of the Distressed and Betrayes the Liberties of the People. To ward off such a Censure, a Lawyer must shun all those Indirect Ways of making Hast to be Rich, in which a man cannot be Innocent ...[34]

The gist of Mather's lecture in Boston, minus the suggestion of a death penalty, was a continual refrain among the leaders of the large metropolitan bars for decades: for a lawyer to possess the independence that is essential to rendering correct advice and maintaining legal order, he must isolate himself from commercial pursuits. As Superior Court judge William W. Porter of Philadelphia wrote, the office of the old ideal lawyer was "a modest room adorned with book cases where sits a learned semi-recluse writing to bestow his wisdom in the law and satisfied if his compensation shall come as an honorarium."[35] This monastic standard for elite lawyers was a mark of nobility for them, and it was certainly one of the ways in which a lawyer sought to build a social wall separating himself from the butcher, the blacksmith and the street peddler.

On the Western frontier, the wall was not so impenetrable, and the lawyers were not so monastic. Writing of the Western lawyer of the early nineteenth century, Friedman observes that

> *... [I]t was not so easy to scratch out a living in new soil ... Their practice took patience, luck and skill. They did not bother asking what was or was not fit work for a lawyer. Whatever earned a dollar was fair game. ... [H]ard money was at all times scarce; a lawyer who got his hands on some cash would cast around for the most profitable investment.*[36]

When Thomas Mellon entered the Allegheny County bar in 1838, he was entering the profession within a "Western" frontier post that was rapidly blossoming into an "Eastern" metropolis, one in which the identification with Eastern ideals and standards of propriety and the cultural traditions of Western individuality and self-actualization were increasingly at odds. Certainly some Pittsburgh lawyers of the period viewed law and commerce as appropriately separate arenas, and embraced the Eastern ideal of the monastic lawyer. Henry Warren Williams, a Pittsburgh lawyer who served on the Pennsylvania Supreme Court, for example, advised young lawyers that "It is sometimes possible to seek wealth or position for its own sake and find it, but it is not the best or the surest road to either; and it is never wise for a professional man to take the risks of such a course."[37]

In Mellon's vision of the successful lawyer, however, one may see how the ideal of the American lawyer began to change in Pittsburgh in response to the rise of industry, and how aspects of Mellon's own model of American lawyer became the predominant one by the end of the nineteenth century, even as he left the profession behind to become a full-time capitalist. If the traditional view was that lawyers should separate themselves from commerce, Mellon's view was not only that the most successful lawyers were naturally good businessmen, but also that it was becoming increasingly important within the dynamic economy of Pittsburgh for a lawyer to master the inner-workings of commerce in great detail. In Mellon's view, it appeared, the most fatal weakness of the lawyers of his age was their naiveté concerning the mechanics, methods and motives of commerce.

In his memoir, Mellon writes:

> [T]he lawyer's profession embraces the whole field of human nature and the entire scope of human knowledge. He must be intimate with the objects and feelings which actuate the busy world in every department of life. Hence the more comprehensive and clearer his perceptions the better he is calculated to succeed if he possesses the necessary energy to propel him. ... He is necessarily a man of the world, mingling with all classes and acquainted with all interests ...[38]

By way of illustration, Mellon relates the story of two brothers, Robert and Andrew Burke, who were admitted to the Allegheny County bar in 1822 and 1833, respectively:

> Robert had the propelling energy which Andrew lacked, and Andrew had the easy flow of eloquence which Robert lacked; consequently Robert accumulated considerable estate although he was in practice comparatively a short time when he died, whilst Andrew remained at the bar for nearly forty years, with more education and acquired accomplishments than his brother, and died in poverty. Robert was an energetic business man and industrious; Andrew had no business tact and was indolent. Robert practiced the law as an active tradesman would his work, whilst Andrew spent his time preparing polished addresses in the few cases in which he was retained. Andrew's adversary would usually gain the case, leaving him but the empty honor of a fine speech.[39]

In other words, Mellon's ideal lawyer was one who embraced the thoughts and habits of the successful businessman, and not necessarily the one who could raise the roof with his oratorical gifts. "I never cared to prepare or deliver a set speech to gain applause," Mellon wrote in his memoir. "We only possess a limited amount of mental power, and the result or product therefrom depends on how it is expended. If unexerted and it remains idle, nothing whatever is accomplished; or if exerted in useless ornamentation and display or other frivolity, a proportionate loss accrues to the clients in the management of their business and to the attorney in the amount of his income."[40] During an age when a lawyer's showy speeches were prized, Mellon was undoubtedly impatient with and disdainful of the vast majority of his colleagues at the bar.

It was Mellon's opinion that no amount of rhetorical talent as an orator or examiner of witnesses was likely to produce success "unless the lawyer has first made himself acquainted with all the facts and details of the case, even to the minutest circumstance."[41] Like his colleague Edwin Stanton within the context of trial advocacy, Mellon's habits of thinking prodded him to pursue knowledge of Pittsburgh's businesses in great detail. These habits are reflected, for example, in his advice to his second eldest son James Ross Mellon on how to learn about business:

> ... associate with businessmen in different departments and pump them. You recollect Girard's course in that respect.[a] He squeezed all the information out of every man he met like he would a sponge and did it without their suspecting he had any design in it. By appearing communicative and talking about the business and asking questions you can get any man to give information. This information is not about what they are making particularly, for in this they are apt to lie, but as regards the details of the business—the prices—the freights—the risks—the expenses—the amount sales—or amount consumed, etc., etc. Thus, the coal business is important to be known, where the coal comes from, what it costs to mine, the freight, cost of handling, quantity consumed at the gas works and where obtained and by what route, etc. Learn the modus operandi of the business and merchandising and iron business or other important branches of manufacturing ... Remember a young man can never have too much useful information and everything relating to active life is useful nowadays.[42]

Pennsylvania Supreme Court Justice Henry W. Williams by contrast, had a traditional, somewhat provincial view of the knowledge that a lawyer was required to possess in order to practice effectively. In his *Legal Ethics and Suggestions for Young Counsel*, the former Allegheny County judge acknowledged, like Mellon, that "[t]he practice of law requires a little knowledge of almost every trade, art and science in the whole realm of human learning and labor."[43] However, Williams advised young lawyers not to immerse themselves:

> But 'art is long and time is fleeting' and a lawyer engaged in practice cannot stop his work whenever such a question presents itself and turn his attention to mastery of the details of the branch of labor or of learning thus brought under examination. He needs to be able by some short cut, some comprehensive summary of the subject to leap at once 'in media res' and gather up so much of the needed learning as relates to the points in controversy and is therefore indispensable to the proper trial of the cause in which they are presented.[44]

---

a   The character of Stephen Girard, the financier, who may have been known to Mellon and his son through a biography published in Philadelphia, in which attorney Stephen Simpson writes that when interviewing acquaintances in the business world, Girard "operated like a complete colustrator upon his subject, sifting out of him, little by little, every particle of information ..." Stephen Simpson, Esq., *Biography of Stephen Girard, with his Will Affixed* (Philadelphia: T.L. Bonsal, 1832), 192.

Justice Williams suggested that having dictionaries, digests and encyclopedias on various branches of knowledge on hand was always advisable—a far cry from the investigations and the immersion in the minutiae of business practices that Mellon personally adopted.

By 1859, through investments in coal and real estate, Mellon had amassed a fortune of several million dollars, and he felt that his private and professional business had "increased so rapidly that it became difficult to do justice to either."[45] He had tried taking on law partners, but found the experience unsatisfactory. While contemplating his quandary, he was approached by a delegation of colleagues at the bar—Thomas Mercer Marshall, A.M. Watson and Stephen H. Geyer—about becoming a Republican candidate for the office of assistant law judge of the County Court of Common Pleas:

> *I regarded the proposition rather in the light of a practical joke. I had never entertained the slightest desire for office of any kind, or given a thought to seeking popularity, or indeed taken any share in party politics, and accordingly scouted the idea. But they returned again and again to persuade me of its advisability. I was overwhelmed and oppressed by business at the time, and in a mood to get rid of my law business and last law partners together if I could; and they finally persuaded me that this was the way to do it, and an honorable way of retiring from the profession.*[46]

Mellon had also developed disdain for what he perceived as hypocrisy within the profession among lawyers who "pretended to a disregard of money and exhibited contempt at its accumulation."[47] Perhaps the most telling evidence of his impatience with the legal profession turns up in his later advice to his sons. When his son James expressed an interest in entering a lawyer's office as a clerk, Mellon cautioned that after six months he would probably learn all that was important, and that there were more lucrative pursuits. In order to succeed in the law, Mellon told his son, one required

> *... first class business talents; but if pecuniary success is the object first class business talent can mostly be utilized to better advantage in other pursuits: especially is this the case if the party has any capital of his own to operate with. ...Attention to other people's business is a waste of time when we have profitable business of our own to attend to ...*[48]

One gets the sense from his letters and memoir that Mellon was only too happy to leave behind the practice of law in an age in which a lawyer's need to understand the business of Pittsburgh was not yet fully appreciated or understood.

Mellon was elected to a ten-year term on the Common Pleas bench in 1859, and came to be regarded as an industrious jurist, somewhat more lenient in criminal cases than his senior colleague, Judge William B. McClure. During his time on the bench, however—although he regarded his judicial career as "altogether pleasing and satisfactory to myself"[49]—Judge Mellon developed an even more cynical view of the machinery of justice and the legal profession, noting that the typical jury was not competent to reach proper decisions, and disparagingly observing that there were members of the bar "who pride themselves upon ability to humbug the jury and obtain verdicts by clap-trap."[50]

Upon his retirement from the bench at the age of fifty-seven, with "two bright boys just out of school," Judge Mellon "concluded to open a banking house" rather than going back into the practice of law.[51] On January 2, 1870, Judge Mellon opened the T. Mellon & Sons Bank with two of his younger sons, Andrew and Richard, in a building at 514 Smithfield Street. His acumen and stewardship successfully guided the Mellon Bank through the Panic of 1873, in which more than fifty of Pittsburgh's banks failed, and he made shrewd investments in downtown real estate and coal, as well as a ten thousand dollar loan to Henry Clay Frick which enabled Frick to provide coke for Andrew Carnegie's steel mills. In time, under Judge Mellon's leadership, the Mellon Bank was one of the strongest and most stable banks in the region.

By the time he reached his seventies, Judge Mellon's conversion from "man of laws" to "man of finance" was virtually complete, as further evidenced by his personal war against the building of the new Allegheny County Courthouse. In 1881, Judge Mellon accepted the nomination of the Republicans in the East End of Pittsburgh for a seat on city council, to which he was elected and in which he served for three two-year terms. As a councilman, he assumed the role of the perennial fiscal conservative, opposing on principle the levy of new taxes and the issuance of public bonds as fueling nothing but "folly and extravagance." He cast, for example, the lone vote against the city's acceptance of the offer of his friend Andrew Carnegie to build a library for Pittsburgh on the grounds of the future maintenance expense that would fall as a burden upon the taxpaying public.

When the matter of a bond offering for a new county courthouse arose, Judge Mellon unhesitatingly opposed it, calling H.H. Richardson's courtroom designs too grand for their proposed use. He asserted that rooms "about forty feet square would ... best serve the purposes of justice" and that the grandness of the building would only serve to attract "loafers and hangers on." He was so passionate in his opposition to the courthouse plan that he personally litigated the propriety of the bond issue all the way to the Pennsylvania Supreme Court—where, to his chagrin, he not only lost the cause, but looked on as the city paid two thousand dollars in taxpayers' money to defend the lawsuit.[52]

In 1882, at the age of sixty-nine, Thomas Mellon turned over the active management of Mellon Bank to Andrew and Richard (known as "R.B."), who invested, as an editor of the family letters writes

> *in businesses that were building a new, nationwide industrial economy. Acting as venture capitalists, the brothers helped to develop such industries as aluminum, coke gas, structural steel, and transportation. They bought into plate glass, insurance, street railways, public utilities, electricity, iron castings, silicon carbide, and oil. Their backing launched the Aluminum Company of America (Alcoa), Gulf Oil Corporation, the Koppers Company, the Carborundum Company, McClintic-Marshall Construction Company (builders of locks for the Panama Canal), Pittsburgh Coal Company, and other companies that created jobs for tens of thousands of workers. Andrew and Richard B. Mellon's success was due in part to their circumstances as bankers in a crucial industrial center—and also to the lessons in life, psychology, and business they had learned literally at their father's knee. Thomas Mellon took his parental responsibilities with the utmost seriousness ... and was intent on guiding his children to the best of his singular ability.*[53]

Mellon's habits of mind and his obsession with the intricacies of Pittsburgh business were also being taken on by younger lawyers in Pittsburgh after the conclusion of the Civil War. Even before Mellon exited both law and finance, the major lines of discussion and debate among members of the bar were shifting away from the nature and powers of the State, to the nature and powers of the Corporation. Thus, a new generation of Pittsburgh lawyers, born right into a time and place of explosive change at the noisy nexus of Pittsburgh law and Pittsburgh commerce that was encouraged in no small part by the Mellon Bank itself, were developing business acumen out of necessity—some of them, inevitably, in the likeness of Thomas Mellon. Far from being separate from commerce, far from being encouraged to gain a mere dilettante's command of business, far from being neutral about the forms and institutions of business—the new model of Pittsburgh lawyer that began to emerge after the Civil War would absorb and adopt the principles and objectives of business, and would be a leader in the creation of the Corporation culture of Pittsburgh. Men like John Dalzell, D.T. Watson, George Shiras, Willis F. McCook, Philander Knox and James H. Reed were examples, to varying degrees, of this model, and they helped to make the Pittsburgh bar a forceful institution during the period. It was their way of wielding the axe that their forbearers had wielded in the early years of the Pittsburgh bar. Each of them became wealthy in the process.

What can be seen in practice in Pittsburgh, beginning after the end of the Civil War, became a part of the conventional wisdom of commentators in New York and elsewhere within the Eastern professional establishment by the turn of the century: law is a business, and a successful lawyer, as Mellon had urged, must have first-class business talents. William O. Inglis, writing in *Munsey's* in 1901, observes:

Formerly the lawyer was assumed to be an omnium gatherum of legal information ... He was not supposed to be a man of affairs, or to have property. Indeed, he was farthest removed from the business-man and his methods. Today, to be successful, the lawyer must make his methods those of the business-man, and become an integral part of the business-world. Twenty years ago a man went to a lawyer when he was in trouble. Now a client seeks a lawyer in order to keep out of trouble.[54]

Even then, the idea was certainly not free from doubt. In 1903, James B. Dill, a New York corporation lawyer, gave a keynote address to a political science convention, attempting to prove that "the business lawyer of today is a business man, specialized along the lines of legal principles." Dill declared:

The successful lawyer of to-day is not the man who is the last resort of the business man, to whom the business man appeals when he is on the verge of destruction. On the contrary, he is consulted at the outset and throughout the progress of every enterprise of magnitude, that by reason of his special legal experience upon business lines he may, primarily, make the undertakings of the business man of more profit than without his assistance, and secondarily, may avoid the possibility of attack and litigation. The more nearly the lawyer brings his profession into touch with business methods the greater will be his success, and the profession is to-day beginning to realize the fact and act upon it ... The trend of business is unmistakably toward combination, involving a heavier individual responsibility, a broader sweep of vision—covering the markets of the world—a more complex organization of the business and prompt solution of, or decision upon, intricate problems than had ever been required of the business man of the past. The corporation lawyer to-day is the right hand of the corporation management, an integral part of the body corporate.[55]

The *Central Law Journal*, however, editorialized that the "millionaire corporation lawyer" had "lost all conception of true advocacy."[56]

The progeny of Thomas Mellon extended far beyond the sons who built the banking empire that bears his name and the industries that it financed. In Pittsburgh, he was an important transitional figure—the lawyer who acknowledged Business (with a capital 'B') as the central engine of his career—and whose habits presaged those of a generation of Pittsburgh lawyers who were, in their way, helping to define the identity of the American lawyer during the Gilded Age.

THE CORPORATION MEN

The first modern, complex business institutions in America, and in Pennsylvania in particular, were railroads. As Alfred D. Chandler, Jr. wrote:

> *The men who managed these enterprises became the first group of modern business administrators in the United States. Ownership and management soon separated. The capital required to build a railroad was far more than that required to purchase a plantation, a textile mill, or even a fleet of ships. Therefore, a single entrepreneur, family, or small group of associates was rarely able to own a railroad. Nor could the many stockholders or their representatives manage it. ... Only in the raising and allocating of capital, in the setting of financial policies, and in the selection of top managers did the owners or their representatives have a real say in railroad management.*[57]

As Chandler suggests, the existence of the nation's railroads depended, to a large degree, upon the indulgences provided by the corporate form of entity—principally, the ability to raise a large amount of passive equity capital while affording the investors with a "veil" of insulation from the corporation's liabilities. The trick of the veil enabled the railroad tycoons of the era to enlarge the scale of private industry in ways that would have been unimaginable without it.

Not surprisingly, the most important railroad in Pennsylvania, the Pennsylvania Railroad, was founded and organized, as a corporation, on April 13, 1846.[58] By 1880, with thirty thousand employees and forty million dollars in capital, the Pennsylvania Railroad was the world's largest corporation, and it was a center of political power in Pennsylvania.[59] The old joke was that the legislature of Pennsylvania only adjourned when the Pennsylvania Railroad had no more business for it to transact. The close ties between the Railroad and politicians, as facilitated in many cases by the Railroad's corporate lawyers, became the stuff of popular legend around Pittsburgh. At a South Side labor meeting in 1877, one of the speakers told the following story:

> [T]he railroad company wanted Eighth street—which now forms part of the metal yards—vacated. They made their proposition to [City] Councils... but people raised a hubbub, and Councils refused to pass a bill. But Will A. Stokes, then solicitor of the company, said he would fix the Councilmen, and he did. He got up a big supper at the Monongahela House, stuffed the Councilmanic stomachs with oysters, sweet-meats and wine till they lost their brains. The next night Councils met in regular session, the bill was passed and Eighth street was vacated.

The *Pittsburgh Post* reported that the story met with laughter and applause.[60]

The Pennsylvania Railroad, as a hive of commercial activity and a frequent target of litigation, provided a laboratory for the earliest Pittsburgh corporation lawyers to learn their craft—particularly for John Henry Hampton, the son of Judge Moses Hampton, who was first appointed as an outside "assistant solicitor" for the western division of the Railroad at the age of twenty-six in 1854. Following the resignation of the aforementioned William A. Stokes, a Philadelphia lawyer who had earlier moved to Greensburg to assist the Pennsylvania Railroad with its expansion west to Pittsburgh, Hampton was appointed as outside district solicitor for Pittsburgh from 1858.

As Hampton's private practice grew, much of it around railroad and streetcar activity, he gained a reputation as a lawyer's lawyer—a brilliant cross-examiner and jury trial lawyer, with a flair for the theatrical. "Sarcasm and invective were often his weapons," noted one colleague, "but the humorous was his more congenial vein. By homely stories, irresistibly funny, told with a masterful art, mellow witticisms, and most grotesque similitudes, he often laughed his opponent out of court."[61] The job of a Pittsburgh-based Pennsylvania Railroad lawyer, however—though not a boardroom advisor, since the corporation was largely an Eastern Pennsylvania invention—involved a great deal more than defending the Railroad from lawsuits, as the Stokes anecdote illustrates.

The birth of the Pennsylvania Railroad itself was a lawyerly slog through the state legislature: the Baltimore & Ohio (B&O) Railroad had been working toward securing Pittsburgh as its western terminus, and had a corporate charter that permitted it do so until 1843. Philadelphia lobbyists convinced the legislature to refrain from extending the B&O's charter on the grounds that the western trade would go to Baltimore, while Pittsburgh politicos urged for extension so that Pittsburgh would finally have a rail passage to the East. In the end, the legislature voted to recharter the B&O, but only if the Pennsylvania Railroad, the new state creation, could not obtain one million dollars in capital and build thirty miles of track towards Pittsburgh by July 30, 1847. The "Pennsy" sprang into action, and beat the B&O charter renewal, going on to build a working line between Harrisburg and Philadelphia by 1854.[62]

The efforts of rival railroads did not end with the B&O's charter expiration. The B&O, as well as other railroad companies, did their best to frustrate the extension of the "Pennsy" to Pittsburgh by tying up land when possible, and by enlisting the aid of local politicians in throwing up roadblocks. One of Hampton's greatest legal achievements was winning a case before the Pennsylvania Supreme Court, *Pittsburgh v. Pennsylvania Railroad* (1865),[63] that established the principle that the power of the Pennsylvania

Railroad to establish branch lines, by the terms of its corporate charter, was as large as the power it had been granted in its charter for the construction of the main railroad, and that therefore, the Railroad essentially had the right to engage in "digging, excavating, and piling up dirt, stones, &c., in several of the streets of Pittsburgh" to extend the rails to more one or more convenient locations within the city of Pittsburgh. Through the efforts of John Hampton, relying upon the grant of powers within its charter, the Pennsylvania Railroad secured the franchises and easements necessary to establish itself as the principal means of long-distance transportation in Western Pennsylvania, forcing competitors to take odd crooked routes to Pittsburgh.

The *Pittsburgh* case, by focusing upon the scope of the charter of the Railroad, was fought and won on what would become one of the primary battlefronts for Pittsburgh's pioneering corporate lawyers. Corporate charters had initially been granted by the legislature to undertake, on an exclusive basis, specific major projects that had traditionally been a part of the state's function, such as the building of roads, bridges or canals, or banking. In order to survive in a competitive environment, however, corporate charters were being fashioned into vehicles for purposes that inured to the benefit of private investors. In a time when there was no such thing as a corporation with general powers to undertake any activity, the art of being a corporate lawyer required the ability to draft a corporate charter that advanced the business plans of one's client, while at the same time continuing to honor the fiction that a corporation was a public institution—all the while, without necessarily exposing the future plans of one's client to nosy competitors. Pittsburgh lawyers had long been called upon to be clever in drafting a deed or a pleading. But in drafting the charter of a corporation, the Pittsburgh lawyer was now forced to be a student of his client's entire business—from the broad plan for its future to the minutiae of its daily activities—in order to be effective.

The dazzling success of the Pennsylvania Railroad as a corporation inevitably led Pittsburgh businessmen to emulate its structure and the advantages that came from the corporate form. By the 1870s, legislators were besieged with requests for new corporate charters and charter amendments. On behalf of lesser businesses than the "Pennsy," the art of being a corporate lawyer also required the ability to convince a legislator to take such a charter to the floor. The backslapping John Henry Hampton, the hale lawyer well-met with a touch of the barracuda, was perfectly suited to the task.

Two of the most important Pittsburgh corporation lawyers of the age studied with John Henry Hampton in his offices at the east side of Grant Street: Yale's John Dalzell and Harvard's David Thompson Watson. The diminutive Dalzell would go on to become Hampton's law partner before eventually being election to Congress, while D.T. Watson—whom Dalzell described as "a tall young man with high shoulders, fine head and face, and a modest bearing"—opened his own office, also on Grant Street. As Watson's biographer, Francis R. Harbison, relates, their meeting in Hampton's offices was a fated beginning:

Had some crystal gazer witnessed the meeting of these two young men in their early twenties, what a tale he could have spun. Gazing into the future, two parallel careers would have appeared, sometimes associated, more frequently opposing one another at the Bar. Dalzell pitted against Watson for the Pennsylvania Railroad against Vanderbilt and his ambitious ventures for the New York Central towards Pittsburgh; Dalzell for Carnegie and Watson for Frick in the greatest lawsuit ever filed in Pennsylvania. The two traveled side by side daily in the elevator in their new St. Nicholas Law Building to adjoining offices; and one could almost hear Watson murmur to Dalzell, "John, you'd better tell Carnegie to get down off his high horse, for over here, men are still free and equal."[64]

One very high-profile imbroglio, emanating from a period when the Pennsylvania Railroad's corporate structure was still the exception rather than the rule, became an object lesson for the flaws of doing "big business" outside the corporate form. It was the cluster of lawsuits that came to be known as the "Bull Ring Cases."

An oil boom had begun in Western Pennsylvania following Colonel Edwin Drake's discovery of oil at Titusville in 1859. It was the first strike of its kind in North America, and it attracted a gallery of lively characters to the region that came to be known as "Petrolia"—wildcatters who were learning how to drill for oil by trial and error; entrepreneurs in the oil refining trade; men of capital who came to consolidate operations; and of course, speculators. In 1869, a collection of prominent oil entrepreneurs—Charles Lockhart and his partner Major William Frew, successful drillers and refiners whose Phillips No. 2 well held the record for production in the region for over twenty years, and whose Philadelphia-based distribution business was the chief trader of oil on the East coast; Byers and Company, led by A.M. Byers, an iron manufacturer who became distracted by the prospect of oil profits in the 1860s and established a refining and trading business; oil operator Captain Samuel Lewis; and Dr. Arnold Hertz of the Fairview Refinery—gathered in the office of the long-bearded Dr. David Hostetter, a purveyor of medicinal bitters and the publisher of *Hostetter's Almanac*, and hatched a plan to buy up all the crude oil in storage in the Western Pennsylvania oil fields and hold it back from trade until prices rose. They organized as a partnership, the Pittsburgh Petroleum Company, borrowed capital and started buying crude oil on a scale never before seen in Petrolia.

Despite the Company spending almost four million dollars, oil prices did not rise. Their own purchases of oil appeared to be supporting the market through the end of 1869; and when they found themselves unable to borrow additional capital, the price actually started to drop. The Company began to receive margin calls for borrowings secured by oil as the beginning of the Franco-Prussian War in 1870 wiped out the possibility of a European market for their product.

By July, they were merely trying salvage what they could. They divided the oil among them, each of them disposing of it in their own way; and then they began to sue each other. Without the protection of a corporate veil, every partner in the scheme was vulnerable to each other and all their creditors. Captain Lewis sued Byers; the Iron City Banking Company followed; Hostetter sued Lockhart & Frew and their Atlantic operation; Byers sued Lockhart & Frew; Lewis sued Lockhart & Frew; and other creditors came out of the woodwork and sued everyone else. Each of the oil spill's protagonists engaged a leading member of the bar: David Reed, the uncle and preceptor of James H. Reed, represented Captain Lewis; John Barton represented Hostetter; John Hampton represented Lockhart & Frew; and George Shiras, Jr. and D.T. Watson represented Byers & Company.

As Harbison writes, "The parties were inextricably mingled. Co-plaintiffs in one suit were opponents in others; and co-defendants in some cases likewise opposed each other in another ..." The taking of testimony in just the Lewis and Hostetter cases took two years, from December 20, 1872 to December 14, 1874, tracing through "a labyrinth of purchases and sales of oil" and "the mingling of orders and substitutions." Finally, in March 1875, the "Bull Ring" cases were consolidated in a proceeding before three special masters, J.H. Miller, Jacob F. Slagle and F.N. Magee, and in May 1878, a decision came down, netting out the damages among the parties. The total losses of the Company were $904,130.14, equal to perhaps hundreds of millions today; Dr. Hertz died and left an insolvent estate; Captain Lewis was bankrupt; and Dr. Hostetter ended up owing money to Byers and Lockhart & Frew. The trials drew large public crowds, although the public was generally unsympathetic toward all the parties. As Harbison observes, "the plotters' losses was a case of the biter being bitten."[65]

Although the "Bull Ring" affair was a stain on the reputation of the Pittsburgh oil business and somewhat of an embarrassment to the legal community, at least D.T. Watson emerged as a star talent. His thumping of Lockhart & Frew on behalf of Byers attracted the notice of Lockhart & Frew's some-time associate, John D. Rockefeller, the founder of Standard Oil. Other important work would follow. William H. Vanderbilt engaged Watson to help him to dig a rail tunnel through the complexities of Pennsylvania corporation law as the Pennsylvania, McKeesport & Youghiogheny Railroad and its related entities attempted to reach Pittsburgh in the 1880s. Watson also successfully took on the almost herculean task of keeping Captain J.B. Ford in control of the Pittsburgh Plate Glass Company when early shareholders threatened to break it apart, and he was rewarded with the opportunity to invest—one of the main reasons that Watson died among the wealthiest men in Pittsburgh.

Meanwhile, if the success of the Pennsylvania Railroad was not enough to convince Pittsburgh's lawyers and businessmen that the corporation was a preferred structure for doing business, the "Bull Ring Cases" were no doubt a cautionary tale that seized the imaginations of Pittsburgh's business lawyers and cried out for the establishment of a different business culture.

In the model of the "Pennsy," the successful iron and steel entrepreneur of Pittsburgh—a man such as Henry Clay Frick (the former coke entrepreneur who became manager of Carnegie's operations), Benjamin Franklin "B.F." Jones, Sr. (the founder of Jones & Laughlin) or Henry W. Oliver (of the Oliver Iron and Steel Company)—would deploy vast amounts of private, passive equity capital to erect his own vertically-integrated enterprise. Such a corporation, as James Howard Bridge describes in his "inside" history of Carnegie Steel, assembled "its own mines, dug its ore with machines of amazing power, loaded it onto its own steamers, landed it at its own ports, transported on its own railroads, distributed it among its many blast-furnaces, and smelted it with coke similarly brought from its own coal-mines and ovens, and with limestone brought from its own quarries" and consolidated "these disorganized units into a solid, compact, harmonious whole, whose every part worked with the ease and silent motion of the perfectly balanced machine."[66]

Pittsburgh's elite corporation lawyers would fall in with that "ease and silent motion," but for a variety of reasons—because lawyers were generally well-educated, because they were affluent, and because the corporation itself was a legal device that required a lawyer's care and feeding—they often did so as the peers of Pittsburgh's increasingly sophisticated industrialists. Unlike many of the managers and superintendents employed by these industrialists, who passed messages back and forth to the top executives via middle managers, the top lawyers dealt directly with the top industrialists. For example, when Henry Clay Frick sought advice from D.T. Watson regarding his equipment and supply sales activities, Watson was as blunt as an elder brother: "Your H.C. Frick Coke Company," Watson wrote, "has no power to legally engage in the purchase and sale of general merchandise. You have taken out a charter for the Union Supply Co. Ltd. It has no capital but you use its name as a mere cover for doing 'what your company cannot do legally.' Pay in the capital stock and make your Union Supply a legal corporation."[67] George B. Gordon, one of Dalzell's junior partners and later the head of the successor firm of Gordon & Smith, was known to have enjoyed working sessions with such tycoons as Andrew Mellon and Alcoa's Arthur Vining Davis, sitting by while they read long, complicated contracts or briefs and discussing the essential points and weaknesses of them.[68] Some of these corporation lawyers would participate even more directly in the affairs of their commercial colleagues. Willis F. McCook, who was captain of the Yale Bulldogs' first-ever football squad before returning to Pittsburgh and becoming Frick's personal business lawyer, was among the seven co-founders, an initial investor, general counsel, and ultimately a president and chairman, of Pittsburgh Steel Company,[69] one of the antecedents of Wheeling-Pittsburgh Steel.

The peerage of executives and lawyers during Pittsburgh's Gilded Age also manifested itself in their social relations. In June 1873, an exclusive "voluntary association" called the Duquesne Club was founded by eleven Pittsburgh industrialists "where," as Winfield Shiras put it, "dinners and banquets could be held more privately than in a hotel."[70] By the 1890s, the Club had its own building on Sixth Avenue, a handsome Romanesque brownstone designed by a successor to the architectural firm of H.H. Richardson, who had designed the courthouse.

An illustrious group of industrialists and lawyers founded an even more exclusive "club within a club" called the "Number Six Club" that lunched every day in Room Number 6 of the Duquesne Club. These men included Thomas Carnegie, Andrew's talented brother; Henry Oliver; Charles L. Fitzhugh, a former Union Army general and president of Shoenberger Steel, along with his brother and financial manager, Robert; John H. Ricketson, a lawyer who had assumed control of his father-in-law's business, the Pittsburgh Foundry; B.F. Jones, Sr.; John Chalfant, one of the fathers of the Pittsburgh steel industry and a manufacturer of steel tubing, along with his partners Charles Spang and Campbell Herron; the iron broker Albert H. Childs; another iron manufacturer, Maxwell K. Moorhead; A.E.W. Painter of the J. Painter & Sons Iron Works, later president of the People's National Bank; Judge William G. Hawkins of the Orphans'

Court; corporate lawyers Solomon Schoyer, Jr. and George Shiras, Jr.; Captain Frank H. Phipps, a high-ranking ordnance officer and later the commandant of the Allegheny Arsenal; and Henry S.A. Stewart, an oil and real estate magnate.[71] While soot from the steel mills blackened Pittsburgh's downtown streets outside, the mustachioed men of the Number Six Club dined, smoked cigars, and discussed the nation's business.

Lawyers, tycoons and their families socialized in other ways. Lawyer Ricketson's family and those of Jones and Childs were enthusiastic participants in the annual Pittsburgh Horse Show.[72] Shiras counted Chalfant and Childs as particularly close friends; Childs was Shiras' younger fraternity brother at Yale, and Shiras took a weekly Sunday walk with Chalfant, "often crossing the bridge from Allegheny bridge and tramping through the deserted streets of downtown Pittsburgh," according to Winfield Shiras.[73] Childs' daughter Clara would subsequently marry Shiras' son Winfield.[74] Later, Philander Knox and James H. Reed, the founders of the law firm that later became Reed Smith, were among the regular attendees of Henry Clay Frick's poker nights, along with Judge Mellon's son Andrew, George Westinghouse and Robert Pitcairn, superintendent of the Pennsylvania Railroad.[75] Frick's poker companions, Andrew Carnegie, and other members of the Number Six Club were prominent members of the South Fork Fishing and Hunting Club, the club that later became notorious for its alleged role in the Johnstown Flood of 1889. Other Pittsburgh lawyers who frequented the Club along with the "pig-iron aristocracy" of the day included Hilary B. Brunot; Cyrus Elder, chief counsel for the Cambria Iron Company; Westinghouse's patent advisor George Christy; Alexander C. Crawford; and Major James McGregor.[76]

The elite Pittsburgh lawyer's social standing gave him the ability to leave his imprint on the corporation culture of the age, but he was also required to be an innovator and a thought leader, particularly with respect to the metaphysical questions of the status and the powers of the corporation—the shape of the corporate soul—that inevitably arose in dealing with the government that permitted their creation.

One such question that vexed Pittsburgh corporation lawyers was the seemingly simple one of whether a corporation was a "person" under the law. Willis McCook found himself arguing in the affirmative in 1898 on behalf of the Peter Schoenhofen Brewing Company, an Illinois corporation that had applied for a license to sell liquor in Pennsylvania, but was denied one on the grounds that it was a foreign corporation. McCook argued that the Pennsylvania licensing law merely referred to "applicants" or "persons" without any reference to domicile or residence, and that a corporation should be entitled to equal protection under the law under Article IV, Section 2 of the U.S. Constitution. The Pennsylvania Superior Court did not agree[77]; and neither, apparently, did D.T. Watson—at least, in connection with a corporation's political identity. When Elbert Gary, the first chairman of the United States Steel Corporation and a lawyer himself, asked Watson about whether U.S. Steel could provide contributions to its preferred candidates for political office, Watson took a very formulaic approach to the nature of a corporation in his advice, reminding Gary that corporate property was a trust fund for its stockholders. Watson went on to advise: "Your charter does not, in plain language, give you the right to make such contributions, and if they exist you must find them in your implied power. ... The law did not give you a right to vote. ... If you cannot vote, and thus directly influence an election, how can you safely imply your right to influence it indirectly by campaign contributions ... Our Government is one of men. The power resides with the people. ... The people saw fit to give you certain rights, and in some respects regard you as a person or citizen, but you never became one with the people in a political sense."[78]

McCook noted in 1895, however, that the trend was favoring the grant of "omnibus charters" that gave corporations unlimited scope. "The more liberal the scope of the charter," he observed, "the greater immunity of the stockholder," recognizing the power that was being granted to corporations. He noted that omnibus charters could be so broad that a corporation might be designed "under which a steamship line was operated on the Atlantic seaboard" and "next used as the contractor to construct an interstate railway in the Southwest" and later "used to supply a large city with gas."[79] He was predicting the rise of the modern corporate conglomerate. All the signs pointed toward the liberation of the corporation, and from the 1870s through the first decades of the twentieth century, this was exactly what would occur: a corporation came to be seen as being more like a person.

While Pittsburgh's lawyers held adamant opinions about the rules and limitations of the corporation, they were nonetheless protectors of the "liberty of contract," the phrase later made famous by the U.S. Supreme Court in *Lochner v. New York* (1905).[80] Like each of the top Pittsburgh corporation lawyers on Grant Street, D.T. Watson promoted the laissez-faire perspective of his corporate clients: businessmen should be positioned to be free to conduct business as they saw fit.

Watson took on the specter of the so-called "public interest" regulation of business almost as a crucible following his disappointing loss before the U.S. Supreme Court in *Powell v. Pennsylvania* (1888).[81] W.J. Powell was cited for selling oleomargarine as "imitation butter"—clearly marked as such—in contravention of a state law recently enacted at the demand of Pennsylvania dairy farmers. Watson took the case first to the Pennsylvania Supreme Court, then to the U.S. Supreme Court, losing in both—although Associate Justice Stephen J. Field agreed with Watson that a "law does not necessarily fall under the class of police regulations because it is passed under the pretense of such regulation, as in this case by a false title." The influential Watson, grudgingly recognized as one of the nation's foremost corporation lawyers even by his colleagues in the Philadelphia bar, later railed against the decision in a speech before the Sharswood Club of Philadelphia in December 1904, urging that, within the courts, the burden of establishing the necessity of so-called "public interest" laws should be shifted to the legislatures who would pass them:

> [B]oth the Supreme Court of Pennsylvania and the Supreme Court of the United States held by that the General Assembly of the State of Pennsylvania has the supreme control in determining the articles of food which any citizen of the state may sell or possess, and all that is necessary to validate the law is for the statute to state on its face that it is an act passed to protect the public health. This declaration bars all investigation of facts. ... I do ask you to consider whether it may not be wise by conservative action to so provide that such laws ... shall in some appropriate way come under the closer scrutiny

of the courts, and that by some appropriate remedy it shall be the duty of the courts, when properly invoked, to investigate and see that such laws have a real and substantial and bona fide bearing on, and relation to, public health or peace or morals, and not merely an unsubstantial, artificial or simulated one. Give the individual whose liberty is assaulted in such cases a chance to be heard. Let the Courts investigate and determine the facts instead of standing helpless before a Legislative declaration ... Never forget that it is individual cases of violated constitutional rights which make the aggregate of successful usurpation of power.[82]

Even if a corporation could not vote, a business had rights under the Constitution, which Watson passionately sought to protect. Harbison recalls that it was "difficult to portray the iconoclastic mind" of Watson in regard to his "attitude toward the Bill of Rights. It was something akin to the devotion with which the Sons of Levi guarded the Ark of the Covenant ... It was the anchor of the democracy he loved." Watson warned his younger associates against "the tide of clamor toward the destruction of the right to own and preserve one's property." The "right to own" was not in itself, the superior right, but, for Watson, it was "the emblem of all which the Bill of Rights secured to humanity, the emblem of democracy, the 'thou shall not touch' of the American conception of life."[83]

"Thou shall not touch" was the credo of the American tycoons; it was the commandment that would enable them to deploy resources—both capital and labor—without governmental interference. Watson, McCook and their brethren in the Pittsburgh bar were all at once immersed in and helping to create the powerful corporation culture that helped to fuel American business during the Gilded Age. More than one hundred years before the Supreme Court's ruling in *Citizens United v. FEC*,[84] Pittsburgh's lawyers were even immersed in the question of the citizenship rights of the corporation. Men with capital counted on the creativity of these corporation lawyers to take hold of the corporate form, originally designed to enable humble Pennsylvania towns to build modest Pennsylvania bridges over little Pennsylvania streams, and to mold and shape it into a vehicle for building empires and amassing great wealth.

WHAT A STRIKE LOOKS LIKE

It was the height of the summer of 1877, and many of Pittsburgh's lawyers were away on holiday. On Saturday, July 21, attorney Joseph S. Haymaker had just returned to his office in Pittsburgh from Ben Avon, where he had been at home sick for a few weeks. Walking out to 28th Street in the Strip District around two o'clock in the afternoon, he saw a "very considerable crowd of men" and approached some of them to find out what was going on. He quickly learned that a railroad strike, foreshadowed in the city's newspapers, was in progress. Seeing the arrival of a detachment of the state militia from Philadelphia, he was concerned that there would be shooting, so he climbed onto the hillside above the tracks where the crowd was gathered.

Just as he had feared, a battle commenced very shortly afterwards. According to Haymaker, it seemed to start with a few stones being thrown from the direction of a nearby watch-house. Then, there was a pistol shot, which was answered by a few more pistol shots, followed by loud, scattering of rifle fire lasting about a minute and a half. "Right by me, on my right hand an old man, and a little girl on my left hand, were shot dead," he recalled. "I got into the ditch."

When later asked what business he had there, Haymaker replied, "None at all; but I had never seen a strike before, and I went up to see what it looked like."[85]

Up to that time, that was about as close as any lawyer had gotten to an actual workers' strike in Pittsburgh. Although there had been labor strikes, labor law as we now understand it was non-existent; the workers had no right to strike. In the 1814 cordwainer cases, striking Pittsburgh shoemakers were charged with "criminal conspiracy" for confederating "by direct means to impoverish or prejudice a third person [i.e., the employer], or to do acts prejudicial to the community." The court at that time was typical in taking the position that any organization that forced an employer to hire only members of that organization was illegal as well.[86] The only notable proceedings arising from the millworkers' uprising in Allegheny City in 1848 were the criminal trials in which Edwin Stanton and Charles Shaler managed to obtain the conviction of thirteen textile workers.

The Railroad Riots of the summer of 1877, which occurred not only in Pittsburgh but in West Virginia, Maryland, Philadelphia, Chicago and elsewhere, represented a watershed event in the history of American labor. They were the first notable occasion during which laborers in a single industry employed by more than one company communicated their demands en masse to corporate decision-makers across the nation.

Poverty that already existed in Pittsburgh was exacerbated by the Panic of 1873, and the period of bank failures and high interest rates that followed, causing employers to tighten their belts. During 1875, the Pittsburgh Association for the Relief of the Poor, founded in 1862, was inundated with requests for food, clothing and coal, and strained its resources to the limit to meet such requests. In its appeal for contributions in January, the Association told of "[c]hildren ... crying for bread, mothers starving themselves to feed their little ones, young men and old walking the streets seeking employment in vain, whose families shivering with cold for lack of fuel and comfortable clothing ..."[87] Noting that Pittsburgh had become the scene of "a population of beggars who surged and swarmed through the city like birds of prey," the Association disbanded in December, unable to carry on with limited staff and resources.[88]

Pittsburgh's economy, with its iron industry on the rise, seemed to recover more quickly than the rest of the country. Nonetheless, the 1876 presidential election kept all Americans on "the ragged edges," as the *Wheeling Register* declared,[89] ending with a dispute over electoral votes between Democratic New York governor Samuel J. Tilden and Republican Ohio governor Rutherford B. Hayes. The election was ultimately decided on March 2, 1877 in Hayes' favor by an electoral commission—but not without the backroom bargaining of John Henry Hampton's client, Thomas A. Scott, president of the Pennsylvania Railroad, who proposed a compromise that would also conveniently pave the way for federal support of the development of his planned Southern transatlantic railroad, the Texas and Pacific Railway.[90]

The 1877 strike began on July 14 in Martinsburg, West Virginia, where railroad workers blocked the lines after being informed of the second wage cut in a year, amounting to more than a dollar a day, by the B&O Railroad. Violent clashes ensued in Martinsburg and Cumberland, Maryland, as state militia and federal troops skirmished with supporters of the strike; ten people were killed and twenty-five were wounded, while President Hayes sent the Marines to Baltimore to restore order.[91]

Like the B&O, the "Pennsy" cut wages by ten percent at the beginning of 1877, and then announced in June that it would be cutting wages by another ten percent. "Pennsy" workers responded by taking control of the railyard switches at 28th Street and shutting down the system on Thursday, July 19. One of the strikers, Andrew Hice, explained that "it was a question of blood or bread." He said, "If I can go to the penitentiary I can get bread and water, and that is about all I can get now." David Watt, the assistant superintendent of the Railroad, went to City Hall and asked Mayor William McCarthy to come to the railyard with a squad of police. Mayor McCarthy declined, excusing himself on account of illness. When Watt asked for ten policemen, McCarthy again declined, citing the fact that budget cuts, precipitated by Pittsburgh's perilously low credit rating, had forced him to lay off half of Pittsburgh's police force. There was probably truth in both of his responses, but McCarthy, like most of his constituents, was not particularly sympathetic to the Pennsylvania Railroad. Watt managed to find ten laid-off policemen and approached the protesters who stood at the switches, only to get his eye blackened by one of the strikers. Then the lawyers began to arrive on the scene.[92]

Watt retreated to an outer depot and sent for John Scott, the Pittsburgh-based general counsel of the Railroad.[b] The Railroad's outside lawyers, John Henry Hampton and John Dalzell, wasted no time in preparing warrants on behalf of the Railroad for the arrest of certain identified protesters, to be carried out by the Pittsburgh police.[93] When Watt explained to John Scott that the city seemed unable or unwilling to provide protection, however, Scott and Watt visited Allegheny County Sheriff R.H. Fife on Thursday evening, and urged him to call out a *posse comitatus*, i.e. a temporary police force. With the sheriff's counsel on holiday, John Scott took the liberty of advising Fife that legally, if he could not get the crowd to disperse after a mere pro forma call for peace, the sheriff would be within his rights to call upon Governor John W. Hartranft for state troops.[94] By this time, Thomas Scott, vacationing in Delaware, began to receive word of the Pittsburgh shutdown. He suggested that the workers should be given "a rifle diet for a few days and see how they like that kind of bread,"[95] and the word went out that the Pennsylvania Railroad was requesting troops from the state's Adjutant-General, Major General James W. Latta.

Major General Latta immediately sent General Alfred L. Pearson—the former Allegheny County District Attorney who would receive the congressional medal of honor in 1897 for his brave service at the Battle of Lewis Farm during the Civil War, and who was now in command of the Sixth Division of the Pennsylvania National Guard—to investigate the situation at 28th Street. Sheriff Fife, Watt and General Pearson all arrived at the scene and assessed the crowd, which now numbered in the hundreds. After meekly calling for the crowd to disperse, Sheriff Fife asked General Pearson for his legal advice. General Pearson also advised calling a *posse comitatus* and suggested that he notify Latta of the situation. John Scott, sensing that Fife was still uncertain how to proceed, wrote a form of dispatch requesting Governor Hartranft to send troops to Pittsburgh, and Fife signed it. With the governor on a junket in Wyoming in a luxury railroad car provided by the Pennsylvania Railroad, Latta was left in charge of the Pennsylvania National Guard. Already expecting the request, Latta wired General Pearson and ordered him to call out a regiment.[96]

On Friday, the crowds only grew larger and bolder. Some observers noted that there seemed to be a number of men from the iron mills, standing in sympathy with the Railroad employees; others remarked that they suspected that a large contingent of the crowd was from out of town. The leaders of the strike sent a list of demands to Railroad superintendent Robert Pitcairn, Thomas Scott's right-hand man, but Pitcairn refused to even send them on to the Railroad president.[97] General Pearson, meanwhile,

---

b   Scott, the ex-U.S. senator representing Pennsylvania, had no known family connection to the Railroad's top executive, Thomas Scott.

convinced that a regiment would not be enough, called out the whole Sixth Division; but when he could only muster 130 men and began to express concerns about whether in any event Pittsburgh soldiers would fire upon fellow Pittsburghers, Railroad officials called upon Major General Latta to send a Philadelphia division of the Pennsylvania National Guard by special overnight train to Pittsburgh. Six hundred Philadelphia troops, under the command of General Robert M. Brinton, arrived at one o'clock in the morning on Saturday, fixing for a fight. Old animosities between Pittsburgh and Philadelphia—stemming not only from some of the same territorial conflicts and class biases that existed as early as the Whiskey Rebellion, but also from the fact that Pittsburgh politicians frequently argued against the Pennsy's interests during the early years when the B&O Railroad was also trying to extend to Pittsburgh—bubbled to the surface among the Philadelphia soldiers, some of whom boasted that they were going to "clean up" Pittsburgh.[98]

Later on the morning of July 21, Hampton and Dalzell sent their young associate, M.H. Houseman, to visit Mayor McCarthy's clerk, Henry Metzgar, to suspend the execution by the Pittsburgh police of the warrants they had sworn on Thursday. According to the lawyers' instructions, the Railroad's demand for arrests would now be handled by Allegheny County Sheriff R.H. Fife, who had thus far demonstrated more interest in protecting the interests of the Railroad.[99] Subsequently, as others continued to try to get Mayor McCarthy to act, McCarthy fell back on the excuse that the entire affair had been taken out of his hands by Hampton & Dalzell, and that the authority to deal with the rioters had been placed by them in the hands of Sheriff Fife.[100] Even if the city police could have intervened, Mayor McCarthy had a handy excuse to stay out of the conflict.

By midday Saturday, the day that Joseph Haymaker came out to see what a strike looked like, the crowd had grown to several thousand. The Pittsburgh militia had begun to blend into the crowd, notwithstanding orders, some sitting on the hillside above the 28th Street crossing with friends or family members. Three hundred Philadelphia troops guarded Railroad facilities as the remaining three hundred went to the crossing to face the crowds. As the standoff persisted, taunts were exchanged; and then, rocks started to fly. Reacting to pistol shots from the hillside, the Philadelphia soldiers, without an order to fire, unloaded their guns in all directions, and ultimately, to the hillside where Joseph Haymaker watched the confrontation unfold.[101]

Haymaker rushed to the aid of the little girl who was hit nearby and with his handkerchief made a tourniquet on her knee to stop her bleeding; nonetheless, doctors amputated her leg later that evening, and as far as Haymaker knew, she died soon thereafter.[102] In five minutes of shooting, twenty people were killed and approximately seventy were wounded. The Philadelphia militia retreated quickly to the 26th Street roundhouse; but they were followed by the enraged rioters, who sent a burning coke car in. Before the roof caved in, the militia evacuated the roundhouse, but they immediately became subject to heavy fire from protesters, many of whom had stolen their guns from a nearby gun shop. Brinton's men retreated to the Allegheny Arsenal, but were turned away for fear that the angry mob would overtake them and raid the Arsenal itself. General Brinton ultimately led his troops to Sharpsburg, to safety, across the Allegheny River.[103]

Throughout Saturday night and Sunday, the crowds continued their assault on the property of the Railroad. By the end of the melee, they had destroyed more than a thousand railroad cars, 104 engines, forty-six passenger cars, and all thirty-nine buildings of the Pennsylvania Railroad in Pittsburgh, including the Union Depot and the Union Depot Hotel.[104] It would be days before the Railroad could establish full control over its own lines. On the following Wednesday, Hampton & Dalzell (on behalf of the Pennsylvania Railroad, the Cleveland and Pittsburgh Railroad, the Pittsburgh, Cincinnati and St. Louis Railway, and the Pittsburgh, Virginia and Charleston Railroad Company) stated to Sheriff Fife that the property of the railroads was "in immediate and constant danger of destruction at the hands of a body of rioters and disaffected workmen, which may at any time become a mob ..." Welty McCullough, a young protégé of George Shiras, did the same on behalf of the Baltimore & Ohio Railroad.[105] The Sheriff, who was still unsuccessful in his own efforts to summon a *posse comitatus* to suppress the disturbances, applied for more aid from the state, while a citizens' group, led by attorney John Ricketson among others, met on Market Street and put out a call for funds to pay for the organization of a supplemental private police force to patrol the city streets.[106]

The disturbances in Martinsburg, Baltimore and Pittsburgh were the first bloody links in a chain reaction of railroad riots that ultimately spread from Philadelphia, where rioters burned much of Center City, to Chicago, where twenty people were killed and dozens were wounded in clashes between rioters and police. By the time order was restored in Pittsburgh and the first "Pennsy" freight trains finally resumed service on July 29, railroad men from coast to coast were agitating, and numerous sympathy strikes were cropping up among miners and laborers all around the country.

There were rumors that General Alfred Pearson had been killed in the battle of 28th Street. At around nine o'clock on Saturday evening, however, during the most intense moments of the battle, General Pearson managed to walk from the roundhouse to the Union Depot Hotel, in full military regalia, without being touched by the mobs. There he was greeted by Adjutant-General Latta, who ordered him to leave the scene. Pearson quickly changed into his street clothes, resuming his identity as a mild-mannered Pittsburgh lawyer, and departed. In his rush, he accidentally left his pocket book behind, which was burned, along with the Hotel itself, later that evening. Meanwhile, a mile or so away, Mrs. Pearson was evacuated from the Pearson home on 39th near Butler Street, where an angry mob turned up with an empty coffin, vowing to put General Pearson in it.[107]

Justice moved swiftly against the most visible supporters of the strike. Six of the rioters were arraigned in the court of President Judge Thomas Ewing on August 2. William Reardon[c] had the defense on most of them, along with old John Barton. One rioter,

---

c   Reardon, a native of County Cork, was a well-known Pittsburgh criminal defense lawyer. Thomas Mercer Marshall could not help taking a poke at his young colleague, telling the story that Reardon once came into court at the beginning of a major criminal trial and was informed that the court had appointed "three members of the bar" to represent the defendant. "Defended by three members of the bar?," Reardon asked, according to Marshall. "Why didn't he think to appoint a lawyer?" Thomas Mercer Marshall, "Address of Hon. Thomas M. Marshall delivered before the Allegheny

George Kensel, was represented by both William Reardon and William C. Moreland. Within several weeks after the riots, Reardon was nominated by the local Greenback-Labor Party to run for District Attorney, but he lost the election. Major Moreland was a popular, somewhat charismatic politico who would later serve as city solicitor, with infamously unfortunate results. Moreland had tentacles in all directions when it came to the Railroad strike: as John Henry Hampton's partner for a few years in the 1860s, Moreland had served as Hampton's assistant solicitor to the Western Division of the Pennsylvania Railroad. Sometime before the riots, Major Moreland had served on the staff of General Pearson with the western division of the Pennsylvania National Guard. He had also run against Pearson for the post of Allegheny County District Attorney in 1868, losing the election by just one vote.[108]

Judge Ewing's statement at the arraignment sealed the fates of the prisoners:

These men appear to labor under a complete misapprehension as to their rights in the premises. Clearly they had a right to quit work if they wished to do so, and without giving any reason for their action. It was immaterial to the public what their reasons were. After ceasing work, however, they had not right to remain on the ground of their employers. If they did so it was trespass, and they were liable to legal action. If they gathered in force and consulted together to interfere with other employees in pursuance of their labor, it was conspiracy. If they were in sufficient force to create terror, or if three or four acted in such a manner as to create terror, they were rioters, and if others looked on without making endeavors to keep the peace, they were also guilty. There can be no innocent spectators at a riot. There are but two parties—the rioters and those who consent to the riot, and it is often difficult to decide which is the more guilty.[109]

Seventeen of the rioters ending up receiving long sentences, including Matthew Marshall, who was sentenced to six years and ten months in the penitentiary for lighting up the coke cars.[110]

The day after the preliminary hearings in Judge Ewing's courtroom, General Alfred L. Pearson was restored to his command at the head of the sixth division of the Pennsylvania National Guard by Governor Hartranft. However, the public, already prejudiced against the Railroad, began to place the blame for the dead and wounded with General Pearson, who had remained in hiding for some days after the riots subsided. On July 25, General Pearson had issued a statement for the newspapers in which he insisted that no member of the Pennsylvania militia gave any orders to fire on the crowd, and in fact, that he himself had "issued positive orders to General Brinton not to fire a shot if he could help it."[111] He was, however, the de facto commander of all troops stationed in Pittsburgh on Saturday night, and was seen to be in conference with Railroad officials on a constant basis during the height of the riots, so it was perhaps inevitable that General Pearson would be charged with some crime.

County Bar Association, on Saturday afternoon, November 14, 1896," (lecture, Allegheny County Bar Association, Pittsburgh, PA, November 14, 1896), 30.

On the morning of September 27, Pearson was arrested and charged with the murder of Nicholas Stoppel at the battle of 28th Street. The General waived his hearing and occupied a cell at the Allegheny County Jail for a few hours while his legal team, led by the unstoppable Thomas Mercer Marshall, arranged for a bail hearing in Common Pleas Court No. 2 before Judge John Kirkpatrick; they secured Pearson's release on a ten thousand dollar bond. Pearson was publicly defiant:

The charge and arrest are mere spite work on the part of the Mayor. The Mayor during the time of the riots acted in a very imbecile manner, and it is to cover up his lack of action at that time that he does this. He knows that I am shortly going to make an official report to the Governor and in that report it will express the Mayor's imbecility, and so it is to cover that up that he proceeds in this manner against me.[112]

A month later, the grand jury issued subpoenas to Major General Latta and General Brinton, and to Governor Hartranft, who refused to appear on the grounds that he denied "the right of a coordinate branch of the Government to compel the attendance of the executive officers or investigate the manner in which, in their discretion, they have performed their official duties."[113] The investigation thus hampered, the grand jury issued its presentment, declaring, "We believe that the riots followed inevitably from the conduct of the military, too largely controlled in its movements by the railroad officials,"[114] but ultimately ignored the bill against General Pearson whom, it was ultimately established, was in the telegraph office at the roundhouse when the shooting began. Not long afterward, Governor Hartranft reorganized the Pennsylvania National Guard, mustered out General Pearson, and "relegated fancy uniforms to the museum," according to historian Robert V. Bruce.[115]

Meanwhile, a great deal more legal thought, time and attention was bestowed upon the question of whether the county—and not the city of Pittsburgh, despite Mayor McCarthy's alleged "imbecility" and inaction, nor the Railroad—ought to bear responsibility for the loss of property that resulted from the riots. Within days after the riots, property owners started to clog the county offices with claims on the basis that in 1841, the Pennsylvania legislature had passed a law holding counties financially responsible for the consequences of failing to maintain the peace and protect the property of private owners. As the newspapers surmised, however, "many of them undoubtedly are without a shadow of validity."[116]

George Shiras was retained by the County to defend against a suit brought by a Philadelphia company, Gibson's Son & Co., for the loss of sixty barrels of whiskey destroyed (or consumed) by the rioters; at trial, the verdict was for the plaintiff in the amount of $3,131. The County decided to appeal the decision to the Pennsylvania supreme court, with County solicitor Stephen H. Geyer, Judge Daniel Agnew and Shiras arguing on behalf of the County, and D.T. Watson, Marcus W. Acheson and Thomas Mercer Marshall arguing on behalf of the plaintiff. In *County of Allegheny v. Gibson*, Justice Paxson handed down an opinion which, after tracing the origins and precursors of the Act of May 31, 1841 through English statutory law to the reign of King Edward I in the thirteenth century, sustained the verdict of the trial court and upheld the validity of the Act.[117] The three thousand dollar Supreme Court case confirmed a torrent of check-writing by the County, culminating in John Henry Hampton securing a million-dollar County settlement in favor of the Pennsylvania Railroad, and the payout of over millions of dollars to miscellaneous other claimants.[118]

To the Pittsburgh lawyers on Grant Street, what did a strike look like in 1877? It looked like a violent mob, a hail of bullets, and flagrant instances of arson and looting. It looked like sidebar conferences with law enforcement officials and the generals of the National Guard, in the heat of battle; and it looked like a series of arrest warrants and criminal prosecutions of strikers, and claims for property damage. It did not yet look like a forum for typical lawyerly discourse, especially not for any lawyer looking to create precedents that might advance the cause of labor. That would come later.

A GENIUS DEVISES A LEGAL ENGINE

"Westinghouse detested legal suits, which were inconsistent with his Puritan roots, yet a lot of his business career was spent in courtrooms."

—Quentin R. Skrabec, Jr.[119]

Of George Westinghouse, Andrew Carnegie once observed:

Fine fellow, George ... And a great genius. But he is a poor businessman. A genius and a businessman are seldom found in one individual. Now Westinghouse is of too much value to the world, in originating ideas and developing them, to have one whit of energy wasted in business work and worries. You see, all of his business activity would never get him individually a noticeable success, whereas his genius, at play, would keep home an outstanding figure in the world. He should have a good businessman, so that he never would have to bother about business details.[120]

Carnegie's back-handed compliment of his some-time friend has become a standard trope in assessments of George Westinghouse's talents as a mogul, seemingly confirmed by the forced reorganization of the Westinghouse companies following the Panic of 1907, in which he lost control of his organization to the superior gamesmanship of arguably the greatest financial mind of the age, J.P. Morgan. True, Westinghouse was slow to build the kind of sharp and visionary financial team that might have saved him from that fate, and he could sometimes demonstrate a poor aptitude for delegation; but to dismiss Westinghouse as a mere "inventor" is a failure to recognize the extent to which, in thirty years of work, Westinghouse managed to build a successful international conglomerate, with dominance within a number of product areas, of arguably far greater scope than anything Carnegie had ever dreamt. "Look at all these jobs I created," Westinghouse would exclaim. "Does that mean I'm a bad manager?"[121]

Historian Steven W. Usselman suggests a new view of Westinghouse—seeing him as a harbinger of twentieth and twenty-first century American industrial organization theory and practice, an engineer who was "attuned to economics, readily able to accept financial constraints on technical possibilities." According to Usselman, Westinghouse "brought a discipline to his own innovative activities very much like the discipline that corporate research directors would at times impose on their creative personnel. As a businessman, Westinghouse demonstrated remarkable persistence and thoroughness in gaining entry to markets and securing control over technology. He built comprehensive, integrated organizations dedicated to particular lines of enterprise. In the process, he displayed an impressive array of tactics, including a sophisticated manipulation of patent rights."[122] With the mind of an engineer, Westinghouse had a peculiar facility for understanding the systems, fields and forces that were at play, and their sometimes significant cross-impacts, within his areas of commercial interest.

Perhaps it is no coincidence that history hands us so many instances in Westinghouse's life in which he relies on the aid and counsel of one or another lawyer—and there are a number of individual "characters" in these narratives who are referred to as "Westinghouse's lawyer." Such stories, which are far more abundant and varied than those surrounding other moguls of the nineteenth century, including Carnegie himself, would seem to indicate Westinghouse's sophistication as a consumer of legal advice. In a sense, Westinghouse's methodical approach in choosing the elements of his legal team mirrors his habits as a student of systems, fields and forces, as if he understood that American business law was an organic field—comprising objects, systems and sets of rules, not unlike thermodynamics or electromagnetism, that interact to produce equilibrium or conspire to unleash spontaneous processes. In other words, he appears to have perceived American business law as a field within which he would be required to design and organize an effective, synthetic system, or "engine," in order to harness it in the service of his objectives.

In this case, the "engine" took the form of a team of legal advisors with strengths in a variety of distinct disciplines, both inside his company and out, in Pittsburgh (his headquarters), in New York (the financial capital) and abroad. In doing so, Westinghouse provides us with the best, earliest example in Pittsburgh legal history of some of the key defining characteristics of the modern corporate legal team—a comprehensive, integrated organization, to paraphrase Usselman, dedicated to particular lines of enterprise in the service of Westinghouse's legal needs.

At the age of nineteen, Westinghouse's debut with American business and American law was not auspicious. He had invented a cast steel "frog" for replacing derailed trains, and he found a couple of investors in Schenectady, New York who agreed to back him in the manufacture and sale of the device. He made a few sales, but the device was so durable that he had trouble doing repeat business, and his investors quickly became impatient. They told the boy inventor that the business was too small for three partners, and they asked Westinghouse to buy them out, or turn over the rights to the device to them for free. Westinghouse petulantly refused, but realized his "frog" business was imperiled. Having heard about a steel facility in Pittsburgh that could cast the device more cheaply than in upstate New York, he decided to visit and see if he could work up a business plan that his partners would find more attractive.[123] Westinghouse's focus was, however, "derailed" when he witnessed a railroad accident that, from his perspective, could have been avoided if only the trains had sufficient braking systems.[124]

When he came to Pittsburgh in the 1860s, Westinghouse happened to arrive in a city that arguably had among the most sophisticated patent bars in the country, even if it was relatively small. In 1889, among the approximately thirty-eight hundred patent attorneys active in the United States, 977 were located in New York, but almost fifty were active in Pittsburgh.[125] Spurred on by a local economy that attracted inventors and innovation, William Bakewell had started his practice in Pittsburgh in 1845,[126] and had been the mentor or preceptor to a line of Pittsburgh patent attorneys. Westinghouse was familiar with patents and had worked with patent attorneys in upstate New York, but his experience in Schenectady certainly taught him additional lessons about the practical value of a patent. When he began to consider seeking patent protection for the technologies embedded within his latest line of railroad safety device, the air brake, his inquiries in Pittsburgh led him to Bakewell and his firm, then known as Bakewell & Christy (and subsequently as Bakewell, Christy & Kerr). George Westinghouse began to work with William Bakewell's younger partner, George Harvey Christy.[127]

The two Georges—Christy and Westinghouse—were very similar in physical appearance: both men were broad-shouldered and bull-necked, exactly six-feet tall, with full faces, massive leonine heads, luxuriant hair, and blue or grey-blue eyes.[128] Skrabec says that Westinghouse looked like a walrus with his Victorian moustache and long coat[129]; it is possible that together, the two Georges looked like a pair of walruses. Christy could be accused of having an abrupt manner and a habit of being glibly candid,[130] which probably blended well with Westinghouse's intellectual curiosity, quickness and intensity. Both men also shared a solid grounding in mathematics as well as the experience of having served the Union during the Civil War. Christy, a native of Ohio, was educated at Western Reserve University, and subsequently taught mathematics there. He arrived in Pittsburgh just before the Civil War, and began a law preceptorship with Judge James Veech while serving as a postal clerk; but with the outbreak of the War, Christy enlisted in the Union artillery, assuming the role of quartermaster in Knapp's Batallion and later serving as a Lieutenant and Adjutant in the 22nd Regiment, U.S. Colored Troops, under Colonel Joseph B. Kiddoo, another future member of the Pittsburgh bar. Christy served with the Regiment as it assumed a post of honor at President Lincoln's funeral, followed the Regiment to Texas, and then resigned, resuming the study of law and entering the bar in 1866.[131] Nine years older than Westinghouse, the thirty-two year-old Christy had been practicing law for three years when Westinghouse first met him.

Christy served as the lead patent attorney for Westinghouse's "Improvement in Steam-Power-Brake Devices" (granted in 1869), and thereafter would handle most of Westinghouse's early mechanical patents. Through his close working relationship with Westinghouse, Christy must be credited with helping Westinghouse develop, at least initially, the strategies for Westinghouse's "sophisticated manipulation of patent rights," both as his outside advisor and as the vice president and general counsel of Westinghouse Air Brake Company, a position he assumed in 1873.[132]

The concept of the "company solicitor" had been floating around Pittsburgh since before the Civil War, but in practice it bore little relationship to today's notion of the chief in-house lawyer, sitting in an executive capacity within a large corporation. The early "general counsels" of Pittsburgh would never be "vice presidents," nor would they even be employees of their clients. When, for example, Robert McKnight wrote in his journal on March 17, 1846 of being "elected Solicitor" for the Bank of Pittsburgh in exchange for a periodic retainer, the expectation was that McKnight would be called upon to assist the Bank of Pittsburgh with respect to all of its significant legal matters,[133] but that McKnight would continue to practice through his own firm, Magraw & McKnight, in his own office, and that he would continue to take other client engagements. Westinghouse clearly saw the value, apparently well before most of the other Pittsburgh moguls, of installing a lawyer on a desk within his own company, on a full-time basis, who could be counted on to take a more direct entrepreneurial interest in the company's objectives and provide high level strategic advice. Christy served this task ably for a few years, before returning to private practice with inventor/patent attorney J. Snowden Bell. Despite leaving Westinghouse's employ, Christy remained a key member of Westinghouse's legal team for the rest of his life, handling fewer of Westinghouse's new patents, but spending a good deal of time in courtrooms protecting Westinghouse's intellectual property portfolio. It was said that Christy, throughout his career, was Westinghouse's "last tribunal as to whether … suits would be brought" against potential infringers.[134]

Following Thomas Edison's early successes with the incandescent light bulb in the 1870s, Westinghouse began to investigate the possibilities of large-scale electric power distribution. Among his advisors in electrical matters was a New York-based telegraph pioneer named Franklin Leonard Pope. Pope worked with Westinghouse and his chief engineer in Pittsburgh, William Stanley, on a system for high voltage electrical transmission, although Pope advised Westinghouse against Alternating Current, believing that it was too dangerous for practical use.[d][135] While Westinghouse disagreed with Pope and proceeded with his own plans, he continued to rely on Pope for advice. Pope had by this time formed his own patent law firm in New York, Pope & Edgecomb; and seeing Pope as a leader in the field (it did not hurt that Pope had also spent time working with Westinghouse's rival, Thomas Edison[136]), Westinghouse gave all of his electrical patent work to Pope and his young partner, Charles A. Terry—despite Westinghouse's close association with Christy and Christy's former law firm.[137] Around the same time, Westinghouse opened a New York base of operations—no doubt viewing New York/New Jersey as a center for electric innovation—and hired one of Christy's former partners, William Bakewell's nephew Thomas Bakewell Kerr, as the "inside"

---

d   Ironically, Franklin Pope died by electrocution in 1895 when he went into his basement to fix the power in his own home during a storm. "Death of Franklin L. Pope," *The New York Times*, October 14, 1895.

general counsel of the Westinghouse Electric Company. Kerr moved from Pittsburgh to Englewood, New Jersey, across the Hudson from Manhattan, in 1888.[138]

Kerr followed the mold fixed by Christy in assuming a role of personal advisor to Westinghouse. Westinghouse placed enough trust in Kerr's abilities that he sent Kerr along with the vice president and general manager of the Electric Company, Henry M. Byllesby, to visit the laboratory of Nikolai Tesla in May 1888, to assess Tesla's AC motor—a matter of great importance to Westinghouse. While Byllesby was on hand to provide an opinion about the efficacy of the motor, Kerr's purpose would be to come back with advice on how Westinghouse could strike a deal to acquire Tesla's patent. Tesla's business partners were demanding a high price for the patents: two hundred thousand dollars plus a royalty of $2.50 per horsepower for each motor installed. Kerr and Byllesby nevertheless recommended that Westinghouse press for a deal in order to broaden his coverage within the domain of Alternating Current. Kerr, Byllesby and another Westinghouse inventor, Oliver Shallenberger, succeeded in negotiating the deal with Tesla based on an upfront payment of twenty-five thousand dollars in cash and fifty thousand dollars in notes, plus royalties.[139] The Tesla acquisition ultimately resulted in Westinghouse's development of the first U.S. electric power distribution scheme, using Tesla's proposal of three-phase AC at 60 Hz.

Intellectual property, of course, was not Westinghouse's sole concern when it came to legal advice. He also required a strong corporate law advisor, and very early on he engaged John Dalzell, John Henry Hampton's junior partner. Small and slight in stature, immaculately dressed, mustachioed and coifed, with a fondness for silk hats[140]—and a Yale man to boot—Dalzell was made to order as an advisor to the captains of industry in Pittsburgh's Gilded Age. He rarely displayed emotion, to the point of being called "cold" by his acquaintances, and was not known to enjoy social occasions.[141] He was a tough, straight-up strategist, prized for his ability to think several steps ahead of both his clients and his adversaries. With Hampton, Dalzell had built one of the premier law firms in Pittsburgh—Hampton & Dalzell, subsequently known as Dalzell, Scott & Gordon— and enjoyed one of the best corporate client lists in town. Not coincidentally, Dalzell and Hampton represented the Pennsylvania Railroad; unquestionably, Westinghouse realized that his lawyer's close association with the executives of the most important railroad in the region would prove to be invaluable in furthering the progress of the Air Brake Company.

Dalzell, however, offered more than just ready access to potential customers. Dalzell knew how to get things done, and he had probably assisted Westinghouse on more than one occasion in his acquisitions of stock in numerous small companies that possessed patent rights in his areas of interest. Dalzell's acumen would come in handy in a significant way with respect to Westinghouse's interest in natural gas. In the early 1880s, Westinghouse became increasingly interested in the potential of fueling factories and city lights with natural gas; he took note of the discovery of gas in Murrysville, east of Pittsburgh, in 1882, which suggested there was more natural gas underneath the Pittsburgh region than geologists had originally estimated, and he began prospecting for gas on the grounds of his home, known as "Solitude," in the Homewood/Point Breeze section of Pittsburgh. By 1884, Westinghouse had devised a plan for the distribution of natural gas within Pittsburgh, but his existing corporate charters were narrowly tailored to the types of business in which he was already operating—not as a public utility. The Fuel Gas Company, a rival confederation in Pittsburgh comprising some coal gas companies and banks, was stirring up political opposition to the idea of granting a charter to anyone else for the purpose of distributing natural gas in Pittsburgh.

Dalzell knew that several companies had obtained charters to become "public utilities" under the old charter system, and had since gone inactive without losing the powers granted under their charters. Dalzell went to Harrisburg and consulted with his contacts there, who produced an old charter secured by the Pennsylvania Railroad, called the Philadelphia Company, that was created for the purpose of building a branch line to the Pennsylvania system. The proposed line was never built, and the charter, which "was so drawn that under it you can do almost anything you care to except engage in the business of banking," fell into the hands of another party, who ultimately proved to be a delinquent taxpayer. At Westinghouse's instruction, Dalzell put a bid on the charter, and secured it for thirty-five thousand dollars. On August 4, 1884, the Philadelphia Company unveiled its new prospectus for a stock offering, showing George Westinghouse as president, with John Dalzell serving on its board.[142] Westinghouse succeeded in launching his new company, with a patent written by George Christy for a "system for conveying and utilizing gas under pressure"[143]; and by 1888, the Philadelphia Company was supplying gas to over twenty-five thousand homes and seven hundred factories.[144]

Dalzell was elected to Congress in 1886, and although he was nominally still involved with his practice in Pittsburgh, the demands of Capitol Hill soon robbed Westinghouse of one of his most trusted advisors. Westinghouse would ultimately fill the void through his association with two New York lawyers—Charles A. Terry, Franklin Pope's young partner, and Paul D. Cravath.

Around the same time that Thomas Bakewell Kerr relocated to Englewood, Westinghouse asked Charles Terry to relocate to Pittsburgh to assume stewardship, as an employee of the Westinghouse companies, for the Westinghouse portfolio, now comprising technologies ranging from air brakes to railroad switch and signal systems, from electric railways and natural gas pipeline distribution systems to the AC projects. Terry had some of the patrician bearing of Dalzell. A descendant of William Bradford of the Plymouth Colony, Terry graduated from Amherst, where he was president of the football club, before taking up the study of law in New York with Franklin Pope while simultaneously attending Columbia Law School. He was admitted to the New York bar in 1883, and joined Pope's firm as a partner, taking a leading role with respect to the Westinghouse electrical patents. When Terry moved to Pittsburgh, because he was in-house with Westinghouse, he apparently saw no reason to apply for admission to the Allegheny County bar, although he did join the Duquesne Club. Nonetheless, when Kerr left Westinghouse in 1890 to return to private practice, establishing the firm of Kerr & Curtis in Englewood, New Jersey, Terry stepped into Kerr's shoes as general counsel of Westinghouse Electric. Westinghouse's confidence in Terry's abilities, particularly his understanding of electricity, was high—as evidenced by the fact that he chose Terry to represent Westinghouse in the "feeder and main" lawsuit against

Edison before a commission in Glasgow, in which Terry was charged with the duty of examining Lord Kelvin, the eminent physicist, as an expert witness.[145]

Paul Drennan Cravath was not yet the lion of the Manhattan bar when he first encountered George Westinghouse. Many years later, Cravath's name would be honored and sometimes taken in vain as the originator of the so-called "Cravath system," the tradition around which Cravath's own law firm, Cravath, Swaine & Moore, would be developed. The "system" was "designed to produce lawyers with breadth, sophistication and a deep working knowledge of a wide variety of practice areas"[146] and it involved hiring fresh young law students from the best law schools (Harvard, Yale and Columbia law review editors were their first choices), training them in the Cravath methods at the beginning of their careers, and setting their eyes on "partnership" as a long-term career goal. "Our partners come from the ranks of our own associates,"[147] according to the system, meaning that the firm would preserve its culture and the quality of its legal services by growing it from the inside, rather than hiring in partners from the outside. Cravath's influence as the leader of a law firm would ultimately extend to Pittsburgh law firms, as well as other elite firms around the country—at least for a time.

Cravath was twenty-eight years old when he met Westinghouse. Cravath's uncle, Caleb Jackson, was an officer in one of Westinghouse's companies, and he recommended Cravath to Westinghouse in 1889, when Cravath was but three years at the bar. Westinghouse was having trouble with local authorities in New York with respect to overhead wires for electrical transmission. "Cravath was in the thick of the extremely bitter fight," Cravath's colleague Robert Swaine writes. "He knew no regular hours; and when George Westinghouse came to New York in October, 1889, and set up quarters in the old Brunswick Hotel on Fifth Avenue, Cravath moved his force of men there and worked day and night and all day Sundays."[148] Although Westinghouse ended up losing the battle—he was ordered to place the wires in conduits—he was impressed by Cravath's shrewdness and work ethic. During the Panic of 1893, it was Cravath who helped coordinate Westinghouse's reorganization, in which he persuaded his creditors to accept stock in liquidation of their claims. Westinghouse had come close enough to surrendering the company to receivership that Cravath had actually drawn up the receivership papers, keeping them locked in a safe in the event they would be needed quickly.[149]

While Cravath provided the sophisticated corporate finance advice that Dalzell had once provided to Westinghouse, Terry ultimately became Westinghouse's shadow, his "chief of staff"[150]—one of his closest strategic commercial advisors and confidants.

Westinghouse's use of multiple lawyers from multiple law firms in multiple cities was not necessarily novel, but by the force of his personality, Westinghouse managed to get the most out of it. The rivalry between the Pittsburgh bar and the New York bar could be bitter—even more so than any potential rivalry between the Pittsburgh and Philadelphia bars—due to the preeminence of New York's financial industry, against which Pittsburgh's unrivaled industrial economy often seemed to play the foil. Individual lawyers have always been, by nature, jealous of their rivals from different firms who practice in the same subject area. Westinghouse's insistence on spreading his work around could have resulted in chaos, subterfuge and clashes among the members of his team, but in fact, Westinghouse proved to be a devoted client over many years. His earliest close advisors—Christy and Kerr—were provided with work for as long as they wanted it. As was the case with Christy, even after Kerr quit his position as Westinghouse's general counsel, Kerr and his firm were Westinghouse's primary New York litigation counsel in his patent wars with Edison.

As biographer Henry G. Prout observed, "Westinghouse valued consultation; that was one of the reasons why he was so well served."[151] He demonstrated his appreciation for faithful and efficient service by demanding more of it, and "[t]oward the group upon whom he specially leaned he had as strong a sense of loyalty as they had toward him."[152] In short, around his best advisors he created a kind of extended, cooperative workshop—like the ones in which his teams of engineers flourished—that, despite all the market forces that might conspire to drive them apart, inspired his lawyers to act in a coordinated fashion to advance Westinghouse's goals.

One celebrated example of this coordination took place at Christmas time in 1892. Westinghouse had been awarded the contract to light the Chicago World's Fair as a display of his alternating current system. Edison, however, held the patent for the incandescent bulb, and was refusing to sell bulbs to Westinghouse for use at the Fair. Not to be discouraged, Westinghouse's engineers came up with a new design for a light bulb that sidestepped Edison's patent technology. Sitting on an upbound Manhattan elevated train with Charles Terry, Westinghouse encountered Grosvenor P. Lowrey, Edison's chief patent counsel. Exchanging pleasantries, Lowrey let slip that Frederick P. Fish, another of Edison's lawyers who was the founder of the Boston firm of Fish & Richardson, was visiting Pittsburgh that day. Westinghouse politely bid adieu to Lowrey and tugged at Terry's sleeve. Standing on the platform of Fourteenth Street station, Westinghouse instructed Terry to track down Kerr and his partner, Leonard Curtis, and to tell them that Edison was launching an assault on Westinghouse. Terry found Curtis first, and Curtis immediately wired George Christy in Pittsburgh, "warning him," as Leupp tells the story, "to look out for whatever was in the wind."[153]

The next morning was Christmas Eve. As Frederick Fish entered the United States Circuit Court room in Pittsburgh, Christy was there waiting for him. Fish had applied the day before for an injunction against Westinghouse's sale or use of its competing lamps. Judge Marcus Acheson, seeing Christy in the courtroom, said that before he ruled on Fish's petition, he would like to hear from Westinghouse's counsel. Christy's off-the-cuff presentation succeeded in delaying Acheson's ruling until the New Year, by which time Christy and Kerr were able to show, with blueprints revealing the details of Westinghouse's lamp, that Westinghouse had not infringed Edison's patents.[154] The long association each of these attorneys—Terry, Curtis, Christy and Kerr—had with Westinghouse and with each other prior to 1892, enabled each of them to jump into the fray without hesitation. They each knew Westinghouse and his objectives well, and could operate independently yet collaboratively without waiting for Westinghouse's specific instructions, like a well-oiled engine.

The Panic of 1907 represents an unfortunate conclusion to Westinghouse's relationship with lawyers. In March 1907, Westinghouse was announcing record quarterly earnings and was prepared to pay a dividend of over two million dollars. Reactions to new federal regulation, however, triggered some steep declines in the price of certain stocks, railroad stocks in particular; the Dow Jones average lost twenty-five percent of its value by the end of the month. Westinghouse had previously issued millions of dollars in bonds to investors, who began to panic over the dwindling liquidity of securities in the market. In order to calm investors, Westinghouse struck a deal with French investors in the summer of 1907 to borrow a little over twelve million dollars. The covenants for $8.7 million of the French collateralized notes required that the collateral needed to be maintained at a certain level of value.

When the stock market plunged in October, causing an abrupt fall in the value of Westinghouse's collateral, Westinghouse found himself in default on all twelve million dollars. On October 22, Westinghouse called Paul Cravath, who rushed to Pittsburgh and attempted to organize bridge financing from among the Pittsburgh banks. The Panic, meanwhile, had begun to freeze lending in Pittsburgh as well, and Cravath wired back to New York that the Pittsburgh "banks concluded they were not strong enough to cope with situation" and "the protection of all concerned requires immediate receivership."[155] Once the receivers were appointed, the Pittsburgh firms of Reed, Smith, Shaw & Beal, and Gordon & Smith—the latter being one of the successors to John Dalzell's old firm upon its dissolution the year before—were appointed as counsel for the receivers.

Robert Swaine's account of Westinghouse's personal involvement in effecting the year-and-a-half long reorganization of the Westinghouse companies shows some of the mastery of his financial thinking, and his indefatigable energy resources—zooming back and forth between Pittsburgh and New York, meeting with banks and creditors' committees, and structuring settlements. He was, in a sense, attempting to recreate the reorganization that he successfully concluded during the "mini-panic" of 1893, a crisis which had propelled Westinghouse's reputation as a first-rate financier, in addition to being a great engineer. Cravath was with him through most of the ordeal, even lending his personal capital, and some of his fees in the case, to help preserve some of Westinghouse's equity position in the companies. Witnessing Cravath's dedication to Westinghouse, the receivers and their lawyers, Reed Smith and Gordon & Smith, followed suit and agreed to apply a portion of their fees toward Westinghouse's equity subscription. Cravath later said of him:

> *For twenty-five years ... I saw [Mr. Westinghouse] intimately under almost every conceivable condition ... It is my sober judgment that no man I have known combined so many of the qualities that make for greatness as George Westinghouse. ...Besides being a great inventor Mr. Westinghouse was a great organizer ... Besides being a great inventor and a great organizer, Mr. Westinghouse was in my estimation a great financier ... I don't say he was a prudent financier, especially if judged by the standards of Wall Street or orthodox banking circles in Pittsburgh, but I do claim he was a great financier. If he had been what we are pleased to call a prudent financier he would not have been a great one.*[156]

When the reorganization became operative in November, Westinghouse was still president, but the New York banks, backed by J.P. Morgan, insisted on the creation of a Chairman of the Board. Near the end of 1909, a board committee appointed Robert

Mather, former chairman of the board of the Rock Island Company, as the Chairman of Westinghouse, prompting Westinghouse to launch a tirade and character assault against Mather, hoping to cause him to be ousted. His fifty-eight-page statement was delivered to the board with a cover letter from his new personal lawyers, John G. Johnson of Philadelphia and Salmon O. Levinson of Chicago. Both were well-known, highly-skilled lawyers who, unfortunately, had little history with Westinghouse or his companies. It was a half-formed plan, uncharacteristic of Westinghouse's efforts—and as to the fifty-eight pages, probably a solo effort.

As advisor to the corporate entity, and not to Westinghouse personally, Cravath was forced to take a stand, writing to Westinghouse: "My obligation is to the Westinghouse Company and I think you have gone back on the arrangement you have agreed to. I think my duty is to the Board of Directors and to the Company and to the plan of reorganization to which you assented and which I was instrumental in carrying through." Westinghouse's campaign failed; and although he and Cravath remained cordial, they never again enjoyed each other's confidence.[157]

Westinghouse still remained on the board, but he rarely made himself seen or heard after losing control of the Company. Charles Terry, who had since moved back to New York from Pittsburgh but remained as vice president of Westinghouse Electric, was Westinghouse's personally designated proxy to attend board meetings. When Westinghouse died in 1914, the handpicked trustees for his interests, valued at fifty million dollars at the time of his death, were his brother, Henry Herman Westinghouse, W.D. Uptegraff, a long-time director of the Air Brake Company, and Charles Terry.[158] Terry took his own seat on the board of directors of the Westinghouse Company in 1928, and Westinghouse Electric in 1933; and at the time of his death a few years later at age eighty, Terry was heralded as having spent fifty years with Westinghouse Electric[159]—which is as much proof of Terry's loyalty to George Westinghouse as it is a testament to Westinghouse's vision of the breadth and depth of a lawyer's role within a modern corporation.

ABSCONDING ATTORNEYS

Historians have referred to the Gilded Age as a particularly corrupt period in American politics and business, almost to the point of cliché. Whether or not, statistically, the Gilded Age was a more corrupt era in Pittsburgh history than any other is difficult to quantify, but it was certainly the case that contemporary commentators smelled corruption in Pittsburgh. The muckraker Lincoln Steffens, writing in 1903 and looking back upon the Magee-Flinn years in Pittsburgh, argued:

> *Minneapolis was an example of police corruption; St. Louis of financial corruption. Pittsburg is an example of both police and financial corruption. The two other cities have found each an official who has exposed them. Pittsburg has had no such man and no exposure. The city has been described physically as "Hell with the lid off"; politically it is that same with the lid on.*[160]

Undoubtedly it may also be observed that the Gilded Age in Pittsburgh was a period of an unprecedented expansion of wealth; and that during similar periods in history, the opportunities for corruption seem to become more plentiful. Pittsburgh lawyers were not immune from greed, and their status as members of a profession that was enthusiastically embracing the entrepreneurial spirit of Pittsburgh business inevitably gave them access to temptations. Even in the absence of an exposing official (to paraphrase Steffens), however, there were a couple of Pittsburgh lawyers who ended up being exposed in grand fashion for their crimes.

One notable example was Samuel "S.B.W." Gill. Gill was admitted to the bar in 1851 and by the end of the Civil War he had not only established a large practice in Pittsburgh, but also "possessed the confidence of the community."[161] Like Judge Mellon, D.T. Watson and other members of the bar, in the mid-1870s Gill had begun to supplement the income from his practice by investing in the Pittsburgh mortgage market. In a typical transaction, he might offer to provide purchase money, or pay off an existing mortgage, and become the direct mortgage lender to a purchaser of land. On the back end of these transactions, Gill began to solicit investments in his mortgages from clients and other acquaintances. Thus, in March 1877, Gill paid off an existing mortgage given by Hamilton Lacock and his wife in exchange for a new mortgage in his favor. Later that month, Rev. Matthew M. Pollock gave Gill one thousand dollars to invest in one of Gill's mortgages, for which Gill assigned him a portion of the Lacock mortgage. In this case, however, Gill then took the liberty of purportedly selling the mortgage again the following month to William C. King—without accounting for his partial assignment of the mortgage to Rev. Pollock.[162]

By the pattern of Gill's other conduct, later revealed in a tangled snarl of proceedings in Common Pleas Court and ultimately in federal bankruptcy court, Gill's sale of a previously assigned mortgage to William C. King was not an isolated incident, but an example of a greater habit of fraud encompassing trading in bogus mortgages, overselling legitimate ones, embezzling funds and committing forgery over a period of four years. He was even accused of attempting to push questionable schemes through the Orphans' Court on more than one occasion, looking for an official stamp of approval for some of his allegedly underhanded dealings.[163]

Gill apparently conducted his activities with a keen sense of stagecraft, as the newspapers would later report:

His affectation of honesty proved one of his most successful instruments of fraud. An Allegheny lady one time deposited with him $10,000 worth of bonds. In return he gave her $1,100 cash. She asked if it would not be proper for him to give her a note for the balance, when he indignantly replied, "Madame, you have no confidence in me. Here, take back your bonds, for I can not do business with you." The lady was abashed at the statement and ... told her counsel that she actually felt so much ashamed of her question that she apologized to Mr. Gill and begged him as a favor to keep the bonds. ... If any client would make a complaint he would fish out in $1,000 bills the amount due the client, and with an injured air demand that the money be accepted and that all business relations be closed between them. He wanted to 'do business with no person who did not have perfect confidence in his integrity.'[164]

Around the beginning of September 1877, a law student of Gill's noticed that "the attorney was busily engaged, a great deal of his time, in a careful study of the extradition treaties between the United States and different foreign countries."[165] T. Walter Day, another attorney whose office was in the same building as Gill's and who would become one of Gill's creditors, would later swear that, to his knowledge, "on or about September 17, 1877 ... Gill did depart out of and from the State of Pennsylvania, of which he is an inhabitant, with the intention ... of defrauding his creditors."[166] It became apparent that Gill had skipped the country as his creditors began to close in and question their dealings with him. Gill had turned over most of his court business to Day before he left town.

The mess that Gill left behind was ugly and deep, and ultimately tragic for some. Within a week after Thanksgiving, some sixty of Gill's unsuspecting victims had come to Common Pleas Court with their petitions for amounts totaling close to three hundred thousand dollars.[167] Among his "marks" were at least two clergymen, and a number of elderly men and women, including one "old lady," Mrs. Rosanna Hamilton of Carroll Street in the Bloomfield neighborhood, who allegedly committed suicide by hanging herself after Gill had defrauded her of twelve hundred dollars.[168] On January 11, 1878, the Court of Common Pleas took the apparently unprecedented step of striking Gill's name from the rolls of practicing lawyers in Allegheny County, with Gill still in absentia.[169] As late as 1881, the Pennsylvania Supreme Court was still hearing cases involving Gill's fraud,[170] and his creditors ultimately received less than ten cents on the dollar.

The story would have been closed with the disposition of the last pennies of Gill's sorry estate were it not for revelations by a former Pittsburgher, Thomas Gillespie, living in Belfast, Ireland in 1886. As reported by the *Reading Times*, Gillespie had become acquainted with a "mysterious American stranger" in Belfast by the name of "S.B. Wallace." According to the *Times*

> ... [W]hen he discovered that Gillespie was an old Pittsburgher [Wallace] exhibited great interest in him. Upon better acquaintance Wallace informed Gillespie that he, also, was a native of this city. He frequently inquired about prominent persons living here, and one day asked if anything had ever been heard of S.B.W. Gill. Gillespie said no, but added that if he was ever found he would get his just deserts. After that Wallace avoided the subject.

Wallace took ill with fever early in November 1886, and died in Belfast on November 19. Gillespie took charge of Wallace's effects, and discovered therein a number of legal documents and books marked with the name of "Gill." According to Gillespie, Wallace was in actuality Gill, having eluded discovery for nine years and apparently dying without being held accountable for his crimes.[171]

Nine years after Gill's death in Belfast, the discovery of financial misdealings by another prominent Pittsburgh attorney rocked the Pittsburgh legal establishment. William C. Moreland, who had succeeded Thomas Bigelow as city solicitor in February 1882,[172] was one of the more beloved members of the bar. Silver-tongued and silver-coiffed, he was "bright, witty and fresh"[173] as an after-dinner speaker and served as Pittsburgh's unofficial toastmaster for a number of years, acting as master of ceremonies at many of Pittsburgh's public and patriotic gatherings. At age thirteen, he was a messenger for the Atlantic & Pacific Telegraph Company, working with several very illustrious future Pittsburghers; Thomas Scott of the Pennsylvania Railroad, Scott's associates Robert Pitcairn and David McCargo, and even Andrew Carnegie himself all began their careers as teen messengers alongside Moreland. It was no doubt a point of pride among members of the bar that the same proving ground begat both Pittsburgh's most successful industrialist, and one of its favorite lawyers. Although he never served in the Union Army, his opponent in the 1868 District Attorney election, General Alfred Pearson, appointed Moreland to the post of judge advocate general of the Western Division of the National Guard of Pennsylvania, with the rank of major. Thus, he would be known to all as "Major Moreland."[174]

In October 1895, the finance committee of the councils of the City of Pittsburgh empowered a subcommittee to investigate the financial operations of the city's law department, and it quickly became apparent that Moreland and his assistant, William H. House, had been engaged in some questionable, not very well hidden financial transactions involving the city treasury. In what the newspapers called "an apparently systematic method of embezzlement,"[175] all money collected by Moreland and House on city claims and assessments was apparently deposited by House, not in the city treasury, but in one of Moreland's personal bank accounts at one of four banks in town. Moreland had no separate personal accounts, and without knowing how much House had deposited into his accounts or how much interest had been earned on city funds in his accounts, he would sometimes deposit his own funds, and freely draw upon the contents of the accounts.

Meanwhile, if that were not enough, in May 1885, House began to enter into loan arrangements with Booth & Flinn, the city's most active general construction contractor, using money from Moreland's account. The company's founder, William Flinn, who was leader of Pittsburgh's Republican machine with Christopher Magee, approached House with the complaint that city disbursements for construction projects were running behind, and that he needed to make payroll. According to later court records, House told Flinn that collections "were slow in coming in, but that he could help tide them over, by loaning the money."[176] For ten years, Flinn and House traded thousands of dollars in loans and repayments. When making the loans, House would write out the checks on Moreland's account to himself, which Moreland would sign, and House would subsequently endorse them to Booth & Flinn.[177]

Immediately upon the discovery of these transactions, and the deposits in Moreland's account, Moreland resigned as city attorney, and was replaced by Clarence Burleigh. House followed suit. On October 15, Moreland and House were arrested on a warrant from District Attorney John C. Haymaker[e] and charged with three counts of collecting interest on public money. The indictments detailed approximately forty-eight thousand dollars in improper interest payments. The indictments were subsequently expanded to include several more counts.[178] A quick trial on one of the counts resulted in a "not guilty" verdict in February 1896, but the remaining counts were said to be more difficult for Moreland and House to surmount.

When the second trial was set to begin on July 14, 1896, it was expected that Moreland, through his lead attorney J. Scott Ferguson, would fight the charges tooth and nail, just as he had in the first trial. Instead, Moreland pulled a last minute surprise, as reported by the *Post*:

> *[Moreland] was dressed in a natty suit of pongee, and greeted everyone that entered his office with his accustomed smile. However, there is a noticeable difference from the time when the exposure was not anticipated. He has lost his springing gait, and though his handshake is just as cordial as of yore, there is a sadness in his manner entirely new*

---

e   The younger brother of Joseph Haymaker, known as the lawyer-witness to the Pennsylvania Railroad riots in 1877.

to those who have known him for years. But so much of his old self remains that those who have not seen him nor known him before the exposure would not believe that he could have pleaded guilty of a crime. …

The court opened yesterday with Judges Porter and Kennedy on the bench. Every seat in the room was occupied before the roll of jurors was called. While this was going on District-Attorney Haymaker was in consultation with John S. Robb and William Yost, who had been engaged, with the permission of the court, to assist him in the trial. While they were preparing the evidence against Moreland, J. Scott Ferguson and H.L. Goehring, Moreland's attorneys, entered the room and went to Judge Porter. After they had talked earnestly for some time Judge Porter turned to D.F. Patterson, who represented W.H. House, and asked for a plea. Mr. Patterson said "not guilty," and Mr. Ferguson left the room. When he had disappeared H.L. Goehring electrified the courtroom by saying in a loud, clear voice:

"If your honor please, we wish to enter a plea of guilty for Mr. Moreland."

Nothing could have been a greater surprise. For a moment the district-attorney was non-plused. He had not anticipated such a move and had so prepared his case that it would be difficult to try only one of the defendants. House blanched when he heard it, but straightened up immediately, probably seeing in the plea of Moreland an advantage to himself. The court took the plea and Mr. Goehring left the room, leaving House and his attorneys to fight the array of indictments themselves.[179]

While Moreland awaited sentencing, House became emboldened by this turn of events, taking as his defense strategy that Moreland was completely at blame, and that everyone else was lying. House was, nonetheless, convicted at trial[180]—quite possibly because people had come to believe that it was House's negligence and stupidity that led to Moreland's downfall.

On the day of sentencing, Judge John M. Kennedy's courtroom was "thronged … with spectators," *The New York Times* reported, and "[e]very person in the courtroom during the proceedings was a personal friend and co-laborer" with Major Moreland.[181] As the *Post* reported:

Moreland advanced to the bar where he had seen thousands arraigned before without nervousness, but when he realized that he was in the position of a felon about to receive sentence he bowed his head upon his hands and restrained a flow of tears by biting his lip. It was a moment of expectation that enforced quietness in the court room without the presence of deputy sheriffs or court tipstaves.

Ferguson gave an appeal for leniency. "Mr. Moreland has filled the office of city attorney for fourteen years and has personally acted in thousands upon thousands of actions against the city," he declared. "He had no time to keep accounts, his time being fully engaged in court. His actions, to which he is now to be held accountable, were brought on by carelessness. I don't believe that any of us that knew William C. Moreland think that he intended to commit a wrong. There was a loose method of conducting business in that office, and poor bookkeeping is responsible for it all. I say, and God help us, there was no intention to do wrong. ... I ask for leniency. Mr. Moreland is upward of 60 years old, and the punishment he had undergone since this thing began ... is greater than any your honors can inflict."

Judge Kennedy's voice faltered as he passed sentence on his old friend. "Major Moreland, I am unable to express in words the painful duty I am called upon to discharge. I have given your case the most careful consideration, and in passing sentence shall give due regard to the fact that you have pleaded guilty and saved the county the expense of trying you. The sentence of the court is that you pay a fine of $26,653.74, the costs of prosecution and undergo imprisonment in the Western Penitentiary, there to be kept, clothed and fed, as the law directs, for and during a period of three years."[182] *The New York Times* observed that "the scene was ... impressive and remarkable."[183]

House received a lighter sentence, but less sympathy in the courtroom, as he and his attorneys readied his appeal. Meanwhile, Moreland was immediately taken out of the courtroom and across the Bridge of Sighs to the County Jail. Later, at the Western Penitentiary on the banks of the Ohio, then known as "Riverside," Moreland was said to have broken down in tears as his curly silver locks were cut short, and he was required to exchange his "natty suit of pongee" for "a suit of prison stripes."[184]

After serving eighteen months of his prison sentence, Moreland received a pardon from Governor Daniel H. Hastings. In the letter to the governor from the Board of Pardons, dated January 29, 1898, it was noted that "[t]here was no secrecy about his office in any way, and the books of account, receipts and disbursements, were open to the inspection of anyone. ... [W]hen the auditors came to adjust his accounts they found a large discrepancy and this fact was made public. He was not informed that the auditors were going over his books, nor had he an opportunity of going into the accounts with them for the purpose of explaining the discrepancy. When this discovery was first announced, the press took hold of the matter and published exciting stories as to the amount involved, and public feeling was very much aroused, as the amounts said to have been appropriated by the applicant was very much exaggerated."[185]

Accompanying the recommendation of the Board of Pardons was a voluminous series of petitions:

> ... two petitions from the Allegheny county bar, one signed by 177 members, and the other by 42 members, who strongly urge the liberation of the applicant. Also, a petition from 34 members of the Fayette county bar, 57 members of the Butler county bar, 48 members of the Beaver county bar, 48 members of the Westmoreland county bar, 18 members of the Washington county bar, and 31 members of the Greene county bar, who ask that a recommendation for Executive clemency may be made. Another petition is signed by 37 clergymen of Allegheny county. There is also filed a petition from 168 of the officers and clerks of Allegheny county. There are two petitions signed respectively by 175 and 73 of the business men of Allegheny county; three petitions signed respectively by 79, 91 and 72 of the business men of Pittsburgh; three petitions signed respectively by 77, 66 and 78 of the business men of Allegheny. Another petition by 135 of the business men from the Fifteenth and Seventeenth wards of the city of Pittsburgh. The petition

of 146 citizens of Allegheny city; another petition of 110 citizens of Allegheny city; the petition of 54 Pittsburgh railroad clerks; 46 Allegheny councilmen; 110 of the Allegheny county telegraph operators; 84 professional men of Allegheny county, four petitions signed respectively by 107, 58, 51 and 144 of the citizens of Pittsburgh. Another signed by 29 members of select and 28 members of the common council of the city of Pittsburgh. Another petition signed by 240 firemen of the city of Pittsburg [sic]. Another petition signed by 58 members of the Senate and House of Representatives of Pennsylvania, including those of Allegheny and surrounding counties. Another petition signed by 14 of the largest manufacturers of Allegheny county. Another petition signed by 30 of the officers and 173 of the employes of the Jones & Laughlin Company of Pittsburgh. Another signed by 71 of the business men of McKeesport, and another signed by 19 of the business men of Tarentum.

There were also 133 personal letters by prominent citizens, including B.F. Jones, General Alfred Pearson, the Honorable John Dalzell and D.T. Watson. In closing, the Board wrote: "The imprisonment that he is serving, he claims, is not greater punishment than the fact of his disbarment and his being shut out from the society of the judges and lawyers with whom he has associated for so many years. To a man of his character and life the imprisonment brings a degree of agony and humiliation beyond that suffered by the common criminal."[186]

When news of the governor's pardon reached the Penitentiary, Warden Wright sent for Moreland; and while "indulging in a hearty handshake" with the prisoner, Wright whispered in his ear, "Billy, you are pardoned, and within another day you will perhaps be again with your family."[187]

Moreland returned to his Forbes Avenue home and died four years afterward, on May 2, 1902.[188] Although Moreland was disbarred following his conviction, his colleagues apparently were loath to allow that fact to be recorded for posterity. To the contrary, his memory continued to be honored. Jones & Laughlin Steel named a steamship for him in 1910.[f] Archibald Blakeley pointedly mentions S.B.W. Gill's disbarment in his roll of Allegheny County lawyers for the publication *The Twentieth Century Bench and Bar of Pennsylvania* (1903), but for the late William Moreland he merely states that he "was for many terms in succession solicitor for the city of Pittsburgh."[189] In a subsequent profile in *History of Pittsburgh and Environs* (1922), Moreland is lauded for bringing a "wealth of talent and surpassing ability to the promotion of the general welfare" and states that "[h]is conception of his profession was high, and he regarded the law as a science offering vast benefits to men in its just and proper interpretation."[190] In perhaps yet another measure of both the power of the bar and the camaraderie among its upper echelon during this age, neither publication mentions Moreland's resignation, conviction, prison sentence or disbarment.

---

f   After four uneventful cargo runs, the *William C. Moreland* struck a reef off the coast of Michigan and sank in October 1910. It was the largest vessel lost on the Great Lakes up to that time. "Ship of the Month No. 4 Parkdale," *The Scanner, Monthly News Bulletin of the Toronto Marine Historical Society* 2, no. 3 (December 1969).

NEW PIONEERS

For the first seventy-eight years of the Pittsburgh bar, the legal profession was almost entirely closed to all but white, Anglo-Saxon, Christian men—and for the entire nineteenth century, the bar was dominated by them. Pittsburgh was relatively slower than some other cities to accept diversity among its lawyers, particularly in creating the conditions in which Jews, African Americans and women could practice in its courts. Samson Simpson paved the way for Jews to establish themselves as lawyers with his admission to the New York City bar in 1802[191]; Macon Bolling Allen became the first African American lawyer in the nation when he entered the Portland, Maine bar in 1844, entering the Boston bar the following year[192]; and Arabella Mansfield became the first woman lawyer in the United States when she was admitted to the Iowa bar in 1869, although she never practiced.[193] The comparable "firsts" in Pittsburgh would not be achieved until 1866, 1891 and 1895, respectively.

In general, the lack of educational opportunities available to African Americans and women held back their progress in most American cities, and the rise of the law school was one of the most significant factors in the "democratization" of the bar, in that control over whom would be educated in the profession was no longer held by lawyers themselves. Pittsburgh's failure to establish a law school until the 1890s no doubt had a significant impact on the halting progress of its bar's diversity. In urban Jewish communities, however, early educational opportunities were often quite abundant; for Jews hoping to enter the profession, however, it is apparent that ethnic prejudices against non-native English speakers limited their advancement.

Jews started settling in Pittsburgh in large numbers by the 1850s, and initially most of them came from the German states of Baden, Bavaria and Wurttemburg; later, many came from Eastern Europe.[194] Josiah Cohen, who was born in Plymouth, England in 1841, had a distinct advantage over other Jewish immigrants who may have aspired to enter the bar at mid-nineteenth century in that English was his first language, and he had been educated in at the Institute of Jewish Learning in London before arriving in the U.S. with his parents, Henry and Rose Cohen, when he was sixteen. Upon his subsequent arrival in Pittsburgh in 1860, he was hired to teach English grammar, spelling, reading, writing and arithmetic to German Jewish immigrants at Rodef Shalom. In the years that followed, Cohen assumed a leadership role within the Rodef Shalom community, and was frequently called upon to serve as the community's spokesman in the greater Pittsburgh community—a circumstance through which he ultimately fashioned a great deal of personal goodwill in Pittsburgh at large.[195]

While continuing to teach, in 1863 Cohen registered as a law student with John M. Kirkpatrick, then serving as Allegheny County District Attorney, and Kirkpatrick's partner and deputy, John Mellon—arguably one of the leading Roman Catholic attorneys in Pittsburgh. Following the normal examination, led by George Shiras, Jr., he was admitted to the Allegheny County bar on January 4, 1866. The following day, the *Pittsburgh Evening Chronicle* made the following comment on Cohen's admission:

We noticed yesterday that on motion of John M. Kirkpatrick, Mr. Josiah Cohen was admitted to the practice of law at the various county courts. Mr. Cohen is the first Jew admitted to the Pittsburgh bar. He has been a resident of our city for the past six years, and most of the time has been engaged as Principal of the English Department of the Hebrew School on Hancock street, in which position he won the esteem and friendship of the large and wealthy congregation which supports the school, by his scholarly attainments and genial qualities. We wish him success in a profession which he is so fitted to adorn.[196]

Despite his admission to the bar, Cohen had not initially planned to go into practice. As Cohen tells it:

Shortly after my admission that famous character, that man of wonderfully magnetic personality, Thomas M. Marshall, who was then a leading member of the bar, sent for me. I was at that time teaching school. He said, "I understand you have been admitted to the bar." I replied, "Yes, sir." "Well, why don't you go into practice?" said he; to which I replied, "While the grass grows the horse starves." "What do you mean," said he. "Why, I mean, I am earning $700 a year as a teacher." To which he responded, "Come into my office and I will pay you $1,000 a year."[197]

As a native English speaker, the obviously talented and well-respected Cohen was immediately embraced by the Pittsburgh legal community. From the outset of his brief association with Marshall & Brown, Cohen worked on cases involving the non-Jewish majority in Pittsburgh, as well as matters that directly involved the Jewish community of Pittsburgh; the first petition he presented in the Court of Common Pleas, before Judge Thomas Mellon, was for a corporate charter for a Jewish burial ground.[198]

Subsequent Jewish lawyers in Pittsburgh were not immediately as successful as Cohen. Magnus Pflaum was born in Prussia and was educated at the famous Gymnasium zum Grauen Klosters in Berlin before arriving in the U.S. in 1863. Pflaum's brother, Maurice Pflaum, is thought to have been the first Jewish physician in Pittsburgh. While serving as a notary, Magnus Pflaum registered as a student with attorney James M.

Stoner two years after Cohen's admission to the bar, and was admitted on the motion of John Mellon in 1871. Pflaum set up his own practice without fanfare, and eventually built a respectable practice among the German Jewish community and otherwise; but Pflaum was also a gentleman and scholar, busying himself with personal investments and, notably, with investigations into the natural sciences as a leader of the American Microscopical Society.[199]

The next several Jewish members of the Allegheny County bar were American-born. Solomon L. Fleishman followed Pflaum into the bar a few months later, but practiced only sporadically as he built his retail business in Pittsburgh. Louis A. Heidelberg (admitted in 1873) left Pittsburgh before 1881; Benjamin Winternitz practiced in New Castle; and Louis Rosenzweig practiced in Erie. Abraham Israel and Joseph M. Friedman were admitted in 1881; Israel became Cohen's partner for seventeen years before returning to his native New York City, shortly before Cohen was appointed as a judge of the Orphans' Court of Allegheny County.

Before the end of the century, two other Jewish members of the bar would emerge as leaders: Joseph Stadtfeld (admitted in 1886), who served as the first Jewish president of the Allegheny County Bar Association (1927-28) and subsequently as a judge on the Pennsylvania Superior Court; and A. Leo Weil, a native of Titusville and a University of Virginia Law School graduate who was admitted to practice in Bradford, Pennsylvania in 1880 and entered the Pittsburgh bar in 1886, opening a downtown office and taking Standard Oil as a client.[200]

George Boyer Vashon, the son of Pittsburgh African American leader John Vashon, grew up amid his father's activities in the anti-slavery movement and the beginnings of the Underground Railroad. At sixteen, he began studies at Oberlin College, gaining facility in Sanskrit, Hebrew, Persian, Greek and Latin. He graduated with honors in 1844, and returned to Pittsburgh to work in the law office of Walter Forward while contributing to Martin R. Delany's African American newspaper, *The Mystery*. In truth, he had probably attained a level of erudition greater than most of his white peers who were studying for the bar around the same time. When he completed his studies in 1847, Vashon applied for admission to the Allegheny County bar; but the examining committee would not consider his application, citing the fact that the 1838 revision of the Pennsylvania Constitution restricted suffrage to white men—despite the good efforts of his preceptor Walter Forward to open the vote to African American men.[201]

Vashon left Pittsburgh and entered the New York bar. As the New York correspondent for the *Philadelphia Enquirer* reported:

> *Geo. Vashon ... does not, however, intend to practice his profession here; he merely took out his credentials from our Courts, and intends to practice at Cap Haitien, where they will act as a powerful letter of recommendation, and where he can plead without being sneered at.*

> *... The education of young Mr. Vashon was of the most liberal character—such as to draw from his Professors encomiums of praise. His qualifications for legal proficiency were certified to by our most eminent and erudite lawyers. Yet under the present constitution*

and organization of our Courts, he could not be permitted to pursue the line of life for which he had labored so assiduously to prepare himself. New York has extended the courtesy due to his merit, regardless of the complexion of the applicant.[202]

Vashon lived in Haiti for a time, but eventually returned to the United States, practicing law in Syracuse before returning to Pittsburgh as president of Avery College, a school for African American children in Allegheny City.[203] In July 1867, the year after Josiah Cohen was admitted to the bar and two years after Jonathan Jasper Wright, an African American, was admitted to the Susquehanna County bar, Vashon again applied for admission to the Allegheny County bar. Judge P.C. Shannon of the Allegheny District Court (the late Walter Forward's successor on the bench) moved for Vashon's admission in the Court of Common Pleas before Judge Mellon and Judge Edwin H. Stowe. According to the *Pittsburgh Commercial Journal*, attorney James Herron Hopkins, a future Democratic congressman from Pittsburgh, stated that Vashon's application

should be referred to the [examination] committee. His Honor Judge Shannon replied, he thought not. It was unusual to do so unless some objection to made to the character or qualifications of the applicant. In this case the whole objection related, it would seem to be the man's color. This appeared to be the only difficulty. Mr. Hopkins added in reply the course he advocated was the usual and proper course; and he did not wish to see special and unusual privileges extended to a colored person, over and above those extended and allowed to white persons. He wished in this matter all treated alike.

The bar was in full attendance at the Saturday hearing, taking a "lively interest in the proceedings." The Court concluded by granting a rule to show cause why Professor Vashon should not be admitted to the bar.[204]

When the argument resumed the following week, it was apparent that, through back-channel communications, the case would not be a referendum on whether an African American man was permitted to enter the bar. The *Gazette* reported:

We learned that the question of citizenship as regards to color will not be touched. This takes away much of the importance which at first seemed to attach to the proceedings, as all that remains to be inquired into is as to the qualifications of Mr. Vashon, or as to his right to admission on the strength of the certificate of the Supreme Court of New York.[205]

Vashon's application was again denied, this time ostensibly on the grounds that he had not practiced law at any time for the previous three years.[206]

In 1865, the Thirteenth Amendment to the U.S. Constitution, prohibiting slavery and involuntary servitude, was ratified; in 1868, there followed the Fourteenth Amendment, which granted citizenship to former slaves and their descendants; and in 1870, the Fifteenth Amendment theoretically granted the right to vote to African American men. The stage had been set for African Americans to enter the bar in large numbers, and by 1890, nearly every state had admitted a "first" African American lawyer.

On December 20, 1891, the *Pittsburgh Commercial Gazette* reported that "W.M. Randolph of New York and J. Wilfred Holmes [sic] of Baltimore, both colored men, were admitted to practice law in Allegheny county," upon the motion of Judge Charles S. Fetterman, the chair of the examination committee.[207] John Welfred Holmes, a big, burly twenty-four year-old, was a Georgia native who grew up on a farm in Virginia. In 1890, he graduated from Howard Law School in Washington, D.C. A national newspaper, the *Colored American*, discussed Holmes' disadvantages in coming to the Pittsburgh bar:

> *With neither friend nor relative and without a single letter of introduction he landed in Pittsburg, Pa., which prior to this time had no lawyer with Negro blood in his veins. Here another difficulty presented itself. The Allegheny County Bar Association zealously guarding the high calling of the law made it obligatory upon those who would practice before its courts, that they first demonstrate their fitness by two examinations ...*

Holmes' first examination was a general education exam that included English grammar and Latin, and the second was a law exam.[208] The *Gazette* observed that, during the prior summer, "he applied for admission to the bar here, but failed for lack of knowledge of Pennsylvania law."[209]

In December, Holmes entered the examination in Common Pleas Court No. 2, room 2, with another African American law school graduate, William Maurice Randolph. Randolph, twenty-five, was born in Richmond, Virginia. He attended public schools in New York City, clerked with New York lawyers Henry Freeman and Mason W. Tyler, and entered the City bar on May 8, 1888, graduating from the law school of the University of New York a few days after his admission.[210] After their admission to the Allegheny County bar, Holmes and Randolph hung out their independent shingles while sharing space on Fourth Avenue,[211] and began to attract a primarily African American clientele.

The success of Holmes and Randolph paved the way for other African American lawyers in Pittsburgh. The following year, Walter E. Billows entered the bar. William Henry Stanton, whose brother Edward was a file clerk and doorman at the Dalzell firm and later at Gordon & Smith and its successor firms,[212] studied law with former federal judge Charles W. McKenna and entered the bar in 1895. Like Holmes and Randolph, Stanton came to be known as an expert criminal lawyer, and he was the first lawyer of any race to be appointed by a court in Pittsburgh to defend a pauper charged with murder, with the County paying for his services. Frank R. Stewart, known locally as "Captain Stewart," also entered the bar in 1895. After 1895, however, the progress of African Americans at the bar came to an abrupt halt; these five men and a sixth, William N. Butler, who moved to Washington County, were the only African Americans to be admitted to the bar in the nineteenth century, and the next, Robert Lee Vann, would not be admitted until 1910.[213]

Each of the first five Pittsburgh men, however, would become highly-visible leaders in the Pittsburgh African American community, much like Josiah Cohen would be within the Pittsburgh Jewish community. Holmes served as the president of the Afro-American League of Western Pennsylvania and was part of a delegation that urged President William McKinley to pursue justice on behalf of African Americans who had been victims of racially-motivated murder; Randolph served as first president of the Loendi Club, the center of the Hill District's African American social and literary life, and was active in the Republican Party and the Afro-American League; William Stanton served as counsel to many high-profile local African American businesses, such as the

Douglass Loan and Investment Company, and was an active member of the Knights of Pythias, an African American fraternal group; Walter Billows advocated against segregated Pennsylvania public schools; and Frank Stewart was a perennial candidate for the state legislature and unofficial "ward boss." They organized public campaigns and appeared as protectors of the African American community, which ultimately helped them secure a loyal clientele within the African American community.[214]

The path of women to the bar was more arduous, in a way, than that of African Americans.

In March 1899, the following announcement appeared in a Pittsburgh newspaper:

Miss Agnes Fraser Watson's marriage Thursday evening to Herbert Lee Stitt of Pittsburgh, which took place at her mother's residence on Locust Street, Allegheny, was a pretty little ceremony, witnessed by about 50 guests and solemnized by Rev. Henry D. Lindsay, pastor of the North Presbyterian Church. There were but a two flower children in attendance, little Helen Barnes, a niece of the groom, and Harold Watson, a small nephew of the bride. The floral decorations were exceedingly handsome throughout the house. White azaleas, palms and maidenhair fern were used in the drawing room, white carnations in the dining room and all the other apartments were done in pink tulips and spring flowers. The bride wore a wedding gown of white pearl-tinted satin trimmed with duchess lace, in her hair she wore a white aigrette and plume, and she carried a bouquet of white carnations, her favorite flowers.[215]

The marriage of Agnes Fraser Watson to Herbert Lee Stitt, just before the close of the nineteenth century, marked the retirement of Pittsburgh's first woman lawyer.

Agnes Fraser Watson was born in Pittsburgh in June 1867 to a Scottish immigrant, Andrew Watson, who worked as a boilermaker, and his second wife Susan. Andrew Watson died when Agnes was ten years old. While Watson was still a youngster, the newspapers headlines were full of the actual trials and tribulations of pioneers like Myra Bradwell and Arabella Mansfield: Bradwell passed the Illinois bar examination in 1869, but was refused admission, even when the matter came before the Illinois Supreme Court; Mansfield passed the Iowa bar examination in the same year, and had to win the right to be admitted before the Iowa Supreme Court. Bradwell was later finally admitted to the Illinois bar.[216] In 1886, Carrie Kilgore of Philadelphia became the first woman lawyer in Pennsylvania, but only after the same kind of protracted litigation to secure the right of women to practice that Myra Bradwell and Arabella Mansfield had gone through.[217]

In Pittsburgh in the nineteenth century, sons followed fathers into the profession. The trend began before the Civil War, but it was responsible for staffing the "Gilded Bar" with some of its most prominent practitioners. Moses Hampton's son John Henry Hampton was a leading member of the late nineteenth century bar, as were Stephen C. McCandless, son of Wilson McCandless; Richard Biddle Roberts, son of E.J. Roberts; John A. Lowrie, son of Walter H. Lowrie; and W.S. Purviance, son of Samuel A. Purviance. The Fetterman brothers had, between them, three sons who entered the County bar before the Civil War: G.L. and Wilfred B. Fetterman, sons of W.W. Fetterman, and Charles

S. Fetterman, son of N.P. Fetterman. The trend continued as the century wore on: notably, T.J. Bigham's sons Joel and Kirk entered the bar in 1870 and 1880, respectively; George Shiras, Jr.'s sons George III and Winfield K. entered the bar in 1883 and 1884, respectively; C.B.M. Smith's sons Albert Y. and Edwin W., in 1880; and William Bakewell's sons James and Thomas, in 1879 and 1883, respectively. John Barton, who took the Allegheny County bar exam two or three times before being admitted by certification from Clarion County in 1845, had three sons who entered the Allegheny County bar between 1876 and 1881; and even Harry Blair Gill entered the profession from which his father, S.B.W. Gill, was expelled. There were many other fathers and sons in the Pittsburgh bar during the late nineteenth century, including the James Buchanans, the Julius Koethens, the James Sterretts, the Carnahans, the Colliers, the Browns, the Robbs, the Kerrs, the Schoyers, and so on.[218]

The trend was unmistakable, but not surprising. In the United States, before law school attendance became the norm rather than the exception, fathers managed the education of their sons directly, and could not be faulted for providing them with an education that would inevitably lead them to join their fathers' profession. In a very real sense, early nineteenth century lawyers—members of the founding generation of Pittsburgh's legal traditions—saw the cultivation of legal aptitude in their sons as their most important legacy, and in meaningful numbers, their sons seem to have readily embraced this legacy. Moreover, as gatekeepers of the profession, it was both the right and the privilege of the nineteenth century Pittsburgh lawyer to bring his sons into the guild, and to be cautious about otherwise expanding the membership of the bar. Sons of farmers, clerks and mechanics were undoubtedly making their way into the profession in significant numbers, but the sons of lawyers had every advantage in getting there.

In 1893, when Agnes Fraser Watson entered the University of Michigan Law School, one of the earliest law schools in the nation to support the education of women as lawyers,[219] the Pittsburgh bar remained largely closed to white men, and there were still only handfuls of women lawyers throughout the United States.

Meanwhile, Pittsburgh experienced difficulties in establishing its own law school. It had been almost fifty years since the University of Pittsburgh's first ill-fated experiment in providing legal instruction had been terminated by the effects of two fires and a lack of approval by the Pittsburgh bar. The vacant law professorship was filled for a year by Judge Moses Hampton in 1862, and subsequently by Judge Henry W. Williams. The University's "professorship" did not, however, blossom into a full-fledged degree program.[220]

Harvard had established its law school in 1817; an independent law school became affiliated with Yale some time by the 1840s; and the University of Pennsylvania had formally established its law school in 1852. In 1860, while only twenty-one law schools were in operation in the United States and no state recognized a law school education as a prerequisite to bar admission,[221] it was also clear that in Pittsburgh a law school education could be a mark of prestige, as some members of the young elite of the Allegheny County bar were law school-educated, including D.T. Watson (Harvard Law, '1866) and George W. Guthrie (Columbian Law, now George Washington, '1869).[222]

Responding to the emerging demand, in 1870, Western University's chancellor, George Woods, attempted to initiate a formal, two-year Bachelor of Laws program, hiring Hill Burgwin to lecture on real property and on practice and pleadings of common law, W.T. Haines to lecture on criminal, domestic relations, insurance and commercial law, and William Bakewell to lecture on equity jurisprudence and practice, constitutional law, patents, contracts, corporations and federal law. As Dean Sell writes, however:

> *Only three years later, the program collapsed. ...When the University's program was instituted, it met with great opposition from some of the city's lawyers. One of these opponents was a University trustee. These individuals were opposed to any system which would undermine the traditional system of 'reading law' and training as law clerks to established lawyers. ... They alleged that the University had no right to seek consideration of the courts [in sanctioning a formal legal education as an appropriate step toward attaining Bar membership] and that no special privilege should be accorded their graduates with respect to the admission to the practice of law.*[223]

Woods attempted to mediate a solution with the leaders of Pittsburgh's legal community, but Burgwin, Haines and Bakewell ultimately resigned, and the University's second attempt to establish a law program was terminated in 1873.[224]

In the years between 1873 and 1895, the number of law schools around the country increased dramatically, from thirty-one in 1870 to sixty-one in 1890.[225] At the same time, as the use of the typewriter in law offices increased, the demand for law clerks as long-hand scribes began to decline. Chief Justice Morrison Waite of the U.S. Supreme Court was giving voice to a prevailing mood within the legal profession when he wrote in 1881 that "[t]he time has gone when an eminent lawyer, in full practice, can take a class of students into his office and become their teacher. Once that was practicable, but now it is not. The consequence is that law schools are a necessity."[226] Thus, the climate was already changing in favor of introducing a home-grown law school education when a Western University of Pennsylvania curriculum committee lamented to the trustees in 1894 that "Pittsburgh is the only large city in the United States as yet without a law school. It is manifestly the function of a university," the committee declared, "to provide such a school."[227]

In order to assuage any lingering disapproval over the creation of a law school in Pittsburgh, Chancellor William J. Holland invited the judges of the Allegheny County Court of Common Pleas to a dinner at the Duquesne Club, asking them to appoint a committee of the bar to work with the University trustees to establish a law school. In October 1895, the Department of Legal Instruction was founded at the Western University of Pennsylvania under the leadership of John D. Shafer; it would be this program that would eventually come to be known as the University of Pittsburgh School of Law (Pitt Law School). The first graduates received their Bachelor of Laws degrees after a two-year course of study, in 1897; for all subsequent classes, a three-year course of study was required. Organization, the great "lever of the age," had begun to overtake the education of lawyers in Pittsburgh, wresting that function away from individual lawyers and vesting it in an institution of higher learning. Soon after Shafer's appointment, the University's first law faculty was assembled from among some of the leaders of the bar, including Samuel Mehard, Thomas Herriott and District Attorney Clarence Burleigh.[228]

The first graduating class, in 1897, had thirty students, of whom two joined the Pittsburgh bar in March 1897—Henry Atwood and Ralph Longenecker. Four more followed in June 1897; and by September 1900, twenty-three of the thirty graduates from the first class of the Department of Legal Instruction had become members of the Pittsburgh bar.[229] By 1900, the percentage of new Allegheny County bar admittees who had attended some law school—Harvard and Michigan, in addition to Pittsburgh, were prevalent—was nearing fifty percent.[230] The mold of the new Pittsburgh lawyer, educated in a law school, was setting.

In Pittsburgh, and in other cities, it was not law school *per se* that directly fostered the introduction of women into the legal profession. Rather, it was technology. The steel-nubbed pen continued to be the lawyer's most important tool prior to the end of the 1870s; but the increasing tempo of business during the period challenged a number of inventors to work on a machine that could improve upon the sluggish pace set by longhand writing, allegedly clocked at a mere maximum of thirty words per minute in an 1853 test.[231] In 1873, a sewing machine company, E. Remington & Sons began the production of the first commercially successful typewriter, with a QWERTY keyboard layout,[232] a development that eventually led to the disappearance of the handwritten document within the legal profession. If there were some older lawyers—like the ones observed by John Foster Dulles when he arrived at Sullivan & Cromwell in New York in 1911, who "felt that the only dignified way of communication between members of the legal profession was for them to write each other in Spencerian [sic] script"[233]—protesting that an element of their written expression would disappear and that the dramatic undertones of the handwritten word upon the page were being replaced by the cold uniformity of typewritten correspondence, they were in the minority. Court stenographers first jumped on board the typewriter bandwagon in order to increase their speed, followed rapidly by the rest of the legal profession itself.

The typewriter, however, did more than mechanize the writing process for greater speed, accuracy and uniformity; it actually launched the entry of women into the white collar workplace, and in Pittsburgh law firms more specifically. In 1870, women held only about five percent of all stenographer positions,[234] when stenography was still generally held to be the practice of taking shorthand dictation and writing letters and instruments in longhand. Typewriters really began to flood the workplace in the 1880s; and by 1890, women held about sixty-four percent of all positions classified as typists or stenographers in the United States.[235] Typical among them in Pittsburgh were Lucy Dorsey Iams, better known today as the social reformer she eventually became, who went to work during the 1880s as a secretary in her husband Franklin P. Iams' downtown law office; and Clara I. Houston, an unmarried Beaver County woman who joined Dalzell, Scott & Gordon as a stenographer in the 1890s. The feminization of stenography as a trade in Pittsburgh is also evident from the listings of stenographers in the *City Directory*; by 1899, thirty out of forty-two independent stenographers and "typewriters" (as typists were then known) were women.[236] Still, the city's largest firm, Knox & Reed, did not get around to hiring its first female staffer until around 1915.[237]

Some employers rationalized the hiring of women based on the assumption that "a woman could operate typewriter keys more easily than a man could, because a woman's fingers are more dexterous,"[238] not to mention that women were "easier to control than young men, and cheaper to employ."[239] Women office workers earned approximately half of what their male counterparts earned at the end of the nineteenth century.[240] Despite these inequities, however, the typewriter was a mighty force that turned the environment of the law office from an all-male domain—with male lawyers, male students, office boys and male messengers—to a place where young women might actually catch a glimpse of the inner-workings of the legal profession.

After concluding her studies at Michigan in the fall of 1895, Agnes Fraser Watson quietly applied to take the bar exam. She was accepted for the exam by Noah W. Shafer, the chair of the examination board—promiment as the Register in Bankruptcy under the Bankruptcy Act of 1867, and somewhat of a progressive. The *Pittsburgh Post* headline on September 14, 1895 was simply "Miss Watson Passes." Out of twenty-six applicants, only ten passed the bar exam—nine young men (including William Henry Stanton) and "the Plucky Western Girl," as the papers called her, twenty-nine year-old Agnes Fraser Watson.

The *Post* reported: "Miss Agnes F. Watson, the first woman who has ever passed the final examination for admission to the Allegheny County bar, was admitted to practice in the various courts of the county yesterday ... in Common Pleas No. 1, the nine young men were sworn in first, and then Miss Watson was called up. Mr. Shafer moved for her admission." Judge Edwin Stowe leaned forward over the bench to study Miss Watson. "Mr. Shafer," he inquired, "has the Supreme Court of Pennsylvania decided the right of women to be admitted to practice?"

"Why, yes Your Honor," said Mr. Shafer, "it had been decided in the case of Miss Kilgore of Philadelphia."

Judge Stowe sat back in his chair, his expression unchanged. "I want to say if the Supreme Court had not decided the question, I would not consent to any women practicing law in this court. But if women want to practice law and ride bicycles, I suppose it is none of my business. Let her be sworn."[241]

On the same day the *Post* announced Miss Watson's admission, in separate stories it reported that a woman postmistress was appointed at Kennon, Ohio; that it was decided that women would be allowed to attend the national conference of the Methodist Episcopal Church; that women would now be admitted to the Catholic University of Washington; and, among a few column inches of filler, the newspaper published the following statement: "A woman lawyer is a woman still, and when the right petitioner comes to court with a good case he will get a favorable decision."[242]

Agnes Watson set up her office at 413 Fourth Avenue, and practiced by herself for a little over three years. A few weeks before her marriage to Herbert Lee Stitt in 1899, she closed the doors of her practice, and as the papers reported it, following the wedding, she spent weekdays in Blairsville, took carriage rides back to Allegheny on Saturdays to be with her mother, "determined to abandon her profession and center her attention on homemaking."[243] By the time the next woman was admitted to the bar in Allegheny County, Agnes Watson had already retired.[g]

While Jewish and African American lawyers were naturally affiliated with ethnic communities that were ready and willing to engage them to assist them with their legal problems, the legal affairs of most women—representing approximately half of the population of Pittsburgh—were handled by men. Indeed, it is probably more accurate to say that a woman's legal problems did not belong to women in the nineteenth century, but to the men who were financially responsible for them, if such problems were recognized at all. Thus, women such as Agnes Fraser Watson did not have a community ready, willing or able to engage them for legal services. Unlike the experiences of Cohen, Holmes, Randolph and the others, Watson did not have a ready base of women's institutions through which to gain influence in a theoretical "women's community"; such a community did not really exist in 1895 in any way that could have been helpful to a young woman trying to build a law practice on her own.

Each of these groups—women, African Americans and Jews—continued to face challenges as the twentieth century unfolded.

---

g Agnes Fraser Watson Stitt died at the age of 92 in Springfield, Pennsylvania in 1960, and was buried in Arlington National Cemetery next to her husband, who served in the U.S. Army at the end of World War I. Pennsylvania Department of Health, death certificate, no. 36, file no. 18308, distr. no. 46938-423 (1960), Agnes Stitt; digital image, *Ancestry.com*, accessed March 23, 2017, http://ancestry.com; "Pennsylvania County Marriages, 1845 - 1963," index and images, *Ancestry.com* (http://www.ancestry.com : accessed March 23, 2017), entry for Herbert L. Stitt-Agnes F. Watson, Allegheny County, March 30, 1899, series C, no. 22295; citing microfilm publication of the Pennsylvania Historial and Museum Commission, Harrisburg, PA.

MIGHTY CASEY AT THE BAR

Pittsburgh has been one of the nation's foremost "sports towns" since the rise of professional sports, so it is perhaps no surprise that the Pittsburgh bar should have had so many significant run-ins and entanglements with professional baseball, the grand-daddy of professional sports. Pittsburgh lawyers have owned the Pittsburgh Pirates baseball club, exercised management control over it, and played significant roles in keeping them in Pittsburgh over the years. One even pitched for the ballclub. The Pittsburgh Pirates' relationship with the bar began with the very name of the club, as early as 1890, and it closed out the nineteenth century with one of the most talked about pieces of litigation the city had seen.

The National League of Professional Baseball Clubs was established in 1876, but the American League was not established until 1903. Before the birth of the American League, however, the National League established a rivalry with another professional league of baseball clubs known as the American Association—not the current minor league by that name, but a genuine major league with top-flight talent—and the two leagues had an agreement to put their best teams to a proto-typical "world series"-type championship contest, which they did from 1884 to 1890.[244] Pittsburgh's first entry into major league baseball was as a founding member-club of the American Association in 1882, with a franchise known simply as the "Alleghenys," started by Robert McKnight's son H.D. "Denny" McKnight.[245] At the time of the club's organization, Allegheny City was still a separate entity from the city of Pittsburgh, and the club played its home games in either Recreation Park or Exposition Park, both on the North Side.

After several mediocre seasons in the American Association, team owner W.A. Nimick, a genial fellow who served as president of the Pittsburgh Transfer Company when he wasn't dabbling in baseball, decided to move his club to the National League for the 1887 season—a surprise that certainly antagonized his American Association peers, including the mercurial owner of the Association's St. Louis Browns, saloon proprietor

Christian Frederick Wilhelm Von der Ahe.[246] Once in the National League, Nimick renamed the club the "Pittsburgh Alleghenies." In 1887, even after the team's exit from the "Beer and Whiskey League," as the American Association was known, members of the Pittsburgh establishment were by no means impressed with the Alleghenies. That year, Common Pleas Judge J.W.F. White lectured a defendant in a larceny case about the moral ambiguities of baseball:

You should never go to a ball game. The majority of the persons connected with base ball bet on the result of the games, and all betting is gambling. Base ball is one of the evils of the day.[247]

The 1890 season was a dismal one for Pittsburgh baseball fans. John Montgomery Ward—a New York pitcher/shortstop who had graduated from Columbia Law School and formed the first professional baseball players union—led the creation of the Players' League as a rival to both the National League and the American Association during the 1890 season, with a revolutionary profit-sharing system for ballplayers. Most of the stars of the Alleghenies—including future Hall of Famers Ned Hanlon, Jake "Eagle Eye" Beckley and Pud Galvin, the team's ace hurler—jumped to the Players' League franchise in Pittsburgh, the "Burghers," and the two teams competed against each other for fans, if not on the field.[248] The Alleghenies, who finished in last place in the National League in 1890, did manage to pick up one notable player in the middle of the season from the Chicago Colts—a tall, right-handed hurler from Penn State named Robert Gibson, who pitched and lost three games for Pittsburgh that season. He would be notable for what he accomplished after his playing career was over: after entering the bar in 1894, Gibson served as assistant U.S. attorney, special assistant to the U.S. Attorney General, assistant district attorney in Allegheny County, and finally as a judge on the U.S. District Court for the Western District of Pennsylvania.[249][h]

Both Pittsburgh clubs ultimately played bad baseball in 1890. Even with all of that talent, the Burghers finished sixth out of eight teams in the Players' League. Although the Players' League was modestly successful as a whole, it was undercapitalized from the start. In the offseason, the Players' League collapsed, and talks began for the consolidation of the Alleghenies and the Burghers as a National League franchise. In the ensuing meetings, which took place in the downtown law office of Solomon Schoyer, Jr., a member of the august "Number Six Club" inside the Duquesne Club, in December 1890, Nimick ended up with a minority stake in the consolidated team, and the new owners enlisted the services of J. Palmer O'Neil, an intense, wily insurance executive and gun manufacturer, as team president.[250]

In the chaos that followed the collapse of the Players' League, with both remaining leagues scrounging for ex-Players' League players to add to their rosters, Pittsburgh would become the epicenter of some of the rumblings and legal machinations that ultimately led to the demise of the American Association. By the end of January, O'Neil was bragging

---

[h] Another Burgher pitcher, John Tener, retired after the end of the 1890 season. He entered banking as a cashier for the First National Bank of Charleroi, and was later elected governor of Pennsylvania in 1910.

to the press that he was determined on signing some Players' League refugees,[251] and then made headlines with the revelation that he had managed to coax former Philadelphia star second baseman Lou Bierbauer into joining Pittsburgh for the 1891 season.[252] The management of the Philadelphia Athletics, the Association club for whom Bierbauer had played during the 1889 season, said it was not possible that Bierbauer could be signed by Pittsburgh.[253] The Association's Baltimore manager Billy Barnie, fearing other defections, filed a formal protest with the Association, claiming that, in light of the demise of the Players' League, the Philadelphia club should have the right to re-sign Bierbauer.[254]

The newly-elected president of the American Association was a Columbus lawyer named Allen W. Thurman—the son, incidentally, of Allen G. Thurman, who had entered the Allegheny County bar in 1860[255] before becoming Grover Cleveland's running mate in the 1888 presidential election.[256] The younger Thurman was riding high following his role in resolving the Players' League war in the Association's favor, earning the nickname of "The White Winged Angel of Peace"[257]; but without taking a breath, he found himself having to deal with this new controversy between the National League and the American Association.

Under the agreement between the two remaining leagues, a board of control had been established to deal with such disputes, and it consisted of Thurman; Col. John I. Rogers, a Philadelphia lawyer and owner of the National League's Philadelphia Phillies[258]; and Louis C. Krauthoff, a Kansas City lawyer and president of the Western League, who later moved to New York and came to be regarded as one of the finest Manhattan corporate lawyers of his generation.[259] The parties met at the Auditorium Hotel in Chicago to present their arguments on the Bierbauer matter on February 13, 1891. The lawyers on the board of control deliberated until three o'clock in the morning, when Thurman invited the parties into the smoke-filled room and read his opinion that Bierbauer would play for the Pittsburgh National League club. Thurman and Rogers ruled in favor of Pittsburgh based on what the American Association regarded as a mere "technicality"—the Athletics' failure to place Bierbauer's name on their reserve list—and Krauthoff dissented, primarily because he believed the board did not have jurisdiction over the claim.[260] The majority report concluded, "Undoubtedly the Pittsburg Club has the legal right to the man, but morally it has not. It ought to withdraw its claim; but as it does not we must reluctantly decide in favor of Pittsburg."[261]

It was a lawyerly solution, faithful to the facts and accepted principles of contract, but the American Association owners exploded with anger over the result. Within a couple of days, they moved to impeach Thurman and to secede from the Association's agreement with the National League; there would be no more championship games between the two leagues.[262] An Association executive stated, "The action of the Pittsburgh club in signing Bierbauer was piratical."[263] A few days later, O'Neil was in New York, emerging from Parlor F of the Fifth Avenue Hotel, when someone started singing a few lines from Gilbert and Sullivan's opera, *The Pirates of Penzance*:

For I am a Pirate King!
And it is, it is a glorious thing
To be a Pirate King![264]

O'Neil, though scornful of those who accused him of piracy, loved the idea of being a "pirate king," and thus the Pittsburgh ballclub debuted in 1891 with a new nickname—the Pittsburgh Pirates.

The fallout, however, had just begun. O'Neil turned around and signed Mark Baldwin, a right-handed pitcher from the South Side who had won thirty-four games with the Chicago Players' League club in 1890, stealing him from the Columbus AA club. O'Neil immediately sent Baldwin to St. Louis to try to convince pitcher Silver King to break his American Association contract and join the Pittsburgh club. King agreed to jump to Pittsburgh; but the St. Louis Browns' owner, Chris von der Ahe, caught wind of Baldwin's activities and prevailed upon St. Louis assistant prosecutor Thomas Estep to issue a warrant for Baldwin's arrest on "conspiracy" charges. Baldwin was arrested, but he was quickly released and the flimsy charges against him were thrown out.[265]

Baldwin returned to Pennsylvania, and sued Von der Ahe in Philadelphia court for malicious prosecution and false imprisonment, asking for ten thousand dollars in damages.[266] Three years later, on the day that Baldwin's lawyers moved the case to Allegheny County, Von der Ahe was visiting Pittsburgh. He walked onto the grounds at Exposition Park and was promptly arrested by a deputy sheriff and held on a writ of capias, i.e., to take the body of the defendant and to keep him to answer the plaintiff in a plea.[267] Having received service of Baldwin's complaint, Von der Ahe looked to W.A. Nimick, the former Pittsburgh ballclub owner, to come to his rescue. Nimick posted a two thousand dollar bond for Von der Ahe's release.[268]

After two trials, Baldwin was finally awarded $2,525 on his claims against Von der Ahe in 1897, and the decision was affirmed by the Pennsylvania Supreme Court in 1898. Von der Ahe carefully avoided returning to Pittsburgh, however, foiling Baldwin's efforts to collect on the judgment.[269] Nimick, meanwhile, thought it would be a mistake to let Von der Ahe's non-appearance lead to the forfeiture of his two thousand dollar bond, so Nimick hatched a plan with his attorney, Richard Brown Scandrett, to bring Von der Ahe back to Pittsburgh.

Scandrett, a cousin of the long-time team secretary Alfred K. "Al" Scandrett[270] and a protégé of Solomon Schoyer, was admitted to the Allegheny County bar in 1888. A politically well-connected North Sider, Scandrett befriended the powerful state Republican boss Matthew Quay while working as a page in the state senate. Scandrett's political connections would ultimately extend through his wife, Agnes Morrow,[271] the sister of future U.S. Senator Dwight Morrow, who as a youth clerked in Scandrett's Pittsburgh law office and canvassed for him in his election to the Allegheny board of school control. Dwight Morrow's famous daughter, Anne Morrow Lindbergh, the future wife of aviator Charles Lindbergh, was a family intimate; Scandrett's son, Richard B. Scandrett, Jr., would later come to be known as Anne Morrow Lindbergh's favorite cousin. Dwight Morrow's biographer, Harold Nicholson, writes that the elder Scandrett's "interests were concerned rather with local politics and business than with the exact profession of the law."[272]

No doubt it was the chutzpah of a politician and a businessman, to a greater degree than "the exact profession of the law," that served as Scandrett's stock in trade in the adventure that followed. While Scandrett obtained a warrant for Von der Ahe's arrest from A.J. McQuitty, the County prothonotary and a loyal Republican Party man, Nimick hired a private detective, Nicholas Bendell, to go to St. Louis to execute the warrant and forcibly remove Von der Ahe to Pittsburgh. Von der Ahe received a mysterious telegram from a "Robert Smith of New York" inviting Von der Ahe to dine with Mr. Smith at the St. Nicholas Hotel in St. Louis on the evening of February 8. When Von der Ahe arrived at the appointed hour, Bendell grabbed Von der Ahe and threw him into a carriage, which circled the city a few times before it was time to board the train to Pittsburgh.[273]

On February 9, 1898, Bendell deposited the bedraggled Von der Ahe with warden Peter Soffel at the Allegheny County Jail. J. Scott Ferguson, the mutton-chopped big-case trial lawyer who had represented Major Moreland in his embezzlement prosecution, arranged for Von der Ahe's release on bail, and Von der Ahe slept at Ferguson's home that night.[274] Meanwhile, the front pages of newspapers across the country riveted their attention on "Von der Ahe—Prisoner on a Train," and the legal machinations that were to follow in Pittsburgh. After a decade of bad performance on the field by Von der Ahe's rebooted St. Louis Browns National League franchise, the *St. Louis Post-Dispatch* wrote: "A wave of joy would sweep across a half a dozen towns/ should some good friend of ours kidnap the old St. Louis Browns/ We shouldn't mind the loss at all; we'd gladly part with Chris/ if some Philanthropist would do a favor such as this..."[275]

At ten o'clock the next morning, U.S. District Court Judge Joseph Buffington heard a petition for the issuance of a writ of habeas corpus. Von der Ahe was represented by Ferguson; Scandrett and Arthur "A.O." Fording appeared on behalf of Nimick, and Charles A. O'Brien appeared on behalf of Baldwin. Ferguson argued forcefully that his client had been illegally kidnapped. He told the press, after the hearing: "I can't believe the law will countenance the abduction of a man, and I fully expect the Court to pronounce the capture illegal ... Half a century ago, it would have been perfectly legal to kidnap the body of a man at the instance of the bail, but the act of 1848, abolishing imprisonment for debt, and the thirteenth amendment of the Constitution, abolishing slavery, have since come into effect. Von der Ahe's arrest," Ferguson declared, "was purely a violation of the thirteenth amendment." Scandrett was coy, merely telling reporters that the case was now in the hands of Judge Buffington, but he referred with some pride to "the intense interest" that the case had excited.[276]

Buffington rendered his decision on Saturday. After giving an exhaustive review of state and federal case law on bail that continues to be cited to this day, Judge Buffington noted that the authorities held that an arrest on a bail is the exercise of a contractual right between the parties, and not a governmentally-imposed sanction without due process:

> *Irrespective of any views this court might entertain of the question, were it new, and nor affected by former decisions, we are constrained, under stress of these decisions, and particularly in view of that of the supreme court of the United States, to hold that Von der Ahe could lawfully be arrested in the state of Missouri by his bail, and removed to Pennsylvania.*

As quickly as Von der Ahe could leave the Federal Courthouse, he was arrested again, and was then held not only to answer for his debts to Baldwin and Nimick, but for Bendell's expenses in bringing him to Pittsburgh, as well as for the costs of fighting his habeas corpus petition.[277] The following Monday, Von der Ahe's Missouri attorneys arrived with payment of Nimick's bail money, and Baldwin finally received his damage award from Von der Ahe the following September.[278]

Within another decade or so, Von der Ahe was "down and out," tending bar in small saloon on the outskirts of St. Louis, having declared bankruptcy in 1908.[279] Mark Baldwin had left baseball and was a successful physician in Homestead.[280] And Richard Brown Scandrett continued to practice law in Pittsburgh in his way—infused with a blend of local politics and personal business interests—as one of the leading business lawyers in the city, until his death in 1918.

GILDED TWILIGHT, IN FOUR ACTS — I. BILLY

Little remembered are the sympathy strikes that sprung up around Pittsburgh in the days that immediately followed the Railroad Riots in 1877. One relatively peaceful local strike began in the Riots' aftermath and lasted almost two months. On July 24, 1877, while the scent of burnt buildings could still be detected in the Strip, the laborers at the American Iron Works of Jones & Laughlin on the South Side made their demands for a thirty-nine percent increase in pay, from roughly ninety cents per day to $1.25. The machine department foreman told them that B.F. Jones was not on hand just then to discuss their demands with them, and asked them if they would continue to work until he could be consulted. The laborers agreed; but by two o'clock that afternoon, having heard nothing from Mr. Jones, nearly five hundred men and boys threw down their tools and left the Iron Works. At a meeting in Kaney's Hall near 27th Street, a five-man committee of the laborers—made up of one each of the ethnic English, Irish, Welsh, German and Polish men at the Iron Works—resolved to keep sober and show the public that they only wanted their rights.[281]

As the strike wore on, the laborers reached out to the machinists to have them join, but they resisted.[282] Nonetheless, there was one young machinist working at the Iron Works who took a special interest in the plight of the laborers. By 1877, twenty-six year-old William J. Brennen had lived most of his life in the shadow of the Iron Works. His father, John Brennen, was a millwright in the Iron Works; and as the eldest of thirteen Brennen children, William left public school at age eleven and went to work as a "pull up boy" in the Jones & Laughlin machine department. He left the Iron Works briefly at fifteen to attend a Christian Brothers school, but rejoined the Works as a machinist's apprentice, continuing his education by helping to establish the Mechanics' Library—reading and studying, and debating with the avid young men who collected there.[283] In addition to his debating skill, the barrel-chested Brennen was also known as the strongest man for his weight at the J&L mill, with a pair of speedy fists when the occasion would demand.[284]

By 1872, Brennen had become a capable machinist and was presented with a kit of tools by the Iron Works, although he received a temporary setback when he lost the sight in one eye after the breaking of a drill sent a piece of steel into it. Indefatigable, and unmarried (he would remain so for his entire life), he found time to teach night school to fellow ironworkers, prepared a manual for fellow machinists called *The Machinist's Guide*, and became captain of the Ormsby Hose Company, a volunteer fire company on the South Side, as well as president of the South Side branch of the No Rent Manifesto Land League, a group formed to protest the imprisonment of the Irish nationalist Charles Stewart Parnell by the British. Brennen's love of debate had spurred him to become involved with Democratic Party politics, and at twenty-four, the bright, articulate young man had served as one of the youngest delegates to the 1876 Democratic National Convention in St. Louis that had nominated Samuel Tilden for president.[285]

At the height of the laborers' strike at Jones & Laughlin, which ultimately included two thousand "men and boys" despite the fact that the machinists refused to join, "Billy" Brennen became a frequent participant in the "labor meetings" that began to occur around Pittsburgh—largely an outgrowth of activists from the po-paper currency Greenback movement seizing the opportunities for public sympathy laid bare by the violence of the Railroad strike. On August 17, 1877, a crowd of about fifty labor supporters gathered on a stormy night in the Twenty-Fourth Ward for the purpose of organizing the local "Labor Party" for the upcoming city and county elections. Brennen, the twenty-six year-old machinist, responded to calls for a speech. He apparently saw the cause of labor, through the lens of his Roman Catholic faith, as something much greater than disagreements about hours and wages; and against a backdrop of rain and thunder, according to a reporter from the *Pittsburgh Post*, he delivered a homily about the purpose of labor's agitation:

> *During his remarks he said it had been stated in some of the papers that the workingmen had no object to attain. This he thought absurd. The object to be obtained is that for which Christ came among us—for the elevation of mankind. In closing he hoped the movement would succeed and that the workingmen would step forward and join the organization.*[286]

The Jones & Laughlin strike petered out barely a month later, with the laborers resuming their work at the American Iron Works at the old wages.[287] Brennen, however, carried on the fight by getting elected to city council in 1878 on the Democratic-Labor ticket, and immediately becoming minority leader. In 1880, he ran for the board of aldermen and was declared the loser; however, alleging fraud at the polls, he engaged a lawyer and managed to be seated after waging what turned out to be a three-year legal battle.[288] Assuming leadership within the Democratic Party on the South Side, Brennen very publicly fought the battle, to borrow a phrase from historian Paul Krause, of mobilizing Pittsburgh's workers "to wrest the reins of government from the supporters of 'organized capital.'"[289]

Hand-in-hand with entering local politics, Brennen also assumed leadership within the labor circles. He served as president of the Machinists' and Blacksmiths' Union, helping to merge it with the Knights of Labor, and established the Knights of Labor Local 731; he was a delegate to the 1881 International Trades and Labor Congress in Pittsburgh; and in 1883 he served as the clerk to the U.S. House of Representatives' first-ever committee on labor, which was being chaired by James Herron Hopkins, a Democrat.[i] During Brennen's ongoing aldermen election battle, however, he became fascinated by the machinations of the law; and in July 1884, Billy Brennen became a member of the Allegheny County bar, joining his preceptor, J.K.P. Duff as the junior partner of the firm of Duff & Brennen. His experience made him an instant expert in election law, and subsequently he served as counsel to the Democrats in almost every important election controversy in Pittsburgh for a number of years.[290] Most significantly, however, Billy Brennen became labor's first advocate within the bar of Pittsburgh.

Around the same time, another young laborer in Western Pennsylvania was leaning toward a career in the law, but he would follow a very different path from Brennen. David R. Jones was born on a farm near Swansea, Wales in 1853. He immigrated to northeastern Pennsylvania as a young man and began working as an anthracite miner and underground hoisting engineer. In his twenties, he attended Mount Union College in Alliance, Ohio with his earnings from the mines and from teaching, and moved to the Six Mile Ferry mining settlement near the borough of Homestead, about seven miles southeast of Pittsburgh, in 1878. While studying law with Edward Purnell Jones—a Pittsburgh native whose surname incidentally attracted a large Welsh immigrant clientele—David Jones became engaged in organizing coal miners on behalf of the Knights of Labor. In 1879, he played a key role in gaining concessions from mine owners when, as the miners were about to quit a strike, he overheard mine operators at the Pittsburgh Coal Exchange, saddled with a backlog of coal orders, whisper that they were on the verge of acceding to the miners' demands.[291]

Jones became general secretary of the Miners' Association and had racked up a series of successes in wage negotiations with the operators when, in 1880, he was arrested and indicted on conspiracy charges for organizing miners employed by the Waverly Coal and Coke Company—which happened to be owned by a partnership that included Judge Thomas Mellon. Jones was convicted and sentenced to pay a one hundred dollar fine and serve twenty-four hours in jail. Not satisfied, Mellon and his partners filed a seventy thousand dollar libel suit against Jones, the *National Labor Tribune* where Jones had a regular column, and the *Tribune's* proprietors, Thomas Armstrong and Thomas Telford, hoping to bankrupt the *Tribune* and break the backs of the leading voices of miner unionism. Mellon was ultimately unsuccessful on the libel case, but not before dragging Jones and his colleagues before the Pennsylvania Supreme Court in 1883.[292]

---

i Hopkins was also, incidentally, the Pittsburgh lawyer who voiced the initial objections to the admission of George Vashon to the bar in 1867.

Jones clearly found his adventures in the union movement to be a little too exciting. After entering the bar in March 1882, Jones by all accounts exited overt union activism and settled into a very typical, and generally lucrative, law practice in Homestead. As Thomas Mellon's descendant and biographer James Mellon writes

> [O]nce admitted to the bar, Jones sundered his connections to labor, quickly succeeded in his law practice, made a grand tour of Europe with his wife, and wrote a travel log. During the bitter and sanguinary Homestead Strike of 1892, as volleys of gunfire rent the air, Jones was not to be seen on the barricades. ...Like Andrew Carnegie, also a genteel progressive, Jones had concluded that absence of body was better than presence of mind.[293]

Jones participated in local politics, served for a time in the Pennsylvania House, and was supportive of labor, but would never again take the risk of being seen as a leader of labor.

For Billy Brennen, by contrast, the problem of labor represented an irresistible opportunity for a young lawyer and politico, albeit through more conventional approaches than Jones had employed through the Miners' Association. Being Pittsburgh's labor advocate, in Brennen's case, meant fulfilling a variety of roles. It meant being the steward of the organizational machinery of the new entities, the labor unions, that were being born during the period in response to, and in the mirror of, the corporations that were their adversaries, becoming counsel to the Amalgamated Association of Iron and Steel Workers, the American Flint Green Bottle Glass Workers and the United Coal Miners' Union, among others.[294] More importantly, however, being labor's advocate meant helping to define, by shades and degrees, the manner and methods of organized labor's argument with organized capital during a time when labor still had almost no tools recognized by statute or by common law at its disposal. Even the right to strike itself was an unsettled question; despite the fact that the Pennsylvania legislature had passed laws in the 1870s purporting to protect the right to strike, Pennsylvania courts would continue to define most labor organization activities as criminal during the 1880s, as David Jones' experience would confirm.

In 1888, Brennen represented alleged agents of the Knights of Labor in a case involving one of the nascent techniques of organized labor, the boycott. In what became known as the "Brace Boycott Case," the Brace Bros. Laundry had discharged eleven young girls out of a staff of 90 who worked in its steam plant. The agents of the Knights of Labor demanded that the girls be reinstated or "it would be to the injury, if not the ruin, of plaintiff's business." Soon thereafter, the agents began to hand out circulars detailing the firing of the girls and asking patrons to cease doing business with Brace Bros.; followed the Brace Bros. wagons, noted down their customers, and paid personal visits to them to dissuade them from dealing with Brace Bros.; put a big sign in a window of a Pittsburgh building reading "Headquarters Brace Bros. Boycott Committee;" drove buggies through the streets with banners on each side reading "Boycott Brace Bros.;" and generally harassed the Brace Bros. wagon drivers wherever they found them.

Judge Jacob F. Slagle, in an exhaustive opinion in Common Pleas Court, ruled in favor of Brace Bros.' request for an injunction against the agents on the grounds of overt acts of intimidation and coercion on the part of the defendants that "tend[ed] toward violence"; but significantly, the court would not rule on, and left open the possibility that, "the defendants in this case might, individually or collectively, refuse to employ Brace Bros., and advise their friends and neighbors and such of their patrons as they could reach, not to do so, or ... distribute circulars, giving a truthful account of plaintiffs' trouble with their employees."[295]

In *McCandless & Kinser v. O'Brien* (1891), Brennen argued and the Court held that an organization of workingmen formed to secure the payment of higher wages was not, in and of itself, unlawful. The Court further held that when "by words and acts, their numbers, their manner, their movements, by annoyance and intimidation, the members of such an organization undertake to practically compel other workmen to cease work, they are guilty of acts which constitute a nuisance and they may be enjoined."[296]

For Billy Brennen, any progress in defining the manner and method of the protests of organized labor was a matter of two steps forward, one step back—an exercise in puncturing pinpricks in the notion, deeply embedded in Pennsylvania law, that "labor was 'a vendible commodity,' like beans or potatoes," as James Mellon observed,[297] and that organized labor was an illegal conspiracy to fix commodity prices. Brennen's persistence, at a time when the *Pittsburgh Legal Journal* did not even recognize "Labor Law" as an index category, was a drumbeat that kept the concerns of organized labor in the daily conversation, in the courtrooms as well as the newspapers of Pittsburgh. Through the sum total of his work, he was conjuring up a refined, decriminalized vision of what a strike might look like.

GILDED TWILIGHT, IN FOUR ACTS — II. JOHNSTOWN

In the days that followed the Railroad Riots in the summer of 1877, Billy Brennen—the barrel-chested machinist from the South Side—embarked on a course that would make him a leading legal and political advocate for Pittsburgh's workers. Meanwhile, at the same time across the Monongahela, a pair of young men, James Hay Reed and Philander Knox, were beginning their own downtown law partnership—one focused on building one of Pittsburgh's most illustrious collections of corporate clients.

One might have chuckled to see these fellows walking down Fifth Avenue. James Hay Reed, age twenty-three in the summer of 1877, would have been more familiar to most Pittsburghers. The son of a physician, Reed had been shadowing his uncle, the late former U.S. Attorney David Reed, for the last several years, and could also occasionally be seen around town in the company of his schoolmate at the Western University, Judge Mellon's son Andrew. At 5 foot 10-1/2, Reed was noticeably the taller of the pair of young men standing outside of their offices at the corner of Fifth Avenue and Scrip Alley, with a long nose and chin, and soulful grey eyes. His new partner, Philander Chase Knox, age twenty-four, was barely five foot five inches tall, with a round face and a high forehead[298]—"a porcelain egg of a man," as historian Edmund Morris described him.[299] At least physically speaking, there was a "Mutt and Jeff" quality to the pair.

Reed would come to be known for quiet traits, such as the sobriety of his judgment and his ability to build consensus. Pittsburgh attorney and Republican congressman James Francis Burke would say that Reed "probably prevented more litigation than any other man in the Allegheny County bar."[300] By contrast, Phil Knox was all kinetics and attack. He had a hard time sitting still. He loved contests and the outdoors—riding horses, fishing, and later, engaging heartily in the emerging leisure obsession of the wealthy, golf. At the age of forty-seven, Knox would set an amateur world record driving his pair of trotting horses on the racetrack at Brunot Island.[301] The irrepressibly active President Theodore Roosevelt would later come to call his Attorney General his "playmate," and Knox's love of riding led him to become a particular favorite of the Roosevelt children.[302] John Hays Hammond, the gold miner and diplomat, frequently played golf with Knox at Chevy Chase outside of Washington when Knox would later serve as President Taft's Secretary of State, observing that Knox "was a great fellow to bet on every conceivable angle of play and was always concocting some scheme to get a wager out of me. He would enjoy winning a box of cigars from me more than a high stake in diplomacy."[303]

The son of a bank cashier, Knox was from Brownsville in Fayette County, thirty-five miles south of Pittsburgh, and was a boyhood friend of Henry Clay Frick.[304] He had briefly attended the West Virginia University as an undergraduate—some say he was thrown out for playing billiards—and later went to Mount Union College in Alliance, Ohio before pursuing law studies at Albany Law School in New York. He returned from Albany to Brownsville to read law with Seth T. Hurd, a some-time lawyer known primarily as the owner and editor of the *Brownsville Clipper*, but soon angled himself into a preceptorship with Henry Bucher Swoope, the U.S. Attorney in Pittsburgh, where he had the opportunity to help prepare Swoope for federal court trials. Swoope died in 1874, and the new U.S. Attorney, James Reed's uncle David, took him on.[305] Reed was also studying with Knox at the time, and the two of them entered the bar on the motion of Uncle David—Knox in January 1875, and Reed in July. Knox was an assistant U.S. Attorney until Uncle David died in February 1877, when Knox and Reed decided to form their own law partnership.[306]

The connections of their youth—Mellon and Frick—undoubtedly helped to propel the two young lawyers rapidly to the forefront of the corporate bar of Pittsburgh, as did their incidentally advantageous marriages: in 1878, Reed married Katherine Jones Aiken, the daughter of the influential Pittsburgh landowner David Aiken; and in 1880, Knox married Lillie Smith, whose family's iron business would later become part of the Crucible Steel Company, subsequently an important client of the firm. They were entering the right social circles, and would soon have the personal wealth to move in them comfortably. As Reed Smith historians Brignano and Fort recount:

> *Knox was never timid about charging for his notably successful litigation services, and as early as 1882 he typically received $1,000 on account for a case. And as a counselor, Reed brought in a retainer of $2,700 a year—increased to $5,000 in 1888—from the Pittsburgh & Lake Erie Railroad, an important subsidiary of the Vanderbilt's New York Central system. In 1888 the firm first recorded a monthly fee of $500 for its services as general counsel of Carnegie Brothers.*
>
> *The partners collected fees of over $12,000 in 1880, $48,000 in 1885 and $110,000 in 1889. They divided the money down the middle—in a time when the average American employee earned less than $500 a year.*[307]

Their engagement by Andrew Carnegie was a particular coup, since by the end of the 1880s, Carnegie Steel was the largest producer of pig iron and steel in the world. Although Carnegie brought in the recently-admitted Michigan law graduate Gibson D.

Packer as an in-house lawyer in 1889,[308] Knox and Reed had already come to be known as the primary Carnegie legal strategists, especially with the ascension of Knox's friend Henry Clay Frick as chairman of Carnegie Steel in 1889.

Their association with Frick was soon to become a very public matter. Prior to his partnership with Carnegie, Henry Clay Frick had built his small operation for turning coal into coke used in steel manufacturing into the world's largest coke company, largely through acquisitions of weaker coke companies during and after the Panic of 1873 with loans from Judge Mellon and his bank. In 1879, the thirty year-old millionaire bought a few shares of a newly-chartered corporation, the South Fork Fishing and Hunting Club of Pittsburgh, through which a coke salesman named Benjamin F. Ruff intended to develop a country retreat on a man-made lake, Lake Conemaugh, in the Allegheny Mountains about fifteen miles northeast of Johnstown.[309]

The lake, and the dam that created it, were built by the Commonwealth of Pennsylvania between 1840 and 1853 in order to supply water to the "Main Line" canal transportation system, connecting Philadelphia to Pittsburgh. However, shortly after the construction of the South Fork Dam, the Pennsylvania Railroad finally completed its rail line from Philadelphia to Pittsburgh, rendering the canal system a quaint artifact of the pre-Railroad era. The Railroad bought the dam and largely left it to ruin, until John Reilly, a former Railroad official who was elected to represent Pennsylvania's 17th District in Congress, bought the lake and dam for $2,500 in 1875.[310] Four years later, the one-term congressman sold the 160-acre property to Ruff at a loss, for two thousand dollars (but not before removing some iron discharge pipes from the dam and selling them for scrap), and Ruff assigned it to the Club, which began repairs on the dam and construction of the clubhouse.[311] For a membership fee of eight hundred dollars, a select group of wealthy Pittsburghers (sixty-one of them, by 1889) and their families were permitted to stay at the clubhouse, or in a cottage that they might purchase on the premises, and fish for black bass—originally stocked in the lake by rail car in the summer of 1881—sail or paddle on the lake itself, or hunt in the nearby woods.[312] In time, Frick's new business partners, Andrew Carnegie and his financial watchdog Henry Phipps, Jr. were admitted as members, as were Andrew Mellon, Robert Pitcairn of the Pennsylvania Railroad, iron producer Marvin Scaife, and Benjamin Thaw, a coke producer and brother of the ill-fated playboy, Harry K. Thaw. Frick's friend Phil Knox also enthusiastically joined the Club and became its secretary, and Reed followed suit.[313]

On Memorial Day, May 31, 1889, the manager of the Club wired Phil Knox at home to report on the heavy rainfall the Club was experiencing that morning. He was concerned that the water was rising in the lake at a troubling rate. Attorney Ralph Demmler, another Reed Smith historian, reports that Knox, who was under the weather at the time, tried to catch the *Day Express* train to Johnstown to survey the situation himself as the Club's secretary, but his horse threw a shoe on the way to the station and Knox missed the train.[314] Later that day, the Dam burst, unleashing a torrent of nearly five billion gallons of water, weighing twenty million tons,[315] downstream on the South Fork Creek and the Little Conemaugh River, directly at the city of Johnstown. By the time the waters calmed, over 2,200 people were killed in the Little Conemaugh River valley, including at least thirty-seven passengers of the *Day Express* train that Knox had missed,[316] and most of Johnstown and several nearby towns were completely destroyed.

A few days after the flood, the future Allegheny County Common Pleas judge and chief justice of the Pennsylvania Supreme Court, Robert S. Frazer, "was trampling among the ruins looking like a miner" in search of his sister and her four children. When he found them, they told him how they narrowly escaped drowning.[317] Meanwhile, Cyrus Elder, counsel for the Cambria Iron Company and the only Johnstown "local" who had privileges at the South Fork Club, would not be as fortunate. He was unable to find his wife and twenty-three year-old daughter after the flood came through, and in time it became apparent that they perished when his home on Walnut Street was destroyed.[318]

Back in Pittsburgh, however, it was not altogether clear that the South Fork Dam had burst. Whether he had initially intended to do so or not, James Hay Reed found himself getting out in front of the press coverage of the Johnstown flood as a member of the South Fork Club, at a time when the identities of most of the members other than Henry Clay Frick remained a mystery. In an interview with the New York Herald, Reed claimed that "in the past he himself had climbed all over the dam, studying it closely, and that 'in the absence of any positive statement I will continue to doubt, as do many others familiar with the place, that it really let go.' Perhaps, he then suggested, it had been a dam at Lilly [about twenty-two miles northeast of Johnstown] which broke."[319]

Trickling anecdotes from the scene continued to suggest, however, that it was indeed the South Fork Dam that burst, leading one anonymous "prominent lawyer practicing in Allegheny County" to tell the *New York World* on June 2: "I predict there will be legal suits with possible criminal indictments as a result of this catastrophe. I am told that the South Fork Club has been repeatedly warned of the unsafety of its dam, and it comes from good authority."[320] Meanwhile, most of the rest of the members of the Club, having met to discuss strategy on the evening of the day after the flood, decided not to speak to the press at all, and authorized the donation of one thousand blankets to the Johnstown victims.[321]

On June 3, reporters reached the dam and confirmed that the South Fork Dam had failed, leading the press to piece together a not altogether pretty history of the concerns about the dam, and the relations between the members of the "Bosses' Club" at South Fork, and the citizens of Johnstown. By late Monday, as historian David McCullough confirms, "an angry crowd of men had gone up to the dam looking for any club members who might have been still hanging about. When they failed to find anyone, they broke into several of the cottages. Windows were smashed and a lot of furniture was destroyed." The newspapers later reported that a lynch mob went to the farm of Colonel Elias Unger, the president of the Club, bent on killing him, but that by that time Colonel Unger had left for Pittsburgh.[322]

The members of the Club stepped up their contributions to the relief effort. The Carnegie Company gave ten thousand dollars; Frick instructed his coke company to give five thousand dollars; and the Mellons gave one thousand dollars.[323] Meanwhile, as the *National Labor Tribune* reported:

> *All honor to the warm hearts of the mill men of Homestead, who, with a contest for wages on their hands, ignoring the fact that Johnstown mills were never within the jurisdiction of the labor organization, and never a thought but of broadest humanity, met on Sunday last and contributed a day's wages (some $7000) to aid the rescued and give sepulchre to the dead. This and the general subscription in Homestead indicates heart enough in that mill town to swell over the borough boundaries. ... On the first day of the fourteenth annual (June 4) convention of the Amalgamated Association of Iron and Steel Workers the earliest action following the details of organization was the adoption of a series of resolutions of sympathy and the appropriation of $2000 from the Association treasury for the relief fund.*

The *National Labor Tribune* also noted, pointedly, that "[a]n old directory of Johnstown, if attainable, may aid in giving the names of old residents lost in the flood, but in our opinion nothing short of the pay rolls of the Cambria, Gautier and other manufacturing firms will reveal the loss among the working people."[324]

For some, the flood itself had begun to be a metaphor for the struggle between capital and labor. Amid the increasing anger at the "Bosses' Club" was the charge that the Club and its known members in Pittsburgh had not given enough to the cause. As the *New York Graphic* put it: "As they are almost all millionaires, the sum is not staggering. ...It was through their indifference that this great disaster was precipitated upon the residents of the peaceful valley. Remorse, if nothing else, should lead them to alleviate to the fullest extent of their wealth the suffering they have caused."[325]

Meanwhile, the Allegheny County Bar Association, after a vote taken at its annual picnic at Rock Point, appointed attorney Samuel A. McClung to head a committee for the donation of one thousand dollars from the treasury of the Association "for the purpose of aiding the members of the Cambria bar resident in Johnstown."[326]

On June 6, the Cambria County coroner's office announced, after an inquest, that the cause of death of one of the victims was "death by drowning;" that the cause of the drowning was "the breaking of the South Fork dam"; and, finally, that the cause of the dam failure was that "the owners of said dam were culpable in not making it as secure as it should have been, especially in view of the fact that a population of many thousands were in the valley below." The coroner's report went on to say, "[W]e hold that the owners are responsible for the fearful loss of life and property resulting from the breaking of the dam."[327]

With coroners' inquests and newspapers already holding the Club and its members responsible for the death and destruction in the Little Conemaugh Valley, Knox and Reed, as counsel to the Club, were on the spot. Mellon, Frick, Carnegie and the other members were counting on them to make sure there were no criminal indictments of anyone connected with the Club. Reed, whose early interview had elevated him to the role of spokesman for the Club, proceeded to take every opportunity to educate the public on the inherently limited liability of the shareholders of corporations. On June 6, he went on record denying the existence of a two million dollar bond that was rumored to have been given by the Club, and, when asked about the Club's intentions with respect to the damaged lake and resort, told the *Pittsburgh Dispatch*, "I do not know that I am authorized by the club to answer that question, but I will venture to say that the dam will not be rebuilt by the South Fork Fishing and Hunting Club."[328] By June 11, the newspapers began to report the rumor that members of the South Fork Club, which already had a twenty thousand dollar mortgage on its land, had begun to take steps toward its ultimate dissolution.[329]

As if the point of the Club being judgment-proof due to its lack of capital were not already becoming clear, in advance of the filing of any lawsuits, Reed began to argue his case in public, telling the *Dispatch* on June 24:

> *It is no surprise to us to hear that suits are to be brought, as we have been confident that a test case would be made by one of the many who were financially injured by the disaster. The members of the club, while deeply deploring the widespread ruin caused by the flood, have felt no uneasiness as to any financial responsibility resulting to either the club as a corporation or the stockholders as individuals. ... The stockholders of the club have paid in the full amount called for by their subscriptions, and as stockholders owe the company nothing, and consequently owe nothing which could be attached for debt ... The logical inference, therefore, is most certainly that suits for damages would be futile, if brought.*[330]

Reed's previews of legal arguments for the benefit of the press were not unprecedented, but they were highly unusual coming from a lawyer representing large corporate interests in Pittsburgh in the 1880s. Little by little, though, through Reed's statements and other press comments, a populace generally ignorant of the nature of the corporation under Pennsylvania law was beginning to understand the implications of it in connection with the question of whether justice would be done for the victims of the Johnstown Flood. Even the *National Labor Tribune* would admit, in a seemingly unrelated essay regarding the use of the word "Limited" in the name of a corporation on July 13, that "[m]ost American corporations are constituted on the principle of limited liability, and but few, if any, of the states enjoin the companies formed under their laws to append the word 'limited,' to their corporate titles. The matter is so generally understood in this country by business men, however, that it is not deemed necessary, though many companies do it of their own accord."[331] Businessmen understood the limited liability of the corporation; workers were now learning about it in their daily newspapers.

The lawsuits would come, nonetheless, but there would be no deluge of them. The first to be filed, at the end of July, was by Nancy W. Little, a Sewickley widow and mother of eight children whose husband John, a traveling salesman, had been killed when the flood hit the Hulbert House hotel on Clinton Street in Johnstown. She asked for fifty thousand dollars in damages. In response, Knox and Reed entered a plea in the Court of Common Pleas of "not guilty" with respect to Little's allegations.[332]

In addition to the limited liability of the corporate entity, Knox and Reed had another advantage available to them. Under Pennsylvania law, the plaintiff would be required to show actual negligence by the Club and/or its officers or shareholders in order to gain recovery. Three years before, the Pennsylvania Supreme Court had specifically rejected an alternative theory of liability in such cases in *Pennsylvania Coal Co. v. Sanderson*,[333] a Lackawanna County case in which a landowner complained of damage by minewater runoff from the Pennsylvania Coal Company. In the absence of facts supporting negligence, the plaintiff's attorney had argued that Pennsylvania should accept the authority of a controversial English case called *Rylands v. Fletcher* (1868)[334]. In *Rylands*, the Exchequer Chamber held, in the absence of traditional causes of action under trespass, negligence or nuisance, that a textile manufacturer would be held liable for damage to a neighboring coal mine when a dam built by the manufacturer collapsed and flooded the mines. Justice Blackburn's opinion in the English case announced the principles of what has come to be known as the theory of strict liability:

> *[T]he person who for his own purpose brings on his lands and collects and keeps there anything likely to do mischief if it escapes, must keep it in at his peril, and, if he does not do so, is prima facie answerable for all the damage which is the natural consequence of its escape.*[335]

Thus, under *Rylands*, in a case involving inherently dangerous circumstances, the burden of proof would essentially shift from the plaintiff, trying to establish the culpability of the action or inaction of the defendant, to the defendant, who would be required to establish an alternative source of causation or an assumption of risk by the plaintiff in order to avoid liability. In August 1889, a note in an influential legal journal, the *American Law Review*, urged the Pennsylvania courts to adopt *Rylands* in cases concerning the Johnstown Flood. The anonymous author of the note explained:

> *It is good enough for the practical purpose of charging with damages a company of gentlemen who have maintained a vast reservoir of water behind a rotten dam, for the mere pleasure of using it for a fishing pond, to the peril of thousands of honest people dwelling in the valley below. It is enough that they are prima facie answerable. That takes the question to the jury. The jury will do the rest. They can be safely trusted to say whether or not it was the plaintiff's default, that is the fault of some poor widow in Johnstown, whose husband and children were drowned while she was cast ashore and suffered to live.*[336]

Since Pennsylvania had to date rejected *Rylands*, however, Knox and Reed were free to argue, as Demmler relates, that "the Flood was an Act of God," and not the responsibility of the Club.[337] After several years of fighting, neither Mrs. Little nor any of the handful of other plaintiffs managed to win their lawsuits, and the only recorded settlement by the Club amounted to a five hundred dollar payment for the benefit of a Johnstown lumber dealer.[338]

The perceived injustice of the Johnstown Flood cases not only embittered the public against the "Bosses" and their corporate vehicles, but it focused some attention within the legal community on *Rylands*, and the Pennsylvania Supreme Court's prior ruling on the case. Though Knox and Reed had won the battle in fighting off Mrs. Little's claim, one could argue that they lost the war. In 1891, while representing Andrew Carnegie's company in *Robb v. Carnegie Bros.*,[339] Knox and Reed were ironically on the losing end of the Pennsylvania Supreme Court's first application of the *Rylands* doctrine. In a unanimous decision in which three of the justices who had voted against applying *Rylands* in *Sanderson* were now voting in favor of applying it against Carnegie, the Court distinguished *Sanderson* weakly on the grounds that the coal mining in *Sanderson* was a "natural" activity, whereas further development of the coal by the Carnegie Brothers in *Robb* was an activity that supported the need for a shift in the burden of proof from the plaintiff to the defendant.[340]

In the aftermath of Johnstown, the failure of the "Bosses" to be held accountable for the bursting of the South Fork Dam was one of the first national object lessons of the impenetrability of the corporation, one that would be seared into the American cultural memory. Strict liability—though not available for the benefit of Mrs. Little, the other families of the 2,209 who perished, or any of the people who lost property—was now available to plaintiffs as a theory for damages in Pennsylvania. Johnstown had entered the American legal and political bloodstream, changing the chemistry thereof in subtle ways, both nationally and locally.

GILDED TWILIGHT, IN FOUR ACTS — III. HOMESTEAD

The men at Homestead who so identified with the non-union workers of Johnstown that they gave up a day's wages for the victims of the Johnstown Flood were engaged in an ongoing wage contest with the "Bosses"—namely Andrew Carnegie and his steel company—even as the Johnstown recovery effort was under way. Barely a month after the flood itself, on July 1, 1889, the workers found themselves locked out of the Homestead mill.

The Homestead men of the Amalgamated (or AAISW) were arguably the most virulently unionized steel workers in the region, and the Homestead steel mill had experienced a troubled history of labor relations. Opened in 1881 by a Carnegie rival, the Pittsburgh Bessemer Company, the AAISW and management skirmished several times over wages until in January 1882, management of the mill attempted to unseat the union by calling on skilled workers to resign from the AAISW and sign an "ironclad" contract prohibiting strike activities. When the workers refused, management locked the doors of the plant, beginning a ten-week standoff, marked by some pockets of violence, that ultimately led to a capitulation by management, a complete victory for the AAISW. Within months, however, depressed product prices threatened to set the stage for another disagreement over wages. This time, the board of directors of Pittsburgh Bessemer, rather than go through another embarrassing and costly fight with the AAISW, voted to sell the company. Carnegie was only too happy to take a promising competitor out of the picture, and in 1883, the Homestead mill became the property of the Carnegie, Phipps & Co.[341]

Carnegie had his own problems with the AAISW at Homestead, however. Determined to break the influence of the AAISW in Homestead, and while Frick was finding his sea-legs as chairman of Carnegie Brothers and Company, Carnegie turned to his other young protégé, William L. Abbott, the chairman of Carnegie, Phipps & Co., and gave him instructions on how to handle the upcoming expiration of the AAISW contract at Homestead on June 30, 1889: they would attempt to replay the American Bessemer strategy from 1882. On May 18, 1889, Abbott summoned the AAISW's mill committee and told them that on July 1, the day after the expiration of the contract, a new sliding scale would be imposed on the steel workers that would reduce wages by twenty-five percent and place the entire work force on a twelve-hour day. All positions in the mill would be declared vacant as of the beginning of June, Abbott declared. Current employees would have to reapply for their jobs, and if accepted, would be invited to sign individual three-year "ironclad" contracts, thus effectively removing the AAISW from the bargaining table.

Over the objections of William A. Weihe, the union president, who advocated further talks with management, on June 27 the steel workers unanimously voted to reject Carnegie's proposals and walked out. Abbott responded by locking the doors of the mill behind them. In short order, the strong alliances of the steel workers with the residents of Homestead enabled them to counter by seizing possession of the town. Armed steel workers patrolled the entrances to the town and closed it off from Carnegie's attempts to bring in replacement workers. When trains carrying replacements and sheriff's deputies arrived, a few thousand Homestead residents—including children, grim-faced old women with rolling pins, and men who otherwise had little to do with the mill—faced them down, forming a mile-long human column that kept the scabs from approaching the mill. Not incidentally, the crowds beat up a few of the scabs just to prove their point. While the steel workers remained on guard at the mill, the AAISW negotiated and concluded a new three-year contract that reinstated the workers and accepted Carnegie's lower wage scale, but also provided the AAISW with a great deal of control over the direction of operations on the mill floor through fifty-six pages of AAISW-proposed work rules. The AAISW celebrated on July 14, marking the lockout as a tactical success; management had conceded that the AAISW essentially ran the Homestead mill, and union membership there quickly doubled.[342]

By the fall of 1889, the lawyer for the AAISW, Billy Brennen, was coming into his own as a social and intellectual leader among Pittsburgh's Democrats—the party out of power in Pittsburgh. He served as the unofficial dean of the "Steps," later known as the "Amen Corner," a group of "political philosophers" who congregated daily in the late afternoon or evening around a doorway of a pharmacy at the corner of Liberty and Market downtown, generally after the adjournment of the courts, to discuss and debate a wide array of topics in a semi-public forum, all in a friendly fashion—everything from "the state of the weather to the next probable Democratic President." On warm summer evenings, in particular, large crowds gathered to hear Brennen and his compadres speak from the doorway.[343]

Sleekly coifed, mustachioed and dressed to the nines, Brennen was unabashed about displaying his relative affluence, his cultivated learning and appreciation for theater and the arts, even as he defended the causes of steel workers or miners; but the courtly formality of tone and address that he adopted—always calling people by their formal titles, for example—was distributed as equally among the steel workers and miners as it was his many affluent Republican friends. His ability to communicate gracefully with such a diverse array of classes and types was undoubtedly one of the keys to his success as a trial lawyer, as well as at the negotiating table.[344] Brennen had, as David L. Lawrence's biographer Michael P. Weber wrote, an "unusual ability to deal successfully with affluent, Protestant, Republicans while at the same time acting as the spokesman for organized labor."[345] His egalitarian grace and ease at crossing the partisan chasm also did not hurt him with the local Democratic Party, which in 1889 was beginning to look hopefully at the 1890 congressional elections.

In the 1888 election, the Republicans succeeded in taking down the Democratic incumbent, President Grover Cleveland—the first Democrat elected to the White House since before the Civil War—and replacing him with Benjamin Harrison, the former governor and senator from Indiana, and the grandson of a president. In the process, the Republicans also gained twenty-seven seats to take back a slim majority in the House of Representatives. Thus emboldened, the Republicans in Washington proceeded to enact almost every plank of the Party's 1888 platform during their first 303-day session, including the controversial McKinley Tariff. Proposed by future president William McKinley, a congressman from Ohio and the chairman of the House Ways and Means Committee, the Act raised average duties on imports to nearly fifty percent as a way of protecting American manufacturing interests from foreign imports, but inevitably it resulted in higher average prices to consumers during a period of deflation that was generally good for the wealthy, but tough on farmers and workers whose incomes were declining.[346]

The enactment of spending programs by the Republicans, including a lavish pension for dependents of Civil War veterans, led the 51st Congress to be dubbed by its critics as the "Billion Dollar Congress." In answer to such critics, the Republican Speaker of the House, Thomas B. Reed of Maine, quipped, "This is a billion-dollar country."[347] For struggling farmers and workers, Speaker Reed's flippancy seemed to confirm that he was in the pocket of the "Bosses." Around the country, populist movements were becoming more visible, such as the Farmer Alliance groups and the People's Party, agitating for the remonetization of silver to counter the deflationary effects of the gold standard. Meanwhile in Pittsburgh, where the antagonism of labor and capital was already more than a decade old, the distrust of the alliance between moneyed interests and the Republican Party was only exacerbated by the rupture of the South Fork Dam and the response of the "Bosses' Club." As the next election neared, the Johnstown Flood's injuries to the working man became a kind of rallying cry among Democrats. "'He didn't have any Johnstown Flood, did he?,' asked a member of the crowd, sarcastically, while listening to a popular Democrat criticizing the record of a Republican politician.[348] The prospects of Democratic gains across the country in 1890 looked promising.

John Dalzell, the lawyer for the Pennsylvania Railroad and Westinghouse among other corporate interests, was the Republican two-term incumbent in the 22nd Congressional District, which included greater Pittsburgh. As another member of the powerful House Ways and Means Committee, Dalzell was not just a supporter of the McKinley Tariff, but was a prime mover in its passage. On October 2, 1890, the *Pittsburgh Post* reported that William Brennen, a "strong party worker" with "a large circle of friends among the Republicans, and also among the labor organizations," had announced his candidacy for the Democratic nomination to face Dalzell in the general election.[349] Meanwhile, in the neighboring 23rd Congressional District, the Republicans had just endured a battle between George Shiras III, the son of the future Supreme Court justice, and the future governor, William A. Stone, that resulted in Colonel Stone seizing the Republican nomination for the seat being vacated by former District Attorney Thomas Bayne. As reported by the *Post*:

> *In the Twenty-third congressional district the chances for a Democratic candidate are perhaps better than any of the others. The friends of George Shiras III, are still sore about the methods used by Colonel Stone to defeat their choice, and they will support a Democrat in preference to Stone almost to a man. D.T. Watson was the first spoken of and several strong Shiras workers are authority for the statement that he could easily be elected. Mr. Watson, however, does not care for congressional honors and will not allow his name to be used in that connection. It was stated yesterday that the committee next Monday would choose Thomas M. Marshall as Colonel Stone's opponent. Mr. Marshall's well-known favoritism to the Democratic State ticket this fall probably led to this statement. However, when it is remembered that 'Glorious Old Tom' has time after time refused to run for political offices which he could have secured with scarcely any opposition, the fallacy of the statement can be seen. In fact a very close friend of Mr. Marshall stated to a Post reporter last night that the report was without foundation and that Mr. Marshall would enter no political contest.*[350]

A few days later, the Democrats met and anointed Brennen as the candidate to face Dalzell, and chose D.T. Watson, in spite of previously raised concerns about his willingness to accept the nod, to face Colonel Stone. "David T. Watson," said the *Post*, "is a Democrat of excellent record and has hosts of friends. Aside from the following he has in his own party he will receive the support of a large number of the discontented Shiras followers who are still sore over Colonel Stone's methods of securing the nomination. Mr. Watson has previously declined to put himself forward as a candidate for nomination but it was stated positively yesterday that he would accept."[351] No doubt uncomfortable, as a corporation lawyer, with the party rhetoric which assailed corporate greed and corruption at every opportunity, D.T. Watson did ultimately decline the nomination; and by late October, Morrison Foster, the brother of composer Stephen Foster, was tapped to run against Colonel Stone in Watson's place.

Dalzell, who was not a particular favorite of Senator Matthew Quay's statewide Republican political machine in Pennsylvania, for the most part avoided campaigning for himself or his party in his own state, let alone his district, during the heat of the campaign, preferring to stump for his colleague on the Ways and Means Committee, William McKinley, in nearby Canton, Ohio. The Democrats, meanwhile, were keen to roll out Brennen as labor's friend, and Brennen was only too happy to oblige. Dalzell, wrote the *Post*, "is generally accepted as the representative of capital and corporation interests, and there can be no question Mr. Brennen stands for labor. He is a graduate of the iron furnace, self educated and well endowed with good common sense and professional arguments. Here is a chance for labor to assert itself."[352] On October 25, Brennen took his "professional arguments" to the millworkers' neighborhoods during eight open-air meetings, laced together by a colorful parade of carriages and band wagons decorated with flags and lanterns, moving from Fifth Avenue across the Point Bridge and through the South Side. The favorite son of the flats told the crowds at his first stop:

> *Mohammed felt that if the mountain would not come to him he would go to the mountain and I feel the same way about my friends on the Southside. While my opponent is shaking hands with the brokers and gamblers in the stock exchange at Cincinnati I am here to speak with you. I feel that a candidate should neither be ashamed to be seen nor afraid to be heard. The question is whether you, my fellow laboring men, will elect a corporation lawyer or a man who has been reared among you on the Southside... I pledge my word to you that if I am chosen the humblest citizen of the district will always be treated by me with that courtesy which one gentleman owes to another, and when a committee of the Amalgamated association calls on me I will not turn my back on it and walk into the house as my opponent did.*

When he reached 26th Street, an enthusiastic crowd of two thousand had assembled to hear him. As the *Post* reported:

> *Mr. Brennen looked happy at the evidence of his popularity and smilingly remarked: "This is the place where I can truly say I am among friends." "You're dead right there, Billy," came from the audience. In that crowd there were scores of big, muscular mill men who could remember a few years back when they worked side by side with the orator of the evening, sweating over the pots of molten metal together. They sent up cheer after cheer for their favorite, while the red lights and rockets from the windows and the roofs of the neighboring houses lit up the entire scene. Mr. Brennen could scarcely get away to keep the next appointment, so many wanted to grasp his hand ...*[353]

Meanwhile, after his Ohio sojourn John Dalzell returned to Washington, without fanfare, just before the election.

On November 4, in spite of all the red lights, rockets and band wagons, Dalzell handily beat Brennen, sixty percent to thirty-eight percent.[354] Ultimately, despite a national Democratic landslide that resulted in the return of the House to Democratic hands as well as the unseating of Dalzell's Ways and Means colleague William McKinley, the 22nd District was still overwhelmingly Republican. Brennen's former Capitol Hill patron, James Herron Hopkins, would be the only Democrat to serve the 22nd District from the 1840s to the beginning of the twentieth century (1874-76 and 1883-85). Now in the House minority, however, Dalzell was slated to have little influence, as the *National Labor Tribune* surmised, as he had "embittered the opposition against him in the [prior] Fifty-first Congress by his prominently bitter partisanship."[355]

Unsuccessful at wresting "the reins of government from the supporters of 'organized capital,'" at least locally, less than two years later labor would be left to make another desperate stand against organized capital—on the banks of the Monongahela, back at Homestead. With the latest sliding scale contract scheduled for expiration on June 30,

1892, the AAISW began negotiations with Frick at Homestead by proposing a wage increase in February 1892. Frick, lying in wait, saw the expiration of the sliding scale contract as an opportunity to rid Carnegie Steel of the most effective union opposition it had yet encountered—the Homestead lodge of the AAISW—and he began to deploy the plan for its demise, with passive support, arriving periodically by telegram, from Andrew Carnegie from his extended vacation in Scotland. Frick countered the AAISW's offer with a twenty-two percent wage decrease and a contract structure that would remove a number of positions at the mill from collective bargaining altogether. He then announced, on April 30, that he would only engage in negotiations with the AAISW for another twenty-nine days and that if no contract were reached, Carnegie Steel would cease to recognize the union.[356] A few days after talks broke off, on June 4, 1892, the *Pittsburgh Post* reported, "Developments now indicate that Homestead will be the scene of a great conflict between capital and labor."[357] There was a palpable sense around Pittsburgh that the oncoming clash between the AAISW and Mr. Frick was going to be momentous. By June 24, Frick ordered the construction of a twelve-foot high, three-mile long fence, topped with barbed wire, around the Homestead Works.[358]

In some local circles, Frick's lawyer Phil Knox was given the credit, or the blame, for the idea of bringing private police hirelings from the Pinkerton Detective Agency to act on behalf of Carnegie Steel in Homestead in 1892—although the sad history of the Pinkertons' involvement in Homestead is most often used as "Exhibit A" by those who would say that Henry Clay Frick was one of the worst CEOs in American history, or that Andrew Carnegie, the "angel of the workingman," was a hypocrite on the subject of the nobility of labor. Ralph Demmler, who had no reason to bask in Philander Knox's role in the Homestead strike, recounts the eyewitness testimony of a Knox & Reed office boy, Robert T. Rossell, who allegedly recalled hearing "Henry C. Frick in the Firm's office excitedly, loudly and acrimoniously blame Mr. Knox for originating what had turned out to be the ill-advised and ill-fated plan" of sending the Pinkertons in a barge down the Monongahela River to engage the steel workers at the Homestead Works.[359]

The truth of the matter was that the Carnegie companies had already deployed Pinkerton detectives on the front lines in the successful defeat of the Knights of Labor at the Edgar Thomson Works in Braddock in 1887-88, and the AAISW had seen the owners of the Allegheny Bessemer Steel Works bring in the Pinkertons at Duquesne in 1889.[360] Frick himself had deployed hired Pinkertons during the previous year when, in February 1891, ten thousand coke workers went on strike against the H.C. Frick Coke Company, a joint enterprise of Frick and Carnegie, in Connellsville. In that conflict, by March 26, 1891, with no resolution imminent, Frick "invited" the workers to return to their jobs at a reduced wage, but they refused. Instead, they resolved to march on the coke works, which were being guarded by Pinkerton men and sheriff's deputies. During the ensuing confrontation, the Pinkertons shot and killed seven workers. The standoff continued until April 21, when Frick directed the successful landing of one hundred Pinkerton men at the Leisenring No. 2 mine and had them sworn in as sheriff's deputies. The Pinkertons stood guard as a special train carrying fifty Italian replacement workers arrived to begin work. With production back on the rise, the frustrated workers called off the strike on May 27, 1891.[361] Frick had succeeded in busting the union at Connellsville, and the Pinkertons had become a staple of the Carnegie-Frick union busting strategy.

During the 1877 Riots, the Railroad bosses, managers and lawyers alike were caught flat-footed by the upheaval, and were responding in a reactive way to each next reported maneuver by the angry mobs collected at the 28th Street crossing. By contrast, the well-oiled machine of a company over which Frick presided had developed some successful techniques for taking the fight to the workers, rather than waiting for them to move. In order to be ahead of the game at Homestead as the expiration of the sliding scale approached, Frick and Knox worked together closely to implement their plans, using the tools of the corporate machinery and, learning from the patterns that developed during the 1877 Riots, engaging the local government in ways that provided cover for the tactics they devised. As Krause observes,

> *In the view of both Carnegie and his chief executive, Frick, Knox was indeed the consummate corporation lawyer. He provided more than just expert advice; he functioned as a field lieutenant who could handle unseemly details in utter confidence while simultaneously maintaining a gentlemanly public posture. It was, in fact, Knox who surreptitiously helped plan and execute the firm's legal and military strategy during the Homestead Lockout of 1892 and who secretly arranged with local authorities for the Pinkerton's riverboat landing.[362]*

On June 26, shortly after Frick had concluded the engagement of three hundred Pinkerton men from the Agency, Phil Knox met with the Allegheny County sheriff, William H. McCleary, to discuss the details of the "secret plan" for the deployment of the Pinkerton men at Homestead. In the aftermath of the 1877 Riots, of course, the County had been saddled, retroactively, with the responsibility for the protection of the Railroad's private assets. Knox offered Sheriff McCleary the chance to accept the three hundred Pinkerton men as his own "posse" to guard the Homestead Steel Works and to swear them in as sheriff's deputies for that purpose[363]—just as Frick and Knox had asked the Fayette County sheriff with respect to the Pinkerton men who guarded the Leisenring No. 2 mine at Connellsville. Sheriff McCleary, however, was conflicted: while a large section of his voting constituency in the County was unsympathetic to the Bosses, McCleary himself was the beneficiary of the support of the Republican political boss of Pittsburgh, Frick's fickle friend Christopher Magee. McCleary stopped short of reassuring Knox that he would deputize the Pinkerton men, saying he would only do so if "there was liable to be destruction of property or loss of life."[364] Knox took McCleary's response under advisement, while Knox and Frick continued their plans for a Pinkerton landing at Homestead.

Meanwhile, operating without knowledge of the specifics of Knox and Frick's plans but rather possessing great familiarity with their strike-breaking tactics, Billy Brennen stood at the side of the AAISW. William A. "Honest Bill" Weihe, known to his friends at the Lewis, Oliver & Phillips mill on the South Side as the "Giant Puddler," was the outgoing national president of the AAISW, having served since 1884.[365] He and Brennen were both veterans of the mills, and during their ascendant years they lived only a few blocks from each other on the South Side.[366] When Brennen took his congressional campaign to the labor clubs of the South Side in 1890, Weihe was undoubtedly a member of his honor guard. Weihe relied heavily on Brennen's advice, and certainly there was no one better equipped than Billy Brennen to advise the AAISW on how to act under the circumstances; Brennen had lived and breathed the minutiae of legal restrictions imposed upon the tactics of labor unions, both as an advisor to the AAISW through its prior strikes, as well as in his attempts to extend the capabilities of concerted union actions in his trial court arguments.

Against that backdrop, and with the firmly imprinted memory of the 1877 Riots, Brennen's advice was designed to follow the law, such as it was, and to use the leverage of the workers' numbers and solidarity to preserve opportunities for cool-headed dialogue. In 1877, there was no one who could have played Brennen's role: there was no strong union presence among the angry mobs that burned down the Pennsy roundhouse, no institution that could be counseled and no chain of command that could be used to direct the energies of the strikers. There were no labor lawyers. The fact of the existence of a strong, successful union itself gave the Homestead strikers the ability to hear the advice of counsel, and to coordinate actions to some degree thereafter; coordination, after all, had won the day for them in 1889. Nevertheless, Brennen found himself straddling, often uncomfortably and sometimes unsuccessfully, the wall between the objectives of labor and his local political ambitions, despite the fact that both causes, for Brennen, represented chances to improve the lot of the working man in Pittsburgh. By contrast, Philander Knox, as the lieutenant of Frick and an operator of the corporate machinery of the Carnegie Company, had no such conflicting concerns.

As the contract deadline approached at Homestead, meanwhile, Weihe had lost some his sway with the rank and file. It had never been out of the ordinary for him to urge for the retreat of the AAISW in order to keep the lines of communication between union leadership and management, and now, serving in a lame duck capacity, it would prove difficult for him to orchestrate the behavior of the hot-blooded rank-and-file who regarded him as too conservative, too soft for the battle in which they wanted to engage. The union's executive committee, concerned about the ability of the union leadership to keep the peace in Homestead from the top down, elected a Homestead "advisory committee" from among some of the most strident representatives of the eight local union lodges, including Hugh O'Donnell, a thirty year-old former newspaperman who worked as a heater at the 119-inch plate mill, serving as committee chair, and the elected burgess (mayor) of Homestead, John McLuckie, who worked in the Bessemer converting mill.[367]

Despite the shift in authority to the advisory committee, the new committee itself adopted a conservative posture designed to insure observance of the law. Although there was fire in their rhetoric—McLuckie would imply, for example, that the workers had a property right in their jobs, and he would declare that Carnegie had no right to import scabs into Homestead, and that "we will have [our rights] if it requires force to get them"[368]—like Weihe, the committee members knew that a chess match was better than a war. They proceeded to put on a show of force. O'Donnell organized the union rank-and-file and the townspeople of Homestead on a "truly military basis," as he put it, with three eight-hour watch shifts posted at the gates of the plant, at all inbound roads and railroad stations around Homestead, and at several points along the Monongahela River. The committee chartered a steamboat, the *Edna*, to patrol the river, along with about fifty skiffs from the town, and ordered the taverns to curtail excessive drinking that would lead to reckless behavior. O'Donnell's goals were to form a blockade around the Homestead plant, in order to prohibit the entry of replacement workers, and to keep the peace. In the latter effort, Krause refers to O'Donnell and his fellow committee members as "amateur lawyers" who had guided the lockout.[369] While Weihe's absence from the resistance planning meant that Brennen, too, would be largely absent from that process, the committee was undoubtedly infused with Brennen's hand-me-down insights about the legality of their tactics—Brennen was at the forefront of such knowledge, and O'Donnell's instructions to his troops, as well as their later efforts to obtain his counsel, showed the benefit of it.

Brennen, meanwhile, was distracted throughout June. On June 7, while three hundred delegates to the seventeenth annual convention of the AAISW were convening at Turner Hall on Forbes Street to discuss the lockout at the Homestead Works, Billy Brennen was chairing the opening of the new local Democratic headquarters in the old University Building on Diamond Street.[370] On June 16, Brennen was in Chicago, attending the Democratic National Convention, while the AAISW negotiated with the Shenango and Mahoning valley steel manufacturers, who were expediting their talks to reach an agreement in advance of the coming showdown with Carnegie Steel at Homestead.[371]

On June 30, while the sliding scale contract was expiring and Frick was initiating the lockout of the workers at Homestead, Brennen was speaking to the local ratifying convention of the Democratic Party, addressing County Democrats on the merits of the new presidential ticket of ex-President Grover Cleveland for president and Adlai Stevenson for vice president. He did, however, keep his clients' hopes at the forefront of his concerns. As the *Post* would report, "Mr. Brennen said while he had doubted Mr. Cleveland's availability before the convention, he saw at Chicago that the word was flying from all sections to nominate Cleveland, and he was for him now. He said the working people were getting their eyes open on the [McKinley] tariff, and had seen enough of its effects at Homestead, where high tariff means high fences with port holes." The *Post* would go on to observe, "The acts of the Carnegie were denounced and brought out great applause."[372] On the following day, July 1, the Homestead Works were silent and still, and Frick and Knox privately looked forward to a non-union reopening on July 6.

On July 4, Pittsburghers celebrated Independence Day. City solicitor Major William Moreland, standing on the speaker's stage as the chairman and master of ceremonies for the city's Fourth of July celebrations at Schenley Park (three years before he would be indicted in connection with the embezzlement scandal), was his usual effervescent self in introducing Thomas Mercer Marshall as the first of the day's speakers, calling him "the Pittsburgh Gladstone" in reference to Great Britain's famous Liberal orator and prime minister. Marshall began his Fourth of July speech by addressing the great industrial progress of Pittsburgh and, in a rhetorical move probably not unlike that which he might employ when addressing a jury, Marshall acknowledged a young African American boy listening intently to him near the stand, and used the moment as a departure to discuss equality under the nation's Constitution.[373] Then, as the *Dispatch* reported, his mind turned toward Homestead:

> ... Gentlemen, I am sad to-day. Just across this hill lies Homestead. Outside the works are the men encamped, inside are the managers. They say this is a conflict between labor and capital. Not so. The workmen are the creators. The managers inside are the employers. They are not capitalists. I hope some great statesman will soon solve this problem for us that this great country may not perish by intestine broils ... Men are not the sons of toil, but the sons of God by direct descent. I would admonish you men to be patient. If I could speak at Homestead I would say for God's sake be patient. Be patient until a settlement can be made that recognizes the manhood of man, until it can be said of us that we dwell beneath our own vine and eat our own bread.[374]

Meanwhile, in Homestead, there was no public Fourth of July celebration, and the streets, as the *Post* reported, "were as quiet as though it was Sunday."[375]

Marshall's well-received utopian sentiments at Schenley Park betrayed the public's ignorance of the intense behind-the-scenes preparation for the coming confrontation on both sides of the conflict. Knox met with Sheriff McCleary again on July 4 and the following day, reiterating his request that the Sheriff deputize his "secret" Pinkerton army, and each time, McCleary declined.[376] Meanwhile, with knowledge of Knox and Frick's plan, McCleary and several deputies arrived at Homestead by train at ten o'clock in the morning on July 5, saying they wished to provide protection to the plant. They were met by Hugh O'Donnell and his advisory committee, who gave the Sheriff a tour of the perimeter of the Works and assured him that the citizens of Homestead were prepared to protect the plant themselves. O'Donnell asked Sheriff McCleary to deputize his men, a request that Frick would later decry as "the men who were interfering with the exercise of our corporate rights, preventing us from conducting our business affairs, request[ing] that they be clothed with the authority of deputy sheriffs to take charge of our plant." When Sheriff McCleary refused, O'Donnell responded dramatically:

> Sheriff, the last meeting of the Advisory Committee of the AAISW. We, as members of that committee, have, after due deliberation, resolved to formally disband this committee. The Advisory Committee from now on will not be responsible for any disorder or lawless act perpetrated either in Homestead Borough or Mifflin Township. Do you understand— our responsibility ceases from this very moment. I now declare the Advisory Committee to be dead.[377]

As Sheriff McCleary left town, members of the disbanded committee sent urgent telegrams to Weihe and Brennen in Pittsburgh, asking them to pursue an injunction against the pursuit of "measures that will result disastrously to the quiet and peace of Homestead and Mifflin township" and to restrict Sheriff McCleary's ability to send deputies to Homestead. They expected that McCleary would deputize whomever Frick had decided to bring in. Weihe and members of the union's executive committee found Brennen at the courthouse, and Brennen invited them to the rooms of the Bar Association, where they held a long consultation. As the *Post* reported, "Mr. Brennen informed them that there was no legal way of preventing the sheriff sending deputies to Homestead or anywhere else, if it appeared to him that their presence was necessary to protect citizens in their full enjoyment of their property. The sheriff was compelled to take such action," Brennen explained, "to protect the peace, when formal application of the nature of that presented by the Carnegie Steel Company was made, as in his judgment was necessary."[378]

O'Donnell's troops remained at their posts that evening. At around one o'clock in the morning, July 6, union scouts posted at the Smithfield Bridge saw two barges—the *Iron Mountain* and the *Monongahela*—being towed by two little tugs down the river toward Homestead. Philander Knox urged Sheriff McCleary, one last time, to send a deputy to the embarkation point, at Bellevue, near the Davis Island Lock and Dam on the Ohio—where the three hundred Pinkerton men were transferred from railcars at half past ten the previous evening to the barges—in case McCleary were to change his mind and decide to deputize them. Chief Deputy Joseph Gray duly met the Pinkerton detectives at the riverside, but again, on behalf of Sheriff McCleary, refused to deputize them.[379] As they floated down the river in their armament-laden barges under cover of darkness, much to the disappointment of Phil Knox, the Pinkertons would be mere private agents.

The news of the impending arrival of the barges went to Homestead by horseback and telegram. O'Donnell sent the *Edna* up to engage the barges, while a Homestead lookout sounded a huge steam whistle that the committee had installed to warn the residents of an attack. As the *Edna* fired a couple of stray warning shots, to no avail, the entire town of Homestead assembled en masse for the imminent conflict. Shots rang out from the riverbank as the remaining tug boat (the other one became disabled during the excursion) brought the *Iron Mountain* and the *Monongahela* to shore near the Homestead Works. At this point, as Krause observes, what was left of O'Donnell's former committee—the group that had carefully crafted the intelligence and response network that led the citizens of Homestead to this moment in a deliberate and colorably legal fashion—lost all control. They cautioned against violence; however, as the *Chicago Tribune* reported, "There was no organization, but suddenly the cry arose, 'Charge on them' ... There was no method, no leadership apparent ... It was the uprising of a population." Hundreds of men, women and children headed to the shore and up to the gates of the Homestead Works itself to form the town's defenses. They pulled down parts of Frick's wooden fence and erected barricades.[380]

At four-thirty in the morning, O'Donnell, still hoping to restore calm, made an appeal to the townspeople, which was ignored, and also to the Pinkertons. "On behalf of five thousand men," said O'Donnell to the Pinkerton men on the barges, "I beg you to leave here at once. I don't know who you are or whence you came, but I do know that you have no business here, and if you remain there will be bloodshed. We, the workers in these mills, are peaceably inclined. We have not damaged any property, and we don't intend to. If you will send a committee with us, we will take them through the works, carefully explain to them the details in this trouble, and promise them a safe return to their boats. But in the name of God and humanity, don't attempt to land! Don't attempt to enter these works by force!"

Captain Frederick Heinde, the Pinkerton officer in command of the *Iron Mountain*, shouted back. "We were sent here to take possession of this property and to guard it for this company ... We don't wish to shed blood, but we are determined to go up there and shall do so. If you men don't withdraw, we will mow every one of you down and enter in spite of you. You had better disperse," Captain Heinde demanded, "for land we will!"

Heinde threw down a gangplank and proceeded to lead an advance guard, armed with billy-clubs and Winchesters. There was a skirmish between Pinkertons and workers on the shore with oars and clubs, and then, suddenly, shots rang out. Over 120 years later, no one can say who fired the first shot, but rifle fire now poured down onto the barges from all sides. The Pinkerton men broke out through the windows of their barges with their Winchesters and tried to return fire. Bullets flew in every direction, as workers aimed a cannon at the barges from across the river and fired away.[381]

News of the battle reached Pittsburgh, and as the sun rose thousands gathered on the hills above the conflict to watch the fighting. The fighting continued for hours as the barges drifted. By the afternoon, at least two Pinkertons were mortally wounded and several of the strikers were killed in the melee. Dozens more were wounded, many of them badly. The Pinkertons attempted to raise the white flag of surrender a few times, but the firing continued.[382]

Sheriff McCleary sent three requests to Governor Robert Pattison in Harrisburg, pleading with him to send the militia to restore order, but the governor refused.[383] There was talk that the citizens of Homestead might keep up their onslaught until the Pinkertons, trapped on board the barges, were annihilated. McCleary and Christopher Magee asked William Weihe of the AAISW to go to Homestead and try to convince the workers to let the Pinkertons be escorted out of town. Around four in the afternoon, as mill worker reinforcements from the South Side, Braddock and Duquesne arrived to support the Homestead workers, all six-feet-two-inches of Weihe mounted a boiler in one of the mill yard buildings and began to address the assembled crowd of almost four thousand people. He told them that he supported Sheriff McCleary's plan to allow the Pinkertons to surrender on the condition that they would not be permitted to return. The crowd jeered him down.

Then O'Donnell, grabbing an American flag, mounted a pile of steel beams, and suggested his own plan to the crowd. As each Pinkerton man left the barge, O'Donnell submitted, he would have a warrant sworn out against him for murder, and they would all be prosecuted for murder.[384] O'Donnell's suggestion met with greater approval, but the crowd still wanted blood. After O'Donnell went to the barge to negotiate their surrender, the Pinkertons slowly began to emerge onto the shore, while angry citizens yelled "Kill the detectives!" A gauntlet formed around the Pinkertons as they scrambled up the riverbank toward the mill, and the crazed mob showed no mercy to them: they hit them with sticks and clubs, battered their skulls and punched them in their faces. Many of the Pinkertons were bloodied and bruised, and others were beaten senseless during their walk to the mill, and again on their walk from the mill to the Homestead Opera House, which would serve as their temporary jail. Then the crowd turned and set fire to the barges.[385]

While the ex-members of the advisory committee discussed the conditions on which they believed the Pinkertons should be released to Sheriff McCleary, their authority was being usurped across town. Weihe, M.M. Garland, Weihe's successor as president-elect of the AAISW, the union secretary Stephen Madden, and attorney Billy Brennen were meeting with Sheriff McCleary and Magee, conducting their own set of negotiations. After several hours, including a break for supper, the group boarded a special train from Pittsburgh to Homestead at a quarter past ten in the evening. Rumors circulated that McCleary was on his way to Homestead to arrest the detectives, and newspapers began to print that the arrests had already been made. At half past midnight, the Pinkertons were escorted onto the special train and taken, somewhat ironically, to the Pennsylvania Railroad yards at Eighteenth Street in the Strip, where Magee and McCleary announced to the press from the station platform at around two o'clock in the morning that the Pinkerton men would simply be taken out of the city.[386]

Billy Brennen stood by Magee and McCleary on the platform, and wearing the hat of the consummate politico that he was, he concurred. Magee was a Republican, but as a city politician in the "go along to get along" milieu of Pittsburgh machine politics, Brennen could not afford to have Magee as an enemy. "What else can be done except let these fellows go?" he asked, stating that it was not possible to know who was responsible for the deaths of the workers at Homestead.[387] Brennen would live to regret his public support for the plan, however. By sending the detectives out of town, there would certainly be no easy way to prosecute the vast majority them; and as he would later find out, he could expect no *quid pro quo* from Frick and Knox for members of the AAISW.

In the immediate aftermath, although the events of July 6, 1892 went horribly off-course for both the AAISW as well as for the Carnegie Company, there was briefly a sense among the citizens of Homestead that they had been victorious, and that they had staved off Frick's attempt to break the union. Although they had theoretically won the battle of Homestead by keeping the Pinkertons away, it later unfolded that they had lost the war.

As Weihe, Brennen and the ex-members of the committee (now the "reconstituted committee," with Hugh O'Donnell again as chair) began to look a few steps ahead, they could see that the main objective had shifted away from attempting to gain a better contract. The main objective was now to hold on to union recognition at all costs, and they began to recognize that the prospects for this objective were growing dim, especially as it became clear that Sheriff McCleary or Magee would eventually succeed in getting Governor Pattison to send the militia to Homestead. As much as the union might hope otherwise, the arrival of the militia would not be there to act as a neutral security force, but rather in the service of giving Frick and his replacement workers access to the Works. With replacement workers on the scene, the AAISW would quickly lose its negotiating leverage.

Publicly, Brennen attempted to justify the workers' opposition to the deployment of the militia in Homestead by claiming that the Carnegie Company already enjoyed control of the works. "Why ask the governor to protect a works of which the owners have [full] and absolute possession? That is the condition today. I might as well ask to have my office protected."[388] Two days after the battle, however, the situation on the ground was very different from Brennen's description; the union still controlled the gates of the Works, refusing even to permit the plant superintendent, John Potter, to enter.

Brennen, at a meeting of two hundred workers in Homestead on July 8, spelled out on behalf of the AASIW leadership what he saw as the only "tactic" the workers had left to them: embrace Sheriff McCleary's desire to secure the Works without the necessity of calling the militia, and hope that the Carnegie Company would see this as a gesture of goodwill. Brennen told the crowd:

If the sheriff's officers are not admitted to the works, and the property turned over to the firm, the militia must be summoned, and it is their duty to obey orders, regardless of their sympathies or of the results. The present condition of affairs cannot be allowed to continue. When the military come they will be here in force and well armed. They will surround the works. New men will be put to work under military guard, and if anyone attempts to interfere with them he will be shot, for the militia must do their duty.

Bloodshed and a conflict with the troops must be averted. If any man imagines that the State troops will be brought here to stand around like posts or be on dress parade that man is mistaken. They will be brought here to act, and the men will act as they are directed to do. They will shoot you down. The history of the riots in the coke regions shows this to be true. The owners know that whatever the moral position of the men they have the law on their side, and that the sheriff must put them in possession of their property. The people are against the Pinkertons, but they will not be with you in resistance to the sheriff. He and his posse are the legal representatives of the peace, and are not like the Pinkertons, a hired band who are to act as their employer directs.

Another Homestead worker echoed Brennen's sentiments. "Our lawyer has told us what we may expect if the militia comes," the worker said. "If he can't be trusted, who can be? The Amalgamated Association knows that it won't amount to a row of pins if it loses this fight, and our officers would not ask us to take this action if they did not believe it would be best. We cannot win by violence. We either have to let the sheriff take possession of the mill in a friendly, peaceable spirit, or resist him, and then the troops will be called out, and who will gain?"[389]

The workers would not be budged, however. Back in Pittsburgh the next day, acting as chairman of the county Democrats, Brennen called for the adoption of a resolution supporting the efforts of the Homestead men to "maintain American and resist European pauper wages" and sending their condolences to the families of men "shot down by the hirelings of a greedy and arbitrary combination of capital," which passed unanimously.[390]

Meanwhile, on the Republican side of the aisle, Brennen's former congressional opponent, John Dalzell, was taking the brunt of the anger against the "Bosses" in Congress. "Corporation Dalzell," who was then contesting the Pennsylvania Senate seat held by Matthew Quay, had a passionate showdown with Congressman Benton McMillin of Tennessee when McMillin suggested that Homestead proved that the McKinley Tariff reduced instead of increased wages. Dalzell "hotly denied it" and told McMillin that he didn't know what he was talking about, offering "to prove to anyone who would listen that the tariff had no more to do with the Homestead affair than the cholera epidemic in Baku." McMillin countered with a recitation of the glowing promises made by the Republicans about higher wages under the proposed Tariff, and a catalogue of cuts in wages since the law had taken effect. Dalzell accused McMillin of "gloating over the dying men at Homestead," at which point the House broke out into an uproar. He added, under the din of the chamber, that "only two classes of people took advantage of the Homestead affair, and those two classes were anarchists and political demagogues." Shortly thereafter, the Democrats passed a largely symbolic resolution to repeal the tariff on tin plate, "Mr. Dalzell's pet law."[391]

By July 12, McCleary had prevailed upon Governor Pattison to bring in the state militia to restore order in Homestead. At the direction of O'Donnell and the committee, the citizens of Homestead cheered their arrival, but they were quickly made to understand by Major General George R. Snowden, in no uncertain terms, that the militia had come to protect the property rights of the Carnegie Company. Shortly after the arrival of the militia, replacement workers began to arrive and were escorted into the Homestead Works, and by the end of July 15, smoke began to rise from the stacks at the Works, indicating that steel production would shortly resume.[392] Although the AAISW maintained that the strike was still alive, each day the Works turned out product, the strike died a little more.

To add insult to injury, Philander Knox hired John S. Robb and David F. Patterson, two well-known criminal lawyers in Pittsburgh, to assist him in writing criminal "informations," or indictments, against the leaders of the strike. On July 18, Carnegie company secretary Francis Lovejoy issued the first of these formal accusations against a number of strikers—including murder charges against Hugh O'Donnell and Burgess John McLuckie, for the deaths of two Pinkerton detectives. "We have good cases against 1000 of these men," declared Lovejoy, "and from now on from twelve to fifteen informations will be made every day. The laws of Pennsylvania," he continued, undoubtedly scripted by Knox, "are very broad on this subject. Persons who were on the premises at the time of the shooting are liable not only as accessories, but as principals."[393] When Pittsburgh constables arrived at Hugh O'Donnell's house with a warrant for his arrest, however, he could not be found. *The New York Times* suggested that O'Donnell had fled the law.[394]

O'Donnell, at the clever urging of Republican leaders, had secretly departed from Homestead on July 17 for New York to visit with President Benjamin Harrison's new running mate, Republican vice-presidential candidate Whitelaw Reid, the editor and publisher of the *New York Tribune*. Reid, perhaps an unwitting accomplice in the trap being laid for O'Donnell, had already expressed his concern that Homestead would end up being a nail in the coffin of the Harrison re-election campaign, and was eager to hear O'Donnell's message. Meanwhile, O'Donnell believed that Carnegie and Frick depended upon Republican support of tariff legislation to such a degree that they might be persuaded to agree to a compromise with the AAISW, if requested by the presidential ticket. At Reid's suggestion, O'Donnell dictated a formal request to Reid, saying that the workers were prepared to "waive every other thing in dispute, and submit to whatever you think it right to require," if Carnegie would reopen the sliding scale negotiations and recognize the union. In essence, he was offering complete capitulation in exchange for a public embrace of the AAISW. Reid cabled Carnegie and forwarded the request; but in the blink of an eye, O'Donnell's secret offer of across-the-board concessions—through Republican channels, no less—became public, and it became clear that the AAISW's resolve had weakened. O'Donnell's appeal through the Republicans also drove a wedge among AAISW members, many of whom were looking to the Democrats for help. The AAISW in Homestead was becoming even more leaderless and chaotic.[395]

In the meantime, however, O'Donnell returned to Pittsburgh and turned himself in to authorities. Brennen ultimately represented all of the AAISW defendants, assisted by John F. Cox, an ardent Republican lawyer from Homestead who had been a reliable pro-labor vote in the state legislature. Brennen and Cox successfully argued for the release of the first defendants on bail in the sum of ten thousand dollars each.[396]

McLuckie, upon his release, immediately declared that the AAISW would be preparing papers for the arrest of Frick and other company officials on similar charges. Initially, however, Brennen and Cox were cautious about preferring counter-charges. On July 21, Cox told the press, "We have reasons for holding off awhile, and at present we can't tell when the action will be commenced."[397] Brennen and Cox were both holding out hope that either through O'Donnell's conversations with Republicans leaders, or with demonstrations of goodwill (such as delaying counter-charges), the AAISW could entice Frick back to the bargaining table. Brennen continued to emphasize cooperation rather than counter-offensive. Only once O'Donnell's trip to New York had proven to be a major miscalculation, did Brennen begin to suggest to the press that indictments of Frick and other company officials would follow in due course.[398]

Knox's progress in securing additional indictments of strikers and Brennen's stage management and proffering of charges, however, were both temporarily violently interrupted when, on July 23, in Mr. Frick's second floor office in the Chronicle-Telegraph Building, which stood near Pentland Street on Gazette Square in Pittsburgh, Frick was shot and stabbed by a Russian immigrant and self-avowed anarchist named Alexander Berkman. Despite multiple wounds (including two bullet wounds in the neck), Frick survived the attack, but the incident might have been even more catastrophic were it not for the discovery, as Berkman was being apprehended, of a mercury fulminate capsule lodged between Berkman's teeth. Had Berkman managed to detonate the capsule, all present might have been blown to smithereens.[399] For Berkman, the attempted murder of Frick was his avowed "Attentat"—a politically motivated assault designed to inspire the workers to unite and overthrow the capitalists.[400]

In an instant, much of the sympathy engendered by the Homestead workers and their fight against hired Pinkerton detectives and "European pauper wages" was erased;

Berkman, although not a Homestead man, was identified in the public mind with the union cause, and Frick, recovering from the brutal attack, was suddenly seen as a victim. O'Donnell observed that "[i]t would seem that the bullet from Berkman's pistol, failing in its foul intent, went straight through the heart of the Homestead strike."[401]

The ink on Berkman's arrest booking at the County Jail was barely dry when the attack on Frick yielded a new legal controversy. Later in the day on the 23rd, as the news of the attack on Frick reached an encampment of Pennsylvania guardsman in Homestead, a nineteen year-old private from Greene County, W.L. Iams, exclaimed, "Three cheers for the man who shot Frick!" A colonel overheard the remark; and after Iams admitted making it, Lieutenant Colonel J.B. Streator ordered Iams to apologize before the regiment. Iams refused, and Colonel Streator sent Iams to the guard house, where he was subjected to punishment without the benefit of a court-martial proceeding: he was strung up by his thumbs "with notice that he would be cut down as soon as he apologized." Iams endured the punishment for about fifteen minutes before losing consciousness, refusing to retract his statement. General Snowden then ordered that Iams "be disgraced and drummed out of camp." In short order, Iams' head and face were half-shaved, he was stripped of his uniform and given an old pair of overalls, an old hat and an old shirt to wear, while he was led out of camp to the tune of the "Rogue's March," being permanently excluded from the National Guard and disenfranchised.[402]

Iams went to Pittsburgh and announced his intention to seek the prosecution of the officers who gave him his punishment. Several Pittsburgh lawyers offered to represent Iams, but out of familial duty, Iams' cousin Frank Iams led Private Iams' team, along with John D. Watson, the son of prominent Pittsburgh lawyer Alexander M. Watson. As journalist Arthur Burgoyne observed:

> *Within twenty-four hours the Iams case became a National cause celebre. It was discussed everywhere from Maine to California. Military authorities waxed warm over it. Legal authorities squabbled over it. Professional publicists were interviewed concerning it. Editors made it the subject of tremendous publications. Pictures of Iams, hairless, mustacheless and defiant, appeared in the illustrated weeklies.*[403]

Iams' company commander Colonel Alexander L. Hawkins, Colonel Streator, and the company surgeon, Dr. William Simpson Grim, were indicted for aggravated assault and/or assault and battery. Their defense team consisted of Colonel J.R. Braddock, Greensburg-based state senator Edward E. Robbins, and J.M. Braden and Albert Sprowls of Washington, Pennsylvania. In the highly politicized trial that followed, the military men would all be acquitted.[404]

Meanwhile, on September 19, Alexander Berkman was led from his prison cell at the Allegheny County jail into the courtroom of Judge Samuel A. McClung to begin his trial for the attempted murder of Henry Clay Frick and related charges. District Attorney Clarence Burleigh led the prosecution, with Philander Knox sitting behind him at the counsel's table.[405] Judge McClung asked Berkman if he had counsel, or whether he wished to have counsel appointed for him. An organization called the Allegheny Defense Committee for Comrades sent two lawyers to defend Berkman—

Joseph M. Friedman, one of the first several Jewish lawyers in the Allegheny County bar, and Colonel William D. Moore, a former Presbyterian minister and chaplain in the Union Army during the Civil War—but Berkman responded that he intended to represent himself.[406] Later, in her memoir, Berkman's friend and comrade-in-arms Emma Goldman explained that he represented his own case "as true Russian and other European revolutionaries did ... It was inconsistent for an anarchist to employ lawyers."[407] Mr. Frick testified for the prosecution, and Berkman cross-examined him with only one question—had Frick seen him shoot at Frick's manager, J.G. Leishman, who had also been involved in the fracas in Frick's office? Frick replied that he was not sure.[408] Berkman mounted no defense, but with the help of an interpreter, he attempted to read a statement to the court:

> *I address myself to the People. Some may wonder why I have declined a legal defense. My reasons are twofold. in the first place, I am an Anarchist: I do not believe in man-made law, designed to enslave and oppress humanity. Secondly, an extraordinary phenomenon like an Attentat cannot be measured by the narrow standards of legality. It requires a view of the social background to be adequately understood. A lawyer would try to defend, or palliate, my act from the standpoint of the law. Yet the real question at issue is not a defense of myself, but rather the explanation of the deed. It is mistaken to believe me on trial. The actual defendant is Society - the system of injustice, of the organized exploitation of the People.*

At that point, Judge McClung interrupted Berkman and terminated his statement.[409] The jury spent little time returning a guilty verdict, and Berkman was sentenced to twenty-two years in prison.[410]

The Berkman and Iams cases were destined to be distractions in the summer of 1892. Attempting to bring the focus back to the strike itself and in particular the continued recognition of the AAISW, on August 2 Billy Brennen presented before Judge Ewing a petition, signed by sixty-seven steelworkers of Pittsburgh and Homestead (none of whom had yet been the target of criminal charges), requesting the issuance of a license for the establishment of a "voluntary trade tribunal" in accordance with Pennsylvania Voluntary Trade Tribunal Act, passed in 1883, to arbitrate disagreements between steel employers and workers.[411] By its terms, however, the Act provided that the imposition of the jurisdiction of such a tribunal required the acceptance of both sides. After presenting the petition in court, Brennen announced to the press that unless the officials at the Carnegie Steel Company consented to arbitration under the Act, the AAISW would press for their arrest for conspiracy, bringing armed men into the state, and murder. "These [Carnegie] men," said Brennen, "have invoked the law and so will we. It is our intention now to give them all the law they want. They commenced the criminal prosecutions, and we will now see whether they had a right to bring armed men into the State and shoot men down. Possibly both sides are wrong."[412]

It was a last ditch attempt by Brennen to bring Frick back to the negotiating table with both a carrot and a stick. Lovejoy summarily rejected it on behalf of the Carnegie almost immediately, however, stating publicly that "[t]he question of recognizing the

Amalgamated Association cannot be arbitrated." An unidentified representative of the Carnegie told the *Post*: "The time for arbitration is past. We endeavored to adjust the scale with the Amalgamated Association from January to the middle of June, but it was a failure. These men in their application to the court style themselves 'employes.' They are not employes of the Carnegie Steel Company, and it is not likely that any of the men whose names are signed on the petition ever will be again. We gave these men notice that if they did not return to work within a stipulated time, their names would be stricken from our lists of employes. They did not return, and hence are in no sense our employes."[413] The response was predictable: the Act was toothless, and with no restriction on the Carnegie's ability to fire the union members at will, Brennen and the AAISW had little leverage left to them, other than the impact of public opinion.

The following day, August 3, was a momentous day for Henry Clay Frick. His infant son Henry, Jr., who was born just two days after the battle of Homestead, died.[414] And he received news that he was being charged with murder.

The workers made good on Brennen's threats and had retaliated. Hugh Ross, one of the ex-committee members who had also been indicted for murder upon information provided by Francis Lovejoy, made information before Alderman King of the South Side, charging Henry Clay Frick, Francis Lovejoy, brothers William and Robert Pinkerton of the Pinkerton National Detective Agency, and several other corporate officers and supporters of the Pinkertons (a total of twelve men in all), with the murder of four Homestead workers. Interestingly enough, Philander Knox was not charged. It would not be unreasonable to assume that Knox's good fortune was a result of professional courtesy.

Brennen and Cox made some effort to see that the Carnegie partisans received the same humiliating treatment that the workers had received—a night in jail, at least, followed by a bail hearing—but Knox and his team expedited the bail hearing before Judge Thomas Ewing, the same judge who had dispensed with the defense's theories on behalf of the railroad rioters in 1877. Lovejoy, Leishman and another Carnegie official arrived in court with their attorneys, Phil Knox, John Robb, David Patterson and E.Y. Breck, and waived preliminary examination in order to expedite the bail hearing; in light of Mr. Frick's physical condition after the attack on his life and of the death in his family, Judge Ewing permitted Knox to appear in Mr. Frick's stead.

Judge Ewing asked District Attorney Burleigh the grounds for holding the accused, and Burleigh quickly deferred to Brennen. Brennen began with those who were directly involved in the battle:

Mr. Brennen: Well, we are informed that four of these men that are charged here—possibly five of them—were on the boat.

The Court: If you wish me to take judicial notice of common rumours and newspaper stories, I suppose I understand what you are talking about. ... What is your ground for holding anybody?

Mr. Brennen: Well, that there were four men killed; and that eight of those men (the defendants) were on the boat.

The Court: Where were the men when they were killed—what were they doing?

Mr. Brennen: Well, we say they were not doing anything. ...

The Court: What question was to be decided between these parties? One had an undisputed right to their property; the other had none whatever.

Mr. Brennen: Well, that was a matter that, it seemed to me, would have to be determined in some other way than summarily.

The Court: Well, was there any question about that? That is not the case of one party in possession of a piece of property under claim of right—and the party who claims it, instead of bringing his ejectment or bringing him personally before the magistrate, goes with force to thrust him out. That is not the case.

Mr. Brennen: Well, it occupies a very close relationship to that.

The Court: No, none at all. If you would come home and find me in possession of your house, and holding it where I never had a claim—

Mr. Brennen: Well, your honor does not undertake to say that a man can go out and arm 200 or 300 men and come in and take possession?

The Court: You can take possession of your house, and if I use violence I have to look out for it.[415]

Judge Ewing found a ready distinction between the Carnegie partisans and the workers that justified different treatment: "The former were exercising their rights; the latter were rioters and trespassers, whom it was proper to oppose with arms." Thus, in most cases, prior to their actual arrest, each Carnegie defendant was admitted bail in the sum of ten thousand dollars. The Mellon brothers—Andrew and Richard—posted bail on behalf of Frick and his men. Brennen was cool and detached, at least publicly, stating that "[i]t was proper to release them on bail. We never claimed anything more than murder in the second degree" for Frick and the other Carnegie officials.[416]

Philander Knox, meanwhile, had one more trick up his sleeve. On the suggestion of General Snowden, Frick and his team began to work closely with Pennsylvania Supreme Court Chief Justice Edward M. Paxson, a former Bucks County lawyer and Philadelphia Common Pleas judge who had been serving as chief justice since 1874, on the preparation of charges of treason against thirty-three members of the AAISW's Homestead advisory committee. In a brief submitted for confidential consideration by Chief Justice Paxson, Knox asserted that under the Pennsylvania Crimes Act of 1860, a never before invoked Civil War-era piece of legislation aimed at aiders and abettors to the Confederate cause, the men should be charged with treason because—in Krause's words, "by virtue of their usurpation of civil authority prior to the arrival of the state militia, their denial of the rights of new workers to find employment in the mill, and their abrogation of Carnegie Steel's property rights"—they had waged "war, insurrection, and rebellion against the Commonwealth of Pennsylvania." The maximum sentence under the Act was twelve years in prison.

The Chief Justice took the unusual step of handing down the charges himself at an Oyer and Terminer session in the Allegheny County Court on September 30, delivering a long statement on their underpinnings. "We can have sympathy with a mob driven to desperation by hunger, as in the days of the French Revolution, but we can have none for men receiving exceptionally high wages in resisting the law and resorting to violence and bloodshed in the assertion of imaginary rights, and entailing such a vast expense upon the taxpayers of the Commonwealth," the Chief Justice declared, at once giving an accurate statement of then-current labor law and dismissing Brennen's prior assertions of "European pauper wages." Chief Justice Paxson went on:

> *If we were to concede the doctrine that the employe may dictate to his employer the terms of his employment, and upon the refusal of the latter to accede to them to take possession of his property and drive others away who were willing to work, we would have anarchy ... When a large number of men arm and organize themselves by divisions and companies, appoint officers, and engage in common purpose to defy the law, to resist its officers, and to deprive any portion of their fellow citizens of the rights to which they are entitled under the Constitution and the laws, it is levying war against the state, and the offense is treason.*

He declared bail to be set at ten thousand dollars for each of the defendants, including Hugh O'Donnell and John McLuckie.[417]

Brennen made light of the charges. "I do not believe that the charge will ever be sustained," said Brennen, "because there was no element of treason in the acts of the men. The authorities are plain on the question. There must be a general purpose to destroy and resist all rightful and legal authority. The single act of an individual, or of a mob of men in a case like we have had at Homestead, is described by the laws of the State as riot and as the acts of a mob. ... There must, I say, be a general intent to supplant the authority of the government."[418] Nonetheless, the charges were having the desired impact on the men and on the Homestead community. As the *New York Tribune* observed: "The thought of the State of Pennsylvania interfering in the struggle is frightening the sturdy workers. They would accept with derision murder, riot, or conspiracy suits brought by the Carnegie Steel Company, but to be arrested by the State, and on a charge of treason, is different."[419]

Meanwhile, legal scholars began to thunder at the inappropriateness of the treason charges. In the *American Law Review*, for example, one editorialist was incredulous at the charges. "How the case of the committee of an organized society of laborers in directing a strike, some of the incidents of which involved violations of the law and even a resistance to the constituted authorities of the State, can be dignified into the crime of treason, passes professional comprehension ... We have read the indictment, and it is a mass of stale, medieval verbiage, drawn seemingly from some old precedent not dating later than the reign of William and Mary."[420] Such commentators charged that the indictment was proof of nothing less than the aggrandizement of the private objectives of the Carnegie as public rights.

On October 11, a grand jury empaneled to consider all of the charges and counter-charges in the Homestead case brought in true bills on all counts—murder charges against Frick and his men, and murder and treason charges against O'Donnell, McLuckie and the other strikers.[421]

The strikers turned their attention to national politics as the end of October approached, joining a massive Democratic parade in Pittsburgh and hosting another major parade in Homestead in Grover Cleveland's honor on October 23.[422] Although Pennsylvania went for Harrison, Cleveland decisively carried Homestead in the election on November 8,[423] and was re-elected after a four-year absence from the White House. Pittsburgh Republicans "Corporation" Dalzell and William Stone held onto their seats in Congress (Dalzell had abandoned his run against Senator Quay), while nationally the Democrats held onto a deep majority in the House and gained control of the Senate. Opposition to the McKinley Tariff, with or without attendant "gloating over the dying men at Homestead," had carried the tide for the Democrats.

Ten days after the election, the AAISW released two thousand mechanics and laborers from their pledges to support the strike and permitted them to return to work at Homestead. On November 21, 1892, the Homestead members of the AAISW voted 101 to 91 to give up the strike.[424]

On November 24, Sylvester Critchlow, the first of the Homestead workers to be tried, was acquitted of murder charges. By then, Brennen's team had grown to include Thomas Mercer Marshall and William Reardon, two legendary criminal defense lawyers in Pittsburgh, Major Edward A. Montooth and W.E. Erwin.[425] Critchlow's acquittal set the tone for what would follow in February 1893, when striker Jack Clifford, McLuckie and O'Donnell were all acquitted of murder charges, despite the judges' hostile instructions to their respective juries.

After O'Donnell's acquittal, the *Post* editorialized sarcastically about the treason indictments: "The public, and particularly the legal doctors, would now like to see the treason cases taken up, and a thorough examination by courts and juries of the dictum laid down by Chief Justice Paxson, which has been freely criticized and condemned in the leading law magazines of the country. This legal battle should not end without a treason case. It will be a novelty to the bar and very entertaining to the public, especially as no one believes a conviction would be possible. The chief justice, it is the general opinion, went off at half-cock."[426] With neither side having much to gain from further trials, however, the parties quietly reached a compromise after O'Donnell's murder acquittal, and all remaining charges against both Frick and his men and the strikers were buried. "Homestead's Anxious Dream is Ended," went the headline in the *Post*.[427]

Following the heat of the battle of Homestead, Brennen attempted to use every meager advantage available to him to prolong the acceptance of the AAISW at the Works, but Frick and Knox had managed to outmaneuver him in grand fashion, eventually getting the machinery of justice, at opportune moments, to equate the property rights of the Carnegie Steel Company with the Constitutionally-derived civil rights of United States citizens.

Frick and Knox had fought the most virulent union presence within the Carnegie portfolio, and had won decisively. As historian Jesse S. Robinson observed:

The contest was hard fought, but the Union was crushed. Homestead was its Waterloo.

The organization never rallied its spent forces from this defeat. Gradually it was driven from one mill and then another, until its complete dethronement in the East was consummated by the year 1901.[428]

From its peak membership of twenty-four thousand workers in 1891, by 1898 the AAISW had fallen to ten thousand members.[429] Thereafter, Frick's unrestrained ability to manage the cost of his workforce was a principal driver in the creation of the value of the Carnegie Company, and of the wealth of Frick, Carnegie and their partners. Meanwhile, the union's defeat at Homestead—while inspiring a rash of feverish protests among hardcore labor organizers around the country—thoroughly demoralized the labor movement in the United States. It had proven to the rank and file that the deck was stacked against them, just in time for the Depression of 1893 and the rising unemployment that followed.

Pittsburgh's Carnegie Steel Company, the most important company in the world, had weathered a terrific battle against organized labor. Now, with its lawyers in tow, it would face an arguably even greater challenge—internecine strife. Carnegie and Frick were squaring off for their own battle.

GILDED TWILIGHT, IN FOUR ACTS — IV. THE GREATEST LAWSUIT, AND THE DEAL OF THE CENTURY

In September 1893, James H. Smith, a little-known Pittsburgh lawyer with a modest practice, paid a visit to President Cleveland's new Secretary of the Navy, Hilary A. Herbert. Smith carried with him a letter of reference that confirmed that he was "reputable." The lawyer explained to Secretary Herbert that he represented himself and four employees of the Carnegie Steel Company who had in their possession "information which would be valuable to the Government, relating to frauds then being perpetrated" and that they would provide such information to the Government for a fee.[430]

Apparently Smith had already delivered a note to Henry Clay Frick himself, making a similar offer, but Frick dismissed the proposition, believing it to be a specious blackmail threat from a group of disgruntled Homestead employees.

Secretary Herbert told Smith that there was no money available, but offered that if the information led to the recovery of money from the Carnegie, a portion of that money might be paid to the informants. Smith, who stressed that if the identity of the employees were known to the Carnegie they might be subject to reprisals, proceeded to furnish the information to Secretary Herbert.

Carnegie never liked working on government contracts—he was impatient with the red tape and the bureaucratic rigidity—but President Harrison had appealed to Carnegie's patriotism and convinced him to take on a large contract for armor plating for the U.S. Navy.[431] To fulfill the contract, an armor plate mill was installed at Homestead just prior to the strike. Smith and his clients presented documents to Secretary Herbert which allegedly proved that the superintendents in the armor plate mill at Homestead were filling in fissures in the steel plates and re-treating the ones that were to be inspected by the Naval inspectors. While the activity violated government specifications, as historian David Nasaw asserts, the fissures did not mean that the plates were weak, and all "blowholes" were routinely plugged in the steel production process to create a smooth surface.[432] Nonetheless, because the secret re-treating led to premiums being paid to Carnegie Steel for superior work, Secretary Herbert set up his own board of inquiry to investigate the charges, and levied a fine of fifteen percent of all money Carnegie had received on the declined armor, and all premium payments, amounting to about two hundred thousand dollars.

Frick went to Washington in December to meet with Secretary Herbert, where he received word of the fine. He immediately made a personal appeal to President Cleveland. Andrew Carnegie, at home in New York after months away in Europe, was outraged. He joined Frick, attorney Philander Knox and his armor expert, Millard Hunsiker, on a trip to Washington on December 17 to meet with Secretary Herbert and President Cleveland. Carnegie and his team were particularly incensed that Smith's information was accepted without an opportunity for counter-argument. "We have been accused, tried, found guilty & sentenced without ever having been heard," Carnegie wrote in a personal follow-up note to President Cleveland. The Democrat, reluctant for political reasons to show any indulgence to the company that brought the Pinkertons into Homestead, nonetheless dropped the fine to ten percent, or about $140,000.[433] Smith and his clients collected $35,121.23 as bounty for their information, and it seems that Smith himself probably took over six thousand dollars of the reward.[434]

The "armor fraud" incident was irresistible fodder for the press, already hungry for more dirt about the tyrannical steel firm, and Congress felt moved to launch its own investigation of Carnegie Steel's practices. Carnegie Steel was under a microscope now, and Andrew Carnegie blamed Homestead. "It had to come out, our enemies—Amalgamated Association—bound to use it," Carnegie wrote to Frick. "The ghost of Homestead is not yet laid."[435] The scandal upon scandal began to weigh on Carnegie, who felt particularly aggrieved, having begun to imagine himself, in his semi-retirement, as an industrial philosopher capable of empathizing with both employee and employer. He was even planning a book on the proper relations between labor and capital. Homestead indelibly tarnished his reputation. While he continued to congratulate Frick on his great victory at Homestead, he privately began to apologize to his correspondents for the tragedy of Homestead—including his friend, the former British Prime Minister William Gladstone, to whom he wrote that the decisions made at Homestead were Frick's alone and that he was kept out of the loop.[436] As his reconstruction of events became more and more public, the chasm between Carnegie and his once trusted business partner began to open like a sore.

For the next several years, although he spent significant periods away from Pittsburgh and the day-to-day operations of the steel business, Carnegie seemed determined to nudge Frick toward taking more vacation or permitting his role in Carnegie Steel to be reshuffled. One of Carnegie's gambits was to propose that Frick permit the merger of H.C. Frick Coke Company, Frick's one-time start-up enterprise in which Carnegie had taken a stake back in 1882, with that of a competitor, William J. Rainey. Among

Carnegie's objectives, of course, was to dilute Frick's ability to control the Coke Company. Frick was incensed when he learned that Carnegie had met with Rainey privately in Washington, D.C. to discuss the matter without telling Frick, and on December 18, 1894, Frick tendered his resignation as chief executive officer.[437] During the discussions that followed, Carnegie mistakenly sent a letter intended for Henry Phipps about Frick to Frick himself, declaring that Frick was "not well" and that he was "breaking down and ... not of former power."[438] Frick unleashed upon Carnegie in a response to the misdirected correspondence:

> *I desired to quietly withdraw, doing as little harm as possible to the interests of others, because I had become tired of your business methods, your absurd newspaper interviews and personal remarks and unwarranted interference in matters you knew nothing about. It has been your custom for years when any of your partners disagreed with you to say they were unwell and needed a change, etc. I warn you to carry this no further with me but come forward like a man and purchase my interests, and let us part before it becomes impossible to continue to be friends.*

Frick's resignation was finally accepted by the Board of Managers of Carnegie Steel on January 11, 1895, and he was succeeded by his aide John Leishman (who was in turn succeeded by a Carnegie loyalist, Charles Schwab, two years later), but Frick remained as chairman. A portion of his holdings was liquidated to cover some debts he owed to Carnegie for his acquisition of partnership interests, leaving him with six percent of the Company.[439] The two titans, Carnegie and Frick, settled into a somewhat awkward if cordial détente.

That détente, however, was defined, at least in Carnegie's mind, by legal relations that were put in place in 1887. Shortly after the death of Carnegie's brother, Thomas, from pneumonia, Carnegie was suffering from a case of typhoid fever, and the partners in Carnegie Brothers & Co. decided that they needed to do something to protect the viability of the partnership in the event of Andrew Carnegie's death. Phipps brought in D.T. Watson to draft a limited partnership agreement that came to be known as Carnegie's "Iron Clad Agreement." The distinctive feature of Watson's agreement was an airtight "ejecture clause" that provided that a departing or ejected partner's interest could be acquired at book value, upon the vote of three-quarters of the other partners, both by number and in-interest. Carnegie purposely engineered a relatively low book value for Carnegie Steel; partners estimated that the book value of the Company was set at perhaps one-fifth to one-third of the market value of the firm, which would have permitted the partners to provide for a relatively inexpensive and orderly buyout of Carnegie's estate in the event of his death.[440]

In Carnegie's hands, however, the "ejecture clause" proved to be handy leverage for weeding out undesirable partners relatively inexpensively. Moreover, depending upon how much of the partnership was being acquired under the ejecture clause, the Company was permitted to pay for the interests in annual installments. Thus, not only were departing partners theoretically underpaid for their interests, but they had to wait years for their money. Finally, as the agreement evolved, Carnegie's own interests were protected from the effect of the ejecture clause, so the agreement became more of a unilateral mechanism for Carnegie's periodic reconsolidation of control over the Company—cycling in loyal junior partners, and forcing out more senior partners who had ceased to contribute or had gotten too big for their britches, in his view.

In 1892, however—just before the battle of Homestead—the partners began to realize that the existing partnership structure was becoming unwieldy and undercapitalized as the Company grew. Thus, a new partnership was formed, called Carnegie Steel Company, Limited, that consolidated all of the Carnegie steel production assets under one partnership with a greater paid-in capital. Carnegie attempted to install another "Iron Clad Agreement" at that time, but several of the partners (Phipps in particular) were against the idea and never executed it. Nonetheless, the firm continued to follow the custom of buying out departing partners at book value, although the partnership did not attempt any ejectures after 1892. As far as Carnegie was concerned, the custom prevailed, even if there was no agreement in place that reflected it. But in 1897, Carnegie decided to hedge his bets on the matter and sent instructions from abroad to the Board of Managers attempting to have a new "Iron-Clad Agreement" formally adopted by the partners. Carnegie's signature was the only one ever appended to the document.[441]

Against this backdrop—with Frick still serving as chairman with day-to-day authority over the running of the business, but with Carnegie continuing to wield influence over the firm from New York or abroad, in part due to a change in the partnership's by-laws, written by Philander Knox at Carnegie's request, that gave Carnegie a veto over any decision of the partnership's Board of Managers[442]—Frick and Carnegie continued to levy their petty offenses against each other for several years.

Concerned about future deadlocks in decision-making, by the entry of J.P. Morgan into the steel market as a well-capitalized, vertically-integrated competitor in 1897, and finally by the prospect of the Company having to pay out untold millions out of its operating funds to the Carnegie estate in the event of Carnegie's death, Frick was anxious to propose a negotiated, fully financed buy-out of Carnegie's interests. In January, after being confronted at his New York residence on "Millionaire's Row" at 5 West 51st Street by Frick, Phipps, Schwab and other another partner, Carnegie's cousin Dod Lauder, Carnegie tacitly agreed to a reorganization.[443] No offer had yet been made, however. Despite the fact that custom dictated that departing partners should be paid book value, Frick knew he would have to do better than book value to satisfy Carnegie, and it appeared that there was a buyer who was willing to pay a great deal more.

Frick received such an offer from William H. Moore, a flamboyant Chicago lawyer with a reputation as a corporate speculator—not at all the kind of buyer Carnegie would have desired to carry on the mission of his industrial child. Yet the opportunity to reorganize the ownership of Carnegie Steel and to continue to participate in its ownership and management without the restrictions imposed by Carnegie appealed to Frick, and so in March 1899, Frick approached Carnegie to suggest a possible sale of Carnegie Steel to an "anonymous" suitor who would value his 58 ☐% interest at $157,950,000, rather than the $29,250,000 he would have received at book value. The suitor, Frick explained, was also requesting a ninety-day exclusive option in order to provide adequate time to make arrangements to complete the deal. Carnegie countered by saying that he was taking a chance by signing an agreement to sell his interests without knowing who the buyer was or whether the buyer had the capital to complete the deal, so he demanded a nonrefundable two million dollar payment for the option. When pressed, Moore and his associate, John "Bet-a-Million" Gates, were unable to come up with more than one million dollars toward Carnegie's demand, but Frick and Phipps each contributed eighty-five thousand dollars (cash that Carnegie promised to refund to his partners, despite the terms of the option), for a grand total of $1,170,000, deposited with Carnegie on May 4, 1899—corresponding to Carnegie's 58 ▢% share of the Company. With the ninety-day option in hand, Moore then proceeded to try to complete the financing necessary for the acquisition.

Unfortunately, two circumstances threw the fate of Moore's bid into turmoil: first, the fact of Moore's identity as the mystery buyer reached Carnegie at his Scottish retreat at Castle Skibo; and second, a prominent member of Moore's syndicate, former three-term New York governor and respected capitalist Roswell P. Flower, had a heart attack after a hearty lunch at the Eastport Country Club and died unexpectedly, putting the Manhattan financial market into a mild panic and making the support for Moore's bid uncertain. Not only was Carnegie incensed by the news that Moore and Gates, whom Carnegie despised as unscrupulous, were behind the acquisition and that Frick and Phipps allegedly stood to gain from the connection, but now it appeared that Moore's financing plan was collapsing. While Moore attempted to recover by casting a wider net for support, Frick understood that it would be necessary to ask Carnegie to extend the ninety-day option, and invited Moore to accompany him to visit Carnegie in Scotland. Moore declined. In June, Frick and Phipps made the long trip to Scotland to convince Carnegie to extend the option past August 4, but Carnegie refused, viewing Frick's collaboration with Moore, in the words of Charles Schwab's biographer Robert Hessen, "as an act of deceit." "Not one hour," Carnegie told them. After the expiration of the option, without any financing for the acquisition in sight, Carnegie pocketed the entire amount of the deposit. He would later brag that his one million dollar renovation of Castle Skibo was a "nice little present from Mr. Frick."[444]

With Carnegie Steel profits soaring toward twenty million dollars near the end of 1899, Carnegie was feeling confident that Frick's assistance would no longer be required to keep Carnegie Steel flourishing. He wasted no time in attacking. At an October 25 meeting of the board of directors of the H.C. Frick Coke Company, Thomas Lynch, the president of the company, announced that officials of Carnegie Steel had informed him that they had "been advised by Mr. Carnegie that he made a permanent contract with Mr. Frick at a fixed price"—alleged to be $1.35—"per ton, commencing January 1st last," and that Carnegie Steel had no intention of paying the higher rates, some as high as $3.25 per ton based on market pricing, that the company had been billing in the interim months. Lynch, however, noted that no written record of any such contract existed, and that Carnegie was apparently alleging that as a partner of H.C. Frick Coke and a partner of Carnegie Steel, he had authority to make such contracts on behalf of both partnerships. Spurred on by Frick's objections, the board passed a formal resolution rejecting Carnegie Steel's claim, and a copy of the meeting minutes went to Carnegie, who regarded the resolution as a "declaration of war."

Meanwhile, Frick had recently acquired some land that he was offering to sell to H.C. Frick Coke Company for $3,500 per acre, $500 per acre less than the appraised price. From the sidelines, Carnegie mumbled that Frick's profit was excessive in light of his partial ownership of the Coke Company. Incensed by the suggestion, Frick countered by saying that he would only go through with the sale if Carnegie offered an apology. "Harmony is so essential for the success of any organization that I have stood a great many insults from Mr. Carnegie in the past, but I will submit to no further insults in the future."[445] Carnegie responded in a letter with a fumbling denial; but behind the scenes, Carnegie confided to Cousin Dod that he had always put up with Frick's outbursts in the past because he needed him to run the Company, but now that Charles Schwab had stepped into the role of president so successfully, there was no reason to remain tolerant of Frick. Carnegie told Dod: "I [have] decided to tell Mr. Frick that I mean divorce under 'Incompatibility of Temper' ..."[446] On December 5, 1899, Frick beat Carnegie to the punch, somewhat ill-advisedly and mostly out of anger, and formally resigned as chairman of the Board of Managers.[447]

Carnegie's response was to move swiftly on the Coke Company, effecting a reorganization of the Board that gave him five out of seven seats. He now sat in control of the coke pricing issue.

Carnegie arrived back in Pittsburgh from New York on the evening of January 7, 1900, and was met at the Union Station by Dod Lauder, as well as by a reporter from the *Pittsburgh Post*. Asked if he planned any management changes, Carnegie replied that "[e]verything is moving along as smoothly as I could wish for. There is nothing whatever in connection with the company's business worth discussing."[448] A few days later, however, the papers finally caught wind of Frick's resignation. "FRICK OUT OF OFFICE" was the headline in the *Post*, although Carnegie was quick to go on record that Frick had "not been retired" by the Board, and that the office of Chairman was being abolished "at Frick's suggestion."[449]

The next day, at a meeting of the Carnegie Steel Board of Managers—without Frick or Phipps present—Carnegie's attention turned back to the unsigned "Iron Clad" Agreement. He proposed that the Board formally withdraw the 1897 "Iron Clad" agreement—the one that had not been signed by any partner other than Carnegie—as it was non-binding. Then, he requested that all partners who had joined the Company since 1892 sign the 1892 "Iron Clad" agreement that Phipps had refused to sign. Now, between the 1892 agreement, and the old, virtually identical "Iron Clad" agreement executed by the partners in Carnegie Brothers & Co., he had a passel of signatures on versions of the "Iron Clad," and an awkward argument that he had the ability to eject Frick as an owner of Carnegie Steel in the event Frick failed to cooperate quietly on the question of the coke prices to be charged by the Coke Company.[450]

The next day, January 9, at the meeting of the Board of Managers of the H.C. Frick Coke Company, Carnegie's five directors outvoted Frick and Thomas Lynch on the question of fixing coke prices at $1.35 per ton for sale to Carnegie Steel, and Frick abruptly quit the room. Carnegie found Frick working in his office in the Carnegie Building the following morning, and attempted to convince Frick to voluntarily accept the fixed price contract. Frick said no, and Carnegie reminded him that he had enough votes to do whatever he wanted anyway. Frick responded by asking Carnegie if he would be willing to sell his interest in the Coke Company at a price fixed by independent appraisal, or if he would be willing to buy out Frick's interests for such a price. Carnegie declined, and added that if Frick persisted in attempting to do harm to the interests of Carnegie Steel, he would have no choice but to call for Frick to be bought out of Carnegie Steel at book value.

Then Frick unleashed himself. As Carnegie later recalled, he "jumped up and clenched his fist and said, 'Why, I expected that, now you will see what a fighter I am,'" thereupon proceeding to hurl a "tirade of personal abuse." "He became wilder," Carnegie reported, "and I was forced to leave."[451] It would be the last time the two titans would ever meet each other face to face.

At an emergency meeting of the Carnegie Steel Board of Managers, Carnegie made good on his threat, extracting from the partners a resolution and notice to Frick requiring his ejecture at book value. The notice, as delivered to Frick, read:

Under the provisions of a certain Agreement between The Carnegie Steel Company, Limited, and the partners composing it, known as and generally referred to as the 'Iron Clad' Agreement, we, the undersigned, being three-fourths in number of the persons holding interests in said Association, and three-fourths in value of said interests, do now hereby request Henry C. Frick to sell, assign and transfer to The Carnegie Steel Company, Limited, all of his interest in the capital of The Carnegie Steel Company, Limited, said transfer to be made as at the close of business January 3, 1900, and to be paid for as provided in said Agreement.[452]

The price under the alleged "Iron Clad" for Frick's interests would be book value, or approximately five million dollars, not the $16,238,000 he might have received under the Moore offer.

The notice was signed by thirty partners of Carnegie Steel Company, Limited, with Carnegie, Dod Lauder, Charles Schwab and Gibson Packer, the Carnegie Steel Company in-house lawyer, at the top of the signatures. Packer's place in the list would indicate that he probably had some hand in drafting the notice, no doubt at Carnegie's request, although it may be assumed that Packer had little independent influence over Carnegie's choice of tactics. James Howard Bridge reports how one unnamed young Carnegie partner explained the apparent willingness of the other partners to join Carnegie in attempting to unseat Frick: "We were simply a band of circus horses, and we all jumped at the crack of the ring-master's whip."[453] Packer, as the son of a Centre County, Pennsylvania farmer, was, like many of the other partners, from a family of modest means; for these junior partners, it was nothing short of miraculous to be invited to be an owner of the greatest company in the world, and yet the miracle came with handcuffs. Even Frick's own secretary, George Megrew, was cowed into signing the notice. Although Packer would have understood the weaknesses of Carnegie's position, he ultimately faced the perennial dilemma of the lawyer who owns equity in his client's business. He had little choice but to fall in line when it came to his personal interest in the matter, and to assist his "client," the Company, in playing its hand.

Conspicuously missing from the approving partners, however, were Frick himself, of course; Henry Phipps; former furnace superintendent H.M. Curry, who, on his deathbed, refused to sign because, as he told Carnegie, "Mr. Frick has never humiliated me;" and Francis Lovejoy, the Company's secretary and a Frick loyalist. Lovejoy did, however, sign an accompanying certification that the notice was a true and correct copy of the original on file with the office of the Company.[454] Ten days later he resigned as secretary, and was replaced by Andrew M. Moreland, the former Company auditor who was the nephew of the ex-city solicitor William C. Moreland.

Carnegie may have been operating without the benefit of strong, independent counsel, but Phipps and Frick had retained their own. Early on Frick had turned to his personal attorney, Willis McCook, as well as engaging John G. Johnson, the well-known Philadelphia corporation lawyer, for ongoing advice. Henry Phipps, meanwhile, who sided with Frick's point of view that the "Iron-Clad Agreement" was no longer valid, retained D.T. Watson, the author of the original "Iron-Clad," for what he saw as an inevitable coming storm. On December 9, 1899, well before the arrival of the buyout notice, Frick also engaged Watson as his counsel. Johnson wrote to Watson: "I had feared that you were to be against Mr. Frick in the fight with Carnegie, and was delighted beyond measure to find that we are to act together."[455] Immediately after receiving the notice from the Company, the well-lawyered Frick wrote and asked for a copy of the alleged "Iron Clad" Agreement under which he was being required to redeem his interests, "the existence of which I deny."[456]

A few days later, Frick responded again with a more formal letter to the Company:

... This is to notify you that all the said action on January 8th, 1900, was taken without my knowledge or consent and I do hereby protest against and object to the same. In some respects the recitals or statements therein contained are untrue in fact ... At the instigation of Andrew Carnegie you now speciously seek without my knowledge or consent and after a serious personal disagreement between Mr. Carnegie and myself, and by proceedings purposely kept secret from me to make a contract for me under which Mr. Carnegie thinks he can unfairly take from me my interest in The Carnegie Steel Company, Limited. Such proceedings are illegal and fraudulent against me, and I now give you formal notice that I will hold all persons pretending to act thereunder liable for the same.

H.C. Frick

The only response he received was a terse note from Charles M. Schwab, dated February 1, 1900, informing him that "pursuant to the terms of the so called 'Iron Clad Agreement' and at the request of the Board of Managers, I have to-day acting as your attorney in fact executed and delivered to The Carnegie Steel Company, Limited, a transfer of your interest in the capital of said Company."[457] The Company had, in effect, just purported to take Frick's equity from him, his payment of roughly five million dollars (based on a book value of $75.6 million) to be made to him whenever Frick might deign to accept it.

For several days, Carnegie appeared to be the victor in his squabble with Frick. Behind the scenes, however, as early as January 23, Frick was working with his dream team, D.T. Watson of Pittsburgh and John G. Johnson of Philadelphia, to prepare a lawsuit—one that would ultimately be nicknamed "The Greatest" of all lawsuits.

Carnegie was aware that a fight was brewing, however, and his first instinct was probably to turn to his most trusted outside lawyer, James Hay Reed. In an interesting display of symmetry, while Frick had come to choose Philander Knox, his headstrong boyhood friend, poker partner and co-developer of the Pinkerton union-busting strategy, as his favored Company legal advisor, Carnegie had come to develop a close kinship with Knox's partner, the prudent and deliberative James Hay Reed.

Judge Reed had come back to the Knox & Reed partnership from a short stint on the federal bench just prior to the battle of Homestead, and Knox & Reed had moved its offices into the Carnegie Building in March 1895. Carnegie handpicked Judge Reed to serve as counsel to his Pittsburgh, Bessemer & Lake Erie Railroad Company. After being less than impressed with the performance of its founder and president, Colonel Samuel B. Dick, in January 1897, Carnegie asked Judge Reed to assume the helm of the Railroad at an annual salary of thirty thousand dollars. Reed continued to practice law, but managed to lead the Railroad successfully during its crucial building stage, extending the reach of its lines 125 miles from Lake Erie to Pittsburgh with the heaviest freight trains in the world, capable of carrying twenty-five freight cars of iron ore, and essentially turning Pittsburgh into a "lake port" for the purposes of Carnegie Steel. Carnegie pushed Judge Reed and his employees hard, but as Carnegie biographer Joseph Frazier Wall observes, the "patient and hard-working" Judge Reed knew what to expect from Carnegie as an employer, and fell into line accordingly. "I know the 'Carnegie' policy is no credit for what has been done but constant spurring up for the future," Judge Reed admitted, and he strove to cultivate Carnegie's trust in his judgment and abilities.[458]

Under the circumstances, however, Knox and Reed had a giant dilemma on their hands. Both their conflicts of interest as counselors to the Company and their personal relationships with Frick and Carnegie, respectively, kept them from playing a direct role in the dispute. Scrambling to find a first-rate legal team, Carnegie visited John G. Johnson in Philadelphia, only to find that Johnson had already been retained by Frick.[459] He settled on retaining George Gordon and William Scott from Congressman Dalzell's firm, Dalzell, Scott & Gordon, as his lead counsel.

On February 13, 1900, the "Greatest Lawsuit" was filed in the Allegheny County Court of Common Pleas. In the suit, Frick asked that the "pretended transfer" of his interest be declared null and void; that the Company be enjoined from interfering with Frick's protection of his ownership interests; that Carnegie be enjoined from conducting the business of the Steel Company without Frick's participation; and ultimately, asking for the Steel Company to be placed in receivership and charging Carnegie with any losses accruing to Frick "by his illegal and fraudulent conduct."

D.T. Watson drafted and released an explanatory statement to the press, large sections of which were picked up verbatim by the Associated Press and reprinted in newspapers and steel industry trade journals around the country. In it, Watson portrayed Carnegie as a mercurial absentee owner, continually interfering with Frick's successful run as president and chairman of the board of Carnegie Steel, and attempting to steal Frick's ownership away through questionable means—"the pretended existence of the so-called 'iron-clad' agreement." In both the press statement and the pleadings, of which he was the principal draftsman, Watson masterfully used the ill-fated 1899 reorganization as evidence of the Company's value, and of Carnegie's greed, by pointing out that Carnegie was attempting to buy Frick's interest at a fraction of the valuation that he himself had agreed upon for his own buyout. Emphasizing the charge of fraud was also central to Watson's strategy, as he confided to Johnson, "even if we get no relief on it, it aids the other parts of the case." Before the suit was filed, he wrote to Johnson:

> [Frick] ought to have the sympathy of the business men of Pittsburgh with him ... I am convinced that the strength of our case lies, in the end, in the proposition that Carnegie is attempting to cheat Frick, that he is attempting to take from him his interest in the Carnegie Steel Company, Limited, at less than its value; that he is doing this dishonestly, and fraudulently and with malevolence toward him. This, if it is true, would tie the business men of Pittsburgh, at least, to Frick, and would, also, be influential with the court.

Not surprisingly, Watson's statement of the case for the press seemed to be aimed at the "business men of Pittsburgh" as an audience. "[F]or Carnegie to attempt this in 1900, through the guise of proposed agreements," wrote Watson in the press statement, "which looked to the honor and well-being of the firm, to gratify his personal malice, was most vicious and fraudulent misconstruction and misuse of the same."[460]

George Gordon declined to spar with Watson in the press, but he did point out that each partner of the Steel Company would have to be personally served with the lawsuit—even the armor expert, Millard Hunsiker, who was in London, and Carnegie himself, who was in Florida visiting his widowed sister-in-law, Lucy Carnegie, at Dungeness, on Cumberland Island.[461]

While the partners were receiving their copies of Frick's pleadings, news of the lawsuit burst out onto the front pages of the nation's newspapers. The *Pittsburgh Times* called the suit "A WAR OF GIANTS ... one of the most startling engagements ever contested in the courts of Allegheny county, or in the courts of the world." Reciting the valuations of the Carnegie Steel Company from the text of the lawsuit, the paper noted that "[t]he figures stagger the imagination. No one can conceive of the enormous sum involved. Leaving out all figures as to the value of the stock, the mere fact that a property can earn $40,000,000 net annually ... makes it a prize that will be fought for in lordly manner. No legal talent is so high-priced but that it will be engaged if it can be of use, and no strategy known to law will be overlooked in the contest."[462] The *San Francisco Call's* headlines blared that Carnegie "SOUGHT TO SWINDLE HIS PARTNER."[463] On the "fabulous profits" of Carnegie Steel, *The New York Times* consulted John W. "Bet-a-Million" Gates of the American Steel and Wire Company, who fueled the fire, stating, "Astonishment is shown at the profits of the Carnegie Steel Company because the average New Yorker has not yet got on to the fact that there are big profits in steel and iron" and opining that that forty million dollar profit estimate for 1900 was, in his opinion, "a very conservative one."[464]

Meanwhile, the labor press seized on the facts and figures of the suit to make the case that the Steel Company's workers were still being treated unfairly. "These profits," wrote an editor of Chicago's *Worker's Call*, "represent all that these workingmen produced and didn't get ... Did Frick and Carnegie produce any of this profit? No. Do they labor? Yes. In what then does their labor consist? In appropriating to their own use the surplus value produced by labor, in fighting between themselves over its division, and occasionally preaching the virtue of 'honesty' and the 'blessings' of poverty for the benefit of those whose product they secure."[465] The *New York People* pointed out that when Mr. Frick felt aggrieved "as a partner," he could fight his battles in the courts, but when four thousand workingmen "partners" felt aggrieved, "[t]hey could not; the mechanism of capitalist law provided no wheel for THEM to turn in their favor. The only wheels that could at all turn in that instance were not accessible to them; these were the police and the militia; and these did turn, and with a vengeance, and ground the 'partner' workingman to dust."[466] The *Haverhill Social Democrat* wearily demurred, however: "[A]s there will be no cessation of the labor-skinning process, whichever one of them wins, the workingman can have no concern as to the outcome of the trial."[467]

Carnegie barely had time to regain his composure from Frick's lawsuit against the partners of Carnegie Steel, and the picture that was being painted of him in public, when he received news from the counsel to the H.C. Frick Coke Company, James S. Moorhead of the Greensburg firm of Moorhead & Head,[j] that the minority shareholders of the H.C. Frick Coke Company were launching a second lawsuit against the Company in Westmoreland County over the coke contract controversy.[468] Faced now with two lawsuits, Carnegie met with Judge Reed and his company team to again discuss the question of appropriate counsel, still stinging from his inability to secure Frick's dream team. "Who is the best trial lawyer we can get?" he asked. Judge Reed suggested that A. Leo Weil of the firm of Weil & Thorp, Rockefeller's Pittsburgh attorney, "might be available immediately and had an outstanding reputation as a trial lawyer." Carnegie immediately sent for Weil, who asked pointed questions that had been on the minds of many members of the Pittsburgh industrial elite. "Can Carnegie Steel Company afford to have everyone in the country, including the Amalgamated Iron and Steel Workers, know that it made $20,000,000 in 1899 and is expected to double that amount in 1900? Next question, do you really want to wash your dirty linen in public? And finally, which one of you gentlemen wants to volunteer to answer questions from the dozens of newspaper reporters at the close of each day's testimony?"[469]

Carnegie did not hire Weil (he ultimately hired the renowned Philadelphia trial lawyers George Tucker Bispham and Richard C. Dale, along with city solicitor Clarence Burleigh, who had prosecuted the Homestead rioters and Frick's assailant Alexander Berkman, to join George Gordon and William Scott on his team), but Weil's queries struck the prevailing chord. The whole of the American industrial and financial elite, it seemed, wanted the giants to settle—from the editors of *The New York Times* to the leaders of the Republican Party. Even George Westinghouse was moved to write to

---

j   The old joke that ran through the Pittsburgh bar was, "If you're in Greensburg and you need a smart lawyer, see Mr. Head. If you need a smarter lawyer, get Moorhead."

Carnegie urging a settlement. Observing that the objective of the suit was to determine the value of Frick's interest, Westinghouse wrote "I believe such a step will be almost a calamity by reason of the fact that the private affairs of your company will undoubtedly be made public. Can I be of any assistance to you in an attempt to adjust the matter? ... Will you allow me to say, at the risk of being considered officious, that this matter is looked upon by mutual friends as not only very harmful to your own interests but to Pittsburgh generally." Westinghouse added: "Mr. Frick has recently spoke to me in such terms that I feel there must be a way to adjust matters between you and him."[470]

Although there was little that an unseated labor union could do with the information about Carnegie Steel's profits, the debate about the tariffs, even after the McKinley Tariff had been repealed in 1894 and replaced with milder protection for the steel industry, was still a political lightning rod. President McKinley himself was now engaged in a reelection campaign; in 1896, he had faced a "free trade" Democrat, William Jennings Bryan, and was likely to face him again in this November's election. With profits such as those being described in the newspapers, did the steel companies still need the protection of a tariff on foreign goods? The "Greatest Lawsuit" was bad business for everyone in the manufacturing and steel industries, bad news for the financiers on Wall Street, and bad news for the president.

Nonetheless, there would be no talk of settlement until Carnegie had an opportunity to answer Frick's charges for the benefit of the public. Despite his initial efforts surrounding hiring the right lawyers, with Judge Reed out of the picture, the *Pittsburgh Post* reported that Carnegie was "not trusting the management of his suit entirely to his counsel." He had taken charge of dictating the answer to Frick's complaint, said the *Post*, with "the attorneys simply taking his suggestions and putting them in legal form."[471] However, according to Ida Tarbell, Carnegie showed his original draft answer to Judge Elbert Gary, president of the rival Federal Steel Corporation, during a chance meeting on a railway trip. Judge Gary observed that it was "too abusive" to Frick, and advised Carnegie not to file it in that form. Though disappointed, Carnegie apparently took Judge Gary's advice and scaled back his excoriations.[472]

The final result was a twenty-thousand-word document, filed on behalf of Carnegie and seven of his partners, that purported to meet every detail of Frick's argument with a counter-argument, including an analysis of Henry Clay Frick's temper and its effect on the Company. The answer as filed stated that since January 1895, Frick's functions were largely advisory, and that the partners "would be glad to have him continue the business of the association, had not he himself forced trouble and rendered such a condition impossible." Carnegie charged that Frick had an "imperious temper, and attempted to make a personal matter of business differences, giving way to violent outbursts of passion," and that he was not happy with anything less than "absolute power" over the Company.[473] If his own name was to be publicly dragged through the mud, Carnegie was determined to see to it that Frick's would end up just as muddy.

Filing for extensions of time on behalf of some of the other defendants, George Gordon's partner William Scott precipitated remarks from Judge Edwin H. Stowe that the trial would likely not be placed on the calendar until October,[474] setting the stage for settlement talks. Outwardly, however, there seemed to be no hope of bringing the parties to the table. Determined to keep the pressure on Carnegie, D.T. Watson readied yet another lawsuit—this one on behalf of Henry Phipps, calling for an injunction against Carnegie Steel from using company funds for the purchase of Frick's interests. It was Phipps' meeting with Carnegie, however, that laid the groundwork for the beginning of settlement talks. He did not share the same objectives as Frick—as George Harvey writes, Phipps' "grievance was his own, as he had indicated plainly to Mr. Frick himself, and it was based, not upon legal rights, but upon personal honor, mutual friendship and identical interests"[475]—and thus he was the perfect messenger to urge that Carnegie consider putting aside emotions and sitting at the table to determine a fair solution. "I only want what is fair," Carnegie told Phipps.

Watson would not need to file the third lawsuit. Ultimately, Phipps may have softened his old friend Andy for compromise, but Carnegie was also primed with intelligence from the front. Knox and Reed, as partners to each other and as close advisors to Frick and Carnegie, respectively, played an indispensable role in bridging communications on both sides. After huddling with Frick, Knox was candid and firm in his conversations with Carnegie company officials. In a letter to Carnegie, Charles Schwab writes:

> *Knox told me this morning that he had decided to leave for California tonight as he was satisfied that Frick could not be brought to any reasonable position ... The only thing Frick will say is that he thinks the property is worth 250 m. and would rather buy than sell at that figure ... Knox very strongly advised settlement with F on any reasonable basis. Says that if at any time we want to dispose of our reorganized stock[,] proceeding in court to show a low valuation will injure us. Knox evidently gets this from Frick. My own impression is that Frick is much more anxious for a settlement than we are. But I can't help think that reorganization at an early date is the proper step.*[476]

Meanwhile, as Carnegie seethed over Frick's betrayals, Judge Reed acted as Carnegie's paragon of balance and objectivity. Although he would not represent Carnegie in the conflict, Judge Reed visited Carnegie at Dungeness after the suit was filed,[477] and remained in tight communication with Carnegie as Carnegie considered his options. Just how influential Judge Reed's presence in the background discussions was would not be revealed until the settlement agreement itself was ultimately signed.

Frick, upon hearing from Phipps that a window of opportunity had cracked open, said that an offer to buy or sell Carnegie Steel by either party was "useless," and that "the fair thing to do is to make a consolidation of the two companies [Carnegie Steel and H.C. Frick Coke Company] upon terms agreed to by everybody a year ago before the Moore offer was received." In 1899, Frick had proposed that the two companies should merge for a total combined capitalization of something north of $250 million, but Carnegie had at that time turned down the offer. Frick concluded: "That will solve the whole problem justly and honestly. I am willing."[478]

By way of follow-up, on Saturday, March 17, Frick's lieutenant Francis Lovejoy went to New York and joined Schwab, Phipps and Carnegie for a meeting at Carnegie's home on Millionaire's Row. There Phipps proposed, in broad terms, the consolidation of Carnegie Steel and Frick Coke. Carnegie agreed to negotiate upon that concept, and the parties proceeded to plan a secret meeting at the majestic Hotel Brighton on the boardwalk in Atlantic City rather than in New York, where the press would be lying in wait. Carnegie invited the members of the Board of Managers to leave for the shore on Sunday night—preferably with their wives, to disarm suspicion. Frick remained in Pittsburgh, sitting by the telephone to receive updates on the discussions from Francis Lovejoy.[479]

Lovejoy drafted the settlement agreement on Sunday, and the partners met at the Hotel Brighton on Monday morning to review it. With minor modifications, it was accepted by both sides.

The next day, the agreement was ready for execution by the assembled parties, and according to Bridge, Carnegie Steel's newly-engaged corporation lawyer, James B. Dill of New York—the same "millionaire corporation lawyer" who would be accused of losing "all conception of true advocacy" according to the *Central Law Journal* for saying that "the business lawyer of today is a business man"—arrived by train from New York just as the final signature was being placed on the document, to advise the company on how to carry out the settlement that had been reached. *The New York Times* was quick to build a legend around one of the city's own lawyers. Despite the fact that he had arrived after the inking of the settlement, the *Times* reported that "Mr. Dill, it appears, acted at the conference more in the position of arbitrator than as counsel for either side. He labored for days to bring representatives of the opposing interests together, and succeeded with the meeting at Atlantic City ... Mr. Dill briefly reviewed the situation and pointed out the great necessity for avoiding costly litigation." It then described a conversation with Phipps and Carnegie in which he allegedly negotiated a fair price among the parties. The paper also suggested, wholly fancifully, that Frick showed up at the Hotel Brighton to shake Carnegie's hand and sign the agreement himself.[480]

The settlement agreement itself, on the other hand, shows that the parties had affirmatively placed their trust in another lawyer. Being lean on mechanics, Lovejoy's settlement agreement referred to the appointment of a committee "to carry out the details of this Agreement to consist of C.M. Schwab, G.D. Packer, F.T.F. Lovejoy and A.M. Moreland, who shall act by unanimous consent." Failing unanimous agreement on the details of implementing the settlement, the agreement read, "all differences if any will be referred to Judge J.H. Reed, whose decision shall be final."[481] More than simply a gesture, it was a substantive provision that revealed the trust that each of the parties had placed in Judge Reed, and that paid homage to his role in keeping the peace. The contemporary press failed to mention it, but years later his role would be credited, at least in the Pittsburgh newspapers: in 1908, the *Pittsburgh Gazette Times* would report, "Many Pittsburghers having inside knowledge of the now famous clash between Mr. Carnegie and Mr. Frick will always give credit for the final settlement to Judge Reed,"[482] and the *Pittsburgh Leader* in 1913 would identify him as "the final arbiter in the conflict," observing that "it was due almost entirely to his efforts that the movement for peace was so successful."[483]

Dill's contribution to the effort was largely in executing the combination of the two companies. Lovejoy's settlement agreement provided for the merger of H.C. Frick Coke with Carnegie Steel, and for a recapitalization of the new combined company in the amount of $320 million. The value of Carnegie's interests in the new entity, a combination of stock and five percent senior bonds, was to be approximately $175 million, whereas Frick's share was to be approximately $31 million, substantially more than the five million dollars he was being offered for his portion of Carnegie Steel. Five days after the settlement agreement was signed, Dill obtained a charter in New Jersey for the new corporation, the Carnegie Steel Company. With the revelation that the new corporation would be chartered in New Jersey rather than in Pennsylvania, the *Pittsburgh Post* lamented, "[T]he shortsightedness of the State Legislature" and its corporate tax policy "has caused a serious loss to the commonwealth. The cost of the Carnegie Company's charter in New Jersey was $33,000, and it will have to pay yearly to that State $11,750." [484]

Meanwhile, it was rumored that Dill received a cool million dollars in fees for his role in carrying out the reorganization. Judge Reed was on retainer, but certainly received nothing for his role in the settlement, for which he was not under any official engagement. On the other hand, it appears that Watson and Johnson had trouble collecting from Frick on a $250,000 flat fee, even after Frick's interest in the new Carnegie Steel Company was valued over thirty million dollars. "I learn from outside sources our friend was almost paralyzed by our letter," wrote Johnson to Watson. After some embarrassment, the Pittsburgh lawyer and the Philadelphia lawyer ended up settling for a total of $150,000—one hundred thousand dollars to D.T. Watson for his role in both the Carnegie Steel and Frick Coke cases, and fifty thousand dollars to John G. Johnson.[485]

As part of the settlement, Frick gave up any right to manage the corporation and was not named to the new board of directors. Charles Schwab was named president and chief executive officer, and Carnegie, although also missing from the list of directors, stood hovering over Schwab's desk as the largest stockholder of the corporation.

Rather than precipitating his retirement, the settlement with Frick seemed to reinvigorate Carnegie. Watching Judge Elbert Gary's furtive vertical integration of raw materials, transportation lines and crude steel production with finished steel manufacturing over at Federal Steel, funded by J.P. Morgan, Carnegie caught the threat in the prevailing winds. Frick, of course, had already worked tirelessly to combine Carnegie's raw materials, transportation and steel production businesses into one smooth-running machine. Schwab, however, began to project that Carnegie Steel would begin to lose its dominance as a supplier to a rival with captive markets for its steel. In July, the overall market for steel tumbled, cutting Carnegie Steel's revenues in half. Carnegie's reaction was to cable Schwab from his telegraph office in the lodge at Castle Skibo. "Crisis has arrived," he wrote, "only one policy open; start at once hoop, rod, wire, nail mills … Extend coal and coke roads, announce these; also tubes. Prevent others building … Have no fear as to result, victory certain. Spend freely for finishing mills, railroads, boat lines."[486] His bitter war with Frick at an end, Carnegie was now waging a commercial war for steel supremacy against Judge Gary, Federal Steel, and J.P. Morgan. At his direction, Carnegie Steel began to build a tube mill at Conneaut, Ohio to compete with the Federal Steel affiliate, National Tube Company in McKeesport, and he even threatened to build a railroad from Chicago to the Atlantic coast to rival the New York Central and Pennsylvania networks.

Viewing Carnegie's activities from afar, Judge Gary tried to convince J.P. Morgan to offer to acquire Carnegie Steel—or to at least combine it with Federal Steel, if "to acquire" the world's greatest corporation may not have been the correct terminology. "I would not think of it," was Morgan's reply. Morgan was skeptical that he could even finance such a move.[487]

On January 9, 1901, eighty-nine men who became millionaires, at least on paper, through the settlement of the Greatest Lawsuit and by the combination of Carnegie Steel and H.C. Frick Coke in April 1900, gathered for a lavish banquet at the Hotel Schenley, between Fifth and Forbes on the edge of Schenley Park in the Oakland section of Pittsburgh. Inside, mounds of American Beauty roses were heaped on the massive T-shaped banquet table, and the arched ceiling of the Hotel Schenley banquet hall was festooned with giant ferns. On the rear wall of the hall, garlanded by fern leaves and palm branches, was a large oil painting of Carnegie himself, who did not attend the event. There would be no sign of Frick or Phipps that evening, either. Judge Reed served as the affable toastmaster during the long night of jubilant toasts in honor of Andrew Carnegie and his great corporation, including one entitled "Expectations," delivered by the company's president, Charles Schwab.[488]

It is quite possible that Judge Reed and Schwab were the only ones among the assembled banqueters, however, who fully realized just how fortunate the eighty-nine Carnegie millionaires were, and who had any inkling as to the prize that awaited them. A mere few weeks before this ostentatious celebration, on December 12, 1900, another very significant dinner was held at the University Club at the corner of West 54th Street and Fifth Avenue in Manhattan. Given in Charles Schwab's honor by two powerful New York bankers, Charles Stewart Smith and J. Edward Simmons (both of the Fourth National Bank), the invitees were a select group of prominent New York bankers, including the most important financier in New York, J.P. Morgan. Judge Reed was also in attendance at the University Club dinner. Schwab, boyish at age thirty-nine, sat next to Morgan—the sixty-four year-old, bull-necked, purple-nosed plutocrat—during dinner, and Reed undoubtedly witnessed the two of them in deep discussion.

When it came time for a speech from the guest of honor, "Mr. Schwab started out by saying that he could not talk about anything but steel," Judge Reed later recalled. "I remember that because he always starts every speech that way." Schwab then proceeded to detail a daring vision for the future of the steel industry. "I talked about the advantages that might be derived from doing a manufacture business of a larger scale than had been attempted," Schwab remembered. "Instead of having one mill make ten, twenty or fifty products, the greatest economy would result from having one mill make one product, and make that product continuously." According to Ida Tarbell, Schwab "talked of metallurgical, mechanical, transportation economies that could be effected by large scale production, and a better location of markets. He talked of the possibilities of expanding the export business." In short, he provided Morgan with the first sensible reasons and road map for a combination of the world's greatest steel production assets that had ever tickled J.P. Morgan's fancy.[489] After Schwab's speech, Morgan took Schwab by the arm, and the two conferred for another half hour.[490]

Several days later, Morgan asked Schwab to prepare a list of the companies—currently controlled by Carnegie or Morgan or whomever (including William H. Moore's National Steel Company)—that should be included in an ideal combination of the country's greatest steel production assets. Schwab assembled his list, with estimates of the value of each company, and presented it to Morgan. After reviewing the list, Morgan told Schwab, "If Andy wants to sell, I'll buy. Go and find his price." Carnegie, though reluctant at first to engage Schwab on the topic after a game of golf at St. Andrews in Westchester County near the end of January, decided to sleep on it, and ultimately wrote down the figure of $480 million on a sheet of paper, with a broad sketch of terms, and handed it to Schwab.

Morgan glanced at Carnegie's handwritten sketch of a deal and told Schwab, "I accept this price." A few days later, Morgan called Carnegie on the telephone at his home on Millionaire's Row and invited Carnegie to come down to his office at 23 Wall Street to shake hands on the proposed transaction. Carnegie, however, thought it "unbecoming" for him to go to Morgan's office, and suggested to Morgan that "it is just about as far from Wall Street to Fifty-first as it is from Fifty-first to Wall. I shall be delighted to see you here at any time." The lucky suitor arrived at 51st Street shortly thereafter and met with Carnegie privately for a mere fifteen minutes. As he left Carnegie's home, he turned and grasped the hand of his host.

"I want to congratulate you," said J.P. Morgan to Andrew Carnegie, "on being the richest man in the world."[491]

At the beginning of February 1901, the great combination being not yet public, Carnegie called his trusted advisor in Pittsburgh, Judge Reed, and asked him to come to New York to negotiate the mortgage that would secure the $225 million in senior bonds that Carnegie would be receiving in the combination, as well as the documents for the acquisition of the rest of the interests of Carnegie Steel. Judge Reed arrived in New York and ensconced himself within Morgan's Wall Street offices for the next several weeks, working closely with Morgan's lawyer, Francis L. Stetson of Stetson, Jennings & Russell (subsequently Davis Polk & Wardwell) and popping "in and out of Mr. Morgan's office all the time," as he recalled.

As February wore on, rumors of the impending combination began to leak into newsprint. Meanwhile, as Morgan and his team worked to complete deals with the other participants in the combination—including National Steel, American Steel Hoop Company and American Tinplate Company—Morgan suddenly realized that all he had with Carnegie was a handshake. "[H]e had not a scratch of the pen from Mr. Carnegie with which he could hold him or his estate if he died," said Judge Reed. "You men go up the street as fast as you can and get me something," Morgan told Reed and Stetson. When the lawyers arrived at 51st Street, Carnegie led them into his library, where in a small side room they found a young man from Carnegie Steel who was going through basketfuls of "begging" letters—"from people wanting wooden legs, everything imaginable," Judge Reed said—and asked him if he was a stenographer. He said that he was and Carnegie told him, "You take a letter for these gentlemen." The lawyers dictated a letter of intent to the young man, occasionally interrupted by Carnegie with his own interlineations, and Carnegie signed it. "[W]e took the original down with us to Mr. Morgan," recalled Judge Reed, "and he seemed quite relieved."[492]

On March 1, 1901, a series of agreements with J.P. Morgan & Co., as underwriter, and the United States Steel Corporation, a newly-formed New Jersey corporation, providing for the issuance of preferred and common stock and bonds to the holders of interests in each of the constituent companies, were signed and accepted by the representatives of Federal Steel, Carnegie Steel, National Steel and the rest of the parties to the great combination. The new company, which came to be known as U.S. Steel, had an initial capitalization of $1.1 billion. It was the first billion dollar company in the history of the United States, and on the day of the closing its capitalization represented seven percent of the gross national product. Carnegie's bonds, along with those of Cousin Dod and his brother's widow Lucy—totaling almost three hundred million dollars in value—were deposited in a custom vault at the Hudson Trust Company of Hoboken. Frick's interests would be valued at $61.5 million, and the wealth of the eighty-nine Carnegie millionaires who had toasted the night away at the Hotel Schenley in January had nearly doubled in one year.

Several days after the closing, Andrew Carnegie stopped by 23 Wall Street to bid adieu to his life's work before beginning a European holiday. Judge Reed accompanied him, "as a sort of bodyguard." Again, the meeting between the two tycoons was short. Judge Reed recalled, "I remember Mr. Carnegie saying as he left the room, 'Now, Pierpont, I am the happiest man in the world, I have unloaded this burden on your back, and I am off to Europe to play.'"[493]

Judge Reed, for his part, was on a train back to Pittsburgh, the burden of steel still on his shoulders. "It is said, perhaps apochryphally [sic], that Reed had been offered the presidency of the Steel Corporation," according to Ralph Demmler[494]; another rumor suggested that he was Charles Schwab's choice to serve as chairman of the board.[495] He nonetheless accepted Morgan's invitation to serve as a director of U.S. Steel, at Carnegie's suggestion, and in 1903 he assumed the chairmanship of Carnegie Steel, its major subsidiary. Schwab would serve as the first president of U.S. Steel, and Judge Gary would serve as its first chairman of the board.

Reed was, for the time being, more concerned about the future of his law firm. Only a couple of weeks after Andrew Carnegie left Morgan's office and headed to Europe, Judge Reed's partner Philander Knox accepted the re-elected President McKinley's invitation to serve as United States Attorney General. Both Frick and Carnegie had recommended Knox for the post, but Knox was already well known to McKinley. Perhaps fittingly, they had first met around 1871 when McKinley, who was serving as District Attorney in Alliance, Ohio, put young Philander Knox on the witness stand as a "victim" of illegal alcoholic beverage sales to Mount Union College students in the prosecution of a local tavern owner.[496] Shortly after Knox's appointment, on July 1, 1901, the firm sent out an engraved announcement that the remaining partners had decided to rename the firm as "Reed Smith Shaw & Beal."[497] Even if it were true that Judge Reed had been offered the leadership of the first billion dollar corporation, it was apparent that the Judge felt a great deal of personal loyalty and obligation to his law partners in Pittsburgh.

Around the Pittsburgh bar, the shockwaves from the formation of U.S. Steel began to be felt, at first almost imperceptibly to some. For Billy Brennen, the formation of

U.S. Steel posed an urgent question: how would this unprecedented concentration of market power in the steel industry impact the slow but steady renewal of the AAISW? He would face the uncomfortable answer soon enough. Meanwhile, A. Leo Weil saw the handwriting on the wall as early as 1899, when he was approached by two clients for whom he served as outside general counsel, the American Sheet Steel Company and the American Tinplate Company, to prepare option agreements for their potential sale to a third party. In the thick of the activity surrounding Morgan's combination in the early months of 1901, Weil was asked to prepare and review documents providing for the acquisition of these companies as part of the formation of U.S. Steel. "Leo knew that once they became a part of U.S. Steel," wrote his grandson Andrew, "they would no longer be his clients. The attorneys for the U.S. Steel Corporation would take over."[498]

Other Pittsburgh lawyers were undoubtedly having this same feeling, as though a giant ship were sailing away and leaving them behind on the dock to watch. Even the James H. Smiths of the world would be affected, their potential bounties being reduced as their proximity to industrial power began to recede. Over the next several decades, as the sphere of influence over the steel industry gradually shifted from Pittsburgh to New York—from Carnegie and Frick, to J.P. Morgan and the New York Stock Exchange, from the era of building an industrial powerhouse and its corporate machinery to the era of feeding the cosmopolitan financial empire around the provincial industrial core—the elite members of the Pittsburgh corporate bar would ultimately experience a humbling change in their identity. As Leo Weil may have seen it, there were still many important companies headquartered in Pittsburgh, but a pattern had been established; an entrepreneur's most likely exit, his chance to go "to Europe to play," was going to be routed through Manhattan. There would still be important work to be done for the steel corporations in specialties of the law that were more germane to the locale, such as those connected with the people (labor) and the land bound up in steel production in and around Pittsburgh and in the Monongahela and Ohio valleys. And there were an inordinate number of ill-framed, white-vested millionaires now walking around Pittsburgh, each with their own wills, trusts, divorces, scandals, and sundry other legal issues.

For one brief, shining moment, however, before the full effect of such a shift would be felt, the corporation bar of Pittsburgh did, in fact, enjoy national power and prestige that was unmatched by almost any other group of lawyers anywhere in the country, save for Manhattan. Their almost biblical exploits—their expert navigation through an apocalyptic flood in Johnstown, a bitter war on the Monongahela, and a battle of two terrible giants standing astride Grant Street, only to emerge on the lofty summit of a billion-dollar Mount of Olives—gave them a kind of legendary status, for a time, as the twentieth century opened.

PART III

THE PROGRESSIVE ERA BAR, 1902-1942

THE PROGRESSIVE ERA BAR, 1902-1942

On Independence Day in 1902, an estimated half million people gathered at Pittsburgh's Schenley Park to see and hear President Theodore Roosevelt, who made his way from Union Station to the speaker's stand in a jubilant holiday parade. As *The New York Times* reported:

> *Flags and bunting fluttered everywhere along the course of the parade. People hung themselves from windows of tall skyscrapers, yelling themselves hoarse in greeting of the Nation's Chief Executive. The greatest ovation came as the line passed up canyon-like Fifth Avenue to the top of Grant's Hill. Tall buildings on either side of the street offered fine vantage points for spectators. Every window in the immense buildings was filled with enthusiastic people, women predominating ... As the President and those in carriages passed in review the band struck up the stirring strains of "Hail to the Chief." The music was fairly drowned by the cheering of the multitude of 200,000 persons in the stand and occupying vantage points on the amphitheatre-like hillside which rose in front.[1]*

After a half century in which Pittsburgh industrialists such as Carnegie, Frick and Westinghouse created the world's largest corporations and amassed dizzying wealth and power amid the strife borne of Johnstown, Homestead and the "world's greatest lawsuit," Roosevelt sounded a clarion call, almost unnoticed, that would change the course of the legal profession. The Republican president observed:

> *Especially great, especially difficult, are the problems caused by the growth and concentration of great individual, and above all, great corporate fortunes. It is immensely for the interests of the country that there should be such individual and corporate wealth as long as it is used right, and when not used right then it becomes a serious menace and danger.*

The instruments and methods with which we are to meet these new problems must in many cases themselves be new, but the purpose lying behind the use of these methods of those instruments must, if we are to succeed, be now, as in the past, simply in accord with the immutable laws of order, of justice, and right.

He continued: "We may need, and in my belief, will need, new legislation conceived in no radical or revolutionary spirit, but in a spirit of common sense, common honesty, and a resolute desire to face facts as they are." Fervent applause by the assembled Pittsburghers punctuated his remarks.[2]

Perhaps no more perfect irony was connected with the celebration than the fact that sitting at the president's right hand during his rhetorical testing of the appetite for legal and economic reform in America was his Attorney General, Pittsburgh's own Philander Chase Knox—the man who helped Henry Clay Frick send a barge full of Pinkerton detectives down the Monongahela to do battle with the union at Homestead. Knox's sponsor to the job, President William McKinley, was assassinated by a man who called himself an anarchist in September 1901, and now Knox served at the pleasure of a chief executive who wanted to stimulate reform.

There was no avoiding the fact that Pittsburgh corporate lawyers had come to occupy a preeminent station in American life by the beginning of the twentieth century. In 1902, there was a Pittsburgh corporate lawyer on the United States Supreme Court (George Shiras), a Pittsburgh corporate lawyer on the House Ways and Means Committee (John Dalzell) and a Pittsburgh corporate lawyer serving as United States Attorney General (Philander Knox). Another young Pittsburgh lawyer, Henry M. Hoyt, Jr., was serving as Solicitor General. Pittsburgh lawyers inhabited powerful positions within each of the three branches of the federal government, and it was anything but a coincidence. The meteoric rise of Pittsburgh as the nation's industrial mecca, and the roles played by Pittsburgh lawyers in facilitating, nurturing and protecting that rise, had garnered the members of the nineteenth century Steel Bar a measure of respect that would be only be matched, in their day, by the respect shown to the members of the Manhattan bar. Over the prior twenty-five years, Pittsburgh lawyers had played a major role in defining the rules and the culture of the corporation as an institution within American business, as evidenced not only by their parts in the sculpting of the Pennsylvania Railroad and the Carnegie Steel Company, and U.S. Steel—three of the largest corporate businesses the world had ever seen—but in countless others. They had shown themselves to be among the most sophisticated practitioners in the country, capable of outmaneuvering labor's armies at every turn. They had essentially mapped the battlefield between capital and labor, and they had prepared the scene for the extraordinary changes that were then formulating in the mind of President Theodore Roosevelt.

What would follow, through the Roosevelt and subsequent presidential administrations during the next decades, would be a period in which federal legislative reform would be the driving force that would not only change the way the nation viewed corporations, labor, wealth and capital, but that would also shape the Pittsburgh bar. Led by profound changes in such areas as labor law and antitrust law, Pittsburgh would become a ferocious battleground for lawyers, perhaps the country's most active battleground—with big firm Pittsburgh lawyers who would continue to defend the battlements of the tycoons' legacies, lawyers from Pittsburgh who joined forces with the government to make reform a reality, radical Pittsburgh lawyers who would shape their practices into political statements, and small-firm and sole practitioners in the city, who found in the new federal legislation a new catalogue of rights, new areas of specialty within the law, new causes of action, and new opportunities for individual clients seeking to redress wrongs that had not even been recognized by the jurisprudence of the prior century.

In the first few decades of the twentieth century, Pittsburgh was an "onward and upward" city of business, and this spirit was both reflected and magnified by the city's changing downtown landscape. Where once the 249-foot courthouse tower and the thirteen-story Carnegie Building dominated the downtown skyline, the businessmen of Pittsburgh—like the medieval patricians of San Gimignano—built a forest of towers to celebrate their successes. Henry Clay Frick jammed his twenty-story Frick Building right next to the Carnegie Building, blocking its view of the courthouse, in 1902. The twenty-seven-story Farmers Bank Building opened that same year at the corner of Fifth Avenue and Wood Street, as did the thirteen-story Bessemer Building on Sixth Avenue. Thereafter, new construction went rampant: George Jay Gould erected his Wabash Railroad Terminal and office building at Liberty and Ferry in 1904; in 1906, the Frick Annex and the Benedum-Trees Building, nineteen stories each, and the twenty-one-story Commonwealth Building, were built; in 1907, the twenty-one-story Union National Bank Building and the twelve-story Century Building; in 1908, the Jones & Laughlin Building on Ross Street; in 1910, the twenty-five-story Oliver Building; in 1912, the sixteen-story First National Bank Building; in 1913, the twenty-story Bell Telephone Co. of Pennsylvania Building; in 1916, the William Penn Hotel; and in 1917, the Union Trust Building and the Chamber of Commerce Building. The twenty-one-story Law & Finance Building and the twenty-four-story Lawyers Building were both completed in 1928. By the time of the stock market crash of 1929, the skyline was topped by two more giant structures: the thirty-seven-story Grant Building and the thirty-two-story Koppers Building.[3]

With the Great Depression came an increase in the federal presence in Pittsburgh that also transformed the look and feel of downtown, most formidably in the federal stone fortresses that weighed down, almost as a symbolic counterbalance, the north end of Grant Street—the massive U.S. Post Office and Courthouse, commenced in 1931 and completed in 1934, and the Art Deco-style Pittsburgh branch of the Federal Reserve Bank of Cleveland, begun in 1930 and opened in 1933. The entire socio-political drift of the era could be seen, if one were paying attention, in Pittsburgh's downtown construction sites.

The mechanisms of that drift, the works of "new legislation" that President Theodore Roosevelt prophesied in his 1902 Pittsburgh speech, were already having an impact on the attorneys of Pittsburgh, and not just in the area of labor and antitrust, well prior to the Great Depression and the New Deal of Theodore Roosevelt's fifth cousin, President Franklin D. Roosevelt.

Probably the most far-reaching federal enactment, creating a whole industry of Pittsburgh lawyers with the stroke of a pen, was the ratification of the Sixteenth

Amendment to the United States Constitution, paving the way for a permanent federal personal income tax. Interestingly enough, it was that "porcelain egg" of a Pittsburgh corporation lawyer, Philander Knox, who, serving as President Taft's Secretary of State in 1913, stood in the position of declaring that the Sixteenth Amendment had been cleared by the requisite state approvals and had become the new law of the land. In doing so, Knox has earned a century's worth of ire from anti-tax polemicists, some of whom have claimed that Secretary Knox declared the ratification of the Sixteenth Amendment "fraudulently"—in that his departmental solicitor, J. Reuben Clark, Jr., had provided him with a sixteen-page memorandum detailing defects in various state ratifications—notwithstanding that the memo itself, however, does conclude with the recommendation that the Secretary should "issue his declaration announcing the adoption" of the Amendment.[4] The legend has lived on as a stridently presented artifact in a few unsuccessful tax appeal decisions.

Whether or not Secretary Knox personally usurped constitutional authority (and the courts have not bought the argument[5]), some of his good friends among the white-vested millionaires of Pittsburgh did not fare well by it. One of Knox's poker companions, the former Secretary of the Treasury Andrew Mellon, was a casualty of federal tax enforcement during a two-year civil suit beginning in 1935, when it was charged that Mellon's three million dollar gift to a trust in 1931 did not support a charitable tax deduction. By the 1930s, the Reed Smith firm had already begun to build a practice area around federal tax law, led by William Seifert, who recruited not only lawyers but tax accountants to assist the firm's wealthy individual clients in both litigation and planning with regard to federal income, estate and gift tax matters. When Andrew Mellon went to court to defend his 1931 charitable deduction, he did so keeping Seifert, his partner William Wallace Booth and a Reed Smith tax accountant, Alvar G. Wallerstedt, busy for a few years, along with Paul G. Rodewald from the Smith Buchanan firm and a battery of Washington attorneys from the Hogan firm. Mellon was eventually exonerated by the Board of Tax Appeals, a few months after his death, in 1937.[6]

Philander Knox was back in the U.S. Senate when another sweeping piece of federal legislation was passed, the act proposing the Eighteenth Amendment to the United States Constitution, providing for a nationwide ban on the sale and production of alcoholic beverages. Although personally opposed to the idea of Prohibition,[a] Knox was nonetheless one of the last minute swing votes in favor of the submission of the Eighteenth Amendment to the states,[7] and it was deemed to be ratified in January 1919. Before liquor would be declared contraband, however, Knox did take home twenty cases of Old Overholt Whiskey from his friend Henry Clay Frick, whose family owned an interest in the distillery.[8]

Prohibition meant more work for Pittsburgh's lawyers of every stripe. Edwin W. Smith and George Shaw of Reed Smith helped to secure the Pittsburgh Brewing Company's right to produce and sell near-beer, thus helping it to eke out an existence and survive

---

[a] We may recall that Knox met his political sponsor, William McKinley, after a night of binge-drinking in Alliance, Ohio.

the Prohibition era.[9] Billy Brennen, noted for his skills as a criminal defense lawyer since the labor conspiracy cases of the 1880s, scored an acquittal for Sam Engelsberg—the brother of druggist, politico and noted Pittsburgh bootlegger Joe Engelsberg—who was accused of selling 150 gallons of whiskey in one of the earliest cases brought in the Western District of Pennsylvania under the Wartime Prohibition Act, the predecessor of the enabling legislation for the Eighteenth Amedment, known as the Volstead Act.[10] The crime wave that surrounded the activities of some bootleggers in Pittsburgh—including the murders of rival bootleggers that splashed across the headlines of Pittsburgh newspapers—kept local prosecutors and defense lawyers busy as well.

Despite numerous federal prosecutions under the Volstead Act locally, as well as the creation of a large national apparatus for enforcement—a Prohibition Bureau of 2,278 employees by 1930[11]—Prohibition was spectacularly unsuccessful in Pittsburgh. Two successive attorney-mayors of Pittsburgh, William A. Magee (serving his second non-consecutive term in office, from 1922 to 1926) and Charles Kline, both did little to help to enforce the Volstead Act locally. Kline was openly disrespectful of the law, claiming that Prohibition was "regarded as abnormal from Maine to California."[12] As a consequence, Pittsburgh was considered to be an open city, "wet enough for rubber boots," as one commentator put it.[13] In June 1928, federal frustration with Pittsburgh's local noncooperation came to a head, when the chief agent of the Fourth District of the Prohibition Bureau, Captain John D. Pennington, working with U.S. Attorney John D. Meyer and his staff, secured indictments against 167 individuals throughout Pittsburgh in what came to be known as the "Rum Ring" conspiracy cases. The accused—among whom numbered the superintendent of the Pittsburgh police, three police inspectors, two police magistrates, ten police lieutenants, five ward chairman and an assortment of city workers and local politicians—were said to be part of a well-oiled machine that helped to shield from prosecution the friendly liquor purveyors who paid the appropriate bribes to city officials, and to harass and focus enforcement efforts on those who did not.[14] The inquiry, which represented the most notable exercise of federal authority aimed at local officials in the Pittsburgh area since the Whiskey Rebellion, fell short of prosecuting Mayor Kline; it would be left to local prosecutors to launch their own inquiry into Mayor Kline's activities.

By the end of the 1920s, even some of Pittsburgh's leading temperance advocates, such as attorney Simon T. Patterson, leader of the Pittsburgh chapter of the Crusaders, were coming out against Prohibition, actively working for its repeal so that the issue could be regulated at the state and local level.[15] While Pennsylvania's governor, Gifford Pinchot, was an ardent "dry," Pennsylvania became one of the last of the required number of states to ratify the Twentieth Amendment on December 5, 1933. Four days before the sale of liquor became legal again in Pennsylvania, Governor Pinchot called a special session of the general assembly to consider the creation of a Pennsylvania Liquor Control Board to "discourage the purchase of alcoholic beverages by making it as inconvenient and expensive as possible."[16] Although the federal prosecutions would cease, Pennsylvania's tough replacement regulations created "liquor law" as an area of legal specialization in the state.

One of the lasting legacies of both the ratification of the Sixteenth Amendment and the Prohibition era in Pittsburgh, however, was the creation of a growing permanent class of professional federal government lawyers in Pittsburgh—somewhat hermetically sealed from the bar at large, pitched against the interests of Pittsburgh lawyers representing Pittsburgh clients on issues relating to the new federal regulations. The trend began in 1896, when Congress provided for U.S. Attorneys to be paid regular salaries by the federal government rather than earning their fees on a case-by-case basis.[17] In 1909, the federal prosecutor's office in Pittsburgh consisted of the U.S. Attorney, two assistant attorneys and one clerk; in 1916, the office had been enlarged to include the U.S. Attorney, three assistant attorneys, two clerks and two "special assistants" hired to help with specific cases; and by 1929, there were at least five assistant attorneys in the U.S. Attorney's office.[18]

Although some government lawyers enjoyed careers in private practice in Pittsburgh following their government service, career mobility was often interdepartmental. A young lawyer named L.B. Griffith, for example, who was serving as a junior attorney in the Internal Revenue Service stationed in Pittsburgh, was transferred in 1926 to serve as counsel for the Fourth Federal Prohibition District in Scranton.[19] Louis Graham, U.S. Attorney for the Western District of Pennsylvania from 1929 to 1933, was formerly chief counsel to the Prohibition Bureau in Pittsburgh[20]; he later served in Congress. Many of the rest of the U.S. Attorneys from the period were not Pittsburgh attorneys, but were appointed from other parts of Western Pennsylvania—E. Lowry Humes from Meadville, R. Lindsay Crawford from Greene County, D.J. Driscoll from St. Marys, Horatio Dumbauld from Uniontown[21]—thereby creating something of a sense of distance between the resident chief federal prosecutors and the members of the Pittsburgh bar, an unavoidable "us versus them" posture when it came to federal issues that would continue to grow thematically throughout the twentieth century.

Meanwhile, the infrastructure that was feeding new attorneys into this new array of federal cases was undergoing some significant changes at the beginning of the twentieth century. During the eighteenth and nineteenth centuries in Pittsburgh, elite members of the bar maintained tight control over who might be admitted to practice—first, by deciding who would and who would not be permitted to read law in their offices (i.e., who would be permitted to be educated in the law), and second, by administering the examinations, interviews and character reviews that preceded a new attorney's admission on a local level. With no system for state admission to practice, the local members of the County bar could effectively decide for themselves who would be permitted to practice in the local courts.

The old personal apprenticeship system began to wither away with the rising popularity of law school education during the last half of the nineteenth century, however, leaving local administration of the exam process as the final barrier of defense for those among the elite who jealously guarded the gates of the bar. Law schools, meanwhile, were an instrument of class mobility; while the sons of established practitioners continued to be well-represented among the ranks of students at the law schools, the schools were also populated by the sons of industrious middle-managers from the mills of Pittsburgh, as well as the occasional woman, African American or newly-arrived Italian American. Democratization of the Pittsburgh bar was assisted not only by the growth of the Pitt Law School beginning in 1895, but also by the establishment of the law school at Duquesne University of the Holy Ghost in 1911, with the express mission of accommodating "individuals who might otherwise be unable to study law in a traditional, full-time day program," through an offering of night classes.[22]

In the midst of these organic changes, some leaders of the Pennsylvania bar—among them, George Wharton Pepper, the leading Philadelphia lawyer and a professor of law at the University of Pennsylvania—grew concerned that the apparent arbitrariness in both locally-administered curriculum and admission procedures throughout the state was tarnishing the reputation of the Pennsylvania bar, particularly in light of the movement in other states such as New York and Massachusetts to centralize these matters at the state level. For Pepper, one of the chief aims of centralization was to supply "local examining boards with the results of all that is latest and best in legal education science ... [so that] the local board will be enabled without expenditure of time and labor which it is impossible for them to make, to lay before their students a comprehensive and graded course of studies, and finally to subject their students to a fair but searching examination ..."[23] Meanwhile, Chief Justice Paxson, when asked about the movement toward centralization and uniformity in the admission process, declared, "I consider it extremely desirable that the subject be left in the control of the inferior or local courts ... who are most familiar with the needs of their communities and of the personal fitness of applicants"[24]—not bothering to hide his distress over the democratization of the bar.

These questions were among the primary topics for discussion at the first meetings of the newly-created Pennsylvania Bar Association, in 1895 and thereafter. Initially, much of the discussion focused on potentially adopting both a standard curriculum as well as a state admissions system, but the curriculum debate proved to be too controversial. Reviewing an early curriculum proposal at the 1897 annual meeting of the Pennsylvania Bar Association, Judge Robert Archbald of Lackawanna County complained that he doubted "whether there is any gentleman in this room—I confessedly will admit the same with regard to myself" who could pass the proposed exam,[25] and Judge Morgan Greer of Butler County declared that the proposal "would have ruled out Abraham Lincoln or Ben Wade[b] from practicing law in the State of Pennsylvania."[26]

The supporters of centralizing admissions eventually gave up on the curriculum battle and, in May of 1902, the Supreme Court of Pennsylvania established a State Board of Law Examiners,[27] with the ultimate aim, as described by Robert Snodgrass, a Dauphin County lawyer who led the state bar association's committee on legal education, "to practically dispense with the local Boards of Examiners."[28] At the outset, however, local courts still retained the right to admit lawyers to practice before them; so the new rules initially resulted in a bifurcated system of admissions rather than a centralized one. In Pittsburgh, the local Board of Examiners, chaired in 1902 by John D.

---

b Benjamin F. Wade (1800-1878), lawyer and U.S. senator from Ohio who served as president pro tempore of the U.S. Senate, next in line for the presidency, during the impeachment trial of Andrew Johnson.

McKennan,[29] continued to administer local examinations and to rule on the fitness of various candidates for admission, while giving some measure of deference in admitting new lawyers who had been admitted to practice by the State Board of Law Examiners.

Such deference was not a rubber stamp, however. In 1906, for example, John H. Musgrave, a native Pittsburgher and Yale Law graduate who had practiced in Chicago and Minneapolis before applying for admission in Allegheny County, was denied admission to the bar—despite the fact that he had been issued a certificate of admission by the State Board of Law Examiners—on the basis that he had been living in Pittsburgh for the prior year and a half and could not have been legally actively engaged in the practice of law during that time.[30] Arguing the case before the Pennsylvania Supreme Court, County Board chairman Charles P. Orr and Board secretary E.E. Chalfant also pointed out that Musgrave did not, in the alternative, attempt to comply with local rules which required applicants to either certify that they had passed the state bar examination, or that they had been in active practice in another state for at least five of the prior six years. Since Musgrave's state admission appeared to be premised upon his prior admissions in Illinois and Minnesota, no such certifications were a part of his record. The Supreme Court sided with Allegheny County, and Musgrave was denied admission to the local courts.[31] Musgrave was eventually admitted in 1916,[32] after Allegheny County's local rule on proof of examination or continuous practice, as applied to state certificate holders, was eclipsed by the passage of the Act of 1909, which set up the presumption that a candidate admitted by the Pennsylvania Supreme Court was nominally qualified to be admitted in the courts of Pennsylvania's counties.[33] Thereafter, it would be next to impossible for the local courts to refuse to admit someone on the basis of a lack of professional credentials if the State Board had granted the candidate admission to the state bar.

All through the period, however, even after the passage of the Act of 1909, the Allegheny County Board of Law Examiners continued to scrutinize the "good moral character" of its applicants, and there are numerous instances recorded in the Board's minutes in which a candidate's admission was delayed or denied over a character inquiry. In 1927—perhaps in response to a decade in which the bar experienced an explosion of class mobility, and not a small amount of concern over the emerging sects of "reds" and radicals during the period—the state gave shape to the local Boards' attention to the "moral character" issue when the State Board of Law Examiners issued elaborate new rules that essentially codified the role of the local Boards as gatekeepers of the profession. Under the new rules, the local Boards were permitted to put each candidate through an exhaustive investigation of moral qualifications at the time a candidate registered as a law student within the county; local Boards were to administer a system of preceptorship by which a law student would be required to be registered with a preceptor from within the ranks of the local bar during his or her entire course of study; and local Boards would administer the requirement that each student complete a six month clerkship in a law office prior to admission.[34]

The latter two elements of the rule were obviously a way of restoring, artificially, the gatekeeping function that was lost when "reading law" in a local law office fell out of favor; just as in the nineteenth century, a prospective candidate would find him or herself being weeded out by the marketplace if no practicing attorney were to agree to take them on as a preceptee or law clerk in satisfaction of the requirements. Apart from permitting lawyers to weed out undesirable candidates, there was little content to the preceptorship/clerkship system; it fell far short of the definition of the word "preceptor" as "teacher," or of living up to the ideal atmosphere of learning and questioning that the old apprenticeship system had been at its best. Henry Hoffstot, Jr., who was admitted to the bar in 1942, was registered with his family's lawyer, Robert Dodds, Sr. of Reed Smith, as his preceptor in 1939. Recalling his preceptorship, Hoffstot noted: "I had very few conferences with Mr. Dodds ... I remember in one of those sessions, he started off with an 8-1/2" x 14" paper and said, 'How would you fold this?' He also asked me what the capital of Kentucky was."[35]

Rather than inching toward the original goal of eliminating the local Boards of Examiners altogether, on the whole the admission reforms of the first half of the twentieth century did more to keep the Allegheny County Board of Law Examiners in business for years to come.

Meanwhile, very few newly-minted lawyers attempted to join the Allegheny County Bar Association during the earliest years of the twentieth century. One of the rare exceptions, David Aiken Reed, the son of Judge James Hay Reed, was admitted to the Allegheny County bar in June 1903 and was accepted as a member of the Bar Association in October 1905.[36] By contrast, a review of the accepted applications reveals that it was fairly common for lawyers who had been admitted to practice during the nineteenth century, even as early as the 1870s, not to apply for or be accepted to the Bar Association membership until the first dozen or so years of the twentieth century—some twenty years or more into their careers. The practice of admitting younger lawyers began to accelerate in the run up to World War I, just prior to some of them enlisting in the military. While the leaders of the local bar were losing some control over the admission of new lawyers to the local bar, they exercised detailed control over acceptance to membership in the Bar Association. All applicants required a reference from a member of the Association, and some applicants were excluded on "character" grounds or on the grounds that they were not actively engaged in private practice in the County; a lawyer working in the trust department of a bank, for example, was said to be unqualified for membership on the basis that he was not engaged in practice.[37] Early in the century, there were no women or African American members of the Bar Association. A surviving 1905 sepia-toned group portrait of the Bar Association now adorning the hallway of its headquarters—actually a collage of individual portraits made to appear as though it had taken place in one room—is a sea of white male faces in dark suits.

The fact that the membership in the Bar Association was not anywhere close to being co-extensive with admittance to the County bar during this period may have had a great deal to do with prevailing attitudes about the mission of the Bar Association among its senior leaders. The Bar Association's charter, in fact, began with a description of its purpose that included "the elevation of the character" of the bar, and the "superintendence of the general interests ... of the profession of law."[38] Thus, purporting to stand at the top of the profession and acting as its stewards in Pittsburgh, the Bar

Association tackled issues such as the expansion of the local courts to meet increasing demand (resulting in the state legislature increasing the number of Common Pleas courts to four in 1907, and the consolidation of the four separate Common Pleas courts of equal jurisdiction into one integrated court system in 1911)[39]; the recommendation of local procedural reforms[40]; the endorsement of qualified judicial candidates[41]; the adoption of the American Bar Association's Canons of Professional Ethics, with the addition of locally inspired canons, in 1934[42]; and adding their recommendations to the discussion about the manner of education and admission and, in some cases, recommending the disbarment of lawyers in the County.[43] There was undoubtedly a sense that these were all matters that required the deliberation of experienced practitioners—not callow youths—and that for the recommendations of this body to be valuable and credible to the legislature or other enacting body, there must appear to be the sense that they were the recommendations of the elite members of the bar, the best and the brightest that Pittsburgh had to offer.

This sense of elitism carried through to Bar Association elections. As a group of lawyers with a sense of solidarity among themselves, apart from the rest of the bar, the leadership elections were rarely contested. Only twice between 1902 and 1942 was there a choice of candidates for election to the presidency; in forty-one years, the vice presidency is only recorded as being contested eight times—twice in a row during the last two years of the period.[44] Throughout the period, the tradition was that each president served two consecutive years, until John Buchanan, the Bar Association's president in 1940, announced during his inaugural speech that he would only serve for one year, thus beginning a tradition of one-year service for future presidents.[45] (Incidentally, the number of stories about major decisions that were made or about initiatives that were launched following a persuasive speech by John Buchanan—perhaps the Pittsburgh bar's greatest talker of his era—is actually rather astounding.) The orderly transition of power, built around a general consensus on the most important contemporary issues, helped to promote the Bar Association's conservatism during the period.

The Bar Association did promote a few rather progressive ideas during the period, however. One was its suggestion to the city and County that they should acquire the land bordered by Grant, Fourth, Ross and Diamond (now Forbes) Streets as the site for a new local government building, anticipating the growth of local government and the court system. The Association first made this recommendation in 1907, and it was ignored by the County and by the contentious city legislature, then locked in battle with the reform mayor, attorney George W. Guthrie, a member of the Bar Association. After the adoption of the new city charter reduced the bicameral city councils from 155 members to one council of nine members in 1912, the Bar Association again offered the recommendation, and this time it was executed upon by the County commissioners.[46] Construction on the new ten-story, neo-classical City-County Building on that site, designed by architect Henry Hornbostel (with input on the new courtrooms coming from members of the Association), began in 1915 and was completed in 1917, whereupon the Bar Association moved its offices from the County Courthouse next door to the ninth floor of the Building.[47] Another somewhat progressive move by the Bar Association was its brief support of an arbitration forum, the Lawyer's Court, from 1909 to 1911, in another move to relieve docket congestion in the County; ultimately, however, the endeavor collapsed under the weight of complaints over the fees of the lawyer-arbitrators and the inability to stop losing parties from appealing to the courts.[48]

Another measure to reduce the burden on the County Common Pleas courts was the creation of the County Court of Allegheny County in 1911, designed to take the smallest cases off the Common Pleas Court's dockets, with jurisdiction over controversies not exceeding $1,500. The court had one judge for every two hundred thousand inhabitants of the County (six judges, at inception), and was supposed to hold sessions at locations throughout the area; eventually, however, the idea of a traveling small claims court was abandoned, and the County judges eventually moved into the County Courthouse. The legislation establishing the County Court was challenged on the grounds that the legislature had no power to create a court that was not conceived of by the state constitution. D.T. Watson argued the case on behalf of the County in the Pennsylvania Supreme Court, which upheld the enacting legislation, thereby affirming the authority and jurisdiction of the County Court.[49]

With the increase in federal legislation during the period, the federal court infrastructure also expanded. Up until 1909, only one judge at a time served in the U.S. District Court for the Western District of Pennsylvania; in that year, Judge James S. Young was joined by Charles P. Orr, and together they formed the first panel of that court. Upon Judge Orr's retirement in 1922, two judges were appointed—Robert M. Gibson (the former ballplayer) and Frederic P. Schoonmaker—enlarging the panel to three. The expansions helped to alleviate the pressure on the District Court introduced by the Judicial Code of 1911, which redefined the Circuit Courts as appellate courts ("Circuit Courts of Appeal") rather than as trial courts. When Marcus W. Acheson, the Third Circuit's only judge resident in Pittsburgh, died in 1906, he was replaced by Judge Joseph Buffington, who was promoted from the District Court.[50] Judge Buffington served until his death in 1947; however, the "aging, deaf and nearly blind" judge took "senior status" in 1938, after being caught up, innocently it would seem, in a scandal involving another Third Circuit judge, John Warren Davis, who was resident in New Jersey (not to be confused with John W. Davis, the U.S. Solicitor General and founder of the Davis Polk firm in New York City). Judge Davis had allegedly written opinions for which he had received bribes and in turn had procured Judge Buffington's signature on them; although Judge Davis was acquitted of the charges, he also took senior status and retired from the bench shortly thereafter.[51] Charles Alvin Jones joined the Third Circuit as a resident of the Western District in 1939.[52]

Following President Theodore Roosevelt's call for regulation came an increase in the enforcement of the Sherman Antitrust Act of 1890, and the passage of various trade regulation laws; during the Taft administration, the passage of the Clayton Antitrust Act and the ratification of the Sixteenth Amendment; during the Wilson administration, the creation of the Federal Reserve System and the beginning of Prohibition; during the Harding and Coolidge administrations, an expansion of the federal apparatus for enforcement of all that had come before; and finally, Franklin Roosevelt's New Deal, with an increase in the regulation of management in labor disputes and sundry other expansions of federal regulation. In barely the blink of an eye, vast areas of the regulation of Pittsburgh business life that were once the province of custom, designed by the peerage of executives and elite corporation lawyers of Pittsburgh over lunches at the Duquesne Club, were now being crowded by an onslaught of young attorneys coming into the bar—the unwashed horde—waving federal laws instead of torches and pitchforks. One can almost imagine the bearded lawyers of the Gilded Age looking up from their escaloped potatoes in surprise and wondering, "Where did they all come from?" Rather than being on the offensive, now Pittsburgh's elite lawyers were forced to play defense, locked in a series of ground-preserving, figurative "fights to the death" over the inexorable creep of federal authority and the waning ability of their clients among the local gentry to set their own rules of conduct. It was a phenomenon that was occurring all over the United States, but in Pittsburgh, the fall to be experienced by the city's industrial behemoths was perhaps among the hardest. The "federal" versus the "local" would become the theme of the age for the Steel Bar.

THREE RIVERS, RUNNING DIRTY

The forces of change literally lit up the skyline in Pittsburgh in 1906. On a brisk night late in February, a huge throng gathered to watch silent motion pictures and slides projected onto the side of a building on the corner of Smithfield and Diamond. Kaufmann's department store turned off its lights for the occasion. Thunderous applause broke out when a picture of George Guthrie, Greater Pittsburgh's newly-elected mayor, flashed onto the screen—owl-like, professorial in round spectacles and a bushy moustache.[53] Guthrie, a lawyer who campaigned against the entrenched political machines that controlled Pittsburgh at the turn of the century, won by the largest vote ever polled by a mayoral candidate. The crowds roared for progress; and after the way that City Hall seemed to have been yanked to and fro by bosses and would-be bosses playing machine games for the several years leading up to Guthrie's election, the spontaneous eruption of warmth for Guthrie undoubtedly grew out of some optimism that the lawyer would finally set things right in the city.

For George Wilkins Guthrie, his election as mayor may have seemed like a long time coming, particularly for one who seemed so destined to lead the city. He was the scion of one of Pittsburgh's more well-connected founding families. His father, John Brandon Guthrie, was a frequent federal appointee (he served as the equivalent of the Assistant Secretary of the Treasury under four presidents) and was mayor of Pittsburgh from 1851-52. George's maternal grandfather, Magnus Murray, was the last lawyer to serve as mayor of Pittsburgh during the nineteenth century, during 1828-29 and 1831. After preparatory education in public and private schools in Pittsburgh, George attended the Western University of Pennsylvania, obtaining his A.B. with honors at age eighteen, and then followed in Grandfather Murray's footsteps, pursuing a law degree at Columbian College (now George Washington University) in Washington, D.C. He was admitted to practice in Washington, but returned to Pittsburgh to begin his law career in 1869—initially in partnership with Col. James W. Kerr, and after Kerr's death in 1876, with Malcom Hay.[54] Relatively early on, Guthrie's pedigree propelled him to represent and establish relationships with corporations, the clients at the cutting edge of the profession during the Gilded Age—in particular, banks, such as Germania Savings Bank and Dollar Savings Bank, and on at least one occasion in 1887, the German National Bank of Pittsburgh.[55]

Like his father, Guthrie was a Democrat, although for the better part of his professional life he was a Democrat in a city controlled by a Republican political machine. The typical orientation of the elite lawyer in Pittsburgh—even a Democratic corporation lawyer such as D.T. Watson, or even a lawyer who happened to be a Democratic Party leader such as Billy Brennen—was to mind one's own business, and that of one's own clients, and to operate in tolerance of the Republican machine. It was perhaps an easy choice for a lawyer to make, given how effective the Magee-Flinn Ring was during the last quarter of the nineteenth century.

While William Flinn, the founder of the Booth & Flinn construction business and the local Republican chairman, made millions of dollars through corrupt public construction bargains, Christopher Lyman Magee was the glue that held the machine together—a charming, full-faced handsome creature; diplomatic; and, in the opinion of some contemporary observers, a public policy visionary. As a young man, after serving two terms as city treasurer learning at the knee of his powerful uncle, city Republican leader and councilman "Squire Thomas" Steel, Christopher Magee then studied the "Gas Ring" in Philadelphia and the New York Tammany political machine in detail, and consciously designed his planned Pittsburgh ring to correct some of their weaknesses. Under Pittsburgh's home rule charter at the time, the office of the mayor occupied a relatively weak position. Without holding a significant city or county office, then, Magee controlled Pittsburgh politics from the neighborhoods to the 155-member common and select city councils by dispensing political appointments to working-class immigrants in the downtown wards and holding public purse strings, essentially owning councilmen, controlling all legislation, and protecting lucrative vices, such as gambling and prostitution, that could be depended upon to fuel contributions to his discretionary fund.[56]

As the muckraking journalist Lincoln Steffens wrote in "Pittsburg: A City Ashamed" in *McClure's Magazine* in 1903, despite the machine's dictatorial excesses, Magee's control of legislation in Pittsburgh meant that Pittsburgh businessmen were inclined to fall into step as well:

> *The manufacturers and merchants were kept well in hand by many little municipal grants and privileges, such as switches, wharf rights, and street and alley vacations. These street vacations are a tremendous power in most cities. A foundry occupies a block, spreads to the next block, and wants the street between ... [In Pittsburgh, the foundry owner] went to Magee, and I have heard such a man praise Chris, 'because when I called on him his outer office was filled with waiting politicians, but he knew I was a business man and in a hurry; he called me first, and he gave me the street without any fuss.'*[57]

For a lawyer trying to get public business done for a paying client, the existence of the Magee-Flinn Ring could be an efficiency. Going through the Ring—the prevailing way of transacting business with the city, unseemly at times though not always strictly illegal—was certainly more effective for some lawyers with time-pressed clients than fighting City Hall, or the powers behind City Hall, on their behalf. In return for Magee's favors, the businessmen of Pittsburgh might make voluntary contributions to Magee's personal "campaign fund," which Magee used in turn to continue to consolidate his power.[58] All the while, Magee enhanced his legitimacy by playing the role of benevolent civic leader, as a board member and sponsor of such institutions as the Carnegie Fine Arts and Museum Fund[59] and the Tuesday Music Club,[60] as well as putting in his appearances at meetings of the Chamber of Commerce, and at the Press Club, the Duquesne Club and the Shadyside Presbyterian Church.[61]

Support for Magee and Flinn was not, of course, unanimous. In the 1880s, at the height of the Ring's power, another well-connected scion of a founding Pittsburgh family, a rug and furnishings merchant named Oliver McClintock, began to question publicly why Booth & Flinn seemed to win every asphalt contract. McClintock waged an unsuccessful war against the Republican chairman's construction firm in court, showing evidence of the firm's non-competitive high prices and photographs of the firm's shoddy workmanship. "This single citizen's long, brave fight," as Steffens called it, was ultimately thrown out of court, however, by a judge who was whispered to be "Ring-controlled."[62]

Apart from McClintock's one-man crusade, a growing citizens' movement against the Magee-Flinn Ring could be found among the religious congregations of Pittsburgh's East End, such as the Calvary Episcopal Church on Penn Avenue in East Liberty (subsequently at Shady Avenue and Walnut Street in Shadyside). Oliver McClintock was not strictly speaking an East End reformer; McClintock's family church was the Second Presbyterian, downtown on Penn Avenue and Seventh,[63] although his participation in the Civic Club of Allegheny County, whose modest objectives were "better municipal government, improved social conditions, increased educational opportunity and a more beautiful city in which to live,"[64] put him touch with other reform activists in the East End, not only at Calvary Episcopal, but from the Christ Methodist Episcopal Church and its Society for Aid to the Poor, and the First Unitarian Church, located at the current site of St. Paul's Cathedral in Oakland, among others.[65]

Calvary Episcopal Church was the epicenter of the movement's quaking rhetoric, however. The rector there, the Reverend Dr. George Hodges, a silver-haired man with a beatific gaze and a clenched jaw, preached a kind of muscular social gospel, denouncing the activities of the Magee-Flinn machine, especially insofar as they perpetuated institutions such as prostitution and gambling that exploited the impoverished and lined the pockets of the bosses. He designated machine politics—the "admirably disciplined army of the devil—the allied forces of intemperance, of impurity, or corrupt politics, of fraud and falsehood, of theft and murder"—as the "chief hindrance" against fixing the ills of Pittsburgh. Reverend Hodges went beyond an analysis of causes, however; he saw the religious community as a militia of good government, called to arms to effect change. "There is an idea, derived from much experience," Rev. Hodges observed, "that religion and politics do not go well together ... But if politics is defined as the application of the principles of Jesus Christ to the alternatives of daily life, public as well as private," he argued, "then the two belong together. Politics properly understood is a part of religion. The primary and the polls are as close to the path of duty as the prayer-meeting."[66]

George W. Guthrie, the elite downtown corporate lawyer who was a leading member of Hodges' flock, was morally committed to political reform, inspired by Hodges' vision of social justice. "As the Christian owes his duty to God," Guthrie would say, "no less does he owe his duty to the government and the community in which he lives."[67] While a muscular social gospel was his true wind, Guthrie's grounding in the law was his tiller. It gave him the tools to undertake a structural analysis of corrupt activities, and to cast them in the light of legal principles, clothed in the language of civic rights and freedoms. Guthrie's critique naturally was focused on legal institutions, such as the existing city charter, created by the politically pliable state legislature. He blamed the state's grubby grip on the content of the charter for restricting the ballot in Pittsburgh, propping up an "absolutely unnecessary and indefensible" bicameral system of city councils made up of 155 potential patronage beneficiaries,[68] and turning a blind eye to a confusing, opaque system for the public accounting of funds, arguing that the boss-drawn charter essentially stripped the people of their power to frame their own government. "Let our cities ... be given the power to frame a government of their cities in such form as they think wise. They are able to do it," he would declare. "Let them, subject to the general laws of the state, have all the powers necessary to carry out the purposes of municipal life."[69]

At street-level, when it came to the lack of transparency of city government in the hands of the Ring, Guthrie would argue that "no private company would tolerate" the uncontrolled discretion left in the hands of the Department of Public Works to award public contracts in accordance with "the grossest favoritism."[70] The "municipal corporation," as Guthrie would occasionally refer to the city, should be governed under a strict adherence to rules, procedures and processes designed to ensure transparent fairness and parliamentary order—the way that private corporations were run, at least ideally, vis-à-vis their shareholders. Thus, the "municipal corporation" would putatively benefit from a corporation lawyer's expertise.

The rhetoric of Guthrie and other parishioners of Calvary Episcopal—including other reform leaders such as H.D.W. English, an insurance man and the president of the Chamber of Commerce, lawyer George R. Wallace and Orphans' Court Judge Joseph Buffington—came to irritate the partisans of the Machine, who referred to them as "that damned Calvary crowd."[71] This growing movement—Oliver McClintock's higher end clientele, and the men and women who were communicants at Calvary Episcopal and the other reform-minded churches—came largely from the middle-class families who had migrated from downtown to the quieter garden paradise of the East End, but who kept one foot in downtown each day by virtue of their status as downtown business and professional leaders. Like Guthrie, they were "young lawyers, engineers, and college-bred managers," as Bauman and Muller would describe them, who were interested in "healthfulness" and cosmopolitan beauty in both architecture and greenery, and who had "a growing acceptance of environmentalism."[72]

Thus it was an environmental health issue—Pittsburgh's dirty drinking water, downtown and in the suburbs—that not only provided a rallying point for the East

End reform movement, but was also a flashpoint for the picaresque course of political reform from 1895 to the time of Guthrie's election as mayor in 1906. In addition to industrial dumping and acid runoff from the active mines in the greater Pittsburgh area during Pittsburgh's industrial revolution, over 350,000 residents of seventy-five upriver cities discharged untreated sewage into the Allegheny and Monongahela rivers.[73] One indication of the poor quality of Pittsburgh's drinking water during the period was Pittsburgh's extraordinary rate of typhoid disease. Pittsburgh earned the distinction of being the typhoid capital of the western world, with one out of every six residents suffering from typhoid fever during the period from 1883 to 1908, accounting for 8,149 deaths during the twenty-five-year period.[74] In a 1909 study, Pittsburgh's mortality rate per one hundred thousand residents during the period from 1898 to 1909 was 130, as compared to 59.9 for Washington, D.C., 54.7 for Philadelphia, 18.2 for New York, and 11.7 for London during the same period.[75] Flooding in Pittsburgh was an aggravating factor. In its 1912 report, the Pittsburgh Flood Commission reported that from 1890 through the end of 1905, Pittsburgh had suffered twenty-five floods, including the devastating floods of February 1891, March 1902 and January 1904.[76] With floods, in addition to the water damage to property, came the potential health concerns associated with the backflow of untreated sewage during the flood. Regarding the Pittsburgh flood of April 1901, *The New York Times* reported: "Where the flood has subsided, it has left behind a greasy yellow scum two or three inches deep."[77]

As early as 1893, chemists and other experts, with the support of the First Unitarian Church in Oakland, began exploring the connection of Pittsburgh's polluted drinking water to the inordinately high death rates in the city due to typhoid fever. They concluded that sand filtration would effectively remove organic matter that was prone to carry typhus, and to illustrate the point, the Church installed a model sand filtration plant on a corner of the Church lawn, offering small quantities of free water to residents. However, leaders of the Ring dismissed the conclusions of the Church's study, arguing that the conclusions were incorrect and that in any event the criticism of the city's water threatened to discourage investment in Pittsburgh.[78] In 1895, following a mass meeting held in protest of the Magee-Flinn Ring, Oliver McClintock, George Guthrie and others formed the Citizens' Municipal League, specifically to take on the Magee-Flinn Ring over the issue of city water filtration.[79]

During the 1896 mayoral election, the League took on the guise of a local political party and nominated George W. Guthrie as its candidate, pitting him against the Republican, Henry P. Ford, the founder of a saw blade manufacturing company. The Democratic Party chose to stay out of the fray, and the prospects of getting Guthrie elected seemed positive. As a member of the downtown corporate elite and a founding family of Pittsburgh, Guthrie was a candidate made to order for dividing the Republican vote, although Congressman John "Corporation" Dalzell did his best to rally Republican solidarity by arguing that a local Republican defeat would weaken the effort to elect Pittsburgh's old friend, William McKinley, as president.[80] On election night, while Guthrie appeared to be winning the vote from the reported election returns, sometime during the wee hours "all returns ceased suddenly," as Steffens reported,[81] and ultimately Guthrie lost to Ford by a narrow 1,292 votes out of 39,812. The Ring was said to have privately bragged about how it stuffed the ballot boxes in the 1896 election, but election laws were such at the time that ballot boxes could not be opened for the investigation of alleged voter fraud.[82]

The near-election of George Guthrie in 1896 was undoubtedly considered to be a close call for the Magee-Flinn forces, who then attempted to appease the reform movement by pushing through an ordinance creating a "Filtration Commission" in the summer of 1896. Flinn, director of public works Edward M. Bigelow (Magee's first cousin, another nephew of "Squire Thomas" Steel) and Robert Pitcairn of the Pennsylvania Railroad would be among the members studying the effect of Pittsburgh's water on public health, and the advisability of building a filtration plant.[83]

The following year, Guthrie and another attorney, William B. Rodgers, the former city solicitor of Allegheny City, continued to assail the Machine's inner-workings by following up on an article in the *Pittsburgh Leader* about Joseph "J.O." Brown, the director of public safety, and the "queer set of specifications" for the construction contracts on the new Public Safety Building at Sixth Avenue and Cherry Way. Using a "lowest *responsible* bidder" scheme, Brown was apparently colluding with Flinn's firm to narrow the specifications of the new Building to include materials to which Booth & Flinn had exclusive access—"Ligonier block," for example, "of a bluish tint rather than a gray variety"—solely to exclude all other bidders. Although Guthrie and Rodgers were able to force an investigation of Flinn's practices in the city councils similar to the one undertaken by McClintock in the 1880s, since the councils were largely controlled by the Ring, once again the efforts of reform were unable to bring Flinn or J.O. Brown to justice.[84]

Meanwhile, the erstwhile Filtration Committee, having strung out its deliberations for over two years, issued a strategically timed report in January 1899, just before the upcoming mayoral election. Not surprisingly, the Committee was forced to concede that "the present water supply [was] objectionable" and that with the proper filtration, water-borne diseases would be greatly lessened. The Committee concluded that the city should build a sand filtration plant, at a cost estimated at three million dollars, including land acquisition and a metering system.[85] In the February election, the Ring backed William J. Diehl, an oil and gas businessman and a former deputy sheriff, against the Democrats' choice, John C. O'Donnell, a Strip District grocer who had been served as postmaster of Pittsburgh during the Cleveland administration. With no clear option available for the East End reformers, Diehl beat O'Donnell by over ten thousand votes.[86]

As the Diehl administration began, Guthrie and the reformers had some reason to believe that the conclusions of a Filtration Committee led by both Flinn and Bigelow would be acted upon, and a bond issue of $2,500,000 was authorized for the purpose of building the filtration plant.[87] The fragility of the alliances that held the Magee-Flinn Ring together was exposed, however, when Christopher Magee decided to take a leave of absence from his place at the head of the Ring for health reasons. Magee's cousin, the usually pliable director of public works Edward M. Bigelow, took charge of the process of letting the public contracts for the building of the filtration plant and, asserting his own authority, refused to award any of the contracts to Booth & Flinn. Flinn retaliated quickly, ordering the city councils to remove Bigelow from office.[88]

Enter Bigelow's elder brother, attorney Thomas Steele Bigelow—a burly Gilded Age lawyer with prodigious sideburns who had served as Pittsburgh city solicitor before Major Moreland, during the earliest days of the Magee-Flinn partnership. Although Bigelow had a lucrative practice, during the heyday of the Ring his "attention had been turned to outside enterprises." Undoubtedly his proximity to the initiatives of the Ring provided him with superior inside knowledge and ample opportunity for ground-floor investments around the city, even if he found himself clashing with Magee from time to time. By 1900, he was a millionaire.[89]

Enraged by his brother's firing, Thomas Bigelow called upon Matthew Quay—the head of the state Republican machine, whom Bigelow had been supporting while Quay fought to regain his U.S. Senate seat following Quay's alleged involvement in a scandal involving the misappropriation of state funds—to enlist his aid. Coincidentally, the 1900 Census had shown that the city of Scranton had grown in population and now qualified as a "second-class city" under state law. As Pittsburgh was the only other "second-class city" at the time, the legislature's review of city charter legislation occasioned by Scranton's growth would affect Pittsburgh as well. Bigelow saw the legislative review, coming on during Magee's illness, as an opportunity to unseat the Magee-Flinn machine; so in the name of civil reform, Bigelow enlisted the aid of the genuinely reform-minded attorney William B. Rodgers, Guthrie's compadre during the Public Safety Building investigations, to draft emergency charter legislation. Quay, who had also been looking for an opportunity to neutralize his greatest rivals for the control of the state, used his influence in Harrisburg to get the so-called "Ripper Bill"—named for giving the governor the power to "rip out" the mayor and replace him with a "recorder" who was empowered to appoint city department chiefs, thus performing an end-run around the Machine's control of the city councils—passed by the state legislature. The Act took effect on March 7, 1901,[90] and two days later, the newspapers reported the death of Christopher Lyman Magee in Harrisburg at the age of fifty-two.[91]

With the birth of a new city charter giving the state even greater control over the fate of Pittsburgh, and the demise of the old boss, it would have seemed that the Machine era was finished. There followed, however, a period of chaos at City Hall that did nothing to promote the cause of water filtration and did little to solve the problem of municipal corruption.

Almost immediately, the Ripper Act was challenged in the courts, with a complaint against the new chief executive of Scranton to show cause by what authority he undertook to assume power. The lawyers opposing the Act argued that it was "unrepublic in form and substance, a fraud on the people, and not within the proper scope and power of legislation, being passed for the benefit and advantage of a partisan faction and not for the good of the people." Judge Robert W. Archbald of Lackawanna County[c], in upholding the constitutionality of the Ripper Act, commented "As we have taken pains to point out, the question of expediency is not before us. This bill may be good or bad; time alone will demonstrate, and none of us can anticipate its judgment."[92]

---

c   Later, as a federal judge, Archbald suffered the distinction of becoming the third federal judge in the history of the United States to be impeached and removed from office, amid charges that he had improperly solicited and accepted gifts from litigants in his courtroom.

With the Act upheld in court, now the power to take action rested with the governor. William A. Stone, a Tioga County-born practicing Pittsburgh attorney, had become the first Pittsburgher to be elected governor of Pennsylvania in 1898. Not squarely within either the Magee-Flinn or Quay camps, Stone was thought to aspire to the vacant U.S. Senate seat to which Quay was battling to return. Without consulting Quay, in April Governor Stone announced that Mayor Diehl was to be removed and that Major Adam Mercer Brown, the seventy-four year-old one-time first president of the Allegheny County Bar Association, would be the new "recorder" of Pittsburgh. While Quay was initially convinced that Major Brown was going to continue to represent the Flinn faction, after his inauguration as recorder at the end of May, Brown moved quickly to remove some of the key Flinn appointments and replace them with new men, "according to merit and skill."[93]

Significantly, one of Major Brown's moves was to re-install Edward Bigelow as director of public works.[94] Whatever his associations with the old Machine, the younger Bigelow had enjoyed great stature with East End reformers such as Guthrie, who admired Bigelow's work in developing Pittsburgh's lavish, expansive park system, a "necklace" of green parks surrounding the urban area similar to the system of parks Frederick Law Olmstead had envisioned for Boston around the same time. The reformers were also cognizant of the fact that Bigelow's removal came as a response to his attempts to submit the filtration plant bids to public competition.

As quickly as it had appeared that the winds had shifted in favor of the Bigelow brothers, however, in November 1901, Governor Stone used his power under the Act to remove Major Brown, replacing him with Flinn's old director of public safety, J.O. Brown (no relation). At the bottom of his order to install J.O. Brown as recorder, Governor Stone wrote, without any apparent irony intended, "P.S. I was not bribed." Recorder J.O. Brown then quickly undid Major Brown's work, forcing Edward Bigelow's resignation as well as that of Major Brown's choice for Director of Public Safety.[95] The beleaguered new recorder accomplished very little, and certainly nothing significant toward the cause of clean water.

In 1903, Allegheny County District Attorney John C. Haymaker was nominated by the Republicans to face William B. Hays in the election for the new recorder, as mandated under the Ripper Act. Hays, also a Republican, was supported by the Bigelow brothers through the newly-created Citizens' Party. Meanwhile, the Democrats, now led by the new County chair, the union lawyer Billy Brennen, again declined to run a candidate, and confusion reigned among those who wanted reform. While some reform elements saw the Citizens' Party as an opportunity to extinguish the remaining influence of the Magee-Flinn machine, some representatives of the newly-founded Voters' Civic League favored Haymaker based on his record as an honest prosecutor; and prior to the election, some newspapers were already referring to the Citizens' Party candidates as representatives of a new "Bigelow machine." In the end, Hays took enough votes from the Republican Party to beat Haymaker by about 8,000 votes, and the Citizens' Party secured a majority in the Common council.[96] With an element of wishful thinking, perhaps, Guthrie and other East End reformers initially chose to celebrate Hays' election as a victory for reform.

Before Hays could take office, the incumbent recorder, Flinn's lieutenant J.O. Brown, submitted his resignation, to take effect on March 15; however, when the day of his effective resignation came, Brown suddenly died, his death record stating that the cause was "heart failure super-induced by long, continued mental strain and worry," although *The New York Times* blamed "the unusually perturbed condition of politics" in Pittsburgh.[97] The soon-to-be-inaugurated Hays was appointed interim recorder by the new governor, Samuel W. Pennypacker, and Hays immediately announced a wholesale clean-up of the public payroll, delivering notice to three thousand city employees that their services would not be needed after April 1.[98] A Richmond newspaper called it "the cleanest official sweep on record,"[99] but it would prove to be a sweep in favor of the Bigelow brothers. Legislation was passed a few weeks later re-establishing the recorder as the "mayor" of Pittsburgh, and Edward Bigelow was re-appointed as director of public works, as were a number of Bigelow partisans to key positions within the administration.

Meanwhile, Thomas Bigelow, as the de facto boss of Pittsburgh was, according to Zahniser, "pushing aside the concerns of the reformers who had helped to get Citizens' Party candidates elected."[100] In particular, the way toward the construction of the water filtration plant continued to be delayed through "injunctions and other obstacles," while engineers finally concluded that it would now cost roughly seven million dollars to complete the plant.[101] As Steffens observed, "[T]he best men in Pittsburg put it: 'We have smashed the ring and we have wound another around us.'"[102]

And still, the rivers ran dirty.

Thomas Bigelow died in his sleep in his North Highland Avenue mansion during the summer of 1904,[103] and while the grimy infrastructure of machine politics in Pittsburgh remained viable, the question of who controlled it became less certain. With a vacuum of power at the boss' seat, it appeared that the time was ripe, finally, for the implementation of reform, for George Guthrie's vision of the "municipal corporation," defined by rules that would encourage reason and fairness, rather than by politics.

In the run-up to the mayoral election of 1906—the first mayoral election of Greater Pittsburgh, formed by the union of Pittsburgh and Allegheny City under the auspices of legislation drafted by D.T. Watson and George Guthrie—George Guthrie was nominated by the local Democratic Party as its candidate for mayor, endorsed by the chair of the County Democrats, Billy Brennen, as well as by Edward Bigelow and what was left of the Bigelow brothers' Citizens' Party, now little more than a citizens' committee.[104] Guthrie, the corporation lawyer, accepted the nomination, saying, "The city belonged to the people and should be administered as any well-run corporation for the benefit of the people, its stockholders."[105] The Republicans passed over the late Christopher Lyman Magee's nephew, lawyer and former state senator William A. Magee, and instead selected Alexander M. Jenkinson, heir to the multi-million dollar "Pittsburg Stogies" cigar manufacturing fortune, who entered the race at the urging of R.B. Mellon and Henry Clay Frick, and who was supported by what was left of William Flinn's machine.

Guthrie seized upon non-partisan government and civil service reform as his main campaign theme, telling a gathering of the city policemen:

The moment I take office the employees of the city shall be put on a civil service basis. Promotion on the force will depend on honesty, fidelity, courage and intelligence ... I shall have drawn and presented a constitutional bill that will place you outside of politics. It will be an act of justice to you and to the taxpayers of Pittsburgh.[106]

On the night of the election, Billy Brennen stood by like a proud papa as Guthrie sailed easily to victory, but maintained publicly that Guthrie's election represented not "a Democratic, but a non-partisan victory."[107] Guthrie, although a Democrat, would soon hold Brennen to his words.

In his inaugural address on April 2, 1906, Guthrie focused again on taking politics out of the municipal corporation. "There can be no doubt," he declared, "that it is the will of the people of Pittsburg that city affairs should be taken out of partisan politics, and as a public servant it will be my duty as it certainly will be my pleasure to carry out their wish ..."[108] He also gave a nod to the East End reform movement's dissatisfaction with the way that public works had been administered, stating:

Of course, neither favoritism in the selection of contractors, nor the changing of specifications after bids have been received, is compatible with honest administration ... Every citizen is interested in having the streets kept clean and in repair, and the sanitary and police laws properly enforced. Too often, the greatest sufferers from the violation of these laws, or the neglect of those charged with their enforcement, find it difficult to make their wrongs known to those who would rectify them. They should have every opportunity afforded to them to obtain relief.[109]

In choosing his cabinet, Guthrie ignored the County Democrats entirely, instead choosing a group of independent Republicans. Billy Brennen was publicly supportive, if a bit tepid: "I would have been better pleased if the Democratic party had been recognized by Mr. Guthrie in his appointments as the party expected to be ... Mr. Guthrie is a man who has his own ideas, his own belief as to the way in which a municipal administration should be conducted. He was elected without making a single pledge. In making his appointments he is doing what he, no doubt, considers for the best. The more than 20,000 Democrats who voted for Mr. Guthrie hope that his administration will be a success."[110] Guthrie placed an exclamation point on his appointments, saying, "No man under me need feel that his position depends upon political service. I will issue no political orders myself, nor will I permit department heads or bureau heads or foremen to issue orders. The time for such outrageous methods is going by rapidly."[111]

Guthrie's principal success as chief executive of the municipal corporation was in creating, however briefly, an atmosphere for reform in Pittsburgh, both by attempting to take politics out of the equation and by changing the conversation about civic advancement, with the help of his friends in the Voters' League, the Civic Club of Allegheny County, and the Chamber of Commerce, and in the churches and missions of the East End.

Perhaps the greatest legacy of that change of conversation was the monumental *Pittsburgh Survey*. In June 1906, Alice Ballard Montgomery, at one time Pennsylvania's first full-time probation officer in Philadelphia who was then serving as chief probation officer of the Allegheny County Juvenile Court, approached Paul Kellogg, the managing editor of *Charities and the Commons*, a New York City journal, and asked him, "Would it be possible for you to appoint a special investigator to study and make a report of social conditions in Pittsburgh and vicinity? ... We feel that the people of Allegheny County are not as yet wide awake to the needs of the poor, and it is almost impossible with our limited corps of workers, to make the systematic investigation and presentation that is needed."[112] Montgomery had a formidable background, spending much of her professional time in the Allegheny County courts convincing judges to keep children out of adult jail cells; it was a lawyer's work in all but name and certification.[113]

Kellogg jumped at Montgomery's suggestion to undertake a survey of this kind with official support, and began to assemble national philanthropic backing, led by the Russell Sage Foundation, while the East End reformers, including Mayor Guthrie himself, contributed additional financial and moral support. What began as Mrs. Montgomery's modest call for a "special investigator" blossomed into a seminal undertaking within the history of American social reform, one of the earliest and most exhaustive studies of American urban social conditions ever attempted. Kellogg sent seventy-four people "into the field" in Guthrie's Greater Pittsburgh to spend the better part of the year interviewing Pittsburgh residents and collecting data, culminating in the publication of six volumes of material between 1909 and 1914, ranging in subject matter from "Women and the Trades," to "Work Accidents and the Law," to coverage of steel workers and the community of Homestead, to the Pittsburgh downtown district and its wage earners.[114]

One of Kellogg's field investigators was another young woman who had aspirations of appearing in the courts. Crystal Eastman, who had previously received a bachelor's degree from Vassar and a master's in Sociology from Columbia, went to New York University to study law in 1906, one of sixteen women out of a class of 156, and earned her LL.B the following year. Eastman passed the bar examination and found it almost impossible to find work as a lawyer in New York City, but her friend Paul Kellogg was happy to engage her to go to Pittsburgh to focus on the human toll of a legal construct—the then-current state of employer liability to workers for accidents and dangers of the workplace in Pennsylvania. Eastman embraced the project whole-heartedly, spending hours reviewing death certificates in the Allegheny County Coroner's Office, and supplementing her research by interviewing families, co-workers and employers of the deceased, and touring mills and factories. Working from the Pittsburgh Law Library, she also wrote an article, "Employers' Liability in Pennsylvania," published in the *Albany Law Journal*, on the law of personal injury as applied to workers in the workplace, which in an even-handed fashion ultimately exposed how Pittsburgh courts had routinely recognized implied contractual terms in the employer-worker relationship, holding that workers legally accepted ordinary risks and extraordinary dangers of the workplace and therefore could not hold employers liable for accidental injuries. While "Employers' Liability" shed light on legal circumstances, her contribution to the *Pittsburgh Survey*, titled "Work Accidents and the Law," provided the heart and soul of the practical argument, examining not only the causes of workplace accidents, but also the secondary effects of them—the loss of income, the problems of injured workers, and the impact of accidents on homes and communities.[115]

Writing to her mother from the Pittsburgh Law Library in the fall of 1907, Eastman was enthusiastic about entering the profession of the law, based on her experiences in Pittsburgh. "[Practicing law] interests me so much that I am dead sure I want to stop this investigating at Xmas time and get at my profession ... there is a joy in doing things, fighting fights."[116] We are left to wonder if Eastman, had she stayed in the city where she had found her voice as a legal scholar, might have had a direct impact on the Pittsburgh bar during a time in which only one woman, Suzanne Beatty (admitted in 1902), was actively practicing law. After the publication of her law review article and "Work Accidents and the Law," however, Eastman achieved considerable critical notoriety, and was appointed by Governor Charles Evans Hughes of New York, the future Chief Justice of the U.S. Supreme Court, to serve as the only woman on the state's Employers' Liability Commission, where she drafted the first workmen's compensation law for the State of New York.[117] The law took effect in the fall of 1910, only to be overturned by the New York Court of Appeals in 1911 as being unconstitutional. The day after the Court overturned the law, 146 employees of the Triangle Shirtwaist Factory, most of them women, died in a terrible fire. The ensuing outrage over the acquittal of the factory owners, who had locked the exits in an attempt to keep union organizers out of the building, and their meager financial responsibility for the lives of their employees (amounting to seventy-five dollars per victim), led to the passage of the 1914 Workmen's Compensation Law in New York.[118]

In what can only be described as another indirect measure of Crystal Eastman's influence in Pittsburgh—born in an atmosphere of reform created by the administration of Mayor George Guthrie, reared at a table in a darkened file room inside the Allegheny County Coroner's office, and lit up by the flames of a holocaust near Washington Square in Manhattan—Pennsylvania's first workers compensation law was enacted in 1915, thereby fundamentally altering the previously accepted principles of employer liability in Pittsburgh.

Crystal Eastman did not, however, pursue a career as a lawyer in Pittsburgh. Instead, Eastman went on to be a leader in the women's suffrage and peace movements, serving as one of the authors of the Equal Rights Amendment and as one of the founders of the Women's International League for Peace and Freedom. Along with Roger Baldwin and Norman Thomas, Eastman helped to organize the National Civil Liberties Bureau, originally established to defend conscientious objectors during World War I, which was eventually transformed into the American Civil Liberties Union, or ACLU.

Meanwhile, Mayor Guthrie managed to push through some other significant initiatives during his three-year term. He passed a merit-based civil service law that took effect in July 1907.[119] After the defeat of a strong smoke abatement ordinance in July 1906, Guthrie's administration presided over a compromise that established a Bureau of Smoke Regulation that, for the first time in Pittsburgh, empowered an officer of the city whose sole responsibility was to regulate the emission of smoke in the city. As historian Robert Dale Grinder observed, "engineers and contractors now had a person to 'see' in city hall." (Unfortunately, the ordinance was declared unconstitutional by the state Supreme Court in 1911.)[120] Guthrie also succeeded in getting the Pennsylvania Railroad to remove railroad tracks from the center of Liberty Avenue in downtown—tracks that were installed during an atmosphere of graft and political wish-granting, and that compromised both the safety and aesthetics of downtown—by assessing the Railroad with charges for street cleaning between the tracks.[121] The move turned out to have a profound and lasting influence on Pittsburgh's cultural life, as it influenced downtown produce merchants to move to the Strip District so that they could be nearer to the Pennsylvania Railroad yards.

Finally, and most significantly, under Guthrie's leadership, by October 1908, a large portion of Pittsburgh's water supply began to be filtered. The first filtered water was delivered through the Pittsburgh water filtration plant east of Aspinwall on the Allegheny River on December 18, 1907, and the first filtered water was delivered on the South Side by February 1908. By the end of Guthrie's term, Pittsburgh was recording its lowest ever mortality rates, and the incidence of typhoid was reduced dramatically.[122] The East End reformers' dream of clean water, expressed through the founding of the Citizens' Municipal League in 1895, had finally been achieved, at least in part, for a time.

Clean government, however, still remained beyond the grasp of Guthrie and the reformers. The vacuum of power left by the death of Thomas Steele Bigelow was not simply erased by the election of George W. Guthrie. "There is no doubt," wrote the National Municipal League's Clinton R. Woodruff, "if the mayor had been willing to do so, he could have purchased support by judicious distribution of patronage, but he did not choose to do so."[123] Mayor Guthrie may have refused to play the role of political boss of Pittsburgh, but Pittsburgh's "weak mayor" charter still made it difficult for Guthrie to pursue a full-throated agenda for structural political reform. Specifically, where Chris Magee controlled Pittsburgh's political agenda by buying city councilmen—now certain leaders within the 155-member common and select councils of Pittsburgh began to play the role of boss, buying back-benchers within the city councils and acting as brokers for favorable legislation for paying customers.

Near the end of his term as mayor, Guthrie became particularly incensed by the passage of a suspicious city bank ordinance in 1908. If there was one area of Pittsburgh business about which George Guthrie was intimately familiar, it was banking, as many of the mid-sized banks of Pittsburgh had numbered among his clients before he became mayor. In June 1908, the Common Council passed legislation, on a vote of seventy-six to one, designating six local banks as the official depositories of city funds—the Farmers' National, the Columbia National, the Second National Bank of Pittsburg, the Workingmen's National Bank of Allegheny, the Second National Bank of Allegheny, and the German National Bank of Pittsburg—but Guthrie quickly observed that the banks that were chosen offered only two percent interest on daily balances, whereas a number of other reliable banks were paying at least 2-1/2%, some as much as three to four percent. Mayor Guthrie publicly declared that the city would be losing more than $150,000 a year on deposits if he signed the ordinance. He vetoed the bill, but the city councils promptly overrode Guthrie's veto, the Common Council by seventy-three to two, the Select Council by forty-two to six.[124]

Guthrie was convinced there was no reason other than bribery that the councils would favor the banks paying the lowest interest rates, and his suspicions were confirmed when the city auditor, Frank Kimball, came to him with a story about how his friend, a downtown saddler, had reported that Councilman John F. "Smiling Johnnie" Klein bragged to the saddler about how he had received thirty thousand dollars to sway the councils in favor of the requested bank ordinance. Further gossip suggested that a pool of over one hundred thousand dollars was distributed among various councilmen, and that Smiling Johnnie, as one of the councils' so-called "Big Five," was the bagman who collected funds for distribution to the key voters within the councils.[125] The mayor wanted to conduct an investigation, but because his civil service reform project was still in its infancy, he did not yet have a high level of trust in the city detectives; so he turned to the Voters' League for help. Guthrie set up a secret meeting with his friend A. Leo Weil, the president of the Voters' League, at the law offices of Weil & Thorp on the eighth floor of the newly-completed Frick Building.[126]

Leo Weil, the trial lawyer whom Judge Reed had attempted to refer to Andrew Carnegie at the outset of the "World's Greatest Lawsuit," was known to be one of the toughest lawyers in Pittsburgh, as well as one of its most visible Jewish leaders. His junior partner, Leo Ruslander, described him as "nonsettling, noncompromising, aggressive" and at all times, an "able" fighter.[127] His later foe, William A. Magee, would say that Weil was a "human bloodhound" with "the instincts of a headsman."[128] Nonetheless, Weil believed it was the natural role of the lawyer to fix what was wrong with American cities. "More than any other body of men," Weil observed in an address to the state bar association, "the lawyers of our cities have the power to curb and to check ... tendencies to evil in our municipal conditions."[129] His sense of professional duty, as well as his desire for civic justice and fairness, led him to establish the Voters' League. By 1908, Weil and the Voters' League had already scored a modest success, joining with attorney Starling W. Childs—the son-in-law of Justice George Shiras and the son of Shiras' good friend Albert Childs—in seeking injunctions in state and federal court against the grant of railway easements along Bigelow Boulevard, alleging bribery, and forcing the railway company to abandon its easement claims.[130]

Coincidentally, only a week before Mayor Guthrie contacted him, Weil and several of his colleagues on the executive committee of the Voters' League—H.D.W. English and attorney George R. Wallace from the Calvary Episcopal congregation, Winfield K. Shiras (a Yale-educated lawyer, the brother-in-law of Starling Childs and the son of Justice George Shiras) and Frick's personal lawyer Willis McCook—met with a news reporter from the *Pittsburgh Leader*, who told them a fascinating story about graft that he had uncovered almost by accident. Since a number of people around city hall made a habit of joking about bribes being paid to councilmen, the reporter decided to play a prank on a prominent councilman, walking up to him with a roll of $250 in bills and saying "[I]t sure took a long time before they got around to me when they divided up the banks' swag," referring to the suspicious bank legislation. The councilman demanded to know where the reporter got his money, to which the reporter replied,

"I haven't the slightest idea, unless it's because I don't write unfavorable articles in the paper." At that, the councilman seemed to acknowledge that there was a fund to "take care of" newspapermen who wrote favorable articles.

Guthrie arrived unseen at Weil's office around half past six on the appointed evening and told his friend, "I am fed up with the corruption in the councils and their indifference to public opinion. I want to put a stop to the payment of bribes to councilmen for the awarding of contracts. In order to accomplish this, it will be necessary to obtain proof of the bribery and I have no confidence in being able to succeed using our city detectives. Any investigation must be kept a secret known only to a handful of people."

Weil told Guthrie that it was fortuitous that the mayor would call upon him just now, in that the Voters' League had just authorized Weil to head up an independent citizens' investigation of city council corruption based on the story they heard from the *Leader* reporter. Weil told Guthrie that he planned a sting operation with the help of a fellow who had been leading the fight against municipal corruption in Scranton.[131]

The Scranton associate was a machinist-turned-Christian-evangelist named Robert Wilson, a blue-eyed, square-jawed fellow described as being "utterly without fear ... a man of superb physical proportions, quick and agile as a panther, but cool as ice." A leader of poverty missions in Scranton, Wilson had helped to bring down several Scranton city councilmen, playing detective and even brawling with gamblers during the raid of a gambling parlor to collect evidence for the slew of convictions that followed.[132] Wilson came to Pittsburgh with his sidekick, a detective named T.S. Hufflings, to talk strategy. While Wilson and Hufflings launched their undercover operation, Weil would consult with the federal government on reviewing the books of the banks who were awarded deposits under the suspicious ordinance.

Wilson, posing with permission as a particular executive from Scranton's United States Lumber Company to whom Wilson bore a rather striking resemblance, checked into the Hotel Duquesne on Smithfield Street in early November and set up a meeting with Smiling Johnnie Klein. Wilson introduced Klein to two of his "salesmen," Herbert Jones and William Bates (actually two of Hufflings' detectives), and explained to Klein that he was interested in getting Klein's help to convince the city councils to award him a contract to pave a street in Pittsburgh with wood blocks. Klein smiled and told Wilson he would do what he could, and Wilson left Jones and Bates in Pittsburgh to continue to meet with Klein. For the next several weeks, Jones and Bates then proceeded to wine and dine Klein, who was sometimes accompanied by another member of the "Big Five," the president of the Common Council, William Brand. Klein continued to offer encouragement to Jones and Bates, telling them "I think I can get the Councils to go along provided we handle it in the right manner." Wilson came back into town and met with Klein and Brand, and Brand explained that the "Big Five" were capable of pushing legislation through the councils "if they got the steam." Wilson smiled politely, but did not take the bait.[133]

Brand and Klein were beginning to get frustrated with this "bunch of hicks from Scranton" who obviously didn't understand "how these things are done in the big city." They called Wilson back to the city for a meeting during the first week in December, and Wilson agreed to meet them, this time in the Fort Pitt Hotel at 10th Street and Penn Avenue. Through the assistance of the Hotel's lawyers from Weil & Thorp, Wilson and his detectives checked into a quiet corner of the hotel in adjoining rooms with a connecting door, drilled several small holes in the door, and fitted the holes with small paper cones, to act as megaphones. Jones and Bates stayed in the adjoining room with a stenographer, while one of Leo Weil's associates, Charles B. Prichard (subsequently Pittsburgh's director of public safety and a city solicitor), sat just behind the bathroom door, which also had holes and cones to help him hear from his listening post.

At the appointed time, Brand and Klein arrived at Wilson's room with another man, Joseph C. Wasson, another city councilman and member of the "Big Five." Klein asked Wilson, "How would you like to pave Fourth Avenue?" A stunned Wilson said he would be delighted to pave one of Pittsburgh's main thoroughfares with wood-block—it was more than he had asked for. Klein explained, "If we want Fourth Avenue paved, one of us introduces the bill, someone else moves that we suspend the rules, another moves to adopt an ordinance and bang, bang, bang, it passes just like that."

"However," Brand chimed in, "there are a lot of councilmen that have to be taken care of." He explained to Wilson that the councilmen would expect to receive from Wilson ten percent of the paving contract, or eight thousand dollars.

"That's no problem," said Wilson. "How do we handle payment?" Klein said Wilson could pay him directly in cash, that he acted as the "angel of charity" in these matters to make sure that the appropriate councilmen were receiving their payments. Wilson gave them a one thousand dollar down payment in cash and told them he would deposit the rest in a Pittsburgh bank account to be paid out after the council passed the ordinance. He asked them to give him the name of a Pittsburgh banker they trusted.

"William W. Ramsey, president of the German National Bank," Klein answered, and he proceeded to tell Wilson how they were paid approximately twenty-five thousand dollars by each of six banks that were included in a special ordinance earlier in the year. It was almost more than Wilson and his undercover team could have hoped for, but Klein continued his explanation, producing a list of councilmen and pointing out which ones could not be bought, "because it was easier to check them than the crooked ones."[134]

Meanwhile, with stenographer's notes and several eyewitnesses to Klein and Brand's incriminating statements in hand, Leo Weil worked on corroborating the evidence, to show the payments emanating from the banks. Through his connections, Winfield Shiras arranged an appointment for Weil, Shiras and George R. Wallace to visit President Theodore Roosevelt, the self-avowed "muckraking" political reformer who was then serving in the last months of his final term in office, to ask for the president's help in getting federal bank examiners to investigate the German National Bank. Weil in particular thought it would be a good idea to see "the man at the top" to avoid "middlemen who can throw a hundred obstacles in your way and who may have loose tongues." They went to Washington and were admitted to the oval office, where they met Charles J. Bonaparte, the Attorney General, and Lawrence O. Murray, the Comptroller of the Currency. Weil described the meeting:

The President, dressed in his tennis clothes, had just come in from a game of tennis which he had won and was feeling particularly fit and vigorous. After brief introductions, the President slapped Winfield on the back and said, 'How is your dad? I am a great admirer of your father. Give him my best regards.' Turning to me without waiting for an answer from Shiras, the President said, 'Now what can I do for you? I've been told that you are the one who wants some help in Pittsburgh, something about graft. From what I have been told about you, I can't imagine your needing anyone's help.' I immediately seized the opportunity and said, 'We have become 'muckrakers.''

'Muckrakers!' the President shouted, roaring with laughter and slapping me on the back. We couldn't help but laugh, so infectious is the President's laugh. ...

I explained the problem as briefly as I could. I must admit that he seemed fascinated with what he heard. When I was finished, the President asked the attorney general, 'Is Weil's request for a federal bank examiner legal and proper?'

Receiving an affirmative answer, Roosevelt told the controller [sic] of the currency, 'See that the best bank examiner we have available is sent to Pittsburgh immediately and before he begins his examination have him get in touch with Weil. How does that sound to my muckraking friends?' the President inquired, laughing again and giving me another slap on the back. Before we could answer, President Roosevelt put his face close to mine and threatened, 'Now if this whole thing turns out to be a wild goose chase, it won't be a goose but it will be your head that I'll serve up on a platter!" I pictured my head on a platter surrounded with roasted potatoes. Looking directly at me and gritting his teeth, the President added, 'I have the utmost scorn and contempt for any man who brings false charges.'

I replied, 'Mr. President, I want you to understand that I take the entire responsibility in this matter.'

'You needn't say it,' he answered. 'I liked the way you looked at me when I threatened you. You never blinked.'

Back in the city councils, Klein and Brand were performing as promised, pushing through the Councils a preposterous piece of legislation to pave Fourth Avenue in wood-block to be purchased from the United States Lumber Company. Leo Weil advised Mayor Guthrie to veto the ordinance. "Don't worry," said the mayor. "I would never sign the contract even if they passed the ordinance over my veto."[135]

Meanwhile, Harrison Nesbit, the federal bank examiner—a lawyer by training who had served as a special attorney in the Bureau of Corporations in Washington and as assistant law officer in the Department of Commerce and Labor—arrived in Pittsburgh on December 7 and met briefly with Weil. He then arrived at the offices of the German National Bank in the Granite Building on Sixth Avenue, showed his credentials, and began to review the bank's books in what the bankers would have considered to be a routine audit proceeding. Before long, however, Nesbit found an entry for a note for $17,500 given by the bank's president, William W. Ramsey, with the notation "councilmen." When asked about the meaning of the entry, Ramsey went pale and stammered something about a personal loan. "That is a violation of the banking law, and I don't believe you," said Nesbit. During the cross-examination that followed, Ramsey admitted that the money had been paid to Smiling Johnnie Klein in order to have the bank included in the city depositary ordinance.[136] Nesbit ordered Ramsey to call a meeting of the Bank's board of directors to confess to the bribe; and the directors immediately asked for his resignation, as well as that of the cashier, August A. Vilsack—who was, incidentally, the brother-in-law of Billy Brennen's younger sister Stella.

On the following Monday, a few days before Christmas 1908, city detectives, armed with warrants, arrested all of the members of the "Big Five"—Smiling Johnnie Klein, William Brand, Jacob Soffel, Jr. and Joseph C. Wasson of the Common Council, and T.O. Atkinson of the Select Council—as well as a couple of other councilmen, William H. Melaney and Hugh Ferguson, and William W. Ramsey and August A. Vilsack, formerly of the German National Bank.

Weil gave the scoop to the reporter at the *Pittsburgh Leader* who had met with him back in November. As the *Leader* reported, Weil, who was to be acting as prosecuting attorney before the grand jury along with Willis McCook and William B. Rodgers, declared that the investigation had been initiated by the Voters' League, and that all evidence had been collected and submitted to the venerable D.T. Watson and the law firm of Patterson, Sterrett & Acheson for their review and evaluation before charges were filed.[137]

At the preliminary hearing before Police Magistrate F.J. Brady on December 22, in a packed courtroom with Mayor Guthrie sitting in the gallery, Allegheny County District Attorney William Blakeley turned the prosecution over to Leo Weil. Weil stunned the city council defendants as well as courtroom onlookers with a meticulous laying out of the evidence. One by one came the witnesses—from Robert Wilson, to Jones and Bates, to the stenographer from behind the hotel door, to young Prichard from the hotel bathroom, to Harrison Nesbit, the bank examiner—presenting both eyewitness testimony of the wood-block bribes and documentary evidence of the bank ordinance bribery scheme. At the end of Weil's presentation, Magistrate Brady ordered all nine defendants held for trial, the bail for the seven councilmen totaling $178,000.

Klein, Wasson and Brand, protested their innocence in the press, saying the charges were a political ploy by the Voters' League. Meanwhile, another councilman was seen at Union Station being escorted off of a train to New York by a detective. There were some who were clearly worried. Others were just puzzled by the swift turn of events. Public Safety director Edward Lang said, "The first time that I became aware of the investigation was when I was given the warrants and told to have my officers serve them." He was surprised that the Voters' League could have conducted an investigation in the city, with out-of-town detectives, without anyone in his department knowing about it.[138]

Amid the disruption to business and political custom, the reactions of the people of Pittsburgh ranged from shock, to horror and disgust, mixed with a bit of distrust of the motives of the reformers. As journalist Albert Jay Nock wrote:

Press and people—the press covertly and suggestively, the people openly—impugned their motives. "What do these fellows want?" was the continual question. "Does Weil want to be judge? Well, let's elect him and stop this mess; it's ruining the town." "Does Blakeley want to be governor? Well, let's give it to him and cut all this stuff out; it hurts business."[139]

Nevertheless, Klein, Brand and Wasson were all convicted of accepting bribes (despite an attempt by John and Charles Colbert, brothers who were brokers from Tarentum, to bribe the jury in Klein's case; they were later found guilty and sentenced to two years in prison) and the councilmen were sentenced to prison, as was William W. Ramsey of the German National Bank. The bank's cashier, Mr. Vilsack, turned state's evidence, pleaded no contest, and ended up in jail for eight months. Klein, Brand and Wasson attempted to have their convictions overturned, but in April 1909, Judge Robert Frazer threw out their appeals and sentenced them. Klein received three years and six months, and Brand and Wasson each received eighteen months in prison.

Meanwhile, Weil continued his work with the grand jury, and focused a great deal of attention on getting Klein to confess. At first, Klein was defiant, as he had been at the forefront of the council's culture of not "squealing," raising a fund just a year or so before for the defense of another convicted councilman, William Martin, in order to keep him from talking; but after a time Klein realized that his friends had scattered, and there was no one willing to step up and help his wife and twins during his time in jail.

During a courtroom appearance on one of his appeals, Smiling Johnnie Klein was sitting next to Weil and said, "I rather wish now that I had made a clean breast of this thing, and got in out of the wet ..." to which Weil replied, "Maybe it is not too late."[140]

Late one night, Weil received a "personal, confidential and private" note from Smiling Johnnie. A few days later, Klein was sitting in the law offices of Weil & Thorp in the Frick Building, giving two hundred pages of testimony to Weil and two stenographers. District Attorney Blakeley was astounded. "I never met a man who could remember the details of incidents with such precision. He recalls his every move and we know his memory is perfect for it fits with precision with the evidence we have."[141]

The floodgates were opened. Following Klein's confession, District Attorney Blakeley invited all bribe-takers to confess in open court. The following day, ten councilmen volunteered their confessions and resigned from council, including Dr. W.H. Weber, who had been Mayor Guthrie's principal foe against the smoke abatement ordinance. In three more days, twenty-four councilmen offered confessions and resignations. Then came more indictments against the bankers and businessmen who were allegedly involved in the scandal, including Frank N. Hoffstot, president of the Pressed Steel Car Company and the German National Bank of Allegheny, who was charged with giving $52,500 to councilman Charles Stewart in connection with the bank ordinance; Charles W. Friend, vice president of the Clinton Iron and Steel Company; and Emil Winter, president of Workingmen's Savings & Trust.[142] Hoffstot was ultimately acquitted. In all, however, as the grand jury concluded its work, there had been 186 indictments filed against 116 individuals; over sixty percent of the members of city council had been accused of criminal activity. More than sixty of them pleaded no contest and were fined. At least twenty were in jail.[143]

Mayor Guthrie, who sounded the alarm at the crooked bank ordinance and gave his secret stamp of official approval to its investigation by the Voters' League, saw a former client, the German National Bank of Pittsburg, have its reputation dragged through Pittsburgh's muddy streets and watched as two of its executives went to the penitentiary. He suffered the awkwardness of standing by while the brother of the brother-in-law of one of his most visible political patrons, Billy Brennen, lost his career and his freedom. Although he went on to greater things in public service, Mayor Guthrie's law practice was never the same.

Meanwhile, Weil's partner, Charles Thorp, asked Weil if he feared for his life. "Aren't you afraid that one of these days an angry councilman is going to hire someone to take a shot at you?" Weil laughed and told Thorp that he slept with a gun beneath his pillow. One night, he used it, shooting twice into the darkness as an unidentified intruder lingered in his bedroom doorway. One of his bullets struck the mantle. "We ought to look for a man with splinters in his face," said the investigating policeman.[144] Weil and his colleagues also suffered a professional toll from their involvement in the bribery cases. As Weil's grandson Andrew writes:

> *The members of the Voters' League had achieved a success far beyond what they had imagined when they initiated their investigation but were not cheering and congratulating each other ... Leo Weil, W.K. Shiras and Willis McCook were particularly disconsolate that several of their friends were among the bankers and businessmen caught in the net.*[145]

Nock alleged that Weil lost more than $150,000 in legal business as a direct result of his involvement in the city council prosecutions.

Another casualty of the city council bribery trials was, ironically, the momentum of reform itself. In the mayoral election in February 1909, the Civic Party candidate, William H. Stevenson, went down in defeat to Chris Magee's nephew, lawyer William A. Magee, the Republican candidate, by more than two to one. The younger Magee, a masterful politician, ran on a pro-growth, pro-business platform and effectively exploited the sense of chaos that had arisen in the wake of the bribery indictments among the white collar downtown crowd, pledging to continue the course of reform, but declaring that the Guthrie administration was ultimately too idealistic and inexperienced to have achieved any lasting progress for Pittsburgh. He said, "the result of three years of reform has demonstrated conclusively that while a mayor can do no wrong, he at the same time may do no good."[146] After Magee's election, according to *The New York Times*, "[t]he word had been passed along that Pittsburgh was to be 'wide open' again and that the reformers had been beaten."[147]

As it turned out, the younger Magee was not made precisely from the same mold as his late Uncle Chris, and his administration would not ultimately be as rife with corruption as everyone imagined. He would outshine Guthrie in his ability to get legislation passed by deftly packaging bond issue projects to serve many key constituencies at once, using his influence to extend water filtration to the rest of Pittsburgh, in addition to adding land to the city park system, widening and paving more city streets, constructing the

Bloomfield Bridge and initiating the cutting of the "hump"—the lowering of Grant's Hill at Fifth and Grant Streets.

Still, while the reformers had brought down some of the people who were involved in corruption, the structure that permitted corruption remained—and Weil and Guthrie were not prepared to rest on their laurels after having come so far.

On April 1, 1910, over three thousand Pittsburghers pushed their way into Exposition Hall, at the Point, to protest the continuation of corruption even after the bribery convictions. Mayor Magee shared the dais with ex-Mayor Guthrie and Leo Weil, representing the Voters' League, as well as a number of other civic and religious leaders. When Weil rose to speak, however, the fact that Mayor Magee was sitting behind him on the stage did nothing to cause him to edit his remarks against Magee. He was at a stage in his career, in fact, when he found little reason ever to edit his remarks at the expense of his principles. Turning to Magee, Weil publicly charged the mayor with failing to clean up "the rotten political conditions which exist in the city over which you preside." As historian Barbara Burstein writes, "In the style of Emile Zola, he thundered: 'I accuse the administration of betraying the civil service of this city. I accuse them of handing over the city to vice.'" Magee tried to answer the charges, then and there, but the crowd was with Weil; Weil attempted without success to calm the crowd down and permit Mayor Magee to respond, but in the end, the frustrated mayor walked out of the Hall in disgust.[148]

The stage was set for structural change. Over the next several months, the municipal affairs committee of the Pittsburgh Chamber of Commerce began to study and refine a proposal written by attorney George R. Wallace for the amendment of the city charter. Wallace's proposal was to eliminate the bicameral city council structure and replace it with one council of eight at-large members—with no members of city council representing any particular city ward.

The consideration of Wallace's plan led members of the Chamber of Commerce, along with other civic and religious leaders, to form an unofficial "Charter Committee," with Colonel T.J. Keenan, the son of the founder of the *Pittsburgh Legal Journal* and himself a former owner of the *Pittsburgh Press*, as its chair. The Charter Committee elaborated on Wallace's proposal: not only would the current bicameral city council be replaced with one body of nine at-large members (an odd number, to avoid gridlock), but its members would be elected to four-year terms on non-partisan ballots, and they would each receive a yearly salary of $6,500. By creating a small class of paid, party-neutral professional legislators the Committee intended to not only make it easier for city council members to refuse bribes, but also to eliminate the city council seat as the perk of a wardheeler's loyalty to a partisan boss. Bribing a number of faceless councilmen to martial them towards the passage of private legislation was an easy thing to do in the dark, with too many councilmen for watchdogs to monitor; a smaller group would necessarily be subject to easier public scrutiny. Ultimately, the city council would look a lot more like a corporation board—just as George Guthrie, the promoter of the "municipal corporation," would have it in his perfect world. Also, the new charter would permit ballot initiatives to be introduced by voters, as well as the popular recall of officeholders, and referenda, the ability of voters to block a legislative action by voting against it at the ballot box. These procedures would place the threat of popular revolt just within earshot of the city council, as another governor on corrupt behavior.[149]

Mayor Magee was no great fan of the proposals, although he pressed forward on his own investigations and housecleaning of corruption in the city's schools. The Committee, meanwhile, took every opportunity to encourage support of the "Pittsburgh Plan," issuing bulletins, seeking endorsements and holding rallies. After nearly a year of agitation by the Committee, the proposed charter finally made it onto the legislative calendar in Harrisburg. Pittsburgh's "charter army" of approximately 250 concerned citizens arrived in Harrisburg in March 1911, on the day before the reading of the bill, in eight special train cars, and enjoyed a luncheon with the Scranton delegation, replete with a brass band. Among the citizens speaking in favor of the bill at the Senate and House committee hearings were George R. Wallace; P.J. McArdle, the president of the Amalgamated Association of Iron and Steel Workers; ex-Mayor Guthrie; Rabbi J. Leonard Levy of Rodef Shalom; Bishop Cortland Whitehead of the Anglican diocese of Pittsburgh; F.R. Babcock of the Pittsburgh Chamber of Commerce; and, of course, Leo Weil.

Wallace, in a page taken out of Judge Alexander Addison's book, blamed the abuses of the bicameral city council on the "drag wave of the French Revolution" that "swept over this country" during the early nineteenth century, and argued with the precision of a trial lawyer the merits of the "Pittsburgh Plan." Guthrie, noting that this bill was the result of a popular movement and not that of a machine, reminded the legislature that Pittsburgh was not looking for a "Ripper" but merely "the power to govern [our] own city." McArdle declared that municipal corruption was a burden on labor.[150]

It was Weil's address to the legislature that was most anticipated, and he did not disappoint. "By your gracious patience," he began, "I will a round, unvarnished tale deliver, shocking though it may be." Weil then proceeded to fill the chamber with specific allegations and charges of Pittsburgh's notorious "councilmanic graft and incompetence," including a review of the final scorecard of the city council bribery trials and the fact that several current councilmen were still under pending indictment. "The majority of the present councils are wholly unfit for office," he summarized, stating that many of them were "gamblers, ward-heelers, bartenders and the like." Speaking over the warnings of the hearing chairman, Weil also accused Mayor Magee of abetting the ongoing corruption of the councils, leaving accused conspirators in public posts, appointing unworthy and incompetent political favorites to others, entering into corrupt city contracts, and protecting vice in exchange for an annual tribute of one million dollars for the coffers of the mayor's machine. "It would require the genius of a Dante to adequately portray the orgy of vice that prevails in our community, protected by the administration of the city." Even the mayor himself was a monster, according to Weil. "A monthly diary of the doings of the chief magistrate of our city would horrify one whose moral perceptions are not wholly blunted," he claimed.[151]

A number of legislators immediately expressed their outrage over Weil's remarks, some remarking that his personal attacks on Mayor Magee did more harm than good to the cause of reform. Magee, meanwhile, blasted Weil in the evening newspapers, calling him a "slanderer" and a "vicious romancer," responding point-by-point to Weil's charges and questioning the motives of a man who would pretend to assume the role reserved for elected public officials, such as the County District Attorney, to protect the city.[152]

In the end, a new Pittsburgh charter was adopted, but, perhaps predictably, it was a product of compromise. The Republicans opposed the initiative, recall, referendum and non-partisan ballot provisions of the "Pittsburgh Plan." In the bill that was finally passed on May 25, 1911, the new charter provided for a nine-member at-large city council, and for city council members to be paid, but did not contain the other provisions. Governor John K. Tener, the Republican former ballplayer, appointed the first council members under the new charter.[153] With a partial victory in the legislature, Guthrie, Weil and the other reformers had finally achieved at least some of the characteristics of the structural political reform that they had sought in Pittsburgh since the 1880s.

Despite the success of water filtration and the *Pittsburgh Survey*, among other accomplishments, historian Michael Weber called Guthrie's mayoral administration "generally ineffective." However, contemporary supporters of municipal reform nonetheless saw Guthrie as a hero of the movement. As Clinton Woodruff observed, "there are those who are inclined to criticize Mayor Guthrie, because, lawyer-like, he accomplished so many of his important things without taking the public into his confidence until the results were accomplished."[154] It is not surprising that Guthrie would approach his job as mayor in the same way he had achieved success as a corporation lawyer—operating behind the scenes, tinkering with processes and institutional machinery—and leaving the dirty work of political intercourse to others.

Most tellingly, perhaps, it took the very different mayoral administrations of two lawyers, that of both Guthrie and Magee, to achieve the two most prized objectives of the reform movement—arranging the filtration of the entire Pittsburgh water supply, and the dismantling of the corrupt city legislature. The two mayors may be seen as representing two distinct, recurrent strains of lawyer within American legal and political culture. Guthrie was the lawyer who dabbled in politics—a principled man seeking to make big changes, a legal scholar who was carried forward and energized by a moral philosophy; Magee, by contrast, was the politician who was incidentally a lawyer—propelled by a talent for compromise and consensus-building, but able to call upon his knowledge of the legal machinery to reduce his hard political work to practice. Guthrie's strain functions well as a catalyst, Magee's as an implementer.

Interestingly, Magee was able to maintain both a legal practice and a political career after his tenure as mayor, and was eventually re-elected as mayor in 1922. Guthrie's legal career, on the other hand, was effectively finished after his term in office, perhaps as a price for his assault on "business as usual" within the city. Turning his attention to the party he had all but abandoned after taking office in 1906, he squabbled with Billy Brennen over control of the state Democratic delegation during the 1912 presidential primary. Brennen wanted the delegates to enter the Democratic convention undeclared, to be used as a bargaining chip, while Guthrie wanted the delegation to support the candidacy of another professorial, bespectacled lawyer with an enlarged moral compass, Woodrow Wilson.[155] Guthrie ultimately prevailed, and was rewarded by President Wilson with an appointment as United States ambassador to Japan. He died at his post in 1917, after a round of golf with a reporter in Tokyo.

Leo Weil, operating outside official imprimatur, represents a different strain of American lawyer entirely, and a very rare one at that. As a passionate muckraker, he was akin to public interest lawyers such as Ralph Nader, but he was also a corporation lawyer who had made his fortune arguing cases on behalf of the Rockefellers and other tycoons—seeing no conflict in his two halves, even if his clients occasionally did. Weil continued to play at both during the rest of his career, dodging attempts to smear his reputation and continuing to be relied upon within Pittsburgh as a voice of moral authority until his death in 1938.

BIG WORK, BIG WAR

Only a few days after the street celebrations welcoming George W. Guthrie as the new mayor of Greater Pittsburgh, on February 27, 1906, William Scott, the senior partner of Dalzell, Scott & Gordon, died at his home on Bidwell Street on the North Side. For several months, he had been complaining of indigestion and insomnia, and a trip to the shore had only worsened the fifty-six year-old attorney's condition.[156]

Rather suddenly, forty-six year-old George Gordon found himself without his partner of nineteen years. John "Corporation" Dalzell, the former senior partner to Scott & Gordon, was now a career United States congressman, battling the Southern Democrats over canal appropriations. Scott and Gordon had been through many of their own battles together, and had counseled the likes of Andrew Mellon, Andrew Carnegie and Arthur Vining Davis, titans of Pittsburgh's Gilded Age. Gordon was the front-man, the corporation lawyer who went to court when he had to, and William Scott—the son of Pennsylvania's Senator John Scott, the former general counsel for the Pennsylvania Railroad—was the firm's "office lawyer," although Scott's independent reputation was such that he enjoyed a term as the president of the Allegheny County Bar Association as well as being the second Pittsburgh lawyer, after Philander Knox, to serve as president of the Pennsylvania Bar Association.

John Dalzell's son, Yale-educated William Sage Dalzell, had joined the firm in 1893, and had been named as a junior partner of the firm in 1897, the year his father formally retired from the firm.[157] The younger Dalzell, age thirty-eight in 1906, was a passionate and excitable young trial lawyer, known to get so anxious while dictating trial memoranda that he would bite his own lip, bleeding all over himself as he continued to compose.[158] George Gordon and William Scott were cooler customers, gentlemen from another age; and with William Scott's death terminating the old partnership, it seemed like a good time for Gordon and the younger Dalzell to go their separate ways.

Dalzell formed a partnership with Gordon Fisher, an associate who worked with Dalzell, Scott & Gordon, Edwin P. Young, a Cornell-educated Lycoming County lawyer, and Richard H. Hawkins, also an associate of Dalzell, Scott & Gordon and the son of Orphans' Court judge William G. Hawkins, Jr. The younger Dalzell kept the offices of the old firm in the St. Nicholas Building, at the corner of Fourth Avenue and Grant Street, of which his father was a part owner.

George Gordon moved his offices to fifteenth floor of the new Frick Building Annex. In choosing his new colleagues, he gravitated toward men of like qualities. On a superficial level, William Watson Smith, at age thirty-four, shared a great deal with Gordon. They were both tall, thin men; both the sons of the Western Pennsylvania merchant class whose fathers provided them with local schooling before sending them to Ivy League schools. Both had only recently suffered the untimely deaths of their only young sons.[159] Although both were stylistically impassive, their recent losses seemed to make them even more serious men. But at Princeton, classmates knew "Reddy" Smith,[160] nicknamed for his bright red hair, to be something of a cut-up, if only seasonally. For the annual Washington's Birthday festivities, Smith was chosen by the Class of 1892 to deliver the senior address. Smith's text, self-authored, was a piece of fluff called "George Washington's Last Pants," in which he repeatedly interrupts himself to assail his classmates with witty insults such as "'String Beans' Conwell... is a very useful man on a tug-of-war team, as he not only pulls well, but at a pinch he can be used as a rope."[161] By 1907, however, Smith had acquired a reputation among his old classmates for showing exceptional discipline, and for being "very serious." In a reunion publication, they good-naturedly taunted him, writing, "He has no hobby," but he "is looking for a good one and is open to suggestions."[162]

When Smith left Princeton he moved to Pittsburgh ("a first-class place, all reports and New York newspapers to the contrary notwithstanding," he wrote[163]), and took up the study of law with Knox & Reed, the predecessor of Reed Smith Shaw and Beal. Upon entering the bar in 1894, Smith practiced on his own for a few years and in the fall of 1899, he was appointed assistant city solicitor of Pittsburgh,[164] serving under Clarence Burleigh. In the solicitor's office, Smith steadily gained trial experience, and argued before the Pennsylvania Supreme Court on behalf of the city of Pittsburgh on several occasions, but with the onset of the Guthrie administration in 1906, Smith decided it was time to return to full-time private practice.

Despite George Gordon's esteemed reputation and experience, he approached Smith more or less as an equal. In the partnership agreement that established the firm of Gordon & Smith as of April 1, 1906, Gordon and Smith agreed to share equally in the profits and losses, except that after each of them had received twenty thousand dollars in net profits, Gordon had the ability to decide how the excess would be distributed. The two partners immediately hired another experienced attorney known to both of them as their most senior associate. Ralph Longenecker, the thirty-three year-old son of a prominent judge in Bedford County, received his bachelor's degree at Yale and graduated at the top of the class from the law school at Pittsburgh in 1897. According to the tradition of time, Longenecker, as top graduate, was given a teaching fellowship at Pittsburgh where he struck up an acquaintance with William Watson Smith, then serving his own brief stint as a law professor. When he was not teaching, Longenecker was establishing his career in a shared suite of offices in the St. Nicholas Building, not far from George Gordon's old office. Gordon and Smith offered him $416 a month to leave his one-man office, with the possibility of becoming a partner in short order. Rounding out the office were Allen Taylor Caperton Gordon, a shoestring cousin of Gordon's from Virginia, who had been an associate of the Dalzell, Scott & Gordon firm; Alexander Black (Sr.), a Princeton and recent Pittsburgh law graduate who had also taught at the law school; and William K. Johnson, a first-year associate from Pitt Law School.

The former Dalzell, Scott & Gordon bookkeeper and stenographer, Clara Houston, was offered one hundred dollars a month, twice what Black received and four times what Johnson received as associates, to join the new firm. In addition, there were two other stenographers, Ralph Kramer and Emma J. Erck. Personal secretaries were still virtually unheard of in those days, so Houston, Kramer and Erck were utilized as a steno pool by all the attorneys, but Gordon and Smith relied heavily upon Miss Houston. Sadie Ingram was hired as a telephone operator and filing clerk, Edward Stanton, the brother of African American Pittsburgh lawyer William H. Stanton, began his long career with the firm as the doorman/receptionist, and Joe Kennelly was hired as a messenger at five dollars per week.[165] This was the entire firm of Gordon & Smith in 1906: two partners, four associates and six staff employees.

The correspondence arising from the dissolution of Dalzell, Scott & Gordon was cordial, but it did seem to go on endlessly, as Gordon and Dalzell each attempted to collect old bills. While William Dalzell's share of the old partnership was a mere sixteen percent compared to Gordon and Scott's forty-two percent each, Dalzell nevertheless cooperated to the last penny. As late as 1920, when Dalzell's firm unexpectedly received a check for $9.95 in the matter of *John F. Wilcox v. Semet-Solvay Co.* (1905), Dalzell dutifully sent it in to Gordon for distribution. George Gordon himself would send Scott's widow, Anna King Scott, her late husband's share of the periodic collections from the old partnership. The dissolution of the old firm finally concluded seventeen years after Dalzell and Gordon parted company, Gordon sending his last letter to Mrs. Scott regarding old accounts in 1923.[166] The partnership itself had only been in existence for approximately nineteen years. Such was the surprising persistence of the otherwise fragile partnership form.

Meanwhile, in the once towering Carnegie Building, now jammed into a corner between the Frick Building (built in 1902) and the Frick Building Annex, Judge James Hay Reed continued to lead the venerable firm of Reed, Smith, Shaw & Beal with his new partners after the departure of Philander Knox: Edwin Whittier Smith, the deep-voiced trial lawyer; George E. Shaw, the counselor to Mellon Bank and many other Pittsburgh corporations of the first rank; James H. Beal, Sr., the outside general counsel to the Pittsburgh Coal Company; and George B. Motheral, who sacrificed his legal career to function as the firm's business manager—each of whom were granted a fifteen percent share of the partnership, to Judge Reed's forty percent, at its formation in 1901. Shortly thereafter, the partners made room for Chicago-educated Samuel McClay, the real estate lawyer who had been hired before Knox left, and Judge Reed's son, Pittsburgh Law graduate David Aiken Reed, who came on board in 1903. In the five years after the creation of the new partnership, Judge Reed and his partners brought on three other associates—trial lawyer John G. Frazer (Sr.) in 1904; and William McIlvane Robinson (Sr.) and Robert J. Dodds (Sr.), who were partners in their own firm in the Farmers Bank Building before joining Reed Smith in 1905.[167]

By 1908, Gordon & Smith had only added one additional lawyer, Thomas Mellon II, the grandson of Judge Thomas Mellon and son of James Ross Mellon; but he was not particularly interested in the law and was on his way out of the firm as soon as he arrived to spend the rest of his life collecting pages from medieval manuscripts.[168] Reed Smith added two more long-term hires during the same period: associates William A. Seifert and John J. "Jack" Heard, both graduates of the Pittsburgh Law School.[169] Thus, by 1908, Reed Smith had twelve lawyers (seven partners and five associates), and Gordon & Smith had six and a half (three partners, three associates, and Mellon). In 1908, Reed Smith had gross revenues of $334,115, its best year since 1900; with half the lawyers, Gordon & Smith grossed $101,843.[170] Overhead was low, and it is likely that Judge Reed, George Gordon and William Watson Smith each made today's equivalent of around a million dollars or more that year.

While they were competitors, these two of the largest, most patrician firms in Pittsburgh also enjoyed some close familial ties. In 1898, William Watson Smith married Florence Aiken, whose older sister Katherine was married to Smith's preceptor, Judge Reed.[171] William Watson Smith and Judge Reed were brothers-in-law by marriage. Longenecker was also related to Judge Reed by marriage; his wife, Grace, was the sister of Reed's daughter-in-law.[172] The close family relationships between the two firms meant that, despite the fact that they might find themselves on opposite sides of some matters, work might comfortably be passed from one to the other when conflicts arose.

Such was probably at least one of the reasons that Gordon & Smith assumed the role of lead counsel to A. Overholt & Company, one of the largest whiskey manufacturers in the world—owned by Henry Clay Frick and the Mellon brothers, who had all been closely aligned with Reed Smith for a number of years—following a devastating fire. At two forty-five in the afternoon on November 19, 1905, in the town of Broadford, near Connellsville, Pennsylvania, the fire broke out in the main warehouse of the company. Seeing smoke pouring out of a third story window, two employees of the company climbed the outside fire escape of the warehouse and pried open one of its small iron doors, only to be caught in a suffocating cloud of smoke. Within minutes, blue-tinged flames, fed by exploding whiskey barrels, shot up into the sky. Firefighters came from as far as Uniontown and McKeesport to douse the fire, but it was still burning fiercely at midnight, the flashes of flame lighting the countryside for miles around.[173] By the time the fire was finally put out, the main bonded warehouse was completely destroyed, along with an estimated sixteen thousand barrels of rye whiskey, much of it already sold. Preliminary damage estimates were in the range of at least two million dollars.[174] While the insurance companies for Overholt asserted that they were only obligated to pay for the amount of money it would take to reproduce the lost whiskey, instead of its market value, which was considerably higher, William Watson Smith eventually won a verdict for Overholt based on the market value of the whiskey, because, as the appeals court put it, "the age of whisky materially affects its character and quality" and that Overholt's whiskey "has a distinctive character and quality of its own."[175] The case resulted in a substantial recovery for Frick and the Mellons, and was one of the reasons why 1908 was such a good year for Gordon & Smith. Frick would later appoint William Watson Smith as one of the executors of his estate, resulting in a seven-figure receipt to the firm by the time of the estate's final accounting.

While these two firms were receiving significant revenues from some of the most prestigious clients Pittsburgh had to offer, the entire bar of Pittsburgh was a hive of activity, and a number of other firms in town were also enjoying a period of expansion, with the number of potential recruits emerging from Pitt Law School, as well as, from 1913, from the Duquesne University Law School, reaching record numbers. In 1900, the number of local law school graduates in Pittsburgh totaled twenty, but by 1914, with Pittsburgh and Duquesne both adding to the pool, the number of local graduates reached fifty-one.[176] While the number of graduates grew at an outlandish rate, the number of active private practitioners in the downtown Pittsburgh bar grew, as well, at the somewhat more modest but significant rate of around ten percent, from approximately 972 in 1906 to 1,052 in 1917.[177] Many other law school graduates were finding work in the trust departments of banks and in government.

The most definitive development during the period, however, was the concentration of these lawyers into ever larger partnerships. The number of active law firms, on a net basis, grew steadily during the first half of the century, from sixty-eight in 1899 to almost one hundred by the mid-1940s.[178] More importantly, however, as large Pittsburgh corporate clients continued to adopt the principle that "big companies do big work," they tended to bring their legal work to larger law partnerships, firms that had crossed the chasm from being an ephemeral assemblage of one to three partners, each handling their own cases—a scenario typical of the mid-to-late nineteenth century—to something akin to an institution, organized along modern business lines to serve the "big work" of the "big companies" rather than a mere series of unconnected "cases." Teams of lawyers were now required to be available to provide continuity and experientially informed judgment about the current and future "big work" of a client.

The size of firms such as Reed Smith and Gordon & Smith were only two examples of how Pittsburgh firms were reacting to the market demand. The firm of Patterson, Sterrett & Acheson was formed in 1900 by Thomas Patterson, an esteemed big case trial lawyer who was a nephew of Judge Baird of Washington County; Ross Sterrett, the nephew of the former Chief Justice of the Pennsylvania Supreme Court, James P. Sterrett; and Marcus W. Acheson, Jr., the son of Judge Marcus W. Acheson of the Third Circuit federal court. The firm expanded rapidly, such that by 1912, it consisted of nine lawyers—three more lawyers than Gordon & Smith had on its roster, and only one fewer than Reed Smith—including young Charles F.C. Arensberg, a Harvard Law graduate who joined the firm around 1910 after a few years of practicing on his own, at a salary of fifty dollars per month. The expansion of the firm occurred so rapidly, however, that it soon fell victim to instability. As Arensberg explained it, a "country lad" named Fred C. Shoburt had been promoted by Mr. Acheson from stenographer to head clerk of the firm, from which perch he began "directing the young men who were either students or young lawyers employed by the firm and generally making their lives miserable." It was Shoburt's behavior, Arensberg said, that led to the dissolution of the firm at the end of 1912, whereupon Thomas Patterson formed a new firm, two floors below their offices on the nineteenth floor of the Oliver Building, with some of the younger men: James S. Crawford, James R. Miller, Arensberg and Roy Dunn. Sterrett & Acheson kept the offices on the nineteenth floor, two associates, and Fred C. Shoburt.[179] By 1916, the Patterson Crawford firm was composed of eight lawyers, and Sterrett & Acheson of four.

Clarence Burleigh's firm, Burleigh & Challener, also reached eight lawyers by 1916, as did the firms of McKee Mitchell & Alter, led by the future Pennsylvania Attorney General George E. Alter, and Morris Walker & Allen. Leo Weil's firm, Weil & Thorp, grew to seven lawyers by 1916. They were located one floor above Burleigh & Challener in the Frick Building, including his partner Charles M. Thorp, and associates George K. Warn, Leo Ruslander, L. Pearson Scott, Malcolm Goldsmith and Meyer Greenbaum. John M. Freeman, the long-time partner of the late D.T. Watson, who died in 1916, left the name of his firm as "Watson & Freeman"—a habit of a firm choosing to be seen as an institution rather than as a fleeting storefront, rare but prescient in 1916—and had five associates working with him that year.[180]

Whether or not influenced by the "Cravath System," the approach to developing legal talent within a law firm espoused by Paul Cravath at Cravath, Swaine & Moore in New York, some of these firms were adopting elements of that "System"—hiring fresh, young, trainable recruits, eschewing lateral hires, and in general creating their firms in the image of more permanent institutions and building larger teams around the needs of their corporate clients.

The Patterson and Sterrett break-up, however, undoubtedly led Judge Reed and Messrs. Gordon & Smith to ponder questions of stability and sustainability within their own firms during a period of overall growth. While Reed Smith rode a roller coaster of gross revenues from 1908 to 1917 (registering a low of $264,403 in 1909 and a high of $475,062 in 1916), the firm effectively added no new lawyers during the period. During the same period, Gordon & Smith added eight lawyers, or a net of seven lawyers after the unexpected death of Ralph Longenecker, at age forty-two, from a cerebral hemorrhage in 1916. Among the new Gordon & Smith lawyers were the late William Scott's son, William R. Scott, and two veteran practitioners, signed just nineteen days after Longenecker's death: real estate lawyer Edgar Bell and trust and estates lawyer Albert Weitzel.[181]

John Grier Buchanan, a Harvard law graduate, was the son and grandson of prominent Pittsburgh surgeons. While at William Watson Smith's alma mater, Princeton, Buchanan was the editor of the *Daily Princetonian*, the *Nassau Literary Magazine* and the *Princeton Tiger*, as well as a member of the University Debating Team.[182] With "his propensity for syllogisms, his debater's delight in 'talking for victory' and his habit of sharing his encyclopedic knowledge ... with anyone who cares to listen,"[183] it was clear to John and anyone who knew him that unlike his celebrated ancestors he was destined for a career in the law. At Princeton, Buchanan attended courses in jurisprudence and constitutional government taught by Princeton's president, Woodrow Wilson, whom Buchanan later referred to as his "favorite of all Princeton teachers" and "the second greatest teacher" he ever had. After soliciting Wilson's advice on his ambition to become a lawyer, Buchanan entered Harvard Law School in 1909, and joined Gordon & Smith on September 1, 1912 at a salary of fifty dollars a month. He so impressed Mr. Gordon and Mr. Smith that they took the unprecedented step of doubling his salary after his first ten months with the firm.[184] Messrs. Gordon, Smith and Longenecker were all outstanding lawyers, but with his verbal quickness and intellectual energy, Buchanan began to dominate the culture of the law firm even before he was made a partner in 1916.

Throughout the period, Gordon & Smith continued to show growth on the balance sheet. In fiscal 1907, the firm had net profits of $41,046, but by fiscal 1914, net profits soared to $144,000.[185] Smith's new hires were necessary merely to stay on top of the workload, although despite the additions Gordon & Smith remained only the second largest firm in Pittsburgh, after the break-up of Patterson Sterrett & Acheson in 1912.

Among all these firms, there was a large contingent of Princeton alumni: William Watson Smith (Class of 1892) and John G. Buchanan (1909) certainly, but also Gordon Fisher (1895) from the Dalzell firm; Alexander Black (Sr.) (1902), William R. Scott (1910) and James I. Marsh (1911) from Gordon & Smith; David Aiken Reed (1900), Jack Heard (1904), John G. Frazer (1901) and William M. Robinson (1900) from Reed Smith; James S. Crawford (1895), James R. Miller (1903) and James R. Dunn (1893) from the Patterson Crawford firm; Harry Stambaugh (1902) and Robert Woods Sutton (1901) from Watson & Freeman; and Meyer Greenbaum (1912) and Ferdinand T. Weil (1913) from Weil & Thorp.

As was the fate defined by the relatively small world in which these lawyers dwelt, the one-time professor of jurisprudence and political economy and subsequently college president at Princeton until 1910—John Buchanan's "second favorite teacher"—would be a key actor in determining the course of the war in Europe, giving matters of global statecraft a personal element for some of these men.

Woodrow Wilson's political rise was meteoric. He was elected governor of New Jersey in the fall of 1910 and entered the statehouse in January 1911; and following the election of 1912, Wilson moved into the White House in March 1913. The great conflict in Europe started raging in 1914, and initially President Wilson had strenuously urged the nation to remain neutral. In May 1915, however, a German submarine torpedoed a British liner, the *Lusitania*, killing 1,200—including more than 120 Americans. While Wilson labored to keep the United States out of the war, some impatient young American men began to skip across the border to enlist in the Canadian Army and join the conflict. It would only be a matter of time before the impatient young men of the Pittsburgh bar would go to Europe for the fight—and a change of view by President Wilson might make that a virtual certainty.

On March 31, 1917, as the *Gazette Times* reported, "[t]housands of men, women and children, representatives of the highest type of Pittsburgh citizenship and Christian humanity, looked into the pictured faces of Washington, Lincoln and Wilson in a great patriotic mass meeting in Exposition Hall ... and lifted their voices in thundering cheers that took out to the whole world that the 'Workshop of the World' is ready to sacrifice the flower of her manhood and the resources of her hills and valleys to maintain the honor of Old Glory."[186]

The keynote speaker at the mass meeting was Pittsburgh's own Philander Knox, who had recently been reelected to the U.S. Senate representing Pennsylvania, after having finished his tenure as Attorney General and as President Taft's Secretary of State, with a short prior stint in the Senate in between. "By no wrongful act of our own," he told the crowd, "we have been drawn into the rim of the vortex of war, that with whirlpool madness is wrecking the manhood, the resources and the civilization of mighty nations." After detailing the German attacks on ships in the Atlantic that resulted in the loss of American lives, and declaring that Americans had "a right to navigate the seas unrestrained," he asked: "But is that all that is involved? ... All civilizing forces ... are operating for democracy. The old systems finally perish through some concrete act of folly or madness and the people come into their own. The crowning act of madness of autocracy is the present European war of ambition, and God grant that it shall be ended by the people themselves, crushing forever the system and the men who have been its beneficiaries. What a glorious conclusion it would be if those who have endured the agonies and shed their blood in an unholy war should be the divinely selected instruments to effect an enduring victory of liberty and peace."[187]

According to Senator Knox, the U.S. entry into the War would be more than a defense of our maritime rights; it would be to answer our calling as a leading democracy in the world to fight for the liberation of humanity from the bonds of tyranny. It was a war that was to be about good versus evil, a non-partisan cause, as emphasized by the support for the Democratic president's call for American intervention also given in short addresses to the crowd by attorney James Francis Burke, the former Republican congressman representing Pittsburgh, and by William Magee's city solicitor, Charles A. O'Brien.[188] Patriotic fervor in Pittsburgh was building to a fever pitch, inspiring Pittsburgh men to join the fight. "There was a feeling," writes Pittsburgh historian Elizabeth Williams, "that democracy itself rested upon their shoulders. Romanticism of war, the excitement of battle and a deep desire to take part in their generation's one great war" were all part of the magnetism and mystique.[189]

On April 6, 1917, President Wilson signed the joint resolution of Congress declaring war on Germany, following his own request. At Reed Smith, Princeton grad David Aiken Reed enlisted in the Army on May 11. Gordon & Smith's Princeton men also enlisted quickly. Third-year associate William R. Scott left to join David Reed at the Fort Niagara First Officers' Training Camp on May 15; James I. Marsh enlisted in the Navy in June; and partner John Buchanan joined the Army in December. By June, Leo Weil's son Ferdinand T. Weil had enlisted in a coastal defense squad and was on his way to the U.S. Navy, and his friend and fellow associate at Weil & Thorp, Princeton grad Meyer Greenbaum, had joined a volunteer squadron of American pilots attached to the Italian Air Force, subsequently joining the Army in August. Joseph M. Duff, Jr., an All-American guard for Princeton's football team (class of '12), football coach at the University of Pittsburgh (1913-14) and a member of Duff, Marshall & Duff in the Bakewell Building, joined a machine gun unit. Lawrence D. Blair, class of '12, and Bertram L. Sichelstiel, class of '10, both left their solo practices and joined, and John C. Sheriff, class of 1896, left his partnership to do the same.[190] The draw of young Princeton men in the Pittsburgh bar to President Wilson's war effort was, incidentally, reflected in the greater Princeton community, leading to a significant number of Princeton alumni and students—over three thousand in all, including 117 faculty members—to enter the service by December 1917. The immediate effect on Princeton itself was a sixty-three percent decrease in admissions and a university budget deficit of $120,000. The following year, Princeton "opened its campus to the military and became, for all intents and purposes, a military college," according to Princeton's Seeley G. Mudd Library. By the war's end, 6,170 Princeton men and 139 faculty members had served.[191]

The "Princeton effect" notwithstanding, participation in the war effort permeated the entire bar. At Morris Walker & Allen, two out of eight lawyers left for the War. McKee Mitchell & Alter lost associate James Milholland to the Army. Watson & Freeman lost associate Felix B. Snowden to service. Richard H. Hawkins left Dalzell, Fisher & Hawkins to join the U.S. Ordnance Department in Washington, decreasing that firm's numbers from four to three. Two associates, Drayton Heard and Charles Alvin Jones, left Sterrett & Acheson for the War, bringing that firm down from five lawyers to three. Mehard, Scully & Mehard loaned the younger of its two Mehards to the War effort—Samuel's son Churchill B. Mehard. Judge James B. Drew stepped down from the County bench and enlisted in the Army. Harry I. Miller, Pennsylvania Law '15, was at age twenty-four a member of the local draft board; he resigned to enlist in the Army.[192] In addition to losing Buchanan, Scott and Marsh, Gordon & Smith also lost two more lawyers to enlistment—partner Miles England and Frank B. Ingersoll, a Cornell law graduate who had only just joined the firm. Overnight, it seemed, Gordon & Smith went from eleven to six lawyers.[193]

In all, the Pittsburgh bar would (temporarily) yield 129 lawyers or law students to war service, as compared to 115 who entered the Union cause during the Civil War, representing a modest decrease in participation by the bar on a per capita basis.[194] As was the case during the Civil War, many of the World War I recruits from the Pittsburgh bar were younger men—law students, or recent grads who were either trying to build a practice on their own or who may have felt like subalterns within small law firms, men whose career footing was just uncertain enough to make a temporary military career seem like a somewhat solid path for advancement.

The real difference between the enlistments in the Civil War and World War I would be found among the middle-aged lawyers. During the Civil War, of course, a number of middle-aged lawyers left their practices behind in Pittsburgh to enter the Union Army. Men such as city solicitor Oliver Rippey (age thirty-six at enlistment) and prominent trial lawyers such as Samuel W. Black (age forty-five) and J. Bowman Sweitzer (age forty) were icons of that movement; yet Black (who was left to return to the law after the recent expiration of his term as governor of territorial Nebraska) and Sweitzer had practices based on cases rather than on longer term relationships with entities as clients. If they had such relationships, their clients' reliance on them would have prohibited their enlistment, since none of them practiced with regular partners or associates. By contrast, very few middle-aged leaders of the bar, particularly those who were senior members of downtown firms, were drawn to war service in World War I. Two of the Princeton men, David Aiken Reed and John G. Buchanan, were probably the most singular exceptions, in that they were leaders within established firms; they served the roles of practice leaders, team leaders and mentors to a staff of associates, all in the Cravathian model. In a sense, the Cravathian model made it more unlikely that partner/leaders of firms would take a leave of absence, even for a most important cause, because to do so would not only threaten their carefully cultivated client relationships but the identities of their firms. The cultural and professional education of younger partners and associates in the early twentieth century downtown Pittsburgh law firm depended upon the continual attention of senior partners; such concerns were foreign to the gunslinging sole practitioners or siloed, non-coordinating partners of nineteenth century partnerships.

There were a few other exceptions that tended to confirm the contrast between the eras. The partnership of Bialas, Irons & Ryan, for example, was formed in October 1916, and by the end of 1917, partners Joseph Bialas and T.F. Ryan had both gone into the service, leaving poor Harry Irons to run the practice on his own. More specifically, the partners did not have any associates and did not have much time to establish their identity as a firm prior to Bialas' and Ryan's departures. To their credit, the partners did reunite after the War, and practiced together until Irons' death in 1937. Similarly, Elder W. Marshall and Joseph M. Duff, Jr. both left Duff, Marshall & Duff, another partnership that had only recently been formed, to enter the service, leaving John's brother, the future governor and U.S. senator James H. Duff to practice alone; that partnership would not be reformed. Harry Aronson left his brothers Harvey, Leonard and Jacob behind as he joined the fight, leaving the partnership of Aronson & Aronson with a mere three Aronsons—but cultural identity shouldn't have been much of an issue within a firm composed of four brothers.[195] They were, at that stage, firms that shared more with the nineteenth century conception of a law firm than with the Cravathian model.

The "Cravath System" was the furthest thing from the minds of those men who eventually landed in France with the American Expeditionary Forces, however.

In March 1917, David Aiken Reed had just delivered his oral argument before the U.S. Supreme Court in *United States v. United States Steel Corporation,* the Sherman Antitrust Act case against U.S. Steel brought in 1912 in which the government called for the dissolution of U.S. Steel, when scarcely a few weeks later he found himself packing up for Fort Niagara and then Camp Meade, Maryland. With the declaration of war in April, the Court took the case off the docket and resolved to dispose of it after the War. Reed received a commission as Major and, while at Camp Meade, during the summer of 1917 he was placed in command of the Second Battalion of the 311th Field Artillery Regiment. There he took charge of instruction on the French 75mm field guns that would be distributed to the Regiment in France. He accompanied the unit to France in July 1918, and from the Regiment's encampment in Montmorillon, he contributed a couple of light letters about London, the French countryside, food and relations with the locals, that were published by the Union Trust Company of Pittsburgh in a 1918 collection entitled *Service Letters: A Record of Experiences and Achievement.* "I wish you could see the place," he wrote, "for it really is beautiful, and the gardens are still fine, although of course all the men gardeners are in the army now."[196] The Regiment never saw action, and Major Reed was summoned away to serve with the Interallied Armistice Commission at Spa, Belgium on diplomatic detail until the Spring of 1919.

He was awarded the Army Distinguished Service Medal for "his exceptional ability and insight into affairs requiring delicate and diplomatic treatment."[197]

William R. Scott also left Fort Niagara as a commissioned officer, serving as a Captain in the U.S. Army Infantry. While at Camp Meade, Captain Scott became aide-de-camp to Major General Joseph E. Kuhn, Commander of the 79th Division of the American Expeditionary Forces, which comprised about twenty-seven thousand American soldiers. Scott accompanied General Kuhn to France and stood by him during the first and third phases of the Meuse-Argonne Offensive.[198] The Meuse-Argonne front had been in deadlock since September 1914 when the 79th Division came to relieve the 157th French Division in July 1918. Under General Kuhn's command, the 79th Division launched a bitter attack, capturing several German strongholds and eventually penetrating deeper into enemy territory than any other Allied division at the time of the Armistice in November 1918.

Meanwhile, Captain Robert G. Woodside (Pitt Law '02), formerly a law clerk to Dalzell, Scott & Gordon, received the Distinguished Service Cross for his activities with the 38th Infantry Regiment, 3rd Division, at Les Franquette Farm, near Jaulgonne, where on July 22, 1918, he reformed the men of his platoon who were scattering under heavy enemy fire, thereby preventing the Germans from enveloping the battalion.[199]

Major Joseph H. Thompson (Pitt Law, '09), formerly a state legislator and Beaver Falls lawyer, was best known for his former career as a successful college football coach at Geneva College and Pittsburgh; one of Joseph Duff's predecessors at Pittsburgh, Thompson would be inducted into the College Football Hall of Fame in 1971. During the War, however, Major Thompson fought with the 110th Infantry, 28th Division and received the Congressional Medal of Honor for bravery in action near Apremont, France on October 1, 1918, when, five days after his forty-seventh birthday, he rushed in advance of the assaulting line on foot, under heavy machine gun and anti-tank fire, and disabled an enemy machine-gun nest. He was badly wounded on more than one occasion during the War, and died at the age of fifty-six from ailments aggravated by his wounds.[200]

A few Pittsburgh lawyers would not make it home at all. Lieutenant James. P. Over of Company K, 47th Infantry, 4th Division, the son of Judge James W. Over of the Orphans' Court, practiced with his brother Arthur in the Park Building. Lieutenant Over was killed while leading an assault on a machine-gun nest on July 30, 1918 in Sergy Heights, France. He was posthumously awarded a Silver Star for gallantry in action. While Captain Scott was at the nerve center of the Meuse-Argonne offensive, Lieutenant Joseph M. Duff, Jr. was killed in action in the Meuse-Argonne, serving with the 125th Infantry, 32nd Division, on October 11, 1918. Seven days later during the same campaign, First Lieutenant Harvey A. Dean of the 76th Field Artillery Regiment, 3rd Division, formerly a sole practitioner in the St. Nicholas Building, was killed while attempting to perform reconnaissance under fire. Lieutenant Dean was also posthumously awarded a Silver Star for gallantry in action. As the War was winding down, Lieutenant William H. Mulvhill of the U.S. Air Service, University of Pennsylvania Law '16, was killed in an airplane accident on November 27, 1918 at Carlstrom Field in Arcadia, Florida, where he served as an aviation instructor; the cadet who was flying with him survived. George L. Walter, Jr. (Pitt Law '15), the son of a successful Pittsburgh lumber magnate, listed himself as "attorney - not employed" on his draft registration card, but shared office space on the twelfth floor of the Oliver Building. He received commission as a Lieutenant at Officer's Training at Fort Oglethorpe, Georgia, joined the 34th Infantry Regiment at Camp McArthur, Waco, Texas and went to France in August 1918. He died of pneumonia at Briey, France on January 23, 1919, a little more than two months after the Armistice.[201]

John Buchanan and his partner Miles England had quieter duty stateside, eventually becoming Army lawyers. England started as a boot camp instructor, but later was appointed Regimental Judge Advocate of the 72nd U.S. Infantry, 11th Division. Buchanan started in the Sanitary Corps under the Surgeon General—perhaps due to the fact that his father was a surgeon—but was eventually transferred to the Constitutional and International Law Division of the Judge Advocate General's Office in Washington. At the Judge Advocate General's Office, Buchanan was involved in drafting presidential regulations and federal and state legislation regarding wartime activities, and ultimately worked on some of the most important cases facing the office.

For the Gordon & Smith attorneys, life in Washington and Camp Meade, where England was later stationed, was peppered with news of other Gordon & Smith soldiers and occasional visits from old friends. As England wrote to bookkeeper Clara Houston in August 1918:

> *I had letters from James Marsh and William Scott a little while ago… As you know, Mr. [Alexander] Black [Sr.]… paid me a visit a week ago last Saturday and, quite by coincidence, Mr. Buchanan came over from Washington the same afternoon for his first visit to me and the camp… Last Sunday, I was over in Baltimore with Mrs. England, which is my customary Sunday good fortune, and I missed seeing Mr. [Albert] Weitzel, whose card I found on my return.*[202]

"Mrs. England," as it happens, was Miles England's new Virginia bride, the former Miss Helen Lynch.[203] The firm's lawyers related to each other much like family members during their separation and habitually took great interest in each other's activities. Buchanan, after reading some letters from Ken Buffington, a Pittsburgh Law School graduate who had been offered a position with the firm just before the War, wrote to Miss Houston: "[T]hanks for Buffington's fine letters. When one scents the battle from afar, it certainly sounds interesting; but I guess it's hard to realize the troubles of a man who is stuck in the mud."[204]

At Reed Smith, David Aiken Reed's return to the firm as a partner would seem to have been a foregone conclusion, of course, but the departures of Scott, Buchanan and England forced George Gordon and William Watson Smith to consider how their loyal employees and partners would be treated during their wartime service. Associates were given what essentially amounted to unpaid leave, without loss of seniority. In the case of Buchanan and England, a temporary partnership agreement was entered in which Buchanan and England, who prior to their Army enlistments each received five percent of net profits, were to receive an advance of two percent each of net partnership profits during the War.

Both Buchanan and England were surprised by this arrangement and found it to be exceedingly generous. Buchanan wasted no time in writing to Mr. Gordon from his station at the Commission on Training Camp Activities in Washington. On February 4, 1918, Buchanan wrote:

> *Yesterday evening I went over my books, and I believe that one percent of the probable profits of the firm, added to my salary from the Government and other income, will be enough to enable me to keep up my home without impairing my invested capital. I should be glad, therefore, to receive one percent of the profits during the war, to be repaid by deducting one percent of the profits from my share in them after the war until the whole amount paid to me out of profits from January 1, 1918 till the end of the war is made up; if the partnership should terminate before this amount is repaid, it should immediately become due and payable.*
>
> *I am very anxious that I shall not appear ungrateful to the firm for the general proposal embodied in the partnership agreement. I wish to continue to be, and I am glad that my partners wish me to continue to be, associated with the firm. I am glad also that you wish to relieve me from the financial strain which is involved in Government service. But less than the partnership agreement calls for is necessary for that purpose, and I should prefer to receive the share of the profits mentioned above about the expectation of sometime rendering a quid pro quo to the firm.*[205]

As was the prerogative of the senior partner, however, George Gordon simply ignored Buchanan's proposal. That May he sent Buchanan a check for four hundred dollars, representing two percent of the firm's twenty thousand dollars in distributed profits. Lieutenant Buchanan persisted in a May 24 letter to Mr. Gordon:

> *I wish to thank the firm very much indeed for the check. . . . I have already said how generous I think this action on the part of the firm . . . It is very difficult to talk about such things on paper, but I would like to renew the suggestion in case it has not been considered. I assure you that if it is followed I shall feel as grateful as if the larger sum were given to me in accordance with the firm's plan.*[206]

Miles England, on the other hand, sheepishly but gratefully accepted the firm's check. To Mr. Gordon he wrote from Camp Lee, Virginia: "In view of John Buchanan's attitude, I am a little embarrassed in accepting this check, in spite of the marked difference in the pay we presently receive from Uncle Sam . . . I shall retain this check and any others that come pursuant to the new agreement in the hope that the future will give us all a chance properly to adjust these matters."[207] Meanwhile, England, the newlywed, had extra need of the cash. George Gordon eventually wrote back to Buchanan that he would continue to send him his two percent share and that Buchanan could settle up in any way he wished following the war.[208] This seemed to suffice for Buchanan, as he dropped the subject, stating, that he would "try constantly to give better service in view of the firm's generosity."[209] After the war, both Buchanan and England, at their own request, went off partnership participation for a half a year and took a salary in order to recompense, at least in part, the firm's generosity. Buchanan had a little trouble getting out of the Army, however. It was his misfortune to be hailed as a genius by his Army superiors. The Judge Advocate General's Office had handed him an assignment in January of 1919 to compile a new digest of the opinions of the Judge Advocates General—a job that was to have taken over a year to complete. In the end, the Army had to settle for the services of the dean of the University of Chicago Law School, James Parker Hall, as Buchanan plea-bargained his way back to Pittsburgh.[210]

Meanwhile, Scott was made a partner of Gordon & Smith on his first day back to work on July 1, 1919. Ingersoll and Marsh were rewarded with renewed employment, and Ken Buffington entered the firm as a new associate. During the War, the firm suffered through its temporary 5-lawyer deficit by bringing on three more lawyers: seasoned practitioner Robert F. Wendel, who stayed a little over a year; Harvard Law grad Norval Little; and one decidedly un-Cravathian hire—a down-and-out, middle-aged lawyer named Samuel G. Nolin.

Nolin had been Albert Weitzel's math teacher at Allegheny High School, and had entered the bar in 1900. He was Weitzel's preceptor on his entry into the bar in 1909, and by 1915 had carved out a niche in matrimonial cases. By 1918, however, Weitzel and Edgar Bell found him suffering from an addiction to alcohol, his practice in a shambles. Gordon & Smith needed immediate help, so Weitzel and Bell cleaned him up and helped to bring him into the firm as an associate at $125 per month. The genial, intellectually curious Nolin quickly caught on as "man Friday" to George Gordon, doing the legwork for his slightly older contemporary, drafting letters and performing legal research. It developed, however, that Nolin's early education in Rhetoric had made him an excellent writer and draftsman, and Gordon increasingly relied upon him as his ghost writer on briefs. Paul Rodewald recalled that shortly after he arrived at the firm in 1924, George Gordon had asked Rodewald for a memo on certain tax cases in connection with a U.S. Supreme Court case he was arguing, *Llewellyn v. Frick*. As Rodewald related:

> *I collected the cases and I wrote a memo describing every case that dealt with the issue. Mr. Gordon asked to see the memo, so I handed it to him; and to my alarm, he stuck it bodily into the brief. I went to Sam Nolin and said, "Sam, look what he's done. That memo of mine is not ready for printing for the Court. It's just talking about everything under the sun." Sam said, "I'll fix it." He wrote about a page and a quarter and put it into the proof. After the case was argued and decided in our client's favor, the Court reporter summarized the briefs of the parties, including at least three briefs of amici curiae, and generally he cut out most of what was written in the briefs and kept just the conclusions; but that page and a quarter of Sam Nolin's, he printed in full!... Sam Nolin knew how to say things.*

The interruption of the War had provided an improbable second chance for a middle-aged lawyer with little going for him.[211] Sam Nolin remained with the firm until his death in 1934.

David Aiken Reed made it back to the U.S. and was at his desk in the Union Arcade (where Reed Smith had moved in 1917) in time to prepare for the re-argument of the *U.S. Steel* case before the U.S. Supreme Court in October 1919. Frazer, Robinson, Dodds, Seifert and Heard were all made partners of the firm in 1922, just as David Aiken Reed was being appointed by Governor William Sproul to fill the vacancy in the U.S. Senate caused by the death of Senator William E. Crow, who had succeeded Philander Knox on his death in October 1921. No additional lawyers would be admitted to the partnership until 1928, but Reed Smith did hire a few new associates at the Cravathian rate of approximately one per year for the next few years: P[hilander]. K[nox]. Motheral, George Motheral's son, joined the firm as an associate in 1918; William L.G. Gibson in 1919; Maynard Teall in 1921; William Wallace Booth in 1922; and James H. Beal, Jr. in 1923.[212]

Reed Smith and Gordon & Smith, the city's two largest firms, were adding new lawyers at roughly the same rate, but during the 1920s, Gordon & Smith would add only two net lawyers to its partnership agreement. Meanwhile, Reed Smith added five net partners. The differences in leverage (i.e., the ratio of partners to associates) between the two firms in the years leading up to World War II, the next great interruption in the talent pool, would ultimately have an impact on how the firms fared culturally immediately after World War II.

The Great War's interruption wrought changes and disruptions throughout the downtown firms. At Weil & Thorp, neither Mac Goldsmith nor Meyer Greenbaum would return to the firm (Greenbaum, in fact, would leave the profession altogether to join his father's furniture business in Kittanning) and Leo Ruslander departed to begin a twenty-nine-year tax practice with Main & Co. Leo Weil's son Ferdinand did re-join the firm after the War, and Charles Thorp was joined by his son, Charles Thorp, Jr., and his son-in-law W. Denning Stewart. Barely a year after the War, however, Weil & Thorp split, and Thorp formed a firm with his son and son-in-law, Thorp & Stewart. Leo Weil regrouped with his son Ferdinand and J. Smith Christy as Weil, Christy & Weil. When Richard H. Hawkins left Pittsburgh for Washington to begin service with the Ordnance Department, it was effectively the end of his partnership with William Dalzell, who reformed the law firm with Gordon Fisher and his younger brother, Robert D. Dalzell, as Dalzell, Fisher & Dalzell. Shortly after his return from service, Lt. Colonel Hawkins became a full-time professor at Pitt Law School. Felix Snowden, formerly of Watson & Freeman, became a prosecutor. Other firms decreased their ranks of lawyers who had not served in the War effort, either by natural attrition or otherwise.

Meanwhile, at the Morris Walker firm, both of its soldier-lawyers returned to the fold, as did James Milholland at McKee Mitchell & Alter, and Drayton Heard and Charles Alvin Jones at Sterrett & Acheson. James H. Duff carried on after his brother's death, forming a new firm with his other former partner who did return from the War, Elder Marshall, and a Pitt Law graduate and former instructor, Allan Davis. Patterson, Crawford, Miller & Arensberg hired Howard K. Walter, the younger brother of the late Lt. George L. Walter, Jr., right after the War.

By the end of the 1920s, George Gordon, Willis McCook, Phil Knox, Judge James Hay Reed and John "Corporation" Dalzell had all passed away, as had a generation of lawyers who had helped to steer the course of the Pittsburgh bar through an unprecedented American industrial revolution taking place within earshot of the courthouse on Grant Street. Whatever momentum of growth that some of the smaller downtown firms had experienced going into World War I, that momentum was overwhelmed, at least until the middle of the 1920s, by the uncertainty coming out of the European conflict, the post-World War I recession, and the competing desires of welcoming back the men who served their country and the need to operate effectively and efficiently. As the Twenties roared, while record numbers of graduates emerged from the regional law schools, and record numbers of new lawyers were admitted to the Allegheny County bar, each Pittsburgh law firm—whether they were attempting to follow the Cravath System or not—found itself having to wrestle with both the momentum of business growth during the second half of the decade, as well as the knowledge that some unpredictable event—such as an assassination in Sarajevo, or bad omens in the London financial markets—might have a material effect on its future financial health and prospects. The World War reminded them that the issue was not academic—the associates these firms hired with the promise of future potential advancement had careers and families at stake. Lives, in fact—like that of an unemployed lawyer in the Oliver Building choosing to go to war, or a recovering alcoholic lawyer looking for redemption—could be at stake.

For decades, the leading Northeastern voices within the legal profession had carried on the fiction that law was not a business; but as Pittsburgh firms grew bigger during the first half of the twentieth century, the men who ran them had no choice but to be the good businessmen, the "active tradesmen," that Thomas Mellon had once exhorted his younger colleagues to become. As Pittsburgh business grew in volume and complexity, developing further into "big business," so too would Pittsburgh law become "big business."

ANARCHY: INTERRUPTING AND INTERRUPTED

Within days after the U.S. Steel combination hit the newspapers, Billy Brennen already found himself in the thick of a labor dispute with the new one billion dollar behemoth. His client, the old AAISW, had made modest gains in its membership since the disastrous failure of the Homestead Strike in 1892. Early in 1900, the AAISW had enough muscle to organize, quietly, a non-union plant of the American Sheet Steel Company, the DeWees Wood in McKeesport. In April 1901, with the machinery of the U.S. Steel combination under way, the local Sheet Steel management discovered the AAISW activity at the plant, and retaliated by dismissing ten of the union men. In counter-retaliation, the supposedly non-union mill went on strike. By mid-April, Billy Brennen was on the front lines of what looked like it might be a successful peace negotiation between the AAISW and the DeWees Wood plant, in which all of the workers except one—George S. Holloway, a boss heater in the mill and the president of the local union lodge—would be reinstated.[213] Giving his assurances to the newspapers, Brennen was surely most within his element when standing next to a peace agreement.

The new executive committee of U.S. Steel (including Judge Gary and Charles M. Schwab), meeting between April and June 1901, paid little attention to what was happening in McKeesport while it was formulating its company-wide policy toward union activity. In their meetings they concluded that "we are unalterably opposed to any extension of union labor and advise subsidiary companies to take a firm position when these questions come up and say that they are not going to recognize it, that is, any extension of unions in mills where they do not now exist."[214]

Meanwhile, the AAISW was very much aware of the fact that if there were any chance of obtaining further concessions from the companies that were intended to be rolled up into U.S. Steel, the time was now, before U.S. Steel had all the bargaining power. Thus, on June 25, 1901, Theodore J. Shaffer, the president of the AAISW, met with American Tinplate Company, American Steel Hoop Company, and American Sheet Steel Company, demanding that each of these future subsidiaries of U.S. Steel recognize the AAISW at all their plants. While Shaffer was quickly able to reach an agreement with American Tin Plate, the other two companies held out, and the union prepared to strike against them. On July 13, American Sheet Steel, coming off of the peace agreement at DeWees Wood, offered to recognize the union at certain non-union plants, but the AAISW rejected the offer. Taking an aggressive stance, Shaffer ordered a strike against not only American Sheet Steel and American Steel Hoop, but also against American Tin Plate—on the premise that workers at all mills must participate in a strike even if only one mill within a trust had a breakdown in bargaining—effectively breaking the AAISW's successful agreement with American Tin Plate in June. After an unsuccessful conference between Shaffer and J.P. Morgan, the union called a general strike against U.S. Steel. Turnout for the 1901 Steel Recognition Strike, however, was weak throughout most of U.S. Steel's holdings.[215]

Billy Brennen shrugged. On August 22, he glumly reported that the union had no plan to file suit against U.S. Steel regarding discharges of unionized workers.[216] Undoubtedly weary of the union's aggressive approach, Brennen saw little hope for a graceful exit. The AAISW ended up settling the strike in September on far less favorable terms than it had been offered previously.

The subsequent life of Brennen's client, the AAISW, already crippled by the Homestead strike in 1892, was, according to historian David Brody, "a melancholy tale" of a union subsiding "into submissiveness, hoping thereby to conserve the remnants of its former glory."[217] By World War I, it had a mere six thousand members,[218] and eventually, in the 1940s, the union was subsumed by the United Steelworkers.

Brennen's involvement in the Westmoreland County Coal Strike of 1910-1911, brought by rogue lodges of the United Mine Workers of America (UMWA) against several coal companies in the Irwin Gas Coal Basin, was even more tangential. Most of the workers lived in company houses on company property, thus requiring them in many cases to set up tent cities when they went on strike. Private "Coal and Iron Police" as well as local sheriffs' deputies and state and local police prevented workers from leaving their jobs, denied workers the use of the post office and courthouses, prevented them from holding public meetings—even on nearby public roads or property—and in some cases, restricted the movement of all citizens without passes from the local mine managers. Sixteen people were killed in the ensuing clashes, most of them strikers or their family members.[219] While local attorneys in Greensburg fought on behalf of the strikers within an increasingly hostile legal environment, Brennen ultimately only became involved in any meaningful way when he was retained to represent leaders of the UMWA after seven of the coal companies brought criminal charges of conspiracy and intimidation against them in federal court.[220] Because of the public outcry, none of the charges were ever brought to trial; nonetheless, it appeared that one of Brennen's final labor battles resembled some of his earliest, in that they involved fighting against the criminalization of union activity. In the end, Brennen was playing defense once again.

As he approached thirty years at the bar, William Brennen's role as labor lawyer—defined for himself, by himself, out of whole cloth—clearly had begun to show its limitations relative to his time. Throughout his career, but especially in its formative stages, his role was to operate within an atmosphere of complete hostility to unions, and to craft, through trial and error within the local court system, a handbook for unions attempting to prosecute a clean, non-criminal strike. The role was perfectly suited to the habits of his personality. By launching a clean strike, the best one could hope for was an opportunity to hold a dialogue with a receptive management—and dialogue was Brennen's stock in trade. He was a likeable, charming gentleman whose ability to build relationships with people in different classes gave him opportunities to shape compromises between labor and capital, where both parties had the willingness to compromise.

By the time of the 1901 Steel Recognition Strike, in which the AAISW pursued the hardest of lines against the biggest of foes, and the 1910-11 Westmoreland County Miners' Strike, which was a prolonged, brutal battle, there was little hope for Brennen's preference for friendly dialogue. One senses, in Brennen's less and less frequent appearances in these fights, that he saw himself as the last holdout for civility in labor controversies. There was little wonder why the next generation of labor lawyers, the one emerging just after the Mine Strike, would have so little patience for Brennen's approach.

The tone of the era that was commencing as Billy Brennen was fading from view would be defined by another kind of brutality.

Around half past eleven on the night of June 2, 1919, two crude dynamite pipe bombs went off almost simultaneously in two separate locations in the Pittsburgh area. One exploded on the porch of B.J. Cassady, a general manager of Pittsburgh Plate Glass Company, at 5437 Aylesboro Street in the upscale Squirrel Hill section of Pittsburgh; the other, outside the home of Herbert E. Joseph, a railroad dispatcher, on the slopes above West Carson Street in the Sheraden neighborhood, at 2635 Glasgow Street. No one was injured in either bombing, but the explosions did considerable damage to Cassady and Joseph's homes, as well as several of the homes of their respective neighbors.[221]

Information came pouring in from outside of Pittsburgh about at least six similar bombings that evening—targeting the mayor of Cleveland, Harry L. Davis; Massachusetts state representative Leland Powers; Judge Charles C. Nott, Jr. of New York; and the Unites States Attorney General, A. Mitchell Palmer, at his home on R Street, NW, in Washington, D.C,[222] just across the street from the young Assistant Secretary of the Navy, Franklin D. Roosevelt, whose front windows were all blown out by the explosion at Palmer's home[223]—and it became clear that neither Cassady nor Joseph were the intended targets in Pittsburgh. Joseph lived down the street from William W. Sibray, the U.S. Commissioner for Immigration for Pittsburgh, an official who had been involved in the deportation of Italian and Eastern European labor agitators; and Cassady lived next door to Judge W.H. Seward Thomson of the federal District Court for the Western District of Pennsylvania.[224] Judge Thomson, a Beaver County lawyer who had relocated his practice to Pittsburgh and was appointed to the Court in 1914 by President Wilson, was considered to be "broad-minded" and "liberal,"[225] but he had, during World War I, presided over the convictions of thirteen labor agitators under the Espionage Act, and had heard a state law case involving a well-known Italian anarchist, Carlo Tresca.[226]

None of the intended victims were injured by the explosions—although in New York a nightwatchman was killed by the bomb intended for Judge Nott, and the then-anonymous bomber of Attorney General Palmer's residence was killed when his bomb went off prematurely. At each location, authorities found copies of an anarchist publication entitled "Plain Words," which included the following passage:

> *There will have to be bloodshed; we will not dodge; there will have to be murder; we will kill because it is necessary; there will have to be destruction; we will destroy to rid the world of your tyrannical institutions.*[227]

Judge Thomson was at his farm near Cambridge Springs, close to Erie, on the night of the bombing. His immediate thought, when he heard about the explosion by telephone, was that the cause was likely a gas leak. Upon learning of the alleged anarchist connections, Judge Thomson declared:

> *There is no doubt that the motive for such actions was to intimidate government agents and federal and civil officials to the discharge of their duties ... [T]his manner among the lawless element of attempting to gain their end by terrorism and disorder will be fruitless. Law and order have always reigned supreme in the United States. By them we live. And law and order will continue in this country, efforts on the part of these misguided outlaws notwithstanding.*[228]

In other words, the legal institutions of the federal government now found themselves in the middle of a crisis, an ongoing battle between Law & Order, on the one hand, and Anarchy, on the other.

Pittsburgh's public safety director, Charles B. Prichard (the former Weil & Thorp associate who held the bathroom listening post during the city council sting in 1908), working closely with the U.S. Department of Justice's special agent-in-charge for the Bureau of Investigation in Pittsburgh, had little evidence to consider at the outset, so Pittsburgh police were ordered to raid the headquarters of the Industrial Workers of the World, also known as the IWW or the "Wobblies," in the Apollo Building downtown, and generally to round up the usual suspects—most of whom were known as radical propagandists rather than potential terrorists.[229] As the police broke through the door of Suite 301 of the Apollo Building, however, one of the occupants, Edward Johnson, shot his pistol at the authorities, grazing a city detective; he and a few others at the headquarters were quickly apprehended.[230] Around Pittsburgh, police arrested several other known Wobblies, including an auto mechanic known as Louis M. Walsh, and an ex-Westinghouse machinist named Walter Loan.[231]

Loan had something of a history with the law. He had been "implicated" in a 1911 bombing in Wilkinsburg. In March 1915, the twenty-four year-old Loan was accused of assault and battery for shooting and wounding a Wilkinsburg policeman. During the course of the trial—for which Allegheny County assistant district attorney Robert M. Gibson (the former ballplayer who joined Judge Thomson on the federal bench in 1922) served as prosecuting attorney, and over which Judge J.W. Bouton, sitting in from McKean County, presided—the evidence placing Loan at the scene was weak, and Loan appeared to have a reasonable alibi. According to Thomas Loan, Walter's brother, one of the jurors, a deacon and Sunday school superintendent of the Presbyterian Church of Sheraden, was the lone holdout, saying, "I will not leave this room with a verdict of acquittal. A man who denies both God and Government should not be at liberty. This man admitted that he is an Anarchist and all his witnesses refused to swear." Walter Loan was convicted on a compromise verdict, on the assault charge only, and was sentenced by Judge Bouton to one to three years in the Western Penitentiary, saying "You are known to be associated with a group whose teachings are not conducive to the instillation of good citizenship and morals. You are fortunate that you are not being sentenced for murder."[232]

Two months after Loan's 1915 trial, a short piece authored under the pen name of "J.M." appeared in the pages of *Mother Earth*, an anarchist journal edited by Alexander Berkman, Henry Clay Frick's assailant, who had been released from prison in 1906. In the piece, "J.M." admits that Walter Loan is an anarchist, "(b)rave, frank, refined, uncompromising," and describes "Judge B" as "[r]ednosed, bulging eyes, behind spectacles, bald" with a "[c]ynical sneer, chewing tobacco and spitting incessantly." "J.M." goes on to say that in his instructions to the jury, "Judge B" uses language "correct and judicial," but uses a tone and attitude "importunate, demanding conviction." After Loan's guilty verdict is announced, Loan's friends in the corridor of the courthouse say, "What in hell can you expect of a court?" J.M." closes his little narrative with the following:

> *Society, the painted courtesan—overfed, hypocritical smug, propertied society. Indeed thou art a menace to her ease and sloth, her property and security, Walter! Policemen have been shot before, and have, strange to relate, shot others, and yet the culprits hardly merited that exalted phrase, 'menace to society.' No, your crime was not the wounding of the policeman, but a shot at the rotten, filthy, parasitic, blood-drenched, enslaved society ... Walter Loan did not shoot the policeman. He is an Anarchist.*[233]

The author of the piece in *Mother Earth*, who exhibits little but sneering contempt for the Pittsburgh courts, was none other than Walter Loan's defense attorney, Jacob Margolis.

The eldest son of Jewish immigrants from Russian Poland, Jacob Margolis grew up in the Lower Hill district, on Magee Street. Jacob's father Julius, a sewing machine salesman, died when Jake was in his early teens, and his mother made ends meet running a small grocery store and working as a seamstress. Jake saved enough money as a newsboy to attend a few terms at Washington & Jefferson College.[234] His obsession with political and economic philosophy apparently began at least as early as his teenage years. Back home in Pittsburgh in 1905, the confident nineteen year-old Margolis, a member of the Zion Literary Society, chaired a Jewish history class at the Zion Institute on Centre Avenue, during which he "recited the history of the Jewish people from Abraham to Bar Kochba, laying especial stress upon the political, economical [sic] and social conditions that either made or unmade the Jewish people in the various periods of its history."[235] The following year he began reading law in the office of James C. Gray, an assistant city solicitor, and entered Pitt Law School. He graduated in 1909 and was admitted to the bar in March 1910.[236] He married Florence Kaminsky, the daughter of a rabbi, and by 1916, they had two children, a girl and a boy.[237]

Margolis initially developed his law practice from among the community of Eastern European immigrants, principally Russian and Polish Jews, whom he met through his volunteer English teaching at the Irene Kaufmann Settlement and through other Jewish community activities. Much of his work involved immigration or debt collection matters, but soon he gained a reputation as a defender of free speech and workers' rights. Although there were other active leftists in the Pittsburgh bar—notably William E. Schoyer, the son of attorney and Civil War hero Captain Samuel C. Schoyer, and Bernard B. McGinnis, a special assistant U.S. Attorney and later County Democratic chairman—Margolis became the "go to" lawyer in Pittsburgh and surrounding areas for leftists in their run-ins with local and federal authorities. After 1914, he was helped in his practice by another sole practitioner, James J. Marshall, a fellow Pittsburgh Law graduate who shared in Margolis' political convictions. When Margolis moved his practice to the Union Arcade, Marshall moved in with him, and became a member of the radical inner circle that Margolis ultimately developed around his activities. In 1917, while the two of them were providing "free" advice to immigrants with regard to their Selective Service questionnaires, Margolis and Marshall benefited from a pre-paid legal service, sold under the name of the United States Protective League, that purported to provide blanket legal services to immigrants for a flat fee of twelve dollars per year. The two lawyers later found themselves distancing themselves from the League, however, after allegations arose concerning the high-pressure sales tactics of non-lawyer salesmen.[238]

Through the 1910s, Margolis' practice was ultimately quite lucrative, and, perhaps like Brennen before him, he was not shy about the level of affluence it afforded to him and his family. As historian Charles H. McCormick relates, "On principle he refused to own real property, but he dressed ostentatiously, earned a sizeable income, and owned 'a few thousand dollars,' bank stock, and a $27,500 life insurance policy."[239] His association with Marshall undoubtedly became essential after several years, however, as his involvement with leftist organizations became more time-consuming, involving a seemingly endless schedule of night-time local union meetings and weekend rallies. Still, Margolis never sought membership in the Allegheny County Bar Association, nor would it have been likely that he would have been admitted.

While Billy Brennen never had a thought of effecting a change of the prevailing order—some of his good friends were capitalists—Jake Margolis envisioned revolution. As McCormick explained:

> Margolis called himself an anarchosyndicalist, or a direct actionist. ... [H]is ideological positions were consistent and clearly articulated. For him, the only way to realize the Socialist dream was through a two-stage revolution. The first, or negative, stage would destroy capitalist government. The second, or positive, stage would construct a new democratic and decentralization society in the shell of the old. Workers, 'the underlying population' possessing the technical expertise to manage production, would build 'a new society without capitalists, wage workers, or government' at 'the point of production,' the workplace.[240]

Trade unions, such as Billy Brennen's client, the AAISW, or the emerging American Federation of Labor (AFL), were not instruments of revolutionary change in Margolis' view; their members were too easily seduced by "[t]he subtle poison called Democracy"—that is, for Margolis, the prevailing political structures that operated at the behest of the Wall Street capitalists, and the rags-to-riches fantasy that "everyone is equal and everyone has the same opportunity" to make the leap from the working class to the owning class.[241]

In the IWW, Margolis found a home for his vision, even if he never formally joined the union. Founded in 1905 in Chicago, the Industrial Workers of the World was an attempt to unite all workers within an industry—skilled and unskilled, regardless of the technical area of their expertise, regardless of gender, ethnicity or race—to create "one big union" to mirror and take on the monolithic concentration of industrial ownership typified by the U.S. Steel combination. In its early days, the IWW was briefly the hub for American radicalism, bringing Margolis into contact with such radical celebrities as Emma Goldman (who called Margolis her "very able friend"[242]); Frick's assailant Alexander Berkman; Swinburne Hale, the New York civil rights lawyer; Big Bill Haywood, a leading figure in the Colorado Labor Wars and a founder of the IWW; William Z. Foster, the future head of the Communist Party U.S.A., who organized unions through the Syndicalist League of North America during the 1910s; Roger Baldwin, the founder of the National Civil Liberties Bureau, for whom Margolis served on a panel of lawyers available for civil rights cases in Pennsylvania; and Vincent St. John, the IWW's general secretary. A consummate radical networker, Margolis hosted leftist gatherings at his home on Ophelia Street (which could occasionally tax his wife Florence's household patience), as well as in his law office, originally in the Frick Building but later in Room 507 of the Union Arcade; at the IWW Pittsburgh headquarters or the Radical Library, both housed in the McGeagh Building, on Bigelow near Grant Street; in one or another of several downtown saloons or private after-hours clubs; or, as McCormick notes, "in animated debate under smoke-dimmed stars on the corner of Fifth and Grant."[243]

Margolis' chief talent was as a "talker." He never let his law practice get in the way of a speaking engagement, particularly an opportunity to denounce the institutions that he particularly despised (trade unionism; the capitalist-controlled government and courts; and the War) or to teach a crowd about a topic near and dear to his heart, such as "Industrial Socialism" or "The End of Civilization." Although he never enjoyed the national celebrity of some of his radical friends, he frequently traveled to speak at radical assemblies around the country, particularly in northern industrial cities such as Chicago and Detroit, as well as the radical intellectual center of New York City.

Free Speech was, for Jake Margolis, an essential weapon in the revolution. As he explained:

Free Speech is a valuable asset. To be deprived of it means that secret methods must be employed and the latter are hardly ever successful. It goes without saying that it is well nigh impossible to carry on an effective propaganda when the power of granting or refusing a permit to speak on the street is left to the discretion of a police official who may object to the cut of your coat or the color of your necktie.[244]

Margolis was able to burnish his reputation as a radical by supporting members of the Pittsburgh Socialist Party in what became known as the "Homewood Free Speech Fight." Fresh from a minor victory in a strike against the National Tube Company in McKeesport, another subsidiary of U.S. Steel, former Socialist congressional candidate Fred Merrick and his comrade, John McGuire, were arrested and fined during the summer of 1912 for speaking at the corner of Homewood Avenue and Kelly Street in the Homewood section of Pittsburgh—despite the fact that they had obtained a permit from the local magistrate. The following week, the Thirteenth Ward branch of the Socialist Party staged a protest of Merrick and McGuire's arrest at the same street corner, with an estimated ten thousand people in attendance. This time, nine women and eleven men were arrested. When they appeared before a police magistrate the next morning, they were released because, according to the police magistrate, they did not need a permit to hold a meeting. On the following Saturday, fifteen thousand protesters gathered at the same street corner, whereupon police arrested nine women and thirty-six men and placed them in six overcrowded cells at the Frankstown Avenue police station. The next morning, the forty-five appeared before a different magistrate and many were fined before being released from custody.

Margolis and the Socialists decided to make a test case out of the arrest of Samuel Mervis, four days later, who was fined twenty-five dollars for speaking without a permit. Margolis appealed Mervis' case to the County Court. Meanwhile, city solicitor Charles A. O'Brien secured an injunction prohibiting anyone from giving speeches at Kelly and Homewood. Although the County Court declared the city ordinance unconstitutional on the grounds that banning public meetings without a permit was potentially discriminatory, the city council acted quickly to support O'Brien's injunction by amending the permit ordinance to eliminate its overtly discriminatory language.

Margolis lashed out at the city's use of the injunction. "That most pernicious instrument of capitalist law, the injunction," he wrote, "figures again in the struggles of the working class. When the capitalist has exhausted all his efforts along legal lines he resorts to that most potent, certain and speedy weapon, the injunction, and our judges have not been notoriously guilty of refusing to issue it when asked by the capitalist to be used against the workers."[245] Meanwhile, the Homewood Free Speech fight became a touchstone for Socialists around the country, as Big Bill Haywood came to Pittsburgh and addressed a protest meeting of fifteen thousand at Kennywood Park. Margolis chronicled the entire story of the fight in an article published in the *International Socialist Review* in October.[246] As McCormick observed, "Here Margolis savored the victory, advertised his own radical credentials, and proclaimed the existence of an organized revolutionary movement in Pittsburgh."[247]

Unlike some of his anarchist comrades, however, Margolis was a devout pacifist, and he attributed the movement's success in recruiting during the Homewood Free Speech fight to its use of "passive resistance":

> *A great wave of public sentiment in a community, a great demonstration of protest is very much more effective than a court decision, though the courts of Allegheny county and the state of Pennsylvania decide against the workers, they have not lost, for they*

have succeeded in arousing a storm of protest, have succeeded in doing such effective propaganda work by the Free Speech Fight that we can not estimate its value ... [I]t has shown to many workers the value of Mass Action, the value of Passive Resistance and the necessity for organization among the workers of all lines.[248]

During the Great War, Margolis carried his fervent pacifism with him as he allegedly advised workers, fellow radicals and Eastern European immigrants on strategies for gaining exemption from the draft. Although he was not aware of it at the time, he would have good reason to avoid grey areas of the law and ethics, as he was being closely watched.

In May 1917, a postal inspector intercepted inflammatory postcards from the Pittsburgh Anti-Conscription League. Acting on a series of tips as to their source, the Pittsburgh police raided the McGeagh Building and arrested several members of the League, including Margolis. Jake was released due to lack of evidence; but in the wake of the incident the U.S. Department of Justice's special agent-in-charge for the Bureau of Investigation in Pittsburgh—focusing on Margolis' involvement with the Wobblies, who were said to be planning to organize against the steel companies in the region— recommended that the Bureau of Investigation plant a spy close to Margolis. That spy would be Louis Wendell, known as Louis Walsh, the auto mechanic who would subsequently be arrested and released following the anarchist bombings in 1919, and he quickly became a member of Margolis' inner circle, avidly participating in both the housekeeping and the cheerleading of the radical community that surrounded Jake.[249]

Walsh immediately attempted to continue to build a case against Margolis for illegally interfering with the draft. Further tips led to a young witness who said he was advised to meet with James Marshall in the Union Arcade if he wanted to avoid the draft. There, the witness claimed, he was met by a "tall, dark man in a Panama suit" who matched Margolis' description, and who talked to him about ways to avoid conscription, including feigning disabilities or getting a doctor to certify that he was needed at home to care for an incapacitated spouse.[250]

The Bureau of Investigation decided to set up a sting in which ten volunteers from the American Protective League, a quasi-official intelligence group that frequently worked with federal authorities to identify anti-war anarchists or radicals, visited Margolis' office seeking draft avoidance advice, hoping to obtain enough evidence for the Department of Justice to bring charges against Margolis under the Espionage Act. Margolis was cautious, however, and the Bureau was never able to pin anything on him. Walsh, however, did manage to get Margolis' law clerk, Victor Slone, arrested on draft evasion charges after Slone admitted to Walsh that he had failed to register for Selective Service. Slone served a short sentence in the Allegheny County Jail, while another one of Margolis' clerks, Meyer Teplitz, ended up being sent to the conscientious objector disciplinary barracks at Ft. Leavenworth, Kansas.[251] Meanwhile, Margolis had, himself, registered for the draft, apparently without asserting any disability or a case for his disqualification from military service.[252]

Margolis had some other close calls during the period. In February 1918, Margolis and Marshall were summoned by the Allegheny County Bar Association to address charges regarding their handling of certain Selective Service questionnaires for immigrant clients; after Margolis denied the charges, the Bar Association dropped its inquiry.[253] In November, the Military Intelligence Division of the U.S. Army (MID) was said to be preparing to bring charges against Margolis for collecting fees for filing draft exemptions, but reconsidered after a Pittsburgh intelligence officer with the MID reminded authorities that "Margolis has been under constant observation by our confidential agent for many months, and all his activities and utterances are promptly reported to this office." He pointed out that "Margolis is the source of much valuable information regarding the radical labor and socialistic activities in this district."[254] The following month, after Walsh reported that Margolis had admitted to tax evasion, saying he would "be damned" if he would give his money to the federal government to feed U.S. militarism, IRS agents visited Margolis, but turned up nothing.[255]

Florence Margolis was supportive of Jake's political activities, even if she was occasionally disapproving of the company he kept, but she often questioned whether his activities were worth the price they paid in other ways. She had warned him, "You keep this up, and you'll get disbarred."[256]

Just a few days after the anarchist bombings targeted Judge Thomson and William Sibray in June 1919, the state legislature empowered the Allegheny County Bar Association to push the disbarment issue with attorneys that were considered to be undesirable. On June 6, Governor Sproul signed into law a bill that enabled committees of bar associations within the state to compel the attendance of witnesses and the production of documents in investigations of the conduct of lawyers who were accused of unprofessional conduct and against whom disbarment proceedings had been brought.[257]

By June 20, Bar Association president George E. Alter had already named a "Committee on Offenses" to review complaints about the professional conduct of unnamed members of the bar, comprised mainly of lawyers from established Pittsburgh firms: Charles F.C. Arensberg, of the Patterson Crawford firm, chairman; Leander Trautman, a corporate lawyer, vice chairman; and members John M. Ralston of Stonecipher & Ralston, Alexander Black (Sr.) of Gordon & Smith, Roy G. Bostwick of Brown Stewart & Bostwick (soon to leave to form Thorp, Bostwick & Stewart), and William M. Robinson of the Reed Smith firm.[258] The stage was now set for the elite bar to take aggressive action against attorneys such as Jake Margolis. Indeed, from the timing of these lightning-fast moves, coming on the heels of a pair of bombings presumed to have been conducted by anarchists, one has to assume that Margolis' name was at the top of the list of unnamed lawyers against whom complaints had been whispered.

In the meantime, however, following a summer in which no progress had been made in capturing the perpetrators of the June anarchist bombings—a summer of insecurity and borderline panic throughout the country in which even *The New York Times* criticized the Department of Justice for its inability to stop the anarchist threat—the AFL started to stir up trouble in retaliation for the government crackdown on its ability to meet or hold rallies, and unleashed a series of strikes that effectively shut down half the steel industry. Although the AFL had not necessarily laid the groundwork with its organizing, there was serious discontent among steelworkers across the country who had felt that the gains they had made during the Great War—a time of labor scarcity—

were being taken away following Armistice Day. Margolis, at one time, had shared the vision of some of his local Wobbly friends that the IWW should stand at the vanguard of the next great fight with Capital, but by the summer of 1919, most of the leaders of the Pittsburgh Wobblies were in jail for one reason or another. Margolis, therefore, was inclined to support the AFL—despite the fact that it represented mainstream trade unionism rather than being an industrial union—because it would serve as a tool for organizing labor, hopefully for the future benefit of the IWW. To seal the deal, Vincent St. John sent William Z. Foster, at that time one of the principal organizers for the AFL, to speak with Margolis about getting the support of the Wobblies in Pittsburgh, meager though it would be.

The government, specifically J. Edgar Hoover, the new head of the Bureau of Investigation, saw an avenue to discredit Foster by associating him with the most radical elements, thereby discrediting the AFL. Walsh reported to Washington that he believed that Margolis would be a good witness before a Senate committee formed to investigate the strike, because he would tell the truth, unabashedly, about Foster and his radical affiliations, as well as about his own radical philosophy.[259]

On October 16, 1919, Jake Margolis received a telegram summoning him to appear before the Senate Education and Labor Committee in Washington. He sent Marshall to show the telegram to Foster, and Foster sent back a message saying he wanted to meet with Margolis at five in the afternoon under the Kaufmann's Department Store clock at Fifth and Smithfield. Instead, they met in the back of a union hall during a labor meeting, exchanging papers and engaging in a long discussion.[260]

As it happens, two Pittsburgh lawyers were called to testify before the Senate Education and Labor Committee. Listed as "A.J. Brennan" in the official minutes of the hearing, Billy Brennen went to Washington and testified on Sunday, October 12, beginning his statement by saying that he was "an American citizen" and that the actions of the local authorities against the workers he had been called upon to represent aroused his "opposition as an American citizen." When asked how long he had represented the AFL, Brennen replied that he had been "the attorney for the American Federation of Labor, I would say, only since this thing happened." "I am," he said, "and have been a general attorney for the laboring people, but I do not charge them anything ... I do not advise the men to get into trouble. My business is to keep them out of trouble."[261]

On the morning of Monday, October 20, Jake Margolis sat down in Room 201 of the Senate Office Building to testify before the Senate Committee on Education and Labor. The chairman, Senator William S. Kenyon, a Republican from Iowa, began the hearing by telling Margolis that the Committee wanted "to have a pretty frank talk" with him about the general conditions in Pittsburgh, and about whether the strike was really to benefit the workers or whether it was part of a radical element attempting to get control of the AFL.[262]

Soon, Senator Kenyon had drawn Margolis into talking in detail about his opposition to the Great War, after Margolis offered that Judge Charles Orr recommended that he should not apply to practice before the federal bar in view of his well-known anti-war stance. "I do not believe in war under any circumstances," Margolis said. When Kenyon asked him what he would do if the country and his home were attacked, he replied,

"I believe in nonresistance. I believe rather than to arm an army in order to meet the invaders, that nonresistance is more effective than resistance." Senator Kenyon asked, "Even to the point of an enemy attacking the country and taking over the government, you would raise no objection?"

"I would raise no objection," replied Margolis. He admitted that if someone attempted to assault his wife, he would try to persuade them not to do so, and if he could not, he would do nothing.[263]

Senator Thomas Sterling, a Republican from South Dakota, interjected, "What do you believe in?" Margolis replied that "human society can get along without government, and that if certain conditions prevailed the people of this country, or, for that matter, of any other country, can do away with the causes of government, and then they would not have to have any government."[264]

After engaging Margolis in a discussion about anarchism, syndicalism and the IWW, Senator Kenyon asked him, "Just how would you describe yourself?"

"First, syndicalist; I put the syndicalist first, because it is an important thing; syndicalist-anarchist would be my position."[265]

They grilled him on Foster, but Margolis was unwilling to say much more than that Foster was "a good trade-unionist," not a syndicalist or an anarchist.[266]

Seeing that Margolis was not going to be very useful to the Committee on Foster's radical views, Senator Kenneth McKellar, a Democrat from Tennessee, questioned Margolis regarding his admission to the bar. "Did you take an oath?" Margolis replied that he did. "To support and defend the Constitution of the United States?" He did. "And do you think," Senator McKellar continued, "that you are supporting and defending the Constitution of the United States when you advocate principles against this Government and all other government?"

"Senator," replied Margolis, "I have lived up to my oath to support and maintain the Constitution of the United States. I feel, as honestly and as consistently as any lawyer in Allegheny County whoever took the oath ... And furthermore, I try to make myself clear—apparently I have not—that I do not advocate the overthrow of government. I do not advocate that, I say, but I do say that when certain conditions, based upon our industrial life, are modified, as a consequence of that modification and social arrangement will arise a condition which will obviate the necessity of government." Senator McKellar pressed him, saying he did not understand how advocating for a "disappearance of the government" was consistent with his oath. "While the Government is in existence, while the Constitution is in effect," Margolis attempted to explain, "I will do nothing against that Constitution, I maintain and uphold it, but when the new social arrangements come into being, which makes a government obsolete, I leave it."

Senator Kenyon interrupted. "And you have not sworn before God, have you?"

"No; I do not believe in God."

"You are an atheist?"

"I am."[267]

The senators turned particularly sarcastic by the end of the interview:

SENATOR WESLEY JONES (R-Washington): Don't you think you should go to some other place where you could have things more in accordance with your view of what is right in the view of the great majority?

MARGOLIS: There is no such place for me to go.

McKELLAR: You might try a place.

MARGOLIS: I do not know of such a place.

McKELLAR: There may be another world in which that sort of a theory can be worked out. Don't you think it would be well to try that?

JONES: ... Don't you think it would be a good thing for the United States to find an island somewhere and put all the people on it that think as you do?

MARGOLIS: No.[268]

Margolis' appearance before the Committee went on for almost three and half hours in total.[269]

The next day, Margolis' testimony in Washington was making front page news. The *Pittsburgh Gazette Times* gave it a four-column headline, reporting that Margolis, prominently identified as a member of the Allegheny County bar, had not only told "[a] startling tale of extreme radicalism, its sway in Pittsburgh and its insidious influence in the nation-wide steel strike," but that he "[f]rankly" professed himself to be "an 'anarchist syndicalist.'" The newspaper went on to report in a sub-headline that Margolis "Would Not Protect Wife," detailing his pacifism colloquy with the Committee, and that he had "entertained Alexander Berkman and Emma Goldman in his home."[270]

The publicity, with the anarchist bombings still fresh in the public mind, undoubtedly inspired the Bar Association to take prompt action. On the day after Margolis' testimony, the day it hit the local headlines, attorney Arthur "A.O." Fording filed a written complaint against Margolis with the Bar Association stating that Margolis had violated his oath as an officer of the court to support the Constitution.[271] Margolis had well and truly gotten himself caught up in the paradox to which his friend Emma Goldman had alluded while referring to Alexander Berkman's trial for his assault on Henry Clay Frick 27 years before: if "it was inconsistent for an anarchist to employ lawyers," perhaps it was even more inconsistent for an anarchist to be a lawyer. And while Goldman and Berkman were about to be boarded onto the *Buford* and deported to Russia by year's end, it appeared that Margolis would now face a different kind of "deportation" proceeding.

The Bar Association's Committee on Offenses designated two of members of the Bar Association, John C. Bane and Arthur M. Scully, to conduct an investigation on its behalf (using the new powers granted by statute in June), and the two were very well suited to the task, both from a substantive and a symbolic point of view. The fifty-eight year-old Bane, originally a Washington County lawyer, was a popular member of the bar, a Democrat, and a particular proponent of "good character" as a prerequisite for membership to the bar. In an address to the Bar Association in 1908, Bane asserted that Pittsburgh lawyers "should be proud of the fact that admission to the bar is, in effect, a certificate of good character." Although he recognized that there were exceptions, he argued that, on the whole, "when it appears that a man is a member of the bar, in good standing, this is enough, prima facie, to sustain a verdict that he is a truthful and an honorable man."[272] For Bane, the profession represented, and was defined by, "honor, integrity, patriotism, and fidelity to duty."[273] Lieutenant Colonel Scully, at age thirty-three, meanwhile, was a Boy Scout leader, also a Democrat, a member of the vestry of Calvary Episcopal Church, and had been, until the death of his wife in 1917, the son-in-law of a prominent Pittsburgh lawyer from an illustrious family of lawyers, George C. Burgwin. He was, furthermore, something of a war hero, having served for a time on General Pershing's staff as well as the Americans' second-in-command in the U.S. Army intelligence office at Koblenz during the French occupation of the area following the War. He had only been discharged from the Army on October 2.[274] Bane and Scully were, in many ways, almost everything that Margolis was not within the bar.

On the heels of the news that the Bar Association was preparing to consider recommending his disbarment, on October 26, Florence Margolis gave birth to the Margolis' youngest daughter, Louise.[275] Florence was probably a bit too consumed with motherly duties to have said "I told you so" at the time, but Jake undoubtedly began to feel the stress of potentially losing his livelihood.

As Bane and Scully began their investigation, J. Edgar Hoover sought to help the Bar Association to build its case by assigning an assistant to collate all of the evidence on Margolis that was in the Bureau of Investigation's files in Washington, and directing the Pittsburgh special agent-in-charge to provide Scully, the former Military Intelligence man, anything he needed.[276]

In December, Bane and Scully presented their findings at a two-hour meeting of the Bar Association. Taking his Senate testimony as their compass, Bane and Scully described Margolis as "an anarchist, a syndicalist, a communist, an atheist and a supporter and propagandist of the lawless and pernicious doctrines, principles, aims, purposes and practices of divers unions, organizations, societies and associations, including the Union of Russian Workers, the Industrial Workers of the World and the Communist Party of America ... in the propagation of plans and projects for the overthrowing of the government." They recited his associations with Goldman and Berkman, noted that his office in the Union Arcade had become "the rendezvous of members of these unions, organizations, societies and associations," and that he distributed their propaganda literature, and raised money for them. Finally, they asserted that he had "repudiated his oath of office and freely stated that he would not resist and raise no objection to a foreign enemy attacking, invading and overthrowing the government of the United States." They also mentioned that he had said that he would not resist an assault on his home or his wife.[277]

The report ended with a recommendation that Margolis be disbarred from practicing law in the courts of Allegheny County. The chairman of the Committee on Offenses, Charles Arensberg, offered a dissenting report, as he "saw nothing to warrant any such finding," but it was largely ignored.[278] The members, who had turned out in larger than usual attendance for the occasion, voted nearly unanimously to approve the report, with only "three or four lawyers voting in the negative." The *Gazette Times* reported that the "announcement of the decision was greeted with applause." Some argued that, as a matter of procedure, Margolis should have had a chance to defend himself, but the recommendation of the report was that the matter should be referred to trial before the Court of Common Pleas, at which time Margolis was free to mount his defense.[279]

The Bar Association filed its petition for Margolis' disbarment in January 1920, and Margolis hired three lawyers to represent him: S.S. Robertson, a sixty-two year-old native Scotsman who had relocated to Pittsburgh at the turn of the century and earned a reputation as an effective business lawyer[280]; forty year-old George Calvert Bradshaw, who had studied in Judge Thomson's law office before joining the Judge's brother as his partner in the firm of Thomson & Bradshaw[281]; and sixty-three year-old Louis Kossuth Porter, the older brother and law partner of Republican congressman Stephen Geyer Porter, and a distinguished trade union lawyer.[282] Each of them were members of the Bar Association.

While they prepared his case, however, Margolis embarked on a speaking tour, basking in the glow of his instant celebrity and incidentally providing his foes with additional evidence to support Bane and Scully's report—all except with regard to his being a "communist." Margolis was heckled at one of his speaking engagements by Communists who were angry at his assertion that the Soviet leaders were dictators. Margolis was unabashedly anti-Communist, although he did represent Communists in their fights against deportation. He went to Chicago, where he took the stage with Lucy Parsons, widow of Albert Parsons, the Haymarket martyr; and in Detroit and Akron, he denounced the actions of the bosses and the government in the steel strike. According to McCormick, Margolis' audiences "were sprinkled with detectives and stenographers," who took down his words and readied them to be presented at his disbarment hearing.[283]

Margolis' trial opened on April 29, 1920 before President Judge John Shafer, and Judges Thomas Ford and Joseph Swearingen. In Robertson's opening statement within the crowd-packed courtroom, he protested that "this entire proceeding is based on mob action." Bane took testimony from ex-special agent Edgar Speer of the Bureau of Investigation, who walked the court through the information obtained by the Bureau and gave examples of Margolis' distribution of incendiary literature, pointing out that Margolis had been under observation by agents for four years. Charles Prichard, the public safety director, testified that Margolis had argued with Prichard that his clients' free speech was being violated when police raided a meeting and took possession of radical literature; he also noted that Margolis admitted to being a Wobbly and an anarchist. An IRS agent testified that Margolis said that he "wished Germany would be in control of the United States for about 25 years." When on cross-examination Robertson asked whether it wasn't unusual for someone in his position to encounter people who did not want to pay taxes, the IRS agent claimed that "Margolis was the one exception ... The people at that time seemed anxious to pay their income tax—they wanted to help the government. He was the only disloyal one I personally came in contact with." Assistant district attorney John D. Meyer took the stand and told of knowing Jake when he was a law clerk, claiming that Margolis had told him in 1908 or 1909 that "we could get along better without any government at all."[284]

On day two of the trial, the U.S. attorney, E. Lowry Humes, took the stand and claimed that Margolis had once told him that "no man should be compelled or made to obey the conventional law." Two physicians, acquaintances of Margolis, testified that he had said that if a German fleet had entered New York harbor, "that he would just as leave be under the kaiser's rule as under the present government."[285] The allegedly pro-German statements made by Margolis stole the front-page headlines on both days.

The Bar Association lawyers submitted a 192-page trial brief, detailing all that came in as testimony, as well as much of what had been provided by the Bureau of Investigation.[286] S.S. Robertson, in his reply brief before the court, argued that the Bar Association's case was "a thing entirely in the region of ideas" and that the Association had not introduced any fact that was not simply an idea expressed in words. "[T]here can be no injury to our government, National or State, by speech," he argued. He sardonically considered what had been proven at trial—that Margolis "had talked," and that he "talked in doubtful company ... to miscellaneous assortments of the sons of men: Russians, Lithuanians, Poles, Italians, Bohemians, Parthians and Medes and Elamites and the dwellers in Mesopotamia. The worst that could be said of that," Robertson asserted, "would have to be that we might have been better employed." As to his associations with Goldman and Berkman, Robertson asked, "Do we try men for being in bad company?" As to the Bar Association's argument that lawyers are to be held to a higher standard of conduct, Robertson argued that "distinctions based upon this are meaningless except in a case where some infraction of the law is being considered," but that all that was offered here was "mere talk." In closing, Robertson wrote:

> *There is such a thing as due process of law, but it was not for us. We were tried without pleadings. We were tried without evidence. No such pleadings and no such evidence were ever heard of before in an American court. But they lost most of their objectionableness for us when the learned President Judge stated that the proceedings were in the nature of an investigation, which we took to mean that if there should be discovered matter for which we ought to answer we would be formally charged therewith and afforded an opportunity to defend. We have had our investigation, which turned out to be an investigation of others besides Margolis, and now we know something of how the foreigner is handled and why he does not love us.*[287]

Between the end of the trial phase and the court's eventual decision, Margolis continued business as usual, making speeches and attending union meetings. Over the summer, he and Marshall discussed the possibility of launching a lawsuit against officials of the Department of Justice relating to their conduct during raids on Croatian Communists; the intent, according to an informant, was in part to embarrass the local agents of the Bureau of Investigation.[288]

On September 16, the Court of Common Pleas ordered Jake Margolis' disbarment. In its opinion, the Court stated that while "we have no power in this proceeding to inquire into the mere belief of the respondent respecting either religion, government or law," Margolis was charged with more than a set of beliefs; he was charged with "conduct totally destructive of the government which he took an oath to 'support'."

Through his speeches and support of radicals and their activities, they wrote, Margolis "has done his utmost to breed unrest, among the lawless and vicious, and to incite them to acts of violence and disloyalty," and that therefore Margolis "has violated his duty as a lawyer and the obligation of the oath which he took to support the Constitution of the United States and of this Commonwealth."[289]

Although it was never suggested that Jake Margolis had anything to do with the Pittsburgh anarchist bombings, or in fact with any incident of violence, there was possibly some feeling of satisfaction within the community that those who had disrupted Law and Order in Pittsburgh, those who had supported Anarchy during this crisis, were being punished through Margolis' disbarment. The bombers would later be identified, generally, as members of the Galleanists, a group of violent Italian anarchists with whom Margolis had very little contact; no convictions were ever obtained with regard to the June 1919 night of terror.

Margolis was no bomber, but he was an anarchist.

On the day after the ruling, Margolis returned from a trip to New York at Marshall's behest to confer with his attorneys about taking an appeal. One of the Bureau of Investigation's informants said that Margolis told his lawyers that he thought that an appeal would be hopeless, but they insisted that by filing an appeal they could get the disbarment suspended during the appeal period, thereby permitting him to continue to practice law. Later in the day, talking with his friends, Margolis went on an angry, immoderate rant. He said that

> ... he would be G--- D----- if he would spend any money to practice in these G--- D----- courts; that he had no use for law and never did have, and that he had got away with the stuff as long as he could. He said, however, that if his friends were willing to put up the money to have the appeal printed he would not object. He was informed of the threats made by the members of the I.W.W. on Wednesday evening and stated that it certainly would have a wonderful effect if anything like that happened. He said he deplored the killing and wounding of the workers in the New York explosion, but it would have a very salutary effect and set these G--- D----- crooks on Wall Street to thinking and waken them up to the fact that there was something happening in this world. He said further that he would get the gang of wobblies at Gallatin, PA to do this job that the anarchists are talking about, by just saying the word—in fact, that they might do the job without his saying the word. He also stated—that when this Galliani bunch do this kind of job they do it right. ... Margolis stated further—Believe me, I surely will give the gang of G--- D----- crooks hell. I am going to ridicule them from the house tops and believe me, I am going to do the best I can to have the Liberal papers and Radical papers to ridicule them.[290]

Meanwhile, some of his friends, "a number of the English, Hungarian, Croatian and Russian wobblies" meeting at Kestner's saloon on the North Side, discussed retaliation against the judges, according to the Bureau of Investigation's informant. Statements "flew thick and fast" that either the courts or the judges' homes should be blown up. One of the Hungarians said, "We fix the damn Judges—we wait for this for sometime ...

we catch them—we blow them to hell. We get Russian and Hungarian Fellow Workers already to do job—G--- D---- it, we give them hell."[291]

Tempers cooled after the Pennsylvania Supreme Court granted Margolis a writ of supersedeas on September 23 that permitted Margolis to continue practicing law until the disposition of an appeal. "After it was granted," reported the informant, Margolis "stated that he never saw such a bunch of spineless individuals as these G--- D-----Judges. He said although there has never been a case of this kind before in any of the disbarment proceedings, the judges rarely ever granted a writ of supersedeas. He said—just think—these fish granted the writ of supersedeas, not on petition, but on argument, one of the judges drawing the order himself to restore him to practice." Margolis asked his friend "what they would do if they were judges and then answered the question himself by saying—if an anarchist was ever thrown out of my court and came around looking for a writ of supersedeas I would throw him down the courthouse steps and throw his attorneys in jail for contempt of court by asking for a writ. I would tell them to go to the supreme court for their writ." He said that he believed the judges were "yellow and when the fact leaked out that they might get a tin can placed under their porches they became afraid and recanted."[292]

"This granting of a writ of supersedeas," Margolis said, "gives me the privilege of practicing for a year and a half, or more, and by that time I hope and feel that no judges will be in existence to hear my appeal." He ridiculed the judges "in every profane manner possible," as well as the Bar Association, Bane and Scully. "Believe me boys," he said, "this can of beans that they opened on Wall Street has made all of these 'birds' sit up and take notice."[293]

In November, at a meeting of the Metal & Machinery Workers #440 of the IWW and the Pittsburgh Local of the General Recruiting Union, with eleven members in attendance at the International Socialist Lyceum, on the motion of Louis M. Walsh the defense committee voted to spend $75 of the $160 in the treasury to print Margolis' appeal to the Pennsylvania Supreme Court.[294] Margolis had earlier reached out to Roger Baldwin of the National Civil Liberties Bureau, sending him a copy of the court's opinion and Robertson's brief, but Baldwin was tepid, saying that his case, while "interesting," did not "deal with an issue of civil liberty which we could get across to the folks we reach."[295]

Swinburne Hale, who had suggested to Margolis that perhaps he could come to New York and work as business manager to his firm, Hale, Nelles & Shorr, in the event of his disbarment, published a piece in October in *The Nation* entitled "U.S. Steel v. Margolis," excoriating the judges for their flawed logic, recalling instances of Pittsburgh police oppression, and noting, "as an interesting sidelight," the federal espionage that produced much of the evidence against Margolis. Evidently, Hale observed, reading private letters and telegrams and tapping private telephone conversations "has come to be a part of modern American institutions."[296]

On February 14, 1921, in an opinion written by Justice Sylvester Sadler, the Pennsylvania Supreme Court upheld the order of the Allegheny County Court of Common Pleas disbarring Jacob Margolis. The Court was particularly swayed, it seemed, by Bane and Scully's argument that lawyers needed to be held to a higher standard of conduct, citing the U.S. Supreme Court's opinion in *Ex Parte Wall* (1883), in which an attorney encouraged a lynching. In *Wall*, the Court opined:

> *Of all classes and professions, the lawyer is most sacredly bound to uphold the laws. He is their sworn servant; and for him, of all men in the world, to repudiate or override the laws, to trample them under foot, and to ignore the very bands of society, argues recreancy to his position and office, and sets a pernicious example to the insubordinate and dangerous elements of the body politic. It manifests a want of fidelity to the system of lawful government which he had sworn to uphold and serve.*[297]

The fact that Margolis had never been charged or convicted of a crime did not matter, according to the Pennsylvania Supreme Court; the standard for professionalism could not be set so low. As to Margolis' protest that he never advocated the use of violence to overthrow the government, the Court said simply that "this denial was not sustained by the weight of the evidence."[298]

According to McCormick, shortly after the Pennsylvania Supreme Court had rendered its decision, Margolis ran into a pair of Bureau of Investigation agents on the streets of Pittsburgh. He told them he knew he "never had a chance," but what irked him was that he was adjudged to have advocated violence. "You and every man in your Department knows that I never did use that argument. I believe in non-resistance. My friends insist that I am not a Bolshevist on that account."[299]

McCormick writes that after 1921, "Margolis's career went into eclipse."[300] True, his niche of radical philosophy was no longer "in the radical vanguard," but he remained active. His obsession with political and economic issues drove him to continue to speak at leftist gatherings and to help raise money for radical causes. He put his own money into the acquisition of a newspaper, the *Detroit Jewish Chronicle*, and moved his family to Detroit so that he could assume the role of editor, writing on national issues.[301]

Despite his flippant assertion that "he would be G--- D----- if he would spend any money to practice in these G--- D----- courts; that he had no use for law and never did have," Margolis apparently still found an important aspect of his own identity in his former profession, and did not cease trying to get himself reinstated to the bar. In 1924, he petitioned the Pennsylvania Supreme Court to readmit him and "issue a certificate to that effect" so that he might "practice law outside the state of Pennsylvania." In a per curiam opinion, the Court dismissed his petition, stating that all proceedings regarding disbarment were required to be conducted in the "'proper court' of the county where the attorney 'misbehaved himself,' or where 'his office' is located," and that the Court had no jurisdiction over the issue.[302]

On the same day that news of Margolis' failure to gain reinstatement was reported in the *Pittsburgh Post*, the *Post* also reported that William J. Brennen, "Democratic Leader and Noted Attorney," had passed away at the age of seventy-three.[303]

Notably absent from Brennen's obituary in the *Post* was much discussion of his role as a labor lawyer, or any recognition of his role as one of the first, if not *the* first, labor lawyer in Pittsburgh; in fact, in an article of more than 1,800 words (a long obituary, by any standard), the only mention was the following: "His early association with the labor movement and his outspoken support of the unions won the young attorney many cases in the litigation growing out of industrial disturbances in the early 80s, and he was counsel for all the leading labor organizations in Western Pennsylvania."[304] It is quite possible that by 1924, so much had changed about organized labor from Brennen's heyday, so much had changed about being a labor lawyer (even the look of the archetypal labor lawyer had fundamentally changed; Brennen's pomaded hair, frock coat, starched collars and spats looked completely out of place next to Margolis' frizzy mop and Panama suits), that the *Post* obituary writer did not realize he had a labor lawyer in his sights.

Margolis' professional redemption came, finally, in 1928. On November 13, 1928, the *Pittsburgh Press* reported that a committee composed of Judges Richard W. Martin, James B. Drew and Frank P. Patterson of the Allegheny County Court of Common Pleas, appointed following Margolis' most recent petition, had recommended that he be reinstated.[305] By this time, not that it necessarily mattered, but John C. Bane had died, and Arthur M. Scully had settled into a lucrative corporate and municipal finance practice during the "go-go" years of the end of the decade. Scully did ultimately acknowledge to Arensberg that he was wrong about Margolis. "I am sorry I didn't stand by you," he told him.[306] Perhaps most members of the elite bar were just too busy during those years to care. The term "anarchist" had lost some, if not all, of its villainous urgency. In fact, by then, it had taken on a whiff of quaint anachronism.

Shortly after the committee issued its recommendation, Margolis was reinstated. He sold his interest in the *Chronicle* and moved his family back to Pittsburgh, where he resumed the practice of law for a time, representing some of the same usual suspects. But the labor unions he used to know well had all but disappeared, and the ones that replaced them were being represented by a new generation of lawyers. He continued to speak on political issues, although the gatherings—at synagogues or small labor meetings—would never be noted in any history of the radical left. The radical left had moved on.

Eventually, Margolis and his wife retired to Santa Barbara, California, where Jake did manage to keep in touch with some of his comrades from the old days. Roger Baldwin came to visit. His granddaughter Barbara Margolis recalls seeing the big man, her grandfather, sitting on his front porch reading from the newspapers he had stashed there in great stacks; and his letters from his later years—typically a paragraph of pleasantries followed by several pages of trenchant analysis of current events[307]—indicate that he never lost his obsession with politics, even if he had ultimately let his hard-fought connection to his profession recede into the distant, red past.

LAWYER, WHERE DO YOU STAND?

■━━━━━━━━━━━■

Seymour Sikov, one of the deans of the plaintiffs' bar in Pittsburgh from the 1960s until his death in 2013, was the second of three generations of lawyers who graduated from Pitt Law School. His father Meyer Sikov was born in Russia, earned a bachelor's degree at Michigan, received his law degree at Pittsburgh, entered the bar in 1913 and practiced for about forty years. Thus, it might have been a foregone conclusion that Seymour would have developed an ambition to become a lawyer from the experience of his father, but Seymour Sikov maintained that it was just the opposite; he had actually fixed his sights on a career as an engineer until fate intervened and he found himself in the Judge Advocate Corps during World War II and the Korean War. "My father was a lawyer during the Great Depression," Sikov explained. Watching his father trying to create and maintain a law practice, working at other jobs to keep food on the table, Sikov developed distaste for the idea of practicing law.[308]

The newspaper headlines on October 30, 1929, the day after the market crash that sent the American economy into a decade-long tailspin, probably baffled the average Pittsburgher. "All Trading Marks Broken, Bank Group Checks Slump," said the *Post-Gazette*.[309] "Bankers Confident of Stock Rise," said the *Press*.[310] The trickle-down effect from the stock crash and its effect on the availability of capital, however, would have devastating effects throughout Western Pennsylvania over the next several years. As steel mills cut their production by fifty percent or more and coal production fell by the same amount, Pittsburgh's unemployment rate rose to nearly forty-percent by the end of 1932.[311] Private relief agencies exhausted their resources quickly, and for the growing numbers of families with unemployed wage-earners in Pittsburgh, there was no government safety net; there was instead, increasingly, homelessness and malnutrition and human tragedy.

Banks, such as the late Judge Mellon's institution, were the catalysts of the Pittsburgh industrial revolution, the engines behind the engines of job creation, but in the atmosphere of anxiety that existed following the Crash, they stood paralyzed, hoping to avoid the calamity of a "run" on deposits by nervous customers. For some, the calamity was inevitable. Benjamin Roth, a lawyer from nearby Youngstown, Ohio, noted in his diary that in one week in September 1931, ten Pittsburgh banks closed their doors.[312] and by the end of the following month, Roth witnessed the closure of ten more.[313] In January 1933, Roth lamented, "Money continues to be scarce and almost non-existent."[314]

The strength of the banking system was President Roosevelt's first priority after his inauguration on March 4, 1933. On the last business day before Roosevelt's proposed "bank holiday," Pittsburgh's most successful bank braced itself. As Brignano and Fort write:

> *Mellon National Bank in Downtown Pittsburgh opened its great bronze door for business as usual. The normally serene banking floor, anchored with massive marble columns, became a scene of mass agitation as more than ten thousand depositors clamored to withdraw their money between the hours of nine A.M. and twelve-fifteen P.M. The presence of the genial Richard B. Mellon, his usual immaculately dressed, distinguished self, plainly in view and in charge, did much to reassure them. Reed Smith's William M. Robinson stood with the banker that morning, and even the near panic around them could not dampen Mellon's dry sense of humor. "Bill," he reportedly said to his friend and counselor, "I have never seen so many of my customers at one time."*[315]

Reed, Smith, Shaw & McClay was a bankers' law firm. It would be commonplace during the period for Robinson, assisted by partners John G. Frazer and James H. Beal, Jr., and associates Arthur Van Buskirk and Robert Kirkpatrick, to work "into the wee hours in arranging for the rescuing takeover, for example, of the Third National Bank," according to Demmler.[316] Frazer and Beal also represented the receivers of the Bank of Pittsburgh and the Monongahela National Bank, whose liquidations resulted in depositors receiving one hundred percent of their deposits.[317]

"The firm was busy, very busy, during the Depression and the recovery, what with receiverships, reorganizations, foreclosures and the advent of the New Deal," observes Demmler,[318] which explains why, as Brignano and Fort relate, Reed Smith's partners "suffered few privations during the 1930s." Senior partners, who each received distributions of $50,265 in 1929, maintained pretty consistent annual distributions after the crash of 1929, with the exception of the distributions for 1932 ($37,666) and 1933 ($35,065). Even the dip during those years reflected spectacular earnings, as the average American salary was a mere $1,368 in 1932. In 1938, each of the senior partners received $139,906, although, as Brignano and Fort indicate, "hikes in the income tax offset part of the income."[319] The firm managed to avoid layoffs of clerical employees during the period, but there were few raises or bonuses for them.

At the Smith Buchanan firm, although the practice continued to thrive for many of the same reasons that Reed Smith's did, William Watson Smith put the brakes on. Having added eight associates during the 1920s—two in 1924 and two in 1925—the firm parted ways with two of them in 1930, and only added four net lawyers from

1930 to 1935. The standards for associate sustainability were apparently raised once the Great Depression actually began, as while none of the 1920s era hires left the firm until 1930, half of the lawyers hired from 1930 to 1935 left during the decade. While the firm's net profits hovered somewhere between $420,000 and $525,000 each year from 1928 to 1931, the years 1932-34 and 1936 saw a pretty sharp decline in net profits, with the low point being $252,865.96 in 1932, before soaring again in the late 1930s. Under the circumstances, the Smith Buchanan partners had little to complain about even during the low years; the partners having the smallest percentage of net profits under the partnership agreement still received over $7,500 in distributions in 1932, and even one of the eleven female stenographers on staff was given a five dollar annual raise that year.[320] At both Reed Smith and Smith Buchanan, modest annual raises for staff members were commonplace before the Depression; during the worst years of it, staff raises were exceptionally rare.

Meanwhile, at the Patterson Crawford firm, gross revenues plunged from their peak in 1928 of $117,200 to $38,625 in 1932, before rallying modestly. It would not be until 1950 when the firm beat its 1928 record, on a nominal basis.[321]

The Socialist editor Oscar Ameringer wrote about the "brokers, bank clerks, counter-jumpers, A.B.s, M.D.s, Ph.D.s, D.D.s, shoveling snow in the lowly company of bricklayers, cellists, hod carriers, oboists, garment workers, concert masters, stevedores, dramatists, and dock wallopers" during the Great Depression.[322] He could have, perhaps, expanded his motley list to include a lawyer, or an LL.B or J.D. or two. As Christine Brendel Scriabine writes, "Contrary to popular belief that owing to increases in bankruptcies, foreclosures and crime, the law is a depression proof profession and that the New Deal provided endless opportunities for young lawyers, the law was one of the hardest hit of professions" during the period. Even as late as 1935, 1,200 unemployed New York City lawyers mobilized as the Lawyers' Security League, asking the government for more work for lawyers.[323] In Pittsburgh, the growth in the active bar—lawyers in private practice as revealed by the business directories of the time—essentially flat-lined from 1929 (1,328) to 1931 (1,394), despite additional admissions to the bar of eighty-five new lawyers in 1929, one hundred in 1930, and ninety-four in 1931.[324] The numbers would indicate that, in Pittsburgh, there were lawyers who were unemployed, or at least underemployed, working in other jobs, as the Great Depression got under way.

What a Pittsburgh lawyer experienced during this desperate time depended a great deal upon where he or she was standing the moment the music stopped. John Ralston, the co-founder of the firm of Stonecipher & Ralston, was a leader in the Commercial Law League of America, had a nationally respected collections practice before the Great Depression set in, and undoubtedly earned healthy fees collecting debts during the Great Depression. As his granddaughter, Linda Shoop Smalstig, recalled, "He was able to help some other families during the Depression."[325] Meanwhile, where Reuben Fingold happened to be standing was in an oral final exam, facing a panel of teachers, at Duquesne Law School. Entering the bar in 1930, he had no job waiting for him. He shared space with a few other young lawyers in the Jones Law Building on Fourth Avenue, and waited there, almost as in a bullpen, for an established lawyer to come along and ask for help. He managed to earn a small living by doing title searches for other lawyers for ten dollars a search, sometimes accepting even less. "The [deed] books weighed almost as much as me," he remembered.[326]

Another Pittsburgh lawyer was standing at the side of the president.

The weight of the Great Depression on the American economy certainly took its toll on the popular opinion of President Herbert Hoover and the national Republican Party. One Pittsburgh lawyer who was working hard to bear the load of that weight was James Francis Burke. Burke was born in Petroleum Center, Pennsylvania in 1867, the eldest son of Irish immigrants. At fifteen, he "joined" the Republican Party during the presidential campaign of James G. Blaine, marching in a torchlight parade holding a banner that said, "We can't vote, but our Dads can." While studying at the University of Michigan in 1892, Burke was the founding president of the American Republican College League, later known as the College Republicans, and was shortly thereafter elected as the youngest ever secretary of the Republican National Committee. He entered the bar and practiced general corporate law in Pittsburgh, while participating in the national leadership of the Republican Party, until he was elected to Congress as the representative of the 31st District serving portions of Pittsburgh, beating the one-term Independent Republican incumbent, H.K. Porter, a railroad locomotive millionaire.[327] Burke served for ten years before retiring in 1914—just after he tried to block the passage of the Federal Reserve Act.

While Burke served as the director of the War Savings program during the Great War, Herbert Hoover was the head of the U.S. Food Administration, and the two war-time bureaucrats formed a bond. Burke became general counsel to the national Republican Party in 1927, and after Hoover was elected president in 1928, Burke became a "kitchen cabinet" advisor to him, one of his closest political advisors. During the worst days of the Depression, Burke was the first Republican leader to stand in line to tout the re-nomination of President Hoover as a foregone conclusion, despite a short-lived movement to draft former president Calvin Coolidge to pursue the Republican nomination. "The whole world has been going through an economic illness, and the one old-fashioned physician who has remained at the bedside and who has never left the nation's welfare throughout it all is Mr. Hoover," said Burke. "The people are now beginning to realize this and to appreciate just what Mr. Hoover has been doing to keep this nation on a steady keel."[328] Speaking in January 1932 like a man still carrying the heaviest of burdens, the Party's general counsel drew a desperate line in the sand, saying, "If the Republican Party cannot re-elect Mr. Hoover it cannot re-elect anyone."[329]

Nonetheless, Burke was still a Pittsburgh lawyer, and had clients who were suffering from the effects of the Great Depression, even as he tried to keep his political spirits high. In December 1930, for example, Burke was apparently one of several friends of Albert M. Greenfield, the president of the Bankers Trust Company of Philadelphia, to contact President Hoover to secure his help in staving off the takeover of the failing bank by the Pennsylvania Department of Banking. Writing to Greenfield from his office in the Farmers Bank Building after the inevitable closing of the bank, Burke explained, "Our friend [President Hoover] acted promptly. By 830 he had the Reserve and Clearing House people together—but they informed him it was too late. He deeply regretted he did not know before that he might help to the limit of his capacity. I hope you emerge as triumphantly as your all conquering genius deserves."[330] The sweep of events was occurring with such speed that, for some of Burke's clientele, even access to the Oval Office was for naught; the problems they were facing were bigger than Hoover.

Two other Pittsburgh attorneys of the era stood off to the side—outside of the elite bar, and nowhere near the Oval Office.

In August 1927, in Acmetonia, near Harmarville, a Pennsylvania state trooper was shot and killed during a meeting held to protest the impending execution of Nicola Sacco and Bartolommeo Vanzetti, two Italian anarchists who were convicted of killing two men during an armed robbery at a shoe factory in South Braintree, Massachusetts in 1920. The Sacco and Vanzetti case became a national cause célèbre among the American Left, since there were suspicions, in light of weak evidence, that the men were convicted primarily for their political beliefs. Salvatore Accorsi, a Cheswick miner, was arrested and charged with the murder of the state trooper at the Acmetonia protest. Two Pittsburgh lawyers became associated with the successful defense and acquittal of Salvatore Accorsi: one was Jake Margolis, after his reinstatement to the bar, and the other was an obscure young civil rights lawyer, then working with the American Civil Liberties Union, named Henry Ellenbogen.[331] Meanwhile, a little over a month prior to the Acmetonia protest, a series of mass meetings were held in New York to protest and to raise funds for the ongoing defense of Sacco and Vanzetti. Among the speakers were Clarence Darrow, Congressman Fiorello LaGuardia, and Jake Margolis.[332] And one of the busiest lawyers on the front lines of the Sacco and Vanzetti Defense Committee at that time was another Pittsburgh lawyer, Michael A. Musmanno.

Henry Ellenbogen and Michael Musmanno—in later years known to members of the Pittsburgh bar as men with colossal egos, stubborn and autocratic—were coincidentally linked together in their early professional days through the activities of a "red" lawyer who had been disbarred. Both eventually became among the most powerful, and certainly among the most colorful, members of the Pittsburgh bench and bar. Understanding where they stood in the years leading up to the Great Depression, during its worst years and its aftermath, becomes important to understanding how the Pittsburgh bar was beginning to change during the Depression years.

Neither of them, by background, came to the profession through the white, Anglo-Saxon Protestant mainstream.

Henry Ellenbogen was born in 1900 in Vienna, Austria to a "solidly middle-class family," according to historian Kurt Stone.[333] His family's financial stability, despite the death of his father in 1911, enabled him to study law at the University of Vienna, and the industrious young man managed to receive his degree at age nineteen. Shortly thereafter, "feeling there was no future in Vienna for a young Jewish lawyer," Ellenbogen immigrated to the United States to join his mother and younger brother Theodore, who had arrived in Pittsburgh shortly before his graduation.[334]

When he arrived in 1919, Ellenbogen may have had some reason to question whether there was any future in Pittsburgh for a young Jewish-American lawyer. Although Leo Weil and Joseph Stadtfeld were enjoying illustrious careers, there also stood Jake Margolis, hounded on the fringes of the profession. The difference between their status in the bar betrayed a fracture that existed in the Jewish population of Pittsburgh at the time. As historian Kenneth J. Heineman observes, "Pittsburgh's 53,000 Jews were ... sharply divided by class, culture, and regional origins." Heineman recounts how, because of Rodef Shalom's adherence to Reform Judaism, it attracted "assimilated, prosperous" German-American Jews, while the orthodox Tree of Life Congregation "attracted poor Eastern European Orthodox Jews" from Russia, Croatia, Poland, Lithuania and Romania.[335] As attorney Robert Sable recalls, "They used to talk in the Jewish community about the 'Holy Trinity': Rodef Shalom, Concordia, and Westmoreland Country Club—that's where the German Jews belonged."[336] The Concordia Club, founded in 1874 with Judge Josiah Cohen as its first president, barred Lithuanian, Russian, Romanian and Polish Jews from membership.[337]

Assimilated German Jews such as Leo Weil and Eugene Strassburger, Sr. would form firms with Gentiles (i.e, Weil & Thorp, 1895[338]; Strassburger & McKenna, 1920s[339]), but they would also establish German Jewish firms, such as Sachs & Caplan, that would represent the middle and upper-middle class individuals and businesses within the Rodef Shalom community. Columbia-educated David B. Buerger, the son of an assimilated German Jew who served as vice president of Gulf Refining Company, was hired in 1932 by an elite Pittsburgh firm, Smith Buchanan.[340]

On the other hand, Eastern European Jewish lawyers during the pre-World War II era—such as Louis Barach, Meyer Shapira and Jake Margolis, each of whom were beset by troubles with the mainstream bar in one way or another—typically found their clientele among the less prosperous, Yiddish-speaking Eastern European Orthodox Jews in the "insulated Jewish enclaves" of the Hill District[341] or, in Margolis' case, among the radical activists. Their bread and butter was the ethnic downtrodden. As Heineman observes, the Kaufmanns, owners of Pittsburgh's large downtown department store and members of the "Holy Trinity" crowd, "took a dim view of the Orthodox Jews":

> *Chiefly, the assimilated Germans [like the Kaufmanns] were worried that the easterners would provoke an anti-Semitic backlash. After all, their prayer shawls, yarmulkes, and boisterous Yiddish made them look so obviously Jewish. The Germans also half-believed ... that the eastern Jews were dangerous radicals.*

The old-line German Jewish lawyers in Pittsburgh would perform their duty to help the assimilation of Eastern European Jews through their support of the Irene Kaufmann Settlement, but they were generally inclined to return to their lucrative practices, representing prosperous clients.[342] These divisions within the Pittsburgh Jewish legal community would persist, less dramatically over time, into the 1960s.[343]

With a strong desire to assimilate rapidly, Ellenbogen fortunately found a job working as an accountant for Kaufmann's Department Store while attending Duquesne University at night. A mere four years after his arrival in Pittsburgh, Ellenbogen was the proud holder of both a bachelor's degree and a law degree from Duquesne. He entered the bar in 1924, receiving one of the highest scores ever achieved on the bar exam. Despite his score, the Allegheny County Bar Association took issue with his admission on the basis that Ellenbogen was not a U.S. citizen, but Ellenbogen took the

Bar Association to court, and won.[344] Shortly thereafter, Ellenbogen began to represent labor unions and laborers—the ethnic downtrodden.

Ellenbogen's German-language education and middle-class background undoubtedly meant that he would have identified with the German Jews, but unlike the German Jewish families that arrived in Pittsburgh in the nineteenth century, the Ellenbogens were very recent immigrants without any established connections among Pittsburgh's Jewish elite. Ellenbogen committed his career to the underprivileged, with whose concerns he would also empathize, as a first-generation immigrant. His obvious intellectual gifts and his confident physical presence—his dignified bearing, and his broad-jawed, open countenance, with his long, patrician nose and immaculate Ruritanian moustachette—did ultimately recommend him to the Irish Catholic Democrats with whom he studied at Duquesne, even if these qualities did not immediately bring him within the ambit of the elite lawyers of the Bar Association, or even the elite German Jewish lawyers. They were undoubtedly among the qualities, though, that caused David L. Lawrence, the insurance man who was elected chairman of the County Democrats in 1919, to take notice of the young lawyer, asking him to become his "legal advisor and political legman," according to Heineman.[345]

Meanwhile, while Michael Angelo Musmanno was a U.S. citizen, born to Italian immigrants in Stowe Township in 1897, his heritage meant that his entry into professional life was no less challenging than Ellenbogen's. At age fourteen, Musmanno went to work with his father as a coal loader, while continuing to attend school at night. After high school, Musmanno enrolled in Georgetown University in Washington, D.C., but his studies were interrupted by the Great War, during which he served in the U.S. Army infantry. When he returned, he finished his bachelor's degree at Georgetown, then earned bachelor's and master's degrees from George Washington University before obtaining his Master of Laws and Master of Patent Laws degrees from National University and his Doctor of Jurisprudence from American University, in 1923. After law school, he moved to Philadelphia and worked with a general practitioner for a year, gaining quite a bit of trial experience before resigning and sailing to Europe to consider his next career moves.[346] He studied Roman law at the University of Rome, taking a moment to serve as an extra in a Metro-Goldwyn-Mayer silent movie epic that was then being filmed in Rome, *Ben Hur: A Tale of the Christ* (1925), starring Ramon Novarro and Francis X. Bushman.[347] After a nine-year absence, Musmanno returned to Pittsburgh and entered the bar in 1926—two years after Ellenbogen—perhaps the best educated Italian American in the region. All that, and he spoke "without the trace of a foreign accent," as a Washington newspaper would later report.[348]

The Pittsburgh bar had not proven to be the friendliest of environments for upwardly mobile Italians, however. The first wave of Italian immigration to Pittsburgh began in the 1880s, and was fueled in part by labor unrest; during the steel and coal strikes of the latter years of the nineteenth century, unskilled Italian immigrant laborers were often the "scabs" that were brought in by Frick and other industrial tycoons when the unions tried to shut down production. Later, the public mind identified Italians with radicalism, on the one hand, and with bootlegging, on the other. These views were exacerbated by the cultural insularity of the Italian community.[349] The first Italian

American to be admitted to the Pittsburgh bar appears to have been Frank J. Lagorio, a second-generation Italian American from Boston, in December 1905.[350] From the paucity of information available about Lagorio, it would seem that he kept a low profile.

Just prior to Lagorio's admission, however, there was an Italian American candidate who was a much more visible member of Pittsburgh's Italian community, and who would experience some difficulty in gaining admission to the bar. Felidio "Frank" Canuti was born in Allerona, Italy in 1867, and immigrated to the United States with his parents when he was eight years old. In 1887, he published a history, *The Siege and Fall of Constantinople: The Last Roman Struggle in the East*, and three years later founded the Pittsburgh Italian-language newspaper, *I Nostri Tempi*. He continued to publish the newspaper while attending the University of Pittsburgh, where he received his law degree in 1906.[351] Prior to receiving his degree, however, in November 1905, the Allegheny County Board of Law Examiners convened an unusual session to consider "certain complaints" regarding "the conduct of Felidio Canuti, a registered student at law." While the complaints were not detailed in the surviving minutes of the session, the minutes indicate that the Board considered statements from a pair of Oakmont laborers, Salvatore DiFatta and John A. Walgren, and heard translations, made by "Mr. DeRosa of the Union Savings Bank," of several articles from issues of *I Nostri Tempi*. It was also alleged that Canuti had attempted to intervene in a case before the Pardon Board and attempted to file an affidavit of defense in a matter before a local alderman.[352] Witnesses were heard in a second and a third session on Canuti's candidacy, and on November 17, the Board voted to refuse Canuti's application for a final examination, ruling that he would be restricted from making another application for a period of one year.[353] Canuti was ultimately admitted to the bar the following year, sold *I Nostri Tempi* in 1910 (it would eventually become known as *Unione*, the official organ of the Order of the Italian Sons and Daughters of America), and enjoyed a relatively prosperous career as a criminal lawyer.[354]

By the time Musmanno entered the Pittsburgh bar, there was less novelty in the idea of an Italian American lawyer, but some prejudices remained. Judge Ruggero Aldisert recalled an August 1923 clash between authorities in his hometown of Carnegie and the Ku Klux Klan of Western Pennsylvania, in which the Klan defiantly slandered "Catholics, Jewish, Italian and Negro people." The resulting riot left one Klan member dead, several others injured. Aldisert called the event a turning point in the Klan's influence, but that "what was begun in August 1923 took years, indeed many decades, to accomplish" relative to mainstream attitudes about Italian Americans. In 1958, when Aldisert began his campaign as the endorsed Democratic candidate for a seat on the Common Pleas bench, David L. Lawrence suggested that he change his name to "R.L. Aldisert" because "with a name like Aldisert, no one will know whether you are Catholic or Protestant, English or German or old line American … if you go on the ballot as 'Ruggero J. Aldisert' all the Ku Kluckers in the North Hills will cut you. They're good Democrats, but they just don't like Italians or Poles or Jews."[355]

On his return to Pittsburgh, Musmanno had no capital with which to open his own law office, but he did not believe he would have any difficulty finding a spot in an existing law firm in 1926. "Each morning," he recalled, "I boarded a streetcar and jolted over five miles of rough track to the Golden Triangle, only to be jolted successively by well-fed and well-dressed lawyers who informed me, one after the other, that they were not interested."[356] At first without an office, later working from the lobby of a real estate agent, Musmanno began to build for himself a small, local criminal defense practice, often tinged with labor vs. management undertones, around the coal fields of Allegheny County. He made a run for the lower house of the state legislature as a Republican—most of the Italian Americans were Republicans in 1926, the result of Republican patronage, the awarding of city and county jobs to key members of the Italian community—but failing to receive the Party endorsement, he lost.[357]

His experiences with a few capital punishment cases in Pittsburgh led his active mind to wander to the Sacco and Vanzetti case in Boston, then going through appeals. Despite his growing credibility in labor circles, working on behalf of the Italian working men and women of Stowe Township and surrounding areas, Musmanno "did not approve of the political philosophy" of the two men.[358] However, "with an ever-augmenting quantity of evidence supporting the defendants' insistence they were innocent and yet apparently ever diminishing chances for their liberation, I worried as to what was happening to our whole system of jurisprudence," he recalled.[359] He wrote to the lead defense counsel for the men, William G. Thompson, to arrange to meet Sacco and Vanzetti in their prison cells at the Norfolk County Jail in Dedham, Massachusetts. Shortly after those interviews, against advice of a senior colleague at the bar, Musmanno closed his office in Pittsburgh during the summer of 1927 to join the Sacco and Vanzetti appeals team in Boston, bringing as his part of the case a petition for clemency from the Sons of Italy to be laid before Massachusetts governor Alvan T. Fuller.[360]

When Fuller announced that he would not interfere with the sentences, Musmanno filed a motion for a new trial on the basis that the men had never received the fair trial to which they were entitled under the Constitution. On the Friday before the scheduled execution, to be held at midnight on the following Monday, August 10, he jumped on a train to Washington to file an appeal with the U.S. Supreme Court. Finding that he did not have all the necessary papers for an appeal, he promised to send them on Monday morning, and then canvassed the Department of Justice, attempting to convince someone there to open the sealed federal files on Sacco and Vanzetti, to no avail. Back in Boston on August 10, he visited the prisoners. Vanzetti tried to make a gift to Musmanno of something he had been given while in prison, a two volume set of *The Rise of American Civilization* by Charles A. Beard; Vanzetti inscribed it to Musmanno as "my friend and defender." Musmanno told him he would take the books, but only after Vanzetti was a free man.

The governor delivered a temporary stay, pending the last of the state appeals by the Defense Committee. The Massachusetts Supreme Judicial Court ruled against Musmanno's motion for a new trial as being "too late," however, so Musmanno turned his energies toward securing a stay of execution from one justice of the U.S. Supreme Court, pending consideration of the petition for a writ of certiorari that the Committee filed with U.S. Supreme Court. Musmanno applied personally to Justices Holmes and Brandeis and Chief Justice Taft, and then sent a wire to President Calvin Coolidge, who was vacationing in South Dakota, to ask him to request another stay from Governor Fuller pending consideration of the petition. Finding no one else who would issue a stay, on August 22, 1927, the new day set for the executions, Musmanno stood as the last man pleading with Governor Fuller for an additional stay, to no avail. He rushed back to the prison, but arrived too late to say goodbye to his clients, as the official witnesses had already been admitted to the death chamber. Musmanno regretted that he had not had a chance to accept Vanzetti's gift. "I returned to Pittsburgh a failure," he wrote.[361]

Working feverishly at the heart of a case that commanded the attention of the entire nation—and getting no small amount of attention from the press—Musmanno was in his element. The case showed the lengths to which he would go to follow his passion for what he perceived to be justice. He returned to Pittsburgh as a failure in the case, but with a renewed self-confidence from his encounters with the high courts and the well-known politicians, and a determination to fight injustice.

He ran again for the state legislature in 1928, taking on critics who intended to tar him with the political stripes of his Boston clients. He stood defiantly on the political stage with his wild, upswept, maestro-style hair, visually suggesting to those encountering him, even before he might open his mouth and let loose his poetic orations, that he was a man who had a big brain. This time, he won the election narrowly. Among those who voted for him were members of the United Mine Workers, who expressed their support not only for his defense of Sacco and Vanzetti, but also for his battles, case by case, against the dreaded Coal and Iron Police.[362] The Coal and Iron Police were creatures of a Pennsylvania law, enacted in 1865 and amended the following year, that permitted coal, railroad and steel companies to employ private police, with state commissions giving them the powers of state and local police officers for one dollar per badge, to protect corporate property—in theory. As Judge Aldisert later described them, they "rode big black horses up and down the muddy company streets with huge truncheons fastened to their saddles like cavalry sabers" and they were "brought in at the slightest attempt to organize" workers.[363] To the workers, they were state-licensed thugs whom they called "Cossacks," and Musmanno would remark that over the years they "had become increasingly arrogant and brutal."[364] One of the UMW locals passed a resolution encouraging Musmanno's efforts on their behalf, stating "In many ways, the brutal deeds of Coal and Iron Police are in the same classification of injustice as that perpetrated on the workmen, Sacco and Vanzetti."[365]

Shortly after taking his seat in the legislature, Musmanno purportedly drafted legislation banning the Coal and Iron Police. At first, it would not have seemed that such a bill would have had much traction because, as Musmanno observed, the corporations that benefited from the Coal and Iron Police "wielded enormous financial-political power in the state" such that "no legislator dared to oppose" the system.[366] Prevailing fortunes changed, however, on the night of February 8, 1929, when Harold Watts, an inebriated Coal and Iron Policeman hired by the Pittsburgh Coal Company, randomly accosted a miner, John Barcoski, who was walking home alone after his shift near Imperial, Pennsylvania, a town in Musmanno's legislative district about seventeen miles west of Pittsburgh. Barcoski fled to the doorstep of his mother-in-law's home, where Watts caught up with him and pistol-whipped him. Watts then dragged Barcoski to his car and drove him to the Coal and Iron Police barracks, where Watts and the officer in charge, Lt. Walter J. Lyster, savagely beat him to death while trying to extract a "confession" from him. Watts had previously been exonerated in the shooting death of an African American miner in October 1927.

Public outcry from the death of Barcoski was intense, and Governor John S. Fisher, a Republican and a former Indiana County attorney and coal executive, declared that the "viciousness" of the attack on Barcoski "consists of the surrender by the state into private hands of police powers. These powers ought to be jealously guarded by the state and exercised only under its jurisdiction. There ought to be a thorough revision by the legislature of the present methods." The governor's call to action sounded exactly like what Musmanno would have needed to push through his bill, which is why he was surprised when the governor's Attorney General, Cyrus E. Woods—the former attorney for the Mellons—told Musmanno that his legislation had no chance of passing because it was "too drastic." The governor wanted Musmanno to propose a different bill that would keep the Coal and Iron Police system intact as the "Industrial Police," and limit their arresting power to one thousand feet beyond the boundaries of an employer's property. Fearing political reprisals, the threat of which were thinly veiled in his conversations with Woods, Musmanno would later explain that he introduced the governor's bill with the secret intention of amending it to abolish the Coal and Iron Police. With choreographed swiftness, the governor's bill was also introduced by Senator William Mansfield, a Republican of McKeesport, in the Pennsylvania Senate.[367]

Meanwhile, when news of "Musmanno's bill" hit Pittsburgh, Musmanno's name was taken in vain by those who, like Musmanno, wanted the Coal and Iron Police to be banned. The American Civil Liberties Union was particularly bitter in its statement:

> *An explanation is due from Representative Michael A. Musmanno for his change of front. When John Barcoski was murdered, Musmanno expressed abhorrence and introduced a bill calling for the abolition of the coal and iron police. Now he suddenly appears as a champion of an insipid measure, which, according to reports, continues the coal and iron police in full force and power.*[368]

In addition to Henry Ellenbogen, among the members of the Pittsburgh chapter of the ACLU was the pastor of Old St. Patrick's Church in the Strip District, Father James R. Cox. A vigorous man in his 40s who had served in a hospital on the Western front during the Great War and had an affinity for boxing (the middleweight champion, Harry Greb, was a protégé), Father Cox worked in a steel mill as a young man and studied at Duquesne University and St. Vincent College before becoming a priest. From his parish at the edge of downtown, Cox attracted parishioners through his weekly thirty-minute radio broadcasts on WJAS-AM, drawing Pittsburgh's Catholic workers in as a "labor priest," with Pope Leo XIII's 1891 encyclical *Rerum Novarum* (On the Condition of Labor) as his theological guide. As Heineman observes, "Cox realized that in a region where unions had either fallen apart or remained quiescent since the wrenching 1919 steel strike, other institutions would have to bear the responsibility for promoting workers' rights."[369] With John Brophy, a prominent member of the United Mine Workers,

Cox established a local labor school for trade union organizers and, in the late 1920s, as the evils of the Coal and Iron Police increasingly became a flashpoint for reform, Cox became vice chairman, and perhaps the most prominent and vocal member, of the executive committee of the Pittsburgh chapter of the ACLU.[370] Ellenbogen, the Jewish immigrant lawyer, and Father Cox, the Irish Catholic priest, became fast friends and comrades in the fight—"educated by Catholics" at Cox's alma mater Duquesne, as Heineman observed, Ellenbogen "moved comfortably between Hill District *shtetl* and Oakland neighborhood pub,"[371] and the two of them shared deep convictions over the plight of the ethnic downtrodden in Pittsburgh.

By March 1929, the newspapers were still calling the weakened Coal and Iron Police bill "Musmanno's Bill," but were pointing out that it had been prepared by Governor Fisher, and the outcry from labor against it was still going strong.[372] Father Cox and Ellenbogen boarded a Ryan monoplane piloted by James Rutledge at seven fifteen in the morning on March 19 to go to Harrisburg and represent the ACLU before the Judiciary General Committee. There they joined leaders of the United Mine Workers, as well as Rabbi Samuel Goldenson of Rodef Shalom and Rev. Albert Day of Christ Methodist Episcopal Church, in denouncing the governor's token response. Father Cox said he was "well pleased" with their reception by the Committee.

On the return trip later in the day, Rutledge's compass seemed to malfunction, and he lost his bearings. "The first thing I knew," Father Cox recalled, "I looked down and saw we were over the ocean." He turned to Ellenbogen and said, "I think we're lost," to which Ellenbogen replied, "I know we are." The "Flying Pastor," as the papers called him (he had maintained that he was the first priest ever to conduct mass on an airplane flight), and his companions, eventually landed on Kent Island in Chesapeake Bay. A farmer gave them thirty gallons of gasoline to refuel the plane, and the party returned to Harrisburg where, due to the lateness of the hour, Ellenbogen and Cox departed for Pittsburgh by the night train. Father Cox called the incident a "wonderful experience," no doubt basking in the extra publicity he secured for his opposition to the governor's bill.[373]

In the wake of the Committee hearing, Musmanno prepared his amendments to his own bill, which would confine the jurisdiction of the Industrial Police to company property, and provide that all arrested persons would immediately be brought before a public magistrate and if committed taken to a county jail rather than to the private police barracks, and that no private policeman would be permitted to hold a public position. On April 2, the House Committee approved Musmanno's amendments, and the amended bill was approved by the House by a vote of 184 to 0. Musmanno's bill was summarily rejected by the Senate Committee, but after protests reached a fever pitch in Pittsburgh, the Senate suddenly relented at Governor Fisher's instruction and reported Musmanno's bill. The victory for anti-Coal and Iron Police partisans was short-lived, however, as the weaker Mansfield bill was also presented to the governor. Governor Fisher vetoed the Musmanno bill and signed the Mansfield bill.[374]

Although the Coal and Iron Police remained intact with a few minor restrictions, Musmanno's constituents were pleased with his efforts. The *Pittsburgh Press* endorsed his candidacy for reelection to the Pennsylvania House, saying, "He was the author of the industrial police bill which was vetoed by Governor Fisher because it was too strong. He was indefatigable in fighting that measure through the Assembly. His potentialities should not be lost. He injects into the Assembly the spirit of discussion and debate revealing issues to the public, an almost lost art in the Assembly which has come to do too much of its legislation in secret committee session."[375] Musmanno was reelected as a Republican in 1930 with the highest vote among the four winners in his district.[376]

Meanwhile, Governor Fisher retired from public life. His immediate predecessor, Gifford Pinchot, was elected for his second non-consecutive term to succeed Fisher after a tumultuous, protracted Republican primary campaign in which the Pennsylvania Supreme Court had to weigh in on the significance of perforated primary ballots. Pinchot's election gave labor forces some reason to celebrate: unlike Fisher, Pinchot was a progressive in the mold of Theodore Roosevelt (he served as Roosevelt's founding chief of the U.S. Forestry Service), was considered to be labor friendly and supported relief for the unemployed—a class that was, during 1930-31, a growing one. Shortly after the 1930 election, Governor-elect Pinchot invited Musmanno to his home in Milford, and laid out a plan to Musmanno for fixing the Industrial Police problem, hoping to gain Musmanno's support. Pinchot's plan was to permit state police to be "hired out" by corporations for a fee, arguing, according to Musmanno, that "if the police were under state control and jurisdiction they could not be used by corporations for terroristic or strike-breaking purposes." Musmanno objected, saying that the state police would still understand that they were being paid by the corporations, albeit indirectly, and their behavior would be linked to the corporation's interests, not the state's.

Immediately upon his return to the legislature in January 1931, Musmanno presented two bills: House Bill No. 1, the "Property Guard Bill," which would specifically prohibit the state from hiring out its police to private interests, permit corporations to hire property guards but only subject to a number of rules and restrictions, and would subject the corporations to liability for the actions of the guards; and House Bill No. 2, which would repeal the Mansfield Act. Governor Pinchot, through his Attorney General, William A. Schnader, wrote a bill providing for "trade police" under the scheme he had previously described to Musmanno, and had it introduced by Thomas Wilson of McKean County. With heavy lobbying from the coal and iron industries, the Wilson Bill was speeding through committee, while Musmanno's bills were languishing. Musmanno managed to maneuver them into the House for a general vote, and after giving an impassioned speech on the House floor, the House voted in favor of the "Property Guard Bill." There was still the possibility, however, just as had happened with the Mansfield Act, that the legislature would approve the Wilson Bill, giving Governor Pinchot the option of signing one and vetoing the other.[377]

By March 1931, while Musmanno was attempting to get the House to sink the Wilson Bill, Musmanno was still stinging from the ACLU's rebuke over the introduction of Governor Fisher's bill in 1929. Writing to Ellenbogen, Musmanno snarled:

> *I always believe in speaking frankly and I write this letter to tell you that I think the Civil Liberties Union is a very erratic organization. Please do not misunderstand me. I have the greatest respect and regard for you personally, but when you function as a member of the Civil Liberties Union, you frequently use bad judgment. In the present fight for a correction of the coal and iron police evils the Civil Liberties Union has done nothing. It is even worse than that. They acted in such a way that if any serious attention were paid to their attitude, much harm might have resulted.*

Musmanno was particularly upset that the ACLU had not bothered to help in clearing up a misunderstanding over whether the labor leaders might support the Wilson Bill and, moreover, that the newspapers were reporting that the Civil Liberties Union was "equally opposed to 'the Musmanno Bill ... and the Wilson Bill.'" Musmanno signed his letter to Ellenbogen, "With regards for you personally, believe me."[378]

Ellenbogen responded that he was "very much surprised" that Musmanno would charge that the Civil Liberties Union had "done nothing," and that "in all sincerity it particularly hurts—coming from you." Ellenbogen went on to recite the ACLU's involvement in the 1929 fight against the Coal and Iron Police. In particular, Ellenbogen remarked, that he had drafted, on behalf of the ACLU, a bill banning the Coal and Iron Police that had been introduced by Musmanno in the legislature, that it had been the template for all such bills that had followed, and that the ACLU had "never publicly taken credit for our work in this connection, and particularly, have never interfered with any credit that was accorded to you in connection with the fight during 1929, for the reason that our organization is not concerned with credit, but with accomplishment. And for the further reason that you, yourself, had made a splendid fight." If Ellenbogen was referring to Musmanno's first bill on the subject, it is quite true that, even in his autobiography, Musmanno never gave any credit to Ellenbogen or the ACLU for drafting the bill. Ellenbogen returned Musmanno's personal compliments of him, though, saying that he had "the highest regard for you personally and for your efforts and sincerity" and that he hoped he would have the opportunity to persuade Musmanno that the ACLU "is one of the few stars upon a dark horizon."[379]

Neither Musmanno, nor Ellenbogen, nor the ACLU would win the day in 1931. After Musmanno succeeded in publicly ridiculing the Wilson Bill on the House floor, the Senate carved up the Property Guard Bill, turning it, as Musmanno described it, into "the very antithesis of everything for which I had been fighting since 1926." The revised bill was passed and served up to Governor Pinchot for his signature.[380] In June, Governor Pinchot revoked the commissions of the Coal and Iron Police; but instead of Coal and Iron Police, per se, Pennsylvania now had Trade Police.

It was a disappointment to Musmanno. "We were where we had begun," he wrote.[381] Later referring to the legislature as a place of "uninhibited buffoonery,"[382] Musmanno eventually resigned his seat, returned to Pittsburgh, and sought and received nominations by both the Republican and Democratic Parties as a judge of the County Court of Allegheny County in September 1931. He was easily elected to the bench, and when he took office on January 1, 1932, he was the youngest ever Allegheny County judge at age thirty-four.[383]

Meanwhile, Musmanno's friend Henry Ellenbogen would soon be experiencing a similar kind of ascent, through a different campaign.

By 1932, as the Great Depression continued to take hold of Pittsburgh by the throat, a "Hooverville" of homeless unemployed workers grew in the Strip District. Ellenbogen's friend Father Cox, moved by both his support of labor as well as by his greater sense of Christian mission to the poor, responded by establishing a soup kitchen at 14th Street and Penn Avenue at the foot of Polish Hill, serving a thousand meals a day, and by opening his church basement to hundreds of homeless families. Row after row of shacks, made from packing crates and construction scraps, grew up along the railroad, from Penn Station to the 17th Street Incline, and to the poor who took refuge there, Cox became the benevolent "Mayor of Shantytown."[384] Seeking to draw attention to the need to help the poor, and also to steal some attention from certain Communist organizations that were attempting to take advantage of economic conditions to lash out at the Catholic Church, Father Cox started to organize an event that would be a show of support to the nation's poor, an opportunity to petition the president and Congress for public works programs to get his parishioners back to work similar to one he remembered hearing about when he was young. Jacob Coxey, a successful quarry owner from Massillon, Ohio, had proposed a program of road-building to get people back to work during the Depression of 1893 and conceived of a march to "send a petition to Washington with boots on." A month after Coxey began, he entered Washington with approximately one thousand marchers, and was promptly arrested and jailed for twenty days for walking on the lawn of the Capitol Building. Although it had no effect on government policy at the time, "Coxey's March" became the most extensively reported American event between the Civil and the Spanish-American Wars, other than the disputed presidential election of 1876.[385]

Now Father Cox was going to lead his own march to Washington, and he put out the call for volunteers. David L. Lawrence, the chair of the County Democrats, called Henry Ellenbogen and asked him if he would accompany Father Cox, just in case President Hoover were to have him arrested.[386] Lawrence probably also had it in mind that it would be a good idea to have an ear in the room, if indeed something important were to develop. Ellenbogen would not join Father Cox merely as an observer, however; he was a fellow warrior, and in a very short time, he would become a central figure in his own crusade.

On January 5, 1932, Father Cox watched as a crowd of approximately twelve thousand marchers, along with approximately six hundred cars and trucks and two brass bands—from "the idled steel towns of Carnegie, McKeesport, Millvale, and beyond," according to Heineman—converged near his home church, causing a traffic jam in the vicinity of Penn and Liberty Avenues in the Strip District. With much pomp and circumstance, Father Cox led his marchers out of the city, eastward, towards Johnstown and Harrisburg. As they traveled—some by car, others on foot—they picked up more supporters along the way. In Johnstown, Father Cox and Democratic mayor Eddie McCloskey appeared together at a rally at Point Stadium, where they both denounced big business, criticized Hoover (particularly for his willingness to give relief aid to big banks but none to the poor) and proclaimed that Washington needed to help feed the unemployed. In Harrisburg, the following day, Governor Pinchot, the progressive Republican, welcomed Father Cox and his followers with open arms after seeing how many voters were showing up on his doorstep, inviting the crowds to dine in the legislature's private dining room at his expense. Appearing with Cox and McCloskey, Governor Pinchot took the opportunity to tell the crowd that the Philadelphia Republican machine was interfering with his legislative program to provide help to the unemployed. Afterwards, Cox and his followers continued their journey, reaching Gettysburg as night fell, marching in the rain and the dark until, as they reached Wisconsin Avenue in Washington, the sun began to rise.[387]

President Hoover initially made it clear to his aides that he had no intention of meeting with Father Cox, but as he gained intelligence about the size and character of the crowd, he began to find it hard to say no. His aides informed him that the crowd was between fifteen and twenty thousand strong, probably the largest protest march Washington had ever seen; and that approximately twenty percent of Cox's followers had fought in the Great War, and many of them had come to Washington in uniform. They were Catholics, mainly, waving flags and singing patriotic songs—a difficult group to brand as radicals or Communists. President Hoover broke down and decided to meet with a small group from Cox's "Jobless Army," welcoming Father Cox, along with Henry Ellenbogen, Mayor Eddie McCloskey, the Republican U.S. senator from Pennsylvania James J. Davis (a former Pittsburgh steel worker), some labor and small business representatives, and some fellow dressed as Uncle Sam. While Ellenbogen recalled that President Hoover had called Father Cox's petition "inappropriate," the president nonetheless told his guests that he had "intense sympathy for their difficulties" and that he was engaged in "the final campaign against the depression." Returning to Pittsburgh the next day—with aid for train fares and gasoline coming from Andrew Mellon, Hoover's own disaffected Secretary of the Treasury, much to the chagrin of the Republican National Committee—Father Cox was greeted with a hero's welcome as the crowd marched into the city along the Boulevard of the Allies.[388]

A few days after the march ended, Henry Ellenbogen announced to the newspapers that there would be a rally at Pitt Stadium on Saturday, January 16, to back up Father Cox's demand for five billion dollars in public works projects and relief to the unemployed, to be paid for with "higher taxation of large incomes and inheritances."[389] The *Jewish Criterion* proudly intimated that Ellenbogen was the "brains" behind Father Cox's crusade.[390] At the rally, attended by an estimated crowd of 55,000 despite the cold and damp weather, Father Cox told the crowd that "Ours is a battle against Wall Street and Smithfield Street"—the latter, perhaps, being a reference to Mellon Bank, despite Andrew Mellon's generosity—and that "our movement will grow and expand throughout the nation."[391] Father Cox also told reporters at the rally that he was "going to run for President."[392] Plans were laid for a "Jobless/Liberty Party" convention in St. Louis, Missouri in August, billed as a meeting of Father Cox's "Jobless" supporters and the "Liberty Party" of William "Coin" Harvey, an eighty year-old populist from Arkansas who was organizing anti-Hoover unrest in the Southwest.

Meanwhile, in several days after the rally, Ellenbogen announced his candidacy for the 33rd District seat in the United States Congress, representing Pittsburgh, running against former assistant district attorney Harry Estep[393]—a "tall, suave, astute" Republican prosecutor, a member of the Duquesne Club, a Freemason and a Methodist.[394] Estep's 35th District seat was being eliminated through redistricting; the 33rd District incumbent, Republican Clyde Kelly, moved to accommodate Estep by seeking election to the 31st District seat. Ellenbogen stated as his platform that he was "anti-utilities, for the independent merchants" and "in favor of legislation guaranteeing bank deposits and unemployment relief."[395]

The joint "Jobless/Liberty" convention in St. Louis blew apart before it began. While Father Cox and Coin Harvey found they agreed almost completely on a platform, neither man would step aside to allow the other to be the standard bearer, and Liberty Party supporters from the South were skeptical of supporting a Roman Catholic priest. The Jobless Party held its convention as planned at Creve Coeur Park in St. Louis, and Henry Ellenbogen delivered a keynote address just before Father Cox received the Party's presidential nomination.[396] His travels with Father Cox during the spring and summer of 1932—giving speeches from the platform—kept Ellenbogen's name in the newspapers, and maintained his credentials as a critic of President Hoover. Back in Pittsburgh, in a much emulated technique, Ellenbogen had his friends sponsor "house parties" where he could address groups of neighbors, forty to fifty at a time.[397]

David Lawrence had another job for Ellenbogen during the campaign: try to convince Father Cox to end his quixotic quest for the presidency and endorse the Democratic nominee. In July, the Democrats nominated New York governor Franklin D. Roosevelt to face Hoover in the election in November. For the 1932 Democratic nomination, James M. Costin, the editor of the influential *Pittsburgh Catholic,* had supported Al Smith. Smith, who was Roosevelt's predecessor as governor of New York, was the 1928 nominee, but as a Roman Catholic his previous candidacy had fallen victim to an anti-Catholic smear campaign. Roosevelt, on the other hand, was seen by the *Pittsburgh Catholic* as a white-shoe patrician who had usurped Smith's position at the head of the Party. Lawrence hoped that Father Cox's endorsement would neutralize the impact of the *Pittsburgh Catholic* on a key constituency within the coalition that Lawrence was trying to build in Pittsburgh. After a hectic schedule of speeches throughout the summer, Ellenbogen appealed to Cox to consider Roosevelt's candidacy, showing him the text of a speech that Roosevelt had delivered in Detroit on October 2, in which Roosevelt quoted Pope Pius XI's 1931 encyclical *Quadragesimo Anno* (Reconstructing the Social Order), a further call to action on Pope Leo XIII's 1891 encyclical, *On the Condition of Labor.* In response, Father Cox ended his candidacy on October 12, stating that "Mr. Roosevelt has pledged himself to the protection of the interests of the common man ... He has endorsed the principle of large public construction by the federal government in times of depression." Roosevelt came to Pittsburgh on October 19 to speak at a rally of thirty thousand supporters at Forbes Field, with Cox at his side. The tally was impressive, considering that as recently as in the 1930 election, there were only a mere five thousand registered Democrats in the city.[398]

A couple of months before Roosevelt's triumphant Pittsburgh rally, sixty-five year-old James Francis Burke, President Hoover's friend and advisor, was keeping a full schedule working on behalf of the Republican Party. On August 8, 1932, Burke was finishing the second of two meetings with President Hoover in the White House when the president noticed that Burke did not appear to be well. He convinced Burke to allow himself to be examined by the White House physician, Lieutenant Commander Joel T. Boone, U.S.N., who ordered him to go directly to Garfield Memorial Hospital. With Dr. Boone at his side, Burke died that evening of a blood clot in the heart.[399] Said President Hoover the next day, "He labored for the country he loved up to the hour of his death."[400]

The death of the Pittsburgh lawyer—perhaps one of the nation's most fervent Republican boosters for fifty years, occurring after a day of two White House consultations with a beleaguered Republican president—was a most unfortunate omen, or at worst a metaphor, for what was to follow during the election of 1932. Burke's friend Herbert Hoover lost in a landslide to Governor Roosevelt—fifty-seven percent to thirty-nine percent on the popular vote, 472 electoral votes to fifty-nine. Pennsylvania supported President Hoover, but through the hard work of Lawrence, Cox and Ellenbogen among others, Roosevelt carried Allegheny County by thirty-seven thousand votes.[401] Even Musmanno supported Roosevelt.[402] Trouble for the Republican Party was also brewing at City Hall: after almost a quarter century of uninterrupted Republican hegemony, at the time of Roosevelt's victory, Mayor Charles H. Kline was holding on to his office by a thin thread after being convicted on corruption charges. It appeared that Pittsburgh would be experiencing an upheaval of party politics at all levels.

Henry Ellenbogen also benefited personally from the upheaval. In the November election, Ellenbogen, who was endorsed by both the Independent Republicans and the Democrats, defeated the Republican Harry Estep, 34,886 votes to 28,982.[403] Estep challenged the results, however, arguing that Ellenbogen had not been a citizen for seven years at the date of the election, as required by Article I, Section 2 of the Constitution. "I had just missed out by a few months the required seven years of citizenship before my election in November," Ellenbogen later recalled. "I thought I would find that many early Americans became active in political life and were elected to political office before they had been citizens seven years. But I didn't find a single instance of this."[404] In response, Ellenbogen did not present himself for his swearing in until January 1934, almost a year after the opening of the session, once Ellenbogen had been a citizen for almost 7-1/2 years. In the meantime, Speaker of the House Henry T. Rainey did make sure that Ellenbogen was provided with an office on Capitol Hill and a staff, the only hitch being that he could not vote until he was sworn in. On June 16, 1934, the House put any remaining controversy to rest by passing a resolution stating that, like the age requirement, the constitutional citizenship requirement need not be applied until the candidate offered himself to be seated.[405]

It helped Ellenbogen's cause that the Democrats earned a 196-member majority in the House of Representatives in the 1932 election. Ellenbogen immersed himself in the planks of Franklin Roosevelt's New Deal, and visited the president about three times a month to discuss the legislative agenda.[406] He eventually proposed one of the first federal old-age pension measures of the New Deal; and when, after Roosevelt's Committee on Economic Security submitted its recommendation for a Social Security bill, Ellenbogen became a key supporter, even though he thought the Committee's bill fell short in many ways. "I am not satisfied with the provisions of the Social Security

Act," he said in a speech on the House floor, "But the principle which this act of Congress establishes, the decent, human, and social philosophy upon which it is based, is far more important than its specific provisions. We now have the foundation; we can improve and enlarge from time to time the building which we construct upon that foundation ... Ahead of us lies a great ideal."[407] His unemployment compensation bill for the District of Columbia became a model for state unemployment compensation systems,[408] and he was one of two House sponsors for the legislation that created the thirty-year mortgage.[409] Probably his other most important legislative achievement was the bill that was known as the Wagner-Ellenbogen Bill, later known as the Wagner-Steagall Act. Ellenbogen worked closely with Senator Robert Wagner on the bill creating a U.S. Housing Authority that would assist local public housing agencies with federal financing in the clearing of slums and the construction of low-cost housing—in contrast to the approach that some of Roosevelt's advisors favored, which would have given the federal government strict control over local public housing development.[410] He also followed his friend Father Cox onto the airwaves, giving Pittsburghers a weekly radio update of Washington legislative activities on WJAS-AM.

Michael Musmanno, meanwhile, was still sitting as a County Court judge, engaged in a decidedly less lofty, more mainstream, consensus-oriented and parochial campaign against drunk driving in Pittsburgh; but that did not mean that he was finished with his fight for the abolition of the Coal and Iron Police. He decided to write a fictionalized short story about the Barcoski murder, taking as his protagonist the character of Jan Volkanik, a legendary Polish immigrant coal mining hero similar to Pittsburgh's legendary Croatian immigrant super-hero steel worker, Joe Magarac. The two characters, Volkanik and Magarac, had already been memorialized together in a 1915 sculpture by Charles Keck on the North portal to the late Manchester Bridge, which once connected the Point to Pittsburgh's North Side. Musmanno's story focused on Volkanik as a 1920s union leader, and on the brutal killing of one of Volkanik's friends, Mike Shemanski, by the Coal and Iron Police. Although he never published the short story, Musmanno thought he had found an avenue for getting it to the public in March 1933. Reading the column of Kaspar Monahan, the drama editor of the *Pittsburgh Press*, he discovered that the lauded actor Paul Muni (Oscar-nominated star of *Scarface* and *I Was a Fugitive From a Chain Gang*), was appearing at Pittsburgh's Nixon Theatre in a traveling production of Elmer Rice's *Counsellor at Law,* a story about a Jewish lawyer who makes it to the top of his profession, but is abandoned by his wife. Muni had apparently told Monahan that he wanted to return to the screen, but he wanted a strong dramatic role. "I would like to play a Pennsylvania coal miner," he reportedly said, "but I've been searching for a year or more and haven't found the right story."

Musmanno rang Monahan's phone off the hook, excitedly telling him that he had a story that would be perfect for Muni, and asking if he had a way to get it to him. Muni took Musmanno's story and read it on the train to Cincinnati, "liked it, saw in it the role he wanted—and Warner Bros. agreed to produce it." But Muni and the producers thought Musmanno's story was a little thin on its own, so they also bought the rights to an unproduced play by Harry R. Irving entitled *Bohunk*, and engaged a couple of studio writers to complete a screenplay using both sources. Musmanno, meanwhile, was impressed with Muni's preparation for the role; together, Muni and Musmanno "visited coal mines, went down into the shafts, talked to the miners—the actor busy all the time, listening to the Polish dialect, noting the actions and gestures of these husky toilers in the underground gloom," as Monahan writes.[411] While awaiting the debut of his screen credit, Musmanno secured both the Republican and Democratic nominations to a seat on the County Court of Common Pleas for the November 1933 election, easily defeating his challengers.[412]

In 1934, Ellenbogen easily sailed to reelection in Congress, also as the nominee of both the Republican and the Democratic Parties, with 98.7% of the vote.[413] There was enough tumult within Pennsylvania politics, especially with a new coalition of Democratic constituencies emerging from Roosevelt's 1932 landslide—immigrant, Catholic, Jew, African American—that Senator David Aiken Reed now began to see the handwriting on the wall during his reelection campaign in 1934. Senator Reed had been an author and co-sponsor of the Immigration Act of 1924 (also known as the Johnson-Reed Act), a reaction in part to the radical activities of recent immigrants during the 1919 Steel Strike and to the softness of the American economy after the Great War. The Johnson-Reed Act established severe quotas on the entry of Catholic and Jewish immigrants from Southern and Eastern Europe, such that the immigration of such persons declined from 912,000 in 1914 to 21,000 each year after 1924. As Philip Jenkins writes, Reed belonged to the "diehard conservative wing of the party, which regarded even Herbert Hoover as perilously liberal." Challenged from the left by Governor Gifford Pinchot for the Republican nomination, Reed held on, and although he won Philadelphia in November, David Lawrence's variegated coalition of outsiders delivered Allegheny County, and the election, to Reed's Democratic challenger, "his Shadyside neighbor" Joseph Guffey.[414] After the election, Reed returned to Reed Smith and the practice of law, but it would not be accurate to say that, after 1934, he was a leader of the bar. Rather, he assumed the role of ex-politician within the state and national party out of power, and was best known for his affiliations with the "anti-New Deal" American Liberty League and, until World War II, the America First Committee, which sought to keep the U.S. out of the War.[415]

Black Fury, starring Paul Muni and directed by Michael Curtiz (later known for *The Adventures of Robin Hood* with Errol Flynn, and *Casablanca*, with Humphrey Bogart and Ingrid Bergman), premiered on May 18, 1935, with an original story by "Judge M.A. Musmanno."[416] The final product, while critically acclaimed, was very different from Musmanno's story—especially the ending. The main character of Musmanno's story, now known as "Joe Radek," barricades himself in a mine with dynamite after capturing the Coal and Iron policeman who killed his friend, and threatens to blow up the mine unless the owners recognize the union. In Musmanno's story, the hero is prosecuted and sent to prison when he emerges from the mine. In the Hollywood version, the strike is solved with government intervention, and Radek is hailed as a hero when he emerges from the mine, embraced by his girlfriend while the Coal and Iron policeman is led away in handcuffs. As historian Colin Shindler writes, "It might be reasonably supposed that Musmanno would have divorced himself entirely from the finished film since it was so far removed from his original aims." On the contrary, Shindler observes, "he positively embraced it, traveling with it as it was shown throughout Pennsylvania" in order to advocate for a ban of the Trade Police.[417] This time, in no time at all, Musmanno achieved his long-cherished goal. Governor Pinchot's successor, Democrat George Earle, stroked to an easy victory in the 1934 election over William Schnader, Pinchot's former attorney general and the founder of the Philadelphia law firm of Schnader, Harrison, Segal & Lewis. Less than a month after the release of *Black Fury*, Governor Earle signed legislation abolishing the Trade Police.[418]

This time, Musmanno had not failed. This time, he was not disappointed; and he had exercised his influence from the bench, not from a legislature of "uninhibited buffoonery," instead using his unparalleled ability to drum up attention.

Although Ellenbogen's legislative experience in Washington had been more profoundly successful than Musmanno's in Harrisburg, Ellenbogen, urged on by his family, looked longingly at a return to Pittsburgh. His wife was not particularly happy about being in Washington. "Congressmen's wives were such hicks!," Rae Ellenbogen recalled. "There was anti-Semitism in Washington, too. The New Deal was called the 'Jew Deal.'"[419] After winning his third term in Congress, Ellenbogen began to discuss the possibility of running for a seat on the Court of Common Pleas with his old mentor, David L. Lawrence. Winning in a Congressional district was one thing, Lawrence advised. "You can't win this County, because you're Jewish," he purportedly told Ellenbogen. According to Rae, Ellenbogen replied, "That's a very bad feeling to have, and if you feel that way—I must run."[420] In the 1937 election, Ellenbogen led the County ticket, and joined Judge Musmanno, his "frenemy," on the Allegheny County Court of Common Pleas on January 3, 1938.[421]

In 1926, it would have been inconceivable that either Henry Ellenbogen or Michael Musmanno—let alone both of them—would have found himself on the Common Pleas Court, standing shoulder to shoulder as two of the most influential members of the Allegheny County bar. One of the most far-reaching effects of the Great Depression on the bar of Pittsburgh is that—through the Depression itself and the shifting political climate that resulted from the collapse of the Republican Party in Pittsburgh—Ellenbogen and Musmanno were two among many protagonists in what became the re-definition of the elite bar in Pittsburgh during the twentieth century. It was both a generational re-definition, as the era of James Francis Burke and David Aiken Reed receded, and an ethnic re-definition, as Italians and immigrant Jews, among others, were able to take their places in the seats that shaped the legal profession, alongside the inheritors of the legacies of Knox & Reed, Gordon & Smith, and Patterson & Crawford.

It did not happen all at once—both of these men would continue to experience their difficulties within the bar. In 1937, Musmanno's fellow Common Pleas judges— almost all of whom were white, Anglo-Saxon Protestants—were particularly miffed by Musmanno's grandstanding in holding New Year's Eve drunk driving proceedings, and removed him as presiding judge of the criminal court,[422] although he continued to serve on the Common Pleas Court and went on to greater renown in the 1940s and 1950s. The fact that the rise of these two judges began during a time of economic struggle and upheaval, however, says something also about their personal characteristics. While some young lawyers undoubtedly stood helplessly under the Crash of '29 and watched it tumble down upon them, Ellenbogen and Musmanno adopted aggressive stances from which their activism sprang. They could have found easier ways to put food on the table, but they chose instead to conduct rehearsals for the leadership stations they eventually created for themselves—fighting, failing, marching, declaiming on behalf of their ethnic neighbors, the forgotten men and women of Pittsburgh's Great Depression. What they ultimately became depended upon where they stood, and what they stood for.

'THE PLAINEST FACTS OF OUR NATIONAL LIFE'

In the summer of 1934, a series of extraordinary meetings were convened in New York City by John J. Raskob, the former head of finance at General Motors and DuPont and until recently the chairman of the Democratic National Committee, and Jouett Shouse, a former Assistant Secretary of the Treasury and former chairman of the executive committee of the Democratic Party. Some of the meetings were held in the Broad Street offices of John W. Davis—the former Clarksburg, West Virginia lawyer who had risen to fame as a Wall Street appellate lawyer, head of the firm that would become Davis Polk Wardwell Gardiner & Reed, and who had run for president as the nominee of the Democrats in 1924; some were held in the Empire State Building office of Al Smith, the former governor of New York and 1928 Democratic presidential candidate; others in the offices of General Motors near Columbus Circle, or in one or another private dining club around Manhattan. The meetings, as advertised by Raskob and Shouse, were held to discuss the rampant abuses of the New Deal.

The other attendees of these meetings included some of the elite figures of American business and government: Raskob's former bosses, the DuPont brothers, Irenee, Lammot and Pierre; Alfred P. Sloan, Jr., the president of General Motors; former Senator James W. Wadsworth, Jr., now in the House representing Western New York's 39th Congressional District; Michael Benedum, the Pittsburgh-based oil wildcatter and owner of Transcontinental Oil; and Ernest T. Weir, the founder and president of Weirton Steel. Often accompanying Weir was his counsel, a Pittsburgh lawyer named Earl Reed.[423]

Reed, despite the surname, was not related to the late Judge Reed, the millionaire founder of Reed Smith. He was born in Spartansburg, Pennsylvania, a Crawford County farming community with a population of about five hundred, and moved with his family to McDonald, another small town, about eighteen miles southwest of Pittsburgh.

His father was a pumper in the oil fields. Working at odd jobs from the age of eight, Reed put himself through Washington & Jefferson College. Said to be a "math shark" from a young age, Reed taught mathematics in the School of Applied Industries at the Carnegie Institute of Technology while attending Pitt Law School, scraping by only because a friend was willing to loan him tuition money when he was on the verge of dropping out. The War interrupted his studies, but as a private in the U.S. Army, he was assigned to be an Army contract liaison for work being conducted at the Carnegie Institute. He entered the bar in 1918 after only two years of law school, without any apparent advantages, and began the practice of law with the firm of Boyer and Morton. In 1922, he joined Thorp, Bostwick & Stewart, and he became a partner of the firm after only eighteen months.[424]

Hart Hillman, a Pittsburgh tycoon about whom it was said, "Anything that the Mellons don't own, the Hillmans do,"[425] used to send Reed "to all stockholder's meetings where a contest was likely, because of his ability to think fast and swiftly calculate voting odds with pre-computer mathematical ability," Reed's daughter, Virginia Gaffney, recalled. "This mathematical strength was an unusual combination with extraordinary verbal ability: he had a clarity and power of written and spoken language." In addition, "Earl Reed was fearless, gutsy, unawed by anyone" if he felt he was right, according to Gaffney.[426] He had proven himself to his partners and clients as being tough as nails and fast on his feet, but in 1931 he would garner headlines in connection with the corruption trial of Mayor Charles Kline of Pittsburgh.

Charles H. Kline, a dapper-dressing lawyer who had entered the bar in 1899, had served as a Court of Common Pleas judge from 1919 to 1926, the beginning of the Prohibition Era. He was elected mayor of Pittsburgh in 1926 as the Republican candidate, besting his primary opponent William L. Smith, principal of Allegheny High School, and Democrat Carman C. Johnston, by a landslide after the Mellon family had dissuaded the incumbent, William Magee, from seeking another term in office. In exchange for his agreement to step down and support Kline, Magee exacted an agreement that required Kline to retain Magee's twenty-five most important political appointees in office. This left Mayor Kline at somewhat of a disadvantage when he decided to consolidate his power and make a run for another term without either the support or the interference of the Mellons.[427] As Benjamin L. Hayllar, Jr., writes, to take over the Pittsburgh Republican Party,

> [Kline] would have to build his own political organization within three years. However, twenty five of the city's most important patronage jobs had already been given to Magee people. Therefore, Kline had to build his political machine out of the most sordid materials. First, he made alliances with corrupt ward and district politicians. Second, he replaced the regular organization workers and the Mellon's financial contributions with those of the rackets and vice industry. Under his administration, the city police, an already tainted bunch, became increasingly corrupt as they became the force that regulated the rackets empire.[428]

Among the rackets from which Mayor Kline would ultimately benefit was the bootlegged liquor racket. Ironically enough, although Mayor Kline was as vocal a critic of Prohibition as there was, it was Prohibition that gave him the opportunity to use his control over contraband as a source of funds for his political machine. As Hayllar observes, the "absence of known independent racket leaders" during the period "can be explained by the suggestion that control over Pittsburgh vice was not achieved by members of the rackets community," but by Mayor Charles Kline himself.[429]

The corrupt mayor managed to avoid prosecution when, in July 1928, Captain John D. Pennington, the local head of Prohibition enforcement, and U.S. Attorney John D. Meyer, secured 167 indictments against politicians, policemen of all ranks and common racketeers who were apparently working in concert to control the supply and sale of banned liquor within the Pittsburgh area. Because of the accusations against local Republican officials, it was said that Captain Pennington was pressured to wait until after Herbert Hoover's election as president in November 1928 before trying the defendants, in order to minimize the negative impact on Republican voter turnout.[430] Although the trials were mostly a failure (the broad conspiracy charges against the entire group were thrown out, but Meyer did manage to garner convictions in a few individual cases), the evidence showed that bootleg liquor sold through the "rum ring" was priced at three dollars a gallon, even though it only cost thirty-seven cents to make.[431] The Kline machine certainly seemed to be doing well from the rum trade.

In 1929, Mayor Kline won re-election (the first Pittsburgh mayor to serve a second consecutive term under charter provisions adopted during the Magee administration), but only secured the Republican nomination by a plurality of votes during the primary, against Council President James F. Malone, Sr., and Judge Richard W. Martin. His popularity had been weakened by the drumbeat of newspaper stories about official corruption.[432] The beginning of the end for Kline was not an indictment for his involvement in liquor, gambling or prostitution; rather, it came from his handling of an investigation into bidding procedures for the city's grocery contracts for city properties such Mayview Hospital[d]. After irregularities in the bids hit the newspapers, Mayor Kline conducted a superficial investigation and fired his director of the department of supplies, Colonel Bertram L. Succop.[433]

Although Colonel Succop refused to pin blame elsewhere, the newspapers raised an uproar, forcing Allegheny County District Attorney Andrew Park to conduct a full investigation of his own. A citizens' committee raised some money to assist Park, and the committee engaged Earl Reed as its counsel. Reed was a Republican, like Kline, but he took the case, because in his view, "the city was corrupt and everybody knew that." As Reed recalled, as the investigation got underway it very quickly became apparent that "the mayor and the director of supplies were both violating the law, in that they were buying things, automobiles, rugs and other things, without following the law respecting the taking of bids."[434] On June 25, 1931, Kline and Succop were indicted on forty-five counts of making illegal purchases for the city, including one count involving the purchase of an oriental rug for the mayor's office for $1,350.[435]

---

[d] Mayview, formerly known as the Pittsburgh City Home and Hospital at Mayview, was taken over by the Commonwealth of Pennsylvania in 1941 and renamed Mayview State Hospital.

Park was set to prosecute the mayor, but under public pressure Park surrendered to the hiring of Reed as a "special Assistant District Attorney." The defendants succeeded in getting the cases moved to Butler County due to the publicity in Pittsburgh. Meanwhile, as Reed prepared his case, a great deal of "pressure was exerted on me to try to eliminate me as a prosecutor," Reed remembered. "I was getting anonymous telephone calls from thugs in the city, threatening me with various things if I went ahead with the prosecution of the mayor and director. It was so burdensome and intolerable that finally the Citizens Committee provided me and my family with a guard."[436] This was, of course, familiar territory for the senior member of Reed's firm, Charles M. Thorp, who endured the backlash against his former partner, Leo Weil, during the city council investigations of 1908.

Despite the threats, Reed and Park took the cases to trial (after fighting through an attempt at jury fixing), with Reed methodically marching through the testimony of numerous witnesses and presentation of a maze of evidence. Kline was represented by Edward G. Coll and Charles B. Prichard, the former public safety director.[437] On May 14, 1932, Kline and Succop were found guilty of misconduct in office (Kline on one count, Succop on 29)[438], but Kline stayed in office for almost a year more while his appeals worked their way through the courts. Kline was eventually sentenced to serve six months in prison and pay five thousand dollars in fines, but he pleaded poor health and was spared the prison sentence after he resigned on March 31, 1933. He died less than four months later.[439]

Reed's refusal to back down to pressure and his meticulous, forceful presentation of the case against Kline earned him a following; the *Pittsburgh Press* singled him out by name in its editorial on the Kline verdict, saying that the chief counsel of the Citizens' Committee, Earl F. Reed, deserved "the gratitude of the people of Pittsburgh."[440]

Meanwhile, Ernest T. Weir, the founder of Weirton Steel, had taken Earl Reed on as his Duquesne Club lunch partner and close advisor as Weirton Steel began to find itself in difficulties with the Roosevelt administration.[441] Weir had a long history with Charles M. Thorp. Thorp was one of Weir's original investors when, in 1905, Weir and his partner James Phillips acquired the tin plate company that was the cradle of what would eventually become National Steel Corporation, the holding company for Weirton Steel.[442] Thorp would continue to serve as a director on the boards of Weir's companies for many years.[443] Now National Steel's headquarters shared the twenty-eighth floor of the Grant Building with its primary law firm, Thorp, Bostwick, Stewart & Reed.[444]

Like some of the people attending Raskob and Shouse's New York meetings, Weir had initially been supportive of the New Deal. A lifelong Republican, Weir nonetheless believed that by Roosevelt's "conservative use of federal powers," as John D. Ubinger wrote, the president could help lead the country out of the Depression, and Weir was at the outset an active participant in White House meetings on policy. Weir's views quickly changed, however, with the passage of the National Industrial Recovery Act (NIRA) in June 1933, which had been led by Senator Robert Wagner from New York. [445] The NIRA was an ambitious, far-reaching piece of legislation aimed at a number of the ills of the Great Depression all at once, including the creation of a Public Works Administration to push forward public construction projects such as dams, roads and bridges. Section 7(a) of the Act, however, cut into the heart of the management-labor relationship by guaranteeing the right of workers to organize unions, and banning the "yellow dog" contract, whereby an employee would be forced to agree not to belong to a union in exchange for employment. Under the authority of the National Recovery Administration, also created by the NIRA, a National Labor Board was established in August 1933 to handle labor disputes under Section 7(a).[446]

Weir had always been extremely anti-union,[447] and had designed Weirton Steel in particular to minimize the risk of unionization. First, he chose rural northern West Virginia, in the village of Holliday's Cove, about thirty-six miles west of Pittsburgh, as the site for his new sheet and tin mill in 1908 on the basis that cities were "if not breeders... certainly magnifiers of discontent among workers," according to Ubinger, because of the segregation of workers' homes in lower-income city districts. Although not a company town, "Weirton," as the town was eventually re-named, was certainly a company-dominated small town, in which the children of the workers and managers attended the same schools and everyone participated in the same community activities. Secondly, Weir generally paid higher wages to his workers than the other steel companies were accustomed to paying, placating his workers with wages just high enough to avoid protracted wage bargaining.[448]

After at least fifteen years without any labor organization or strikes at Weirton Steel, Weir attempted to preempt enforcement of the NIRA by establishing a captive "company" union, the Employee Security League, and imposing it upon the workers at his mills.[449] In response to Weir's attempt to keep independent unions out, and certainly as a way of testing the authority of the NIRA and the National Labor Board, the AAISW (now known as the Amalgamated Association of Iron, Steel and Tin Workers, or AAISTW), managed to convince ten thousand workers from Weirton Steel's Weirton, Clarksburg and Steubenville, Ohio mills, to walk out, calling a strike on September 26, 1933, and demanding that the AAISTW be recognized. In the disturbances that followed, the West Virginia state police shot tear gas into a striking crowd of three to four thousand people to open an entrance into the mill, and "rioting strikers" in Steubenville were also dispersed with tear gas. While Weir insisted that the strike was really the product of "a few racketeers," after two weeks he acceded to the pressure, at least initially, by signing a standard settlement with the Board, providing that the strike would be ended, that all strikers would be re-employed without prejudice, and that a union election would be held in December under the supervision of the National Labor Board to determine which union would win the right to organize Weirton Steel.[450]

After the workers returned, Weir and Reed began to negotiate with the National Labor Board over the content of the so-called "fair" union elections. On December 11, representatives of the Board arrived in West Virginia to supervise the election, but Weir took the opportunity to repudiate the settlement, declaring that "the election will proceed in accordance with the rules adopted by" the company union. The Board accused Weir of bad faith and threatened him with prosecution, to which Weir replied, "That's fine with me. I have complete confidence in the courts. If I am wrong, I'll go to jail."[451] At the election four days later, a slate of company union representatives was elected. The Board claimed that workers were coerced into approving the company union. In February 1934, the Board sent a representative, Milton Handler, to speak with Weir and Reed, asking if Weirton Steel would relent and consider holding another election under the Board's supervision. According to historian Irving Bernstein:

> *Reed told Handler that NLB agents would not be permitted on company property, could not have payrolls to check against petitions, could not set up polling places or ballot boxes, could not post notices, and could not conduct an election. 'May I learn,' Handler asked, 'whether the company will cooperate in any form, shape or manner?' 'We will not cooperate,' Reed replied.*[452]

With Weirton Steel now in open defiance of federal law, the Board filed suit against Weirton Steel in the federal District Court in Delaware to enforce the settlement. In the interim, Reed had been appointed as a special prosecutor in some federal voting fraud prosecutions in Pittsburgh, but in light of the Weirton case, he tendered his resignation to Attorney General Homer Cummings.[453] On May 29, 1934, after argument by Earl Reed, with local counsel from the Wilmington firm of Richards, Layton & Finger, Judge John Nields refused to grant a preliminary injunction to the Board on the grounds that both sides had raised the question of the constitutionality of NIRA in their arguments, and that was a legal question that needed to be resolved in a final, rather than a preliminary hearing.[454] In June 1934, before the final hearing, President Roosevelt issued an executive order abolishing the ineffective NLB and replacing it with a "national labor relations board,"[455] a board that would presage the board that would be created by the Wagner Act a year later.

A similar sequence of events was unfolding at the Aliquippa plant of Jones & Laughlin Steel, about twenty-five miles down the Ohio River from Pittsburgh. Shortly after the enactment of NIRA, Jones & Laughlin established its own company union, much like Weirton Steel's Employee Security League, in order to head off union organization efforts. When the AAISTW began its organization drive in Aliquippa in August 1934 as predicted, the Aliquippa Borough police department engaged in a variety of crackdown activities—raiding the home of one organizer, putting him and others under surveillance, and refusing to protect union organizers from getting beaten by company thugs.[456]

One case that garnered considerable attention was that of George Issoski, a former employee of the mill who had suffered a back injury in 1916 when a platform on which he was standing collapsed and dropped him twenty-five feet into a steel pit. Unable to win his workers compensation claims against Jones & Laughlin, the company nonetheless assigned him to light duty until he was laid off in 1931.[457] The AAISTW approached Issoski in the summer of 1934 and asked him if he would help register his former co-workers in the union. At first, he was merely harassed by some Jones & Laughlin company police; but then, on the night of September 11, 1934, after a friend of his bought him a couple of drinks, he was arrested by a borough policeman, who questioned him about his registration activities and punched him a few times before taking him to the local jail, where he was beaten again. The next day he was moved to the Beaver County jail, where his wife came to visit him. The authorities refused to let her see him, telling Mrs. Issoski that George was "very crazy." After a trumped up sanity hearing, on September 19, Issoski was transported to Torrance State Hospital for the Insane, located about sixty-five miles east of Aliquippa in Westmoreland County; and for a few weeks, his family had no idea where he had gone. A state labor mediator, Clint Golden, finally found Issoski at the Torrance Hospital and managed to see him, concluding "Issoski is as sane as I am."[458]

Golden informed the state secretary of labor, Charlotte Carr, as well as Cornelia Bryce Pinchot, the wife of the governor. The union was prepared to press the temporary national labor relations board to take action against Jones & Laughlin for intimidation against union organizers under Section 7(a) of NIRA, but the October meeting of the board was postponed at the last hour. On October 4, Governor Pinchot ordered state troops into Aliquippa to protect the organizers; Mrs. Pinchot visited Aliquippa on October 14 and spoke encouragingly to the town's first-ever labor rally, with four thousand in attendance; and on October 24, after a state psychiatrist interviewed Issoski and confirmed Golden's conclusions, Governor Pinchot ordered Issoski's release. The union received no satisfaction from the board, but state troops did permit union organizers to continue their activities.[459]

In both the Weirton Steel and Jones & Laughlin situations, local authorities, presumably acting under their municipal charters, were essentially carrying out the work of the companies that dominated their towns. One of Henry Ellenbogen's arguments to Michael Musmanno, during their spat in March 1931, was that no measure abolishing the Coal and Iron Police would ultimately ensure that workers would secure their rights to "free speech, free assemblage, to be secure in their life, liberty and homes, and with their right to organize and strike" because the corporate bosses "would resort to the appointment of thugs and gangsters as deputy sheriffs, as they have done in the past."[460] The pattern was repeating itself, disturbingly, in the wake of the NIRA.

Earl Reed, meanwhile, argued his case again before the federal District Court in Delaware at the final hearing on the government's proposed Weirton Steel injunction, in a trial that lasted several weeks and involved thousands of pages of testimony. On February 27, 1935, Judge Nields affirmed his earlier decision on the preliminary injunction motion, this time on the merits, declaring that the NIRA was unconstitutional as applied to Weirton Steel because "the commerce clause cannot be construed so as to bring within the regulatory power of the federal government the manufacture of goods intended for shipment in interstate commerce and *a fortiori* the entire economic life of the nation."[461]

The government appealed the *Weirton* decision to the U.S. Supreme Court, but in May, the U.S. Supreme Court ruled that NIRA was unconstitutional in another case, *Schechter Poultry Corp. v. United States*. In *Schechter*, Chief Justice Charles Evans Hughes wrote on behalf of a unanimous court that NIRA contained several fatal flaws. The most serious flaw, however, was its attempt under Section 3 of NIRA to impose uniform national "live poultry" standards and workplace regulations, including fixing the hours and wages of poultry workers, on a poultry slaughterhouse that occasionally obtained live poultry from other states but did not sell poultry into interstate commerce. Chief Justice Hughes called it an invalid attempt to regulate interstate commerce as permitted by the Constitution:

> *It is not the province of the Court to consider the economic advantages or disadvantages of such a centralized system. It is sufficient to say that the Federal Constitution does not provide for it. ... [T]he authority of the federal government may not be pushed to such an extreme as to destroy the distinction, which the commerce clause itself establishes, between commerce 'among the several States' and the internal concerns of a state.*[462]

In effect, the U.S. Supreme Court unanimously threw out one of the crowning achievements of President Roosevelt's first one hundred days, one that had come to be identified, through the ubiquitous logo of the National Recovery Administration that was also created by NIRA—the defiant Blue Eagle holding a gear in one talon, symbolizing industry, and a lightning bolt in the other, symbolizing power—with the New Deal itself. Moreover, the Court had done so on a fundamental constitutional issue, the interpretation of Congress' "commerce" power that had largely been unchanged, with few exceptions, since the nineteenth century.

The White House called May 27, 1935, the date of Justice Hughes' opinion, "Black Monday." Nervous about his ability to enact other centralized economic regulations to strengthen the New Deal, President Roosevelt took to the press, referring to the Court as being stuck in "the horse-and-buggy age."[463]

The defiance of federal authority by Ernest Weir and Earl Reed at Weirton was effectively rewarded by the *Schechter* decision. Meanwhile, even a year before the *Schechter* ruling, the great and powerful men who were meeting with Raskob and Shouse in various board rooms around New York City in the summer of 1934 had begun to rally around Ernest Weir's defiance, attaching to it, as Weir himself had begun to do, loftier principles. Raskob envisioned the formation of a group he called the "Union Asserting the Integrity of Persons or Property,"[464] that would provide education about the Constitution, encourage individual initiative, and "preserve the ownership and lawful use of property when acquired."[465] Several other names for such an organization were suggested, such as the "National Property League" and the "Defenders of the Constitution," but eventually Jouett Shouse incorporated an organization called the "American Liberty League," after a suggestion by John W. Davis, on August 15, 1934, in the District of Columbia.[466] At a press conference on August 22, Shouse read a prepared statement of the purpose of the American Liberty League at the National Press Club, stating

> *The particular business and objects of the Society shall be to defend and uphold the Constitution of the United States and to gather and disseminate information that (1) will teach the necessity of respect for the rights of persons and property as fundamental to every successful form of government and (2) will teach the duty of government to encourage and protect individual and group initiative and enterprise, to foster the right to work, earn, save and acquire property, and to preserve the ownership and lawful use of property when acquired.*[467]

In a declaration that was aimed directly at the kind of troubles Weir had experienced with the NLB, Shouse stated:

There is no justification, under the traditional American system of government, for permitting an executive bureau to issue orders having the force of laws and subjecting citizens to criminal or civil penalties ... The American Liberty League believes that Congress, having been elected to represent the people, should not shirk its task by delegating authority to bureaus to promulgate arbitrary regulations having the force of laws. Likewise, the League believes that Congress should not attempt to delegate judicial power to executive bureaus. The courts of the nation and not government bureaus should pass upon questions of civil justice.[468]

As the League continued with its launch and publicity barrage, its list of financial contributors and supporters would expand to include Raymond Pitcairn of Pittsburgh Plate Glass, William S. Knudsen of General Motors, J. Howard Pew of Sun Oil, the film producer Hal Roach, and Edward F. Hutton, chairman of General Foods.[469]

Shouse was named president of the League, and he hired as his assistant a Pittsburgh lawyer named Ewing Laporte.[470] A somewhat shadowy figure, Laporte was born in Normandy, France and studied at Yale and George Washington Law School, entering the District of Columbia bar in 1917. He served as an Assistant Secretary of the Treasury under both Presidents Wilson and Harding, succeeding Shouse in the position, before moving to Pittsburgh to serve briefly as financial secretary to the University of Pittsburgh, under Chancellor John Gabbert Bowman. He entered the Pittsburgh bar in 1923, but seems to have been involved in Democratic Party matters more than in the practice of law. Although he applied for membership in the Allegheny County Bar Association, he abandoned his application when asked for references within the Pittsburgh bar. "Better drop it," was his terse written reply to the committee on admissions.[471] Until recently, he had served with Shouse as the executive secretary of Democratic National Committee.[472]

While the *Schechter* decision was a great victory for the newborn League (even if it had no right to claim it as its own achievement), New York senator Robert Wagner had already begun to appreciate that the labor provisions of NIRA were weak on matters of enforcement. On February 21, 1935, six days before Earl Reed would be handed his victory before the District Court in Delaware in *Weirton Steel*, Senator Wagner introduced a National Labor Relations bill. The bill proposed the creation of a new independent agency, the National Labor Relations Board, to be made up of three members appointed by the president, to enforce employee rights—with no role in the mediation of disputes. The bill would also reinforce the protections granted by Section 7(a) of NIRA—requiring employers to bargain with unions selected by the majority vote of employees within a given bargaining unit—and defined a list of prohibited "unfair labor practices," focusing on activities that companies had historically used in anti-union campaigns, such as hiring discrimination and various other coercive tactics.

Senator Wagner, in his speech on the Senate floor during his introduction of the bill, was quick to try to preempt the type of criticism that could be expected to come from the American Liberty League and other opponents of the New Deal. "Nothing could be more unfounded than the charges that the Board would be invested with arbitrary or dictatorial or even unusual powers," Senator Wagner declared. "Its powers are modeled upon those of the Federal Trade Commission and numerous other governmental agencies. Its orders would be enforceable not by the Board, but by recourse to the courts of the United States, with every affected party entitled to all the safeguards of appeal."[473]

In a pamphlet released in April, the American Liberty League began to lay out the position that even partisans of the bill had feared—that it would also be found to be unconstitutional. "The new bill makes a gesture toward avoidance of Federal encroachment upon the rights of the States," the League observed, "However, the definition of what constitutes interstate commerce is exactly the same in the new bill as in the present law."[474] Even President Roosevelt thought the measure went a bit too far substantively. As Frances Perkins, Roosevelt's Secretary of Labor, would say, "It ought to be on the record" that Wagner's bill was "not part of the President's program. It did not particularly appeal to him when it was described to him."[475] Roosevelt stood by as the Senate voted in favor of it on May 16, 1935 by a vote of sixty-three to twelve,[476] eleven days before the *Schechter* decision was announced; after *Schechter*, the president finally offered his endorsement of the bill. The bill was speedily passed by the House, and the conference report on the bill was agreed to by both houses on June 27. President Roosevelt signed the bill on July 5.[477]

On August 23, 1935, the White House nominated an obscure law professor from Pitt Law School, J. Warren Madden, to be seated as the first chairman of the National Labor Relations Board under the National Labor Relations Act (NLRA). He was approved by the Senate without comment on the following day.[478]

There were a number of ironies associated with Roosevelt's choice of Madden to be the chairman of the new independent commission. First, Madden was a real property professor who avowed during an interview with the Secretary of Labor, Frances Perkins, that he "didn't know anything about labor." "Well, that's fine," she replied, according to Madden. "We want somebody who hasn't any particular preconceptions about the thing."[479]

Second, the University with which he was affiliated was not known for its tolerance of "liberal" philosophy. One of its trustees, incidentally, was Ernest T. Weir. In addition, the University's chancellor, John Gabbert Bowman—Ewing Laporte's former employer—had gotten into a well-publicized clash with the ACLU and leftist commentators when he disbanded a student-formed "Liberal Club" and expelled two of its leaders in 1927. In 1933, Bowman again courted controversy when he dismissed several faculty members who were regarded as "Communist," including Ralph Turner, who had become chair of the Pennsylvania Security League, which advocated for federal old-age pensions and unemployment insurance.[480] The action became a cause célèbre in leftist magazines across the country; and locally, Representative Henry Ellenbogen, the former ACLU lawyer, expressed his concerns about Turner's dismissal in a July 9, 1934 letter.[481] The Chancellor responded to Ellenbogen that the circumstances of Turner's firing were "not concerned at all with the New Deal" but with his "attitude toward faith," in that he made fun of students who attended Sunday School.[482] In his letter, Ellenbogen had not specifically asked about the "New Deal."

For his own part, J. Warren Madden—"a very tolerant man," according to his former law clerk, Peter Adomeit[483]—was charitable in his assessment of the charge that Bowman was hostile to liberals. Rather, he understood that Bowman needed to "make a good impression for potential rich donors" to the University.[484] Any public controversy involving "socialists" or "communists" on campus was likely to be returned with threats by these major donors to change their bequests. Weir himself, in fact, had inquired of Bowman regarding the problem of Communists on campus in a March 1934 letter, and in response Bowman reassured him that among the "10,000 students at the University I doubt if there are fifty who subscribe to the communistic theory ... [and] if there are that many, most of them, I think, approve just to be 'smart,' rather than because they are convinced."[485] In general, Madden said, Bowman "was as considerate of the privilege of professors to be liberal or even make fools of themselves as it was possible to be."[486]

Madden had some cause to consider the question of Bowman's conservative outlook. From 1917, after three years of practicing law, he had bounced around the country teaching in various law schools from Ohio State to Oklahoma. He served as the dean of the West Virginia University College of Law for six years beginning in 1921, before arriving on the Pitt Law faculty in 1927. In 1933, Madden's next door neighbor, a fellow Pittsburgh professor from the Economics department named Marion O'Kellie McKay, gave Madden's name to Governor Gifford Pinchot for a non-statutory advisory committee which he was forming to study the Coal and Iron Police. Pinchot had already selected Francis Biddle, the Philadelphia lawyer, and John Kane, a Pittsburgh-based union activist who had recently been elected to the state legislature, and was looking for one more member from Pittsburgh to round out the committee. Madden said that when he asked a vice president of the University if it would be alright for him to serve, the vice president gave his approval, but said, "I wouldn't trust Pinchot around a corner."[487] The committee's conclusions were not universally loved by the region's business interests, but as Governor Pinchot did not move to ban the Coal and Iron Police completely—much to the disappointment of the leader of the abolition crusade, Michael Musmanno—the work of Madden's committee was somewhat forgotten.

Very soon afterwards, in the spring of 1934, Madden was drawn into a contract dispute between Philadelphia Company-controlled Pittsburgh Railways Company and a union of operating employees. The contract provided that if the parties could not agree on a new agreement, they would submit the contract renewal to arbitration. The operators chose John Kane as their arbitrator, while the company chose its in-house lawyer, Philip Fleger—who happened to have been Madden's student at West Virginia. Madden read about the arbitration in the newspaper and remarked to his wife, "I'm the only man in town that Phil Flager [sic] and John Kane both know." A few weeks later they called him and asked him if he would serve as the chairman of the arbitration panel, and he agreed. After six weeks of hearings that Madden would describe as "very deliberate, completely calm, and completely judicial," Madden submitted a decision on the arbitration that shortened hours for the employees while raising slightly their pay. "Altogether, I suppose it was a rather liberal sort of decision," Madden recalled. "At any rate, certainly the company thought it was." The street railway arbitration, as well as his time with the Coal and Iron Police committee, gave Madden "something of a reputation in Pittsburgh," he admitted, "as knowing something about labor, and as being somewhat sympathetic to the labor side of things." Nonetheless, Madden maintained that neither experience caused him to lose any standing at the University.[488]

Madden would ultimately speculate that his appointment to the National Labor Relations Board was the result of serendipitous social relationships. He had been acquainted with Lloyd K. Garrison, the dean of the University of Wisconsin Law School, when the two of them taught for the summer term at Stanford in 1933; in June 1934, President Roosevelt had appointed Garrison to be the chairman of the pre-NLRA version of the national labor relations board, after the abolition of the NLB. After a few months, Garrison returned to Wisconsin and was replaced by Francis Biddle, whom Madden had known through his work on the governor's Coal and Iron Police committee. After the passage of the NLRA, newspaper reports hinted that Charles Clark, the dean of Yale Law School, might be chosen for the new chairman position. Madden also knew Clark, and he had met Charlton Ogburn, the general counsel of the American Federation of Labor, during the Pittsburgh Railways arbitration. While the National Labor Relations Board was intended to be an independent commission, outside of the ambit of the Department of Labor, Frances Perkins was in effect leading the search effort. There was no doubt in Madden's mind that some combination of conversations with Garrison, Biddle, Clark and Ogburn, and possibly even with John Kane, had led Perkins to him.[489]

Since Madden was unknown to Washington, there was no controversy about his nomination, and his confirmation sailed through in a late-night Senate vote. Edwin Smith, a former Massachusetts commissioner of labor, and John Carmody, a former chief engineer for the Civil Works Administration, were selected as the other members of the new Board.[490]

Although there is no evidence on this point, it is tempting to believe that President Roosevelt may have been aware of the fact that his appointee was coming from an institution on whose board Ernest Weir served; and, at the very least, he understood that the Pittsburgh region was likely to produce controversies that would be relevant to the mission of the new Board—after all, it had already produced the *Weirton Steel* debacle. It is also tempting to believe that President Roosevelt's well-known sense of humor might have been tickled by such circumstances. Whether Roosevelt was prescient enough to believe that Pittsburgh would be the scene of the next controversy or not, one of the most significant labor controversies of the era would burst forth, just downriver from Pittsburgh, almost immediately after the NLRA came into being.

Four days after President Roosevelt signed the National Labor Relations Act, Jones & Laughlin Steel began to dismiss various employees who were affiliated as leaders of the local AAISTW in Aliquippa. On July 9, 1935, the company fired Martin Dunn, a crane operator who was a charter member of the local AAISTW, for leaving his crane key on a bench in violation of company rules. Next, on July 20, the company fired Harry Phillips, the president of the local, for failing to answer a whistle while he was using the restroom. On July 31, the company fired Angelo Volpe, the vice president, for using "head signals" rather than "hand signals" while operating a crane. Over the next six months, Jones & Laughlin dismissed at least nine more union leaders for a variety of minor infractions, and demoted another.[491]

Before the Jones & Laughlin dismissals would become a controversy before the Board, however, the American Liberty League would go on the offensive. On June 10, 1935, Shouse announced the formation of a "Lawyers' Vigilance Committee" by the League, to be chaired by Raoul E. Desvernine, a Wall Street lawyer from the Hornblower Miller firm (predecessor to Willkie Farr & Gallagher). The list of lawyers associated with the committee was like a who's who of American corporate law—including George Wickersham, a former U.S. attorney general, with the Cadwalader firm; John W. Davis; Joseph Proskauer of Proskauer Rose; Frederic R. Coudert, Jr., of Coudert Brothers; Frank Hogan of Hogan & Hartson; and David Aiken Reed and John J. Heard of Reed Smith.[492]

Through Weir's influence, Earl Reed was named chair of the Lawyers' Vigilance Committee's subcommittee on Industrial Relations and Labor Legislation. On September 18, 1935, Reed and Desvernine stood before a room of about fifty newspaper reporters in the Willard Hotel in Washington, D.C. to discuss the subcommittee's newly-released "Report on the Constitutionality of the National Labor Relations Act." As the *Pittsburgh Press* would report, Reed and Desvernine "spent an uncomfortable hour and a half undergoing cross-examination" on the Report's conclusion that the NLRA was unconstitutional. "Several of the lawyers on the committee" contributed to the Report, Reed allowed, "but I put the material together." Reporters questioned Reed on whether his involvement with the Weirton Steel matter in 1934 permitted him to be "unbiased" in his view. Unruffled, Reed explained that his experience was helpful, but as a lawyer he could objectively reach the conclusion that the Act was unconstitutional.[493]

Earl Reed then told the assembled crowd, "When a lawyer tells his client that a law is unconstitutional, it is then a nullity, and he need not obey that law."[494]

The press conference, and Reed's suggestion of civil disobedience, became the subject of editorials and opinions across the country. The *United States Law Review* questioned the purpose of the subcommittee report. "We are just a little incredulous," said the editors, that all of the "Fifty-Eight Lawyers" named as members of the Lawyers' Vigilance Committee "would actually subscribe a round robin or resolution for use in the newspapers, declaring that legislation duly enacted by the Congress, and approved by the Executive, to be unconstitutional before it has found its way into the courts or received judicial interpretation ... Whether the purpose of such emanations is to influence the federal courts when such legislation shall be presented for consideration, or whether it is to arouse public sentiment so that confidence in the courts will be impaired should the legislation be held constitutional, is not clear. But neither purpose has anything to commend it."[495]

In an editorial entitled "A Conspiracy of Lawyers," the editors of *The Nation* wrote:

> *Propaganda can be legitimate and even desirable, but when disguised as objective service to the general interest it is a menace against which the public has little protection. Gratitude, therefore, is due to the Washington news men for tearing off the trumpery costumes of the corporation lawyers who prepared for the Liberty League a unanimous legal opinion that the national Labor Relations Act is unconstitutional. These lawyers paraded as objective judges, and as such they helped to impress the community. But the press conference at which the opinion was launched never got down to a discussion of*

> the brief. Instead the Liberty League and its legal committee were occupied in resisting a barrage of questions as to the authorship of the brief and the right of the men who wrote it to be regarded as anything but special pleaders. These questions developed the fact that not a professor of law and not a lawyer distinguished for service to labor had been invited to join the committee. It was made up exclusively of lawyers known for their work for big corporations.[496]

The Nation singled out Reed's comment that clients "need not obey the law" for special comment, saying that "If this is the ethics of the profession many lawyers will call for a drastic purge," and noting that while the content of the brief itself did not receive much press, the work of the Liberty League's subcommittee did result in the circulation to many employers across the country, free of charge, a brief that "would have cost a single corporation at least $100,000." "A $50 lawyer may now file it in his local court," *The Nation* lamented.[497]

Meanwhile, shortly after the headlines on the subcommittee's report appeared, the Ethics Committee of the American Bar Association, apparently feeling that there was enough controversy surrounding Reed's report that it required comment, declared that "no ground for criticism exists as to the conduct of the fifty-eight lawyers."[498] While the Roosevelt administration remained silent on the Report, the Secretary of the Interior, Harold Ickes, charged that issuing such a report before the Supreme Court had a chance to rule on the Act was "evidence per se of disrespect of the court."[499]

On January 28, 1936, the AAISTW filed charges against Jones & Laughlin Steel for its allegedly retaliatory firings. Rather than turning to a "$50 lawyer," the steel company hired Earl Reed as its counsel. Thorp Bostwick had not been the company's usual law firm; it had routinely been represented in Pittsburgh by Wilson & Evans, or by the Challener firm in workers compensation matters. Reed's association with the subcommittee report also appeared to have the effect of galvanizing the "Little Steel" companies of the Ohio Valley around Reed and his firm, and Reed began to position the companies to lead the charge for the nullification of the NLRA, occasionally convening roundtable meetings with all the "Little Steel" companies to make sure that their legal positions were consistent going into the next big battle. It happened that the complaint against Jones & Laughlin Steel offered the earliest opportunity for Reed to build a test case around it.

On Monday, March 2, 1936, J. Warren Madden, chairman of the National Labor Relations Board, and his fellow board member, John M. Carmody, convened case number C-57, "In the Matter of Jones & Laughlin Steel Corporation and Amalgamated Association of Iron, Steel & Tin Workers of North America, Beaver Valley Lodge No. 200," in courtroom number 6 of the Federal Post Office Building on Grant Street in Pittsburgh.[500] The Board's lawyers, who assumed the primary role in presenting the case, were Robert Burnham Watts, an associate general counsel of the Board, and the Board's regional attorney, Robert Kleeb. Representing the AAISTW were Alexander H. Schullman of Pittsburgh, a New Dealer who in 1934 had unsuccessfully sought the Democratic nomination for Congress from Pennsylvania's 32nd District representing the North Side, and California lawyer Aaron Sapiro, a leader in the agricultural cooperative movement who was best known for having once sued Henry Ford for libel, a suit that ended with an apology by Ford and a mistrial in 1927.[501] Appearing on behalf of Jones & Laughlin Steel were Earl Reed and his young associates, John E. Laughlin, Jr. (no relation to the company's founder), a Harvard lawyer with a photographic memory, and Donald W. Ebbert, street-smart son of a coal company treasurer from Crafton Borough, west of Pittsburgh.[502]

After some skirmishes with the government lawyers over foundational evidence, Reed interrupted the proceedings, asking Watts, "Is this going into the merits of the labor controversy or this jurisdictional phase of it?" "I haven't any particular line," Watts replied. "If the Board please," Reed said, turning his attention to Chairman Madden, "we have entered a special appearance here and raised the question of the jurisdiction of the Board on the theory that the company is not engaged in interstate commerce ... We are entitled to a preliminary determination of that question." Watts protested, but Madden sided with Reed, and Reed proceeded to present a few company witnesses on Jones & Laughlin Steel's "manufacture" of steel, directing attention to the argument that "manufacture" is not "commerce," as Judge Nields had written in his opinion in the *Weirton Steel* case.[503]

At the close of his evidence, Reed declared, "We move to dismiss, on the ground that ... the business of the respondent is not interstate commerce, and any labor controversy, therefore, would not be within the jurisdiction of the Board. Further, the complaint only complains of matters of hiring or discharging employees, which is a matter that is not interstate commerce, even if it related to any agency in interstate commerce, and it seems clear to us that there is no jurisdiction in this case."

Chairman Madden replied, "It would be very interesting, Mr. Reed, to hear you argue this question, but I suppose you do not care to do it, and I doubt whether we can take the time to do it. We are quite definitely committed," he went on, "to the doctrine that an enterprise such as has been shown ... is in a situation where its labor relations do affect interstate commerce ... and so your motion to dismiss is denied."

"With respect to the specific complaints relating to employees," Reed argued, "the respondent takes the position that it is the sole judge of the right to hire and fire, and that it is not subject to the Board in that respect." He told Madden that he declined to offer any testimony on the merits, and that he was withdrawing from the hearing. And with that, Reed, Laughlin and Ebbert left the court room.[504] Consistent with his approach at Weirton, Reed was baiting the government into a course of judicial review, hoping to get to the Supreme Court on the jurisdictional issue as quickly as possible.

Madden, meanwhile, re-convened the hearing on Jones & Laughlin Steel on seven subsequent dates in Pittsburgh and Washington, hearing testimony on the merits as well as testimony from several economists on the impact local actions with respect to labor on interstate commerce. None of the witnesses were subject to cross-examination, and by the end of the hearings, the only people left in the room other than the witnesses were Madden, his fellow Board members, and the Board's lawyers. On April 9, Madden signed an order requiring Jones & Laughlin Steel to "cease and desist from in any manner interfering with, restraining, or coercing its employees in the exercise of their rights to self-organization" and to re-hire its terminated employees in the respective positions formerly held by them.[505]

Madden and his staff, including Charles Fahy, the general counsel of the NLRB, were very much aware that *Schechter* had been a bad case upon which to consider the constitutionality of the NIRA; Madden said that the poultry regulations the government had to defend in *Schechter* led the NRA's legal team to argue "that it was necessary to draw upon the vast arsenal of the national power in order to bring under control a situation which could, in fact, be quieted with a pop-gun."[506] The team was being extra careful about which case might reach the Supreme Court first this time. The first case to get close was against the Pennsylvania Greyhound Lines, which the team thought would be viewed favorably in light of the *Texas & New Orleans Railroad* interstate commerce case from 1930. But when the NLRB petitioned to have the Greyhound case enforced by the Third Circuit, it languished. Next up was a case against the Associated Press, a company that operated in interstate commerce through its use of telegraph and telephone wires to transmit news. Liberty Leaguer John W. Davis defended the Associated Press before the Second Circuit, but the Board managed to win, based on the *Texas & New Orleans Railroad* case, in an opinion handed down on March 17.[507]

Robert Watts suggested that he might be able to get a quick, favorable ruling out of the Fifth Circuit on Jones & Laughlin Steel Corp., so after confirming that Jones & Laughlin had operations in Louisiana (the company owned a structural steel fabricating shop in New Orleans), the Board filed a petition for enforcement of the order in the U.S. Circuit Court of Appeals for the Fifth Circuit in Louisiana.[508] In this case, the team hoped to argue that the fact that Jones & Laughlin's raw materials were brought in through interstate commerce, and its products were sent out into interstate commerce, would be enough to establish the constitutional connection between the regulation and Congress' authority. Watts faced Earl Reed in arguments before the Circuit Court on June 1, and telegrammed back to Madden that the "Court appeared friendly but anxious to see way clearly on constitutional issue." Two weeks later, the team learned that the Circuit Court ruled against the NLRB.[509] Earl Reed now had two wins against the government, and was gunning to dispose of the NLRB in the Supreme Court.

Meanwhile, three other NLRB cases were also on their way to the Supreme Court, two focusing on the raw materials/product line of thinking, and one on the *Texas and New Orleans Railroad* line of thinking—one against the Fruehauf Trailer Company, a manufacturer of truck trailers; another against the Friedman-Harry Marks Clothing Company; and the third against the Washington, Virginia and Maryland Coach Company. On October 26, writs of certiorari were granted by the Supreme Court in *Associated Press* and *Washington, Virginia and Maryland Coach*. On November 9, the Court also agreed to hear appeals in *Jones & Laughlin*, *Fruehauf*, and *Friedman-Harry Marks*. Arguments in all five cases were set to begin on February 9, 1937.[510] Madden's future tenure as the chief of the NLRB would either live or die with what he and colleagues could do in February.

In the run-up to the intervening 1936 election, at the Democratic National Convention, President Roosevelt criticized "economic royalists" who were using their wealth to obstruct the progress of recovery and the era of social pioneering that the New Deal was launching.[511] Ernest T. Weir took the comments personally, writing in *Fortune*:

> *I believe I am warranted in the assumption that I am one of the men whom Mr. Roosevelt calls economic royalists. I have personal means; I am the chief executive of a large corporation; and I have been and am opposed to the policies and actions of the Administration. I deny that these things, in themselves, make me an antisocial force, or that I have ever used them in an antisocial manner.*

Referring to other self-made men, such as Walter P. Chrysler, Henry Ford, Charles Schwab and John D. Rockefeller, Weir asked, is it not appropriate to wonder "whether men such as these ... have a more genuine and practical interest in the common people than a man like Mr. Roosevelt, whose whole experience in the creation of jobs has been limited to the expansion of government payrolls?"[512]

The debate between President Roosevelt and the "economic royalists" appeared to have little impact on the views of the voting public. On November 3, President Roosevelt beat Governor Alf Landon of Kansas, the Republican nominee, by an even greater landslide than he achieved in his 1932 victory over President Hoover. Governor Landon carried just two states, Maine and Vermont, to Hoover's six in 1932, and garnered just 36.5% of the popular vote, versus President Hoover's 39.7%. Roosevelt carried Pennsylvania this time, and repeated his dominance in Allegheny County.[513] He also won in Aliquippa by a two-to-one margin.[514]

With the amount of work to be done in preparation for the five NLRB cases before the Supreme Court, it stood to reason that the duties of briefing and argument would be divided among several NLRB lawyers, as well as a few in the office of Stanley Reed (no relation to Earl or to Judge James Hay Reed), the Solicitor General. However, the Solicitor General was "quite taken aback" when J. Warren Madden made his request to argue the *Jones & Laughlin* case before the Supreme Court. After all, Madden was the chairman of the NLRB—in effect, a party in interest before the Court. Second, he had been the trier of fact in the first stage of the case. Third, Madden had been a law professor for almost twenty years; he was not an experienced appellate litigator. "After he thought it over," Madden recalled, "he said it was alright." Ultimately, perhaps out of sheer necessity given the workload the team faced, the Solicitor General relented, and agreed to split the argument in *Jones & Laughlin Steel* with Madden.[515]

Earl Reed's brief on behalf of Jones & Laughlin Steel Corp. was much more than the filing by a "$50 lawyer" of the American Liberty League Report; however, Reed did lift passages, large and small, directly from the Report and place them, with minor edits, into the brief.[516] By necessity, the brief for the Supreme Court would cover many items that were not intended to be covered in the Report—not the least of which was the theoretical application of the NLRA to Jones & Laughlin Steel Corp.—as well as being a response to the arguments that the NLRB had made in the Fifth Circuit. The fact that there were indeed sections of the Report that made it relatively unscathed into Reed's Supreme Court brief is further evidence, however, of how confident Reed was in his conclusions. He was resting on what he believed to be a well-considered argument based on sound precedent. Not only did he have complete confidence in himself, but as Weir had said in 1934, he had "complete confidence in the courts."[517]

Despite the best laid plans of teams of lawyers laboring on all sides of the five NLRB cases, President Roosevelt would drop a bombshell right into the middle of the proceedings on February 5, 1937, four days before arguments were set to begin. Cloaked in the notion that "the personnel of the Federal judiciary is insufficient to meet the business before them," the president sent to Congress a plan for legislation that would allow the president to appoint one new judge for each judge with ten years of service who did not leave the Court within six months after attaining the age of seventy.[518] In effect, in response to "Black Monday" and the *Schechter* decision, among others, Roosevelt desired to expand the Court to include new blood that would be open to more expansive interpretations of congressional authority.

The then current make-up of the Court included six Supreme Court justices who were over the age of seventy: Brandeis (eighty-one), Van Devanter (seventy-eight), Chief Justice Hughes, Sutherland and McReynolds (each seventy-five), and Butler (seventy-one). Justices Van Devanter, Sutherland, McReynolds and Butler were considered to be the "conservative bloc" on the Court. Justice Owen Roberts and Chief Justice Hughes functioned as the potential swing votes, while Justices Brandeis, Cardozo and Stone represented the "liberal bloc." Under Roosevelt's "court packing plan," the president would be entitled to add up to six more justices to effectively outvote the conservative bloc without the help of the swing voters. If he was not too explicit about these aims when he unveiled the plan, by the following month the president was openly criticizing the Court's majority for its narrow readings of the Constitution, declaring that action was required "to save the Constitution from the Court, and the Court from itself."[519]

Perhaps not surprisingly, bar associations around the country began to issue their statements against the president's plan, ranging from tepid examinations of Congress' authority to effectuate the plan to full-blown outrage. On March 4, the Pennsylvania Bar Association announced the results of a referendum on President Roosevelt's proposal, with 3,638 Pennsylvania lawyers (members and non-members) voting against the proposal, and just 764 voting for it; among Allegheny County lawyers, the vote was 813 against, and only 150 for.[520] Eight days later, at a meeting of the Allegheny County Bar Association, John G. Buchanan introduced a resolution denouncing the plan. Judge Michael Musmanno moved to amend the resolution to state that the resolution should specify that it was the action only of those who were present at the vote, and not of the entire bar, but his amendment was defeated. After some discussion, Buchanan's resolution passed, seventy-four to nineteen, and it was forwarded to the president, as well as Pittsburgh's congressmen (including Henry Ellenbogen) and Pennsylvania's senators in Washington.[521] The American Liberty League largely stayed out of the quarrel, as the president seemed to have enough critics from his own party on the subject.

These reactions would come in the weeks after President Roosevelt's plan was unveiled. Today, no one seriously disputes that in the immediate aftermath of his proposal, the justices of the Supreme Court understood the importance of what was being proposed, and that at the very least, President Roosevelt's "chin music" was the debut of a bold overture, unavoidably to be heard just as the Court was about to consider the fate of the NLRA.

After a day of argument on the *Associated Press* case, at 3:05 in the afternoon on Wednesday, February 10, 1937, the Jones & Laughlin and NLRB teams assembled at the Supreme Court of the United States for their argument. Earl Reed was accompanied by Charles Rosen, a New Orleans appellate lawyer who worked on the Fifth Circuit case; W.D. Evans of Jones & Laughlin's primary Pittsburgh firm, Wilson & Evans; and John Laughlin; Reed, however, would be their sole presenter. For the NLRB, J. Warren Madden and the Solicitor General, Stanley Reed, entered their appearances.[522]

Madden opened the argument. Shortly after he began, one of the NLRB staffers saw Justice Brandeis call one of the page boys over to him and hand him a note. A moment later, the page returned with what looked to be a copy of *Who's Who in America*. While Madden continued his argument, Justice Brandeis perused the book, wrote something down on a piece of paper and handed it to Justice Butler, who was sitting next to him. "I thought so," Butler said to Brandeis. The staffers surmised that Brandeis and Butler were confirming that Madden was a law professor, rather than an appellate lawyer.[523] The Court nevertheless gave Madden a long runway in establishing the circumstances of the case, after which he launched into the "commerce clause" arguments. At one point, he observed the irony in Jones & Laughlin Steel threatening to make use of federal antitrust enforcement against striking laborers because strikes "disrupt the commerce of the Nation," but denying that the causes of the strike would have anything to do with interstate commerce.[524] After about 50 minutes, Madden handed the case to Stanley Reed, who took up where Charles Fahy and one of the Justice Department lawyers, Charles Wyzanski, left off in their arguments the day before against John W. Davis in the *Associated Press* case on the power to regulate, emphasizing that "collective bargaining is not the ultimate end of this act ... It is, from our point of view, a regulation of commerce. It deals with labor relations as they directly affect commerce."[525]

The Court adjourned for the day after Stanley Reed's argument, and Earl Reed opened the proceedings when the Court reconvened at noon on the next day.[526] Madden remarked that Reed "was no John W. Davis,"[527] but Reed was as blunt and penetrating in his arguments as any of the other company lawyers in the five cases, Davis included; Davis' style, at age sixty-three, was from an earlier age of appellate argument, most charitably described by historian Peter H. Irons as "florid."[528] Reed, by contrast, attacked the NLRB and its case against his client for almost an hour and a half like an unleashed pit bull, beginning his argument by observing that "the persuasive oratory of Government counsel has magnified this discharge of twelve persons into some national calamity to stop the streams of commerce."[529] He referred to the "mass of hypothetical testimony" in the Board proceeding and said that what the Board's petition amounted to was that "Mr. Madden and his Labor Board did not agree with the superintendents of the company as to the sufficiency of the causes for which they discharged the employees."[530] He pointed out that the Board appealed to the Fifth Circuit—where the company has a warehouse in which none of the dismissed men had ever set foot—for enforcement of the Board's ruling before the company even knew about it.[531]

Reed observed that the government's case was not ultimately made on constitutional grounds, but on economic grounds:

It seems to me that the Government's argument comes down to an economic argument. 'It would be a good thing,' says Mr. Madden, 'If the Federal Government could control the labor relations of industry.' But that is not the law, and never has been. He may think that the States are handling it 'stupidly', as he says. He may think that a centralized government in which the Federal Government controls all of the labor relations of industry is desired. That is not the law and never has been.[532]

He concluded by asking the Court not to throw away "the traditions and precedents of a century" because "things that for a century have not been the business of the Federal government are now to be subject to regulation, because of the remote possibility that these discharges and things of this kind may obstruct commerce."[533] Reed's argument was not solely a legal argument, either—it was about the traditions and precedents of Pittsburgh business and entrepreneurism, and, urgently, about preserving a world in which "a man had a right to hire whom he wished."[534]

Press coverage of the arguments mostly focused on *Associated Press*, for somewhat obvious reasons, as well as the fact that John W. Davis was the best known lawyer among the eleven who argued in the five NLRB cases. However, the "Pittsburgh angle" to the arguments before the Supreme Court was not lost on the *Pittsburgh Press*, whose headline read, "MADDEN, REED DEBATE J. & L. WAGNER CASE—Pittsburgh Lawyers Argue Before Supreme Court in Important Test."[535]

Madden had noted that there were few questions from the bench during the argument of the case. "The bench was a little paralyzed by the whole situation," he observed. "It was quite certain that Mr. Roosevelt's [court packing] plan was not going to go through. But I think that whole uproar had left the Court in a considerable wonderment as to whether it was out of step with what was going on in the country and what had to be done."[536] On March 29, the Court upheld a minimum wage statute in *West Coast Hotel Co. v. Parrish*, overruling the Court's previous opinion in *Adkins v. Children's Hospital* (1923), in which the Court held that a federal minimum wage law was an unconstitutional infringement of the freedom to contract.[537] It was a significant decision, and one which indicated that the Court was ready to permit the wholesale federal regulation of the workplace.

On April 12, the Court delivered its opinions in the five cases. The *Associated Press* case was decided 5-4 in favor of the NLRB. In an opinion by Justice Roberts, the narrow ruling held that the NLRB's actions, as applied to an editor who gathered news but who did not transmit news through interstate commerce, were valid.[538]

Next came the *Jones & Laughlin Steel Corp.* decision, also in favor of the NLRB by a 5-4 margin. The opinion was read by Chief Justice Hughes, and would extend the sweep of the NLRB's jurisdiction even further. Hughes called the "right of employees to self-organization and to select representatives of their own choosing for collective bargaining" a "fundamental right." Hughes went further to ask, in recognition of the way in which the business world had changed since 1901, when Charles Schwab had prophesied the fully-integrated steel conglomerate, that "[w]hen industries organize themselves on a national scale, making their relation to interstate commerce the dominant factor in their activities, how can it be maintained that their industrial labor relations constitute a forbidden field into which Congress may not enter when it is necessary to protect interstate commerce from the paralyzing consequences of industrial war?" Undoubtedly fully informed by Pittsburgh's labor history, Hughes also observed, "Experience has abundantly demonstrated that the recognition of the right of employees to self-organization and to have representatives of their own choosing for the purpose of collective bargaining is often an essential condition of industrial peace. Refusal to confer and negotiate has been one of the most prolific causes of strife." In the strongest departure from the rigid nineteenth century view of what constituted interstate commerce, Hughes said that the Court would not "shut our eyes to the plainest facts of our national life and to deal with the question of direct and indirect effects [on interstate commerce] in an intellectual vacuum."[539]

In the opinions for the other three NLRB cases, the Chief Justice also announced the Court's support of the NLRB. The NLRA would stand, and *Jones & Laughlin Steel Corp.* turned out to be the lead opinion.

There exists a difference of opinion as to whether the court-packing plan had a direct effect on Justice Owen Roberts' shift to the liberal bloc in *Parrish* (most agree that *Parrish* was actually decided before the Roosevelt unveiled his court-packing plan) or on his support for the NLRB in the five cases.[540] Nonetheless, Roberts' shift has become the stuff of legend, "the switch in time that saved nine," rendering the Roosevelt court-packing plan unnecessary in the wake of a Court that was willing to give the New Deal a chance. There is perhaps better evidence to indicate that Hughes and Roberts, who both voted to strike down NIRA, may have awakened to certain of the "plainest facts of our national life" on the day after Election Day 1936, and realized that public opinion was drastically different then it had been when they began their service on the Court.[541] All that can be said for certain is that the timing of President Roosevelt's court-packing announcement, just before the arguments on the five NLRB cases, was calculated by the White House.

Stepping away from the politics of the Court, though—before *Jones & Laughlin Steel Corp.*, the state of labor and management relations in the United States could be summarized in the following observation by historian Roy Lubove: "Company power to control working conditions was reinforced by political influence in the mill towns and by divisions within the labor force between skilled and unskilled, American- and foreign-born."[542] After *Jones & Laughlin Steel Corp.*, a large measure of that power would now be surrendered to the federal government.

Pittsburgh corporate lawyers, or at least Earl Reed and his colleagues at Thorp Bostwick Reed & Armstrong, would not go quietly into the night. The ruling in *Jones & Laughlin Steel Corp.* was undoubtedly greeted with shock and dismay, and not a little anger. If the Report of the Lawyers' Vigilance Committee was meant to be a publicity ploy to influence the wheels of justice, it turned out the Roosevelt's court-packing plan was a better one. If the NLRB was going to be the new sheriff in town, Reed and his colleagues were going to make sure the government would have to fight to earn every notch in the handle of its gun.

Undoubtedly with relish, the NLRB turned the government's attention back to Earl Reed's client, Weirton Steel Company. On July 6, 1937, barely two months after the Supreme Court's opinion in *Jones & Laughlin Steel Corp.*, the Steel Workers Organizing Committee (SWOC), formed by the Congress of Industrial Organizations (CIO), filed a complaint against Weirton Steel with the NLRB alleging, among other things, that the company had dominated the Employee Security League, discouraged membership in the SWOC, and "by bribery, threats, loyalty pledges, espionage, lawless acts, and ejections, and by other means ... interfered with, restrained, and coerced its employees in the exercise of rights guaranteed in Section 7" of the NLRA.[543]

This time, neither Reed nor Madden would participate in the hearings on the complaint, which were set to begin in New Cumberland, West Virginia on August 16. The NLRB assigned sixty-nine year-old Edward Grandison Smith, a Clarksburg lawyer who was president of the West Virginia University board of regents, to serve as hearing examiner. The government's case was presented by Isidore "Shad" Polier—a tallish, broad-shouldered thirty-one year-old Harvard Law grad who had assisted in the preparation of the briefs in the U.S. Supreme Court appeal on the conviction of the Scottsboro Boys in 1932 and was active on behalf of the NAACP. His wife, Justine Wise Polier, daughter of an activist rabbi, was a Yale lawyer who had become the first woman judge in New York in 1935.[544] Taking the reins of Weirton's case was Earl Reed's junior partner, Clyde A. Armstrong—a lanky, distinguished-looking Pitt lawyer from New Kensington, a former Westminster College football player.[545] Armstrong was made a "name" partner of the firm in 1934, although Armstrong later claimed it was a Depression cost-saving measure; as a partner, he was only entitled to a share of the profits, and the firm would not be obliged to pay him a salary.[546] Laughlin and Ebbert again filled out the rest of the Thorp Bostwick team.

The hearings had barely begun when they were first covered in the national press. In the September 6, 1937, issue of *Life*, there appeared a four-page photo spread, depicting the packed, humid scene within the "neat little ivy-covered Hancock County Court House" in New Cumberland, West Virginia, the lawyers shown in their shirt-sleeves at their respective counsels' tables, brows furrowed.[547] On both sides of the *Weirton* case, the lawyers were true believers in their clients' causes, and they conducted themselves like gladiators, fighting to the death. Armstrong, a smooth courtroom tactician who nevertheless would evidence a hot temper and a sharp tongue, was ferociously conservative, politically, and he was encouraged by Reed and their neighbor on the 28th Floor, Ernest Weir, to view the NLRB's activities as political. During the course of the hearings, he would occasionally break out into a tirade against the Left, at one point remarking to the hearing examiner, "I'll be satisfied if Mr. Polier states that he doesn't condone Communism."[548]

Polier replied that "if ever the day should come that I should have to state my personal belief in response to questions by a man like Mr. Armstrong, I'll be a very unhappy person."[549] As a progressive lawyer working in pro bono or government roles prior to joining the NLRB staff, Polier was completely committed to the government's purpose in *Weirton*. In a letter to his father-in-law, Polier referred to Armstrong and his team as a "dishonorable group of legal knaves." As to his purpose for being there, he was just as unwavering as Armstrong: "[T]his is a matter of importance transcending just another Board case. This is the United States against Weirton Steel Company, U.S. v. [Tom] Girdler [of Republic Steel] and Weir, U.S. v. 'Little Steel,' U.S. v. the most arrogant and ruthless aggregation of wealth in the country. And if I never do another thing in my life I'll be satisfied if I can help to bring these tyrants before the law."[550]

With ideologies as backdrop, tempers ran high throughout the case. During one day of testimony, Armstrong became especially enthusiastic in his cross-examination of a government witness, leading Polier to object. Armstrong exploded, telling Polier he had no right to judge "his conduct" and that he was making specious objections in order to "make a record against him."[551] On another occasion, Don Ebbert accused Polier of coaching a witness on the stand. Polier responded that Ebbert was "a liar," at which point, Polier recalled, Ebbert "started for me, and of course Armstrong grabbed him," joined by a company tough who sat with the defense team inside the counsel table area. After calm was restored, Polier moved to have the bodyguard removed, to which Smith simply replied that he would take the motion under advisement.[552] Around the same time, another Thorp Bostwick lawyer, Kenneth G. Jackson, traded punches with Benjamin Gordon, an NLRB attorney, outside a federal courtroom in Pittsburgh during an NLRB hearing on a petition against another Thorp Bostwick client, Moltrup Steel Products.[553] This new kind of proceeding, the labor relations hearing—not a traditional courtroom, not overly concerned with traditional common law—was proving to be a pressure cooker for both Thorp Bostwick and the government.

In the *Weirton* case, dirty tricks and coercion also abounded—both from the company as well as from the SWOC. The government had trouble keeping track of its witnesses. Polier told of having to drive thirty miles to interview a witness who had "disappeared" three times before finally giving the government her full story. "Lord, were they surprised when today's witness appeared," he wrote.[554] Outside of the hearing site in Steubenville, a crowd of onlookers formed, some of whom held anti-NLRB signs, taunting Polier with the slogan "*Comrade PoLiar.*"[555] The NLRB and the SWOC did everything they could to avoid handing over the SWOC records of membership, fearing reprisals during the case, and Armstrong accused the government of putting witnesses on the stand merely to establish what could be established if the membership records were entered into evidence. According to a Thorp firm associate, Don Ebbert claimed that Weirton Steel had installed a bug in Edward Grandison Smith's hotel room, and that the company caught the hearing examiner talking with the SWOC organizers and their counsel "colluding as to how they were going to proceed" in the case. Meanwhile, as one of his associates remembered, Clyde Armstrong claimed that the SWOC sent "armed goons" to his front porch in Shadyside to try to intimidate him during the case.[556]

On January 4, 1938, Polier wrote to his wife Justine, "There was enough excitement today to make your hair stand on end—and none of it 'on the record.'" Armstrong requested a conference outside the main hearing to go over certain records that had been subpoenaed. "It lasted three hours," Polier wrote, "and he finally yielded every single point despite his melodramatic threats to walk out on us several times." During the entire conference, Polier's "star witness" was sitting on the witness stand back in the hearing room—"or so I thought," wrote Polier, until an assistant ran into the conference and informed him that "two deputy sheriffs have grabbed your witness and started out with him."

Polier ran through the crowded corridors and saw them at the bottom of some steps. The deputies were about to handcuff his witness. "Where in the hell do you think you're taking that man?," he shouted. One of the deputies offered that he had a warrant for the witness' arrest for passing a bad check. "I said, 'this is a state process—you have no right to serve it in a federal building and moreover this man is here under subpoena. You're interfering with the government of the U.S. and if you take that man I'll have you and your buddy put in jail so fast you won't know what's what.'" Polier conferred with the U.S. marshal and then demanded that the deputies bring the witness back. "I said to the witness—go back in the courtroom—and to the deputies so everyone could hear—and you stay the hell out of there. They asked what are we to do about him and I said you'll have to wait until he's through testifying." Polier observed that after inspecting the warrant he realized the deputies had had it for two weeks, and that their appearance was designed for maximum press coverage.[557]

As the hearings lengthened into late spring, Polier wrote to his wife, "The practice of law among gentlemen is certainly a pleasant experience—I look forward to returning to it."[558]

After the first anniversary of the ongoing hearings was marked, the heat of the summer apparently made Armstrong testy again. During an argument over a witness in the Federal Building at Steubenville, Ohio, the latest locale for the seemingly never-ending hearings, Examiner Smith ordered Armstrong to sit down. As related by the *Pittsburgh Press*, the colloquy proceeded as follows:

Mr. Armstrong: If it is a request, I will, Mr. Examiner, but not an order.

Trial Examiner Smith: It is my request and it is my order.

Mr. Armstrong: I won't sit down on an order, but I will sit down on a request. I am not going to sit here and listen to charges of corruption of this witness.

Trial Examiner Smith: Nothing further. The remarks of Mr. Armstrong on the subject are expunged, and the remarks of Mr. Polier on the subject are expunged.

Mr. Armstrong: I would like to make a special request that they remain on the record.

Trial Examiner Smith: The order has been made. The proposition here presented will be taken under advisement until tomorrow morning. This witness may retire from the stand until tomorrow morning.

Mr. Armstrong: Mr. Examiner, every time—

Trial Examiner Smith: The order has been made.

Mr. Armstrong: Every time we put a witness—

Trial Examiner Smith: The order has been made.

Mr. Armstrong: I want to explain my position. I do not care whether it is right or not.

Trial Examiner Smith: Sit down. We will not hear any such comments.

Mr. Armstrong: I am going to explain my situation as to this witness. I have a right to do it, and I am going to do it.

TrIAL EXAMINER SMITH: Sit down. I say right now!

Mr. Armstrong: Mr. Examiner, I will not sit down under instructions of that kind.[559]

Smith adjourned the hearing over Armstrong's objections. The following Monday morning, Smith opened the hearing, declaring:

On Thursday last an incident occurred in this courtroom, in this hearing, which was the direct result of the defiant and contumacious behavior of Clyde A. Armstrong, one of the attorneys for the respondent ... Immediately thereafter, as a direct result of said conduct of said Armstrong, some of the spectators in this courtroom became exceedingly noisy and exhibited an attitude toward the Trial Examiner and the Board which cannot and will not be tolerated. Since that time, Mr. Armstrong has not indicated to the Trial Examiner any remorse or repentance for his definitely defiant, contemptuous and contumacious conduct ... This Trial Examiner is convinced that Mr. Clyde A. Armstrong's defiant, contemptuous and contumacious conduct on July 7, 1938, makes it impossible for him further to participate in this hearing, and he is accordingly barred and excluded from further participation as one of respondent Weirton Steel Co.'s counsel in this hearing.[560]

"CHIEF COUNSEL EJECTED," ran the headline in the *Pittsburgh Press*, with a photo of Armstrong prominently featured.[561] Polier confided to his wife, "My back was toward Armstrong throughout" the ruling, but his colleagues were able to watch him. "Both say he was both stupefied and on the verge of tears."[562] Weirton Steel appealed Armstrong's ejection, but after a special hearing in Washington on July 20, the Board affirmed Smith's ruling,[563] and Armstrong's senior partner Roy Bostwick was forced to step in to help close the case out.

The final decision from the Board came on June 25, 1941. The transcript from the proceedings, some thirty-nine thousand pages through the completion of all testimony, cost approximately eighty thousand dollars to complete. The Board found that Weirton Steel was guilty of propping up a company-dominated union, and under a cease and desist order, the Employee Security League was disbanded.[564] While the Board probably expected that this would have resulted in the SWOC becoming the incumbent union, some of the officials of the Security League immediately formed a new organization called the Weirton Independent Union (WIU). The costly fight over that union would persist through the end of the 1940s, and none too successfully for the WIU. Ironically, though, after all was said and done, Weirton Steel still managed to be the one steel company in the United States whose workers were represented by an independent union during the last half of the twentieth century.

By 1936, even before the re-election of President Roosevelt and the *Jones & Laughlin Steel Corp.* Supreme Court decision, the American Liberty League was besieged by threats of investigation and unfavorable press, and shortly after the 1936 election in November, the League started to shut down its operations. Ewing Laporte conducted a final audit of the books of what would be considered one of the most lavishly funded yet least successful political organizations of the day.[565] After *Jones & Laughlin Steel Corp.* and the first *Weirton Steel* NLRB case, Earl Reed, aided by his younger colleagues, would continue as the trusted counsel to Ernest Weir and his companies; indeed, at its peak, National Steel represented almost half of the revenue of Thorp Reed & Armstrong, as the firm became known after the death of Roy Bostwick in 1947—a precarious circumstance for any law firm, even if it yielded the firm's partners a nice income during the muted prosperity of the mid-twentieth century steel industry.[566] Reed would find other things to occupy his time, including more state and municipal political investigations (he became, ironically, David Lawrence's most trusted legal advisor) and his personal acquisition of radio and television properties; he was a part owner of WTAE-TV when he died in 1963.[567]

Meanwhile, J. Warren Madden, the former Pittsburgh real property professor, remained one-for-one in U.S. Supreme Court arguments over his lifetime—he never represented the Board before the U.S. Supreme Court after *Jones & Laughlin Steel Corp.*[568] His tenure at the NLRB became rocky near the end of his five-year term, as he was accused by the House Un-American Activities Committee of staffing the NLRB with Communists. It turned out to be true in at least a few instances, though Madden would protest that it was not intentional. Nor, he would argue, would Communists get any satisfaction out of the work of the NLRB. "I have tried to figure out how a thoughtful Communist would have viewed the Board and what it was doing, and how he could have made use of his position there to further the cause of the Communist party," he said in retrospect. "It seems to me that his actions there were in rather complete contradiction to what would be long range Communist aims. If the Wagner Act served its purpose, as it was intended to do ... to make labor strong, to raise wages and improve the condition of working people, that would not in any sense serve the cause of communism."[569]

In 1940, President Roosevelt nominated Madden for a seat on the U.S. Court of Claims, but this time he was a known quantity, and Senator Robert Taft attempted to block his confirmation. Madden was eventually confirmed, and he ultimately served out his federal judicial career sitting by designation with the Ninth Circuit in San Francisco.[570] Despite the fact that he left the NLRB in the midst of a cloud of controversy, labor historian James A. Gross believes that Madden's record as chairman of the NLRB was that of a "vigorous enforcement of the Act unmatched in the history of administrative agencies."[571] Madden quietly observed, with his mastery of understatement on display, that his era at the NLRB achieved its aims:

> *For better or for worse, the Wagner Act was, in my judgment, an almost unqualified success. It's the only fundamental piece of federal legislation that I have ever heard of that largely accomplished it purpose. It was intended to make workmen free to organize, and to make unions strong. It did both those things. I think along with a lot of other*

things, the effect of it has been quite inflationary. The bargaining strength of unions has had a very inflationary effect on the economy—whether that's good or bad I don't know. Certainly most of our people have lived very well under it.[572]

There was no counterpart, during this era of revolution, to a labor lawyer like William J. Brennen, trying to keep his union members out of trouble, or like Jacob Margolis, taking righteous stands on the freedom to speak and to assemble. The union lawyers milling around Pittsburgh during this period had almost nothing to say, either on the record or otherwise. They were effectively eclipsed for a brief period by hirees of the federal government like J. Warren Madden and Shad Polier, who were trying to establish the authority and legitimacy of the government over what had previously been the domain of the "traditions and precedents" of Pittsburgh business. Unlike Madden, most of the government lawyers would not have much of a connection to Pittsburgh. Pittsburgh's union lawyers would eventually regroup and redefine themselves as tacticians and negotiators after the revolution took hold.

Jones & Laughlin Steel Corp. was a turning point for Pittsburgh corporate lawyers. Labor law in Pittsburgh would cease to be the province of hard-boiled corporate field marshals such as Earl Reed; the successful management-side labor negotiators who would develop in Pittsburgh after *Jones & Laughlin Steel Corp.*, and even those within Reed's own law firm, would have to demonstrate other skills—like the ability to enjoy a shot and a beer with a union president, to engender face-to-face trust at the bargaining table at which they were forced to sit. Additionally, it would never hurt for them to summon up some of Earl Reed's guts and fearlessness when it came time to hash out the details of a collective bargaining agreement.

THE EARLY BAR

DAVID BRADFORD, a lawyer and leader of the Whiskey Insurrection. Gallatin called him "an empty drum, as ignorant, [indolent] & insignificant as he is haughty & pompous."

HUGH HENRY BRACKENRIDGE, Pittsburgh's first lawyer, America's first novelist: "[H]ow to be both free and orderly ... consumed the life of Hugh Henry Brackenridge at the beginning of the democratic experiment."

JUDGE ALEXANDER ADDISON: Pittsburgh's first judge "learned in the law" was impeached when the Democratic-Republicans assumed power in Pennsylvania.

President Washington, gathering with his troops near Fort Cumberland, Maryland, before heading West to quell the Whiskey Rebellion, from a 1795 painting. Brackenridge made jokes at Washington's expense at a gathering of rebels at Mingo Creek in 1794 and was, at least initially, targeted for arrest in connection with the Rebellion.

THE EARLY BAR

"THE GREAT TRIUMVIRATE"

HENRY BALDWIN, future congressman and U.S. Supreme Court justice.

TARLETON BATES: The county prothonotary, who died in Pittsburgh's last duel.

WALTER FORWARD, Baldwin's protégé – a future congressman, Secretary of the Treasury, ambassador to Denmark, and county judge.

Pittsburgh's first courthouse, on the Diamond, where Market Square is located today.

THE EARLY BAR

THOMAS J. BIGHAM, the "Sage of Mt. Washington," secured convictions against "runaway slave" kidnappers and was a clandestine leader of the Underground Railroad in Pittsburgh.

THOMAS J. KEENAN, a pioneer of international commercial law, founded the *Pittsburgh Legal Journal*, the second oldest legal periodical in the U.S., in 1853.

COL. SAMUEL W. BLACK, whom Judge Mellon called "impulsive and passionate," was a great orator of the Pittsburgh bar before his death in the Union cause at the Battle of Gaines Mill.

EDWIN M. STANTON, later the U.S. Attorney General and Lincoln's Secretary of War, was an influential member of the Pittsburgh bar during the late 1840s and 1850s.

THE GILDED BAR

THOMAS MELLON, lawyer and judge, was a forerunner to the business-oriented Pittsburgh lawyers of the Gilded Age, as founder of T. Mellon & Sons – the bank that helped to launch Pittsburgh's industrial heyday.

JAMES HAY REED and **PHILANDER C. KNOX** were the founders of the present-day law firm of Reed Smith. Through their representation of tycoons Andrew Carnegie and Henry Clay Frick, they played major roles in the controversies surrounding the Johnstown Flood, the Homestead Strike, the "World's Greatest Lawsuit," and the founding of U.S. Steel. Knox went on to serve as U.S. Attorney General under President Theodore Roosevelt and was influential in setting the government's antitrust policies.

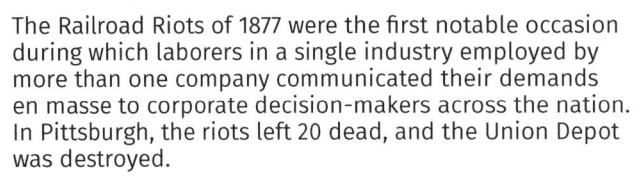

The Railroad Riots of 1877 were the first notable occasion during which laborers in a single industry employed by more than one company communicated their demands en masse to corporate decision-makers across the nation. In Pittsburgh, the riots left 20 dead, and the Union Depot was destroyed.

The present day Allegheny County Courthouse, designed by H.H. Richardson, was completed in 1887.

THE GILDED BAR

GEORGE WESTINGHOUSE and his patent lawyer **GEORGE H. CHRISTY**: "Skrabec says that Westinghouse looked like a walrus with his Victorian moustache and long coat; it is possible that together, the two Georges looked like a pair of walruses."

JOHN "CORPORATION" DALZELL: Made to order as an advisor to the captains of industry of Pittsburgh's Gilded Age; later, a long-time member of the House Ways and Means Committee.

D.T. WATSON, the brilliant philosopher of corporation law who helped Frick beat Carnegie, was the brains behind Knox's antitrust victory over *Northern Securities*, and argued for a "rule of reason" in antitrust cases in *Standard Oil*.

The attempted assassination of Henry Clay Frick by anarchist Alexander Berkman occurred at the height of the Homestead Strike of 1892, during which Philander Knox, for Carnegie Steel, and William Brennen, for the steelworkers, waged a behind-the-scenes battle over whether the union would continue to be recognized.

WILLIAM J. BRENNEN: A former pull-up boy and machinist at Jones & Laughlin Steel, Brennen became the first union lawyer in Pittsburgh. He also served as head of the County Democrats for many years, and as mentor to a young David L. Lawrence.

NEW PIONEERS

J. WELFRED HOLMES and **WILLIAM MAURICE RANDOLPH** (left) were admitted to the Pittsburgh bar in 1891. **AGNES FRASER WATSON** (right) was admitted in 1895.

JOSIAH COHEN, admitted in 1866, served as a common pleas judge from 1907 to 1930.

SARA SOFFEL, first woman judge in Pennsylvania.

ELLA GRAUBART, partner of the firm that became Tucker Arensberg.

ANNE X. ALPERN: first woman solicitor of a major city, first woman state attorney general; also a state supreme court justice and common pleas judge.

GEORGE B. VASHON, already admitted to practice in NY, was blocked by the Pittsburgh bar in 1847 and 1867.

ROBERT LEE VANN, lawyer and publisher of the *Pittsburgh Courier*.

HOMER S. BROWN, first African American judge in Pittsburgh, was a parliamentary genius behind Pittsburgh Renaissance legislation.

THE PROGRESSIVE ERA BAR

Lawyer at home, c. 1938: **JOHN G. BUCHANAN** (2nd from right) and his family outside their Murray Hill Avenue home. Left to right: eldest son John, Jr.; wife Charity Packer (niece of Carnegie lawyer Gibson Packer); youngest son, James; and middle son Gibson.

WILLIAM WATSON SMITH He and his firm began sparring with the U.S. government over Alcoa and the Sherman Act in 1911; he entered his last appearance for Alcoa in 1957, at age 86.

GEORGE W. GUTHRIE, first lawyer to be elected mayor of Pittsburgh since the early 19th century, ushered in a wave of municipal reform.

Princeton alumnus at War: Major **DAVID AIKEN REED**, son of James Hay Reed.

Asked at a congressional hearing how he would characterize himself politically, **JAKE MARGOLIS** (right) testified, "First, syndicalist; I put the syndicalist first, because it is an important thing; syndicalist-anarchist would be my position." He was disbarred in 1920, but later reinstated.

321

THE PROGRESSIVE ERA BAR

MICHAEL A. MUSMANNO (above), "with his wild, upswept, maestro-style hair, visually suggesting to those encountering him... that he was a man who had a big brain." He wrote *Black Fury* about the excesses of the Coal and Iron Police; it was later turned into a Hollywood movie, starring Paul Muni (above).

ACLU attorney **HENRY ELLENBOGEN** (right) barnstormed with **FATHER JAMES COX** and his "Jobless Army" before being elected to Congress and helping to lead the enactment of New Deal programs. He subsequently served on the common pleas bench for 40 years.

EARL REED (above, with steel tycoon **ERNEST T. WEIR**, right), led the efforts of the American Liberty League to have the National Labor Relations Act declared unconstitutional. Meanwhile, Pitt law professor **J. WARREN MADDEN** (right, with Secretary of Labor **FRANCES PERKINS**), was named as first chair of the NLRB, and argued against Reed in the seminal *Jones & Laughlin* case.

THE POST-WAR BAR

JIM MCARDLE: Railroad workers wrote his name and number on railroad cars.

NICHOLAS UNKOVIC: Instructions on swallowing a toad.

DAVID FAWCETT, JR. (left) and ACBA executive director **JIM SMITH** (right). Their leadership created one of the strongest local bar associations in the nation.

"Generals" of the Pittsburgh Renaissance: (left to right) **ARTHUR VAN BUSKIRK**, VP of T. Mellon & Sons, R.K. Mellon's right-hand man; **LELAND HAZARD**, VP of PPG and founder of WQED-TV; and **LEON HICKMAN**, VP of Alcoa.

Targeted as Communist Sympathizers: (left to right) **RUGGERO ALDISERT** defends **ALDO ICARDI**; **MARJORIE MATSON**, suspended from DA's office during "pink" inquiry; **HYMEN SCHLESINGER** (with moustache), testifying before Congress, with attorney **M.Y. STEINBERG**, at right.

THE POST-WAR BAR

EDGAR SNYDER

DICK THORNBURGH

ROZ LITMAN celebrates with her client, NBA star Connie Hawkins.

BOB DUGGAN

DR. CYRIL WECHT

After publicly feuding, it would fall to medico-legal adviser Cyril Wecht to determine Bob Duggan's cause of death.

DEALMAKERS

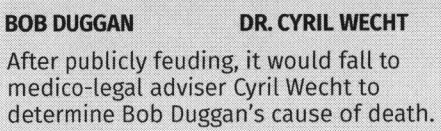

CHUCK QUEENAN

CARL BARGER

BILL NEWLIN

MARLEE MYERS

K. LEROY IRVIS

BYRD BROWN

WENDELL FREELAND

All images courtesy of the Allegheny County Bar Association, with permission of living subjects, except for the following: **Brackenridge**: painting by Clayton Braun, after Gilbert Stuart (1953), courtesy of Dickinson College Archives and Special Collections; **Bradford**: portrait of David Bradford, unattributed, from R.M. Devens, *Our First Century: being a popular descriptive portraiture of the One Hundred Great and Memorable Events of perpetual interest in the History of Our County* (Easton, Pa.: C.A. Nichols & Co., Mass., J.W. Lyon, Easton, Pa., 1876); **Whiskey Rebellion**: painting attributed to Frederick Kemmelmeyer (c. 1795), Metropolitan Museum of Art collection; **Addison**: from Bausman, *History of Beaver County, Pennsylvania and its centennial celebration* (New York: The Knickerbocker Press, 1904); **Courthouse at the Diamond**: lithograph by L. Braun, "Old Pittsburgh market & court house, taken down 1852," from a sketch by J.P. Robitzer, published c. 1866 by A. Krebs & Bro.; **Baldwin**: painting by Thomas Sully (1834), collection of the Supreme Court of the United States; **Bates**: miniature portrait by Charles Balthazar Julien Fevret de Saint-Mémin; University of Virginia Visual History Collection, Special Collections, University of Virginia Library; **Forward**: portrait by the Bureau of Engraving and Printing, Washington, D.C.; **Stanton**: photograph, c. 1860-70; Library of Congress, "Selected Civil War Photographs" collection; **Bigham**: from Coster, *A history of Grace Church parish, Mount Washington, Pittsburgh, Pa.* (Pittsburgh: Wm. G. Johnston, 1903); **Keenan**: from *Twentieth Century Bench and Bar of Pennsylvania* (Chicago: H.C. Cooper, Jr., Bro. & Co., 1903); **Black**: photograph, c. 1862, printed in *The University of Pittsburgh Record*, October 1926, Vol. 1, No. 1, p. 13; **Mellon**: from *Twentieth Century Bench and Bar of Pennsylvania* (Chicago: H.C. Cooper, Jr., Bro. & Co., 1903); **James Hay Reed**: courtesy Reed Smith collection; **Knox**: courtesy Reed Smith collection; **Railroad Riots**: "Destruction of the Union Depot," *Harper's Weekly* (August 11, 1877); **Allegheny County Courthouse**: author's collection; **Westinghouse**: photograph by Joseph G. Gessford, c. 1900-14; Library of Congress; **Dalzell**: Photograph by Clinedenst, from *National Magazine*, March 1905; **D.T. Watson**: photograph from Smith, *Notable Men of Pittsburgh and Vicinity* (Pittsburgh: Pittsburgh Printing Company, 1901); **Brennen**: from *National Cyclopedia of American Biography*, Current Volume B (New York: James T. White Company, 1927); **Frick Assassination Attempt**: Drawing from *Harper's Weekly* (August 6, 1892); **Holmes**: from *The Colored American*, Vol. IX, No. 39 (January 24, 1903); **Randolph**: from *The Crisis*, Vol. 24, No. 5 (September 1922); **Agnes Fraser Watson**: from *Pittsburgh Daily Post* (April 2, 1899), p.10; **Cohen**: courtesy of Rauh Jewish Archives, Heinz History Center; **Soffel**: photograph by Parry Pgh, courtesy of ACBA; **Vashon**: courtesy of Moorland-Springarn Research Center, Howard University, Associated Publishers collection; **Vann**: courtesy of Moorland-Springarn Research Center, Howard University, Associated Publishers collection; **Homer S. Brown**: photograph (c. 1939) from *Opportunity: Journal of Negro Life*, Vol. XVII. No. 1 (January 1939); **Guthrie**: Photograph (c. 1906-09) from Pittsburgh City Photographer Collection, 1901-2002, University of Pittsburgh, University Library System; **David Aiken Reed**: photograph from Library of Congress, George Grantham Bain Collection; **John G. Buchanan family**: courtesy Thomas G. Buchanan; **William Watson Smith**: photograph, c. 1918, from *Report of the Twenty-fourth Annual Meeting of the Pennsylvania Bar Association* (June 1918); **Margolis**: courtesy Barbara Margolis; **Musmanno**: courtesy of Duquesne University Archives and Special Collections; **Black Fury**: Lobby card for re-release by Dominant Pictures Corp., c. 1956, National Screen Service Corp., author's collection; **Ellenbogen and Cox**: courtesy of Rauh Jewish Archives, Heinz History Center; **Weir and Earl Reed**: ACME photograph (April 5, 1934), author's collection; **Madden and Perkins**: photograph by Harris & Ewing (Dec. 6, 1938); Library of Congress, Harris & Ewing Photographs; **Aldisert and Icardi**: United Press Telephoto, author's collection; **Matson**: courtesy of ACBA; **Schlesinger testifying**: reprinted from *Youngstown Vindicator*, November 29, 1956, © The Vindicator Printing Company, 1956; **Thornburgh**: Thornburgh for Governor Committee - Dick Thornburgh Papers, AIS.1998.30, Series 18: Photographs, Sub-Series 7. Campaign for Governor; **Wecht**: courtesy *Pittsburgh* magazine; **Snyder**: copyright ©, *Pittsburgh Post-Gazette*, 2019, all rights reserved. Reprinted with permission; **Litman and Hawkins**: photograph by Gary Renaud, from *Life*, June 27, 1968; **Queenan**: courtesy of Charles Queenan, Jr.; **Myers**: courtesy of Marlee Myers.

OUT IN THE OPEN

Between 1902 and 1942, among the hundreds of new lawyers who entered the profession in Pittsburgh, a total of sixty-five white women and thirteen African American men were admitted to the Allegheny County bar.[573] However, the political upheaval of the 1930s, the fights for civil liberties and the new political coalitions that helped to raise the status within the ranks of the bar of Henry Ellenbogen and Michael Musmanno and, by degrees, to bring their brethren among the ethnic Eastern European Jews and Italians in Pittsburgh into the mainstream, did not do the same thing for women and African Americans in the Pittsburgh bar. While the ambient forces of social and political assimilation could erase many of the differences in the brethren of Ellenbogen and Musmanno as perceived by white, Anglo-Saxon Protestants, the plainly visible differences of gender and race left the women and African Americans in the bar with no ability to step into the mainstream without somehow redefining it.

Ellen Crayne Hoge and her older cousin, Guy Hoge, both grew up in Waynesburg, about fifty miles south of Pittsburgh in Greene County. Guy graduated from Waynesburg College in 1913, and Ellen, from California (Pa.) State Teachers' College two years later. Ellen went to work as a grade school teacher in Greene County. Guy went straight on to Pittsburgh Law School and graduated in 1916, eventually practicing estates and trusts law with Reed Smith in Pittsburgh. A number of years later, Ellen began attending Duquesne Law School, and in 1930, Ellen entered the bar at age thirty-four, working as a stenographer to her preceptor, attorney E.M. Borger, the president of Peoples Natural Gas Company. Eventually she earned the right to be called an attorney there, was admitted to the Allegheny County Bar Association in 1940, participating, along with other women lawyers from Pittsburgh, in the National Association of Women Lawyers.[574] One corporate reorganization later, however, and by July 1956, Ellen Hoge was writing a letter to Josephine McDonagh, a secretary at the Bar Association, asking what the "average pay" was "for experienced legal secretaries who take a new position in Pittsburgh." She wrote, "In October I came to Seattle and since April I have been working in one of the big law firms for one of the partners whose secretary is on leave of absence for a trip to Europe. She may not return to this office and I may be offered a permanent position."[575] She eventually retired to Phoenix, where cousin Guy and his family moved after he retired from Reed Smith.

We have no way of knowing, of course, whether Ellen Hoge was a good lawyer, or a good legal secretary. We do know, however, that many features of Ellen Hoge's story were not unusual for women lawyers during the first half of the twentieth century. She came to the law late, as a middle-aged single woman, after working in a profession that was more typical of her gender in that era; she had a male relative in the bar; she found her highest status as a professional in a position that was largely tucked away from the public, in an in-house environment; and, despite her degree, she spent some part of her post-law school career working as a stenographer or a legal secretary rather than as a lawyer.

From 1902 to 1920, most of the women who were admitted to the Pittsburgh bar did not actually end up practicing law, at least not around Pittsburgh. A few of them were married shortly after they were admitted, much like Agnes Fraser Watson, Pittsburgh's first woman lawyer, and did not attempt to enter private practice. Mary Callan, who was admitted in 1918, married another Pittsburgh lawyer, James J. Cosgrove, as did Paula Cohen, who was admitted in 1920 and married Ben Lubic.[576] On the other hand, Suzanne Beatty, a Clarion College graduate who read law with James H. Osmer and was admitted in 1902, opened an office in the Frick Building which she shared with her sister, a contract stenographer. She maintained a largely unheralded law practice until she retired in 1940, supplementing her income by serving as a part-time assistant city solicitor under Mayor Charles H. Kline. Another single woman, Hanna Patterson, began her post-admission career in 1914 as a broker in the "women's department" of a Pittsburgh stock brokerage firm, and in 1919 served as Assistant Secretary of War.[577]

Government work was among the better opportunities available for women who wanted to practice law. For an ambitious woman lawyer in Pittsburgh in the 1910s, it was practically the only way to be noticed. From this era, Sara Mathilde Soffel was the one woman of the Pittsburgh bar who would be so noticed.

Soffel, known in her youth as "Sadie," was the daughter of Jacob Soffel, a Civil War veteran who worked for thirty-five years as a crier and interpreter in the Allegheny County Court of Common Pleas—introducing judges, calling witnesses to the stand, and so on—and later served as an alderman.[578] Her mother died when she was four. Sadie's elder cousin was Peter K. Soffel,[579] the warden of the Allegheny County jail—best known today as the hapless husband of "Mrs. Soffel." Kate Dietrich Soffel fell in love with a convicted murderer, Ed Biddle, and then helped Ed and his brother Jack break out of jail on January 2, 1902. A Pittsburgh detective, Lt. Buck McGovern, tracked the three of them to a farm in Butler County, and after a gun battle, the Biddle Brothers were dead, and Mrs. Soffel was wounded.[580] Mrs. Soffel was convicted for her role in the prison break and served two years in the Western Penitentiary; Peter divorced her and remarried. The tragic tale became headline news, of course, and eventually became the basis of a 1982 film, *Mrs. Soffel*, starring Diane Keaton and Mel Gibson.

Sadie was sixteen years old at the time of the jail break. After serving as valedictorian of her class at Central High School, she obtained her bachelor's degree, her letter in field hockey and her Phi Beta Kappa key at Wellesley College. After graduation she taught Latin at her alma mater, Central, and at Crafton High School. While teaching, she attended law school classes in the afternoon at Pitt Law School, and in 1916, at the age of thirty, Soffel graduated with highest honors. The tradition of the time was that the graduate at the top of the class was given a cash prize and a teaching fellowship at the law school; Ralph Longenecker, Richard Hawkins and Louis Caplan, for example, were among these award winners. In Sara Soffel's case, the School refused to give her the teaching fellowship, although they did pay her the money. Unable to find employment in a downtown firm, she opened her own practice in the Frick Annex Building; her first case came as a referral from her father, and she managed to settle it out of court to her client's benefit. In 1922, she was hired as an assistant city solicitor under Mayor William Magee—actually preceding Suzanne Beatty as the first woman lawyer in the city law department. Governor Fisher appointed her director of the Bureau of Women and Children in the Pennsylvania Department of Labor and Industry in 1929, and the following year, he appointed her to a seat on the Allegheny County Court to fill the vacancy created by the resignation of Judge Sylvester Snee, who was moving up to the Court of Common Pleas. Sara Soffel became the first woman judge in Pennsylvania.[581]

On August 27, 1930, dignitaries gathered in the fifth floor assignment room of the Allegheny County Courthouse for the investiture of Sara M. Soffel as a County Court judge. As Soffel greeted her guests, shots rang out just outside the courtroom, diagonally from the direction of the "desertion and non-support" office across the hall. Moments before, a twenty-one year-old woman, Clara Palschak, had entered the office and asked the attendant if she could see her husband Steve, who was waiting there for their court proceedings to begin. The two spoke briefly. Then, Mrs. Palschak pulled a pistol from her purse and fired it three times, hitting her husband in the abdomen.[582] He died soon afterward. As the papers reported, the Palschaks' divorce was to be the first case on Judge Soffel's docket. The newspapers were not immune to the ironies. "WIFE SHOOTS HER SPOUSE AS WOMAN JUDGE TAKES OATH," ran one headline.[583]

The greater irony would not be available to be identified until Judge Soffel's judicial career was underway. Judge Soffel was spectacularly successful at holding on to her post—she was elected to full term on the County Court the following year, beating a field of thirty-one candidates with the highest vote total ever polled by a judicial candidate. In 1941, she was elected to ten-year term on the Court of Common Pleas, and was re-elected in 1951. Predictably, she would be assigned to hear divorce, child custody, and juvenile criminal cases during much of her career.[584] She would not enjoy her electoral success on the back of a program of reform or women's rights. Her views on marriage were quite traditional. On the failure of so many marriages in their first few months, the stone-faced Judge Soffel cited that in her experience many young women go into marriage "blindly, as a 'gay lark,' wholly lacking in the knowledge of what it takes to make a home ... Many of them," she observed, "can't cook, or bake, or sew."[585] She advocated pre-marriage and pre-natal examinations "to further the battle against syphilis," training from the cradle for the duties of married life, and uniform marriage and divorce laws by constitutional amendment.[586] The greater irony, lost on smirking city editors in 1930, was that Steve Palschak would likely have received a fair hearing from Judge Soffel, in case anyone was expecting anything different. At that time, she would not attain the status of an elite member of the bench and bar by standing at the head of a parade of women demanding progress.

During the 1920s, there were several women who entered the bar and went into private practice with their husbands: there was Gertrude Friedlander Markel, who practiced with her husband Jacob after entering the bar in 1925; Mary Gaughan, who practiced with her husband Martin; Rebecca Davis Talenfeld, who practiced with her husband Samuel; and Ruth Levy Goldstein, who practiced with her husband George until their divorce. Several others worked for trust or loan companies; Potter Title and Trust Company hired at least three Pittsburgh woman lawyers during the 1910s and 20s.[587]

Two women who entered the bar in 1927 seemed to share a natural gravitas, as well as a natural sense of self-promotion, perhaps, that helped them to burst out of the conventions of their time.

One was Ella Graubart. In 1927, Ella Graubart was a thirty year-old homemaker and mother, married to an electrical engineer named Henry Richter and living in the Pittsburgh suburb of Mount Lebanon. A graduate of Hunter College in New York, Mrs. Richter received her LL.B from Pitt Law School, and entered the bar with her sword drawn. As Anne Weiss, society editor of the *Pittsburgh Press,* wrote in a 1933 profile of Graubart, "When a married woman applies for admission to the bar, it is customary for her to sign the application papers with the name of her husband, plus the 'Mrs.' prefix. But Mrs. Henry Richter wanted to practice law under her maiden name—Miss Ella Graubart." Graubart prepared a brief, "citing English and American authorities," and submitted it to the State Board of Law Examiners.[588] Her victory was covered by *The New York Times.*[589] (Unfortunately, the ruling in Graubart's case apparently had no precedential value. The next woman to attempt to be admitted under her maiden name, Marjorie Hanson, was turned down by the State Board in 1937 and rebuffed by the Pennsylvania Supreme Court. She had to enter the bar under her married name, Marjorie Matson.[590])

Having begun her career with a flourish of confidence, Graubart opened her own office and rapidly gained a reputation as an effective trial and appellate lawyer. In 1934, Graubart was invited to join the firm of Patterson, Crawford, Arensberg & Dunn as an associate. Patterson was an elite firm, and for a firm of its caliber, hiring a woman attorney was unprecedented in Pittsburgh. In Graubart's *Press* profile, she nonetheless towed a conservative line, declaring, "I am a mother first and a lawyer second ... There is no question as to which is more important—my home or my profession." She also noted that "[i]t requires patience as well as ability if a woman hopes to succeed in a profession that was, until a short while ago, man's exclusive field."[591] Within a few years after the *Press* profile was published, however, Ella Graubart and Henry Richter divorced, and in 1940, Graubart was elected as a partner of the Patterson firm, making her the first woman partner in a major Pittsburgh law firm.[592]

In addition to providing her with access to important Pittsburgh clients, the platform of such a firm—the resources that she had at her disposal within an important Pittsburgh law firm—also gave Graubart the opportunity to publicize her expertise within the profession in ways that were often reserved for elite members of the bar, as the author of numerous articles on trusts and trial procedure, and as chair of various committees within the Allegheny County, Pennsylvania and American Bar Associations—the committee on "modernization of writs," for example, or the committee on procedural rules. Her intellectual curiosity stubbornly ran well outside the parameters of so-called "women's" legal issues. Her image, finely honed, was also one that embodied community leadership—as the first woman president of the First Unitarian Church in Shadyside and a director of Point Park Junior College.[593] We may observe that participation in these kinds of activities is almost mundane today, something we might generally expect to see in the resume of any lawyer of any race or gender, but it conveyed a different thought about a woman partner of an important law firm in the 1940s; in context, these activities lent additional proof that a woman could independently, willingly and capably take ownership of the role of an elite lawyer, in all its public facets. Graubart would not be hidden away.

Charles F.C. Arensberg's first wife, Emily, died in July 1948,[594] while Graubart was just returning from traveling through Eastern Europe on behalf of a client, "making a study of the Russian satellite states," as the *Press* reported. In August 1949, Arensberg and Graubart were married at the First Unitarian Church, with a reception following at the Pittsburgh Golf Club. A photo caption in the *Sun-Telegraph* read, singularly, "Ella Graubart weds law partner."[595] Graubart was fifty-two, Arensberg was sixty-nine, but they seemed well-suited to each other—they were both "Renaissance" people, with ravenous appetites for *scientia gratis scientiae*, "knowledge for knowledge's sake." Graubart continued practicing at Patterson (subsequently known as Tucker Arensberg) until she and Arensberg retired to Florida in 1965.[596]

The other woman who shared something of Graubart's gifts for moving through the ranks, who also entered the bar in 1927, was Anne X. Alpern. A smarmy 1946 *Collier's* profile of Alpern, the "Portia of Pittsburgh," described her this way:

> *Aside from the smoke the most noteworthy thing about Pittsburgh, Pennsylvania, at this writing is probably its city solicitor. That functionary is unique in a lot of ways: (1) She's a lady. (2) She's still in her thirties. (3) She has a facility for making judges change their minds. (4) She gets more than her allotment of wolf whistles. Her name is Anne X. Alpern and she has succeeded in reversing the Horatio Alger formula for success: Born into a well-to-do family, living on fashionable Beechwood Boulevard and happily married, she has managed to turn a potential life of ease into a 20-hour-a-day grind.*[597]

Alpern's legend, preserved in press clippings, is full of colorful stories and factual vagaries, and one wonders sometimes where the truth lies—a tribute to Alpern's mastery at framing her own identity. According to Census records, however, Alpern was born in the Ukraine and immigrated to the U.S. with her mother and four of her siblings when she was five years old, a couple of years after her father and older brothers had landed and established a wholesale hosiery business near Washington, Pennsylvania. Her father, from Poland, met and married her mother in Lithuania. The entire family spoke Yiddish before they arrived in the U.S., but, so the legend goes, her father became an avid reader of English. Anne grew up hearing about the exploits of Clarence Darrow, one of her father's heroes. "From the time I was a little girl," Alpern recalled, "it was his wish that I become an attorney and like Darrow, help the unfortunate." She attended the Pennsylvania College for Women (now Chatham University), then finished her bachelor's degree at the University of Pittsburgh, going on to receive her LL.B at Pitt Law School.[598]

She was hired out of law school by the downtown firm of Cunningham, Galbraith & Dickson, located on the thirteenth floor of the Park Building on Fifth Avenue and headed by some-time state senator Kenneth R. Cunningham. Alpern would say, "I was never really discriminated against because I was woman. Of course, they didn't pay me as much as a man ... And where mediocrity was accepted in a man, it wasn't in a woman. So as a woman, I had to work harder to prove my capabilities." Alpern was a gifted writer with the gift of spoken gab as well. Cunningham slated her to write briefs, but she wanted courtroom work. In response, she was handed the "office lemon," the unwinnable appeal that the firm was nonetheless bound to take on due to its relationship with a client. The client had refused to pay for a set of awnings on delivery because of a small rip on one of them. The judge asked Alpern—who walked into court on one evening's preparation without books or notes, citing cases from memory—why a minor rip should render the awning unfit. She drew a gender-based analogy, straight out of the family business. "If you are familiar with a run in a woman's stocking," she said, "you will understand the nature of the damage." The story goes that the blushing judges found in her client's favor.[599]

Alpern's rise was ultimately achieved through politics, but her entry into political life was somewhat accidental. After years of running unsuccessfully for office, attorney William N. McNair, a Democrat, was elected mayor in 1933, following the resignation of disgraced Republican mayor Charles H. Kline. David L. Lawrence, head of the County Democrats, tepidly embraced the erratic candidate, although Lawrence regarded him as a loose cannon. Once in office, McNair chose a Lawrence comrade, Cornelius Scully, as his city solicitor.[600] After only a few months, McNair fired Scully, which prompted four members of Scully's staff—assistant city solicitors Austin Staley, A.L. Wolk, Manuel Kraus and James L. O'Toole, Jr.—to resign, leaving the city short on lawyers. "I'll carry on the law department's work," McNair fumed. "Why not? I'm a lawyer. I can handle it."[601] Rather than attempt to fulfill the duties of the city solicitor's office himself, however, McNair hired a new solicitor, Ward Bonsall; and among the "temporary" assistant city solicitors he brought in were Kenneth Cunningham's partner, Wilbur F. Galbraith, and, as "third assistant city solicitor," Anne X. Alpern, initially "without pay."[602] The next several months would see considerable turmoil in the city solicitor's office, as Bonsall died in June 1935, and Bonsall's replacement, William D. Grimes, would be pressured by McNair into resigning in March 1936. Alpern had, by then, graduated to "first assistant," and was asked to assume the duties of the solicitor until Grimes' replacement, Gregory Zatkovich, was named.[603]

Gregory Zatkovich was a colorful character in his own right. Born in Austria-Hungary, he immigrated to Pennsylvania with his parents at age two. His father was the editor of an activist journal supporting Rusyn-Americans, an ethnic group from Carpathian Ruthenia, an area now within Slovakia and western Ukraine. Zatkovich grew up in Pittsburgh, received his bachelor's degree from the University of Pennsylvania in 1907, and earned his law degree there three years later. He entered the Pittsburgh bar in October 1910. In July 1918, as the Austro-Hungarian monarchy was on the verge of collapse, Rusyn-Americans began to agitate for the independence of Carpathian Ruthenia. As a leader of the Rusyn movement, Zatkovich was convinced by members of the Wilson administration that merging Carpathian Ruthenia into a new Czech state was the only viable option, and he was convinced to sign the "Philadelphia Agreement" with Czech president Tomas Masaryk, upon the promise that Carpathian Ruthenia would be granted autonomy within the new Czech state. Masaryk appointed Zatkovich governor of the province on April 20, 1920. He served for a little less than a year, resigning on April 17, 1921 over disagreements on the border with Slovakia, and returned to his practice in Pittsburgh. He has the distinction of being the only American citizen to have presided as governor over a province that would later become a part of the Soviet Union.[604]

Meanwhile, in October 1936, in the middle of a deadlock with the city council over financial matters, William McNair suddenly submitted his resignation. City council immediately accepted it and elected attorney Cornelius Scully, the Council president installed by David Lawrence after Scully was fired as city solicitor by McNair in 1934, as McNair's successor. About a week later, McNair attempted to rescind his resignation, with Gregory Zatkovich arguing that the city council could not have properly accepted McNair's resignation without posting a proposed ordinance on it for twenty-four hours prior to taking action.[605] McNair, however, would not be permitted to return to his post. Acting Mayor Scully fired Zatkovich and hired his own former law partner, war hero Churchill B. Mehard, as city solicitor.[606] Alpern, still the first assistant, somehow escaped the axe. After Scully's re-election as mayor in 1937, Mehard was accused of taking bribes in exchange for quick, lucrative out-of-court settlements on lawsuits against the city. Attorney Morris Levy confessed that he acted as the bag man for $11,499 in bribes to Mehard over a six month period. After a long investigation and trial, during which Alpern functioned as acting city solicitor, Levy was convicted and sentenced to nine months in prison, and Churchill Mehard was convicted and sentenced to three years, of which he would serve fifteen months.[607] Mayor Scully won re-election again in 1941, barely, and after several years of the city enduring a revolving door of city solicitors, a collection of circus-like headlines and a cauldron of corruption, Scully promoted the dependable Alpern to the city solicitor's position in 1942. "Miss Alpern finally became City Solicitor … after doing much of the work of that post for eight years," noted the *Press*.[608]

For Alpern, it was only the beginning. In 1937, she had married a fellow assistant city solicitor, Irwin Swiss ("City Hall's dark-haired Portia, First Asst. City Solicitor Anne X. Alpern, and Irwin A. Swiss, another city solicitor, will leave Pittsburgh today for New York to be married," gushed the *Press*[609]); two years later, she gave birth to her daughter Marsha, with only a brief interruption of her work for the city.[610] When David Lawrence was elected mayor in 1945, he kept Alpern in place as city solicitor, and backed the enormously popular woman lawyer when she decided to run for a seat on the Allegheny County Court of Common Pleas in 1953. "'X' marks the spot," was her rallying cry, although she would never exactly go on the record about her mysterious middle initial. "It stands for 'X' on the ballot," she would say, although some would maintain that she added the "X" to her name in law school "to add a little color."[611] She won both the Democratic and Republican nominations, and took her place on the bench, alongside Judges Soffel and Ellenbogen, and others, in 1954. Her publicity, now moving beyond remarks about "wolf whistles," portrayed her as a homemaker wearing a judge's robes. "She's a dandy cook," said the *Press*. "Her Yankee pot roast is famed far and wide, and people who have tasted her chicken-and-steak rolls say there's nothing like them this side of paradise."[612] Such patronizing portraits did, however, provide more texture to Alpern's reputation as a lawyer and a jurist who was aspiring to be seen as a defender of "the consumer."

After David Lawrence was inaugurated as governor of Pennsylvania in 1959, he chose Alpern as the first woman Attorney General of the Commonwealth of Pennsylvania, and then, in 1961, as the first woman justice on the Pennsylvania Supreme Court. She lost her re-election bid, but Lawrence re-appointed her to the Court of Common Pleas, where she served until 1974.[613] Lawrence may have been squeamish about throwing support behind ethnic types, from time to time, but he knew a magnet for publicity when he saw one.

Although Alpern flourished in electoral politics and Graubart earned respect in the male-dominated corridors of the American Bar Association and the downtown bar, both did so through an expert manipulation of their respective public images. They both endeavored to show their superior intellects while at the same time continuing to appear as paragons of womanly virtues. And neither of them would tackle women's rights in any controversial fashion.

Meanwhile, the maze of federal agencies that grew up during the 1930s and '40s bestowed employment upon a number of Pittsburgh women lawyers who entered the bar during that period. Mary Lemon Schleifer's husband Elmer died in December 1929, leaving her with a baby daughter to support. She was a private school substitute teacher while he was alive, but in 1930 she decided to go to law school.[614] While at Pitt, she worked with Judson Crane on a new edition of the *Restatement of the Law of Agency*. At age twenty-nine, she entered the bar and within a few years she found herself working as a staff attorney with the NLRB in Washington under J. Warren Madden. By the 1950s, Schleifer was associate chief counsel of the Wage Stabilization Board.[615] Katharine Loomis also worked in the NLRB, as well as in the Office of Alien Property at the Department of Justice.[616] Agnes Dodds, the daughter of Reed Smith's Robert Dodds, Sr., served as chief of the British Colonies section of the Lend-Lease Administration.[617] Rose Daniels, Rosina Beck and Dorothy Grote all worked in the Office of Price Administration.[618]

On the whole, the choices for women during the first half of the twentieth century were largely limited to taking up junior partnerships with lawyer-husbands, in-house roles, or government—or, not practicing at all. Almost none of the established Pittsburgh law firms were entertaining the idea of hiring women as lawyers. The real problem for women trying to sustain one-woman law firms was still the lack of a natural community available to them as a clientele. Women were non-autonomous as clients. Women who lived within the elite economic ranks in Pittsburgh tended to visit elite male lawyers; working class Italian American women would see male Italian American lawyers; and so on—so most women who operated their own practices usually spent a portion of their careers supplementing their income with government work. As opportunities opened within federal practice with the New Deal, women lawyers were attracted to them because for the vast majority of these women lawyers, there was still nowhere else to go.

As Robert L. Vann, a Pittsburgh African American attorney and business leader, told a meeting of the National Bar Association in August 1937, the increase in federal agency authority was "tending to place social problems under bureaus and boards. It is not tending to increase litigation." It did not necessarily follow, for a group of lawyers whose bread and butter came from clients within an autonomous, albeit somewhat segregated community, that the activity created by the New Deal offered any great opportunity for advancement. The problems facing male African American lawyers were very different from those of white women lawyers, and they were inextricably related to the development of the African American community in Pittsburgh. Vann argued that the "Negro lawyer must take leadership in the economic life of the community. He must interest himself in modest enterprises, modestly financed, so that in the next quarter century he may find himself inheriting clients of a new type. Negro lawyers should lead the economic life of a community toward Negro industrials."[619] It was to be a source of great disappointment for Vann that a full-blown African American economy, capable of sustaining the efforts of the small, segregated African American bar to build a practice, had not already arisen by 1937 within Pittsburgh.

When William M. Randolph and J. Welfred Holmes were admitted to the Pittsburgh bar in 1891, Pittsburgh's African American population was nearing the end of a dramatic increase, from approximately two thousand in 1870 to twenty thousand in 1900.[620] The "Old Pittsburghers" or "OPs,"—who, according to Vann's biographer Andrew Bunie, were "members of the local black elite comprised of early settlers who were prosperous enough to support a middle-class lifestyle"[621]—built and supported a number of important cultural institutions around Pittsburgh, including, as Laurence Glasco has observed, "an AME (African Methodist Episcopal) church, an AME Zion church, four benevolent societies, a private school, a cemetery, a militia company, a newspaper, and a temperance society," as well as a number of social clubs, such as the Loendi, the White Rose Club and the Goldenrod Social Club, and literary societies, such as the Aurora Reading Club and the Wylie Avenue Literary Society.[622] Randolph and Holmes were not from Pittsburgh originally, but by dint of their educational and professional attainments, they were welcomed within the ranks of the OPs and took their places within the leadership of black Pittsburgh.

The community that the OPs managed to create may seem idyllic in retrospect, but segregation in places like restaurants and theaters, as well as employment discrimination, were cold realities during the period. There were important exceptions to this rule, however. Pittsburgh had a desegregated school system from 1875 onward, although the School Board would not be required to hire African American teachers until the

1930s.[623] Also, some members of the African American middle class in Pittsburgh held employment that placed them into contact with whites on a daily basis. Among the eighty-five black-run businesses in Pittsburgh in 1909, some African American barbers had downtown establishments with almost exclusively white patrons, as did the caterers Spriggs and Witt and the wigmaker Proctor, as well as several grocers and restaurant owners.[624]

While the OPs may have created a "black metropolis" within Pittsburgh, there was only one bar and one system of local courts. When Randolph and Holmes launched their practices, they did so downtown, on Fourth Avenue—not in Allegheny City, where many of the OPs had settled over the years, or in the Hill District, where the black population was then growing. Likewise, William Henry Stanton had an office on Fourth Avenue, and Walter Billows and Cap Stewart opened their practices on Grant Street.[625] Their proximity to the courts, their relatively small numbers among the white bar, and the relatively small African American population in Pittsburgh generally during the period—as well, perhaps, as the observation among white lawyers of the success of the cultural institutions of the OPs, and a recognition of the African Americans of Pittsburgh as an emerging voting bloc—all actually seemed to operate to encourage, for a time, the limited integration of this small band of African American lawyers within the legal profession during the first decade of the twentieth century. For example, Walter Billows briefly served as an assistant district attorney under District Attorney John C. Haymaker, and Mayor William Magee appointed William M. Randolph as assistant city solicitor, a post he held from 1909 to 1914, and again from 1922 to 1934.[e][626]

Sometimes the political motivations of the white bar were all too apparent. At a 1909 meeting of the Pennsylvania Odd Fellows, an African American fraternal order, city solicitor Harry M. Irons addressed Pittsburgh's African American elite, referring to the Republican Party as the party of "liberty and freedom" and lauding Mayor Magee's policy "of encouraging worthy and representative Negroes by appointment to office, as in the appointment of Wm. M. Randolph" to the solicitor's office. Irons concluded his remarks by saying:

> *On behalf of the Mayor, the city is now yours so long as you walk in the straight and narrow path, and should you stray from it call on the city fathers and we will do what we can for you as the sun sometimes refuses to shine in Pittsburg. I give you both the key and canteen.*[627]

For Randolph, the post was anything but ceremonial; he did appear to assume significant authority over city litigation, and was a visible member of the city law department.

---

[e] It has been asserted that a "William Randolph Grimes" was the first African American to be appointed as a city solicitor; see Trotter & Day, eds., *Race and Renaissance: African Americans in Pittsburgh Since World War II* and Bunie, *Robert L. Vann of the Pittsburgh Courier: Politics and Black Journalism*. In fact, William Maurice Randolph was appointed in 1909, and the name "William Randolph Grimes" does not appear on the Allegheny County attorney rolls during the period. There was a "William D. Grimes" who served as city solicitor during 1935-36, but census records indicate that this Grimes was white. His daughter, Martha Grimes, is known as the author of the "Richard Jury" series of detective novels.

Around the time Robert Lee Vann was admitted to the bar in 1910—the first African American to be admitted in fifteen years, and the second to be admitted in the twentieth century—the African American community in Pittsburgh was at the precipice of significant change. As Glasco relates:

Economic expansion and the war-related cut-off of European immigration forced northern industries to open up factory jobs for the first time to black Americans. This touched off a migratory wave from the South that, between 1910 and 1930, increased the northern black population by more than five hundred thousand. Newly opened jobs at places like Jones & Laughlin Steel enlarged Pittsburgh's black population from twenty-five to fifty-five thousand, while hiring by Carnegie Steel plants in Aliquippa, Homestead, Rankin, Braddock, Duquesne, McKeesport, and Clairton raised the black population in those neighboring towns from five to twenty-three thousand.[628]

While the "Great Migration" fueled a Hill District renaissance in nightlife (on Wylie Avenue and its side streets), music (nurturing such jazz greats as Billy Strayhorn, Kenny Clarke, Lena Horne, Mary Lou Williams, Earl Hines and Art Blakey), and baseball (led by the independent Negro baseball clubs, the Pittsburgh Crawfords and the Homestead Grays, and their stars, such as Josh Gibson, Cool Papa Bell, Satchel Paige and Oscar Charleston), the influx of African Americans from the deep South caused rifts in Pittsburgh's African American community and, paradoxically, may have contributed to setbacks in the limited integration of African Americans in the mainstream life of Pittsburgh between World Wars I and II.

The newly-arrived African Americans from the deep South were largely unskilled workers from impoverished backgrounds, looking for work at the mills, in contrast to the OPs and other members of Pittsburgh's black middle class, who were barbers, waiters, butlers and janitors, if they were not professionals or entrepreneurs. As Heineman and Bunie both recount, middle class African Americans found the blacks from the deep South to be "uncouth," and through middle-class institutions such as the *Pittsburgh Courier*, they "chastised" them for their "anti-social behavior"—divorce, drinking, and violence.[629] Like the German-American Jews of Pittsburgh who were afraid that the newly-arrived Eastern European Jews would lead to increased anti-Semitic sentiment, the middle-class African Americans feared that the behavior of the new arrivals would increase racism against all African Americans. It would seem that they had reason to feel that way, as black employment opportunities began to be marginalized, away from downtown. As Glasco writes, "In 1900 blacks operated most of the city's prestigious downtown barbershops; by 1930 they operated almost none. In 1900 they had driven most of the city's taxis, hacks, buses and trucks; by 1930 they drove mainly garbage trucks."[630] African American opportunity seemed to be on the decline in Pittsburgh as Pittsburgh's African American population grew.

The city's African American lawyers, in some sense, fared no better as the Great Migration took its toll on Pittsburgh. The assistant's chair granted to African Americans in the city law department would remain a fixture for much of the rest of the century, although it would not be awarded with as much fanfare as suggested by Harry Irons' speech to the Odd Fellows in 1909; when Robert Vann held the position in 1918, it would be diminished by being given the designation of "fourth assistant city solicitor," and then temporarily eliminated by budget cuts in 1921.[631] Sara Soffel and Anne Alpern would move from the city law department to the County bench as a result of a gubernatorial appointment or other political favor, but during this period there were no such offers for Pittsburgh's African American lawyers. And while for a time, a number of the more prominent African American lawyers of Pittsburgh would continue to maintain their offices downtown, little by little they would find themselves most significantly represented at 806 Wylie Avenue or in the Descalzi Building at 1004 Wylie Avenue, professional buildings in the Hill District, where African Americans represented from seventy-three percent to ninety-five percent of the population, depending on the neighborhood, by 1950.[632] The African American bar had become, by 1942, even more practically segregated than it had begun the century.

Robert Lee Vann, meanwhile, would benefit in his business life, to some degree, from the consequences of segregation (or perhaps its flipside, "congregation"), as the publisher of an African American newspaper and a business leader in his community—even if his law practice was beset by the same troubles as his black colleagues at the bar. He was born to a single young woman who was working as a family cook on a farm in rural Hertford County, North Carolina. She gave her son the surname "Vann" after the first family for whom she worked, the same surname as several prominent white families in the area. Both he and his mother were light-skinned, and Vann also had a "strong straight nose" from his half-white grandmother, and "elegant good looks"—all of which, suggests Bunie, "would facilitate his later acceptance in a world of business and politics as yet unprepared to embrace the most African blacks."[633] From the age of fourteen, Vann worked as a janitor, postal clerk and tobacco field hand to save enough money to attend a private school for young African Americans in Hertford County. He graduated as valedictorian, then attended Wayland Academy, the preparatory school of Virginia Union University in Richmond, Virginia, and then Virginia Union itself for a couple of years before heading north to Pittsburgh and enrolling in 1903 at the University of Pittsburgh as a sophomore with an Avery Scholarship of one hundred dollars. Through the family with whom he boarded, he was introduced to the social circles of the OPs.[634]

While at Pitt, he became known as an orator and student journalist—as a member of the Tri-State Debating League championship team, winner of 2nd Place in the Senior Oratorical Contest, and finally, as the first black editor of the student body journal, *The Courant*. He also ventured into politics, campaigning for the local Republican candidate, Alexander M. Jenkinson, the Stogie heir, against George Guthrie for mayor in 1906. "Despite his age, his poverty, and his blackness," writes Bunie, at age twenty-seven, Vann managed to receive his bachelors degree later that year. While he considered going to the Pulitzer School of Journalism in New York, he elected to stay in Pittsburgh and enter its Law School, in the same class with Jacob Margolis, working as a white-jacketed dining car waiter on night runs of the Pittsburgh and Lake Erie Railroad to pay for his first-year room and board. His diligence impressed Elder Marshall, the teaching fellow, who noted that "the professors were delighted that he had the necessary ambition to study law and become a lawyer, rather than continue in the dining car service." Through the intercession of an OP, he received a patronage job in the mercantile assessor's office the following year, and he clerked with William Henry Stanton. He finished courses in June 1909, passed the bar, and opened his own office at 433 Fifth Avenue.[635]

There was approximately one African American attorney for every five thousand African American residents in Pittsburgh in 1910.[636] Nonetheless, Vann found it difficult to build a practice quickly, according to Bunie:

> ... the average black who migrated from the South to Pittsburgh remembered the great handicap lawyers of his race suffered there, because of discriminatory courts and inequitable law and custom. He therefore thought twice about hiring a black attorney ... Most blacks could barely afford a lawyer's fee, and if they had to pay a sizable amount of hard-earned money, they preferred to have a white attorney who, because of the inherent advantage of color, stood a better chance of winning their cases than a fellow black. The black lawyer almost inevitably encountered prejudice on the part of white judges and juries, even in the North.[637]

Influenced by Stanton, Vann decided to be a criminal lawyer. "I might as well go into criminal law," he once remarked, "since all of my people are criminals." However, the first-degree murder cases were most often handled by white lawyers, so along with handling lesser offenses, Vann also worked on wills, deeds and property claims.[638]

In March 1910, he was asked by a few acquaintances to represent them in the incorporation of a new weekly newspaper for the local black readership, to be called the *Pittsburgh Courier*. The paper was the idea of a Heinz plant guard named Edwin Nathaniel Harleston, but Harleston quit the paper in the fall of 1910, leaving the remaining partners to ask Vann if he would assume the editorship. He agreed to do so, for an annual salary of one hundred dollars, payable in *Courier* stock. To a large degree, in addition to his coverage of the lives and lifestyles of the OPs, the *Courier* gave Vann an opportunity to tout his own professional expertise—covering his courtroom exploits as news—but also to drive his political viewpoints, not only by covering such issues as the fight for better education, improved housing and equal employment for Pittsburgh's African Americans, but also by supporting political candidates.[639] Though the newspaper had its financial ups and downs over the years, by 1937 the *Courier* had become one of the leading black newspapers in the U.S., with a national circulation of 250,000.[640]

Vann himself played a significant role in the 1917 mayoral campaign. Vann was, like most African Americans of the day, a loyal Republican. In Pittsburgh, of course, that meant being loyal to the (William) Magee machine, even after the reform movement led by George Guthrie and Leo Weil uncovered massive corruption in the Republican ranks. Vann did not appreciate the insinuations of reformers that the Republicans courted illegal black votes, or, as Bunie describes, that blacks were "brutes, keepers of white women, proponents of vice, gambling, and physical violence."[641] During the 1912 presidential election, in which Republican incumbent William Howard Taft faced a challenge from the independent Republicans by way of his old political patron, Theodore Roosevelt, Vann was adamant. "Anything but a Democrat," he wrote. "Brethren, black Democrats will not be in style this fall." During the 1913 mayoral contest, Vann supported the unsuccessful Magee faction Republican candidate, Stephen Geyer Porter, working with the white Irish boss of the heavily African American Fifth Ward, James F. Malone, Sr., to bring black voters to Porter.[642]

In 1917, William Magee decided to run for mayor again. Magee had been popular within the African American community for his appointment of William Randolph as assistant city solicitor in 1909. But he was being faced by an independent Republican named Edward V. Babcock, a lumber magnate who had been appointed by Governor John Tener to serve as one of the first nine city councilmen under the reorganized Pittsburgh city council in 1911. Vann made a decision to drop Magee and support Babcock after Babcock promised to appoint him to a city position in exchange for his help in securing the African American vote in Pittsburgh. The fact that Babcock also advertised in the *Courier* did not hurt. Vann assisted Malone in the Fifth Ward and wrote long pro-Babcock editorials. Babcock carried the day in the general election, 40,604 to 36,174, and Vann was given credit for helping to carry two out of three wards where black voters were the majority.[643]

Following the election, Babcock appointed Vann as "fourth assistant city solicitor" at a salary of $2,650 per year, and Vann's business manager at the *Courier*, Ira Lewis, was given a clerkship in the office of the newly-elected sheriff, another Babcock candidate. Although he was initially only given routine cases that involved African Americans, city solicitor Stephen Stone began to give Vann more complex cases. "I tried these cases for four years before juries," Vann said, "chiefly all white—certainly the judges were all white and the witnesses were all white—and was not reversed a single time. I was taken to the [State] Supreme Court only once and won the case before that tribunal, making a perfect score for my years as attorney for the City of Pittsburgh."[644] In 1921, however, the city council, still loyal to Magee, cut Vann's position, ostensibly due to budgetary concerns, and Vann's city government career came to an abrupt end.[645] Moreover, when Magee reemerged as a successful mayoral candidate in 1921, Vann effectively lost his local political power. Magee reappointed William Randolph to his old post as assistant city solicitor after he won the next mayoral election and took office in 1922.[646]

Just about the time that Vann was leaving the city law department, Homer Sylvester Brown was half way toward finishing his LL.B from Pitt Law School. Brown was born in 1896 in Huntington, West Virginia, the third son of seven children of a Baptist minister and his wife. When he was seven, the family moved to Roanoke, Virginia, where he attended public schools. As Homer reached his mid-teens, the family resolved to move to Pittsburgh, where opportunity was more plentiful, but his father secured funds to place Homer into Wayland Academy, the preparatory school in Richmond that Robert Vann had attended. He entered Virginia Union at the age of eighteen, majoring in political science and singing in the University Double Quartet. During the summers he followed his family to Pittsburgh and worked in steel mills. After a brief stint in the U.S. Army, he entered the Law School, and in 1923 became its third African American graduate, along with his friend Richard F. Jones, from Lynchburg, Virginia. Jones graduated at the top of their class and was the first African American to be inducted into Pittsburgh's chapter of the Order of the Coif. Brown's connections with Wayland and Virginia Union caught the eye of Robert Vann, who invited Brown to join his practice. Brown demurred, however, preferring to set up his own law firm with Richard Jones, eventually setting up offices in the Descalzi Building.[647]

The year after he entered the bar, Brown assumed the presidency of the Pittsburgh chapter of the National Association for the Advancement of Colored People (NAACP), which had been active, though not robust, under the leadership of Pastor J.C. Austin of the Ebenezer Baptist Church for about a decade. Brown energized the group. Not only did the position give Brown the opportunity to supplement his income from his legal practice, but it put him on the front lines of the fights over racial segregation in Pittsburgh—in public schools (his partner Richard F. Jones would win a case against the Pittsburgh Board of Education in 1937, resulting in the employment of Pittsburgh's first black teacher), housing and in public places—and catapulted him into a circle of energetic, younger black activists throughout the country, such as Ralph Bunche, Thurgood Marshall and Roy Wilkins.[648] Although Vann and Brown were ostensibly good personal friends during Brown's early years with the NAACP, as Brown gained credibility as a voice for African American civil rights in Pittsburgh, however, their interests would begin to diverge and they grew distant from each other.

Vann had lost his preeminence as a local political power broker on behalf of the African American community when the independent Republicans lost to William A. Magee in the 1921 mayoral race. Homer Brown entered the fray in 1929, supporting Judge Richard W. Martin, one of two independent Republicans seeking to unseat Mayor Charles Kline (the other being James F. Malone, Sr.) and a member of the panel that reinstated Jacob Margolis to the bar. Once again, however, the Republican machine was victorious.[649] Meanwhile, from his editorial rostrum at the *Courier*, Vann had by this time turned his attention to national politics; but after working hard for both Coolidge in 1924 and Hoover in 1928, without receiving a hoped-for federal appointment, his patience was wearing thin, and he was beginning to consider "turning Lincoln's picture to the wall" and defecting to the Democratic Party.[650] Vann would remain a Republican for one more campaign, in which former governor Gifford Pinchot was running as an "anti-machine" Republican. Vann led the *Courier* in endorsing Pinchot, and Pinchot ended up winning every African American ward in Pittsburgh in the 1930 election. Statewide, Pinchot's margin of victory was small enough that Vann could credibly claim that his activism was a decisive factor in the results; however, the most he would receive from Governor Pinchot for his efforts was a "little note of appreciation for his assistance in the campaign."[651]

After 1930, Vann was finished with the Republican Party. Next would come an outright conversion to the Democratic Party, which oddly enough would be precipitated by a meeting with Michael Benedum, the Pittsburgh oil wildcatter. Benedum, who would later turn on Franklin Roosevelt by helping to form the American Liberty League, was as anti-Republican as anyone in 1932, having suffered through a federal prosecution under the last three Republican administrations concerning an alleged seventy-nine million dollar tax delinquency. Benedum asked Vann, "What had the Negro ever gotten by voting the Republican ticket?," which was in fact Vann's very same question to himself. "Nothing," Vann replied. Vann snapped into action in an odd way, by contacting the black beautician who served Mrs. Emma Guffey Miller and asking her to convey the message that Vann wanted to speak with her brother, Joseph Guffey, one of the state's Democratic leaders and a strategist for Roosevelt. Vann convinced Guffey that "he could personally help the Democrats capture the state's black votes," which by 1932 potentially numbered around 275,000.[652]

Vann was invited to help to establish the "Colored Advisory Committee" of the national Democratic Party, through which he worked behind the scenes helping the Party network with black leaders across the country.[653] In September 1932, Vann delivered a key address at the St. James Forum in Cleveland. His support for the Democrats was now full-throated and public, and it earned national coverage. In his address, against the backdrop of the Depression and its effects upon the nation's African Americans, Vann gutted the idea of a partnership between African Americans and the Republican Party:

> *So long as the Republican party could use the photograph of Abraham Lincoln to entice Negroes to vote a Republican ticket they condescended to accord Negroes some degree of political recognition. But when the Republican party had built itself to the point of security, it no longer invited Negro support ... The Republican party under Harding absolutely deserted us. The Republican party under Mr. Coolidge was a lifeless, voiceless thing. The Republican party under Mr. Hoover has been the saddest failure known to political history ... The only true gauge by which to judge an individual or a party or a government is not by what is proclaimed or promised, but by what is done ... In those years, the early years, when Negroes held the highest offices, the literacy of the Negro was only ten percent. Today, when the literacy of the Negro in this country is eighty-four percent, that same Republican party not only declares the Negro unfit to hold office, but organizes Lily-Whitism as an excuse and justification for keeping Negroes out of office ... It is a mistaken idea that the Negro must wait until the party selects him. The only true political philosophy dictates that the Negro must select his political party, and not wait to be selected ... I see millions of Negroes turning the picture of Lincoln to the wall. This year I see Negroes voting a Democratic ticket ... I, for one, shall join the ranks of this new army of fearless, courageous, patriotic Negroes who know the difference between blind partisanship and patriotism.*[654]

Vann's speech was widely distributed, reprinted in black weeklies around the country and published in a widely circulated pamphlet.[655] On October 8, Vann followed his St. James Forum speech with a scathing editorial in the *Courier*, entitled "And There Stood the One Hundred," about a meeting arranged at the White House between a "panic-stricken" President Hoover and one hundred "old line" black Republicans. Vann depicted the group as subservient, pleading with the president, who had previously reportedly refused to have his photo taken with African American groups, "Give us your photograph and tell us Lincoln still lives and we will do the rest." An accompanying cartoon by Wilburt Holloway showed Hoover wearing a top hat and looking out the White House window at the visiting delegation, saying "I love to hear the darkies sing."[656] Vann later spoke at the October 19, 1932, rally in Pittsburgh, at which Father Cox had also delivered his endorsement of Roosevelt.[657]

Meanwhile, Brown had all but given up on the idea of receiving patronage in exchange for supporting white candidates, and was determined to run for office himself—although he had not yet determined to follow Robert Vann's lead out of the Republican Party. He filed as a Republican candidate in the state House election for a seat from the First District, but lost to a white opponent, John O. Scorzo, by almost 1,500 votes, after Earl Sams, another African American candidate, put own his name on the ballot and split the vote. A Republican loyalist, Sams had previously been put forth as a candidate by James F. Malone, Sr. in 1925, in order to split the African American vote and deprive alderman Robert Logan of a seat on the city council, leaving Malone's candidate, a white man named Martin Griffin, to win. Vann's recollection of that episode probably encouraged him to be even more strident in his critique of the election results than he would normally be. "The Pittsburgh Negro," he wrote, "is absolutely in a class by himself when it comes to civic and political advancement ... It is a thankless task to try to tell Negroes in Pittsburgh what is best to do or even how to do it. They are too dumb to see the picture after it has been painted. This thing has been going on for years and years. It is sickening."[658]

Vann had reason to celebrate the national election results. Vann maintained that African American voters tipped the balance of power in Allegheny County in favor of Roosevelt, with an estimated thirty-five thousand African Americans voting for the Democratic Party for the first time. The *Courier* proudly alleged that 2 million black votes had tipped the election in Roosevelt's favor in fourteen states, although the estimate was probably just a bit inflated.[659] Nevertheless, Joseph Guffey went to the president-elect at Hyde Park and lobbied him for a particular job for Robert Vann—special assistant to the U.S. Attorney General. "Before you say anything about Bob Vann," Guffey told him, "I ought to tell you he's colored." Roosevelt expressed concern that conservative Southern Democrats might give him trouble if the appointment was required to be confirmed by the Senate. Guffey assured Roosevelt that confirmation would not be required, and Roosevelt agreed to give Vann the job.[660]

Before the inauguration, however, Vann and Brown would become embroiled in a local controversy. On the night of January 20, 1933, forty African American men and women were arrested for "disorderliness" during a chitterling supper and dance in the home of Mrs. Virginia Heath in the town of Industry, about thirty-five miles west of Pittsburgh in Beaver County. Beaver County police raided the home and beat several of the people in attendance before lining up all fifty-six African American guests and asking them for payment of $2.50 in order to avoid going to jail. Those who paid were released; those who did not were taken to the Beaver County jail, where they had to sleep on bare jail cell floors. The next day, the women were loaded into a Ford sedan and the men were put in open truck beds, and all of them were driven to Waynesburg, where they were turned out of the vehicles and told by the police to walk to the West Virginia border—that they were required to leave Pennsylvania or face two years in jail. Outraged by the "shanghaiing" of the group, Homer Brown approached the Beaver County District Attorney, A.B. DeCastrique, and demanded action against the Beaver County police. DeCastrique replied that "the officers could not be convicted in Beaver County and that the 'shainhaing' of these negroes [sic] was merely a mistake." It later unfolded that Beaver County commissioner Howard A. Hunter had decided that the detainees could be "deported" to save the cost of jailing them, since most of them were only in the County to help in the construction of the new Montgomery Locks and Dam, near Monaca.[661]

After Governor Pinchot's investigation of the incident, his Attorney General, William Schnader, recommended that those who were involved in the kidnapping of the detainees be prosecuted, but the Beaver County prosecutor still refused, citing lack of evidence. Acting separately from the NAACP and citing his frustration with the lack of action in the case, Vann launched his own campaign on the issue, telling the press that he intended to file his own charges against the Beaver County commissioners for kidnapping, false arrest and false imprisonment, and that he would to do so in federal court if necessary. Vann's grandstanding, however, provoked Brown, who wrote to Walter White, the head of the national NAACP, that Vann's statement to the press "will hurt our position in that it will give Pinchot and Schnader an opportunity 'to get out' on the grounds that if Mr. Vann is going to do so much," in his role as a federal lawyer, "then they will turn the matter over to him. Mr. Vann did not consult with me," Brown complained, and he observed that "it certainly gives the people here the idea that we are lying down on the job." Vann emerged from the incident looking like a man of action, although, as predicted by Brown, nothing further was ever done with respect to the case.[662]

On June 10, 1933, Vann sat at the speakers' table at a Democratic Party banquet at the William Penn Hotel with Joseph Guffey, Secretary of the Interior Harold Ickes, Michael Benedum, David Lawrence, and Roosevelt's campaign manager, Jim Farley. The banquet was convened to honor Ickes' visit to the city, but Vann acknowledged what it meant for him to attend. "I felt that I should have been recognized in such a manner twenty years ago," he said. "But during all those years, while a worker in the Republican party, I was not only never asked to sit at a speakers' table but was never invited to a banquet."[663]

It would, unfortunately, be one of the last times Vann felt moved to celebrate his connection to the Democratic Party. Vann arrived in Washington in July 1933 to take up his position as special assistant to Attorney General Homer S. Cummings, a white, old-line Democrat from Connecticut. Right and left, Vann's hopes for the position were being blasted away. Vann had thought that his place in Washington would have given him some influence over federal political patronage with respect to African Americans, but his communications with Farley and other patronage chiefs within the administration were ignored. Worse yet, the position he had earned seemed to be devoid of content, and he was being shown little respect. He was shunted off to a tiny inconspicuous office, and, as he recalled, "It was about six weeks before I got a desk to my liking ... It was some time before I could have a stenographer assigned to me. In fact, I was in the department about a month before they knew I was there." Stenographers, once assigned to him, sometimes refused to take dictation from him because he was African American, and, to his utter dismay, he never received a word of welcome from Cummings. In fact, he had difficulty getting an appointment to see him. Although he would serve on some federal commissions, most of his work involved "meager, insignificant, routine tasks" such as "investigating and verifying titles" for future post office sites and Indian schools. As Bunie writes, "It must have seemed a terrible comedown for the shrewd lawyer who had planned and delivered successful defense pleas at murder trials which had had all Pittsburgh agog."[664] Vann resigned and returned to Pittsburgh to resume his role with the *Courier* in 1935. In a well-established pattern, Vann was succeeded in his post by another Pittsburgh African American lawyer, Theron B. Hamilton.[665]

Back in Pittsburgh, Brown ran again for a seat in the state legislature in 1934 after being approached by independent Republicans, and this time he won, as the candidate of both party tickets. Robert Vann had opposed his nomination, however, prompting Brown to say that he "received more Democratic votes in Pittsburgh when I was elected to the Legislature, because Vann opposed me than I would have if he had favored my endorsement." Although Brown was still registered as a Republican when he arrived in Harrisburg in January 1935, he was nominated by both parties, meaning that under a new state law that required him to declare his party he had a choice to make. Understanding that the new governor, George Earle, was determined to liberalize employment laws in the spirit of Roosevelt's New Deal, Brown made the decision to take his seat in the General Assembly as a Democrat.[666]

In 1936, Brown would make headlines joining Representative Marshall Sheppard of Philadelphia in a petition to request the impeachment of Judge B.C. Atlee on Lancaster, Pennsylvania. On July 10, 1936, Judge Atlee remarked to a black defendant who was up for sentencing on charges that he had "enticed" two teenage girls that "If they had lynched you they would have been justified." He told the courtroom that south of the Mason Dixon line no court would have needed to be involved. The remarks were published in the *Philadelphia Record*, which also published an editorial calling for his impeachment. After Brown and Sheppard's petition, a subcommittee of the judiciary general committee of the Pennsylvania state legislature heard testimony on the matter and established the truth of the newspaper account; on a close vote, the subcommittee recommended that Judge Atlee be impeached. After the judge's lawyers asserted that Judge Atlee was "a lover of law and order" and "hated lynching," however, a political compromise was struck, and Judge Atlee was ultimately censured by the legislature and forced to apologize. He delivered his apology in person to the legislature, reading it aloud and then signing it in the presence of the judiciary committee. The papers reported that "the whole proceedings are regarded as invaluable in demonstrating the power and the temper of the state's Negro citizens."[667]

In 1937, Vann stole back some headlines by criticizing the Roosevelt administration, through the *Courier*, over its choice of Hugo L. Black as an associate justice on the U.S. Supreme Court upon the retirement of Justice Van Devanter, primarily due to Black's failure to support, while serving as a senator from Alabama, the Wagner-Costigan anti-lynching bill. President Roosevelt himself had refused to speak out in favor of the bill over concerns that he would alienate the Democrats in the South; and, ironically, some Senate Democrats actually objected to Black's nomination on the grounds that, as an enthusiastic supporter of the New Deal, Black was deemed to be too liberal.[668] Meanwhile, shortly after Justice Black was sworn in, *Pittsburgh Post-Gazette* reporter Ray

Sprigle broke the story that Hugo Black had joined the Ku Klux Klan in 1923 and had been given a life membership.[669] There had been conjecture about Black's supposed ties to the Klan, but Sprigle brought the evidence forward, causing a national controversy over the newly-installed Supreme Court justice. Vann immediately sent a telegram to President Roosevelt, which he also ran on the front page of the *Courier*:

> *ROOSEVELTIAN COURAGE AS THE AMERICAN PEOPLE KNOW IT DEMANDS YOUR DISAVOWAL OF THE APPOINTMENT OF SENATOR BLACK TO THE SUPREME COURT. THE MORAL ISSUE NOW RAISED FAR TRANSCENDS EVERY POSSIBLE POLITICAL EXPEDIENT.*[670]

President Roosevelt never joined the argument, and Justice Black gave a radio address explaining that he had resigned from the Klan in 1925, that the life membership had been "unsolicited," and that he intended to oppose groups like the Klan that would purport to interfere with the constitutional rights of others. The dispute faded.[671]

When Justice George Sutherland retired in 1938, Vann's name was put forward as his potential successor on the U.S. Supreme Court, though mainly by the National Bar Association and several other African American groups. Columnist H.L. Mencken, a long-time acquaintance of Vann's, weighed in with his own flippant endorsement, saying, "If the white Crackers of the South, in return for their votes, deserve to have a reliable agent in the Supreme Court, then why should the colored faithful of both North and South, not to mention East and West, be denied? If a Ku Kluxer is good enough for the ermine, then what is to be said against a respectable colored Elk?" Vann sent Mencken a note telling how much he laughed over the column.[672] Justice Sutherland was ultimately replaced by the Solicitor General, Stanley Reed. Robert Lee Vann died of abdominal cancer on October 24, 1940.[673]

Brown, meanwhile, was fighting the battle for equal rights in the Pennsylvania legislature. In addition to launching hearings on the Pittsburgh Public School system that ultimately aided Richard F. Jones' successful litigation against the schools on the hiring of African American teachers. In 1937, Brown successfully shepherded an amendment to an important piece of legislation in Governor Earle's "Little New Deal," the Pennsylvania Labor Relations Act, that provided that any union that discriminated in its membership would not be afforded the protections of the Act. The AFL and CIO lobbied against it, but the House passed the bill unanimously with Brown's amendment, and a compromise committee passed the bill in January 1938. Brown's parliamentary effectiveness began to be known and respected throughout the Commonwealth, a talent that would serve him through the 1940s with regard to a number of important pieces of legislation.[674]

The Allegheny County Bar Association had, until this period, steadfastly refused to admit African American members. William Henry Stanton and P.J. Clyde Randall both applied for membership in the 1920s, and, apparently responding to the inaction on their applications, withdrew them in March 1927.[675] During the term of James H. Gray, the former Common Pleas judge, as president of the Bar Association, the membership committee spontaneously took action to correct its past behavior. Eight applications from among the African Americans in the Pittsburgh bar—Oliver L. Johnson, Theron B. Hamilton, Joseph W. Givens, Homer S. Brown, Thomas E. Barton, Wilbur C. Douglass, William Wendell Stanton (son of the late William Henry Stanton) and Richard F. Jones—were approved (a handwritten designation—*"(Colored)"*—being affixed on most of them) and the eight lawyers were admitted to the Bar Association in April 1943.[676] P.J. Clyde Randall was later admitted in August 1945.[677] There were still no African American judges, and still no African Americans affiliated with downtown law firms; the African American bar was as segregated as it ever would be, physically and socially, in 1943—but at least, at that moment, the Bar Association had been willing to recognize the achievements and professional worth of eight African American men.

For any category of human, there will always be some individuals who aspire to reside within the mainstream—in effect, to hide there, to dwell comfortably among the average. To some extent, it is the desire to have a place within which to hide that actually defines the outlines of any mainstream movement. To be outside the mainstream, by contrast, is to be out in the open. Successive generations of ethnic groups in America have almost always managed to get lost inside the mainstream—perhaps not for all purposes, but pretty much at will, with the shedding of ethnic accents and other public marks of ethnicity. Not so with women and African Americans during the first half of the twentieth century. To be an average lawyer, for them, was tantamount to being unemployed as a lawyer.

For the most ambitious women and African American lawyers of the period—Soffel, Graubart, Alpern, Vann and Brown among them—talent and hard work alone would not define a successful career. In an era in which the professional attainments of women were few, the women who succeeded in the Pittsburgh bar did so without reference to campaigns for women's rights; even in Alpern's case, where her success was political, she succeeded by largely avoiding women's issues. Management of publicity, however, would be key to the success of each of the top women lawyers of the Pittsburgh bar. The path of the successful African American male lawyers during the period would diverge significantly from that of the women. They would pursue African American civil rights loudly and defiantly as they won a measure of respect of their fellow members of the bar—although, admittedly, not anything like the votes of confidence ultimately given to Ellenbogen and Musmanno in their similar struggles. What was shared among both groups, ultimately, was that for an ambitious woman or African American lawyer to rise within the profession, their only choice, rather than to seek a comfortable hiding place, was to burn bright, be bold and be noticed.

BAD COMPANY

Even as Philander Knox sat on the stage at Schenley Park on Independence Day 1902, while President Theodore Roosevelt talked about "the problems caused by the growth and concentration of great individual, and above all, great corporate fortunes,"[678] Knox—the former Pittsburgh corporation lawyer, now serving as President Roosevelt's Attorney General—had already begun to carry out the president's declaration of war on the nation's biggest corporate "trusts." The repercussions of this war would be felt within the Pittsburgh bar for several generations.

Roosevelt had actually fired his first salvo in the war against the trusts in his first annual message to Congress on December 3, 1901, barely three months after the assassination of his predecessor, William McKinley. After a note of mourning for the late president, Roosevelt said:

> *The tremendous and highly complex industrial development which went on with ever accelerated rapidity during the latter half of the nineteenth century brings us face to face, at the beginning of the twentieth, with very serious social problems. The old laws, and the old customs which had almost the binding force of law, were once quite sufficient to regulate the accumulation and distribution of wealth. Since the industrial changes have so enormously increased the productive power of mankind, they are no longer sufficient ... There is a widespread conviction in the minds of the American people that the great corporations known as trusts are in certain of their features and tendencies hurtful to the general welfare.[679]*

Roosevelt had been all too aware of the ineffectiveness to date of the federal government's attempts to enforce the Sherman Antitrust Act of 1890, which purported to prohibit businesses from engaging in anti-competitive or monopolizing activities. While it had occasionally been used effectively by the government to stop labor union activity, its use against corporations was spotty. The leading U.S. Supreme Court case under the Act, *U.S. v. E.C. Knight Co.* (1895),[680] in which the government attempted to break-up the nearly complete monopoly on sugar production owned by the American Sugar Refining Company, resulted in a holding that the federal government had only limited power to regulate the interstate activities of corporations. Roosevelt was certainly looking for new regulations, new weapons in his arsenal, to attack pernicious trusts, but he also very much wanted the Sherman Act to have its teeth restored. He desired to send a signal to Wall Street.

An irresistible target arose in November 1901, just before Roosevelt's message to Congress. The Great Northern Railway, controlled by James J. "Empire Builder" Hill, and the Union Pacific Railroad, controlled by E.H. Harriman, fought each other as rival suitors for the control of the Chicago, Burlington & Quincy Railroad, which had lines that would have helped each of them connect to Chicago. After stock raids on the open market brought the two to a stand-off, Hill and Harriman decided to meet and settle their differences. The result was a plan by Hill, Harriman, J.P. Morgan, John D. Rockefeller and other prominent stockholders to combine the Great Northern, Burlington and Northern Pacific Railroads in one great trust. The plan, unveiled in November, effectively gutted the considerable stock speculation that had been induced by the independent activities of Hill and Harriman in the market, and there was considerable outcry about the back-room deal that was going to result in the concentration of ownership of a large portion of the railroad lines of the Northwest in one trust, the Northern Securities Company, the "second largest corporation in the world" after U.S. Steel. With all of these railroad assets now within one company, there was also concern that eventually all trans-Mississippi rail lines would end up in Hill, Harriman and Morgan's back pockets.[681]

Roosevelt went to his Attorney General, Philander Knox, in January 1902 and asked him if a Sherman Act case could be made against Northern Securities.[682] Knox, of course, was a McKinley man—or more importantly, a Henry Clay Frick man, who had aligned himself by life and livelihood with the massive accumulation of market power, as counsel to Frick and Carnegie. On the other hand, he and Roosevelt had grown to be avid companions in a very short time—they shared an inability to sit still and a love of being outdoors—and Knox was not himself unmindful of the political impact of being involved with a revival of the Sherman Act, so long as its uses would not be aimed indiscriminately. Knox had political ambitions of his own, and he understood, as Roosevelt did, that the symbolism of tackling J.P. Morgan, of all people, in such a case would resonate with the American public.[683] At venues such as E.F. Proctor's 125th Street Theatre in Manhattan, vaudeville comedienne Bonnie Thornton was at about that time singing a ditty with a chorus that went, "It's Morgan's, it's Morgan's, the great financial gorgon!"[684] According to the song, Morgan owned *everything*.

Knox agreed to look into the matter. In the meantime, the Interstate Commerce Commission had already begun its own investigation of the formation of Northern Securities Company, and perhaps even more importantly, the attorney general of the state of Minnesota, Wallace Barton Douglas, had already appeared before the U.S. Supreme Court, moving for leave to file a complaint against Northern Securities to stop the combination of the rail lines.[685] While Minnesota awaited its decision from the Supreme Court, Knox provided the results of his analysis to the president; he told him that he believed the formation of the company was in violation of the Sherman Act, and Roosevelt directed that a suit be filed. They decided, however, that in order to maintain calm in the markets, they would announce the lawsuit to the public before its filing. Knox called a press conference on February 19, 1902, after the close of the market, to announce that the federal government was preparing a lawsuit to "test the validity of the merger." Knox stated, matter-of-factly, that he believed that the Northern Securities combination "violates the provisions of the Sherman Act of 1890."[686] On February 20, the market went into a mini-panic, leading the *New York Tribune* to report that "[n]ot since the assassination of President McKinley has the stock market had such a sudden shock as was caused by the announcement on Wednesday night of President Roosevelt's purpose to proceed" against Northern Securities.[687]

J.P. Morgan would not let the president's plan proceed without a personal appeal. He came to Washington to meet with President Roosevelt. Knox, whom Morgan knew of through Knox & Reed's involvement in the U.S. Steel combination, was also present. Morgan told the president that he felt particularly injured by the president's failure to contact him before announcing the plans. "That is just what we did not want to do," Roosevelt replied. Morgan protested that this was just not the way things were supposed to be done. "If we have done anything wrong," he said, indicating Knox, "send your man to my man and they can fix it up." Although Knox was well aware that that was how things were done, he toed the line of his client. "We don't want to fix it up," replied Knox. "We want to stop it." Startled, Morgan inquired, "Are you going to attack my other interests, the Steel Trust and the others?" The President replied, "Certainly not—unless we find out that in any case they have done something we regard as wrong." As Morgan left, President Roosevelt chuckled, telling Knox that Morgan had just perfectly illustrated "the Wall Street point of view ... [he] could not help regarding me as a big rival operator, who either intended to ruin all his interests or else could be induced to come to an agreement to ruin none."[688]

Knox filed his lawsuit on March 10. While Knox began the work of building the government's case, Hill, Harriman and Morgan assembled their team of lawyers, including Francis Stetson, Morgan's New York counsel who had faced Knox & Reed in the negotiations on the U.S. Steel merger; Knox's immediate predecessor as Attorney General, New Jersey lawyer John W. Griggs; and John G. Johnson, the Philadelphia lawyer who had represented Henry Clay Frick alongside D.T. Watson in the "Greatest Lawsuit of the Century."[689] The defense team was openly disparaging of Knox's position, one of their members (probably not Stetson or Johnson) declaring to Roosevelt's good friend, reporter Joseph Bucklin Bishop, that President Roosevelt had been led into a losing cause on the advice of an "unknown country lawyer from Pennsylvania."[690] Upon later hearing about the remark, Roosevelt fumed, "They will know this country lawyer before this suit is ended."[691]

At the conclusion of almost nine months of pre-trial planning and investigation, however, Knox became concerned that he needed some additional help. Knox was known as an agile trial lawyer with a fine business mind, but he was no great legal scholar, and a revival of the Sherman Act—with the prestige of the White House and perhaps Knox's own political future at stake—required a corporate lawyer with a superior jurisprudential intellect. Knox contacted D.T. Watson in Pittsburgh to engage him as special counsel for the United States. As Watson's biographer Francis Harbison writes:

> D.T. Watson's integrity was unchallenged. He was an outstanding Democrat. He had been frequently proposed for appointment to the United States Supreme Court. He was in the confidence of leaders of both political parties. The Democrats would never assail Knox for the loss of the case if Watson represented the United States. He, probably better than any other man, knew Watson's ability in court for often [Knox] had been forced to drop his shield before [Watson].[692]

Before he began work, however, Watson consulted with Henry Clay Frick, Knox's friend and his own some-time client, about the propriety of entering into the representation. Frick promptly replied, "You are perfectly free in my opinion to act for the United States in the case mentioned in your letter nineteenth" of January, 1903.[693]

With the trial set to begin on March 18, 1903, Watson jumped into the case with "round-the-clock labor." Only by the middle of February, with the assistance of Knox's staffer, former U.S. Attorney for the Eastern District of Pennsylvania James M. Beck, did Watson manage to marshal the extensive facts of the case in order to frame the attack. On March 5, Watson reported that he was "still working on our brief, but have been led into so many by-paths of investigation that it is yet unfinished." The following day he asked Beck if he thought it would be proper in this case to print the brief after oral argument rather than submitting it to the Court beforehand; and the day after, Watson answered his own question. Submitting a complete portion of the brief on the question of monopolistic intent, with significant assistance from his junior partner John M. Freeman, he noted, "I have not as yet closed up the other portion of the brief. It is such a hugh [sic] work that it has taken three times as much attention as I supposed it would. I see no benefit to be derived from printing in advance."[694]

The defense's primary argument against the application of the Sherman Act to the Northern Securities merger was, as Harbison said, "in railroad parlance," that the railroad parties had gotten "the tracks down first" and were now fighting "for the right of way"—the merger was already completed, and the government could not be given the opportunity to "prohibit doing that which is already done."[695] For Watson, however, the government's case was inextricably linked to the question of the intent of Hill, Harriman and the others in entering into the combination. "As I understand the defendant's theory, it is that they did not organize the Northern Securities Company for the purpose of being able to control the freight rates and prevent competition on these two competing railroads and they made a decided point on that," he told Beck. "I regard the arguing of that question in the opening of the case with persistence and vim as exceedingly desirable. I cannot fail to impress the Court with the flimsy nature of the defense and the exceedingly technical and subtle means by which the Anti-Trust Act is attempted to be evaded." By the last week before the argument, Watson was even more certain of the approach. "If we can show, as I think a good argument will, that the real purpose of the formation of the Northern Securities Company was to control and to be able to stifle competition, then I feel we are far on our journey to a decree," he told Beck.[696]

Knox had chosen to file the case in the Eighth Circuit in St. Louis, Missouri, before Judges John B. Sanborn, Jr., William C. Hook, Amos Madden Thayer and the future Supreme Court Justice, Willis Van Devanter. At the close of the case for Northern Securities, argued by John W. Griggs, D.T. Watson argued for two days on behalf of the government. As Harbison writes, "Watson's argument was popularly conceded to have won the case. ... [O]ne present, representing interested parties, was reported to have left the court room at its close and wired to his principal: 'Watson has just closed his argument and he has won the case.'"[697] Watson mobilized a team of stenographers to file government's brief three days later. He told Knox:

> *Perhaps I misjudged the attorneys for the defendants, but after listening to them for two days, I was satisfied that they intended to ridicule the case, as we used to say you will remember in Pittsburgh: "laugh it out of court." That impressed me so that I completely realigned and changed my arguments and endeavored to impress upon the Court that there had been a plain and palpable violation of the words of the Anti-Trust Act, and the only question to be decided was whether the defendants had done so adroitly and subtly that the government was powerless in the premises ...I want to say to you that I am more thoroughly convinced than I ever have been that your opinion in this case was correct and that ultimately, the Supreme Court of the United States will so decide.*[698]

On April 9, 1903, the Eighth Circuit delivered its opinion, and it came in as a complete victory for the U.S. government, a vindication of President Roosevelt's new war on the trusts. Quizzed by the press, Watson was loyal and generous. He said, "The credit for the victory belongs to Attorney General Knox. He first thought the case through ... [and] positively advised the president and instituted the case ... He has courageously and honestly pressed the case, and the unanimous decision of the court fully sustains him in his course."[699]

The defendants immediately appealed the case to the U.S. Supreme Court. Knox knew that the president would have preferred that a Republican could have been fully credited for the victory in the Circuit Court, so Knox took control of the Supreme Court argument and, although Watson was not credited, Knox argued and won the case substantially on Watson's brief. Northern Securities was ordered to divest itself of its railroad holdings.[700]

During the divestiture, E.H. Harriman tried to retain D.T. Watson to represent him in a claim against the other Northern Securities parties, as the method of divestiture was leaving him as a minority investor in lines which he had contributed to Northern Securities as a majority investor. Watson ultimately declined to take the engagement, saying that as he thought Harriman's case through, "I necessarily always go back to the original case where I (with others) represented the Government ... [B]ecause of that I might find myself in a divided allegiance which would not only be humiliating to me, but might embarrass the Harriman interests."[701]

Watson found himself in a similar position in 1906, when the U.S. government filed a lawsuit against Standard Oil Company of New Jersey under the Sherman Act. John D. Rockefeller and the Standard Oil interests had been clients of D.T. Watson's going back to 1878, beginning with a couple of local counsel engagements in Butler and Clarion Counties. Watson later distinguished himself by winning a major tax case for Standard Oil before the Pennsylvania Supreme Court.[702] In 1881, Standard Oil's chief counsel, S.C.T. Dodd, reached out to D.T. Watson, asking him to review Dodd's draft of what would become the Standard Oil Trust of 1882. Among Watson's suggestions was to include a clause restricting the right of the Trust's beneficiaries to bring suit against the trustees, and he raised the issue about whether a corporation had the necessary power to execute the Trust. Prophetically, he also pondered whether

> ... these people [could] be indicted for conspiracy? and if so, where? I hardly see how the question can be directly answered. If the broad language used in many cases ... is accepted, then doubtless it would be a question of fact for the jury under all the evidence to determine the intent ...

The state of Ohio enjoined the Standard Oil Company of Ohio from performing the Trust agreement in 1892, causing a reorganization that resulted, in 1899, in the Standard Oil Company of New Jersey becoming the vehicle for the ownership of all of the Standard Oil properties.[703]

On November 15, 1906, citing the 1899 reorganization as the offending transaction (since the creation of the original Trust took place before the enactment of the Sherman Act in 1890), Charles Bonaparte, Philander Knox's second successor as President Roosevelt's Attorney General after Knox left the cabinet in 1904 to fill a vacancy as one of Pennsylvania's U.S. Senators, filed the Sherman Act case in St. Louis. Bonaparte deliberately chose the Circuit Court there for the Standard Oil case as that was where D.T. Watson had argued successfully on behalf of the government in *Northern Securities*.[704] Bonaparte relied, to a large degree, on factual assertions made by James R. Garfield, the late martyred president James A. Garfield's son and President Roosevelt's head of the Bureau of Corporations, who had been investigating Standard Oil and had issued a report in October 1905, based in turn on evidence compiled by journalist Ida Tarbell and published in a series of magazine articles called "The History of Standard Oil." Tarbell and Garfield both believed, and Bonaparte now asserted in his lawsuit, that Standard Oil had acquired almost all of the oil refining capacity in the United States, and that it absolutely controlled the price of oil, in part by freezing competing oil producers out of its refining operations.[705]

Prior to launching its Sherman Act case against Standard Oil, the government also pursued a criminal prosecution of Standard Oil in the federal District Court for the Northern District of Illinois under the Elkins Act, which prohibited railroads from offering rebates to significant shippers, and prohibited shippers from accepting them. Bonaparte charged that Standard Oil used its market power to demand rebates on the shipping of its oil on rail lines, thus driving up the cost of shipping for competing oil shippers. John S. Miller, Standard Oil's Chicago lawyer, handled the defense, and the case was heard by the colorful Roosevelt appointee, Judge Kenesaw Mountain Landis—known subsequently as the man who articulated the so-called "anti-trust exemption" of major league baseball, who was subsequently named as the first commissioner of baseball, and who later banned Shoeless Joe Jackson and the 1919 "Black Sox" from the sport. Landis gave his ruling as if he were delivering a political convention speech, eliciting applause in the courtroom for his tongue-lashing of Rockefeller as well as his lawyers, and levying a fine of $29,240,000 against Standard Oil.[706]

Landis' opinion was eventually overturned by the Seventh Circuit,[707] but when the Sherman Act case was launched, Standard Oil had no desire to relive the public relations disaster it had encountered in Landis' courtroom. For all the same reasons that Philander Knox desired to have D.T. Watson on his side in *Northern Securities*, Rockefeller and Standard Oil desired to have their trusted counsel with them in their Sherman Act case. Once again, Watson was concerned about his prior connection to the *Northern Securities* case; although Watson did believe that while *Northern Securities* was decided correctly, he admired Standard Oil as an organization. Watson asked his friend and some-time adversary, John G. Johnson, for advice. Johnson wrote: "I think that any defense in the Standard case must start with the acceptance of the Northern Securities law as final, and must differentiate and seek to destroy the foundation of facts averred in the Bill. Your own connection long ago with the Standard Oil would make your retainer in the present a fitting sequence."[708] Johnson also joined the defense, along with John G. Milburn of the New York firm of Carter Ledyard & Milburn.

The trial record grew like no case before it, eventually comprising almost fifteen thousand pages, divided into twenty-three volumes, covering forty years of Standard Oil's business. In the early spring of 1909, as the case was finally coming to its end, D.T. Watson went to Atlantic City to prepare his argument. On April 6, 1909, Milburn began the defense's close before the Eighth Circuit by laying out the facts as the defendant saw them, and on April 8, D.T. Watson took up the legal argument, insisting that Standard Oil's facts were distinctly different from those found in *Northern Securities* and declaring that "under no stretch of the imagination could they be deemed identical." Moreover, he argued, *Northern Securities* did not stand for the proposition that citizens such as Mr. Rockefeller and his associates did not have the legal right to combine their businesses. It therefore followed, Watson argued, that the appropriate legal inquiry here was whether Standard Oil was acting in restraint of commerce or engaging in unfair competition, and that Standard Oil "could not be held for their conduct of years past," referring to the failed 1892 trust. Although his client was extremely pleased with Watson's oral argument—Standard Oil vice president H.G. Folger, Jr. wrote to him that he agreed that "no other man living" could have presented the legal argument with as much credibility—the Circuit Court handed down a decree that the nineteen subsidiaries of Standard Oil of New Jersey were required to be divested from the parent and divided among the parent company's stockholders.[709]

Standard Oil appealed the ruling to the Supreme Court, and kept its legal team in place for the oral argument, set for March 14, 1910. Among the three lawyers—Milburn, Johnson and Watson—Watson was given 40 minutes out of the four hours set aside by the Court to address the argument that the stock sale that comprised the Circuit

Court's order was not a feature of the *Northern Securities* decision and therefore would be inappropriate, given the fact that the government purportedly premised the rest of their case on *Northern Securities*.[710]

After some consideration, the Supreme Court asked for a re-argument of the case. Buoyed by the thought that the Court was struggling with an expansion of the application of the Sherman Act, Watson and the team revised their brief, surmising that Watson's argument drove at the biggest weakness in the government's case. Watson argued the stock sale issue again on January 16, 1911, as well as making perhaps the most important point of all—that the vast holdings of Standard Oil were never owned by multiple parties:

> *All these were built by whom? By one group. There never was a division. They were built by one group, by one great partnership. ... [T]hey organized as partners. Then they organized as a corporation. Then they were organized as a trust in 1879. Then, in 1882, it went into a formal trust; and then, in 1899, it was conveyed to the Standard Oil Company of New Jersey. But it was always owned by one group of owners. There never was a diversity of ownership. There never was competition among these people.*

Despite the soundness of Watson's argument, the Supreme Court affirmed the lower court on May 15, 1911, with some modifications that removed some of the onerous features of the Circuit Court's decree. Still, Standard Oil of New Jersey was ordered to be divided into pieces—pieces that would eventually become, by the end of the twentieth and beginning of the twenty-first centuries, Exxon, Mobil and Amoco. As Harbison writes, "The New Jersey Company was punished for the sins of its antecedents."[711]

D.T. Watson's only consolation was that two of the main points of his argument—that the mere fact of the organization of the business under a New Jersey corporation was not a *per se* violation of the Sherman Act, and that the dissolution of the corporation was not to be carried out under the continued direction of the court under threat of punishment (only a subsequent proceeding on a violation of the decree could produce such sanctions)—were tacitly adopted by the Court in its opinion. The Court's rejection of a *"per se"* violation upon Watson's argument essentially formed the basis of what became the Court's new Sherman Act doctrine—the adoption of a "rule of reason" when analyzing a combination of businesses. That is, even though the government won its case against Standard Oil, Watson had convinced the Court to adopt a standard for analyzing future antitrust claims that would greatly diminish the power of the Sherman Act; the Court had called Standard Oil's combination an "unreasonable" restraint of trade, in contrast to "reasonable" restraints that the Act would permit[712]—and indeed, that President Roosevelt himself would support.

Theodore Roosevelt had left office in March 1909, content to be known as a "trust buster" who had revived the Sherman Act and had succeeded in busting J.P. Morgan's Northern Securities Company, and who was well on the way to busting John D. Rockefeller's Standard Oil trust. His hand-picked successor, William Howard Taft, was a former federal judge and one-time Cincinnati prosecutor. It was inevitable that Taft would pick up where his mentor had left off, although Roosevelt would not ultimately profess to be happy with Taft's progress. In fact, Taft's next big move in the antitrust arena—a move against a Pittsburgh behemoth—caused a permanent rift between the two that would result not only in the fracturing of the Republican Party, but in the face of a divided G.O.P., the election of Democrat Woodrow Wilson as President in 1912.

J.P. Morgan well remembered the meeting he had with President Roosevelt and Philander Knox early in 1902, during which he asked the two men if U.S. Steel would be considered to be a target of Roosevelt's "trust busting" in the future. "Certainly not," was the president's reply, "unless we find out that in any case they have done something we regard as wrong."[713]

Although Knox would have wished to repudiate the idea that a tycoon could ring up the president and ask him to pass on a potential transaction before he might spend his time and money on it, in order to avoid the hassle of unwinding it after a prolonged government prosecution, Morgan did just that with respect to a proposed transaction by U.S. Steel in October 1907. During the week of October 6, the stock market experienced a moderate crash which caused the failure of two major Wall Street financial firms. Roosevelt's Treasury Secretary, George Cortelyou, went to Wall Street to meet with Morgan and other prominent financiers, offering assistance to them "in every feasible and possible way." In the days that followed, a series of "frantic" investor meetings took place in J.P. Morgan's Madison Avenue residence over the fate of the Tennessee Coal and Iron Company, which at that time was beginning to emerge as a major competitor to U.S. Steel. Large blocks of the stock of Tennessee Coal and Iron had been pledged against loans at the time of the crash, with one firm in particular, Moore & Schley, having five million dollars of the stock as collateral. With fears that Moore & Schley and other firms might go under if the market were to sag any further, Morgan sent Judge Gary and Henry Clay Frick as his special emissaries to the White House, where they argued that if U.S. Steel were permitted to acquire Tennessee Coal and Iron, thereby confirming a higher price for its stock, it would save Moore & Schley, and the market itself, from collapse. They said they did not wish to make the purchase if the president were to say that they should not. Although Roosevelt understood that he did not have the authority to permit any transaction, he winked at them, saying "while of course I could not advise them to take the action proposed, I felt it no public duty of mine to interpose any objections."[714]

Four years later, in October 1911, Taft's Attorney General, George W. Wickersham, a partner with the Cadwalader firm before and after his public service, with assistance from special counsel Jacob Dickinson, Taft's ex-Secretary of War, filed a lawsuit against U.S. Steel accusing the company of creating a monopoly. Among the allegations in the complaint, the government argued that U.S. Steel's acquisition of Tennessee Coal and Iron was an unreasonable restraint of trade. Moreover, the complaint alleged that President Roosevelt had been hoodwinked. In the relevant count, the government maintained that:

> *The President, taken as he was partially into confidence, and moved by his appreciation of the gravity of the situation and the necessity for applying what was represented to him to be the only known remedy, stated that he did not feel it to be his duty to prevent the transaction.*

If Judge Gary and Frick had told him the whole truth, the government alleged, the president would not have signaled his approval of the transaction.[715]

After the complaint became public, Elihu Root, the New York lawyer who had served as Roosevelt's Secretary of State, said that ex-President Roosevelt "was so mad it dethroned his judgment."[716] In a letter to James R. Garfield, Roosevelt pointed out that Taft was a cabinet member when Roosevelt acted in the Tennessee Coal and Iron matter, and that the decision was explained to him in detail at the time. "It ill becomes him either by himself or through another afterwards to act as he is now acting."[717] In the November 1911 issue of *The Outlook*, Roosevelt plainly declared:

> *I was not misled. The representatives of the Steel Corporation told me the truth as to what the effect of action at that time would be, and any statement that I was misled or that the representatives of the Steel Corporation did not thus tell me the truth as to the facts of the case is not itself in accordance with the truth ... I reaffirm everything ... not only as to what occurred, but also as to my belief in the wisdom and propriety of my action—indeed the action not merely was wise and proper, but it would have been a calamity from every standpoint had I failed to take it.*

He went on to take dead aim at his successor's overall antitrust policy, declaring, "The effort to prohibit all combinations, good or bad, is bound to fail; and ought to fail; when made, it merely means that some of the worst combinations are not checked and that honest business is checked. Our purpose should be, not to strangle business as an incident of strangling combinations, but to regulate big corporations in thoroughgoing and effective fashion, so as to help legitimate business as an incident to thoroughly and completely safeguarding the interests of the people as a whole."[718] Newspapers around the country re-published Roosevelt's attacks against Taft on their front pages, and Roosevelt himself would ultimately credit his *Outlook* editorial on Taft's antitrust policy for bringing him into the presidential campaign of 1912.[719]

None of that was of much consequence or comfort to the heads of U.S. Steel, bracing, presumably, for a forced march of several years through the federal court system, nor indeed to U.S. Steel's Pittsburgh lawyer, David Aiken Reed of the Reed Smith firm. Reed was thrown into a defense team that was constructed on a grand scale, with Richard V. Lindabury, who had previously unsuccessfully represented American Tobacco in a Sherman Act case; Cordenio A. Severance, future president of the American Bar Association and founder of the American Law Institute; Joseph H. Choate, a founder of the New York firm of Evans Choate & Beaman; the redoubtable John G. Johnson; and Mr. Morgan's lawyer, Francis L. Stetson.[720]

Even David's father, Judge James Hay Reed, entered an appearance in the case, but in the end he was only called upon as a witness,[721] to testify that Carnegie was not "forced" to sell out to the combination. As to the Steel Corporation's attitude toward competitors, Judge Reed offered that they were treated with "Christian forbearance."[722]

After the end of the Taft presidency, John W. Davis came in to represent the government as President Wilson's Solicitor General. Over the four years of planning and pre-trial dueling that culminated in the closing statements at trial, the parties had compiled a trial record before the federal District Court for New Jersey consisting of fifty-seven volumes. David Aiken Reed was virtually living in New York, where much of the testimony was taken, while the trial progressed, leading Judge Reed's secretary back in Pittsburgh, Robert T. Rossell, to plead with David in a letter, "It would add to the peace of the whole office if you could devise some plan for withdrawing from the case." On June 3, 1915, the District Court dismissed the government's case, ruling that U.S. Steel was not formed with the intent to monopolize, but was, as Demmler paraphrased the District Court, "a natural consummation of the tendencies of the industry, which required combinations of capital and energy rather than diffusion in independent action."[723]

The Department of Justice appealed the case to the Supreme Court, with oral arguments set for March 1917. Wilson's Attorney General, Thomas Watt Gregory, and John W. Davis led the argument on behalf of the government, and Lindabury, David Aiken Reed, Severance, and the recently-appointed general counsel of U.S. Steel, thirty-nine year-old Raynal Bolling, argued the case on behalf of U.S. Steel.[724]

After the Supreme Court arguments, the War intervened. On April 6, 1917, President Wilson signed the declaration of war. Bolling, a National Guard aviator, was called to active duty twenty-one days later; and David Aiken Reed enlisted in the Army on May 11. While serving in France near Estrées-Deniécourt in the North, on the morning of March 26, 1918, Colonel Bolling's car was ambushed by German machine gunners, and Colonel Bolling was shot and killed while trying to protect his driver.[725] He was considered the first high-ranking officer of the U.S. Army to be killed during the War. Severance served on the Red Cross Commission in Serbia until later that year,[726] and Reed was discharged in February 1919.

The Supreme Court called for a re-argument of the case during three days in October of 1919. By that time, John W. Davis had been appointed U.S. ambassador to Great Britain, and Assistant Attorney General Charles B. Ames, formerly an Oklahoma City business lawyer, took the reins of the case for the government. Lindabury, Reed and Severance argued again for U.S. Steel. On March 20, 1920, Justice Joseph McKenna gave the opinion of the Court. Echoing the principle for which D.T. Watson had argued in *Standard Oil*—the rejection of the concept of a *per se* violation of the Sherman Act based on size alone, the "rule of reason" articulated by Chief Justice Edward White—the Court held that while U.S. Steel was "undoubtedly of impressive size" such that "it takes an effort of resolution not to be affected by it or to exaggerate its influence .... we must adhere to the law, and the law does not make the mere size an offense or the existence of unexerted power an offense." The Court upheld the District Court's dismissal of the case.[727] Passed from lawyer to lawyer (from Wickersham to Dickinson to Davis to Ames) by a government increasingly disinterested in the Sherman Act, the government's nine-year case against U.S. Steel ended with nary a whimper.

Beginning with the Wilson administration and continuing through those of Wilson's Republican successors, Harding, Coolidge and Hoover, the government virtually shut down its active enforcement of the Sherman Act, although the passage of the Clayton Act in 1914 gave the government additional weapons to attack anti-competitive behavior, including price discrimination, exclusive dealing and tying arrangements.

But one Pittsburgh corporate giant continued to receive the attention of the government throughout the first half of the twentieth century. The Aluminum Company of America, known as Alcoa, was formed in 1888 as the Pittsburgh Reduction Company by inventor Charles Martin Hall and metallurgist Alfred E. Hunt, with an experimental aluminum smelting operation on Smallman Street in the Strip District. Andrew Mellon was one of its early investors, and he eventually acquired about one-third of the company. Because of its patents, Alcoa functioned as the only legal supplier of aluminum in the U.S. until 1909. In 1911, after the expiration of the key patents, the Department of Justice came after Alcoa.[728]

The company, advised by George B. Gordon of the Pittsburgh firm of Gordon & Smith (later Smith, Buchanan & Ingersoll) entered into a consent decree with the government in 1912, whereby Alcoa agreed not to participate in foreign cartels or enter into certain restrictive contracts.[729] In 1921, the government attacked Alcoa again under the Clayton Act and ordered it to divest itself of the stock of a competitor that it had acquired, Cleveland Metals Company, resulting in a supplemental consent decree in 1922.[730] The even-tempered Gordon advised relatively quick settlements, thereby hoping to avoid a costly, multi-year government suit such as those experienced by Northern Securities, Standard Oil, and U.S. Steel. Nevertheless, in 1922, the Federal Trade Commission launched what became an eight-year investigation into Alcoa's alleged anti-competitive practices, first in the cooking utensil business and later in their sheet and sand casting, secondary scrap, ingot and raw materials businesses. At its conclusion, investigators charged that Alcoa had violated its 1912 consent decree, but in 1930, the Coolidge-appointed, pro-business chairman of the FTC, William E. Humphrey, dismissed the complaint. The investigation had cost Alcoa more than one million dollars.[731]

As economist and historian George David Smith relates, "Alcoa had become the very model of industrial concentration, and its principal owners had become exemplars of the kind of corporate barony that seemed distant, powerful and dangerous to the popular mind." Moreover, its "vulnerability to antitrust was heightened by its reputation as a 'Mellon Company.'"[732] During the Great Depression, Alcoa's association with Andrew Mellon, the former Secretary of the Treasury and, like J.P. Morgan, a symbol of corporate America, whose policies were blamed in some popular circles for the Depression itself,[733] meant that it attracted the attention of private antitrust plaintiffs. The defense against such suits was now left largely to Gordon's partner, William Watson Smith, as Gordon had passed away in 1927. Smith won the largest case, brought by the Baush Machine Tool Company, on technical grounds, after which Alcoa entered into a settlement with Baush, conditioned upon receiving a letter from the government that they would not use the settlement as the basis for further federal prosecution.[734]

Meanwhile, the prevailing mood in Washington regarding the Sherman Act began to shift during the presidency of Franklin Roosevelt. As George David Smith writes, "After first trying to stabilize depressed American industry through Government-sponsored cartelization (the NRA) and through suspension of antitrust pressure on matters of production, price setting, and employment, the Roosevelt administration veered toward antitrust as a political tool for controlling industry."[735] Robert H. Jackson, then the head of the Antitrust Division of the Department of Justice, sought to implement the administration's basic philosophical viewpoint—that it was detrimental to the recovery that big corporations, by definition, had the power to control sectors of the American economy—by filing a new lawsuit against Alcoa in 1937, calling for the company's dissolution. In effect, Jackson and the DOJ would now attempt to persuade the courts to dispense with the "rule of reason" for which D.T. Watson had argued in *Standard Oil* in favor of a "big equals bad" interpretation of the Sherman Act.[736]

Alcoa apparently found it to be a bit sinister that Roosevelt's Attorney General, Homer Cummings, was the lead lawyer on the complaint, as Cummings' Connecticut law firm had been counsel for Baush Machine Tool Company during its fight with Alcoa.[737] Cummings, however, played almost no role in the suit. Instead, much of the case would be handled by Walter L. Rice, a Harvard-trained former New York prosecutor who had been hired as a special assistant to the Attorney General, and later by Thurman Arnold, a Harvard lawyer-turned Wyoming political maverick—later the founder of the Washington, DC firm of Arnold & Porter—who arrived at the Department of Justice in 1938 with six-shooters blazing.

William Watson Smith, at age sixty-six—George Gordon's surviving partner who at the time of the suit had the misfortune of spending the most hours in court of any living human being defending Alcoa against antitrust allegations—would again be tapped to defend Alcoa from the latest round of government accusations. At his side would be Frank B. Ingersoll, age forty-four—a blunt-nosed instrument of a corporate lawyer, and a great back-slapping client relationship manager, who had acted as Smith's right hand on Alcoa matters—and Leon Hickman, age thirty-seven—a shrewd Iowa Methodist with a cool and courtly professional manner. Ingersoll, in particular, had over the years become "like a brother" to the heads of Alcoa, according to Smith Buchanan corporate lawyer William J. Kyle, Jr.—men such as Roy Hunt, the company president and son of Alcoa founder Alfred Hunt, and I.W. "Chief" Wilson, Alcoa's vice president in charge of operations.[738]

Cummings and Jackson filed their case against Alcoa in the Southern District of New York on April 23, 1937, and Smith immediately resorted to history to get the case dismissed. He filed a petition six days later in the Western District of Pennsylvania, where the twenty-five year-old 1912 consent decree was entered, arguing that the new case was a carbon copy of the 1912 case, that the consent decree foreclosed the demand for dissolution, and that jurisdiction should in any event be retained by the Western District of Pennsylvania. Judge Robert Gibson of the Western District of Pennsylvania issued a preliminary injunction against the government's New York proceedings.[739]

While this skirmish was under way, Ingersoll's partner, Paul G. Rodewald, wandered into Ingersoll's office in the Union Trust Building and told Ingersoll about a dream he had had the night before. Rodewald dreamed that "the Supreme Court, after Judge Gibson had ruled in our favor, issued a writ, reviewed the case, reversed it, and sentenced the officers of Alcoa to terms in prison." Ingersoll sat back in his chair and shook his head. He said, "Roy A. Hunt is not going to like this."[740]

They had a good laugh, but Rodewald's dream turned out to be a premonition of sorts. The government sought a hearing on the merits of the injunction before a "special expediting court" made up of a panel of Third Circuit judges acting as the District Court. Judge Joseph W. Thompson vacated Judge Gibson's preliminary injunction on the basis that the 1912 suit and the 1937 suit "were not so similar as respects parties, subject-matter, issues or relief" as to entitle Alcoa to have the case thrown out of the Southern District of New York.[741] Smith and his team appealed the ruling to the Supreme Court, and in December 1937, Justice McReynolds gave the opinion of the Court that upheld Judge Thompson's ruling, meaning that Alcoa would have to stand trial in New York.[742]

The trial began on June 1, 1938 at the then relatively new federal courthouse in Foley Square in lower Manhattan before Judge Francis G. Caffey. Caffey was sixty-nine years-old at the beginning of the trial—a native Alabaman and a veteran of the Spanish American War who had attended Harvard, practiced in New York and eventually served as U.S. Attorney for the Southern District of New York under Woodrow Wilson before ascending to the bench.[743]

One might have been forgiven for feeling sorry for William Watson Smith at the outset of the trial: an old Pittsburgh lawyer with a pair of middle-aged assistants—one portly and surly (Ingersoll), the other slight and somewhat stiff (Hickman)—facing a young, vigorous New York prosecutor (Walter L. Rice) and his twenty or so industrious young federal assistants. A look at Smith's grave countenance and one could not be blamed, as William Kyle suggested, for believing that the old lawyer might have been "susceptible to 'leg-pulling.'"[744] With a judge of his own generation presiding, however, Smith was able to deploy his own dry sense of humor—seasonally evident, ever since his Princeton days—to undermine the Judge's view of the humorless government team. Irving Lipkowitz, a Department of Justice economist, bittersweetly recalls that watching Smith during the trial was a "pleasure," and that his sense of courtroom psychology was "marvelous." As George David Smith relates, Lipkowitz recalled how Smith "deftly played on the difference between the generations of young attorneys in the Antitrust Division and the septuagenarian Woodrow Wilson appointee on the bench." "The judge and [Smith] were the old guys," Lipkowitz recalled. "They had wisdom. They had judgment. And we had a bunch of kids over here, scurrying around ... [Smith was] able to refer to us as Boy Scouts, and not be reprimanded by the court. He had built it up gradually, to the point where this was the atmosphere."[745]

Smith's methods were evident even during the opening days of the trial. Walter Rice put on a dead-panned opening statement on behalf of the government that lasted for two and a half days, filled with excruciatingly painful detail about prices, markets, market segments, alloys, raw materials—a fire hose stream of factual data, during which Judge Caffey continually interrupted, admonishing Rice by saying he needed to understand the "forest" before hearing about the "trees."[746] "I have no place to put the trees unless I have the forest," the Judge would say.[747]

In his opening, Smith told the Judge, "The other day you suggested to Mr. Rice that he should first point out to you the forest before indicating the trees. As I view it, for two and a half full days you did not get the forest at all; you got nothing but trees, and even huckleberry bushes."[748]

Turning to the government's underlying argument, that Alcoa's concentration of power in the aluminum market was a burden on the economy, Smith began his opening by graphically referring to how "other substances compete with aluminum," indicating the "little reading desk" he had brought into the courtroom, composed of "pure aluminum ... made [by Alcoa] for our use in this trial, in the company's plant in New Kensington, Pennsylvania, a short distance above Pittsburgh on the Allegheny River." Smith went on, in his understated way, to point out that "Mr. Rice has a reading desk made of wood. No doubt he thinks that is equally good. I do not agree with him, but that is a matter of opinion." Judge Caffey now had a constant visual reminder throughout the trial that the American economy was much bigger than the aluminum market.

Smith also wasted no time in building his "rule of reason" case:

The men in charge of this company's affairs throughout its history have been ordinary American citizens. With good reason they have been proud of the job they have done of the useful employment they have given to many thousands of workers, of the great service they have rendered to the public in reducing the cost of this useful metal, from a jeweler's price of $8 per pound to 20 cents in the course of the company's history. These men, your Honor, have not only done that, but they have developed and used this metal in scores of useful ways in industry and commerce. Your Honor will have an opportunity to see these men on the stand, to hear their testimony and observe their demeanor. And I submit it is too great a strain upon your Honor's credulity to ask you to believe that these men were ever such business pirates and cutthroats as they have been charged to be by the Government in this case.

I marvel at a Government which could make these sweeping charges, in that book of 104 paragraphs, and never give us the benefit of an honest motive in a single instance. We have never done an honest thing of substantial importance in the 50 years of our life if you believe the averments of the Government's petition ... The company has done a fine job and contributed materially to the welfare of the nation. I hope your Honor will understand that while I cannot take the time to deny every statement made by Mr. Rice, we nevertheless do deny practically every statement which he has made as to the purpose and intent of the Aluminum Company and a multitude of assertions of fact which he has made. We emphatically deny every single charge ...[749]

As the trial progressed, Thurman Arnold joined the government's team as the head of the DOJ's Antitrust Division. Understanding that he had to dismantle Smith's "rule of reason" case, Arnold waged an aggressive second battlefront in the newspapers, driving home the idea that Alcoa was a bad actor. In November 1939, Arnold released a statement outside New York City to the effect that Judge Caffey had passed on the merits of the case in a ruling from the bench that had indicated that Alcoa had been guilty of conspiring with German and other foreign manufacturers to divide the world markets. Pulitzer Prize-winning reporter Alva Johnston, covering the Alcoa case for the *New Yorker*, wrote that the New York reporters "who were following the trial ... instantly would have recognized the statement as a hoax. They knew that the Judge had not decided that Alcoa was guilty of anything" and that "Alcoa had not yet placed a single witness on the stand." The effect of the ruling, rather, was that the Judge permitted certain documents to be placed in evidence. In August 1940, after the taking of testimony in the case had been concluded, Arnold presumptuously pushed out to the press a twenty-eight-page "decision," written by the government, in which the government had won on every single count of its case.[750] Alcoa, by contrast, refused to fight on Arnold's turf; Alcoa's chairman, Arthur Vining Davis, was openly hostile to the concept of public relations, preferring to let Alcoa's work speak for itself.[751]

Arnold's efforts on the "newspaper" front had little effect on Judge Caffey, however, other than irritation. As Johnston reported, when a witness mentioned during the trial that "everybody knew" a certain fact, Judge Caffey interrupted, "Everybody knows it? I don't know it. I don't trust anything I see in the newspapers about anything."[752]

Another Arnold press release discussed the scope of the trial, which concluded in August 1940:

The record of the testimony has reached the unprecedented figure of more than 40,000 pages, in addition to nearly 10,000 pages of exhibits. As the trial has progressed, counsel have been obliged to bring new tables and shelves into the courtroom to hold the growing volumes of the record. When the trial ended today the record covered thirty-two feet.[753]

One hundred and fifty-five witnesses testified at trial; Arthur Vining Davis testified for six weeks, covering 2,105 pages on direct and cross-examination.[754] Johnston reported that the transcript of testimony weighed 325 pounds, "or more than three times as much as the Encyclopedia Britannica," contained fifteen million words, "or more than thirty times as many as 'Gone With the Wind,'" and was printed, along with the rest of the trial record, in 480 separate volumes. Arnold apparently took unusual delight in pointing out England's longest trial, the Tichborne Case of 1874, lasted "only" 188 days, while the Alcoa case lasted for 364. It was the longest trial in the history of Anglo-Saxon jurisprudence. "If the period of preparation is included," Johnston wrote, "the Alcoa case"—that is, even just up to the moment of Judge Caffey's decision—"outlasted the Civil War."[755]

Judge Caffey took several months to study the massive record, which included new briefs prepared by the parties after the closing of the trial, and summoned the parties back to the courtroom to hear his decision. The Judge read his ruling aloud over the course of nine days in October 1941. In summary, Judge Caffey stated that it was necessary to show evidence of Alcoa's intent to monopolize in order to hold Alcoa guilty of illegal monopolization. There were approximately 140 charges involved in the government's case, and one by one, Judge Caffey found that Alcoa's success in coming to dominate certain markets was due to acceptable commercial activities and good business practices. Furthermore, Judge Caffey found no monopoly at all in the supply of bauxite, one of the important sources of aluminum; no monopoly in the product markets, such as cooking utensils or automobile engine pistons; and no monopoly in Alcoa's electrical power generation activities.[756] The existence of viable competition seemed only to be proved by the departure of Walter Rice from the prosecution team during the case—to accept an offer of employment from Reynolds Metals. Rice, it seemed, had learned enough about the aluminum industry to get a good job in it, with a competitor of Alcoa.[757]

After the entry of the judgment dismissing the government's complaint in July 1942, the Department of Justice appealed to the Supreme Court. However, the Supreme Court could not come up with a quorum to hear the case. Three Justices—Frank Murphy, Stanley Reed and Robert H. Jackson (newly appointed in 1941)—had participated directly in the Alcoa case while they were inside the DOJ, and one, Chief Justice Harlan Stone, had been Attorney General during the Coolidge administration, and had recommended a monopoly suit against Alcoa at that time. Six justices were required to hear the government's appeal.[758] The case sat more or less idle for two years, until a special act of Congress was passed designating the Second Circuit Court of Appeals in New York to hear the case.[759]

The parties went to New York to argue the government's appeal in January 1945 before a three-judge panel consisting of Learned Hand, Learned's elder cousin Augustus Hand, and Thomas Swan. The three judges were definitely contemporaries of William Watson Smith, who at age seventy-four would lead the argument on behalf of Alcoa; but in the context of the appeal there would be no opportunity for Smith to repeat his tactic of making the government's team, this time represented by Solicitor General Charles Fahy, age fifty-three, look like callow youths. Still, Smith had the winds at his back: he had a categorical dismissal of the government's case by the court below, based on firm antitrust precedent—the "rule of reason"—that would date all the way back to Chief Justice Edward White's opinion in *Standard Oil*, based on D.T. Watson's argument.

If Judge Caffey's categorical dismissal of the Alcoa case was a surprise, the partial reversal of Judge Caffey's decision by Judge Learned Hand, sitting with the authority of the highest court in the land, was a shock. Judge Hand went through each of the charges of the government with respect to whether or not Alcoa had a monopoly and upheld Caffey's dismissal of all of them, except for one—in the aluminum ingot market. Purporting to review Alcoa's aluminum ingot business only up to August 14, 1940, when testimony in the original trial ended, the Court concluded that Alcoa was supplying ninety percent of the U.S. market. In an oft-paraphrased line from the decision, Judge Hand wrote that while ninety percent "is enough to constitute a monopoly ... it is doubtful whether sixty or sixty-four percent would be enough; and certainly thirty-three per cent is not." When considering Alcoa's intent and conduct, Judge Hand took pains to detail the company's effectiveness over the years, and concluded, "We can think of no more effective exclusion [of competitors] than progressively to embrace each new opportunity as it opened, and to face every newcomer with new capacity already geared into a great organization having the advantage of experience, trade connections, and the elite of personnel." In finding Alcoa guilty of anticompetitive behavior in the aluminum ingot market, Judge Hand said, signaling a departure from the *Standard Oil* "rule of reason":

> *... it might have been thought adequate to condemn only those monopolies which could not show that they had exercised the highest possible ingenuity, had adopted every possible economy, had anticipated every conceivable improvement, stimulated every possible demand. No doubt, that would be one way of dealing with the matter, although it would imply constant scrutiny and constant supervision, such as courts are unable to*

provide. Be that as it may, that was not the way that Congress chose; it did not condone 'good trusts' and condemn 'bad' ones; it forbad all.

In effect, Alcoa would be held to be guilty under the Sherman Act for being really good at its business.[760]

Hickman would later tell George David Smith that, in an atmosphere in which public policy apparently carried greater weight than precedent, Alcoa did not stand a chance:

I can see why Judge Hand felt that no matter how we got where we were, that it wasn't in the public interest that we be in such a dominant position. If you kept that in mind, then you worked back from that. 'What do I pin on them?' Well, he principally pinned on us the fact that we were the first in every market that opened up. But actually, look at the reverse of that. Suppose that we had acted as a monopoly is supposed to act and we simply sat back and took our profits and hadn't developed the market. You would say now there is a monopoly of action. There is a great need for new markets and new uses for aluminum and you aren't meeting it. So, in a way, from his approach, we had no escape. He'd get us either way.[761]

The government had asked for Alcoa to be dismantled, but Judge Hand stopped short of granting that relief. Whatever shortcomings there may have been in his analysis (a young Alan Greenspan wrote that Hand's opinion was "disastrous" in that it "led to the condemnation of the productive and efficient members of our society *because* they are productive and efficient"[762]), Judge Hand limited his ruling to the state of affairs that existed on August 14, 1940. After that date, as Judge Hand acknowledged, the War and government intervention in the aluminum market might have changed things; thus, the Court directed that whatever remedial relief was to be afforded the government would need to be decided upon a review of those effects.

In 1947, Alcoa applied to the District Court for the Southern District of New York for a determination that it no longer had a monopoly. The government attempted to quash the District Court proceedings and return the case to the Second Circuit, and the trial on Alcoa's monopoly position after 1940 was postponed while appeals ran up to the U.S. Supreme Court, and back down through the Second Circuit. Finally, in March 1949, the parties gathered in the District Court room in Foley Square, this time before Chief Judge John C. Knox (apparently, no relation to Philander Knox). Smith, Ingersoll and Hickman, accompanied by their young partner William Unverzagt, continued to represent Alcoa; Leonard J. Emmerglick, special assistant to the Attorney General, argued on behalf of the government. Alcoa argued that Reynolds and Kaiser had become formidable competitors, thereby terminating Alcoa's monopoly on aluminum ingot production.[763] After a six-month trial, in an opinion filed in June 1950, Judge Knox agreed that Alcoa no longer had a monopoly on aluminum ingots, but that those persons who owned stock in both Alcoa and Aluminum, Ltd., Alcoa's non-wholly-owned Canadian subsidiary, were obliged to sell their stock in one or the other company in order to remove any appearance of collusive action in the ingot market in the future. Further proceedings focused on the stock disposal plan filed by the major stockholders; and finally, Judge

Knox indicated that the government should retain jurisdiction for another five years to petition the Court for additional relief "if conditions so warrant."[764] In sum, there would be no dissolution of Alcoa.

In 1957, William Watson Smith, age eighty-six, entered an appearance before Judge John M. Cashin in the federal District Court for the Southern District of New York, on a petition by the U.S. government asking for the Court to retain jurisdiction over Alcoa for an additional five years in order to petition the courts for additional relief "if conditions should so warrant." Along with his partner George Gordon, Smith had been in the firm's defense of the client from government parries since 1911—for forty-six years. Now leading the defense, however, was Smith's former partner Leon Hickman, who in 1951, after working at Smith's side on the *Alcoa* case since 1937, was hired by Alcoa as its first vice president and general counsel.[765] Hickman was joined again by William Unverzagt, who had been hired by the Smith Buchanan firm in 1938, and who had subsequently been brought into Alcoa by Hickman as an assistant general counsel.[766] The *Alcoa* case had virtually represented Unverzagt's entire career as a lawyer up to 1957.

In his opinion, Judge Cashin reviewed what he believed to be the uncertainties about the aluminum market in 1950 that led Judge Knox to suggest that the court should continue to retain jurisdiction for five years after his decision, and determined that "within the framework of [Judge Knox's] opinion," the facts did not sustain an application for an extension of jurisdiction. "Judge Knox's opinion," he wrote, "and the resultant final judgment of 1950, is the law of the case."[767]

United States v. Aluminum Company of America, April 23, 1937, to June 28, 1957. Twenty years of battling, and in the final analysis, neither side could really claim victory. Twenty years of battling to a Pyrrhic draw.

The case itself, in George David Smith's words, "changed the whole focus of antitrust law for more than three decades."[768] Meanwhile, the *Alcoa* case also left its mark on the firm of Smith Buchanan. Hickman's departure for Alcoa in 1951 caused ripples within the firm that would magnify into waves within months after the case had ended. But the collective impact of *Alcoa* and its ancestors—*Northern Securities, Standard Oil, U.S. Steel*—on the bar of Pittsburgh is perhaps a bit more subtle, but material nonetheless.

Not many cities in the U.S. had as much of an opportunity to participate in, much less define, the "Anti-Trust" battlefield as Pittsburgh. In some respects it was because of that history that successive generations of lawyers in Pittsburgh, from the 1940s to the 1970s, continued to develop and maintain an active antitrust practice in the city—lawyers such as Paul Winschel and Gilbert Helwig at Reed Smith; Clayton Sweeney and Tom Van Kirk at Buchanan Ingersoll; Walter Braham and Thomas Pomeroy at Kirkpatrick Lockhart; David Armstrong of Dickie McCamey, who was in-house counsel at Westinghouse during the electrical price fixing cases; Frank "Zeke" Seamans at Eckert Seamans; Paul Titus at Koppers Company, and subsequently, with Tom Kerr at Titus, Marcus & Shapira; and William Wycoff at Thorp Reed.[769] Although antitrust cases would never necessarily represent full-time work for any of them, it was natural for these lawyers from among the elite firms and corporations in Pittsburgh to step into the footprints of their mentors and forbearers, continuing to participate in defending against the federal regulatory onslaught on big business (both *American* business and

Pittsburgh business) that began at the outset of the twentieth century. The large scope and scale of antitrust cases, their procedural complexities and their factual and economic intricacies, and the occasional necessity of gearing up for the spillover of these cases into the arena of white collar criminal defense, was also excellent conditioning for these trial lawyers, who were considered to be among the best of their respective generations in Pittsburgh, within any commercial litigation context.

Finally, in an era of decline and painful re-definitions, as the elite bar of America seemed to begin largely to recede to a few cities on the coasts of the continent (plus Chicago), Pittsburgh's antitrust legacy was one which kept many Pittsburgh lawyers clashing either at the side of or against the top trial lawyers from the top firms of the country on a regular basis. There would, perhaps, be fewer and fewer circumstances in which that would be the case as the rest of the twentieth century unfolded.

PART IV

WWII AND THE POST-WAR BAR, 1942-1988

WWII AND THE POST-WAR BAR, 1942-1988

Pittsburgh during the War years was a study in contrasts, none of which necessarily pointed to any comfortable conclusions about the future of the city. It had just endured the worst of the Great Depression. Industrial production fell fifty-nine percent from the 1929 average during the 1930s,[1] with unemployment in the city hitting as high as twenty-five percent.[2] Moreover, the steel industry at large had slowed its investment in the old Pittsburgh mills beginning in the decade after U.S. Steel was formed in 1902, as new competitors were popping up and new steel plants were being built in places like Cleveland, Detroit and Gary, Indiana. In the wake of general economic conditions and the gradual relocation of the industry, Pittsburgh became increasingly dilapidated, with vacant, decaying downtown buildings, abandoned rail tracks, blighted neighborhoods, and debris along the river banks.[3] The last great downtown building, the Gulf Tower, had been completed in 1932.[4]

Meanwhile, the enlistment of the old mills of Pittsburgh for wartime production beginning in 1941 was an adrenalin shot for the region's economy. As one of the main centers of the American "arsenal of democracy," Pittsburgh produced more steel than Germany and Japan combined, and unemployment fell nearly to zero. Thousands of young men and women went off to the War, however, leaving the region short-handed to meet the demand for workers.[5] The relentlessness of wartime manufacturing also impacted the legal profession, which had lost its own share of young men to wartime roles. "The grueling pace of the war years," recalled Ralph Demmler of Reed Smith, "was something that had to be experienced to be believed," as Reed Smith broke the two million dollar barrier in revenue in 1944.[6] It was a breathless time—breathless for the near inability of Pittsburghers to keep up with wartime requirements, but also for the heavy clouds of black, sooty smoke that hung low throughout the city.

Yet, with all of that wartime activity, all of that new industrial expansion, all of that wealth being created, there had been no time to restore Pittsburgh. When the veterans returned from the bombed-out landscapes of Europe and Japan at the end of the War, they encountered Pittsburgh with an eerie sense of déjà vu. They found that their own neglected hometown also needed rebuilding, both physically and spiritually. Pittsburgh needed its own "Marshall Plan" after the War.

Judge Joseph F. Weis, Jr., of the federal Third Circuit recalled a moment of eerie panic when he entered practice shortly after returning from the War. He walked into a County courtroom in which Judge Premo Columbus and Judge Henry Ellenbogen were presiding, en banc. Seeing them perched on the dais, side by side—the completely bald Columbus, with his heavy forehead and doughy nose, and Ellenbogen, with his straight, severe comb-over and fussy little moustache—Weis would later remember, snickering, "I swear to God, it looked like Mussolini and Hitler ... it really took my breath away to see that!"[7]

It is a wonder that Joe Weis was not even more traumatized. Weis was twenty years old, a sophomore studying pre-law courses at Duquesne, when he entered the Army and joined the Third Army's Fourth Armored Division in Germany in 1943. While in France, driving toward the Battle of the Bulge in November 1944, Weis was wounded in the leg with shrapnel from a tank shell. He returned to combat on the same day, but was more seriously wounded when a mortar round exploded behind him. He suffered extensive injuries to his back, leg and pelvis, and, according to *Post-Gazette* reporter Torsten Ove, "when he opened his shirt, he saw his intestines." Another soldier, a fellow Pittsburgher named Chester Wernecke, carried him onto a jeep, which sped through enemy fire to a battalion aid station.[8] For the next three years, his Army service consisted of being an Army patient in one Army hospital after another. In 1947, he came home and, while continuing to be nursed back to health by his mother, he finished college at Duquesne, taking half-days at school and resting for the remainder of the day. He was afforded the benefits of the G.I. Bill, and finished law school at Pitt. "I still hadn't recovered from my wounds," Weis remembered. Shortly after he entered the bar, he recalled, "I was trying a case before Judge Henry O'Brien, and my condition worsened. I had to go to the Mayo Clinic for emergency surgery. ... I was feeling pretty poorly towards the end of that trial, and just barely made it through to the charge to the jury. I wasn't even there for the final verdict."[9] Weis would regain his health, enjoying an illustrious career as a trial lawyer and both a trial and appellate judge before his death at the age of ninety-one.

The G.I. Bill that spurred Weis to finish his education, despite his condition, came down like a miracle from on high to so many War veterans who would never have had the opportunity to go to law school without it; it was undoubtedly an important element of Pittsburgh's "Marshall Plan." The local law schools, Pitt and Duquesne, after a few years of smaller than normal classes during the War, were only too happy to oblige the returning veterans. The number of law graduates had shrunk by fifty percent from 1938 to 1942 at Duquesne, and from forty-seven graduates in 1938 to just seven in 1944 from Pitt Law. Meanwhile, the number of new lawyers admitted to the Allegheny County bar in 1941 was sixty-five, while in 1945, just nine new lawyers were admitted. With the G.I. Bill fueling the fire, the number of new lawyers who entered the bar jumped from twenty-nine in 1948 to sixty-five in 1949, and ninety-six in 1950. Pitt Law's graduating class in 1950 was seventy-six students.[10] "In those days they were taking an abundance of people with the idea that these people would cop out in the first year," remembered Jack Feeney, a Pitt Law grad and a veteran of the Navy. "Four or five years later," Feeney observed, "they [the local law schools] changed that whole program; they decided to be tough on admissions."[11] They also became tough on continuing students, with Pitt imposing a requirement of maintaining a weighted average grade scoring of at least sixty-nine, without failing a single course, to advance to the next year.[12] While that toughness had a momentary effect—bar admissions took a tumble down to fifty-three in 1957—the 1950s saw an average influx of eighty new lawyers per year entering the Allegheny County bar.[13]

With the addition of so many young lawyers during the period—the numbers only increased after 1960—it was an era in which the figure of the Pittsburgh lawyer was, in many ways, cut down to human size. Because of the availability of scholarships and financial aid, many of the young men and women who entered the bar during the period did not come from particularly wealthy backgrounds. Many of them, in fact, were the first in their families to graduate from college. They moved into modest suburban homes, a far cry from the mansions that were the homes of the elite lawyers from the Gilded Age or the early years of the twentieth century. While some from the new crew would surely attain those heights, lawyers in Pittsburgh became more generally accessible to their neighbors. In an extension of the democratization of the bar that began in the 1890s, the Pittsburgh lawyer had become a member of the middle class. By dint of the sheer increase in their numbers, over the course of forty years the lawyers went from being seen as members of an exclusive professional intelligentsia who carried with them the mystique of their guild, operating behind dark wood-paneled walls, to being encountered as fellow commuters who answered their own telephones and watered their own lawns—across the street from the home construction contractors, engineers and salesmen who were also increasing the population of the Pittsburgh middle class during the years of relative economic stability that followed the War.

Immediately after the War, however, the Pittsburgh bar was still a relatively small tribe, mostly consisting of lawyers who had managed to survive the Great Depression, and whose successes depended to some degree upon their skills, but also upon disciplined, cordial social interactions. For a variety of professional and spiritual reasons, the collegiality of the bar was highly-prized by these lawyers, and their efforts to build institutions around it—to preserve it in the face of the growth in the numbers of lawyers that was beginning to occur after the War—were reflections of the value that was placed on it.

If there was one lawyer in Pittsburgh who typified the collegiality of the bar immediately after the War, and probably did much to continue to stimulate it, it was James P. "Jim" McArdle. Jack Feeney, who worked in McArdle's firm for ten years, described him as "a real down-to-earth, Mt. Washington Irishman"[14] whose father, P.J. McArdle, was president of the Amalgamated Association of Iron and Steel Workers during the 1900s and a long-serving Pittsburgh city councilman. Jim went to Duquesne Law School, and then studied in the office of Judge James Gray. During the 1930s, McArdle took over the plaintiffs' negligence practice of John Egan, who became a Common Pleas judge,[15] and built his own law firm which rivalled Evans, Ivory and Evans, as the premier plaintiffs' firm in Pittsburgh.

McArdle became particularly well-known for representing railroad workers from the steel company "short line" railroads in Federal Employers Liability Act (FELA) cases—so well-known, in fact, that railroad workers used to write his name and phone number on the sides of rail cars in chalk so that everyone would know the lawyer they should call in case of an on-the-job injury.[16] At a time when most Pittsburgh lawyers did not decorate their offices with expensive furnishings for fear, as David Fawcett, Jr., would recall, that clients "would think you were too expensive and wouldn't come to you," McArdle moved his practice into the Frick Building and outfitted his offices lavishly. His clientele was committed to him because of who he was. "He didn't care whether they thought he was wealthy or not—and he did become wealthy," said Fawcett.[17] As a trial lawyer, the 6'-3" tall McArdle was "flamboyant," as Judge Weis remembered, a one-man circus who would steal the attention of juries with his pranks on opposing counsel, such as putting goldfish in defense lawyer Samuel Bredin's water pitcher.[18] Feeney remembered that McArdle had another "gimmick," in which, back in the days when smoking was permitted in the courtroom, he would let the ash on his cigarette grow so long while the defense put on its case that jurors would become distracted over when the ash would fall.[19a] As David Fawcett, Jr. recalled, McArdle was a "tremendous trial lawyer" in his own right. "He had a knack with jurors," Feeney asserted, because he "talked like them."[20]

At the same time, McArdle "was friendly with everybody," Weis remembered,[21] and he extended every courtesy to opposing counsel. It was second nature to McArdle to enjoy lunches and drinks with his opponents outside the courtroom—not only because he worked in a small trial bar where it did not make sense to burn bridges, but also because friendships among plaintiffs and defense lawyers were a good grounding for settling cases. Judd Poffinberger, a Kirkpatrick & Lockhart trial lawyer who represented the interests of the railroads in many of McArdle's FELA cases, told of the time that the two of them were locked in battle on one particular case. At the end of the day, McArdle approached Poffinberger and said, "C'mon across the street, let's have a drink." Poffinberger told him, "Jim, I'd like to go, but my mom is in Magee Hospital, she's been operated on, and I promised I'd go out and see her." By the time Poffinberger arrived at his mother's hospital room, his mother was admiring a bonsai tree that had just been delivered. "Who is Jim McArdle?," she asked, looking up from the card. McArdle, recalled Poffinberger "was my old buddy."[22] McArdle's way of getting along within the bar set the tone for other trial lawyers. Certain downtown lounges, such as the Cork and Bottle on Smithfield, the Grant Street Tavern, the old bar at the William Penn Hotel, and the cocktail lounge at the Carlton House, the hotel that once stood where One Mellon Plaza now stands, were favored as lunchtime and after-work settings for

---

a   Jim McArdle's nephew, Pittsburgh lawyer Jerry Mansmann, contended that McArdle accomplished the trick by inserting a wire into the cigarette before lighting it; thus, the ash stuck to the wire as the cigarette burned. J. Jerome Mansmann, interview by the author, September 14, 2015.

the impromptu social activities of members of the bar. As Judge Weis recalled, "The trial bar was very congenial. They talked to each other ... and drank together and had dinner together, and so they were all friends. So it was not difficult at all to get them together to work on a problem where they had common interests."[23]

The collegiality among members of the trial bar in Pittsburgh in the 1950s did not extend to the judiciary, and the conflicts between them reached a boiling point in 1958. By then, the Allegheny County courts had developed a paralyzing backlog of civil cases—growing, as Judge Weis would later suggest, from the "booming economy of the post-war 40s and the early 50s" which "dumped millions of cars onto an inadequate road net" causing accidents to increase dramatically. The ensuing litigation, brought by a quickly expanding bar, was slowed by insurance companies that were unprepared to handle the flood of new claims, and the fact that the courts were understaffed.[24] Criticism of the court backlog was already in the air and in the newspapers when Judge Henry Ellenbogen, ever the skillful self-publicist, blamed the trial lawyers in an interview in the Sunday newspaper, saying that damage cases moved at a "snail's pace" because only "a dozen law firms" had locked up "80 per cent of these cases."[25]

Concerned about the effect of the interview on a new jury being empaneled that Monday morning, four lawyers—Jim McArdle; Joseph Weis, who was then practicing with his father's insurance defense firm, Sherriff, Lindsay, Weis and McGinnis; Sanford "San" Chilcote, a defense lawyer from the Dickie McCamey firm; and T. Robert "Bob" Brennan, another plaintiff's lawyer from the firm of Brennan & Brennan—went before President Judge William McNaugher, complaining that Ellenbogen's harsh criticism of the lawyers would prejudice the juries, and they asked Judge McNaugher to dismiss the panel. The judge denied their request, but told the trial lawyers that any of them who did not want to pick a jury from that panel would be excused. "Most of us did walk out," recalled Weis, and the cases were continued to a later date.[26]

With the battle lines having been drawn by Judge Ellenbogen, the four lawyers met for lunch to discuss the formation of an organization, separate from the Allegheny County Bar Association (ACBA), to represent the common interests of Pittsburgh trial lawyers, especially vis-à-vis the local judges. "We felt that the trial bar wasn't adequately getting its message across to the public or to the judges" and that the fallout was "affecting all of us." Weis was charged with organizing a meeting of the city's trial lawyers, which was ultimately convened at the University Club in February 1959, with about sixty lawyers in attendance.[27] Out of that meeting was born the Academy of Trial Lawyers, an "invitation only" organization initially comprising fifty-five lawyers—"evenly divided" between defense and plaintiffs' lawyers, explained plaintiffs' lawyer Seymour "Sy" Sikov, without a hint of irony.[28] "One of our first projects," says Weis, "was an aggressive campaign of public relations to bring our side of the court controversy to the community."[29] The show of strength by the trial bar caught the attention of the judiciary, as the trial lawyers and the Common Pleas judges began to engage in substantive discussions about procedural revisions in an effort to streamline the pre-trial phase, and began to call in cases for intensive conciliation, mediation and settlement.

As the trial lawyers and the Common Pleas judges began to reach agreement through the work of the Academy, it soon became clear that another battle was raging in the background—this one between local judges and federal judges. "Trouble was brewing," Weis commented, as Judge Ellenbogen succeeded Judge McNaugher as President Judge of the County Common Pleas courts in 1963. Weis explained:

> [B]oth the federal and state courts were drawing upon the same pool of trial lawyers and both courts were led by strong personalities who understandably were each more concerned with the state of their own court's docket than that of the jurisdiction at the other end of Grant Street. Caught squarely in the middle of these competing institutions were the trial lawyers. They were being figuratively torn limb from limb by [the judges] to try cases in their respective courts. Neither court took kindly to an excuse that a lawyer was in trial at the other end of Grant Street ... Tempers flared, and it is only a slight exaggeration to say that posses of sheriffs from common pleas and platoons of marshals from the federal court passed each other on Grant Street en route to bring lawyers from one court to the other for a contempt proceeding.[30]

Sy Sikov enjoyed telling the story that the straw that finally broke the camel's back in the fight between the federal and County courts was when attorney Allen Brunwasser, "of all people," was hauled out of Common Pleas court by federal marshals and ended up spending the night in jail on a contempt citation for failing to appear for a simultaneous federal court proceeding.[31]

Certainly Allen Brunwasser was no stranger to controversy. Judge James B. Craven, Jr., of the Fourth Circuit once famously wrote in his opinion in *Brunwasser v. Suave* (1968), that, "To Lawyer-Appellant Allen N. Brunwasser of Pittsburgh, Pa., life is a battle."[32] In a legal career spanning over six decades, the Harvard Law-trained Brunwasser became notorious in Pittsburgh as the city's most relentless combatant—frequently representing himself as plaintiff, waging war against every person or institution who had ever slighted him, from suing TWA over cancelling a direct flight between Pittsburgh and London,[33] to launching a complaint against the firm of Reed, Smith, Shaw & McClay for "illegally" using the names of deceased partners as a trade name in violation of the code of professional responsibility,[34] to objecting to class action fee applications for members of the city law department who had pursued him personally in an unrelated case for the payment of back business privilege tax bills.[35] "Brunwasser sues people for the same basic reasons that a Bengal tiger will bite," wrote *Post-Gazette* reporter Thomas Hritz, "sometimes because he's angry, sometimes because he's hungry, and sometimes just for the hell of it."[36] "Anytime you ran into Brunwasser you were likely to be sued," concurred Weis.[37] "If he can't win a case," Hritz wrote, "he will keep asking for writs of whatever forever, tying it up hopelessly. Judges cringe when he appears in their courtrooms."[38]

However, Judge Weis asserts, "Sy's memory was wrong on that"—it wasn't Brunwasser's imprisonment on contempt charges that provoked a response from the Academy of Trial Lawyers[b]; rather, in 1963, members of the Academy drew up a plan to bring the

---

b   Brunwasser was jailed on a contempt charge for showing up late to a federal hearing in Judge Hubert Teitelbaum's courtroom, but that was in 1970; the ACBA did take up Brunwasser's cause, and several colleagues from the bar bailed him out. The characteristically frugal Brunwasser allegedly

two arms of the judiciary together, growing out of a "general dissatisfaction" with how the two courts were making the trial lawyers' lives miserable over scheduling conflicts. "Jim McArdle had acquired an ancient launch somewhere," Weis recalled—he thought McArdle might have received the old "scow" in payment of a debt—"and brought it to Pittsburgh. I don't recall its real name but it was appropriately referred to as the 'African Queen,'" and it was not thought to be unlike the tramp steamer from the 1951 movie in its alleged seaworthiness. The Academy, represented by McArdle, Weis and plaintiffs' lawyer Jim Evans, arranged an evening cruise along the three rivers of Pittsburgh on the "African Queen," with President Judge Henry Ellenbogen of the Court of Common Pleas and Chief Judge Wallace S. Gourley of the United States District Court for the Western District of Pennsylvania both in attendance, each accompanied by their seconds—Judge Ruggero Aldisert of the Common Pleas Court, and Judge Herbert P. Sorg of the federal District Court. Although the dour jurists treated each other somewhat coldly at first, soon Gourley began to address Ellenbogen as "Henry," and Ellenbogen began to call Gourley "Wally." "[O]n the peaceful waters of the Allegheny an accord was reached," Weis recalled, that the head judges would send their chief clerks to meet with each other "in the Carlton House, half-way between the two courthouses in the demilitarized zone," to coordinate the schedules of jury trials on a regular basis. It helped, Weis later observed, that the hard-nosed judges were a captive audience for mediation on McArdle's old boat as they traversed up and down the rivers.[39]

The same crisis that inspired the "African Queen" cruise of Judges Ellenbogen and Gourley up and down the rivers of Pittsburgh at the behest of the Academy of Trial Lawyers also led to the inaugural Bench-Bar Conference, held on June 21 and 22, 1963 at Seven Springs Mountain Resort, about an hour southeast of Pittsburgh in the Laurel Highlands of Somerset County. William Challener, Jr., the president of the ACBA in 1962, suggested that a larger group of trial attorneys ought to have an opportunity to meet on an informal basis with some of the local and federal judges—preferably outside the city, for at least one entire day, so that productive conversations could be had more easily. In order to establish its credibility as a forum for discussing serious issues, Challener and his Bench-Bar committee (which included Feeney and Sikov) decided that the first Bench-Bar conference would be an "invitation-only" event.[40] The carefully choreographed inaugural event proved to be a success—both the judges and the lawyers took it seriously, despite the cocktails and the campground setting— paving the way for greater communication between the judges and the trial bar in the years to come.

While the leaders of the ACBA were attempting to solve the problems of the trial bar (its leadership also argued for a system of compulsory arbitration to help reduce the court backlogs), the late 1950s and early 1960s were a time when the ACBA also undertook internal improvements. In a trend that began around World War I and was encouraged by the racial integration of the Association in the 1940s, it soon became

---

remarked upon his release that the food in jail was not half bad, according to Weis. Judge Joseph F. Weis, Jr., interview by the author, July 29, 2011; Jessup v. Clark (Appeal of Allen Brunwasser), 490 F.2d 1068 (3rd Cir. 1973).

clear that membership in the Bar Association would eventually become coextensive with membership in the bar, rather than existing as the lobbying arm of elite middle-aged and senior lawyers. The Association became a corporation, and restructured its by-laws to provide for a "board of governors" rather than an "executive committee" in recognition of a greater desire for transparency and democracy.[41] It also purchased, in 1962, the century-old *Pittsburgh Legal Journal* from its owner, Ross Blair, and began to publish it as an Association organ.[42] Furthermore, in light of its rapidly swelling ranks after the War, Thomas Pomeroy, one of the founders of the firm of Kirkpatrick & Lockhart and the president of the ACBA in 1959, "strongly emphasized" the need to recruit and hire a full-time administrator, both to serve and to help organize Pittsburgh lawyers for important initiatives.[43] Up to that time, the Association had survived with the help of one secretary, most recently Josephine McDonagh,[c] for decades. In the fall of 1962, during the presidency of William Challener, Jr., a search committee turned up a promising recruit—a tall, lanky, thirty-two year-old Notre Dame graduate from Ohio named James Ignatius Smith, III.[44]

Jim Smith's grandfather had founded the Esmeralda Canning Company in Circleville, Ohio, south of Columbus, and after graduation and Air Force service, Smith was forced to take his turn running the family business; but after only two years he knew he needed a position that better suited his gregariousness, and he went to work as a reporter with the *Circleville Herald*. His articles on jury duty won an award from the Ohio Bar Association, followed by a job offer when the Association established a public relations position.[45]

Smith moved to Pittsburgh and, on January 1, 1963, he began his thirty-eight-year tenure as the first executive director of the ACBA. As the *Post-Gazette's* Lawrence Walsh wrote, "He brought a tireless work ethic, an endless supply of ideas, a manual typewriter that he poked with two fingers, a penchant to address everyone by their last name, borrowed cigars, a shaky golf game, dry Manhattans and a no-pleasantries phone greeting: 'Smith!'"[46] Not an attorney, he nonetheless became the champion of attorneys in the community, and earned enough respect within the profession to become recognized as a mentor to younger lawyers, a referee between lawyers and judges, and occasionally as a mediator among arguing attorneys. Robert Sable remembers that when Sable was a young lawyer, Smith was always accessible and willing to discuss the progress of Sable's career. "You're doing fine," Smith told him during one interview. "I could probably get you a job in another firm where you would make another $500 or a thousand dollars a year, but you are with a firm that is growing ... But," Smith told him, "don't wait too long to find out if you're going to be a partner"—which Sable considered to be good advice.[47] The files of the ACBA are filled with the patient correspondence of Jim Smith, functioning as an ombudsman when clients had complaints about their lawyers, or trying to work out issues in connection with the unpleasant dissolution of a law partnership, as well as his typewritten, affectionately compiled drafts of the newspaper obituaries of each Pittsburgh lawyer.

---

c The former railroad stenographer and long-time secretary of the ACBA, who never married, later bequeathed a portion of her estate in 1981 to establish a scholarship for Duquesne Law students.

After the success of the first Bench-Bar Conference in 1963, Smith promoted the second and subsequent annual Bench-Bar Conferences at Seven Springs as Thursday-through-Sunday events, eventually open to all members of the bench and bar, featuring an annual golf outing, notable guest speakers and home-grown comedy and musical shows, in addition to educational seminars and working sessions. With the initial crisis that had stimulated the idea of the Conference being a faint memory by the 1970s, the Conference continued as an opportunity "to get together," explains David Blaner, Smith's successor as ACBA executive director, "to talk about common problems that occur between the bench and bar throughout the year, and to resolve them in a social setting that is relaxed, so that people can really talk through the problems and resolve the problems"—all within a friendly, open environment that, among other gatherings of lawyers in large metropolitan areas, was "unique to Allegheny County," according to Blaner. After more than fifty years, the ACBA Bench-Bar Conference is now considered to be one of the longest running bar association conferences held anywhere in the United States.[48]

Jim Smith's energy and vision for what the ACBA could be coincided with a youth leadership movement that was bubbling to the surface within the Bar Association, culminating in the 1965 election of David Fawcett, Jr., age thirty-eight, to the presidency. David's father, David, Sr., had entered the bar in 1926, and had served as an assistant district attorney as well as a "big time" supervisor of college basketball and football referees. David, Jr., was a high school football and basketball hero in Oakmont, served briefly in the Navy in the Pacific at the tail-end of World War II, and after his return earned his B.S. from Bucknell. While attending Pitt Law School on the G.I. bill, the defense firm of Dickie, McCamey, Chilcote, Reif & Robinson hired the younger Fawcett as a "paper server," then hired him to join the firm when he entered the bar in 1954. Urged on by other young Pittsburgh lawyers such as Jack Feeney, Jack Plowman and Sy Sikov, Fawcett rose rapidly through the ranks of the Bar Association while developing a reputation as an excellent trial lawyer, and in 1965 he was then and for many years afterward the youngest elected president of a major metropolitan bar association in the country. Smith, the still relatively new executive director, was thirty-four.[49]

The new lawyers who emerged from law school after World War II "were vitally interested in improving the way law was practiced and improving the way lawyers were viewed," Fawcett observed. "They were interested in emphasizing the profession's obligation to the community at large. They were interested in improving the Court system and the way Judges were selected. They were interested in providing information to the public concerning when lawyers were needed." Fawcett recalls that while the Association had been led by many distinguished lawyers, its "activity and reach were quite limited." The young World War II veterans who were joining the bar "had no fear," said Fawcett, "in shaking up the Association and making it more active, representative and efficient."[50]

Together, Smith and Fawcett, along with other young lawyers and a few key supporters from the older generation—such as James M. Houston, the "bantam rooster" from Rose, Houston, Cooper & Schmidt, and Alexander Unkovic, co-founder of the firm of Meyer, Unkovic & Scott—embarked on a remarkably productive year for the Bar Association.[51]

One over-arching theme of Fawcett's presidency was the way in which the ACBA sought to build bridges outside the Pittsburgh legal community—not just to the larger Pittsburgh community (through the introduction of a lawyers' speaker bureau and courthouse tours for the general public), but to the national legal community. A review of Fawcett's personal files from the era reveals a dizzying calendar full of banquets, speeches and summits—including outreach meetings with representatives from other professions, such as the clergy, the press and doctors. Smith also insisted on taking the ACBA on the road, traveling with Fawcett to national bar association meetings and touting Pittsburgh's cutting-edge activities and plans, as well as its youthful leadership and energy, to bar associations across the country. Another urgent area of focus was improving the court system by focusing on developing more qualified candidates for the bench. In addition to the Bar Association referenda on judicial candidates that had been ongoing, Fawcett and the Association leadership began to reach out to the local Republican and Democratic organizations to recommend outstanding lawyers for judicial office; created more permanent liaison committees between the Bar Association and the courts to work jointly on improvements and innovations; and advocated for the assignment of more County judges to the Criminal Division in order to deal with the backlog in criminal cases.[52]

Meanwhile, in 1963, the U.S. Supreme Court had ruled in *Gideon v. Wainwright*[53] that the Fourteenth Amendment required states to provide counsel in criminal cases where a defendant was unable to pay for his or her own counsel. In Allegheny County, providing counsel to indigent defendants had been ad hoc; while there was a "Volunteer Defender" program that had been initiated by the Association, Fawcett recalled that it was not unheard of for a lawyer to be sitting at his or her desk and to receive a phone call from a judge telling him or her to report to criminal court to represent a defendant. Under Fawcett's leadership and with the avid participation of a young Kirkpatrick & Lockhart lawyer named Dick Thornburgh as vice chair of the Association's "Public Defender Committee," the Association drafted and lobbied for the passage of the Allegheny County "Public Defender Act," which created an Allegheny County public defender's office in June 1965.[54] The office, which opened that November, was initially headed by George H. Ross.[55] Later, when Dick Thornburgh and K. Leroy Irvis served as delegates to the Pennsylvania Constitutional Convention of 1967-68, they co-drafted the provisions that made the office of public defender a constitutional office of the Commonwealth.[56]

"The next logical step," explained Dick Thornburgh, "was Neighborhood Legal Services."[57] In 1964, Congress passed the Economic Opportunity Act, establishing the Office of Economic Opportunity (OEO), as part of President Lyndon Johnson's "War on Poverty." Sargent Shriver—brother-in-law to the late President Kennedy and Attorney General Robert F. Kennedy, and the first director of the Peace Corps—was named by President Johnson as the first director of the OEO. Although Shriver's initial focus was on other poverty initiatives, Shriver's executive assistant, Yale law graduate Edgar Cahn, convinced Shriver to request funding for legal services for the indigent. In February 1965, the American Bar Association, then led by future Nixon Supreme Court appointee Lewis F. Powell, Jr., met and endorsed Shriver's plan for government funding "for the development and implementation of programs for expanding availability of legal services to indigents and persons of low income."[58]

In Pittsburgh, legal representation for the poor was a hit-and-miss affair, much like finding counsel for criminal defendants had been. There was an all-volunteer Legal Aid Society, incorporated in 1908 by H.V. Blaxter, Allen Kerr and William K. Johnson and members of the Pittsburgh Civic Club,[59] which could provide counseling but did not have the capacity to appear in court. In eviction, collection and domestic proceedings, the poor were left to convince a local lawyer to take their case at no charge, or represent themselves in court. Following the lead of the ABA, the Public Service Committee of the ACBA, chaired by Thornburgh, began a pilot program for providing more comprehensive legal services to the poor in July 1965. Later that year came word that Pittsburgh was to become one of five cities to receive targeted community action funds from the OEO, and the success of the ACBA's pilot program prompted the federal government to offer an additional $222,000 to turn the pilot into a full-fledged community service institution. With federal funding promised, the board of governors of the ACBA voted to establish the Neighborhood Legal Services Association (NLSA), with the ACBA as its operating agency. "It was a simple thing," said Fawcett, a lifelong Republican. "If criminal indigents are entitled to representation, certainly innocent, law-abiding citizens that are indigent are entitled to representation."

Then, however, there came a petition from members of the ACBA to hold a hearing on the matter before the full membership.[60] The hearing was held on a winter evening early in 1966, in the 9th floor auditorium in the City-County Building. It was the most well attended meeting anyone could remember. David Fawcett, Jr., as the immediate past president of the ACBA and a member of the board of governors, chaired the meeting.[61] As the speakers rose, it quickly became apparent that there was considerable opposition within the bar to the creation of Neighborhood Legal Services. The opposition came from two distinct camps. As Livingstone Johnson remembers, "A lot of people were opposed to it because the trial bar felt that ... [government-paid] lawyers ... were going to compete with them for legal fees and clients."[62] The other camp, according to Wendell Freeland, were "those people who were opposed to 'socialized law'" as a matter of political principle.[63] "A lot of people felt there should not be a legal services organization at all," recalled Tom Hollander. "Many favored 'judicare,' which would fund lawyers in private practice to provide those services on a case-by-case basis. Instead of having lawyers who regularly practiced poverty law and would become experienced and expert in it, they would have people doing it as needed."[64]

The prospects for the passage of a resolution supporting the creation of the NLSA seemed dim when Fawcett recognized John G. Buchanan, Sr.—the seventy-seven year-old, ruddy-complexioned, Republican senior partner of Buchanan, Ingersoll, Rodewald, Kyle & Buerger. As Buchanan began his speech, Fawcett later admitted, "I didn't know which side he was on!"[65] Justin Johnson, Livingstone's younger brother, remembered: "I would have guessed that he [Buchanan] intended to drive the final nail into the NLSA coffin. But he surprised me, and I believe he surprised most of the lawyers there assembled. He spoke fervently about the need to form the Legal Services group and about the responsibility of the Bar Association in assuming the leadership role in that formation."[66] "He really turned the tide," said Fawcett. "That was a great, great speech."[67] When Buchanan was finished, the resolution was put to a vote, and it passed by a slim margin. "John G. Buchanan—God rest his soul—was neither black nor poor," said Justin Johnson. "I will always remember that, but for the head of one of Pittsburgh's most conservative law firms putting his personal endorsement behind the project, it most certainly would not have passed that day."[68]

Dick Thornburgh drafted the incorporation documents, and on March 10, 1966, a diverse group of incorporators from the ACBA filed for the incorporation of the NLSA: Wendell Freeland, the dean of the African American bar, who was named as the NLSA's first board president; David G. Hill, the assistant U.S. attorney in charge of civil litigation; Justin M. Johnson, a young African American lawyer from the firm of Johnson, Johnson & Johnson, the son of one of the first African American members of the ACBA; Maurice Louik, the County solicitor; Thomas F. Quinn, the dean of Duquesne Law School; Irwin M. Ringgold, leader of the Pittsburgh workers compensation bar; George H. Ross, the County public defender; W. Edward Sell, the new dean of Pitt Law School; James I. Smith, III, the ACBA's director; Eric W. Springer, an African American lawyer who taught at Pitt Law and the University's Graduate School of Public Health; David W. Stahl, the former Pennsylvania Attorney General then serving as city solicitor; Wayne Theophilus, president of the Legal Aid Society; Dick Thornburgh from Kirkpatrick & Lockhart; and Alex Unkovic, the ACBA president, from Meyer, Unkovic & Scott.[69] Big firms and small, academia, government, whites, blacks, Democrats, Republicans, the bar had demonstrated that it could come together—in a spirit of optimism and generosity, on a bipartisan, racially integrated basis—to minister to the needs of the poor, from whom, by definition, they could expect no economic benefit. In the late 1960s and 1970s, under the leadership of R. Stanton "Tony" Wettick, the NLSA would become, perhaps unexpectedly, a force to be reckoned with, leading class action fights and challenging the status quo on segregated public schools and prison overcrowding, in addition to providing vital basic legal services to what had been a lost and hapless segment of the community.

In the early 1960s, during a period of relatively consistent growth in the American economy, there was a sense that poverty was solvable, that something like the NLSA could be an ingredient in the eradication of the malady—just as Jonas Salk's vaccine, developed at the University of Pittsburgh School of Medicine and announced to the world in 1955, had all but eradicated polio. The lawyers who fought for the NLSA in 1965 and 1966 would have had no idea how important institutional safety nets would soon become, nor were they able to predict the magnitude of the economic tragedy that was about to befall Pittsburgh beginning in the late 1970s.

Steel, the industry that defined Pittsburgh, flew the highest and fell the hardest during the post-War period. At the center of the Pittsburgh economy, steel's collapse in the late 1970s and 1980s—pushed over the edge of the cliff by "many complex, interrelated forces" as John P. Hoerr relates, such as "structural shifts in the international steel industry; the growth of foreign steel and the resulting excess of steelmaking capacity over demand by 1986; the increasing use of plastics" and other materials; "and the rise of American minimills with modern equipment and low labor costs"—destabilized everything around it.[70] Over 115,000 Pittsburgh manufacturing jobs disappeared overnight; the total number of unemployed rose above two hundred thousand in 1983.[71]

At the beginning of the period, the industry was still mired in labor-management issues. The launch of the NLRB was a costly period for the steel companies as the lawyers who represented management during the 1930s, such as Earl Reed and Clyde Armstrong, fought the NLRB with everything they had so they could go back to being corporation lawyers, in virulent denial that there would ever be a need for labor lawyers. At the outset of World War II, however, both the American Federation of Labor (AFL) and the Congress of Industrial Organizations (CIO) pledged that there would be no strikes while the War continued.[72] The United Steelworkers (USW), formed in 1942 from SWOC and what was left of the Amalgamated Association, was affiliated with the CIO and largely followed suit (with minor exceptions) under its leader, Philip Murray, seeking to engage the steel companies in cooperative dialogue through "labor management committees." During the same period, management backed off of its heavy-handed anti-union stance that had been so costly and time-consuming during the end of the 1930s. Amid the interregnum of industrial calm, union membership throughout the United States doubled, from 7.2 million workers in 1940 to 14.5 million by the end of the War.[73]

With five years' worth of pent-up disputes awaiting resolution, the "no strike" pledges collapsed quickly after the War. Japan's surrender to the Allies occurred on August 15, 1945. Barely a month later, forty-three thousand CIO oil workers went on strike. In November, 225,000 members of the United Auto Workers walked out. In January 1946, the strike wave hit Pittsburgh, as members of the United Electrical, Radio and Machine Workers walked out of Westinghouse Electric's plants in East Pittsburgh and Trafford, followed by the Steelworkers. In all, 4.3 million workers participated in strikes during the period.[74] President Truman, siding with labor in recognition of its loyalty to the War cause, advised management to settle with the unions. In the November 1946 elections, however, the Republicans took back Congress and passed the Taft-Hartley Act over President Truman's veto, which expanded management's right to oppose unions and limited the unions' ability to strike at will.[75]

At Reed Smith, which still represented U.S. Steel, the combative Jack Heard had geared up to lead the fight against the NLRB during the 1930s, in the mold of Earl Reed and Clyde Armstrong over at Thorp Reed, but was instructed to stand down by U.S. Steel's chairman and CEO, Myron Taylor, who decided to settle with the unions, granting a substantial wage increase to workers in 1937.[76] With clients desiring to mediate their differences with the unions in order to avoid costly legal battles, a different kind of management-side labor lawyer was now required after the War, and Nicholas Unkovic, who joined Reed Smith in 1942 after practicing with his mentor, H. Fred Mercer, Sr., and as a sole practitioner for ten years, would come to define what a management-side labor lawyer would be. Nick's father, Kosto "Constantine" Unkovic, was a graduate of Duquesne Law School. He never practiced law, but rather made his living as an interpreter and acted as consul for the Kingdom, and subsequently the Republic, of Yugoslavia. Nick was the oldest of nine children (ACBA president Alexander Unkovic was one of his younger siblings), and was therefore provided with the opportunity to be sent away to school; he received his A.B. from Harvard in 1928, studied one year at Harvard Law School and finished his legal education at Dickinson in 1932. "About that time," recalled Nick, "labor law started getting important and the average lawyer didn't want to do any labor law because he didn't want to deal with unions ... many lawyers felt it was not really law business."[77]

Despite his white-collar, cosmopolitan background, Harvard education, and his finely-tailored wardrobe, Nick Unkovic turned out to be tailor-made for dealing with unions on behalf of management. "He was a man of the people. He could talk to the unions," recalled Charles R. "Dick" Volk, who served as a management-side labor lawyer with Thorp Reed for a number of years. Volk suggested that at least part of Unkovic's appeal was his Slavic surname, during a time when so many union leaders still identified themselves as ethnic Eastern Europeans,[78] but Unkovic was also universally regarded as a straight talker—direct, informal and to the point—and an honest broker. One of his colloquialisms has floated around the Pittsburgh bar for a few generations: "If you have no choice but to swallow a toad, get it over with. It won't do you any good to just sit there and look at it." It was a folksy saying, but it was also consistent with the pointed advice Unkovic gave to other negotiators. "Tell the truth even when it hurts," he would say, as well as "When you must tell a union, 'no,' say it promptly. Don't beat around the bush."[79] The new management-side labor negotiator would not solely function as a combatant; his aim was to earn the trust of union officials in the service of minimizing conflict, while at the same time staying single-mindedly focused on his clients' goals.

There would be one further disruption in the steel industry before Unkovic's approach would take hold. In July 1950, President Truman sent U.S. troops into Korea, and, just as it had been during World War II, Truman called for defense mobilization in the steel industry. The latest agreement between the USW and the steel companies was set to expire on December 31, 1951, and negotiations were stalled. The Wage Stabilization Board produced a compromise report that was acceptable to the union, but not to management, and the USW called for a strike to begin on April 9, 1952. Prior to the walk-out, and in light of the nation's war-time footing, President Truman directed the Secretary of Commerce to take possession of the steel industry—refusing to invoke the Taft-Hartley Act to stop the strike, as he believed that the impending strike was management's fault. The steel companies called Truman's move an "abuse of power" that amounted to "tyranny," and they quickly sought an injunction against Truman's order. After a temporary restraining order was obtained, with Reed Smith's John C. Bane, Jr.—the son of the lawyer who had pressed for the disbarment of Jacob Margolis in 1920—representing Jones & Laughlin Steel in the effort, the case was presented on an emergency basis to the U.S. Supreme Court. Bane stepped aside to permit the heralded appellate lawyer John W. Davis, who had been engaged by U.S. Steel (ironically, since Davis had led the fight as President Wilson's Solicitor General to break up U.S. Steel in 1915), to argue the case in May, but Bane was nonetheless an active member of the team that prepared a 175-page brief for the Supreme Court. The decision, which came down on June 2, 1952, was five to three against the constitutionality of the president's order, and shortly thereafter the USW went out on strike for over fifty days before an agreement could be reached.[80]

After the Steel Seizure case, the USW and the major players in the industry—U.S. Steel, Bethlehem, Jones & Laughlin, National, Republic, Armco, Inland and Allegheny Ludlum—looked for ways to simplify the process of negotiating wages, and among competitors in the industry, to take wages out of competition. As the largest employer, headquartered in the same city as the headquarters of the USW, U.S. Steel dominated the proceedings, and Nick Unkovic, as the trusted front-line negotiator for U.S. Steel, became the effectuator of industrywide bargaining, beginning in 1956. "They would have these meetings in ... the William Penn [Hotel], and you would have outside the door—Inland, Bethlehem, Youngstown Sheet and Tube and all these other[s] ...—and they would literally wait to be told what the deal was," said Dave Robertson, former counsel to the Independent Steelworkers Union, the independent union at Weirton Steel, and later, after the ESOP sponsored by the steelworkers' acquired Weirton Steel, the company's vice president. "U.S. Steel would tell them what was going to happen, and they would follow in line like little ducks," said Volk.[81] Following the conclusion of Unkovic's negotiations with the USW, each of the smaller steel companies, with the industrywide wage agreement in place, would focus on resolving non-wage controversies and management issues, each of them represented by their own teams.

For a few decades, centralized wage bargaining had the effect of helping to minimize disruptions in the steel industry. The sole major USW strike during the period occurred in 1959, when USW members walked out for 116 days over work rule disagreements. President Eisenhower invoked the Taft-Hartley Act to force the workers back to the work, and the strike was settled with minor concessions, although not before the U.S. Supreme Court upheld the constitutionality of the Act.[82] By the time Nick Unkovic retired in 1976, labor litigation had again become the focus of Reed Smith's activities, rather than collective bargaining, and Unkovic's protégé, the accomplished labor litigator Leonard Scheinholtz, became the chair of the firm's labor group.[83] The unique role that Unkovic had established, as the honest broker in the bargaining room, had begun to diminish as early as the 1960s, as management bureaucracies grew larger within both the USW and U.S. Steel and cannibalized the mechanics of bargaining. Meanwhile, while industrywide bargaining resulted in less labor strife, placing wage decisions in the hands of U.S. Steel ultimately weakened the smaller steel companies. Nationwide bargaining in the steel industry simply collapsed by 1985, as several of the smaller steel companies began to fail.[84] By that time, the lawyers from outside law firms (as opposed to lawyers on the payroll of the steel companies) were almost completely absent from the room.

Elsewhere in Pittsburgh, the local unions of the International Brotherhood of Teamsters, Chauffeurs, Warehousemen and Helpers of America were active and contentious during the early years after World War II. In 1951, the Teamsters Local 249 had relations with 723 employers in the region, including businesses in construction, food processing, auto parts, paint, refrigeration, laundry, coal, ice, lumber, roofing, wrecking, beverage, meat packers, department stores, electric supplies, drugs, tobacco and paper industries, among others. The newspaper truck drivers became such a large segment of the local membership that they broke away and formed their own local (Local 211), as did the taxicab drivers (Local 433).[85] Ben Paul Jubelirer, a Pitt Law graduate from McKeesport who had attended Harvard as an undergraduate a few years before Nick Unkovic, represented the Teamsters as early as the 1930s.[86] "Their idea of a strike," recalled Carl Hellerstedt, a management-side labor lawyer who was a partner at Thorp Reed, "was that you didn't move any goods." When the Teamsters conducted a walk-out, it could have a paralyzing effect, as the products and businesses that were involved were frequently staples of daily consumption—dairy goods, groceries and newspapers.[87] Physical stand-offs at Teamster picket lines frequently turned violent, and, in the well-worn footsteps of Billy Brennen and other early Pittsburgh union lawyers, Jubelirer frequently found himself representing criminal defendants, fresh from the picket lines, as well as assisting the union locals in their wage negotiations. He also handled their small claims, wills, divorces and adoptions, becoming a part of the fabric of the union community.[88]

Jubelirer was succeeded by his younger partner, Joseph J. Pass, Jr.—a Duquesne Law graduate from McKees Rocks, Vietnam War veteran, and former clerk to Judge Ellenbogen—who ultimately expanded the practice of Jubelirer, Pass & Intrieri to include representation of AFL-CIO and public worker unions. Pass was particularly successful in his work with the Amalgamated Transit Union, resulting in what one study called the highest paid transit workers in the U.S., adjusted for cost of living.[89][d] His formula as a union-side negotiator was similar to that of Unkovic as a management-side negotiator: "You [have to] be as forthright and honest as you can—not only to the other side, but to your own people, who sometimes don't want to hear."[90] Honesty, of course, is an imperative of the ethics of the profession, but collegial relations with the opposition was both a prerequisite and a by-product of the trust that was required to reach a successful accommodation. Even in the most contentious matters, the long-standing relationships between the two halves of the employment bar helped to sustain a sense of order amid combat—like Ralph the Wolf and Sam the Sheepdog in the old Warner Brothers cartoons, wishing each other good morning each day as they clocked in before engaging in battle during work hours.

Pass was also at the center of the protracted Teamsters Local 211 negotiations with the Pittsburgh Press Co., shortly before the ninety year-old daily *Pittsburgh Press* newspaper was sold to the *Post-Gazette* and ceased publication in 1992.[91] The extinction of the *Press* was emblematic of the time, capping a decade of diminishing regional resources, business failures and disappearing jobs.

Where jobs were being lost by the hundreds in many industries throughout the region during the 1980s, the hope of collegial bargaining washed away quickly, replaced by frowns, calculators and awkward silences. The period from the 1980s to the present day, in fact, is one marked by discontinuities—an ever-changing cast of transient corporate managers, unencumbered by codes of professional responsibility; a constant tumble of buyouts and bankruptcies; a jumbling of corporate identities so jarring that one cannot tell the players without a scorecard. "The guys I used to deal

---

[d] It should be noted that Pass himself bristles at that specific contention, saying that the distinction—"highest paid transit workers in the U.S."—is used by foes of the union to justify smaller wage increases.

with were a hell of a lot better," Pass says. "They were a lot more reasonable. They understood the nature of the business. They understood that we had to make peace, because it's going to continue." They were "lifers" who believed they were going to be involved in the next round of negotiations, and the next, for decades to come. "They get these kids in there who think they're going to reinvent the wheel, and they're going to fight on everything."[92] In that context, collegiality, at least at the bargaining table, almost became an anachronism.

"When I first got started," says Pass, reflecting on his career, "I never thought about how many hours I'm going to bill, or [how to] make a living. That never entered my mind. Today, I think we have businesses, not professions."[93] The concept of law firms as businesses, of course, was something that was on the minds of Pittsburgh lawyers since the days of Thomas Mellon, but in the atmosphere of uncertainty that overtook the Pittsburgh economy during the 1970s and 80s, law firms were rather obviously attempting to respond to market forces, in a business-like manner.

As Pittsburgh businesses continued to feel financial pressures, Pittsburgh lawyers—who had been accustomed to charging monthly retainers for their work, in some cases providing a one-line, unitemized bill for "services rendered" at the end of a long, extraordinary matter, and having their invoices paid without question—were with increased frequency asked to justify their charges. Out of the strained dialogue between lawyers and client fiscal managers, hourly billing evolved as the rule by the end of the 1980s, rather than the exception that it had been at the beginning of the 1940s.

The threats to the way lawyers were accustomed to billing for their services were not only coming from the general state of the economy. Trust and estates lawyers, in particular, suffered when in the early 1970s the U.S. Justice Department began to attack "minimum fee schedules"—guidelines published by the bar that placed a floor on what could be charged for the drafting of a will, for example—as illegal restraints on trade.[94] After the Allegheny County bar announced that minimum fee schedules were no longer in effect,[95] the elite estate bar—previously consolidated in the hands of a few, fairly powerful practitioners who reaped very high "percentage-based" fees, based on the graduated minimum schedule, from the great estates of Pittsburgh—suddenly faced an onslaught of competition from low-cost providers. "One of the things [the schedules] allowed people to do," observed Robert B. Wolf, the late estates and trusts lawyer and head of the firm of Tener, Van Kirk, Wolf & Moore, "was to represent more modest-sized estates, and to charge a modest fee. You didn't make money on it, but it was okay because you were able to make it up on other things." The banning of the schedules impacted more than just fees, however, according to Wolf. Since the schedules took some of the economic pressure away from the estates practice, senior estates lawyers could take more time to train younger estates lawyers. "It freed you as a practitioner to be a better mentor." In addition, Wolf asserts, the minimum fee schedules were "helpful from the point of view of lending a bit of gentility to the practice."[96] The inability of such lawyers to convert effectively to hourly billing downgraded the importance of estates lawyers within the larger Pittsburgh firms and, by the end of the century, the practice area that historically had often been one of the most profitable segments of downtown law firms in Pittsburgh had all but disappeared from the roster of services provided by these firms.

One strategy that Pittsburgh firms adopted early on in the face of fiscal threats was diversification. The old model of downtown law firm, composed of a mixture of transactional lawyers and trial lawyers, general practitioners in each camp, was now beginning to shift to add areas of "specialization" that had not existed in downtown law firms before. Indeed, in Reed Smith's 1942 lateral recruitment of Nick Unkovic to fill a perceived need for management-side labor lawyers, one can see a recognition of circumstances that Nick Unkovic saw when he entered the profession—that "this might be like taxes were twenty years before, a field for the future," as Unkovic had put it.[97] Unkovic was a big proponent of diversification, as Ralph Demmler observed in a eulogy he delivered at Unkovic's Common Pleas Court memorial service in 1983. "[H]e was always forward-looking ... [H]e pressed the firm to be prepared to meet the challenge of new fields of law, civil rights, discrimination, environment, wage and price controls, public employee's collective bargaining, pensions and the like."[98]

The bankruptcy practice was, similarly, an area of expansion for the downtown firms. Prior to the passage of the Bankruptcy Reform Act of 1978, most bankruptcy lawyers operated in smaller firms, some of them considered to be "low rate" collections firms, to whom the larger downtown firms, uninterested in pursuing these matters themselves, would often refer work. One of the primary reasons was that the old Bankruptcy Code limited the compensation of bankruptcy lawyers to rates that were significantly below that of most lawyers. With the rise of business failures in Pittsburgh, the ongoing interests of regional banks in the assets of such businesses, and a liberalization of the standard for payment under the 1978 Act, the large downtown firms began to see that there were significant fees to be earned in corporate reorganizations, and they began to develop bankruptcy practices.[99] Reed Smith started its bankruptcy group in 1979, led by Paul Singer, and three years later represented its long-time client, Mesta Machine Company, in a Chapter 11 reorganization.[100] By 1988, two of the top ten largest corporate reorganizations in the nation were being litigated in the U.S. Bankruptcy Court in the Western District of Pennsylvania—Wheeling-Pittsburgh Steel and Allegheny International. M. Bruce McCullough at Buchanan Ingersoll, who started his career as a commercial lawyer, was tapped to be lead counsel for both of the debtors,[101] and almost every major downtown firm had someone spending significant time in bankruptcy court on these cases.

Intellectual property lawyers, too—always residing in their own ghetto of small firms through the mid-twentieth century (patent lawyers were even listed separately from the rest of the lawyer population in the old Pittsburgh phone directories[102])—were, at the end of the 1980s and early 1990s, enticed to join large downtown firms as those firms attempted to find more legal services that intersected with their clients' interests. In the early 1980s, Eckert Seamans brought on Walter Blenko, Jr., and Arnold Silverman from the patent firm of Buell, Blenko, Ziesenheim & Beck, one of the successors to the pioneering patent practice of William Bakewell[103]; a few years later, after hiring a few individual patent lawyers, Buchanan Ingersoll acquired what was left of the Buell Ziesenheim firm.[104] Notably, among the established patent firms only the Webb Law

Firm—another firm tracing its roots to Bakewell—remained independent, benefiting from referrals from law firms who did not build their own patent practices.[105]

Inevitably, diversification also became a geographic matter. Dan Booker, Reed Smith's managing partner from 1992 to 2001, called the phenomenon "delocalizing."[106] Multi-office practices in the Pittsburgh bar, before some Pittsburgh law firms began to adopt "manifest destiny" as a guiding principle beginning in the 1970s, were often simply the outgrowth of the personal vision of one lawyer—such as Thomas Keenan's European and American Law Agency in the 1850s, and Edwin Stanton's march across southern Ohio into Pittsburgh during the same era. As Judd Poffinberger explained, "with the impact of federal legislation in so many areas of business and individual livelihoods, more lawyers began to think of their practice and concomitant legal abilities as having a national scope or, at least, a regional one." With the rise of federal regulation, naturally, as Poffinberger observed, "Washington was a necessary locale or point of tangent," in order to add regulatory lawyers to the roster who practiced right outside the walls of the federal agencies.[107] Reed Smith led the way to Washington, D.C. among Pittsburgh law firms, acquiring the firm of Whitlock & Tait in 1970, and Gall Lane & Powell in 1976.[108] Thorp Reed opened an office there around 1974[109]; the Baskin firm and Buchanan Ingersoll made their initial forays into Washington in 1977[110], and Kirkpatrick followed in 1981 with the acquisition of Hill, Christopher & Phillips.[111]

The idea of the regional practice was the next natural extension, leading Reed Smith, Buchanan Ingersoll and Baskin to open offices in Philadelphia, in 1978, 1985 and 1986, respectively.[112] Florida, a haven for Pittsburgh retirees, was another natural fit: in the mid-1970s, Thorp Reed opened offices in Tampa and Sarasota (fronted, for a time, by baseball manager/lawyer Tony LaRussa)[113] and Buchanan Ingersoll briefly added a Boca Raton office in 1981, followed by a West Palm Beach office in 1990.[114] In the 1990s, Pittsburgh firms began to market their expertise beyond the mid-Atlantic and Florida rapidly thereafter, most often tugged along by major corporate clients who were also "delocalizing," opening offices in New York, California, and eventually, abroad. Meanwhile, despite the assertion of David J. Armstrong, head of Dickie, McCamey & Chilcote, in 1987 that big firms from other cities were not interested in Pittsburgh "because nothing very exciting is going on here"[115]—a comment undoubtedly betraying the weariness of some members of the local bar in the face of the region's economic woes in the late 1980s—Pittsburgh also became the object of geographical expansion, beginning with Jones Day's entry into the market in 1989.

Diversification wreaked havoc on the "Cravath model" in Pittsburgh, the practice of developing home-grown talent from the best law schools and eventually advancing them to partnership, as it most often required Pittsburgh firms to draw in lateral partners, either for new areas of specialization or for lawyers in other cities. While the largest downtown firms continued, for a time, to emphasize the development of young associate talent, competing among themselves for and amassing large stables of lawyers-to-be in summer associate programs and welcoming ten to twenty new lawyers into the fold with each graduating class during the 1980s, the influx and outflux of laterals stretched and reshaped the sometimes carefully-crafted cultures of these Pittsburgh firms, and led to more internal haggling over compensation as the old lock-step compensation programs became less and less relevant, and the compensation of home-grown talent fell out of step with the premium prices that would be paid for lateral partners.

In light of these changes, just as the major downtown firms were reaching the one hundred-attorney mark, "smaller" appeared to be "better" to some lawyers who had been trained in the big firms. The firm of Manion Alder & Cohen—subsequently known as Alder, Cohen & Grigsby, and now Cohen & Grigsby—spun out of Reed Smith in 1981. Its co-founder, Charles "Chuck" Cohen, known to be one of Pittsburgh's foremost securities lawyers, "wanted to be more entrepreneurial," to work directly with decision-makers at growth-oriented, middle-market companies, rather than "the big, old-line manufacturing firms," and to provide "better service at lower cost."[116] Similarly, the firm of Babst, Calland, Clements and Zomnir was formed when several lawyers left Thorp, Reed & Armstrong in 1986, bristling at the entrenched culture of the larger firm and desiring to form an environmental and energy law boutique.[117] Eventually, both of these firms grew to become among the larger "full service" firms in downtown Pittsburgh.

By the 1980s, the plaintiffs' bar had also grown, certainly beyond the wildest dreams of Jim McArdle, Bob Brennan and Evans, Ivory and Evans. It had always been strong in Pittsburgh, in part because of the availability of contingent fee arrangements, which existed in Pennsylvania at least since the early nineteenth century; Hugh Henry Brackenridge referred to them by name in his common law treatise in 1813[118]—although, as evidenced by the opinion of Pennsylvania's chief justice, George Sharswood, in the 1850s that lawyers who employed contingent fee arrangements would "be tempted to make success, at all hazards and by all means, the sole end of his exertions ... [and become] blind to the merits of the case,"[119] such fee arrangements were looked down upon by at least the eastern Pennsylvania bar. A variety of other forces gave impetus to the plaintiffs' bar after World War II, among them: the creation of the Equal Employment Opportunity Office under the Civil Rights Act of 1964, which launched private lawsuits on pay disparities and wrongful terminations allegedly based upon membership in "protected classes;" the 1966 revisions to the Federal Rules of Civil Procedure, which gave birth to the modern class action suit[120]; the ballooning of toxic tort litigation following the seminal opinion in the field in *In re Agent Orange Products Liability Litigation* in New York federal court[121]; and the re-discovery of medical malpractice claims during the 1960s as lawyers were able to use "non-local" experts who were willing to testify against fellow physicians, thus breaking the "conspiracy of silence" among local physicians.[122] Still, the rise in the variety of plaintiffs' work did not necessarily translate immediately into greater opportunity for plaintiffs' lawyers. Before 1977, plaintiffs' lawyers still had to rely upon word of mouth, or occasionally upon some favorable newspaper coverage, to reach a fragmented, disparate clientele.

Up until the late twentieth century, the idea of lawyers as salesmen, touting their services to businesses and the general public, was considered unseemly for members of a learned profession. Like most states, Pennsylvania had banned lawyers from advertising in any form for a number of years. George Flinn, managing partner of the Pittsburgh corporate firm of Moorhead & Knox, took the ban quite literally, and refused to carry business cards for many years.[123] To the senior lawyers at Reed Smith in the years immediately after World War II, "the concept of 'marketing'—of purposely going out to create business" was "an anathema," according to Brignano and Fort.[124] In 1977, however, the U.S. Supreme Court ripped away the restrictions on lawyer advertising in *Bates v. State Bar of Arizona*[125], holding that advertising was commercial speech that was entitled to protection under the First Amendment.

Edgar Snyder, who had been a successful criminal defense lawyer after serving in the County public defender's office during the early years of his career, was one of the earliest and most successful lawyers to advertise around Pittsburgh. In 1979, Snyder recalls, Hyatt Legal Services, a nationwide chain of low-cost law firms founded by Joel Hyatt from Cleveland, began to advertise on Pittsburgh television stations. Snyder, whose marketing was led by his then-wife Sandy, owner of a small advertising agency catering to other professionals such as dentists, ran a small newspaper ad with the headline, "Know Your Rights." In 1983, Pennsylvania overhauled its "driving under the influence" laws. Before then, most DUI cases were handled by local magistrates, and they rarely resulted in anything more than a fine; after the new laws were passed "all of a sudden," Snyder recalls, "white collar people who drank too much could end up going to jail." Snyder's newspaper ad targeted drunk driving defendants, and within one year, he had developed the largest drunk driving practice in Pittsburgh. "That was the genesis of the entire advertising phenomenon for me."[126]

Snyder and his associate, Cynthia Danel, grew restless of the penny-ante DUI cases, however, and Edgar and Sandy started to develop TV ads for personal injury cases in Johnstown and Altoona, where TV spots were inexpensive. The skinny, bald, bespectacled Snyder starred in his own ads, uncoached, his arms waving about somewhat carelessly as he spoke, finishing his message with his signature move, which eventually developed into a slogan—as Snyder, smiling and pointing at the camera, chin to shoulder to fingertip, would promise, "There's never a fee unless we get money for you." "Overnight, the whole course of my business life changed," Snyder said. His firm quickly became a personal injury/plaintiff's case factory. He began to hire more attorneys as quickly as he could to keep up with the demand, but he also hired analysts from the insurance industry, who assisted in assessing potential cases, with the aim of taking the ones that could be settled quickly, without incurring large investments of time and money in courtroom activity by the law firm. Snyder organized his law firm to maximize income from contingent fee cases by reducing the risk of taking bad or difficult cases. He says he did not originate the business model, but he made it work for him. By 1988, he made enough money to pay for Pittsburgh TV spots and better, more polished video productions, and soon he became a Pittsburgh pop icon, the most recognizable lawyer in town.[127]

Nonetheless, Snyder took his lumps from his colleagues in the profession. After his initial ads in the outlying counties, he says, "In areas like Johnstown and Altoona and Erie, I was persona non grata ... I was taking business that they had traditionally had and referred to Pittsburgh lawyers like [Jim] McArdle's law firm.[e] They made more

---

e   Hard-living Jim McArdle died in 1969 at the age of 59, but he left behind an army of Pittsburgh plaintiffs' lawyers who had been schooled in his law firm.

money referring out that business than they did in their own practice of law, and here was some carpetbagger coming in ... taking all this business away." He infamously applied to be a member of the Cambria County Bar Association, about seventy-five miles east of Pittsburgh, and was refused—the first time, to his knowledge, that any member of the state bar had been denied admission to the Association. His visibility as a TV pitch man also meant that he could not appear in court anymore, because he quickly came to realize jurors would have instant opinions about him—either good or bad—that might impact their views of a case. For someone who was so good at conducting jury trials to be sidelined by his own notoriety was ironic; but in the process, Snyder became a law magnate.[128]

Snyder says, "Those were the golden days of advertising because I had major recognition [and] I had a competitive advantage because people wouldn't do what I was doing ... They said what I was doing is unprofessional and you are a disgrace to the legal profession. I was hopeful that it would stay that way forever," because no one else was eating into his market share through competitive advertising. Although he was ostracized professionally, Snyder would say that he was "laughing all the way to the bank." Advertising, he says, really "never bothered anybody, except lawyers," something that Jim Smith, the ACBA's executive director, also understood. "Jim Smith stood up for me when no one else would," Snyder remembers, telling people "'Edgar is a good lawyer and you're all jealous.'" At some point, the tide of opinion turned in Snyder's favor; the bar accepted advertising as a fact of life, and by the beginning of the 1990s, Snyder began to be asked to conduct seminars on advertising for lawyers. He was also invited to serve on the Pennsylvania Bar Association's task force on advertising as the state's reigning expert on lawyers' television ads.[129]

Meanwhile, the larger downtown law firms began to flirt with promotional activities, although not specifically with newspaper, radio or TV ads. In 1984, Buchanan Ingersoll took a chance on creating a full color, glossy brochure, and achieved some unwelcome notoriety for it. At the time, under the leadership of Bill Newlin, Buchanan was seen as a "most unlawyerly of law firms," according to a local business magazine—entrepreneurial, with an internal organization that "resembles that of, horror of horrors, most other American business," and a clear emphasis on growth.[130] The firm engaged Hill & Knowlton, an international public relations firm, to create a twenty-eight-page brochure with a dramatic color close-up photo of a gavel on the cover. Inside were solemn photos of Buchanan's lawyers, in groupings of two, three or four, with accompanying platitudes about Buchanan's practice capabilities. In disseminating the brochure to its partners in January 1984, the firm's operating committee wrote, "Firms striving to build an image or increase their share of market can use a variety of communications to achieve that end ... The fact is that, with all of today's modern technology, there are still only two ways a client/prospect can learn about Buchanan Ingersoll. Someone can tell them. Or they can read it. There are no other choices. Our new corporate brochure is needed to help reach and inform selected clients and prospects about our capabilities. By promoting awareness of and preference for Buchanan Ingersoll use of the brochure can lead to new or continued work for the firm."[131]

Buchanan's new color brochure landed on the desk of Steven Brill, the founder of *The American Lawyer* magazine and subsequently the driving force behind the original CourtTV television network. In the April 1984 issue of *American Lawyer*, Brill skewered the brochure:

> *Recently I found in my "in" box what looked like a routine, if rather flashy and expensive annual report from a corporation calling itself Buchanan Ingersoll. I didn't remember buying stock in such a company and couldn't figure out why I'd received this heavy-gloss 9" x 12" all-color booklet. So I peeked inside—only to find that this wasn't an annual report but a marketing brochure, and that Buchanan Ingersoll isn't a corporation but a law firm. It is in fact a 109-lawyer, Pittsburgh-based firm with a reputation for competent legal work and aggressive management that belies its staid 125-year history. However, it is also a firm that has produced the tackiest, least effective, most professionally embarrassing brochure I've seen.*[132]

Brill acknowledged Hill & Knowlton's role in the brochure's creation and went on to call it "expensive, beautifully photographed garbage" that engaged in "arrogance" and "puffery," as well as labelling it a "triumph of form over substance."[133] Buchanan may have taken it on the chin for being one of the first off the press with their firm brochure, but large firms (both in Pittsburgh and around the country) tended to follow Buchanan's example rather than shying away from it, producing their own thick, high-gloss brochures; they became a staple of large firm marketing in the 1980s and the early 90s, before the Internet. Meanwhile, says Newlin, "The thing that always bugged me was that *American Lawyer* kept trying to say, 'Law firms—be more like businesses. Get outside advice.' We go hire one of the best national PR firms to make sure that we do it correctly, and it gets screwed up. And then he [Brill] says, 'you screwed up.'"[134]

During the late 1980s Buchanan and other firms were also developing relationships with local newspapers and magazines to encourage earned media attention—through news coverage or expert interviews—getting the name of the firm in front of readers at a time when law firm names were most often left out of news articles as a matter of journalistic convention. Meanwhile, the *Pittsburgh Press'* business reporter, David Ranii, began to insert law firm names into the public consciousness as he began to cover law firms as businesses in the late 1980s.[135] Other downtown firms embraced advertising and marketing through sponsorship of charity or cultural events (inaugurating the tradition of placing sponsor ads in programs for the Pittsburgh Symphony or the Ballet, for example). By the mid-1990s, it was commonplace to see downtown law firm names and even their logos (which, themselves, were creatures of the post-*Bates* world in the Pittsburgh bar) alongside those of banks, utility companies, supermarket chains and other major Pittsburgh businesses on sponsorship banners for events such as the Three Rivers Arts Festival and the Pittsburgh Regatta. Law firms were becoming visible members of the downtown business community in ways that would have been unthinkable thirty years before.

The Post-War years in the Pittsburgh bar, led by returning war veterans and the generations of lawyers that immediately succeeded them, were years of rebuilding and rebirth; they were the years of Renaissance I immediately after the War, and Renaissance II, the more amorphous community rebuilding initiative that straddled the worst-ever decline in the economy of the region. The lesson of the War, and the spirit that pervaded the age, was that big projects were worth pursuing, and they could be completed successfully by young men and, later, young women, who possessed a combination of energy, ingenuity, selflessness and drive. The Pittsburgh lawyers of the era not only participated in those "big projects," but often provided key leadership in creating what would eventually become "America's Most Livable City" by the end of the 1980s.[136] At the same time, the human-sized lawyers of the period were also fighting their own internal battles to preserve something of the native institutions and distinct character of the bar and the legal landscape in Pittsburgh, despite the seemingly unstoppable dilutive effect of the growth in its own numbers, and the influences of federalization, local economic uncertainty and the tentative adoption of a modern business outlook—the latter, not solely in the service of their clients now, but in the management of their own livelihoods.

WON'T YOU BE MY NEIGHBOR?

One might just imagine Leland Walker Hazard arriving in the white-marbled lobby of the Frick Building to take his post as the new general counsel of the Pittsburgh Plate Glass Company in 1938: the chubby little forty-five year-old man with a round face and blue eyes behind round spectacles, beaming with anthropological appreciation and optimism on his first day in Pittsburgh. Hazard was fresh off the train from Kansas City, Missouri, and moving to Pittsburgh was, for Hazard, a move to the big city—the city of industrial tycoons and corporate giants.

Hazard was born in Kansas City, the son of a secretarial school owner. He studied at William Jewell College, a little Baptist school in Liberty, Missouri, then at the University of Missouri. A month after the United States declared war on Germany, Hazard was at Officer's Training Camp at Fort Riley, Kansas, and then he went to France in 1918 as a first lieutenant and assistant adjutant in the 89th Division. After the War, he studied at Harvard Law School for one year before returning to Missouri and entering the bar. Beginning somewhat aimlessly as a title lawyer for hire, he caught on with a downtown law firm. In Kansas City, Hazard developed a habit of taking on lost causes (such as representing a college professor terminated over an unpopular sex education questionnaire) or losing battles (such as opposing the local Pendergast political machine). An early Depression-era episode in which he filed for receivership for a steel trading client brought him into contact with a Pittsburgh lawyer, Arthur Van Buskirk of the Reed Smith firm, who visited Kansas City on behalf of his client U.S. Steel and saw in Hazard a quick-thinking, "can-do," business savvy lawyer. A few years later, in 1938, Van Buskirk wrote to Hazard telling him that he had proposed Hazard to fill the role of general counsel for Pittsburgh Plate Glass Company.[137]

Although Arthur B. Van Buskirk, age forty-two, had worked in Pittsburgh for almost fifteen years, he was not a native Pittsburgher, either. His parents were outstanding citizens of Pottstown, thirty-two miles northwest of Philadelphia. His father ran the family hardware business, founded a generation earlier, and his mother was known for her work with the local library board and the needlepoint club and for teaching the women's Bible class at Transfiguration Lutheran Church. Arthur went to Yale, and after serving in the Great War, he obtained his law degree at the University of Pennsylvania. He clerked for Pennsylvania Supreme Court Chief Justice Robert von Moschzisker for a couple of years before accepting an invitation to go to Pittsburgh to join the Reed Smith firm in 1924.[138] Over the course of fourteen years in private practice, Van Buskirk had developed close relationships with the top executives at U.S. Steel and Mellon Bank, and obviously had enough influence with Pittsburgh Plate Glass to secure the general counsel office there for Leland Hazard.

Hazard and Van Buskirk had both come to a city that seemed to be long on economic opportunity for educated men of ambition, but short on livability. On his arrival, Hazard later wrote, "We came to Pittsburgh; and it was dark at noontime—black and yellow with smoke and acrid with sulphur smell; and the ladies at cocktail parties said, 'We love the smoke and smell,' adding, 'There was good air in Pittsburgh during the Depression but no business in the mills. We like it this way.'"[139]

Pittsburgh's reputation as the "Workshop of the World" was being threatened by its very success. *Life* magazine appeared for the first time in 1936, and through its crisp photojournalism, Pittsburgh was observed by the rest of the nation to be "grimy, gray, dirty, and of course, smoky."[140] In addition to the ubiquitous smoke, floods—such as the St. Patrick's Day Flood of 1936—seemed to occur every year, and property values in downtown Pittsburgh began to dip dramatically as a result. Huge sections of downtown, especially at the Point, where the Allegheny, Ohio and Monongahela Rivers meet, were blighted with decrepit buildings and industrial detritus; the most recognizable feature of the Point, visible in contemporary photos taken from Mt. Washington, were the rusted, hulking Point and Manchester steel bridges extending asymmetrically from the North and South shores to the apex of the city's downtown triangle. Housing in the city and in neighboring suburbs was substandard, and cultural assets were perceived to be limited. Managers and engineers—corporate talent—were becoming less attracted to Pittsburgh for its economic opportunity because they did not want to raise their families in these conditions.[141] Frank Lloyd Wright, who had come to town in 1935 to build Fallingwater in the nearby Laurel Highlands for department store magnate Edgar Kaufmann, was asked how he would rebuild Pittsburgh. "It would be cheaper to abandon it," he replied.[142] By 1945, some of the large corporations that had built Pittsburgh, and had been built by Pittsburgh—such as Westinghouse, Alcoa and U.S. Steel—were beginning to think the same thing, according to Adolph Schmidt (R.K. Mellon's cousin-in-law and president of the A.W. Mellon Educational and Charitable Trust), taking options on properties in other cities and "laying plans to build skyscrapers there and move their offices."[143]

During the late nineteenth century, while reformers made slow progress in improving Pittsburgh, the city's great industrialists—Carnegie, Frick, the Mellon brothers, Westinghouse—occasionally proved themselves to be visionaries. Their execution of their industrial plans effected massive changes on Pittsburgh, its landscape, its economy and its society—sometimes to the city's detriment, sometimes to its benefit—but they also used their unprecedented personal wealth, in the words of historian Olivier Zunz, "to both envision and fashion the common good" in their philanthropic activities. Their philanthropic projects, like those of wealthy benefactors in other cities in the country, "were acts of generosity and hubris on a scale never before entertained."[144] Andrew Carnegie was the most influential philanthropist of his age, writing in his *Gospel of Wealth* that "the duty of the man of wealth" was "to consider all surplus revenues which come to him simply as trust funds, which he is called upon to administer, and strictly bound as a matter of duty to administer in the manner which, in his judgment, is best calculated to produce the most beneficial results for the community."[145] For Carnegie, this duty was meant to be fulfilled during the lifetime of the wealthy man, not simply by bequests.

Thus, Carnegie set in motion during his lifetime the investment of fifty-six million dollars in building 2,509 libraries throughout the world—including over twenty in the greater Pittsburgh area—as well as establishing the Carnegie Museums of Pittsburgh, and the Carnegie Technical Schools, which morphed into a four-year college and eventually merged with the Mellon Institute for Industrial Research, established by the Mellon brothers, to become Carnegie Mellon University.[146] Carnegie's friend and partner, Henry Phipps, gave millions for the establishment and upkeep of Pittsburgh public parks, gardens and playgrounds, as well as building the Phipps Conservatory and Botanical Gardens[147]; and Carnegie's nemesis, Henry Clay Frick, gave the start-up funds to build the Allegheny Observatory and bequeathed 151 acres of woodlands to the city for the establishment of Frick Park.[148] Even George Westinghouse, who hated the notion of charity, nevertheless "saw employee living conditions and corporate productivity as interlinked," according to Skrabec, and he supervised the creation of an "ideal" industrial community around his new Air Brake plant in Wilmerding in the 1890s, with public green spaces, clean water and inexpensive power.[149] Mary Schenley, not an industrialist but a land heir, gave three hundred acres to the city for the establishment of another of its great urban parks, after being coaxed by planner Edward Bigelow and his attorney Robert B. Carnahan. She later sold the city an additional 120 acres.[150] Most of these gifts did not require much cooperation or affirmative action by the corrupt municipal governments of the day, but occasionally, when the efficiencies of a corrupt government and visionary planning and philanthropy were in step, as in the creation of Schenley Park, the results could be spectacularly successful.

By the 1930s, Pittsburgh's larger-than-life nineteenth century industrial philanthropists were gone—some had moved on to New York even before they died—and while some of their trusts remained intact, the force of personality that inhabited these men while they were living, the uncontainable confidence of men in mid-career who believed that they could actually make great changes for the betterment of the world with their wealth, had gone with them. In their place were a number of large, increasingly multi-regional corporations, governed by executives and boards largely from out of town, and to a great degree, their focus was on public stockholders, not on the communities in which their executive offices were located. The predominant questions on the minds of many Pittsburghers during the 1930s, exhausted by both the Depression and the prevailing conditions of the town, must have been—where would the new benefactors come from? Who would lead?

In the image of Judge Gary of U.S. Steel, there were several lawyers in top executive positions within Pittsburgh's corporate community during the period. U.S. Steel's chairman and chief executive officer until 1938, Myron H. Taylor, started out as a small-town lawyer; during the 1950s and 60s, another lawyer, Roger Blough, held the post. The lawyer who hired Leland Hazard, Clarence Brown, served as chairman of Pittsburgh Plate Glass (PPG) from 1931 to 1955. Gwilym Price, a Pitt Law graduate who practiced with Judge Richard W. Martin before becoming a bank executive, was named president of Westinghouse in 1946. Philip Fleger started as a law clerk in the Philadelphia Company before eventually becoming chairman of Duquesne Light in 1950. Another Pitt Law graduate, first in a class of 102 in 1932, Robert C. Downie, served as president of Peoples First National Bank (later Pittsburgh National Bank).[151] When the crowned heads of corporate Pittsburgh convened during the late 1940s and early 1950s, it wasn't quite a room full of lawyers (there were a number of engineers and salesmen there as well), but their notable presence did demonstrate that stockholders, during a period of rapid expansion in federal regulatory oversight over corporate America, had grown comfortable with the idea of relying upon lawyers to assume the helms of major businesses.

Out of necessity, the role of lawyers who actually functioned as lawyers within these businesses became elevated during the period. Clarence Brown was all too aware, as an old lawyer himself, of the challenges brought on by the "the New Deal laws," as Hazard described them, "controlling the stock market; sale of securities; labor-management relations; minimum wages; maximum hours; trade practices of almost every kind." Brown hired Hazard to work closely with the business units of the company—to keep them coloring inside the lines of federal regulation—and to build a law department inside PPG, developing on an on-site stable of specialized talent.[152] Leon Hickman, who had been immersed for fifteen years in the details of the Alcoa anti-trust case before joining Alcoa as vice president and general counsel in April 1951, was more explicit about his task—and perhaps a bit more systematic in his approach. Hickman saw himself in the role of general counsel as a vice president of the company "who is given complete responsibility for the legal affairs of his company," someone who is "not uncommonly a member of the board of directors," sitting "in the innermost councils of the company," and managing the corporate law department "much as a general law office is, with careful recruitment of personnel from the best law schools, training very similar to that of the large law offices, good law libraries, and with more professional independence than most general practitioners enjoy."[153] In short, Hickman—who was formerly a partner of one of Pittsburgh's largest and most venerable law firms—saw himself in the role of building a law firm within Alcoa.

The public company general counsel in the 1940s and 50s had become a completely different species from the "'kept' counsel" (Hickman's phrase)[154] who often occupied the role in the days of Gibson Packer, Carnegie's in-house man, in the late nineteenth century. Hazard, Hickman and their contemporaries became corporate executives, bearing a deeper understanding of some of the most daunting complexities then facing corporate America, with a seat at the table in the boardroom, and the ability to form agendas and to set and execute policy.

By the end of World War II, Arthur Van Buskirk had also become an in-house man, too, after a fashion. Before the War, his client, Edward Stettinus, who had succeeded Myron Taylor as chairman of U.S. Steel in 1938, had secured a promise from Van Buskirk that if the United States were to enter the conflict, Van Buskirk would come to Washington to work with Stettinus in the Roosevelt administration.[155] As Hazard put it, although Van Buskirk was a Republican, "he was nonetheless in Pittsburgh and Pennsylvania a liberal. He could live with the New Deal when others of his era spent their time in futile fulmination."[156] After Pearl Harbor, Van Buskirk made good on his promise and joined Stettinus as his deputy administrator at the Lend-Lease Administration,[157] the vehicle for President Roosevelt's effort, based on questionable legality, to be the "Arsenal of Democracy," providing munitions, vehicles and ships to the Allied powers before the United States declared war on Germany and the Axis powers. At its height, incidentally, the Lend-Lease Administration was arguably one of the greatest law firms in the country, consisting of such leading legal lights as Oscar Cox, a former Cadwalader lawyer and assistant corporate counsel for the City of New York who authored the Lend-Lease Act; Yale property law professor Myres McDougal; Adlai Stevenson's law partner George Ball, a future Secretary of State; Cravath lawyer Lloyd Cutler, subsequently White House counsel for Presidents Carter and Clinton; Joseph Rauh, a Harvard lawyer later known for his civil rights work and as a founder of the Americans for Democratic Action; Eugene Rostow, a Yale law professor who would later serve as dean of Yale Law School; and the dean of Cornell Law School, Robert Sproule Stevens.[158] The Lend-Lease Administration may, in fact, have been the pinnacle of elite lawyer public service during the earliest days of World War II.

Van Buskirk returned to Pittsburgh in 1944. "[A]t that time," he recalled, he "was strikingly impressed with the very sad condition of affairs—the smoke, the floods and the lack of faith in the community." One of his firm's clients, R.B. Mellon's son Richard King Mellon, was a colonel in the U.S. Army, and had served in Washington as assistant chief of the War Department's international division. Mellon had asked Van Buskirk if after the War he might have an interest in joining the Mellon Securities Corporation, the family's most active business, as a kind of chief of staff. "I knew that when he returned from the Army it was his intention to do something about the city," Van Buskirk said, "and his wife fully shared this feeling. It also struck a sympathetic note with me."[159] R.K. Mellon's interest in Pittsburgh as a community may have come from what Hazard described as "a suggestion of his father that a man should live and work in the community where he had made his money (a precept which the Carnegies and the Fricks with the New York Fifth Avenue places had not followed)."[160] Van Buskirk accepted Mellon's invitation, and later maintained that he ceased practicing law the moment he joined Mellon in 1944; but as a minister without portfolio, he continued to serve in the lawyer's guise of "wise counsel" to Mellon, as well as serving as Mellon's chief delegate in his civic activities.[161] Similar to Hazard and Hickman from their posts atop "law firms" existing within major corporations, Van Buskirk would hold a position of powerful civic influence—arguably greater than those held by the leading private practitioners of the time, because it was backed by the patient indulgence, the capital and might of Pittsburgh big business. In addition, unlike many of the executives with whom they worked, these men were also members of a strong local professional institution, the County Bar Association, that grounded them to some degree in local concerns.

While Mellon and Van Buskirk remained in Washington during the War, Wallace Richards carried the Mellon torch back in Pittsburgh. Richards was a former Indianapolis newspaper reporter who had worked with Rexford Tugwell, head of the U.S. Resettlement Administration, on the development of the federal cooperative community in Greenbelt, Maryland until 1936. Richards then came to Pittsburgh to run the Pittsburgh Regional Planning Association, an organization founded by R.K.'s father, Richard B. Mellon. As Mellon's proxies, Richards and Park H. Martin, an engineer, established the Allegheny Conference on Post-War Planning as a non-profit, non-partisan vehicle for inviting Pittsburgh's corporate elite to participate in the revitalization of Pittsburgh in 1943.[162] Charles F.C. Arensberg served as the incorporating attorney.[163]

Van Buskirk and Richards both surmised by 1945, however, that the success of the Allegheny Conference (later renamed as the Allegheny Conference on Community Development, or ACCD) and the future of Pittsburgh revitalization depended upon the cooperation of David L. Lawrence, who was elected mayor in November, and the Democratic Party. As Lawrence's biographer Michael P. Weber observed, "David L. Lawrence and Richard King Mellon were so powerful in their respective fields that resistance on the part of either could destroy the best planning. The business community could not act without the city's power to condemn land, build roads, revise zoning and so forth. ... But the city could not act without the support of the business community, which would finance most of the redevelopment and maintain the businesses and corporations vital to the welfare of the city." Mellon functioned as a kind of baron of the realm, and he and his family had seats on the boards, and influence within the boardrooms, of such companies as Westinghouse, Gulf Oil, Koppers, Consolidation Coal, Jones & Laughlin Steel and PPG.[164]

R.K. was not interested in politics, nor in being caught in the limelight[165]; but after Mellon returned from the War, Richards, Arthur Van Buskirk and Adolph Schmidt convinced him that he had to meet with Mayor Lawrence. Van Buskirk advised Mellon: "The generous offer would be for you to leave your office and go over and visit the mayor."[166] The idea that the scion of Pittsburgh's wealthiest family—the family that had controlled Republican politics in the region from behind the scenes, and that had been Lawrence's main political irritant in the years before the Democrats took city hall—would emerge in shoe-leather in broad daylight and pay a call on the mayor in his office, seemed preposterous on its face. Mellon hesitated, but after some convincing, he permitted his aides to cook up an excuse to see the mayor involving the donation of a small parcel of family land for a park and recreation center that was to become Mellon Park at Fifth and Beechwood Avenue in Shadyside. On the appointed day, Mellon left his office in the Mellon Bank building at Fifth Avenue and Smithfield Street and walked up to Mayor Lawrence's office on the 5th floor of the City-County Building on Grant Street to enlist the mayor's support for the Conference's redevelopment plans. Schmidt remembered that "Lawrence was duly embarrassed"—perhaps this was Van Buskirk's objective—but the ploy worked. The next time, Mayor Lawrence came to visit

Mellon. The two never became intimate friends—in fact, they did not meet all that often—but the rules of engagement were quickly defined. As Weber says, sometimes projects were initiated by the city, sometimes by the ACCD, sometimes by a private party, but "[a]s work progressed, and it became clear that Lawrence was an irreplaceable asset, all favorable publicity was carefully shifted in the direction of the mayor."[167]

Mellon, meanwhile, was to be a powerful but mostly invisible presence. He would not even actually join the ACCD himself. Instead, as Leland Hazard explained, Arthur Van Buskirk, Mellon's principal confidant, carried Mellon's portfolio as chairman of the ACCD beginning in 1945. "[Van Buskirk's] voice," wrote Hazard, "was the last word. When he was enthusiastic, the resolutions were affirmative and the project moved. When he said 'W-e-l-l-l, let's think that one over,' everyone knew that he was either uncertain himself or uncertain about R.K.'s reaction on the issue."[168] Lawrence observed that Van Buskirk was a man of "suavity, subtlety, intelligence and underlying strength of purpose," and that he was "a master hand in a meeting, quick to summarize essentials, adept at the courteous trades and concessions which bring agreement among equals."[169] Edgar Kaufmann, Edward Weidlin from the Mellon Institute, Robert Doherty from Carnegie Tech and J. Steele Gow from the Falk Foundation were among the first members of the Conference's small executive committee; Van Buskirk invited Leland Hazard to join after a couple of years, along with presidents of several other major Pittsburgh corporations.[170]

Van Buskirk was also responsible for giving a name to the initiatives on which they were about to embark. Studying preliminary plans for a park at the Point during a meeting, Van Buskirk thought about some background reading he had been doing on Italian art, and, as he explained it, he "kept reading again and again about the Renaissance in Europe and the impact of it in various countries. And there passed through my mind the thought that if we could do what we proposed, this would be a renaissance of the city, and I said that to the meeting." Among the attendees that day were some executives from the local newspapers. The name stuck—this project of theirs would be known, for better or worse, as the "Pittsburgh Renaissance."[171]

Meanwhile, the plans for the redevelopment of the Point took shape, encompassing not only a thirty-six-acre state park located in the lower Point, but a proposed twenty-six-acre real estate development adjoining the park in the upper Point area. The latter idea began to gain ground after David Lawrence had occasion to watch the destruction by fire of the once-grand Wabash Terminal Building, at the intersection of Liberty Avenue and Ferry Street in the upper Point, from the roof of the Pittsburgh Press Building on March 22, 1946. "We enjoyed the fire," said the mayor's executive secretary Jack Robin. "What the hell, we knew the fire was helping us."[172] As Van Buskirk explained, the Point Park would only be successful "if the area adjoining the park on the east"—an area with many old dilapidated structures—had "attractive approaches to the park" and if there was an "architectural unity" between the park and "whatever is built that will face upon the park." Otherwise, the "band of blight" between the park and the rest of downtown would render the park somewhat isolated and useless.[173] In the summer of 1946, Van Buskirk led a team composed of himself, Wallace Richards, Park Martin and the president of the Pittsburgh and West Virginia Railroad, Charles J. Graham, to New York City in search of a developer for the area. Graham had an interest in moving the project forward, since his company owned what was left of the burnt-out Wabash Terminal. Their first stop was the Metropolitan Life Insurance Company, whose executives told the group that their commitments to Manhattan real estate made it impossible for them to participate. Graham suggested that the team pay a cold call upon his friend Thomas Parkinson, president of the Equitable Life Assurance Society. After the Pittsburgh delegation told him of the efforts already under way to deal with smoke and floods, Parkinson admitted he was intrigued and agreed to have his team review the plan.[f][174]

In 1945, the state legislature had enacted the Urban Redevelopment Act, which authorized the creation of local redevelopment authorities and gave them the power to acquire blighted areas and to contract out their redevelopment to private or government developers[175]; but development of the office complex by the Equitable, not to mention future revitalization initiatives, required certain additional legislative action. Thus, Van Buskirk and his executive committee at the ACCD called for the drafting of new state legislation designed to carry out the Renaissance program, to be known as the "Pittsburgh Package." The ACCD's new outside lawyer, Theodore Hazlett, was given the task of drafting the bills, with assistance from Lawrence's city solicitor, Anne X. Alpern, and the solicitor to the Pittsburgh Housing Authority, Al Wilner. Hazlett, a Harvard lawyer and the son of a Squirrel Hill physician, had gotten his first taste of the Renaissance while working as a clerk for Charles F.C. Arensberg, helping to draft the documents for changing the ACCD's name from the "Allegheny Conference on Post-War Planning." After law school he clerked with Chief Justice James Drew of the Pennsylvania Supreme Court for a year, and then opened his own practice in Pittsburgh, soon to be brought into the Burgwin Churchill firm. His first independent client was the ACCD, through which he was hired by Park Martin to work on the "Package."[176] The "legal architect of Pittsburgh's Renaissance" as he would be called in his 1979 obituary, was a fresh-faced first-year lawyer who later admitted that he "probably

---

[f] In 1941, during the mayoral administration of Lawrence's protégé Cornelius Scully, the Pittsburgh city council passed a smoke abatement ordinance, requiring businesses and homeowners to invest in smokeless fuel burning machines, following a particularly smoky coal-heating season; after Pearl Harbor, however, enforcement of the new ordinance was put on hold until after the War. Upon his election in 1945, Lawrence declared that the War was over and that it was time to implement the smoke ordinances, amid protests from coal producers as well as the United Mine Workers. After considerable backroom bargaining designed by the ACCD to give Lawrence political cover, the city council voted to begin enforcement of the smoke abatement ordinances on commercial users on October 1, 1946, with residential users to follow the year after. During the exceptionally cold winter of 1947/48, however, the price of low volatility coal rose dramatically, causing protests over smoke abatement. The mayor responded by directing enforcement activities at the coal suppliers and easing up on enforcement in the poorer neighborhoods. When the results of smoke abatement began to roll in, by the summer of 1948, opinion polls showed that a majority of city residents noticed the improvement in air quality; and while the smoke problem was not by any means completely resolved, voices of protest grew faint. Nonetheless, Lawrence barely squeaked by in the 1949 mayoral Democratic primary election when he was challenged by Eddie Leonard, a city councilman who took on Lawrence over the smoke regulations. Meanwhile, flood control initiatives began as early as 1936; over the next 20 years, the Corps of Engineers built 10 new dams in the Upper Ohio Valley. Lawrence, *Rebirth*, 386-402; Weber, *Don't Call Me Boss*, 243-254; Lubove, *Twentieth-Century Pittsburgh I*, 119-120.

would have left the city" if it weren't for the chance to become involved with such an exciting project.[177] He was exactly the kind of talented individual that the Pittsburgh Renaissance was being created to retain.

Ten bills were presented by the Lawrence administration to the state legislature in 1947. The diverse package included an extension of Allegheny County's smoke abatement regulations to railroads; the creation of County authorities for refuse disposal and sewage treatment; the creation of a city department of parks and recreation; the creation of a city parking authority to develop parking facilities through revenue bond issuances; the establishment of a commission to study mass transit; more local control over suburban subdivision plans; completion of the Penn-Lincoln Parkway (Interstate 376, connecting downtown Pittsburgh with the Pennsylvania Turnpike); County authority to pursue grievances against the Public Utility Commission; the operation of bridges on state highways by the state; and the expansion of the Pittsburgh tax powers beyond levying taxes on real estate. An additional bill permitted insurance companies to invest in redevelopment areas, something that was required in order to get the Equitable project off the ground.[178]

Portions of the "Pittsburgh Package" were controversial. The Parking Authority bill would expand the eminent domain powers of the locality, and was considered yet another threat to private property; the expansion of the smoke control ordinances revived the opposition of both the corporate community and the United Mine Workers; and the expansion of the tax base was yet another lightning rod for criticism.[179] On behalf of the ACCD, Ted Hazlett spent almost six months in Harrisburg as part of the Pittsburgh "lobbying" team, along with Richards, Martin, and Robert Bassett, the assistant to the president of the Joseph Horne department store company, one of the ACCD's lead corporate supporters.[180]

The ACCD also approached Homer Brown, the Hill District lawyer and president of the Pittsburgh chapter of the NAACP who entered the state assembly in 1935 and was now serving as the chair of the Democratic delegation of Allegheny County, for assistance in the passage of the "Pittsburgh Package." While R.K. Mellon used his influence, through U.S. Steel, to convince the Pennsylvania Railroad to cease its opposition to the anti-smoke bill, Brown became particularly important as floor manager on the Parking Authority bill. Although it was voted down upon first consideration, through Brown's well-timed arguments on the constitutionality of proposed dilutive amendments and his deployment of parliamentary tactics—such as insisting that each proposed amendment to the bill be dealt with separately—he ultimately secured passage of the Parking Authority bill by a margin of 186-4 in the House, and 44-5 in the Senate. By the end of the session eight of the ten bills, plus the insurance investment legislation, passed. Robert D. Fleming, a fellow Pittsburgh-area representative, said that "it is questionable whether these bills would have gotten through" without Brown's expert navigation of the legislature, "and if so, it probably would have been more quarrels for two years getting the bills passed."[181]

Meanwhile, taking advantage of the Urban Redevelopment Act, Van Buskirk and Martin asked Mayor Lawrence to form a city redevelopment authority, which would have the ability not only to acquire blighted land for the project, but to raise money for the acquisitions through private financing. Lawrence agreed and asked if Van Buskirk would serve as chairman. Van Buskirk countered that Mayor Lawrence should serve as chairman. "Arthur, that's ridiculous!," exclaimed Lawrence. "I don't think there's a case in all the history of this country where any man ever appointed himself to the job." Again, Van Buskirk was doing his best to push Lawrence to the political forefront of the Renaissance effort, and also calculated that "the prestige of the Mayor's office" would be useful to the Authority. The two men settled on Lawrence taking the chairmanship, with Van Buskirk as vice-chairman. William Alvah Stewart, an attorney and Democratic city councilman, along with Republicans Edgar Kaufmann and Carnegie-Illinois president J. Lester Perry, rounded out the ostentatiously bi-partisan board of directors of the new Urban Redevelopment Authority of Pittsburgh (URA).[182]

As the building blocks of public-private cooperation in Pittsburgh were coming together, the negotiations with the Equitable continued for four years after the first meeting of Van Buskirk's team and Thomas Parkinson in the summer of 1946. The first suggestion for the upper Point real estate development—apartment housing—was rejected by the Equitable's real estate people, but they agreed that Pittsburgh had considerable demand for new office space, since few new downtown office buildings had been built during the last decade. During one trip to New York, Lawrence, Van Buskirk and other members of the team were having breakfast in Van Buskirk's room at the Ambassador Hotel on Park Avenue, and in the course of discussing the Equitable deal—the basic structure would be that the URA would purchase the land and sell it to the Equitable for the URA'a acquisition cost—Van Buskirk suggested to Lawrence that the URA should consider charging a "toll" to the Equitable for the privilege of developing the area. "Do you realize we're giving them the value and the prestige and the power of the act of assembly that gives the Authority the right of eminent domain"? Lawrence took a moment to grasp the concept—up until then it had felt like they had been coming to New York with their hats in their hands, still a bit worried about reaching a deal—and asked Van Buskirk, "What kind of figure are you thinking about?" "Well, said Van Buskirk, "why not a round million dollars, say $50,000 a year for twenty years." Edgar Kaufmann volunteered two million dollars as a conversation starter.[183]

When the Equitable and the URA finally reached their preliminary accord, the Equitable agreed to pay fifty thousand dollars per year for forty years as a developer's fee. In return, the URA agreed to make sure that Pittsburgh's corporate community had pre-agreed to lease a minimum of two-thirds of the space in the new office development, to be known as Gateway Center. Van Buskirk and R.K. Mellon judiciously applied their pressure on Jones & Laughlin Steel, Westinghouse, PPG, Peoples Natural Gas and others to sign long-term leases. When they began to fall slightly short of the goal, the URA was in a position to bargain away a portion of the development fee to encourage the Equitable to reduce its rental prices.[184]

The Equitable had one additional condition, which was that the land should be obtained quickly, without exorbitant costs associated with litigation. Setting the untested powers of the Urban Redevelopment Act in motion, the City Planning Commission declared the entire fifty-nine acres of the Point to be a blighted area in March 1947—"unfit for human habitation" not for "prolonged vacancy" or "dilapidation,' but due to the more nuanced concept of "obsolescence."[185] The entire scheme of eminent domain proposed by the Act, however, had been subject to attack by critics on constitutional grounds, that the use of eminent domain to take private property from one private party so that it could be used differently by another private party was, according to opponents, an unconstitutional infringement of private property rights. Fortunately for the URA, a constitutional challenge was already under way against the Redevelopment Authority of the City of Philadelphia. After the Philadelphia Common Pleas Court dismissed the suit, the plaintiff appealed to the Pennsylvania Supreme Court. The URA, represented by William Eckert from the Smith Buchanan firm, and the City of Pittsburgh, represented by Anne X. Alpern, joined the defense of the appeal. On July 29, 1947, the Pennsylvania Supreme Court affirmed the lower court, holding that the Urban Redevelopment Act was constitutional.[186]

Still, both the URA and the Equitable expected challenges as they began the process of acquiring the properties, and they were determined to acquire as many of them as possible without involving the power of eminent domain. In the lower Point, the area for the proposed park was occupied in part by the abandoned Exposition Hall, already owned by the city, and Mayor Lawrence had already pledged the cooperation of the city in vacating the public streets in the lower Point. The remainder was a collection of warehouses and railroad tracks largely owned by the Pennsylvania Railroad. After prolonged negotiations between Van Buskirk and Charles D. Young, the Pennsy's vice president in charge of real estate, the parties settled on a selling price of $4.25 million, with the state kicking in the purchase price in accordance with its commitment to build the park as a state park.[187]

The acquisition of the upper Point area proved slightly more difficult. According to Ralph Demmler from Reed Smith, in addition to the ruins of the Wabash Terminal and some vacant lots, the upper Point was occupied by

> *some small relatively run-down shops and stores, some boarding houses and some houses to which male patrons made short visits. But there was also a hotel [the Mayfair, originally built in 1895] which had once been occupied by the Pittsburgh Club ... a professional building filled largely with doctors' offices ... the Congress of Women's Clubs in a rehabilitated old residence ... and there were some substantial mercantile buildings ...*[188]

About seventy parcels were involved. Businesses would need to be relocated. People would need to be moved. The URA decided that it would encourage the launch a "friendly" lawsuit to establish, in short order, the URA's power to clear the area. While thirty independent property owners were getting themselves organized to fight with the URA, Albert W. Schenck, the owner of a three-story building at 420-22 Penn Avenue, engaged his son-in-law, Robert Van der Voort—then the president of the Allegheny County Bar Association—to file a lawsuit in December 1949, to attack the constitutionality of the Urban Development Act as applied to the Gateway Center project. Van der Voort petitioned the Pennsylvania Supreme Court to hear the case in the first instance, and in response the Court cleared the docket for argument on January 5, 1950. Three "unfriendly" plaintiffs also joined the suit. Meanwhile, representing the city, once again, was Anne X. Alpern; the URA's new general counsel, Ted Hazlett, appeared on behalf of the Authority; and from Reed Smith, Robert Dodds, Sr. (a board member of the Equitable), former Pennsylvania Superior Court judge Charles Kenworthey, and Demmler appeared for the Equitable.

The Pennsylvania Supreme Court wasted no time in affirming the constitutionality of the Act. On January 11, Justice Horace Stern delivered a sweeping opinion in favor of the Act, affirming as its purpose "to give wide scope to municipalities in redesigning and rebuilding such [blighted] areas within their limits as, by reason of the passage of years and the enormous changes in traffic conditions and types of building construction, no longer meet the economic and social needs of modern city life and progress." Rehearing on the case on petition of the landowners was denied nineteen days later, and the URA had survived its greatest challenge, quickly and efficiently.[189] As Dodds had put it, "[I]t was necessary to bring all the trains into the station at the same time, the agreements to lease, the municipal approvals, and the redevelopment contract." The contracts between the parties, providing for a commitment of fifty million dollars from the Equitable, were signed on February 14, 1950.[190]

Still, the wrangling continued. In April, approximately twenty other landowners and stakeholders filed actions in state and federal court, seeking to re-examine the Pennsylvania Supreme Court's decision. The state court suits were summarily dismissed, and in the U.S. District Court for the Western District of Pennsylvania, a three-judge panel also dismissed the attempt to overturn the state court ruling. The plaintiffs' attorneys in the federal case—a trio of lawyers from the Grant Building, James A. Danahey, a thirty-eight year-old Pitt Law grad; Gilbert Morecroft, age forty-one, the some-time solicitor for the Boroughs of Crafton and Bellevue; and Maurice J. Arnd, age forty-four, a real estate lawyer—appealed the case to the U.S. Supreme Court. Anne X. Alpern and Arthur Van Buskirk were on the brief for the city interests. On October 9, 1950, the Supreme Court affirmed the lower court without opinion. By that time, almost half of the buildings in the upper Point had already been demolished.[191]

The first three buildings in the Gateway Center complex opened in 1952. Point State Park took shape more gradually as state and local authorities worked together to replace the Point and Manchester Bridges and rework traffic patterns across the new, streamlined Fort Duquesne and Fort Pitt Bridges near the Gateway Center development; by the end of 1970, the Park looked much as it does today, and the iconic fountain at its apex, which sprays water from an underground aquifer up to 150 feet in the air, was finally dedicated on August 30, 1974.[192] The tremendous vista of Pittsburgh that dazzles visitors to the city to this day as they ascend the Duquesne Incline had finally taken shape.

In the meantime, for Van Buskirk and the planning minds within the ACCD and the URA, success was a heady thing. "Van was happy," wrote Leland Hazard. "In those days there was a bounce in his step and his energies seemed boundless."[193] R.K. Mellon continued the momentum by donating a park and underground garage in the heart of downtown between Smithfield Street and Cherry Way—later named Mellon Square—which would become a focal point for two new privately-developed skyscrapers, the forty-one-floor 525 William Penn Place (1951), shared by Mellon Bank and U.S. Steel, and the thirty-floor Alcoa Building (1953). The URA undertook a novel capital expansion project in Hazelwood with the enlargement of a Jones & Laughlin Steel Plant in 1952. Deploying many of the same tactics as those that were used in the clearing of the Point, beginning in 1955 the URA acquired and cleared ninety-five acres in the Lower Hill District, adjacent to downtown, displacing more than 1,500 families and four hundred businesses, in order to build a Civic Arena with a retractable roof, to serve as a home for the Civic Light Opera and sporting events. Edgar Kaufmann, a Light Opera enthusiast, donated one million dollars in start-up funds for the Arena.[194]

In the midst of its early success, the Pittsburgh Renaissance also had its critics. In May 1951, the *Atlantic Monthly* published an article on the city's redevelopment phenomenon. The author, Karl Schriftgiesser, was a former drama editor for *The New York Times* and a book editor for *Newsweek*. Schriftgiesser wrote: "In the minds of some thoughtful Pittsburghers there lurks the suspicion that the work of the Conference has laid too much emphasis on the materialistic side, that it has neglected the fields of social welfare and cultural development. There is no question of the truth of this accusation."[195] The members of the ACCD who read the piece were left feeling as though there was a misunderstanding about the city that needed to be cleared up. Van Buskirk approached his friend, Leland Hazard, at a cocktail party in Ligonier, about sixty miles east of Pittsburgh, where both men had summer homes, and charged him with delivering an address to the mid-fall annual ACCD dinner. "Gwilym Price ... will address us on the industrial future of Pittsburgh, and then you will charge us with our cultural responsibilities." Hazard—an enthusiastic cultural omnivore, a lover of theatre, art, literature and philosophy who enjoyed dropping Shakespearean quotations into normal conversation—initially felt some dread over the thought of being invited to play the role of "scold to a community." He noted, to himself, that a writer in *Harper's* in 1930 had referred to Pittsburgh as "on the whole, barbaric."[196]

Nonetheless, on the evening of September 15, 1952, at the Carnegie Music Hall, the vice president and general counsel of PPG took on a singular role within the Pittsburgh Renaissance, as its intellectual herald and thoughtful publicist. Paying tribute to the success of the Point project, Hazard said:

> *It takes more than a park, more than the rescue of a noble site of land to make culture. If Pittsburgh is to become pre-eminent in spirit, she must make herself a place where tolerance is stronger than fear of dissident thought and taste; where untruth will be looked in the face and talked, not shouted, down; where what is right is more sought after than what is wrong.*[197]

He touted libraries and education, and referred to an inventory prepared by the ACCD of Pittsburgh cultural institutions—featuring a Dickens Fellowship, a Society of Sculptors, a Homestead Russian Orthodox Male Chorus, the Goose Lookers (who followed the migration of the Canada Goose), the Old Westmoreland Rifles (devoted to collecting old muzzle-loading rifles), and on and on through the categories of art, ballet and dance, drama, literature, music, garden clubs, historical societies and women's clubs.[198] Pittsburgh was not barbaric; but its cultural future depended upon "an organized and effective conscience," drawn not only from people within the industrial and business segments of the community, but also the civic and educational segments, with their "differing hopes and insights with respect to community development." He asserted, "the community must not expect accumulated wealth to do everything"—a nod to the passing of the age of Carnegie. Instead, he insisted that the future of Pittsburgh, quoting the local Carnegie Tech poet Haniel Long, "lies in the future of its least citizen; its least citizen is bound by tears and blood to its greatest citizen ... Pittsburghers, what is Pittsburgh? It is the total of the relationships of us who live in Pittsburgh: is nothing else, now and forever."[199]

One might imagine that some of the 350 Pittsburgh leaders who gathered for the dinner may have been unmoved, but R.K. Mellon—"never given to perfunctory praise," Hazard observed—told him immediately afterward, "This was a little bit different tonight. Some people had tears in their eyes."[200]

Van Buskirk promptly formed a standing committee of the ACCD on cultural affairs—widely known as "Committee No. 4"—and appointed Hazard as its chairman. From that post, Hazard received invitations from across the country—Boston, St. Louis, Dallas—to come and speak about urban renewal and its broader social meaning and possibilities. In Pittsburgh, he spoke to small gatherings around town with great excitement about the new Civic Arena, about how "private philanthropy, city, county, state, and federal funds would be commingled to erect at the heart of a former slum area a civic arena to house summer light opera, sports events, circuses, sunrise prayer meetings, Billy Graham, hockey, Jehovah's Witnesses, and every good or great event which could attract 14,000 people or any substantial portion of that number."[201] Later, he would tacitly acknowledge that his enthusiasm sometimes got the better of him; the Civic Arena, he would observe, "became largely a sports arena"[202] (its eventual anchor tenant, the Pittsburgh Penguins National Hockey League franchise, would not be established until 1967, by Jack McGregor—a Pitt Law grad, former Reed Smith associate, and Pennsylvania state senator).[203] Hazard also had to admit "[h]ow little we understood in those days that there was more to a slum than met the eye,"[204] referring to the decline of Hill District after the Civic Arena was implanted in the midst of its former thruways to downtown.

If Hazard's enthusiasm for the bricks and mortar aspects of the Pittsburgh Renaissance was not always rewarded, another Renaissance project captured his mind and heart in a much more personal way.

In 1948, the Federal Communications Commission (FCC) had announced a "freeze" on new television station licenses due to the need to sort out technical allocation issues in the face of hundreds of new station applications. Although the freeze was only supposed to last for six months, the Korean War gave the FCC a handy excuse to take more time to develop a "master blueprint" for television in the United States— one which would include a standard for color television, as well as a reservation of channels for educational purposes. Meanwhile, David Lawrence was a vocal proponent of non-commercial television for educational purposes, and when the freeze was being lifted in 1952, he used his pull with President Harry S Truman, as one of the few local Democratic party bosses who had given Truman unqualified support in 1948, to secure for Pittsburgh one of the new educational station licenses.[205] The FCC came through with a proposed new non-commercial Channel 13 in Pittsburgh, on the condition that Pittsburgh could meet the minimum financial requirements. Across downtown, however, Gwilym Price at Westinghouse was in the market for a new commercial license in Pittsburgh; the company that owned TV stations across the country did not have a station in the city of its headquarters. Lawrence knew that the support of the ACCD would be critical in realizing his dream, so he turned to his friend Leland Hazard, chairman of Committee No. 4, for assistance.[206]

Hazard became the driving force behind the project. He promptly applied to the ACCD board for a resolution of support. "There was opposition," Hazard recalled. "Who would manage the station, what influences, subversive, Communist, Democratic or otherwise objectionable, might gain control?"[207] It was precisely the kind of "fear of dissident thought and taste" to which he would refer in his address to the ACCD annual dinner. Moreover, Gwilym Price and Westinghouse were conspicuously absent for the first discussion of the non-commercial TV station. Hazard called Price afterwards and asked him point-blank, "Bill, do you say I should abandon my efforts for educational television in Pittsburgh?" Price replied, "No, Leland, I don't." Based on a feasibility study presented to the ACCD by Park Martin, the ACCD gave its tacit, if underwhelming, approval in July 1952, and Hazard went off to raise money for the nonprofit venture—$250,000 from A.W. Mellon Educational and Charitable Trust, the Ford Foundation and the Arbuckle-Jamison Foundation. All but seventy-five thousand dollars were spent on studios and equipment. Westinghouse, meanwhile, contributed to the new non-commercial station the tower it had built in anticipation of acquiring the Channel 13 license; it ultimately bought its way into the Pittsburgh market, paying over ten million dollars for the struggling Dumont network affiliate on Channel 2, and promptly renaming it KDKA, after its flagship radio station call letters. The call letters of the new educational station would be WQED—q.e.d., for "*quod erat demonstrandum*," Latin for "that which is to be proved." WQED would prove to be, as it brags today, the "fifth public broadcasting station in the nation, the third educational-based station, and the country's first community-supported station."[208]

Hazard would later write that his "penchant for lost causes" is what drew him to educational television.[209] He became the first president of WQED, while still serving as vice president, general counsel and a director of PPG; and although he took a deep interest in programming and community outreach, he also used his platform to slash away at opponents who complained that non-commercial television was doomed to failure, or unnecessary in any event. He wrote:

> *I believed then, as I do now, that intellectual minorities, for whom advertising agencies do not care at all, should have their fair share of television. Such minorities in all ages have made the critical difference. They have ever been the leaven of society. And they cling always to a precarious position—threatened with what de Tocqueville called the tyranny of the majority.*[210]

WQED began broadcasting on April 1, 1954, with its own locally-produced programming fare that would never have seen the light of day on commercial television of the time: *Your Marriage*, featuring a husband and wife psychology team; *Shop Talk*, a do-it-yourself repair show; *Ein Zwei Drei*, a German language course; and a documentary on dance legend Martha Graham, a Pittsburgh native, called *A Dancer's World*.[211]

Through the creation one of WQED's earliest programs, *Children's Corner*, Hazard presided over the career-birth of the closest thing Pittsburgh has ever had to a secular saint. Fred Rogers, from nearby Latrobe, was a toothy, skinny, nasal-voiced, recently-married graduate of Rollins College who was working for pennies as an assistant producer for NBC in New York. As a college senior, he had developed the view that children's commercial television was entirely too cruel and hostile. At his father's suggestion he returned to Pittsburgh and interviewed with Leland Hazard for the job of program manager at WQED. Soon Hazard found the musically-talented Rogers running around with various puppets—referred to as Daniel S. Tiger, X the Owl, and King Friday the 13th, among others—playing the piano and singing, sometimes in the persona of Daniel, "with a scratchy, miniscule voice." "We had no idea what the audience was," recalled Hazard. "We knew we were getting letters from mothers, saying, 'Thanks for the baby-sitting.'" When the station decided to have an open house for Daniel S. Tiger, they were surprised to find a blocks-long queue of fans waiting for the doors to open.[212]

Re-tooled as *Mister Rogers' Neighborhood* in 1968, Rogers would make 895 episodes before retiring in 2000, while earning a Masters in Divinity from the Pittsburgh Theological Seminary and becoming an ordained minister, the first Presbyterian minister ever to be ordained without serving a church pastorate. "His programs express to children the Christian concept of the worth of the individual," wrote Hazard. "He says to his young audience—everyday, 'You make each day a special day by your just being you. There is only one person in the whole world like you and I like you just the way you are.' No person so precious and so powerful as Fred Rogers could ever have survived on commercial television."[213]

Hazard was often demonstrably inspired, in his work with the ACCD, by his personal enthusiasm for truth and beauty. However, he would also write, "I have been moved in work, whether in private or public affairs, by the conviction that social inertia (the tendency of people to think and act as they have been thinking and acting) is a necessary object of attack. The people," he explained, "will not rise up and do the right thing."[214] It was the obligation of a person of Hazard's talents and public status to fight social inertia, to make the right thing happen. Van Buskirk, meanwhile, was inspired in his work by ideals that he would chart as elements of the success of the earliest American colonists. Quoting Dr. Benjamin Rush, a signer of the Declaration of Independence, Van Buskirk proclaimed that "Every man is public property. His time and talent—his youth—his manhood—his old age—nay more, his life, his all, belong to his country." He suggested to listeners at a National Business Conference in Boston in 1959 that "we must develop new techniques by which our best citizens may voluntarily be enlisted to aid public officials in the solution of our civic problems at the municipal and state level ... The whole of our body of citizens must know that the price of freedom is service."[215]

Leon Hickman, the vice president and general counsel of Alcoa, saw a more definitive relationship between the corporation and the communities in which it resided that played a role in inspiring him to become involved in the Pittsburgh Renaissance. "I would say that all the top officers of the period ... were convinced that corporations had to play a role in solving the urban problem. To begin with, we were partially creating it."[216] He noted that large corporations

> *have become public institutions ... Today's corporation which has achieved a regional or national stature accepts basic responsibilities with respect to housing, schooling and municipal development. That is not so because one or two men or a few companies have willed it so; rather it stems from the fact that these companies that serve large markets so profoundly affect the wellbeing of so many people that they are recognized as public institutions and act the part. ... [The corporation] must satisfy the people who work for it, not only in the matter of wages and salaries, but in working conditions which makes for a full life ... Let it fail in any of these areas and public retribution is swift and often vengeful.*[217]

For Hickman, participation in the renewal of Pittsburgh was a matter of fiduciary necessity for Alcoa.

Alcoa also had a more direct business interest involved when Leon Hickman led the company into its experiments in developing real estate in Pittsburgh in the 1950s and 60s. Hickman perceived that Alcoa's competitor, Kaiser Aluminum, was considering going into housing, but that Alcoa was better positioned to profit by it due to its experience in manufacturing building materials.[218] It began its foray into real estate development with high-profile projects in Century City, California and in the United Nations Plaza project in New York City, but neither were "redevelopment" projects.[219] After those projects, Hickman was convinced "that Alcoa was in a unique position to participate profitably in the rebuilding of a number of important American cities ... and to contribute ideas and stability to the urban redevelopment movement which started in Pittsburgh at the end of the war and became a Congressional-sponsored national concept in 1949."[220] By 1964, as Hickman would tell the Mortgage Banking Association of America, "Alcoa [was] in urban redevelopment up to its neck."[221]

For Alcoa's projects in Pittsburgh, Hickman walked the company into two massive, controversial redevelopment initiatives. In addition to the Civic Arena project, the cleared ninety-five-acre section of the Lower Hill District was slated for a redevelopment plan that was to include a new cultural center, the Pittsburgh Center for the Arts, housing an opera venue, theater and art museum, in addition to a hotel and apartment buildings.

In the context of that plan, Alcoa built the 388-unit, twenty-four-floor, I.M. Pei-designed Washington Plaza apartment high-rise, further up Centre Avenue across from the Arena. The building was originally intended to be the first of three adjacent towers; but both Alcoa and Heinz, which was sponsoring the Center for the Arts, halted their plans, demanding that the URA and the city put together a plan for the 50 blocks east of the Lower Hill's redevelopment area, from the deteriorating, impoverished Crawford-Devilliers section of the Hill all the way to Oakland. Heinz representatives wanted "to make certain that the proposed cultural center is not built next to a seething slum" and they wanted additional renewal for the Upper Hill "to protect their donations."[222] Hickman told URA director Robert Pease that "if the Upper Hill is not to be improved in a major way, it will stop us in our tracks."[223] At the same time, there began to be a backlash against redevelopment within the African American community in the Hill District, culminating in the charge by the *Pittsburgh Courier* that the city intended to push blacks entirely out of the Hill; local leaders complained that even if they were forcibly moved out, there was a shortage of low-income housing in Pittsburgh to accommodate the relocations, and housing discrimination was still rampant.[224] By 1966, the only completed projects in the Lower Hill District were the Civic Arena, the Chatham Center hotel and apartment complex, and Washington Plaza building #1. The rest of the cleared land was consigned to surface parking lots, or was otherwise left undeveloped for some time.

Alcoa became involved as majority owner of the seventy-nine-acre Allegheny Center redevelopment in 1964. The focal point of the redevelopment project was the construction of an indoor mall, replacing the old open-air public square surrounded by substandard housing and dilapidated retail space in an area in which the population had declined by ten thousand residents from 1950 to 1960. In addition to the 250,000 square feet of retail shopping space in the mall, which architectural critics took to calling the "Northside Kremlin," the project included three office buildings, fifty townhouses, four six-floor apartment buildings, and a three-acre public square. Additional redevelopment plans would have resulted in office buildings and middle-class housing between Allegheny Center and the Allegheny River, but apart from Three Rivers Stadium (which ultimately was surrounded by a sea of surface parking lots), the plans never got off the ground. Although the Mall opened in 1965 with anchor tenants such as Sears, Ames and Woolworth's department stores, it generally failed to bring suburbanites back to the North Side; after the retail stores pulled out in the mid-1990s, the Mall became an office complex. Despite the failure of the redevelopment projects to cause a revitalization of the neighborhoods in which they were built, both Washington Plaza and Allegheny Center Mall remain occupied (the latter, by a data center and commercial offices, with plans to open a shared workspace for start-up companies) and financially viable today.[225]

Hickman lamented the failure of the Allegheny Center redevelopment plan, however, noting that "the diffusion of authority" in the political sector meant that "they can't really concentrate on cleaning up the North Side ... If they do an Allegheny Center, they have to do an East Liberty or something on the South Side before they can come back and put any money on the North Side." As a result, Hickman pointed out in 1970, "Allegheny Center today is sort of an island, and in a way it doesn't make sense to improve Allegheny Center and let the blight exist on either side of it."[226] In the absence of a David Lawrence, who left Pittsburgh to become governor of Pennsylvania in 1959 and died in 1966, there was no one with enough political clout to focus the redevelopment activities of a public-private partnership and to silence the competing political voices of the region. Frustrated that low income housing was lagging, and the lack of it was dragging down redevelopment projects, Hickman joined the board of directors of ACTION-Housing, Inc., a nonprofit housing developer.

Leland Hazard was making some of the same observations about the collapse of the downtown political and business coalition, embodied by the ACCD, that cleaned up the Point. He, too, would cite "political fragmentation" and observed that without "Mr. Mellon," the ACCD was almost inert.[227] Nonetheless, while he was aware of the disappearing ingredients, Hazard waged a quixotic fight to develop public rapid transit in Pittsburgh.

Hazard once remarked that his friend Van Buskirk "tended to belong to the group of people who believe that anyone who doesn't own a Cadillac ought to walk."[228] By contrast, Hazard had developed a passion for the idea of public transit in Pittsburgh. As a member of the County Port Authority Transit (PAT) board of directors and the chairman of its rapid transit committee, Hazard helped to strike up a partnership in 1963 with Westinghouse Electric for a demonstration project involving Westinghouse's Transit Expressway System, better known as Skybus. Unlike traditional streetcars, the rubber-tired, driverless Skybus was designed to run on dedicated, elevated concrete roadways, which Westinghouse engineers claimed would be better than steel rails for the varied terrain of Pittsburgh. The demonstration project was a nine thousand-foot circuit on the Allegheny County Fairgrounds at South Park, but as part of a proposed "Early Action Plan," the first Skybus route was contemplated as an eleven-mile course from South Hills Village to downtown Pittsburgh via the unused Wabash Tunnel.[229]

At a closed meeting of the executive session of the PAT board in the summer of 1969, another Pittsburgh corporation, Westinghouse Air Brake Company (WABCO, which had been acquired by American Standard in 1968) made a last-minute proposal to PAT for an alternative rapid transit plan involving WABCO's competing rail car technology: a twenty-eight-mile, steel-wheel line from East Liberty to downtown to the South Hills, using existing trolley car tracks. WABCO contended that its plan would be less expensive and would rely on existing technology. Hazard and his compatriots, operating as the ACCD had operated in its hey-day, virtually ignored the WABCO proposal and approved the Skybus Early Action Plan a few days later.[230]

Democratic mayoral candidate Pete Flaherty, a city councilman and former assistant district attorney, had recently beaten the establishment Democrat, Judge Harry Kramer, in the primary election, touting himself as "Nobody's Boy." Flaherty cried foul at PAT's announcement of the adoption of the Skybus plan, as did Dr. William Hunt, a Republican Allegheny County commissioner. Both politicians criticized the elitist character of the PAT board and its secretive decision-making process. "In short," said Flaherty, "the whole issue of rapid transit up until now has been ... a private affair of the PAT board ... Their tone is not one of 'the public be damned' but rather 'We know best.'" Flaherty insisted that since public tax dollars would be going into the project, that the public had a right to disclosure and participation in the decision-making process. He also raised doubts about the safety of Skybus.[231] Pete Flaherty was easily elected mayor in 1969 over his Republican challenger, John Tabor of the Kirkpatrick & Lockhart law firm, whose co-founder, George Lockhart, had been a member of the ACCD. Flaherty became a powerful opponent of Skybus, as well as the paternalistic habits of Hazard and the "experts" at the ACCD, from his office in the City-County Building.

Meanwhile, the business community that could usually be counted upon to speak with one voice through the ACCD became fractured over the Skybus-WABCO controversy, which put two Pittsburgh companies at odds with each other. Because of design considerations, moreover, it was said that U.S. Steel preferred WABCO's steel-wheel design, while Alcoa supported the aluminum-sheathed Skybus.[232] By this time, R.K. Mellon, in ill-health and in the last year of his life, was in no position to step in and force consensus. For some time prior to the controversy, the city's business boosters were touting Pittsburgh to be for rapid transit what Detroit was to the automobile. Now, as one transportation official noted, "The industry wants to see if the community that bills itself as the transit capital of the world can solve its own mass transit problems."[233]

Although federal funding had come through and was close to making Skybus a reality, opponents tied up the project in litigation—Common Pleas Judge Anne X. Alpern issued an injunction against the project in 1972, later overturned—and eventually even the most ardent institutional supporters of Skybus, from the ACCD to the state, quietly began to withdraw their support. In 1976, PAT adopted the findings of a consultant's report recommending the abandonment of Skybus in favor of a system of exclusive bus lanes, an upgrade of the South Hills trolley line, and a downtown mini-subway loop.[234] There is little doubt today that the discord over Skybus had the lasting effect of leaving Pittsburgh behind other cities when it came to the development of public rapid transit. The wheels had finally, definitively, come off what had been termed Pittsburgh's "first" Renaissance.

In a 1972 interview, a defeated Hazard would blame the impending failure of Skybus not only on the disintegration of political power within the region, but on the declining influence of accomplished leaders from the private sector. "I must say right now I do not hold with participatory democracy as it is offered in song and dance and in disordered disruption of school boards, corporation boards and other institutional assemblies in the 1970s," he said. "I do not believe that the poor are the only competent analysts of the cause and cure of their plight, nor do I believe that the uneducated are the best curriculum designers for their education. I do believe in expertness."[235]

Appreciation for the "expertness" of the in-house lawyer was on the decline, as well. Hazard left PPG in 1958 to become a professor in the Graduate School of Industrial Administration at Carnegie Mellon University. Van Buskirk gradually retreated from his public role during the 1960s, and Hickman retired from Alcoa in 1967. With their respective departures from their corporate posts, the days of the in-house lawyer as top corporate leader in Pittsburgh receded with them, the rare exception being Martin McGuinn, the Sullivan & Cromwell-trained, one-time general counsel of Mellon Financial Corporation who rose to be its chairman and chief executive officer in 1999.[236] Hazard and Hickman were both members of the boards of directors of their respective employers while they served as general counsel; Van Buskirk served on the board of governors of T. Mellon & Sons. As of 2016, only one of the top twenty-five publicly-traded companies in Pittsburgh had its chief legal officer as a member of its own board of directors (John McGonigle at Federated Investors), and he has since retired.[237] No longer occupying an independent seat of power within the community at large—no longer special just for being themselves, to paraphrase Fred Rogers—the power that the Pittsburgh public company general counsels retained was largely internally-focused, concerned with the choice of outside law firms, the supervision of the internal staff of lawyers, and the calibration of the mixture between using inside lawyers and outside firms. The public company general counsel became invisible within the community, invisible to the markets.[g]

"This decline was set in motion by one fact," writes Carl D. Liggio, the former general counsel of New York-based Ernst & Young, "—the emergence of the business school as a training ground and desirable discipline for senior management. Suddenly, marketers and financial types became the new 'wunderkinds.'"[238] According to Liggio, while seventy-five percent of the chief executive officers of major corporations in the U.S. were lawyers in the late 1930s, only five percent of them were lawyers as of the beginning of the twenty-first century.[239] Liggio also suggests that the rise of the Harvard MBA was met with "a corollary decline in the esteem the corporate America held for employed counsel. This translated itself into a reduced reliance on and consultation with employed counsel." Neither would senior corporate counsel continue to be among the most highly paid executives in the corporation; by the 1970s, their pay had decreased to about thirty percent of the chief executive officer's income.[240] And, of course, the corruption of the "employed counsel" of the White House amid the Watergate scandal did not do the image of the "kept counsel" any favors during the 1970s.

The rise of the MBA may also be seen as reflecting the next logical step in Wall Street's complete and total conversion of public corporations into entities that fundamentally resided on the New York Stock Exchange, and not in the locales of their headquarters; the aim of the business, after all, was to provide financial returns to the public investor, not to be a well-regulated, good corporate citizen, or to be a good corporate neighbor. The common wisdom of that perspective was so ingrained by 1983 that the Pennsylvania legislature, in response to a wave of corporate takeovers, felt moved to adopt an amendment to the state's corporation law providing that in discharging their fiduciary duties, directors of a Pennsylvania corporation were allowed to "consider the effects of any action ... upon communities in which offices or other establishments of the corporation are located."[241] Public corporations, however, were given the ability to opt out of the new provision, and by October 1990, ninety-one of the state's three hundred public companies had done so.[242] Not only had the in-house lawyers become somewhat fungible, but communities were now fungible as well.

By the end of the 1960s, Pittsburgh had been transformed by the experiment of its first Renaissance. Some projects, such as the URA's East Liberty redevelopment in the early 1960s—which wiped out remaining retail activity in a declining area with an ill-

---

g Greg Jordan, the general counsel and chief administrative officer of PNC and former managing partner of Reed Smith, takes issue with this characterization. The highly visible Jordan cites the hiring of Thomas VanKirk, William Newlin's successor as CEO of Buchanan Ingersoll, as chief legal officer at Highmark Blue Cross Blue Shield, and of Thomas McGough, a former senior partner at Reed Smith in Pittsburgh, as chief legal officer at UMPC, as contrary examples. Gregory B. Jordan, interview by the author, August 28, 2014. Interestingly, PNC, Highmark and UPMC all have large retail interests in Pittsburgh—which may distinguish them and their natural roles in the Pittsburgh community from the chief lawyers of other large Pittsburgh companies that have no retail presence in Pittsburgh—such as U.S. Steel or Alcoa, for example.

advised pedestrian mall project—were inevitably viewed as failures of the paternalistic approach to city planning. Others were considered to be a mixed bag. As for the Point Park/Gateway project, as historian Rachel Balliet Colker observes, "few would argue that the overall plan was not a success. The large-scale urban renewal experiment succeeded in revising the perception of Pittsburgh as a smoky, dirty city."[243]

One is left to wonder, furthermore, if public and private instrumentalities had not moved mortar and earth to rebuild the Point during those earliest post-War years, would they have had the political might or the financial resources available to do so during the late 1970s or early 1980s, when Pittsburgh's industries were in decline and the city was losing its base of the biggest public corporations in the nation? If not, then would Three Rivers Stadium, or the stadiums that have since replaced it, have even been desirable, across from the decaying warehouse and railroad yards that might have still inhabited the Point? Would the downtown Cultural District, across the bridges from those arenas further down along the Allegheny River, have come alive? Would anyone have been able to imagine Pittsburghers living downtown again, in the outdoor "café culture" that has emerged in the 2010s, without the success of what had come before? Travel writers who write glowingly about Pittsburgh's "striking renaissance" today tend to discuss the city in terms of its renewal only since the crash of the steel industry; in contrast to other rust-belt cities, however, it is an almost inescapable conclusion that the revolutionary use of eminent domain and the revitalization of the Point, from 1946 to 1952, were the essential first steps in preparing Pittsburgh to be the city it is today, well before "the wolf finally came" for "big steel."

Scarcely a generation of the in-house lawyers of Pittsburgh's major corporations ever had the power to set policy and "run plays" with the full encouragement and backing of their corporate sponsors. Leland Hazard, Arthur Van Buskirk and Leon Hickman—each of them transplants to Pittsburgh from other parts of the country—were naturally inclined to be good Pittsburgh neighbors, by philosophy and disposition. More than that, though, they shared with the city's nineteenth century industrial philanthropists a hubristic propensity for envisioning and fashioning the common good in their adopted hometown, on a grand scale. What they helped to accomplish with their leadership and their focus on long-term community goals, driving the details of each step to a conclusion with single-minded intensity as lawyers will often do, would have a lasting impact on the city. Indeed, some of their Renaissance works are gifts that keep on giving even today—for better or worse, in failure and in success.

RED TO THE WORLD

At the end of World War II, Ernie Adamson was a transportation lawyer from Carrollton, Georgia who was living in Mount Lebanon, a South Hills suburb of Pittsburgh, and working as counsel for a local storage and trucking company. In March 1945, he was appointed as the part-time counsel to the House Committee on Un-American Activities (HUAC), which had just become a permanent standing committee chaired by Representative Edward J. Hart of New Jersey, a Democrat. In December 1946, after assisting HUAC in its investigation of seditious activities for a year and a half, Adamson released his own unofficial report to the public, without securing the approval of HUAC, which described a massive Communist conspiracy to overthrow the government, charging among other things that seventeen CIO unions were "dominated by" Soviet agents, that "Communist-led" unions had "gained control" of the Panama Canal Zone, and that the Library of Congress was a "haven for aliens and foreign-minded Americans." When J. Parnell Thomas of New Jersey, a Republican, took control of the Committee in 1947, Adamson was summarily fired.[244]

The subsequent sordid folk history of the actions and attitudes of HUAC (Congressman Richard Nixon's flamboyantly led pursuit of Alger Hiss, Whitaker Chambers and the "pumpkin papers," the blacklisting of the Hollywood Ten, and so on) would indicate that, apart from his insubordination, Adamson's other major sin was that he was merely too early to the anti-Communism soiree. However, Adamson's rabidly anti-Communist perspective, evidenced scarcely a few months after the Yalta Conference, is perhaps indicative of the milieu in which he worked in Western Pennsylvania.

As described by historian Philip Jenkins in his book *The Cold War at Home*, Western Pennsylvania was a cauldron of anti-Communist sentiment which ultimately exploded, during the 1950s, into the "Mecca of the inquisition." Jenkins and others speculate that among the reasons that anti-Communism seethed so intensely within a state whose politics were generally not marked by extremism was the generally held view that "[i]f there was a subversive threat, then all logic suggested that a primary target would be the defense-related industries of Pennsylvania, its steelworks and coal mines, electrical plants and shipyards," coupled with the fact that labor union activism and unvarnished Communist-organizing activities continued to take place in the shadows of these industrial targets.[245]

Harry Alan Sherman was a Pittsburgh lawyer who was on the front lines of fighting Communist influences inside labor unions. The fourth of five children born to a North Side Russian Jewish tailor and his wife, Sherman entered the newspaper business as a reporter with the *Pittsburgh Post-Gazette* at the age of nineteen, but he graduated from the University of Pittsburgh four years later in 1929, and from Pitt Law in 1932. With the Great Depression in full swing, Sherman continued working on newspapers until 1935, when he hung out his shingle as a sole practitioner doing plaintiffs' work. Around 1940, probably helped by his reporting background, he began to catch on as a counselor to small local union chapters, such as the Pittsburgh local of the United Electrical, Radio and Machine Workers of America (UE), acting as part business advisor, part lawyer. At first his work centered on purging unions of racketeering influences, pitting him against grafters and extortionists in the Teamsters and other unions.[246]

During World War II, however, Sherman began to focus on Communists. The national UE had adopted a patriotic "no strike" stance in order to help boost wartime production, but in 1943, the UE Local 615 held a work stoppage at the Equitable Meter plant in Homestead, seeking a wage increase across the board and higher wages for nighttime work. Sherman blew the whistle on the group in a letter to the FBI, claiming that the Pittsburgh UE was involved in subversive activities. The leadership of the UE responded by firing Sherman. In November 1944, Sherman sued the UE Local 615 officers, claiming that he was illegally expelled by the union as part of a conspiracy to overthrow the United States government and set up a "Communist dictatorship" in its place. Sherman continued to try to interfere with the UE leadership until the UE obtained a restraining order against him in January 1945. Sherman's suit against the UE was finally thrown out in March by Judge Harry H. Rowland of the County Common Pleas Court, who declared that at least half of Sherman's complaint "constituted impertinent, irrelevant, and scandalous material."[247]

Sherman, along with Judge Blair Gunther of the County Court, founded an activist group called Americans Battling Communism in November 1947. Judge Gunther, who was born in rural Cambria County, about eighty-five miles east of Pittsburgh, suffered a hardscrabble youth. He arrived in Pittsburgh in 1924 on his way to Oregon to become an apple farmer. Instead, he lost his savings in a Pittsburgh poker game and, stranded, eventually decided to attend Duquesne Law School. A glad-hander, described by historian Daniel J. Leab as a "witty zesty man," Gunther landed a job as a state Deputy Attorney General in the Earle administration, then sought various elected offices—first as a Democrat, then as a Republican—before getting appointed to the County Court in 1942 by Governor Arthur James. His initiation in the anti-Communism cause grew out of his involvement in 1942 in the founding of the American Slav Congress (ASC), a fraternal organization variously described as being created "with Government blessing" as an anti-fascist group, or as a Communist-controlled "pro-Soviet" front. As a prominent member of the Polish National Congress, Gunther was named the first chairman of the ASC; but after several months, Communists in the ASC ousted Gunther, calling him "a stooge for former Nazi puppets." "The Commies are taking over," lamented Gunther.[248]

It was Judge Gunther who, in October 1947, convened a public meeting of "civic leaders" in his courtroom (including former U.S. Attorney Raymond D. Evans, Judge Harry Montgomery and attorney Malcolm Hay, Jr., a leader of the Young Republicans) to discuss the adoption of a "Pittsburgh plan against Communism." Highlighting the duty to educate the public about the evils of Communism, Gunther called the plan "an ABC movement." Sherman duly filed the charter for the Americans Battling Communism, or "ABC," the following month.[249]

Meanwhile, a familiar face on the Pittsburgh political scene reemerged after World War II wearing his Naval officer's dress khaki uniform and speaking at union election rallies against the Communist leadership of the UE—Judge Michael Angelo Musmanno. Antsy, perhaps, after serving on the Common Pleas bench for a few years, Musmanno enlisted in the U.S. Naval Reserve just after war broke out in Europe in 1939. He was called for active duty a month after Pearl Harbor, and mobilized for the Allied campaign in Italy. Injured at Minturno, after the liberation of the Sorrento Peninsula, Musmanno was nonetheless named military governor of Sorrento. His grandstanding there (he allegedly illegally commandeered a ship to give olive oil to the citizens of Sorrento, for example) apparently embarrassed the Navy, which transferred him to Vienna where he served as presiding judge of the United States-Soviet Board of Forcible Repatriation.[250] While in Vienna, he developed an intense loathing for Soviet authorities who were trying to repatriate wartime expats who were certain, in Musmanno's words, to "face firing squads, Siberian exile, forced labor camps or other drastic punishment for having committed the unpardonable offense of declining the proffered 'paradise' of Sovietland."[251] The Navy then transferred him to Nuremburg, where he served as a judge on the International War Crimes Tribunal on the trials of Goering's deputy, Field Marshal Erhard Milch, and of the Einsatzgruppen, the Nazi paramilitary death squads.[252] Commander Musmanno received a hero's welcome when he returned to Pittsburgh in September 1946, telling the assembled crowd that Pittsburgh's plumes of smoke represented "the plumes of triumph—without guns and ammunition produced here, the world still would be struggling ... America now is accepted as the hope of the world—and it is the Pittsburgh furnaces which will keep that hope warm." His seat on the Common Pleas Court was waiting for him on his return.[253]

The anti-Communist activities of the ABC and Musmanno would converge in the public debut of Matt Cvetic in February 1950. Cvetic joined the Pittsburgh branch of the American Communist Party during the 1940s and served as both a low-level party member and a low-level paid informant for the FBI for almost ten years. Near the end of his run, the FBI began to be concerned about his increasingly erratic behavior, including an arrest for drunkenness during which he protested, "You can't do this to me, I work for the FBI!" Rumors around downtown newsrooms about Cvetic's relationship with the FBI filtered to staffers at HUAC, however, who saw in Cvetic an opportunity to publicize the extent of Communist infiltration in America.[254] Before he went to Washington to testify, however, Cvetic began meeting with Harry Alan Sherman, who prepped him extensively for his testimony, and Judge Blair Gunther, who "secretly 'deposed'" Cvetic on February 7. Although Cvetic was scheduled to testify before HUAC on February 21, Gunther released his "deposition" to the press on February 18, along with a photo of himself and Cvetic from their meeting.[255] The ABC team followed up by producing a special thirty-minute radio broadcast portraying Cvetic as an FBI hero.[256] Timing was everything: Senator Joseph McCarthy, a Wisconsin Democrat, had just been in nearby Wheeling, West Virginia on February 9, where he delivered a speech on the "Enemies from Within" in which he charged that he had a list of 205 names of members of the Communist Party who were working in the U.S. State Department (later revised to fifty-seven in the *Congressional Record*).[257] Cvetic's now even more topical HUAC testimony on February 21, 22 and 23 produced sensational headlines around the nation. He returned for four more days of testimony in March.

Now out in the open, Cvetic was no longer the FBI's responsibility. The ABC provided financial support to Cvetic and secured free lodgings for him at the William Penn Hotel, and Sherman became Cvetic's agent. Basking in reflected notoriety, Judge Gunther was appointed to the Pennsylvania Superior Court by fellow anti-Communist Governor James H. Duff in April 1950. In mid-July, Cvetic's story was being retold on an episode of the NBC human interest TV show, *We the People*, hosted by Dan Seymour, and in a three-part *Saturday Morning Post* serial. The *Post* serial formed the basis of a Warner Brothers movie, *I Was a Communist for the FBI* (1951) starring film noir B-player Frank Lovejoy as Cvetic. The film, directed by *Little Rascals* director Gordon Douglas, was a heavily fictionalized account of Cvetic's undercover work, but, oddly enough, was nonetheless nominated for an Oscar for "Best Documentary."[258]

Judge Musmanno had his own interest in making use of Cvetic's new-found notoriety. During the impaneling of a grand jury in March 1950, Judge Musmanno brought in Cvetic, fresh from giving testimony in Washington, to confirm the identity of one of the prospective jurors, Alice Roth. Cvetic identified Roth as the secretary of the East Pittsburgh branch of the Communist Party. Judge Musmanno summarily dismissed Roth from the grand jury, publicly declaring that her Communist affiliation, "her surly attitude, her indecorous language, her disrespectful demeanor and her unwillingness to affirm her devotion to the United States Constitution" made her unfit for service.[259] Roth appealed her dismissal to the Pennsylvania Supreme Court with support from the ACLU; and in a per curiam opinion on March 30, the Court held that Judge Musmanno had attempted to exercise "power beyond the jurisdiction of any judge under existing law," reversing Musmanno's decision.[260] Meanwhile, Musmanno had been positioning himself as a possible candidate for the Democratic nomination for governor, but David Lawrence supported Philadelphia mayor Richardson Dilworth. Dilworth agreed to accept the headline-grabbing anti-Communist judge from Pittsburgh as the Democratic candidate for lieutenant governor in May.[261]

One of Alice Roth's lawyers was Hymen Schlesinger, a forty-six year-old Princeton and Duquesne Law-educated left-wing plaintiff's attorney who also represented maritime unions—a short man who always seemed to wear suits that were too long for him, according to Judge Joseph Weis, Jr. Schlesinger entered the bar in 1927, and his younger sister Sylvia followed in 1933. By May 1950, Schlesinger had become notorious as a lawyer who represented individual members of the Pittsburgh branch of the Communist Party.[262] During the jury selection phase of a routine slip-and-fall case in federal court, Gertrude Berger, the court clerk, asked several prospective jurors if they would be influenced by the newspaper and radio publicity given to Schlesinger in connection with his representation of "Communists or left-wingers." Berger referred to a newspaper article in which it was reported that attorney John W. Cost, a Bellevue sole practitioner, had introduced a resolution to expel Communists from the Allegheny County Bar Association.[263] J. Garfield Houston, the president of the Bar Association, later indicated that the resolution had been submitted to the Association's executive committee, which decided that it could not act on the resolution until the Association's Committee on Offenses—the same committee formed just before the disbarment of Jacob Margolis in 1920—could rule on the question.[264]

Meanwhile, on June 30, John Gilfillan, chairman of the Committee on Offenses, had already secretly initiated a complaint against Hymen Schlesinger, alleging that he was "a member of the Communist Party" and that he assisted in carrying out its policies, "especially with reference to the organization and control of basic industries in the Pittsburgh district." The language of the complaint was similar to accusations about Schlesinger that Cvetic had made to Musmanno, so one might fairly assume that Cvetic was the original source of Gilfillan's information for the complaint. The secret complaint called for an investigation, report and recommendation to be made to the Court of Common Pleas.[265] As Judge Musmanno campaigned for higher office and continued his assault on the Communist threat in Pittsburgh, Hymen Schlesinger—already a target of the Bar Association—would soon get caught in the crossfire between Musmanno and local Communist Party leader Steve Nelson and his comrades.

Undaunted by the setback in the Pennsylvania Supreme Court over the Roth decision, Judge Musmanno was already moving on to his next battle. During his HUAC testimony, Cvetic had named dozens of Pittsburghers who were either party members or sympathetic to the Communists, but he focused on the alleged activities of Steve Nelson—a Croatian, born Stjepan Mesaros, who had bounced in and out of the U.S. for some years beginning in 1920, attended the Lenin Institute in Moscow, fought against Franco in the Spanish Civil War, socialized with J. Robert Oppenheimer in Berkeley during the War, and arrived in Pittsburgh in 1948 to be named head of the Pittsburgh branch of the Communist Party.[266] Nelson's office, the party headquarters, was in the Bakewell Building, across Grant Street from the City-County Building on the corner of Grant and Forbes. Judge Musmanno wrote:

> ... I experienced each day, as I came out of the courthouse[,] a sense of frustration and almost despair. Despite the increasing concerted attempted of the whole western world to push Communism back to its Asiatic frontiers, the Communist Party in Pittsburgh had set up its headquarters right across the street from the Courthouse! Less than 100 feet from the very room in which I renewed my court sessions, the Russian agents had planted what amounted to the equivalent of an advance post of the Red Army. Here the foreign agents planned to make our law courts things of the rubbled past.[267]

Judge Musmanno had attempted to persuade local and federal prosecutors to take action against the red threat, confirmed by Cvetic's HUAC testimony, but they moved slowly and uncertainly. Judge Musmanno then took matters into his own hands. Acting, in his own words, "as a private citizen," Musmanno swore out a warrant for the arrest of Steve Nelson, along with two Party functionaries, Andy Onda and Jim Dolsen, for violating the little used Pennsylvania Sedition Act of 1919. On August 31, 1950, Nelson, Onda and Dolsen were arrested; and on the same day, with a sheriff's search warrant, Judge Musmanno, Matt Cvetic and Assistant District Attorney Sidney Sanes—with press photographers in tow—burst into the headquarters of the Pittsburgh Communists, seizing further evidence of their alleged sedition in the form of Communist pamphlets and books.[268]

At the arraignment of the Communists, Hymen Schlesinger argued to Judge A. Marshall Thompson that Judge Musmanno should be barred from testifying in light of his judicial position. Judge Thompson overruled the motion, and entertained an argument from Judge Musmanno on a request that Steve Nelson's bond should be set at one hundred thousand dollars (his bail was ultimately set at ten thousand dollars, after an appeal from the original fifty thousand dollars).[269] Schlesinger, who was under pressure to answer the secret complaint filed against him by the Committee on Offenses, brought his argument against Musmanno to the Pennsylvania Supreme Court, charging that Judge Musmanno had committed unethical conduct, violating the American Bar Association canon of ethics, by acting as prosecutor, witness and judge. He asked that Musmanno "be suspended from his judicial duties until determination of the criminal proceedings."[270] Before the Court could rule, however, Judge Musmanno "suspended himself" from his judicial duties on the Common Pleas Court until November 1, without pay, citing the burdens of his campaign for lieutenant governor.[271] The Democratic ticket of Dilworth and Musmanno would fall to the Republican ticket in the November election, led by John S. Fine; yet Musmanno remained on leave to prepare for his testimony in the Sedition Act trials.

The trial of Nelson, Onda and Dolsen began in January 1951. While John T. McTernan, a prominent left-wing attorney from Los Angeles, came to Pittsburgh to lead the defense, with Schlesinger sitting by his side, Nelson decided to act as his own counsel during much of the trial that would follow. The prosecution was led by Assistant District Attorney Loran Lewis, along with another assistant district attorney, Gil Helwig.[272] Meanwhile, in that same month, one of Lewis and Helwig's colleagues, Assistant District Attorney Marjorie Hanson Matson, became the target of a separate investigation by Pennsylvania Attorney General Charles J. Margiotti, because of her alleged "Communist sympathies."

The Punxsutawney-born Margiotti was the son of poor Italian immigrants. He had quit school at fifteen to help support his family, but he was awarded a senatorial scholarship and earned his law degree at the University of Pennsylvania. He entered the bar in Jefferson County in 1914 and later practiced in Pittsburgh, quickly gaining a reputation as a dynamic criminal trial lawyer—"[f]ast-talking, quickminded and contentious," according to historian Paul Beers. "Margiotti had a Manichean personality, generously supportive of friends but vindictively hostile to enemies … he was a brilliant prosecutor and defense attorney, but when he applied his antagonistic methods to politics he met with little success." In 1934, he ran for governor in a crowded Republican primary—the first Italian Catholic and first Republican Catholic to do so—only to finish third. In his pique, he switched to the Democratic Party, and the successful Democratic candidate for governor, George H. Earle, named him as his Attorney General. In 1938, Margiotti launched a Democratic primary campaign for governor while still serving as Earle's Attorney General, slinging scathing attacks at the Earle administration, but again placed third. Earle fired him following the primary, whereupon Margiotti went public with accusations of corruption within the Earle administration that resulted in an unsuccessful prosecution of David L. Lawrence, then the state Democratic chairman, for conspiracy, blackmail and election law violations.[273]

Lawrence called Margiotti a "smear artist."[274] Lawrence once found himself sitting at the speakers' table of a banquet with Margiotti sitting two seats down, separated from Lawrence by Monsignor Andrew J. Pauley, Margiotti's pastor at St. Paul's Cathedral. Monsignor Pauley, sensing the chill between the two men, tried to break the ice by telling Lawrence, "You know, Charley and I have a contract. He has agreed to keep me out of jail and I have contracted to keep him out of hell." Lawrence replied, "Margiotti has the easier job."[275]

Margiotti returned to Harrisburg as Attorney General when his friend, Pittsburgh attorney James H. Duff, was elected governor as a Republican in 1947. Issues regarding the use of Pittsburgh city employees to perform private work had hit the headlines around that time, and bowing to public pressure, Allegheny County District Attorney William S. Rahauser, another Lawrence protégé, had begun a grand jury probe into the alleged corruption. When Margiotti returned to office, he immediately informed Rahauser that he would be superseded in his investigation by the State Attorney General's office, and Margiotti launched his own state probe of corruption in the administration of Pittsburgh Mayor David L. Lawrence.[276]

In the midst of his corruption probe, Margiotti contacted Rahauser on January 8, 1951, accusing Assistant District Attorney Marjorie Hanson Matson of "Communistic tendencies which make her unfit to hold the office she does," and calling for her immediate dismissal. Through his lieutenant who was handling the corruption probe, W. Denning Stewart, and three State police officers, Margiotti presented his alleged evidence of Matson's Communist ties. Margiotti wasted no time in issuing his ultimatum in public. In a statement to the press, Margiotti declared that he "gave Mr. Rahauser some of the information State Police have gathered against Mrs. Matson, but not all. Some of the information bears on other matters now under investigation. But," said Margiotti, Rahauser had "sufficient [evidence] to act upon and that is what I expect him to do."[277]

While District Attorney Rahauser conducted his own internal investigation, Matson decided to take matters into her own hands. On January 11, she submitted a request to Rahauser for an unpaid leave of absence and entered the Common Pleas courtroom of Judge Samuel A. Weiss, petitioning the court to appoint a committee of lawyers to hear all of the relevant evidence on the charges made against her and to recommend appropriate action by the court. "As long as I am under this cloud," she said, "I cannot function as an officer of the court." In her appearance, Matson affirmed under oath that she was not then, nor had she ever been, "a member of the Communist Party, a Communist sympathizer or knowingly a member of any Communist front organization." Matson observed that her religious background was contrary to all Communist beliefs, and that Margiotti's unsubstantiated public charges embarrassed her, deprived her of a livelihood, and even subjected her ten year-old daughter to schoolyard taunts. Matson also filed notice of her intent to sue Margiotti personally for libel and slander.[278]

Later that same day, Rahauser's response to Margiotti was made public. In it, Rahauser asserted that he had investigated Margiotti's factual allegations—that Matson had had conversations with known leftist lawyers (including Hymen Schlesinger) or taken Communist positions in civil rights cases outside of Pittsburgh in the course of her work with the ACLU—and declared "to this date I have been unable to find any evidence" to support Margiotti's charges. He went on to say:

> *During her period of work as Assistant County Solicitor and Assistant District Attorney, Mrs. Matson has had the highest reputation. During her three years here she has had a perfect record of attendance and of carrying out the orders of this office. Her briefs filed in all cases handled by her, showed painstaking care to set forth the law; and her trial[s] showed equal care to see to it that every piece of evidence was placed before the court and jury ... As a public prosecutor, elected by the people to safeguard their rights, I will not condone or tolerate disloyalty or subversion to our Government. On the other hand, as a man and as a public servant, I will not now or ever permit myself to become a medium of crucifying a woman on the basis of suspicions, rumors, or innuendos.*[279]

While Rahauser was throwing down the gauntlet before Margiotti, Judge Weiss granted Matson's petition, appointing a five-person committee to hear evidence on Margiotti's charges against her beginning on Monday, January 15. The committee consisted of former judge James Milholland; William H. Eckert of Smith Buchanan & Ingersoll; former Allegheny County Bar Association president Harold Obernauer; former judge Roy T. Clunk; and Emily Wilson, a sole practitioner known as a tax and family lawyer. After convening on January 15, the Milholland Committee decided to postpone its work until Margiotti could appear personally and present his evidence against Mrs. Matson.[280]

Three days later, Margiotti responded to the Milholland Committee by announcing that his office was going to open its own public hearing on Matson's "Communist sympathies," set for Monday, January 22 at ten o'clock in the morning in Courtroom 5 on the 7th Floor of the City-County Building. The Attorney General appointed one of his deputies, Samuel H. Jackson, to act as hearing examiner, and another, Robert L. Kunzig of Philadelphia, to act as prosecutor. "The public is entitled to be informed of all the facts in this matter," Margiotti declared, adding that Rahauser and Matson would also be entitled to participate. He declined to appear before the Milholland Committee, stating that such an appearance "would create a precedent and lower the dignity of the office of Attorney General."[281]

With dueling hearings now scheduled, speculation focused on whether Matson would attend and defend herself in the Margiotti hearing. Matson would not say, but took the opportunity to again publicly denounce Communism, adding that her work in support of free speech for Communists did not "mean sympathy or leaning to Communism."[282] Rahauser, meanwhile, said that "it is shocking that one holding the high office of Attorney General, after having formed an opinion on the issue, would pretend to hold an impartial adjudication on the same matter through its own agencies."[283]

On Monday, January 22, Deputy Attorney General Samuel H. Jackson convened the Attorney General's probe and gave the floor to Deputy Attorney General Kunzig for his opening statement. Rahauser's first assistant district attorney, Robert Van der Voort, appeared as the official observer of the District Attorney's office. Matson was not present. At the conclusion of Kunzig's statement, Michael von Moschzisker (son of Pennsylvania Supreme Court Chief Justice Robert von Moschzisker) entered the courtroom and announced that he and another Philadelphia lawyer, Thomas B. McBride, were present as defense counsel to Matson. Meanwhile, McBride was in Judge Weiss' courtroom, arguing for a preliminary injunction against the Margiotti hearing on the basis that, in addition to the irregularity of appointing a hearing officer from Margiotti's own staff, Margiotti may not have even been the legitimate Attorney General of Pennsylvania. Although Margiotti was appointed by Governor Duff, following his inauguration on January 16, Duff's successor John S. Fine was now required to appoint a new cabinet—and Margiotti's position was the only one for which Governor Fine had not yet submitted a name for consideration by the Democratic-controlled state legislature. Margiotti had personally advised Governor Fine that since his re-appointment was during a recess in the state legislature, no approval would be necessary, but the Democrats in Harrisburg, fomented by Mayor Lawrence, were crying foul about Margiotti's legitimacy. Judge Weiss ordered that the Margiotti hearing be delayed, pending argument and decision on the merits of McBride's argument. Weiss ultimately ordered a stay of the Margiotti hearing, which Margiotti appealed.[284] Meanwhile, the Milholland Committee decided to await the resolution of the Margiotti's appeal.

The turmoil over Governor Fine's inaction on Margiotti's reappointment as Attorney General became too much for Fine to bear by the beginning of February, and on February 24, 1951, Margiotti finally resigned as Attorney General.[285] Yet the Matson case continued.

During the summer, Judge Musmanno blazed back into the headlines—not only for his thirty-one-day testimony in the Onda and Dolsen trials (Nelson's trial was postponed after he suffered injuries in an auto accident), or his new bid for election to the Pennsylvania Supreme Court, but for his latest courtroom antics. On May 24, 1951, Hymen Schlesinger entered courtroom 4, presided over by Judge Musmanno, on a damage suit against the Borough of Wilmerding. Judge Musmanno claimed that Schlesinger appeared seventy minutes late for the trial, without explanation. After excusing the jury, the witnesses and the parties, Judge Musmanno questioned Schlesinger:

> *Judge Musmanno: Before we proceed in this case, I want to interrogate, and my duties require that I interrogate, counsel for the plaintiff.... Hymen Schlesinger, have you ever been a member of the Communist Party; Are you a member of the Civil Rights Congress;*

... Did you or did you not form the Civil Rights Congress, which is a Communist Front Organization, in your office—the Civil Rights Congress which is a part of the movement to overthrow the Government of the United States by force and violence.

Attorney Schlesinger refused to answer these questions.

Judge Musmanno: *We have formally adjudged you unfit to try a case in this Court as of today, morally unfit. You do not possess an allegiance to the United States.*[286]

A few days later, Judge Musmanno summoned Schlesinger back to court with the intention of sentencing Schlesinger for contempt of court, but Schlesinger refused service of the summons. Schlesinger's attorney, William S. Doty, filed an appeal with the Pennsylvania Supreme Court. As Chief Justice James Drew's order was hitting Judge Musmanno desk, however, deputies found Schlesinger outside the office of the prothonotary and hauled him before Judge Musmanno. Judge Musmanno acknowledged the Chief Justice's order, but stated that it applied "only to matters which occurred before this day," and sentenced Schlesinger to be held in the Allegheny County Jail. After conferring with Chief Justice Drew, however, Judge Musmanno stayed the contempt proceedings for further review.[287] Then, on June 11, Matt Cvetic made out a complaint against Schlesinger, alleging that Schlesinger had violated the Pennsylvania Sedition Act, the same Act that Schlesinger's clients were on trial for violating. A constable arrested Schlesinger around half past six that evening on the basis of Cvetic's complaint and committed him to the County Jail. McTernan managed to obtain his release on bond around one-thirty in the morning on June 12 after a bitter colloquy with Cvetic's attorney, Harry Alan Sherman, before a local magistrate.[288]

Schlesinger's sedition charges were later thrown out by the Common Pleas Court, stating that Schlesinger "was denied his state constitutional and statutory rights" when he was thrown in jail in June.[289] Stinging from the rebuke he received from the Supreme Court over his attempt to hold Schlesinger in contempt, Judge Musmanno publicly urged the Bar Association to take action to disbar Schlesinger, saying that "It is incredible and intolerable that Schlesinger—formally accused of being a Communist, formally accused of advocating revolution ... should continue to practice in our courts."[290]

At the end of June, the Pennsylvania Supreme Court rendered its decision on Margiotti's appeal in the Matson case. Speaking for a unanimous court, Justice Horace Stern wrote that the Margiotti hearing was "a proposition, the very statement of which illustrates its inherent absurdity," and that to allow the hearing "would be equivalent to holding that the attorney general is vested with the power to conduct hearings as to the political, economic and social views of every public officer in the commonwealth ... ." The Court added that such a hearing would not give the accused a right of "appeal for protection against unfair interrogation" and that the accused could be "subtly and maliciously attacked and irreparable damage sustained by him without any right or possibility of legal redress. ... We do not think that authority to conduct proceedings or hearings of the nature here in question is conferred upon the attorney general by any provision of the administrative code, an authority that would be contrary to the spirit of all our laws which so jealously guard the rights of individuals."[291]

Matson, though grateful for the derailment of Margiotti's hearing, was still on unpaid leave from the District Attorney's office, and now looked to the Milholland Committee to proceed with its investigation in order to clear her name. Margiotti's successor, Judge Robert E. Woodside of Millersburg, Dauphin County, promised to turn over all of the state's evidence against Mrs. Matson to the Milholland Committee, so long as the Milholland Committee agreed to conduct its proceedings in public; and for his part, District Attorney Rahauser put to rest any question of the authority of the Milholland Committee by agreeing to be bound by its decision.[292]

On September 6, Deputy Attorney General Robert Kunzig gave his opening statement before a packed house. "We are not out to prove Mrs. Matson is a Communist," Kunzig stated. "We merely are trying to show that by her associations, acts and utterances she is unfit to hold such an important public trust."[293] Kunzig's case relied heavily on what the newspapers described as "sensational testimony" from witnesses who claimed to have seen her in conference with attorneys who represented Communists, to her services as an attorney for the Soviet consul general, and to her denunciation of the 1949 Smith Act trials, in which eleven top U.S. Communist Party officials (including William Z. Foster and Gus Hall) were charged with sedition following an investigation by FBI director J. Edgar Hoover. Witnesses and counter-witnesses disputed whether they had seen Matson in a night club with a known Communist, and whether Matson owned a beige dress with red print flowers. Testifying in defense of Matson's character were Mayor Lawrence; Arthur Garfield Hays, the general counsel to the ACLU; and District Attorney Rahauser. As the case drew to a close, Milholland Committee member Emily Wilson asked Matson, "If you were reinstated and were back in the district attorney's office, would you continue your past course of action?" To which Matson replied: "As far as American civil liberties are concerned, I would. Absolutely I would not appear on the opposite side of a case in which the district attorney's office is interested."[294]

On December 4, 1951, almost eleven months after Margiotti initially leveled charges against Matson publicly, the Milholland Committee presented a twenty-nine-page report to Judge Weiss which exonerated Marjorie Matson of charges that she was pro-Communist, but stating that Matson had been "indiscreet" in her ex parte involvement in certain cases being prosecuted by the District Attorney, and advising her that she "should conduct herself in all her activities with every caution, discretion and judgment so as not to give the public the wrong impression. This can be done without surrendering her ideas of protection of the civil rights and liberties of American citizens."[295] Matson immediately returned to work in the District Attorney's office; however, the election that occurred the month before had heralded the arrival of a Republican District Attorney, James F. Malone, Jr., to replace Rahauser, who won election as an Orphans' Court judge. Thus, Matson resigned from the District Attorney's office a little over a month after her return, and returned to private practice as a criminal defense lawyer. Matson was grateful for the outcome of the case, but noted that it came at great personal cost to her by way of depriving her of her livelihood for the duration, having to spend thousands of dollars on her defense, and feeling like a social pariah in her community.[296]

During the long, hot summer of 1951, another person accused of having Communist ties would have his own run-in with the Pittsburgh bar. Aldo "Ike" Icardi was, according to his friend Judge Ruggero Aldisert, "a very popular undergraduate at the University of Pittsburgh, head cheerleader and catcher on the baseball team." As a member of the ROTC, he joined the war effort immediately upon graduation from the University, and, as Aldisert says, "he returned from the war a decorated hero" before joining Aldisert as a Pitt Law student. After his graduation from law school, Icardi and his young wife Eleanor and family moved to Peru, where he passed the Peruvian bar examination and went to work with Panagra, an airline joint venture between Pan-American Airlines and Grace Steamship Lines. He had returned to New York City, in the summer of 1951, to assume the role of in-house counsel to Panagra. He had already passed the Pennsylvania bar examination and was awaiting word from the Allegheny County Board of Law Examiners about whether he could dispense with the preceptorship requirement in light of his law service in Peru in order to be admitted to the bar in Pennsylvania.[297]

"On the evening of August 15, 1951," as Aldisert wrote, "his world caved in." Icardi was in his New Jersey home, and as Eleanor cleared the dinner table and his children played in the yard, he was listening to the radio:

> *All at once, the radio was blaring! The announcer was screaming. He was talking about me! Telling how I had master-minded the fantastic and brutal murder of my commanding officer in Northern Italy in 1944. I sat paralyzed, unable to believe what I heard. Yet the announcer cited my name, Aldo Icardi ... He said that Aldo Icardi engineered the murder of Major Holohan for $100,000 in gold, that Aldo Icardi was a Communist and Holohan opposed Communist partisans in Italy.*[298]

The source for the radio report turned out to be the U.S. Department of Defense. Upon receiving an advanced copy of an article in a crime/gossip tabloid called *True Magazine*, in which *True* was going to be critical of the Defense Department for supposedly suppressing information about the Holohan case, the Defense Department jumped in front of *True* with a press release of its own.[299]

The story hit headlines across the country. The Allegheny County Board, which had initially approved the waiver, instantly withdrew its approval.[300] It was not the first time the Board had taken up questions about the possible Communist ties of its bar applicants. In December 1947, the Board examined the file of an applicant who was voluntarily withdrawing his application and petitioning the Board for a refund of his fees after a "Citizen Sponsor" named by the applicant as a character reference refused to answer a portion of the character questionnaire or recommend the applicant on the grounds of having personal knowledge of the applicant's membership in the Communist Party and of his having held "Communist meetings at his home." The Board did not review the applicant's credentials, but merely voted to send his file to the State Board of Law Examiners for further disposition.[301] In January 1951, two more cases arose relating to applicants who were allegedly members of the Communist Party. With regard to the first, the Board avoided taking any action on the application on the grounds that the applicant was said to have "left Pittsburgh in June of 1950 and ... will not return to Pittsburgh to practice law ...." At that same meeting, another applicant's case was reviewed in which "the applicant became a member of the Communist Party during the second World War and attended meetings of the society until he went to sea in 1943." The minutes went on to state that "[r]ecords show that he has never actually resigned from the party," and the Board decided "that the application for registration be approved subject to the applicant writing a letter to the Board before his being permitted to take the Bar Examinations, disavowing any communist tendencies."[302]

Icardi's case was a little more complicated. Not only was he being charged publicly with being a Communist (which he denied), but he was also being accused of the murder of a U.S. Army officer, while himself wearing a U.S. Army uniform (which he also denied).

Lieutenant Icardi had parachuted into enemy territory near Como, Italy in September 1944, before the arrival of Allied liberation forces in that area, as a member of the U.S. Army's Office of Strategic Services (OSS), along with mission commander Major William V. Holohan (a Harvard lawyer who worked with the Securities and Exchange Commission during the 1930s), Lieutenant Victor Giannino, Sergeant Carl LoDolce and three Italian agents. The aim of their mission, code-named "Mangosteen," was to organize resistance movements in advance of the arrival of U.S. troops.[h] Major Holohan was carrying sixteen thousand dollars in various currencies to aid their efforts. Among the anti-Fascist groups in this area of northern Italy, the Communists represented about seventy-five percent of the partisans; they would undoubtedly be required to take part in any successfully organized resistance. Meanwhile, the Mangosteen team had many close calls with hostile German forces roaming the area.

On December 6, 1944, the Mangosteen team members were in hiding in Villa Castelnuovo on Lake Orta, east of Lago Maggiore and Como. A pair of priests came to the Villa to warn them that they were about to be ambushed. The men left under the cover of darkness, but suddenly they found themselves under fire, and they shot back into the darkness. They had agreed to split up if there was trouble and to meet at the headquarters of a local resistance commander. When the team was reconstituted, Major Holohan was missing.[303] After an inconclusive investigation by the OSS, Icardi and the rest of the team were transferred to Milan, where they served out the War conducting other espionage activities. Lieutenant Icardi received the Silver Medal, the second highest military honor of the new Italian government, and the U.S. military gave him a Legion of Merit citation. Before he returned to the U.S. in August 1945, he was questioned once again about the disappearance of Major Holohan. "With apologies for the inconvenience," Icardi wrote, "the investigators told me that I was free to go home and become a civilian citizen again." He was honorably discharged from service.[304]

In August of 1947, while Icardi was in law school, he was contacted again by an agent of the Civil Investigating Division (CID) of the U.S. Army. The disappearance of Major Holohan was clearly becoming an uncomfortably unsolved case within the Pentagon. The agent told Icardi that there were rumors circulating in Italy that Major

---

[h] Before the Mangosteen operation, Icardi acted as driver and interpreter to Moe Berg, the former major league catcher who was working for the OSS in Rome, attempting to bring Italian nuclear physicists back to the U.S. See Nicholas Dawidoff, *The Catcher Was a Spy: The Mysterious Life of Moe Berg* (New York: Knopf, 2011), 181.

Holohan had been murdered by his allies in order to steal some one hundred thousand dollars in gold that he had kept with him. Icardi said that he was not aware that Major Holohan had anything more than the sixteen thousand dollars in cash with which the Mangosteen team had been initially entrusted, and he had provided the OSS with an accounting of that money in 1944. The CID agent admitted, "Frankly, we checked your financial situation ... quite closely. We looked over your bank account, and your father's and mother's. We've checked your relatives and close friends. We haven't found a shred of evidence to back up the charges the Italians make." Nevertheless, the CID asked Icardi to take a lie detector test on questions about whether he murdered Major Holohan and stole money from him. He passed with flying colors.[305]

Icardi had not given the matter another thought until the public allegations came out in the summer of 1951. The *True Magazine* article seemed to have been based on an alleged account of Major Holohan's murder given by Sergeant LoDolce to a CID agent in 1950, as well as corroborating statements by Vincenzo Moscatelli, a leader of the Communists in the Como area and now a senator in the Italian parliament. According to LoDolce's alleged statement, Icardi and LoDolce planned Major Holohan's murder over Major Holohan's refusal to support the Communists. LoDolce and Icardi supposedly flipped a coin over which one of them would actually perform the murder; LoDolce lost the coin toss and shot him. The recovery of Holohan's body from Lake Orta by ex-partisans of the resistance in 1950, evidencing two gunshot wounds to Holohan's skull, seemed to add credence to LoDolce's alleged statement. After the *True Magazine* article was published, however, LoDolce denied the accounts of his involvement in a murder plot.[306]

Under fire from the public attention, Icardi and his family moved back to Pittsburgh and went to live with his parents. He enlisted the aid of two of his law school classmates, Ruggero Aldisert and Samuel Rodgers, to attempt to clear his name and obtain admission to the bar. Meanwhile, the news came from Italy that Icardi and LoDolce were being charged with murder, and that the Italian government was requesting their extradition for trial. Icardi—supported not only by Aldisert and Rodgers, but by Mayor David L. Lawrence (who asked the Pennsylvania Attorney General to refuse extradition), the Sons and Daughters of Italy, and Icardi's local American Legion Post—managed to escape extradition, as did LoDolce, on the grounds that under a 1943 Armistice between Italy and the U.S., later confirmed by a post-War peace treaty, members of the U.S. Armed Forces had a "right of passage" in Italian territory, and that such "right of passage" implied a "waiver of jurisdiction" over all American troops in Italy.[307]

After successfully fighting Icardi's extradition, Aldisert and Rodgers managed to get the Board of Law Examiners to begin to reexamine the Icardi matter. In October 1952, the Board appointed a four-man committee to prepare a report for the Board. In December, the Board resolved to hold a hearing at which time Icardi would be invited to present evidence and witnesses in defense of his application; Robert Kirkpatrick of the Kirkpatrick & Lockhart firm, Carl Glock of Reed Smith and Charles P. Walter were appointed as a special subcommittee for the hearing.[308] The local proceedings were delayed, however, by the Italian trial, *in absentia,* of Icardi and LoDolce for the murder of Major Holohan in 1953. At the trial, Italian witnesses testified that they helped Icardi and LoDolce plan the murder of Major Holohan in order to divert more aid to the Communists and to abscond with between $45,000 and $150,000 that Major Holohan had kept for funding covert operations. The Italian court found the two Americans guilty of the murder of Major Holohan in November 1953. LoDolce was sentenced to seventeen years in prison, and Icardi received a life sentence.[309]

On February 15, 1954, Charles Walter and Carl Glock reported to the Board of Law Examiners on an interview they conducted with Carl LoDolce in his home in Rochester, New York a few days before. The account of their presentation to the Board, preserved in the February 15, 1954, meeting minutes, states that both lawyers "outlined for the Board their reactions to the demeanor and conduct of Carl Lo Dolce throughout the interview and to the various statements that he made to them during the interview." The Board asked for a written report from the Icardi subcommittee, and tabled the issue of his application to the bar. On May 26, 1954, Carl Glock presented the report of subcommittee, which included as exhibits a March 1, 1954 article about the Italian trial from *True Magazine*, "Guilty" by Michael Stern; Glock and Walter's report on their interview with Carl LoDolce; and a copy of Michael Stern's book *No Innocence Abroad*. After discussion of Glock's report, the Board decided to vote, by secret ballot, on the question, "Are you satisfied that Aldo L. Icardi has the fitness and general qualifications (other than scholastic) for admission to the Bar." When the votes were tabulated, one member of the Board had voted "yes," and twelve voted "no." Icardi was again denied admission to the bar.[310]

The anti-Communist crusaders suffered a number of setbacks beginning around 1954, when Senator Joseph McCarthy's red-baiting tactics were denounced publicly by Joseph Nye Welch during the Army-McCarthy Hearings, followed by McCarthy's censure in the Senate on December 2, 1954. The prosecution of Steve Nelson and his Pittsburgh comrades for sedition was also dealt a couple of fatal blows. Although the Pittsburgh Communists were ultimately convicted for violating the Pennsylvania Sedition Act, the U.S. Supreme Court overturned the convictions on the basis that the federal Smith Act of 1940, which made it illegal to advocate the overthrow of the U.S. government by violence, preempted state law.[311] In 1953, Nelson and five others were prosecuted and convicted under the Smith Act, but in 1956 the U.S. Supreme Court granted the Communists a new trial when it was discovered that testimony by one of the paid government informants, Joseph Mazzei, was falsified.[312] The government declined to retry them. By 1955, even Matt Cvetic's veracity was being questioned around Washington; the Subversive Activities Control Board, created by the McCarran Act, recommended in April 1955 that Cvetic should "not be used as a Government witness unless ... [his testimony] is corroborated from independent sources ... ."[313]

In retirement in Santa Barbara, California, Jake Margolis, the anarchist lawyer who was disbarred by the Allegheny County Bar Association in 1920, was philosophical about the "red hysteria," and about the discrediting of sources and red-baiters. Long unsympathetic to the Communist cause, Margolis wrote to his daughter and son-in-law in November 1953 that "Communism is a dead horse and all the floggings by all the super patriots will not put life into it. There is much more danger from the Fascists of the McCarthy et all stripe [sic], but that danger too is minimal and nothing to keep me awake at night." Regarding the efforts of undercover agents and sources, Margolis wrote that "I have always had a very low regard for secret police and when one of them is glorified as was Edgar Hoover, the chief of America's secret police, I sort of gag." He added: "As far as my own experience goes I knew that many of their so-called 'reliable sources' were just simply tale weavers, snoopers, vindictive neighbors, blathermouths, neurotics and notoriety seekers."[314]

However, for Aldo Icardi, as well as for Hymen Schlesinger, red hysteria continued to be a living, breathing circumstance, even after McCarthy and Cvetic fell into decline.

The Bar Association's Committee on Offenses continued its back-and-forth with Hymen Schlesinger over the question of his possible disbarment following Judge Musmanno's call to action in June 1951—just prior to Musmanno's election to the Pennsylvania Supreme Court in November. The Committee on Offenses granted Hymen Schlesinger a hearing on his proposed disbarment by notice dated May 1, 1953, with the principal charge being that he was a member of the Communist Party, "one of the major aims and purposes of which party is the overthrow of the Government of the United States by force and violence;" but Schlesinger secured a delay in the hearing date on the basis that he was unsuccessful in his attempts to find counsel to represent him. The hearings nonetheless proceeded during January, February and March of 1954, with Schlesinger being unrepresented. The hearings continued in February and March of 1955 for the purpose of allowing Schlesinger to present evidence in his own defense, and again, Schlesinger was without counsel.[315] Years later, Chief Justice Charles Alvin Jones of the Pennsylvania Supreme Court would state, "It is a lamentable commentary, but none the less true, that, in the existing frame of the public mind, a lawyer who undertakes voluntarily the legal representation of a person charged with being, or even pointed at (in *J'accuse* fashion) as, a Communist runs the risk of a disruption of his law practice and the impairment of his own professional reputation."[316] Schlesinger petitioned the Bar Association for assistance in obtaining counsel in June 1955, and was offered the services of a sole practitioner who handled divorces.[317]

Several leading members of the bar saw the matter of securing Hymen Schlesinger appropriate representation as a matter of principle. As Judge Joseph Weis recalled, "A lot of us thought he should be disbarred, but everybody agreed that he had to get a good defense" so that the proceedings "would stick." According to the Bar Association's executive director, Jim Smith, John G. Buchanan—as a "champion of a person's rights to a defense regardless of the charges or the times"—decided to organize a group of the bar's top lawyers to form Schlesinger's defense team. In June 1956, the Committee on Offenses filed an order in the Court of Common Pleas appointing as Schlesinger's counsel Charles F.C. Arensberg and Richard B. Tucker, Jr., of the Patterson Crawford firm; John G. Buchanan of Smith, Buchanan Ingersoll; Louis Caplan; Thomas N. Griggs of Griggs, Moreland; Louis Glasso, a prominent trial attorney; James Craig Kuhn, Jr., of Wilner, Wilner & Kuhn; and John K. Tabor of the Kirkpatrick & Lockhart firm.[318] Arensberg, of course, had served as the lone dissenter on the Committee on Offenses that recommended the disbarment of Jacob Margolis in 1920.

Before Schlesinger's disbarment proceedings would land in the Court of Common Pleas, however, Aldo Icardi found his cause derailed by another set of proceedings. In

March 1953, while Icardi was focusing on his petition before the Board of Law Examiners, a two-man subcommittee of the House Armed Services Committee—consisting of Congressmen W. Sterling Cole, a red-baiting Republican from New York,[319] and Paul Kilday, a Democrat from Texas who was elected to Congress after charging that his opponent was a "friend and ally of Communism"[320]—came to Pittsburgh and interviewed Icardi. Aldisert counseled Icardi not to accept their invitation to speak with them. "These characters are not out to do you any favors," he said; but Icardi believed he could use the Committee as a forum to clear his name. Aldisert stood by his client as, again, he denied any involvement in the murder of Major Holohan.[321]

On August 29, 1955, however, Aldo Icardi was indicted by a federal grand jury on six counts of perjury, on the basis of the statement he gave to Congressmen Cole and Kilday in 1953.[322] Aldisert and Rodgers brought Icardi to Washington to recruit Edward Bennett Williams[i]—whom Aldisert described as "a bold young 34-year old lawyer" who represented Senator Joseph McCarthy during the Watkins Committee hearings that led to McCarthy's censure—to serve as Icardi's lead defense counsel at the trial.[323] As Williams' biographer Evan Thomas writes,

> *By the time [Icardi] came to Williams's office in August 1955, he already 'stood convicted in the court of public opinion and sentenced to infamy," Williams wrote. The small, bespectacled, bald-headed man was desperate and despondent. ... His neighbors were calling him a 'dago murderer' and, worse in that era, hinting that he was a Communist. If convicted, he faced up to forty years in prison.[324]*

Aldisert told Williams, who was also a sole practitioner like Aldisert, that Icardi had no money, but "there are things that a lawyer has to do because it's the right thing to do." Williams replied, "Well, I guess you're right ... I'll take the case and we'll all go broke together."[325]

Aldisert and Williams, along with Williams' friend Robert Maheu[j]—Williams' debate partner at Holy Cross and an ex-FBI agent who had just established his own private investigation agency—traveled to Italy to interview witnesses. There they obtained photos of Major Holohan's corpse, which showed that his hand had been chopped off, which Aldisert explained was "the gruesome signature of the Communist underground in Northern Italy." During their interview with Senator Moscatelli, the Communist partisan who had once accused LoDolce and Icardi of the murder, Moscatelli "freely told them that he decided to remove Major Holohan ... because he was a liability to the partisans. Icardi, he said, had nothing to do with the murder."[326]

Although Williams was prepared to litigate the substance behind Icardi's statements to the subcommittee, based on Aldisert's legal research, Williams wanted to establish that Cole's subcommittee had no legislative purpose for its interview with Icardi—that, in effect, it was conducting its interview in an effort merely to establish the basis for

---

[i] Williams later established the Washington law firm of Williams & Connolly. He also later became the owner of the Washington Redskins and the Baltimore Orioles.
[j] Maheu is better known as the CIA operative who ran Howard Hughes' Nevada operations during the 1950s and 60s.

a perjury indictment of Icardi. As Aldisert explained, "You do not violate the federal perjury statute if the oath was not administered by a 'competent tribunal.' And a committee of the legislature that sets up a hearing for the purpose of setting up a witness for a perjury rap is not a 'competent tribunal.'" During his cross-examination of W. Sterling Cole, Williams managed to get the congressman to admit that he had discussed the possibility of a perjury indictment with committee counsel prior to taking Icardi's testimony. "Bingo!" wrote Aldisert. "Congressman Cole said the magic words without realizing it ... This testimony effectively killed the government's case." Williams moved for a directed verdict at the end of the government's case, and on June 17, 1956, Judge Richmond Keech of the U.S. District Court for the District of Columbia directed a verdict of not guilty. "There were tears in Ike's eyes as he embraced all of us," Aldisert recalled.[327] Icardi—free of indictment, free of conviction by an American court—was now, again, free to pursue admission to the bar.

While Hymen Schlesinger's dream defense team skirmished with the Committee on Offenses, meanwhile, Schlesinger was called to testify before HUAC. On November 26, 1956, in a hearing convened in Youngstown, Ohio, HUAC counsel Richard Arens and committee chairman Harold Velde, a Republican congressman from Illinois, quizzed him about whether he was a member of the Communist Party. Schlesinger replied:

> *Mr. Chairman, in view of the fact that there are pending proceedings against me in which I have claimed the fifth amendment as to that very question, in view of the fact that certain paid professional informers, such as Joseph Mazzei and Matthew Cvetic have stated that I am a Communist, I am claiming the fifth amendment.*[328]

After fifteen minutes or so of additional wrangling and Fifth amendment invocations, Congressman Velde concluded, "I have nothing further to say except to make a remark for the record, that a professional man, especially a lawyer, is a very dangerous person if he is a member of the Communist conspiracy. Certainly it appears to me that the witness we have just heard is a member of the Communist conspiracy."[329]

On April 15, 1957, the Committee on Offenses filed its final report with the Common Pleas Court, recommending the disbarment of Hymen Schlesinger, and the dream team filed exceptions to the report, arguing them before the Court on December 18, 1957. Three years later, on May 3, 1960, the Court finally ruled on the report, recommending that Hymen Schlesinger should be disbarred. On May 10, the board of judges of the Common Pleas Court entered its order disbarring Schlesinger.[330]

Richard B. Tucker, Jr., a member of Schlesinger's dream team, recalled:

> *Since we lost in the Common Pleas Court, we had to ask the Supreme Court for a supersedeas to stay his disbarment from practice pending the decision of that Court on the merits. The Supreme Court was in Harrisburg and we all drove over in one car—Hymie Schlesinger, Mr. Buchanan and I with Mr. [Robert] Rundle who represented the Grievance Committee and who was morally certain that Hymie had an armed bomb in his pocket. In Harrisburg facing us from the bench was a furious Justice Musmanno ... Nevertheless, the rest of the Court granted a supersedeas and the four of us returned to Pittsburgh without Hymie's bomb going off.*[331]

The dream team, led by John K. Tabor and Richard B. Tucker, Jr., argued Schlesinger's appeal before the Pennsylvania Supreme Court on March 17, 1961. On July 18, 1961, Chief Justice Charles Alvin Jones delivered the opinion on the Court, holding that not only was the evidence insufficient to prove professional misconduct worthy of disbarment—i.e., stating that Schlesinger was a member of the Communist Party, whether or not true, "would not support an inference that he did not have good moral character," quoting *Konigbserg v. California*—but that the procedural path of the case was fundamentally flawed. The Court noted that the "functions of prosecutor, judge and jury were combined in one body, namely the Committee on Offenses, which lodged and prosecuted and, through its Subcommittee of three of its own members, adjudicated the charge of unprofessional conduct whereon the Court of Common Pleas, without any hearing of witnesses, ultimately entered the order disbarring the appellant." The proceedings basically deprived Schlesinger of due process of law, according to the majority. Justice John C. Bell, Jr. dissented, stating that "I am convinced that Communism is the mortal enemy of our Country, that it has organizations in the United States (and indeed in most of the world) which are completely directed, dominated and controlled by Russia and constantly plan and plot the overthrow and destruction of our Government and our free way of life by force and violence, and whenever necessary, by insurrection, revolution and war."[332]

The gulf between Justice Bell and the majority could not be wider, as he himself said in his dissent; but Schlesinger was finally left to practice law without the cloud of disbarment over his head for the first time in over ten years. Judge Joseph Weis, Jr., who had supported his disbarment, would later admit, "He was not a bad egg. If he was the best that the Communists could send against the country, we were pretty safe."[333]

In September 1960, Aldo Icardi petitioned the Pennsylvania Supreme Court for leave to reapply to the state board for admission to the Pennsylvania bar, but was rebuffed without an opinion. He applied directly to the state bar in 1967, and when he was refused, he appealed to the Pennsylvania Supreme Court. By this time, Ruggero Aldisert had been appointed to the Court of Common Pleas (and later, to the U.S. Court of Appeals), so his friend Samuel Rodgers handled the appeal. The case was argued on October 6, 1969; and on January 9, 1970, Justice Henry X. O'Brien delivered the opinion of the Court, stating that since Icardi never had a chance to cross-examine his accusers in the hearing before the Allegheny County Board of Law Examiners subcommittee in 1953, he was deprived of due process. The Court ruled that County Board of Law Examiners should be directed "to conduct a hearing, on reasonable notice to the petitioner containing a plain and concise statement of the particular charges against him on account of which his character and fitness to practice have been disapproved, with opportunity to him to be confronted by and to cross-examine the witnesses against him and that in default thereof, he be granted a certificate to permit his admission to the Bar."[334] Justice Musmanno had passed away in 1968, and there was no mention of Communists by the Court in its opinion.

In May 1971, Aldo Icardi was finally admitted to the Pennsylvania bar.[335] The County Board of Law Examiners had long since disbanded. For twenty years, Icardi had survived and supported his family in a succession of odd jobs—driving a cab, working as a law clerk, searching real estate titles. He was eventually able to obtain a real estate brokerage license and engaged in a little real estate development, building a few houses on Eutaw Street on Mt. Washington. Hoping, finally, to engage in the practice of law, he moved to Florida to join his brother Dario's law firm, but had to engage counsel to fight his way into the Florida bar as well. He was admitted there in 1972, at the age of fifty-one, and practiced in Maitland, north of Orlando—first with his brother, then with his daughter and son—until the age of eighty. In twenty years of hostile proceedings, it appears that the gentle core of Icardi's personality had been ignored. "My Dad," said his son, Jeff Icardi, "if you knew him, you would know that he was just not a slick enough operator, at age twenty-three no less, to mastermind a plot to kill an officer and steal a bunch of gold ... and the family, my grandparents who were immigrants from Italy, they were certainly anti-Communist."[336]

By 1972, of course, Communism was no longer the flashpoint that it had once been. In that year, President Richard M. Nixon—once one of the leading anti-Communists in the country as a member of HUAC—visited Mao Zedong in China, opening the door to the United States giving full recognition to the Communist Chinese government in 1979. Nixon's political rise in the late 1940s and early 1950s has often been attributed, in part, to the soapbox that public red-baiting had provided him. This was also true of some adept political operators within the Pittsburgh bar; the anti-Communist crusades were largely a project of perennial political candidates of both major parties, such as Musmanno, Gunther, Duff and Margiotti. Although Musmanno never gained the statehouse or a seat in the U.S. Senate (he lost the Democratic nomination in 1964), he was elected to the Pennsylvania Supreme Court twice; James Duff went from serving as governor of Pennsylvania to U.S. senator; Judge Gunther ultimately won election as an Allegheny County commissioner.

The shared methods of Musmanno, Gunther and Margiotti—in addition to their liberal requisition of newsprint—frequently involved the use of irregular legal proceedings: secret depositions, ex parte interrogations, citizen's arrests, tribunals in which staffers acted as prosecutors, judges and juries. The public excesses of these activities during the McCarthy Era in the Pittsburgh bar had their counterparts, even their antecedents, within the quasi-public sphere of the County Bar Association. The institutions that had been created during the century's previous red scare—the County Board of Law Examiners' morals inquiries and the disbarment activities of the Committee on Offenses—were ultimately gutted by the decisions in the *Icardi* and *Schlesinger* cases, but it would probably not be appropriate to see those results simply as a reaction to the tactics of anti-Communism. Rather, the anti-Communist movement in Pittsburgh occurred during a time when the Pittsburgh bar's normative control over its own membership was already disappearing. Democratization of the bar was the larger movement during the period, enveloping the grasping attempts of the anti-Communists to exercise control over who could practice law in Pittsburgh.

CONTINUITY AND LOSS IN THE GOLDEN TRIANGLE

In 1952, the law firm of Smith, Buchanan, Ingersoll, Rodewald & Eckert sent out an engraved "change of address" card announcing its relocation from the 10th floor of the Union Trust Building, where it had operated since 1923, to the thirteenth floor of the new Alcoa Building on the corner of Sixth Avenue and William Penn Place. Harold B. Tanner, the senior partner of the Providence law firm of Tillinghast, Collins & Tanner, used the occasion to write to John G. Buchanan with a question:

> *Reading your firm name makes me think again of my own problem. Mr. Tillinghast and Mr. Collins are dead, and I am nearly sixty-five. Question, should we start out again incorporating the names of a few of the older among my partners, or should we, as our friends Edwards & Angell, perpetuate the name of Tillinghast, Collins & Tanner? The Tillinghast part of the name gives us a sort of claim for continuity back to about 1825, and it would seem both sentimentally and practically inadvisable to drop either the Tillinghast or the Collins name ... In Providence we have not often had a firm name of more than three elements.*[337]

Buchanan did not hesitate in providing his answer, which was based on his own experience with the naming of the Smith Buchanan firm over the years:

> *It has been the regular practice of our firm to change its name regularly after the deaths of partners, and sometimes on other occasions. Since I have become a member of it, on July 1, 1916, the name has been successively Gordon & Smith; Gordon, Smith, Buchanan & Scott; Smith, Buchanan, Scott & Gordon; Smith, Buchanan, Scott & Ingersoll; Smith Buchanan & Ingersoll; and the present name ... I don't know what we should have done if we had had a name going back to 1825, but I rather think we should have followed*

our present practice of recognizing the living in the firm name. I take it that your firm once followed a like practice, or your name would not have been in its present name. Why shouldn't you change the name of your firm and merely retain the names of your deceased partners, with their dates, on your letterhead. [338]

Buchanan was an avid promoter of his version of the Smith Buchanan law firm's historical roots, going back in a mostly unbroken chain to the partnership of Moses Hampton & Son, founded in 1850. However, Buchanan's desire to see the firm's name changed with each departure—which would persist into the late 1970s, when six months after the death of his long-time partner Frank B. Ingersoll he suggested to the partnership, to no avail, that it was time to drop Ingersoll's name from the firm style[339]—had its underpinnings in the nature of the partnership as an entity. The law firm, as a partnership, was theoretically required to be reconstituted as a new partnership each time a partner would die or otherwise depart from the firm. Buchanan's view was one that was unimpeachably consistent with partnership law, yet, paradoxically, his pride in the firm's history recognized that these successive separate partnerships formed a line of continuity.

By contrast, after the departure of Philander Knox in 1901, the Reed Smith partnership clung to its name long after the last Reed, David Aiken Reed, and Edwin Whittier Smith had both died. Its final name change during the twentieth century was from "Reed, Smith, Shaw & Beal" after the death of James H. Beal, Sr. in 1922, to "Reed, Smith, Shaw & McClay." Demmler called the name change the "attainment of a long-term ambition" of Samuel McClay, and observed that "the elimination of Mr. Beal's name was cruelly abrupt."[340] The firm would subsequently subordinate the marquee ambitions of its partners in favor of the development, over time, of brand recognition—even if none of its lawyers would have deigned to use such "commercial" terminology during the era. During a time when advertising or marketing was, within the profession, ethically impermissible, the decision to keep an old name with each periodic reconstitution of the partnership was a subtle and continual reminder to current and future clients, as well as opponents, of the grand and dignified history of the law firm. The Reed Smith firm's decision was one that infected the thinking of Earl Reed at Thorp, Reed & Armstrong, who refused to permit a change of the firm's name after the death of Charles M. Thorp, Sr., in part also because he wished to avoid confusion between a "Reed Armstrong" firm and a "Reed Smith" firm.[341] Perhaps there was already confusion enough in downtown Pittsburgh over a "Reed Smith" and a "Smith Buchanan" firm.

The power of the brand name has long been palpable within the law. Philip E. Beard, a freshly-minted Pitt Law graduate who joined Stonecipher & Cunningham as an associate in 1960, would experience that power first hand. The firm, which originally had called itself Stonecipher & Ralston in 1904 after its founders, Frank W. Stonecipher and John M. Ralston,[342] and came to be known as Stonecipher & Cunningham some time after Ralston's death in 1936.[343] Stonecipher died in 1952[344]; but the firm's long-held leadership in the Commercial Law League of America, through which the firm's lawyers received referrals of debt collection lawsuits from across the country, led the firm's remaining lawyer, Bill Cunningham (the son of Frank Stonecipher's partner

Charles L. Cunningham), to decide not to change the firm's name, despite the fact that by 1960, Bill Cunningham was a sole practitioner. In 1962, when Beard was the sole associate, Cunningham suddenly died, after routine surgery, at the age of forty-six.[345]

Beard was legally the owner of nothing; he had been an employee of a now-nonexistent sole proprietorship. "I was left ... with four secretaries, all of whom knew more about the practice of law than I did," Beard recalled; and yet the referrals from the Commercial Law League continued to roll in. Beard called his law school classmate, Joseph Schmitt, who was then practicing in Erie, and asked him for help. The two worked out an arrangement with Cunningham's widow, Dorothy, to provide her with a percentage of the firm's profits for a time—though she declined them at first—and the two young lawyers left the firm's name as "Stonecipher & Cunningham," eventually adding "Beard & Schmitt" to the end of the name. On the strength of the firm's brand within the Commercial Law League, Philip Beard and Joe Schmitt were swept right along, developing their own successful debt collection and bankruptcy practices, with their brand name leading the way. Old branding habits die hard; Beard had never even met Frank Stonecipher, but now the firm that has been Philip Beard's life's work is generally known as the Stonecipher Law Firm. Beard shrugs, "It is an odd name," but people "remember it."[346]

Philip Beard's experience is a reminder that underneath the porous veil of a partnership agreement or behind the hubris of a "d/b/a," there exist human lives. In 1942, at the two largest law firms in Pittsburgh—Reed Smith and Smith Buchanan—most of the human lives, the attorneys, were named something other than Reed or Smith or Buchanan. Human needs will occasionally trump the merits of branding, as the histories of these firms affirm.

At Reed Smith, there were a handful of young attorneys arriving at the firm in the years prior to World War II who were sons of partners of the firm: Robert J. Dodds, Jr., William A. Seifert, Jr., Joseph I. Marshall (son of Judge Elder Marshall, who came to the firm in 1938), John G. Frazer, Jr., and Donald B. Heard (son of John "Jack" Heard). Each of them, however, joined one branch of the military or another during the early years of World War II, as did the more senior associate, Joseph Robinson, son of William Robinson, and a number of other associates of various levels of experience. To deal with the manpower shortage as the associates went to war, Reed Smith's managing partner, Jack Heard, hired approximately fifteen experienced Pittsburgh lawyers and three new recruits, and beefed up the firm's staff of tax accountants.[347] As Brignano and Fort observe, "The 'temporary' associates had fitted in smoothly. They rose quickly to Reed Smith standards and picked up its culture and pace."[348]

Among the associates who left for the War, there were seven who saw a good deal of each other while they were away. John G. "Jack" Frazer, Jr., left Reed Smith to enlist in the Army in August 1942 and served in the Judge Advocate General's Corps, and Robert L. "Kirk" Kirkpatrick entered the Army as a captain on November 1, 1942. Kirk was a corporate finance and tax lawyer from Butler County, by way of Harvard Law School. As warm, informal and casual as Kirk could be, Jack Frazer—another Harvard lawyer—was quiet and austere. Jack's father had been managing partner of Reed Smith, but he died of a heart attack only four months before Jack left for the War; Jack's grandfather was Robert S. Frazer, Chief Justice of the Supreme Court of Pennsylvania, and his grandfather on his mother's side was the firm's founder, Judge James Hay Reed.[349]

Another Reed Smith associate, George Lockhart, left in January 1942 to join the Navy, but was initially kept out due to poor eyesight. After he worked for the Navy for a while as a civilian, the Navy reconsidered and gave him a proper commission. Lockhart, a Pitt Law graduate and an estate and trust lawyer, was Jack Frazer's brother-in-law; his grandfather was an oil magnate, one of Rockefeller's original partners in Standard Oil, and though George grew up amid great wealth, he was known to be gracious and humble. Tom Johnson, by contrast, was a force of nature. His grandfather on his mother's side was T.W. Phillips, founder of another oil and gas fortune and a bitter rival of Rockefeller. The Phillipses were a busy family, serving in Congress and the Senate and endowing several colleges, and they were even the major benefactors of a Christian denomination, the Disciples of Christ. A corporate lawyer with an entrepreneur's energy, Johnson entered the Naval Reserves in 1944. Thomas W. Pomeroy, Jr., a tall and distinguished-looking Harvard-trained trial lawyer and a good friend of Lockhart, joined Johnson in the Naval Reserves around the same time. Rounding out the crew were Naval officers W. McCook "Cookie" Miller, the Pitt-trained grandson of Frick's lawyer Willis McCook, and Harvard-trained Stuart Nye Hutchinson, Jr., the son of a Presbyterian pastor.[350]

The seven, whom Brignano and Fort described as being "practically the entire middle level of pre-war Reed Smith," all spent the War in Washington, at desk jobs.[351] This seemingly mismatched yet generally well-connected crew "had been good friends and their families were socially compatible before the Washington sojourn," as John U. Anderson, Jr., their future partner, would write. "They continued to socialize on occasion in Washington ... It was perhaps inevitable that some of the discussions in Washington turned to a critique of how the firm of Reed Smith was organized and managed."[352]

Jack Heard, Robert Dodds, Sr., William Robinson and William A. Seifert, Sr. served as the firm's management committee, and "they operated with a cabal-like secrecy," according to Brignano and Fort. In a revised partnership agreement of wartime vintage, they retained sole control of "the management of the partnership, the determination of its policies, the employment and compensation of all employees and the capacities in which they are to serve."[353] Nepotism was the order of the day, and when the sons of the senior partners returned from war duty, each of them was offered a junior partnership of three percent, culled from their fathers' respective shares of the firm. None of the other returning lawyers, including Jack Frazer, Jr., the son of the former managing partner, were given an offer of partnership.[354] According to Brignano and Fort, in fact, Heard and his colleagues "seemed at a loss to know quite what to do with all this talent. Worried about a post-war economic downturn, they feared that the market might not support them all. And the concept of 'marketing'—of purposely going out to create business—would have been an anathema to these old school attorneys."[355] Upon the return of the seven from Washington, Heard, whose opinions were rarely secret and could often be seen in the expression on his face, led the returning veterans to understand that he believed that they had done the firm a disservice by going to

War when client demands were at an all-time high, according to Anderson. In any event, Heard told the seven that they would be returning to be paid the same salaries they had received when they left.[356]

Tom Johnson already had one foot out the door. When he returned, he started working for several clients from home, including Standard Steel Spring (later known as Rockwell Spring and Axel). Lockhart, as well, had made a furtive move toward the exit by working from home rather than returning immediately to the firm's offices.[357] Heard's attitudes were not altogether surprising to them, and during those wartime social conversations about the firm's future—some over cocktails in the Kirkpatricks' kitchen, some "around the kitchen table of Kate Reed Frazer," Jack Frazer's mother, who was both the daughter of the founder of Reed Smith and the widow of the firm's late managing partner—the group had begun to talk about setting up their own law firm.[358] A few of them, however, including Robert Kirkpatrick and Tom Johnson, decided to get an audience with Heard one more time to discuss the possibility of raises for the returning men. Kirkpatrick made a case for salary increases based on the fact that each of the returning lawyers gained significant experience as military lawyers. Heard reportedly frowned and replied, "Lawyers are a dime a dozen these days. There will be no increases." Legend has it that Tom Johnson's response was to toss a dime onto Heard's desk, telling him, "Here's a dime. Go buy a dozen, because you just lost seven."[359]

Whether or not the legend is true (and it is one of those stories that ought to be true, even if it is not), the seven approached their departure in a most respectful fashion. On September 28, 1946, the founding partners of the firm of Kirkpatrick, Pomeroy, Lockhart & Johnson, signed a statement that they submitted to the management committee. They announced their decision to leave and declared:

> *Our decision has been made on the basis of a mutual desire to practice in a small office of our own, wherein we will all experience the satisfaction (as well as the tribulations) of building and running a law firm. It is only fair to say, however, that this desire has been forged into a decision at this time by reason of what we conceive to be problems at Reed Smith Shaw & McClay for which no satisfactory solution in the near future seems possible. These have been brought to your attention at various times by some of us, commencing in November 1945, but there is no occasion to detail such matters at this time, since they have become academic in view of our irrevocable decision to leave.*[360]

The attorneys of the new firm asserted that they had no intention to raid the files of Reed Smith in their departure, although as their later partner Judd Poffinberger would observe, "They banked on the goodwill and loyalty of earlier clients and friends."[361] Chuck Queenan, another of their subsequent partners, noted that "most spinoffs take a significant client mix with them, [but] these guys had been in the War for four years without client contact." Said Queenan: "I think that for the first six months or so, they sat around and looked at themselves." With their personal family wealth, Johnson and Lockhart, in particular, were able to guarantee that each of the other five partners would receive partnership profits that would at least equal the salaries they had received at Reed Smith. The partners dealt with their first set of "tribulations," however, when they settled into "borrowed" quarters inside the Lockhart family offices in the Union National Bank Building at the corner of Fourth Avenue and Wood Street. "There was not sufficient furniture or space in that office to accommodate seven sedentary lawyers," said Poffinberger in 1986. "George Lockhart still wonders how the chock-a-block group got any legal matters done there." Shortly after the beginning of 1947, the partners signed a lease for offices on the 11th floor of the Oliver Building.[362]

The firm weathered its first years handily. Just a month before the group sent their departure notice to Reed Smith, Tom Johnson had joined a business partnership consisting of Frank McKinney, an Indianapolis banker, real estate investor John Galbreath, and Hollywood crooner Bing Crosby in acquiring the Pittsburgh Pirates baseball club, as well as its stadium in the Oakland section of town, Forbes Field, from the Dreyfuss family (McKinney later sold his share to the other partners, leaving Galbreath as the lead owner). Johnson's connection with the club made him a household name in Pittsburgh, and not only was the deal a mark of what would be perceived as Johnson's entrepreneurial spirit (and, by extension, that of the new law firm), but it was a figurative demonstration of the type of "middle-market" business work that would become its bread and butter for a time. Meanwhile, through connections developed in Washington, Kirkpatrick was engaged by the investment bank First Boston to handle its work in Pittsburgh, and through that relationship he would end up sitting at the table opposite his former colleagues at Reed Smith, performing sophisticated financing work for out of town clients that, according to Queenan, blended well with the firm's entrepreneurial practice.[363]

Back at Reed Smith, some of the older lawyers were incredulous at the decision of the seven to leave Pittsburgh's top firm—to the leave the "Reed Smith" brand behind—to form their own small firm. The act was more or less unprecedented in the Pittsburgh bar, let alone in Reed Smith's history. Some Reed Smith partners even took to referring to them as the "Mexican League," mostly in jest.[364] Ralph Demmler, writing in the 1970s, charged that the problems to which the men referred in their departure announcement "were not so serious as they conceived and were more readily soluble than they thought."[365] Brignano and Fort, however, conceded that the departure of the Kirkpatrick lawyers was a kind of wake-up call. "The exodus of these experienced, able lawyers shook Reed Smith—and improved its governance," they wrote. Reed Smith adopted a new partnership agreement in 1948, taking the centralized control of the firm away from the management committee, requiring regular partnership meetings, and providing for the election of the managing partner by majority vote of the partners.[366] Jack Heard would nonetheless remain as managing partner until 1957.

Relations between the firms, though they may have been strained at first, at last settled into the kind of mutual respect that was the hallmark of all elite lawyers' relations during the period. When the Kirkpatrick firm needed to borrow a book from the Reed Smith library, or use its copy machine on a weekend, says Kirkpatrick partner Woody Turner, Reed Smith would oblige. "There was no real sense of animosity" between the two firms, Turner said, except on the football field. During intramural flag football games between the associates of the two firms, things would get a little rough, especially when the games would pit Blair McMillin, a Reed Smith associate, against his cousin Ed McMillin, a Kirkpatrick associate. During those meetings, things got out of control quickly, Turner recalled, so eventually the firms stopped playing the games.[367]

Meanwhile, at the Smith Buchanan firm, the partners seemed to survive World War II a bit more gracefully than Reed Smith had done. Twelve of the nineteen lawyers in the firm had all been hired by 1932, and were all past the appropriate age for military service by 1941; of the remaining seven, six entered military service (including John Buchanan's son, John Buchanan, Jr., who was hired in 1941), meaning that during World War II, Smith Buchanan lost the services of slightly less than one-third of its lawyers. During the War, the firm temporarily hired a couple of older practitioners in their 60s to fill the gaps, and cautiously added a few younger lawyers as the War years waned.[368] At the beginning of the War, the firm also extended offers to a pair of Harvard Law classmates, Carl Cherin and George Heinitsh, who would serve in the Army and Navy, respectively, before actually settling down to assume their roles as Smith Buchanan associates. Cherin had turned down a clerkship with Justice Felix Frankfurter to accept the job in Pittsburgh, for family reasons, before entering the Army.[369] At any rate, by the end of the War, the Smith Buchanan firm had grown comfortably to approximately twenty-six lawyers, including the six returning lawyers.[370]

The firm's 1941 partnership agreement remained unchanged until 1947. In that year, the firm decided for the first time to separate economic percentages from voting percentages; thus, while William Watson Smith, at age seventy-six the firm's senior partner and leader, was willing to lower his economic portion of the partnership from sixteen percent to ten percent in order to share more profits with the firm's active middle-aged partners—Paul Rodewald, William Eckert, Leon Hickman and William Kyle—he retained the sixteen partnership votes that he had had in the 1941 agreement. While senior partners John Buchanan and Frank Ingersoll each continued to enjoy fifteen percent of the profits and fifteen partnership votes in both the 1941 and 1947 agreements,[371] everyone knew that Smith ruled the firm as an autocrat. At the end of each year, the partners would gather in a room, and Smith would tell the partnership, "I wish to reform the partnership as of January 1, with the following partners receiving the following partnership percentages ..." Invariably, the lawyers would fall in line without argument. Smith's word was as good as law.[372]

Rodewald and Eckert joined the firm on the exact same day in 1924—Rodewald from Harvard Law School, Eckert from Pitt—and they could not have been more different. Rodewald was an ebullient raconteur who—though he was a devout man and like Buchanan, a lover of ancient classical literature—also loved a good old-fashioned ribald joke. As his tenure with Smith Buchanan lengthened, he began to gather around him a group of loyal associate acolytes who were both charmed by him personally and dazzled by his professional mastery and erudition. Eckert, meanwhile, became heralded as a trial lawyer who also practiced in the estates area; but unlike Rodewald, he was a bit of a close-mouthed hermit, a socially ill-at-ease man without any avocations or many friends, who went through each year committing two thousand-plus hours to legal work, even as a partner. Gregg Kerr, an associate at Smith Buchanan, said that Eckert, the son of a Crafton butcher, "was never quite sure he was good enough," generally speaking; and Smith and Buchanan did him no favors on that score by placing Rodewald's name before Eckert's on the firm's letterhead.[373] Alex Black, Jr., a Smith Buchanan partner, said "they flipped a coin" to determine the order, but the outcome reinforced the perceptions within the firm that John Buchanan thought Harvard should prevail over Pittsburgh.[374]

John Buchanan, at this stage of his career, was known as one of the nation's top appellate lawyers—a frequent visitor at the U.S. Supreme Court who could call to mind the salient points about almost any Supreme Court case, if pressed—and a lion of the Allegheny County bar. Meanwhile, the remainder of the active senior team—William Watson Smith, Frank Ingersoll, Leon Hickman and William Kyle—were devoting themselves, in some measure, to serving Alcoa. Bill Kyle, a corporate finance lawyer and boardroom advisor in the mold of Frank Ingersoll, was a handsome, immaculately-dressed fellow with broad shoulders who looked like he could have stepped right into the cast of *Mad Men*; when Clayton Sweeney's wife Sally first met Bill after Clayton was hired in 1962, she told Clayton, "*That's* what I want you to be when you grow up."[375] Kyle worked on Alcoa's first registration statement before the Securities and Exchange Commission, but he also acted as an advisor to some of the firm's other major corporate clients, such as Allegheny Ludlum Steel, Armstrong Cork and the Union National Bank.[376] The rest of the team—Smith, Ingersoll and Hickman, along with associates William Unverzagt and Frank "Zeke" Seamans—spent long hours with each other over the years in New York, fighting the gargantuan Alcoa antitrust case. When Cherin and Heinitsh came on board after the War, they fell right into the tax and trust & estates group with Paul Rodewald, along with one of the other returning servicemen, Don McCaskey. During the early 1950s, the firm hired additional associates as two lawyers died and others retired. By the end of 1957, the firm had thirty-two lawyers—sixteen partners and sixteen associates.[377]

It came as a surprise to the downtown legal community when on January 31, 1958, eight lawyers—one-fourth of the firm—announced that they were forming a new partnership under the name of Eckert, Seamans & Cherin, with "the honor of having Mr. William Watson Smith as counsel to their firm."[378]

Sifting through the memories of lawyers who were on hand to witness the event—known to the Buchanan partisans as "the split," a phrase whispered mournfully through the hallways for decades afterwards, and to the Eckert partisans as "the founding of the firm"—one is struck by the fact that there were almost as many opinions as to why the event occurred as there were survivors who had witnessed it. Though the facts are simple enough to process, the event itself was a bit more complex, a bit more cataclysmic than seven young lawyers leaving Reed Smith in 1946 to form a new law firm. The Eckert lawyers were a mix of partners (one of them quite senior) and associates, and they were taking with them the largest client of the firm, Alcoa. With the departure of William Watson Smith, the "Smith Buchanan" law firm brand that had built its equity in the Pittsburgh bar over a period of thirty-one years, was shattered.

Alcoa figures largely in the chronology that led to the event, beginning as early as 1951. Urged by its bankers to hire a general counsel, Alcoa naturally turned to the Smith Buchanan team that had been representing it in the antitrust case and hired Leon Hickman on William Watson Smith's recommendation. Hickman quickly acceded to a position of influence within Alcoa, not only as a lawyer, but as an executive officer and director of the company. Bill Kyle remembered, however, that "Frank Ingersoll was very close to a lot of people at Alcoa, like Chief Wilson, Roy Hunt ... he was like a brother to all the heads at Alcoa." According to Kyle, the fact that Hickman received the nod "was a disappointment" to Ingersoll; not that Ingersoll actually needed the job for himself, but it was indicative of the way that Smith and Ingersoll "were growing farther apart" during the course of the Alcoa trial.[379] Smith had initially envisioned that Ingersoll would play a larger role in trying the case, but it became clear to Smith in 1938 that while Hickman seemed to have the right touch in dealing with Judge Caffey, Ingersoll was more like a bull in a china shop. The year after Hickman went to Alcoa, Hickman's chief lieutenant on the case, William Unverzagt, also left the partnership to join Hickman as assistant general counsel at Alcoa. As Alcoa completed its new aluminum clad, thirty-floor building on Sixth Avenue, across from the new Mellon Square development, the firm of Smith, Buchanan, Ingersoll, Rodewald & Eckert moved into the thirteenth floor.

In 1957, two events caused William Watson Smith to reassess the circumstances of his career. First, early in the year, Alcoa sent its notice to the firm that the rapid expansion of its headquarters staff required the company to take back the thirteenth floor of the Alcoa Building; the Smith Buchanan firm would be required to find new space. At age eighty-six, however, Smith was loath to move his offices yet again.[380] Second, on June 28, the federal District Court for the Southern District of New York relinquished its jurisdiction over Alcoa in the government's antitrust case, effectively ending the twenty-year long battle.[381] No longer beholden to the proceedings that had represented the primary reason why he had extended his career for two decades past the age of sixty-six, Smith quietly informed the partnership that he was ready to retire.

On January 2, 1958, by all outward appearances the machinery of the firm's management was locked into gear; a memorandum on that date invited the partners to the first of what was anticipated to be a regular monthly meeting of the firm's partners, to be held at twelve fifteen in the afternoon on January 8 in Room 3G of the Duquesne Club. The meeting would be presided over by John G. Buchanan, at age sixty-nine now the firm's most senior partner. The memo noted that "Mr. Smith does not wish to participate."[382]

Over the holidays—perhaps at William Watson Smith's urging, although the sources differ—William Eckert set about attempting to gain support among the partners for a significant reorganization of the firm. Alex Black, a real estate lawyer who also had an insurance litigation practice, recalled that Eckert proceeded to call in each of the younger partners to meet with him, one by one. "When I was called in," he said, "the people sitting there were Eckert, Frank Seamans, Carl Cherin and Paul Rodewald." They handed Black a list proposing that the partnership shares should be divided in such a way that would eliminate the shares of Buchanan and Ingersoll, who would be named as "of counsel," and that would elevate the partners sitting before him to be the leading economic partners and the leaders of the firm, which would be renamed with Eckert's name at the head. Carl Cherin had prepared the percentages himself, based on his review of the "client billing lists and which partners were responsible for such billings." Alex Black could barely contain his shock. Alex's father, Alex Black,

Sr., had once been John Buchanan's partner, and after his father died in 1924 at the age of forty-four, Buchanan had treated Alex, Jr., almost like a son and had seen to his education. "I remarked that when I had gone to Harvard Law School, I was the recipient of a [Buchanan] scholarship." "Everyone here owes a great deal to Mr. Buchanan," said Rodewald. "I didn't say anything," said Black, "but what I thought was, 'This is no way to show it.' I just told him, 'Well, I'll think it over.'"[383]

"No sooner was I out of the meeting and back in my office," Black remembered, "then young John Buchanan [John Buchanan, Jr., John G. Buchanan's son] came in and he said, 'Well, what did you think of that?' I saw then it just wasn't going to come down."[384]

At the partnership luncheon, Eckert's proposal was voted down by the partners, twelve to four—the four being Eckert, Seamans, Cherin and Milton Lamproplos, a forty-seven year-old partner of the firm who was known as "Eckert's shadow." Paul Rodewald, who had initially intended to go along with the plan, switched his vote, as did several of the younger partners who had previously expressed support for it.[385]

Leon Hickman became a key figure in what followed; Kerr, in fact, called him "an author of the event."[386] Carl Cherin, who did tax work for Alcoa, and Zeke Seamans, who had worked closely with Hickman on the Alcoa litigation almost from the beginning and who lived across the street from Hickman, saw the writing on the wall immediately after the vote. The Eckert plan would need to be abandoned, but the only way they were going to see themselves properly rewarded for their work was to leave the lockstep compensation system of the Smith Buchanan firm behind and establish their own new firm. After the defeat of his proposal, however, Eckert had apparently seriously considered just staying with the old partnership and continuing with business as usual. According to an Eckert Seamans staffer, it was Hickman who argued to Eckert that a new firm needed to be created, and that it would not survive unless Eckert, who had been paid well within Smith Buchanan for many years, would support it. Eckert, Hickman asserted, was "the only one with real money" to help start the partnership. Most importantly, however, Hickman pledged to move the Alcoa work to the new firm. Eckert eventually agreed.[387]

Hickman's motives are now lost to the ages. However, given Frank Ingersoll's disappointment over Hickman's role at Alcoa, it would not be surprising to learn that the irascible Ingersoll might have taken every casual opportunity to undermine Hickman with the heads of Alcoa, his "brothers." Clayton Sweeney recalled, matter-of-factly, that "Ingersoll and Hickman hated each other."[388] Hickman's systematic approach to building a "law firm within the corporation" yields other clues. In an address on "The Need and Utilization of Retained Counsel" in 1959, Hickman discusses the advantages of occasionally using outside law firms if they are "familiar enough with the corporation's work to be able to lend a hand to corporate lawyers" in times when the in-house workload "becomes abnormally heavy." Yet in describing seven situations in which it is advisable for a general counsel or in-house department to seek the advice of an outside firm, Hickman's attitude reveals an understandable desire to control the environment of the in-house/outside counsel relationship. While, in Hickman's words, "it is a great mistake for corporate [in-house] counsel to deny retained [outside] counsel access to any papers or individuals that should be seen to form a proper policy or program ... It is equally fatal to a satisfactory relationship for retained counsel to go around corporate counsel and deal with corporate officials on his own. This brings retained counsel and corporate counsel into competition, and, when that happens, there can be but one outcome."[389]

Given the public stature of the general counsel in the guise of Leon Hickman during the era, it is also quite natural that Hickman would feel that it was within his power to shape his "retained counsel" to Alcoa's specifications so that it could better serve the company. With Seamans and Cherin in charge of the relationship—younger and more directly beholden to Hickman—it was undoubtedly more likely that he would achieve such an objective than if the relationship were to stay with Ingersoll and Kyle. Gregg Kerr recalled that the element of control was there in later years, for example, when Eckert Seamans might specifically recruit a lateral attorney after Hickman said he thought the firm needed more expertise in a particular area.[390]

Over the next week and a half after Hickman threw his support to the new firm, the Smith Buchanan offices were in turmoil as Eckert, Seamans and Cherin began a series of one-on-one meetings and phone calls with various lawyers within the firm, attempting to convince them to join them in their new law firm, while Buchanan and Ingersoll were doing the same thing to convince people to stay.

Now Paul Rodewald sat on the pivot. Over the years, Paul and Carl Cherin and George Heinitsh became a close-knit team, not only as tax practitioners but as friends and peers. Moreover, Rodewald had many connections within the leadership at Alcoa, and the prospect that Alcoa would leave and become a client of the new firm was unsettling. "I had the feeling at the time that maybe Rodewald had some idea of going to the other firm," recalled Edward Schoyer, a corporate finance lawyer who worked closely with Ingersoll and Kyle.[391] If Rodewald were to decide to leave and join the new firm, it might have changed the calculus somewhat. Thomas M. "Tom" Thompson, who arrived at the Buchanan firm several years after the split, noted that Rodewald had the ability to make "new associates feel completely at ease," whereas John Buchanan was "somewhat aloof" and Frank Ingersoll was "hard-nosed" and "a pragmatist to the bone."[392] Rodewald was popular with the younger men, and some of them might have decided to follow him; or perhaps the partners would have gone back into negotiations. But Rodewald, mindful that whichever way he decided to go would result in a great sacrifice, decided to stay. "I still remember seeing him at the meeting breaking down in tears," said Black. "It was a nervous strain."[393]

When the music stopped, most of the lawyers decided to stay. All of the partners who had voted against the Eckert plan at the January 8 meeting stayed. The four associates who decided to go—Cloyd "Mel" Mellott (who was named as a partner in the new firm), Gregg Kerr, John Morgan and Roderick Norris—were attracted in part by Zeke Seamans' dynamism and Carl Cherin's technical brilliance, packaged in a relatively youthful accessibility and informality that represented the exact opposite of the personae that Buchanan and Ingersoll inhabited. The old firm seemed "stodgy" to them, according to Kent May, who joined Eckert a few years after the firm's founding and served as managing partner for a time. Kerr said that he received a call on January

22 from Zeke Seamans asking him to join the new firm. Both sides courted him, but in the end, Kerr—a child of the Depression who did not come from a wealthy or socially-connected background—"was going to get in my life only what I could get for myself. I thought it would play out differently in the other firm."[394] William Watson Smith, though still committed to retiring from practice, announced to John Buchanan that he had agreed to serve as counsel to "the small firm," saying, "I feel sorry for those boys." "There was really no reason to be sorry for them," Buchanan wrote to Donald Shepard, a Washington lawyer and co-executor of the estate of Andrew Mellon, "since they made an effort to lead the firm," and that effort failed.[395] According to Alex Black, Smith told Buchanan that he felt bad about the way it had all turned out. "He had apparently expected that everything would go along the way he thought it ought to be, but he wasn't aware of the opinions we all held about Mr. Buchanan," Black said.[396]

John G. Buchanan convened a meeting of the twenty-four remaining attorneys. He gave a speech about the reformation of the partnership, to be known as "Buchanan, Ingersoll, Rodewald, Kyle & Buerger," and remarked as he looked around the room that "these are the men with whom I want to be engaged in the practice of law." Then, as Edward Schoyer recalled, "Mr. Buchanan congratulated all present for standing by him and Mr. Ingersoll ... and put on his hat and coat, shook hands with us all, then left the room, only to return, somewhat embarrassed because he had mistakenly exited in Mr. Ingersoll's private bathroom."[397] A pall of awkwardness persisted over the existence of the two firms as they continued to occupy the same space on the thirteenth floor of the Alcoa Building, with two receptionists at two reception desks, jockeying over who controlled files and so on, until the eight Eckert Seamans lawyers took a fifteen thousand square-foot lease on the tenth floor of the H.K. Porter Building on Grant Street.[398] Facing the termination of the Alcoa Building lease, Buchanan Ingersoll eventually moved to the eighteenth floor of the Oliver Building. Meanwhile, in February 1958, John Buchanan wasted no time in claiming the historical lineage of the Smith Buchanan firm for Buchanan Ingersoll, penning an article for the *Pittsburgh Legal Journal* that reaffirmed his firm's origins in 1850 and detailed the departure of the eight Eckert lawyers following Smith's announced retirement.[399]

Eckert Seamans rocketed to an early success, rapidly devouring Hickman's Alcoa work and hiring new associates steadily from 1958 through 1966; by 1972, the firm had forty lawyers.[400] Carl Cherin's son Steve, a Pittsburgh attorney, recalled that the financial effect upon his family was swift and significant; shortly after the new firm was formed, he recalled, his family moved from a modest half of a duplex to "a mansion with a big yard" a few blocks away in Point Breeze.[401] Buchanan Ingersoll, the larger firm, by contrast, suffered some lean years. While the firm continued to represent some major corporate clients, due to the connections of Frank Ingersoll and Bill Kyle, Alcoa work had represented a large percentage of the firm's revenues, and the litigation group was decimated by Eckert's departure. The firm stopped hiring new associates until 1962, when John Buchanan brought in Clayton Sweeney from Duquesne Law School as well as Judge Sara Soffel, who was retiring from the bench. The firm's litigation group had to be rebuilt through the independent work of James D. "Jim" Morton, who joined the firm in 1955, and Clayton Sweeney.[402] Meanwhile, many of the Buchanan Ingersoll partners credited Paul Rodewald's tax work for various officers of Alcoa for keeping the firm afloat from a revenue standpoint during the immediate aftermath of the "split."[403]

Speaking about "the split" thirty-five years later, at age ninety-three, Paul Rodewald—normally jovial, almost elfin—reduced his voice to a hush. His eyes moistened. To that day, he still carried the emotional burden of the event, saying, "I was at the center of it." He believed that his decision to break away from the Eckert plan sent the negotiations into a tailspin.[404] But for Paul Rodewald, this was not merely a matter of lost client fees or a broken firm name; it was a loss of friendship, and a crack in the collegiality that he had enjoyed for thirty-four years at the Smith Buchanan firm and that seemed to be the core of his professional life. It was tantamount to a divorce, or a death in the family; it was shocking, in that law firms did not break apart like that, not in that day. Others, too, suffered their losses. Carl Cherin and George Heinitsh had been close friends since their Harvard days, but after the "split," says Steve Cherin, the Cherins and the Heinitshes no longer socialized. Don McCaskey was "broken-hearted" over his good friend Zeke Seamans' departure, according to Clayton Sweeney. "I don't think you can underplay what kind of a trauma that was," Gregg Kerr reflected.[405]

Kerr, who would later serve on the management committee of Eckert Seamans, was philosophical about the causes of the tension that inevitably led to the formation of his firm. He recalled attending a banquet in 1952 for the 40th anniversary of John G. Buchanan's admission to the bar shortly after being hired by the firm. "In light of what happened later, think about what kind of an experience it must have been for John G. Buchanan to be the number two lawyer in a firm for that length of time ... Later I drew some conclusions about Mr. Buchanan's participation in that turmoil based on the supposition that he fully expected to be the number one lawyer in the big firm when Mr. Smith retired." But Kerr also conceded that had the events played out somewhat differently, perhaps the firms need not have split from one another. "My take on it," said Kerr, was that when Smith announced his retirement "he was leaving behind him a group of lawyers, each of whom deservedly was impressed by his own importance, but they had never had an opportunity to bargain with each other." It probably didn't help that, as Kerr said, Eckert was "no expert at personality interplay."[406]

Eckert Seamans and Buchanan Ingersoll addressed the issues of firm stability in different ways in subsequent decades. In 1985, Eckert Seamans scored a four-column headline in *The American Lawyer* when twenty-two of twenty-nine partners voted to dissolve the partnership, only to reform a day later, minus seven "non-producing" partners.[407] The firm has since reorganized as a limited liability company, a slightly more durable form of existence. Buchanan Ingersoll reorganized as a professional corporation in 1980—one of the first law firms "of a certain size" to do so in the United States, according to William Newlin. "We always advised our clients to adopt a certain method of operation if it made good sense for them," Newlin explained. "Yet we, like most law firms, frequently didn't listen to our own advice. In this case we studied it intently, and we concluded that an overall firm incorporation made good financial and business planning sense."[408]

The incorporation of the firm ended the practice of changing the firm's brand name with each departure, the practice that John Buchanan seemed to tout as an advantage in his letter to the Providence lawyer way back in 1952. The firm's name would now be frozen as "Buchanan Ingersoll" until a majority of the shareholders would otherwise vote. Moreover, incorporating the firm certainly saved the partners from dealing with reforming the firm each time a partner left it. The incorporation also had the effect of focusing leadership in a "chief executive officer" and a "board of directors"—certainly still democratic, in a way, because the CEO and the board would be elected by the voting shareholders, but the CEO would nonetheless be a position, defined by corporate law, which carried enough clout that, on a good day, would enable the inhabitant of the office to make decisions as though he were a William Watson Smith. On a good day, the CEO's word was as good as law. Other large firms, whether they incorporated themselves or not, began to "corporatize" their management in similar fashion, in reflection of their clients' ways of doing business.

By the 1980s, other large, old firms in Pittsburgh were beginning to break apart, for a variety of reasons, and their brands disappeared from the downtown bar. The firm of Rose Schmidt Hasley and DiSalle, which could trace its origins back to the early part of the twentieth century, was a firm that Bill Rodewald, Paul Rodewald's son and a partner at Buchanan Ingersoll for a number of years, described as being "like the Mexican government—in a constant state of revolution."[409] Rose Schmidt was primarily a litigation firm, known for its expertise in the coal industry. By the early 1980s, the firm had reached its zenith, with more than seventy lawyers and offices in Washington, DC and Detroit. Around that time, a group of younger partners attempted to mount a coup against the old line management in order to reorganize partnership percentages in favor of younger productive partners, but were unsuccessful. Instead of going off to form their own firm, a number of partners and associates trickled out the door to different firms; even more left after the death of its long-time managing partner Harold Schmidt. The joke around town was that Rose Schmidt had one of the best alumni lists in the city. By 2004, the firm had just five attorneys in Pittsburgh, who kept the "brand" alive, despite the fact that the surviving Schmidts and Roses were practicing elsewhere in Pittsburgh, until 2010, when the firm disbanded. Fran DiSalle, one the firm's last lawyers, noted that by then the brand wasn't good enough ultimately to be sustained any longer. "People would say, 'I thought you guys went out of business.'"[410]

Two of the fastest growing Pittsburgh law firms of the 1970s and 80s were firms that had begun their lives as "Jewish law firms." In a continuation of the divisions within the segregated Jewish bar that began the early twentieth century, German Jewish law firms represented upper- and upper-middle class Pittsburgh Jewish families and their businesses—such as "the Falks, the Reiszensteins, probably the Dreyfusses—where the real money was," as attorney Robert Sable observed, whereas the Eastern European Jewish law firms would represent the less well-to-do members of the Jewish community.[411] The firm of Berkman, Ruslander, Pohl, Lieber & Engel—which had its beginnings as Ruslander, Ruslander and Lieber, founded in 1948 by S. Leo Ruslander, who began his career an associate to A. Leo Weil at Weil & Thorp—became the leading German Jewish firm in Pittsburgh after World War II, representing some of the leading Jewish businesses around Pittsburgh, including the specialty steelmaker Ampco Pittsburgh which was founded by Allen Berkman's brother Louis.[412] The firm of Baskin, Boreman, Wilner,

Sachs, Gondelman & Craig—which was originally formed in 1954 by brothers Philip and Seymour Baskin—typified the post-War Eastern European Jewish law firm, although it built up its downtown credibility in part by doing referral work from "white-shoe" firms such as Reed Smith on matters that those firms did not typically get involved with: bankruptcy, collections, divorces and even criminal work.[413] Both firms began growing during the 1970s by "ecumenicalizing," as former Berkman Ruslander partner Lee Keevican put it—by hiring non-Jews, such as Keevican himself.[414]

Sable, a partner in the Baskin firm during the early 1970s, was once asked whether the firm was a partnership. "I said we were a monarchy," he recalled.[415] Philip Baskin, invariably described by his colleagues and clients as "tough," "rough-and-tumble" or "scrappy," was born in Washington County, and he grew up in an orphanage with his brothers in Erie after his father died. After working his way through Pitt, he joined the Air Force during the War and served as a bomber navigator in thirty-one European missions, then attended Harvard Law School on the G.I. bill. While his firm was establishing its bona fides as the challenger firm in the Jewish community, Baskin served as an assistant County solicitor, getting involved in the post-War Pittsburgh Renaissance initiatives before winning a seat on city council.[416] Baskin's mantra seemed to be "go big or go home," and he was aggressive in developing the firm. As Sable remembers, the firm formed its own REIT in the early 1970s; "Baskin said we're not going to get the big clients, so we have to form our own clients."[417]

At the end of his tenure in the council in 1969, Baskin began to conceive a vision to grow his firm, as Jack Feeney, who was a Baskin partner during the early 1980s, explained, "into a multi-city firm when there were none in Pittsburgh."[418] In 1977, Baskin went to Washington, touting his firm's regional political connections, and brought into the partnership John Sears, a key figure in Nixon's presidential nomination in 1968 and Ronald Reagan's campaign manager during his unsuccessful run for the Republican nomination against President Gerald Ford in 1976. The firm of Baskin & Sears grew rapidly, and by 1981 had 150 lawyers.[419] However, Sears' well-publicized representation of the apartheid government of South Africa was causing problems with Baskin's lucrative representation of various instrumentalities of the City of Pittsburgh; a group called Pittsburghers Against Apartheid demanded that Baskin & Sears be dismissed as bond counsel because of Sears' connections.[420] Thus, in 1984, Baskin and Sears split the firm, and Baskin renamed his firm "Baskin & Steingut" in favor of his new New York partner, Stanley Steingut, a former speaker of the New York Assembly.[421] By then, the firm had offices in Pennsylvania, New York, Florida, Maryland, Virginia and Washington, DC. When that alliance unwound two years later, acrimoniously, with Baskin suing Steingut for diverting legal fees, Baskin renamed the firm "Baskin Flaherty Elliott & Mannino," reflecting the political weight of his Philadelphia partners, John Elliott and Edward Mannino, and his Pittsburgh partner, Jim Flaherty, a former County commissioner and the brother of former mayor Pete Flaherty.[422]

Feeney left the firm in 1984 for a seat on the Common Pleas Court, but he saw the direction in which the firm was headed. The offices, he said, "were never integrated, they never worked," and all Baskin really offered by way of synergies was that "we could do their books for them."[423] With all but the Pittsburgh, Harrisburg, Philadelphia,

Washington and Cherry Hill, New Jersey, offices left by 1990, the Pittsburgh presence began to shrink, to thirty-five lawyers, while the Philadelphia office grew to 80 lawyers. The internal dissension between the Pittsburgh and Philadelphia factions was becoming a newspaper sideshow, with partners on both sides of the state commenting openly to the press about the problems in the firm, until April 1991, when Baskin announced that the Pittsburgh office was separating from the rest of the firm. Ultimately, the Pittsburgh lawyers scattered into other downtown firms, and Baskin retired.[424]

Berkman Ruslander, says Keevican, "was a firm that should have worked." It had a top-flight client list, it performed sophisticated corporate and banking work and, unlike other firms that experienced tension between younger, more energetic business-getting partners and the old guard, "it was a firm that allowed you to rise as far as your talent would take you." Keevican was among a group of younger partners that catapulted into firm management and were compensated well, based on their success. By the mid-1980s, the firm had grown to seventy lawyers and was among the top five largest firms in Pittsburgh.[425] Then, in January 1988, the firm was rocked by a scandal. Edward K. Strauss, a Berkman Ruslander bond lawyer, entered into a plea agreement, admitting guilt to federal charges of misprision of a felony in connection with fraudulent bond offerings underwritten by a Wall Street investment bank called Matthews & Wright, led by Arthur Abba Goldberg. Matthews & Wright had spent a few years exploiting a loophole in the tax code, convincing government officials to issue tax-free bonds on infrastructure projects that they never intended to initiate and investing the money, making millions in taxable dollars before returning the money to bondholders after three years. There was enough money being made in the spread of 350 basis points or more to accommodate kickbacks to the government officials.

In order to facilitate the transactions, Matthews & Wright came to Pittsburgh and asked Ed Strauss to provide legal opinions on them. Keevican surmises that Matthews & Wright "really didn't want to deal with the New York firms. You had to have somebody that if you dangled that much money in front of them, they won't really dig into what's behind it." Strauss was another young partner on the firm's management committee, and the firm was making money hand-over-fist doing bond deals. "We should have seen the signs," says Keevican. "We should have seen it. It was too much, too fast, too easy." The reaction to Strauss' plea—which he accepted, without informing the firm, in order to avoid jail time—was that many of the business clients of the firm, especially the banks, began to retreat. Bad legal opinions were bad for Berkman Ruslander's business. Not only were Strauss' bond deals gone, but the transactional side of the practice was falling apart as well. The firm did not have any debt, but the loss in revenue led to layoffs, and the firm hired management consultants to figure out how to turn the tide. According to Keevican, the consultants came back with two recommendations: the firm had to change its name, and it had to change its business—meaning, it had to get out of the bond, banking and corporate finance business, which had been the traditional strengths of the firm, and lean toward litigation and bankruptcy. As a result, twelve transactional lawyers left to form Doepken Keevican & Weiss; the Berkman firm recruited two lateral partners from Eckert Seamans, Edward Klett and William Schorling, to bolster its litigation and bankruptcy experience; and the firm changed its name to Klett Lieber Rooney & Schorling. "It was a new firm," Keevican said, "different vision, different focus, different leadership." And it had a different brand.[426]

The Berkman implosion was an anomaly, brought on by a catastrophe. Meanwhile, the departures of Klett and Schorling from Eckert Seamans made headlines in 1989, as did the departures of Arthur Schwab and Pamela McCallum from Reed Smith to join Buchanan Ingersoll in 1990[427]—a scenario between those two "white-shoe" firms which would have been unthinkable during the golden age of the Golden Triangle. The downtown bar, after decades of loosely following the dictum of the Cravath model ("no lateral hires"), was caught by surprise by these early lateral moves, but a trend was brewing; and by the end of the twentieth century, lateral defections became a tsunami. By then, it became so commonplace for groups of several lawyers to move from one firm to another in Pittsburgh that such events began to occur without generating much more than a half an inch of newsprint about routine "comings and goings."

Whether you called them "splits" or "defections," the events that created Kirkpatrick Lockhart from out of Reed Smith and that resulted in Buchanan Ingersoll and Eckert Seamans occurred during a time when the two original firms were growing at breakneck speed after the War. They were partnerships—large ones, to be sure, but still intimate enough that the disagreements between those who ruled and those who left were personal and philosophical, even if they were also about money. They were about nepotism, about stodginess, about an unwillingness to let younger partners assume the mantle of leadership. The downtown bar, it may be argued, was merely reflecting the zeitgeist of the age—even if, characteristically, the legal profession was a few decades slow on the uptake. When at the end of the nineteenth century, the partnership form began to show its weaknesses as a vehicle for large businesses, Pittsburgh lawyers were the first to recommend to their clients doing business under corporate charters, but also the last to take their own advice, as William Newlin had observed. Because Reed Smith and Smith Buchanan were old-style general partnerships whose managing partners governed by conversation and sometimes by consensus, it is perhaps easy to see how they were fragile and unstable enough, in the face of accelerated growth, to experience some jarring breaks.

Corporatization of the bar has given great advantages to the leaders of law firms. It has certainly stabilized the branding of law firms by freezing their names in place; and by requiring the delegation of firm management to a CEO and a board of directors, it has permitted the leadership of a firm to exercise a tighter grip over business planning— over issues such as budgeting, and about which areas of expertise need to be grown and which need to be jettisoned—in exchange for electoral accountability to the rest of the firm. It permitted firms to become exponentially larger while minimizing the risks of instability. The more that a corporatized management has become the norm within larger Pittsburgh law firms, however (whether these firms operate as professional corporations, professional limited liability companies, or limited liability partnerships), and the larger the firms became, the more alienated the non-management lawyers have become from the management lawyers. Out of necessity, to the leaders of large corporatized law firms with hundreds of lawyers, individual attorneys begin to look more like ledger entries than members of a team.

Meanwhile, the tsunami of lateral moves within the Pittsburgh bar since 1990 has largely been about compensation, not about actual disagreements, *mano a mano*, between dissenters and management about culture or philosophy. Neither personal differences nor questions of loyalty are even part of the equation, in most situations. "Today it's almost customary," says Judge Robert Cindrich, once the head of the firm Cindrich & Titus, "for a partner to build up a huge book of business, demand more than the other partners will let him take out as compensation ... and then leave. Well, we did it to ourselves." And branding? "So I say to my client," Judge Cindrich says, "the reason you should be with our firm is it's not just me. It's all these other people, this team we have together. It's the ethos and the culture. It's the commitment to you. But tomorrow I may be in that [other] firm, and I'll tell you the same thing about them."[428] Thus, ironically, the more stable the branding of the firm through corporatization, the less meaningful it has become. Not only have lawyers become fungible in the eyes of management, in Cindrich's view, but to some degree law firms have become fungible in the eyes of lawyers.

Even if that is correct—and it certainly is to some degree—it is not the whole story. Pittsburgh lawyers are still practicing in large law firms in an age in which, by dint of the Internet and mobile technologies, lawyers have theoretically never needed less physical infrastructure in order to serve clients; and these law firms are named for real human beings, living or deceased. There is still a palpable suggestion of some undefinable quality associated with some of these names. For some, there is still some sense of pride attached to being a part of the traditions associated with such names, still some need to be connected to a professional ancestry and pedigree—even if just temporarily, on the way to the next firm.

The idea of Jack Frazer leaving his grandfather's firm and establishing its biggest rival in the Pittsburgh bar, or the gutting loss of camaraderie and collegiality that Paul Rodewald felt when his colleagues left to form Eckert Seamans, now seem like quaint folk stories, ephemera from a bygone era, like Buchanan's engraved announcement card; but they also mark the last moments before a turning point in the Pittsburgh legal profession. They represent the canaries in the coal mine, if you will, at the moment when the legal profession in the Golden Triangle was becoming a modern business, dragging with it a host of continuities, as well as a sense of loss, along the way.

YEARS FOR INCHES

⸻

K. Leroy Irvis, an African American public school teacher in Baltimore, wanted to be a pilot during World War II, but because he built and flew model airplanes, the War Department instead hired him to teach aircraft assembly to women factory workers.[429] After the War, Irvis was looking for something a little closer to the action. At the recommendation of Lester Granger, the national executive secretary of the Urban League, Irvis was invited to join the Pittsburgh chapter of the Urban League to do "a job that had never been done before," according to Arthur Edmunds—"public relations for black people."[430]

In Pittsburgh, the Urban League had achieved modest success over the prior thirty years by encouraging vocational training and working with businesses to expand employment opportunities for African Americans. There was a ceiling, however, on the type of employment opportunities available for African Americans; while they might be offered jobs as janitors, food service workers or stock boys in a downtown department store such as Kaufmann's, qualified applicants were systematically being turned away from sales jobs with better wages. The attempts of the Urban League to engage the department stores in dialogue had been met either with silence or frustrating delays.

In November 1946, the downtown department stores—Kaufmann's, Horne's, Gimbel's, Frank & Seder and Rosenbaum's—began hiring sales clerks for the Christmas rush. The Committee for Fair Employment in Pittsburgh Department Stores, formed by members of various African American support organizations including the Urban League, saw an opportunity to test the stores. Ten "capable and qualified Negro women" applied for sales jobs in response to the stores' want ads, accompanied by a member of the Committee and a reporter for the *Courier*. Rosenbaum's rejected the applications entirely, telling the applicants that "the girls might try the tea room" of the store instead. The rest of the stores accepted the applications, but never followed up with any of the women. While the newspapers began to cover the story, the stores nonetheless continued their course.[431]

Members of the Committee began to organize a "poster walk" for Monday, December 9, 1946—a peaceful picket of the department stores to protest their hiring policy. Irvis and his wife, Katharyne, handled recruiting for the protest, while the Committee consulted with Hymen Schlesinger, attorney for the ACLU, and applied for a permit from the Department of Public Safety. They made no secret of their intentions. Meanwhile, Mayor David Lawrence expressed his concern, saying that the protest would "give our city a black eye ... I implore you to cancel this 'Poster Walk' for the good of the city and of all concerned." The Committee agreed to attend a meeting with representatives of the stores in the mayor's office on Monday before the appointed time. All of the stores except Rosenbaum's attended the meeting. By eleven in the morning, no agreement had been reached, and the "poster walk" proceeded as planned, with about forty men and women, both African American and white. Hearing the news, the department stores refused to negotiate until the walk was called off, but the Committee rejected the demand. It was not until January 24, 1947, that the department stores finally put out an affirmative announcement that "[t]here will be no discrimination in upgrading or employing of Negroes from this day forward."[432]

Although the "poster walk" had the desired effect (the actual hiring of Africans Americans would only gradually begin to occur after the announcement), the Urban League ultimately found itself in the position of disowning the "walk," as the League received much of its funding from white-owned downtown businesses. For his success in mobilizing the protesters, Irvis was fired by the League. "I was a young firebird who was upsetting things around the nest," Irvis recalled. "I had offended the white man downtown."[433] He stayed in Pittsburgh, however, working at several odd jobs—including, for a time, in a steel mill—until he entered Pitt Law in 1951. He graduated fourth in his class in 1954, and accepted a clerkship with Judge Anne X. Alpern.[434]

The wartime experience had proven to be empowering for so many young white men who returned to Pittsburgh and entered the bar. For young African American men who had been consigned to the fringes of economic life in the North, the wartime experiences were life-changing, and the African American soldier literally became an emblem of the civil rights movement in Pittsburgh, emblazoned on the letterhead of the NAACP with the words "Back 'em up" and "a just peace at home."

Wendell Freeland's wartime experience was more dramatically concerned with the civil rights struggle. Born in Baltimore, Wendell Freeland had fair skin, blue eyes and light brown hair; and even though he could have easily "passed" as white, he "was raised to be proud of his African-American heritage and was largely unaware of his light complexion as a boy," according to writer Ytasha Womack. "We were just poor and Black," Freeland said.[435] He received a scholarship to attend Howard University. In 1943 he was drafted and entered flight school at Tuskegee. "And I didn't know a damned thing about airplanes," in contrast to Irvis' background. Nonetheless, he trained as a bombardier at Tuskegee as well as in an integrated gunnery school. He joined the all-African American 477th Bombardment Group just as it was being transferred to Freeman Army Airfield near Seymour, Indiana. Although Army regulations provided that there should be no discrimination among officer personnel by reason of race, creed or color, "We learned that the members of the 477th who had gone there had been told that the [Field's only] officer's club had been made the white officers' club, and the white NCO [i.e. non-commissioned officers'] club"—a converted shack—"was now going to be the officers' club for Negroes," Freeland recalled. "We decided that we weren't going to put up with that."[436]

As they arrived at Freeman Field by train in March 1945, the African American officers of the 477th, as well as those of the 332nd Fighter Group, went one by one directly into the whites-only officers' club. Nineteen of them, including Freeland—who "went in, sat down and read a *Newsweek* magazine"—were arrested and confined to quarters at the first instance of the protest; and in all, sixty-one officers were arrested for entering the club against orders over two days, April 5 and 6, 1945. In the aftermath, Freeland and one hundred others were arrested and held for about a month for failing to sign a statement regarding the rules of the base. After receiving an administrative reprimand, Freeland and one of his comrades typed out ninety-nine individual responses to it, containing a list of grievances, after which the entire crew were released back into the 477th. William T. Coleman, the future Secretary of Transportation, was in the middle of Harvard Law School, and had been with the 332nd Fighter Group during the protests; along with Ted Berry, the future mayor of Cincinnati, Coleman helped to obtain the acquittal of the group on the more serious charges.[437] A couple of years later, President Harry S Truman issued an executive order providing for the racial integration of the United States Armed Services.

Freeland was ultimately trained too late in the War to see any combat action. After the War, he graduated from Howard, and then became one of the first African American graduates of the University of Maryland School of Law in 1950. He was recruited to Pittsburgh by Richard Jones, the former partner of Homer Brown, who had just been elected to the County Court of Allegheny County.[438]

The African American bar in Pittsburgh into which Wendell Freeland and K. Leroy Irvis entered in the early 1950s was as segregated as it had ever been. There were still no African American lawyers working in the same firms with white lawyers. Homer Brown had only just ascended to the County Court bench. While Wilbur Douglass and Thomas Barton were fulfilling the traditional roles as the only African American assistant County and city solicitors, respectively,[439] Russell H. Adams appointed Oliver L. Johnson as the second African American assistant district attorney in 1942,[440] and Freeland would eventually succeed him in that office. These were still part-time positions, supplementing the relatively modest incomes they each received as general practitioners. In 1952, almost all of the African American lawyers were clustered in just two locations near the Courthouse downtown. Richard Jones, with his partners Wendell Freeland and Henry R. Smith, Jr., occupied offices on the fourth floor of the broken down Bakewell Building along with Everett Utterback, Judge Brown's brother-in-law, who had just become general counsel for the Pittsburgh Housing Authority—across the street from the courthouse, in the building where Judge Musmanno had found his nonplussed Communists. On the third floor, Douglass, Joseph Givens and William Wendell Stanton shared space. Meanwhile, Oliver Johnson, Thomas Barton,

Theron Hamilton and Paul Jones shared space ("ramshackle" space, said Livingstone Johnson), upstairs over a bar at 527 Fifth Avenue. Only Arthur D. Stevenson, beset by financial problems and living under a lingering ethical cloud, practiced alone in the Upper Hill. This group of lawyers was effectively segregated from the white members of the profession by real estate, by law firm, by tokenism, and by clientele—although, as Livingstone Johnson remembers, his father Oliver used to have some white clients, among them "several families down in Coraopolis of Italian American background."[441]

Oliver Johnson's eldest son, Oliver, Jr., was killed just before his twenty-second birthday at the Battle of the Bulge. "That took the starch out of my dad and mother," recalled Livingstone Johnson, the second eldest. From 1945 until 1957, he said, "Dad was just hanging on emotionally ... When I came out of law school, that rejuvenated him."[442] When Dick Jones lost his partner of twenty-seven years to the bench, along came Freeland and Smith to keep him on his game. The younger generation were inspired by what Robert Vann, Homer Brown and Dick Jones were able to accomplish for their civil rights before the War, and the older lawyers were energized by the new blood, emptying out of the law schools, fresh from war service (Livingstone Johnson was a navigator/bombardier in the Korean War; Byrd Brown, Homer Brown's son, had served in the U.S. Army just after the Korean War[443]) or stiffened by the opportunities that the integrated military had given to their African American brethren. The new breed was outspoken, and they understood the power of symbols held up as signs of things to come to white downtown Pittsburgh. *Brown v. Board of Education*, in which the NAACP's Thurgood Marshall argued that state-sanctioned segregated public schools violated the Equal Protection clause, was originally filed as a class action lawsuit against the Topeka, Kansas school board in 1951. When the U.S. Supreme Court handed down its decision in *Brown* in 1954, it provided a road map for Pittsburgh African Americans. Together, the older lawyers and their young protégés were to help to usher in a new chapter of civil rights activism.

Jones, Freeland and Smith came out swinging in 1951. Dick Jones was at the time the president of the local chapter of the NAACP, taking over the leadership role previously held by Judge Homer Brown, and in the new head of the local Urban League, Alexander J. "Joe" Allen, the holder of a Divinity degree from Yale, he found a kindred spirit. Allen began his tenure in Pittsburgh in 1950 asking the question, "What does the Urban League *do*?" League chapters around the country were under fire for their emerging activism, and local "Community Chests" were agitating to exclude them from their philanthropy for being "advocacy" organizations rather than "support/safety net" organizations. Allen had nonetheless decided that it was time for the Urban League to stand up for more than "case work," and instead lead the fight to overcome the Pittsburgh Negro's status as "second-class citizen."[444]

According to Arthur Edmunds, "Interracial swimming, it seemed, was second only to interracial dating in the resistance it generated" among white Pittsburghers. For years, the city had an informal policy of segregation, and had even opened smaller, alternative pools for African Americans—Sully's in the South Hills, and the run-down Washington Boulevard pool in the East, known as the "Inkwell." In the summer of 1948, the Young Progressives of America, led by Nathan Albert, the secretary of the

Squirrel Hill Club of the Communist Party, arrived at the Highland Park pool in one of the tonier sections of the East End of Pittsburgh with a group of African American youths on three separate days. On the third day, a group of "several hundred" white counter-protesters arrived, and it took 160 police officers to quiet down the disturbance. Albert was arrested, charged with inciting a riot, and sentenced to four years in the county workhouse. The newspapers emphasized his Communist connections.[445]

Nonetheless, Joe Allen, a former Red Cross lifeguard, decided that the community should rally around a renewed effort. Hoping to avoid the disastrous aftermath of the Albert affair, in the summer of 1951, Allen met with Dick Jones of the NAACP and his team, Wendell Freeland and Henry Smith, to figure out the legal strategy to back them up. According to Freeland, Thomas Barton, who was then serving as an assistant city solicitor under Anne X. Alpern, also sat in the strategy meetings. The group, joined by several other local organizations such as the League for Civic Improvement, the Frontiers Club and the Bethesda United Presbyterian Church, met with the city and demanded equal access, but received only a vague reply. Then on a hot day in June, Allen decided to put equal access to the test by arriving at the Highland Park pool to swim. A gang of white teenagers summarily ejected him. When he returned a second time, they threw stones at him.[446]

On behalf of the legal redress committee of the NAACP, Dick Jones went before Judge Clarence B. Nixon and, after the "calm, articulate, and infinitely credible" Joe Allen (as observed by Arthur Edmunds) testified most compellingly as to his treatment at the pool, Jones argued that the city had a duty to keep all pools open for everyone, regardless of race, or shut them down as a "public nuisance." Judge Nixon abruptly broke off the argument and asked Alpern, "You can't make this place safe?" The normally quick-witted Alpern had no answer, and Judge Nixon ruled in favor of Allen and the NAACP, forcing the integration of the Highland Park and Paulson Avenue pools. African American policemen were assigned to guard the pools, and Allen himself took half-day vacation days to serve as a lifeguard. Mayor David Lawrence, who was on a "three-I" political junket at the time (Ireland, Italy and Israel), was livid about the disturbance when he returned. Thereafter, he referred to his fellow Democrat, Dick Jones, as "the number one ingrate." Despite the favorable ruling in 1951, according to Freeland, African Americans met with difficulty again in the summer of 1952 when they attempted to use the Kennywood, West, North and South Park pools; so Freeland took up where Jones had left off in court, deploying the same "integrate or close" strategy. Ultimately, however, Kennywood avoided interracial swimming by restricting its pool to row-boating, and the city decided to fill in the West Park pool rather than desegregate.[447]

Freeland, whose parents were Republican and who, as a child, wore an Alf Landon sunflower pin during the 1936 presidential election, had no party affiliation of his own as an adult until he was asked by Republican James F. Malone, Jr., who was elected Allegheny County District Attorney in 1951, to join the D.A.'s staff.[448] Thereafter, Freeland ascended within the Party to become an advisor and confidant to Republican kingmaker Elsie Hillman. Meanwhile, K. Leroy Irvis, who emerged from his clerkships with Judges Anne Alpern and Loran Lewis to serve as assistant district attorney (as successor to Freeland, after the election of Democrat Edward Boyle as District Attorney), had no thought immediately of going into electoral politics. However, Paul F. Jones, an African American lawyer and Democrat who served as Pittsburgh's first black city councilman, planted the seed with Irvis as early as 1947, saying that Irvis reminded him of a little boy standing outside of a greenhouse throwing rocks. "Did you ever figure how easy it is to break up the greenhouse glass," he asked, "and how tough it is to grow the flowers?" When Irvis decided to run for a seat in the state House of Representatives in 1958, surprisingly enough even Mayor Lawrence, who had fumed over Irvis' role in the department store protests in 1946, became his supporter. Once in office, Irvis fell heir to Homer Brown's former role as civil rights spokesman within the legislature, as well as becoming a highly regarded parliamentarian.[449]

Irvis' election came as David L. Lawrence and R.K. Mellon's Renaissance initiatives began to visit the Hill District. After the URA had requisitioned a major portion of the Lower Hill for the Civic Arena, thereby cutting the heart of the Hill from downtown, it became very clear that Alcoa and Heinz, who were leading the Lower Hill developments, had designs on the Middle and Upper Hill areas—heavily populated with low-income African American families—from Crawford-Devilliers to Oakland. Judge Homer Brown, while serving in the legislature, had ironically made it easier for Alcoa and Heinz to achieve their goals through his support of the "Pittsburgh Package"; now it was left to his successor, Leroy Irvis, to deal with the consequences. Irvis turned his attention to eradicating housing discrimination, an especially important issue if the people of the Hill District might find themselves looking for new housing. The prevailing discrimination in rentals gave landlords the ability to gouge black families on prices, forcing families to double and triple-up within cramped, substandard accommodations in segregated neighborhoods.[450] Meanwhile, the East End Multilist, which controlled the vast majority of Pittsburgh real estate listings, excluded African American brokers, which effectively blocked them from showing properties that were represented by white brokers. Wendell Freeland, because he moved within both white and black circles, would occasionally be engaged to find white "straw buyers" to purchase houses on behalf of middle-class black clients in neighborhoods where restrictions were enforced.[451][k]

Irvis supported adding housing protections to the job protections that Brown fought hard to win during the 1950s, by way of a Fair Housing bill, but faced strong opposition from Pittsburgh housing developers who argued that the adoption of anti-discrimination laws would result in fewer new low-income homes. Senator Robert Fleming, who had lauded Brown's deft handling of parliamentary tactics during the adoption of the "Pittsburgh Package," attempted to derail the Fair Housing bill by proposing that it should only apply to counties in which voters had approved it by

---

[k] Tom Johnson, a founding partner at the Kirkpatrick firm and co-owner of the Pittsburgh Pirates, once asked Tony Wettick, then a young Kirkpatrick associate, if he would employ subterfuge to help procure an apartment for Willie Stargell and Donn Clendenon, two African American players on the Pirates, on the assumption that the landlord would not rent to black men. "It turned out that one of them had a dog," Wettick recalled, and since pets were not allowed in the particular building they had targeted, "we couldn't do it." Judge R. Stanton Wettick, interview by the author, September 2, 2010. After he retired from baseball, incidentally, Donn Clendenon earned his law degree from Duquesne, and practiced in Dayton, Ohio. Richard Goldstein, "Donn Clendenon, 70, M.V.P. for the 1969 'Miracle Mets,' Dies," *The New York Times*, September 19, 2005.

referendum.[452] Ultimately, however, with Irvis leading the fight and Governor David Lawrence himself bringing along a solid Democratic coalition, the Fair Housing Act of 1961 was enacted, and the "Pennsylvania Fair Employment Practices Commission" was renamed the "Pennsylvania Human Relations Commission."[453]

While Irvis was tackling a fundamental issue of civil rights and public policy in aid of the residents of the Hill, Wendell Freeland, president of the Urban League, and Judge Brown's son, Byrd Brown, president of the NAACP, were leading the fight on the front lines of the Pittsburgh Renaissance. In 1960, Byrd Brown and other NAACP activists put up a billboard at the corner of Crawford Street and Centre Avenue, just east of Alcoa's proposed Washington Plaza development, that said, "Attention: City Hall and the U.R.A. / No Development beyond this Point! / We Demand Low Income Housing for the Lower Hill."[454] For them, "Development" meant "downtown, white development," because blacks living in the affected neighborhoods were not being included in the decision-making process. Their demand was for increased housing opportunities. Wendell Freeland, who launched a campaign, as a Republican, for election to the state legislature in 1963, noted that the demolition of the Lower Hill beginning in 1955 for the construction of the Civic Arena had led to even more overcrowding in the Middle and Upper Hill areas, prior to the passage of the Fair Housing Act. "The Negroes who were removed went over to the North Side [but] moved back to the Hill within six months or a year," he recalled. Freeland and his partisans were skeptical about whether the Fair Housing Act would actually erase housing discrimination in the short term.[455] Integration was a game of inches and years, as Freeland's swimming pool fight, for example, had proven.

While Freeland lost in the general election, his draw among the African American electorate and his endorsement by the normally Democratic-leaning *Pittsburgh Courier* were enough to scare Lawrence's local successor, Mayor Joseph Barr, and the leaders of the Pittsburgh Democratic coalition into submission on the question of the redevelopment of the Hill. Washington Plaza, right across Crawford Avenue from the protest billboard, would ultimately represent the easternmost outpost of the Pittsburgh Renaissance's proposed remaking of the Hill District, and the corner of Crawford Street and Centre Avenue would become known as Pittsburgh's "Freedom Corner," the rallying point for future civil rights marches.

A younger generation of the African American bar was assuming full leadership in the cause of civil rights in Pittsburgh during the eventful summer of 1963. The charismatic Byrd Brown had already emerged, of course, during the urban renewal protests, but the Johnson brothers—Livingstone, who was appointed assistant County solicitor in 1962, and Justin, who entered the bar in 1962 after serving several years in the Air Force—were also beginning to assume prominent roles as the era dubbed as "Pittsburgh's Modern Black Freedom Movement" by historians Joe Trotter and Jared Day, began that summer.[456]

On the morning of June 11, 1963, Governor George C. Wallace of Alabama made a public display out of keeping African Americans out of the University of Alabama by standing in the doorway of the University auditorium, blocking the entrance as prospective African American students Vivian Malone and James Hood approached, accompanied by U.S. Deputy Attorney General Nicholas Katzenbach. Later that evening, after directing the Alabama National Guard to secure the entrance of the students, President John F. Kennedy delivered a televised address from the Oval Office calling for Congress to enact legislation aimed at eliminating racial discrimination in public schools and places of public accommodation, such as hotels and restaurants, and in voter registration. Speaking in language unmistakably calculated to reach the men and women who fought for freedom during World War II, the president said: "We preach freedom around the world, and we mean it, and we cherish our freedom here at home; but are we to say to the world, and, much more importantly, for each other, that this is a land of the free except for the Negroes; that we have no second-class citizens except Negroes; that we have no class or caste system, no ghettos, no master race, except with respect to Negroes? Now the time has come for this nation to fulfill its promise."[457] It was the first time the president—not just President Kennedy, but any president of the United States—had gone so far in public support of African American civil rights since Abraham Lincoln. Privately, in a conversation with Walter Fauntroy of the Southern Christian Leadership Conference, the immediate reaction of Rev. Dr. Martin Luther King, Jr., the pastor of the Ebenezer Baptist Church in Atlanta and the spiritual leader of the civil rights movement in America, was one of elation. "Can you believe that white man not only stepped up to the plate, he hit it over the fence!," he exclaimed.[458]

Within a few short hours after Kennedy's address, however, shortly after midnight on June 12, Mississippi NAACP leader Medgar Evers was shot and killed as he returned home from a rally in Jackson. Later that day in Pittsburgh, the local NAACP announced that it was preparing to picket at a downtown construction site, where, in the words of the local NAACP spokesman, there were "shockingly few" African Americans employed. Asked for comment about the Evers murder, the spokesman said, "A man was shot in the back. What kind of a comment can you make to that?"[459]

Although President Kennedy had not directly addressed employment discrimination in his call to action, King and other leaders of the national movement had been planning a march on Washington in August, to culminate at the steps of the Lincoln Memorial, "for Negro job rights." After President Kennedy's speech, it seemed appropriate to supplement the call for jobs with an echo of President Kennedy's call for comprehensive civil rights legislation to protect public school integration, voting rights, and integrated public accommodations. The full name of the march would be the "March on Washington for Jobs and Freedom," set for August 27.

Meanwhile, with both fair employment and marching—"nonviolent direct action"—front and center in the minds of national leaders in June and July, Byrd Brown was emboldened, along with union activist Jim McCoy, Livingstone Johnson, and, as Johnson described him, "a milk truck driver from up around Beltzhoover" named Charlie Harris, to form the United Negro Protest Committee—an attempt to coordinate the various pockets of Pittsburgh civil rights activism and channel them toward expansion of African American employment opportunities in downtown Pittsburgh. "It was to be an amorphous body," said Johnson, "so that if somebody said, 'OK, we're going to sue the United Negro Protest Committee,' they'd have nothing to sue." Also, Johnson noted, the Committee would be free to act without having to worry about the policies or trigger points of the national NAACP or the national Urban League. The Committee was designed to be a quick and aggressive force.[460]

Byrd Brown came up with the idea of targeting Duquesne Light Company. He told the Committee that, as a utility, Duquesne Light was "the perfect target" because it was "a virtual monopoly" that could be subject to government sanctions, by the Public Utility Commission for example, in a more direct way than other private corporations. Their headquarters building, at the corner of Sixth Avenue and William Penn Way, was a good location for a picket, and was strategically close to Mellon Square, where more supporters could gather.[461] Finally, it had a notably poor record of hiring African Americans: only fifty-four out of 3,700 Duquesne Light employees were African American, and approximately twenty-five of them were coal miners in the furthest southern reaches of Allegheny County; others served in janitorial positions.[462]

The Committee met with Duquesne Light on August 9 and announced its intention to start picketing Duquesne Light's headquarters on Monday morning, August 12. The group chose Livingstone Johnson to be the lead negotiator with Duquesne Light. Douglas Perrin, Duquesne's manager of employee relations, held one set of talks with Johnson, but they broke off on Friday without any agreement. A meeting for Monday was called off by the Committee, and around eleven o'clock on Monday morning, approximately 3,000 supporters of the United Negro Protest Committee encircled Duquesne Light's offices. Perrin asked if they could resume their discussions at nine in the morning on Tuesday, but Johnson insisted that they begin at six o'clock in the evening. On Tuesday, the crowds came again and marched outside the headquarters, singing "We Shall Overcome." The sheer number of them made it difficult for people to get in and out of the building, but a Duquesne Light spokesman insisted that the company would not be attempting to seek an injunction against the protestors. Nonetheless, at around two o'clock in the afternoon on Tuesday, Byrd Brown, Jim McCoy and Lain Lee, another organizer of the march, were arrested for using a loudspeaker. The crowd chanted, "We want Byrd Brown!" and "Let's All Go To Jail!" The three men were later released, and Johnson and Perrin made little progress in their meeting on Tuesday night. The demonstrations resumed on Wednesday and Thursday; and finally, on Thursday night, Johnson reached an agreement with the company, by which the company agreed to cooperate with local African American organizations on recruiting. The crowds persisted for four days, and Duquesne Light's president, Phil Fleger, admitted that it had "gone on long enough," according to Johnson.[463]

No sooner had the Committee concluded its agreement with Duquesne Light when Johnson received a call from an acquaintance who was the director of personnel at Equitable Gas. He told Johnson, "I don't think there is any need for the UNPC to have the demonstrators around our building down here on the Boulevard ... We're prepared to sign the same agreement that Doug Perrin and you just signed." Several other downtown businesses would also reach agreements with the UNPC over the course of further protests.[464] A few months later, Byrd Brown would say, "You cannot deny that the direct approach is correct. We have gotten more jobs in the last two months than we got in the last two years without demonstrations."[465] Nonetheless, the activist community went back to Duquesne Light in 1967 when the leaders felt that the company still had not done enough.[466]

A little less than two weeks after the end of the Duquesne Light protests, Byrd Brown accompanied other Pittsburgh leaders—including Arthur Edmunds of the Urban League, Molly Yard of the YWCA of Pittsburgh (subsequently, the president of the National Organization for Women), city councilman Jim Jordon, and Wendell Freeland's law partner Henry Smith, among others—on a specially chartered fifteen-car train to Washington to participate in the March for Jobs and Freedom. By train and in thirteen chartered buses, 1,100 people from Western Pennsylvania ("About sixty per cent ... Negro, about 40 per cent white," reported the *Post-Gazette*), joined two hundred thousand others from around the country to march from the Washington Monument to the Lincoln Memorial.[467] There, on the Mall, they listened to speeches all day.

Surprisingly, Brown was about to leave when King began to speak. TV stations across the country broke into their regular programming to broadcast King, who departed from his prepared text to tell the world:

> *I have a dream that one day this nation will rise up and live out the true meaning of its creed—we hold these truths to be self-evident: that all men are created equal ...*

"All of us just somehow turned around and crowded back to the podium," Brown remembered, "and by the time he was finished I was crying like a baby."[468]

The watershed moments of 1963 gave way to the reality that in Pittsburgh, as in most of the rest of the country, racial discrimination was still a reality. It was encouraging, at least, that Mayor Barr's administration, through the city solicitor, David Craig, decided to intercede on behalf of an African American physician, Oswald Nickens, who was denied the opportunity to buy a lot in a new development in Stanton Heights by the Stanton Land Company. Craig, a former partner with Moorhead & Knox, was mentored by Judge Homer Brown while serving as a clerk to the Court of Common Pleas at the beginning of his career. Gil Helwig of Reed Smith represented the developer, arguing that African Americans lowered property values, and that Pittsburgh's Fair Housing Law of 1957 was an unconstitutional violation of private property ownership rights. Craig was able to refute the property values "defense" with statistical information from the City Planning Department. In his November 30, 1963, decision, Judge Frederick Weir of the Court of Common Pleas held that the Fair Housing Law was a valid and constitutional exercise of the authority of the city council. "Segregation in housing," he wrote, "which was not envisioned as a proper concern of government in 1901, is now widely regarded as such ... A national poll need not be taken ... Ours is a republican form of government. It is only necessary that segregated housing be a serious social problem to invest the City Council with the right to deal with it in its own wisdom ... ."[469]

The diversity that the *Post-Gazette* observed in the Western Pennsylvania delegation in the March on Washington reflected the fact that, in Pittsburgh, the civil rights struggle of African Americans had become a multi-racial issue, and this was also evident within the bar. The examples set by the activism of the World War II generation of

African American lawyers provided inspiration for some young white lawyers who desired to channel their desire for social and political change through their profession.

R. Stanton "Tony" Wettick, Jr., the son of a steel company middle-manager, attended Amherst as an undergraduate and received his law degree from Yale in 1964. He was drawn to civil rights as a vocation while he was still in law school. He interviewed with the civil rights division of the U.S. Department of Justice. "That's where I wanted to work, but then it became fairly clear that they weren't going to get money" to fund a position for him. Instead, he ended up interviewing at Kirkpatrick, Pomeroy, Lockhart & Johnson, a firm inhabited by staunch Republicans. He was the first Democrat they ever hired, in fact, and the partners jokingly referred to him as "our little Communist"—but they were nonetheless extraordinarily tolerant of Wettick's political persuasions. When Tom Johnson's male secretary came around one day to collect donations for the Republican Party, Wettick protested, "I'm a Democrat!" The partners all had a good laugh over the fact that Johnson's secretary thought he was empowered to be so persistent.[470]

Shortly after he joined the firm, Wettick went to Judd Poffinberger, whom he perceived as the most liberal of the Kirkpatrick partners, and discussed the possibility that he might take a six-week unpaid leave of absence to work as a consultant on a "Head Start" early childhood education program in Mississippi through the U.S. Office of Economic Opportunity. Poffinberger came back to Wettick a little while later, saying, "Hutchinson wants to see you." Stuart Hutchinson, whom Wettick says was one of the most conservative of the Kirkpatrick partners, expressed some alarm over the fact that Wettick had a wife and family to support. "We voted you down," Hutchinson told him. "It has to be a *paid* leave of absence."[471]

Wettick left the firm after three years to become a full-time professor of law at the University of Pittsburgh Law School, but in 1968 he was quickly pressed into service by the ACLU to handle bail hearings during the riots in the aftermath of the assassination of Martin Luther King, Jr.

The night after Martin Luther King was murdered in Memphis, Tennessee, on April 5, over two hundred Pittsburgh black community leaders met at the Ebenezer Baptist Church, on Wylie Avenue at Devilliers—ostensibly to plan a memorial to King, but also to address the anger that was imminently boiling over in the African American community. Anti-white sentiment was running high even in the meeting, as the fair-skinned Wendell Freeland and a white staffer from the Urban League had trouble getting in the door. Once in the meeting, Freeland and Irvis resolved to call Governor Raymond P. Shafer and urge him to close the bars and liquor stores in Pittsburgh—Freeland as a fellow Republican, Irvis as a representative of the local Democratic leadership. Shafer demurred, saying he would not take any action unless Mayor Joseph Barr, a Democrat, called him to request it. Freeland knew that was unlikely to happen, due to the political divide between the two officials. While Irvis returned to speak to the meeting, Freeland left and walked down Devilliers to Centre Avenue, to a state liquor store on the corner. He saw the sales clerks there, nervously hunkering down, and he asked them, "Do you want to close up?" They told him they did. "Well, I just talked with the governor," he said. "Close up." Freeland laughed to recall the moment—it was true that he had spoken to the governor, but he certainly had no authority, from the governor or otherwise. Nonetheless, the clerks closed the store.[472]

Violence broke out in the Hill about an hour after Freeland's encounter at the liquor store. "Roving gangs of young Negroes in racial unrest," as the *Post-Gazette* described them,[473] worked their way up and down the streets of the Hill District, as well as in the Homewood-Brushton, Oakland, Hazelwood, Lawrenceville and Manchester sections of town, targeting white-owned businesses with vandalism, fire-bombing and looting over the course of almost eight days.

As Pittsburgh police, state troopers and National guardsmen tried to quell the riots, on Sunday afternoon, April 7, Byrd Brown attempted to lead an NAACP-sponsored march from Freedom Corner on the Hill to Point State Park. David Craig, the former city solicitor who was now serving as Mayor Barr's Director of Public Safety, was a friend of Brown's, but nonetheless interrupted the start of the march, stating that he could not "permit your safety and the safety of this city to be endangered." Although Craig had been under some pressure from downtown leaders to shut down the march entirely, fearing the spread of violence to downtown, after a half hour, when Craig determined that there were enough police available to guard the route, Craig announced over a bullhorn that the march could continue.[474]

During the heaviest days of rioting, amid suggestions that police should be given shoot-to-kill orders, Craig urged restraint on the part of the police. "Not a shot was fired by police that weekend," Craig recalled, although thousands were peacefully arrested. Craig also gave permission to counter-rioting youths to wear "red vests" and patrol the streets—a move which some critics called "crazy, saying it was tantamount to giving militants firearms," according to historian Michael Sean Snow, but which proved effective in stopping looters in Homewood. Later, Leroy Irvis toured the Hill with Governor Shafer, helping to reduce tension during the governor's visit to survey the area. "Pittsburgh officials' handling of the riots in 1968 demonstrated the power African-Americans had accumulated in just six years via their growing political network," wrote Snow; while "hundreds of people died" in riots in cities across the country following the death of King, only one person died in Pittsburgh.[475] In the aftermath, however, white-owned businesses never re-opened in the worst hit areas of the riots, leaving bombed out and abandoned storefronts in the Hill for decades.

Tony Wettick, meanwhile, was on call for the ACLU as the arrests from the riots mounted. Having no experience in criminal law, he slogged through bail hearings for a day, returning the next day as a veritable criminal law veteran accompanied by a "rookie," his former Kirkpatrick colleague Dick Thornburgh, who had introduced Wettick to the local ACLU. As Wettick worked side by side with lawyers from the Neighborhood Legal Services Association (NLSA), which had been founded by the County Bar Association in 1966 to provide the poor with access to subsidized legal representation, he quickly became appalled by what he perceived to be their substandard performance. Many of them, Wettick recalled, were part-time staff lawyers who had never spent any time in court before. "They were ineffective," he said, and some "were really bad."[476]

When the proceedings subsided, Wettick went to Tom White, assistant associate dean at Pitt Law School and the board president of the NLSA, and told him, "Tom, you have such a crappy program." A week later, White asked Wettick if he wanted to run the NLSA as executive director. Without blinking, Wettick told him he would, and in an instant, Wettick found himself in a position to set the course for the sleepy organization during an era in which progressive change had infected the zeitgeist.[477]

Wettick faced opposition to his vision of what the NLSA could be at the outset, however. "The Bar Association had a lot of control over who was on the board" of the NLSA, "and the board did not want" the NLSA "to do anything that was going to upset anyone," Wettick recalled. In Wettick's view, however, providing poor people with access to the law meant providing them with all of the tools of the law. Class action lawsuits, for example, could impact "thousands of people's lives" rather than simply trying to solve one individual's problem, and watching the same problems march into the office over and over again. Wettick essentially defied the NLSA board by bringing a class action lawsuit very early in his tenure. Soon he was faced with a complaint from a board member who said that there was a board resolution on the books that prohibited the NLSA from bringing a class action without board permission. "Boards don't practice law," Wettick told the member. "When I think that a class action is in the best interests of my client, that's what I'm going to do." The board member moved to censure Wettick, but the resolution narrowly lost. A follow-up resolution to rescind the motion also lost. "That's how divided we were," Wettick recalled.

New board members eventually tipped the balance of the NLSA in Wettick's favor, however, and Wettick soon had both the funding and a free hand to turn the Association into an activist organization. Two of the most controversial cases he personally handled during his tenure at NLSA were a case on abortion rights (in which the NLSA challenged, on behalf of several plaintiffs, the state's refusal to provide reimbursement for the cost of abortions under the Pennsylvania Medical Assistance Program) and school desegregation (in which the NLSA's clients alleged that school district reorganizations during the 1960s had resulted in de facto school segregation along racial lines, even though officially sanctioned school segregation in Pittsburgh had theoretically ended in 1875). "The funny thing is," Wettick said, "people accused the NLSA of casting plaintiffs for causes, saying, 'You went out and hustled these cases,'" but in both of these matters, the cases were brought to the NLSA by third parties. The abortion case, *Doe v. Wohlgemuth*, arose when two partners from a large downtown firm brought a plaintiff to Wettick's attention; and in the famous Woodland Hills school desegregation case, the matter came to the NLSA when Monsignor Charles Owen Rice, Pittsburgh's well-known "labor priest," took Wettick to lunch at the Press Club to push the matter on behalf of a beleaguered school administrator. The *Doe* case ultimately went before the U.S. Supreme Court as *Beal v. Doe*, in which the Court upheld abortion as a right, but refused to strike down Pennsylvania's restrictions. The Woodland Hills case, in which the Court ordered the formation of a new school district, went on for years, with federal jurisdiction over the district finally being lifted in 2000. Another civil rights class action eventually forced Allegheny County to build a new jail to address prisoner overcrowding.[478]

Wettick recruited for the NLSA while teaching part-time at Pitt Law, increasing the staff from sixteen lawyers when he arrived to seventy by the time he left in 1976.

The highly-publicized civil rights work that the NLSA did become attractive among the "long hairs" during the late 1960s and early 1970s, Wettick recalled. Other young, "long haired," white lawyers and law students, while sympathetic with the aims of the NLSA, charted a different course for themselves—even as they enjoyed partying with the like-minded NLSA staffers at the pool at the big mansion on Richland Place in Point Breeze where several NLSA attorneys were renting during the early 1970s.[479]

Passions that had previously been reserved for the civil rights cause spilled over to the peace movement as the U.S. involvement in the war in Vietnam escalated. In September 1969, the Weather Underground, a "militant" splinter from a national student protest organization called the Students for a Democratic Society, attempted to stage an anti-war protest at South Hills High School in Mt. Washington, sending fifty or sixty protesters to Pittsburgh to urge students to leave the school. Police arrested twenty-six women, all from out of town, on charges of inciting to riot and disorderly conduct—as well as, in two cases, assault and battery on a police officer. Harry Swanger, a former All-Ivy guard at Brown who later graduated from Duquesne Law School, agreed to represent them but, according to attorney Paul Boas, found himself to be *persona non grata* at his regular job shortly afterward as a result of his affiliation with the Weather Underground.[480]

Along with a group of Pitt Law students who were interested in social change, he decided to form, instead of a law firm, a "law collective" similar to other progressive law groups that were being formed in New York, Chicago and elsewhere. In the "Commune," as Boas now prefers to refer to it, decisions were made collectively, with consultation among lawyers, students and secretaries alike, as opposed to "the traditional elitism in law offices where secretaries are lesser human beings." Secretaries, in fact, might make more money in the Commune than a young single lawyer if they were supporting a family—each according to his or her need. Their office was above a pinball arcade, and the attorneys and law students typically wore jeans to work, while keeping a suit and a tie handy for court appearances. Each lawyer performed some area of what they called "shit work"—wills, divorces, real estate closings—to pay the bills while pursuing social justice through litigation, often on a pro bono basis. "In a landlord-tenant dispute, you represent the tenant; in a criminal case, you represent the defendant; in a labor matter, you represent the union. You represent the rank-and-filers against the union ... There's a right side of issues," Boas would explain. They often consulted with Hymen Schlesinger at the end of his career, and eventually took over some of what was left of his practice as he wound it down before his death in 1975.[481]

Len Sharon and Jim Logan were both Pitt Law students graduating in 1970, and they joined the Commune as lawyers; Boas graduated in 1972. Paul Boas' father, Edward, had been a lawyer, practicing with Markel & Markel in the Grant Building. Edward Boas died young, however, at the age of forty-two, when Paul was about five years old. He moved to Cleveland with his family before attending college at Tulane, studying political science and spending his free time "on the radical fringe." While Boas was in Louisiana, a prominent leader of the Student Nonviolent Coordinating Committee, H. Rap Brown, was arrested in Baton Rouge on charges of possessing firearms while under indictment (he had just previously been indicted for inciting a riot in Maryland).

William Kunstler, the famed "radical lawyer" who had defended the "Freedom Riders" in Mississippi and the comedian Lenny Bruce when he faced obscenity charges, had come to Louisiana to represent Brown. "I decided, 'I've got to see this,'" Boas remembered. "So I went to every minute of that trial, and when it was over I knew I wanted to become just like Bill Kunstler, a *movement* lawyer." [482]

Boas returned to Pittsburgh after graduation and entered Pitt Law School. Late in the evening on May 18, 1970, Boas was participating in a "National Draft Week" protest by standing in front of the home of a local draft board member in a silent vigil. After several attempts to break up the vigil, the police arrested twenty or so student protesters. By the morning the students had made phone calls to their supporters, so when Judge Robert Dauer convened their preliminary hearing, there were about fifty people in the courtroom, including Boas' brother Ken, just back from his honeymoon, who had come to make bail for his younger brother. During the hearing, one of the defendants, Cappy Ascheim, began to glare at one of the arresting officers, which inspired the court tipstaff to yank Cappy's pony tail violently, barking at him to "face forward." The spectators in the front row behind the defendants all jumped up and yelled, trying to call Judge Dauer's attention to what had happened. Judge Dauer interrupted them. "I've had enough of this," he said, instructing the officers to clear the courtroom of all spectators so that he could resume the hearing. While the spectators were in the anteroom outside the court, however, someone turned out the lights, and a melee ensued. "The next thing I know," Boas recalled, "they're dragging people through the courtroom, including my brother, with blood pouring down his head. It was a police riot—I mean, this was a nonviolent group of people. The police just exploded."[483]

Boas and the vigil defendants were acquitted, but five of the injured spectators—including Ken Boas—were charged with aggravated assault, resisting arrest and inciting a riot. The Commune reached out to William Kunstler, who agreed to come to Pittsburgh to represent the "Pittsburgh Five," so-named as an echo to Kunstler's other famous clients, the "Chicago Seven." Kunstler, with the Commune assisting, filed a "*Dombrowski v. Pfister*" claim on behalf of the defendants, a federal civil rights petition seeking to enjoin local prosecution, alleging that it was part of a pattern of harassment to deter the exercise of free speech. Although Kunstler had successfully argued such cases in the past, Judge Joseph Weis ruled against the Pittsburgh Five; according to Boas, Judge Weis allowed that he was "quite shaken" by the allegations, but that in this case, the plaintiffs had not met all the elements for the cause of action. Eventually, after the defendants were fined one hundred dollars for disorderly conduct, the charges against them were set aside.[484]

Gradually, by the end of the 1970s, what was left of the Commune became more like a traditional law firm, albeit a very "progressive, civil rights-oriented" firm, representing the same types of clients—including victims of police assaults, the Black Panthers, the United Farmworkers, an insurgent group within the Teamsters, and so on. Boas subsequently became best known as a criminal defense lawyer; Logan practiced independently as a plaintiff's employment lawyer; Swanger and Sharon both moved away.[485]

The NLSA, like other groups of its type around the country, may have been a victim of its own success. Its progressive run was interrupted in the mid-1970s as the federal government began to place restrictions on the activities of these federally-funded legal service providers. Ultimately, Wettick complained, they told these groups that "they can't do class actions, they can't do constitutional challenges, they can't represent a tenant in an eviction if the eviction's based on drug use." According to Wettick, the progressive mandate of the NLSA was being gutted. "Basically," he said, "they took away lawyers for poor people." He left the NLSA in 1976 when he was appointed to the Court of Common Pleas.[486]

Meanwhile, after the King riots, the "civil rights movement" in Pittsburgh seemed to begin to outpace the progressive outlook of the African American bar in speed and intensity. Byrd Brown, Wendell Freeland and the Johnson brothers and other lawyers continued to play their traditional leadership roles, especially in the older organizations such as the Urban League and the NAACP, but the "movement" was increasingly being conducted through ad hoc organizations led by students and non-professional laborers, members of the Nation of Islam, the Black Panthers, and the growing Black Power movement in general.

Another phenomenon was to have an even more significant impact on African American lawyers in Pittsburgh. New corridors of opportunity for young black lawyers in Pittsburgh were beginning to open.

In 1963, Duquesne Law School—then led by Dean Thomas Quinn—quietly hired Ronald R. Davenport, a young African American with a law degree from Temple and a Yale LL.M, to teach wills, property and criminal law. As a part-time NAACP staff attorney, while at Duquesne, Davenport wrote the brief in *Abernathy v. Alabama*, in which the U.S. Supreme Court ultimately overturned the convictions of certain "Freedom Riders" in Mississippi. In 1967, Thurgood Marshall joined the U.S. Supreme Court; and in that same year, when Dean Quinn delivered his resignation, two of Davenport's colleagues offered the thirty-one year-old's name as a candidate to be Quinn's replacement. The job instead went to fellow professor Lou Manderino, who served until 1970. Davenport succeeded Manderino in 1970, at age 35 becoming one of the youngest law school deans in the country, as well as the first African American dean of a major law school. One area of immediate focus for Davenport was increasing scholarship aid and making more opportunities available at the Law School for women and blacks.[487]

Other signs of a gradual climate change began to appear. Lawrence Moncrief, a 1962 Duquesne law graduate, was hired as assistant counsel to the H.K. Porter Company in 1970, breaking the corporate color barrier.[488] The following year, Eric Springer, an NYU Law graduate who had been hired by the University of Pittsburgh in 1965 as a joint faculty appointment in the Law School and the Graduate School of Public Health, co-founded a health and hospital law firm with John Horty and Clara Mattern—notable not only as an early successful foray into health care law as a specialty, but also as the first integrated downtown law partnership in Pittsburgh, with not only an African American and a white man, but a white woman, among its founding partners.[489] Martha Richards Conley, a Pitt Law graduate, became the first African American woman admitted to the Allegheny County bar in 1972, and two years later she was hired as a staffer in the labor arbitration department at U.S. Steel.[490] 1972 also saw two other significant milestones: Garland H. McAdoo, Jr., another Pitt Law graduate who, like Moncrief, had worked for a few years as an engineer before graduating from law school (in McAdoo's case, as a nuclear engineer for Westinghouse), was hired as a first-year associate by the downtown law firm of Tucker, Arensberg, Very & Ferguson—the same firm that had pioneered in the hiring of a woman lawyer when it hired Ella Graubart in 1934; and Thorp Reed & Armstrong, another established downtown firm, hired Glenn R. Mahone as a part-time clerk while Mahone completed his third year at Duquesne.[491]

Mahone likes to call himself an "accidental lawyer." "I didn't grow up dreaming to be a lawyer... It was sort of a means to a general end that I was looking for, which was being able to eat on a regular basis." Mahone was born in relatively impoverished circumstances, in rural Eastern Kentucky, and moved with his parents and seven siblings to New Kensington, an eastern suburb of Pittsburgh, when he was about five years old. Although moving to the Pittsburgh area meant that the next generation of Mahone children would not have to be coal miners, Mahone recalls that during the early 1960s, "there was no opportunity" in Pittsburgh for an ambitious young black man. "I don't think there were five black people in Pittsburgh that would be downtown every day with a suit on." He worked his way through Penn State, located in rural central Pennsylvania, which essentially meant that he had no access to the atmosphere of protest that existed in the big city. He studied psychology, hoping to go to medical school and become a psychiatrist. After college, however, looking for the quickest route to further opportunity, Mahone joined the Army and went to Vietnam, where he ultimately became a platoon leader for an engineering unit. Once again, he had effectively isolated himself from the civil rights movement by leaving the country, at a time when there was ambivalence in many young African Americans about joining the military and serving the nation that had failed to deliver on its promise of freedom. "I missed all that," he says.[492]

Although he still had it in his mind to return to the U.S. after his tour of duty and enter medical school, he saw an announcement that the Law School Admission Test (LSAT) would be given at a U.S. military base in Nha Trang, Vietnam, for a five dollar admission fee. On a whim, he signed up. "I was just looking for an opportunity, just looking for a door to open. I thought, let's see how that goes—maybe something will come of that. It only costs five bucks." As the test date grew nearer, Mahone was encamped at Pleiku, about two hundred miles away from Nha Trang, but fairly close to an Air Force base. Receiving permission to go to Nha Trang, he hitched rides on various Air Force cargo flights, flying in rainy weather during the monsoon season, finally entering the appointed location for the test—fifteen minutes late, in combat gear, "smelling like a goat, walking around looking like a mud turtle." He took the test, and promptly forgot about it.

Upon his discharge from the Army and return to Pittsburgh in August of 1970, without pausing, he went to visit a teacher on the University of Pittsburgh medical school faculty to talk about gaining admission. The teacher advised Mahone that he should work in a medical lab for a year and take some courses first, to ease his way back in to academic life. Mahone then started doing some math. He was twenty-five years old; if he waited a year before entering medical school, he would be thirty years old when he graduated, followed by a residency period. "I would be thirty-four years old before I started making any money. That's a long, long time," he thought. Seeking advice from another friend, a student counselor at Carnegie Mellon, Mahone's attention was turned to law school. Ron Davenport had just been named as the dean of Duquesne Law School. Before he knew it, Mahone says, he was being whisked over to meet with Davenport, and he was telling him about his LSAT score and other qualifications. His Carnegie Mellon friend said to Davenport, "I know you have at least one 'dean' admission in your pocket. I want you to give it" to Mahone. Davenport agreed that he would. Outside, Mahone said, "Wait a minute, I'm still thinking about medical school." "Do you want to do this or not?," his friend asked. "If not, I will call Davenport and tell him it was all a hoax." Eight days after having left Vietnam, Mahone was sitting in a law school class, embarking on the rest of his career.

Had he given his decision a little more thought, he admits, he might not have gone to law school at all. In August of 1970, there was little indication that a law degree would have given him anything more than an opportunity to practice law in a segregated "Negro bar" in Pittsburgh, perhaps picking up additional income as a part-time civil servant. "A recipe for starvation," Mahone observes. "I was looking at a timeline to revenue." As he awakened to that reality, he consoled himself by saying that law school would be a stepping stone. "I'll keep punching, I'll keep moving, doing the right thing, keep my nose clean ... whatever's out there, I'm going to break something off. ... I could not have, in that era, set myself up to say, 'I'll go here and these things will open for me.'"

He worked under Wettick at Neighborhood Legal Services for one summer, then served as an intern with Congressman John Heinz in Washington during his second summer. Then Garland McAdoo was hired at Tucker Arensberg, and Mahone was given an offer to work at Thorp Reed as a clerk during his third year. With the utmost diplomacy, Mahone observes that the firm was "not in readiness to hire an African American in Pittsburgh." However, Thorp Reed had opened an office in Detroit to help serve National Steel there, and the firm made an offer to Mahone to become an associate in Detroit after graduation.

"But for Reed Smith," Mahone says, "I would have gone to Detroit." John M. Duff, Jr., chairman of Reed Smith's New Associates Committee, spearheaded an effort to hire a black associate, at the forefront of a group several young partners who championed the idea within the firm, and he reached out to Ron Davenport for advice. Davenport recommended Mahone for the job. Once on board, Mahone says, "I was very fortunate. I had three or four, maybe five guys who either determined that I was smart enough to play or that they were going to help me to be smart enough to play. And I consistently got good work from them and good developmental experiences." Big law, the collection of law firms that Reed Smith was used to dealing with during the 1970s, was not altogether prepared for the presence of an African American lawyer in the room. Mahone laughingly recalls the first time he visited Sullivan & Cromwell in New York after negotiating a document over the phone with one of that firm's lawyers. When the lawyer came to the reception area looking for "Mr. Mahone from Reed Smith in Pittsburgh," he stared at Mahone, standing in the lobby in his blue suit—stared right through him—and said to the receptionist, "I thought you said Mr. Mahone was here." "It never occurred to him that I could be black. After all, Mahone is an Irish name."

After a couple of years at Reed Smith, Mahone decided to follow Davenport's advice and example by going to Yale and studying for his LL.M in corporate finance and taxation. Reed Smith encouraged him and gave him a small stipend as he moved to New Haven, with a promise that his job would be waiting for him when he returned.

As it happens, there was something else waiting for Glenn Mahone on the day he was moving back to Pittsburgh after completing his degree. In the early morning of Saturday, May 29, 1975, Mahone and his pregnant wife Andrea were driving in their car on East Street on the North Side, with his brother Harvey following behind in a rented U-Haul truck containing their furniture and belongings. Mahone, the former Army platoon leader, had timed their arrival in Pittsburgh specifically so that they could make an appointment at nine o'clock in the morning with the elevator at the Mahones' new apartment building. Driving through the North Side after a long night on the road, however, Harvey was pulled over by two Pittsburgh policemen, who accused him of tailgating their patrol car in the U-Haul. Glenn Mahone pulled over just ahead of them, and watched as the policemen, now accompanied by two other officers, hurled racial epithets and verbal abuse at his brother. He signaled to Harvey to stay in the truck and keep his cool—"Let's make our elevator appointment," he remembers thinking, "I'm going back to work on Monday." Impatient, Harvey got out of the truck to ask the first policeman what he was being charged with and how long it was going to take. Glenn and Andrea watched in horror as the policemen started to thrash Harvey with their "hands, fists, and nightsticks." "I got out just to keep him from getting killed," Mahone said, but soon he found himself under attack as well. Before long, they were handcuffed and thrown into the back of a police van. "We had done nothing," Mahone said. "No fool, no black man, would tail a police car."[493]

Mahone managed to fish out his last remaining Reed Smith business card and, in an instant, everything changed as he handed it to one of the officers. "Apparently he knew what Reed Smith was," remembered Mahone. "He says, 'Oh, shit!'" Immediately they uncuffed the brothers and announced that they would be taking them down to the station and charging them with traffic violations. Andrea called a friend of theirs, Wendell Freeland, who represented them in their preliminary hearing later that day. At the hearing, Freeland saw a high-ranking police official and told him that his clients were stopped by these particular police officers. The official told him, "No, it can't be *that* officer—he's one of the good ones. Now, these two *other* officers are the ones who are bad ..."[494]

Mahone returned to Reed Smith on Monday and went straight to see the managing partner, Robert Dodds, Jr. The two had previously bonded over the fact that Dodds was an Army platoon leader in World War II, and he had been very supportive of Mahone during his first years at Reed Smith. Mahone told him what had transpired over the weekend. Dodds responded that it was "disgraceful," and asked if he needed any assistance. Mahone—who had feared that such an incident, which was likely to attract press coverage, would be enough to cause the firm to question why it had hired an African American lawyer to begin with—told him that he was going to sue the city for civil rights violations, and that Wendell Freeland and Garland McAdoo would be representing him. Dodds replied, "Okay, we'll back you up 100%." Dodds sent for Gil Helwig—the Reed Smith trial lawyer who had fought against the city's Fair Housing Law on behalf of the Stanton Land Company twelve years earlier, and who was considered to be one of the most talented trial lawyers in the city. When Helwig, a former assistant district attorney, heard Mahone's story, he was outraged, and immediately joined Mahone's legal team.[495]

The Mahone brothers sued the city for damages on the grounds that they were deprived of their civil and constitutional rights, alleging that the city was directly liable for its "alleged negligence or wanton recklessness in failing to train and supervise the two individual defendants and in permitting them to act as police officers notwithstanding the City's prior knowledge of their propensity to harass and mistreat black citizens"—a reference to Freeland's conversation with the police official on the day of the Mahones' preliminary hearing. The federal District Court dismissed the claims on the basis of municipal immunity, but Freeland, McAdoo and Helwig won the case on appeal to the Third Circuit in *Mahone v. Waddle*, setting an important precedent for claims against municipalities based of the tortious acts of their police officers.[496] Their financial recovery was nominal in the end, but they had won a moral victory. However, Freeland later encountered one of the lawyers who represented the policemen, and told him he hoped they had learned something from it all. "Yeah," said the lawyer, "we learned something ... Don't beat up that guy at Reed Smith."[497]

The putative list of "black guys the police shouldn't beat up" was growing as African American lawyers began to achieve more downtown notoriety. Henry Smith was elected as a Common Pleas judge in 1969. Rose Schmidt had hired Leroy Irvis, and in 1977, Irvis was chosen by acclamation as the first African American speaker of the Pennsylvania House of Representatives—the first African American speaker of the House in any state legislature since Reconstruction. Livingstone Johnson was appointed to the Court of Common Pleas in 1973, and won re-election to a ten-year term. In 1978, Paul Simmons was appointed to the federal District Court by President Jimmy Carter. That same year, Berkman Ruslander hired Justin Johnson, and two years later he was appointed as a judge on the Pennsylvania Superior Court. Buchanan Ingersoll hired Ron Davenport in 1984.[498]

The judiciary became an especially important field for the advancement of African American women lawyers, providing them with higher visibility than they would receive within downtown law firms during the period. Doris Smith-Ribner served as an interim appointment to the Court of Common Pleas during 1984 and 1985, and in 1987 she began her twenty-two-year tenure on the Pennsylvania Commonwealth Court. In 1989, Cynthia Baldwin became the first black woman to be elected to the Court of Common Pleas in Allegheny County, and in 2006, she was appointed to serve on the Pennsylvania Supreme Court. As of this writing, Kim Berkeley Clark now serves on the Court of Common Pleas, and Cheryl Lynn Allen serves on the Pennsylvania Superior Court.[499]

Like the Negro Baseball Leagues of yore, the concept of a segregated Negro bar in Pittsburgh was beginning to thin out and fade away; and yet, the premises underlying police violence against black men, the social circumstances which the *Mahone* case fiercely demonstrated—the preternatural, ingrained fears and prejudices that drive a wedge between whites and blacks in Pittsburgh and elsewhere in America, whether violently or silently expressed—persisted even as the integration of the downtown bar was occurring with some speed in the 1970s and 1980s, and they still do persist. Asked if the "Negro bar" still existed in Pittsburgh in 2008, Wendell Freeland—still working, mostly as a sole practitioner at age eighty-three—was cleverly oblique. "I think there's still white firms and Negro lawyers."[500]

Brian Parker, an African American lawyer who served from 2011 to 2015 as the managing partner of the Pittsburgh office of McGuireWoods, an international law firm based in Richmond, began an address to the Second Annual Corporate Equity and Inclusion Roundtable in Pittsburgh in 2014 by observing that in 1993, when he started practicing law, there were four African American partners in the top twenty-five largest downtown Pittsburgh firms. "As I stand in front of you today," he observed, "there are still only four African American partners in the top 25 law firms" in Pittsburgh.[501] "We've gotten very good at recruiting African Americans," says James Barnes—an African American lawyer who served from 2007 to 2009 as managing partner of the Pittsburgh office of Reed Smith and subsequently practiced with Pepper Hamilton and Blank Rome in Pittsburgh—"but we've made no progress beyond getting African Americans in the door." Barnes maintains that, although he received excellent mentoring and was exposed to all the best opportunities to do complex corporate finance and securities work as an associate at Buchanan Ingersoll, many African American lawyers leave big firms within four years because of a more subtle form of racial discrimination, in that they do not receive the same opportunities for mentoring and participation as white recruits. "Some of them, coming from Harvard, Stanford, Yale—they are not used to failure," but year after year, Barnes says, they fall further and further behind. "It is a shame that there are only four African American partners in large law firms in Pittsburgh. I worry more about there being zero African American senior associates in large law firms in Pittsburgh."[502]

Mahone also laments the lack of progress. "There have been only two African American partners at Reed Smith in 40 years. How can that be?," he asked in 2014. However, Mahone cites forces that make it difficult to achieve progress. Competition for good work—everywhere, no matter what type, no matter the race or the status of the lawyer in question—has never been tougher than it is today, Mahone surmises. The prospects for an African American lawyer developing his or her own client business in Pittsburgh can also unfortunately be defined, sometimes, within racial boundaries; while Pittsburgh's African American business community is not insignificant, it is not as robust as similar communities in cities like Atlanta or Washington, D.C. Fortunately for Mahone, Barnes and Parker[1], the cache and reach of their law firm affiliations has given them the opportunity to develop business without regard to race, and indeed has provided them with the platform for generating good client business outside of Pittsburgh. Mahone further points out the difficulties he has seen over the years in developing the necessary relationships between white senior lawyers and younger lawyers of color; social occasions, such as going out to a bar after work or having dinner, generally advance working relationships between senior and junior lawyers,

---

[1] Parker has since moved to Charlotte, North Carolina.

but in the 1970s and early 1980s in Pittsburgh, whites and African Americans did not mingle much in public, which made this aspect of the mentoring process awkward.[503] Most of the overt obstacles to developing such social relationships have disappeared, but some of the awkwardness remains. The wedge still exists.

"What we've seen is frustrating for us," says David Blaner, the executive director of the Allegheny County Bar Association. Diversity has been an important mandate of the Bar Association at least since the late 1980s, he says, but he has seen too many situations in which African American lawyers in bigger firms get to a certain level and then are asked by their firms to accept a transfer to another city—often, a city where there is more diversity to begin with. Blaner says that often the Bar Association's diversity initiatives feel like "rolling a stone up the hill, only to have it slide back down on top [of you]." He argues that while the bar can be as good at the diversity game as it can be, "until the region embraces diversity, it's going to be very difficult to achieve those goals." "We're still committed," he says, "... but you will measure our progress in decades—not months, days or years."[504]

Decades for inches, then—not just years.

The bar's involvement in Pittsburgh's "protest era," the era of the 1960s and early 1970s, grew directly out of the emboldening tests and minor victories from the World War II era, and—although it would also spawn the beginnings of a broader progressive agenda through experiments such as Wettick's tenure at the NLSA and grass-roots phenomena such as the Pittsburgh Law Collective—it would be focused mainly on the unsettled relations between whites and blacks in Pittsburgh. As Martin Luther King and his activist counterparts within the bar of Pittsburgh—such as Irvis, Freeland, Brown and the Johnson brothers—were working towards expanding economic opportunity for African Americans during the "protest era," after its decline, "economic opportunity" would become a dominant narrative element for African American lawyers entering the Pittsburgh bar in the 1970s and 1980s. Initially, "economic opportunity" would be a slogan, cheering on the successes of young black lawyers breaking barriers in the downtown law firms, while later that slogan would become an apprehensively posed, open-ended question for blacks contemplating a career in the Pittsburgh bar, subsequently and perhaps for decades to come.

SELF-INFLICTED

On Friday evening, September 17, 1971, U.S. Deputy Attorney General Richard Kleindienst stood before a gathering of Pittsburgh Republicans at a swanky fifteen-dollar-a-plate fundraising dinner at the Hilton Hotel and grandly extolled the prosecutorial record of the incumbent Allegheny County District Attorney, whose reelection campaign was to benefit from the evening. Robert Duggan was running for his third term in office, and Kleindienst spoke glowingly of the "1,800 racket arrests" that had occurred under Duggan's watch during the previous eight years of his tenure as DA. Duggan wasted no time in returning the compliment, telling the crowd that "it took a long time to achieve an attorney general and a deputy attorney general" like John N. Mitchell and Richard Kleindienst—two men who restored law and order to the Department of Justice after eight years of Democratic administrations.[505]

Duggan and Kleindienst had a bit of a history. At the 1964 Republican National Convention, when Pittsburgh RNC member Elsie Hillman and Senator Hugh Scott, leaders of the moderate wing of the Party, were attempting to lead the Pennsylvania delegation to sing in unison for its favorite son, Governor William Scranton, for the Republican presidential nomination, Duggan broke from the establishment to support the conservative candidate and eventual nominee, Senator Barry Goldwater from Arizona.[506] Kleindienst was Goldwater's field manager in 1964.[507] In 1968, Duggan and his close friend and political protégé Richard Mellon Scaife, an heir to the billion-dollar Mellon bank fortune, had come out fiercely for Richard Nixon, while the moderate wing of the Pennsylvania Republicans, led by Scranton's successor, Governor Raymond P. Shafer, had supported Nelson Rockefeller for the presidential nomination.[508]

As the 1972 election approached, rumour had it that Kleindienst would soon be elevated to U.S. Attorney General, assuming that President Nixon's friend and confidant John Mitchell would resign in order to take the leadership of the Committee to Re-Elect the president. Duggan was a good soldier for Nixon, and Kleindienst made sure that Pittsburgh Republicans understood that. Meanwhile, as if to emphasize the point, Dick Thornburgh, the U.S. Attorney for the Western District of Pennsylvania who was appointed by President Nixon at the behest of the Hillman-Scott faction of the Pennsylvania Republican Party, did not receive a visit from Kleindienst on that trip.[509]

Within a few short years, however, President Nixon, Kleindienst, Mitchell and their lieutenants would all suffer a sharp decline in their fortunes, as would their friend Bob Duggan. Their shared fervor for "law and order," and their public support of a powerful federal apparatus for achieving "law and order," would emerge as tragic ironies in the stories of their downfall.

Bob Duggan came from a politically-active Irish Pittsburgh family that had built its fortune in ice. The patron, Thomas A. Dunn, had been in the ice business since the 1880s, and had served as the original general manager of the Consolidated Ice Company, Pittsburgh's largest supplier of ice back in the days when the only way to keep perishable food in Pittsburgh was in iceboxes, stocked with ice harvested from places such as Lake Chautauqua near Buffalo and brought by rail to the Strip District. Dunn eventually took over as the head of the multi-million dollar company.[510] He ran unsuccessfully as a Democrat for mayor of Pittsburgh in 1929, and served as one in a revolving-door parade of public safety directors under the mercurial Democratic mayor William McNair.[511] Bob Duggan's father, Frank Duggan, was Dunn's younger cousin, and Dunn had hired him as a messenger boy in 1900. Like Dunn before him, Frank Duggan eventually became president of Consolidated, while the company transitioned into the merchandise storage business as refrigeration ate into its market share. Frank Duggan served on city council, but as a Republican, and was for several years the president of the Chamber of Commerce of Pittsburgh. The Duggan family lived in moderate luxury, and they had a thirty-acre summer home in Ligonier.[512]

Bob Duggan was the youngest of Frank and Blanche Duggan's three sons. As Mellon family biographer Burton Hersh reported, Duggan used to turn up at the Scaife residence in Ligonier, trying to take out Dick Scaife's older sister Cordelia "when both were barely teen-agers," but Cordelia's mother, Sarah Mellon Scaife, would put a stop to it when she could. To her, said Joseph Hughes, a Mellon in-house lawyer, "Duggan was a little Catholic boy from down in the village."[513] Nonetheless, Duggan graduated from the prestigious Shadyside Academy, served in the Army Air Forces at the tail end of World War II, and came home after his father's death to attend the University of Pennsylvania for one year, followed by college and law school at Pitt. He entered the bar in 1951, and became associated with a small group of lawyers in the Frick Building.[514] In 1953, District Attorney James F. Malone, Jr., a Republican, hired Duggan as an assistant district attorney. The newspaper coverage trumpeted the young lawyer as "the son of the late Frank L. Duggan, former City Councilman and president of the Chamber of Commerce."[515] Malone, however, was beaten in his reelection bid in 1955 by the personable Democratic U.S. Attorney, Edward C. Boyle, a close friend of David L. Lawrence, and Duggan went back to full time private practice.[516]

Edward Boyle—a regular on the glad-handing Pittsburgh political banquet circuit, known for "wearing pinstripe suits, heavily-starched shirts, and polka-dot bow-ties," according to author Jim Fisher[517]—was popular enough as District Attorney to be re-elected in 1959 over Republican John V. Snee[518]; but by the time Boyle was up for his third term in 1963, he had acquired a reputation as being lazy, or, at worst, calculatedly indifferent to the activities of Pittsburgh's underground numbers racketeers. Fueling that reputation were two series of investigative reports published by the *Pittsburgh Post-Gazette*, the latter appearing in the month prior to the 1963 election, which dubbed him "Easy-Going Eddie." The articles cited the fact that while Malone and his County detectives, a force administered by the DA's office, made 1,402 rackets arrests during his four-year term, Boyle's crew had made only 120 arrests from 1956 to 1963.[519] A *Post-Gazette* reporter also monitored Boyle's arrivals and departures to and from the DA's office during a two one-month periods during late 1962 and early 1963 and found that Boyle was fond of rolling in between eleven in the morning and two in the afternoon, and departing at four in the afternoon, if he showed up at all.[520]

The police and a succession of DAs had been waging a half-hearted war against the numbers rackets since at least the 1920s, and public opinion had often been ambivalent, at best, about the laws against "numbers" gambling in Pittsburgh. The numbers racket, sometimes known as the "policy game," was essentially an underground lottery, in which a customer would choose a three-digit number from 000 to 999 on which to lay a bet with a local bookie, usually for a nickel or a dime. On the appointed day of the bet, customers and bookies would look to the newspaper for the last three digits of a number that was published on a daily basis, such as the exact total number of stock sales on the New York Stock Exchange. The game was "off-the-books," an opportunity for a steel town working man to make six hundred to one on a nickel bet, tax free. In Pittsburgh, bookies were often trusted local business owners—the fellow at the candy store, the grocer around the corner, or the guy at the newsstand or the tobacco shop—although in order to support winning bets, these bookies often became functionaries of numbers "bankers" who controlled larger territories within the city or the suburbs. Some numbers racketeers ploughed a portion of their riches back into the community, offering scholarships to local kids. Gus Greenlee, the Hill District numbers king, enriched the cultural life of African Americans and the Hill District considerably through his Crawford Grill nightclub and his Negro League baseball team, the Pittsburgh Crawfords, all funded in part by the numbers racket.[521] On the other hand, the numbers racket was seen by many community leaders as the engine that helped to drive a myriad of other illegal activities, from prostitution and pornography to money-laundering and political corruption.

With the newspaper attacks on Boyle's weak record against the numbers rackets becoming more pronounced, Wendell Freeland, another of Malone's former assistant district attorneys, observed, "It became obvious to the Republican Party that any clean cut, attractive lawyer could beat Boyle."[522] Aided by Scaife's financial support and Malone's political advice, Duggan maneuvered himself into the Republican nomination for District Attorney for the 1963 election. Duggan wasted no time in adding his voice to the chorus of criticism over Boyle's lack of interest in pursuing the rackets. Pointing to a gambling trial against Henry Katz and his associates that was going on during the campaign—one that had been propped up on evidence provided by federal, rather than local, law enforcement agents—Duggan said that the DA's failure to pursue charges of police corruption that could be based on evidence presented at that trial proved that Boyle was not "truly interested in cleaning up the county." "If a defense attorney," Duggan asked, "can bring this out in open court, why could not the district attorney's office have uncovered the same thing many months before it had access to the evidence?"[523]

Meanwhile, the Duggan campaign received an assist from newly inaugurated Republican governor William Scranton, David L. Lawrence's successor, who encouraged his state Attorney General to launch state police raids on suspected rackets in Allegheny County. On October 16, 1963, a few weeks before the election, the state police arrested over twenty people in numbers raids in Bridgeville, East Pittsburgh, Pitcairn and Rankin; and on that same day, the IRS arrested thirty-one people on income tax evasion charges relating to gambling income. A few days later, state police arrested sixty-two people in twenty or so locations on the North Side, the Hill District, and as Benjamin Hayllar notes, "to the embarrassment of city police and the district attorney, downtown clubs located a block from the Court House where Boyle had his offices." A reporter from the *Post-Gazette* was allowed to tag along for the arrests. Boyle, Mayor Joseph Barr and Philip Baskin, the Democratic Party campaign manager, all cried that the arrests were politically motivated, but the publicity over the arrests had the effect of suggesting to the electorate that Boyle had no intention of doing anything about crime that was almost literally taking place right underneath his nose. A few days later, Duggan demanded the launch of a grand jury probe to investigate city and County vice, a sentiment echoed by Scranton's Attorney General Walter Alessandroni, who stated that he was considering a grand jury probe "of serious breakdown in law enforcement in Allegheny County.[524]" Duggan, meanwhile, asserted that there would be no need for a grand jury probe if he were elected on November 5. "I am certain that under my administration it will never be necessary to turn to a grand jury for assistance in order to carry out the duties of my office," he declared.[525]

On November 6, the day after the election, the DA's race was considered too close to call, with Boyle maintaining a shrinking lead over Duggan with the votes of half of the districts counted.[526] Robert Duggan ultimately became the only Republican in Allegheny County that year to break through the hold of Lawrence's Democratic machine and its significant voter registration advantage, beating Boyle by more than twenty-seven thousand votes out of over half a million votes cast.[527] After his swearing-in in 1964, Duggan—a thirty-seven year-old bachelor—was named the "Young Republican of the Year" by the Allegheny County Republicans[528] and, much to the satisfaction of his friend Richard Scaife, was beginning to be touted as a potential future governor of Pennsylvania.[529]

The new District Attorney had carte blanche when it came to choosing his staff, so almost immediately after Duggan took office, a number of part-time assistant district attorneys, as well as some full-time County detectives, were handed their walking papers. Initially, Duggan appointed Louis Bowytz, a sixty-six year-old former assistant district attorney under Malone, as his "first assistant district attorney," and George W. Collitt, a former state trooper, as the head of the County detectives,[530] but after the fanfare of his inauguration passed, he made a few changes. Not long afterward he replaced Collitt with Robert Butzler, a colorful and highly-decorated Pittsburgh

Police lieutenant who gained fame in the 1950s working undercover for the Chicago Crime Commission.[m] Butzler was known for wild exploits, such as taking his police horse, Napoleon, up a building in an elevator, and kidnapping a suspect in Cleveland without obtaining extradition orders.[531]

Just as Butzler's swashbuckling style was a reflection of Duggan's own flashy persona—his snazzy suits; his "bandstand mannerisms," as Hersh described them[532]; his jet-setting lifestyle with his high-flying friends, Dick Scaife included—Duggan went in search of some vibrancy for his legal staff as well, and hired his cousin, Jimmy Dunn, to replace Bowytz in 1965. "We were out drinking one night in a bar in Shadyside ... the Hollywood Social Club, a very active after hours club on Walnut Street where the politicians all used to hang out," Dunn recalled. The Hollywood Social Club was the club that stars such as Bob Hope, Frank Sinatra and Sammy Davis, Jr. would visit while staying in Pittsburgh, as well as being a favorite among Pittsburgh celebrities such as Art Rooney. "I said to Duggan one night at three o'clock in the morning, 'What you need are some sharp young assistants.' He said to me, 'I don't think I could hire you, your father would go through the roof because I'm a Republican and you're a Democrat.'" The diminutive Dunn—Duggan's sartorial doppelgänger, his "mini-me"—was the grandson of Thomas A. Dunn, the Democratic patron of the family ice fortune; Jimmy's father, lawyer H. Stewart Dunn, had been a special assistant city solicitor and advisor to David Lawrence and Joseph Barr, and had succeeded Frank Duggan as president of the ice company after Duggan's father died. Jimmy's father had passed away in 1963, however; so putting party affiliations aside, Dunn became Duggan's first assistant district attorney, with full authority to hire and fire prosecutors and to act as general administrator of the work of the DA's office.[533]

Another early assistant DA hire made by the image-conscious Duggan, before the arrival of Jimmy Dunn, was a "medico-legal advisor" with degrees in both law and medicine—the brilliant, quirky, mercurial Cyril Wecht. Wecht's fraternity brother, Jim Morton from Buchanan Ingersoll, was active in the Republican Party, and he brokered the initial meeting between Duggan and Wecht, who was a Democrat. Dr. Wecht was a curiosity at the time, and Wecht himself admits that he made up his occupation all on his own. "Nobody really knew a goddamned thing about 'legal medicine'" in those days, Wecht recalls. His father, a lower Hill District grocer, had essentially told his son that he was going to become a physician, but during his undergraduate years at Pitt, he found himself so absorbed in leadership roles in numerous campus organizations (he served as president of the student body, president of his fraternity, a varsity debater, business manager of the *Pitt News*, concertmaster of the Pitt orchestra, etc.) that his classmates naturally assumed he must have been a pre-law student. His first real contact with the concept of a legal-medical expert was during medical school, when he went to a conference in New York, the first-ever co-sponsored by both the American Bar Association and the American Medical Association, where he briefly met Dr. Louis

---

m Butzler was the biological father of subsequent Allegheny County District Attorney Robert Colville. Butzler and Colville's mother were divorced when Colville was a toddler, and Colville never knew Butzler until much later.

Regan, a Los Angeles-based specialist in "legal medicine," a physician who had received an LL.B degree through a correspondence course after practicing medicine for a number of years. "That was dramatic," Wecht said; from then on, he was driven to carve out a niche in this new field, inventing his role without guidance from anyone "because there was nobody" who could speak with any authority on how the professions could be combined.[534]

Wecht ended up getting his medical degree from Pitt, served as an Air Force pathologist, and finished law school while simultaneously serving as a forensic pathologist for the chief medical examiner in Baltimore and as a pathologist at the Veterans Administration hospital in Pittsburgh (he ultimately ended up with legal degrees from both Pitt and the University of Maryland). After he entered the bar, he joined the firm of Litman & Litman, the husband-and-wife partnership of David and Roslyn Litman, while also serving as the acting chief of the lab service at the VA hospital.

Having Wecht on his staff undoubtedly catered to Duggan's desire to portray his office as new, modern, and impeccably ethical and scientific in its approach to crime; however, it wasn't long before Wecht and Duggan's egos jousted, and Dunn ended up firing Wecht, for what Dunn claimed was insubordination, in 1965.[535] Wecht, for the record, says he left after Duggan started calling him "Sonny," a name Wecht's family used to call him when he was growing up in the Hill District. "It became very nasty ... I referred to him as 'Dixie,'" Wecht said, after the comic strip heroine "Dixie Dugan," a fictional Hollywood showgirl/government secretary. "That was pretty biting."[536]

The staff of assistant district attorneys that Dunn did help to build, however, was a young, energetic and capable group that ultimately included at least four prominent future judges: Carol Los Mansmann, who later served as both federal District Court judge for the Western District of Pennsylvania (1982-85) and as a judge for the U.S. Court of Appeals for the Third Circuit (1985-2002); Robert "Bob" Cindrich, who served as U.S. Attorney for the Western District of Pennsylvania (1978-81) before his tenure as a federal judge in the same District; D. Michael "Mike" Fisher, who served as Pennsylvania Attorney General (1997-2003) and was appointed as a judge to U.S. Court of Appeals for the Third Circuit by President George W. Bush in 2003; and Terry McVerry, a federal District Court judge for the Western District of Pennsylvania (2002-13).[537]

Underneath the patina of swash and shine, however, the DA's office was hiding some rather disconcerting pockmarks.

First, after a brief honeymoon period during which the local newspapers recounted how Duggan's County detectives were working side-by-side with the state police on numbers raids, by 1967, the state troopers began to refuse to cooperate with the County detectives for fear that they were tipping off the targets.[538] Also in 1967, when information surfaced about the involvement of an assistant superintendent of the Pittsburgh Police, Lawrence Maloney, in taking protection bribes from numbers writers, Duggan indicted Maloney, but only after the statute of limitations had passed on bribery and extortion charges. The case against Maloney was summarily dismissed. Later, he would let similar charges grow stale against members of his own County detective staff when evidence of their alleged receipt of bribes surfaced in other criminal trials.[539]

There were also questions about Duggan's competence as an attorney, although they were not well-aired publicly until after his second re-election as District Attorney in 1971. In 1972 it was revealed publicly for the first time that Duggan's legal malpractice insurance had been cancelled by the Reliance Insurance Company just before he took office in 1964; an independent lawyer had investigated a number of lawsuits brought against Duggan in his role as a lawyer in private practice "and found his legal ability seriously wanting," according to Benjamin Hayllar.[540]

One of the areas in which a measure of Duggan's competence in the DA's office was laid bare was in his highly publicized campaign against "dirty movies" in Pittsburgh. In June 1965, Duggan ordered his detectives to raid five theatres showing a Jayne Mansfield movie called *Promises, Promises* in which, according to Duggan, Mansfield appeared "'ninety-nine' per cent nude." Judge David Olbum of the County Court of Common Pleas threw out the charges and barred Duggan from further interfering with the showing of the film on the basis that he had not first given the theatre owners a constitutionally-mandated hearing on whether the movie was obscene. Three years later, Duggan sent the detectives to raid the Guild Theatre on Murray Avenue in the Squirrel Hill section of the city, seizing the film *Therese & Isabelle*, based on a lesbian episode from Viollet-le-Duc's novel *Ravages*, but again was shot down on the grounds that no prior obscenity hearing had been conducted. Identical constitutional problems were raised in his attempted seizures of *The Female* (1969), *Rubber Anniversary* (1972), *Money Honey* (1972) and *Deep Throat* (1973). "If nothing else," Hayllar writes, "he was a very slow learner."[541]

Apart from his failed "dirty movie" crusade, Duggan showed poor attention to detail in other matters, such as personally failing to administer a *Miranda* rights warning appropriately during the interrogation of two murder suspects, leading to the overturning of their convictions in *Commonwealth v. Dixon* and *Commonwealth v. Kontos*[542]; presiding over the mass dismissal of 800 criminal cases by Judge Samuel Strauss in 1973 under a state Supreme Court rule that required such dismissal after two years of inactivity (which the clerk of courts, a fellow Republican named Robert Peirce, denounced as "a break for scofflaws")[543]; and charging twenty people with "surety of peace," an offense which, as Judge Henry Ellenbogen observed in dismissing the cases, had been declared unconstitutional. "I'm surprised the district attorney hasn't learned about it yet," Judge Ellenbogen said.[544]

Nevertheless, Duggan remained popular, and continued to have a reputation as a racket buster, despite the fact that he never really initiated the reforms he had promised during his first campaign against Edward Boyle. Over the course of his tenure, he shifted his rhetoric away from the rackets, suggesting that "kids" were the number one crime problem in Allegheny County, and he publicly downplayed the significance of the rackets, dismissing a state crime commission report that stated that the gross income from numbers rackets in the County was in the range of forty million dollars per year. The same report also suggested that some four to six million dollars of that revenue ended up in the hands of police and government officials as protection money. When asked if he would convene a special grand jury investigation of bribery and corruption, Duggan replied, "Absolutely not. What purpose would it serve? The grand jury isn't the panacea for all our problems."[545]

Meanwhile, after Duggan had given his conspicuous support to Richard M. Nixon during the 1968 Republican primary campaign, Nixon won election to the White House, beating Vice President Hubert Humphrey in a close race. The Republicans now held the presidency for the first time since the Eisenhower administration. Gustave Diamond had served as U.S. Attorney for the Western District of Pennsylvania since being appointed to the post by President Kennedy in 1963, but now President Nixon would have the opportunity to place a Republican in the position. Nixon's loyal supporter, Bob Duggan, put forward the name of his cousin, Jimmy Dunn, for the job. When Bob Duggan was elected president of the National District Attorneys Association, Jimmy Dunn came along as the recording secretary of the organization, and together Duggan and Dunn met local prosecutors from across the country. According to Dunn, sixty-seven of them joined in a petition supporting Dunn's candidacy to President Nixon. Senatorial privilege, however, was in the hands of the moderate Republican, Senator Hugh Scott, who had, along with Elsie Hillman, supported Rockefeller against Nixon in the primaries. "Scott and Hillman said no way," Dunn said.[546]

Instead, Scott and Hillman chose Dick Thornburgh, and President Nixon obliged. Lean, tall, bespectacled, and without a hint of flash or swagger, Thornburgh, thirty-seven years old at the time of his appointment, was a direct descendant of the *Mayflower* pilgrims through his mother's line. Prep school educated at Mercersburg Academy, Thornburgh was an undergraduate at Yale destined for a career in engineering, following in the footsteps of the elder Thornburgh men, until epiphanies—his discovery of his own love of language, for one, evident in his carefully constructed sentences and habitual use of brainy clichés and metaphors—led him to enroll in Pitt Law School. His first job out of law school in 1957 was working in the Alcoa legal department under Leon Hickman, but little more than a year later, after turning down an unsolicited job offer from the new Eckert Seamans firm, he accepted a position at Kirkpatrick, Pomeroy, Lockhart & Johnson. There he learned at the elbow of Thomas Pomeroy, a future justice on the Pennsylvania Supreme Court and an active member and president of both the state and local bar associations—although unlike Pomeroy, Thornburgh eventually evolved into a corporate finance lawyer. He had married his high school sweetheart, Virginia Hooten, during law school, and the two had three sons by 1960, when fate cruelly intervened: Virginia, with their three sons in the car, was involved in a terrible accident on the McArdle Roadway. Virginia was killed, and their youngest son Peter suffered a debilitating brain injury. While Thornburgh continued to practice with Kirkpatrick, his children were being raised by nurses until he met his second wife, Ginny Judson, at a colleague's wedding in 1963.[547]

In the model of Tom Pomeroy, Thornburgh was irresistibly drawn to bar activities, becoming intensely involved in the Junior Bar Section of the ACBA and gravitating toward issues involving legal services for the indigent, in the wake of the U.S. Supreme Court's landmark decision in *Gideon v. Wainwright* (1963)[548]. He worked with colleagues on securing legislation establishing a permanent public defender's office in Allegheny County and was one of the founding incorporators of the NLSA. "Frankly, I was spending far too much time on these activities," Thornburgh recalls, but they were a clue to his future interests in policy and politics. In 1964, with the nomination of Barry Goldwater for president, Thornburgh, the moderate—some would say "liberal"—Republican began to complain to his friends about how the right-wing was taking over the party. Two years later, Thornburgh ran for Congress against the popular incumbent Democrat, William S. Moorhead, Jr.—formerly a partner in his father's downtown firm, Moorhead & Knox—and was trounced. Bob Duggan had been one of his supporters. Nonetheless, his efforts were also noticed by Elsie Hillman, who put forth Thornburgh's name when Senator Scott asked her for potential U.S. Attorney candidates. Thornburgh notes that the Kirkpatrick firm was very supportive of his "extracurricular" activities within the bar and in politics throughout the 1960s, but he admits "I think they heaved a great sigh of relief when I finally ... became the U.S. Attorney." As an associate with the firm, he admits, "I really wasn't terribly productive."[549]

He walked into an office where he had a large trial docket and only nine assistants, so it was virtually required that Thornburgh would actually try cases. As Thornburgh wrote in his autobiography, *Where the Evidence Leads*:

To learn the litigation ropes, I had haunted the federal courtrooms for months. This made my assistants very nervous, as they thought I was monitoring their trial performance. In reality, I was learning where to stand in the courtroom and how to enter documents into evidence.[550]

However, Thornburgh says, "I had always had a desire to try cases ... and by the time I got through [as U.S. Attorney], I had tried a dozen or so cases. I was a pretty good trial lawyer by the time I was through."[551]

Nothing could really prepare Dick Thornburgh for what he learned during his early briefings by the Internal Revenue Service when he took office as U.S. Attorney, however. In 1969, undercover state troopers claimed that the new chief of the County detective bureau, Samuel G. Ferraro, had been receiving protection money from numbers writers, and was purportedly "attempting to gather a large amount of money ... to set up a numbers operation" which he could control after he left the bureau.[552] IRS agents informed Thornburgh that eleven members of the DA's County detective bureau had asserted their constitutional privilege against self-incrimination under the Fifth Amendment during an investigation by the IRS of allegations of bribes being made to Ferraro.[553] The swashbuckling Butzler had quit the bureau in 1966 to become chief of police of Ross Township, a northern suburb of Pittsburgh, and Ferraro was his hand-picked successor.[554] Now, with the heat of an IRS investigation breathing down his neck, Ferraro resigned from the bureau and accepted a position, which Thornburgh assumed had been created by Jimmy Dunn in his guise as solicitor of Hampton Township in the North Hills, as Hampton's first public safety director.[555] Thornburgh began to use his office's resources on the matter by preparing to bring the detectives before a federal grand jury on potential charges of obstruction of justice.

The U.S. Attorney's office issued subpoenas to the County detectives. On August 4, 1970, an agitated Duggan asked Thornburgh to meet him—in Duggan's private law office in the Frick Building to avoid reporters—protesting that Thornburgh should have given him advance notice before sending the subpoenas to his detectives. They sparred, but Thornburgh told him he would continue to pursue the matter. Duggan broke off the meeting, saying "We will just have to see where the investigation leads." Thornburgh agreed. As he departed, Thornburgh left a letter with Duggan about the status of the investigation, stating, "Mindful of your earlier request that I apprise you of any seeming wrongdoing by employees of your office, I am transmitting this information to you for such action as you may see fit." Thornburgh had hoped that Duggan would use the information "in cleaning up his own office"; however, as Thornburgh wrote, "No response was forthcoming."[556] The following week, a federal grand jury indicted Americo Picone, one of the County detectives, on perjury charges in connection with the IRS' investigation of Sam Ferraro.[557]

In 1970, Duggan and the DA's office were fresh from one very high-profile success in the case against Stanley B. Hoss, Jr.—a case that incidentally pitted Duggan against Thornburgh in both County and federal court over jurisdictional issues. Hoss, a twenty-six year-old from Tarentum, east of Pittsburgh, was being held in the Allegheny County Workhouse in Blawnox, awaiting sentencing for the rape of a seventeen year-old girl, when he and another prisoner escaped on September 11, 1969, using knotted bedsheets to go over the wall. Eight days later, armed and driving a stolen yellow Chevy, Hoss was approached by a Verona patrolman, Joseph P. Zanella, who ordered him out of the vehicle. Without turning, Hoss used his rear and side mirrors and aimed a small caliber pistol, also stolen, and mortally shot Zanella in the heart. Hoss fled the scene to nearby Lower Burrell, where he kidnapped a twenty year-old woman, stole her car, and drove to Wheeling, West Virginia. He let the woman go, but continued on to Western Maryland, where he kidnapped a twenty-one year-old woman, Linda Peugeot, and her two year-old daughter, Lori Mae. For the next few weeks, Hoss drove from town to town through the Midwest, committing armed robberies to fund his flight. After a nationwide manhunt, Hoss was arrested at a restaurant across from a police station in Waterloo, Iowa on October 4. The most hated man in the nation, at least for that month, had been captured, but Peugeot and her daughter were nowhere to be found.[558]

The FBI had hovered over the search for Stanley Hoss. The Bureau's mission had slowly changed over the years from providing technical assistance to local law enforcement before World War I to becoming the star of its own fifty-state law enforcement show, aided by decades of federal legislation that directly expanded the FBI's jurisdiction over crimes—from the Mann Act, to the Crimes Aboard Aircraft Act, to the Civil Rights Acts of the 1960s, to the Racketeer Influenced and Corrupt Organizations Act (RICO). Still led by the publicity-conscious J. Edgar Hoover, the FBI took over the case in Iowa. Hoss confessed to FBI agents that he had shot Zanella, that he shot Linda Peugeot somewhere along the line, and that several days later he suffocated and shot Peugeot's daughter Lori Mae. He was stubbornly vague and self-contradictory, however, about where he disposed of the Peugeots' bodies.[559] Duggan, meanwhile, was focused on bringing Hoss back to Pittsburgh—first, to face sentencing on the rape charge, and then to stand trial on the murder of Patrolman Zanella. When Hoss was brought back to Western Pennsylvania, to the Allegheny County Airport in West Mifflin, Duggan attempted to gain custody of Hoss immediately, but Hoss was spirited away by federal marshals.[560] After heated encounters between Duggan and the feds, Hoss landed in the Western

Penitentiary, and was subsequently sentenced by Judge Robert Van der Voort to ten-to-twenty years on the rape conviction.[561]

The FBI was still convinced that they could get Hoss to tell them where he left the bodies of the Peugeots. Thus, under orders from Hoover, Dick Thornburgh, the rookie U.S. Attorney, presented a petition in Common Pleas Court before Judge Van der Voort to have Hoss released into the custody of the FBI so that Hoss could lead them to the bodies. Duggan demanded that the search party include members of the County detective bureau, but when the FBI declined to permit it, Judge Van der Voort ruled against Thornburgh's petition. Near midnight on the next day, Thornburgh quietly obtained an order signed by federal District Court Judge Wallace Gourley for Hoss' release to the FBI. During the pre-dawn darkness of October 17, Hoss was snatched out of the Western Penitentiary by the FBI and taken to Ohio, where it was presumed Linda Peugeot had been killed. As the news of Hoss' release became public, Judge Van der Voort issued an order that Hoss be returned, then issued an order for the FBI to show cause why they should not be held in contempt for violating his original order. Hoss was returned to the Western Penitentiary to await trial on the murder of Patrolman Zanella.[562]

Duggan assigned the Zanella murder trial to an assistant, Edward "Ted" Fagan—a Duquesne Law graduate, and a grizzled, somewhat humorless veteran of the County prosecution staff, a holdover from the Boyle years—and a junior assistant, Don Minahan. Hoss, having no money, was to be represented by the County public defender's office, and there the case was assigned to a twenty-nine year-old, two-year veteran of the office, Edgar Snyder, assisted by his colleague Fred Baxter. Snyder, years before he would become famous in Western Pennsylvania as a TV law firm pitch-man, threw himself passionately into the unpopular cause, despite receiving death threat letters and having his car's windshield shot out one evening by an anonymous gunman who apparently was no fan of Hoss.[563] At the trial in March 1970 before Judge Samuel Strauss, Fagan brought in fifty-two witnesses, including an FBI agent who had heard Hoss' confessions, and Dr. Cyril Wecht, who by this time was now serving in his first term as the elected County Coroner—achieving some notoriety outside of Pittsburgh for his consultations on the Robert Kennedy assassination investigation, the Manson Family/Tate-LaBianca murders, and the investigation of the death of Mary Jo Kopechne in an auto accident with Senator Ted Kennedy at the wheel near Chappaquiddick, Massachusetts.

After Fagan rested the prosecution's case, Snyder announced that the defense also rested its case, without introducing any evidence or testimony. In his closing argument, with a bulldog's determination, Snyder spent more than an hour picking apart the circumstantial nature of the state's case. Fagan delivered a fifteen-minute summation, and the jury deliberated for three hours before returning its guilty verdict. The next day, Hoss was sentenced to death. The penalty was reduced to life imprisonment on appeal.[564]

The bodies of Linda Peugeot and her young daughter were never found. While serving his life sentence, Hoss stabbed another inmate and was later convicted of murdering a prison guard. On December 6, 1978, Hoss was found dead, hanging from the neck by a blue shoelace, a suicide note nearby.[565] Edgar Snyder, however, never accepted the ruling that he took his own life. "He was not capable of committing suicide," Snyder asserts. "He was capable of killing, or being killed."[566]

The lawyers, at least, did well by the whole wretched Hoss affair. "That case gave me fame," said Snyder. Despite being on the losing side, it established him "as a young lawyer who everybody knew," and affirmed his reputation as a cagey, aggressive trial lawyer.[567] Meanwhile, Duggan was able to bask in the glow of a success—he and his staff fought with the federal government and won, avenged the death of a policeman, and put away a monster who had terrorized Western Pennsylvania. Even with the first public indications that something was wrong in the County detective bureau with the conviction of Detective Picone in January, in the 1971 election, Duggan achieved a somewhat narrow re-election victory over Democratic candidate Leonard Martino, whom Duggan had insinuated was affiliated with Pittsburgh organized crime.[568] Pointing to the allegedly poor record of the DA's office on reform and other matters, however, Hayllar argues: "The news media, perhaps in part, because of their early support of his candidacy, did almost no investigation of his legal abilities, his cases, or his administration of office."[569] Without a groundswell of vocal criticism, Duggan was set to enjoy a third term as District Attorney and possibly an opportunity to seek higher office.

Perhaps the only public figure in Pittsburgh to voice any complaints about Duggan at the time was Dr. Cyril Wecht. In October 1971, just before the election, Wecht publicly announced that he was requesting a federal and state investigation of the District Attorney's office and, in the interests of objectivity, an investigation of his own office as County coroner. Wecht noted, in particular, his concern that Duggan's arrest of three Jewish physicians at Magee Women's Hospital on charges of performing illegal abortions reflected "Duggan's anti-Jewish attitude." He went on to say that "many allegations have been made by responsible officials that organized crime could not flourish and operate to the extent and magnitude that it does without the knowledge and complicity of some public officials and law enforcement agents." "Ho hum," Duggan replied for publication. "It's that time of the month again, you know—there was a full moon two days ago—and that's really more than I want to say about him," Duggan said, referring to Wecht. The *Pittsburgh Press*, in reporting on Wecht's announcement, noted that "Thornburgh already is investigating the county detective bureau."[570] In general, however, the press at this stage treated Wecht's public jibes at Duggan, and Duggan's bitter rejoinders, as nothing more than partisan jabs, or, at worst, a personal conflict being played out in public. As Hayllar reports, the opening line of a *Post-Gazette* piece in 1972 read, sardonically, "District Attorney Robert W. Duggan, a Republican, and Dr. Cyril Wecht, Allegheny County Coroner and Democrat, yesterday engaged in vituperation at 40 paces. This time the continuing feud revolved around testimony at a coroner's hearing Wednesday ..."[571]

Wecht had no way of actually knowing that the net of Thornburgh and the IRS was already closing in on Duggan.

The "nickel-and-dime prosecution" of Detective Picone, as Thornburgh himself referred to it, was meant to send a message to the other "Fifth Amendment" County detectives that the U.S. Attorney's office had no intention of letting up on them.[572] Using the newly enacted Organized Crime Control Act of 1970, Thornburgh next decided to compel testimony from the other detectives based on the condition that none of their testimony could be used against them in a criminal proceeding. Detective James Hockenberry was compelled to testify before the grand jury, but denied receiving protection payments or having any knowledge of payoffs. In January 1972, Hockenberry was convicted of having lied to the grand jury, based on the testimony of a Turtle Creek numbers writer, Charles Navish, who said that he was forced to pay $1,500 per week to Sam Ferraro, and that Hockenberry was the bag man.[573]

At that point, the newspapers began to sit up and taken notice. After a third detective was indicted on perjury charges in March 1972, the *Post-Gazette* published an editorial entitled "Conspiracy of Silence," highlighting the fact that Duggan had failed to comment publicly on the conviction of Hockenberry or the new indictment. "Why," asked the editorial staff, "has Mr. Duggan undertaken no investigation of his detectives' refusal to cooperate with federal officials? Why has Mr. Duggan not pursued the serious implications under Pennsylvania criminal law of the testimony concerning payoffs to Mr. Ferraro?... It is especially damaging to the public's confidence in the honesty and competence of the District Attorney's office when these same detectives have as their job the conducting of investigations into the sensitive area of organized crime."[574] Under pressure from the press, Ferraro was relieved of his Hampton public safety post the following month. Duggan's response, rather, was directed privately at Thornburgh, and it amounted to the words "I said stonewall this thing," as Thornburgh recalled.[575] "We kept getting calls from Washington, from Mitchell's people," Thornburgh told Hersh. "Kleindienst was their closest contact, Scaife and Duggan were talking to him."[576] Nonetheless, Thornburgh moved on to build their case against Ferraro.

Unfortunately for Ferraro, and ultimately for Duggan, Thornburgh managed to obtain some help from an unlikely source: Pittsburgh numbers king Tony Grosso. Anthony Grosso, age fifty-eight, was, according to reporter Paul Maryniak, "Horatio Alger from the wrong side of the tracks." Cutting a swath in silk suits while at the same time putting forth "the image of a confused and barely literate immigrant" (even though he was born within walking distance of the Courthouse on Grant Street), Grosso had been playing cat-and-mouse games with law enforcement since the 1930s while reputedly building his Pittsburgh numbers business into a twenty-five million dollar a year concern employing over five thousand people, suspected to be one of the largest underground criminal franchises in the country.[577] When he was arrested on a federal gambling charge in 1964, Grosso wasted no time in offering testimony against one of the police officials he had bribed, assistant police superintendent Lawrence Maloney—the same official whom Duggan had failed to prosecute on local bribery charges until after the statute of limitations had run. However, Grosso's testimony that he had paid $250,000 in bribes to Maloney did not result in Maloney's conviction on federal charges, either—a U.S. tax judge said that it was likely that Maloney "was merely a conduit through which funds passed to others," while Grosso appealed his conviction and won a landmark Supreme Court ruling against the constitutionality of the so-called federal "gambling tax," thereby avoiding jail time.[578] In 1972, however, Thornburgh managed to secure Grosso's conviction on racketeering charges based on court-approved wiretaps, a relatively new law enforcement tool made possible by the passage of the Omnibus Crime Control and Safe Streets Act of 1968 (also known as the "Wiretap Act").[579] True to form, just after he began to serve his ten-year prison sentence in Lewisburg Penitentiary in January 1973, Grosso offered to help the U.S. Attorney's office with the Ferraro case.[580]

On February 13, 1973, Sam Ferraro was indicted for income tax fraud stemming from his failure to include twenty-thousand dollars in illegal payoffs from racketeers from 1966 to 1968. With additional information from Grosso, Thornburgh's office managed to obtain a superseding indictment of Ferraro in August 1973 claiming that Ferraro had received over $289,000 in unreported income, including payoffs of $4,950 per month over a six-year period from Grosso for the "protection" of his numbers empire, as well as an additional count under the Organized Crime Control Act of 1970 alleging a conspiracy to obstruct law enforcement.[581] Meanwhile, the IRS went public with its investigation of Duggan when he was ordered to present the records of his real estate title company, Abstracts, Inc., to a grand jury in July 1973. The *Post-Gazette* said that the District Attorney "cooled his heels in a waiting room at the Federal Courthouse ... while a federal grand jury opened a tax investigation of his business activities."[582] By this time, of course, Mitchell, Kleindienst and the rest of the Nixon administration were busy with their own problems. Kleindienst, who had become U.S. Attorney General in June 1972, resigned on April 30, 1973.[n] That same day, Nixon aides H.R. Haldeman and John Ehrlichman resigned, and White House counsel John Dean was fired, after U.S. Attorneys alerted Nixon that they had evidence of Haldeman, Ehrlichman, Mitchell and Dean's involvement in the Watergate affair. There would be no more heat coming from Washington over Thornburgh's investigations into the affairs of the County detectives or Duggan himself.

While the IRS built its case on Duggan, Thornburgh concentrated on the Ferraro trial. One of Gustave Diamond's former assistants in the U.S. Attorney's office, Samuel Reich—the prosecutor who had secured a conviction against Tony Grosso in 1964 that was later overturned, and who had tendered Grosso as a witness in the federal trial of Lawrence Maloney—represented Ferraro in the trial before federal Judge Hubert Teitelbaum. Thornburgh took the lead for the prosectiuon. Chuck Navish, the Turtle Creek numbers writer who was the star witness in the Hockenberry trial, came back to the witness stand in the Ferraro trial, essentially repeating his testimony, followed by Detective Hockenberry himself, who not only substantiated Navish's testimony, but told how he delivered envelopes filled with cash directly to Ferraro.[583]

The "main attraction," however, as Thornburgh recalled, was the appearance of Tony Grosso, "[h]is Florida tan ... diminished by the hospitality of Lewisburg to a sallow pallor." He testified that he had met Ferraro through Robert Butzler, the former County detective chief, and confirmed that he paid $4,950 per month to Ferraro for protection. On cross-examination, Reich asked Grosso when his payments to Ferraro began, and

---

n   Kleindienst would later plead guilty to "failing to fully testify" in a matter related to Nixon's ITT campaign contribution scandal. His 30-day sentence was suspended, and he returned to Arizona to private practice. Ann T. Keene, "Kleindienst, Richard G.," American National Biography Online, accessed March 10, 2017, http://anb.org/articles/07/07-00730.html.

Grosso answered that they began in June 1966. "How do you know that it was then?'" Reich asked. "Butzler was leaving the county detectives division. After he left, he took me to Sam Ferraro ... I only carried over what Butzler had assessed." Grosso went on to confirm that he had paid Butzler for protection for a few years, beginning from the time that Duggan had appointed him as the chief of the County detectives.[o] Although Reich proceeded to try to undermine Grosso's credibility as a witness with questions about his past misdeeds and admitted perjury, but Thornburgh said the effect was "somewhat disingenuous ... as [Reich] had utilized Grosso as his principal witness" in the unsuccessful prosecution of Maloney.[584]

In his closing argument, Thornburgh pointed at Ferraro and charged, "This man is living a lie. He has been living a lie since he joined the Racket Squad in 1965. He has been living the lie of a law enforcement officer who has betrayed his badge, betrayed his fellow police officers, and betrayed the society he was hired to protect." He concluded, "You have heard from this very witness stand, from the depths of the troubled predicament and shattered career of Jim Hockenberry, that you can only live a lie so long. That time is up for Sam Ferraro. That lie is finished." The jury received the case at half past three in the afternoon on November 1, 1973, and by noon the next day had returned a guilty verdict on all six counts. Judge Teitelbaum sentenced Ferraro to a thirty thousand dollar fine and six years in prison.[585]

Having secured Ferraro's conviction, Thornburgh hoped that Ferraro would turn and testify as to the greater details of the bribery scheme, but at least initially Ferraro remained silent. Going back to the well of the 1970 Act, Thornburgh attempted to compel Ferraro to testify to a grand jury on a promise of immunity from prosecution, but Ferraro would not budge, and he was held for contempt in the Washington County jail. Then federal agents took Ferraro on an uncomfortable odyssey in the course of transferring him from Washington County to a Florida prison camp—depositing him, in a series of one-night stays, in various rural Southern jails for three weeks, forcing him, as Hayllar writes, "to spend the night with drunks, unwholesome street criminals, and it was inferred, black people." According to one reporter, it was Ferraro's prison odyssey that broke him down. Asked by Hayllar if that was a strategy of the U.S. Attorney, Thornburgh pleaded ignorance but did not deny that prison gave Ferraro a change of heart.[586]

Meanwhile, even before the Ferraro indictments, Thornburgh and the IRS had been undertaking a painstaking review of Duggan's finances, pursuing what they termed to be a "net worth" case against Duggan by comparing his holdings and his spending against his relatively meager income from his position as District Attorney ($20,400 a year) and from what remained from his private practice. Even given the fact that Duggan had received a $250,000 fee for serving as a co-executor of the estate of Sarah Mellon Scaife, who died in 1965, Thornburgh would assert that Duggan's expenditures on his lavish lifestyle were far outpacing any reasonable tally of what he could be earning from legal activities. He had grown the family's summer home, Bell

---

o   Butzler was never prosecuted, despite Grosso's revelations; the statute of limitations was the likely impediment.

Acres, from a thirty-acre spread into a 240-acre estate, called Lochnoc Farm, in what IRS Special Agent Keith Hyatt, in a November 1973 summary report on the Duggan investigation, characterized as "an exclusive area of private estates, country and hunt clubs known as the Rolling Rock area of Ligonier ... the exclusive and private domain of several of the wealthiest families in the United States." Hyatt also stated that "Duggan has allegedly cultivated his taste for mingling with the Rolling Rock gentry since adolescence." He hired a groundskeeper to live at Lochnoc, owned three cars and kept a private chauffer.[587]

In addition to Lochnoc Farm, Duggan kept a high-end apartment in the King Edward Building on Bayard Avenue in Pittsburgh, had purchased a seaside condominium, with boat access, at The Billows in Naples, Florida, and a thirty-one-foot Chris Craft Sedan Cruiser. He had memberships in the Duquesne Club, the Pittsburgh Field Club, the Pittsburgh Athletic Association, "and in various hunt and country clubs" in Ligonier, as well as the Royal Poinciana Country Club and the Country Club of Naples, Florida, and the Sea View Country Club in Absecon, New Jersey. Upon further investigation, he had expanded the Farm with cash purchases of land, paid his personal assistants in cash, bought his boat with cash, and bought his Florida condo with a check drawn on an Abstracts, Inc. bank account which, as further investigation revealed, had received regular cash deposits until right about the time Sam Ferraro left the County detective bureau in April 1970.[588] Duggan's travel "was so frequent," wrote Thornburgh, "that he became known as an 'absentee prosecutor.'"[589] Chuck Watkins, another assistant district attorney, subsequently a founder of the firms of McClure & Watkins and Barnes Dulac, recalled that Duggan almost never came to the office. "I think I saw him twice, professionally, in four years," he recalled.[590]

While Thornburgh felt fairly secure about the "net worth" case against Duggan, his office developed concerns about the extent to which his friends, siblings Dick and Cordelia Scaife, might have extended their own fortunes to Duggan for his use.[591] As Hersh reports, in September 1971, government agents sent Cliff Jones, an executive of the Manufacturers Association of Pennsylvania and a state Republican leader, to present the case for Duggan's misconduct to Dick Scaife. "He showed me police records," Scaife said. "Suddenly it all made sense." Scaife, who had been treasurer of Duggan's latest re-election campaign, remembered being handed an envelope with $9,900 in fifty and one hundred dollar bills, coincidentally exactly twice what Grosso would later testify paying to Ferraro for protection, accompanied by a memo from Duggan saying that the cash was from staff members and that he would supply the names later. The whole exchange was beginning to make Scaife uneasy, and, as he would point out, "By then Bob Duggan was spending money, as my grandmother used to say, like a drunken sailor ... He used the death of my mother to explain all this," Scaife said. Scaife had already confronted Duggan at a lunch at the Duquesne Club. "Well," Duggan said, "I see they've finally gotten to you." Scaife told Hersh, "I said, 'If you mean the good guys, the noncorrupt politicians of the world, yes.'" Duggan asked him if he had told his sister Cordelia, and Scaife said he hadn't. "Tell me that you won't tell her," Duggan asked him. Scaife said he wouldn't as long as she didn't become involved. Duggan resigned as a trustee of Scaife's Allegheny Foundation and Scaife resigned as

Duggan's campaign treasurer. By the time Jones came to present the full case to Dick Scaife, Scaife and Duggan had already broken their ties.[592]

With Cordelia, such was not the case. Dick Scaife thought of Duggan as his de facto "brother-in-law," as he and Cordelia had been "dating" for years. Cordelia had been married, very briefly, to Herbert May, Jr., in 1949, although no one knew that they had divorced until May's second marriage was announced to the press. Cordelia was sent by the family to hide in Palm Beach, Florida, for a while, but eventually she and Duggan began to see each other again. Duggan was especially understanding and helpful as Cordelia struggled to conquer her alcoholism, as Hersh details. "I think he was the most wonderful human being I ever met, out of a fairly large acquaintance," she told Hersh. During her drinking bouts, she said, "Bob was so hopeful, so positive. He'd say, that's why pencils have erasers."[593]

On August 27, 1973, the IRS initiated contact with Cordelia Scaife's personal attorney, former U.S. Attorney D. Malcolm Anderson, about arranging an interview with Miss Scaife concerning financial matters relating to Robert Duggan, and Anderson agreed to schedule the interview for September 6, 1973. On the appointed date, Anderson asked to reschedule, to September 20. On the 20th, however, Anderson showed up unaccompanied. Anderson told Thornburgh that a few days before their first scheduled appointment, Duggan appeared in Anderson's office and stated that he did not want his "wife" to testify before the IRS. He stated that he and Cordelia Scaife had been married on August 29 in Tahoe County, Nevada, before a justice of the peace. Anderson went on to state, however, that it was "highly improbable" that Cordelia Scaife could be the source of any "cash hoard" to explain the increases in Duggan's assets.[594]

By the time news of the marriage of one of America's wealthiest heiresses to Duggan had hit the press in November, Dick Scaife had hit the roof, and it apparently caused a rift between the two siblings that took years to heal. Cordelia, however, remained loyal to Duggan and steadfast about her spur-of-the-moment decision. "I had been determined not to become a politician's wife," she told Hersh. "He asked me to marry him I don't know how many times ... But by then efforts were being made to portray Bob as a homosexual."[p] Hersh writes that Cordelia "insists that her unexpected marriage to Duggan became inevitable just then, a gesture of confidence."[595] Thornburgh was

---

p   Robert Duggan's sexual orientation has been a matter of considerable commentary, although there is not much evidence to suggest that Duggan's "enemies" were about to reveal any information publicly at that time. Cyril Wecht says "it was already out that he was a homosexual" during the 1960s—a well-known secret, and part of the subtext underlying the popularity of Duggan's nickname, "Dixie." Dr. Cyril H. Wecht, interview by the author, May 27, 2014. Mellon family biographer David Koskoff writes, "Quiet rumor named him as the silent backer of one of Pittsburgh's better known gay clubs." David Koskoff, *The Mellons: The Chronicle of America's Richest Family* (New York: Thomas Y. Crowell Co., 1979), 538. Maryniak treats Duggan's alleged underground lifestyle as a narrative of hypocrisy. "[W]hile trumpeting the raids on filth," Maryniak writes, "Duggan was leading a queer private life ... In certain Pittsburgh and Florida bars that catered to closet gays, and on special occasions in Westmoreland County where he actually resided, Duggan dressed in women's clothes and hosted sexual orgies for elite men friends." Maryniak, *Liar's Poker*, 77. Hersh states that "Thornburgh, tracing evidence, cites nothing to substantiate the imputations of homosexuality," and they certainly were not relevant to Thornburgh's case against Duggan. Hersh, *Mellon Family*, 548. Oddly enough, the only published first-hand confirmation of overt behavior on Duggan's part comes from Dick Scaife himself, who told Hersh about an incident in 1969 when Duggan was

able to solve the puzzle without the testimony of Cordelia Scaife, by getting a subpoena for Cordelia's financial records in the possession of her accountant.[596]

After the Ferraro conviction, the heat was on Duggan. Both the *Press* and the *Post-Gazette* were scathing. "Just what is it going to take to convince District Attorney Robert W. Duggan that all has not been on the up-and-up in the County detective bureau that is a part of its office," wrote the *Press* editorial staff. Until he prosecutes graft-takers "within his own official family," the *Press* continued, "the district attorney cannot expect to be regarded as a very credible guardian of law and order in Allegheny County."[597] The *Post-Gazette* asked, pointedly, "Did all the money end in Mr. Ferraro's hands, or was he just a conduit for at least part of it? If so, where did the money go?"[598] Furthermore, in January 1974, the state crime commission released a report on fundraising irregularities in connection with Duggan's 1971 re-election campaign, charging that he had failed to report over thirty-six thousand dollars that was illegally "maced" (i.e., extracted, almost as a tithe) from 177 employees of the DA's office and parked in an undisclosed campaign account in the Potter branch of the Pittsburgh National Bank.[599] "Macing" employees had apparently been a quietly persistent, although illegal, tradition in county government for years under both Democratic and Republican administrations (Livingstone Johnson recalls experiencing it while he served as assistant County solicitor[600]), and assistant district attorneys generally knew about the practice in Duggan's office, referred to as Duggan's "Flower Fund." Bob Cindrich remembered that he was questioned about the Fund. "They said, 'Were you coerced?,' and I said, 'No.' I guess what they couldn't grasp is that if you work in a place, you shouldn't be there unless you had at least some sense of loyalty to it ... Politics was different then."[601]

On February 24, Duggan took to the airwaves for an interview with Bob Sprague and Don Cannon on WTAE's *Close-Up* program. He claimed that the DA's office had been conducting its own investigation of the County detectives all along, and charged that Thornburgh was motivated by personal political aspirations. "[B]y making charges against another individual it does give you publicity ... perhaps being a product of the political climate that Mr. Thornburgh is, he has perhaps—he has other aspirations and this is one way to get the necessary publicity."[602] Two days later, Pennsylvania Attorney General Israel Packel informed Duggan by letter that charges would be pursued against him on the campaign financing violations.[603]

By March, Ferraro had made a full statement to the U.S. Attorney's office that, as Thornburgh writes, "the racket payoff money had, in fact, been paid over to Duggan," and that he would tell that to a grand jury. Thornburgh called Duggan's counsel, James E. McLaughlin, on Monday, March 4, 1974, and told him that he expected to seek the indictment of his client on the following morning. McLaughlin later confirmed to Thornburgh that he conveyed the message to Duggan, who was nonetheless seen around five thirty that night, in high spirits, joking with colleagues in his office downtown. On Tuesday, March 5, Ferraro gave his testimony to the grand jury, and at

---

too drunk to get to his bedroom on his own, and that Duggan kissed Scaife as Scaife was putting him to bed. "At the time I thought the guy was, just, you know, being friends," Scaife said. Hersh, *Mellon Family*, 544.

eleven o'clock in the morning, the grand jury returned an eight-count indictment of Duggan on tax evasion charges stemming from unreported income received through the bribery scheme.[604]

Thornburgh returned from the federal courtroom to his office, where a press conference had been scheduled to announce the indictment. Reporters and TV crews stood nearby, awaiting Thornburgh's statement. A few minutes later, Thornburgh received shocking news. The moment was captured by an AP photographer, and the look on Thornburgh's face could not have revealed him to be any more blankly, any more gravely stunned.[605]

Cyril Wecht parked his car that day in his reserved parking space on the Third Avenue side of the stone, fortress-like building where the County morgue was located. He recalls:

> *I came up the back steps, as always, to see what the bodies were and talk with the pathologist on duty ... and they say, 'Oh, we have Duggan on a table' ... Well, you know, those are the kind of jokes that you tell. ... I said, 'Sure, sure, sure,' and then—there he is.*[606]

No one, apparently, had heard the shot.[607] Duggan's groundskeeper, Floyd Hoffer, found Duggan's body near a split-rail fence on Lochnoc, and alerted state police around ten o'clock in the morning; the Westmoreland County coroner's office received a call at ten forty-five, and the news began to spread. Jimmy Dunn rushed out to Ligonier with the new chief of detectives, John Stack.[608]

Hoffer and Duggan had spoken by phone that morning, and Duggan had indicated that he wanted to inspect a small dam on the property that was being damaged by muskrats. Duggan was wearing "outdoor clothes" and ear plugs. A twelve-gauge shotgun, its right barrel emptied, was found between seven and ten feet from the body. The mortal wound was to Duggan's chest. Cordelia later made the official identification of Duggan's body. They had spent their "usual weekend together," Hersh wrote, and then Duggan returned to Pittsburgh. She called him Monday evening. "We talked of the future. He was worried, but not to the point of being really depressed ... ."[609]

The Westmoreland County coroner sought assistance from Wecht, who performed the autopsy with Dr. Galicano Inguito, a pathologist from the Westmoreland County coroner's office. He noted powder burns on Duggan's clothes and skin, and that the impact area on Duggan's body was not much larger than the diameter of the right barrel of the shotgun, all of which indicated a close-range shot. Also, the left barrel left an imprint on his skin. From trigger to muzzle, the shotgun measured 28-3/4"—short enough that a man of Duggan's height could have used the gun to fire it into his own heart. Wecht's conclusion was that it was a self-inflicted wound, but that it was impossible to say whether the shot was intentional or accidental. The Westmoreland County coroner marked his official conclusion as "undetermined."[610]

Bob Cindrich observes that a shotgun "would not be the weapon of choice" if you were going to shoot yourself. "The proper way to take a firearm through a fence—you learn in the Army, you learn when you're a hunter," Cindrich says, "you put the firearm across, then you cross the fence. You don't try to carry the firearm while you're stepping over or climbing over the fence, because that's how you get killed." Having seen him in an upbeat mood only a few days before his death, Cindrich tends to believe that Duggan's death might have been an accident, more so than he would believe it to be a suicide.[611] To this day, however, Wecht—notoriously contrarian, never shy about taking the side of the conspiracy theorists, as he did in criticizing the Warren Commission report or reaching conclusions about the death of JonBenet Ramsey—remains steadfast in his opinions. Even the local officials, he says, "the state police, they agreed—they knew damned well it was a f—king suicide."[612]

Wecht laughs, somewhat squeamishly, that it should have fallen to him to be the judge, after so much acrimony between the two men. "I mean, this has got to be made up, right? Who the f—k would make up this?"[613]

"I never believed that" he shot himself, Jimmy Dunn says. "I still don't ... I just don't think, knowing the person as I knew him, that he would've committed suicide." As to the many conspiracy theories that have circulated over the years, Dunn remains mum. "You could say Bugs Bunny and I wouldn't say anything," Dunn says—although, when asked about the theory that the mob killed him to prevent him from talking, Dunn says quietly, "I've heard that, but I don't know."[614]

Thornburgh later wrote: "Many of his friends and admirers were unable to accept the notion that he was a crook and they cast about feverishly for some other explanation of his demise. No evidence ever came to light, however, to indicate that it was anything other than a suicide."[615] It is not hard to see how a man might rather take himself out than to live through the disclosure of all his worst secrets, even if he were not guilty of the crimes of which he was being accused.

Jimmy Dunn, as Duggan's first assistant, was named acting District Attorney by the Common Pleas judges until a month later, when the judges reconvened and chose Jack Hickton, a former deputy County solicitor, as the new District Attorney.[616] Thornburgh's investigation, resulting effectively in the indictment of a dead man, was also dead. Nevertheless, the indictment hung out there, in the late winter air of Downtown Pittsburgh, like an unfinished declarative sentence, an admonishment without punctuation. Cindrich remarks, "It caused a great deal of bitterness among those of us who were supporters of Bob. Because he never had a trial, we don't know if he was guilty of anything."[617] Meanwhile, local TV news reports simultaneously covered Duggan's death, Thornburgh's case on Duggan, the "Flower Fund" allegations in Harrisburg, and later, Duggan's elaborate and well-attended funeral at St. Paul's Cathedral in Oakland.

KDKA anchorman Bill Burns intoned, on the noon news, on March 5, 1974, "It would not be letting the cat out of the bag to say that Mr. Thornburgh and Mr. Duggan were political enemies."[618] It was not the first time that local television news pointed its cameras at the house burning down but missed the story. True, the "Young Republican of the Year" for 1964 would not be elected governor of Pennsylvania; and Dick Thornburgh *was* elected governor, just four years later. They were both Republicans, however, members of a party under siege nationally as the Watergate dominoes tumbled toward President Nixon's resignation in disgrace five months after Duggan's death. In the broader partisan context, Thornburgh had no good reason to damage the reputation of his own party any further; but as Duggan had all but challenged him to do, Thornburgh pushed on to see where the investigation would lead.

Maeve Victoria Geddis, a Democrat whose tenure as an assistant district attorney straddled the Boyle and the Duggan administrations, knew Bob Duggan in law school and worked with the same group of attorneys with whom Duggan worked as a lawyer in private practice. Asked about Duggan's downfall, she says, "I thought it was all a political thing, frankly"—while at the same time noting that people in the DA's office during previous administrations were known to take money from racketeers. "It was accepted—this was how you dealt with" them, she says.[619] Her point of view seems to echo that of Bob Cindrich, also a Democrat, when he says, in broad observation, that "Politics was different then."[620] It is important to understand that neither Geddis nor Cindrich, by any stretch of the imagination, could be held out as condoning this corruption, but as junior functionaries during a bygone era, their observations consist of the facts of political life as it once existed in Pittsburgh. Even Thornburgh acknowledges that the behaviors he scrutinized in his investigations were endemic in the status quo of city and County politics, not simply limited to the personality, frailties and predilections of one District Attorney. "Back in Dave Lawrence's day, the Democratic organization was half politicians and half racketeers—and everybody was happy." He recognizes that some variation of what he purportedly uncovered in Duggan's office may have been going on for decades. "It was kind of an emolument of office ... It was the way the system worked."[621]

The Duggan affair occurred at a time when the old way of politics was already on the ropes. David L. Lawrence, the former mayor of Pittsburgh and governor of Pennsylvania, died of a massive stroke he suffered at a campaign rally on the eve of the 1966 election. In 1969, another one of Eddie Boyle's assistant DAs, Pete Flaherty, beat the Democratic machine candidate, Judge Harry Kramer, to achieve the Democratic nomination on his way to getting elected as mayor. A revolution was occurring. Even the numbers racket itself, ironically, was set for decline as an institution, with the passage of the Pennsylvania Lottery Act in 1971, creating a legal alternative to the underground sweepstakes. The machine was winding down at the same time that Thornburgh, as U.S. Attorney, showed up with the mightiest arsenal of weapons theretofore available to federal law enforcement officials—the ability to compel testimony under immunity, a new federal wiretap statute, the RICO Act. As Jimmy Dunn notes, "The feds and the locals never got along," but acknowledges that during the 1960s and 70s, the tension between the two became worse because of the increased power of the federal government and the intense scrutiny the feds directed toward local government.[622]

Just as the steel barons of the early twentieth century and their lawyers found themselves, by degrees, immersed within the jurisdiction of federal courts applying new federal laws regarding labor-management relations and the concentration of monopoly power, the bosses and municipal officials of Pittsburgh found themselves being told that the old way of running things would not apply, that Pittsburgh would be held to a national standard of good government, rather than a local one. The Duggan affair may indeed have been, as one contemporary lawyer put it, "a sorry episode ... a kind of F. Scott Fitzgerald type story" involving "the rich and powerful, the politically ambitious, and the guy from the wrong side of the tracks." It was also, however, a story about the aftermath of the Progressive era, the continued growing preeminence of federal laws and a federalized bar that persists through today, and about methods and templates that were even being turned on the White House itself during a period of self-examination and loss of confidence, during a season of self-infliction.

BACKWARDS AND IN HIGH HEELS

Clifford Fergus was the assistant cashier at Mellon Bank—a higher position than it sounds. He was prominent as a manager of Mellon's foreign desk and also served, in his spare time, as the treasurer of the University of Pittsburgh. One day in 1941, Fergus invited prominent partners from the two largest law firms in Pittsburgh to lunch. Fergus asked John Buchanan, a senior partner of the Smith Buchanan firm, if he would serve as preceptor to his daughter, Nellie, who was then attending Pitt Law School. Buchanan declined on the grounds that his partners would not be receptive to the idea of having a woman lawyer in their midst.

Robert J. Dodds, Sr., a senior partner of Reed Smith, was also at the table. Known for his negotiating prowess, he was not used to finding himself backed into a corner, but after Buchanan declined Fergus' request, that is exactly where Dodds was. Not only was Mellon Bank an important client of Reed Smith, but Dodds could not make the claim that his partners would be unreceptive to having a woman lawyer. In 1940, Dodds' own daughter, Agnes, served her six-month required pre-admission clerkship with Reed Smith, and his partners were actually a bit surprised when Agnes declined to stay with the firm once she passed the bar. Dodds was not especially fond of the idea that his own daughter had chosen to enter the profession, but he reluctantly agreed to take Nellie on during her preceptorship.[623]

Nellie Fergus, Clifford and Annie Fergus' oldest child, grew up in the suburb of Mt. Lebanon and was the valedictorian of her high school class. She went to Mount Holyoke College, showing up for her first day of classes with a black eye from a fishing accident. She met her future husband, Templeton "Temp" Smith, a Harvard student and also a future Pittsburgh lawyer, while in college. Remembering her during those days, Smith wrote that Nellie "was good looking, athletic for a girl though fragile, brighter than she realized, diligent and self-disciplined almost beyond belief, and basically qualified to be almost anything she wanted to be." After winning a debate in high school, Nellie's teacher told her she would make a good lawyer, which she "filed away for future reference"; but immediately after college, she considered going into social work, and applied to the social work school at Pitt. Just before the term was to begin, however, she confided to her father that she wished she had applied to the law school instead. While meeting with John Gabbert Bowman, the chancellor of the University, Bowman asked Clifford Fergus how his daughter was faring. He told Bowman that she was going to start her studies in the social work school but she regretted not applying to law school. "Two days later Nellie got a letter from Bowman stating that she had been accepted at the Law School and enclosing an application form," wrote Smith. "She later observed, 'I think the Chancellor wanted to see a woman go to law school.' Being a good Presbyterian, she felt this must be what's to be."[624]

It was not just divine providence that landed Nellie in law school. With the onset of World War II, the University of Pittsburgh Law School implemented a number of changes designed to make it easier for men called to service in the armed forces to complete their degrees. In May 1941, in response to war clouds on the horizon, the School changed its academic year from two semesters followed by a summer break, to a year-round, four-quarter term, resulting in the ability of a law student to attain a degree in two years rather than three. By 1942, it became apparent to the new dean, Judson Crane, that the supply of male law students was running low, and the University made an extra effort to support the admission of more women to law school classes. "They welcomed you with open arms" in order to offset the loss of revenue, recalls Elizabeth Bailey, who took a Contracts course with Nellie Fergus at Pitt during the summer of 1943. In that course, there were three women and no men.[625] Nonetheless, Crane had a habit of telling ribald stories to the men in his classes, and he refused to edit himself simply because there were now more women around. When some of the male students put Nellie up to complaining to Dean Crane about his jokes, Crane replied, "Miss Fergus, you must remember that this is not Mt. Holyoke female seminary."[626] Fergus finished her degree in two years, graduating in a relatively small class of thirty students, four of whom were women. There had been forty-five students in the class of 1942, three of whom were women. Fifty-three men who had entered the Law School with Nellie in 1941 had interrupted their studies for the War. The class of 1944 consisted of just seven graduates, three of whom were women. At Pitt Law School during the War, women had gone from being seven percent of the graduating class, to being forty-three percent of the graduating class.[627]

One of the other women who graduated from Pitt Law during the War was Jane Schanfarber Strassburger, the wife of Eugene B. Strassburger, Jr., and eventually the mother of Judge Eugene B. "Gene" Strassburger III and E.J. Strassburger, the subsequent head of the Strassburger McKenna firm. Jane's father and aunt were practicing attorneys in Columbus, Ohio, and while Eugene, Jr., was finishing law school at Harvard and subsequently entering service with the U.S. Navy, Jane was studying law at Ohio State. A classmate of hers later told Gene Strassburger that his mother was taking law school exams while she was pregnant with him, and had a nurse stationed outside the exam room, "just in case." Ultimately, Jane obtained her law degree at Pitt in 1943, and shortly thereafter approached her husband's father, Eugene Strassburger, Sr., the co-founder of

Strassburger McKenna, asking if she could come to work with the family firm while her husband was away in the service. According to E.J. Strassburger, his grandfather answered "Absolutely not! How would that look? It would make it look like my son couldn't support his family." Jane Strassburger unfortunately never had another opportunity to practice law.[628]

Meanwhile, when Nellie Fergus showed up in the offices of Reed Smith to begin her pre-admission clerkship in 1943, she recalled that Robert Dodds seemed surprised to see her. It had been two years since he had agreed to be her preceptor. "I guess he probably had not told his partners that he had taken on a woman," she surmised. While it had not been customary for Pittsburgh law firms to pay their clerks, the big New York firms had just begun to do so. A month into the clerkship, one of Fergus' male colleagues, Jack Smith, told Fergus "that he thought I ought to know he had been paid." Fergus went straight to Dodds' office and said, "Mr. Dodds, how come Jack Smith was paid and I wasn't?" Fergus remembered:

He turned red in the face and asked "Who told you?" I said "Never mind who told me; I want to be paid" and I walked out the door before he could say anything more. I was paid by the end of the day. Margaret Vance, who ran the office at that point and had charge of the payroll, kept me advised from then on I was even with the men in pay scale.[629]

Fergus was assigned to a desk in the library, initially, with all of the other clerks, and eventually ended up with her own office when she was invited to stay on after her admission to the bar. One item of standard furnishing she could never get used to were the water-filled spittoons that lined the aisles of the library and that were installed under the desks in each office.[630] "When I first got my own office," Fergus remembered, "there was one under my desk which I was continually forgetting about and kicking and the water would spill all over things ... They were disgusting things which weren't kept clean." Reed Smith did not have a women's restroom at that time, either—despite the fact that there were "55 or so" women secretaries and bookkeepers working in the firm, yet there were two men's restrooms on the 7th Floor of the Union Trust Building. The women had become accustomed to taking the elevator to another floor of the building to find a restroom. One day, one of the older women on the staff fainted, and William Seifert instructed some of the other women to take her to the lady's room. Fergus told him, "Mr. Seifert, there is no lady's room." Seifert was somewhat stunned, and perhaps a little embarrassed that he did not know it. "Within a week," Fergus recalled, "we had a ladies' room at Reed Smith."[631]

Elizabeth Bailey's route to entering the profession was more circuitous. Her father was a principal at Oliver High School, and after receiving her bachelor's degree from the University of Pittsburgh in 1941, Bailey followed her father into education, teaching English and History to eighth graders in West View. When the War was on, she took the summer Contracts course at Pitt to see how she would like the law. She liked it, but incurred the wrath of Dean Crane when she returned to teaching in the Fall; Crane wanted full-time students, not dilettantes. She recalled that Crane had not liked her much, anyway. The other two women in the class "were much better looking than me," she asserted, but she received the best test scores. Bailey then enrolled in the Duquesne Law School night school program—teaching by day, going to law school classes every weeknight from 5 to 7 p.m. When she needed to find her preceptor, Bailey's father called on one of his former teachers at Oliver High School, attorney James C. Tallant. After entering the bar in 1948, Bailey quit teaching and joined a title company for a time, but ended up joining Tallant's practice in the Law & Finance Building as a full-time legal secretary.[632]

Bailey might have remained a legal secretary for the rest of her career, were it not for a phone call she received from a woman in California sometime in the early 1950s. "I don't know how she found me," Bailey says, speculating she must have seen Bailey's name in a list of members of the bar. Eleanor Buckner had been married to a sailor, Kenneth Eastman, at sixteen, and had two children. In 1948, Kenneth and Eleanor separated, and Eastman took the couple's six year-old son, Lawrence, to live with the daughter of Robert and Leona Barr, who ended up taking custody of the boy in Pittsburgh. Robert Barr was the brother of Joseph Barr, then a Pennsylvania state senator and head of the Pennsylvania Democratic Party who would later become mayor of Pittsburgh. Bailey suspects that Eleanor Buckner was specifically looking for a woman attorney. In any event, Bailey won custody of the boy for her client in Common Pleas Court, but Barr's attorneys appealed the order to the Superior Court, which also ruled in favor of Eleanor Buckner. The Barrs appealed again to the Supreme Court of Pennsylvania, and Bailey enlisted aid from Regis Nairn, a former B-17 navigator during World War II, former County police detective and Duquesne Law night school graduate, to prepare for the argument. Bailey won the case again before the Supreme Court, with the Court noting that Bailey's client had actively sought custody of the child during the whole time the Barrs had the boy, and that the Barrs "may not successfully contend that their custody should continue because of the length of time during which their affections have widened and deepened, where they have been instrumental in prolonging final decision of the court." Thereafter, Bailey was in demand as a lawyer on adoption cases, although much of her practice later became involved in estate and Orphans' Court matters.[633]

For a number of years, Tallant maintained a "night hours" office in Murrysville, just over the Allegheny County line in Westmoreland County. Many downtown Pittsburgh lawyers gained a significant middle-class, suburban clientele through the opening of night-time practices in the suburbs around Pittsburgh during those years: David Fawcett, Jr., of Dickie McCamey kept a night-time practice in Verona, near his hometown of Oakmont, for example; David Litman had one in his hometown of Braddock; Joseph J. Pass, Jr., of the Jubelirer firm had one in Kennedy Township; and Edgar Snyder kept one in Duquesne, near the Duquesne Steel Works and the Dorothy 6 blast furnace.[634] In 1978, Tallant closed his downtown office and moved his practice to his nighttime office in Murrysville. Bailey followed him. Tallant's wife Lucille passed away in 1983; and after Tallant retired, Bailey, who never married, became Tallant's caretaker, moving into his house in 1992 ("I needed someplace to live and he needed help," she explains) and seeing to it that he had in-home care, rather than having him placed in a nursing home, until he died in 1994. Meanwhile, Bailey took over Tallant's practice, and became

Murrysville's favorite lawyer, practicing law well into her nineties while also practicing yoga and Tai Chi, and playing in a Thursday morning golf league during the warmer months.[635] Giving an address to the Allegheny County Bar Association on the sixtieth anniversary of her admission to the bar in 2008, she told the fifty-year honorees, "To all of you young men who have been practicing law for only 50 years, the next 10 years are the best."[636]

Nellie Fergus, meanwhile, left Reed Smith in 1952. When in 1948 she married Temp Smith, who was working as an in-house lawyer at Koppers Company, she was advised by the lawyers at Reed Smith not to change her name, "because of the possible confusion with the firm name ... Reed SMITH." After the birth of their son, Temp, Jr. (another future Pittsburgh lawyer), Nellie decided to leave the firm to concentrate on her family, although she resumed her practice as a sole practitioner, handling wills, estates, adoptions and property tax disputes, retiring in 2001.[637]

Both Fergus and Bailey were helped, at the outset, by indulgent, supportive fathers who had connections with lawyers. Roz Margolis Litman, who graduated from Pitt Law School first in her class, with highest honors, in 1952, was a different breed. She had grown up in New York City, born to parents who were from Pittsburgh and who were working in the garment trade. Although she received a full scholarship at Cornell after high school, her parents prevailed upon her to go to the University of Pittsburgh, where she met her future husband, David Litman, in a Modern American Drama class. David entered Pitt Law School in 1948, and Roz was inspired, while reading his casebooks, to follow him the next year. "Law school, to me, was such a natural thing" from an academic point of view, she recalled, though while she excelled in her studies, she could not help but be aware that she had entered an environment that was not particularly welcoming of the idea of women lawyers. Dean Crane, she remembers, was "not very nice to the women in the class," but ultimately gave Roz respect because of the quality of her work. When she scouted for a preceptor, despite the fact that she was at the top of her class, she came up empty-handed, and she asked David if he would ask his preceptor to take her on. "His preceptor kind of bumbled around, fumbled around, and said, 'Well, I don't think it would be such a good thing for her ... picking up books, [they] would be too heavy'" for a little woman like her—she stood a mere 5 foot 2-1/2 inches tall.[638]

Roz ultimately entered the bar with Leo Kostman as her preceptor, and she and David, by then married, opened their office together in the Jones Law Building on Fourth Avenue. Roz built a reputation as an effective plaintiff's personal injury lawyer—again, in spite of prevailing prejudices. "There was the myth that was attempted to be perpetrated back then that women jurors would resent women lawyers," Roz observed. "I never found that to be the case," she said; in fact, her clients were generally "proud that a woman was their lawyer." She also began a sixty-plus year career as an ACLU volunteer lawyer and local ACLU leader, culminating in her election to the national board of the ACLU in 1985.[639]

During the 1960s, she stumbled onto a case that would take her out of the "red car, blue car" cases into legal matters of great complexity. In 1961, David Litman's brother, Lennie, was the owner of the Pittsburgh Rens, a franchise of the American Basketball League. While attending the games at the Civic Arena, David and Roz became acquainted with a nineteen year-old, 6′ 8″ forward/center phenom from Brooklyn named Connie Hawkins. Hawkins, who was dazzling on the court but perhaps a bit naïve about the ways of the world, won the League's most valuable player award with the Rens during the League's first season, and played with the Rens until the entire league folded half-way through the next season. It turned out, the Litmans discovered, that the only reason that Hawkins was playing in the broken-down ABL was that he had been blackballed by the NBA due to his alleged "association" with a college point-shaving scheme. After high school, Hawkins had earned a scholarship to play at the University of Iowa. During a New York City investigation of point-shaving, his name turned up as someone who had dealt with Jack Molinas, an attorney and former pro basketball player who was accused of procuring players to throw games. Striking up a relationship with Hawkins during his freshman year, Molinas loaned Hawkins $250, but never asked him to throw any games (it would have been impossible for him to do so as a freshman, since he was ineligible to play until his sophomore year under NCAA rules), and Hawkins' brother repaid the loan before the scandal broke. When it did break, Hawkins was expelled by Iowa and banned by the NBA—without ever being formally accused of a crime.[640]

Acknowledged as one of the best players in the country, Hawkins was nonetheless relegated to playing on the Harlem Globetrotters for laughs, and in secondary leagues such as the ABL, and subsequently, for the Pittsburgh (later Minnesota) Pipers of the American Basketball Association, where he again won the most valuable player award. Roz and David had virtually adopted the young man during his time in Pittsburgh, and seeing the injustice that he had been dealt, they filed a six million dollar lawsuit against the NBA in 1966, charging that the NBA had organized a boycott against Hawkins and had refused to give him a chance to clear his name—effectively striking at the presumed "antitrust exemption" of the NBA, a construct that was diligently guarded by the Association. During depositions, Roz Litman was particularly relentless in her questioning of NBA officials, and as the proceedings moved to settlement, it was Roz who played the leading role, proving to be a master manipulator of the board room. Eventually, the NBA called with a settlement offer. When it was over, the Litmans had put in over ten thousand hours on a case for which their client had no means to pay if they had not succeeded. But they did succeed, and Hawkins received a substantial amount of cash and a contract with the Phoenix Suns in the NBA. In June of 1969, *Life* magazine featured a photo of the gigantic Hawkins and the diminutive Roz, flashing peace signs and celebrating their victory. Connie Hawkins ended up playing seven seasons in the NBA and eventually entered the Basketball Hall of Fame; and Roz ended up with a new practice involving antitrust law, which eventually evolved into a plaintiffs' class action practice in which she found herself facing off in court against lawyers from the large downtown firms on a regular basis.[641]

Those older, larger downtown law firms were starting to hire women lawyers, but only very slowly. During the 1960s, Rita Kelly, who had been practicing with Rose Schmidt since 1958, was one of the founding partners of the firm Houston, Cooper, Speer & German; by 1973, her name was added to the letterhead of the downtown firm, which would ultimately come to be known as Sherrard, German & Kelly. A former schoolteacher known for her expertise in estate planning and transactional work, she signed her letters "R. Kelly" in order to take attention away from her gender[642]. In 1967, Linda Leebov Goldston joined the Baskin firm and became known not only as a general business lawyer, but as one of Pittsburgh's foremost liquor lawyers.[643] At Reed Smith, seventeen years after Nellie Fergus' departure, the firm hired Kathleen Merry Mills from Duke Law in 1969.[644] But with the slow increase of women lawyers finding work in downtown law firms came some increased tension over career expectations.

Marcella Phelps Hanson graduated from Pitt Law School in 1970 at the age of forty-four, after previously obtaining a pre-med degree from Michigan in 1947 and serving for some time as a blood bank director.[645] Her husband Raymond was a salesman for National Steel and, in part because of the close ties between National and Thorp Reed & Armstrong, she was hired as a first-year associate at the firm. Although the old guard at Thorp Reed was still somewhat dubious of the idea of a woman lawyer in their midst, they hoped she might make an impact as an estate and trust lawyer. When the firm decided to take an additional floor in the Grant Building, four years after Hanson had joined, a number of lawyers were moved into new offices. Feeling that she had attained some seniority as an associate at the firm, and assuming that she was growing nearer to becoming a partner of the firm, she casually mentioned to Ken Jackson, one of the mercurial senior lawyers of the firm, that she was hoping to receive a budget from the firm to hang curtains on the windows and redecorate her office. Jackson exploded into a tirade, telling her to forget about the curtains—adding, "And you know you're never going to be a partner here!" Hanson promptly filed a sex and age discrimination suit against Thorp Reed; but shortly after she told the firm that she had filed the lawsuit, Hanson was told by the partners not to hold herself out as an "associate" of the firm, that she was being put on indeterminate leave with pay, and that she should not take any "firm clients" during her leave. She countered by filing a second lawsuit, this time alleging that the firm had retaliated against her.[646]

Just one year after Hanson filed her lawsuits, Roz Litman was elected as the first woman president of the Allegheny County Bar Association, having previously served as the chair of the Association's antitrust and class action sections.[647] Litman's success and Hanson's disappointment were circumstances that co-existed awkwardly together within the space of one year. Hanson's lawsuit was eventually settled out of court,[648] but the pioneering case became a warning shot fired over the bow of downtown bar, and the mid- to late 1970s were a watershed period in the hiring of women by larger downtown law firms. Reed Smith added Johanna O'Loughlin from Pitt and Martha Munsch, a classmate of Hillary Rodham and Bill Clinton, from Yale in 1973, Kerry Kearney from Temple in 1975, and Allison Barnes from Penn in 1976. After a stint as a member of the Pitt Law faculty, Munsch returned to Reed Smith and became the first woman partner in the firm's Pittsburgh office in 1983. Buchanan Ingersoll hired Martha Zatezalo from Dickinson Law School as an associate in 1974, Cathy Gerhold from Pitt Law in 1976, and Sue Friedberg from Pitt Law and Karen Barrett from Harvard Law, in 1977; Friedberg and Barrett became the first women partners at the firm in 1984. Samantha Francis Flynn, a College of William & Mary Marshall-Wythe Law School graduate, was hired by Eckert Seamans in 1975, and the firm anointed its first woman partner, Janice Bowers Wolk, another William & Mary graduate, in 1980. Joy

Flowers Conti was the first woman lawyer hired at Kirkpatrick Lockhart in 1974, but left the firm for a couple of years to serve as a professor at her alma mater, Duquesne Law School; she returned to become a partner of the firm in 1983. Janice Hartman joined the firm in 1975 from Pitt Law and became Kirkpatrick's first woman partner in 1982. Marlee Myers, who graduated from Pitt Law *summa cum laude*, was hired by Kirkpatrick in 1977 and became a partner in 1984.[649]

Meanwhile, the Baskin firm added Karen Baskin and Joann Panzar from Duquesne, and Joan Feldman from Pitt; Estelle Comay joined Titus, Marcus & Shapira in 1975; Nora Barry Fischer joined Meyer Darragh in 1976; Rose Schmidt hired Gail Gratton and Mary Kate Laffey; and Berkman Ruslander, which had invited retired judge Anne Alpern into its ranks in 1974, added Sandy Metosky in 1975 and Margaret Angel in 1977. Beverly Gazza had joined Tucker Arensberg from Pitt in 1973; subsequently Tucker named Lynette Norton as a partner in 1985. Nancy Lamont joined Meyer Unkovic from Dickinson Law in 1978. In 1979, Dickie, McCamey & Chilcote hired Ingrid Lundberg and Katherine Benesch, both from Duquesne; Lundberg became the firm's first woman partner in 1988. Thorp Reed, recovering from its early gaffe with Marcella Hanson, hired Jane Lewis (Volk) in 1976 and Louise Yoder in 1978.[650]

"There was some pressure" to hire more women, recalls Sue Friedberg, now a shareholder with Buchanan Ingersoll & Rooney. "We all got offers from Thorp Reed," in the wake of the Marcella Hanson debacle, Friedberg said.[651] At the same time, said Marlee Myers, a classmate of Friedberg's and subsequently the founding managing partner of the Pittsburgh office of Morgan Lewis & Bockius, said, "We were all children of the '60s. I think we had a strong sense of just running through walls. I don't think we expected it to be easy."[652] For many of the women joining the profession at that time, it was not easy; the prospects for the employment of women lawyers in Pittsburgh were still quite limited. A review of the *ACBA Lawyers Pictorial Register* from 1980 shows that, while there are photos of approximately 259 women lawyers in the directory, a little over one per average page of sixteen lawyers, the vast majority of them were still inhabiting positions that were the typical, limited outlets for the professional ambitions of women lawyers since the early twentieth century—in the smallest downtown or suburban partnerships, in government, and in court clerk positions, banks and public interest jobs. The number of women lawyers obtaining in-house positions was on the rise, but it came during a time when the number of in-house employers—the major corporations of Pittsburgh—was decreasing. Forty-nine of them listed their positions as "Self," meaning they were functioning as sole practitioners, perhaps some of them underemployed as lawyers as a result. Only a little over ten percent of the women in the directory were in larger, older downtown firms.[653]

Despite the increase of women lawyers in downtown law firms, an underlying awkwardness in professional relations still prevailed between young women, with law degrees on their walls and bows on their silk blouses, and many grizzled male veterans, whose response to making room for women lawyers could range from hostility to indifference to social immaturity. While Nellie Fergus was excluded from celebrating the holidays with her male colleagues at the Duquesne Club (instead, she had holiday lunch with the Reed Smith women staffers at a dining room at Kaufmann's

Department Store), one Buchanan partner recalls the absurd drama of smuggling Martha Zatezalo into the Club through the back entrance for meetings during the late 1970s.[654][q] There were the interview questions, unthinkingly inappropriate—*Who is your father and what does he do? Are you married? Do you plan to have children? When?*—and the assumption that getting coffee for the meeting and carrying bags to the courthouse were peculiar elements of the young woman's job description as a lawyer, and not so much of the young man's job description. Scrutiny of women lawyers by their male colleagues and female staffers alike (the latter, from positions of institutional seniority) extended to their workplace wardrobe, including the question of whether it was appropriate for women to wear pants in the workplace. In 1976, Assistant District Attorney JoAnn D'Arrigo was dismissed from County Criminal Court by Judge Nicholas Papadakos for wearing a pantsuit—although the judge received a stinging rebuke from the *Post-Gazette* editorial writers, who declared that he was "wrong in his sartorial rigidity to begin with" and "doubly wrong in wasting the time of the criminal justice system to satisfy his apparent desire to be the final arbiter of female fashion."[655]

And there was also career pigeon-holing. The idea that women were somehow better suited for handling estate and trust matters was a decades-long conceit; a newer one was the concept that it would be a good idea to have women as second-chair in litigation on the defense side of employment discrimination cases, in an effort to balance the jurors' perspective of a woman plaintiff, perhaps represented by a woman plaintiffs' lawyer or a woman government lawyer. Marlee Myers turned down one offer from a large downtown firm because she had no interest in becoming an employment discrimination lawyer. "I thought, 'You know, I don't really want to be the 'skirt.'" Myers said. "'I don't want to be the woman; I want to be the man ... I want to go out there and be the star.'"[656]

Although all the awkwardness, tension and outright gender comedy was palpable, to many women entering the profession it became evident that most male lawyers who began their careers in the 1940s or 50s in the man's world of downtown Pittsburgh were ill-equipped to initiate any change. Rather, it was the young women lawyers who found themselves cultivating strategies—on the fly, while simultaneously trying to advance their careers—for dealing with the gender insensitivities, ranging from suffering in silence, to departing the field, to (occasionally) directing the attention of male lawyers to their foibles in some meaningful and socially acceptable way and hoping that the raising of consciousness would stimulate different behavior the next time around. It brings to mind the old line about Ginger Rogers that she did everything that Fred Astaire did, "except backwards and in high heels." As Laura Ellsworth, who entered the Pittsburgh bar in 1983, recalled:

---

[q] The Duquesne Club admitted its first woman member in 1980; the similarly restricted Harvard-Yale-Princeton Club also began admitting women that year. Sandra Salmans, "Pittsburgh's Top Brass All Love the Duquesne Club," *The New York Times*, August 9, 1981; Marylynne Pitz, "Allegheny Harvard Yale Princeton Club: Ivy League haven welcomes all and plots a course for the future," *Pittsburgh Post-Gazette*, April 15, 2012.

> When I was a young lawyer, I went into court and there was this really important Common Pleas judge, and he saw me come in and he said to me, "Now, we're not going to have a lot of silly objections from you, are we?" And I said, "Your honor, that all depends on whether counsel for the other side asks a lot of silly questions." We all laughed about it, and after the trial was over I went to the judge and I told him, "We had a great trial here, I really respect your work, but I want you to know that your remarks at the beginning of the trial really put me at a potential disadvantage ..." ... He didn't know. He didn't realize. And later he was one of the primary supporters of women in the bar.[657]

Sometimes, an earnest attempt to raise consciousness could work. Sometimes it could not.

Arguably the height of the bar's unintended gender comedy occurred during the summer of 1988. Barbara Wolvovitz and Jon Pushinsky were representing plaintiffs in an employment-related racial discrimination case before Judge Hubert I. Teitelbaum of the U.S. District Court for the Western District of Pennsylvania. At age seventy-three, Judge Teitelbaum had enjoyed a long and eminent career as a special agent with the FBI, based in Bolivia; as an official with the U.S. military government in Germany following distinguished service as a Captain in the U.S. Army at the Battle of the Bulge; as an assistant U.S. attorney under Malcolm Anderson and then acting U.S. attorney for three years; and, following his appointment to the bench by President Nixon in 1970, as a federal judge.[658] The case was against PPG Industries, represented by David Fawcett, Jr. Wolvovitz recalled that in the three weeks before the day's proceedings that would end up exploding in the newspapers, Judge Teitelbaum had made "very unusual comments" about women, and had been treating her and the other women in the courtroom in a way that was "disparaging"—including, as she recalled, patting her on the head after a sidebar.[659]

The foolishness began in earnest when Judge Teitelbaum rebuked Pushinsky for using "Ms." instead of "Mrs." when referring to PPG's director of human resources, Renee Burke. "[I]t's a bad habit," Judge Teitelbaum told Pushinsky, "and don't do it in my courtroom." The judge then turned his attention to Wolvovitz, who was married to Pitt Law professor Jules Lobel. "You don't like to use your married name here, do you?," the judge asked. "Your honor," Wolvovitz replied, "my name is not a married name. I have just one name, as I explained to you on another occasion." "You don't pay much attention to the laws, do you?," he asked, in open court. "Under that," Wolvovitz replied, "my married name is Ms. Wolvovitz." As Fawcett called the next witness to the stand, attempting to break the tension he offered that the next witness was male, and there would be no reason to argue about "Ms." or "Mrs." Judge Teitelbaum turned his attention back to Wolvovitz. "I ordinarily do not allow anyone to use that 'Ms.' in this courtroom. Your name is Mrs.," he asked Wolvovitz, "what was it?" "My name is Barbara Wolvovitz," she replied. "My husband's name is Jules Lobel. That's not my name. That last name, I have not ever, never used it."[660]

"From here on in," Judge Teitelbaum declared, "in this courtroom you will use Mrs. Lobel. That's your name." "Your honor," Wolvovitz retorted, "I have to object." "Do what I tell you," the judge interrupted, "or you're going to sleep in the county jail tonight.

You can't tell me how to run my courtroom." Then, openly in front of the jury, Judge Teitelbaum declared, "That is your name under the laws of the state of Pennsylvania, and that's what I want you to be, to call yourself from here on in this courtroom." Fawcett recalled that, in a sidebar conversation, he pleaded with Judge Teitelbaum to stop—as he felt the case was going well for his client, and he didn't want a mistrial

As testimony continued, the Judge called on Wolvovitz, referring to her as "Mrs. Lubin," and then asserting (inaccurately) that in Pennsylvania, when a woman marries, her husband's name becomes hers and that if she wanted to use her maiden name she had to go through a procedure to obtain court consent. "Your honor," replied Wolvovitz, "I was not married in the state of Pennsylvania, and under the laws of New York, I was not required to take action with respect to my name."

"In Pennsylvania you are, and we're going to call you Mrs. Lubin until you get a court order from the Common Pleas Court." "Your honor," she replied, "I cannot answer to that name. I'll have to ask for a mistrial, because I cannot continue to respond to a name that is not my name." The judge told her again that she would by "Mrs. Lubin" in his court. "That's not my husband's name, either," she said. "What is your husband's name?," Teitelbaum asked. "Lobel." "Lobel," he said, "all right. Mrs. Lobel."

After Wolvovitz cross-examined the witness, Pushinsky rose and protested, asking to postpone his own cross-examination until after the upcoming weekend. "At the risk of incurring the court's wrath," he said, "I think it is not appropriate to force someone to go by a name that they have ..." Judge Teitelbaum responded by saying it was none of Pushinsky's business, and that for his "officious intermeddling" he was being found to be in contempt of court. With the jury excused, Judge Teitelbaum sentenced Pushinsky to thirty days in jail, to begin after the end of the trial.[661]

By the following Monday, the legal community was abuzz with the details of Judge Teitelbaum's astonishing colloquy with Barbara Wolvovitz. On reconvening the proceedings, Judge Teitelbaum vacated his contempt order against Pushinsky, but turned to Wolvovitz and asked, in a ham-handed attempt to lighten the mood, "What if I call you sweetie?" Before Wolvovitz could answer, Judge Teitelbaum interrupted and offered that he would be calling Wolvovitz "counsellor" for the duration of the trial. Judge Teitelbaum still seemed genuinely confused by the attention; Wolvovitz recalled Judge Teitelbaum saying to her, "I really like you. *Why are you doing this to me?*"[662] By the time Judge Teitelbaum apologized publicly, stating that "This is the way my generation was taught," the incident had hit the press—not only in Pittsburgh, but in *The New York Times, Time* magazine and the *Washington Post.*[663] "He was of an advanced age at that point," said one observer from the bar, echoing the view of many, "and these actions weren't normal for him."

"I was stunned by the amount of attention it received," Wolvovitz later recalled. "It was on almost every front page in Europe and in Sydney and Melbourne in Australia."[664] The incident became a cause célèbre that summer. Wolvovitz' friend, Pitt Law graduate and political folksinger, Anne Feeney, wrote a song about the affair, called "Ms. Ogyny, or the Ballad of Barbara Wolvovitz," in which she expressed the silent view of women in the bar, singing, "Now, you might think this story/ Is an isolated case/ But misery in the courtroom/ is all too commonplace ..."[665]

The incident was something of a turning point in the Pittsburgh bar. It exposed for the first time publicly, for many men who had not realized their own errors, how flat-footed, disrespectful and anachronistic their own habits in dealing with women members of the bar could be. It was not only a mass consciousness-raising event among male lawyers and judges, but it also galvanized the women's bar in a way that had not occurred before. Tom Hollander, who was president of the ACBA at the time, recalled that it had been very difficult to find a woman lawyer who would take a leadership role on the "Women in the Law" committee, suggesting to him in retrospect that, prior to that incident in the summer of 1988, "it was still not very favorable for women to appear in that role" of being the advocate for women's issues within the bar.[666] Or, perhaps, to put it another way, it was not very consistent to brand oneself as the bar's leading advocate of women's issues when the identity struggle that women were facing in day-to-day practice was, to paraphrase Marlee Myers, to be the man and not the skirt.

Nonetheless, the need for advocacy was brewing. As attorney Susan Ruffner recalled, several women in the Pittsburgh bar had only recently petitioned the board of governors of the ACBA to permit them to write and present an amicus brief on behalf of the ACBA in a Pennsylvania Supreme Court case in which the privilege of rape victims' statements to their counselors was being challenged. With the ACBA's refusal to permit the Bar Association to become involved in the issue, followed by the Teitelbaum incident and the realization that there were no women in the ACBA's governing body at the time, the ACBA began to seem, in Ruffner's words, "irrelevant." Ruffner, a former assistant district attorney then serving as staff counsel to Allegheny County commissioner Barbara Hafer, and several other Pittsburgh women lawyers—including plaintiff's class action lawyer Ellen Doyle (a former director of the local ACLU), divorce lawyer Carol Kowall, trial lawyer Wendy Newton from Buchanan Ingersoll, and criminal defense lawyer Caroline Roberto, banded together to form the Ad Hoc Committee to Eliminate Gender Bias, which eventually became the Women's Bar Association of Western Pennsylvania (WBA).[667] Although since that time the participation of women in the leadership of the ACBA has become considerably more common and the Bar Association has introduced numerous measures in support gender equality, the WBA continues today as a separate, women-led organization addressing women's issues through education and public service projects. In contrast to the experience of African American men, fighting discrimination in the bar and in the community at large, the Women's Bar Association remains the closest thing to a protest movement among women in the Pittsburgh bar for 125 years.

Throughout the 1990s, a generation of new lawyers had the experience of seeing women in leadership positions within the Pittsburgh bar, which expedited the shift in attitudes among young men who entered the bar during that decade as much as it did for young women. Among the downtown firms, Marlee Myers left Kirkpatrick & Lockhart in 1996 and established, as managing partner, the Pittsburgh office of Philadelphia-based Morgan Lewis & Bockius, and Mary Milie Jones began her ten-year turn as managing partner of Meyer Darragh in 1998. Johanna O'Loughlin became general counsel at Fisher Scientific in 1986, and then joined Equitable Resources as its general counsel in 1996; Helen Pudlin became general counsel at PNC Bank in 1994;

Linda Drago assumed the role of general counsel at Duquesne University in 1995; and Nancy Wynstra served as general counsel at Allegheny Health for most of the decade. Marion Finkelhor and Eunice Ross completed their long runs as Common Pleas judges in 1987 and 1993, respectively. In addition to Judge Kim Berkeley Clark on the Common Pleas Court, Cheryl Allen on the Superior Court, Judge Doris Smith-Ribner on the Commonwealth Court, and Justice Cynthia Baldwin on the Common Pleas Court and the state Supreme Court, Kate Ford Elliott was elected to the Superior Court in 1989; Judith L.A. Friedman and Donna Jo McDaniel were elected to the Common Pleas court in 1985; and Joan Orie Melvin, Kathleen Durkin and Kathleen Mulligan joined the Common Pleas Court in 1990, 1992 and 1997, respectively. On the federal side, Carol Los Mansmann was installed as District Court judge for the Western District of Pennsylvania in 1982, and was elevated to the Third Circuit in 1985, serving until her death in 2002. Donetta Ambrose, a former Westmoreland County Common Pleas judge, was named to the federal District Court in 1993. She later served as Chief Judge for the Western District of Pennsylvania.[668]

If the credibility gap, the one that kept women in larger numbers from gaining positions of authority within the legal profession in Pittsburgh, was beginning to be closed, there remained other gaps with which they had to contend, gaps that seem to persist for women lawyers today. In 1990, the Women in the Law Committee of the ACBA commissioned a study of men and women of the Pittsburgh bar to explore gender bias. Twenty-nine percent of the bar responded. The study determined that "females earned less than males, reported differential treatment, and assumed a greater share of domestic responsibility" at home, and that "years of practice, area of practice, number of children under eight years old, and marital status" did not adequately explain the differences in income between men and women, in which women were earning about forty percent less than men on average.[669] The same committee commissioned a follow-up study fifteen years later, in 2005, in which twenty-one percent of the bar participated. The 2005 study revealed that, among respondents, women were about twice as likely as men to be employed part-time; and that the women were more likely to move out of private practice (the overwhelmingly most popular area for both men and women to begin their careers) to "alternative settings, including non-profit, corporate, judicial, or government positions." The income picture had not changed much: there were no female law graduates from the 1990s earning as much as $250,000 per year, while ten percent of the male graduates of the same vintage were earning above $250,000. For male lawyers with children, their spouses were the main providers of child care, while women lawyers with children were more likely to use paid child care outside the home.[670]

Laura Ellsworth, who served as managing partner of Jones Day's Pittsburgh office from 2003 to 2015, is not bashful about her opinion of the 2005 study. Although there is no greater advocate for the advancement of women in the Pittsburgh bar, Ellsworth dismisses portions of the study. "I was on the committee," she explains, "and I told them that it was flawed, that it didn't weed out the 'confounders,' the people who self-select. ... So a lot more women are part-time—did we ask whether they chose that for themselves?" Ellsworth has trained her focus, along with a group of other successful women in the Pittsburgh bar, on talking to younger women lawyers about what it takes to be successful and to advance to partnership. At the top of her list of advice is that success requires sacrifices. It is undoubtedly painful, at times, to organize your life and the lives of your family members in such a way as to make the same professional choices that men make—choices they have always seemed to make without breaking stride—but the legal profession is a demanding one. Ellsworth admits to her sacrifices, and proves her point by example; married, with one son, she was the managing partner of the seventy-six-lawyer Pittsburgh office of Jones Day, the sixth highest ranking firm on the AMLAW 100, and is considered to be one of the top commercial litigators in the country.[671]

The next generation of women lawyers, the one following those women leaders into the profession, have found themselves in a rapidly changing industry. Less urgently concerned with being "the man," they have tended to have a different outlook. They have tended to ask the question: amid all of that rapid change, are there opportunities for women to have an impact on the ways in which the profession will work in the future—will we change the profession, or will the profession ultimately change us? The collapse of the "Cravath system," such as it had been applied by Pittsburgh firms up until the late 1980s, provided the next generation of women with the ability to chart alternative routes to achieving rank and prosperity in downtown firms. Outside of a lock-step approach to training, advancing and paying young recruits, individual differences could be taken into account. Although child-bearing and child-rearing might have interrupted their commitments to the practice of law from time to time over the long term, star female performers were sometimes able to negotiate a rewarding path—even if it required considerable effort.

Amy Pandit was born in Detroit, but largely grew up in Pittsburgh. Her parents—immigrants from India during the Vietnam War, each carrying eight dollars in their pockets, the maximum permitted by the Indian government to be carried by travelers outside of India—entered the U.S. as skilled physicians—her mother, an OB/GYN; her father, a cardiologist. Eventually they settled in amid the burgeoning Pittsburgh health care industry. When Amy left Pittsburgh in 1986 to go to college at Northwestern, however, she thought she had left Pittsburgh behind for good; it was a time, during the decline of the Pittsburgh economy, when the educated children of Pittsburghers saw little future in the city. While she attended law school at Boston University, her husband, also a Pittsburgh native, attended medical school at Tufts University. As he began his residency in New York, Amy joined the New York firm of Weil Gotshal & Manges as an associate in the corporate and securities department. In the days when Scott Turow's *One L* was required reading for law students who would pursue a career in the dog-eat-dog environment of a big New York City law firm, Pandit says that Weil Gotshal's reputation was encapsulated in a popular parody of its name: "We'll Getcha and Mangle ya." It was "a tough lifestyle" but, nonetheless, it was "an exciting time" to be at Weil Gotshal practicing securities law, with IPOs for Planet Hollywood and Estee Lauder among others, and the Macy's bankruptcy. After her husband finished his residency, however, the couple elected to return to Pittsburgh and start a family.

Already pregnant with her first child when she joined the corporate finance department of Buchanan Ingersoll—which in 1997, according to Pandit, was arguably "the strongest group" in Pittsburgh with a securities practice, the "most like what I was leaving in New York"—Pandit told the firm that she wanted to pursue an alternative work schedule. While the partners were open to the idea, "there was no real path for that. It was a one-off kind of thing." They eventually settled on a schedule in which she would spend two days per week in the office, and three days at home. While initially there were lawyers at the firm who were uncomfortable with her schedule and who were predisposed not to involve her in their projects, the technologies that would enable all lawyers to work from home—essentially, a modem, a personal computer, email and the Internet—were just beginning to emerge, and soon she found that rather than working two days a week and not working for three days a week, she was actually working something close to a full schedule, with technology making her experience of working from home "more or less seamless for everyone." "I was fine with the idea of working from home," Pandit recalls, but while "my hours were full-time, my compensation was not commensurate." The labeling of her situation as "alternative" actually "hindered my ability," she says, "to be fully recognized as a full time contributing member, from a compensation standpoint ... I was certainly contributing as much as anybody."

When it came time to discuss Pandit's promotion from associate to a higher level within the firm, her "alternative work schedule" became the source of a "big disconnect" between herself and management. Until she expressed her disappointment on being passed over for a promotion, despite the fact that she was carrying a full workload, "no one wanted to have the conversation" about what her expectations were for advancement, she observed. "It was easier not to have the conversation." A year and a half later, however, she was promoted to non-equity shareholder, and was eventually promoted to equity shareholder while still only coming to the office for three days a week. Subsequently as a partner at another firm, Pandit went into the office four days a week, and worked from home one day a week.

While the prior generation of women lawyers still emphasizes the requirement of outright sacrifice in order to succeed, Pandit's experience showed that it was now possible to forge another path—albeit not without earning "scars," as she admits. Upon reflection, Pandit's advice to younger women lawyers with family obligations is "to just shut up and do what you need to do, and don't advertise it." She says that one of her female colleagues has noted that "as women we always feel the need to tell everybody everything we're doing. 'I'm going to pick up my child, I'll be back,' 'I'm going to go for a quick run to the grocery store, I'll be back.' And men just ... take off for golf, and don't say anything. So," says Pandit, "I think it is sort of this in-grown, from-the-day-you-were-born, guilt thing, where you feel like you always have to be accountable for every move that you make." By revealing less about the time you take for home responsibilities and still meeting all of your work responsibilities, perhaps a woman avoids the perception that she is "not contributing as much, when in fact you are doing the same thing that all your male counterparts are doing [but] you're just being far more open about it."

She also advises that "if you choose to modify your work schedule because of other life demands, it is important to have the conversation with your employer to make sure that you and your employer are on the same page" about your complete career track. "At one point," she recalls, "there was a real risk that I would leave Buchanan because I really perceived that the firm wasn't valuing me. I don't think that was the case at all—I just don't think they knew what to do with me, and they didn't want to deal with that, and so they just sort of put it off, put it off, put it off ...No one should have that excuse today," Pandit says. "Firms should be prepared to have those discussions."[672]

Pandit's experience might seem extraordinary in some respects, but there were variations throughout the bar, beginning in the 1990s—flex-time, work-from-home, job-sharing initiatives—that permitted some talented women to maintain a measure of job security, to keep them in the game long enough, amid the other inevitable personnel disruptions that law firms now routinely experience on a regular basis, to ascend to partnership or leadership. They have been imperfect solutions. Indeed, despite the advantages of the "fall of Cravath" in promoting ad hoc employment arrangements for women, the lack of a lock-step system has completely confused the question of whether women are being paid on an equal basis. The question is further complicated in the Pittsburgh market by the fact that some law partnerships have adopted so-called "closed" compensation systems, touted as progressive in that they eliminate competitive envy. Theoretically, in such firms, no one knows how anyone else is being compensated.

Finally, the advancement of women lawyers to the status of "partners" in law firms has paradoxically made it more difficult in some cases to enforce equal pay. In 2010, the Third Circuit threw out a claim for equal pay by a female partner of a downtown Pittsburgh law firm, saying that the lawyer could not sue her firm for sex discrimination because she was a shareholder and director of the firm, and she was given the opportunity to share in the firm's profits.[673] And while greater acceptance of women in leadership and partnership roles is evident, it is also evident that women lawyers in Pittsburgh have not been immune from sexual harassment. An early instance of the #metoo movement arose in 2010 when a female partner of a large Pittsburgh firm brought suit against the firm on the basis that "work was diverted ... to female attorneys who were willing to engage in sexual relations" with a male partner at the firm. The case, which had both income disparity and harassment within its core allegations, was settled out of court, and neither the plaintiff nor the male attorney remained at the law firm.[674] Despite progress, there continue to be women who feel that they have been mistreated, ill-used and left behind, and at any given moment, a snapshot reckoning of a given downtown law firm may well show income and advancement disparities between men and women, if not worse.

To sum up: here in Pittsburgh in the twenty-first century, we are no longer concerned that a woman can study law and yet must end up working, for any part of her career, as a legal secretary rather than as a lawyer, as Elizabeth Bailey did; we are no longer concerned that downtown firms will treat the hiring of women lawyers as some kind of begrudged obligation, as Marcella Hanson experienced, or that such firms won't hire women in large numbers, or that they won't be considered for advancement. And for the most part, we're no longer concerned that women lawyers will end up celebrating the holidays with the women staff members at a department store dining room, rather than at the Duquesne Club with all the male lawyers, as Nellie Fergus did. There still lingers, however, a concern that women are sometimes not paid as well as men, and that because women bear a disproportionate role in child-rearing at home, there still seems to be greater attrition among the ranks of women lawyers—far more of them, it seems, find it easier to leave traditional career paths within the law, and perhaps to leave the profession altogether, when the pressures of home become too great. Despite the fact that law schools have for some time routinely reported that women make up roughly half of the student population, the female population of the downtown bar, measured by the number of women who are members of the Allegheny County Bar Association, is stagnant, hovering around thirty percent for the last decade.

Yet, as one woman partner of a downtown Pittsburgh law firm quips, "It would be a shame if the story of women in the bar ended up being all about 'work-life balance.'"

With the elimination of the most blatant barriers to the entry of women into the profession, perhaps it should now become possible to speculate on how the increased participation of women in the profession will ultimately improve it—to move the question of diversity from being asked from a solely defensive posture, a posture that implies victimization, to asserting it as an imperative for the future of the profession, and a "competitive edge" for firms that embrace it. It should be possible now to recognize that the addition of women in increased numbers will enhance the capabilities of a law firm, and the bar as a whole, as they will bring with them a distinct perspective that is missing, and that they will enrich the values of the legal profession—support for the principle of the rule of law, independent thinking, service, integrity, a concern for justice and fairness—by bringing a different character to such values. It should be possible now for both men and women to answer the question asked by women over the past several decades in Pittsburgh—will we change the profession, or will the profession ultimately change us?—with the resounding answer that not only have they changed and will they continue to change the profession, but that the profession needs to be changed by them.

A number of studies over the past twenty years have called attention to the unique character of women's leadership qualities and the success of institutions that have placed women at the top. A 2008 McKinsey & Company report, *Women Matter 2: Female Leadership, A Competitive Edge for the Future*, summarized much of that research, pointing out that studies by Eagly, Bass and Avolio had concluded that women use five of nine classic leadership behaviors that are essential to organizational success more than men do—"people development," "expectation and rewards," "role model," "inspiration," and "participative decision making"—and that men tend to adopt two of the classic leadership behaviors more than women—"control and corrective action" and "individualistic decision making." Ultimately, said the McKinsey report, "we have demonstrated that companies with more women in their management teams score more highly, on average, on their organizational criteria than companies with no women in senior positions. Moreover, the gap increases significantly once a certain critical mass is obtained ..." The report concludes: "Gender diversity is not just a social concern. Our new study suggests that it could also create a competitive edge to address the global challenges that corporations will face in the near future."[675]

Peter Kalis, the former managing partner of the two-thousand-lawyer, Pittsburgh-based global law firm of K&L Gates, expressed this view in an April 2015 op-ed piece for *The Lawyer* called "Women, teamwork and innovation." He charts the simultaneous rise of Title IX, the federal law enacted in 1972 that prohibits discrimination based on gender in federally funded education programs and activities—including athletics programs—and the rise in numbers of women entering large law firms, and observes that a common element of both is the participation women in team-oriented activities. "Law has always been a team sport," Kalis writes. "[O]nly law firms can screw that up with their silly ego-driven internal borders and barriers—but until recent times half the population was excluded from the team." Kalis' principal point, however, is as follows:

Now that more women are adding their skill and insight to the team game of law, the profession stands on the cusp of greatness ... every once in a while it's possible to stand back and say we're on the cusp of seismic change and, if we're lucky, greatness. This is how I feel about the legal profession and the practice of law. And I feel that way largely for three reasons: women, teamwork and innovation.[676]

"How much richer the collaboratively woven tapestry is now," Kalis concludes, "and will be in the future. For women and men alike, there has never been a better time to become a lawyer. Greatness awaits."[677] Whether or not one agrees with Kalis that there is any correlation with Title IX, the head of one of the world's largest law firms sees a future in which women have a significant impact on the improvement of the legal profession.

The profession of the law is notoriously resistant to change—it is perhaps one of its greatest merits as well as one of its most pernicious weaknesses. While the legal profession in general has arguably done more than any other American institution to advance the causes of stamping out discrimination and eliminating gender-based pay and advancement inequalities, to paraphrase William Newlin's remarks from a different context, lawyers have often been the last to apply their own advice to themselves. The 2008 McKinsey report makes the point that "Achieving gender diversity in corporations, at all levels, is a long and demanding journey, which requires the involvement of the whole company and the strong commitment of top management."[678] In companies where it has been achieved, it has "amounted to nothing less than a cultural revolution."

As Kalis, Ellsworth, and others in the Pittsburgh bar continue to make the point that our law firms and our profession will rise and become better as the inculcation of women's habits and perspectives become a more significant part of the intellectual mix, such statements represent signs that the profession has, at the very least, the awareness necessary for change.

BEYOND RENAISSANCE

During a snowstorm in the early 1950s, an era when traveling men wore suits and ties, a twenty-something-year-old Chuck Queenan, Jr. was on a train heading back to Hanover, New Hampshire to resume his studies in business and engineering at Dartmouth College. His companion for half the trip was a lawyer to whom he had been introduced by his father, a Rockwell executive. It was Nick Unkovic, the brilliant and charismatic Reed Smith labor attorney, who was on his way to Corning, New York to visit his client, Corning Glass. As their train chugged its way through snow-blanketed upstate New York, Unkovic made his pitch to the young Queenan. "Have you ever thought about a career in law?"

Queenan had never intended to do anything but "enter industry," but he consulted his father about his chat with Unkovic. The elder Queenan confessed that he had always been intrigued by lawyers, and wondered why "these Wall Street lawyers" wielded so much power. "Go to law school," Charles, Sr. advised, "and find out what makes these guys tick."[679] Queenan went to Harvard Law School and was hired by the Kirkpatrick law firm in 1956. His training in engineering was evident in his style of deal-making, combined with a builder's sense of self-confidence, and in no time at all Queenan enjoyed a reputation for designing some of Pittsburgh's most sophisticated transactions. He took particular delight in navigating obscure provisions in the tax code and adding extra dollars to his clients' bottom lines, giving them better deals than even they thought they had bargained for. As Dick Thornburgh recalled, thinking of associates' meetings at Kirkpatrick in which everyone would take their turn discussing their current projects: "Queenan would always have some esoteric deal that he was working on that none of us understood."[680]

At the height of his career as a deal lawyer, in 1980, Queenan was engaged by Dick Simmons, the president of Allegheny Ludlum Steel, to represent the management of the specialty steel company in a management buy-out. The chief executive officer of the parent company, Allegheny Ludlum Industries, was the Bronx-born Robert J. Buckley, who had been an executive at General Electric and Ingersoll Milling Machine, and had been brought on by Allegheny's board of directors to lead the company into becoming a diversified conglomerate. He started, with the aid of Clayton Sweeney—the former Buchanan Ingersoll lawyer who had functioned as the firm's managing partner prior to joining the company in 1977 as Buckley's second-in-command—by buying Standard-Thomson Corp. (a maker of car thermostats), Jacobsen lawn mowers and True Temper golf clubs. With Allegheny Ludlum Steel suffering weak demand and falling revenues, in 1978, the board gave Buckley the go-ahead to sell the steel company, and Buckley ordered Simmons to find a buyer. Simmons searched everywhere—throughout the U.S., in Canada, Japan, Europe and South Africa—but no one was interested. Buckley then announced to Simmons that he had a financier for a management buyout: Victor Posner, a shady Miami corporate raider who already owned Sharon Steel.[681]

When that deal failed to materialize, Buckley brought in Clint Murchison, Jr., an heir to a Texas oil fortune who was the founding owner of the Dallas Cowboys, and set the price at $195 million plus liabilities, for a closing to occur on December 26, 1980. Murchison was supposed to put up nineteen million dollars in cash, and Simmons and his team—mortgaging themselves to the hilt—would put up one million dollars; the remaining $175 million would be debt and preferred stock to be held by Allegheny Ludlum Industries. In November, Murchison started to suggest that he might do the deal without putting up the cash, and Simmons began to feel uneasy about Murchison. Simmons told him that unless he came up with the nineteen million dollars, Simmons wanted no part of Murchison's deal.

With three weeks left before Buckley's scheduled closing date, Murchison was still trying to get the deal done—but without Simmons. Simmons meanwhile turned to Queenan and told him, "Find me somebody else." Although it was, according to Bill Dietrich, a request that "was both impractical and unreasonable," Queenan "pulled a $19 million rabbit out of the hat" by bringing in his client, George Tippins. Tippins was a steel mill equipment manufacturer who had over twenty-five million dollars in revenues sitting in a company bank account that needed to be distributed or it would be subject to an excess accumulation penalty tax of seventy percent; on the other hand, if he did distribute it to himself, he would have to pay a seventy-percent dividend tax. Queenan's plan was to have Tippins invest nineteen million dollars in Allegheny Ludlum as a "related investment," thus sparing Tippins the tax liability, and giving Simmons a new partner. Tippins loved the idea, as almost the whole investment would be "found money"; he was, in effect, paying $6.4 million for eighty percent of a company that had six hundred million dollars in annual revenue.

On December 26, the Murchison team and the Simmons team showed up at Buchanan Ingersoll, which represented Allegheny Ludlum, and prepared for a showdown. Simmons announced to Murchison that if he succeeded in buying the company, Simmons and every member of his sixteen-man management team would resign. Murchison pulled his deal, and Tippins, Simmons and the management team emerged from the firm that day as owners of a steel company in the then largest-ever management buyout. "[I]t's hard to overstate the contribution Queenan made to the Allegheny Ludlum buyout," wrote Dietrich. "In all likelihood, no Queenan, no deal."[682]

It is the story of a great deal, well-told by Dietrich in a 2009 article for the *Pittsburgh Quarterly*. It also serves to illustrate two important phenomena that Pittsburgh began to experience during the 1980s.

First, Bob Buckley's desire to lead Allegheny Ludlum Industries (which was renamed Allegheny International after the Simmons deal) out of the steel business was a desire that was shared by the other CEOs among Pittsburgh's steel and other manufacturing companies during the late 1970s and early 1980s. Although Allegheny had invested some money in updating its plants before the steel company sale, most of the steel companies in the region were questioning whether it made economic sense to modernize Pittsburgh's aging steel plants—and were being urged by bankers, shareholders and consultants to deindustrialize and diversify. National Steel went into the savings and loan and oil distribution businesses; Armco went into insurance.[683] U.S. Steel took a particularly bold step. As Lubove observed, "No episode more dramatically symbolized the disinvestment process than U.S. Steel's acquisition of Marathon Oil in the early 1980s. David Roderick, who became chairman in 1979, was committed to major diversification because the company's thirty-five million tons of steelmaking capacity was excessive, 'looking at profit margins and inflation.' It was imperative, from his viewpoint to seize a 'growth opportunity' to compensate for the shrinking steel component."[684] For the unions and the communities that had lived on steel, diversification—investing in businesses other than steel—looked like a slap in the face to loyal stakeholders.

The subsequent stories of Allegheny International and Allegheny Ludlum revealed both the worst that diversification could do for a company, as well as the continuing hope of a resurgent steel industry. Buckley continued his buying spree, buying out minority shareholders of Wilkinson Sword, a well-known razor brand, in 1980, following Allegheny's investment in the company in 1978; acquiring Sunbeam, a leading home appliance brand, in 1981; making some lackluster energy investments; and binging on large-scale commercial real estate, including the Dover Hotel in New York and an office tower in Houston. Although Sunbeam and Wilkinson tripled Allegheny International's revenue over its steel industry days, it was drowning in debt. Meanwhile, Buckley's appetite for the trappings of a conglomerate empire seemed insatiable, as he bought five corporate jets and luxurious corporate condos, and had the corporate offices in Two Oliver Plaza redecorated like an imperial palace, with parquet floors, brass doorknobs and a marble bathroom suite. Clayton Sweeney, who once enjoyed a position of trust with Buckley, resigned in 1985. "I ended up quitting because it got to the point where he wouldn't listen to me anymore." Sweeney told his wife, "This company is going to get into real trouble and I'm not going to sit there and watch it." The board threw out Buckley the following year, and by the end of 1988, Allegheny International had become the debtor in one of the top ten largest bankruptcies in the country.[685]

Meanwhile, Dick Simmons, over at Allegheny Ludlum Steel—benefiting from a thirty-one million dollar modernization of its Brackenridge, Pennsylvania flat-rolled steel plant in 1977—navigated the rough waters of high inflation and a prime rate at twenty-percent to post record steel sales in 1984; he bought out Tippins in 1986 for $190 million; bought back Allegheny International's paper at a discount during the former parent company's time of desperation; and took Allegheny Ludlum public during a narrow window in 1987, just before the October crash, at a market capitalization of $605 million. Simmons' personal investment of $325,000 in the deal was worth $218 million immediately after the IPO, and well above that a few years into the twenty-first century.[686]

The second phenomenon that pops up in Dietrich's telling of the Allegheny Ludlum story is Queenan's expanded role in the transaction. Queenan is modest about it, saying that he was just "looking to combine capital and talent," calling it "a classic investment banker's role," but admitting, "I never got paid for it." Nevertheless, Queenan regarded his quasi-investment banking activities as part-and-parcel of his purpose as a corporate lawyer in private practice. "You know, you wanted to see things happen." Helping to find the resources that would ensure the success of enterprises that produced goods and wealth was an essential part of the service he was supposed to be providing, in his view, all toward "aiding and abetting the 'Productive System.'" And by taking on that larger role, Queenan says, being the lawyer "became fun" and "utterly rewarding."[687] The consequences of the waning of steel and other manufacturing in Pittsburgh in the 1980s would require some lawyers, in the image of lawyers like Chuck Queenan, to go beyond merely negotiating and papering deals. It would require them to undertake expanded roles, to do the bigger things.

At the end of the 1970s, Pittsburgh was the "City of Champions." The University of Pittsburgh Panthers football team, led by head coach Johnny Majors and Heisman Trophy-winning running back Tony Dorsett, won the NCAA national championship in 1976—although the team lost Majors to his alma mater, Tennessee, the following year. The Pittsburgh Pirates baseball club, led by its happy-go-lucky manager Chuck Tanner, slugger Willie Stargell and submarine-throwing relief pitcher Kent Tekulve, came back from a three-to-one deficit to win the 1979 World Series, beating the Baltimore Orioles in the seventh game at Baltimore's Memorial Stadium on October 17, 1979. Back in Pittsburgh, fans took to the streets, singing "We are Family," the Sister Sledge disco hit that had become the Pirates' theme song that year. At age thirty-nine, Willie Stargell, known as "Pops," became the oldest World Series MVP. The Steelers—another family affair, Art Rooney's NFL football team, which shared space with the Pirates at Three Rivers Stadium—won the Super Bowl in 1974, 1975 and 1978, led by head coach Chuck Noll. They successfully defended their title in the 1979-80 season, beating the Los Angeles Rams in the Rose Bowl in January 1980. Pittsburgh was a town that seemed to know how to win.

The new mayor, Richard Caliguiri, had previously served as city parks director and as city council president. He was also working to seize some of that winning energy. After his predecessor, Mayor Pete Flaherty, left office to accept appointment as President Carter's U.S. Assistant Attorney General in 1977, Caliguiri returned to the strategy of partnering with Pittsburgh corporate interests, a strategy that Flaherty had stubbornly resisted, to carry out building projects in the spirit of the David Lawrence days. Without a Richard King Mellon to speak monolithically for the corporate interests, however, the initiatives were not part of a grand civic plan, but were more ad hoc, and more definitively commercial. For example, early in Caliguiri's tenure as mayor, PPG Industries wanted to build a new corporate headquarters in downtown Pittsburgh, and approached the mayor. As the URA's general counsel Joseph I. Gariti III recalled, PPG "identified an area they wanted for a headquarters [and] the area was deteriorated." PPG funded the URA in its acquisition of land for the site—both through the use of the URA's eminent domain powers and through negotiated purchases, similar to the assembly of parcels required for the revitalization of the Point during the 1950s. In exchange for the use of the URA's authority to clear the land, Gariti remembered, PPG "had to agree to build their headquarters in accordance with the plans and specs" that the URA approved.[688]

U.S. Steel which had already built a fortress-like, sixty-four-story headquarters tower on Grant Street between Sixth and Seventh Avenues back in 1971,[689] relied upon the URA to assemble land across Sixth for a tower that it would develop without any intention of occupying it. The new fifty-five-story skyscraper, for which construction began in 1980, was dubbed "Dravo Tower" after its intended tenant, the construction and shipbuilding company, until just before the building's completion, when Dravo backed out of its commitment, essentially swapping space with Mellon Bank to maintain its corporate headquarters in One Oliver Plaza. The resulting building, which opened in 1984, became known as One Mellon Bank Center (now BNY Mellon Center).[690] Similarly, Allegheny International struck a deal with the URA and the Pittsburgh Cultural Trust to develop land between Penn and Liberty Avenue for a new corporate headquarters. After Allegheny filed for bankruptcy, the thirty-two-floor Art Deco-inspired building became known as CNG Tower, after its new anchor tenant Consolidated Natural Gas, opening in 1987.[691]

The result of Caliguiri's "Renaissance II" public-private partnerships was a shiny, brand new skyline for Pittsburgh, now featuring the iconic PPG Place—an office and retail campus of six towers with the tallest tower, One PPG Place, designed by architect Philip Johnson as an all-glass visual "quotation" of London's neo-Gothic Victoria Tower at the Palace of Westminster—as well as One Mellon Bank Center; CNG Tower; the forty-six-floor, steel and glass One Oxford Centre (1983), developed by the DeBartolo Company and Oxford Development; Liberty Center, featuring the twenty-seven-story Federated Investors Tower and a 615-room Vista International Hotel (1985)[692]; and the thirty-one-story Fifth Avenue Place (1988), with its distinctive pyramidal roof and 178-foot mast, which became the headquarters for Blue Cross of Western Pennsylvania (Highmark).[693] In five years, from 1983 to 1988, the image of downtown Pittsburgh as a dreary, complacent steel headquarters town began to shift to that of a modern, diversified corporate center. In 1985, Pittsburgh received Rand McNally's "most livable city" award.

It has become a cliché to say that Renaissance II marked the beginning of Pittsburgh's economic and cultural recovery. In retrospect, however, it should also be observed that Renaissance II, while successful in helping to rehabilitate the image of Pittsburgh by focusing on its downtown curb appeal, was also a leading example of corporate diversification in Pittsburgh, occurring during the most devastating series of plant closings that the Pittsburgh region would face. Real estate, as Buckley had convinced his board at Allegheny International, was a hedge against inflation.[694] PPG Industries, while it had not yet closed its Ford City plant as it began to consider the development of PPG Place, had already begun to close outmoded manufacturing plants throughout the U.S. in the late 1970s.[695] PPG Place was a modest opportunity for PPG to invest in real estate and to be a landlord in its headquarters town, as its plan never called for PPG to occupy the entire space. U.S. Steel's development of One Mellon Center, through its real estate division, came simultaneously with its closure of the Rankin blast furnace and its decision to postpone an upgrade to the Edgar Thomson plant in Braddock. The year after the building opened, U.S. Steel announced that it was going to demolish the Dorothy 6 blast furnace in Duquesne, which was followed by its closure of the Homestead Works in 1986 and its McKeesport plant in 1987.[696] The company had renamed itself "USX," a nod to its status as a diversified conglomerate, in 1986.[r]

Meanwhile, Crucible Steel in nearby Midland was closed in 1982; troubled Dravo closed its Neville Island barge works in 1984; LTV, the successor to Jones & Laughlin Steel, closed its plants in Hazelwood and the South Side and a large portion of its Aliquippa site in 1985; Wheeling-Pittsburgh Steel closed its Monessen plant in 1986, after filing for its first Chapter 11 bankruptcy reorganization; Westinghouse closed its facilities in East Pittsburgh in 1988; and American Standard closed Westinghouse Airbrake and Union Switch & Signal in 1989.[697] Other key corporations with Pittsburgh headquarters, such as Gulf Oil, Rockwell International and Koppers, disappeared from Pittsburgh, in the blink of an eye, as they were consumed in corporate acquisitions. The region hemorrhaged jobs, losing 125,000 in just a few years, turning once vibrant factory communities around Pittsburgh into ghost towns and many of their inhabitants into the walking dead. In the words of Franklin Tugwell and his co-authors, "outside of the Soviet Union, few places on earth have undergone such profound economic change in time of peace."[698]

In the heat of these cataclysmic events, an organized resistance to deindustrialization did develop. By 1970, Staughton Lynd had already built a long and heralded (some might have said "infamous") career as a fiery leader of the American radical left, as a socialist academic at Spelman College and Yale, a conscientious objector during World War II, a civil rights activist in Mississippi, and as an anti-Vietnam War tax resister. At the age of forty-four, Lynd entered the University of Chicago Law School with the aim of fighting for workers' rights. As a newly-minted lawyer at age forty-seven, Lynd moved to Youngstown, Ohio in 1976, where he stood up for workers during the closure of three major steel mills.[699] During that fight, and recognizing that similar circumstances were cropping up in the northern panhandle of West Virginia and in southwestern Pennsylvania, Lynd helped to establish the Tri-State Conference on the

---

[r] PPG Industries sold PPG Place in 1999. PPG Industries, Inc., "Hillman Interests Buying PPG Place; To Remain PPG Headquarters," *PR Newswire*, April 19, 1999, accessed March 10, 2017, http://www.prnewswire.com/news-releases/hillman-interests-buying-ppg-place-to-remain-ppg-headquarters-74096582.html. U.S. Steel sold One Mellon Center to a real estate investment partnership before Mellon even entered the premises, the year after it had sold its headquarters building; the two sales were said to be the largest real estate sales in the history of Allegheny County as of 1983, together putting over $300 million into U.S. Steel's coffers. Associated Press, "U.S. Steel Sells Office Tower in Pittsburgh," *Toledo Blade*, February 17, 1983.

Impact of Steel, along with workers, members of the clergy and other community activists. Through the Tri-State Conference (although without, strictly speaking, a client paying his way), Lynd began to argue for the creation of a "community steel corporation," to be financed by the federal government in the model of the Tennessee Valley Authority, that would permit communities to take over steel mills that were being closed by major corporations and operate them with local management. At the first general membership meeting of Tri-State, on January 21, 1981, the group concluded its mission statement by stating: "Our motto is simple: generations of Mon[nongahela] Valley steelworkers have made the big steel corporations rich over the years and aren't just getting up and walking away!"[700]

After the Youngstown Sheet and Tube, U.S. Steel and Republic Steel plants had closed in Youngstown, Lynd's focus shifted to Pittsburgh. Jay Hornack met Lynd when Lynd was a guest speaker at Rutgers-Newark Law School, where Hornack was a student, in 1981. Lynd invited Hornack—a Cleveland-area native who had worked in steel mills during the summer months and had developed a first-hand sense of empathy for what the steel workers went through to put food on their families' tables—to help Lynd and Tri-State on a volunteer basis to research the possibilities of using eminent domain to save Pittsburgh's mills. After graduation, without a job waiting for him, Hornack came to Pittsburgh and continued to volunteer for Lynd. At Midland, Pennsylvania, where Colt Industries had announced in the summer of 1982 that it was planning to close the Crucible Steel Works, with five thousand jobs at stake, the unassuming, bespectacled Hornack found himself addressing a mass meeting, standing alongside Pittsburgh's "Labor Priest" Father Charles Owen Rice, describing how eminent domain could work as a strategy for saving the mill.[701] Midland borough officials found the idea "too big and scary," however, according to Mike Stout, a steelworker, singer and activist aligned with Tri-State, and the Crucible plant closed in October 1982.[702]

Playing an increasingly visible role in the movement, however reluctant he may have been to be in the limelight, Jay Hornack was on hand to help Tri-State achieve one of its greatest victories. Nabisco, headquartered in New York, had operated a plant in Pittsburgh's East End since 1918. Around the same time the Crucible plant closed, Nabisco announced that it was going to close the profitable plant in early 1983, which would result in 650 workers losing their jobs. Tri-State, along with other community organizers, formed the "Save Nabisco Action Coalition" or "SNAC" and threatened several boycotts—a national boycott of Nabisco's brands, as well as the threat that over a thousand depositors would close their accounts with Equibank, Nabisco's local banker. Mayor Caliguiri propelled himself to the front of the protest, supporting the snack food boycott (promising to curtail his own cookie and cracker habit) but also threatening to use the URA's eminent domain power to take over the plant, echoing the strategy made popular by Lynd, Hornack and Tri-State. Nabisco was sufficiently chastened by the public uproar and the official threats to keep the plant open, which it did until 1998.[703]

In the wake of the Nabisco episode, Hornack was involved, along with SNAC, in the promotion and drafting of a Pittsburgh plant closing notification law, which was passed by city council and which would have required employers to notify the city of closings or layoffs of more than fifteen percent of their work force. At the time, there was no analogous federal law; the Worker Adjustment and Retraining Notification (WARN) Act would not be enacted until 1988. Although Caliguiri had gone as far as saying that the city was willing to do "everything possible" to make sure that Nabisco would remain open permanently, he quickly announced his opposition to the Pittsburgh plant notification legislation. "Council is not building a wall around the city to keep business in," the mayor declared. "Their wall is going to keep business out."[704] Moreover, the broad sweep of the law would have undoubtedly put the mayor at odds with Pittsburgh-based corporate citizens, such as U.S. Steel, with whom he was then working on downtown development.

When the law was passed by city council, Caliguiri informed the council that the city solicitor, Dante Pellegrini, would not be made available to defend the law against the legal challenges that almost instantly arose against it, led principally by the Small Manufacturers' Council, the Tri-State Manufacturers Association and the Greater Pittsburgh Chamber of Commerce. City council hired Hornack to defend the law, facing off against Jacques Wood from Berkman Ruslander, James B. Brown from the Baskin firm and David McClenahan of the Kirkpatrick firm, before Common Pleas judges Nicholas Papadakos and Emil Narick. Judge Narick had once been an attorney for the NLRB and had served as assistant general counsel to the United Steelworkers, so Hornack had hoped that there was a good chance the judges would be receptive to the law, but as Hornack recalls, "They were extremely hostile during oral argument." The law was struck down by the Common Pleas Court on constitutional grounds (interference with interstate commerce) as well as because it violated Pittsburgh's home rule charter; the Commonwealth Court affirmed the latter point, and the law was wiped off the books.[705]

"It was a time when there was just a lot of panic," recalled Hornack, and there was considerable disagreement among stakeholders about the best way to fight the plant closures. While Tri-State continued to try to get existing municipal authorities interested in the "eminent domain" concept, the United Steelworkers expressed their concern about raising the ire of U.S. Steel and making matters worse, branding the Tri-State group as "outsiders" and troublemakers. Lynd, meanwhile, was critical of the lack of democracy within the United Steelworkers.[706] And further out on the fringe was a group called the Denominational Ministry Strategy (DMS), founded by radical members of the local Lutheran clergy, which focused on Mellon Bank's role as a leader of deindustrialization and a financier of foreign steel expansion. DMS waged public stunts against the Bank, including depositing stinky dead fish into Mellon safe deposit boxes.[707]

At the end of 1983, U.S. Steel's David Roderick announced that the Duquesne blast furnace, known as the "Dorothy 6" after the wife of former U.S. Steel president Leslie Worthington, was going to be shut down. The twenty-one year-old plant had just won a company productivity award. The Dorothy 6 blast furnace absolutely dominated the community of Duquesne, located ten miles southeast of Pittsburgh on the Monongahela River. The announced shutdown sent dumbfounded members of the USW exploring the possibility of an employee stock ownership plan (ESOP) in the nature of the one that the members of the Independent Steelworkers Union were in the process of creating to acquire Weirton Steel, but the USW did not enjoy any success with the idea.

The plant closed in May 1984; but when U.S. Steel announced in October 1984 that it intended to demolish the plant the following month, it stimulated the formation of an all-star coalition, consisting of an uneasy alliance between the USW and Tri-State, as well as political leaders and droves of unaffiliated citizens throughout the region. Their "Save Dorothy" campaign "swept through the Mon Valley like a tornado," as John Hoerr writes. Hornack was involved in pitching Tri-State's ideas to politicians on Grant Street who were otherwise busy with downtown development projects. "We were trying to get them to get involved in our project, our activity," Hornack recalls, "and I think we all recognized that at the same time they were spending money on these other things ... okay, maybe some diversification is good, but we also need to save manufacturing as well," Hornack observed. "[C]an't you do some work in that area in addition to improving the skyline?" The USW, Allegheny County commissioners (led by Tom Foerster and Pete Flaherty, who had returned from Washington after losing a Senate bid to Arlen Specter, and was elected commissioner in 1983) and Pittsburgh city council jointly sponsored a $150,000 feasibility study of the possibility of local employee ownership of the plant, while Roderick, though irritated by the efforts, agreed to delay the demolition and permitted workers to inspect and winterize the mothballed plant, pending the results of the study. The workers established "Fort Duquesne" outside the gates of the plant, standing guard to make sure that U.S. Steel honored its promise and did not try to remove machinery and equipment from the site.[708]

As the citizen-soldiers of the Mon Valley battled over the closure of the Dorothy 6 in the midst of the most alarming decline in the economy that Pittsburgh had ever experienced, the newspapers reported the grim news that John Galbreath, the eighty-seven year-old lead owner of the Pittsburgh Pirates, was trying to sell the ballclub. In November 1984, Dan Galbreath, John Galbreath's son and the president of the Pirates, acknowledged that the owners were soliciting bids for the team. John Galbreath, it seemed, had attained his goal of winning another World Series in 1979, and now the air was coming out of the team's tires. After the 1979 World Series, the Pirates finished third in the NL East; during the following two seasons, they dropped to 4th; in 1984, they were last in the NL East. After eight months of trying to find a local buyer, in the middle of the 1985 season Dan Galbreath announced that the ownership was open to considering out-of-town bids.[709] Making matters worse, the Pirates had become implicated in a federal cocaine prosecution that summer; six current and former Pirates—including Dave Parker, one of the stars of the 1979 World Series—as well as the guy who wore the Pirate Parrot mascot costume, testified before the grand jury and admitted to buying and using illegal drugs.[710] With the Pittsburgh economy in freefall, the team slumping on the field and its image damaged by the drug trials, there could not have been a worse time for Pittsburghers to try to figure out how to retain their major league baseball team.

Kent May, a partner at Eckert Seamans, frowned at the news that the Galbreaths might be looking for an out-of-town buyer. Concerned that no one in the community seemed to be stepping up to keep the Pirates in Pittsburgh, he went to one of the members of Eckert's management committee, Gregg Kerr, with an unusual proposal.

"Why don't we volunteer to represent any group that wants to buy the Pirates—free, not charge them for it—so long as they agree that they'll keep the team in Pittsburgh?," May asked. Remarkably enough, Kerr agreed. The firm reached out to the local office of Price Waterhouse and to Ketchum Communications to provide accounting and publicity services on the same basis. It soon became clear, however, that the lure of owning a baseball team and the public offer of free professional services attracted too many unqualified suitors, so the firm enlisted its senior corporate partner and recently-elected managing partner, Carl Barger, to run a different strategy: to provide free legal services to a buyer, or a buyer's group, that the firm would take the lead in creating.[711]

May and Barger were both baseball fans. As a teenager, Carl Barger used to hitchhike from his home in Lewistown in central Pennsylvania to Forbes Field in Pittsburgh to see games. He and his father were sitting in the left-field bleachers at Forbes Field when Bill Mazeroski hit his game-winning home run in the seventh game of the 1960 World Series. "I think of that day often," Barger recalled. "I remember walking around the Downtown streets afterward. It was like VJ Day and VE Day and the Fourth of July all at once." Barger, who went to Dickinson Law School after getting his degree at Shippensburg State, was Eckert Seamans' first true corporate deal lawyer. In that capacity, Barger traveled the world making deals for Alcoa—his manic energy fueled by cigarettes and cocktails—armed with a positive thinking and enthusiasm for the project at hand that was combustible enough to blow the doors off of most boardrooms. As the *Post-Gazette*'s Bill Utterback wrote, "Barger refuses to believe that anything's impossible ... [and he believes that] impossibility wears down under baseline-to-baseline pressure."[712] The charismatic Barger had "only one speed: overdrive," according to his friend, Alcoa general counsel/chairman's counsel Richard Fischer.[713] "Carl loved big projects," said May,[714] and he was ready-made for the big project of marshaling large corporate resources to save an important artifact of Pittsburgh's cultural identity.

Barger and May met with the Galbreaths in Columbus to discuss a price for the team, and then Barger launched headlong into putting together a deal.[715] After one group led by Jim Roddey, a local businessman and chairman of the Port Authority board, fell apart, Barger went to Douglas Danforth, the chairman of Westinghouse, for help in lining up larger players in the Pittsburgh corporate community.[716] Barger himself played a significant role in selling the idea to two of his long-time clients, Ryan Homes and Alcoa. The CEO of Ryan Homes, Malcolm "Mac" Prine—a former prosecutor in Columbus before joining the company—was also a college football referee, and was particularly excited about the idea of becoming involved with a professional sports franchise. He became the *de facto* head of the group. Meanwhile, Danforth and David Roderick, as representatives of the ACCD—which had predictably remained on the sidelines of the plant closure battles—approached Mayor Caliguiri for additional funding in the event an ownership group could be formed. The price for the team, as conveyed by the Galbreaths to Barger, would be around twenty-two million dollars, which was lower than the purported market value, but was something that John Galbreath had conceded because he wanted the team to stay in Pittsburgh.[717] That meant raising approximately two million dollars each from thirteen buyers—not much more than a line item in the typical "advertising budget" of a large Pittsburgh corporation, asserted

May.[718] Meanwhile, the leaders of the ownership team required the city to put up another twenty-five million dollars for working capital.

Caliguiri's original plan was to raise the city's share through a sale of Three Rivers Stadium to New York investors, but the deal fell through. Ultimately, the city raised twenty million dollars through a bond issue, and the money was loaned by the URA to the ownership group, known as "Pittsburgh Associates," on highly favorable terms (a fifteen-year note payable, as Gariti observed, only from "positive cash flow" from team operations) in exchange for an "equity option agreement" from the owners, providing that if they ever decided to put the team up for sale, the URA would have the right, for three months, to find a local buyer for the team.[s][719] Ultimately, with Barger and the ACCD leading the way, in addition to Ryan Homes, Alcoa, Westinghouse and U.S. Steel, Pittsburgh Associates' investors represented some of the cream of Pittsburgh's corporate crop: PNC, Mellon Bank, National Intergroup (formerly National Steel) and PPG. Carnegie Mellon University received a share of the team, reportedly as a donation from members of the Heinz and Mellon families, and four businessmen bought their shares of the team individually: Harvey Walken, the high-profile Chicago real estate developer who built One South Wacker Drive in the Loop; Eugene Litman, Roz Litman's brother-in-law and a successful Pittsburgh-area real estate developer; Frank J. Schneider, chairman of a successful engineering and construction firm; and John McConnell, chairman of Worthington Industries, a Columbus steel manufacturer. Mac Prine was named president of the team and Danforth was named chairman after the sale closed in April 1986.[720]

Kent May recalled that the public-private deal was extremely difficult to put together, with a number of moving parts, not to mention that Peter Ueberroth, the commissioner of Major League Baseball, was initially skeptical of the idea of an "ownership group," preferring to deal with a single owner and a single voice.[721] "And you're doing this with the eyes of the entire community watching you," as Barger emphasized.[722] Meanwhile, although many people did not necessarily see a connection between the building of new skyscrapers in downtown Pittsburgh and the deindustrialization of the region, the Pirates deal certainly had its local critics. The newspapers quoted presumed average citizens asserting that the deal was "a public handout for what should be a private affair," and that "the taxpayers didn't get themselves into trouble ... The Pirates got themselves into trouble."[723] Tom Flaherty, a Duquesne Law graduate and later Common Pleas judge then serving as city controller, had been a supporter of SNAC during the Nabisco fight; he said the Pirates deal was the result of "cronyism" and called it "the biggest ripoff I've ever seen."[724] Barger's response to critics was that the Pirates generated significant tax revenue for the city, delinking the effort from the efforts to save industrial jobs. "The unemployed in this area have to find jobs," Barger said. "You can't resurrect the steel industry. You can't wish it back. So you have to do whatever possible to keep what we have."[725][t]

---

s   The remaining $5 million for working capital was allegedly "promised" by Caliguiri to come later in the event the Stadium could be sold or refinanced. When it did not come, the "promise" became the subject of a years-long conflict between the City and the Pirates. See e.g., Pittsburgh Baseball v. Stadium Authority, 630 A.2d 505 (Pa. Cmnwlth. Ct. 1993).

t   Carl Barger assumed the presidency of the Pittsburgh Pirates in 1987, after Ryan Homes pulled out

Back in Duquesne, the citizen-soldiers were still doing whatever they thought was possible to save Dorothy 6 On January 18, 1985, Rev. Jesse Jackson, gearing up for his second presidential run, brought the national press to Duquesne to see him address a crowd of five hundred during a snowstorm at the plant gates, declaring that that the Mon Valley was "the Selma of the plant shutdown movement."[726] A couple of weeks later, nearly seven hundred people packed into the basement of the Sts. Peter and Paul Church in Duquesne to hear the results of the coalition-commissioned study on the viability of Dorothy 6, which concluded that it would cost ninety million dollars to restart the furnace, but that it could net thirty-five million dollars in profits in three years. The coalition kept its hopes for the plant alive while U.S. Steel sought to discredit the study, releasing its own study saying that it would cost half a billion to reopen the plant and that it would lose $110 million in the first three years. The USW then announced that it was hiring the New York investment bank Lazard Freres & Company, the same group that was working on the friendly sale of Weirton Steel to an ESOP by its owner, National Steel, to see if financing could be obtained for local ownership and operation of Dorothy 6. The USW Local 1256 and U.S. Steel continued their standoff at the gates of Dorothy 6 until Lazard returned with its verdict in January 1986: in the words of Jim Smith, an assistant to USW president Lynn Williams, "If people worked for free, the project still wouldn't succeed." The USW withdrew its support for the "Save Dorothy" campaign, and U.S. Steel demolished the facility in 1988.[727]

Lynd, Hornack and Tri-State did manage to get one significant benefit out of their participation in the "Save Dorothy" coalition. Their long-held goal of establishing an independent regional authority that could credibly threaten to acquire plants slated for shutdown through the use of eminent domain, as had been successfully done within Pittsburgh city limits in the Nabisco episode, received support from all factions within the coalition during 1985. The city of Pittsburgh donated fifty thousand dollars in seed funding to the effort, while the municipalities of Munhall, Homestead, McKeesport, Glassport and others in the industrial region southeast of Pittsburgh passed resolutions in support of the creation of a Steel Valley Authority (SVA) under the state Municipal Authorities Act of 1945. Hornack worked with Joe Gariti at the URA in creating the charter and the intermunicipal agreements necessary for the incorporation and launch of the SVA. In January 1986, just as the Lazard report was shutting down the "Save Dorothy" movement, the SVA was officially created, with Frank O'Brien, the former president of the USW Local 1843, as its first chairman, and Hornack as its solicitor.[728]

The SVA had scarcely seen the light of day before it was involved in what finally became the last hurrah of the anti-plant shutdown movement. In July 1985, American Standard announced that it was planning to close its Union Switch & Signal and

---

of the ownership group. He worked with his long-time client, Wayne Huizenga, on the creation of a National League expansion team, the Florida (Miami) Marlins, and became the new team's first president in 1991. However, at the 1992 Winter Meetings of Major League Baseball, Barger collapsed and died after suffering an aortic aneurysm. Robert McG. Thomas, Jr., "Carl Barger, 62, Team President With Pirates and Florida Marlins," *The New York Times*, December 10, 1992. The Marlins played their first game at the beginning of the 1993 season.

Westinghouse Air Brake plants in the community of East Pittsburgh, which it had acquired from Westinghouse in 1968. With two thousand jobs at stake, the SVA filed an injunction against American Standard, to prevent the company from dismantling the plants, and its legitimacy as a state-sanctioned municipal authority enabled it to use a variety of delaying tactics—reports and appraisal activities—to stall the closings, until federal Judge Barron McCune stated the obvious in siding with American Standard: the SVA had neither a buyer nor any financing to save the plants. Subsequent efforts by the SVA to come up with a credible financing plan for any plant revival project were also unsuccessful, and today the SVA largely concerns itself with displaced worker assistance and manufacturing business attraction and retention activities. Hornack has continued to serve as its solicitor for over thirty years.[729]

Jay Hornack was aware of the efforts of some people in the greater Pittsburgh community to focus on the stimulation of a homegrown entrepreneurial, technology economy during the plant shutdown years, but in a sense it only strengthened his commitment to saving steel and manufacturing. "From the standpoint of the communities who had these good paying jobs" at the manufacturing plants, Hornack recalled, "there was just a concern that if something else was going to come along, it was going to take a long time to get set up, and then in the meantime, these great middle class jobs were going to be disappearing ... We wanted to save as many of the good-paying jobs as possible."[730]

Other Pittsburgh lawyers were becoming experts at corporate anti-takeover law. When Gulf Oil became the target of corporate raiders as its stock price began to fall below its breakup value in the early 1980s, William P. Hackney at Reed Smith, among others, helped to design and push through a state anti-takeover law that broadened the scope of factors that management could consider in exercising its fiduciary duties, required supermajority votes for certain fundamental transactions, and created a shareholder right to demand to be bought out by a corporate raider at a "control premium" over market price. Factions of the corporate bar, Dean Edward Sell at Pitt Law among them, criticized the law as probably unconstitutional and otherwise bad corporate policy. In the midst of a 1988 overhaul of the Pennsylvania corporate statute, the state legislature enacted more anti-takeover protections. At that time, Vincent Deluzio at Buchanan Ingersoll was successfully guiding Lancaster-based Armstrong World Industries through an attempted takeover by the Belzberg family.[731]

Meanwhile, William R. "Bill" Newlin, the head of Buchanan Ingersoll, had a different perspective. "I didn't think [saving old-line companies] was the solution" for the region, Newlin remembered. "I thought the reality was that the destruction had occurred ... I had a genuine belief at the time that technology was the future of Pittsburgh."[732]

Pittsburgh's two major universities—the University of Pittsburgh and Carnegie Mellon University (CMU)—were quietly emerging as major employers in the region as well as scientific research powerhouses. The Mellon Institute, an independent science school focusing on applied chemistry, physics and biology established in 1910, had fallen on hard financial times and merged with Carnegie Tech in 1967, to become CMU. Five years later, when economist Dr. Richard Cyert became president of CMU, it received only thirteen million dollars in research funds; by 1990, Cyert had led the

University to a more than eight hundred percent increase in its research funding (to $123 million), including fifty million dollars in Department of Defense funding. Under Cyert's leadership, CMU experienced an extraordinary transformation. With corporate funding, Cyert was able to establish a CMU Robotics Institute in 1978 and a Magnetics Technology Center in 1982; and in 1984, the University was awarded a five-year, $103 million Defense grant to establish a federal research lab known as the Software Engineering Institute to study computer security and develop best practices in the design of operating systems. In 1982, CMU joined together with Pitt, then being led by Wesley Posvar, entered into a partnership with IBM to create the jointly operated Pittsburgh Supercomputing Center.[733]

Meanwhile, Posvar, who had become president of the University of Pittsburgh in 1967, was presiding over a similar period of extraordinary growth: in 1967, the University's total budget was ninety million dollars, and by 1990, it had expanded to $630 million—or $1.1 billion, if you included the University of Pittsburgh Medical Center (UPMC) hospital system. UPMC, which was closely affiliated with Pitt's medical school, became a world-class center for organ transplantation after the arrival of surgeon Thomas Starzl in 1981. UPMC also laid the groundwork for becoming a leading center for cancer research with the establishment of the University of Pittsburgh Cancer Institute in 1984, with a substantial grant from the R.K. Mellon Foundation. The Cancer Institute would pursue research in molecular biology and genetics in collaboration with both Pitt and CMU, where the beginnings of a computational biology program were being established. Also, in the aftermath of Chevron's acquisition of Gulf Oil, in 1985 Chevron made a gift of Gulf's research lab campus in nearby Harmarville, along with forty million dollars in equipment, to the University of Pittsburgh as an applied research center, with incubator space for small technology firms.[734] When one stops and considers how long science-oriented institutions such as MIT and Caltech have enjoyed their reputations as leading research centers in the U.S.—since at least the 1940s in MIT's case, perhaps a decade earlier in the case of Caltech—the rise of the national reputations of CMU and Pitt during the early 1980s was meteoric.

Dr. Cyert—who was embraced by the downtown community as a director of such companies as Heinz, American Standard, Allegheny International and the Pittsburgh Pirates—became a prophet of the future of Pittsburgh technology, and in particular on the role that computer science would play in the transformation of Pittsburgh. High Tech, said Cyert, "will change our lives the way automobiles did." He articulated a development strategy that would begin with "a campus saturated with computing," and touted Pittsburgh as a future "software capital of the world."[735] There was no question that Pittsburgh had been developing the raw materials for a new industry built around technology. No one yet, however, had a specific vision how technology businesses could become significant employers in Pittsburgh—or how you could take all those zeros and ones, and go from zero to one.

Bill Newlin was a young man in a hurry when he became president of Buchanan Ingersoll Professional Corporation in September 1980. Born in Pittsburgh, his family moved frequently when he was growing up—he attended thirteen different schools as they relocated from Pittsburgh to West Virginia, to Philadelphia, New Jersey and New York, and back and forth again to Pittsburgh several times, before the family settled in the Pittsburgh suburb of West View, in his grandparents' home above the West View amusement park. While at West View High, Newlin accumulated more national forensic league points than anyone in the country, and was a state and national-level debater. With the intention of going on to law school, he went to Princeton and undertook such gritty pursuits as majoring in philosophy and battling as a member of the wrestling team (only a few years behind another, similarly combative and intense Princeton wrestler, Donald Rumsfeld). On the advice of a family friend, Carl Brandt of the Brandt, Riester, Brandt and Malone law firm, he turned down slots at Michigan and Penn law schools to attend Pitt, based on the assumption that he would be settling in Pittsburgh since he had just married his Princeton girlfriend, Ann, who was also from Pittsburgh. After working for a summer with the local branch of the IRS, Newlin landed at Buchanan Ingersoll in the summer of 1964.[736]

When he arrived at Buchanan Ingersoll as a full-time lawyer in 1965, he encountered the firm that Kent May had described as "stodgy," still reeling a bit from the "split" with the Eckert Seamans group and the loss of Alcoa as its client. After the split, the firm had no managing partner for a time. "You had a chairman of the meeting that rotated to a new partner every meeting, which meant nothing got done ... which a lot of people liked," Newlin recalls. "It was a situation where no one wanted any real management. You hired an office manager to do it." With nothing getting done, however, the firm was stagnating financially. He began to realize, at partner compensation time, that major discussions were occurring "over a tenth of a point that amounted to almost no money whatsoever." There was no growth, and to Newlin, "it was shocking." As a partner, he became actively involved in management—organizing a securities law practice group at the firm, talking about setting up an advisory committee, and forcing uncomfortable discussions about growth. He recalls one of the senior corporate partners, Elmer Myers, rather impatiently confronting him, asking, "Don't you have anything better to do?" He nonetheless cut through the generational differences in style and became the chief executive officer of the firm at age thirty-nine, with the aim of taking Buchanan Ingersoll back to its traditional place as "a really powerful law firm" with "a powerful business base."[u]

---

[u] Before Newlin became the leader of the firm, Buchanan Ingersoll did have three managing partners in succession: Glenn Reed, Edward Schoyer (who was actively assisted by a deputy, Clayton Sweeney), and Robert Patton. With the exception of Sweeney, perhaps, their styles of management, operating as caretakers rather than captains, were influenced by the need to appeal to the older, more senior partners and their desire for less management control. Sweeney and Patton in particular—both of whom moved on to executive roles in large Pittsburgh corporations—are most appropriately viewed as the generational bridge to the more hands-on, "corporate" style of management that Newlin would deploy in his tenure. Clayton Sweeney, interview by the author, October 24, 2008; Robert Patton, *An Ordinary Life* (Lincoln, NE: iUniverse, 2006), 114-117.

Where that "powerful business base" would come from was not altogether apparent in 1980. The firm had some larger legacy clients, such as Allegheny Ludlum and Armstrong Cork, for whom it worked on securities, acquisitions and financings. The firm, however, "didn't have an endless list of corporate clients," Newlin recalled, and Pittsburgh's corporate base was contracting, making the competition for additional corporate legal work fiercer. Eventually, Newlin's love of deal-making led him to attract "small, aggressive-growth companies" as clients. Often, they were technology companies, and often, Newlin was invited to sit on their boards of directors as a key business advisor.[737] Two of his early tech client successes from the 1970s were Online Systems, a mainframe computer time-sharing platform company founded by John Godfrey and Jack Roseman, which went public and was eventually sold to Sprint in 1980, and Duquesne Systems, a mainframe systems management company founded by Glen Chatfield that went public and then merged with Morino Inc. to form Legent Corp. in 1989.[738]

This new generation of companies was being led by risk-oriented entrepreneurs who understood technology and technology markets, but who sometimes had little C-level or upper management experience. They had different problems than companies like Alcoa and Allegheny Ludlum: they were often fighting for product acceptance within immature industry segments, or within mature industries that had not yet experienced the computer revolution; they had exceedingly lean-and-mean management teams compared to old-line businesses; rather than dealing with labor issues, unions and environmental matters, intellectual property and basic commercial guidance were key concerns; and they were constantly in fundraising mode, but because banks were squeamish about lending to new technology companies, these companies were looking for private angel investors and venture capital money. The companies changed and moved at a rapid pace, and their leaders resisted constraints—legal, financial or otherwise—that could slow them down. In guts and vision alone, they were Newlin's kind of people.

Newlin understood, however, that while there was the potential that these kinds of companies might become significant employers in Pittsburgh, Pittsburgh itself was missing some key components that could help these companies launch, mature and grow. Fortunately, there were a number of like-minded people who began to meet and discuss these matters. Tom Murphy, a former Peace Corps volunteer in Paraguay who was a community organizer on the North Side, then serving in the state legislature as a Democrat, was inspired by Dr. Cyert to think about "how you build an entrepreneurial culture in Pittsburgh." James R. "Jim" Colker, a Pitt physicist/engineer who had worked at RCA, General Electric and Westinghouse before buying a New York-based optical company which eventually became Contraves Goerz Corporation, was also interested in developing the next generation of Pittsburgh businesses. Others included Dr. Angel Jordan, the CMU provost, who had helped to attract the Software Engineering Institute and led in the establishment of the CMU School of Computer Science; Jay Aldridge, president of the Penn Southwest Association; and Gary Golding, the business development director for Penn Southwest.[739]

"I remember Dr. Cyert rattling off a list of companies [that] were started at CMU, or the people had gone to CMU, and then they moved," Murphy said. "They were our failures."[740] Another example of a big technology company with Pittsburgh roots was Genentech: its Nobel Prize-winning founder, Dr. Herbert Boyer, was born in the little town of Derry, about 40 miles east of Pittsburgh, studied biology and chemistry at St. Vincent College in Latrobe, received his PhD at Pitt, and then moved to California, where he taught at UCSF and founded Genentech in 1976.[741] When Boyer left Pittsburgh in 1963, there was little commercial interest in biotechnology and not much in the way of support for what Boyer would eventually accomplish. The group began to lay out plans for building some of the infrastructure that would keep the future Boyers in Pittsburgh, building the next Genentechs.

Pittsburgh's technology sector received a boost from Governor Dick Thornburgh early on. In 1979, Thornburgh formed the Commission on Choices for Pennsylvanians, spearheaded by Walt Plosila, to study the future of job growth and economic renewal in the state. The Commission urged the governor to devise policies, as Lubove relates, "to promote the service and advanced technology component of the economy." Based on the Commission's recommendations, Governor Thornburgh proposed a funding mechanism for the co-development of new technologies by universities and private sector partners.[742] Legislation creating the Ben Franklin Partnership, introduced by Tom Murphy and Republican Rick Geist from Altoona, was passed in 1982.[743] The goal of the state-wide Partnership, whose Pittsburgh arm would eventually be called Innovation Works, was to encourage universities to collaborate with private companies and commercialize university research by providing a source of early-stage funding for new technology businesses.

Newlin supported the effort to create the Ben Franklin Partnership, but noted that there were still a number of things that Pittsburgh needed in order to encourage an entrepreneurial culture—"all the other ingredients that you need in order to" take the technology that was being created in Pittsburgh and "really make it a business." Newlin ticked down the list. "The entrepreneur. The infrastructure. The public support. The government support, tax-wise and otherwise. Then, eventually, the banks, the lawyers, and the venture capitalists." He, Jim Colker, Jay Aldridge and others began to feel strongly that the "disconnected technology bases" around Pittsburgh needed their own institution where they could hang their hats, and from which leaders in the new industry could articulate needs and showcase success. "And you have to give it an independent standing or you suffocate it," Newlin opined. "In other words ... it's so hard to start a real entrepreneurial idea in a much larger organization, even in a company today. So it had to be separate, so it could be identified that way, it would attract attention that way. The newspapers would pay attention. It needed its own standing to have a chance at success."[744]

In 1983, Colker and Newlin formed the Pittsburgh High Technology Council (later renamed as the Pittsburgh Technology Council), with Colker as its first president and Timothy Parks as its first executive director. "[The] view was if you assemble [new technology startups] into a trade organization and partner with the universities, it could become a very significant economic player in the region, and it did," Newlin said.[745] The Council eventually became, by membership, the largest regional technology trade association in the nation,[746] offering basic business services as well as serving as a platform for regional business development, government relations and talent retention.

Meanwhile, Colker and Newlin began to consider the viability of launching a venture capital fund. In 1983, there were a few venture capital firms operating in the Pittsburgh region, but most were either family office funds—such as Hillman Ventures (formed in 1976), Fostin Capital (1982) or Robinson Venture Partners (1982)—or they were private investment arms of banks, such as the PNC Venture or Security Pacific venture capital groups, and they had not yet become focused on the technology sector in Pittsburgh.[747] Newlin knew very little about venture capital at the time. "I knew how to finance companies, but I hadn't really dealt that much with the venture capital ... [I] certainly didn't really understand yet the business of venture capital, which as we all know is very complex, to actually set up a fund and run it and attract people and make the decisions." Nonetheless, recognizing the need for venture capital in Pittsburgh, Colker and Newlin began to draw up a plan for establishing a new local venture capital fund, eventually known as the CEO Venture Fund, that would focus primarily on Western Pennsylvania technology investments as well as providing hands-on management advice to start-up entrepreneurs. To augment the team, they brought in Glen Chatfield of Duquesne Systems and Gene Yost, founder of Black Box Corporation, a seller of data communications hardware, as general partners.[748]

Before beginning to seek investment for their first fund in 1985, however, Newlin and Colker led the effort to amend state pension laws so that, through Act 95 which passed in 1984, state pension funds would be permitted invest up to one percent of their holdings in "alternative investments" such as venture capital funds. CEO Venture Fund, and the Pittsburgh technology community, became beneficiaries of the change.[749] The first and second CEO Venture Funds were significant players in the Pittsburgh entrepreneurial community, becoming the lead investors in such companies as Formtek (acquired by Lockheed), Extrel (acquired by Millipore Corporation), Biological Detection Systems (acquired by Amersham Biosciences) and Neolinear (acquired by Cadence Design Systems), and they helped pave the way for later venture capital entrants in Pittsburgh, such as Draper Triangle and Birchmere Ventures. The indefatigable team of Colker and Newlin also helped to launch a "CEO network," in order to cultivate a corps of executives "with some experience in taking a chance, becoming entrepreneurs [and] taking technical risks," as Colker explained, and matching them with opportunities in Pittsburgh start-ups; and in 1989 they formed the Pittsburgh Biomedical Development Corporation, the region's first pre-seed fund focused exclusively on biomedical technology.[750]

While "doing something that I felt added to the stability of the region, the economic base" was Newlin's primary motive, it was no coincidence that he positioned Buchanan Ingersoll to take advantage of the wave of activity.[751] However, that was not as simple as putting his lawyers to work on technology clients—it also meant retooling the firm to be equipped to deal with the very different needs of start-ups. The middle-aged corporate lawyers in Buchanan Ingersoll were, at the time, more accustomed to working with clients like Allegheny International—mobilizing large teams of lawyers to negotiate international acquisitions and launch public offerings, working with the decision-making of public boards and the dictates of seasoned executive officers—and getting well-paid for it, until these clients began to disappear. Working with technology start-ups required the firm to structure its client teams differently—lean-and-mean, one partner working with one young associate on more established technology ventures, sometimes an associate managing the relationship in the case of a true start-up. Getting associates involved at an earlier point in their careers not only served the objective of making sure that lawyers received important training, but it gave the firm a less expensive way of bearing payment risks associated with start-ups—associates billed out at lower hourly rates, and if a start-up never received adequate funding, the firm lost less money on the representation.

Working with these clients required the firm to develop new disciplines—greater depth in private placement regulations, an understanding of the structure of venture capital equity rounds, greater emphasis on intellectual property and the commercial law surrounding "technology transactions"—and where the discipline could not be cultivated from within, it was acquired, as with the acquisition of the Buell Ziesenheim patent group in 1988 and the lateral hiring of a pharma/medical device regulatory group from Akin Gump in 2000.[752] Working with start-ups also often required the lawyer, rather than the client, to design the project. And to succeed, every technology start-up lawyer would ultimately be required to grow into the trusted counselor to the entrepreneur on matters other than the law—on management, finance and/or product or service markets—based on the sum total of their experiences in dealing with new technology start-ups; in their advice, they would have to demonstrate their ability to adjust to the level of risk tolerance being undertaken by an entrepreneur, while still maintaining their integrity as lawyers.

Within the firm, partners would say that Buchanan Ingersoll lawyers were being trained to be "more entrepreneurial," and that their objective as lawyers was "not to throw up roadblocks" but to "get the deal done." This self-consciously entrepreneurial culture produced a small army of lawyers who became identified with Pittsburgh technology company growth during the era, including Carl Cohen, Robert Devlin, Sheryl Clark Stoll and Susan Hartman, among others. Although larger firms in Pittsburgh were still ambivalent about taking on the revenue risks of representing start-up clients, the impact of what Buchanan Ingersoll was doing was not lost on its rivals. As Greg Jordan, who would later serve as managing partner of Reed Smith, recalled, "I looked at Buchanan and they were out-performing us. They were out-growing us, they were out-recruiting us."[753] To Jordan, it seemed, for a time, that Buchanan Ingersoll was the exciting place to practice law in Pittsburgh.

"There's no question Bill's interest in the entrepreneurial side of Pittsburgh transcends his legal practice. His passion for the entrepreneurial side of Pittsburgh is because he believes in its potential," said Tim Parks in a 1995 interview.[754] "I felt like the only way that it was going to happen was if the people on their own go out and make it happen more dramatically," said Newlin, "—that we had to actively participate in creating things in Pittsburgh that became at least part of the solution" to rebuilding Pittsburgh's economy.[755] It was not immediately apparent, however, to many executives and institutions in Pittsburgh that an entrepreneurial economy was a good thing, nor were other law firms in Pittsburgh devoting the unpaid time and resources to the effort that Newlin brought to these activities in the early 1980s. "The headwinds at the time were significant," recalls Tom Murphy. "It's true with every change, the difficulty of getting people to imagine something other than what's there. It's always a challenge, particularly when you're talking about shifting resources to something very unknown."[756] For undertaking such an experiment—for becoming publicly identified with it as the founder of key start-up organizations, for spending valuable time away from paying projects, for re-designing a large portion of the firm as an engine for representing entrepreneurial companies—one might have expected greater protest from the ranks of the partners of Buchanan Ingersoll during the period. But the experiment worked; and, in any event, as Newlin admits, he "never asked" permission.[757] In 2000, the *National Law Journal* had named Newlin one of the "100 Most Influential Lawyers in America."[758]

Another Pittsburgh lawyer who became identified with representing technology companies in Pittsburgh was Marlee Myers, initially at Kirkpatrick Lockhart and later at the Pittsburgh-office of Philadelphia-based Morgan Lewis & Bockius, which she founded in 1996. Myers, who grew up in impoverished circumstances, won a full scholarship to CMU, but ended up "dropping out" twice—once, temporarily, to accept a job as a bookbinder at the Harvard Museum of Comparative Zoology, and again when she married Jim Myers, a former CMU English instructor and copywriter, at the age of nineteen. As a newlywed, contemplating her future while teaching herself cooking, music and symbolic logic, she hit upon the idea of returning to college—this time at Pitt—and shortly thereafter, to pursue a career teaching children suffering from autism, at that time a relatively rare and little known disease. After doing some volunteer work with autistic children, however, she decided she didn't like it and, in a further epiphany, decided to go to law school. Graduating from Pitt with a double major in English and history and earning recognition as the University's outstanding graduate in literature, she entered Pitt Law, and ended up graduating first in her class in 1977.[759]

When she joined Kirkpatrick, she gravitated toward the corporate/tax group, working with Chuck Queenan and one of the younger lawyers, Robert Anestis, a 1971 Harvard Law graduate. "It was after I started practicing," Myers recalled, "that I realized that … what I really wanted to do was work with entrepreneurs." In 1978, Anestis was representing a member of a wealthy Pittsburgh family who wanted to invest in a materials technology start-up. Myers came up with the idea of structuring the investment through a research and development partnership, which would give the investor some tax advantages; it was the sort of clever, tax-driven construct for which Queenan had become famous around Pittsburgh. As she worked on the deal with the Silicon Valley-based inventors on the other side, she bonded with them, and ended up doing all of their work after the transaction. Back in Pittsburgh, she gave presentations on R&D partnerships and began to get a trickle of local tech clients. It was a different exercise for Myers than the earthmoving processes launched by Newlin and his community colleagues, however. "He was before his time in this town," Myers observes, but she points out that as a managing partner of a major firm, Newlin had the gravitas and the platform to achieve the larger projects involved in building a technology industry. "I was just an associate, I just went out and did it. Nobody said you can't, and I didn't ask anybody if I could."

Like Newlin, though, Myers saw the tech industry as a way to improve Pittsburgh's prospects. "We were in devastation-mode, [and] this was a way to reinvent the whole city," she recalls. Working with tech entrepreneurs was also a perfect match for her restless, relentlessly knowledge-seeking and intellectually inventive habits. "These people were exciting. ... I really liked working with people who were the smartest people, who were inventing new things, who were seeing the world in new ways, [and] being able to help them be able to create something where nothing was before, was extremely exciting and gratifying," she said. Myers surmises, "They also liked the characteristics that I brought to the table, that had been problematic in a more hidebound environment" of old school law and old school business in Pittsburgh. "I'm quick, I'm creative, I like to think of new ways of doing things." The tech entrepreneurs of the 1980s and 1990s were, out of necessity, among the first businessmen in Pittsburgh in generations to free themselves from the intellectual and social shackles of the old boys' network of corporate Pittsburgh; they had no connection to it, owed little to it, and it never occurred to most of them that they would get anything out of it, except perhaps late stage capital investments. Thus, importantly for Myers, a woman lawyer during an era of transition, "They didn't mind that I didn't look like lawyers usually looked."[760]

Myers has enjoyed an extraordinarily successful career as a lawyer for tech companies. Included among her client successes were two of Pittsburgh's biggest tech engagements before the dotcom bubble burst: FORE Systems, a computer network switching equipment company that was sold to General Electric Corp. plc for $4.5 billion in April 1999, and FreeMarkets, an online global supply auctioneer, whose market capitalization soared to nearly thirteen billion dollars after its 1999 IPO before it was sold to Ariba for $493 million.[761] Like Newlin, she has also populated the Pittsburgh bar with a number of acolytes who learned how to work with tech companies by her example, and like Newlin, she began to play a leadership role in the Tech Council during the late 1980s, serving on its board, leading seminars and seizing opportunities to promote and celebrate the achievements of Pittsburgh technology entrepreneurs for a wider audience.

During the "go-go" 1990s, Pittsburgh's technology industry created a significant amount of jobs and wealth, and also incidentally heightened the importance of the people—including the lawyers—who were involved in it.

In 1993, state legislator Tom Murphy was elected mayor of Pittsburgh, and before he was even inaugurated, he received a call from Vincent Sarni, the retiring chairman of PPG and the then current chairman of the Pittsburgh Pirates. One of Sarni's last official acts as PPG chief was the closing of PPG's Ford City plant, which once employed 4,400 workers, in July 1993—a significant withdrawal from the region, after a prolonged labor dispute.[762] Sarni told Murphy that the Pittsburgh Pirates were unhappy with their lease at Three Rivers Stadium, and were contemplating a sale. Murphy called Newlin for help. For seven years, Newlin and his team worked closely with the Murphy administration on almost every aspect of the next phase of the Pirates' existence in Pittsburgh—from the negotiation of a new Three Rivers Stadium lease, to finding a new "local" ownership group under the URA's "equity option agreement," closing the sale of the team to the new group (led by Kevin McClatchy, heir to a California newspaper fortune, with close ties to the Rooney family), leading the analysis in the selection of a site for a new ballpark, working on the financing plan for a new ballpark, and ultimately negotiating the construction agreements and new lease for what became PNC Park, which opened in 2001 on the North Shore, at the foot of the Sixth Street Bridge, newly rechristened as the "Clemente Bridge" after Pirates legend Roberto Clemente. The work was further complicated by a misfire with a first potential buyer—the Rigas family, owners of Adelphia Cable—and by the defeat of a ballot initiative to authorize a regional sales tax increase to help pay for the new ballpark and the new stadium also then being demanded by the Pittsburgh Steelers.

The new ballpark for the Pirates was required by Major League Baseball as a condition to the sale to the new group, and as Murphy admitted, Pittsburgh could not afford to lose the team. "These teams are symbols of Pittsburgh. They're a symbol of moving forward or backward. Something is at stake far bigger than what they're worth financially. The larger value is being a major league city," he said. "People can get mad at it and not like it, but the reality is that sports are international. It becomes a defining element of your city. Pittsburgh is thought of as a major league town, even though we're the same size as Oklahoma City and Dayton and Birmingham, Alabama, because of our sports teams." By the end of the process, the North Shore of Pittsburgh was completely transformed, with a new river walkway, two new stadiums, and a vibrant micro-community of new corporate headquarters buildings, new retail space and new residential units.

It was, both literally and figuratively, a changing of the downtown guard. Stepping up to the plate to solve the problem were two of the most prominent proponents of the new economy of Pittsburgh—Murphy and Newlin. While PNC, U.S. Steel and Westinghouse initially retained small interests in the team (with H.J. Heinz Company joining the new group), the new ownership was now largely a collection of individual leaders of successful regional middle-market businesses—not technology companies, but definitely not the old-line companies that had carried the weight of civic improvement during most of the twentieth century. Most of the large corporations who banded together to support the Pirates in 1986 no longer had any interest in the team, and many of them had fewer commercial ties to the region by 2001.[763]

The tech industry continues to thrive in Pittsburgh. Large companies such as Google and Uber have established campuses within close proximity of Pitt and CMU (Google moved into Bakery Square, a retail-and-office redevelopment of the old Nabisco factory space), as did Steve Jobs when he opened an "Eastern headquarters" in Pittsburgh for NeXT, Inc. in 1990. New startups emerge regularly from the halls of academia, or out of the studios of Pittsburgh's growing stable of serial entrepreneurs. A modest wave of commercial success in biotechnology has also taken place, beginning as early as the mid-1970s with Respironics, which introduced the first CPAP machine for the treatment of sleep apnea (acquired by Philips for five billion dollars in 2007) and continuing with Renal Solutions, a maker of a sorbent dialysis therapy technology, which was sold to Fresenius for two hundred million dollars in 2007.[764]

Buchanan Ingersoll, meanwhile, remained a dominant player in the technology industry into the 2000s, and though its clientele was diversified, like many law firms of its size it was hobbled a bit by the bursting of the dot-com bubble in 2000. Newlin retired from the presidency of the firm in 2003 to join Dick's Sporting Goods as its chief administrative officer, and has served on and off as chairman of the board of directors of

Kennametal, Inc., a long-time client.[765] Buchanan Ingersoll went on to merge with Klett Lieber Rooney & Schorling in 2006, becoming Buchanan Ingersoll & Rooney.[766] Marlee Myers' Pittsburgh office of Morgan Lewis contracted slightly in size during the years following the bubble, but began another growth period, and Myers has continued to be a strong advocate for entrepreneurs and the Pittsburgh technology industry. Larger law firms in Pittsburgh, while recognizing that working with good startups often leads to higher rate work when startups mature, have been cautious about devoting too many resources to working with early-stage technology companies. By contrast, many smaller firms and sole practitioners have assumed the role of early-stage advisors, bending their practices toward the entrepreneurial community and developing expertise in emerging areas such as cybersecurity, data protection and social media.

During the 1980s, Jay Hornack fought the battle of the plant closures without being paid for his efforts. He found a job at a workers compensation firm a year or so after he arrived in Pittsburgh, one that paid the bills while he continued to do legal research and make speeches for Tri-State. He would eventually receive a small stipend from the client he helped to create, the Steel Valley Authority. Carl Barger and Kent May did not receive any fees when they put together the deal that kept the Pirates in Pittsburgh in 1985. "It was debilitating at times in terms of the amount of effort that we put into this," Barger said in a 1986 interview. "We had the complete support of all the partners in the firm and from top to bottom our people believed in this. As a firm, we've put many, many hundreds of hours into this project, with many, many hundreds of hours to come. Right now we have seven lawyers in the firm working on various tax, labor and corporate aspects of the deal."[767] Bill Newlin essentially worked for free while plowing the ground and seeding Pittsburgh with some of the infrastructural elements required by the tech industry, and during the seven years Buchanan Ingersoll worked to close the deals that kept the Pirates in town when the corporate owners moved on, the Buchanan team labored unpaid for years at a time, until the deal was ultimately successful—a state of affairs that would be now be considered disastrous to firms that distribute most of their profits to partners at the end of each year. Marlee Myers has given hundreds of hours to the education and promotion of the tech industry. Even Chuck Queenan admitted that he didn't get paid for the investment banking component of the Allegheny Ludlum deal.

The common denominator between Hornack, May, Barger, Newlin and Myers, ultimately, was their desire to participate, aggressively, in the betterment of the community on a large scale—to "make things happen" in a region which had fallen upon tragically hard times. "It was important as an obligation to go out and participate and try to build things that would be good," says Newlin. "Now, should you try to leverage them also so that they work out fine for your business? Absolutely. So it always... fit like hand in glove. But it wasn't only to develop business. It was both."[768] Private practice lawyers, especially some lawyers within big firms in Pittsburgh—firms large enough in scale to bear some of the costs and risks associated with participating in big community projects without the expectation of immediate institutional benefit—began to fill the roles that had been filled, during "Renaissance I," by lawyers such as Arthur Van Buskirk, Leland Hazard and Leon Hickman, the powerful general counsels from large Pittsburgh corporations. By the end of the 1980s, some of the big Pittsburgh-based corporations had either been acquired, gone out of business, or had significantly retreated from bearing responsibility for the state of the Pittsburgh region; to the extent they stayed and survived, they became, for all intents and purposes, citizens of the stock exchange, not of Pittsburgh.

In some respects, the larger law firms of Pittsburgh that provided leadership during the crisis years of the 1980s have also lost some of their connection to the communities in which they operate. With hundreds of lawyers in offices across the nation or the globe, in the twenty-first century they reside, rather, on the AMLAW 100 list, less so in Pittsburgh. They have become, as Dan Booker put it, "delocalized"—geographically diversified. Their need to keep their "revenues per lawyer" and their "profits per equity partner" higher than those of their competitors on the list has turned their focus inward, out of necessity. It has frequently meant that fewer visionary risks, fewer longer-term flights of fancy, are initiated by their leaders. For businesses that operate from year to year, there is little incentive for such activity, and not much room for failure.

Pittsburgh has been fortunate since its years of crisis. As President Obama observed in 2009, when he announced that Pittsburgh would be the site of the G20 Conference that year, "Pittsburgh stands as a bold example of how to create new jobs and industries while transitioning to a 21st century economy ... a city that has transformed itself from the city of steel to a center for high-tech innovation including green technology, education and training, and research and development..."[769] During the Great Recession of 2008 and the bursting of the housing bubble, its job and housing markets remained relatively stable—not too frothy during the good times, not too desperate during the bad times. The engine has been running pretty smoothly, and the region hasn't needed too much in the way of grand repair plans. The "overnight success" of the city—planned, developed and executed by a group of civic leaders, including big company lawyers, to rescue the city from the excesses of the Second American Industrial Revolution during Renaissance I from the 1940s through the 1960s, paving the way for the important work of other civic leaders, including the essential contributions of big firm lawyers during the 1980s—is beheld with a sense of awe by those who visit today. The city has its problems and deficits, to be sure; but it is undeniable that some of the brightest features of Pittsburgh have the fingerprints of its Steel Bar upon them.

Did Chuck Queenan ever figure out what makes these lawyers tick? "I would say they are scoundrels and they're bullshitters!," he jokes. However, as he points out, "The good lawyers can see the changes coming; they have their antennae out." They have "the kind of training" that gives them "a sense of relevance" as they wade through the myriad of forces that can propel or block a major initiative or project. The good lawyers "understand from a political standpoint" how these forces develop and how they can be navigated in the service of making things happen. "You could say knowledge is power," Queenan observes.[770] Although it remains to be seen where the next band of civically-engaged lawyers will come from when the next Pittsburgh crisis arises, it would be foolhardy to bet against them. The profession is no longer what it once was, and has many challenges facing it, but Pittsburgh's lawyers have shown an enormous capacity for caring about the reinventions of Pittsburgh, and an enormous capacity to reinvent themselves.

LAW CITY: AN EPILOGUE

Pittsburgh, January 2017

From the observation deck near the Monongahela Incline on Mt. Washington, across the river from downtown Pittsburgh, among the various lighted signs that shine from atop the city's downtown buildings, the names of two law firms may be seen: "Reed Smith," in red and white letters atop the Reed Smith Centre on Fifth Avenue, and "K&L Gates" in white letters at the top of the thirty-nine-floor One Oliver Plaza, now known as K&L Gates Center. Today, Reed Smith is a global law firm of more than 1,700 lawyers with offices in New York, London, Beijing and Dubai, among other world cities.[1] In 2007, the Kirkpatrick Lockhart firm merged with the Seattle-based law firm of Preston Gates & Ellis (whose named partner, William H. Gates, Sr., is the father of Microsoft founder Bill Gates), to be renamed as K&L Gates. The firm now has almost two thousand lawyers on five continents.[2] Both Pittsburgh-based law firms reside near the top of the vaunted "AMLAW 100" list, published annually by *The American Lawyer*. Other AMLAW 100 firms have opened offices in Pittsburgh over the years, including Jones Day, Morgan Lewis, McGuireWoods and Littler Mendelson.

It is a rare enough sight, though, in cities across the United States, to see the names of law firms emblazoned on the tops of downtown skyscrapers. In a city whose industrial might—its steel, coal, oil, aluminum and glass—used to be its brand, under the marquee lights of Reed Smith Centre and K&L Gates Center, Pittsburgh is Law City. Law, the Steel Bar in its most unabashedly commercial form, is one of the city's definitive industries in the twenty-first century.

Greg Jordan, who presided as the Pittsburgh-based global managing partner of Reed Smith during its years of massive growth, from 2001 to 2013, grew up in modest circumstances—in a Greek ethnic household in Warwood, West Virginia, a tiny steel town suburb an hour's drive southwest of Pittsburgh. Coincidentally, Peter Kalis, the

Pittsburgh-based chairman of K&L Gates from 1997 to 2017, is also a second generation Greek-American from Warwood. "Pete's father is from the Greek island of Samos," says Jordan. "My father's from the Greek island of Icaria ... Samos is right next to Icaria, and Pete's father and mine both ended up in Warwood." When Jordan was a summer associate at Reed Smith, he lived in Peter Kalis' house in Pittsburgh while Kalis took a sabbatical from Kirkpatrick at Oxford. When Kalis returned, he suggested to Jordan that he should come to work at Kirkpatrick. Jordan told Kalis, "The Reed Smith guys were nice to me. I sort of feel like I should go there." Had he gone to Kirkpatrick, Jordan jokingly speculates, "My view is, you know, I would have moved Pete out years ago, and I would have been running the firm." Contemplating the presence of the lighted signs of their respective firms as features of the Pittsburgh skyline, Jordan laughs it off, saying it demonstrates what happens when you have "two Greeks" who have "enough competitive ego" to engage in a battle over illuminated letters.[3]

The fact that Jordan and Kalis are both of Greek ethnic heritage is trivia, a comic trope in this case, but it does reveal a characteristic that has come to define the Pittsburgh bar in the years since the mid-twentieth century. The old industrial power of Pittsburgh was built on the backs of immigrant families; the new Pittsburgh, suffering as it has for decades as a net exporter of population, has retained its multitude of ethnic identities, and its working class heritage.

At the conclusion of the Iowa Republican Presidential Caucus on January 3, 2012, former Pennsylvania senator Rick Santorum, in a dead-heat to be crowned the winner that evening, addressed the crowd about the journey that had brought him to that moment. He described how his Italian grandfather had "made a sacrifice" coming to Southwestern Pennsylvania to work in the coal fields, saving his wages and bringing the rest of the family to America when his father was seven years old. His grandfather dug coal in the mines until he was seventy-two. "I'll never forget the first time I saw someone who had died," Santorum told his supporters. "It was my grandfather. And I knelt next to his coffin. And all I could do—eye level—was look at his hands. They were enormous hands. And all I could think was those hands dug freedom for me." The next morning, pundits and commentators lauded Santorum's speech as the high point of his campaign for the presidency. "Wow," exclaimed Joe Scarborough on MSNBC's *Morning Joe*, commenting on how moving it was. John Heilemann, the *New York* magazine reporter and co-author of the 2008 presidential campaign memoir *Game Change*, noted that Santorum "talked about his biography in a very moving and compelling way," hitting "very hard on blue collar themes." Scarborough concurred, observing, "Say what you will about him, he is a guy, in an age of pre-packaged political candidates and pre-packaged messages ... a guy that is all heart."[4] They were responding, with a mixture of awe and astonishment, to Santorum's unscripted, or non-teleprompted, authenticity, in stark contrast to the carefully planned eloquence of the eventual Republican nominee, Mitt Romney.

Santorum's start was as a Pittsburgh lawyer at Kalis' firm, then still known as Kirkpatrick & Lockhart.[5] The many sons and daughters of first and second generation immigrants and other working class families crowding the halls of the Pittsburgh bar in the mid-1980s made Santorum unremarkable there; yet it made him, "say what you will about him," for one fleeting moment in Iowa in 2012, an unusual and unexpected figure on the national political stage. An authentic sense of gratitude for what one's family has become, through toil and sacrifice, is something palpable throughout Pittsburgh's parochial citizenry. An atmosphere of pride and gratitude permeates its bar to this day, even among its "old family" white Anglo-Saxon Protestants; its examples, beyond the experiences of Jordan, Kalis and Santorum, are everywhere. It is no stretch to say that "presence of heart" as much as "presence of mind" is a defining characteristic of Pittsburgh lawyers—with all that such a combination suggests, both the bad and the good, from a sometimes morose stubbornness, to a capacity for passionate commitments to their communities, and a high quotient of emotional intelligence. From their working class roots, they also have a bit of the lay-engineer in them, standing over the job site and working out how to get the project built. At their best, their culture has provided them with an atmospheric legacy of technical precision and kinetic practicality. The antecedents of these modern lawyers can be found in countless examples in Pittsburgh's history: from Billy Brennen to Leo Weil, from Musmanno to Alpern, from Unkovic to Freeland.

Unleashing the proud, sensitive sons and daughters of generational destiny who inhabit the Pittsburgh bar into the churning maelstrom of soul-shattering, fundamental change and turmoil that is the American legal profession today seems almost like a cruel punchline. Here in the twenty-first century, the profession is experiencing a number of trends that would seem to be conspiring to strip Pittsburgh lawyers of many of their traditional roles in society. Many of these are trends that lawyers across the country will recognize—they are national, if not global trends.

Undoubtedly one the most significant trends of the twenty-first century among Pittsburgh law firms was the further "delocalization" of Pittsburgh firms—law firms opening offices in multiple locations across the country or across the world. While the impetus for multi-jurisdictional law firms may have been a response to increased federal regulation and a need to follow institutional clients into markets that were important to them, the "regional" and "national" Pittsburgh law firms were enabled by the astonishing wave of technological changes that has washed over Pittsburgh's lawyers from 1980s onward. More than any generation preceding them, the generations of lawyers practicing since the 1980s have experienced the most significant technology-induced changes in the way they experience and conduct their day-to-day practices. Some of the changes have created almost miraculous improvements in attorneys' ability to get things done; others clearly represent threats to the way attorneys have practiced law over the past fifty years.

James M. Houston, Pitt Law class of 1934, a former partner with the Rose Schmidt firm and the co-founder of Houston Harbaugh, wrote in 1995:

> *It was only yesterday that we used to say, 'Miss Edwards, please make three copies of this letter.' She would proceed to pull out three sheets of paper, two carbons and type out the copies on her Underwood. ... More exciting than document copying was the development of equipment to create and manipulate text. We were among the pioneers to test it. The term 'word processing' hadn't appeared, but some ingenious person figured that if*

you could play a piano by punching holes in a paper roll, you ought to be able to run a typewriter using the same technique. It was called the Autotypist. You punched your own rolls on a piece of equipment that sounded like an AK-47. Each roll held about a page of typing, but it was still faster than retyping everything. Later came the Selectric typewriter from IBM, a distinct improvement, and finally, of course, the modern word processor in the form of a computer ... I'd enjoy a brief reincarnation in the year 2055 to visit some law offices and court rooms of that day. Will yellow tablets still be around?[6]

In the blink of an eye, the downtown bar has gone from letter-press wet copying, to carbon copies, to multifunction copying machines; from manual typewriters, to PCs and laptops, to touchscreen tablets and voice recognition dictation; from switchboards, to direct dial phone numbers, to bulky mobile phones, to smartphones; from telegram to telex to fax to email; from paper account ledgers to Excel spreadsheets; from business cards to glossy brochures, to websites, blogs, Youtube and Twitter; and from voluminous paper files to digital storage in the cloud.

Technology has changed the human shape of law firms as well. In 1989, at Buchanan Ingersoll, three lawyers out of over 120 located in Pittsburgh had PCs on their desk; older lawyers would remark that there was no reason for younger lawyers to have this technology "unless they want to be secretaries." In 1997, when the firm moved from the U.S. Steel Building to One Oxford Centre, sentiments had changed such that all lawyers were provided with PCs at their desks, as well as email accounts. By 2015, the firm's "IT department," which had consisted of one-and-a-half persons in 1989 (before the term "Information Technology" or "IT" even became common parlance), had grown to include almost sixty staffers, administering one thousand personal computers and laptops, over five hundred firm-provided smartphones and over two hundred personally-owned and connected iPads and other tablets.[7] While lawyers have now become accessible to the outside world on a twenty-four-hour/seven-day-a-week basis through cellular phones, IP telephony, texts, emails and a myriad of other communications platforms, they do indeed perform more of their own "secretarial work," as the old fogies of the 1980s once predicted—now redefined as part-and-parcel of the manual arts that all lawyers are expected to be able perform. It is a far cry from the eighteenth century Pittsburgh lawyer's essential manual arts—horsemanship, surveying technique and oratory—and, more to the point, it has resulted in the unsung role of the traditional "legal secretary" morphing into more of an information processing center, an "administrative assistant" rather than a typist. One additional result is that since lawyers have less traditional work for their administrative assistants, and they are hiring fewer of them overall.

Legal research has undergone similarly dramatic changes. Libraries of leather-bound law reports and treatises, and their pocket-part supplements, are nearly extinct today, replaced by online services such as Lexis and Westlaw, and by the Internet. The digitization of the body of words that make up the law has not only transformed the way lawyers think about research, but has raised a constant challenge from Googling clients who can now easily take a stab at finding out about legal questions on their own—not always with great precision or accuracy. At the beginning of the century, online companies such as California-based LegalZoom.com started to cut into the business of lawyers who write wills and form corporations, but the march toward outsourcing and technologization continues. In 2014, for example, some Pittsburgh lawyers began to receive emails from a New Delhi, India-based legal outsourcing company called Effectual Services, which purports to offer "a comprehensive range of Legal Support services" including "Legal Research & Drafting; Contract/Lease abstraction; Review and Red-lining of Contracts/Lease Agreements; Drafting and Negotiation of Commercial Contracts" and so on. For legal research and drafting services, their India-based team will charge twenty dollars per hour—approximately ten percent of the lower-end of Pittsburgh lawyer hourly rates.[8] Such an offer would have been impossible before today's inexpensive, ubiquitous communications technologies.

Meanwhile, a Carnegie Mellon start-up venture called LegalSifter, which received financial support from the Pittsburgh-based early-stage seed fund, Birchmere Labs, in 2013, purports to enable users to upload contracts to its website and, after application of an analytical algorithm, to provide a score indicating how "fair" various contractual terms might be. The service is available for free until the company achieves its larger vision—"an intelligent contract management system for legal documents" for the Global 1000.[9] Chuck Queenan confessed that he had a fantasy of matching wits with a law computer. "You have chess players playing chess against an IBM machine ... [I] would have enjoyed if someone could put that kind of concept in a computer to match wits to see if I could come up with a better solution quicker."[10] The legal profession at large is now coming closer to having to deal with that challenge on a daily basis. As Birchmere's managing general partner Ned Renzi delights in saying, "The legal profession as we know it will be extinct by 2025."[11]

Technology has not been the only force exerting pressure on the legal profession.

John Gismondi is known as one of the preeminent personal injury/medical malpractice lawyers in Pittsburgh. Born in Uniontown, his father was a radio sports reporter-turned-stock broker. He inherited from his father a gift, common among good play-by-play announcers, for smooth, impromptu narration; he is a confident storyteller, which has probably helped to make him a great trial lawyer. After law school at Pitt, Gismondi clerked for Judge Gustave Diamond on the Western District of the U.S. District Court for three years before taking a position with Gilardi and Cooper, a union-side labor firm that also happened to handle a lot of personal injury cases. During his first week of private practice in 1981, Dick Gilardi wandered into Gismondi's office, Tareyton cigarette dangling from his mouth, with a case file. "John," he said, "I forgot this case was on the trial list. Can you pick a jury tomorrow?" The case was a maritime damages case for an out-of-town client. Gismondi obtained a continuance of the case until the following week, and then—by himself—picked the jury, gave the opening statement, tried the case, and won a verdict for the plaintiff. It was the stuff of legend around the office, and that year, the firm handed him nine more cases that he tried to verdict. "Never did I second seat for anyone," Gismondi recalls. Subsequently, Gismondi opened his own personal injury firm, and since the late 1980s, he has typically practiced as a sole owner of the practice, with two associates and a medical expert, usually now a nurse practitioner.[12]

"The biggest single change affecting trial lawyers in this community," Gismondi says, "is the disappearing jury trial." Gismondi notes that the Allegheny County Court of Common Pleas had five trials terms per year, and used to have 750 cases or more on the trial list for any given term. "Now we're lucky if we get 350," says Gismondi, and lucky "if more than 15 or 20 of them go to verdict." The upshot, he says, is that it is very difficult for Pittsburgh lawyers to get trial experience anymore. "I got a call from a lawyer the other day," he says, who has been practicing for seven years, and he "has never tried a case to verdict ... I could never get off to the start in my career now that I got off to in 1981. It wouldn't happen."

The change, in Pittsburgh, has some local roots. First, a change in state law in 1990 has done away with the absolute right to a jury trial in all but the cases with the most serious injuries. Gismondi, however, observes that the most dramatic changes have emerged due to the rise of mediation. Generally speaking, he says, the structure of the local court system has never historically been conducive to achieving settlements: rather than having an individual docket for each case, Allegheny County has a master calendar. "What happens in Common Pleas Court," Gismondi says, is that "you never have a settlement conference until you have a pre-trial conciliation two weeks before picking a jury. That conciliation is given a 20-minute time slot." Most of the time, under such circumstances, neither party was interested in settling. One local judge, however, Judge David Murphy, was well-known for his interest in working with parties to achieve a settlement. After his retirement from the bench in 1997, Murphy opened a full-time mediation practice, known as Justus ADR Services. Hired jointly by the parties to a lawsuit on an hourly basis, Murphy started to deploy his talent for settling cases in private engagements, turning his passion into a lucrative post-bench career. Others soon followed in Murphy's footsteps; but the real impact was felt when UPMC, led by a couple of risk management executives who were trained as lawyers, Richard P. Kidwell and Robert G. Voinchet, Jr., started offering mediation in most medical malpractice cases. Plaintiffs love it, Gismondi observes, because they receive cash sooner than they do in litigation—although they trade away "home run verdicts," which have become more rare in Pittsburgh courts, anyway, for the certainty that they will receive some settlement rather than nothing. Seeing UPMC, "the big dog on the block," re-orient itself toward mediation has inspired other institutions, such as medical malpractice insurance carriers and auto insurance carriers, to rely heavily on mediation. The number of trials involving these parties, as a result, has decreased dramatically.[13]

Justus ADR Services advertises that mediation works "because people feel invested in the settlement," and because "[n]obody 'won,' but nobody 'lost' either ... it is a resolution that everyone can live with."[14] John Gismondi, however, laments the fact that trial skills and tactics, falling into disuse, are becoming extinct in Pittsburgh. For Gismondi, these skills represent the essence of what it means to be a lawyer. By tradition, the complex, formal dialectic of trial practice is the lawyer's definitive battleground, and experience in conducting a trial is hard-earned in the heat of battle; furthermore, it is not necessarily an intuitive process, particularly with regard to the tactics that a lawyer deploys outside of a courtroom—making decisions about whom to sue, whom to depose, and so on. While today's lawyer is involved in a different dialectic in a mediation conference, "negotiation," Gismondi says, is a skill that is "a lot easier to learn" than "trial advocacy." Gismondi puts his own time and money to use in educating the future trial lawyers of Pittsburgh through endowing and teaching in the John P. Gismondi Civil Litigation Certificate Program at Pitt, an intensive collection of courses within the Law School designed to give students the practical experience of litigation within a classroom setting.[15]

Perhaps most non-lawyers do not see fewer civil jury trials as being any great loss to society. However, a dramatic shift away from jury trials in criminal cases possesses a more sinister undertone.

Robert J. Cindrich, once an attorney in the public defender's office and an assistant County prosecutor, was appointed U.S. attorney for the Western District of Pennsylvania by President Carter in 1978, and, after co-founding the firm known as Mansmann, Cindrich & Titus (later, just Cindrich & Titus), he was appointed by President Clinton as a federal judge, succeeding Judge Gustave Diamond on the District Court for the Western District of Pennsylvania in 1994. Judge Cindrich enjoyed being on the court, calling it "a genteel life" where "the lawyers laugh at your jokes." In 2004, however, Judge Cindrich quit the bench—a rare move from a position that comes with a lifetime appointment; he was only the second to do so in the Western District. Although he left to join UPMC as its General Counsel, Judge Cindrich says that the main motivation for his departure was his unwillingness to continue to enforce strict minimum sentencing guidelines.[16]

In the 1980s, Congress passed the Sentencing Reform Act, which created the U.S. Sentencing Commission and tasked it with reforming criminal sentencing in federal cases—specifically, to attempt to achieve some consistency in sentencing across similar types of cases. What came out of the exercise was a codified system of mandatory minimum sentences, which in many cases took discretion in sentencing away from federal judges. In addition, as Cindrich observed, it led to almost ninety-five percent of criminal indictments ending up in a plea bargain, rather than a trial. As Cindrich explained, prosecutors would say, "If you plead guilty you'll only get 15 or 20 years, and if you don't, then we'll apply this, and this, and this, and it'll be 40 years." Few wanted to take the risk of going to court, because a guilty verdict in essence would mean a mandatory sentence that might represent the rest of a defendant's life. "Who can risk going to trial when the stakes are so high?" In Cindrich's view, rather than fixing sentencing disparities, the system created "a subterfuge." The preferred criteria for fixing a sentence, now arising out of a backroom negotiation, are no longer the real criteria, "which had been bargained away." Without the real criteria on the record, there is no real way to compare sentences to see if they are consistent. "Worse," said Cindrich, "these deals are made not in a court. They're made solely with the government, who holds all the aces. So, how could they be fair?"

Moreover, Cindrich saw patterns in how the mandatory sentences were constructed. "I began to see what we're doing to young people as immoral—unethical and immoral ... I saw the destruction that we were doing to the poor community."[17] As defense attorney Paul Boas states, the sentencing guidelines were "weighted much, much heavier on crimes that poor people commit, and much lighter on crimes that people with lots of money commit." Boas explains that "you could have 5 grams of crack and get 5 years in prison ... and you could embezzle $2 million and get 18 months. The rich guy who steals money from his company, or cheats all the consumers, or rips off the people [whose] investments [he's handling], isn't going to be selling crack. The poor black guy is not going to be embezzling some trust fund; he's going to be selling crack."[18] Cindrich says, "I was going to have to answer for this, which I began to think of as an atrocity—the mass imprisonment of poor people. It is difficult to find a solution for the problem of intractable poverty, but I can tell you now that imprisoning them won't help. And there's too many to imprison, and the cost is too high, and what's left in the community is even worse off than before you started your mass imprisonment." He concludes, "I just said one day, 'I can't—I won't—do this anymore.'"

In addition, according to Cindrich, the guidelines were having an effect on the profession. Not only were defense lawyers getting fewer chances to try cases, but so were prosecutors. More to the point, the sentencing guidelines were interfering with the constitutional right, according to the Sixth Amendment, to "a speedy and public trial, by an impartial jury of the State and district wherein the crime shall have been committed ...to be confronted with the witnesses against him ... and to have the Assistance of Counsel for his defence." "The founders had a reason for inserting the Sixth Amendment into the Bill of Rights," says Cindrich. "[A]ll our efforts to eliminate the right to jury trial [are] counter to that reason. They wanted people to have an opportunity to be heard." With all the incentives pointing toward deciding not to take that opportunity for one's case to be heard by a jury of one's peers, and fewer lawyers with "heat of battle" experience in providing "Assistance" within such grave and important circumstances, it had become clear to Cindrich that the constitutional system was not working as it should be.[19]

Mandatory sentences did become a target for reform, and following the Supreme Court's decision in *U.S. v. Booker* (2005), the guidelines have become fully advisory, except where Congress has set a mandatory minimum sentence.[20] From Boas' perspective, however, the impetus for reform has not been about restoring constitutional rights, "because who gives a shit about criminal defendants?" Boas concludes, "The only reason right now there might be some changes in some of these mandatories is because they're too cheap to cough up for the prisons that are needed to house these people ... It's purely economics."[21]

The elimination of lawyers from their natural habitat—by way of technology, mediation, mandatory sentences, or otherwise—is thematically part of another dominant strain of American culture, encapsulated by the concept of good ol' American self-reliance. "Give me a set of tools," says the Western frontiersman, "and I'll do it myself." The attitude is not purely American, however; it also plays into currents of thought that have been around for ages. The dream of a lawyerless society—as proposed by everyone from St. Paul in his "Letter to the Galatians," to Shakespeare's henchmen in *Henry VI, Part II* (the ones who want to "kill all the lawyers"), to William Penn, to the Marxist legal theorist Evgeny Pashukanis—has been put forward by those who see lawyers merely, or mostly, as obstructionists, as actors with their own professional political agendas, or as needlessly inefficient cost centers.

There are other forces at play that compromise the traditional roles of Pittsburgh lawyers based on the fact that they are Pittsburghers. In early 2015, when H.J. Heinz Co. agreed to merge with Kraft Foods Group, Heinz was not represented by Reed Smith, the firm that had represented Heinz for much of its history, going back to the nineteenth century. Instead, the company chose Cravath, Swaine & Moore, based in New York, and Kirkland & Ellis, based in Chicago.[22] In 2013, when Heinz was acquired by Berkshire Hathaway and 3G Capital, Davis Polk & Wardwell represented Heinz, and Wachtell Lipton Rosen & Katz represented the company's board of directors.[23] Where once it was commonplace for the leading Pittsburgh law firms to be the leading lawyers on billion dollar transactions involving Pittsburgh corporations, board members of these "delocalized" corporations have come to expect management to choose major New York City or "national" law firms on the AMLAW 100 to represent them. Pittsburgh-based law firms such as Reed Smith and K&L Gates are on the AMLAW 100, and they have New York offices, but they don't tend to fall within the short-list of firms that directors and general counsels choose for such "bet the company" work. Their New York presence is small by comparison to Cravath, Wachtell and other "board-preferred" New York law firms, and their brand was made in Pittsburgh, not in New York, Los Angeles or Chicago.

The trend has some obvious roots in a tension that has always existed between the bars of New York and Pittsburgh, beginning in the nineteenth century. Because of the large corporation base in Pittsburgh, the city of industry has frequently bumped up against the city of finance over the decades. Even when Pittsburgh lawyers were considered among the most important lawyers in the country at the end of the nineteenth century, there were always some New York City lawyers who had an outsized view of their own relative sophistication as practitioners. According to the narratives of these New York lawyers, Pittsburgh lawyers were always the "rubes." One may recall, for example, the New York defense team for Hill, Harriman and Morgan who referred to Attorney General Philander Knox as an "unknown country lawyer from Pennsylvania."[24]

In Pittsburgh narratives, on the other hand, New York lawyers often receive their comeuppance. One such story—a classic—involves Ed Schoyer, the venerated Buchanan Ingersoll corporate finance lawyer about whom Annie Dillard once wrote, "He was always the bemused scholar, mild and democratic," with a "calm, ironic voice."[25] In the mid-1960s, before the days of word processing and inexpensive Xerox copying, Schoyer was handling a corporate financing for a publicly-traded client. Across the table from him representing the underwriter was an "arrogant senior associate" from a "leading Wall Street firm," who was "chagrined to have to leave Manhattan in the first place" and "spent most of the session condescendingly lecturing Ed on just how these deals were done." Schoyer, then in his late forties, was characteristically patient. He ignored the associate's taunts, continuing to work on the voluminous closing documents, and having them signed by his client. The New York associate departed with the signed documents. Later that evening, Schoyer received a panicked call from the associate, who "confessed that he had strapped the closing documents on the back of his motorcycle for his trip from Laguardia to the office only to have the package blown off the side of the Tri-Boro bridge." The associate asked Ed, "What do I do? I'm going to lose my job over this." Ed calmly told him that he should get back on a plane to Pittsburgh and they would re-create the whole packet. They worked all night and Ed sent the associate back to New York with the new signed documents in the morning, "all without ever flaunting the sweetness of the turn of events."[26]

Such tensions even exist now within Pittsburgh law firms that have New York City offices, and in Pittsburgh-based corporations. Says one Pittsburgh securities lawyer: "We can do a five hundred million dollar 144A offering [in Pittsburgh], and get little recognition inside the firm for it. Meanwhile, the New York office closes a little ten million dollar merger and you won't hear the end of it."[27] Tremors were felt throughout the city bar when in 2015 the new general counsel of a major Pittsburgh-based corporation systematically replaced a legal department full of experienced, home-grown lawyers with lawyers who largely had New York or national law firm pedigrees.

But if the roots of the Pittsburgh lawyer's dethronement can be found in old myths and a conflict of egos, the momentum that continues to push Pittsburgh lawyers out of their roles as advisors to the biggest Pittsburgh corporations has to do with the way work is now secured from these clients. For generations, the senior partners of stable Pittsburgh law firms had Pittsburgh clients who were loyal to their law firm as an institution and loyal to the lawyers who advised them; the senior partners would pass their relationships down to the junior partners, and the connections would continue. Now, of course, partners flit from firm to firm like ravenous, cartoon butterflies, thus dampening the importance of the institutional relationship; neither law firms nor their large corporate clients are apt to view the locale of their relationships as having much meaning, as neither law firms nor corporations are as "localized" as they once were; and specialization, the phenomenon that began to have a major impact on the legal profession in the mid-twentieth century, has effectively derailed the notion of lawyers retaining client allegiances based solely on the merits of a long-term "relationship."

Lawyers have been promoting themselves on the basis of their "specialties"[a] with an increasing urgency over the last fifty years. Clients have responded by demanding more narrow specialties and more experienced specialists. Greg Jordan, now the General Counsel for PNC, illustrates the effect on client attitudes. Clients look for "a more laser-like fit" than they used to, he observes. "In the old days, the general counsel of Mellon called Walter McGough [at Reed Smith], saying 'Hey, Walter, we have a problem in Harrisburg ... Send someone over.' That doesn't happen now. Now ... I might call Dan Booker [at Reed Smith] and say, 'Hey Dan, PNC has a problem in Chicago. It's *this* kind of problem ... Do you have somebody who's done *x, y* and *z*, or not? And if the answer is yes, I'd like to talk to them. If the answer is no—you know, let's have a drink sometime, because I'm going to get someone else.' Because, you know, it's a much more targeted hiring. And that increased specialization," Jordan concludes, "is challenging for lawyers who resist specialization."[28] The larger national/international firms have chassis that

---

a   They do so only in cleverly disguised ways, as Rule 7.4(a) of the Pennsylvania Rules of Professional Conduct states that "A lawyer shall not state that the lawyer is a specialist" except with respect to patents, admiralty law or with regard to an area of practice in which an attorney has been certified as a specialist by an organization approved by the Supreme Court of Pennsylvania. As to the latter, there are currently very few of such approved specialties.

can sustain very narrow specialties, and their advantage begins to be self-perpetuating. James Barnes, a securities lawyer formerly with Reed Smith now practicing with Blank Rome, concedes, "I have to say, when I'm doing a deal with a Latham or a Kirkland & Ellis, they are really good lawyers. They are doing big deals every day, and it shows. They have guys who do nothing but $100 million-plus debt deals ... [you can ask them] 'Do you equity deals?' [and they will say,] 'No, I only do bonds.'"[29]

Those national/international law firms who thrive on such rarefied microspecialties ultimately have an additional specialty or two that are left unsaid, but are very powerfully attractive to some clients: they specialize in being "board-preferred" firms; they specialize in being Wall Street firms. The closing of ranks within the upper reaches of the AMLAW 100 nationally has had an impact on how the Pittsburgh offices of AMLAW firms have altered their targets; while once they might have aspired to handle the biggest matters that Pittsburgh business had to offer, now they reach further down market, to middle market companies or start-ups—which, in turn, has had the effect of occasionally unseating the smaller players who have traditionally represented that segment of the market. "There are only a few choices," says one senior Pittsburgh corporate lawyer. "You can either be so big that you cannot be ignored, or you can choose to be small, quick, nimble and entrepreneurial—to be a boutique—and try to appeal to businesses that are the same. Or," the attorney concludes, "you can settle for commodity work, where your only differentiating factor is the price that you charge."

The definition of "commodity work," such as the residential title searches that Reuben Fingold did for ten dollars a pop during the Depression, has now begun to encompass a myriad of lawyer tasks—collections, foreclosures, "red car/blue car" insurance defense litigation, mineral title opinions (which became something of a "commodity du jour" in Pittsburgh with the increase in oil and gas activity surrounding the Marcellus and Utica shale plays in the late 2000s), bank loan closings—and even a few services that never used to be considered as such. James Barnes observes, "A lot of the work we do now is commodity work. The 1934 Securities Exchange Act work used to be considered to be pretty good work, but now it is a commodity. You hold on to it, hoping you will get to do some deals. But then when a big deal comes in, they give it to Latham, or Kirkland & Ellis."[30] With intense competition among highly competent lawyers all looking for the same kinds of work, almost anything can end up being a commoditized service. That which can be commoditized, will be, eventually.

Some are attempting to embrace commoditization in clever ways. Ralph Baxter, the now-former managing partner of the San Francisco-based, thousand-plus-lawyer international firm of Orrick Herrington & Sutcliffe, was born in Wellsburg, West Virginia, just outside of Pittsburgh. Searching for ways to add more dollars to the bottom line, he hit upon the idea of setting up the firm's back office operations in nearby Wheeling in 2002—a struggling steel community where the cost of living was comparatively low, wages are comparatively low and the price per square foot of office space is relatively low. Moving IT, internal tax, general ledger, billing, collections and payroll functions to the Wheeling "global operations center" was so successful, that Baxter started hiring lawyers in Wheeling in 2011 to perform routine document review and due diligence projects—including some newly-minted lawyers from Pitt and Duquesne Law Schools.

"Make no mistake: These are full-fledged lawyers, not paralegals, and they do the same work traditional legal associates do," said *The New York Times*. "But they earn less than half the pay of their counterparts—usually around $60,000—and they know from the outset they will never make partner." In a market in which there is an oversupply of lawyers in general, Baxter figured out how to make the law of supply and demand for first-year lawyers work for Orrick.[31]

The idea that a segment of Pittsburgh lawyers who have gone through four years of college and three years of law school just like the higher paid ones would be consigned to lower wages, operating in a back office temp pool, is evidence to some of a dramatic, disturbing bifurcation of the profession—kind of like the dystopian sci-fi set-up of the leisure-loving Eloi and the sweaty, subterranean Morlocks from H.G. Wells' *The Time Machine*. The truth, however, is that the Pittsburgh bar has always experienced divisions between the self-professed elite members of the profession and the rank-and-file. The greater fear now is that an entire bar—once known for its corporate lawyers defining the American corporation and leading its most complex and sophisticated transactions, and for some of the nation's most influential antitrust, labor, civil rights and in-house lawyers—has somehow fallen below the line. The greater fear now is that the Pittsburgh lawyer, at large, is becoming a subaltern, the more that legal services become commoditized.

Meanwhile, Pittsburgh lawyers are no strangers to the phenomenon that is perhaps the most influential and fundamental change that the legal profession has experienced over the last sixty years: the expression of value, by the elite lawyers on down, in terms of hours. Since the mid-twentieth century, law firms have built their infrastructure around counting and collecting hours; they use "hourly rates" and projections of billable hours for budgeting purposes; they scrutinize hours in order to compare and evaluate their lawyers' performance; and the size of associates' bonuses are often determined by the number of hours that they bill. A whole workforce of middle managers has been created within law firms in order to process and analyze hours—generally, without context, wholly divorced from their content. But senior practitioners raise a note of alarm about the emphasis on hours. "As a professional," Bob Sable argues, "your work should define who you are .... Engaging in your profession is not a job, it is who you are. ... You can't just look at it as a way to make a living." As a result of the hours-based culture, Sable says, "young people get the idea that their job is to bill hours, not to be a professional ... not to achieve a result."[32]

The objections, however, are not coming solely from that generation of practitioners who remember what it was like to practice law before hours were counted. Clients who use apps on their smartphones for instant results have come to expect speed and efficiency from their service providers, counted in deliveries by the nanosecond. Lawyers, betraying their backwardness, are continuing to sell work expressed in hours, when the world is buying solutions expressed in moments.

The view of Law City, from the observation deck near the Monongahela Incline on Mt. Washington, across the river from downtown Pittsburgh, is a bit murky today—and it has nothing to do with steel plant smoke. There isn't any. With all of the encroachments on lawyer territory, with the status quo of the profession in Pittsburgh receiving threats from all quarters, it is the future of Law City that is difficult to see. That murky view is inspiring some soul-searching among the lawyers of the Steel Bar, down in Law City, as they scratch their heads and ask: What are we selling now? Who are we?

Some leaders of the bar are facing the future, without hesitation, by raising quality and excellence as primary virtues, as values of the bar. For Marlee Myers, for example, the idea of providing nothing but the best services is a line drawn in the sand. Although there is pressure in the marketplace to lower fees, Myers asserts, "I never thought that was the way to build a practice. If someone wants free service, they don't want excellent service … People who want free legal services, don't value legal services, by definition. Those are people who will never value them." She observes, "I think in the longer run, there's going to be a certain tier of law firms that are sought after because of their excellence, and if you're below that you're going to have to be a commodity, and you're going to have to compete on price alone, because that's what a commodity is." Not all of the larger law firms will survive, she surmises, because it is not easy to be excellent. "You have to pick your spots where you can actually deliver excellence. You have to deliver it. You have to be worth it."[33]

In addition to delivering excellence, the most forward-thinking of Pittsburgh's lawyers have always succeeded the same way that Pittsburgh drivers succeed in driving on steep Pittsburgh roadways in icy weather: by fixing their eyes on the horizon and "turning into the skid." They have succeeded by recognizing the changes in the environment and running toward change rather than running away from it. If clients have become impatient with paying by the hour, if technology threatens to eliminate your livelihood … then it is probably time to stop trying to sell documents and filings and other relatively ministerial tasks as your main stock-in-trade, and it is probably time to sell one's experience and judgment in ways that stimulate a client's appreciation of their value. It is probably time to imagine ways in which those emerging analytical algorithms and intelligent systems can be turned to the lawyer's advantage—to become the lawyer who wields technology, rather than the lawyer who is superannuated by it. It is probably time to turn into the skid, rather than protesting that the road is icy.

Turning into the skid admittedly requires a bit of courage, as well as the focus and capacity to make quick little innovations and adjustments on the fly. But over the long term, lasting, impactful innovation requires an atmosphere that tolerates failure. That kind of atmosphere is very difficult to establish within an industry in which almost one hundred percent of the value of a law firm is pushed out to its partners at the end of each fiscal year. Opportunities abound for lawyers to reconnect with clients and their ever-evolving needs through innovation. However, law firms, large and small, will all have to fight off rigidity and complacency in order to survive with a measure of commercial relevance.

Perhaps all of that helps us to understand and answer the unavoidable question of what Pittsburgh's future lawyers may be selling in order to earn their livelihoods, but there remains the question of what makes the Pittsburgh lawyer, or any lawyer, distinctly necessary in Pittsburgh or in American society. History, in this case, does permit one to see shapes and colors in the murky landscape of Law City a little more clearly.

With all due respect to accountants and despite the fact that accountants now own the largest law firms in Europe,[34] accountants have never been known to be catalysts for socio-political change. If I want someone to fight for my rights, or for fairness, or for political order, I'm not likely to turn to an MBA, a McKinsey consultant, or, for that matter, to a computer program or a robot. Pittsburgh lawyers, since the days of Brackenridge and Baldwin, have been uniquely positioned as important "stewards of democracy"—an honorific title used by legal historian Paul Carrington to describe de Tocqueville's assessment of the role of lawyers in the American society that de Tocqueville experienced in the early nineteenth century. As Carrington wrote, de Tocqueville saw parallels between feudal barons and American lawyers—not in terms of their wealth or entitlements, but in "their role in mediating between the ruling democratic majority and the monied class or other minorities who may at times be found in opposition to the majority. Like the aristocracy, the democratic legal profession served to stabilize an otherwise fragile social order."[35]

No small part of that role, both in Pittsburgh history and American history, has been the lawyer's ability to shape the dialogue between dissent and authority, and to chart the path of orderly change within the bounds of the Rule of Law—a Rule of Law that consists of a constitution and laws that exist to liberate Americans from the brutal forces of the arbitrary and the capricious, and that is made practical and powerful in our society through the thousands of things a lawyer does each day in fulfilling his or her professional duties. Though lawyers have proven to be imperfect beings from time to time, with their own appetites and frailties, they remain members of the only profession that is schooled to look at every human transaction and circumstance through the lens of the Rule of Law; they are the only profession in America that is armed with the civil status, the ethical framework and the critical thinking to identify and call out the arbitrary and the capricious in both public and private dealings, and to do so in a way that avoids a descent into chaos.

The lawyer's strength as a civic leader, as an arbiter of fairness and justice, has also been deeply intertwined throughout American history with his or her connection to a locale. This is perhaps another way in which the role of the lawyer has been diminished through the trend toward "delocalization." Earlier in the history of the Pittsburgh bar, it is easy to see the relationship between the status of the lawyer and the local nature of his or her activities; witness George Guthrie and Leo Weil, for instance, simultaneously using and uplifting their status as members of the community through their local reform activities. The same can be said, more recently, of the "Renaissance" development activities of Van Buskirk, Hazard and Hickman, and the post-"Renaissance" activities of Barger and Newlin. These are all examples of how the previously elevated status of lawyers and their personal commitments to Pittsburgh have sometimes come together for the improvement of the city and the lives of its inhabitants. A renewed commitment to the communities in which elite lawyers operate—not simply through philanthropy, but through their hands-on activities—will undoubtedly contribute to the elevation of the public status of such lawyers in the future.

Judge Cindrich states:

We are here to serve. We are here as lawyers to make a society work in a just and equitable way. All the highest functions of the law really deal with that. When you think about what we have accomplished as lawyers ... Great lawyers fought for civil rights, risked their lives, battled the courts, battled public opinion, ended up in the Supreme Court eventually in Brown v. Board, after many, many losses before, and won. That was lawyers that did that. And almost every other fight for equality and justice has been led by lawyers. We need to reclaim that.

Even if a lawyer is merely helping someone to plan an estate, or to start a business or make sense of a contract, or representing someone's son or daughter in a minor scrape with the law, Judge Cindrich says, that is not to say that these are not also "important things." They are things that help a society to function. "It doesn't always have to be the idealistic thing, like marching in Selma ... Do some small thing right," says Cindrich. "A client comes in, and they're all distraught ... and they feel like the future's uncertain, you sit them down and talk to them, lead them down the right path ... We can do some small thing right. If we would just get back to that."[36]

Meanwhile, the stories of the Steel Bar remind us that the profession of the law is still a noble one, one that "qualifies for political eminence" as Hugh Henry Brackenridge wrote in 1814. The need for the patriotic spirit of that eminence, that wide-awake sense of stewardship, has perhaps never been greater. Doing the small things right, taking on the big projects, pointing out that damned line between freedom and chaos—are unpopular and unprofitable even under the best circumstances.

As easily as we may picture a triumphant Hugh Henry Brackenridge standing on Grant's Hill, receiving the adulation of a crowd cheering three times and tossing their hats in the air, unfortunately we can also recall him ready to face a firing squad for his insolent dissent, or experiencing public isolation for his principled stances in favor of democratic order. As admired as Philander Knox came to be by his industrialist cronies during the nineteenth century, he inspired their wrath when he became a trustbuster in the twentieth century; and while Billy Brennen's status as a friend of the working man was unimpeachable at Homestead, his steadfast loyalty to the Rule of Law and maintaining the peace left him outflanked by the radical Left by the time of the 1919 Steel Strike. Leo Weil might have been the counselor to the Rockefellers, but his pursuit of municipal corruption made him a pariah in the Pittsburgh business community. John Buchanan represented big corporations in the nation's highest court, yet rose to speak truth to the power of the collective bar to propose that an accused Communist receive counsel, or that the poor needed free legal services—undoubtedly leaving some of his friends at the Duquesne Club perturbed. That alleged Communist, poor Hymen Schlesinger, took the Fifth Amendment and faced disbarment rather than submit to questions about his political views. Ruggero Aldisert took on two powerful institutions, Congress and the Department of Defense, in search of justice for his friend, Aldo Icardi. Dick Thornburgh let his investigation go where the evidence led him, even though it was not the easy thing to do within the close confines of the local Republican Party in 1973. The list goes on and on. There can be a serious tension between popularity and the principled behavior of a lawyer. There's no guarantee of friends, or wealth for that matter, if one does it correctly. Even if one does figure out what one is selling.

Law City may be a modern metropolitan marketplace, but it was built and rebuilt and spruced up again upon what was once a mingling of steeps hills where a few unpromising wisps of stove smoke once floated over the muddy confluence of three lazy rivers. In a sense, Law City is still on the frontier, a fly-over wilderness with a risky, uncertain future. It stands waiting, as it has since it was founded, for the next generation of stubborn, proud men and women to rise and assume the mantle of the Doers of Small Things Right. The Takers-on of Big Projects, and of Unpopular Opinions. To become the Stewards, and the Line-Drawers. And the Patriots.

ACKNOWLEDGMENTS

It takes a great deal of support to write a book of this size and scope. I owe much gratitude, first and foremost, to David Blaner and the Allegheny County Bar Foundation for their generous donations of openness, time and treasure — the latter in the form of funding for my occasional assistants on this book: Megan McKee, Sarah Steers and Andrew S. Morgan. To those assistants, and to Kevin Eddy for his occasional research help, I am most grateful for your hard work and dedication to this project.

I wish to thank Ken Gormley for calling me in 2008 and asking me if I would consider writing this book, and also Mark Shepard for putting him up to it. With their encouragement, and the encouragement and enthusiasm of the Bar Association's History Committee, I have had the opportunity to take an incredible journey through Pittsburgh's history. Thanks also to four of the wisest men with whom I've had the privilege to practice law over the years, for sharing their patience and experience with me: Tom Thompson, Bob Sable, Dave Robertson and Carl Hellerstedt. In addition to these good men, I have been fortunate to have a really good group of readers, in addition to the four wise men and Messrs. Eddy and Morgan, who have dipped in and out of the pages of this book and provided excellent suggestions, including: Sally Edison, Mary Snyder, Cris Hoel, Kimberly Kirk, George Cass, Judge Mark Hornak, James Baldwin, Pat Stewart, Andre Lacouture, Dan Thompson, Dick Jewell, and Michael Walsh. Among my draft readers, my greatest thanks goes to Bernard Hibbitts, who convinced me that this could be a real book, and helped me, time and time again, to find the arc of the story I was writing. Thanks also to my "literary" lawyer, William A. Newman, for suggesting the title of this book, which is about as great an example of "value added" service from a lawyer as I can think of. And finally, thanks to Florence Stauber, for always believing; and to the people who helped me bring this home as an honest-to-goodness book—Melissa Neely, Alex Shvartsman and Victoria Blanco—you saved my life.

My sincere thanks goes to some of the people I've met during the writing of this book who have provided me with key bits of research or content direction, including Devon Cross, Barbara Margolis, Rob Ruck, Bill Wycoff, Jeff Icardi, Linda Shoop Schmalstig, David Murdoch, Woody Turner and Joel Fishman. I can't write a line without thinking of the teachers who helped me to learn how to write, and how to think about writing, including Dick Battelle, Hal Golden, Bill Cole, Bob Davis, Jack Coogan, Martha Andresen, Dick Barnes and Scott Warren; as well as my parents, Bill and Irene, my sister Nancy, and brother-in-law Paul, without whom I may not have been interested in reading books let alone writing them.

Despite the training of good teachers, I have never learned how to write successfully in silent isolation. It also seemed to me that if I were going to write about Pittsburgh, I would be required to spend quality time out and about in the city. Therefore, like Walter Benjamin, on this book I adopted the maxim that the "ale-house is the key to every town ... to know where German beer can be drunk is geography and ethnology enough" to know a town well. Except in my case, there were other items on the menu than just German beer. To that end, I would like to thank the bartenders and servers of some of my favorite writing spots, including: at Pizzaiolo Primo in Market Square, Gina (now at The Commoner), Lee, Kendra and Alena; the Urban Tap on the South Side; Seth, formerly at the Capital Grill in downtown Pittsburgh; Redbeard's, downtown; Pops, Emily I and II, Kyna, Kimberly, Sarah and the team at the former Easy Street at One Oxford Centre; Nicole at the cigar bar at Cioppino in the Strip District; Las Velas; Hough's in Greenfield; Butcher and the Rye; the Sharp Edge in downtown Pittsburgh; the Bigham Tavern on Mount Washington; Amanda and that strange collection of folks at the former Bar 110 on Smithfield Street; the former Mexico City on Wood Street; and the former Kiva Han, Oakland, Pittsburgh; during the long march of footnoting, Local on the South Side; and, more recently, Olive at Union Standard, and Nami and Nick at The Boulevard at the Distrikt Hotel. Special shout-out to Ray from McKees Rocks, who had recently lost his brother to a heroin overdose, and who typified Pittsburghers' inherent politeness by apologizing to me needlessly yet repeatedly for interrupting my work while sitting at the bar.

Finally, much gratitude to Kerstin, who has come to hate this book as much as other spouses hate garages that need to be cleaned out and sock drawers that need to be sorted. "Fine, then, go play with your dead lawyers," she would often say; but she has been the best promoter of the stories contained herein that anyone could ask for, and the one person on whom I can always count for a great idea.

SELECTED BIBLIOGRAPHY

Writing a history no one has previously synthesized is largely an undertaking built from the ground up. This project involved many hours of personal interviews and archival research in both public and private collections (the collection of the Allegheny County Bar Association being a primary source of research), as well as through genealogical databases and the fruits of Freedom of Information Act requests, in order to give shape to the book's overall narrative. These sources are in each case identified in the endnotes that follow.

The closest thing to a history of Pittsburgh's legal profession prior to this book is a collection of brief biographies compiled by Pittsburgh lawyer Archibald Blakeley in a very long chapter on "Allegheny County" in the two volume set, *Twentieth Century Bench & Bar of Pennsylvania, Vols. I and II* (Chicago: H.C. Cooper, Jr., Bro. & Co., 1903).

Also very helpful for basic research were J.W.F. White, "The Judiciary of Allegheny County," *The Pennsylvania Magazine of History and Biography* 7:2 (1883); James H. Gray, "Allegheny County Common Pleas Court Law Judges, 1791-1939," *Western Pennsylvania Historical Magazine* 24, no. 3 (September 1941); Joseph A. Katarincic, "The Allegheny County Bar Association, 1870-1960," *Western Pennsylvania Historical Magazine* 43, no. 4 (December 1960); David Murdoch, "Profiles in Leadership: Allegheny County's Lawyer-Generals in the Civil War," *Pittsburgh History* (Winter 1998/1999); Lincoln Steffens, "Pittsburg: A City Ashamed," *McClure's Magazine* (May 1903); Allegheny County Bar Association, "Tribute: First One Hundred Women Attorneys in Allegheny County," (banquet program at the William Penn Hotel, April 29, 1992); Allegheny County Bar Association, "Tribute to African American Lawyers" (banquet program at the Vista Hotel, February 22, 1995); Stanley M. Stein and David L. Meister, *A Court for the People, prepared for the Allegheny County Court of Common Pleas, Bicentennial Celebration* (Pittsburgh: The Allegheny County Court of Common Pleas Bicentennial Committee, 1988); and Benjamin Hayllar, Jr., "The Accommodation: The History and Rhetoric of the Rackets-Political Alliance in Pittsburgh" (PhD diss., University of Pittsburgh, 1977).

In addition to these works, listed below are what the author would consider to be the key publications reviewed in preparation for writing of this book. For the remainder, all helpful in their way, the author would refer the reader to the endnotes.

Books

Alexander Addison, *The trial of Alexander Addison, esq. President of the Courts of Common Pleas, in the circuit consisting of the counties of Westmoreland, Fayette, Washington, and Allegheny, on the impeachment by the House of Representatives, before the Senate of the Commonwealth of Pennsylvania. Taken in shorthand by Thomas Lloyd* (Lancaster, PA: Lloyd & Helmbold, 1803).

Ruggero J. Aldisert, *Road to the Robes: A Federal Judge Recollects Young Years & Early Times* (Bloomington, IN: AuthorHouse, 2005).

John U. Anderson, Jr., *Kirkpatrick & Lockhart LLP: The Early Years: Reflections* (Pittsburgh: Kirkpatrick & Lockhart, 1996).

Henry Baldwin, *A General View of the Origin and Nature of the Constitution and Government of the United States* (Philadelphia: John C. Clark, 1837).

John E. Bauman and Edward K. Miller, *Before Renaissance: Planning in Pittsburgh, 1889-1943* (Pittsburgh: University of Pittsburgh Press, 2006).

Jack Beatty, ed., *Colossus: How the Corporation Changed America*, (New York: Crown Publishing, 2001)

Paul B. Beers, *Pennsylvania Politics Today and Yesterday: The Tolerable Accommodation* (University Park, PA: Penn State University Press, 2010).

Robert R. Bell, *The Philadelphia Lawyer: A History, 1735-1945* (Selinsgrove, PA: Susquehanna University Press, 1992).

Irving Bernstein, *Turbulent Years: A History of the American Worker 1933-1941* (New York: Houghton Mifflin, 1970).

Joseph Bucklin Bishop, *Theodore Roosevelt and His Time, Vol. I* (New York: Charles Scribner's, 1920).

Hugh Henry Brackenridge, *Incidents of the insurrection in the western parts of Pennsylvania, in the year 1794*, vol. 2 (Philadelphia: John M'Culloch, 1794).

James Howard Bridge, *The Carnegie Millions and the Men Who Made Them* (London: Limpus Baker & Co., 1903).

James Howard Bridge, *The Inside History of the Carnegie Steel Company: A Romance of Millions* (Pittsburgh: University of Pittsburgh Press, 1903).

Mary Brignano & J. Tomlinson Fort, *Reed Smith: A Law Firm Celebrates 125 Years* (Pittsburgh: Reed Smith, 2002).

Robert V. Bruce, *1877: Year of Violence* (Chicago: I.R. Dee, 1959).

Andrew Bunie, *Robert L. Vann of the Pittsburgh Courier: Politics and Black Journalism* (Pittsburgh: University of Pittsburgh Press, 1974).

Arthur G. Burgoyne, *The Homestead Strike of 1892* (Pittsburgh: University of Pittsburgh Press, 1979).

Barbara S. Burstein, *Steel City Jews: A History of Pittsburgh and its Jewish Community, 1840-1915* (Pittsburgh: privately published, 2008).

Paul Carrington, *Stewards of Demcoracy: Law as Public Profession* (Boulder, CO: Westview Press, 1999).

Richard C. Cortner, *The Jones & Laughlin Case* (New York: Knopf, 1970)/

Thomas Cushing, *History of Allegheny County, Pennsylvania including its early settlement and progress to the present time ; a description of its historic and interesting localities ; its cities, towns and villages; religious, educational, social and military history ; mining, manufacturing and commercial interests, improvements, resources, statistics, etc. ; also, biographies of many of its representative citizens, Vol. I* (Chicago: A. Warner & Co., 1889).

Ralph H. Demmler, *The First Century of an Institution: Reed Smith Shaw & McClay* (Pittsburgh: Demmler, 1977).

Eric Leif Devin, *Crucible of Freedom: Workers' Democracy in the Industrial heartland, 1914-1960* (Lanham, MD: Rowman & Littlefield, 2010).

Annie Dillard, *An American Childhood* (New York: Harper & Row, 1989).

Duquesne University School of Law, *One Hundred Years of Excellence*, 1911-2011 (Pittsburgh: Duquesne Press, 2011).

Samuel W. Durant, A. Merrill and Pliny Durant, *A.History of Allegheny Co., Pennsylvania* (Philadelphia: L.H. Everts, 1876).

Arthur J. Edmunds, *Daybreakers: The Story of the Urban League of Pittsburgh* (Pittsburgh: Urban League of Pittsburgh, 1999).

Joseph J. Ellis, *After the Revolution: Profiles of Early American Culture* (New York: W.W. Norton Co., 1979).

Lawrence M. Friedman, *History of American Law* (New York: Touchstone 1986).

Russell Ferguson, *Early Western Pennsylvania Politics* (Pittsburgh: University of Pittsburgh Press, 1938).

Frank Abial Flower, *Edwin McMasters Stanton: The Autocrat of Rebellion, Emancipation and Reconstruction* (New York, Chicago and Akron: Saalfield Pub. Co., 1905).

Laurence Glasco, *The WPA History of the Negro in Pittsburgh* (Pittsburgh: University of Pittsburgh Press, 2004).

Laurence Glasco, "Double Burden: The Black Experience in Pittsburgh," in *City at the Point*, ed. Samuel P. Hays (Pittsburgh: University of Pittsburgh Press, 1989).

Leland Hazard, *Attorney for the Situation* (New York: Columbia University Press 1975).

James G. Hollock, *Born to Lose: Stanley B. Hoss and the Crime Spree That Gripped a Nation* (Kent, OH: Kent State University Press, 2011).

Doris Kearns Goodwin, *The Bully Pulpit: Theodore Roosevelt, William Howard Taft and the Golden Age of Journalism* (New York: Simon & Schuster, 2013).

Maurice W. Greenwald and Margo J. Anderson, eds. *Pittsburgh Surveyed: Social Science and Social Reform in the Early Twentieth Century* (Pittsburgh: University of Pittsburgh Press, 2011).

Francis Harbison, *D.T. Watson of Counsel* (Pittsburgh: Davis & Warde, 1945).

Dale A. Hathaway, *Can Workers Have a Voice?: The Politics of Deindustrialization in Pittsburgh* (University Park, PA: Penn State University Press, 1993).

Kenneth Heineman, *A Catholic New Deal* (University Park, PA: Penn State University Press 1999).

Burton Hersh, *The Mellon Family: A Fortune in History* (New York: William Morrow & Co., 1978).

John P. Hoerr, *And the Wolf Finally Came: The Decline of the American Steel Industry* (Pittsburgh: University of Pittsburgh Press, 1988).

Aldo Icardi, *American Master Spy* (Pittsburgh: Stalwart Enterprises, Inc., 1954).

Peter H. Irons, *The New Deal Lawyers* (Princeton, NJ: Princeton University Press, 1993).

Philip Jenkins, *The Cold War At Home: The Red Scare in Pennsylvania, 1945-1960* (Chapel Hill, NC: University of North Carolina Press, 1999).

Philip Jenkins, *Hoods and Shirts: The Extreme Right in Pennsylvania, 1925-1950* (Chapel Hill: University of North Carolina Press, 2009).

James A. Kehl, *Ill Feeling in the Era of Good Feeling: Western Pennsylvania Political Battles 1815-1825* (Pittsburgh: University of Pittsburgh Press, 1956).

David E. Koskoff, *The Mellons: The Chronicle of America's Richest Family* (New York: Thomas Y. Crowell Co., 1978).

Paul Krause, *The Battle for Homestead, 1880-1892: Politics, Culture, and Steel* (Pittsburgh: University of Pittsburgh Press, 1992).

Daniel J. Leab, *I Was a Communist for the FBI: The Unhappy Life and Times of Matt Cvetic* (State College, PA: Penn State University Press, 2000).

Francis Leupp, *George Westinghouse: His Life and Achievements* (London: John Murray,1919).

Stefan Lorant, ed., *Pittsburgh: The Story of an American City* (Esselmont, 1999).

Roy Lubove, *Twentieth Century Pittsburgh Volume 1: Government, Business, and Environmental Change* (Pittsburgh: University of Pittsburgh Press, 1996).

Roy Lubove, *Twentieth-Century Pittsburgh, Volume Two: The Post Steel Era* (Pittsburgh: University of Pittsburgh Press, 1996).

J. Warren Madden, *The Reminiscences of J. Warren Madden* (1957), 72, Oral History Collection, Columbia University, New York, N.Y.

Daniel Marder, ed., *A Hugh Henry Brackenridge Reader, 1770-1815* (Pittsburgh: University of Pittsburgh Press, 1970).

Charles H. McCormick, *Seeing Reds: Federal Surveillance of Radicals in the Pittsburgh Mill District, 1917-1922* (Pittsburgh: University of Pittsburgh Press, 1997).

David McCullough, *The Johnstown Flood* (New York: Simon & Shuster, 1968).

Thomas Mellon, *Thomas Mellon and His Times* (Pittsburgh: University of Pittsburgh Press, 1994).

Balthasar H. Meyer, *A History of the Northern Securities Case* (Boston: Da Capo, 1972).

Elizabeth Brand Monroe, *The Wheeling Bridge Case: Its Significance in American Law and Technology* (Boston: Northeastern University Press, 1992).

Michael A. Musmanno, *Across the Street from the Courthouse* (Philadelphia: Dorrance, 1950).

Michael A. Musmanno, *Verdict!: The Adventures of the Young Lawyer in the Brown Suit* (New York: Doubleday, 1958).

David Nasaw, *Andrew Carnegie* (New York: Penguin, 2007).

Claude Newlin, *Life and Writings of Hugh Henry Brackenridge* (Princeton: University of Princeton Press, 1932).

Anthony S. Pitch, *"They Have Killed Papa Dead!": The Road to Ford's Theatre, Abraham Lincoln's Murder and the Rage for Vengeance* (Hanover, NH: Steerforth Press, 2008).

Pittsburgh Gazette Times, ed., *The Story of Pittsburgh and Vicinity* (Pittsburgh: Pittsburgh Gazette Times, 1908).

Benjamin P. Thomas and Harold M. Hyman, *Stanton: The Life and Times of Lincoln's Secretary of War* (New York: Knopf, 1962).

George Thornton Fleming, *History of Pittsburgh and environs: from prehistoric days to the beginning of the American Revolution, Vol. II* (New York and Chicago: American Historical Society, 1922).

William Marvel, *Lincoln's Autocrat: The Life of Edwin Stanton* (Chapel Hill: University of North Carolina Press, 2015).

Henry G. Prout, *A Life of George Westinghouse* (New York: American Society of Mechanical Engineers, 1921).

Hilary Rosenberg, *The Vulture Investors* (New York: Wiley, 2000).

S. Leo Ruslander, *The Life and Times of S. Leo Ruslander (A Quasi-autobiography)* (Pittsburgh: privately published, 1964).

Bernard Schwartz, *A History of the Supreme Court* (New York: Oxford University Press, 1993).

W. Edward Sell, *The Law Down: A Century Remembered* (Pittsburgh: privately published 1995).

George Shiras III and Winfield Shiras, *Justice George Shiras Jr. of Pittsburgh* (Pittsburgh: University of Pittsburgh Press, 1953).

Quentin R. Skrabec, Jr., *George Westinghouse: Gentle Genius* (New York: Algora, 2007).

Thomas Slaughter, *The Whiskey Rebellion: Frontier Epilogue to the American Revolution* (New York: Oxford University Press, 1986).

George David Smith, *From Monopoly to Competition: The Transformation of Alcoa, 1888-1896* (Cambridge: Cambridge University Press, 1988).

Templeton Smith, *Pioneer at Law: the Life of Nellie Margaret Fergus and her Experiences as an Early Female Practioner of Law* (Pittsburgh: Gibson Publishing, 2001).

J. Clay Smith, Jr., *Emancipation: The Making of the Black Lawyer, 1844-1944* (Philadelphia: University of Pennsylvania Press, 1993).

Les Standiford, *Meet You in Hell: Andrew Carnegie, Henry Clay Frick and the Bitter Partnership That Transformed America* (New York: Broadway Books, 2005).

Robert A. Swaine, *The Cravath Firm and Its Predecessors 1819-1948*, vol. I (New York: Ad Press, 1948).

Dick Thornburgh, *Where the Evidence Leads: An Autobiography* (Pittsburgh: University of Pittsburgh Press, 2003).

Joe W. Trotter and Jared N. Day, *Race and Renaissance: African Americans in Pittsburgh since World War II* (Pittsburgh: University of Pittsburgh Press, 2010).

Michael P. Weber, *Don't Call Me Boss: David L. Lawrence, Pittsburgh's Renaissance Mayor* (Pittsburgh: University of Pittsburgh Press, 1988).

Andrew L. Weil, *A Passion for Justice* (privately published, 1994).

George Wolfskill, *The Revolt of the Conservatives: A History of the American Liberty League 1934-1940* (Boston: Houghton Mifflin, 1962).

Keith A. Zahniser, *Steel City Gospel: Protestant Laity and Reform in Progressive-Era Pittsburgh* (New York: Routledge, 2005).

Newspapers and Periodicals

ABA Journal
American Law Review
The American Lawyer
The Atlantic
Business History Review
Business Law
Chicago Tribune
Colliers
Congressional Record
Ebony
Executive Report: Pennsylvania's Business Magazine
The Index
International Socialist Review
The Iron Age
Jewish Criterion
The Journal of Negro History
The Kiplinger Magazine
The Lawyer
Life
Literary Digest
McClure's Magazine
Mother Earth
National Labor Tribune
The Nation
New York Age
New York Daily Tribune
New York Times
New York Tribune
New Yorker
The Outlook
Pennsylvania Bar Association Quarterly
Pennsylvania History
The Pennsylvania Magazine of History and Biography
Philadelphia Daily News
Philadelphia Inquirer
Pittsburg Bulletin
Pittsburgh Business Times
Pittsburgh Commercial
Pittsburgh Commercial Gazette
Pittsburgh Courier
Pittsburgh Daily Gazette
Pittsburgh Daily Post
Pittsburgh Dispatch
Pittsburgh Evening Chronicle
Pittsburgh Gazette
Pittsburgh Gazette Times
Pittsburgh History
Pittsburgh Leader
Pittsburgh Legal Journal
Pittsburgh Post
Pittsburgh Post-Gazette
Pittsburgh Press
Pittsburgh Quarterly
Pittsburgh Sun
Pittsburgh Sun-Telegraph
Pittsburgh Tribune-Review
Pottstown Mercury
Saturday Evening Post
Sporting Life
Vital Speeches of the Day
Wall Street Journal
Western Pennsylvania History
Western Pennsylvania Historical Magazine
United States Law Review
University of Pittsburgh Law Review

Allegheny County Bar Association, *Lawyers Pictorial Register* (annual)
Allegheny County Legal Directory, Potter Title and Trust Co. (annual)
R.L. Polk and J.F. Diffenbacher *City Directories* (annual)

ENDNOTES PART I

1. Hugh Henry Brackenridge, *Incidents of the insurrection in the western parts of Pennsylvania, in the year 1794*, vol. 2 (Philadelphia: John M'Culloch, 1794), 75.
2. Claude Newlin, *Life and Writings of Hugh Henry Brackenridge* (Princeton: University of Princeton Press, 1932), 1-7.
3. Newlin, *Life and Writings of Hugh Henry Brackenridge*, 22-24, 37-41.
4. Hugh Henry Brackenridge, "United States Magazine, January-July 1779," in *A Hugh Henry Brackenridge Reader, 1770-1815*, ed. Daniel Marder (Pittsburgh: University of Pittsburgh Press, 1970), 92; Joseph J. Ellis, *After the Revolution: Profiles of Early American Culture* (New York: W.W. Norton Co., 1979), 80.
5. Hugh Henry Brackenridge, "Brackenridge to the Citizens of Greene, Washington and Allegheny Counties," *Pittsburgh Gazette*, July 21, 1798.
6. Newlin, *Life and Writings of Hugh Henry Brackenridge*, 83; *Pittsburgh Gazette*, April 28, 1787.
7. Thomas Slaughter, *The Whiskey Rebellion: Frontier Epilogue to the American Revolution* (New York: Oxford University Press, 1986), 56.
8. Slaughter, *Whiskey Rebellion*, 57.
9. Thomas Cushing, *History of Allegheny County, Pennsylvania including its early settlement and progress to the present time; a description of its historic and interesting localities; its cities, towns and villages; religious, educational, social and military history; mining, manufacturing and commercial interests, improvements, resources, statistics, etc.; also, biographies of many of its representative citizens, Vol. I* (Chicago: A. Warner & Co., 1889) 249.
10. P. McCall, *Discourse Delivered Before the Law Academy of Philadelphia, at the Opening of the Session, September 5, 1838* (Philadelphia: Law Academy of Philadelphia, 1838), 14-15.
11. J.W.F. White, "The Judiciary of Allegheny County," *The Pennsylvania Magazine of History and Biography* 7:2 (1883),144.
12. Ibid., 144-45.
13. Ibid., 148-49; Hugh Henry Brackenridge, "The Trial of Mamachtaga," in *Incidents of the Insurrection*, ed. Daniel Marder (New Haven: College & University Press 1972), 26.
14. Lawrence M. Friedman, *History of American Law* (New York: Touchstone 1986), 99-101; Robert R. Bell, *The Philadelphia Lawyer: A History, 1735-1945* (Selinsgrove, PA: Susquehanna University Press, 1992), 58, 62.
15. *History of Butler County, Pennsylvania, with Illustrations and Biographical Sketches of Some of its Prominent Men and Pioneers* (Chicago: Waterman, Watkins & Co., 1883), 16; Slaughter, *Whiskey Rebellion*, 61-62.
16. See Wiley Sword, *President Washington's Indian War* (Norman, OK: University of Oklahoma Press, 1985), 45-51; Pearl E. Wagner, "Economic Conditions in Western Pennsylvania During the Whiskey Rebellion," *Western Pennsylvania Historical Magazine* 10, no. 4 (October 1927), 193-209.
17. Daniel Agnew, "Address to the Allegheny County Bar Association," *Pennsylvania Magazine of History & Biography* 13 (1889), 32.
18. "Old Toll Gates About Pittsburgh," *Western Pennsylvania Historical Magazine* 3, no. 2 (April 1920), 71-72.
19. Friedman, *History of American Law*, 160.
20. Hugh Henry Brackenridge, *Law Miscellanies: Containing an Introduction to the Study of Law* (Philadelphia, 1814), viii.
21. Marder, *A Hugh Henry Brackenridge Reader*, 5-6.
22. Slaughter, *Whiskey Rebellion*, 36-37.
23. Hugh Henry Brackenridge, "Thoughts on the Present Indian War," in *Incidents of the Insurrection*, ed. Daniel Marder (New Haven: College & University Press 1972), 44.
24. Ellis, *After the Revolution*, 90; Daniel Marder, *Hugh Henry Brackenridge* (New York: Twayne Publishing, 1967), 47.
25. Ellis, *After the Revolution*, 90.
26. Hugh Henry Brackenridge, "To the Inhabitants of the Western Country," *Pittsburgh Gazette*, April 21, 1784, reprinted in Newlin, *Life and Writings of Hugh Henry Brackenridge*, 83-84.
27. Hugh Henry Brackenridge, "Sermons in Favor of the Federal Constitution," in *A Hugh Henry Brackenridge Reader, 1770-1815*, ed. Daniel Marder (Pittsburgh: University of Pittsburgh Press, 1970), 133.
28. Hugh Henry Brackenridge, "Cursory Remarks on the Federal Constitution, Gazette Publications," in *A Hugh Henry Brackenridge Reader, 1770-1815*, ed. Daniel Marder (Pittsburgh: University of Pittsburgh Press, 1970), 126.
29. Hugh Henry Brackenridge, "Sermons in Favor of the Federal Constitution," in *A Hugh Henry Brackenridge Reader, 1770-1815*, ed. Daniel Marder (Pittsburgh: University of Pittsburgh Press, 1970), 134.
30. Marder, *A Hugh Henry Brackenridge Reader*, 13.
31. Hugh Henry Brackenridge, *Incidents of the insurrection in the western parts of Pennsylvania, in the year 1794*, vol. 3 (Philadelphia: John M'Culloch, 1794), 14.
32. J.W.F. White, "Judiciary of Allegheny County," 153-154; Marder, *Hugh Henry Brackenridge*, 41.

33. "Allegheny County List of Attorneys and Law Students, 1788-1981," vol. 1, 1-2, Reel #47.7, Pennsylvania State Archives, Records of County Governments Collection; Archibald Blakeley, "Allegheny County," *Twentieth Century Bench & Bar of Pennsylvania, Vol. II* (Chicago: H.C. Cooper, Jr., Bro. & Co., 1903), 805.

34. James H. Gray, "Allegheny County Common Pleas Court Law Judges, 1791-1939," *Western Pennsylvania Historical Magazine* 24, no. 3 (September 1941), 184.

35. Agnew, "Address to Allegheny County," 3; Leland D. Baldwin, *Whiskey Rebels: The Story of a Frontier Uprising* (Pittsburgh: University of Pittsburgh Press, 1967), 51.

36. Bernard J. Hibbitts, "Lawyering in Place: Topographies of Practice and Pleading in Pittsburgh, 1775-1895," *University of Pittsburgh Law Review* 73, no. 4 (2012), 625-26.

37. *Pittsburgh Gazette*, June 28, 1788.

38. William F. Keller, *The Nation's Advocate: Henry Marie Brackenridge and Young America* (Pittsburgh: University of Pittsburgh Press, 1956), 14.

39. John Pope, *A Tour Through the Southern and Western Territories of the United States of North-America; the Spanish Dominions on the River Mississippi, and the Floridas; the Countries of the Creek Nations; and Many Uninhabited Parts* (New York: C.L. Woodward, 1888), 14-17; "Pitt Founder's Wife Cost $200," *Pittsburgh Post-Gazette*, July 8, 1950; Baldwin, *Whiskey Rebels*, 43-44.

40. Hugh Henry Brackenridge, *Incidents of the insurrection in the western parts of Pennsylvania, in the year 1794*, vol. 2 (Philadelphia: John M'Culloch, 1794), 77.

41. Slaughter, *Whiskey Rebellion*, 95-105; William Hogeland, *The Whiskey Rebellion: George Washington, Alexander Hamilton, and the Frontier Rebels Who Challenged America's Newfound Sovereignty* (New York: Scribner, 2006), 68-69.

42. Slaughter, *Whiskey Rebellion*, 218-19; Hogeland, *Whiskey Rebellion*, 233-35.

43. Slaughter, *Whiskey Rebellion*, 282.

44. Baldwin, *Whiskey Rebels*, 78-79; Slaughter, *Whiskey Rebellion*, 113.

45. Henry Marie Brackenridge, "Biographical Notice of H. H. Breckenridge, Late of the Supreme Court of Pennsylvania," *Southern Literary Messenger* 8, no. 1 (1842), 4.

46. Hugh Henry Brackenridge, "Thoughts on the Excise Law, so far as it respects the Western Country," in *Incidents of the Insurrection*, ed. Daniel Marder (New Haven: College & University Press 1972), 47-50.

47. H.B., "Excise," *National Gazette*, August 18, 1792, reprinted in Philip Marsh, "Hugh Henry Brackenridge: More Essays in the National Gazette," *Western Pennsylvania Historical Magazine* 28, no. 3-4 (September-December 1946), 152.

48. Charles W. Dahlinger, *Pittsburgh: A Sketch of its Early Social Life* (New York: G.P. Putnam's Sons 1916), 56.

49. Myrl I. Eakin, "Hugh Henry Brackenridge - Lawyer," *Western Pennsylvania Historical Magazine* 10:3 (July 1927), 165.

50. Albert Gallatin to Jean Badollet, 9 Mar. 1793, New York Historical Society, *The Papers of Albert Gallatin*, microfilm edition (Philadelphia, 1969), reel 1. Albert Gallatin to Thomas Clare, 9 Mar. 1793, ibid. Letters quoted in James P. McClure, "'Let Us Be Independent': David Bradford and the Whiskey Insurrection," *Pittsburgh History* (Summer 1991), 75.

51. David Bradford to Governor Thomas Mifflin, Oct. 4, 1794, *Pennsylvania Archives*, Second Series, vol. 4, ed John B. Linn and Wm. H. Egle (Harrisburg, PA: Clarence Busch, 1896), 396-97.

52. Baldwin, *Whiskey Rebels*, 117-23; Slaughter, *Whiskey Rebellion*, 177-180; Hogeland, *Whiskey Rebellion*, 145-148.

53. H. M. Brackenridge, "Biographical Notice," 7.

54. David Bradford's account of the Whiskey Rebellion, *David Bradford Papers*, Historical Society of Western Pennsylvania, Pittsburgh, quoted in Jeffrey A. David, "Guarding the Republican Interest: The Western Pennsylvania Democratic Societies and the Excise Tax," *Pennsylvania History* 67, no. 1 (Winter 2000), 53-54.

55. Brackenridge, *Incidents*, vol. 1, 32-35.

56. Ibid., 38.

57. Ibid., 50.

58. Ibid., 71.

59. H.H. Brackenridge to Tench Coxe, August 8, 1794, *Pennsylvania Archives*, Second Series, vol. 4, ed. John B. Linn and Wm. H. Egle (Harrisburg, PA: Clarence Busch, 1896), 119-122.

60. Slaughter, *Whiskey Rebellion*, 196-197.

61. Slaughter, *Whiskey Rebellion*, 193.

62. J.P. Taylor, "Condensed History of the Whiskey Insurrection," *Historical Magazine of Monongahela's Old Home Coming Week, Sept. 6-13, 1908* (Monongahela: 1908), 93.

63. Sylvester Fithian Scovel, *Centennial Volume of the First Presbyterian Church of Pittsburgh, PA, 1784-1884* (Pittsburgh: Wm. G. Johnston & Co., 1884), 142.

64. Brackenridge, *Incidents*, vol. 2, 46.

65. Ibid., 73.

66. Ibid., 74.

67. Ellis, *After the Revolution*, 106.

68. Brackenridge, *Incidents*, vol. 2, 77.

69. Ellis, *After the Revolution*, 107.

70. Newlin, *Life and Writings of Hugh Henry Brackenridge*, 277-278; David Paul Brown, *The Forum; or, Forty years full practice at the Philadelphia bar, vol. I* (Philadelphia: R. H. Small, 1856), 396.

71 Ellis, *After the Revolution*, 101.

72 Ibid.

73 Taylor, "Condensed History", 95.

74 David Bradford's account of the Whiskey Rebellion, *David Bradford Papers*, Historical Society of Western Pennsylvania, Pittsburgh.

75 M. Avis Pitcher, "John Smith, First Senator from Ohio and His Connections with Aaron Burr," *Ohio State Archeological & Historical Quarterly* 45 (1936), 76.

76 J.W.F. White, "Judiciary of Allegheny County," 185; "History | Western District of Pennsylvania | United States District Court", accessed February 6, 2016, http://www.pawd.uscourts.gov/history.

77 Russell Ferguson, *Early Western Pennsylvania Politics* (Pittsburgh: University of Pittsburgh Press, 1938), 168.

78 Ibid.

79 Albert Beveridge, *The Life of John Marshall, Vol. I* (Boston: Houghton Mifflin Co., 1916), 47; J.W.F. White, "Judiciary of Allegheny County," 157; Ferguson, *Early Western Pennsylvania Politics*, 169.

80 Ferguson, *Early Western Pennsylvania Politics*, 169; J.W.F. White, "Judiciary of Allegheny County," 157.

81 Alexander Addison, *The trial of Alexander Addison, esq. President of the Courts of Common Pleas, in the circuit consisting of the counties of Westmoreland, Fayette, Washington, and Allegheny, on the impeachment by the House of Representatives, before the Senate of the Commonwealth of Pennsylvania. Taken in shorthand by Thomas Lloyd* (Lancaster, PA: Lloyd & Helmbold, 1803); Ferguson, *Early Western Pennsylvania Politics*, 170; Beveridge, *The Life of John Marshall*, 46-47.

82 Addison, *Trial*, 137-138.

83 Addison, *Trial*, 153-154; J.W.F. White, "Judiciary of Allegheny County," 158; Ferguson, *Early Western Pennsylvania Politics*, 171.

84 Ferguson, *Early Western Pennsylvania Politics*, 171.

85 Ferguson, *Early Western Pennsylvania Politics*, 171; Gail Stuart Rowe, *Embattled Bench: The Pennsylvania Supreme Court and the Forging of a Democratic Society, 1684-1809* (Newark: University of Delaware Press, 1994), 264-272; Mildred M. Williams, "Hugh Henry Brackenridge as a Judge of the Supreme Court of Pennsylvania 1799-1816," *Western Pennsylvania Historical Magazine* 10, no. 4 (October 1927), 210-223.

86 Hugh Henry Brackenridge, *Modern Chivalry or, The adventures of Captain Farrago and Teague O'Regan*, Book III (Philadelphia: T.B. Peterson & Bros., 1857), 83-84.

87 Tarleton Bates to Frederick Bates, May 10, 1805, reprinted in Elvert M. Davis, "The Letters of Tarleton Bates 1795-1805," *Western Pennsylvania Historical Magazine* 12, no. 1 (January 1929), 51.

88 J.W.F. White, "Judiciary of Allegheny County," 189-90.

89 J.W.F. White, "Judiciary of Allegheny County," 190; *Twentieth Century Bench & Bar of Pennsylvania, Vol. II*, 821.

90 See Tarleton Bates, "To Emily Morgan Neville," *Western Pennsylvania Historical Magazine* 1, no. 3 (July 1918); Elvert M. Davis, "The Bates Boys on the Western Water, Part III," *Western Pennsylvania Historical Magazine* 30, nos. 1-2 (March-June 1947).

91 James D. Van Trump and James Brian Cannon, "An Affair of Honor: Pittsburgh's Last Duel," *The Western Pennsylvania Historical Magazine* 57, no. 3 (July 1974), 309-310.

92 M. Flavia Taylor, "The Political and Civic Career of Henry Baldwin, 1799 to 1830" (master's thesis, University of Pittsburgh, 1940), 13;

93 John Kennedy to George W. Hitner, Dec. 5, 1833, letter quoted in Burton Alva Konkle, *The Life and Speeches of Thomas Williams: Orator, Statesman and Jurist, 1806-1872, a Founder of the Whig and Republican Parties*, vol. 1 (Philadelphia: Campion & Co., 1905) 37-39.

94 Thomas Mellon, *Thomas Mellon and His Times* (Pittsburgh: University of Pittsburgh Press, 1994), 87.

95 Bell, *The Philadelphia Lawyer*, 100.

96 "Allegheny County List of Attorneys and Law Students, 1788-1981," vol. 1, 1-4, Reel #47.7, Pennsylvania State Archives, Records of County Governments Collection; *Twentieth Century Bench & Bar of Pennsylvania, Vol. II*, 812.

97 Bell, *The Philadelphia Lawyer*, 79.

98 Mellon, *Thomas Mellon and His Times*, 89-90.

99 Mellon, *Thomas Mellon and His Times* 90.

100 Taylor, "Career of Henry Baldwin," 12-15; Trump and Cannon, "An Affair of Honor," 310.

101 *Commonwealth*, Dec. 25, 1805.

102 *Commonwealth*, Jan. 8, 1806.

103 *Tree of Liberty*, January 4, 1806, quoted in Davis, "The Bates Boys on the Western Water," 35-36.

104 Taylor, "Career of Baldwin," 21.

105 Agnew, "Address to Allegheny County," 25.

106 Hugh Henry Brackenridge, *Modern Chivalry or, The adventures of Captain Farrago and Teague O'Regan*, Books I-II (Philadelphia: T.B. Peterson & Bros., 1857), 69.

107 Leland D. Baldwin, *Pittsburgh: The Story of a City* (Pittsburgh: University of Pittsburgh Press, 1937), 178-179.

108 T.L. Rodgers, "The Last Duel in Pennsylvania," *Western Pennsylvania Historical Magazine* 12, no. 1 (January 1929), 55; Trump and Cannon, "An Affair of Honor," 311-12.

109 Trump and Cannon, "An Affair of Honor," 313.

110 Michael Franchioni, "The Next Page: When Political Debate Really Was Deadly Serious," *Pittsburgh Post-Gazette*, Oct. 22, 2006.

111 *Pittsburgh Gazette*, January 14, 1806.

112 *Commonwealth*, January 14, 1806.

113 Trump and Cannon, "An Affair of Honor," 314-315.

114 Walter Forward to Frederick Bates, Feb. 14, 1806, letter reprinted in Davis, "The Bates Boys on the Western Water," 38.

115 United States Congress, *Biographical Directory of the United States Congress, 1774-2005, the Continental Congress, September 5, 1774, to October 21, 1788, and the Congress of the United States, from the First through the One Hundred Eighth Congresses, March 4, 1789, to January 3, 2005, inclusive* (Washington: Government Printing Office, 2005) 7.

116 M. Flavia Taylor, "The Political and Civic Career of Henry Baldwin, 1799-1830," *The Western Pennsylvania Historical Magazine* 24, no. 1 (March 1941), 45.

117 Author of the Thirty Years' View, *Abridgement of the Debates of Congress, from 1789 to 1856*, vol. 6 (New York: D. Appleton & Co., 1858), 321.

118 *Pittsburgh Gazette*, March 21, 1823; James A. Kehl, *Ill Feeling in the Era of Good Feeling: Western Pennsylvania Political Battles 1815-1825* (Pittsburgh: University of Pittsburgh Press, 1956) 186.

119 Timothy S. Huebner, *The Taney Court: Justices, Rulings and Legacy* (Santa Barbara: ABC-Clio, 2003) 7, 55; Herbert A. Johnson, *The Chief Justiceship of John Marshall 1801-1835* (Columbia, SC: University of South Carolina Press, 1997), 49.

120 Johnson, *The Chief Justiceship of John Marshall*, 96-100; G. Edward White, "The Internal Powers of the Chief Justice: The Nineteenth-Century Legacy," *University of Pennsylvania Law Review* 154 (2006), 1463; Huebner, *The Taney Court*, 57-58.

121 Ex parte Bradstreet, 31 U.S. 774 (1832).

122 Henry Baldwin, *A General View of the Origin and Nature of the Constitution and Government of the United States* (Philadelphia: John C. Clark, 1837) 1.

123 Baldwin, *A General View of the Origin and Nature of the Constitution*, 25.

124 Baldwin, *A General View of the Origin and Nature of the Constitution*, 36-37.

125 G. Edward White, *The Marshall Court and Cultural Change, 1815-1835*, vols. 3-4 of *History of the Supreme Court of the United States* (New York: Macmillan, 1988), 297.

126 White, *History of the Supreme Court*, 301.

127 Johnson, *The Chief Justiceship of John Marshall*, 49.

128 Carl B. Swisher, *The Taney Period, 1836-64* (New York: Macmillan Library Reference, 1974), 52.

129 Robert McKnight, *Diaries*, vol. II, August 9, 1846, Historical Society of Western Pennsylvania, Senator John Heinz Pittsburgh Regional History Center.

130 W. Edward Sell, *The Law Down: A Century Remembered* (Pittsburgh: privately published 1995), 1.

131 Robert Bocking Stevens, *Law School: Legal Education in America from the 1850s to the 1980s* (Chapel Hill: University of North Carolina Press, 1983), 8; Friedman, *History of American Law*, 607.

132 *Twentieth Century Bench & Bar of Pennsylvania*, Vol. II, 836-37, 846.

133 Sell, *The Law Down*, 2-3.

134 Donald E. Cook, Jr., "The Great Fire of Pittsburgh in 1845, or How a Great American City Turned Disaster into Victory," *Western Pennsylvania Historical Magazine* 51, no. 2 (April 1968), 129; Baldwin, *Pittsburgh: the Story of a City*, 228; Charles F.C. Arensberg, "The Pittsburgh Fire of April 10, 1845," *Western Pennsylvania Historical Magazine* 28, no. 1-2 (March-June 1945), 11.

135 Mellon, *Thomas Mellon and His Times*, 146.

136 McKnight, *Diaries*, April 10, 1845.

137 Ann Royall, *Mrs. Royall's Pennsylvania, or Travels Continued in the United States, Vol. II* (Washington: privately published, 1829) 70.

138 George Thornton Fleming, *History of Pittsburgh and environs: from prehistoric days to the beginning of the American Revolution, Vol. II* (New York and Chicago: American Historical Society, 1922), 360.

139 McKnight, *Diaries*, April 10, 1845.

140 Cook, "The Great Fire of Pittsburgh," 130-137; Marcellin C. Adams, "Pittsburgh's Great Fire of 1845," *Western Pennsylvania Historical Magazine* 25, nos. 1-2 (March-June 1942), 23-24.

141 McKnight, *Diaries*, April 10, 1845.

142 Mellon, *Thomas Mellon and His Times*, 147.

143 Thomas Cushing, *History of Allegheny County, Pennsylvania including its early settlement and progress to the present time; a description of its historic and interesting localities; its cities, towns and villages; religious, educational, social and military history; mining, manufacturing and commercial interests, improvements, resources, statistics, etc.; also, biographies of many of its representative citizens, Vol. I* (Chicago: A. Warner & Co., 1889) 581; Mellon, *Thomas Mellon and His Times*, 148; Arensberg, "The Pittsburgh Fire," 16.

144 Mellon, *Thomas Mellon and His Times*, 148.

145 Cook, "The Great Fire of Pittsburgh," 141.

146 McKnight, *Diaries*, April 11, 1845.

147 Arensberg, "The Pittsburgh Fire," 17-18; Cook, "The Great Fire of Pittsburgh," 146-47.

148 Arensberg, "The Pittsburgh Fire," 18.

149 "Historical Society Notes: The Coming Centennial of the Great Fire," *Western Pennsylvania Historical Magazine* 26, no. 3-4 (September-December 1943), 170-184.

150 Kirk Q. Bigham, *Major Abraham Kirkpatrick and His Descendants* (Pittsburgh: J.P. Durbin, 1911) 43-44.

151 Cook, "The Great Fire of Pittsburgh," 145-146.

152 Sell, *The Law Down*, 1; Fleming, *History of Pittsburgh and environs*, 364. Dean Sell incorrectly states that Heman Dyer died in the Great Fire. *See*, "Heman Dyer," *Appletons Cylopedia of American Biography*, ed. James Grant Wilson and John Fiske (New York: D. Appleton & Co., 1900), 286.

153 Joseph A. Katarincic, "The Allegheny County Bar Association, 1870-1960," *Western Pennsylvania Historical Magazine* 43, no. 4 (December 1960), 310-311.

154 *Twentieth Century Bench & Bar of Pennsylvania, Vol. II*, 871.

155 "Our First Number," *Pittsburgh Legal Journal*, April 23, 1853.

156 Monte Calvert, "The Allegheny City Cotton Mill Riot," *Western Pennsylvania Historical Magazine* 46, no. 2 (April 1963), 108-113.

157 Calvert, "Cotton Mill Riot," 97, 103-104.

158 *Pittsburgh Gazette*, January 16, 1849.

159 Calvert, "Cotton Mill Riot," 106.

160 Benjamin P. Thomas and Harold M. Hyman, *Stanton: The Life and Times of Lincoln's Secretary of War* (New York: Knopf, 1962), 38.

161 See, e.g., Isaac Harris, *Harris' Business Directory of the Cities of Pittsburgh & Allegheny* (Pittsburgh: A.A. Anderson, 1844), 51-53.

162 Mellon, *Thomas Mellon and His Times*, 153.

163 *Twentieth Century Bench & Bar of Pennsylvania, Vol. II*, 822-23.

164 *Memoirs of Allegheny County, Pennsylvania, Vol. II* (Madison, WI: Northwestern Historical Association, 1904), 402; *Twentieth Century Bench & Bar of Pennsylvania, Vol. II*, 829.

165 *Twentieth Century Bench & Bar of Pennsylvania, Vol. II*, 841; *In Memoriam: John Henry Hampton* (Pittsburgh: Jos. Eichbaum & Co., 1892), 14.

166 Thomas Mercer Marshall, "Address of Hon. Thomas M. Marshall delivered before the Allegheny County Bar Association, on Saturday afternoon, November 14, 1896," (lecture, Allegheny County Bar Association, Pittsburgh, PA, November 14, 1896), 13.

167 Thomas and Hyman, *Stanton: The Life and Times of Lincoln's Secretary of War*, 45; Calvert, "Cotton Mill Riot," 122.

168 Frank Abial Flower, *Edwin McMasters Stanton: The Autocrat of Rebellion, Emancipation and Reconstruction* (New York, Chicago and Akron: Saalfield Pub. Co., 1905), 54.

169 James Waldo Fawcett, "Magnus Murray: A Gesture in Appreciation after 131 Year," *Western Pennsylvania Historical Magazine* 50, no. 4 (October 1967), 278-79.

170 Thomas and Hyman, *Stanton: The Life and Times of Lincoln's Secretary of War*, 57.

171 David T.Z. Mindich, "Edwin M. Stanton, The Inverted Pyramid, and Information Control," *Journalism Monographs* 140 (August 1993), 1.

172 Calvert, "Cotton Mill Riot," 127-129; *Pittsburgh Gazette*, January 19, 1849.

173 Calvert, "Cotton Mill Riot," 130.

174 Mindich, "Inverted Pyramid," 24.

175 Elizabeth Brand Monroe, *The Wheeling Bridge Case: Its Significance in American Law and Technology* (Boston: Northeastern University Press, 1992), 41.

176 William Marvel, *Lincoln's Autocrat: The Life of Edwin Stanton* (Chapel Hill: University of North Carolina Press, 2015), 55.

177 *Pittsburgh v. Grier*, 22 Pa. 54 (1853).

178 Elizabeth Brand Monroe, *The Wheeling Bridge Case: Its Significance in American Law and Technology* (Boston: Northeastern University Press, 1992), 50.

179 *Wheeling Gazette*, November 20, 1849.

180 Monroe, *The Wheeling Bridge Case*, 58-59.

181 Flower, *Edwin McMasters Stanton*, 48.

182 Fletcher Pratt, *Stanton: Lincoln's Secretary of War* (Westport, CT: Greenwood Press, 1970), 46.

183 Monroe, *The Wheeling Bridge Case*, 102-107.

184 Thomas and Hyman, *Stanton: The Life and Times of Lincoln's Secretary of War*, 60-62; Marvel, *Autocrat*, 55-59.

185 Benjamin P. Thomas, *Abraham Lincoln: A Biography* (New York: Knopf, 1968), 158-159.

186 Flower, *Edwin McMasters Stanton*, 73-78; Michael S. Lief and H. Mitchell Caldwell, *The Devil's Advocates: Greatest Closing Arguments in Criminal Law* (New York: Scribner, 2006) 335.

187 Laurence Glasco, *The WPA History of the Negro in Pittsburgh* (Pittsburgh: University of Pittsburgh Press, 2004) 118.

188 Hugh Henry Brackenridge, "Thoughts on the Enfranchisement of the Negroes," *A Hugh Henry Brackenridge Reader*, 103-104.

189 Weston Arthur Goodspeed, *Standard History of Pittsburg, Pennsylvania* (Chicago: H.R. Cornell & Co., 1898), 810.

190 Goodspeed, *Standard History*, 812; Glasco, *The WPA History of the Negro in Pittsburgh*, 105-6; John B. Vashon, "Letter to Messers. Garrison and Knapp," *The Liberator*, March 1832, reprinted in Glasco, *The WPA History of the Negro in Pittsburgh*, 123-124.

191 *Proceedings and Debates of the Convention of the Commonwealth of Pennsylvania to Propose Amendments to the Constitution* 10, no. 14 (Harrisburg, 1837-1839).

192 Glasco, *The WPA History of the Negro in Pittsburgh*, 178; *National Enquirer and Constitutional Advocate of Universal Liberty*, July 15, 1837, 1-2.

193 Eric Ledell Smith, "The End of Black Voting Rights in Pennsylvania: African Americans and the Pennsylvania Constitutional Convention of 1837-1838," *Pennsylvania History* 65, no. 3 (Summer 1998), 279.

194 *Pittsburgh Evening Chronicle*, January 3, 1866.

195 Bigham, *Major Kirkpatrick*, 42-48.

196 *Prigg v. Pennsylvania*, 41 U.S. 539 (1842).

197 Goodspeed, *Standard History,* 818.

198 *Pittsburgh Daily Gazette,* April 17, 1847.

199 Irene E. Williams, "The Operation of the Fugitive Slave Law in Western Pennsylvania, from 1850 to 1860," *Western Pennsylvania Historical Magazine* 4, no. 3 (July 1921), 150.

200 Williams, "Operations," 151.

201 Williams, "Operations," 152-153; John Woolf Jordan, *A Century and a Half of Pittsburg and Her People,* vol. 1 (Pittsburgh: Lewis Publishing, 1908), 539-540.

202 Bigham, *Major Kirkpatrick,* 46.

203 Arthur B. Fox, *Our Honored Dead: Allegheny County: Pennsylvania in the American Civil War* (Chicora, PA: Mechling Bookbindery, 2008), 45, 86.

204 Mellon, *Thomas Mellon and His Times,* 130.

205 *Twentieth Century Bench & Bar of Pennsylvania, Vol. II,* 838-39.

206 *Under the Maltese Cross: Antietam to Appomattox, the Loyal Uprising in Western Pennsylvania, 1861-1865* (Pittsburgh: 155th Regimental Association, 1910), 16.

207 Ibid.

208 A.T. Brewer, *History, Sixty-First Regiment, Pennsylvania Volunteers, 1861-1865* (Pittsburgh: Art Engraving & Printing Co., 1911), 147-149.

209 *Under the Maltese Cross,* 26.

210 Samuel P. Bates, *Martial Deeds of Pennsylvania* (Philadelphia: T.H. Davis & Co., 1875), 914.

211 David Murdoch, "Profiles in Leadership: Allegheny County's Lawyer-Generals in the Civil War," *Pittsburgh History* (Winter 1998/1999), 176-177.

212 Murdoch, "Profiles," 174-175.

213 Murdoch, "Profiles," 175.

214 Murdoch, "Profiles," 178.

215 John Robinson, *Michigan in the War* (Lansing: W.B. George & Co., 1882), 514; *Society of the Army of the Cumberland, Twenty-sixth Reunion, Rockford, Illinois, 1896* (Cincinatti: Robert Clark & Co., 1872), 143-45; Murdoch, "Profiles," 180.

216 Murdoch, "Profiles," 182-83.

217 Richard D. Sauers, *Advance the Colors: Pennsylvania Civil War Battle Flags, Vol. 2* (Harrisburg: Capitol Preservation Committee, 1991), 459-60.

218 Murdoch, "Profiles in Leadership," 183. For graphic presentation, see David A. Murdoch, "Allegheny County's Bench and Bar in the Civil War," chart, author's collection.

219 *Twentieth Century Bench & Bar of Pennsylvania, Vol. II,* 895.

220 Edward H. Schoyer, interview by the author, June 23, 1992.

221 *Twentieth Century Bench & Bar of Pennsylvania, Vol. II,* 893.

222 *Twentieth Century Bench & Bar of Pennsylvania, Vol. II,* 852.

223 *Twentieth Century Bench & Bar of Pennsylvania, Vol. II,* 893.

224 Elizabeth B. Custer, *Tenting on the Plains, or General Custer in Kansas and Texas* (New York: C.L. Webster & Co, 1887), 305.

225 *Handbook of Texas Online,* "Kiddoo, Joseph Barr," by James Alex Baggett, accessed January 28, 2016, http://www.tshaonline.org/handbook/online/articles/fki4; *Twentieth Century Bench & Bar of Pennsylvania, Vol. II,* 905.

226 Samuel W. Durant, A. Merrill and Pliny Durant, *A.History of Allegheny Co., Pennsylvania* (Philadelphia: L.H. Everts, 1876), 208.

227 Bernard J. Hibbitts, "Martial Lawyers: Lawyering and War-Waging in American History," *Seattle Journal for Social Justice,* Vol. 13, Iss. 2 (2014), Article 10, 434, and n. 82, quoting Walt Whitman, *States!* in *Leave of Grass* (David McKay ed. 1900), 73.

228 Anthony S. Pitch, *"They Have Killed Papa Dead!": The Road to Ford's Theatre, Abraham Lincoln's Murder and the Rage for Vengeance* (Hanover, NH: Steerforth Press, 2008), 136.

229 Charles Leale, *Lincoln's Last Hours* (Washington: privately published, 1909), 11

230 David Donald, *Lincoln* (New York: Simon & Shuster, 1995), 599.

231 Charles W. Dahlinger, "Abraham Lincoln in Pittsburgh and the Birth of the Republican Party," *Western Pennsylvania Historical Magazine* 3, no. 4 (October 1920), 169-170; Abraham Lincoln, "Abraham Lincoln to John Van Dyke, Sept. 22, 1860," *Collected Works of Abraham Lincoln,* vol. 4, ed. Roy P. Basler (New Brunswick: Rutgers University Press, 1957), 119.

232 Dahlinger, *Lincoln,* 170-172.

233 Ernest C. Miller, "John Wilkes Booth in the Pennsylvania Oil Region," *Western Pennsylvania Historical Magazine* 31, no. 1-2 (March-June 1948), 26-47.

234 Thomas Goodrich, *The Darkest Dawn: Lincoln, Booth, and the Great American Tragedy* (Bloomington: Indiana University Press, 2005), 227.

235 Edwin M. Stanton to Maj-Gen. Winfield S. Hancock, April 16, 1865, Congressional Series of United States Public Documents, vol. 3263 (Washington: Government Printing Office, 1895) 799.

236 Edwin M. Stanton to Maj-Gen Winfield S. Hancock, April 29, 1865, reprinted in Roy Z. Chamlee, *Lincoln's Assassins: a Complete Account of their Capture, Trial and Punishment* (Jefferson, NC: McFarland & Co., 1990), 194.

237 Edward Bates, "The Diary of Edward Bates, 1859-1866," in *Annual Report of the American Historical Association for the year 1930, vol. 4,* ed. Howard K. Beale (Washington: American Historical Association, 1930), May 25, 1865.

238 Job Barnard, "Early Days of the Supreme Court of the District of Columbia," in *Records of the Columbia Historical Society*, ed. by John B. Larner, vol. 22 (Washington: Columbia Historical Society, 1919), 4; *Twentieth Century Bench & Bar of Pennsylvania, Vol. II*, 837; Jo Burgess and Abi Parker, "Biographical Note," *Andrew Wylie, Jr. Family Collection, 1821-1945*, accessed February 6, 2016, http://webapp1.dlib.indiana.edu/findingaids/view?doc.view=entire_text&docId=VAC0754.

239 David V. Baker, *Women and Capital Punishment in the United States: An Analytical History* (Jefferson, NC: McFarland, 2015), 97; Len Barcousky, "Eyewitness 1858: Woman who killed for love, money faces the hangman," *Pittsburgh Post-Gazette*, May 18, 2008).

240 Pitch, *They Killed Papa*, 351.

241 *Philadelphia Inquirer*, July 8, 1865.

242 Ibid.

243 Pitch, *They Killed Papa*, 355.

244 Marvel, *Autocrat*, 462.

245 *Pittsburgh Legal Journal*, Januray 3, 1870.

246 Flower, *Edwin McMasters Stanton*, 412.

247 Edwin M. Stanton to James Adams Hutchinson, Jr., April 15, 1861, Historical Society of Western Pennsylvania, Senator John Heinz Pittsburgh Regional History Center. See also, "Photo and transcript: Edwin Stanton letter," *Pittsburgh Post-Gazette*, April 12, 2011, accessed February 8, 2016, http://www.post-gazette.com/life/civilwar/2011/04/12/Photo-and-transcript-Edwin-Stanton-letter/stories/201104120273

ENDNOTES PART II

1. Anthony Trollope, *North America*, vol. 2 (Philadelphia: J.B. Lippincott & Co., 1863), 75.

2. James B. Richardson, "Pittsburgh Cannons: Silent Sentinels," *Carnegie Magazine* 59 (July/August 1989), 34.

3. Allegheny County Prothonotary, *List of Attorneys and Law Students, 1788-1981*, vol. 1, Pennsylvania State Archives, Records of County Governments, no. 47.4, LR 289, 1-2.

4. 1860 Census, Allegheny County, Pennsylvania, population schedule, aggregate data, accessed February 26, 2016, http://mapserver.lib.virginia.edu/index.html; 1890 Census, Allegheny County, Pennsylvania, population schedule, aggregate data, accessed February 26, 2016, http://mapserver.lib.virginia.edu/index.html.

5. Francis Harbison, *D.T. Watson of Counsel* (Pittsburgh: Davis & Warde, 1945), 43.

6. Lawrence M. Friedman, *A History of American Law* (New York: Touchstone, 1985), 190.

7. W. Edward Sell and William H. Clark, Jr., *Pennsylvania Business Corporations: Law, Practice, Forms* vol. 2 (Philadelphia: G.T. Bisel Co., 1998), 7; Rosalind L. Branning, *Pennsylvania Constitutional Development* (Pittsburgh: University of Pittsburgh Press, 1960), 41. Initially, corporate filings were designated to be made with either a law judge or a recorder of deeds within the county in which the corporation would principally operate, followed by the presentation of a certified copy of the corporate charter with the secretary of state.

8. H. Boone, ed., *Directory of Pittsburgh & Allegheny Cities, the Adjacent Boroughs, and Parts of the Adjacent Townships for 1870-1871* (Pittsburgh: George H. Thurston, 1870); J.F. Diffenbacher, *Directory of Pittsburgh and Allegheny Cities, 1880-81* (Pittsburgh: Diffenbacher & Thurston, 1880); J.F. Diffenbacher, *Directory of Pittsburgh and Allegheny Cities, 1891-92* (Pittsburgh: Diffenbacher & Thurston, 1891).

9. Katarincic, "Allegheny County Bar Association," 311.

10. Ibid.

11. Ibid., 311-312.

12. Bar Association of the City of New York, *Report of proceedings of the Bar Association of the City of New York* (New York: Douglas Taylor Commercial Printing, 1870), v-vi, 2, 33.

13. "Address of A.M. Brown, Esq.," *Pittsburgh Legal Journal*, April 5, 1871.

14. Katarincic, "Allegheny County Bar Association," 313-14.

15. Ibid., 318.

16. Ibid., 317-319.

17. Ibid., 315.

18. George Dixon, "Phone Debut Here in 1877," *Pittsburgh Press*, January 18, 1959.

19. George Shiras III and Winfield Shiras, *Justice George Shiras Jr. of Pittsburgh* (Pittsburgh: University of Pittsburgh Press, 1953), 72-73.

20. Josiah Cohen, "Half a Century of the Allegheny County Bar Association," *Western Pennsylvania Historical Magazine* 4, no. 3 (July 1921), 136.

21. Shiras, *Justice George Shiras*, 68.

22. "Old Toll Gates About Pittsburgh," *Western Pennsylvania Historical Magazine* 3, no. 2 (April 1920), 71.

23. J.F. Diffenbacher, *Directory of Pittsburgh and Allegheny Cities, 1884-85* (Pittsburgh: Diffenbacher & Thurston, 1884), 245.

24. Celinda Scott and George Cass, interview by the author, February 1, 2010; Celinda Scott, e-mail message to the author, June 15, 2010.

25. Stanley M. Stein and David L. Meister, *A Court for the People, prepared for the Allegheny County Court of Common Pleas, Bicentennial Celebration* (Pittsburgh: The Allegheny County Court of Common Pleas Bicentennial Committee, 1988), 13-14.

26. Francis G. Couvares, "The Triumph of Commerce: Class Culture and Mass Culture in Pittsburgh," *Working-Class America: Essays on Labor, Community and American Society*, ed. Michael H. Frisch and Daniel J. Walkowitz (Chicago: University of Illinois Press, 1983), 126.

27. *Twentieth Century*, 854.

28. "History | Western District of Pennsylvania | United States District Court", accessed February 25, 2016, http://www.pawd.uscourts.gov/history.

29. Alice Fleetwood Burner, "Shiras, George, Jr." in *The Oxford Companion to the Supreme Court of the United States*, ed. Kermit L. Hall (Oxford: Oxford University Press, 1992), 783-84; Timothy L. Hall, *Supreme Court Justices: A Biographical Dictionary* (New York: Infobase, 2001), 210-212.

30. Mellon, *Thomas Mellon and His Times*, 148.

31. Ibid.

32. Ibid., 91.

33. Ibid., 96.

34. Cotton Mather, *Bonifacius: An Essay to do Good* (Gainesville, Fla: Scholars' Facsimiles and Reprints, 196), 160-61.

35. Bell, *Philadelphia Lawyer*, 202; William Porter, "The Present Status of the Legal Profession," *Law Academy of Philadelphia* (September 1907).

36. Friedman, *History of American Law*, 308.

37. Henry Warren Williams, *Legal Ethics and Suggestions for Young Counsel* (Philadelphia: George T. Bisel Co., 1900), 15.

38. Mellon, *Thomas Mellon and His Times*, 123.

39. Ibid., 124.

40. Ibid., 126-127.

41. Ibid., 129.

42   David E. Koskoff, *The Mellons: The Chronicle of America's Richest Family* (New York: Thomas Y. Crowell Co., 1978), 23-24.

43   Williams, *Legal Ethics*, 75.

44   Ibid., 75-76.

45   Mellon, *Thomas Mellon and His Times*, 152.

46   Ibid., 154.

47   Ibid., 28.

48   Koskoff, *The Mellons*, 23.

49   Mellon, *Thomas Mellon and His Times*, 181.

50   Ibid., 162.

51   Ibid., 181, 244.

52   Koskoff, *The Mellons*, 45-47.

53   Mary Brignano, ed., *Dear Sons: Letters from Thomas Mellon, 1882-1886* (Ligonier, PA: Mellon Rolling Rock Museum, 2005), 10-12.

54   William O. Inglis, "The Rewards of the Law," *Munsey's Magazine* 25, no. 3 (June 1901), 426.

55   James B. Dill, "The Business lawyer of To-Day," *The Albany Law Journal* 65, no. 4 (April 1903), 111-112.

56   "The Law as a Business versus True Advocacy," *Central Law Journal* 58, no. 1 (January 1, 1904), 14.

57   Alfred D. Chandler, Jr., "The Railroads: The First Modern Business Enterprises, 1850s-1860s," in *Colossus: How the Corporation Changed America*, ed. Jack Beatty (New York: Crown Publishing, 2001), 100.

58   William Bender Wilson, *History of the Pennsylvania Railroad Company: with Plan of Organization, Portraits of Officials and Biographical Sketches*, vol. 2 (Philadelphia: Henry T. Coates & Co., 1899), 8.

59   Bruce Bomberger and William A. Sisson, *Made in Pennsylvania: An Overview of the Major Historical Industries of the Commonwealth* (Harrisburg: Commonwealth of Pennsylvania, 1991), 26.

60   "Grand Rallies by Fifth Ward and South Side Workingmen," *Pittsburgh Post*, August 14, 1877.

61   *In Memoriam: John Henry Hampton* (Pittsburgh: Jos. Eichbaum & Co., 1892), 14-15.

62   Philip S. Klein and Ari Hoogenboom, *A History of Pennsylvania* (University Park, PA: Penn State Press, 1980), 169.

63   Pittsburgh v. Pennsylvania Railroad, 48 Pa. 355 (1865).

64   Harbison, *D.T. Watson*, 38.

65   Ibid., 67-78.

66   James Howard Bridge, *The Inside History of the Carnegie Steel Company: A Romance of Millions* (Pittsburgh: University of Pittsburgh Press, 1903), 169.

67   Harbison, *D.T. Watson*, 48.

68   Charles C. Carr, *Alcoa and American Enterprise* (New York: Rinehart & Co., 1952), 49.

69   Frank Marshall Eastman, *Courts and Lawyers of Pennsylvania: A History, 1623-1923* (New York: American Historical Society, 1922), 277-279.

70   Shiras, *Justice George Shiras*, 69-70.

71   Ibid., 77-79.

72   "The Horse Show," *Index*, September 15, 1906.

73   Ibid., 80.

74   *Obituary Record of Graduates of Yale College* 81 (New Haven: Yale University, 1922), 335

75   Quentin R. Skrabec, Jr., *Henry Clay Frick: The Life of the Perfect Capitalist* (Jefferson, NC: McFarland &Co., 2010), 97.

76   "People - Johnstown Flood", National Park Service, accessed February 25, 2016, http://www.nps.gov/jofl/learn/historyculture/people.htm.

77   In re Application of the Peter Schoenhofen Brewing Company for a Wholesale Liquor License, 8 Pa. Super. 141 (1898).

78   Harbison, *D.T. Watson*, 156-157.

79   Willis F. McCook, "Suggestions on the Organization of Corporations," *Yale Law Journal* 4 (May 1895), 170.

80   Lochner v. New York, 198 U.S. 45 (1905).

81   Powell v. Pennsylvania, 127 U.S. 678 (1888).

82   Harbison, *D.T. Watson*, 109-110.

83   Ibid., 110-111.

84   Citizens United v. FEC , 558 U.S. 310 (2010).

85   Pennsylvania General Assembly, *Report of the Committee Appointed to Investigate the Railroad Riots in July, 1877* (Harrisburg: Commonwealth of Pennsylvania, 1878), 214.

86   John R. Commons and Eugene Allen Gilmore, *A Documentary History of American Industrial Society*, vol. 4 (Cleveland: Arthur H. Clark Co., 1910) 15, 81-85.

87   "The Destitute Poor," *Pittsburgh Daily Gazette*, January 14, 1875.

88   "Relief of the Poor," *Pittsburgh Daily Gazette*, December 11, 1875.

89   Michael A. Bellesiles, *1877: America's Year of Living Violently* (New York: New Press, 2010), 19.

90   C. Vann Woodward, *Reunion and Reaction: The Compromise of 1877 and the End of Reconstruction* (New York: Oxford University Press USA, 1991), 101-105.

91   Frederick T. Wilson, ed., *Federal Aid in Domestic Disturbances, 1787-1903* (Washington: Government Printing Office, 1909), 325-29; J. Thomas Scharf, *History of Maryland from the Earliest Period to the Present Day* 3 (Baltimore: John B. Piet, 1879), 733-42

92   Robert V. Bruce, *1877: Year of Violence* (Chicago: I.R. Dee, 1959), 122-124.

93   "Reign of the Mob!," *Pittsburgh Post*, July 23, 1877

94 Bruce, *1877*, 132.

95 This quote is widely attributed, but poorly documented. See, Christian Wolmar, *The Great Railroad Revolution: the History of Trains in America* (New York: Public Affairs, 2012), 234; Philip Dray, *There is Power in a Union: the Epic Story of Labor in America* (New York: Doubleday, 2010), 117.

96 Bruce, *1877*, 132-134.

97 Ibid., 136.

98 Bruce, *1877*, 135-138; Jack Beatty, "The Next Page: The Railroad War," *Pittsburgh Post-Gazette*, July 6, 2007.

99 Pennsylvania General Assembly, *Report of the Riot Committee*, 170.

100 Ibid., 271.

101 Ibid., 213-214; Bruce, *1877*, 145-146.

102 Pennsylvania General Assembly, *Report of the Riot Committee*, 215.

103 Bruce, *1877*, 149-158; Pennsylvania General Assembly, *Report of the Riot Committee*, 14.

104 "The Great Strike," *Harper's Weekly*, August 11, 1877.

105 Pennsylvania General Assembly, *Report of the Riot Committee*, 284.

106 "Reign of the Mob!," *Pittsburgh Post*, July 23, 1877.

107 "His Dwelling – Mrs. Pearson" *Pittsburgh Post*, July 25, 1877.

108 Fleming, *History of Pittsburgh and Environs*, 83.

109 "The Labor Troubles," *Pittsburgh Post*, August 2, 1877.

110 "Legal Department: Railroad Rioters Sentenced at Pittsburgh," *Railway World* 3, no. 49 (December 8, 1877), 1174

111 "The Censured General," *Pittsburgh Post*, July 25, 1877.

112 "Probing Pearson," *Pittsburgh Post*, September 28, 1877.

113 Commonwealth of Pennsylvania, *Message of John F. Hartranft to the General Assembly of Pennsylvania* (Harrisburg: Lane S. Hart, 1878), 47.

114 "Grand Jury and the Riots," *Pittsburgh Post*, November 20, 1877.

115 Bruce, *1877*, 311.

116 "The Labor Troubles," *Pittsburgh Post*, August 2, 1877.

117 Perry K. Blatz, "Pittsburgh: The Fiery Scape Goat for the Country," *Western Pennsylvania History* (Fall 2011), 57; County of Allegheny v. Gibson's Son & Co., 90 Pa. 397 (1879).

118 "An Active Life Ended," *Pittsburgh Press*, April 13, 1891; Blatz, "Fiery Scape Goat," 58-59.

119 Quentin R. Skrabec, Jr., *George Westinghouse: Gentle Genius* (New York: Algora, 2007), 238.

120 Greater Pittsburgh Chamber of Commerce, *Pittsburgh and the Pittsburgh Spirit: Addresses at the Chamber of Commerce of Pittsburgh, 1927-28* (Pittsburgh: Robert L. Forsythe Co., 1928), 82.

121 Steve Massey, "Who Killed Westinghouse?: In the Beginning," *Pittsburgh Post-Gazette*, accessed February 26, 2016, http://old.post-gazette.com/westinghouse/beginning.asp.

122 Steven W. Usselman, "From Novelty to Utility: George Westinghouse and the Business of Innovation during the Age of Edison," *Business History Review* 66, no. 2 (Summer 1992), 275, 302.

123 Skrabec, *Gentle Genius*, 35-37.

124 Francis Leupp, *George Westinghouse: His Life and Achievements* (London: John Murray,1919), 48-49.

125 Shigehiro Nishimura, "The Rise of the Patent Department: A Case Study of Westinghouse Electric and Manufacturing Company," Working Paper no. 168/12, London School of Economics, August 2012, 10. http://www.lse.ac.uk/economicHistory/workingPapers/2012/WP168.pdf

126 *Twentieth Century, Vol. II*, 855.

127 Henry G. Prout, *A Life of George Westinghouse* (New York: American Society of Mechanical Engineers, 1921), 24.

128 George H. Christy, Application for a U.S. Passport no. 11319, May 21, 1894 *Passport Applications, 1795-1905* (National Archives Microfilm Publication M1372, roll 422), National Archives and Records Administration, digital images, http://ancestry.com; George Westinghouse, Application for a U.S. Passport no. 38829, July 31, 1907, *Passport Applications, Jan. 2, 1906 - Mar. 31, 1925* (National Archives Microfilm Publication M1490, roll 44), National Archives and Records Administration, digital images, http://ancestry.com.

129 Skrabec, *Gentle Genius*, 8.

130 Allegheny County Bar Association, *Meeting of the Members of the Bar of Allegheny County called by the Allegheny County Bar Association Through its Committee on Biography and History to take suitable action with reference to the death of George Harvey Christy, Esq.* (Pittsburgh: L.W. Mendenhall, 1909), 6-7, 14-15.

131 Ibid., 8-10.

132 Ibid., 10.

133 Robert McKnight, *Diaries, vol. II*, March 17, 1846.

134 ACBA, *Meeting on Death of George Christy*, 6.

135 Skrabec, *Gentle Genius*, 101

136 Frederic Taber Cooper, *Thomas A. Edison* (New York: Frederick A. Stokes Co., 1914), 78.

137 "Obituary: Franklin L. Pope", *Electrical Engineer* 20, no. 390 (October 23, 1895), 413.

138 Mitchell C. Harrison, ed., *New York State's Prominent and Progressive Men*, vol. III (New York: New York Tribune, 1902), 177-178.

139 W. Bernard Carlson, *Tesla: Inventor of the Electrical Age* (Princeton: Princeton University Press, 2013), 111-113.

140 Orlando Oscar Stealey, *130 Pen Pictures of Live Men* (Washington: Publisher's Printing Co., 1910), 122-124. An Arthur Burgoyne poem about Dalzell includes the lines "... he's spic and span,/ Well-dressed and neat-mustached—/ A social,

little man ..." Arthur G. Burgoyne, *All Sorts of Pittsburghers* (Pittsburgh: Leader All Sorts Co, 1892), 6. Regarding his height (5'-8"), *see also*, J.S. Henry, "The Success of Little Men," *Saturday Evening Post*, July 20, 1901, 7. He had been described as not being "much bigger than a proverbial pint pot." "When Dalzell Nodded," *Courier* (Harrisburg, PA), March 29, 1908.

141 Stealey, *130 Pen Pictures*, 122.

142 James D. Van Trump, "'Solitude' and the Nether Depths: The Pittsburgh Estate of George Westinghouse and its Gas Well," *Western Pennsylvania Historical Magazine* 42, no. 2 (June 1959), 161-166.

143 George Westinghouse, Jr., "System for Conveying and Using Gas under Pressure," U.S. Patent 301,191, filed June 6, 1884, and issued July 1, 1884.

144 George H. Thurston, *Allegheny County's Hundred Years* (Pittsburgh: A. A. Anderson & Sons, 1888), 207.

145 Richard Herndon and Richard Burton, eds., *Men of Progress: Biographical Sketches and Portraits of Leaders in Business and Professional Life in and of the State of Connecticut*, (Boston: New England Magazine, 1898), 275-276.

146 "The Cravath System," Cravath Swaine & Moore LLP, accessed 26 Feburary 2016, https://www.cravath.com/cravathsystem/

147 Ibid.

148 Robert A. Swaine, *The Cravath Firm and Its Predecessors 1819-1948*, vol. I (New York: Ad Press, 1948), 588-589.

149 Swaine, *Cravath Firm*, 589-90.

150 "By the-Bye in Wall Street," *Wall Street Journal*, April 22, 1933.

151 Prout, *Life of Westinghouse*, 275.

152 Leupp, *Westinghouse*, 243.

153 Ibid., 165-167.

154 Ibid., 167-168.

155 Swaine, *Cravath*, vol. 2, 34.

156 Ibid., 43.

157 Ibid., 41-42.

158 "Geo. Westinghouse Dies in 68th Year," *The New York Times*, March 13, 1914.

159 "Charles A. Terry is Claimed by Death," *Palm Beach Post*, February 20, 1939.

160 Lincoln Steffens, "Pittsburg: A City Ashamed," *McClure's Magazine*, May 1903, 24.

161 Porter v. King, 1 F. 755 (1880).

162 Ibid.

163 "Systematized Fraud," *Pittsburgh Post*, November 21, 1877.

164 Ibid.

165 "The Case of Gill," *Pittsburgh Post*, November 24, 1877.

166 "The Gill Case," *Pittsburgh Post*, November 22, 1877.

167 "Gill's Creditors," *Pittsburgh Post*, December 7, 1877.

168 "City and Country: Things Briefly Told," *Altoona Morning Tribune*, November 8, 1879.

169 "An Order Against Gill," *Pittsburgh Post*, January 12, 1878.

170 Pittsburgh National Bank of Commerce v. McMurray, 98 Pa. 588 (1881).

171 "Lawyer Gill's Fate," *Reading Times*, December 10, 1886.

172 "Department Changes," *Pittsburgh Post*, February 1, 1882.

173 "The Eagle's First Scream," *Pittsburgh Post*, July 5, 1892.

174 Fleming, *History of Pittsburgh and Environs*, 83.

175 "Criminal Prosecution. This is Recommended Against City Attorneys Moreland and House," *Pittsburgh Post*, October 12, 1895.

176 City of Pittsburgh v. Moreland, 47 P.L.J. 195 (1899).

177 Ibid.

178 "Sensational Denouement," *Pittsburgh Post*, October 15, 1895.

179 "Moreland Pleaded Guilty," *Pittsburgh Post*, July 14, 1896.

180 "Penitentiary for Moreland," *Pittsburgh Post*, July 30, 1896.

181 "Sentenced Friends to Prison," *The New York Times*, July 30, 1896.

182 "Penitentiary for Moreland," *Pittsburgh Post*, July 30, 1896.

183 "Sentenced Friends to Prison," *The New York Times*, July 30, 1896.

184 "Penitentiary for Moreland," *Pittsburgh Post*, July 30, 1896.

185 Pennsylvania General Assembly, *Journal of the House of Representatives of the Commonwealth of Pennsylvania for the Session begun at Harrisburg on the Third Day of January 1899* (Harrisburg, 1899), 178.

186 Ibid., 180-182.

187 "Moreland Pardon Signed," *Pittsburgh Press*, February 4, 1898.

188 "W.C. Moreland's Life Has Ended," *Pittsburgh Post*, May 3, 1902.

189 *Twentieth Century, Vol. II*, 872, 890-891.

190 Fleming, *History of Pittsburgh and Environs*, 84.

191 Paul Musselman and Maxwell Baker, *The Jews Come to America* (New York: Bloch Publishing, 1932), 155.

192 J. Clay Smith, Jr., *Emancipation: The Making of the Black Lawyer, 1844-1944* (Philadelphia: University of Pennsylvania Press, 1993), 93-94.

193 Friedman, *History of American Law*, 639.

194 Barbara S. Burstein, *Steel City Jews: A History of Pittsburgh and its Jewish Community, 1840-1915* (Pittsburgh: privately published, 2008), 13-21.

195 "Hon. Josiah Cohen," Allegheny County Bar Association Decedent Files, Allegheny County Bar Association, ACBA Collection; "Biographies of

Newly Appointed Judges," *Pittsburgh Legal Journal* 76, no. 1, January 7, 1928, 10-11; "Hon. Judge Josiah Cohen Dies," *Pittsburgh Legal Journal* 78, no. 24, June 14, 1930, 3-14.

196 "The First Jewish Lawyer Admitted," *Pittsburgh Evening Chronicle*, January 5, 1866.

197 Cohen, *Half a Century*, 129-130.

198 Ibid., 131.

199 *Twentieth Century, Vol. II*, 916 - 917; Jacob S. Feldman and Charles W. Prine, *The Jewish Experience in Western Pennsylvania: A History, 1755-1945* (Pittsburgh: Historical Society of Western Pennsylvania, 1986), 110 - 111; Magnus Pflaum, "Some Notes on Alleged Meteoric Dust," *Transactions of the American Microscopical Society* 17 (1896), 95-97.

200 Feldman, *The Jewish Experience*, 110-111.

201 Catherine M. Hanchett, "George Boyer Vashon, 1824-1878: Black Educator, Poet, Fighter for Equal Rights, Part One," *Western Pennsylvania Historical Magazine* 68, no. 3 (July 1985), 205-208.

202 Glasco, *WPA History of the Negro in Pittsburgh*, 97-98.

203 Hanchett, "Vashon Part One," 208-209; Catherine Hanchett, "George Boyer Vashon, 1824-1878: Black Educator, Poet, Fighter for Equal Rights, Part Two," *Western Pennsylvania Historical Magazine* 68, no. 4 (October 1985), 333.

204 "Motion in the Court of Common Pleas to Admit a Colored Lawyer to the Bar," *Pittsburgh Commercial*, July 15, 1867.

205 Glasco, *WPA History of the Negro in Pittsburgh*, 205-206.

206 Hanchett, *"Vashon Part Two,"* 339.

207 "In the Courts," *Pittsburgh Commercial Gazette*, December 21, 1891.

208 "A Pioneer Lawyer," *Colored American* (Washington, DC), January 24, 1903.

209 "In the Courts," *Pittsburgh Commercial Gazette*, December 20, 1891.

210 *Twentieth Century, Vol. II*, 984.

211 See, J.F. Diffenbacher, *Directory of Pittsburgh and Allegheny Cities, 1891-1892* (Pittsburgh: Diffenbacher & Thurston, 1891), 446, 746.

212 Buchanan Ingersoll, firm ledgers 1906-1942, Buchanan Ingersoll & Rooney, P.C. collection, Pittsburgh, PA; Donald L. McCaskey, interview by the author, July 1992; 1880 U.S. Federal Census, Pittsburgh, Allegheny County, Pennsylvania, 25, digital image s.v. "Stanton, William," *Historic Pittsburgh*, http://digital.library.pitt.edu/cgi-bin/census/census_driver.pl?searchtype=full_record&key=70724&database=Pittsburgh_1880; "Edward Stanton," United States World War I Draft Registration Cards 1917-1918, Pittsburgh City no 4, Pennsylvania, United States, NARA microfilm publication M1509 (Washington D.C.: National Archives and Records Administration, n.d.), no. 1,908,111.

213 Allegheny County Bar Association, "Tribute to African American Lawyers" (conference, Vista Hotel, Pittsburgh, PA, February 22, 1995).

214 Ibid.; Laurence Glasco, "Taking Care of Business: The Black Entrepreneurial Elite in Turn-of-the-Century Pittsburgh," *Pittsburgh History* 78, no. 4 (Winter 1995), 181.

215 "In Society," *Pittsburgh Post*, April 2, 1899.

216 Friedman, *History of American Law*, 639.

217 Rebecca Mae Salokar and Mary L. Volcansek, *Women in Law: A Bio-bibliographical Sourcebook* (Westport, CT: Greenwood Press, 1996), 127.

218 See, e.g., *Twentieth Century, Vol. II*, 802-1020.

219 "The Law School Students," University of Michigan School of Law, accessed February 26, 2016, https://www.law.umich.edu/historyandtraditions/students/Pages/default.aspx.

220 Sell, *The Law Down*, 1.

221 Friedman, *History of American Law*, 607.

222 *Twentieth Century, Vol. II*, 904, 912.

223 Sell, *The Law Down*, 2-3.

224 Ibid.

225 Friedman, *History of American Law*, 607.

226 "Scraps," *Indianapolis News*, October 29, 1881. The quote is widely cited thereafter. See, e.g., James Brown Scott, "The Study of the Law," *American Law School Review* 2, no. 1 (1906), 7; "Law Schools," *Barrister* 3, no. 1 (January 1897), 138.

227 Sell, *The Law Down*, 3.

228 Ibid., 3-4.

229 *Twentieth Century, Vol. II*, 1000-1012.

230 Ibid.

231 James M. Utterback, *Mastering the Dynamics of Innovation* (Boston: Harvard Business Press, 1996), 3.

232 American Society of Mechanical Engineers, *Sholes & Glidden 'Type Writer': A Historic Mechanical Engineering Landmark* (Milwaukee, October 6, 2011), 4-5. https://www.asme.org/getmedia/e34d57c4-fe61-44b4-b263-028b5210e5c2/249-Sholes-Glidden-Type-Writer.aspx

233 Arthur H. Dean, *William Nelson Cromwell 1854-1948: an American pioneer in corporation, comparative and international law* (New York: Ad Press, 1957), foreword by John Foster Dulles, i-iii.

234 Angela Kwokel-Folland, *Engendering Business: Men and Women in the Corporate Office, 1870-1930* (Baltimore: Johns Hopkins University Press, 1994), 30.

235 Ibid; Elyce J. Rotella, *From Home to Office: U.S. Women at Work, 1870-1930* (Ann Arbor: UMI Research Press, 1981), 125.

236 R.L. Polk & Co., *Pittsburgh and Allegheny Directory for 1899* (Pittsburgh: R.L. Polk & Co., 1899), 1668/96-1668/97.

237 Mary Brignano & J. Tomlinson Fort, *Reed Smith: A Law Firm Celebrates 125 Years* (Pittsburgh: Reed Smith, 2002), 58.

238 Eugene Garfield, "From scribes to secretaries in 5,000 years; From secretaries to information managers in 20," *Current Comments* 15 (April 14, 1986), 113 (citing M.W. Davies, *Woman's Place is at the Typewriter* (Philadelphia: Temple University Press, 1982), 217).

239 S.J. Kleinberg, *Women in the United States, 1830-1945* (New Brunswick, NJ: Rutgers University Press, 1999) 112.

240 Jerome P. Bjelopera, *City of Clerks: Office and Sales Workers in Philadelphia, 1870-1920* (Chicago: University of Illinois Press, 2005), 17.

241 "Ms. Watson Passes," *Pittsburgh Post*, September 14, 1895.

242 Ibid.

243 "Society," *Pittsburgh Press*, March 31, 1899; "Cupid Triumphs over Law," *Pittsburgh Post*, March 31, 1899.

244 John Thorn & Pete Palmer, eds., *Total Baseball* (New York: Warner Books, 1989), 11.

245 Ibid., 83; Zeta Psi Fraternity, Semi-Centennial Biographical Catalogue of the Zeta Psi Fraternity of North America (New York: Zeta Psi Fraternity, 1900), 469.

246 Frederick G. Lieb, *The Pittsburgh Pirates* (Carbondale, IL: Southern Illinois University Press, 1948), 9.

247 "Baseball is Wicked," *Pittsburgh Post*, October 8, 1887.

248 William E. Benswanger, "Professional Baseball in Pittsburgh," *Western Pennsylvania Historical Magazine* 30, nos.1-2 (March-June 1947), 11.

249 Thorn & Palmer, *Total Baseball*, 1711; "Robert Murray Gibson," Biographical Directory of Federal Judges, accessed March 9, 2016, http://www.fjc.gov/public/home.nsf/hisj

250 "It is President O'Neil," *Pittsburgh Post*, December 23, 1890.

251 "They are not Reserved," *Pittsburgh Post*, January 27, 1891.

252 "Bierbauer has Signed," *Pittsburgh Post*, January 24, 1891.

253 "Mr. O'Neil in Cleveland," *Pittsburgh Post*, January 28, 1891.

254 "Pittsburgh Will Hold Bierbauer at All Hazards," *Pittsburgh Post*, January 31, 1891.

255 *Twentieth Century Bench & Bar, Vol. II*, 888.

256 United States Congress, *Biographical Directory of the United States Congress, 1774-2005, the Continental Congress, September 5, 1774, to October 21, 1788, and the Congress of the United States, from the First through the One Hundred Eighth Congresses, March 4, 1789, to January 3, 2005, inclusive* (Washington: Government Printing Office, 2005), 2045.

257 David Nemec, *The Beer and Whiskey League: The Illustrated History of the American Association - Baseball's Renegade Major League* (Guildford, CT: Lyons Press, 1994), 221.

258 "Col. John I. Rogers," *The New York Times*, March 14, 1910.

259 "Louis C. Krauthoff Dead," *The New York Times*, October 27, 1918.

260 "Bierbauer Will Go to Pittsburg and Stovey Will Remain in the League," *Sporting News*, February 14, 1891; "Farewell, Old Association," *Pittsburgh Post*, February 19, 1891.

261 "Base Ball," *Sunday Herald* (Washington DC), February 15, 1891.

262 "Farewell, Old Association," *Pittsburgh Post*, February 19, 1891.

263 Lieb, *Pittsburgh Pirates*, 21.

264 "Base Ball Notes," *Pittsburgh Post*, March 5, 1891.

265 "Baldwin in Jail," *Pittsburgh Post*, March 6, 1891.

266 "Baldwin Beats Von Der Ahe," *The New York Times*, January 4, 1898.

267 "Tough on Chris," *Pittsburgh Commercial Gazette*, May 4, 1894.

268 Von der Ahe's Case, No. 1, 20 Pa.C.C. 305 (1898).

269 Baldwin v. Von der Ahe, 184 Pa. 116 (1898).

270 "Pirate Points" *Sporting Life*, May 4, 1912.

271 "Death Record," *Pittsburgh Press*, October 4, 1918, *Twentieth Century Bench & Bar, Vol. II*, 976.

272 Harold Nicolson, *Dwight Morrow* (New York: Harcourt Brace, 1935), 42; Leonard Mosley, *Lindbergh: A Biography* (Mineola, NY: Dover Publications, 2000), 275.

273 "Von der Ahe Prisoner on a Train," *Pittsburgh Dispatch*, February 7, 1898; "Von der Ahe a Prisoner," *Pittsburgh Dispatch*, February 8, 1898.

274 "Chris Von der Ahe Safe in Pittsburg," *Pittsburgh Dispatch*, February 9, 1898.

275 "To Nimick - Please Do us the Favor to Take the Rest of Them," *St. Louis Post-Dispatch*, February 9, 1898.

276 "Claimed that Warrants will be Granted," *Pittsburgh Dispatch*, February 11, 1898.

277 "Chris Von der Ahe Trapped," *The New York Times*, February 12, 1898.

278 "Von der Ahe Bailed," *Pittsburgh Commercial Gazette*, February 25, 1898; "Von der Ahe Finally Settled," *Pittsburgh Post*, September 7, 1898.

279 "Is Down and Out," *Sporting Life*, August 24, 1912; "Von der Ahe is Down and Out," *Chicago Daily Tribune*, February 4, 1908.

280 Brian McKenna, "Mark Baldwin," *Society for American Baseball Research Biography Project*, accessed March 9, 2016, http://sabr.org/bioproj/person/41f65388.

281 "Excitement Waning," *Pittsburgh Post*, July 25, 1877.

282 "The Strike Spreading," *Pittsburgh Post*, August 16, 1877.

283 William Richard Cutler, ed., *American Biography: A New Cyclopedia*, vol. 27 (New York: American Historical Society, 1926), 93-94.

284 "W.J. Brennen Passes Away After Attack of Pneumonia," *Pittsburgh Post*, April 16, 1924.

285 Cutler, *American Biography*, 94.

286 "The Labor Movement," *Pittsburgh Post*, August 18, 1877.

287 "Iron-Workers' Strike Ended," *The New York Times*, September 19, 1877.

288 Cutler, *American Biography*, 94.

289 Paul Krause, *The Battle for Homestead, 1880-1892: Politics, Culture, and Steel* (Pittsburgh: University of Pittsburgh Press, 1992), 8.

290 *Twentieth Century Bench & Bar, Vol. II*, 962.

291 *Twentieth Century Bench & Bar, Vol. II*, 954; Krause, *Battle for Homestead*, 88; James Mellon, *The Judge: A Life of Thomas Mellon, Founder of a Fortune* (New Haven: Yale University Press, 2011), 294-295.

292 Mellon, *The Judge*, 295-304.

293 Ibid., 306-307.

294 Cutler, *American Biography*, 95.

295 Brace Bros. v. Evans, N.S., 5 Pa. Co. Ct. 163 (1888).

296 McCandless & Kinser v. O'Brien, 8 Lanc. Law Rev. 254 (1891).

297 Mellon, *The Judge*, 296.

298 James H. Reed, Application for a U.S. Passport no. 19835, July 23, 1890, *Passport Applications, 1795-1905* (National Archives Microfilm Publication M1372, roll 357), National Archives and Records Administration, digital images, http://ancestry.com; Philander C. Knox, Application for a U.S. Passport no. 2229, July 18, 1895, *Passport Applications, 1795-1905* (National Archives Microfilm Publication M1372, roll 357), National Archives and Records Administration, digital images, http://ancestry.com.

299 Edmund Morris, *Theodore Rex* (New York: Random House, 2010), 61.

300 "Death Ends Career of City's Foremost Jurist in 74th Year," *Pittsburgh Post*, June 18, 1927.

301 Fleming, *History of Pittsburgh and Environs*, 857-58.

302 Morris, *Theodore Rex*, 61.

303 Joe Glass, "When Famous Men Play Golf," *The American Golfer* (June 1934), 24.

304 Brignano and Fort, *Reed Smith: 125 Years*, 23.

305 Edwin W. Smith, "Hon. Philander Chase Knox," *Western Pennsylvania Historical Magazine* 5, no. 2 (April 1922), 122, 127.

306 Ibid., 127-128.

307 Brignano and Fort, *Reed Smith: 125 Years*, 23-24.

308 "Gibson David Packer," *The Successful American* 3 (June 1901), 343.

309 David McCullough, *The Johnstown Flood* (New York: Simon & Shuster, 1968), 49, 55.

310 Robert D. Christie, "The Johnstown Flood," *Western Pennsylvania Historical Magazine* 54, no. 2 (April 1971), 200-201.

311 McCullough, *Johnstown Flood*, 49.

312 McCullough, *Johnstown Flood*, 57; Christie, *Johnstown*, 202-203.

313 Christie, "Johnstown," 203; "People - Johnstown Flood", National Park Service, accessed February 25, 2016, http://www.nps.gov/jofl/learn/historyculture/people.htm.

314 Ralph H. Demmler, *The First Century of an Institution: Reed Smith Shaw & McClay* (Pittsburgh: Demmler, 1977), 18.

315 McCullough, *Johnstown Flood*, 41.

316 McCullough, *Johnstown Flood*, 269, 276.

317 "He Saw the Dam Burst," *Pittsburgh Post*, June 4, 1889.

318 McCullough, *Johnstown Flood*, 85, 253.

319 McCullough, *Johnstown Flood*, 242.

320 Ibid.

321 Ibid., 241.

322 Ibid., 243.

323 Ibid., 255.

324 "Death on the Conemaugh," *National Labor Tribune*, June 8, 1889.

325 McCullough, *Johnstown Flood*, 255.

326 "Liberal Hearted Lawyers," *Pittsburgh Post*, June 13, 1889; "Eleven Hours of Fun," *Pittsburgh Dispatch*, June 18, 1889.

327 McCullough, *Johnstown Flood*, 246.

328 "Defending the Dam," *Pittsburgh Dispatch*, June 6, 1889.

329 "It Will Dissolve," *Pittsburgh Dispatch*, June 11, 1889.

330 "Is the Club Liable," *Pittsburgh Dispatch*, June 24, 1889.

331 "Limited: the Meaning of the Word as Applied to Corporations," *National Labor Tribune*, July 13, 1889.

332 "Fishing Club Pleads Not Guilty," *The New York Times*, August 18, 1889; McCullough, *Johnstown Flood*, 257.

333 Pennsylvania Coal Co. v. Sanderson, 113 Pa. 120 (1886).

334 Fletcher v. Rylands, (1865) 159 Eng. Rep. 737, 740.

335 Fletcher v. Rylands, (1866) L.R. 1 Ex. 265, 279.

336 "The Law of Bursting Reservoirs," *American Law Review* 23 (1889), 643.

337 Demmler, *First Century*, 19.

338 "Suing South Fork Club Men," *The New York Times*, June 20, 1891; McCullough, *Johnstown Flood*, 259.

339 Robb v. Carnegie Bros., 145 Pa. 324 (1891).

340 Jed H. Shugerman, "Fear, Filters, and Fidelity: Judicial Elections and the Making of American Tort Law," Harvard Law School Faculty Scholarship Series Paper 7 (Boston, 2007), http://lsr.nellco.org/harvard_faculty/7.

341 Krause, *Battle for Homestead*, 174-192; David Nasaw, *Andrew Carnegie* (New York: Penguin, 2007), 213; "Andrew Carnegie Succeeded By Knowing Men," *The Iron Age* 104, no. 7 (August 14, 1919), 432.

342 Krause, *Battle for Homestead*, 240-251.

343. "W.J. Brennen Passes Away After Attack of Pneumonia," *Pittsburgh Post*, April 16, 1924.
344. Michael P. Weber, *Don't Call Me Boss: David L. Lawrence, Pittsburgh's Renaissance Mayor* (Pittsburgh: University of Pittsburgh Press, 1988), 12-13.
345. Weber, *Don't Call Me Boss*, 12.
346. See, Homer E. Socolofsky & Allan E. Spetter, *The Presidency of Benjamin Harrison* (Lawrence, KS: University Press of Kansas, 1987).
347. Harry Thurston Peck, *Twenty Years of the Republic, 1885-1905* (New York: Dodd, Mead & Co., 1906), 198.
348. "Issues of the Campaign," *Pittsburgh Post*, October 25, 1890.
349. "W.J. Brennen, Esq., has announced himself in the Twenty-second congressional district against John Dalzell," *Pittsburgh Post*, October 2, 1890.
350. Ibid.
351. "The Winners are Chosen," *Pittsburgh Post*, October 7, 1890.
352. "The Final Ticket," *Pittsburgh Post*, October 8, 1890.
353. "Pattison and Brennen," *Pittsburgh Post*, October 27, 1890.
354. John Fitch Cleveland, ed., *The Tribune Almanac and Political Register* (New York: Tribune Association, 1891), 309.
355. "Notes and Comments," *National Labor Tribune*, November 15, 1890.
356. Arthur G. Burgoyne, *The Homestead Strike of 1892* (Pittsburgh: University of Pittsburgh Press, 1979), 20-21; Krause, *Battle for Homestead*, 284-310.
357. "Fear of a Strike," *Pittsburgh Post*, June 4, 1892.
358. Burgoyne, *Homestead Strike*, 21-22.
359. Demmler, *First Century*, 20.
360. Bridge, *Inside History*, 189-190; Krause, *Battle for Homestead*, 209.
361. Henry C. Frick to Andrew Carnegie, April 20, 1891, Henry Clay Frick Papers, Series VIII: Letterpress Copybooks, 1881-1923, vol. 6, The Frick Collection/Frick Art Reference Library Archives, New York; Nasaw, *Andrew Carnegie*, 392-393.
362. Krause, *Battle for Homestead*, 271.
363. Ibid., 310; Burgoyne, *Homestead Strike*, 47.
364. Krause, *Battle for Homestead*, 27.
365. John Andrews Fitch, *The Steel Workers* (New York: Charities, 1911), 107; "Labor Vote Will Line Up for Tener," *Indiana (PA) Weekly Messenger*, August 31, 1910.
366. In 1874, Weihe lived on Tenth Street and Brennen lived on Sarah Street within the tight-knit South Side community. See, J.F. Diffenbacher, *Directory of Pittsburgh and Allegheny Cities, 1874-75* (Pittsburgh: Diffenbacher & Thurston, 1874), 101, 629.
367. Krause, *Battle for Homestead*, 293-294; Burgoyne, *Homestead Strike*, 37-38.
368. Nasaw, *Andrew Carnegie*, 418.
369. Krause, *Battle for Homestead*, 16, 311; Les Standiford, *Meet You in Hell: Andrew Carnegie, Henry Clay Frick and the Bitter Partnership That Transformed America* (New York: Broadway Books, 2005), 140.
370. "In the New Quarters," *Pittsburgh Post*, June 8, 1892.
371. "Wants Early Conventions," *Pittsburgh Post*, June 30, 1892.
372. Ibid.
373. "He Screamed Sure," *Pittsburgh Post*, July 4, 1892.
374. "Glorious Old Tom," *Pittsburgh Dispatch*, July 5, 1892.
375. "Not So Much of a Fourth," *Pittsburgh Post*, July 4, 1892.
376. Krause, *Battle for Homestead*, 27.
377. "Went by Rail, Back by Boat," *Pittsburgh Dispatch*, July 6, 1892.
378. "Deputies Fired," *Pittsburgh Post*, July 6, 1892.
379. Standiford, *Meet You in Hell*, 156-157; *Investigation of the Employment of Pinkerton Detectives in Connection with the Labor Troubles at Homestead, Pa.*, House Misc. Doc. No. 335, 52d Cong., 1st sess., (Washington, DC: Government Printing Office, 1892), 116.
380. Krause, *Battle for Homestead*, 16-17; *Chicago Tribune*, July 6, 1892; *Chicago Tribune*, July 7, 1892.
381. Krause, *Battle for Homestead*, 18-20.
382. Standiford, *Meet You in Hell*, 171-172.
383. Krause, *Battle for Homestead*, 29-31.
384. "The Pinkertons Surrender," *Times* (Philadelphia), July 7, 1892; Burgoyne, *Homestead Strike*, 81.
385. Krause, *Battle for Homestead*, 34-36.
386. Burgoyne, *Homestead Strike*, 86; Krause, *Battle for Homestead*, 39-41; "They Have Left," *Pittsburgh Post*, July 7, 1892; "Rout of the Hirelings," *Boston Evening Transcript*, July 7, 1892.
387. Krause, *Battle for Homestead*, 41; "They Have Left," *Pittsburgh Post*, July 7, 1892.
388. "Troops Not Necessary," *Pittsburgh Post*, July 8, 1892.
389. "Brennen Advises," *Pittsburgh Post*, July 9, 1892.
390. "Sympathy from Pittsburg," *Times* (Philadelphia), July 10, 1892.
391. "Dalzell Angry," *Pittsburgh Post*, July 9, 1892.
392. Krause, *Battle for Homestead*, 333-338.
393. Burgoyne, *Homestead Strike*, 142.
394. "O'Donnell and Ross in Limbo," *The New York Times*, July 22, 1892.
395. Krause, *Battle for Homestead*, 344-345.
396. Krause, *Battle for Homestead*, 345.
397. "With the Bark On," *Pittsburgh Post*, July 21, 1892.
398. "Keeping Shady," *Pittsburgh Post*, July 20, 1892.
399. Nasaw, *Andrew Carnegie*, 435-436; Burgoyne, *Homestead Strike*, 148-149.

400 Alexander Berkman, *Prison Memoirs of an Anarchist* (New York: Mother Earth Publishing, 1912), 11.

401 Edward W. Bemis, "The Homestead Strike," *Journal of Political Economy* 20 (June 1894), 386

402 Burgoyne, *Homestead Strike*, 152-153.

403 Ibid., 153.

404 Ibid., 165.

405 "Red Berkman Guilty," *Pittsburgh Press*, September 19, 1892.

406 Ibid; Candace Falk, Barry Pateman, and Jessica Moran, eds., *Emma Goldman: A Documentary History of the American Years*, vol. 1 (Berkeley: University of California Press, 2003), 125; Burgoyne, *Homestead Strike*, 295; *Twentieth Century Bench & Bar, Vol. II*, 903, 949.

407 Emma Goldman, *Living My Life (Abridged)*, Miriam Brody, ed. (New York: Penguin, 2006), 70.

408 "Red Berkman Guilty," *Pittsburgh Press*, September 19, 1892.

409 Berkman, *Prison Memoirs*, 89.

410 "The Anarchist Gets 22 Years," *Pittsburgh Dispatch*, September 20, 1892.

411 "Hope Sees a Star," *Pittsburgh Dispatch*, August 3, 1892.

412 "Men to Retaliate," *Pittsburgh Post*, August 3, 1892.

413 Ibid.

414 "Mr. Frick's Baby Dead," *The Wilkes-Barre Evening Leader*, August 3, 1892. See also, inscription on Henry Clay Frick, Jr. memorial, Homewood Cemetery, Pittsburgh, Pennsylvania.

415 "'Twas Tit for Tat," *Pittsburgh Post*, August 4, 1892.

416 Ibid.

417 Krause, *Battle for Homestead*, 331-332; Burgoyne, *Homestead Strike*, 196-199; "The Outlook," *The Christian Union*, no. 17 (October 22, 1892), 717.

418 "Brennen Not Frightened," *Pittsburgh Post*, October 1, 1892.

419 "High Treason the Charge," *New York Tribune*, October 2, 1892.

420 "Treason Trials in the United States," *American Law Review* 26 (November - December, 1892), 912.

421 "Bills in All the Cases," *The New York Times*, October 12, 1892.

422 Burgoyne, *Homestead Strike*, 214.

423 "Majority Going Up," *Pittsburgh Dispatch*, November 10, 1892; Congressional Quarterly, *Guide to U.S. Elections* (Washington: Congressional Quarterly, Inc., 1994), 443.

424 "The Big Strike Ended," *Pittsburgh Press*, November 21, 1892.

425 Myron R. Stowell, *Fort Frick, or the Siege of Homestead* (Pittsburgh: Pittsburg Printing Co., 1893), 257-258.

426 "A Homestead Acquittal," *Pittsburgh Post*, February 19, 1893.

427 "Homestead's Anxious Dream is Ended," *Pittsburgh Post*, February 22, 1893.

428 Jesse Robinson, "The Amalgamated Association of Iron, Steel and Tin Workers: A Study in Trade Unionism," (PhD diss., Johns Hopkins, 1917), 2-3. Text available at https://archive.org/details/amalgamatedassoc00robi, last visited March 8, 2016.

429 Carroll D. Wright, "The National Amalgamated Association of Iron, Steel, and Tin Workers, 1892-1901," *Quarterly Journal of Economics* 16, no. 1 (November 1901), 40.

430 Secretary Hilary Herbert to Hon. Charles F. Crisp, March 26, 1894, in *The Reports of Committees of the House of Representatives for the Second Session of the Fifty-Third Congress* (Washington: Government Printing Office, 1894), 10.

431 Standiford, *Meet You in Hell*, 241-242.

432 Nasaw, *Andrew Carnegie*, 466.

433 Ibid., 467.

434 "The Armor-Plate Fraud," *The New York Times*, March 27, 1894; "The Story Told," *Pittsburgh Post*, March 27, 1894.

435 Nasaw, *Andrew Carnegie*, 468.

436 Wall, *Andrew Carnegie*, 575 (quoting from Andrew Carnegie to William E. Gladstone, September 24, 1893).

437 Nasaw, *Andrew Carnegie*, 491; Standiford, *Meet You in Hell*, 244.

438 Nasaw, *Andrew Carnegie*, 495.

439 Ibid., 495 - 497.

440 Agreement, dated January 10, 1887 (copy of printed "Iron-Clad Agreement, Not Fully Executed), from U.S. Steel Corporation collection; Nasaw, *Andrew Carnegie*, 288; Harbison, *D.T. Watson*, 143. Standiford, *Meet You in Hell*, 69-70;

441 Nasaw, *Andrew Carnegie*, 534 - 535; Bridge, *Inside History*, 338.

442 Nasaw, *Andrew Carnegie*, 507.

443 Bridge, *Inside History*, 300.

444 Standiford, *Meet You in Hell*, 253-258; William Serrin, *Homestead: The Glory and Tragedy of an American Steel Town* (New York: Vintage Books, 1993), 108; Bridge, *Inside History*, 304-306; regarding the death of Flower, see *The New York Times*, May 13, 1899.

445 Bridge, *Inside History*, 321-325; Skrabec, *Frick*, 164-165.

446 Nasaw, *Andrew Carnegie*, 572.

447 Standiford, *Meet You in Hell*, 264-265.

448 "Carnegie Comes Back to Town," *Pittsburgh Post*, January 8, 1900.

449 "Frick Out of Office," *Pittsburgh Post*, January 11, 1900.

450 Nasaw, *Andrew Carnegie*, 574 - 575.

451 Nasaw, *Andrew Carnegie*, 575.

452 Bridge, *Inside History*, 343.

453 James Howard Bridge, *The Carnegie Millions and the Men Who Made Them* (London: Limpus Baker & Co., 1903), 346.

454 Bridge, *Carnegie Millions*, 344.

455 Harbison, *D.T. Watson*, 146.

456 Nasaw, *Andrew Carnegie*, 575.

457 Bridge, *Carnegie Millions*, 345.

458 Joseph Frazier Wall, *Andrew Carnegie* (New York: Oxford University Press, 1970), 619.

459 Standiford, *Meet You in Hell*, 270.

460 Harbison, *D.T. Watson*, 147-149, 152.

461 "Must Find Forty Men," *Pittsburgh Post*, February 15, 1900.

462 "Battle of the Steel Kings," *Wellsboro (PA) Gazette*, February 14, 1900.

463 "Fraud Charged to Carnegie," *San Francisco Call*, February 14, 1900.

464 "Mr. Carnegie's Vast Profits," *The New York Times*, February 15, 1900.

465 Quoted in "Radical Papers on the Carnegie-Frick Dispute," *Literary Digest* 20, no. 10 (March 10, 1900), 293.

466 Ibid.

467 Ibid.

468 "Coke Suit is Begun," *Pittsburgh Post*, February 27, 1900.

469 Andrew L. Weil, *A Passion for Justice* (privately published, 1994), 98-100.

470 Nasaw, *Andrew Carnegie*, 578; George Westinghouse to Andrew Carnegie, February 8, 1900, Andrew Carnegie Papers 1803-1935, vol. 73, Manuscript Division, Library of Congress.

471 "Mr. Carnegie is Not Trusting to Counsel," *Pittsburgh Post*, March 5, 1900.

472 Ida Tarbell, *The Life of Elbert H. Gary: The Story of Steel* (New York: D. Appleton & Co., 1925), 109-110.

473 "Carnegie Answers Frick's Complaint," *The New York Times*, March 13, 1900.

474 "Delay in Carnegie Suit," *The New York Times*, March 17, 1900.

475 George Harvey, *Henry Clay Frick: The Man* (Washington: Beard Books, 2002), 251.

476 Wall, *Andrew Carnegie*, 761.

477 "Must Find Forty Men," *Pittsburgh Post*, February 15, 1900; "Judge Reed Home from Florida," *Pittsburgh Post*, February 28, 1900.

478 Harvey, *Henry Clay Frick*, 254.

479 Bridge, *Carnegie Millions*, 347; "End Big Carnegie Suit," *Chicago Tribune*, March 22, 1900.

480 "Carnegie and Frick Again Combine," *The New York Times*, March 23, 1900.

481 Quoted in Bridge, *Carnegie Millions*, 349.

482 Pittsburgh Gazette Times, ed., *The Story of Pittsburgh and Vicinity* (Pittsburgh: Pittsburgh Gazette Times, 1908), 87.

483 Alexander P. Moore, ed., *The Book of Prominent Pennsylvanians: A Standard Reference* (Pittsburgh: Leader Publishing, 1913), 57.

484 "How Pennsylvania Lost," *Pittsburgh Post*, March 25, 1900.

485 Harbison, *D.T. Watson*, 154-156.

486 Skrabec, *Frick*, 167; Nasaw, *Andrew Carnegie*, 581.

487 Douglas A. Fisher, *Steel Serves the Nation, 1901-1951; The Fifty Year Story of United States Steel* (New York: United States Steel, 1951), 19.

488 "Carnegie's 'Boys' Meet at Table," *Pittsburgh Post*, January 10, 1891.

489 Tarbell, *Life of Elbert Gary*, 110-112.

490 Standiford, *Meet You in Hell*, 277.

491 Nasaw, *Andrew Carnegie*, 586;

492 United States v. United States Steel, 223 F. 55, 120 (D.N.J. 1915); "Carnegie Sale is Described by Judge Reed," *Pittsburgh Daily Post*, June 18, 1913.

493 "Carnegie Sale is Described by Judge Reed," *Pittsburgh Daily Post*, June 18, 1913.

494 Demmler, *First Century*, 26.

495 Brignano and Fort, *Reed Smith: 125 Years*, 36-37; George Motheral to Philander Knox, March 18, 1901, Papers of Philander Chase Knox, Library of Congress, Washington, DC.

496 Quentin Skrabec, *William McKinley, Apostle of Protectionism* (New York: Algora, 2008), 61 - 62.

497 Demmler, *First Century*, 30.

498 Weil, *Passion for Justice*, 103.

ENDNOTES PART III

1. "Crowds in Pittsburgh Cheer the President," *The New York Times*, July 5, 1902.

2. Ibid.

3. "Skyscrapers in Pittsburgh," *The Brookline Connection*, accessed April 27, 2016, http://www.brooklineconnection.com/history/Facts/Skyscraper6th.html

4. William J. Benson and Martin J. "Red" Beckman, *The Law That Never Was: The Fraud of the 16th Amendment and Personal Income Tax* (South Holland, IL: Constitutional Research Associates, 1985), 19-20.

5. See, e.g., U.S. v. House, 617 F. Supp. 237 (W.D. Michigan 1985).

6. Demmler, *First Century*, 101-102

7. Thomas R. Pegram, "Prohibition," in *The American Congress: The Building of Democracy*, ed. Julian E. Zelizer (New York: Houghton Harcourt Mifflin, 2004), 422.

8. Daniel Okrent, *Last Call: The Rise and Fall of Prohibition* (New York: Simon & Shuster, 2010), 113.

9. U.S. v. The Pittsburgh Brewing Co., 67 PLJ 465 (1919).

10. "Acquit Man under Wartime 'Dry' Law", *Pittsburgh Gazette-Times*, January 16, 1924.

11. National Commission on Law Observance and Enforcement, *Report on the Enforcement of the Prohibition Laws of the United States*, vol. 1, no. 2, (Washington: Government Printing Office, 1931), 28.

12. "Ax Swung as Kline Begins his Second Term as Mayor," *Pittsburgh Post-Gazette*, January 7, 1930.

13. "How Wet is Pennsylvania?" *Literary Digest* 79 (November 10, 1923).

14. Benjamin Hayllar, Jr., "The Accommodation: The History and Rhetoric of the Rackets-Political Alliance in Pittsburgh" (PhD diss., University of Pittsburgh, 1977), 125.

15. Chris McGee, "Prohibition's Failure in Pittsburgh," *The Sloping Halls Review* I (1994), 71.

16. Mark A. Noon, *Yuengling: A History of America's Oldest Brewery* (Jefferson, NC: McFarland, 2005), 131.

17. Executive Office of U.S. Attorneys, *Bicentennial Celebration of the United States Attorneys, 1789-1989* (Washington: Government Printing Office, 1989), 5.

18. Department of Justice, *Annual Reports of the Attorney General of the United States for the Year 1909* (Washington: Government Printing Office, 1909), 91; Department of Justice, *Annual Reports of the Attorney General of the United States for the Year 1916* (Washington: Government Printing Office, 1916), 243-44; "Politics in Pennsylvania," *Harrisburg Telegraph*, October 2, 1929.

19. Comptroller General John R. McCarl, *Decision of November 18, 1926*, Doc. Num. A-16236, 6 Comp. Gen. 351, http://www.gao.gov/products/A-16236.

20. "Politics in Pennsylvania," *Harrisburg Telegraph*, October 2, 1929.

21. Executive Office of U.S. Attorneys, *Bicentennial Celebration*, 211.

22. Duquesne University School of Law, *Academic Bulletin 2012-2013* (Pittsburgh: Duquesne University, 2012), 7.

23. George Wharton Pepper, "Legal Education and Admission to the Bar," in *Report of the Annual Meeting of the Pennsylvania Bar Association* (Philadelphia: George H. Buchanan & Co., 1895), 124.

24. "Report of the Committee on Legal Education," in *Transactions of the Fourteenth Annual Meeting of the American Bar Association* (Philadelphia: Dando Printing & Publishing Co., 1891), 307.

25. "Discussion of Address by Robert Snodgrass," in *Report of the Third Annual Meeting of the Pennsylvania Bar Association* (Philadelphia: George H. Buchanan & Co., 1897), 243.

26. Ibid., 245.

27. 59 Legal Int. 225 (May 30, 1902); see Joel Fishman, "The Establishment of the Pennsylvania State Board of Law Examiners, 1895-1902," *Pennsylvania Bar Association Quarterly* 76 (2005).

28. "Report of Committee on Legal Education," in *Report of the Eighth Annual Meeting of the Pennsylvania Bar Association* (Philadelphia: George H. Buchanan & Co., 1902), 129.

29. Board of Law Examiners Meeting Minutes, February 17, 1902, Allegheny County Bar Association, ACBA Collection.

30. Board of Law Examiners Meeting Minutes, June 4, 1906, Allegheny County Bar Association, ACBA Collection; In re Musgrave's Case, 216 Pa. 598 (1907).

31. In re Musgrave's Case, 216 Pa. 598 (1907).

32. Board of Law Examiners Meeting Minutes, June 5, 1916, Allegheny County Bar Association, ACBA Collection.

33. Act of May 8, 1909, P. L. 475, 17 Penn. Stat. Ann. § 1605.

34. Joel Fishman, "The Establishment of the Pennsylvania State Board of Law Examiners, 1895-1902," *Pennsylvania Bar Association Quarterly* 76 (April 2005), 73, 92.

35. Henry P. Hoffstot, Jr. and J. Tomlinson Fort, interview by the author, September 5, 2008.

36. David A. Reed, Application for Admission to Allegheny County Bar Association, October 1905, Allegheny County Bar Association, ACBA Collection.

37 See, Application for Admission to Allegheny County Bar Association, 1905. Allegheny County Bar Association, ACBA Collection.

38 Katarincic, "Allegheny County Bar Association," 326.

39 Ibid., 326-27.

40 Ibid., 331.

41 Ibid., 333-34.

42 Ibid., 339.

43 Ibid.

44 Ibid., 347-48.

45 Ibid., 317.

46 Ibid., 330.

47 Alan B. Tisdale, R.A., City-County Building (Historic American Buildings Survey, HABS No. PA-5193); Katarincic, "Allegheny County Bar Association," 330.

48 Robert G. Leh, "The Lawyer's Court: Pittsburgh's Attempt to Relieve Docket Congestion," *Pennsylvania History* 33 (January-October 1966), 308-331.

49 Katarincic, "Allegheny County Bar Association," 327; Stein & Meister, *A Court for the People*, 16.

50 "History | Western District of Pennsylvania | United States District Court", *United States District Court for the Western District of Pennsylvania*, accessed February 25, 2016, http://www.pawd.uscourts.gov/history.

51 Emily Field Van Tassel, *Why Judges Resign: Influences on Federal Judicial Service, 1789 to 1992* (Washington: Federal Judicial Center, 1993), 22.

52 "History | Western District of Pennsylvania | United States District Court", *United States District Court for the Western District of Pennsylvania*, accessed February 25, 2016, http://www.pawd.uscourts.gov/history.

53 "Vast Throng get Dispatch Election News," *Pittsburgh Dispatch*, February 21, 1906.

54 Eastman, *Courts and Lawyers of Pennsylvania*, 166-67; Valley of Pittsburgh Scottish Rite, *Memorial of ILL: George Wilkins Guthrie, 33☐* (Pittsburgh: Valley of Pittsburgh Scottish Rite, 1917), 10-13.

55 See McNeil v. McNeil, 44 PLJ 129, 130 (1896) (in which Guthrie represents Germania Bank); "George W. Guthrie" in *Who's Who in America (1906-1907)*, John W. Leonard, ed. (Chicago: A.N. Marquis & Co. 1906) (in which Guthrie is listed as vice president and trustee of Dollar Savings Bank Mem.); German National Bank of Pittsburgh v. Farmers' Deposit National Bank of Pittsburgh, 10 Central Reporter 636, 638 (1888).

56 Lincoln Steffens, "Pittsburg: A City Ashamed," *McClure's Magazine* (May 1903), 27-29.

57 Steffens, "City Ashamed," 30.

58 Ibid.

59 Carnegie Museum Pittsburgh, *Annual Report of the Director for the Year Ending March 31, 1898* (Pittsburgh: Carnegie Museum, 1898), 4.

60 Marylynn Uricchio, "Young conductor has big plans for orchestra," *Pittsburgh Post-Gazette*, December 3, 1981.

61 Keith A. Zahniser, *Steel City Gospel: Protestant Laity and Reform in Progressive-Era Pittsburgh* (New York: Routledge, 2005), 32.

62 Zahniser, *Steel City Gospel*, 48; Steffens, "City Ashamed," 33; Fleming, *History of Pittsburgh and Environs*, 5-6.

63 Fleming, *History of Pittsburgh and Environs*, 5.

64 Civic Club of Allegheny County, *Fifteen Years of Civic History* (Pittsburgh: Nicholson Printing Co., 1910), 7.

65 Zahniser, *Steel City Gospel*, 116.

66 Ibid., 42.

67 Ibid., 99.

68 George W. Guthrie, "Some Fundamental Municipal Needs in Pennsylvania," in *Proceedings of the Pittsburgh Conference for Good City Government and the Fourteenth Annual Meeting of the National Municipal League*, Clinton R. Woodruff, ed., (Philadelphia: National Municipal League, 1908), 374

69 Ibid., 373.

70 George W. Guthrie, "Municipal Condition of Pittsburg," in *Proceedings of the Third National Conference for Good City Government and of the Second Annual Meeting of the National Municipal League* (Philadelphia: National Municipal League, 1896), 152, 154

71 Zahniser, *Steel City Gospel*, 35.

72 John E. Bauman and Edward K. Miller, *Before Renaissance: Planning in Pittsburgh, 1889-1943* (Pittsburgh: University of Pittsburgh Press, 2006), 37-38.

73 George Peter Gregory, "A Study in Local Decision Making: Pittsburgh and Sewage Treatment," *Western Pennsylvania Historical Magazine* 57, no. 1 (January 1974), 28.

74 Ibid., 27.

75 Frank E. Wing, "Thirty-five Years of Typhoid," *Charities and Commons* 21 (Feb. 6, 1909), 926.

76 Flood Commission of Pittsburgh, *Report of Flood commission of Pittsburgh, Penna., containing the results of the surveys / investigations and studies made by the commission for the purpose of determining the causes of, damage by and methods of relief from floods in the Allegheny* (Pittsburgh: Murdoch, Kerr & Co., 1912), 44.

77 "Heavy Losses at Pittsburg," *The New York Times*, April 22, 1901.

78 Kathleen R. Parker, "Charles Elliott St. John: Moral Enthusiasm and the Social Question, 1892-1900" (paper presented at the Unitarian Universalist Collegium Annual Conference 2009), 12-15, http://www.test.uucollegium.org/Research%20papers/09paper_Parker.pdf.

79 "It Was a Rouser," *Pittsburgh Press*, November 24, 1895.

80 Bauman and Miller, *Before Renaissance*, 41.

81 Steffens, "City Ashamed," 37.

82 "Pittsburgh Has Had Three Democratic Mayors in 50 Years," *Pittsburgh Press*, June 23, 1934; Steffens, "City Ashamed," 37.

83 Fleming, *History of Pittsburgh and Environs*, 690-91.

84 Steffens, *City Ashamed*, 33-35.

85 Pittsburgh Filtration Commission, *Report of the Filtration Commission of the City of Pittsburgh, Pennsylvania, January 1899* (Pittsburgh: Pittsburgh Filtration Commission, 1899), 2, 7.

86 "Clean Sweep for Diehl," *Pittsburgh Press*, February 22, 1899.

87 Fleming, *History of Pittsburgh and Environs*, 692.

88 Klein and Hoogenboom, *History of Pennsylvania*, 368; Zahniser, *Steel City Gospel*, 82.

89 "In Memoriam: Thomas Steele Bigelow, Esq.," *Pittsburgh Legal Journal* 52, no. 3 (August 3, 1904); Zahniser, *Steel City Gospel*, 82.

90 Zahniser, *Steel City Gospel*, 82-83.

91 See, e.g., "Senator C.L. Magee Surrenders to Death," *Pittsburgh Post*, March 9, 1901.

92 Commonwealth of Pennsylvania, *Official Documents comprising the Department and Other Reports made to the Governor, Senate and House of Representatives of Pennsylvania, 1902*, vol. 8 (Harrisburg, PA: W.M. Stanley Ray, 1903), 88.

93 Zahniser, *Steel City Gospel*, 83.

94 "Bigelow Again Director; Recorder Moir Resigns," *Pittsburgh Commercial Gazette*, June 7, 1901.

95 "Brown Gets Back!," *Altoona Tribune*, November 23, 1901; "New Recorder of Pittsburg Sworn In," *The New York Times*, November 26, 1901.

96 "Record of Current Events," *The American Monthly Review of Reviews and World's Work* 28 (January-June 1903), 411.

97 "Pittsburg Recorder Dead," *The New York Times*, March 16, 1903.

98 "Discharged 3,000," *New York Daily Tribune*, April 19, 1903.

99 "American Affairs," *Richmond Times Dispatch*, March 29, 1903.

100 Zahniser, *Steel City Gospel*, 84.

101 Fleming, *History of Pittsburgh and Environs*, 692.

102 Steffens, "City Ashamed," 39.

103 "In Memoriam: Thomas Steele Bigelow, Esq.," *Pittsburgh Legal Journal* 52, no. 3 (August 3, 1904).

104 "Bigelow Gang with Guthrie," *Pittsburgh Press*, January 21, 1906.

105 Weil, *Passion for Justice*, 143.

106 "Guthrie Talks to Policemen," *Pittsburgh Gazette*, February 20, 1906.

107 "Brennen Claims Big Lead for Mr. Guthrie," *Pittsburgh Gazette*, February 21, 1906.

108 "Guthrie Takes Oath of Office," *Pittsburgh Press*, April 2, 1906.

109 . Id.

110 "Brennen Bears Up Very Well," *Pittsburgh Gazette*, April 2, 1906.

111 "Guthrie to Stick to His New Job," *Harrisburg Daily Independent*, February 22, 1906.

112 Margo J. Anderson and Maurine W. Greenwald, "Introduction" in *Pittsburgh Surveyed: Social Science and Social Reform in the Early Twentieth Century*, Maurine W. Greenwald and Margo J. Anderson, eds., (Pittsburgh: University of Pittsburgh Press, 2011), 7.

113 "Pitiful Scenes in the Court for Juveniles," *Pittsburgh Post*, September 20, 1903.

114 Martin Bulmer, "The Social Survey Movement and Early Twentieth-Century Sociological Methodology," in Greenwald & Anderson, *Pittsburgh Surveyed*, 17.

115 Sylvia A. Law, "Crystal Eastman: NYU Law Graduate," *New York University Law Review* 66 (December 1991), 1963; John Fabian Witt, "Crystal Eastman and the Internationalist Beginnings of American Civil Liberties," *Duke Law Journal* 54 (2004), 705.

116 Law, "Crystal Eastman," 1985.

117 Erin F. Davis, "Love's Labor's Lost?: Crystal Eastman's Contribution to Workers' Compensation Reform," (paper presented to Professor Barbara Babock in Women in the Legal Profession, Stanford Law School, April 5, 2002), accessed April 27, 2016, http://www.ibrarian.net/navon/paper/LABOR__S_LOVE_LOST___Crystal_Eastman_s_Contribution.pdf?paperid=457167

118 Gary Dombroff, "Workers' Compensation at 100, The Fire that Started It All", *New York State Insurance Fund*, accessed April 27, 2016, http://ww3.nysif.com/AboutNYSIF/NYSIFNews/2011/~/media/pdf/Articles/TriangleShirtwaistSeries1.ashx

119 Clinton Rogers Woodruff, "A Mayor with an Ideal," *Outlook* (April 25, 1908), 921.

120 Robert Dale Grinder, "From Insurgency to Efficiency: The Smoke Abatement Campaign in Pittsburgh Before World War I," *Western Pennsylvania Historical Magazine* 61 (July 1978), 187, 199.

121 Clinton Rogers Woodruff, "Guthrie of Pittsburgh," *The World To-Day* 17 (November 1909), 1173.

122 Mark J. Tierno, "The Search for Pure Water in Pittsburgh: The Urban Response to Water Pollution, 1893-1914," *Western Pennsylvania Historical Magazine* 60 (January 1977), 35-36

123 Woodruff, "Guthrie of Pittsburgh," 1173.

124 Frank Moore Colby, ed., *The New International Year Book: A Compendium of the World's Progress for the Year 1909* (New York: Dodd, Mead & Co., 1910), 562.

125 "Pittsburgh's Amazing Story of Graft," *The New York Times*, March 27, 1910.

126 Weil, *Passion for Justice*, 146-47.

127 S. Leo Ruslander, *The Life and Times of S. Leo Ruslander (A Quasi-autobiography)* (Pittsburgh: privately published, 1964), 189.

128. "Mayor W.A. Magee's Hot Reply to A. Leo Weil's Harrisburg Speech," *Pittsburgh Gazette Times*, March 29, 1911.
129. A. Leo Weil, "Modern Municipal Conditions and the Lawyers' Responsibility" (paper presented to the Pennsylvania Bar Association, Cape May, NJ, June 24, 1908), 17.
130. Weil, *Passion for Justice*, 141-142.
131. Ibid., 147-52.
132. William Futhey Gibbons, "An Evangelist of Civic Righteousness," *Outlook* (February 20, 1909), 395-97.
133. Weil, *Passion for Justice*, 155-58.
134. Ibid., 158-162; "Pittsburgh's Amazing Story of Graft," *The New York Times*, March 27, 1910; Albert Jay Nock, "What a Few Men Did in Pittsburg: A True Detective Story of To-Day," *American Magazine* 70 (1910), 808-818.
135. Weil, *Passion for Justice*, 164-66.
136. Ibid., 167-68; "Pittsburgh's Amazing Story of Graft," *The New York Times*, March 27, 1910.
137. Weil, *Passion for Justice*, 168-71.
138. Associated Press, "Pittsburgh's Amazing Story; High Officials Implicated in Graft Trial," *Harrisburg Daily Independent*, Dec, 22, 1908.
139. Nock, "A Few Men in Pittsburg," 816.
140. "Pittsburgh's Amazing Story of Graft," *The New York Times*, March 27, 1910.
141. Weil, *Passion for Justice*, 185-86.
142. Colby, *New International Year Book*, 562.
143. Weil, *Passion for Justice*, 200.
144. Ibid., 191-93.
145. Ibid., 199.
146. Bauman and Miller, *Before Renaissance*, 87.
147. "Pittsburgh's Amazing Story of Graft," *The New York Times*, March 27, 1910.
148. Barbara S. Burstein, *Steel City Jews: A History of Pittsburgh and its Jewish Community, 1840-1915* (Pittsburgh: privately published, 2008), 250-51.
149. Zahniser, *Steel City Gospel*, 125-126.
150. "Reasons Stated for Asking Change," *Pittsburgh Gazette Times*, March 29, 1911.
151. "Mr. Weil's Address in Advocacy of a New Charter for Pittsburgh," *Pittsburgh Gazette Times*, March 29, 1911.
152. "Mayor W.A. Magee's Hot Reply to A. Leo Weil's Harrisburg Speech," *Pittsburgh Gazette Times*, March 29, 1911.
153. Zahniser, *Steel City Gospel*, 131-32.
154. Woodruff, "Guthrie of Pittsburgh," 1173.
155. "Both Factions Claim Victory," *Pittsburgh Gazette Times*, April 15, 1912.
156. Allegheny County Bar Association, *In Memoriam William Scott* (Pittsburgh: Smith Brothers Co., 1906), 15.
157. "William Sage Dalzell," Find A Grave, accessed March 22, 2017, https://www.findagrave.com/cgi-bin/fg.cgi?page=gr&GRid=101584071.
158. Thomas D. Thomson (partner at Thomson Rhodes & Cowie), interview by the author, June 1993.
159. As to the death of Smith's four-year old son, William Watson Smith, Jr., see "Personal and Society–Obituary," *Pittsburg Bulletin*, May 16, 1903, 17; as to the death of 12-year old William Gordon, George Gordon's son in 1902, see Allegheny County Bar Association, *In Memoriam: George B. Gordon* (Pittsburgh: Allegheny County Bar Association, 1927), 10-11.
160. See, e.g., Princeton Alumni Weekly, February 6, 1948, and June 2, 1961.
161. W.W. Smith, "George Washington's Last Pants," *Nassau Herald* (1892), 6.
162. Princeton University, *Quindecinnial Record of the Class of Ninety Two of Princeton University* (New York: Grafton Press, 1907), 201.
163. Ibid., 200.
164. "William Watson Smith, Class of 1892," *Princeton University General Biographical Catalogue, 1746-1906* (Princeton: Princeton University Press, 1908), 298.
165. Gordon & Smith (and successor firms) ledgers and employee rolls, 1906-1942, Buchanan Ingersoll & Rooney, collection, Pittsburgh, PA (hereafter cited as *Buchanan Ingersoll Employee Rolls*).
166. Dalzell, Scott & Gordon dissolution files, 1906-1923, Buchanan Ingersoll & Rooney collection, Pittsburgh, PA.
167. Demmler, *First Century*, 32-36.
168. Charles A. Locke, "Thomas Mellon II - A Memorial," *Western Pennsylvania Historical Magazine* 31, nos. 1-2 (March-June 1948), 18-19.
169. Demmler, *First Century*, 36.
170. Brignano and Fort, *Reed Smith: 125 Years*, 47; *Buchanan Ingersoll Employee Rolls*.
171. See "Personal and Society - Obituary," *Pittsburg Bulletin*, May 16, 1903, 17.
172. See 1900 U.S. Census, Grace C. Humbird and Anica B. Humbird; "The Social World," *The Index* VX, No. 20 (November 17, 1906), 15 (regarding the marriage of Grace Humbird Longenecker's sister Anica to James Hay Reed, Jr.).
173. "Whisky Feeds Raging Flames," *Pittsburgh Post*, November 20, 1905.
174. "Loss to Distillery Set at $2,000,000," *Pittsburgh Post*, November 21, 1905.
175. Frick v. United Fireman's Insurance Co., 218 Pa. 409, 417 (1907).
176. Sell, *The Law Down*, 229; Center for Legal Information, *Duquesne Law Graduates, 1914-2005*, Excel compilation, Duquesne Law School, 2015.

177 Based on review of R.L. Polk & Co., *Pittsburgh and Allegheny Directory for 1906* (Pittsburgh: R.L. Polk & Co., 1906); R.L. Polk & Co., *Pittsburgh and Allegheny Directory for 1917* (Pittsburgh: R.L. Polk & Co., 1917).

178 Based on review of contemporary city directories and annual Allegheny County Legal Directory editions..

179 Charles F.C. Arensberg, "From My Time at the Bar (1956)," Doc. No. ADMIN 278.1, Tucker Arensberg collection.

180 Hubert Rutherford Brown, *The Lawyers' List* (New York: H.R. Brown, 1918), 261-263; R.L. Polk & Co., *Pittsburgh and Allegheny Directory for 1916* (Pittsburgh: R.L. Polk & Co., 1916).

181 *Buchanan Ingersoll Employee Rolls.*

182 Fleming, *History of Pittsburgh and Environs*, 109; "John G. Buchanan, Class of 1909," Princeton University Alumni Records, 1746-1946, answers to questionnaire, Princeton University Alumni Archives.

183 "Class Notes," *Princeton Alumni Weekly* 87, no. 7 (December 10, 1986), 25 (quoting letter from John Buchanan, III).

184 *Buchanan Ingersoll Employee Rolls.*

185 Ibid.

186 "Pittsburghers Pledge Readiness to Fight," *Pittsburgh Gazette Times*, April 1, 1917.

187 Philander C. Knox, *Address of Hon. Philander Chase Knox at a Patriotic Mass Meeting in Exposition Music Hall, Pittsburgh, Pa., March 31st, 1917* (Philadelphia: Allen, Lane & Scott, 1917), 2, 11-14.

188 "Pittsburghers Pledge Readiness to Fight," *Pittsburgh Gazette Times*, April 1, 1917.

189 Elizabeth Williams, *Pittsburgh in World War I: Arsenal of the Allies* (London: History Press, 2013), 102.

190 Based on review of Ancestry.com, *U.S., Department of Veterans Affairs BIRLS Death File, 1850-2010*, http://search.ancestry.com/search/db.aspx?dbid=2441, ACBA decedent files, alumni records, contemporary legal and city directories, and William Elmer Bachman, *The Delta of the Triple Elevens: The History of Battery D, 311th Field Artillery, United States Army, American Expeditionary Forces* (Hazelton, PA: Standard Sentinel Printing, 1920), 22 (record of enlistment of David A. Reed).

191 "Princeton during World War I," Seeley G. Mudd Manuscript Library, Princeton University, accessed April 27, 2016, https://rbsc.princeton.edu/university-archives-2.

192 "Innovation Made," *Pittsburgh Post*, August 3, 1917.

193 Inscriptions, *Members of the Allegheny County Bar in Service of Our Country*, Allegheny County Law Library, City-County Building, Pittsburgh, PA; R.L. Polk & Co., *Pittsburgh and Allegheny Directory for 1916* (Pittsburgh: R.L. Polk & Co., 1916); Brown, *Lawyers List*.

194 Ibid.; Murdoch, "Profiles in Leadership," 183;

195 Ibid.

196 Union Trust Company of Pittsburgh, *Service Letters: A Record of Experiences and Achievement* (Pittsburgh: Union Trust Co., 1918), 8.

197 Bachman, *Delta of the Triple Elevens*, 22.

198 "William R. Scott," Allegheny County Bar Association Decedent Files, Allegheny County Bar Association, ACBA Collection.

199 Robert G. Woodside, *Military Times Hall of Valor*, accessed March 22, 2017, http://valor.militarytimes.com/recipient.php?recipientid=15524

200 "Joseph H. Thompson," *Pennsylvania State Senate*, accessed March 22, 2017, http://www.legis.state.pa.us/cfdocs/legis/BiosHistory/MemBio.cfm?ID=2647&body=S ; Kenneth Britten, *Beaver Falls* (Charleston, SC: Arcadia Publishing, 2000), 79.

201 Fleming, *History of Pittsburgh and Environs*, 212; Polk, *City Directory 1916*; "George L. Walter, Jr.," United States World War I Draft Registration Cards 1917-1918, Pittsburgh City no. 11 G-Z, Pennsylvania, United States, NARA microfilm publication M1509 (Washington D.C.: National Archives and Records Administration, n.d.), no. 2704, https://familysearch.org/pal:/MM9.3.1/TH-1961-26644-30448-43?cc=1968530.

202 Miles H. England to Clara Houston, August 27, 1918, Buchanan Ingersoll & Rooney collection, Pittsburgh, PA.

203 "Miles H. England Answers Last Call," *Pittsburgh Legal Journal* 85 (Pittsburgh: Pittsburgh Legal Journal, Inc., 1937), 230.

204 John G. Buchanan to Clara Houston, August 30, 1918, Buchanan Ingersoll & Rooney collection, Pittsburgh, PA.

205 John G. Buchanan to George B. Gordon, February 4, 1918, Buchanan Ingersoll & Rooney collection, Pittsburgh, PA.

206 John G. Buchanan to George B. Gordon, May 24, 1918, Buchanan Ingersoll & Rooney collection, Pittsburgh, PA.

207 Miles H. England to George B. Gordon, May 26, 1918, Buchanan Ingersoll & Rooney collection, Pittsburgh, PA.

208 George B. Gordon to John G. Buchanan, May 27, 1918, Buchanan Ingersoll & Rooney collection, Pittsburgh, PA.

209 John G. Buchanan to George B. Gordon, January 13, 1919, Buchanan Ingersoll & Rooney collection, Pittsburgh, PA.

210 Ibid.

211 Paul G. Rodewald, interviews by the author, March 1992 and September 5, 1992.

212 Demmler, *First Century*, 214 - 229.

213 David Brody, *Steelworkers in America: The Nonunion Era* (Champlaign, IL:Illinois University Press, 1960), 62-63; "Strike Trouble Settlement," *The Deseret News*, April 18, 1901; "Trouble Averted," *Youngstown Vindicator*, April 18, 1901.

214. Minutes of the Executive Committee of the United States Steel Corporation, June 17, 1901, quoted in U.S. Congress, House Committee on Investigation of United States Steel Corporation, *Hearings before the Committee on Investigation of United States Steel Corporation*, vol. 2 (Washington: Government Printing Office, 1912), 1558.

215. John A. Fitch, *The Steel Workers* (Pittsburgh: University of Pittsburgh, 1910), 133-135.

216. "Steel Mills Use Non-Union Workers," *The New York Times*, August 23, 1901.

217. Brody, *Steelworkers in America*, 68.

218. f *The Oxford Encyclopedia of American Business, Labor, and Economic History*, ed. Melvyn Dubofksy, s.v. "Amalgamated Association of Iron, Steel, and Tin Worker."

219. See Judith McDonough, "Worker Solidarity, Judicial Oppression, and Police Repression in the Westmoreland County, Pennsylvania Coal Miner's Strike, 1910-11," *Pennsylvania History* 64, no. 3 (Summer 1997), 384-406; Stephen H. Norwood, *Strikebreaking and Intimidation: Mercenaries and Masculinity in Twentieth-Century America* (Chapel Hill: University of North Carolina Press, 2002), 125.

220. "Operators Going to U.S. Courts to Fight Union," *Pittsburgh Press*, September 1, 1910.

221. "Homes Damaged by Bomb Explosions," *Pittsburgh Leader*, June 3, 1919.

222. "Persons Bombers Attempted to Kill in Various Cities," *Pittsburgh Sun*, June 3, 1919.

223. H.W. Brands, *Traitor to His Class* (New York: Doubleday, 2009), 134.

224. Charles H. McCormick, *Seeing Reds: Federal Surveillance of Radicals in the Pittsburgh Mill District, 1917-1922* (Pittsburgh: University of Pittsburgh Press, 1997), 102; "Arrests May Have Put Ban on Bomb Work," *Pittsburgh Leader*, June 3, 1919.

225. Fleming, *History of Pittsburgh and Environs*, 40.

226. McCormick, *Seeing Reds*, 102.

227. "Bombers Declare War Against Rich; Pamphlet Found," *Pittsburgh Leader*, June 3, 1919.

228. "Judge Thomson Says Terror Reign of Reds Due to Failure," *Pittsburgh Leader*, June 9, 1919.

229. "'Red' Suspects Being Watched By Police," *Pittsburgh Sun*, June 3, 1919.

230. "Detective Has Narrow Escape From Bullet," *Pittsburgh Sun*, June 3, 1919.

231. "Outside I.W.W. Came Here to Direct Bomb Explosions Police Claim," *Pittsburgh Post*, June 4, 1919.

232. Thomas R. Loan, "Letter to the Editor of The Masses," *The Masses* 6, No. 9 (June 1915), 22; "Walter Loan is Placed on Trial in Local Court," *Pittsburgh Press*, March 2, 1915; McCormick, *Seeing Reds*, 104.

233. J.M. [Jacob Margolis], "Walter Loan," *Mother Earth* 10 (May 1915), 131-133.

234. "Family History" and handwritten family history notes, private collection of Barbara Margolis; Barbara Margolis, interview by the author, October 23, 2012.

235. "Zionist Notes," *Jewish Criterion* 21, no. 22 (November 10, 1905), 12.

236. Board of Law Examiners Meeting Minutes, March 7, 1910, Allegheny County Bar Association Collection, Pittsburgh, PA; *Annual Catalog, University of Pittsburgh, Year Ending June, 1910* (Pittsburgh: University of Pittsburgh, 1910), 443.

237. 1940 census, Warrick Co., Ind., population schedule, Pittsburgh, Allegheny County, enumeration district (ED) 69-389, Sheet 4A, household 76, Jacob Margolis; digital image, *Ancestry.com* (http://www.ancestry.com : accessed September 26, 2016); citing NARA microfilm T627, roll 3663. "United States Social Security Death Index," database, *FamilySearch* (https://familysearch.org/ark:/61903/1:1:JKL2-B22 : 20 May 2014), Judith H Freshman, 17 Mar 1997; citing U.S. Social Security Administration, Death Master File, database (Alexandria, Virginia: National Technical Information Service, ongoing); "United States Social Security Death Index," database, *FamilySearch* (https://familysearch.org/ark:/61903/1:1:J1X6-76T : 20 May 2014), Frederick Margolis, 11 Feb 1991; citing U.S. Social Security Administration, Death Master File, database (Alexandria, Virginia: National Technical Information Service, ongoing).

238. McCormick, *Seeing Reds*, 61.

239. Ibid., 43.

240. Ibid., 38-39.

241. Ibid., 39, quoting Jacob Margolis, "The Orthodox Wobbly and the Borer from Within," *One Big Union Monthly* 1 (October 1919), 27-28.

242. Emma Goldman, *Living My Life*, vol. 2 (New York: Alfred Knopf, 1931), 45.

243. McCormick, *Seeing Reds*, 41-42.

244. Jacob Margolis, "The Streets of Pittsburgh," *International Socialist Review* (October 1912), 315.

245. Ibid., 318.

246. Ibid., 313-320.

247. McCormick, *Seeing Reds*, 39

248. Margolis, *The Streets of Pittsburgh*, 318.

249. McCormick, *Seeing Reds*, 44-45.

250. Ibid., 58.

251. Ibid., 77.

252. "World War I Draft Registration Cards, 1917-1918," images, *Ancestry.com* (http://www.ancestry.com : accessed September 26, 2016), card for Jacob Margolis, serial no. 1516, order no. 220, Local Draft Board 3, Pittsburgh, Allegheny Co., PA; citing World War I Selective Service System Draft Registration Cards, 1917-1918, NARA microfilm publication M1509, roll no. 1908016.

253. McCormick, *Seeing Reds*, 188.

254. Ibid., 189.

255. Ibid.

256 Barbara Margolis, interview by the author, October 23, 2012; Family notes on Jacob Margolis, private collection of Barbara Margolis.

257 "Allegheny Bar Association Bill is Signed," *Pittsburgh Dispatch*, June 7, 1919.

258 "Lawyers' Association to Hold Inquisition," *Pittsburgh Dispatch*, June 20, 1919.

259 McCormick, *Seeing Reds*, 122-130.

260 Ibid., 130.

261 United States Congress, *Investigation of strike in steel industries. Hearings before the Committee on Education and Labor, United States Senate, Sixty-sixth Congress, first session, pursuant to S. res. 202 on the Resolution of the Senate to Investigate the Strike in Steel Industries* (Washington: Government Printing Office, 1919), 809-815.

262 *Investigation of Strike*, 817.

263 Ibid., 819.

264 Ibid.

265 Ibid., 823.

266 Ibid., 827.

267 Ibid., 837-838.

268 Ibid., 857-858.

269 Ibid., 877.

270 "Scheme for Fusion of Reds Here Described by Margolis," *Pittsburgh Gazette Times*, October 21, 1919.

271 "Move in Pittsburgh to Disbar Margolis," *The New York Times*, October 23, 1919.

272 John C. Bane, "Our Critics," *Pittsburgh Legal Journal* 57, appendix (August 1910), 194-196.

273 Ibid.

274 Fleming, *History of Pittsburgh and Environs*, 182; "Arthur Scully, Mellon Bank Official, Dies," *Pittsburgh Post-Gazette*, July 3, 1948.

275 "United States Social Security Death Index," database, *FamilySearch* (https://familysearch.org/ark:/61903/1:1:VM6Y-W3L : 20 May 2014), Louise M Lett, 18 Jan 1996; citing U.S. Social Security Administration, Death Master File, database (Alexandria, Virginia: National Technical Information Service, ongoing).

276 McCormick, *Seeing Reds*, 190.

277 "Lawyers Urge Margolis Lose Practice Right," *Pittsburgh Gazette Times*, December 6, 1919.

278 Arensberg, *My Time at the Bar*, 5.

279 "Lawyers Urge Margolis Lose Practice Right," *Pittsburgh Gazette Times*, December 6, 1919.

280 Minutes of Meeting of Allegheny County Bar Association, March 23, 1928, Allegheny County Bar Association Collection, Pittsburgh, PA.

281 "George Calvert Bradshaw," Allegheny County Bar Association Decedent Files, Allegheny County Bar Association, ACBA Collection.

282 "Death Takes Oldest Lawyer in County," *Pittsburgh Press*, August 25, 1948.

283 McCormick, *Seeing Reds*, 191.

284 "Testimony Sensational in Margolis Disbarment Case," *Pittsburgh Press*, April 29, 1920.

285 "Says Margolis Was Against Man-Made Laws" *Pittsburgh Press*, April 30, 1920.

286 McCormick, *Seeing Reds*, 194.

287 "In Re Petition of Bar Association vs. Jacob Margolis, Brief on the Facts for Respondent," Civil Liberty Cases, 1920/1921, vol. 139, American Civil Liberties Union collection, New York, NY.

288 Bureau of Investigation, "In re: Proposed Suit Against the Department of Justice," July 13, 1920, Freedom of Information/Privacy Act Request, Federal Bureau of Investigation, Washington, D.C.; Bureau of Investigation, "In re: Proposed Suit Against Special Agents H.J. Lenon and F.M. Ames and Attorney General Palmer," June 29, 1920, Freedom of Information/Privacy Act Request, Federal Bureau of Investigation, Washington, D.C.

289 "In re: Margolis," *Pittsburgh Legal Journal* 68 (January 1, 1920 - December 31, 1912), 610.

290 Bureau of Investigation, "In re: Disbarment of Jacob Margolis," September 17, 1920, Freedom of Information/Privacy Act Request, Federal Bureau of Investigation, Washington, D.C.

291 Bureau of Investigation, "In re: Proposed Bombing of Judges Homes," September 17, 1920, Freedom of Information/Privacy Act Request, Federal Bureau of Investigation, Washington, D.C.

292 Bureau of Investigation, "In re: Jacob Margolis Disbarment," September 28, 1920, Freedom of Information/Privacy Act Request, Federal Bureau of Investigation, Washington, D.C.

293 Ibid.

294 Bureau of Investigation, "In re: Metal & Machinery Workers #440 (formerly #300) and Pittsburgh Local – General Recruiting Union – I.W.W.," November 11, 1920, Freedom of Information/Privacy Act Request, Federal Bureau of Investigation, Washington, D.C.

295 Roger Baldwin to Jacob Margolis, January 6, 1920, Civil Liberty Cases, 1920/1921, vol. 139, American Civil Liberties Union collection, , New York, NY.

296 Swinburne Hale, "U.S. Steel v. Margolis," *The Nation* 111 (1920), 498.

297 Ex parte Wall, 107 U.S. 265, *quoted in* In re Margolis, 269 Pa. 112 (1921).

298 In re Margolis 112 A. 478 (Pa. 1921).

299 McCormick, *Seeing Reds*, 198-199.

300 Ibid., 199.

301 Family History" and handwritten family history notes, collection of Barbara Margolis.

302 In re Margolis, 280 Pa. 296 (1924).

303 "W.J. Brennen Passes Away After Attack of Pneumonia," *Pittsburgh Post*, April 16, 1924.

304 Ibid.

305 "May Be Reinstated," *Pittsburgh Press*, November 13, 1928.

306 Arensberg, *My Time at the Bar*, 6.

307 Barbara Margolis, interview by the author, September 11, 2012.

308 Seymour Sikov, interview by the author, September 19, 2008.
309 "All Trading Marks Broken, Bank Group Checks Slump," *Pittsburgh Post-Gazette*, October 30, 1929.
310 Elmer C. Walzer, "Bankers Confident of Stock Rise," *Pittsburgh Press*, October 30, 1929.
311 Kenneth Heineman, *A Catholic New Deal* (University Park, PA: Penn State University Press 1999), 5, 11.
312 Benjamin Roth, *The Great Depression: A Diary*, James Ledbetter and Daniel B. Roth, eds., (New York: Public Affairs, 2009), 26.
313 Ibid., 38.
314 Ibid., 86.
315 Brignano and Fort, *Reed Smith: 125 Years*, 63.
316 Demmler, *First Century*, 92-93.
317 Ibid., 93.
318 Ibid.
319 Brignano and Fort, *Reed Smith: 125 Years*, 64.
320 *Buchanan Ingersoll Employer Rolls*.
321 Patterson Crawford account ledger, summary of revenues 1927-1950, in Tucker Arensberg collection, Pittsburgh, PA. Copy enclosed with explanation by letter, Jeffrey J. Leech to author, October 22, 2013.
322 Oscar Ameringer, *If You Don't Weaken: the Autobiography of Oscar Ameringer* (New York: H. Holt & Co., 1940), 457.
323 Christine Brendel Scriabine, "The Frayed White Collar: Professional Unemployment in the early Depression," *Pennsylvania History* 49, No. 1 (January 1982), 11.
324 *Polk's Pittsburgh City Directory 1929*, Vol. LXXIV (Pittsburgh, Pa: R.L. Polk & Co, 1929); *Polk's Pittsburgh City Directory 1931*, Vol. LXXVI (Pittsburgh, Pa: R.L. Polk & Co, 1931).
325 Linda Shoop Schmalstig, interview by the author, January 2, 2014.
326 Reuben Fingold, interview by the author, June 2, 2009 and June 10, 2009.
327 Fleming, *History of Pittsburgh and Environs*, 31-33.
328 Raymond Z. Henle, "Hoover Sure of Nomination, Burke Asserts," *Pittsburgh Post-Gazette*, September 30, 1931.
329 "Burke Answers Foes of Hoover," *Pittsburgh Press*, January 31, 1932.
330 James F. Burke to Albert M. Greenfield, December 22, 1930, Albert M. Greenfield Papers, the Historical Society of Pennsylvania, Philadelphia, PA.
331 "Accorsi Wins His Battle to Delay Return," *Pittsburgh Press*, July 25, 1929; "Accorsi Goes on Stand for Defense Today," *Pittsburgh Post Gazette*, December 12, 1929.
332 "Sacco and Vanzetti Shall Be Free," *The Villager* (New York), July 7, 1927.
333 Kurt Stone, *Jews of Capitol Hill: A Compendium of Jewish Congressional Members* (Lanham, MD: Scarecrow Press, 2010), 141.
334 Ibid.
335 Heineman, *Catholic New Deal*, 82.
336 Robert G. Sable, interview by the author, July 21, 2008.
337 Heineman, *Catholic New Deal*, 82; "Concordia Club Photographs," Guides to Archives and Manuscript Collections at the Library & Archives at the Heinz History Center, accessed September 26, 2016, http://digital.library.pitt.edu/cgi-bin/f/findaid/findaid-idx?c=hswpead;rgn=main;view=text;didno=US-QQS-msp434.
338 "Thorp Reed and Armstrong," *The Lawyers Directory*, vol. 75 (Miami: The Lawyers Directory, Inc., 1958), 113.
339 E.J. Strassburger and Judge Eugene B. Strassburger, III, interview by the author, September 14, 2010.
340 *Buchanan Ingersoll Employee Rolls*; "Charles B. Buerger – The Man," *Jewish Criterion* (Pittsburgh), September 13, 1929.
341 Heineman, *Catholic New Deal*, 83.
342 Ibid., 83-84.
343 Robert G. Sable, interview by the author, July 21, 2008.
344 Stone, *Jews of Capitol Hill*, 141.
345 Kenneth J. Heineman, "A Tale of Two Cities: Pittsburgh, Philadelphia, and the Elusive Quest for a New Deal Majority in the Keystone State," *The Pennsylvania Magazine of History and Biography* 132.4 (2008), 323.
346 James N. Giordano, "Musmanno, Michael Angelo," *American National Biography Online*, last accessed September 26, 2016, http://www.anb.org/articles/11/11-00620.html.
347 Michael A. Musmanno, *Verdict!: The Adventures of the Young Lawyer in the Brown Suit* (New York: Doubleday, 1958), 31.
348 Musmanno, *Verdict*, 307.
349 Yiorgos Anagnostou, "Film Reviews – The Italian Americans," *Italian American Review* 5, no. 2 (Summer 2015), 152.
350 Board of Law Examiners Meeting Minutes, December 4, 1905, Allegheny County Bar Association, ACBA Collection.
351 Fleming, *History of Pittsburgh and Environs*, 270-271; Stefano Luconi, "The Italian-Language Press, Italian American Voters, and Political Intermediation in Pennsylvania in the Interwar Years," *International Migration Review* 33, no. 4 (Winter 1999), 1035.
352 Board of Law Examiners Meeting Minutes, November 1, 1905, Allegheny County Bar Association, ACBA Collection.
353 Board of Law Examiners Meeting Minutes, November 17, 1905, Allegheny County Bar Association, ACBA Collection.

354 Fleming, *History of Pittsburgh and Environs*, 270; Luconi, "Italian-Language Press," 1035.

355 Ruggero J. Aldisert, *Road to the Robes: A Federal Judge Recollects Young Years & Early Times* (Bloomington, IN: AuthorHouse, 2005), 27-44.

356 Musmanno, *Verdict*, 112-113.

357 Ibid., 201-210.

358 Ibid., 288.

359 Ibid., 269.

360 Ibid., 288-290.

361 Ibid., 302-324.

362 Ibid., 325-27.

363 Aldisert, *Road to the Robes*, 61.

364 Musmanno, *Verdict*, 327.

365 Ibid.

366 Ibid.

367 Ibid., 328-34; "Move to End Coal Police is Sweeping Statewide," *Pittsburgh Press*, February 13, 1929; "Then and Now - Governor Wins Title for Quick Changing of His Mind," *Pittsburgh Press*, April 20, 1929.

368 Musmanno, *Verdict*, 334.

369 Heineman, *Catholic New Deal*, 15-16; Associated Press, "Father Cox Dies at 65," *Reading Eagle*, March 20, 1951; Eric Leif Devin, *Crucible of Freedom: Workers' Democracy in the Industrial heartland, 1914-1960* (Lanham, MD: Rowman & Littlefield, 2010), 167.

370 "Civil Liberties to be Guarded by Local Body," *Pittsburgh Press*, October 28, 1928; e.g., "Liberals Hail Victory in Pitt Reappointment," *Pittsburgh Press*, April 17, 1930.

371 Heineman, *Catholic New Deal*, 18.

372 Mark Shields, "Fight Opened on Coal Police Bill - Pittsburghers Hit Musmanno Bill's Clauses," *Pittsburgh Press*, March 19, 1929.

373 "Flying Pastor Tells of Being 'Lost in Air'," *Pittsburgh Press*, March 20, 1929.

374 Musmanno, *Verdict*, 337-39.

375 "Legislative Candidates," *Pittsburgh Press*, May 18, 1930.

376 Musmanno, *Verdict*, 341.

377 Ibid., 343-44.

378 Michael A. Musmanno to Henry Ellenbogen, Esquire, March 26, 1931, The Honorable Michael A. Musmanno Papers, Duquesne University Archives and Special Collections, Pittsburgh, PA.

379 Henry Ellenbogen to M.A. Musmanno, Esq., March 30, 1931, The Honorable Michael A. Musmanno Papers, Duquesne University Archives and Special Collections, Pittsburgh, PA.

380 Musmanno, *Verdict*, 353.

381 Ibid., 354.

382 Ibid., 369.

383 "Tenth Book by Musmanno Ready Soon," *Pittsburgh Press*, May 5, 1957.

384 Devin, *Crucible of Freedom*, 167; "Father James Cox," St. Patrick-St. Stanislaus Kostka Parish, accessed September 26, 2016, http://www.saintsinthestrip.org/5_3_0.html.

385 See Carlos A. Schwantes, *Coxey's Army: An American Odyssey* (Lincoln, NE: University of Nebraska Press, 1985), 2.

386 Heineman, *Catholic New Deal*, 18.

387 Ibid., 19-22; Robert Taylor, "Cox Leads Jobless Army into Washington in Storm," *Pittsburgh Post-Gazette*, January 7, 1932.

388 Devin, *Crucible of Freedom*, 168; Heineman, *Catholic New Deal*, 23-24.

389 "Cox's Jobless Army, Women Plan Meeting," *Pittsburgh Post-Gazette*, January 12, 1932.

390 "Here and There," *Jewish Criterion*, January 15, 1932.

391 "55,000 Rally to Demand U.S. Aid for Needy," *Pittsburgh Press*, January 17, 1932.

392 "Cox Plans to Make Race for President," *Pittsburgh Press*, January 17, 1932.

393 "Here and There," *Jewish Criterion*, January 29, 1932.

394 "Departed Years," *Mt. Washington News* (Pittsburgh), November 13, 1953; "Harry Estep," Allegheny County Bar Association Decedent Files, Allegheny County Bar Association, ACBA Collection.

395 "Here and There," *Jewish Criterion*, February 12, 1932.

396 "Official Convention Guide, The Father Cox Blue Shirts Jobless-Liberty Convention, Creve Coeur, Mo., August 17th - 18th, 1932," Papers of Henry Ellenbogen, Rauh Jewish Archives, Historical Society of Western Pennsylvania, Senator John Heinz Pittsburgh Regional History Center, Pittsburgh, PA.

397 Ann Butler, "In Congress Or Court, Ellenbogen Did it His Way," *Pittsburgh Press*, January 1, 1978.

398 Heineman, *Catholic New Deal*, 29-30.

399 United Press, "Death of James F. Burke Blow to Republican Party," *Evening Times* (Sayre, PA), August 9, 1932.

400 Gerhard Peters and John T. Woolley, "Herbert Hoover: Statement on the Death of James Francis Burke," *The American Presidency Project*, accessed September 26, 2016, http://www.presidency.ucsb.edu/ws/?pid=23197.

401 Heineman, *Catholic New Deal*, 33.

402 Stefano Luconi, "Building a Democratic Machine in Pittsburgh's Italian-American Community," *Pittsburgh History* (Winter 1994/95).

403 "Estep, Campbell, Erk Lose Seats," *Pittsburgh Press*, November 9, 1932.

404 "Judge Ellenbogen, 25 Years On Bench; Made History in 1933," *Jewish Criterion*, January 4, 1963.

405 Stone, *Jews of Capitol Hill*, 141.

406 Butler, "Ellenbogen Did it His Way."

407 79 Cong. Rec. 13,677 (1935);

408 Butler, "Ellenbogen Did it His Way."

409 Stone, *Jews of Capitol Hill*, 142.

410 John C. Fisher, "Wagner Bill Satsifies Both Housing Groups," *Pittsburgh Press*, May 10, 1936.

411 Kaspar Monahan, "Paul Muni Dedicated to the Art of Acting," *Pittsburgh Press*, September 3, 1967;

411 (cont.) Colin Shindler, *Hollywood in Crisis; Cinema and American Society, 1929-1939* (New York: Routledge, 1996), 174-94.

412 "Heinz Leads Gollmar by 4,000 Votes," *Pittsburgh Press*, November 8, 1933.

413 Stone, *Jews of Capitol Hill*, 142; "Democrats Win All Allegheny Congress Jobs," *Pittsburgh Press*, November 7, 1934.

414 Philip Jenkins, *Hoods and Shirts: The Extreme Right in Pennsylvania, 1925-1950* (Chapel Hill: University of North Carolina Press, 2009), 38-39; Demmler, *First Century*, 91.

415 Ibid., 59, 202; George Wolfskill, *The Revolt of the Conservatives: A History of the American Liberty League 1934-1940* (Boston: Houghton Mifflin, 1962), 119.

416 "Black Fury (1935)," *IMDb*, accessed September 27, 2016, http://www.imdb.com/title/tt0026121/.

417 Shindler, *Hollywood in Crsis*, 189.

418 Robert Taylor, "State Tightens Bill Outlawing Coal and Iron Police," *Pittsburgh Press*, February 13, 1935.

419 Ida Cohen Selavan, ed., *My Voice was Heard*, (Jersey City, NJ: Ktav Publishing House, 1981), 194.

420 Ibid.

421 "3 Judgeships Still in Doubt; Ellenbogen Apparently Sure of Post," *Pittsburgh Press*, November 3, 1937; "Jail Shakeup By Democrats Draws Nearer," *Pittsburgh Post-Gazette*, January 4, 1938.

422 "Aides Await New Outbreak in Judge Feud," *Pittsburgh Press*, January 29, 1937.

423 Wolfskill, *Revolt of the Conservatives*, 25.

424 Virginia Gaffney, "Earl F. Reed," May 24, 1989, unpublished profile, private collection of Devon Cross; "Notes from EFR Tapes: about his early life and education," undated/unpublished, private collection of Devon Cross; "Dictated to me by Aunt Orpha, Earl's mother, at 'Buchanan' house about 1945," November 25, 1968, unpblished, private collection of Devon Cross; Austin Vail McClain, "Nemesis of Election Crooks," *The Cross and the Crescent*, March 1934.

425 Bryan Burrough and Udayan Gupta, "Millions ventured, gained, Henry Hillman also has backed big money-losers," *Pittsburgh Post-Gazette*, October 14, 1986.

426 Gaffney, *Earl F. Reed*, 2.

427 Hayllar, "Accommodation," 112-114; "Expect Mayor to Quit Office," *Schenectady Gazette*, March 27, 1933; "Charles H. Kline", *Pennsylvania State Senate*, accessed March 22, 2017, http://www.legis.state.pa.us/cfdocs/legis/BiosHistory/MemBio.cfm?ID=4873&body=S.

428 Hayllar, "Accomodation," 114.

429 Ibid., 112.

430 See, e.g., "Capital Chiefs Ignore Demand on Pennington," *Pittsburgh Post-Gazette*, August 16, 1928; Hayllar, "Accommodation," 125.

431 "Probe North Side Rum Ring," *Pittsburgh Press*, May 9, 1928.

432 Michael P. Weber, *Don't Call Me Boss: David Lawrence, Pittsburgh's Renaissance Mayor* (Pittsburgh: University of Pittsburgh Press, 1988), 32-33.

433 Hayllar, "Accommodation," 137-138.

434 Earl F. Reed, interview by Virginia Gaffney, undated, private collection of Devon Cross.

435 "Mayor Kline, Succop Indictment Ordered in City Supplies Scandal," *Pittsburgh Post-Gazette*, June 25, 1931.

436 Earl F. Reed, interview by Virginia Gaffney, undated, private collection of Devon Cross.

437 "Court Orders Kline's Trial to be Held in Butler County," *Pittsburgh Post-Gazette*, January 20, 1932.

438 Fred H. Kury, "Kline and Succop Guilty in City Supplies Scandal," *Pittsburgh Press*, May 14, 1932.

439 International News Service, "Former Pittsburg Mayor, Charles H. Kline, Dies After Paralytic Stroke," *The Daily Courier* (Connellsville, Pa.), July 22, 1933.

440 "The Kline Verdict," *Pittsburgh Press*, May 15, 1932.

441 John D. Ubinger, "Ernest Tener Weir: Last of the Great Steelmasters (Part 2)," *The Western Pennsylvania Historical Magazine* 58, no. 4 (October 1975), 488.

442 John D. Ubinger, "Ernest Tener Weir: Last of the Great Steelmasters (Part 1)," *The Western Pennsylvania Historical Magazine* 58, no. 3 (July 1975), 294.

443 William C. O'Neil, "Thorp, Reed & Armstrong," memorandum, August 21, 1981, Thorp Reed & Armstrong Collection, Clark Hill PLC, Pittsburgh, PA, 11.

444 O'Neil, "Thorp Reed & Armstrong," 1.

445 Ubinger, "Weir Part 2," 489-91.

446 "The NLB and 'The Old NLRB,'" *National Labor Relations Board*, accessed January 30, 2017, https://www.nlrb.gov/who-we-are/our-history/nlb-and-old-nlrb

447 John Hennen, "E.T. Weir, Employee Representation, and the Dimensions of Social Control: Weirton Steel, 1933-1937," *Labor Studies Journal* (Fall 2001), 28.

448 Ibid., 28-29; Ubinger, "Weir Part 1," 298.

449 James B. Lieber, *Friendly Takeover: How an Employee Buyout Saved a Steel Town* (New York: Viking, 1995), 23-29.

450 Hennen, "Dimensions of Social Control," 26-27; Lou Martin, *Smokestacks in the Hills: Rural-Industrial Workers in West Virginia* (Champaign, IL: University of Illinois Press, 2015), 82; Irving Bernstein, *Turbulent Years: A History of the American Worker 1933-1941* (New York: Houghton Mifflin, 1970), 177.

451 Ubinger, *Weir Part 2*, 493.

452 Bernstein, *Turbulent Years*, 178.

453 "Earl F. Reed's Resignation is Accepted," *Pittsburgh Post-Gazette*, April 6, 1934.

454 Martin, *Smokestacks in the Hills*, 82; U.S. v. Weirton Steel Co., 10 F. Supp. 55 (Del. 1935).

455 Franklin D. Roosevelt, "Creating of the First National Labor Relations Board," Executive Order 6763 (June 29, 1934), accessed February 5, 2017, http://www.presidency.ucsb.edu/ws/?pid=14708; Stanley Vittoz, *New Deal Labor Policy and the American Industrial Economy* (Chapel Hill: University of North Carolina Press, 1987), 144.

456 Richard C. Cortner, *The Jones & Laughlin Case* (New York: Knopf, 1970), 32.

457 Thomas R. Brooks, *Clint: A Biography of a Labor Intellectual, Clinton S. Golden* (New York: Atheneum, 1978), 133.

458 Brooks, *Clint*, 135; Cortner, *Jones & Laughlin*, 33; David H. Wollman, Donald R. Inman, *Portraits in Steel: An Illustrated History of Jones & Laughlin Steel Corporation* (Kent, OH: Kent State University Press, 1999), 100-101.

459 Associated Press, "Missing Laborer Found in Asylum," *Reading Times*, October 25, 1934; Brooks, *Clint*, 135-36.

460 Henry Ellenbogen to M.A. Musmanno, March 30, 1931, The Honorable Michael A. Musmanno Papers, Duquesne University Archives and Special Collections, Pittsburgh, PA.

461 U.S. v. Weirton Steel Co., 10 F. Supp. 55 (Del. 1935).

462 Schechter Poultry Corp. v. United States, 295 U.S. 495 (1935).

463 Franklin D. Roosevelt, "Press Conference," *New Deal Network*, May 31, 1935, accessed February 4, 2017, http://newdeal.feri.org/texts/780.htm ; Burt Solomon, *FDR v. The Constitution* (New York: Walker & Co., 2009), 73.

464 Sheldon Richman, "A Matter of Degree, Not Principle: The Founding of the American Liberty League," *The Journal of Libertarian Studies* VI, no. 2 (Spring 1982), 145-147.

465 Wolfskill, *Revolt of the Conservatives*, 22.

466 Richman, "A Matter of Degree," 145-147; Wolfskill, *Revolt of the Conservatives*, 26.

467 Jouett Shouse, "American Liberty League," August 23, 1934, Jouett Shouse Collection, Public Policy Archives, Division of Special Collections, University of Kentucky Libraries.

468 Ibid.

469 Wolfskill, *Revolt of the Conservatives*, 63; J. Richard Piper, *Ideologies and Institutions: American Conservative and Liberal Governance Prescriptions Since 1933* (Lanham, MD: Rowman & Littlefield, 1997), 70; Jenkins, *Hoods and Shirts*, 59-60.

470 Wolfskill, *Revolt of the Conservatives*, 57.

471 Ewing Laporte, Application for Admission to Allegheny County Bar Association, November 16, 1926, Allegheny County Bar Association Membership Records, Allegheny County Bar Association, ACBA Collection; Letter of Committee on Admissions to Ewing Laporte, Esq., February 22, 1927, Allegheny County Bar Association Membership Records, Allegheny County Bar Association, ACBA Collection; Wolfskill, *Revolt of the Conservatives*, 57; "Laporte Controls Democratic Funds," *Pittsburgh Press*, September 13, 1928; Willard D. Lutt, ed., *History of the Class of Nineteen Hundred and Twenty-One, Yale College* (New Haven, CT: Tuttle Morehouse and Taylor, 1921), 208-209.

472 Wolfskill, *Revolt of the Conservatives*, 57.

473 Senator Robert F. Wagner, Speech on the National Labor Relations Act, on February 21, 1935, 74th Cong., 1st sess., *Congressional Record* 79, pt. 2371-72.

474 American Liberty League, "The Labor Relations Bill: An Analysis of a Measure Which Would do Violence to the Constitution, Stimulate Industrial Strife and Give One Labor Organization a Monopoly in the Representation of Workers Without Regard to the Wishes of the Latter," pamphlet no. 27, April 15, 1935, Jouett Shouse Collection, Public Policy Archives, Division of Special Collections, University of Kentucky Libraries.

475 Frances Perkins and Adam Cohen, *The Roosevelt I Knew* (New York: Penguin, 2011), 226.

476 Associated Press, "Wagner Measure Passes in Senate By Vote of 63-12," *Pittsburgh Post-Gazette*, May 17, 1935.

477 Dennis W. Johnson, *The Laws That Shaped America: Fifteen Acts of Congress and Their Lasting Impact* (New York: Routledge, 2009), 161.

478 J. Warren Madden, "The Origin and Early History of the National Labor Relations Board," *George Washington Law Review* 29 (1960-1961), 234, 241; "New Labour Board Conference Planned," *The Courier-Journal* (Louisville, KY), August 25, 1935.

479 *The Reminiscences of J. Warren Madden* (1957), 72, Oral History Collection, Columbia University, New York, N.Y.

480 Curtis J. Good, "The Dismissal of Ralph Turner: A Historical Case Study of Events at the University of Pittsburgh," *AAUP Journal of Academic Freedom* 3 (2012), 3-4, accessed January 30, 2017, available at https://www.aaup.org/sites/default/files/Good.pdf.

481 Henry Ellenbogen to John G. Bowman, July 9, 1934, Chancellor of the University of Pittsburgh, John Gabbert Bowman, Administrative Files, University of Pittsburgh Archvies.

482 John G. Bowman to Henry Ellenbogen, July 10, 1934. Chancellor of the University of Pittsburgh, John Gabbert Bowman, Administrative Files, University of Pittsburgh Archvies.

483 Peter Adomeit, interview by the author, February 10, 2014.

484 *Reminiscences of J. Warren Madden*, 69.

485 John G. Bowman to E.T. Weir, Esq., March 19, 1934. Chancellor of the University of Pittsburgh, John Gabbert Bowman, Administrative Files, University of Pittsburgh Archvies.

486 *Reminiscences of J. Warren Madden*, 70.

487 *Reminiscences of J. Warren Madden*, 63-66.

488 *Reminiscences of J. Warren Madden*, 66-69.

489 *Reminiscences of J. Warren Madden*, 70-72.

490 *Reminiscences of J. Warren Madden*, 75; Jason Scott Smith, *Building New Deal Liberalism: The Political Economy of Public Works, 1933-1956* (Cambridge: Cambridge University Press, 2006), 198.

491 Cortner, *Jones & Laughlin*, 83.

492 Wolfskill, *Revolt of the Conservatives*, 71; American Liberty League, "National Lawyers Committee, Advisory to the American Liberty League,"

October 15, 1935, Jouett Shouse Collection, Public Policy Archives, Division of Special Collections, University of Kentucky Libraries.

493 Scripps-Howard Newspaper Alliance, "Labor Relations Act Invalid, Says Liberty League 'Court' Ruling," *Pittsburgh Press*, September 19, 1935; "Reed Explains Wagner Stand," *Pittsburgh Press*, September 19, 1935.

494 Scripps-Howard Newspaper Alliance, "Labor Relations Act Invalid, Says Liberty League 'Court' Ruling," *Pittsburgh Press*, September 19, 1935.

495 "Notes and Comment," *United States Law Review* 69, no. 10 (October 1935), 505-506.

496 "A Conspiracy By Lawyers," *The Nation* 141, no. 3665 (October 2, 1935).

497 Ibid.

498 American Liberty League, "Opinion 148 of the Standing Committee on Professional Ethics and Grievances of the American Bar Association," pamphlet no. 79, November, 1935, Jouett Shouse Collection, Public Policy Archives, Division of Special Collections, University of Kentucky Libraries.

499 Wolfskill, *Revolt of the Conservatives*, 73.

500 Appendix to Petition for Writ of Certiorari at 48, National Labor Relations Board v. Jones & Laughlin Steel Corp., 301 U.S. 1 (1937) (No. 419).

501 "Campaign Briefs," *Pittsburgh Press*, May 11, 1934; "Aaron Sapiro," *Wikipedia*, accessed January 30, 2017, https://en.wikipedia.org/wiki/Aaron_Sapiro.

502 "John E. McLaughlin," Allegheny County Bar Association Decedent Files, Allegheny County Bar Association, ACBA Collection; "Donald W. Ebbert," Allegheny County Bar Association Decedent Files, Allegheny County Bar Association, ACBA Collection; 1920 U.S. census, Allegheny County, Pennsylvania, population schedule, Crafton Borough, Ward 1, E.D. No. 73, sheet 25-A, lines 25-28, Donald Ebbert, digital image, *FamilySearch.org*, accessed February 5, 2017, https://familysearch.org/ark:/61903/3:1:33SQ-GRF7-77T?mode=g&cc=1488411; Carl Hellerstedt, interview by the author, November 29, 2010; David L. Robertson and Carl Hellersedt, interview by the author, January 10, 2014.

503 *J&L NLRB Transcript*, 76-81.

504 *J&L NLRB Transcript*, 129-130.

505 Appendix to Petition for Writ of Certiorari at 973-74, National Labor Relations Board v. Jones & Laughlin Steel Corp., 301 U.S. 1 (1937) (No. 419).

506 Louis G. Silverberg, *The Wagner Act: After Ten Years* (Washington, DC: The Bureau of National Affairs, 1945), 39.

507 Peter H. Irons, *The New Deal Lawyers* (Princeton, NJ: Princeton University Press, 1993), 266.

508 Ibid., 262.

509 Ibid., 268.

510 Ibid., 271.

511 Franklin D. Roosevelt, "Acceptance Speech for the Renomination for the Presidency, Philadelphia, Pa., June 27, 1936", *The American Presidency Project*, accessed February 3, 2017, http://www.presidency.ucsb.edu/ws/?pid=15314.

512 E. T. Weir, "I am What Mr. Roosevelt Calls an. Economic Royalist," *Fortune*, Oct. 1936, 118-20.

513 Congressional Quarterly, *Guide to U.S. Elections*, vol. I (Washington: Congressional Quarterly, Inc., 2010), 783; Associated Press, "Roosevelt Wins by Landslide, Carries City, County, State," *Pittsburgh Post-Gazette*, November 4, 1936.

514 "15 Steel Families Gave $5100 to G.O.P.," *Pittsburgh Press*, November 20, 1936.

515 *Reminiscences of J. Warren Madden*, 96-97.

516 Brief for Jones & Laughlin Steel Corporation, National Labor Relations Board v. Jones & Laughlin Steel Corp., 301 U.S. 1 (1937) (No. 419); c.f. Amerlican Liberty League, *National Lawyers Committee*.

517 Ubinger, "Weir Part 2," 493.

518 Franklin D. Roosevelt, "Judicial Branch Reorganization Plan, February 5, 1937," *The Public Papers and Addresses of Franklin D. Roosevelt 1937* (New York City: MacMillan Company, 1941), 51.

519 Franklin D. Roosevelt, "Fireside Chat on Reorganization of the Judiciary," *National Archives Catalog*, March 9, 1937, accessed February 5, 2017, https://catalog.archives.gov/id/197310.

520 "The Referendum on the Supreme Court Question," *Pennsylvania Bar Association Quarterly* 31 (April 1937), 85-92.

521 "Bar Association Vote On Federal Court Plan Certified to Washington," *Pittsburgh Legal Journal* 85-151-176, no. 12, (March 20, 1937), 4-6.

522 United States Supreme Court, *Arguments in the cases arising under the Railway Labor Act and the National Labor Relations Act before the Supreme Court of the United States, February 8-11, 1937* (Washington: Government Printing Office, 1937), 133 ("J&L Oral Argument").

523 *Reminiscences of J. Warren Madden*, 97.

524 *J&L Oral Argument*, 114.

525 Ibid., 118.

526 Ibid., 133.

527 *Reminiscences of J. Warren Madden*, 97.

528 Irons, *New Deal Lawyers*, 283.

529 *J&L Oral Argument*, 133.

530 Ibid., 135.

531 Ibid., 136.

532 Ibid., 141.

533 Ibid., 142.

534 Ibid., 139.

535 "Madden, Reed Debate J. & L. Wagner Case," *Pittsburgh Press*, February 11, 1937.

536 *Reminiscences of J. Warren Madden*, 97-98.

537 West Coast Hotel Co. v. Parrish, 300 U.S. 379 (1937).

538 Associated Press v. Labor Board, 301 U.S. 103 (1937).

539 NLRB v. Jones & Laughlin Steel Corp., 301 U.S. 1 (1937).

540 See, Daniel E. Ho and Kevin M. Quinn, "Did a Switch in Time Save Nine?," *Journal of Legal Analysis* 2, no. 1 (Spring 2010).

541 See, Solomon, *FDR v. Constitution*, 181 ("The Court had expanded its understanding of interstate commerce to take account the world as it was.").

542 Roy Lubove, *Twentieth Century Pittsburgh Volume 1: Government, Business, and Environmental Change* (Pittsburgh: University of Pittsburgh Press, 1996), 5.

543 In the Matter of Weirton Steel Company and Steel Workers Organizing Committee, 32 N.L.R.B. 1145, 1148 (June 25, 1941).

544 "Guide to the Shad Polier Papers, 1916-1976," *American Jewish Historical Society*, accessed February 4, 2017, http://digifindingaids.cjh.org/?pID=616748.

545 "Clyde A. Armstrong," Allegheny County Bar Association Decedent Files, Allegheny County Bar Association, ACBA Collection; Carl Hellerstedt, interview by the author, November 29, 2010.

546 James E. Kopelman, Esq., "Memories of the Early New Kensington Legal Community," *The Sidebar* (Newsletter of the Westmoreland Bar Association) XXI, no. 1 (February 2009), 11. Also, W. Denning Stewart, Thorp's son-in-law, left to practice elsewhere in 1934, necessitating the removal of his name from the firm's style.

547 "The New Deal Dispenses a New Brand of Justice to Labor and Indsutry," *Life*, September 6, 1937.

548 Shad Polier to Justine Wise Polier, June 13, 1938, Shad Polier Papers, American Jewish Historical Society, New York, NY.

549 Ibid.

550 Shad Polier to Stephen Wise, January 29, 1938, Shad Polier Papers, American Jewish Historical Society, New York, NY.

551 Shad Polier to Justine Wise Polier, December 16, 1937, Shad Polier Papers, American Jewish Historical Society, New York, NY.

552 Shad Polier to Justine Wise Polier, February 16, 1938, Shad Polier Papers, American Jewish Historical Society, New York, NY.

553 "Attorney's Fist Fight Climaxes NLRB Case," *Pittsburgh Post-Gazette*, March 30, 1938.

554 Shad Polier to Justine Wise Polier, October 22, 1937, , Shad Polier Papers, American Jewish Historical Society, New York, NY.

555 Shad Polier to Justine Wise Polier, November 18, 1937, Shad Polier Papers, American Jewish Historical Society, New York, NY.

556 Carl Hellerstedt, interview by the author, November 29, 2010.

557 Shad Polier to Justine Wise Polier, January 4, 1938, Shad Polier Papers, American Jewish Historical Society, New York, NY.

558 Shad Polier to Justine Wise Polier, May 6, 1938, Shad Polier Papers, American Jewish Historical Society, New York, NY.

559 "Weirton Lawyer Wouldn't Sit Down, So He's Barred," *Pittsburgh Press*, July 12, 1938.

560 Ibid.

561 "Chief Counsel Ejected After Many Battles," *Pittsburgh Press*, July 11, 1938.

562 Shad Polier to Justine Wise Polier, July 11, 1938, Shad Polier Papers, American Jewish Historical Society, New York, NY.

563 United Press, "NLRB Upholds Ouster of Weirton Co.'s Counsel," *Philadelphia Inquirer*, July 26, 1938.

564 In the Matter of Weirton Steel Company and Steel Workers Organizing Committee, 32 N.L.R.B. 1145 (June 25, 1941).

565 Wolfskill, *Revolt of the Conservatives*, 146-47.

566 Carl Hellerstedt, interview by the author, November 29, 2010.

567 "Earl F. Reed," Allegheny County Bar Association Decedent Files, Allegheny County Bar Association, ACBA Collection; "Attorney Earl Reed Dies of Heart Attack," *Pittsburgh Post-Gazette*, July 11, 1963.

568 *Reminiscences of J. Warren Madden*, 97.

569 Ibid., 122.

570 Ibid., 147.

571 James A. Gross, *The Making of the National Labor Relations Board: A Study in Economics, Politics, and the Law, 1933-1937* (Albany, NY: State University of New York Press, 1974), 23.

572 *Reminiscences of J. Warren Madden*, 102.

573 Allegheny County Bar Association, "Tribute: First One Hundred Women Attorneys in Allegheny County," (banquet program at the William Penn Hotel, April 29, 1992) (cited hereafter as *First 100 Women*); Allegheny County Bar Association, "Tribute to African American Lawyers" (banquet program at the Vista Hotel, February 22, 1995).

574 "Ellen C. Hoge," Allegheny County Bar Association Decedent Files, Allegheny County Bar Association, ACBA Collection; "Waynesburg Woman Admitted to Bar," *Pittsburgh Press*, August 24, 1930; Laura Mallet, "Obituary of Margaret Hoge Jacobs," *Rootsweb PAGREEN-L Archives*, created January 29, 2002, accessed February 5, 2017, http://archiver.rootsweb.ancestry.com/th/read/PAGREENE/2002-01/1012368475; "Rites Slated for Attorney Guy B. Hoge," *Pittsburgh Post-Gazette*, May 16, 1973; *Women Lawyer's Journal* 32-33 (1946), 61; 1940 U.S. census, Allegheny County, Pennsylvania, population schedule, Pittsburgh, Ward 7, E.D. No. 69-153, sheet 4-A, line 5, Ellen C. Hoge, digital image, *FamilySearch.org*, accessed February 5, 2017, https://familysearch.org/ark:/61903/3:1:3QS7-L9MT-R76V?mode=g&i=6&cc=2000219; "Peoples Gas Awards Thirty-Year Pins," *Pittsburgh Press*, July 29, 1951.

575 Ellen Hoge to Miss Josephine McDonagh, July 10, 1956, Allegheny County Bar Association Decedent Files, Allegheny County Bar Association, ACBA Collection.

576 ACBA, *First 100 Women*; "Married Washington Man," *Pittsburgh Post-Gazette*, April 23, 1922.

577 ACBA, *First 100 Women*.

578 "Obituary News; Jacob Soffel," *Pittsburgh Post-Gazette*, October 29, 1931.

579 "Honorable Sara M. Soffel," *Pittsburgh Legal Journal* 124, no. 11 (November 1, 1976), 44-55. Warden Peter K. Soffel (1864-1938) was the son of shoe merchant Peter Soffel (1838-1921), who was the elder brother of Sara Soffel's father, court crier Jacob Soffel (1843-1931). "Germany, Select Births and Baptisms, 1558-1898," index, *Ancestry.com* (http://www.ancestry.com; accessed March 23, 2017), entry for Peter Soffel, born September 26, 1838, FHL film no. 415640; "Germany, Select

Births and Baptisms, 1558-1898," indenx, *Ancestry.com* (http://www.ancestry.com; accessed March 23, 2017), entry for Jacob Soffel, born June 1, 1843, FHL film no. 415641; "The Death Roll - Peter Soffel," *Pittsburgh Gazette Times*, December 4, 1921.

580 "The Biddles Taken," *Scranton Republican*, February 1, 1902; "Kate Soffel Dead; Loved Murderers," *Vicksburg American* (Vicksburg, MP), September 4, 1909.

581 "Honorable Sara M. Soffel," *Pittsburgh Legal Journal* 124, no. 11 (November 1, 1976), 44-55; ACBA, *First 100 Women*.

582 "Wife Shoots Husband in Quarrel at Court House," *Pittsburgh Press*, August 27, 1930; "Miss Sara Soffel Receives Oath Here As Pennsylvania's First Woman Judge," *Pittsburgh Press*, August 27, 1930.

583 "Wife Shoots Her Spouse as Woman Judge Takes Oath," *Daily Notes* (Canonsburg, PA), August 27, 1930.

584 "Honorable Sara M. Soffel," *Pittsburgh Legal Journal* 124, no. 11 (November 1, 1976), 44-55.

585 "Home Problem a Grave One," *Daily Courier* (Connellsville, PA), January 17, 1939.

586 Ibid.

587 ACBA, *First 100 Women*.

588 Anne Weiss, "Her Home's More Important Than Her Profession," *Pittsburgh Press*, July 12, 1933.

589 "Uses Maiden Name at Bar," *The New York Times*, June 10, 1927.

590 Associated Press, "Woman Lawyer Has to Use Hubby's Name," *Morning Herald* (Uniontown, PA), March 28, 1938.

591 Weiss, "Her Home's More Important."

592 1940 U.S. census, Allegheny County, Pennsylvania, population schedule, Pittsburgh, Ward 7, E.D. No. 69-156, sheet 3-B, line 75, Ella Graubert, digital image, *FamilySearch.org*, accessed February 5, 2017, https://familysearch.org/ark:/61903/3:1:3QSQ-G9MT-R72J?mode=g&cc=2000219; ACBA, *First 100 Women*.

593 Ella Graubart, "Allegheny County Bar Association Biographical Questionnaire," 1943, Allegheny County Bar Association Decedent Files, Allegheny County Bar Association, ACBA Collection; "Woman Attorney to Head First Unitarian Church," *Pittsburgh Press*, January 5, 1950; David Nilsson, "Gave Pt. Park $700,000 Gift, Founder Says," *Pittsburgh Press*, May 30, 1973

594 "Obituaries: Mrs. Emily Arensberg," *Pittsburgh Press*, July 30, 1948.

595 Anne Weiss, "Golf Club Reception Follows Attorney's Church Wedding," *Pittsburgh Press*, August 19, 1949; "Wed" (photo caption), *Pittsburgh Sun-Telegraph*, August 19, 1949; "Woman Peeks Behind the Iron Curtain," *Pittsburgh Post-Gazette*, July 14, 1948.

596 "Obituary News - Charles Arensberg, Lawyer, Civic Figure," *Pittsburgh Post-Gazette*, October 29, 1974; "Ella Graubart Arensberg, former city trial lawyer," *Pittsburgh Post-Gazette*, December 30, 1982.

597 Victor Rubin, "Portia from Pittsburgh," *Colliers* (October 26, 1946), 44.

598 1930 U.S. census, Allegheny County, Pennsylvania, population schedule, Pittsburgh, Ward 15, Block 169, E.D. No. 2-242, sheet 54-A, line 9, Anna Alpern, digital image, *FamilySearch.org*, accessed February 5, 2017, https://familysearch.org/ark:/61903/3:1:33S7-9RZ6-K48?mode=g&cc=1810731; Rubin, *Portia from Pittsburgh*, 48; Anne Alpern, Application for Membership to the Allegheny County Bar Association, December 12, 1932, Allegheny County Bar Association Membership Records, Allegheny County Bar Association, ACBA Collection.

599 Jerry Vondas, "Judge Alpern Remains 'Totally Immersed,'" *Pittsburgh Press*, December 18, 1974; George Swetnam, "X Marks the Ballot," *Pittsburgh Press*, December 27, 1953; Rubin, *Portia from Pittsburgh*, 48-49.

600 Bruce M. Stave, *The New Deal and the Last Hurrah: Pittsburgh Machine Politics* (Pittsburgh: University of Pittsburgh Press, 1970), 85-88.

601 Kermit McFarland, "Four Scully Aides Walk Out," *Pittsburgh Press*, August 10, 1934.

602 "McNair Calls Councilmen to O.K. New City Solicitor," *Pittsburgh Press*, August 13, 1934; Swetnam, "X Marks the Ballot."

603 "Ward Bonsall, Lawyer, Dies," *Pittsburgh Post-Gazette*, July 1, 1935; "Grimes Resigns at Request of Mayor M'Nair," *Pittsburgh Post-Gazette*, March 10, 1936; Kermit McFarland, "Council Names Cabinet Aides," *Pittsburgh Press*, September 4, 1936.

604 "Gregory I. Zatkovich (1886-1967)," *Carpatho-Rusyn American* II, no. 3 (1979), accessed January 30, 2017, http://www.carpatho-rusyn.org/fame/zat.htm.

605 Stave, *New Deal and Last Hurrah*, 138; "M'Nair's Decision Not to Quit Causes Nice Legal Muddle," *Niagara Falls Gazette* (Niagara Falls, NY), October 14, 1936.

606 "Scully, Aides Take Oath of Office Monday," *Pittsburgh Press*, January 2, 1938.

607 "Mehard Case Delays Consent Verdict Trials," *Pittsburgh Press*, September 29, 1939; "Gen. Mehard, World War Hero, Dies in Arizona," *Pittsburgh Post-Gazette*, September 14, 1943; United Press, "State Witness Sentenced for Bribe Scandal," *Daily Notes* (Canonsburg, PA), February 8, 1940.

608 Swetnam, "X Marks the Ballot."

609 "City's Portia Will Marry Colleague in New York," *Pittsburgh Press*, June 13, 1937.

610 Swetnam, "X Marks the Ballot."

611 Vince Johnson, "'X' Is Anne Alpern's Secret," *Pittsburgh Post-Gazette*, December 25, 1953; Swetnam, "X Marks the Ballot."

612 "X Marks the Ballot," *Pittsburgh Press*, December 27, 1953.

613 ACBA, *First 100 Women*.

614 "2 Women Pass Bar Entrance Examinations," *Pittsburgh Press*, October 4, 1933; American Law Institute, *Restatement of the Law of Agency* (St. Paul, MN: American Law Institute, 1936).

615 United States Civil Service Commission, *Official Register of the United States* (Washington: Government Printing Office, 1952), 529; *see, e.g.,* National Labor Relations Board v. H.E. Fletcher Co., 108 F.2d 459 (1st Cir. 1939).

616 ACBA, *First 100 Women*.

617 Agnes Dodds Kinard, *At Home with History:*

600 ENDNOTES PART III

What Did I Do With My Life? (Pittsburgh: Geyer Printong Co., 2013), 155; Agnes Dodds Kinard, interview by author, August 26, 2011.

618 ACBA, *First 100 Women.*

619 Associated Negro Press, "Lawyers Warned Against 'High Hat' Attitude As Bar Association Meets," *Pittsburgh Courier*, August 14, 1937.

620 Charles Franklin Lee, "Pittsburgh" in *Organizing Black America*, ed. Nina Mjagkij (New York: Routledge, 2013), 494.

621 Andrew Bunie, *Robert L. Vann of the Pittsburgh Courier: Politics and Black Journalism* (Pittsburgh: University of Pittsburgh Press, 1974), 32.

622 Laurence Glasco, "Double Burden: The Black Experience in Pittsburgh," in *City at the Point*, ed. Samuel P. Hays (Pittsburgh: University of Pittsburgh Press, 1989), 71, 75.

623 Ibid., 73, 88.

624 Ibid., 74.

625 See, R.L. Polk & Co., *Pittsburgh and Allegheny Directory for 1906* (Pittsburgh: R.L. Polk & Co., 1906). All of them except for Billows were still on 4th Avenue by 1916 as well. R.L. Polk & Co., *Pittsburgh and Allegheny Directory for 1916* (Pittsburgh: R.L. Polk & Co., 1916).

626 ACBA, *Tribute to African-Americans.* Professor Robert Strassfeld of Case Western Reserve, among others, has suggested the idea of greater urban integration among white and African American lawyers during this early period. Robert N. Strassfeld, "How the Cleveland Bar Became Segregated: 1870-1930," May 2009, Case Legal Studies Research Paper No. 09-19, accessed February 5, 2017, http://papers.ssrn.com/sol3/papers.cfm?abstract_id=1401434.

627 "Scored by Odd Fellows," *New York Age*, September 23, 1909.

628 Glasco, "Double Burden," 75.

629 Bunie, *Robert L. Vann*, 32; Heineman, *Catholic New Deal*, 78-80.

630 Glasco, "Double Burden," 83.

631 Bunie, *Robert L. Vann*, 99, 123.

632 See, e.g., Pittsburgh and Allegheny Directory, 1929 (R.L. Polk & Co. 1929), 1931 (R.L. Polk & Co. 1931), and 1945 (R.L. Polk & Co., 1945); population figures from Roy Lubove, *Twentieth-Century Pittsburgh, Volume Two: The Post Steel Era* (Pittsburgh: University of Pittsburgh Press, 1996), 154.

633 Bunie, *Robert L. Vann*, 6.

634 Ibid., 9-21, 27-32.

635 Ibid., 34-40.

636 Ibid., 40.

637 Ibid.

638 Ibid., 41.

639 Ibid., 42-49.

640 Henry Lewis Suggs, *The Black Press in the Middle West, 1865-1985* (Santa Barbara, CA: Greenwood, 1996), 40.

641 Bunie, *Robert L. Vann*, 94.

642 Ibid., 95.

643 Ibid., 95-99.

644 Ibid., 99-100.

645 Ibid., 123.

646 "City Solicitors Named; Seven New, Two Holdovers," *Pittsburgh Post-Gazette*, January 17, 1922.

647 Constance A. Cunningham, "Homer S. Brown: First Black Political Leader in Pittsburgh," *The Journal of Negro History* 66, no. 4 (Winter 1981-1982) 304, 304-305; R.L. Polk & Co., *Pittsburgh and Allegheny Directory for 1929* (Pittsburgh: R.L. Polk & Co., 1929), 438.

648 Cunningham, "Homer S. Brown," 305; Joe W. Trotter and Jared N. Day, *Race and Renaissance: African Americans in Pittsburgh since World War II* (Pittsburgh: University of Pittsburgh Press, 2010), 23.

649 Cunningham, "Homer S. Brown," 305.

650 Bunie, *Robert L. Vann*, 178, 184.

651 Ibid., 184-187.

652 Ibid., 191-192.

653 Ibid., 193.

654 Robert L. Vann, "This Year I See Millions of Negroes Turning the Picture of Abraham Lincoln To The Wall", *Pittsburgh Courier*, September 17, 1932.

655 Bunie, *Robert L. Vann*, 194.

656 "An Editorial - And There Stood the One Hundred," *Pittsburgh Courier*, October 8, 1932.

657 "5,000 Negroes In Huge Crowd Which Greets New York Governor Here," *Pittsburgh Courier*, October 22, 1932.

658 Cunningham, "Homer S. Brown," 305-306.

659 Bunie, *Robert L. Vann*, 197.

660 Ibid., 198-199.

661 Roger Applegate, "The Beaver County 'Shanghai'," *Milestones: The Journal of Beaver County History* 35, No. 1 (Winter 2010).

662 Cunningham, "Homer S. Brown," 306; Bunie, *Robert L. Vann*, 199-200.

663 Bunie, *Robert L. Vann*, 200-201.

664 Ibid., 204-206.

665 Ibid., 221; ACBA, *Tribute to African Americans.*

666 Cunningham, "Homer S. Brown," 306-307.

667 Cunningham, "Homer S. Brown," 307; "Pennsylvania Judge is Censured for Praising Lynching From the Bench," *The Crisis*, September 1936.

668 Bunie, *Robert L. Vann*, 285.

669 Ray Sprigle, "Black's Loyalty to Klan Shown in Fervid Pledge," *Pittsburgh Post-Gazette*, September 15, 1937.

670 Bunie, *Robert L. Vann*, 285.

671 Ibid.

672 Ibid., 285-286.

673 Ibid., 321.

674 Cunningham, "Homer S. Brown," 308.

675 P.J. Clyde Randall, Application for Membership to

the Allegheny County Bar Association, December 3, 1926, Allegheny County Bar Association Membership Application Collection, Allegheny County Bar Association, ACBA Collection ; William H. Stanton to Allegheny County Bar Association, March 31, 1927, Allegheny County Bar Association Membership Application Collection, Allegheny County Bar Association, ACBA Collection.

676 Applications for Membership to the Allegheny County Bar Association, dated April 22-29, 1943, Allegheny County Bar Association Membership Application Collection, Allegheny County Bar Association, ACBA Collection.

677 P.J. Clyde Randall, Application for Membership to the Allegheny County Bar Association, August 31, 1945, Allegheny County Bar Association Membership Application Collection, Allegheny County Bar Association, Pittsburgh, PA.

678 "Crowds in Pittsburg Cheer the President," *The New York Times*, July 5, 1902.

679 Theodore Roosevelt, *Message of the President of the United States Communicated to the Two Houses of Congress at the Beginning of the First Session of the Fifty-Seventh Congress* (Washington: Government Printing Offices, 1901), 6-8.

680 U.S. v. E.C. Knight Co., 156 U.S. 1 (1895).

681 Balthasar H. Meyer, *A History of the Northern Securities Case* (Boston: Da Capo, 1972), 15-22; Doris Kearns Goodwin, *The Bully Pulpit: Theodore Roosevelt, William Howard Taft and the Golden Age of Journalism* (New York: Simon & Schuster, 2013), 297-98.

682 William Letwin, *Law and Economic Policy in America: The Evolution of the Sherman Act* (New York: Random House, 1965), 201, fn. 8.

683 Edmund Morris, *The Rise of Theodore Roosevelt* (New York: Random House, 2010), 88-89. Philander Knox was a distant first runner-up on the first and only ballot at the Republican National Convention in 1908 that selected William Howard Taft as the Republican nominee. Knox also pursued the nomination in 1916, but managed to poll only as high as 9th place before the nomination went to U.S. Supreme Court justice Charles Evans Hughes.

684 "J. Pierpont in Song," *The Inter-Ocean* (Chicago), February 16, 1902; "Plays & Players," *Brooklyn Life*, February 8, 1902.

685 Meyer, *History of Northern Securities*, 28-30, 43-44.

686 "To Test N.P. Merger," *New York Tribune*, February 20, 1902; Theodore Roosevelt to Herschel V. Jones, February 26, 1902, reprinted in Elting E. Morison, John M. Blum and Alfred D. Chandler, Jr., *The Letters of Theodore Roosevelt*, vol. 3 (Cambridge, MA: Harvard University Press, 1951), 289.

687 "Knox Suit Hurts Stocks," *New York Tribune*, February 21, 1902.

688 Ron Chernow, *The House of Morgan: An American Banking Dynasty and the Rise of Modern Finance* (New York: Grove, 2010), 106.

689 See, Harbison, *D.T. Watson*, 163; United States v. Northern Securities, 120 F. 721 (D. Minn. 1903).

690 Joseph Bucklin Bishop, *Theodore Roosevelt and His Time, Vol. I* (New York: Charles Scribner's, 1920), 183.

691 Ibid.

692 Harbison, *D.T. Watson*, 159.

693 Ibid., 163.

694 Harbison, *D.T. Watson*, 164-65.

695 Ibid., 163.

696 Ibid., 165.

697 Ibid.

698 D.T. Watson to Philander Knox, March 24, 1903, quoted in Harbison, *D.T. Watson*, 166.

699 "Wall Street on the Decision," *The New York Times*, April 10, 1903.

700 Harbison, *D.T. Watson*, 167.

701 Ibid., 167-168.

702 Ibid., 219-222.

703 Ibid., 224-226.

704 Steve Weinberg, *Taking on the Trust: How Ida Tarbell Brought Down John D. Rockefeller and Standard Oil* (New York: W.W. Norton, 2009), 250.

705 "Standard Controls Oil," *Boston Evening Transcript*, Octber 21, 1905; Weinberg, *Taking on the Trust*, 251.

706 Ron Chernow, *Titan: The Life of John D. Rockefeller, Sr.* (New York: Knopf Doubleday, 2007), 539-541.

707 Standard Oil Co. of Indiana v. United States, 164 F. 376 (7th Cir. 1908).

708 Harbison, *D.T. Watson*, 227-228.

709 Ibid., 230-231.

710 Ibid.

711 Ibid., 231-235.

712 Bernard Schwartz, *A History of the Supreme Court* (New York: Oxford University Press, 1993), 208-209.

713 Chernow, *House of Morgan*, 186.

714 James C. German, Jr., "Taft, Roosevelt, and United States Steel," *The Historian* (August 1972), 598-599.

715 Petition, United States v. United States Steel Corp., No. 6214 (D.N.J. October 29, 1911), in United States Congress, *Report of the Committee on Interstate Commerce, United States Senate, Sixty-Second Congress, pursuant to S. Res. 98, A Resolution Directing the Committee on Interstate Commerce to Investigate and Report Desirable Changes in the Laws Regulating and Controlling Corporations, Persons, and Firms Engaged in Interstate Commerce*, vol. 1 (Washington: Government Printing Office, 1912), 879.

716 German, "Taft, Roosevelt, and United States Steel," 610.

717 Theodore Roosevelt to James R. Garfield, October 31, 1911, reprinted in Elting E. Morison, John M. Blum and Alfred D. Chandler, Jr., *The Letters of Theodore Roosevelt*, vol. 7 (Cambridge, MA: Harvard University Press, 1954), 430-431.

718 Theodore Roosevelt, "The Trusts, The People and The Square Deal," *Outlook* (November 1911).

719 Goodwin, *The Bully Pulpit*, 669-670.

720 Demmler, *First Century*, 66.
721 Ibid.
722 "The U.S. Steel Corporation Dissolution Suit," *The Iron Age*, June 26, 1913.
723 Demmler, *First Century*, 65-67.
724 Ibid., 67; United States v. Unites States Steel Corporation, 251 U.S. 417 (1920).
725 See Henry Greenleaf Pearson, *A Business Man in Uniform, Raynal Cawthorne Bolling* (New York: Duffield, 1923).
726 James Grafton Rogers, *American Bar Leaders: Biographies of the Presidents of the American bar Association, 1878-1928* (Washington, DC: American Bar Association, 1932), 213.
727 United States v. Unites States Steel Corporation, 251 U.S. 417 (1920).
728 Alva Johnston, "A Reporter At Large, Thurman Arnold's Biggest Case - II," *New Yorker*, January 31, 1942; see also George David Smith, *From Monopoly to Competition: The Transformation of Alcoa, 1888-1896* (Cambridge: Cambridge University Press, 1988), 106.
729 Decree, United States v. Aluminum Co. of America, No. 159 (W.D. Pa. 1912).
730 Petition of Defendant for Modification of Decree, United States v. Aluminum Co. of America, No. 159 (W.D. Pa. October 25, 1922); Supplemental Decree, United States v. Aluminum Co. of America, Case No. 159, (W.D. Pa. October 25, 1922).
731 Smith, *From Monopoly to Competition*, 194, 197.
732 Ibid., 196.
733 Ibid., 198.
734 Ibid., 195-196.
735 Ibid., 199.
736 Ibid.
737 Ibid., 196.
738 William J. Kyle, Jr., interview by the author, July 12, 1992.
739 United States v. Aluminum Co. of America, 19 F.Supp. 474 (W.D. Pa. 1937).
740 Paul G. Rodewald, interview by the author, September 5, 1992.
741 United States v. Aluminum Co. of America, 20 F.Supp. 608 (W.D. Pa. 1937).
742 Aluminum Co. of America v. United States, 302 U.S. 230 (1937).
743 "Bioigraphical Directory of Federal Judges: Caffey, Francis Gordon," *Federal Judicial Center*, accessed January 30, 2017, http://www.fjc.gov/servlet/nGetInfo?jid=347&cid=999&ctype=na&instate=na.
744 William J. Kyle, Jr., interview by the author, July 12, 1992.
745 Smith, *From Monopoly to Competition*, p. 206.
746 Transcript of Oral Argument, United States v. Aluminum Co. of America, 1 F. R. D. 48 (S.D.N.Y. June 1-3, 1938).
747 Transcript of Oral Argument, United States v. Aluminum Co. of America, 1 F. R. D. 48 (S.D.N.Y. June 6, 1938).
748 Ibid.
749 Ibid.
750 Alva Johnston, "A Reporter At Large, Thurman Arnold's Biggest Case - I," *New Yorker*, January 24, 1942, 28.
751 Smith, *From Monopoly to Competition*, 196.
752 Johnston, *Thurman Arnold's Biggest Case*, 28.
753 Ibid.
754 Charles C. Carr, *Alcoa: An American Enterprise* (New York: Rinehart & Co., 1952), 219.
755 Johnston, *Thurman Arnold's Biggest Case*, 25.
756 United States v. Aluminum Co. of America, 44 F.Supp. 97 (S.D. NY 1941).
757 Smith, *From Monopoly to Competition*, 207.
758 Spencer Weber Waller, *Thurman Arnold: A Biography* (New York University Press, 2005), 94.
759 Smith, *From Monopoly to Competition*, 207.
760 United States v. Aluminum Co. of Alcoa, 148 F.2d 416 (2d Cir. 1945).
761 Smith, *From Monopoly to Competition*, 211.
762 Alan Greenspan, *Antitrust* (New York: Nathaniel Branden Institute, 1962), 8.
763 Smith, *From Monopoly to Competition*, 271; "U.S. Presses for Decision on Alco Suit," *Geneva Daily Times* (Geneva, NY), March 30, 1949.
764 United States v. Aluminum Co. of America, 91 F.Supp. 333 (S.D. NY 1950).
765 Ann Rodgers-Melnick, "Leon Hickman: Lawyer whose life was suffused with Methodism," *Pittsburgh Post-Gazette*, June 15, 1999.
766 "Obituaries: William K. Unverzagt," *Pittsburgh Post-Gazette*, March 13, 1989.
767 United States v. Aluminum Co. of America, 153 F.Supp. 132 (S.D. NY 1957).
768 Smith, *From Monopoly to Competition*, 213.
769 Thomas M. Thompson, note to the author, April 28, 2014.

ENDNOTES PART IV

1. John Bodnar, Roger Simon and Michael P. Weber, *Lives of Their Own: Blacks, Italians and Poles in Pittsburgh, 1900-1960* (Champaign, IL: University of Illinois Press, 1983), 185.

2. Michael Weber, *Don't Call Me Boss: David L. Lawrence, Pittsburgh's Renaissance Mayor* (Pittsburgh: University of Pittsburgh Press, 1988), 46.

3. Historic American Engineering Record, *Pittsburgh Industrial District, World War II Structures, Pittsburgh, Allegheny County, PA*, HAER No. 343, 7-9, accessed March 9, 2017, https://www.loc.gov/item/pa3159. Lubove, *Twentieth-Century Pittsburgh I*, 63. See also Stefan Lorant, *Pittsburgh: The Story of an American City* (Pittsburgh: Esselmont, 1999), 306-307, 327-328.

4. "Skyscrapers in Pittsburgh," *The Brookline Connection*, accessed April 27, 2016, http://www.brooklineconnection.com/history/Facts/Skyscraper6th.html

5. Bodnar, Simon and Weber, *Lives of Their Own*, 185.

6. Brignano and Fort, *Reed Smith: 125 Years*, 72, 91.

7. Judge Joseph F. Weis, Jr. interview by the author, July 29, 2011.

8. Torsten Ove, "Joseph F. Weis Jr. - Judge celebrated in court, on battlefield," *Pittsburgh Post-Gazette*, March 19, 2014.

9. Judge Joseph F. Weis, Jr. interview by the author, July 29, 2011.

10. Based on review of Sell, *The Law Down*, 243-246; Center for Legal Information, Duque0sne Law Graduates, 1914-2005, Excel compilation, Duquesne Law School, 2015; Allegheny County Prothonotary, *List of Attorneys and Law Students, 1788-1981*, vol. 1, Pennsylvania State Archives, Records of County Governments, no. 47.4, LR 289.

11. John M. Feeney, interview by the author, September 22, 2008.

12. Sell, *The Law Down*, 70-71.

13. Allegheny County Prothonotary, *List of Attorneys and Law Students, 1788-1981*, vol. 1, Pennsylvania State Archives, Records of County Governments, no. 47.4, LR 289.

14. John M. Feeney, interview by the author, September 22, 2008.

15. "James P. McArdle, 59; Funeral is Tomorrow," *Pittsburgh Post-Gazette*, April 21, 1969.

16. John M. Feeney, interview by the author, September 22, 2008.

17. David B. Fawcett, Jr., interview by the author, September 12, 2008.

18. Judge Joseph F. Weis, Jr., interview by the author, July 29, 2011.

19. John M. Feeney, interview by the author, September 22, 2008.

20. David B. Fawcett, Jr., interview by the author, September 12, 2008.

21. Judge Joseph F. Weis, Jr., interview by the author, July 29, 2011.

22. Judd N. Poffinberger, Jr., interview by the author, November 14, 2008.

23. Judge Joseph F. Weis, Jr., interview by the author, July 29, 2011.

24. "Judge Weis Reminisces About Academy of Trial Lawyers 25th Anniversary Here," *Pittsburgh Legal Journal* 132, no. 5 (May 1, 1984) 3.

25. Sam Hood, "Consolidate Trial Courts - Ellenbogen," *Pittsburgh Press*, June 22, 1958.

26. Judge Joseph F. Weis, Jr., interview by the author, July 29, 2011; *Judge Weis Reminisces*, 3.

27. Judge Joseph F. Weis, Jr., interview by the author, July 29, 2011; *Judge Weis Reminisces*, 4.

28. Seymour Sikov, interview by the author, September 19, 2008.

29. Judge Joseph F. Weis, Jr., interview by the author, July 29, 2011.

30. *Judge Weis Reminisces*, 8.

31. Seymour Sikov, interview by the author, September 19, 2008.

32. Brunwasser v. Suave, 400 F.2d 600 (4th Cir. 1968).

33. Brunwasser v. Trans World Airlines, Inc., 518 F.Supp. 1321 (W.D. Pa. 1981).

34. Al Donalson, "City Law Firm Illegal, Brunwasser Contends," *Pittsburgh Press*, October 8, 1978.

35. E.J. Strassburger and Judge Eugene B. Strassburger, III, interview by the author, September 14, 2010.

36. Thomas M. Hritz, "Jail Failed to Ground Legal Eagle Brunwasser," *Pittsburgh Post-Gazette*, September 30, 1977.

37. Judge Joseph F. Weis, Jr., interview by the author, July 29, 2011.

38. Thomas M. Hritz, "Jail Failed to Ground Legal Eagle Brunwasser," *Pittsburgh Post-Gazette*, September 30, 1977.

39. Judge Joseph F. Weis, Jr., interview by the author, July 29, 2011; *Judge Weis Reminisces*, p. 10.

40. Allegheny County Bar Association, *Bench-Bar Conference of the Allegheny County Bar Association: A Step Back Into History* (Pittsburgh: ACBA Services, Inc., 2004), DVD (hereafter cited as *Bench-Bar Video*).

41. Allegheny County Bar Association, *Lawyers Pictorial Register*, 5th ed. (Pittsburgh: Allegheny County Bar Association, 1980, 21, 24.

42. "Legal Journal Gets New Owner," *Pittsburgh Press*, September 30, 1962.

43. Katarincic, "Allegheny County Bar Association," 343.

44. Seymour Sikov (eulogy, Memorial Service to Acknowledge the Passing of James I. Smith, III, April 21, 2006, Allegheny County Bar Association, Pittsburgh, PA).

45   Arthur Ignatius Judge, *A History of the Canning Industry* (Baltimore: Canning Trade, 1914), 23; Lawrence Walsh, "Obituary: James Ignatius Smith III, Allegheny County Bar Association longtime director," *Pittsburgh Post-Gazette*, February 14, 2006.

46   Lawrence Walsh, "Obituary: James Ignatius Smith III, Allegheny County Bar Association longtime director," *Pittsburgh Post-Gazette*, February 14, 2006.

47   Robert G. Sable, interview by the author, July 21, 2008.

48   Bench-Bar Video.

49   David B. Fawcett, memorandum to author, September 11, 2008 (hereafter cited as *DBF memo*); David B. Fawcett, Jr., interview by the author, September 4, 2008.

50   DBF memo.

51   David B. Fawcett, interview by the author, September 4, 2008.

52   DBF memo; David B. Fawcett, Jr., Correspondence File, Allegheny County Bar Association Activities (1965), author's collection.

53   Gideon v. Wainright, 372 US 335 (1963).

54   "Public Defender Bill for County Signed," *Pittsburgh Press*, June 15, 1965.

55   "Ross Named Public Defender for County," *Pittsburgh Press*, October 19, 1965.

56   Richard L. Thornburgh, interview by the author, May 21, 2009; Pennsylvania Constitutional Convention, *Debates of the Pennsylvania Constitutional Convention of 1967-68*, vol. 1 (Harrisburg: Pennsylvania Constitutional Convention, 1969).

57   Richard L. Thornburgh, interview by the author, May 21, 2009.

58   Earl Johnson, Jr., "A Momentous Event in Legal Services History: ABA's 1965 Endorsement of the Federal Legal Services Program," *Right On* (blog), Georgetown Law Library, February 27, 2015, https://blogs.commons.georgetown.edu/righton/2015/02/27/a-momentous-event-in-legal-services-history-abas-1965-endorsement-of-the-federal-legal-services-program/

59   "Legal Aid Societies' National Convention," *Pittsburgh Post-Gazette*, November 1, 1911.

60   Neighborhood Legal Services Association, *Lighting the Torch: The Architects of Equal Access, Champions of Justice: A Special Tribute to our ACBA colleagues* (Pittsburgh: Neighborhood Legal Services Association, 2010), 2.

61   *Lighting the Torch*, 1-2; David B. Fawcett, interview by the author, September 2, 2008.

62   Judge Livingstone M. Johnson, interview by the author, August 2, 2011.

63   Wendell Freeland, interview by the author, September 18, 2008.

64   NLSA, *Lighting the Torch*, 2.

65   David B. Fawcett, interview by the author, September 4, 2008

66   Justin Johnson, "The African-American Judge and the Rights of the Poor," *Pennsylvania Legal Services Review* (1993), quoted in "Thompson's Corner: A Different Look at John G. Buchanan," *The* (Buchanan Ingersoll) *Bugle* (March 4, 1994), 12.

67   David B. Fawcett, interview by the author, September 4, 2008

68   Johnson, *The African-American Judge*.

69   NLSA, *Lighting the Torch*, 4.

70   John P. Hoerr, *And the Wolf Finally Came: The Decline of the American Steel Industry* (Pittsburgh: University of Pittsburgh Press, 1988), 14.

71   Margaret Cowell, *Dealing with Deindustrialization: Adaptive Resilience in American Midwestern Regions* (London: Routledge, 2014), 54; Bill Toland, "Nowhere But Up," *Pittsburgh Post-Gazette*, January 6, 2013.

72   Dr. Joseph F. Rishel, *Pittsburgh Remembers World War II* (Stroud, UK: History Press, 2011), 13.

73   Leo Troy, *Trade Union Membership, 1897-1962* (New York: National Bureau of Economic Research, 1965), 1.

74   Jeremy Brecher, *Strike!* (Cambridge, MA: South End, 1997), 245-246.

75   Raymond L Hogler, *Employment Relations in the United States: Law, Policy, and Practice* (Thousand Oaks, CA: Sage, 2004), 146.

76   Brignano and Fort, *Reed Smith: 125 Years*, 82.

77   Nicholas Unkovic, interview by Dodie Carpenter, April 17, 1973, transcript, series I, box 3, vol. S-V, p. 2084, Pittsburgh Renaissance Project: The Stanton Belfour Oral History Collection, AIS.1973.24, Archives Service Center, University of Pittsburgh; Center for Legal Information, Duquesne Law Graduates, 1914-2005, Excel compilation, Duquesne Law School, 2015.

78   Charles R. "Dick" Volk and David L. Robertson, interview by the author, August 20, 2012.

79   "Nicholas Unkovic, 77, dies, noted city lawyer," *Pittsburgh Post-Gazette*, October 25, 1983.

80   Demmler, *First Century*, 161-164.

81   Charles R. "Dick" Volk and David L. Robertson, interview by the author, August 20, 2012.

82   Garth L. Mangum and R. Scott McNabb, *The Rise, Fall, and Replacement of Industrywide Bargaining in the Basic Steel Industry* (Armonk, NY: M.E. Sharpe, 1997), 78; Steelworkers v. United States, 361 US 39 (1959).

83   Paula Reed Ward, "Obituary: Leonard L. Scheinholtz, Successful labor law attorney who helped develop Reed Smith into global force," *Pittsburgh Post-Gazette*, July 21, 2014.

84   Mangum and McNabb, *Rise, Fall, and Replacement*, 10.

85   Wiliam Jacobs, "The Story of Teamsters Local 249," *Pittsburgh Press*, October 21, 1951.

86 "Obituaries: Ben Paul Jubelirer," *Pittsburgh Press*, September 13, 1983; Joseph J. Pass, Jr., interview by the author, April 7, 2014.

87 Carl H. Hellerstedt, Jr., interview by the author, April 3, 2014; Wiliam Jacobs, "The Story of Teamsters Local 249," *Pittsburgh Press*, October 21, 1951.

88 Joseph J. Pass, Jr., interview by the author, April 7, 2014.

89 Joe Grata, "Port Authority budget running on fumes," *Pittsburgh Post-Gazette*, June 21, 2008.

90 Ibid.

91 Jim McKay, "From rhetoric to reality: Unions knock out Press," *Pittsburgh Post-Gazette*, January 18, 1993.

92 Joseph J. Pass, Jr., interview by the author, April 7, 2014.

93 Ibid.

94 See, e.g., Thomas D. Morgan, "Where Do We Go from Here with Fee Schedules?," *ABA Journal*, December 1973.

95 Ibid.

96 Robert B. Wolf, interview by the author, November 16, 2010.

97 Carpenter inteviews Unkovic, 2084.

98 "Remarks of Ralph H. Demmler in the Court of Common Pleas of Allegheny County in memory of Nicholas Unkovic, delivered November 22, 1983," 3, Allegheny County Bar Association Decedent Files, Allegheny County Bar Association, ACBA Collection.

99 Robert G. Sable, interview by the author, July 21, 2008.

100 Brignano and Fort, *Reed Smith: 125 Years*, 134-136.

101 Dan Majors, "Obituary: M. Bruce McCullough, Bankruptcy judge credited with keeping Penguins in city," *Pittsburgh Post-Gazette*, November 24, 2010.

102 See, e.g., R.L. Polk & Co., Pittsburgh and Allegheny Directory for 1916 (Pittsburgh: R.L. Polk & Co., 1916), 2844-2845.

103 Eckert Seamans, *Eckert Seamans: Celebrating 50 Years of Service* (privately printed, 2008), 14.

104 Audrey Glickman, "History of the Firm (From Moses to Newlin)," *The* (Buchanan Ingersoll) *Bugle* (May 31, 1991), 13.

105 William H. Logsdon and Russell D. Orkin, interview by the author, January 30, 2009.

106 Paraphrased from Brignano and Fort, *Reed Smith: 125 Years*, 141 ("In Dan Booker's word, the firm 'delocalized.'").

107 Judd N. Poffinberger, Jr., "Kirkpatrick & Lockhart's Firm History, The Early Years" (lecture, Pittsburgh, PA, September 19, 1986).

108 Brignano and Fort, *Reed Smith: 125 Years*, 140-142.

109 Carl H. Hellerstedt, Jr., email to author, May 28, 2015.

110 "Sears Leaves Firm Here to Lead Reagan Drive," *Pittsburgh Press*, March 4, 1979; Audrey Glickman, *History of the Firm*, 13.

111 "2 Law Firms in Merger," *Pittsburgh Press*, November 11, 1981.

112 Terry Bivens, "2 Lawyers confirm they've left Dilworth Paxson," *Philadelphia Inquirer*, March 14, 1986; Audrey Glickman, *History of the Firm*, 13.

113 Carl H. Hellerstedt, Jr., email to author, May 28, 2015; James Warren, Brian Kelly and Joseph Tybor, "Not too bad, for a part-time lawyer from 35th Street," *Chicago Tribune*, July 10, 1984.

114 Audrey Glickman, *History of the Firm*, 13.

115 David Ranii, "Outside law firms don't come courting in Pittsburgh," *Pittsburgh Press*, November 17, 1987.

116 Joyce Gannon, "A Firm Hand," *Pittsburgh Post-Gazette*, June 7, 2006.

117 "Company notes," *Pittsburgh Post-Gazette*, April 8, 1986.

118 H.H. Brackenridge, *Law Miscellanies* (Philadelphia, P. Byrne, 1814), xx.

119 George Sharswood, *An Essay on Professional Ethics*, 3rd ed. (Philadelphia: T. & J.W. Johnson, 1869), 160-64.

120 Nikita Malhotra Pastor, "Equity and Settlement Class Actions: Can There Be Justice For All in Ortiz v. Fireboard," *American University Law Review* 49, no. 3 (2000), 786.

121 In re Agent Orange Products Liability Litigation, 506 F.Supp. 737 (E.D. NY 1979), rev'd, 635 F.2d 987 (2d Cir. 1980), cert. denied, 454 U.S. 1128 (1981); see Robert F. Blonquist, "American Toxic Tort Law: An Historical Background, 1979-87," *Pace Environmental Law Review* 10 (1992), 85.

122 John P. Gismondi, interview by the author, October 26, 2012.

123 Judge Lawrence W. Kaplan (remarks, 50 and 60 Year Practitioners Award Ceremony, Duquesne Club, Pittsburgh, PA, December 1, 2014).

124 Brignano and Fort, *Reed Smith: 125 Years*, 79.

125 Bates v. State Bar of Arizona, 433 U.S. 350 (1977).

126 Edgar M. Snyder, interview by the author, December 16, 2008.

127 Ibid.

128 Ibid.

129 Ibid.

130 "Power of Attorney: Buchanan Ingersoll's Rise to Become Pittsburgh's Second Largest Law Firm Was Strictly Unorthodox," *Executive Report*, May 1987, 19.

131 Buchanan Ingersoll Operating Committee to Attorneys, memorandum re: Brochure, January 26, 1984, Buchanan Ingersoll & Rooney collection, Pittsburgh, PA.

132 Steven Brill, "Tin Rhetoric, High Gloss," *The American Lawyer* (April 1984), 1.

133 Ibid., at 1, 10.

134 William R. Newlin, interview by the author, February 12, 2014.

135 See, e.g., David Ranii, "Administrators keep lawyers on track," *Pittsburgh Press*, May 17, 1987.

136 Richard Boyer and David Savageau, *Places Rated Almanac*, (Chicago: Rand McNally, 1985).

137 Leland Hazard, *Attorney for the Situation* (New York: Columbia University Press 1975), 26-27; 40-128; Leland Hazard, Application for Admission to Allegheny County Bar Association, Allegheny County Bar Association, March 20, 1940.

138 Arthur B. Van Buskirk, Short Biographical Questionnaire, Allegheny County Bar Association, November 24, 1944; "Van Buskirk Firm Dates Back 76 Years," *Pottstown Mercury*, June 19, 1937; "Obituaries: Mrs. Florence (McKinley) Van Buskirk," *Pottstown Mercury*, December 6, 1945.

139 Hazard, *Attorney for the Situation*, 131.

140 Anthony N. Penna, "Changing Images of Twentieth-Century Pittsburgh," *Pennsylvania History* 43, no. 1 (January 1976), 57. See, in particular, footnote 33, stating "Aerial photographs of Pittsburgh taken in 1936 and 1944 by Margaret Bourke-White for *Life* magazine depicted the smoky conditions of the city."

141 Lubove, *Twentieth-Century Pittsburgh II*, 106-107, 112 (photo), 119-120; Demmler, *First Century*, 165.

142 James A. Baubie, "Flings Sneers at Pittsburgh," *Pittsburgh Sun-Telegraph*, June 24, 1935; "City Target of Architect," *Pittsburgh Post-Gazette*, July 1, 1935.

143 Lubove, *Twentieth-Century Pittsburgh I*, 106-107, quoting Adolph W. Schmidt, *The Pittsburgh Story* (booklet, remarks at luncheon in honor of International Press Institute at University of Pittsburgh, April 19, 1958).

144 Olivier Zunz, *Philanthropy in America: A History* (Princeton, NJ: Princeton University Press, 2014), 8.

145 Andrew Carnegie, *The Autobiography of Andrew Carnegie and the Gospel of Wealth* (New York: Penguin, 2006), 333.

146 "Philanthropy of Andrew Carnegie," *Columbia University Libraries*, accessed March 10, 2017, http://library.columbia.edu/locations/rbml/units/carnegie/andrew.html; Florence Anderson, *Carnegie Corporation Library Program, 1911-1961* (New York: Carnegie Corporation of New York, 1963), 57.

147 Martin Morse Wooster, "Henry Phipps Jr.," *Philanthropy Roundtable: Philanthropy Hall of Fame*, accessed March 10, 2017, http://www.philanthropyroundtable.org/almanac/hall_of_fame/henry_phipps_jr.

148 Skrabec, *Frick*, 194.

149 Skrabec, *Gentle Genius*, 152, 214.

150 Fleming, *History of Pittsburgh and Environs*, 640.

151 C. Evan Stewart, "The Man Nobody Knew," *New York Archives*, Summer 2009, 9 (regarding Myron Taylor's early career); Daniel F. Cuff, "Roger M. Blough, 81, Dies; Led U.S. Steel for 13 Years," *The New York Times*, October 10, 1985; "Brown, Clarence Montgomery," *Who Was Who in America (1951-1960)*, vol. 3 (Chicago, IL: A.N. Marquis & Co., 1960), 109; Gwilym A. Price, "Allegheny County Bar Association Biographical Questionnaire," undated, Allegheny County Bar Association Decedent Files, Allegheny County Bar Association, ACBA Collection; "Obituaries: Philip Fleger, 90, former chairman of Duquesne Light," *Pittsburgh Post-Gazette*, November 17, 1993; "Funeral Set Today for Robert C. Downie," *Pittsburgh Post-Gazette*, March 15, 1965.

152 Hazard, *Attorney for the Situation*, 133, 142-44.

153 Leon E. Hickman, "The Emerging Role of the Corporate Counsel," *Business Law* 12 (April 1957), 217; Leon E. Hickman, "The Need and Utilization of Retained Counsel," *Proceedings of Wisconsins Fifth Annual House Counsel Institute* (July 27-28, 1959), 3.

154 Hickman, *Need and Utilization of Retain Counsel*, 3.

155 Arthur Van Buskirk, interview by J. Cutler Andrews, October 28, 1971, transcript, series I, box 3, vol. S-V, p. 2097, Pittsburgh Renaissance Project: The Stanton Belfour Oral History Collection, AIS.1973.24, Archives Service Center, University of Pittsburgh.

156 Hazard, *Attorney for the Situation*, 235.

157 Andrews interviews Van Buskirk, 2097.

158 Randall Bennett Woods, *A Changing of the Guard: Anglo-American Relations, 1941-1946* (Chapel Hill, NC: University of North Carolina Press, 1990), 175 (regarding Oscar Cox's efforts); Richard A. Falk, Rosalyn C. Higgins, W. Michael Reisman, and Burns H. Weston, "Myres Smith McDougal (1906-1998)," *American Journal of International Law* 92, no. 4 (October 1998), 730; "George Ball, Fought Vietnam Policy Under Kennedy, LBJ," *Los Angeles Times*, May 28, 1994; Adam Bernstein, "Consummate Lawyer Played Array of Roles," *Washington Post*, May 9, 2005 (regarding Lloyd Cutler); Wolfgang Saxon, "Joseph Rauh Jr., Groundbreaking Civil Liberties Lawyer, Dies at 81," *The New York Times*, September 5, 1992; Boris Bittker, "Eugene V. Rostow," *Yale Law Journal* 94, no. 6 (May 1985), 1317-1317; Gray Thoron, "Robert Sproule Stevens," *Cornell Law Review* 54, no. 3 (February 1969).

159 Andrews interviews Van Buskirk, 2097-2098.

160 Hazard, *Attorney for the Situation*, 218.

161 Andrews interviews Van Buskirk, 2098.

162 David L. Lawrence, "Rebirth," in *Pittsburgh: The Story of an American City*, ed. Stefan Lorant (Esselmont, 1999), 381, 383-384; Weber, *Don't Call Me Boss*, 233-234.

163 Lawrence, *Rebirth*, 385.

164 Weber, *Don't Call Me Boss*, 236.

165 Ibid.

166 Ibid., at 237.

167 Ibid.

168 Hazard, *Attorney for the Situation*, 235-236.
169 Lawrence, *Rebirth*, 409.
170 Lubove, *Twentieth-Century Pittsburgh I*, 109, fn. 9; Hazard, *Attorney for the Situation*, 233.
171 Andrews interviews Van Buskirk, 2098-2099.
172 Weber, *Don't Call Me Boss*, 255.
173 "Fine New Buildings Are Included in Giant Plan To Redevelop Area Adjacent To Park at The Point," *Pittsburgh Press*, May 26, 1946; Andrews interviews Van Buskirk, 2100.
174 Weber, *Don't Call Me Boss*, 256; Lawrence, *Rebirth*, 428; Andrews interviews Van Buskirk, 2100.
175 Lawrence, *Rebirth*, 423.
176 Theodore Hazlett, interview by Joel Tarr, November 22, 1971, transcript, series I, box 1, vol. Gi-Haz, p. 926-928, Pittsburgh Renaissance Project: The Stanton Belfour Oral History Collection, AIS.1973.24, Archives Service Center, University of Pittsburgh.
177 "Theodore Hazlett Jr., 60, Guide in City Renaissance," *Pittsburgh Post-Gazette*, July 9, 1979; Tarr interviews Hazlett, 927.
178 Lubove, *Twentieth-Century Pittsburgh I*, 121-122.
179 Tarr interviews Hazlett, 929-31; Weber, *Don't Call Me Boss*, 250; "An Angle on City Taxes," *Pittsburgh Press*, March 12, 1947.
180 Tarr interviews Hazlett, 928-929.
181 Cunningham, *Homer S. Brown*, 308-310.
182 Lawrence, *Rebirth*, 426-427.
183 Andrews interviews Van Buskirk, 2100-2101; Lawrence, *Rebirth*, 428-430.
184 Andrews interviews Van Buskirk, 2101-2102.
185 See Plaintiff's Reply Brief to Defendants' Motion to Affirm Order of the United States District Court for the Western District of Pennsylvania, Burt v. City of Pittsburgh, 1950 WL 78381 (1950).
186 Belovsky v. Redevelopment Authority of Philadelphia, 357 Pa. 329 (Pa. 1947).
187 Gregory J. Crowley, *The Politics of Place: Contentious Urban Redvelopment in Pittsburgh* (Pittsburgh: University of Pittsburgh Press, 2005), 55.
188 Demmler, *First Century*, 165.
189 Schenck v. City of Pittsburgh, 364 Pa. 31 (1950); Demmler, *First Century*, 167.
190 Demmler, *First Century*, 165.
191 Rachel Baillet Colker, "Gaining Gateway Center: Eminent Domain, Redevelopment, and Resistance," *Pittsburgh History* 78, no. 3 (Fall 1995), 143-144; Plaintiff's Reply Brief to Defendants' Motion to Affirm Order of the United States District Court for the Western District of Pennsylvania, Burt v. City of Pittsburgh, 1950 WL 78381 (1950); for information about attorneys Morcroft, Arnd and Danahey, see Allegheny County Bar Association Decedent Files, Allegheny County Bar Association, ACBA Collection.
192 "Dedication of Fountain Icing on City's Renewal," *Pittsburgh Post-Gazette*, August 31, 1974.
193 Hazard, *Attorney for the Situation*, 240.
194 Lubove, *Twentieth-Century Pittsburgh I*, 124-126, 128, 131.
195 Karl Schriftgiesser, "The Pittsburgh Story," *The Atlantic*, May 1951, 69.
196 Hazard, *Attorney for the Situation*, 240-241.
197 "Pittsburgh and 'Culture,'" *Pittsburgh Post-Gazette*, September 18, 1952.
198 Hazard, *Attorney for the Situation*, 243.
199 Sterling P. Anderson, "The Best Is Yet to Come, City Planners Report," *Pittsburgh Post-Gazette*, September 16, 1952; Hazard, *Attorney for the Situation*, 243.
200 Hazard, *Attorney for the Situation*, 244.
201 Ibid., at 245-246.
202 Ibid. at 246.
203 "Jack McGregor," *Who's Who in Finance and Industry*, vol. 22 (Chicago: A.N. Marquis & Co., 1981), 438.
204 Hazard, *Attorney for the Situation*, 246.
205 James Roman, Love, *Light, and a Dream: Television's Past, Present, and Future* (Westport, CT: Praeger, 1996), 196; Hazard, *Attorney for the Situation*, 248.
206 "Educational Television," *The Atlantic*, November 1955; "Educational TV, and How It's Coming," *The Kiplinger Magazine*, July 1954.
207 Hazard, *Attorney for the Situation*, 248.
208 Hazard, *Attorney for the Situation*, 248-250; Benjamin H. Simmons, "WQED: We're All In This Together," *Pennsylvania Center for the Book*, accessed March 9, 2017, http://pabook2.libraries.psu.edu/palitmap/WQED.html
209 Hazard, *Attorney for the Situation*, 247.
210 Ibid.
211 Ibid., at 250; *Educational TV, and How It's Coming*, 33.
212 Hazard, *Attorney for the Situation*, 255; Margaret Mary Kimmel and Mark Collins, *The Wonder of it All: Fred Rogers and the Story of an Icon* (Latrobe, PA: Fred Rogers Center, 2008).
213 Hazard, *Attorney for the Situation*, 255.
214 Ibid., at 233.
215 Arthur B. Van Buskirk, "Responsibilities of American Business Leaders," *Vital Speeches of the Day*, vol. 25, no. 22 (September 1, 1959), 692.
216 Leon E. Hickman, interview by Dan Straub, November 29, 1972, transcript, series I, box 2, vol. He-Love, p. 1000, Pittsburgh Renaissance Project: The Stanton Belfour Oral History Collection, AIS.1973.24, Archives Service Center, University of Pittsburgh.
217 Leon E. Hickman, "No Man Is An Island: Basic Characteristics in Business Organizations," *Vital Speeches of the Day* 23, no. 21 (August 1957), 667-669.

218 Straub interviews Hickman, 1001-1002.

219 United States v. Aluminum Company of America, 233 F.Supp. 718 (E.D. Mo. 1964).

220 Leon E. Hickman, "Alcoa Looks at Urban Redevelopment" (address, National Mortgage Banking Conference, Mortgage Bankers Association of America, February 17, 1964, Conrad Hilton Hotel, Chicago, IL).

221 Ibid.

222 William Allan, "Renew Upper Hill, City Planners Told," *Pittsburgh Press*, May 14, 1961.

223 William J. Mallett, "The Lower Hill Renewal and Pittsburgh's Original Cultural District," *Pittsburgh History* 75, no. 4 (Winter 1992-1993), 186.

224 Ibid., 186-187.

225 Frank Hawkins, "Development Report on Allegheny Center," *Pittsburgh Post-Gazette*, July 21, 1969; Justin Streiner, "Allegheny Center Mall: Pittsburgh, PA," January 13, 2010, www.deadmalls.com/malls/allegheny_center_mall.html; Jack Canning, "Allegheny Center: a long history of redevelopment," *Northside Chronicle*, October 5, 2010, http://www.thenorthsidechronicle.com/allegheny-center-a-long-history-of-redevelopment/.

226 Straub interviews Hickman, 1011, 1015.

227 Leland Hazard, interview by Joel Tarr, November 22, 1971, transcript, series I, box 1, vol. Gi-Haz, p. 917, Pittsburgh Renaissance Project: The Stanton Belfour Oral History Collection, AIS.1973.24, Archives Service Center, University of Pittsburgh.

228 Ibid., 918.

229 Ibid, 919; Thomas M. Hritz, "South Hills Skybus May Go Underground," *Pittsburgh Post-Gazette*, December 2, 1967; Ed Reis, "Skybus: Pittsburgh's Missed Chance at Reviving Public Transportation," *Western Pennsylvania History* 97, no. 2 (Summer 2014).

230 Morton Coleman, David Houston and Edward K. Muller, "Skybus: Pittsburgh's Failed Industry Targeting Strategy of the 1960s," (paper no. 15, Center for Industry Studies, University of Pittsburgh, 2002), 25.

231 Coleman et al., *Skybus*, 24, 27; Bill Steigerwald, "True Tales of Transit Folly," *Pittsburgh Tribune-Review*, November 27, 2005.

232 Coleman et al., *Skybus*, 29.

233 Jack Ryan, "Transit Title Is At Stake In Hearings," *Pittsburgh Press*, August 17, 1969.

234 Coleman et al., *Skybus*, 30-31.

235 Tarr interviews Hazard, 925.

236 Patricia Sabatini, "A Kinder, Gentler Chairman," *Pittsburgh Post-Gazette*, January 25, 1998.

237 Based on review of information on Pittsburgh's top 25 publicly-traded companies from Hoover's (U.S. Steel, PNC, PPG, WESCO international, Mylan, Dick's Sporting Goods, Allegheny Technologies, American Eagle Outfitters, CONSOL Energy, GNC, Kennametal, Westinghouse Air Brake, TMS International, Education Management, Atlas Pipeline Partners, EQT, Koppers Holdings, MSA Safety, Matthews International, Black Box, Federated Investors, ANSYS, RTI International, L.B. Foster, Michael Baker Corporation), and of relevant company website investor relations pages.

238 Carl D. Liggio, "The Changing Role of Corporate Counsel," *Emory Law Journal* 46 (Summer 1997) 1201, 1202.

239 Carl D. Liggio, "A Look at the Role of Corporate Counsel: Back to the Future – Or Is It the Past," *Arizona Law Review* 44 (Fall/Winter 2002), 621.

240 Liggio, *Changing Role of Corporate Counsel*, 1202.

241 15 Pa. Cons. Stat. Ann. § 1716(a).

242 Gary M. Holihan, "Pennsylvania's Antitakeover Statute: An Impermissible Regulation of the Interstate Market for Corporate Control," *Chicago-Kent Law Review* 66 (October 1990), 863, 884.

243 Colker, *Gaining Gateway Center*, 144.

244 "Congress Group Set to Battle Alien 'Isms,' Says Adamson," *Pittsburgh Sun-Telegraph*, March 29, 1945; "Thomas Won't Fire Adamson, The Law Will," *Pittsburgh Post-Gazette*, December 28, 1946; Harold L. Nelson, *Libel in News of Congressional Investigating Committees* (Minneapolis: University of Minnesota Press, 1999), 72-73.

245 Philip Jenkins, *The Cold War At Home: The Red Scare in Pennsylvania, 1945-1960* (Chapel Hill, NC: University of North Carolina Press, 1999), 4, 7.

246 James I. Smith, III, "obituary (draft) for Pittsburgh Legal Journal," Harry Alan Sherman, Allegheny County Bar Association Decedent Files, Allegheny County Bar Association, ACBA Collection; Daniel J. Leab, *I Was a Communist for the FBI: The Unhappy Life and Times of Matt Cvetic* (State College, PA: Penn State University Press, 2000), 40-41.

247 Ibid., 41-42; "Court Dismisses Sherman Charges," *Pittsburgh Press*, March 29, 1945.

248 Leab, *I Was a Communist for the FBI*, 35-38.

249 "Form Group To Oppose Communism," *Pittsburgh Post-Gazette*, October 4, 1947; Leab, *I Was a Communist for the FBI*, 44-45.

250 Cliff Tuttle, "Christopher Columbus' American Lawyer," *Pittsburgh History* 77, no. 3 (Fall 1994), 133-134; "Judge Musmanno Wounded in Italy," *Pittsburgh Post-Gazette*, May 1, 1944.

251 Michael A. Musmanno, *Across the Street from the Courthouse* (Philadelphia: Dorrance, 1950), 10.

252 Tuttle, *Columbus' American Lawyer*, 134.

253 "Judge Musmanno Given Rousing Welcome," *Pittsburgh Press*, September 15, 1946.

254 Leab, *I Was a Communist for the FBI*, 7-21.

255 Robert Taylor, "'Commie' Leader Here Unmasks Self as FBI Agent for Nine Years," *Pittsburgh Press*, February 19, 1950.

256 Leab, *I Was a Commuist for the FBI*, 52.

257 Associated Press, "McCarthy Charges Infiltration," *Indiana Evening Gazette* (Indiana, PA), February 11, 1950.

258 Leab, *I Was a Communist for the FBI*, passim.

259 Weber, *Don't Call Me Boss*, 283.

260 Commonwealth ex rel. Roth v. Musmanno, 364 Pa. 359 (Pa. 1950).

261 Weber, *Don't Call Me Boss*, 325.

262 Judge Joseph F. Weis, Jr., interview by the author, July 29, 2011; "Hymen Schlesinger, Activist Lawyer, 72," *Pittsburgh Post-Gazette*, February 9, 1976.

263 "Red Lawyer Issue Aired," *Pittsburgh Post-Gazette*, May 9, 1950.

264 "Musmanno Asks Bar to Tackle Schlesinger Case," *Pittsburgh Press*, June 10, 1951.

265 Court of Common Pleas of Allegheny County, "Complaint In the Matter of Hymen Schlesinger before the Committee on Offenses," June 30, 1950, Hymen Schlesinger Papers, 1927-1990, AIS.1977.33, Archives Service Center, University of Pittsburgh.

266 Jenkins, *Cold War at Home*, 82-83.

267 Musmanno, *Across the Street*, 53.

268 Robert Gorczyca, "Sound and Fury: The Sedition Trial of Communist Steve Nelson," *Western Pennsylvania History* 91, no. 2 (Summer 2008), 47.

269 "Schlesinger Asks 3 Reds Be Freed," *Pittsburgh Post-Gazette*, September 7, 1950.

270 "Bar Musmanno, Reds Ask," *Pittsburgh Post-Gazette*, September 14, 1950.

271 "Musmanno Leaves Court for Political Campaign," *Pittsburgh Press*, September 15, 1950.

272 "Reds' Lawyer Blasts Court, Newspapers At Sedition Trial," *Pittsburgh Press*, January 18, 1951.

273 Paul B. Beers, *Pennsylvania Politics Today and Yesterday: The Tolerable Accommodation* (University Park, PA: Penn State University Press, 2010), 144-146.

274 Ibid., 146.

275 Chester Harris, *Tiger at the Bar: The Life Story of Charles J. Margiotti* (St. Marys, PA:Baumgratz, 1999), 377.

276 Weber, *Don't Call Me Boss*, 311.

277 "DA To Probe Red Charges Against Aide," *Pittsburgh Press*, January 8, 1951.

278 "Mrs. Matson Asks Court for Hearing," *Pittsburgh Press*, January 11, 1951; "5 Attorneys Start Matson Probe Monday," *Pittsburgh Press*, January 12, 1951.

279 William S. Rahauser, "Text of Rahauser Letter Defending Mrs. Matson," *Pittsburgh Press*, January 11, 1951.

280 "5 Attorneys Start Matson Probe Monday," *Pittsburgh Press*, January 12, 1951; "Matson Probe Group Calls Margiotti," *Pittsburgh Post-Gazette*, January 17, 1951.

281 "Margiotti's Office Slates Own Hearing On Matson," *Pittsburgh Press*, January 19, 1951; "Matson Case Hearing Next Monday Morning Ordered by Margiotti," *Pittsburgh Post-Gazette*, January 19, 1951; "Margiotti Fights Matson Ban," *Pittsburgh Post-Gazette*, January 23, 1951.

282 "Mrs. Matson Insists She's 'Against Reds,'" *Pittsburgh Press*, January 19, 1951.

283 "Matt Cvetic Subpenaed [sic] in Matson Case," *Pittsburgh Press*, January 21, 1951.

284 "Matson 'Red' Hearing Halted," *Pittsburgh Press*, January 22, 1951.

285 "Margiotti Resigns as Pennsylvania's Attorney General," *Times Herald* (Olean, NY), February 26, 1951.

286 "Court Holds Schlesinger In Contempt," *Pittsburgh Post-Gazette*, May 25, 1951; Schlesinger Petition, 367 Pa. 476 (1951).

287 "Schlesinger Faces Jail For Contempt," *Pittsburgh Press*, May 31, 1951.

288 "Schlesinger Held for Court After Long Hearing Wrangle," *Pittsburgh Press*, June 13, 1951.

289 "Attorney Schlesinger Free On Charges of Sedition," *Pittsburgh Press*, December 11, 1951.

290 "Musmanno Asks Bar to Tackle Schlesinger Case," *Pittsburgh Press*, June 10, 1951.

291 Matson v. Jackson, 368 Pa. 283 (1951).

292 "Lawyers to Probe Charges Linking Mrs. Matson to Reds," *Pittsburgh Press*, July 2, 1951; "Month's Delay Expected in Matson Case," *Pittsburgh Press*, September 9, 1951.

293 "Public Hearings to Open On Matson Case Thursday," *Pittsburgh Press*, September 4, 1951.

294 "Month's Delay Expected in Matson Case," *Pittsburgh Post-Gazette*, September 9, 1951; "'Private Eye' Tells Bizarre Story," *Pittsburgh Press*, September 10, 1951.

295 Court of Common Pleas of Allegheny County, "Report of the Committee Appointed January 12, 1951, In the Matter of Marjorie Hanson Matson, Esq., No. 408," December 4, 1951, Papers of Marjorie and J. Warren Matson, 1942-1980, AIS 1984:17, Archives Service Center, University of Pittsburgh.

296 "Mrs. Matson Exonerated, Back on Job," *Pittsburgh Press*, December 5, 1951; "Mrs. Matson Resigns Post as Assistant in DA's Office," *Pittsburgh Press*, January 11, 1952.

297 Aldisert, *Road to the Robes*, 307-308.

298 Aldo Icardi, *American Master Spy* (Pittsburgh: Stalwart Enterprises, Inc., 1954), 197.

299 Ibid., 197-198.

300 Board of Law Examiners Meeting Minutes, June 26, 1951, Allegheny County Bar Association, ACBA Collection; Board of Law Examiners Meeting Minutes, September 17, 1951, Allegheny County Bar Association, ACBA Collection.

301 Board of Law Examiners Meeting Minutes, December 12, 1947, Allegheny County Bar Association, ACBA Collection.

302 Board of Law Examiners Meeting Minutes, January 5, 1951, Allegheny County Bar Association, ACBA Collection.

303 Aldisert, *Road to the Robes*, 313-317.

304 Icardi, *American Master Spy*, 178, 187-188.

305 Ibid., 191-194.

306 Ibid., 197-198.

307 Aldisert, *Road to the Robes*, 303-312, 320-327; United Press, "Extradition Fight Waged by Lawrence," *The Daily Notes* (Canonsburg, PA), September 19, 1951;

308 Board of Law Examiners Meeting Minutes, October 17, 1952, Allegheny County Bar Association, ACBA Collection; Board of Law Examiners Meeting Minutes, December 12, 1952, Allegheny County Bar Association, ACBA Collection.

309 Associated Press, "Icardi Convicted of Murder," *Pittsburgh Post-Gazette*, November 7, 1953.

310 Board of Law Examiners Meeting Minutes, February 15, 1954, Allegheny County Bar Association, ACBA Collection; Board of Law Examiners Meeting Minutes, May 26, 1954, Allegheny County Bar Association, ACBA Collection.

311 Pennsylvania v. Nelson, 350 U.S. 497 (1956).

312 Mesarosh v. United States, 352 U.S. 1 (1956).

313 Leab, *I Was a Communist for the FBI*, 101.

314 Jacob Margolis to Judith Margolis Freshman and Dr. Ernest Freshman, November 22, 1953, Barbara Margolis collection.

315 Schlesinger Appeal, 404 Pa. 584 (1961).

316 Ibid.

317 Hymen Schlesinger to Robert A. Rundle, Esq., Charles M. Thorp, Jr., Esq. and Edward R. Lawrence, Esq., June 1, 1955, Hymen Schlesinger Papers, 1927-1990, AIS.1977.33, Archives Service Center, University of Pittsburgh; Harbaugh Miller to Hymen Schlesinger, June 10, 1955, Hymen Schlesinger Papers, 1927-1990, AIS.1977.33, Archives Service Center, University of Pittsburgh. See also, James I. Smith, III, "draft obituary of Zeno V. Fritz for Pittsburgh Legal Journal," December 1984, Allegheny County Bar Association, ACBA Collection.

318 Court of Common Pleas of Allegheny County, "Order Appointing Counsel, In the Matter of Hymen Schlesinger," June 18, 1956, Hymen Schlesinger Papers, 1927-1990, AIS.1977.33, Archives Service Center, University of Pittsburgh.

319 See, e.g., "Cole Holds Reds May Sweep US; Hits New Deal," *The Cornell Daily Sun*, October 31, 1946 (quotes Cole as saying "Threat of a sweep of communism throughout the country is a serious and immediate danger, which has been advanced by the confusion and mismanagement caused by the New Deal policies.").

320 Richard B. Henderson, *Maury Maverick: A Political Biography* (Austin: University of Texas Press, 2010), 177.

321 Aldisert, *Road to the Robes*, 333.

322 Ibid.

323 Ibid., 337-340.

324 Evan Thomas, *Edward Bennett Williams: The Man to See* (New York: Simon & Schuster, 2012), 87.

325 Aldisert, *Road to the Robes*, 340.

326 Evan Thomas, *Man to See*, 87-88.

327 Aldisert, *Road to the Robes*, 344-348.

328 *Communist Political Subversion – Part 1, Hearings Before the Committee of Un-American Activities*, 84th Cong. 6242 (1956).

329 Ibid., 6434.

330 Schlesinger Appeal, 404 Pa. 584 (1961).

331 Richard B. Tucker, Jr., "An Incomplete Supplement to the History of Our Firm (1938-1986)," October 14, 1993, Tucker Arensberg collection, Pittsburgh, PA, 3-4.

332 Schlesinger Appeal, 404 Pa. 584 (1961); see also Konigsberg v. State Bar of California, 353 U.S. 252 (1957).

333 Judge Joseph F. Weis, Jr., interview by the author, July 29, 2011.

334 Icardi Appeal, 436 Pa. 364 (1970).

335 Associated Press, "Washington Attorney Admitted To Bar After 30-Year Struggle," *Evening Standard* (Uniontown, PA), May 27, 1971.

336 Jeff Icardi, interview by the author, July 1, 2014,

337 Harold B. Tanner to John G. Buchanan, October 3, 1952, Buchanan Ingersoll & Rooney collection, Pittsburgh, PA.

338 John G. Buchanan to Harold Tanner, October 11, 1952, Buchanan Ingersoll & Rooney collection, Pittsburgh, PA. Ironically, the Tillinghast firm later dispensed with Mr. Tanner's name entirely. After a series of name changes and mergers, the firm closed its doors in 2008. William Hamilton, "Tillinghast Licht to end 190-year run," *Providence Business News*, May 1, 2008, http://www.pbn.com/Tillinghast-Licht-to-end-190-year-run,31560.

339 Thomas M. Thompson, interview by the author, September 30, 2008.

340 Demmler, *First Century*, 60-62.

341 Virginia Gaffney, "Earl F. Reed," unpublished profile, May 24, 1989, private collection of Devon Cross.

342 "Local News," *Daily Republican* (Monongahela, PA), December 5, 1904 ("John M. Ralston, Esq., of the firm Stonecipher & Raslton, Pittsburg, was a Monongahela visitor Saturday.").

343 "Obituary Notes: John M. Ralston," *Pittsburgh Post-Gazette*, January 25, 1936.

344 "Obituaries: Frank W. Stonecipher," *Pittsburgh Press*, June 7, 1952.

345 "Death Notice: C. William Cunningham," *Pittsburgh Legal Journal*, October 31, 1962.

346 Philip E. Beard, interview by the author, September 20, 2010.

347 Demmler, *First Century*, 109-115.

348 Brignano and Fort, *Reed Smith: 125 Years*, 79.

349 John U. Anderson, Jr., *Kirkpatrick & Lockhart LLP: The Early Years: Reflections* (Pittsburgh: Kirkpatrick & Lockhart, 1996), 1, 4; H. Woodruff Turner, interview by the author, April 5, 2011.

350 Anderson, *Early Years: Reflections*, 4; Charles J. Queenan, Jr., interview by the author, January 14, 2009; H. Woodruff Turner, interview by the author, April 5, 2011.

351 Brignano and Fort, *Reed Smith: 125 Years*, 80.

352 Anderson, *Early Years: Reflections*, 4.

353 Brignano and Fort, *Reed Smith: 125 Years*, 79.

354 Anderson, *Early Years: Reflections*, 5-6; Brignano and Fort, *Reed Smith: 125 Years*, 79.

355 Brignano and Fort, *Reed Smith: 125 Years*, 79.

356 Anderson, *Early Years: Reflections*, 6.

357 Judd N. Poffinberger, Jr., interview by the author, November 14, 2008; H. Woodruff Turner, interview by the author, April 5, 2011.

358 Brignano and Fort, *Reed Smith: 125 Years*, 80.

359 Anderson, *Early Years: Reflections*, 6-7.

360 Ibid., 7.

361 Judd N. Poffinberger, Jr., *The Early Years*, 2.

362 Ibid.; Charles J. Queenan, Jr., interview by the author, January 14, 2009; Judd N. Poffinberger, Jr., interview by the author, November 14, 2008.

363 Charles J. Queenan, Jr., interview by the author, January 14, 2009.

364 Demmler, *First Century*, 116; Richard L. Thornburgh, interview by the author, May 21, 2009.

365 Demmler, *First Century*, 116.

366 Brignano and Fort, *Reed Smith: 125 Years*, 80.

367 H. Woodruff Turner, interview by the author, April 5, 2011.

368 *Buchanan Ingersoll Employee Rolls*.

369 Steve Cherin, interview by the author, July 17, 2014.

370 *Buchanan Ingersoll Employee Rolls*.

371 Gordon & Smith (and successor firms) partnership agreements, 1930-1952, Buchanan Ingersoll & Rooney collection, Pittsburgh, PA.

372 W. Gregg Kerr, Jr., interview by the author, November 10, 2008.

373 Ibid.

374 Alexander Black, Jr., interview by the author, July 16, 1992.

375 Clayton A. Sweeney, interview by the author, October 24, 2008.

376 William Kyle, interview by the author, July 12, 1992.

377 *Buchanan Ingersoll Employee Rolls*.

378 Eckert Seamans, *Celebrating 50 Years of Service* (Pittsburgh: Eckert Seamans, 2008), 1.

379 William Kyle, interview by the author, July 12, 1992.

380 W. Gregg Kerr, Jr., interview by the author, November 10, 2008.

381 United States v. Aluminum Co. of America, 153 F.Supp. 132 (S.D. NY 1957).

382 Memorandum by Frank L. Seamans, Carl Cherin and Edward H. Schoyer to All Partners, "Firm Luncheons," January 2, 1958, Thomas G. Buchanan collection, Pittsburgh, PA.

383 Alexander Black, Jr., interview by the author, July 16, 1992.

384 Ibid.

385 Ibid.; John G. Buchanan to Donald D. Shepard, Esq., March 4, 1958, Thomas G. Buchanan collection; Edward H. Schoyer, interview by the author, June 23, 1992.

386 W. Gregg Kerr, Jr., interview by the author, November 10, 2008.

387 Miles Simon and Thomas M. Thompson, interview by the author July 2, 2014.

388 Clayton Sweeney, interview by the author, October 24, 2008.

389 Hickman, *Need and Utilization of Retain Counsel*, 14-15.

390 W. Gregg Kerr, Jr., interview by the author, November 10, 2008.

391 Edward H. Schoyer, interview by the author, June 23, 1992.

392 Thomas M. Thompson, interview by the author, September 30, 2008.

393 Alexander Black, Jr., interview by the author, July 16, 1992.

394 C. Kent May, interview by the author, September 1, 2011; W. Gregg Kerr, Jr., interview by the author, November 10, 2008.

395 John G. Buchanan to Donald D. Shepard, Esq., March 4, 1958, Thomas G. Buchanan collection.

396 Alexander Black, Jr., interview by the author, July 16, 1992.

397 Edward H. Schoyer, interview by the author, June 23, 1992, quoting from Edward H. Schoyer, "Perceptions of Firm History and Tradition" (address to new associates, September 6, 1991, Buchanan Ingersoll, Pittsburgh, PA).

398 W. Gregg Kerr, Jr., interview by the author, November 10, 2008.

399 John G. Buchanan (attributed), "A History of Buchanan, Ingersoll, Rodewald, Kyle & Buerger and Its Predecessors," *Pittsburgh Legal Journal*, February 17, 1958.

400 Eckert Seamans, *Celebrating 50 Years*, 14.

401 Steve Cherin, interview by the author, July 17, 2014.

402 Clayton Sweeney, interview by the author, October 24, 2008.

403 Thomas M. Thompson, interview by the author, September 30, 2008.

404 Paul G. Rodewald, interview by the author, March 1992.

405 Steve Cherin, interview by the author, July 17, 2014; Clayton Sweeney, interview by the author, October 24, 2008; W. Gregg Kerr, Jr., interview by the author, November 10, 2008.

406 W. Gregg Kerr, Jr., interview by the author, November 10, 2008.

407 Mitchell Pacelle, "Makeover," *The American Lawyer* (March 1985).

408 William R. Newlin, interview by the author, February 12, 2014.

409 Robert Y. Kopf, Jr., interview by the author September 10, 2009.

410 Ibid.; Francis DiSalle, interview by the author, July 24, 2014.

411 Robert G. Sable, interview by the author, July 21, 2008.

412 "Biography," *S. Leo Ruslander Scrapbooks, Guides to Archives and Manuscript Collections at the University of Pittsburgh Library System*, accessed March 12, 2017, http://digital.library.pitt.edu/cgi-bin/f/findaid/findaid-idx?c=ascead&cc=ascead&rgn=main&view=text&didno=US-PPiU-ais199118; "The Berkman Family," *Rauh Jewish Archives of the Senator John Heinz History Center*, accessed March 12, 2017, http://www.jewishfamilieshistory.org/entry/berkman-family.

413 Interview of Philip Baskin, April 29, 1985, transcript, series 28, subseries 2, box 100, folder 17, National Council of Jewish Women (NCJW), Pittsburgh Section Papers, 1894-2003, AIS.1964.40, Archives Service Center, University of Pittsburgh. Robert G. Sable, interview by the author, July 21, 2008.

414 Leo A. Keevican, Jr., interview by the author, July 11, 2014.

415 Robert G. Sable, interview by the author, July 21, 2008.

416 Bob Batz, Jr., "Philip Baskin: Well-known lawyer, former City Council member," *Pittsburgh Post-Gazette*, January 3, 2005.

417 Robert G. Sable, interview by the author, July 21, 2008.

418 John M. Feeney, interview by the author, September 22, 2008.

419 Lynn Rosellini, "Washington Talk; Former Reagan Insider Perceives Signs of Drift," *The New York Times*, October 26, 1981.

420 Albert J. Neri, "Baskin, Flaherty spar on S. Africa tie," *Pittsburgh Post-Gazette*, March 30, 1984; "Baskin without Sears," *Pittsburgh Post-Gazette*, January 25, 1984.

421 "Baskin & Steingut law firm in line to get city business," *Pittsburgh Post-Gazette*, May 31, 1984.

422 "6 sued by law firm for diverting money," *Pittsburgh Post-Gazette*, July 23, 1986.

423 John M. Feeney, interview by the author, September 22, 2008.

424 Albert J. Neri, "Dueling visions, Lawyers split by political issues, business emphasis," *Pittsburgh Post-Gazette*, February 21, 1990; "Baskin leaves namesake firm," *Pittsburgh Post-Gazette*, May 1, 1990.

425 Leo A. Keevican, Jr., interview by the author, July 11, 2014; David Ranii, "Rift Spurs 11 to defect from Berkman Ruslander," *Pittsburgh Press*, August 10, 1988.

426 Howard Goodman and Barbara Demick, "Bond Lawyer Admits Role in Fraud," *Philadelphia Inquirer*, January 15, 1988; Leo A. Keevican, Jr., interview by the author, July 11, 2014; David Ranii, "Rift Spurs 11 to defect from Berkman Ruslander," *Pittsburgh Press*, August 10, 1988; David Ranii, "Law firm gets new partner, name; Berkman Ruslander now Klett Leiber," *Pittsburgh Press*, April 4, 1989.

427 David Ranii, "Law firm gets new partner, name; Berkman Ruslander now Klett Leiber," *Pittsburgh Press*, April 4, 1989; David Ranii, "Schwab leaving Reed Smith for Buchanan," *Pittsburgh Press*, October 6, 1990.

428 Robert J. Cindrich, interview by the author, July 9, 2014.

429 James O'Toole, "K. Leroy Irvis, a man of firsts," Pittsburgh Post-Gazette, March 17, 2006.

430 Arthur J. Edmunds, *Daybreakers: The Story of the Urban League of Pittsburgh* (Pittsburgh: Urban League of Pittsburgh, 1999), 119.

431 James O.F. Hackshaw, "The Committee for Fair Employment in Pittsburgh Department Stores: A Study of the Methods and Techniques Used by the Committee in their Campaign to Secure a Non-Discriminatory Hiring Policy in the Department Stores of Pittsburgh," (master's thesis, University of Pittsburgh School of Social Work, 1949), 26-27.

432 Ibid., at 36; Edmunds, *Daybreakers*, 121.

433 Edmunds, *Daybreakers*, 122.

434 James O'Toole, "K. Leroy Irvis, a man of firsts," Pittsburgh Post-Gazette, March 17, 2006.

435 Ytasha Womack, "'I am not White': for many light-skinned Blacks, identity is more than skin deep," *Ebony*, August 2007, 80.

436 Wendell Freeland, interview by the author, September 15, 2008.

437 Ibid.

438 Ibid.

439 ACBA, *Tribute to African Americans*.

440 "First Negro Prosecutor," *Pittsburgh Post-Gazette*, February 27, 1942.

441 Judge Livingstone M. Johnson, interview by the author, August 2, 2011.

442 Ibid.

443 ACBA, *Tribute to African Americans*.

444 Edmunds, *Daybreakers*, 123-126.

445 Ibid., 128; Jeff Wiltse, "Swimming Against Segregation: The Struggle to Desegregate," *Pennsylvania Legacies* 10, no. 2 (November 2010), 15-16.

446 Edmunds, *Daybreakers*, 128; Wendell Freeland, interview by the author, September 15, 2008.

447 Edmunds, *Daybreakers*, 133; Wendell Freeland, interview by the author, September 15, 2008; Thomas J. Sugrue, *Sweet Land of Liberty: The Forgotten Struggle for Civil Rights in the North* (New York: Random House, 2008), 157.

448 Wendell Freeland, interview by the author, September 15, 2008.

449 Lawrence J. Haas, "On top: Irvis' calm, measured style pleases some, annoys others," *Pittsburgh Post-Gazette*, January 24, 1983.

450 Trotter and Day, *Race and Renaissance*, 65.

451 Wendell Freeland, interview by the author, September 15, 2008.

452 "Lawrence Raps Fleming On Housing," *Pittsburgh Press*, January 25, 1961.

453 "New Fair Housing Law Attacked as Illegal," *Philadelphia Daily News*, September 2, 1961.

454 Michael Sean Snow, "Dreams Realized and Dreams Deferred: Social Movements and Public Policy in Pittsburgh, 1960-1980" (PhD dissertation, University of Pittsburgh, 2004), 93; Laurence Glasco, "The Next Page: That arena on the Hill," *Pittsburgh Post-Gazette*, July 5, 2010.

455 Wendell Freeland, interview by the author, September 18, 2008; Trotter and Day, *Race and Renaissance*, 138.

456 Trotter and Day, *Race and Renaissance*, 90.

457 "Presidential Speeches | John F. Kennedy Presidency | June 11, 1963: Address on Civil Rights," University of Virginia, Miller Center, accessed March 10, 2017, https://millercenter.org/the-presidency/presidential-speeches/june-11-1963-address-civil-rights.

458 Thomas J. Whalen, *JFK and His Enemies: A Portrait of Power* (Lanham, MD: Rowman & Littlefield, 2014), 148.

459 "Job Picketing Planned Here by NAACP," *Pittsburgh Press*, June 12, 1963.

460 Judge Livingstone M. Johnson, interview by the author, August 2, 2011.

461 Ibid.

462 Ibid.; "Picket Plans Surprise Firm," *Pittsburgh Press*, August 8, 1963.

463 Judge Livingstone M. Johnson, interview by the author, August 2, 2011; Edward Jensen, "Duquesne Light Picketed by 300 in Racial Case," *Pittsburgh Post-Gazette*, August 13, 1963; Edward Jensen, "3 Race Leaders Arrested," *Pittsburgh Post-Gazette*, August 14, 1963.

464 Judge Livingstone M. Johnson, interview by the author, August 2, 2011.

465 Len Barcousky, "Eyewitness 1963: Civil Rights advocates emerge in Pittsburgh," *Pittsburgh Post-Gazette*, October 13, 2013.

466 "Negroes Ask Light Firm to Hire 350," *Pittsburgh Post-Gazette*, September 15, 1967.

467 Ingrid Jewell, "Congressmen Meet District March Unit," *Pittsburgh Post-Gazette*, August 29, 1963;

468 Rona Kobel, "Byrd Brown feted by peers" *Pittsburgh Post-Gazette*, January 18, 2000.

469 Vince Johnson, "Negro-Owned Homes Called Value-Cutters," *Pittsburgh Post-Gazette*, July 19, 1963; Leonard L. Karter and David B. Washington, "The Nickens Case a Step Forward in Housing," *The Crisis* 71, no. 3 (March 1964); Snow, *Dreams Realized*, 99, 107.

470 Judge R. Stanton Wettick, interview by the author, September 2, 2010.

471 Ibid.

472 Wendell Freeland, interview by the author, September 18, 2008; "MLK riots: 40 years later, turmoil on the Hill stirs memories," *Pittsburgh Post-Gazette*, April 2, 2008.

473 "Pittsburgh Hit By Gangs in Hill District," *Pittsburgh Post-Gazette*, April 6, 1968.

474 Roger Stuart, "3000 Join In King Tribute," *Pittsburgh Press*, April 8, 1968.

475 Snow, *Dreams Realized*, 106-108.

476 Judge R. Stanton Wettick, interview by the author, September 2, 2010.

477 Ibid.

478 Ibid.; Doe v. Wohlgemuth, 376 F. Supp. 173 (W.D. Pa. 1974); Beal v. Doe, 432 U.S. 438 (1977); Hoots v. Commonwealth, 334 F. Supp. 820 (W.D. Pa. 1971); Eleanor Chute, "Woodland Hills aces court test," *Pittsburgh Post-Gazette*, July 27, 2000; Owens-El v. Robinson, 442 F. Supp. 1368 (W.D. Pa. 1978); Mark Belko, "NLS seeks to punish jail for crowding," *Pittsburh Post-Gazette*, September 10, 1988.

479 Judge R. Stanton Wettick, interview by the author, September 2, 2010; Paul Boas, interview by the author, July 23, 2014.

480 Paul Boas, interview by the author, July 23, 2014; "26 Girls Arrested In War Protest Here," *Pittsburgh Post-Gazette*, September 5, 1969; Roger Stuart, "'Kids Dug Us,' SDS Girl Boasts Of School Fracas Here," *Pittsburgh Press*, September 6, 1969; Harry F. Swanger, Allegheny County Bar Association Questionnaire for Placement Assistance, June 24, 1969, ACBA Collection.

481 Paul Boas, interview by the author, July 23, 2014; John Zingaro, "Times Have Changed But Not Lawyer's Ideals," *Pittsburgh Post-Gazette*, May 31, 1984.

482 Paul Boas, interview by the author, July 23, 2014; Paul D. Boas, Allegheny County Bar Association, Committee on Judiciary, Judicial Candidate's Questionnaire, March 5, 1990, ACBA Collection; "Edward D. Boas (obit)," *Jewish Criterion*, December 5, 1952; Leonard I. Sharon, Allegheny County Bar Association, Membership Application, October 22, 1970, ACBA Collection; James H. Logan, Allegheny County Bar Association Biographical Questionnaire, Septmber 19, 1990, ACBA Collection.

483 Paul Boas, interview by the author, July 23, 2014.

484 Ibid.; Dombrowski v. Pfister, 380 U.S. 479 (1965).

485 Paul Boas, interview by the author, July 23, 2014; Gabrielle Banks, "Support your boss's political cause - or else?," *Pittsburgh Post-Gazette*, May 23, 2011 (regarding Logan's later career).

486 Judge R. Stanton Wettick, interview by the author, September 2, 2010.

487 Duquesne University School of Law, *One Hundred Years of Excellence*, 1911-2011 (Pittsburgh: Duquesne Press, 2011), 36-41; Stephen W. Morris, "Legal Speedster," *Ebony*, December 1970.

488 ACBA, *Tribute to African Americans*.

489 Ibid.; "Horty, Springer & Mattern, P.C. - Firm Profile," *Martindale-Hubbell*, accessed March 10, 2017, http://www.martindale.com/Horty-Springer-Mattern-PC/law-firm-1247917.htm

490 ACBA, *Tribute to African Americans*.

491 Patty Tascarella, "The Oscar Madison of Law," *Pittsburgh Business Times*, June 25 1999; Glenn R. Mahone, interview by the author, September 5, 2014.

492 Glenn R. Mahone, interview by the author, September 5, 2014.

493 Ibid.

494 Ibid.; Wendell Freeland, interview by the author, September 18, 2008.

495 Glenn R. Mahone, interview by the author, September 5, 2014.

496 Mahone v. Waddle, 564 F. 2d 1018 (3rd Cir. 1977).

497 Wendell Freeland, interview by the author, September 18, 2008.

498 ACBA, *Tribute to African Americans*; James O'Toole, "K. Leroy Irvis, a man of firsts," *Pittsburgh Post-Gazette*, March 17, 2006; Al Donalson, "Bigger World Court Role Urged," *Pittsburgh Press*, September 13, 1973 (regarding Irvis' association with Rose Schmidt).

499 Joel Fishman, "Women Judges on the Allegheny County Court of Pleas", *Duquesne University School of Law*, accessed March 10, 2017, http://law.duq.edu/libraries/allegheny-county-law-library/publications/women-judges.

500 Wendell Freeland, interview by the author, September 15, 2008.

501 Brian K. Parker, "Call to Action" (address), Second Annual Corporate Equity and Inclusion Roundtable, Black Political Empowerment Project, Duquesne University, Pittsburgh, PA, June 9, 2014).

502 James J. Barnes, interview by the author, August 19, 2014.

503 Glenn R. Mahone, interview by the author, September 5, 2014.

504 David Blaner, interview by the author, September 8, 2014.

505 "Nixon Aide Lauds DA's Record Here," *Pittsburgh Post-Gazette*, September 20, 1971.

506 Dick Thornburgh, *Where the Evidence Leads: An Autobiography* (Pittsburgh: University of Pittsburgh Press, 2003), 23.

507 Ann T. Keene, "Kleindienst, Richard G.," *American National Biography Online*, accessed March 10, 2017, http://anb.org/articles/07/07-00730.html.

508 Thornburgh, *Where the Evidence Leads*, 33; Frank M. Matthews, "Scaife Heads State's Nixon Fund Drive," *Pittsburgh Post-Gazette*, June 21, 1968.

509 Thornburgh, *Where the Evidence Leads*, 50.

510 "Consolidated Ice Company Factory No. 2," National Register of Historic Places, Regsitration Form, October 3, 2000; William R. Mitchell "Consolidated Ice Co. Has Distributed Approximately $2,600,000 Dividends," *Pittsburgh Press*, January 15, 1928.

511 "Ex-Safety Head Dunn Succombs Suddenly," *Pittsburgh Press*, August 11, 1936.

512 "Frank L. Duggan Taken By Death," *Pittsburgh Press*, June 23, 1946; James H. Gray, Henry Oliver Evans and Charles C. McGovern, "Frank Loughney Duggan - A Memorial," *The Western Pennsylvania Historical Magazine* 29: 3-4, September-December 1946.

513 Burton Hersh, *The Mellon Family: A Fortune in History* (New York: William Morrow & Co., 1978), 539.

514 "The Honorable Robert W. Duggan," unpublished profile, Allegheny County Bar Association Decedent Files, Allegheny County Bar Association, ACBA Collection.

515 "A New Assistant," *Pittsburgh Press*, February 11, 1953.

516 James Helbert, "Boyle Takes DA's Office, Names Adair," *Pittsburgh Press*, December 31, 1955.

517 Jim Fisher, *Fall Guys: False Confessions and the Politics of Murder* (Carbondale, IL: Southern Illinois University Press, 1996), 17.

518 "Boyle Beats Snee For DA On City Vote," *Pittsburgh Press*, November 4, 1959.

519 Vince Johnson, "Easy-Going Eddie: Indifferent D.A. Lets Rackets Have Their Way," *Pittsburgh Post-Gazette*, February 11, 1963.

520 Vince Johnson, "Easy-Going Eddie: Short Work Day Puts No Burden On Prosecutor," *Pittsburgh Post-Gazette*, February 12, 1963.

521 "We've Got Your Number!," *Pittsburgh Post-Gazette*, February 10-13, 1936; Brian McKenna, "Gus Greenlee," *Society for American Baseball Research*, accessed March 10, 2017, http://sabr.org/bioproj/person/fabd8400.

522 Hayllar, *Accomodation*, 305.

523 Hersh, *Mellon Family*, 536; Hayllar, *Accomodation*, 305; "Payoff Tip Hit By Duggan," *Pittsburgh Press*, November 1, 1963.

524 Hayllar, *Accomodation*, 318-322.

525 Vince Johnson, "IRS Weighs Contents of Black Book," *Pittsburgh Post-Gazette*, October 30, 1963.

526 Edward Jensen, "Boyle Holds Shrinking Margin Over Duggan," *Pittsburgh Post-Gazette*, November 6, 1963.

527 Edward Jensen, "'Machine' Fails to Halt Duggan Upset of Boyle," *Pittsburgh Post-Gazette*, November 7, 1963.

528 "Allegheny DA To Speak To GOP Here," *New Castle News*, September 1, 1964.

529 Joseph H. Miller, "Governor Race Touchy For Scranton," *Philadelphia Inquirer*, December 14, 1964.

530 Pat O'Neill, "Duggan Picks Bowytz As His Leading DA Aide," *Pittsburgh Post-Gazette*, December 24, 1963; Pat O'Neill, "Duggan Takes DA Oath Today," *Pittsburgh Post-Gazette*, January 6, 1964.

531 Barbara White Stack, "Robert Butzler, police official, active in politics," *Pittsburgh Post-Gazette*, December 7, 1993.

532 Hersh, *Mellon Family*, 540.

533 James G. Dunn, interview by the author, June 12, 2013; Obituaries, "H.S. Dunn, Legion Founder, Dies," *Pittsburgh Press*, February 24, 1963.

534 Dr. Cyril H. Wecht, interview by the author, May 27, 2014.

535 James G. Dunn, interview by the author, June 12, 2013.

536 Dr. Cyril H. Wecht, interview by the author, May 27, 2014.

537 Jim Davidson, "The Trials and Era of Judge Carol Los Mansmann," *Pittsburgh Press*, October 26, 1986; "Wofford Recommends Cindrich for Federal Bench, Press Release," Senator Harris Wofford press release, April 28, 1994, Biographical File, Allegheny County Bar Association, ACBA Collection (regarding Judge Robert Cindrich's career); Peter J. Shelly, "Democrats in a row over statewide nominations," *Pittsburgh Post-Gazette*, April 16, 1996 (regarding Judge Mike Fisher's tenure in the District Attorney's office); Torsten Ove, "Judgeship is pinnacle of varied legal career," *Pittsburgh Post-Gazette*, September 9, 2002 (on Judge McVerry's career).

538 Hayllar, *Accomodation*, 329.

539 Ibid., 334.

540 Ibid., 332.

541 Ibid., 339-341; Edward D. Yates, "DA Says 'No' To Film Starring La Mansfield," *Pittsburgh Post-Gazette*, June 28, 1965.

542 Commonwealth v. Dixon, 432 Pa. 423 (1968); Commonwealth v. Kontos, 442 Pa. 343 (1971).

543 Robert Baird, "Attorneys Jam Court For Case Dismissals," *Pittsburgh Press*, September 28, 1973.

544 Roger Stuart, "Ellenbogen Raps DA's Bail Remarks," *Pittsburgh Press*, February 17, 1972.

545 Patrick Doyle, "DA Duggan Labels 'The Kids' Public Enemy No. 1," *Pittsburgh Press*, February 9, 1969; "Craig, Duggan Split On Crime In County," *Pittsburgh Press*, February 8, 1969.

546 James G. Dunn, interview by the author, June 12, 2013.

547 Richard L. Thornburgh, interview by the author, May 21, 2009; Sally Kalson, "The Evolution of a Public Man," *Pittsburgh Post-Gazette*, July 4, 1989.

548 Gideon v. Wainwright, 372 US 335 (1963).

549 Richard L. Thornburgh, interview by the author, May 21, 2009.

550 Thornburgh, *Where the Evidence Leads*, 42.

551 Richard L. Thornburgh, interview by the author, May 21, 2009.

552 Jack Grochot and Roger Stuart, "Racket Evidence Often Lost During Ferraro's Reign," *Pittsburgh Press*, August 26, 1973.

553 Thornburgh, *Where the Evidence Leads*, 49.

554 Barbara White Stack, "Robert Butzler, police official, active in politics," *Pittsburgh Post-Gazette*, December 7, 1993; Hayllar, *Accomodation*, 369.

555 Richard L. Thornburgh, Memorandum to File, re: Samuel G. Ferraro, August 5, 1970, Dick Thirnburgh Papers, University of Pittsburgh; Thornburgh, *Where the Evidence Leads*, 49.

556 Richard L. Thornburgh, memorandum to file re: Samuel G. Ferraro, August 5, 1970, Dick Thornburgh Papers, University of Pittsburgh, Pittsburgh, PA; Richard L. Thornburgh to Honorable Robert W. Duggan, August 4, 1970, Dick Thornburgh Papers, University of Pittsburgh, Pittsburgh, PA; Richard Thornburgh, "Where the Evidence Leads" (unpublished original manuscript, Dick Thornburgh Papers, University of Pittsburgh, Pittsburgh, PA), 164 (hereafter cited as *Where the Evidence Leads Manuscript*).

557 Thornburgh, *Where the Evidence Leads Manuscript*, 165; James McCarrow, "Probe Indicts County Sleuth," *Pittsburgh Press*, August 12, 1970.

558 Chuck Biedka, "Stanley Hoss' evil still haunts Valley," *Pittsburgh Tribune-Review*, September 19, 2010.

559 James G. Hollock, *Born to Lose: Stanley B. Hoss and the Crime Spree That Gripped a Nation* (Kent, OH: Kent State University Press, 2011), 150-158.

560 "Secrecy Shrouds Hoss on Return," *Pittsburgh Press*, October 9, 1969.

561 Robert Baird, "State, U.S. Ask Crack At Hoss," *Pittsburgh Press*, October 10, 1969.

562 Hollock, *Born to Lose*, 181-183.

563 Edgar M. Snyder, interview by the author, December 16, 2008.

564 United Press International, "Hoss is found guilty," *Daily Reporter* (Dover OH), March 10, 1970; "Witness Testifies He Owned Hoss Gun," *Pittsburgh Press*, March 5, 1970; Edgar M. Snyder, interview by the author, December 16, 2008; Hollock, *Born to Lose*, 206.

565 Chuck Biedka, "Stanley Hoss' evil still haunts Valley," *Pittsburgh Tribune-Review*, September 19, 2010.

566 Edgar M. Snyder, interview by the author, December 16, 2008.

567 Ibid.

568 William E. Deibler, "Duggan Stages Comeback Win Over Martino," *Pittsburgh Post-Gazette*, November 3, 1971.

569 Hayllar, *Accomodation*, 363.

570 Lawrence Walsh, "Wecht Asks Probe of DA's Office," *Pittsburgh Press*, October 22, 1971.

571 Alvin Rosensweet, "Duggan, Wecht Feuding Over Bullet," *Pittsburgh Post-Gazette*, April 1, 1972.

572 Thornburgh, *Where the Evidence Leads Manuscript*, 165.

573 Ibid., 164-165.

574 "Conspiracy of Silence," *Pittsburgh Post-Gazette*, March 16, 1972.

575 Richard L. Thornburgh, interview by the author, May 21, 2009.

576 Hersh, *Mellon Family*, 542.

577 Paul Maryniak, "Liar's Poker" in *Pittsburgh Characters Told by Pittsburgh Characters*, ed. J.C. Grochot (Greensburg, PA: Iconoclast Press, 1991), 60-61, 112; "Expert in numbers game assists Pa. in its probe of TV drawing fix," *Baltimore Sun*, October 25, 1980.

578 Maryniak, *Liar's Poker*, 71-75.

579 Ibid., 80-81.

580 Thornburgh, *Where the Evidence Leads*, 49.

581 Thornburgh, *Where the Evidence Leads Manuscript*, 167-168.

582 Karolyn Schuster, "U.S. Opens Tax Probe Of Duggan," *Pittsburgh Post-Gazette*, July 5, 1973.

583 Thornburgh, *Where the Evidence Leads Manuscript*, 168-170.

584 Ibid., 171-174.

585 Ibid., 174.

586 Hayllar, "Accommodation," 371-373.

587 Agents Keith W. Hyatt and Robert E. Robertson, "Report to District Director, Internal Revenue Service, Attention: Chief, Intelligence Division, Pittsburgh Pennsylvania," November 8, 1973, Dick Thornburgh Papers, University of Pittsburgh, Pittsburgh, PA.

588 Ibid.

589 Thornburgh, *Where the Evidence Leads*, 51.

590 Chuck Watkins, interview by the author, November 15, 2014.

591 Thornburgh, *Where the Evidence Leads*, 51.

592 Hersh, *Mellon Family*, 542-544.

593 Ibid., 539-540; "Mellon Heiress' Ex-Husband Weds Divorcee," *Pittsburgh Press*, July 1, 1951.

594 Richard L. Thornburgh, memorandum to file re: Robert W. Duggan, September 26, 1973, Dick Thornburgh Papers, University of Pittsburgh, Pittsburgh, PA; Roger Stuart and Jack Grochot, "Duggan, Mellon Heiress Wed Secretly 2 Months," *Pittsburgh Press*, November 6, 1973.

595 Hersh, *Mellon Family*, 548.

596 Thornburgh, *Where the Evidence Leads*, 51-52.

597 "The Defensive DA," *Pittsburgh Press*, November 12, 1973.

598 "The Ferraro Conviction," *Pittsburgh Post-Gazette*, November 6, 1973.

599 Roger Stuart and Jack Grochot, "Crime Panel Ties Duggan To Campaign Fund Coverup," *Pittsburgh Press*, January 30, 1974.

600 Judge Livingstone M. Johnson, interview by the author, August 2, 2011

601 Robert J. Cindrich, interview by the author, July 9, 2014.

602 "Excerpt from Close-Up '73, WTAE-TV, Channel 4, Pittsburgh, PA, February 24, 1973 – 7:30-8:00 P.M," Dick Thornburgh Papers, University of Pittsburgh, Pittsburgh, PA.

603 Sherley Uhl, "Gun Wound Kills Duggan," *Pittsbugh Press*, March 5, 1974.

604 Thornburgh, *Where the Evidence Leads Manuscript*, 179.

605 Ibid.; "Assistant tells U.S. attorney news of Duggan's death"," *Pittsburgh Press*, March 5, 1974.

606 Dr. Cyril H. Wecht, interview by the author, May 27, 2014.

607 Hayllar, "Accommodation," 1.

608 John Golightly, "Duggan Dies of Shotgun Blast," *Pittsburgh Post-Gazette*, March 6, 1974.

609 Ibid.; John Golightly, "'Why' of Duggan Death Unsolved," *Pittsburgh Post-Gazette*, March 13, 1974; Hersh, *Mellon Family*, 550.

610 Deputy Coroner Paul J. Godor, "Death Certifcate of Robert Ward Duggan," March 12, 1974, Westmoreland County Coroner Office, Greensburg, PA; Dr. Cyril H. Wecht, interview by the author, May 27, 2014; John Golightly, "Duggan Didn't Tell Friend of Hunting," *Pittsburgh Post-Gazette*, March 9, 1974.

611 Robert J. Cindrich, interview by the author, July 9, 2014.

612 Dr. Cyril H. Wecht, interview by the author, May 27, 2014.

613 Ibid.

614 James G. Dunn, interview by the author, June 12, 2013.

615 Thornburgh, *Where the Evidence Leads*, 52.

616 "Duggan Cousin Is Acting DA," *Pittsburgh Press*, March 5, 1974; Associated Press, "Democrat Is Appointed Allegheny County D.A.," *Philadelphia Inquirer*, April 5, 1974.

617 Robert J. Cindrich, interview by the author, July 9, 2014.

618 Hayllar, "Accommodation," 379.

619 Maeve Victoria Geddis, interview by the author, October 14, 2011.

620 Robert J. Cindrich, interview by the author, July 9, 2014.

621 Richard L. Thornburgh, interview by the author, May 21, 2009.

622 James G. Dunn, interview by the author, June 12, 2013.

623 Agnes Dodds Kinard, *At Home with History: What Did I Do With My Life?* (Pittsburgh: Geyer Printing Co., 2013), 139. Buchanan later personally recruited retiring Judge Sara Soffel to join the firm as its first woman lawyer in 1962. "Judge Returns to Practice," *Pittsburgh Post-Gazette*, January 2, 1962. Dodds, meanwhile, later sent an unsolicited endorsement of Nellie's work to Clifford Fergus, telling him. "Whenever you and Mrs. Fergus are sitting contentedly in front of the fire counting your many blessings, don't ever forget to count your barrister daughter." Templeton Smith, *Pioneer at Law: the Life of Nellie Margaret Fergus and her Experiences as an Early Female Practitioner of Law* (Pittsburgh: Gibson Publishing, 2001), 66.

624 Smith, *Pioneer at Law*, 55.

625 Sell, *The Law Down*, 56-68; Elizabeth Bailey, interview by the author, February 24, 2010.

626 Smith, *Pioneer at Law*, 55.

627 Sell, *The Law Down*, 244.

628 E.J. Strassburger and Judge Eugene B. Strassburger, III interview by the author, September 14, 2010; John Schmitz, "Jane S. Strassburger: Braille transcriber, longtime volunteer," *Pittsburgh Post-Gazette*, February 6, 1997.

629 Smith, *Pioneer at Law*, 58.

630 Henry P. Hoffstot, Jr. and J. Tomlinson Fort, interview by the author, September 5, 2008.

631 Smith, *Pioneer at Law*, 58-59, 61.

632 Elizabeth Bailey, interview by the author, February 24, 2010.

633 Ibid.; Commonwelath ex rel . Buckner v. Barr, 376 Pa. 9 (1954).

634 David B. Fawcett, interview by the author, September 4, 2008; Roslyn M. Litman, interview by the author, July 16, 2008; Joseph J. Pass, Jr., interview by the author, April 7, 2014; Edgar M. Snyder, interview by the author, December 16, 2008.

635 Elizabeth Bailey, interview by the author, February 24, 2010.

636 Elizabeth Bailey (remarks, 50 and 60 Year Practitioners Award Ceremony, Duquesne Club, Pittsburgh, PA, December 1, 2014).

637 Smith, *Pioneer at Law*, 63; Joyce Gannon, "Obituary: Nellie Fergus Smith - First female attorney at law firm Reed Smith," *Pittsburgh Post-Gazette*, August 8, 2012.

638 Roslyn M. Litman, interview by the author, July 16, 2008.

639 Ibid.

640 David Wolf, "The Unjust Exile of a Superstar," *Life*, May 16, 1969.

641 Ibid.; Roslyn M. Litman, interview by the author, July 16, 2008; David Wolf, "$1 million end to an unjust exile," *Life*, June 27, 1969.

642 Bob Bashaw, interview by the author, April 6, 2015; Jerry Vondas, "Partner at Downtown law firm was role model," *Pittsburgh Tribune-Review*, July 22, 2009.

643 Adam Reinherz, "Linda Goldston leaves legacy of pioneering, philanthropy," *Jewish Chronicle*, November 26, 2014.

644 Demmler, *First Century*, 224.

645 Albert J. Neri, "Hanson hoping to expand her judicial horizons," *Pittsburgh Post-Gazette*, May 7, 1981.

646 Ibid.; Carl Hellerstedt, interview by the author, March 21, 2014.

647 Ann Butler, "Love Leads Bar's 'Portia' To Legal Stardom," *Pittsburgh Press*, February 2, 1975.

648 "Sex suit settled quietly," *North Hills News Record* (Pittsburgh, PA), September 11, 1976.

649 Demmler, *First Century*, 214, 222, 225; "Martha Hartle Munsch," *Reed Smith*, accessed March 10, 2017, https://www.reedsmith.com/martha_munsch; Sue C. Friedberg, interview by the author, March 18, 2015 (regarding herself and others at Buchanan Ingersoll); Eckert Seamans, *Celebrating 50 Years*, 14; "Joy Flowers Conti, Chief District Judge," *United States District Court for the Western District of Pennsylvania*, accessed March 10, 2017, http://www.pawd.uscourts.gov/content/joy-flowers-conti-chief-district-judge; Joyce Gannon, "K&L Gates growth chief eyeing central Europe," *Pittsburgh Post-Gazette*, February 21, 2010 (regarding Hartman); Marlee Myers, interview by the author, April 2, 2015.

650 ACBA, *Lawyers Pictorial Register*, passim; J. Lawrence McBride, *History of Dickie, McCamey & Chilcote, P.C.* (Pittsburgh: Dickie McCamey & Chilcote, 1995), 130-131, 200; Cindi Lash, "Lynette Norton: national known insurance lawyer, twice nominated for U.S. bench," *Pittsburgh Post-Gazette*, March 27, 2002; Carl Hellerstedt, interview by the author, March 21, 2014; Margaret B. Angel, interview by the author, February 8, 2017.

651 Sue C. Friedberg, interview by the author, March 18, 2015.

652 Marlee Myers, interview by the author, April 2, 2015.

653 ACBA, *Lawyers Pictorial Register*, passim.

654 Smith, *Pioneer at Law*, 59; Thomas M. Thompson, interview by the author, September 30, 2008.

655 "Why Pants Don't Suit Judge," *Pittsburgh Post-Gazette*, October 29, 1976.

656 Marlee Myers, interview by the author, April 2, 2015.

657 Laura Ellsworth, interview by the author, October 27, 2014.

658 Carmen J. Lee, "Hubert Teitelbaum, 79, was U.S. district judge 1970-89," *Pittsburgh Post-Gazette*, January 7, 1995.

659 Barbara Wolvovitz (remarks, Women's Bar Association 20th Anniversary Celebration, Omni William Penn Hotel, January 28, 2009) (hereafter cited as *WBA 20th Anniversary*); David Fawcett, interview by the author, March 2009.

660 Ed Phillips, "Lawyer misses with Ms.," *Pittsburgh Post-Gazette*, July 13, 1988.

661 Ibid.; David Fawcett, interview by the author, March 2009.

662 Wolvovitz, remarks, *WBA 20th Anniversary*.

663 Ed Phillips, "Lawyer misses with Ms.," *Pittsburgh Post-Gazette*, July 13, 1988; Associated Press, "U.S. Judge Won't Allow Lawyer 'to Use That Ms.'," *The New York Times*, July 14, 1988; Tara Bradley-Steck, "Judge Ordered Lawyer to Use Husband's Name," *Washington Post*, July 15, 1988.

664 Joyce Gannon, "Legal pioneer: Women's Bar Association marks 20th year with award for trailblazing attorney," *Pittsburgh Post-Gazette*, March 15, 2009.

665 Scott Mervis, "Musicians rally to support ailing Anne Feeney," *Pittsburgh Post-Gazette*, Decemebr 9, 2010; Anne Feeney's song, "Ms. Ogyny" appears on her 1990 album *There's a Whole Lot More of Us Than They Think*. Anne Feeney, "Anne Feeney Recordings," accessed March 11, 2017, http://www.annefeeney.com/Pages/tourbios.html.

666 Tom Hollander, remarks, *WBA 20th Anniversary*.

667 M. Susan Ruffner, remarks, *WBA 20th Anniversary*.

668 Morgan, Lewis & Bockius LLP, "Morgan Lewis Opens Pittsburgh Office, Adds Three New Partners; region's High Technology, emerging Companies Attracted Law Firm," press release, February 19, 1996, PR Newswire, accessed March 11, 2017, https://www.thefreelibrary.com/MORGAN+LEWIS+OPENS+PITTSBURGH+OFFICE,+ADDS+THREE+NEW+PARTNERS%3B...-a018012128; Patty Tascarella, "Women moving up law ranks," *Pittsburgh Business Times*, May 24, 2004; Joyce Gannon, "Only woman among 50 Top-Paid Executives is Equitable general counsel," *Pittsburgh Post-Gazette*, July 8, 2001; "All the way to Pittsburgh, she's making a legal mark," *Philadelphia Inquirer*, January 31, 1991 (regarding Pudlin); "Drago Named Vice President at Duquesne University," *Duquesne University*, October 15, 2009, http://www.duq.edu/news/drago-named-vice-president-at-duquesne-university; "People on the Move," *Pittsburgh Post-Gazette*, August 18, 1983 (regarding Wynstra); Fishman, *Women Judges*; Jim Davidson, "The Trials and Era of Judge Carol Los Mansmann," *Pittsburgh Press*, October 26, 1986; "Donetta W. Ambrose, Senior District Judge," *United States District Court for the Western District of Pennsylvania*, accessed March 10, 2017, http://www.pawd.uscourts.gov/content/donetta-w-ambrose-senior-district-judge.

669 Allegheny County Bar Association, *Report & Recommendations of the Gender Equality Task Force of the Allegheny County Bar Association* (Pittsburgh, PA: Allegheny County Bar Association, 2008), 1-2.

670 Phyllis G. Kitzerow and Virginia M. Tomlinson, *The Legal Profession: A Study of the ACBA Membership, 2005* (Pittsburgh, PA: Allegheny County Bar Association, 2006).

671 Laura Ellsworth, interview by the author, October 27, 2014.

672 Amy I. Pandit, interview by the author, February 3, 2015.

673 Kashmir Hill, "Third Circuit Affirms Dismissal of Female Partner's Discrimination Case," *Above the Law* (blog), July 23, 2010, accessed 3/18/2015, http://abovethelaw.com/2010/07/newsflash-equity-partners-cant-be-discriminated-against/

674 David Lat, "Ex-Reed Smith Partner Drops Sex Discrimination Suit Against Firm," *Above the Law* blog, May 5, 2011, accessed 3/18/2015, https://abovethelaw.com/2011/05/ex-reed-smith-partner-drops-sex-discrimination-suit-against-her-former-firm/

675 Georges Desvaux and Sandrine Devillard, *Women Matter 2: Female leadership, a competitive edge for the future* (Paris: McKinsey & Company, 2008), http://www.mckinsey.com/~/media/McKinsey/Business%20Functions/Organization/Our%20Insights/Women%20matter/Women_matter_oct2008_english.ashx.

676 Peter Kalis, "Women, teamwork and innovation," *The Lawyer*, April 27, 2015.

677 Ibid.

678 McKinsey, *Women Matter 2*.

679 Charles J. Queenan, Jr., interview by the author, January 14, 2009.

680 Richard L. Thornburgh, interview by the author, May 21, 2009.

681 Charles J. Queenan, Jr., interview by the author, January 14, 2009; William S. Dietrich II, "American Grit: The Dick Simmons Story," *Pittsburgh Quarterly* (Winter 2009); Clayton Sweeney, interview by the author, October 24, 2008; "Allegheny Ludlum: Breaking the rules to grow," *Business Week*, July 18, 1977.

682 Dietrich, "American Grit"; Charles J. Queenan, Jr., interview by the author, January 14, 2009.

683 Knight-Ridder, "In Steel Town, USX Runs On Gas, Oil," *Chicago Tribune*, March 12, 1995.

684 Lubove, *Twentieth-Century Pittsburgh II*, 276, n. 33.

685 Hilary Rosenberg, *The Vulture Investors* (New York: Wiley, 2000), 166-170; "Business Week reporting SEC probing AI," *Pittsburgh Post-Gazette*, August 1, 1986; Clayton Sweeney, interview by the author, October 24, 2008.

686 Dietrich, "American Grit."

687 Charles J. Queenan, Jr., interview by the author, January 14, 2009.

688 Joseph Gariti III, interview by the author, August 14, 2008.

689 Geoffrey Tomb, "USS Building Dedicated," *Pittsburgh Post-Gazette*, October 1, 1971.

690 Lubove, *Twentieth-Century Pittsburgh II*, 74; Joseph Gariti III, interview by the author, August 14, 2008; Lorna Doubet, "Mellon Bank to take over Dravo Tower," *Pittsburgh Post-Gazette*, November 12, 1982.

691 Lubove, *Twentieth-Century Pittsburgh II*, 364, fn. 54.

692 Ibid., 62.

693 "Historical Background," *Fifth Avenue Place*, accessed March 10, 2017, http://fifthavenueplacepa.com/fap2/about/bldgfacts/background.shtml.

694 Clayton Sweeney, interview by the author, October 24, 2008; Frederick Betz, *Executive Strategy: Strategic Management and Information Technology* (New York: Wiley, 2002), 460.

695 Jay P. Pederson, *International Directory of Company Histories*, vol. 34 (Detroit, MI: St. James Press, 2000), 436.

696 Bill Toland, "Nowhere But Up," *Pittsburgh Post-Gazette*, January 6, 2013; Lubove, *Twentieth-Century Pittsburgh II*, 7.

697 Bill Toland, "Nowhere But Up," *Pittsburgh Post-Gazette*, January 6, 2013; Cynthia Piechowiak, "Dravo to shut down Neville Island shipyard," *Pittsburgh Press*, December 4, 1984; Lubove, *Twentieth-Century Pittsburgh II*, 7; Jim Gallagher, "Westinghouse E. Pittsburgh plant is sold," *Pittsburgh Post-Gazette*, December 29, 1988; Lubove, *Twentieth-Century Pittsburgh II*, 19.

698 Franklin Tugwell, Andrew S. McElwaine and Michele Kanche Fetting, "The Challenge of the Environmental City: A Pittsburgh Case Study," in *Toward Sustainable Communities: Transition and Transformations in Environmental Policy*, eds. Daniel A. Manzmanian and Michael E. Kraft (Cambridge, MA: MIT Press, 1999), 197.

699 "Biographical Note," Staughton and Alice Lynd Collection, *Kent State University Archives*, accessed March 11, 2017, http://www.library.kent.edu/staughton-and-alice-lynd-collection.

700 Joseph S. Horack and Staughton Lynd, "The Steel Valley Authority," *NYU Review of Law and Social Change* XV (1986-1987), 113-114; Dale A. Hathaway, *Can Workers Have a Voice?: The Politics of Deindustrialization in Pittsburgh* (University Park, PA: Penn State University Press, 1993), 91-94.

701 Jay Hornack, interview by the author, October 8, 2015.

702 Mike Stout, "Eminent Domain & Bank Boycotts: The Tri-State Strategy in Pittsburgh," *Cornell University Labor Research Review* 1 (1983), 13.

703 Lee Hotz, "Coalition's Muscle Keeps City Nabisco Plant Open," *Pittsburgh Press*, December 22, 1982; Toni Locy, "Workers Fight Plant Closing, Rally For Political Support," *Pittsburgh Press*, December 17, 1982; Jay Hornack, interview by the author, October 8, 2015.

704 Albert J. Neri, "Plant-closing law fuels publicity," *Pittsburgh Post-Gazette*, August 15, 1983; Jay Hornack, interview by the author, October 8, 2015.

705 "Council appoints lawyer to defend plant closing law," *Pittsburgh Post-Gazette*, July 19, 1983; Linda S. Wilson, "Riled Papadakos silences crowd at plant law hearing," *Pittsburgh Post-Gazette*, August 17, 1983; Jay Hornack, interview by the author, October 8, 2015.

706 Jay Hornack, interview by the author, October 8, 2015.

707 Associated Press, "Dismissed and Defrocked, Ex-Pastor Still Divides Lutheran Parish," *The New York Times*, April 7, 1988.

708 Hathaway, *Can Workers Have a Voice*, 96-100; Mike Stout, "Reindustrialization from Below: The Steel Valley Authority," *Labor Research Review* 1, no. 9 (1986), 22-25; Irwin M. Marcus, "An Experiment in Reindustrialization: The Tri-State Conference on Steel and the Creation of the Steel Valley Authority," *Pennsylvania History* 54, no. 3 (July 1987), 185-186; Jay Hornack, interview by the author, October 8, 2015; Hoerr, *And the Wolf Finally Came*, 583-586.

709 Bob Hertzel, "Out-of-town bids for Pirates invited," *Pittsburgh Press*, June 17, 1985.

710 Ron Cook, "Pittsburgh Pirates: The Eighties - A terrible time of trial and error," *Pittsburgh Post-Gazette*, September 29, 2000.

711 C. Kent May, interview by the author, September 1, 2011.

712 Bill Utterback, "Anything's possible with Barger at controls," *Pittsburgh Press*, November 30, 1990.

713 Steve Hubbard, "Barger Euologized As Caring, Driven," *Pittsburgh Tribune-Review*, Decmber 15, 1992.

714 C. Kent May, interview by the author, September 1, 2011.

715 Ibid.

716 Henry Lenard, "Barger's Pirate victory, Finessing a franchise to safety," *Pittsburgh Business Times*, October 28, 1995.

717 "Playing for Keeps: Chapter I - How it began: The Galbreath family decides to get out," *Pittsburgh Post-Gazette*, September 1, 1996.

718 C. Kent May, interview by the author, September 1, 2011.

719 Dan Donovan and Jon Schmitz, "Pirates nearing signing on sales," *Pittsburgh Press*, December 22, 1985; Lubove, *Twentieth-Century Pittsburgh II*, 306-307, fn. 70; Joseph Gariti III, interview by the author, August 14, 2008.

720 Asset Purchase Agreement, Exhibits and Schedules between Pittsburgh Associates and Pittsburgh Athletic Company, of December 13, 1985, author's collection.

721 C. Kent May, interview by the author, September 1, 2011.

722 Henry Lenard, "Barger's Pirate victory, Finessing a franchise to safety," *Pittsburgh Business Times*, October 28, 1995.

723 Associated Press, "Money Bonds Pirates to Pittsburgh," *Palm Beach Post*, March 15, 1986.

724 Dan Donovan, "Pirate investors lose Flaherty support bid," *Pittsburgh Press*, March 8, 1986; Craig Stock, "A murky, intricate deal to save a team," *Philadelphia Inquirer*, January 14, 1986.

725 Henry Lenard, "Barger's Pirate victory, Finessing a franchise to safety," *Pittsburgh Business Times*, October 28, 1995.

726 Stout, *Reindustrialization from Below*, 25.

727 Hathaway, *Can Workers Have a Voice*, 100-104; Associated Press, "Union and U.S. Steel Agree: Furnace Not Worth Saving," *The New York Times*, January 9, 1986.

728 Jay Hornack, interview by the author, October 8, 2015; Saughton Lynd, *Living Inside Our Hope: A Steadfast Radical's Thoughts on Rebuilding the Movement* (Ithaca, NY: Cornell University Press, 1997), 183.

729 Jan Ackerman, "Judge rejects authority's plea," *Pittsburgh Post-Gazette*, June 18, 1986; Jay Hornack, interview by the author, October 8, 2015.

730 Jay Hornack, interview by the author, October 8, 2015.

731 John D. Oravecz, "State anti-takeover laws put brakes on hostile corporate bids," *Pittsburgh Press*, March 20, 1988; Thomas M. Thompson, interview by the author, March 15, 2017.

732 William R. Newlin, interview by the author, February 12, 2014.

733 Lubove, *Twentieth-Century Pittsburgh II*, 44-45; Lorant, *Story of an American City*, 624-628.

734 Lorant, *Story of an American City*, 628-629; Mary Niederberger, "Posvar decision to retire at Pitt minor surprise," *Pittsburgh Press*, May 11, 1990; Lubove, *Twentieth-Century Pittsburgh II*, 46; "About Us | University of Pittsburgh Cancer Institute (UPCI)," *University of Pittsburgh Cancer Institute*, accessed March 12, 2017, http://upci.upmc.edu/about/.

735 Lorant, *Story of an American City*, 601; William Y. Arms, *The Early Years of Academic Computing* (Internet-First University Press, 2014), 1.49; Lubove, *Twentieth-Century Pittsburgh II*, 53.

736 William R. Newlin, interview by the author, February 12, 2014.

737 Ibid.

738 Daniel Bates, "The Quintessential Pacesetter," *Smart Business*, July 22, 2002; Willie Schatz, "Legent Corp. Co-Founder Resigns Post," *Washington Post*, March 19, 1990.

739 William R. Newlin, interview by the author, February 12, 2014; Hon. Tom Murphy, interview by the author, May 2013.

740 Hon. Tom Murphy, interview by the author, May 2013.

741 Liz Cousins, "Saint Vincent Opened a New World to Alumnus Herb Boyer, Biotech Founder," *Saint Vincent Magazine*, Fall 2013.

742 Lubove, *Twentieth-Century Pittsburgh II*, 42.

743 "What kind of legislator?," *Pittsburgh Post-Gazette*, May 12, 1982.

744 William R. Newlin, interview by the author, February 12, 2014.

745 Ibid.

746 Pittsburgh Technology Council, "Pittsburgh Technology Council to Feature Firms at Annual Electro-Optics Conference," press release, August 5, 2003, PR Newswire, accessed March 12, 2017, http://www.prnewswire.com/news-releases/pittsburgh-technology-council-to-feature-firms-at-annual-electro-optics-conference-70886407.html.

747 The Enterprise Corporation of Pittsburgh, *A Survey of Venture Capital in Pittsburgh 1989* (Pittsburgh: Enterprise Corporation of Pittsburgh, 1989), 4.

748 William R. Newlin, interview by the author, February 12, 2014; Jim Gallagher, "CEO Venture Fund offers money, advice," *Pittsburgh Post-Gazette*, April 15, 1987.

749 William R. Newlin, interview by the author, February 12, 2014.

750 John R. McCarty, "Local program designed to promote high-tech," *Pittsburgh Press*, November 4, 1985; William R. Newlin, interview by the author, February 12, 2014; Teresa F. Lindeman, "Newlin exits Buchanan law firm for Dick's," *Pittsburgh Post-Gazette*, September 24, 2003.

751 William R. Newlin, interview by the author, February 12, 2014.

752 Audrey Glickman, *History of the Firm*, 13; "Buchanan boosts high-tech," *Pittsburgh Post-Gazette*, June 20, 2000.

753 Gregory B. Jordan, interview by the author, August 28, 2014.

754 Daniel Bates, "Thriving on the Art of a Good Deal," *Smart Business*, April 1995.

755 William R. Newlin, interview by the author, February 12, 2014.

756 Hon. Tom Murphy, interview by the author, May 2013.

757 William R. Newlin, interview by the author, February 12, 2014.

758 "The Business of Pittsburgh," *Pittsburgh Post-Gazette*, March 25, 2001.

759 Marlee Myers, interview by the author, April 2, 2015.

760 Ibid.

761 Malia Spencer, "FORE founders reunite for an evening," *Pittsburgh Business Times*, July 12, 2012; Terzah Ewing, "FreeMarkets' IPO Marks Another Explosive Debut," *Wall Street Journal*, December 13, 1999; Dawn Kawamoto, "Ariba to buy FreeMarkets for $493 million," *ZDNet*, January 23, 2004, http://www.zdnet.com/article/ariba-to-buy-freemarkets-for-493-million/

762 "Shattered dreams, Hollow echoes," *Pittsburgh Post-Gazette*, July 25, 1999.

763 See, generally, "The Home Game: First Inning," *Pittsburgh Post-Gazette*, April 7, 1999; Pirates Acquisition – Closing Documents, February 14, 1996, author's collection; Lease, Operating Agreement and Related Transactions, dated June 2, 2000, author's collection.

764 Associated Press, "For Steve Jobs, Next time is now," *Pittsburgh Press*, October 11, 1988; Foo Yun Chee and Niclas Mika, "Philips in $5 billion Respironics deal," *Reuters*, December 21, 2007; Kim Lyons and Patty Tascarella, "German firm pays $200 million for Renal Solutions," *Pittsburgh Business Times*, November 29, 2007.

765 Teresa F. Lindeman, "Newlin exits Buchanan law firm for Dick's," *Pittsburgh Post-Gazette*, September 24, 2003

766 Joyce Gannon, "Buchanan Ingersoll, Klett Rooney plan to join forces July 1," *Pittsburgh Post-Gazette*, June 14, 2006.

767 Henry Lenard, "Barger's Pirate victory, Finessing a franchise to safety," *Pittsburgh Business Times*, October 28, 1995.

768 William R. Newlin, interview by the author, February 12, 2014.

769 Clare Ansberry, "Why Pittsburgh? Plenty of Reasons," *Wall Street Journal*, September 24, 2009.

770 Charles J. Queenan, Jr., interview by the author, January 14, 2009.

Law City: An Epilogue

1. Reed Smith, "Global Law Firm Reed Smith Sponsors WIN Summit 2017," press release, November 18, 2016, accessed March 15, 2017, https://www.reedsmith.com/Global-Law-Firm-Reed-Smith-Sponsors-WIN-Summit-2017-11-17-2016/.
2. "Firm Overview," *K&L Gates*, accessed March 15, 2017, http://www.klgates.com/about/.
3. Gregory B. Jordan, interview by the author, August 28, 2014.
4. Transcript, *Morning Joe*, MSNBC, Video, January 4, 2012, https://archive.org/details/MSNBCW_20120104_110000_Morning_Joe?q=Morning+joe#start/420/end/480.
5. David L. Michelmore, "Santorum has built a reputation on impatience," *Pittsburgh Post-Gazette*, September 11, 1994.
6. James M. Houston to James I. Smith, III, April 17, 1995, Allegheny County Bar Association Decedent Files, Allegheny County Bar Association, ACBA Collection.
7. Jeremiah G. Garvey, email to author, May 22, 2015.
8. Rakesh Pandey, Sr. Manager, Effectual Services, email to author, September 17, 2014.
9. Frederic Lardinois, "LegalSifter Helps Designers and Developers Read Their Contracts," *TechCrunch*, August 7, 2014.
10. Charles J. Queenan, Jr., interview by the author, January 14, 2009.
11. Ned Renzi, interview by the author, October 4, 2014.
12. John P. Gismondi, interview with the author, October 26, 2012.
13. Ibid.; "History of Justus," *Justus ADR Services*, accessed March 15, 2017, http://www.justusadr.com/company-history.html.
14. "History of Justus," *Justus ADR Services*, accessed March 15, 2017, http://www.justusadr.com/company-history.html.
15. John P. Gismondi, interview with the author, October 26, 2012.
16. Pamela Gaynor and Torsten Ove, "Cindrich quitting to work at UPMC," *Pittsburgh Post-Gazette*, January 6, 2007; Robert J. Cindrich, interview by the author, July 9, 2014.
17. Robert J. Cindrich, interview by the author, July 9, 2014.
18. Paul Boas, interview by the author, July 23, 2014.
19. Robert J. Cindrich, interview by the author, July 9, 2014.
20. U.S. v. Booker, 543 U.S. 220 (2005).
21. Paul Boas, interview by the author, July 23, 2014.
22. Ellen Rosen, "Cravath, Kirland, S&C on Kraft-Heinz Deal: Business of Law," *Bloomberg*, March 26, 2015, https://www.bloomberg.com/news/articles/2015-03-26/cravath-kirkland-s-c-on-kraft-heinz-deal-business-of-law.
23. Steve Schaefer, "Buffett's Ketchup Catch: Berkshire Teams With 3G For $23B Heinz Buy," *Forbes*, February 14, 2013.
24. Joseph Bucklin Bishop, *Theodore Roosevelt and His Time*, vol. I (New York: Charles Scribner's, 1920), 183.
25. Annie Dillard, *An American Childhood* (New York: Harper & Row, 1989), 154.
26. L.J. Marsico and Audrey Glickman, "EHS: ¾ of a Century of Wit and Wisdom," *The* (Buchanan Ingersoll) *Bugle* (December 20, 1991).
27. James J. Barnes, interview by the author, August 19, 2014.
28. Gregory B. Jordan, interview by the author, August 28, 2014.
29. James J. Barnes, interview by the author, August 19, 2014.
30. Ibid.
31. Ralph Baxter, interview by the author, October 10, 2014; Catherine Rampell, "At Well-Paying Law Firms, a Low-Paid Corner," *The New York Times*, May 23, 2011.
32. Robert G. Sable, interview by the author, July 21, 2008.
33. Marlee Myers, interview by the author, April 2, 2015.
34. "Attack of the bean-counters," *The Economist*, March 19, 2015.
35. Paul Carrington, *Stewards of Demcoracy: Law as Public Profession* (Boulder, CO: Westview Press, 1999), 1.
36. Robert J. Cindrich, interview by the author, July 9, 2014.

INDEX

3G Capital **549**
525 William Penn Place (Pittsburgh) **406**

A

A. Overholt & Company **232**. see also Old Overholt Whiskey
A.W. Mellon Educational and Charitable Trust **396, 409**
Abbott, William L. **148**
Abernathy v. Alabama (1965) **470**
Academy of Trial Lawyers (Pittsburgh) **376-377**
Accorsi, Salvatore **269**
Acheson, Marcus W. **66, 69, 95, 104, 203, 233**
Acheson, Marcus W., Jr. **233**
ACTION-Housing, Inc. **412**
Adams, John **18, 19**
Adams, John Quincy **28, 35**
Adams, Russell H. **457**
Adamson, Ernie **417**
Addison, Alexander **9, 10, 14-16, 21, 226**
    impeachment as judge **19-22**
Adelphia Communications Corp. **538**
Adkins v. Children's Hospital (1923) **306**
Adomeit, Peter **297**
Adventures of Robin Hood, The (1938) **284**
AFL-CIO **386**. see also American Federation of Labor (AFL); Congress of Industrial Unions (CIO)
African Americans in Pittsburgh **44, 119, 337**
    African American bar mid-twentieth century **457**
    citizenship and right to vote **44-46**
    early African American lawyers **119**
    first admitted to Bar Association **346**
    first admitted to practice **118**
    gravitation toward Democratic Party **343**
    Great Migration, the **338-340**
    Gus Greenlee and the Hill District **479**
    housing discrimination **460-464**
    Old Pittsburghers, or OPs **335, 337, 339**
    Underground railroad **46**
    Vashon attempts admission to bar **117-118**
Afro-American League of Western Pennsylvania **119**
Agnew, Daniel **95**
Aiken, David **140**
Aiken, Frederick **56-59**
Akin Gump Strauss Hauer & Feld (law firm) **535**
Albany Law School **140**
Albert, Nathan **458**
Alcoa (Aluminum Company of America) **76, 84, 367-73, 396, 398, 414-415, 460-461, 484, 526-527, 531-532, 564**
    and the Buchanan-Eckert split **449-455**
    and urban renewal **414-418**
    U.S. v. Alcoa. see United States v. Alcoa (1945)
Alcoa Building (Pittsburgh) **407, 437, 445, 448**
Alden, Roger, Major **25**
Alder, Cohen & Grigsby (law firm). see Cohen & Grigsby (law firm)
Aldisert, Ruggero **272, 377, 428, 430, 434-435, 555**
Aldridge, Jay **533**
Alessandroni, Walter **480**
Alger, Horatio **331, 489**
Aliquippa, Pennsylvania **293-294, 298, 303, 337, 522**
Allegheny Arsenal **85, 92**
Allegheny Bessemer Steel Works **152**
Allegheny Center Mall (Pittsburgh) **412**
Allegheny City, Pennsylvania **37, 48, 89, 113, 118, 127, 210, 336**
    unified with Pittsburgh **213**
Allegheny Conference on Community Development (ACCD) **403-407, 413, 526-527**
    Committee No. 4 **408**
Allegheny County Bar Association **37, 94, 117, 119, 143, 157, 203, 212, 229, 250, 254, 270, 295, 304, 327, 346, 375, 378, 382, 400, 405, 421, 424, 426, 431-432, 466-467, 476, 503, 505, 510, 515, 559, 565**
    beginnings **68-69**
    Bench-Bar Conference **377, 379**
    Committee on Offenses **254, 258-259, 421, 436**
    elections **202**
    exclusion of women and minorities **201**
    Women in the Law Committee **510-511**
    "Volunteer Defender" program **380**
Allegheny County Board of Law Examiners **199, 200, 428, 430-431, 433, 435**
    and "good moral character" **200**
    and review of Communist ties of bar candidates **428**
Allegheny County Coroner's Office **215, 487**
Allegheny County Court of Common Pleas

and Lincoln assassination 53
decrease in jury trials 546
established 10
expansion 68, 202
first courthouse at the Diamond 10
first judges 10
integrated court system 202
Allegheny County Court of Quarter Sessions 9
Allegheny County Courthouse and Jail 62, 67, 76, 84, 95, 112, 131, 157, 163, 195, 202, 203, 244, 249, 262, 329, 380, 421, 426, 457, 480, 489
Allegheny County District Court
abolished 68
Allegheny County Fairgrounds 413
Allegheny County Juvenile Court 215
Allegheny County Law Library 65, 215-216
Allegheny County Orphans' Court 108, 117
established 68
Allegheny County Port Authority Transit (PAT) 413-414, 526
Allegheny County Public Defender's Office
created 380
Allegheny County, County Court of 203, 252, 278, 457
Allegheny County, Pennsylvania 6, 38, 62, 67, 69, 95, 112, 119, 153, 202, 203, 215, 282, 284, 343, 403, 467, 483
establishment of 8, 9
Allegheny Foundation 492
Allegheny Health, Education and Research Foundation 511
Allegheny International, Inc. 388, 522-27, 530, 534
Allegheny Ludlum Corporation 385, 444, 517-519, 532
Allegheny Ludlum Industries, Inc. see Allegheny International, Inc.
Allegheny Mountains 6, 141
Allegheny Observatory (Pittsburgh) 397
Allegheny River 6, 9, 61, 68, 92, 217, 363, 377, 396, 412, 416
Alleghenys (baseball club) 127
Allen, Alexander J. "Joe" 459
Allen, Cheryl Lynn 474, 511
Allen, Macon Bolling 115
Alliance, Ohio 135, 140, 188, 196
Allison, James 13
Alpern, Anne X. 334-338, 347, 402, 405-406, 414, 456, 459, 506, 543
Alter, George E. 234, 254
Altoona, Pennsylvania 391, 533
Amalgamated Association of Iron and Steel Workers 136, 143, 172, 181, 189, 226, 251, 292-293, 300, 373, 383

Homestead negotiations before 1892 148-149
Homestead Steel Strike (1892) 160-169
Steel Recognition Strike (1901) 247-249
Amalgamated Transit Union 386
Ambrose, Donetta 511
American Association (baseball) 130-131
American Bar Association 300, 358, 380, 481
American Basketball Association 504
American Basketball League 503
American Civil Liberties Union 216, 251, 262, 269, 278, 296, 427, 465-466, 503, 510
American Federation of Labor (AFL) 251, 255, 298, 346, 383
American Flint Green Bottle Glass Workers 136
American Law Review 145, 167
American Lawyer, The 393, 449, 541
American League (baseball) 127-128
American Liberty League 284, 294, 296, 299, 303-304, 312, 341
American Medical Association 481
American Revolution 4, 10, 48
American Sheet Steel Company 189, 246-247
American Slav Congress 418
American Standard Corporation 529-530
American Steel and Wire Company 180
American Steel Hoop Company 187, 246
American Tinplate Company 187, 189, 246
American University 271
Americans Battling Communism 418-419
Americans for Democratic Action 399
Ameringer, Oscar 267
Amersham Biosciences Corp. 534
Ames (department store) 412
Ames, Charles B. 359
Amherst College 102, 465
Ampco Pittsburgh Corporation 450
Anarchist bombings (1919) 247, 254
Anderson, D. Malcolm 493, 508
Anderson, John U., Jr. 440-441
Anestis, Robert 536
Angel, Margaret 506
Appomattox Court House, Virginia 51, 53
Arbuckle-Jamison Foundation 409
Archbald, Robert 199, 211
Arens, Richard 434
Arensberg, Charles F.C. 233, 254, 258, 264, 331, 400, 402, 432
Arensberg, Emily 331
Ariba, Inc. 537
Armco Steel 385, 519
Armstrong Cork Company 444, 529, 532

Armstrong County, Pennsylvania **69**
Armstrong World Industries, Inc. *see Armstrong Cork Company*
Armstrong, Clyde A. **311-314, 383**
Armstrong, David J. **367, 389**
Armstrong, Thomas **135**
Army-McCarthy Hearings **431**
Arnd, Maurice J. **406**
Arnold & Porter (law firm) **361**
Arnold, Thurman **361, 363-364**
Aronson brothers, Harry, Harvey, Leonard and Jacob **238**
Ascheim, Cappy **469**
Aspinwall, Pennsylvania **217**
Associated Press v. National Labor Relations Board (1937) **302-306**
Association of the Bar of the City of New York **67-68**
Astaire, Fred **507**
Atkinson, T.O. **222**
Atlantic City, New Jersey **184, 355**
Atwood, Henry **123**
Atzerodt, George **54-57**
Austin, J.C. **341**
Avery, Charles, Rev. **47**

B

Babcock, Edward V. **340**
Babcock, F.R. **226**
Babst, Calland, Clements and Zomnir (law firm) **390**
Bailey, Elizabeth **500-503, 514**
Bailey, John H. **66**
Baird, Thomas H. **23**
Bakery Square (Pittsburgh) **538**
Bakewell & Christy (law firm) **99**
Bakewell Building (Pittsburgh) **457**
Bakewell, Christy & Kerr (law firm) **99**
Bakewell, James **121**
Bakewell, Thomas **121**
Bakewell, William **99, 100, 121-122, 388**
Baldwin, Cynthia **474, 511**
Baldwin, Henry **22, 31-39, 44-45**
  A General View of the Origin and Nature of the Constitution ... (1837) **29**
  alleged to be mentally unstable **29-30**
  and "middle ground" **29, 31**
  and Andrew Jackson **27-28, 30**
  and dissenting opinions on Supreme Court **28**
  and last duel in Pittsburgh **26**
  and the "Great Triumvirate" **24**
  appointed to U.S. Supreme Court **28**
  death **30**
  in Congress **27**
Baldwin, Mark **132-134**
Baldwin, Roger **216, 251, 262, 264**
Ball, George **399**
Baltimore & Ohio Railroad **80-81, 90, 92-93**
Baltimore Orioles **433, 520**
Baltimore, Maryland **93, 118, 129, 455-456, 482**
Bane, John C. **259-261, 262, 264, 384**
Bane, John C., Jr. **384**
Bank of Pittsburgh **100, 266**
Bankers Trust Company **268**
Bankruptcy Act of 1867 **124**
Bankruptcy Reform Act of 1978 **388**
Barach, Louis **270**
Barcoski, John **274-275, 283**
Barger, Carl **526-528, 539, 554**
Barnes Dulac (law firm) **492**
Barnes, James **475, 551-552**
Barnie, Billy **129**
Barr, Joseph **461, 464-466, 480-481, 502**
Barr, Robert and Leona **502**
Barrett, Karen **505**
Barton, John **83, 93, 121**
Barton, Thomas E. **347, 457, 459**
baseball **130-133, 132, 337, 355, 389, 428-429, 442, 460, 479, 520, 525-528, 537-538**
Baskin & Sears (law firm) **389, 451, 506, 524**
Baskin & Steingut (law firm) **451**
Baskin, Boreman, Wilner, Sachs, Gondelman & Craig (law firm) **451, 505**
Baskin, Flaherty, Elliott & Mannino (law firm) **389, 451**
Baskin, Karen **506**
Baskin, Philip **452-453, 480**
Baskin, Seymour **451**
Bassett, Robert **403**
Bates Street (Pittsburgh) **27**
Bates v. State Bar of Arizona (1977) **391, 393**
Bates, Edward **22, 55**
Bates, Frederick **21-22**
Bates, Tarleton **20-21, 27-30, 44, 55**
Bates, William **219**
Battle of the Bulge, the (WWII) **372, 458, 508**
Baush Machine Tool Company **360-361**
Baxter, Fred **487**
Baxter, Ralph **551**
Bayne, Thomas **150**
Beal v. Doe (1977) **467**
Beal, James H., Jr. **243, 266**

626 INDEX

Beal, James H., Sr. **231, 438**
Beard, Philip E., Sr. **438-439**
Beatty, Suzanne **216, 328-329**
Beaver County Shanghaiing Incident (1933) **343**
Beaver County, Pennsylvania **6, 112, 123, 247, 292, 343, 344**
Beck, James M. **352**
Beck, Rosina **334**
Beckley, Jake "Eagle Eye" **128**
Bedford County, Pennsylvania **6, 230**
Bedford, Pennsylvania **15-16**
Bell, Cool Papa **337**
Bell, Edgar D. **234, 242**
Bell, J. Snowden **100**
Bell, John C., Jr. **435**
Bellevue, Pennsylvania **157, 406, 421**
Beltzhoover (Pittsburgh) **462**
Belzberg family **529**
Ben Avon, Pennsylvania **89**
Ben Franklin Partnership **533**
Ben Hur: A Tale of the Christ (1925) **271**
Bendell, Nicholas **132-133**
Benedum, Michael **287, 341, 344**
Benedum-Trees Building (Pittsburgh) **195**
Benesch, Katherine **506**
Berg, Moe **429**
Berger, Gertrude **421-422**
Bergman, Ingrid **284**
Berkman, Alexander **163, 181-182, 249, 251, 257**
Berkman, Allen **450**
Berkman, Louis **450**
Berkman, Ruslander, Pohl, Lieber & Engel (law firm) **450, 452, 474, 506, 524**
Berkshire Hathaway **549**
Berry, Ted **457**
Bethesda United Presbyterian Church **459**
Bethlehem Steel Corporation **385**
Bialas, Irons & Ryan (law firm) **238**
Bialas, Joseph **238**
Biddle brothers, Ed and Jack **328**
Biddle, Francis **297-298**
Biddle, Richard **40**
Bierbauer, Lou **129**
Bigelow Boulevard (Pittsburgh) **218**
Bigelow, Edward M. **210, 213-215, 397**
  and Pittsburgh parks **212**
Bigelow, Thomas S. **109, 211, 213, 217**
  effort to establish "Bigelow machine" **212**
Bigham, Joel **121**
Bigham, Kirk **121**
Bigham, Maria Louisa Lewis **46**

Bigham, Thomas, J. "T.J." **30, 36, 38, 47-50, 54, 121**
Billows, Walter E. **119-120, 336**
Biological Detection Systems Inc. **534**
Birchmere Ventures **534, 545**
Bishop, Joseph Bucklin **351**
Bispham, George Tucker **181**
Black Box Corporation **534**
Black Fury (1935) **284**
Black Panthers **469-470**
Black, Alexander (Sr.) **231, 235, 240, 254, 446**
Black, Alexander, Jr. **443, 445, 448**
Black, Hugo L. **345**
Black, Samuel W., Colonel **37, 38, 41, 51, 64, 237**
  Civil War service and death **48-49**
Blackburn, Colin, Baron Blackburn **145**
Blackstone's Commentaries **22-23**
Blair, Lawrence D. **236**
Blair, Ross **378**
Blakeley, Archibald **69, 113**
Blakeley, William **222, 223**
Blaner, David **379, 476**
Blank Rome (law firm) **475, 551**
Blawnox, Pennsylvania **486**
Blaxter, H.V. **381**
Blenko, Walter, Jr. **388**
Bloomfield (Pittsburgh) **109**
Blough, Roger **398**
Boas, Edward **468**
Boas, Ken **469**
Boas, Paul **468-469, 548-549**
Boca Raton, Florida **389**
Bogart, Humphrey **284**
Bolling, Raynal **359**
Bonaparte, Charles J. **220, 354**
Bonsall, Ward **332**
Booker, Daniel I. **389, 540, 550**
Boone, Joel T., Dr. **282**
Booth & Flinn (construction firm) **110, 207-208, 210**
Booth, John Wilkes **54-55**
Booth, William Wallace **196, 243**
Boston University **512**
Boston, Massachusetts **4, 72, 104, 115, 212, 272, 273, 408**
Bostwick, Roy G. **254, 311-312**
Bouton, J.W. **248**
Bowman, John Gabbert **295-297, 500**
Bowytz, Louis **480-481**
Boyd, Tommy **68**
Boyer and Morton (law firm) **288**
Boyer, Herbert, Dr. **533**

Boyle, Edward C. **459, 480-481, 483, 487, 497**
Brace Boycott Case **137**
Brackenridge, Alexander **40**
Brackenridge, Henry Marie **8, 12**
Brackenridge, Hugh Henry **3-33, 44, 390, 554-555, 560**
    address at Mingo Creek **14**
    alleged to be "mad" **8, 17-18, 30**
    and American literature **5, 17**
    and the "middle course" **17, 31**
    appointed to Pennsylvania Supreme Court **17**
    celebrates ratification of the Constitution **10**
    death of first wife **9**
    defends African American woman sold into slavery **44**
    defends whiskey tax protesters **12**
    defense of Mamachtaga **6, 8**
    inquisition before Hamilton **3, 11, 16**
    in state assembly **8**
    marries second wife, Sabina Wolfe **11**
    Modern Chivalry (novel) **17, 21, 25**
    opposition to whiskey excise tax **12**
Brackenridge, Pennsylvania **519**
Brackenridge, Sabina Wolfe **10-11**
Braddock, J.R., Colonel **163**
Braddock, Pennsylvania **152, 158, 337, 502, 522**
Braden, J.M. **163**
Bradford, David **9, 15-17**
    and Thomas Jefferson **18**
    calls for rebel milita **14**
    delivers inflammatory address at Mingo Creek **13**
    escapes to Spanish Louisiana **18**
    pardoned **18**
    refuses to prosecute whiskey tax protesters **13**
Bradford, Pennsylvania **117**
Bradford, William (Plymouth colonist) **102**
Bradford, William (U.S. Attorney General) **4, 15-16**
Bradley, Joseph P. **69**
Bradshaw, George Calvert **259**
Bradwell, Myra **120**
Brady, F.J. **222**
Braham, Walter **367**
Brandeis, Louis **273, 304-305**
Brand, William **222-225**
Brandt, Carl **531**
Brandt, Riester, Brandt and Malone (law firm) **531**
Breck, E.Y. **165**

Bredin, Samuel **374**
Brennan & Brennan (law firm) **375**
Brennan, T. Robert "Bob" **375, 390**
Brennen, William J. **135-139, 188-197, 222, 224, 227, 247, 250, 251, 255, 313, 366, 386, 543, 555, 583 n.366**
    alderman election controversy **134**
    as bridge between laborers, Democrats and Republicans **148**
    as first advocate to labor unions **135-136**
    as Jones & Laughlin machinist **134**
    as Pittsburgh Democratic leader **149-150, 155, 206, 212, 214**
    as union leader **135**
    childhood and early education **133**
    death **263**
    elected to city council **134**
    enters Pittsburgh bar **135**
    Homestead Steel Strike (1892) **157-168**
    runs for Congress **151-152**
    Westmoreland County Miners' Strike (1910) **247**
Bridge, James Howard **83, 177**
Bridgeville, Pennsylvania **480**
Brighton Heights (Pittsburgh) **68**
Brill, Steven **392**
Brinton, Robert M., General **92-95**
Brophy, John **275**
Brown Stewart & Bostwick (law firm) **254**
Brown University **468**
Brown v. Board of Education (1954) **458**
Brown, Adam Mercer **66, 212**
    recorder of Pittsburgh **212**
Brown, Byrd **458, 461, 466-470, 476**
Brown, Clarence **398**
Brown, H. Rap **468**
Brown, Homer S. **347-355, 403, 457-458, 460, 464**
Brown, James B. **524**
Brown, Joseph "J.O." **210, 212-213**
Bruce, Lenny **469**
Brunot Island, Pennsylvania **140**
Brunot, Hilary B. **85**
Brunwasser, Allen N. **376**
Bryant, Lucinda **47**
Bryan, William Jennings **182**
Buchanan Ingersoll & Rooney (law firm) **506, 539**
    see also Buchanan Ingersoll (law firm); Buchanan, Ingersoll, Rodewald, Kyle & Buerger (law firm); Smith, Buchanan, Ingersoll, Rodewald & Eckert (law firm); Smith, Buchanan & Ingersoll (law firm); Smith, Buchanan, Scott & Ingersoll (law firm); Smith, Buchanan, Gordon & Scott (law firm); Gordon, Smith, Buchanan & Scott (law firm); and Gordon & Smith (law firm)

Buchanan Ingersoll (law firm) **367, 388-389, 415, 444, 449, 453, 474-475, 510, 513-514, 529, 534-535, 538-539.** *see also Buchanan Ingersoll & Rooney (law firm)*
    brochure controversy **393-394**
Buchanan, Ingersoll, Rodewald, Kyle & Buerger (law firm) **381, 389, 448, 481, 505, 507, 518, 531, 549.** *see also Buchanan Ingersoll & Rooney (law firm)*
Buchanan, James **35, 44, 48**
Buchanan, John G. **202, 238, 241-245, 304, 381-382, 432, 434, 437, 450, 454-462, 499, 555, 616 n.616**
    and World War I **242-245**
Buchanan, John G., Jr. **443, 446**
Buckley, Robert **518-519, 521**
Bucknell University **379**
Buckner, Eleanor **502**
Bucks County, Pennsylvania **166**
Buell, Blenko, Ziesenheim & Beck (law firm) **388**
Buell, Ziesenheim, Beck & Alstadt (law firm) **388, 535**
Buerger, David B. **270**
Buffalo, New York **47**
Buffington, Joseph **69, 131, 203, 208**
Buffington, Kenneth **242-244**
Bull Ring cases **83-85**
Bunche, Ralph **341**
Burgoyne, Arthur **140, 163, 578 n.140**
Burgwin Churchill (law firm) **402**
Burgwin, George C. **258**
Burgwin, Hill **122**
Burke brothers, Robert and Andrew **73**
Burke, James Francis **139, 236, 268, 285**
    death **281**
Burke, Renee **508**
Burleigh & Challener (law firm) **234**
Burleigh, Clarence **110, 123, 163, 165, 181, 230, 234**
Burlington Railroad **350**
Burns, Bill **496**
Burnside, Ambrose, General **49**
Burr, Aaron **25**
Bush, George W. **28, 482**
Bushman, Francis X. **271**
business partnerships **63-64, 82**
Butler County, Pennsylvania **112, 199, 290, 328, 354, 439**
Butler Street (Pittsburgh) **93**
Butler, Pierce **304-305**
Butler, William N. **119**
Butzler, Robert **480, 485, 490**
Byers, A.M. **82-83**
Byllesby, Henry M. **101**

C

Cadence Design Systems, Inc. **534**
Cadiz, Ohio **39**
Cadwalader, John **42**
Cadwalader, Wickersham & Taft (law firm) **299, 357, 399**
Caffey, Francis G. **365-368, 445**
Cahn, Edgar **380**
Calhoun, John C. **28**
California (Pa.) State Teachers' College **327**
California Institute of Technology **530**
Caliguiri, Richard **523-527**
    and "Renaissance II" **521**
Callam, James **38**
Callan, Mary **328**
Calvary Episcopal Church (Pittsburgh) **208-209, 218, 258**
Cambria County Bar Association **392**
Cambria County, Pennsylvania **418**
    bar of **143**
Cambria Iron Company **85, 143-144**
Cameron, J. Donald **69**
Cameron, Simon **44, 48**
Cameron-Quay machine **69, 150, 212-214**
Cannon, Don **494**
Canton, Ohio **150**
Canuti, Felidio "Frank" **272**
Caplan, Louis **329, 432**
Carborundum Company **76**
Cardozo, Benjamin **304**
Carlisle, Pennsylvania **6, 10, 15, 17, 22**
Carlton House (Pittsburgh) **374, 377**
Carmody, John **298, 300**
Carnahan, Robert B. **57, 397**
Carnegie Brothers **140, 146, 173, 176**
    Iron Clad Agreement and ejecture clause **173-174**
Carnegie Building **62, 68, 176, 179, 195, 231**
Carnegie Fine Arts and Museum Fund (Pittsburgh) **207**
Carnegie Institute of Technology *see Carnegie Mellon University*
Carnegie Mellon University **288, 397, 401, 408, 472, 527, 529, 532, 536, 538, 545**
    Graduate School of Industrial Administration **414**
    Magnetics Technology Center **530**
    Robotics Institute **530**
    Software Engineering Institute **530**
Carnegie Museums of Pittsburgh **397**
Carnegie Music Hall (Pittsburgh) **407**

Carnegie Steel **62, 83, 140, 141-142, 188-194, 337**
    attempt to install new Iron Clad Agreement **174, 176-177**
    Homestead Steel Strike (1892) **169-187**
    wage negotiations in Homestead before 1892 **148-149**
Carnegie, Andrew **i, 62, 64, 76, 82-85, 97-98, 109, 136, 146-147, 152, 154, 161, 188-189, 193, 229, 350, 358, 396-399**
    and philanthropy **397**
    and the "Greatest Lawsuit" **185-191, 218**
    attempt to deploy new Iron Clad Agreement **177, 178**
    sells out to J.P. Morgan **187**
    settles "Greatest Lawsuit" **184**
Carnegie, Lucy **180, 188**
Carnegie, Phipps & Co. **147-148**
Carnegie, Thomas **62, 84, 173**
Carnegie-Illinois Steel Company **404**
Carr, Charlotte **293**
Carrington, Paul **554**
Carson Street (Pittsburgh) **247**
Carson, James **9**
Carter, Jimmy **399, 474, 520**
Carter Ledyard & Milburn (law firm) **355**
Casablanca (1942) **284**
Cashin, John M. **367**
Cassady, B.J. **247**
Castle Skibo (Scotland) **175, 185**
Catholic University of Washington **124**
Central High School (Pittsburgh) **329**
Central Law Journal **78, 184**
Centre Avenue (Pittsburgh) **249, 411, 461, 465**
Centre County, Pennsylvania **177**
Century City, California **411**
CEO Venture Fund **534**
Chalfant, E.E. **200**
Chalfant, John **84, 85**
Challener & Challener (law firm) **300**
Challener, William, Jr. **377, 378**
Chambers, Whitaker **417**
Chandler, Alfred D., Jr. **79**
Charities and the Commons (weekly journal) **215**
Charleston, Oscar **337**
Chase, Salmon **44**
Chase, Samuel **5, 21**
Chatfield, Glen **532, 534**
Chatham Center (Pittsburgh) **412**
Chatham University **332**
Cherin, Carl **443, 449-452**
Cherin, Steve **448-449**
Chevron Corporation **530**

Chew, Benjamin **5**
Chicago Colts (baseball) **128**
Chicago Crime Commission **481**
Chicago Seven **469**
Chicago Tribune **157**
Chicago World's Fair (1892) **104**
Chicago, Burlington & Quincy Railroad **350**
Chicago, Illinois **93, 129, 200, 251, 259, 350, 354, 368, 527**
Chilcote, Sanford "San" **375**
Childs, Albert H. **84-85, 218**
Childs, Starling W. **218**
Choate, Joseph H. **358**
Christ Methodist Episcopal Church (Pittsburgh) **207, 276**
Christy, George H. **50-51, 85, 101-102, 104**
Christy, J. Smith **243**
Chronicle-Telegraph Building (Pittsburgh) **162**
Chrysler, Walter P. **303**
Cindrich & Titus (law firm) **454, 547**
Cindrich, Robert **454, 482, 494-497, 548, 554**
Citizens' Party (Pittsburgh) **213-215**
Citizens United v. FEC (2010) **87**
Citizens' Municipal League (Pittsburgh) **209, 217**
City-County Building (Pittsburgh) **202, 381, 400, 413, 421, 424**
Civic Arena (Pittsburgh) **407-408, 411-412, 460, 503**
Civic Club of Allegheny County **207, 214**
Civic Party (Pittsburgh) **224**
Civil Rights Act of 1964 **390**
Civil War, U.S. **iii, 30, 52, 58, 61-63, 65, 68, 77, 99-100, 107, 120, 149, 163, 166, 237, 250, 328, 364, 559**
    Battle at Gaines' Mill **49**
    Battle of Antietam **49**
    Battle of Cold Harbor **51**
    Battle of Fredericksburg **49**
    Battle of Gettysburg **49-50**
    Battle of Hanover Court House **49**
    Battle of Lewis Farm (Quaker Road) **50, 91**
    Battle of Mechanicsville **49**
    Battle of Petersburg **50**
    Battle of Salem Heights **50**
    Battle of Williamsburg **48**
    Yorktown, siege of **49**
Clairton, Pennsylvania **337**
Clampitt, John **55-57**
Clarion County, Pennsylvania **354**
Clarion University **328**
Clark, Charles **298**
Clark, J. Reuben, Jr. **196**
Clark, Kim Berkeley **474, 511**

Clarke, Kenny **337**
Clarksburg, West Virginia **287, 291, 308**
Clay, Henry **27-28, 44**
Clayton Antitrust Act of 1914 **203, 359, 360**
Clemente, Roberto **538**
Clendenon, Donn **460**
Cleveland and Pittsburgh Railroad **93**
Cleveland Metals Company **360**
Cleveland, Grover **129, 149, 155, 172-74, 210**
Cleveland, Ohio **342, 371, 391, 468, 481**
Clifford, Jack **168**
Clinton Iron and Steel Company **223**
Clinton, Bill **399, 505**
Clinton, Hillary Rodham **505**
Close-Up (television show) **494**
Clunk, Roy T. **424**
CNG Tower (Pittsburgh) **521**
Coal and Iron Police **278-283, 283, 293, 297-298**
    Trade Police abolished **285**
Cohen & Grigsby (law firm) **390**
Cohen, Carl **535**
Cohen, Charles "Chuck" **390**
Cohen, Josiah **54, 115-119, 125, 270**
Cohen, Paula **328**
Colbert brothers, John and Charles **223**
Cole, W. Sterling **433-434. 610 n.319**
Coleman, William T. **457**
Colker, James R. "Jim" **532-534**
Coll, Edward G. **290**
College of the Holy Cross **433**
College of William & Mary **505**
Collier, Frederick H. **49-51**
Collitt, George W. **480**
Columbia National Bank (Pittsburgh) **217**
Columbia University **102, 103, 128, 215, 270**
Columbus, Ohio **378, 500, 526, 527**
Columbus, Premo **372**
Colville, Robert **481**
Comay, Estelle **506**
Commercial Law League of America **267, 438-439**
Committee for Fair Employment in Pittsburgh Department Stores **455**
Commonwealth **25**
Commonwealth v. Dixon (1968) **483**
Commonwealth v. Kontos (1971) **483**
Commune, the, or the Law Collective **469-470, 476**
Communists **251, 258, 296, 312, 422-436, 457, 459**
Concordia Club **270**
Congress of Industrial Organizations (CIO) **308, 346, 383, 417**
Conley, Martha Richards **470**

Connellsville, Pennsylvania **152, 232**
Consolidated Ice Company **478**
Consolidated Natural Gas Co. **521**
Consolidation Coal Company **400**
Constitution, United States **i, 3, 9, 11, 12, 23, 29, 46, 52, 85, 87, 118, 156, 196, 420**
    Eighteenth Amendment **196**
    Fifteenth Amendment **118**
    Fifth Amendment **55, 434, 485, 488, 555**
    Fourteenth Amendment **118, 380**
    full ratification **10**
    ratified by Pennsylvania **9**
    Sixteenth Amendment **196-197, 203**
    Sixth Amendment **548**
    Thirteenth Amendment **118, 131**
    Twentieth Amendment **197**
    unpopular in Pittsburgh before ratification **9**
Conti, Joy Flowers **506**
Contraves Goerz Corporation **532**
Coolidge, Calvin **203, 273, 341, 359-360, 365**
Corbett, Boston, Sergeant **54**
Cordwainer Strike (1814) **89**
Cork and Bottle (tavern) **374**
Cornell University **230, 237, 399, 503**
Corning Glass Works **517**
Corporation Act of 1874 **63**
corporations, development of **63-64, 77, 81, 83, 194**
    corporation as "person" **86-87**
    lawyers as heads of corporations **398**
    limited liability **144**
    omnibus corporate charters **86, 102**
    railroads as first corporations **79**
    vertical integration of production **83**
Cortelyou, George **357**
Cosgrove, James J. **328**
Cost, John W. **421**
Coudert Brothers (law firm) **299**
Coudert, Frederic R., Jr. **299**
Coulter, Richard **22**
Counsellor at Law (play by Elmer Rice) **283**
County of Allegheny v. Gibson (1879) **95**
Cox, Father James R. **275-279, 336, 281, 283, 342**
    Cox's March on Washington **280-281**
    runs for president **280**
Cox, John F. **162, 165**
Cox, Oscar **399**
Coxe, Tench **14**
Coxey, Jacob **279**
Coxey's March (1893) **279**
Craft, James S. **40**

Crafton (Pittsburgh) **301, 406, 443**
Craig, David **464, 466**
Craig, Isaac, Major **22**
Craig, Neville **45**
Crane, Judson **334, 500-501, 503**
Cravath, Paul **102-103, 105-106, 234**. *see also Pittsburgh bar - and the Cravath system*
    influential as law firm leader **103**
Cravath, Swaine & Moore (law firm) **103, 234, 399, 549**
Craven, James B., Jr. **376**
Crawford County, Pennsylvania **287**
Crawford Grill (Pittsburgh) **479**
Crawford, Alexander C. **85**
Crawford, James S. **234-235**
Crawford, R. Lindsay **198**
Crawford, William H. (presidential candidate) **28**
Crawford, William, Colonel (soldier) **6**
Crawford-Devilliers (Pittsburgh) **411, 460**
Crimes Aboard Aircraft Act **486**
Critchlow, Sylvester **168**
Cromwell, William Nelson **64**
Crosby, Bing **442**
Crow, William E. **243**
Crucible Steel Company **140, 522-523**
Crusaders (temperance league) **197**
Cumberland County, Pennsylvania **6, 18**
Cummings, Homer S. **292, 344, 361**
Cunningham, Charles L. **439**
Cunningham, Dorothy **439**
Cunningham, Galbraith & Dickson (law firm) **332**
Cunningham, Kenneth R. **332**
Cunningham, William **438**
Curry, H.M. **178**
Curtis, Leonard **104**
Curtiz, Michael **284**
Custer, Elizabeth Bacon **52**
Custer, General George Armstrong **52**
Cutler, Lloyd **399**
Cvetic, Matt **419-421, 426, 431-432, 434**
Cyert, Dr. Richard **530, 532**

D

D'Arrigo, JoAnn **507**
Dale, Richard C. **181**
Dallas Cowboys (football) **518**
Dallas, Alexander J. **20**
Dallas, Texas **408**
Dallas, Trevanion B. **40**
Dalzell, Fisher & Dalzell (law firm) **243**
Dalzell, Fisher & Hawkins (law firm) **237**

Dalzell, John **64, 68, 77, 81-82, 84, 91-92, 105, 113, 149-151, 160, 168, 179, 194, 209, 229, 243, 578 n.140**
    and Westinghouse **102-103**
    as "Corporation Dalzell" **161**
    physical description **101, 578 n.140**
Dalzell, Robert D. **243**
Dalzell, Scott & Gordon (law firm) **101-102, 123, 179, 229-231, 239**
Dalzell, William Sage **229-231, 243**
Danahey, James A. **406**
Danel, Cynthia **391**
Danforth, Douglas **526**
Daniels, Rose **334**
Darragh, Cornelius **35, 37-38, 42**
Darrow, Clarence **269, 332**
Dartmouth College **517**
Dauer, Robert **469**
Dauphin County, Pennsylvania **199, 427**
Davenport, Ronald R. **470, 473-474**
Davis Polk & Wardwell (law firm) **187, 203, 549**
Davis, Allan **243**
Davis, Arthur Vining **84, 229, 364**
Davis, Harry L. **247**
Davis, James J. **280**
Davis, John W. (New York lawyer and politician) **203, 287, 294, 299, 302, 305-306, 358-359, 384**
Davis, John Warren (appellate judge) **203**
Davis, Polk, Wardwell, Gardiner & Reed (law firm) **287**
Davis, Sammy, Jr. **481**
Day, Albert, Rev. **276**
Day, T. Walter **108**
Dayton, Ohio **460, 538**
Dean, John **490**
DeBartolo Company **521**
DeCastrique, A.B. **343**
Deep Throat (1973) **483**
Delany, Martin R. **117**
Deluzio, Vincent **529**
Demmler, Ralph H. **141, 152, 188, 266, 371, 388, 405-406, 438, 442**
Denny, Harmar **28, 34-35, 45**
Denominational Ministry Strategy
    and putting fish in safe deposit boxes **524**
Derry, Pennsylvania **533**
Desvernine, Raoul E. **298-299**
Detroit, Michigan **251, 259, 263, 371, 414, 450, 472, 512**
Devlin, Robert **535**
DeWees Wood mill (McKeesport, PA) **245-246**
Diamond, Gustave **484, 490, 545, 547**

Diamond, the (Pittsburgh) 10, 18, 24, 47, 61, 63, 65, 68, 155, 205
Dick, Samuel B., Colonel 179
Dick, Thomas and Jane, capture of (1791) 6
Dick's Sporting Goods 538
Dickey, Charles C. 67
Dickie, McCamey & Chilcote (law firm) 367, 375, 389, 502, 506
Dickie, McCamey, Chilcote, Reif & Robinson (law firm). *see also Dickie, McCamey & Chilcote (law firm)*
Dickinson College 10, 22, 33, 36, 384, 505, 526
Dickinson, Jacob 357, 359
Dickinson, John 5
Diehl, William J. 210, 212
Dietrich, Bill 518-520
DiFatta, Salvatore 272
Dill, James B. 77, 184-185
Dillard, Annie 549
Dilworth, Richardson 420
DiSalle, Fran 450
Disciples of Christ 440
Dixie Dugan (comic strip by John H. Striebel) 482, 493
Dodd, S.C.T. 354
Dodds, Robert J., Jr. 439, 473-474
Dodds, Robert J., Sr. 201, 232, 243, 334, 406, 440, 499, 501, 616 n.623
Doe v. Wohlgemuth (1974) 467
Doepken Keevican & Weiss (law firm) 452
Doherty, Robert 401
Dollar Savings Bank 206
Dolsen, Jim 422-425
Dombrowski v. Pfister (1965) 469
Dorothy 6 blast furnace 502, 522, 524, 528
Dorsett, Tony 520
Doty, William S. 426
Douglas, Gordon 420
Douglas, Wallace Barton 350
Douglass Loan and Investment Company 120
Douglass, Wilbur C. 347, 457
Downie, Robert C. 398
Doyle, Ellen 510
Drago, Linda 511
Drake, Edwin L., Colonel 61
Dramatic Oil Company 54
Draper Triangle Ventures 534
Dravo Tower. *see One Mellon Bank Center (Pittsburgh)*
Drew, James B. 237, 264, 402, 426
Dreyfuss family 442, 450
Driscoll, D.J. 198

dueling 8, 25-27
Duff & Brennen (law firm) 135
Duff, J.K.P. 135
Duff, James H. 238, 243, 420, 423, 436
Duff, John M., Jr. 472
Duff, Joseph M., Jr. 236, 238-239
Duff, Marshall & Duff (law firm) 236, 238
Duggan, Blanche 478
Duggan, Frank 478
Duggan, Robert 477-498
Duke University 505
Dulles, John Foster 123
Dumbauld, Horatio 198
Dumont Television Network 409
Dungeness (Cumberland Island, Florida) 180, 183
Dunlop, James 23
Dunn, H. Stewart 481
Dunn, James G. "Jimmy" (acting District Attorney) 482, 484-485, 497
Dunn, James R. (Pittsburgh lawyer - Patterson firm) 235
Dunn, Martin 298
Dunn, Roy 234
Dunn, Thomas A. 478, 481
DuPont brothers, Irenee, Lammot and Pierre 287
Duquesne Club 84, 102, 122, 128, 204, 207, 281, 290, 445, 492, 506-507, 515, 555
Duquesne Incline (Pittsburgh) 406
Duquesne Light Company 398, 463, 464
Duquesne Steel Works 502
Duquesne Systems, Inc. 532, 534
Duquesne University 199, 233, 267, 270-275, 327, 372, 373, 382, 383, 386, 418, 420, 448, 460, 468, 472, 487-489, 502, 506, 511, 527, 551, 561
    law school established 199
Duquesne, Pennsylvania 152, 158, 337, 502, 522, 524, 528
Durkin, Kathleen 511
Dyer, Heman 33, 36

E

E. I. du Pont de Nemours and Company 287
E. Remington & Sons 123
Earle, George 285, 345-346, 418, 423
East End (Pittsburgh) 76, 207-210, 215, 217, 459-460, 523
East Liberty (Pittsburgh) 72, 207, 412, 413, 415
East Pittsburgh, Pennsylvania 383, 420, 480, 529
Eastman, Crystal
    and the *Pittsburgh Survey* 215-216
Eastman, Kenneth 502

Ebbert, Donald W. **301, 308-309**
Eckert, Seamans & Cherin (law firm) **444, 448, 454, 484**
Eckert, Seamans, Cherin & Mellot (law firm) **367, 388, 444, 447, 449, 452-453, 505, 525**
Eckert, William H. **405, 424, 443-448**
Eckley, E.R. **39**
Economic Opportunity Act **380**
Economy, Pennsylvania **43**
Edgar Thomson Steel Works **152, 522**
Edison, Thomas **100, 104**
Edmunds, Arthur **458-459, 464**
Edna (steamboat) **157**
Effectual Services (New Delhi, India) **545**
Egan, John **374**
Ehrlichman, John **490**
Eisenhower, Dwight D. **385, 484**
Elder, Cyrus **85, 142**
Elkins Act of 1903 **354**
Ellenbogen, Henry **271, 276-277, 283, 285, 293, 296, 304, 327, 334, 347, 372, 375, 376-377, 386, 483**
    and Father James R. Cox **275-276, 279-283**
    and Social Security **282**
    elected to Common Pleas Court **285**
    runs for Congress **280**
Ellenbogen, Rae Savage **285**
Ellenbogen, Theodore **269**
Elliott, John **451**
Elliott, Kate Ford **511**
Ellsworth, Laura **507, 511-512, 516**
Elwood City, Pennsylvania **67**
Emmerglick, Leonard J. **366**
Employee Security League **291-292, 308, 311**
Engelsberg, Joe **197**
Engelsberg, Sam **197**
England, Helen Lynch **240**
England, Miles H. **237, 240-241**
    and World War I **242**
Englewood, New Jersey **101-102**
English, H.D.W. **208, 218**
Enrollment Act of 1863 **51**
Equal Employment Opportunity Office **390**
Equal Rights Amendment **216**
Equibank **523**
Equitable Gas Company **463**
Equitable Life Assurance Society **402-406**
Equitable Meter Co. **418**
Equitable Resources, Inc. **510**
Erck, Emma J. **231**
Erie, Pennsylvania **47, 117, 248, 391, 439**
Ernst & Young (accounting firm) **415**
Erwin, W.E. **168**

Espionage Act **247, 253**
Estee Lauder Companies **512**
Estep, Harry **281-282**
Estep, Thomas **130**
European and American Law Agency **36, 389**
Evans, Benjamin **40**
Evans, Choate & Beaman (law firm) **358**
Evans, Ivory and Evans (law firm) **374, 390**
Evans, Jim **377**
Evans, Raymond D. **419**
Evans, W.D. **305**
Evers, Medgar **462**
Ewing, Thomas **93-95, 165-168**
Ex parte Martha Bradstreet (1830) **29**
Ex Parte Wall (1883) **263**
Exposition Hall (Pittsburgh) **225, 235, 405**
Exposition Park (Pittsburgh) **127, 130**
Extrel Corporation **534**

F

Fagan, Edward "Ted" **487**
Fahy, Charles **302, 305, 365**
Fair Housing Act of 1961 **461**
Fair Housing Law of 1957 **464**
Falk family **450**
Falk Foundation **401**
Farley, James **344**
Farmers Bank Building (Pittsburgh) **195, 232, 268**
Farmers' National Bank (Pittsburgh) **217**
Fauntroy, Walter **462**
Fawcett, David, Jr. **374, 380-382, 502, 508-509**
Fawcett, David, Sr. **379**
Fayette County, Pennsylvania **11, 112, 140, 153**
Federal Communications Commission **408**
Federal Employers Liability Act (FELA) **374**
Federal Reserve Act **268**
Federal Reserve System, U.S. **203**
Federal Steel Corporation **182, 185-186, 188**
Federal Trade Commission **360**
Federated Investors **414**
Federated Investors Tower (Pittsburgh) **521**
Feeney, Anne **509**
Feeney, John M. "Jack" **373-374, 377-379, 451**
Feldman, Joan **506**
Female, The (1969) **483**
Fergus, Annie **499**
Fergus, Clifford **499, 616 n.623**
Ferguson, Hugh **222**
Ferguson, J. Scott **110-111, 131**
Ferraro, Samuel G. **485-486, 489-495**

Fetterman brothers, Washington and Nathaniel **39, 120**
Fetterman, Charles S. **118, 121**
Fetterman, G.L. **120**
Fetterman, Wilfred B. **120**
Field, Stephen J. **86**
Fife, Henry **56**
Fife, R.H. **91-93**
Fifth Avenue (Pittsburgh) **34, 62, 68, 139, 151, 186, 193, 195, 332, 339, 400, 458**
Fifth Avenue Place (Pittsburgh) **521**
Findley, William **9, 15**
Fine, John S. **425**
Fingold, Reuben **267, 551**
Finkelhor, Marion **511**
Finley, James **16, 23**
First Boston Corporation **442-443**
First National Bank Building (Pittsburgh) **195**
First Unitarian Church (Pittsburgh) **207, 209, 331**
Fischer, Nora Barry **506**
Fischer, Richard **526**
Fish & Richardson (law firm) **104**
Fish, Frederick P. **104**
Fisher Scientific International, Inc. **510**
Fisher, D. Michael "Mike" **482**
Fisher, Gordon **229, 235, 243**
Fisher, John S. **275-277, 329**
Fitzgerald, F. Scott **497**
Fitzhugh brothers, Charles L. and Robert **84**
Flaherty, Jim **451**
Flaherty, Pete **413, 451, 497, 520, 525**
Flaherty, Tom **527**
Flanegin, Francis **37**
Fleger, Philip **297, 398, 463**
Fleishman, Solomon L. **117**
Fleming, Robert D. **403, 460**
Flinn, George **390**
Flinn, William **58, 110, 206, 213-214**
Florida Marlins (baseball) **528**
Florida Territory **18, 27**
Flower, Roswell P. **175**
Flynn, Errol **284**
Flynn, Samantha Francis **505**
Foerster, Tom **525**
Folger, H.G., Jr. **355**
Forbes Avenue (Pittsburgh) **113, 186, 202, 421**
Forbes Field (Pittsburgh) **281, 442, 526**
Ford City, Pennsylvania **522, 537**
Ford Foundation **409**
Ford, Gerald R. **451**
Ford, Henry (auto magnate) **300, 303**
Ford, Henry P. (mayor) **209**
Ford, J.B., Captain **83**
Ford, Thomas **259**
Fording, Arthur "A.O." **131, 257**
FORE Systems, Inc. **537**
Formtek, Inc. **534**
Fort Pitt Foundry **54**
Forward, Walter **22, 24, 27-28, 40, 44-45, 117-118**
Foster, Alexander W. **25**
Foster, Morrison **150**
Foster, Stephen **150**
Foster, William Z. **251, 255, 427**
Fostin Capital **534**
Fourth Avenue (Pittsburgh) **68, 119, 124, 220, 221, 230, 267, 336, 442, 503**
Fourth National Bank **186**
Franco-Prussian War **82**
Frank & Seder (department store) **455**
Frankfurter, Felix **443**
Franklin, Benjamin **25**
Franklin, Pennsylvania **54**
Frazer, John G., Jr. **439-441, 454**
Frazer, John G., Sr. **232, 235, 243, 266, 439-440**
Frazer, Kate Reed **441**
Frazer, Robert S. **142, 223, 440**
Freedom Riders in Mississippi **469-470**
Freeland, Wendell **381-382, 456-461, 464-466, 470, 473-476, 479, 543**
Freeman, Henry **119**
Freeman, John M. **234, 352**
FreeMarkets, Inc. **537**
French Revolution **19, 167, 226**
Freneau, Philip **4, 12**
Fresenius Medical Care **538**
Frew, William, Major **82**
Frick Building (Pittsburgh) **195, 218, 223, 231, 234, 251, 328, 374, 395, 478, 485**
Frick Building Annex (Pittsburgh) **230, 231**
Frick Park (Pittsburgh) **397**
Frick, Henry Clay **i, 76, 82, 85, 140-141, 147, 165, 185-186, 188-189, 193-196, 213, 232-233, 249, 251, 257, 271, 350-352, 357, 396-397, 399, 440**
  and the "Greatest Lawsuit" **179-185**
  assassination attempt **162**
  attempt to negotiate Carnegie buyout **173-178**
  Homestead Steel Strike (1892) **136, 152-153, 157-161, 168, 245-247**
  Johnstown Flood (1889) **85, 142-149**
  resigns as chairman of Carnegie Steel **176**
  testifies at trial of Berkman **164**
Frick, Henry Clay, Jr. **165**
Friedberg, Sue **505-506**

Friedman, Joseph M. **117, 163**
Friedman, Judith L.A. **511**
Friedman, Lawrence M. **7, 63, 72**
Friend, Charles W. **223**
Frontiers Club (Pittsburgh) **459**
Fuel Gas Company **102**
Fugitive Slave Act of 1793 **46**
Fugitive Slave Act of 1850 **46**
Fuller, Alvan T. **273-274**

G

Gaffney, Virginia **288**
Galbraith, Robert **9**
Galbraith, Wilbur F. **332**
Galbreath, Dan **525-526**
Galbreath, John **442, 525-526**
Gall Lane & Powell (law firm) **389**
Gallatin, Albert **13, 15**
Galveston, Texas **52**
Galvin, Pud **128**
Game Change (book by John Heilemann and Mark Halperin) **542**
Garfield, James R. **354, 358**
Gariti, Joseph I., III **521, 527-528**
Garrison, Lloyd K. **298**
Garrison, William Lloyd **45**
Gary, Elbert **85, 182, 185, 188, 245, 357, 398**
Gas Ring machine (Philadelphia) **206**
Gates, Bill (Microsoft) **541**
Gates, John "Bet-a-Million" **175, 180**
Gates, William H., Sr. (lawyer and father of Bill Gates) **541**
Gateway Center (Pittsburgh) **404-406**
Gaughan, Martin and Mary **330**
Gazza, Beverly **506**
Gazzam, Dr. William **44**
Geary, John W. **66**
Geddis, Maeve Victoria **497**
Geist, Rick **533**
Genentech, Inc. **533**
General Electric Co. **518, 532**
General Electric Corp. plc **537**
General Foods **295**
General Motors **287, 295**
Geneva College **239**
George Washington University **121, 271**
Georgetown University **271**
Gerhold, Cathy **505**
German National Bank of Allegheny **223**
German National Bank of Pittsburgh **206, 217, 220-224**

Germania Savings Bank **206**
Geyer, Stephen H. **75, 95**
Giannino, Victor **429**
Gibson, Josh **337**
Gibson, Mel **328**
Gibson, Robert M. **128, 203, 248, 361-362**
Gibson, William L.G. **243**
Gideon v. Wainwright (1963) **380, 484**
Gilardi & Cooper (law firm) **545**
Gilardi, Dick **545**
Gilfillan, John **421**
Gilkinson, James **22**
Gill, Harry Blair **121**
Gill, Samuel "S.B.W." **107-109, 113, 121**
Gillespie, Thomas **109**
Gimbel's (department store) **455**
Girard, Stephen **74**
Girdler, Tom **309**
Gismondi, John **545-547**
Givens, Joseph W. **347, 457**
Gladstone, William **172**
Glasso, Louis **432**
Glassport, Pennsylvania **528**
Glock, Carl **430-431**
Godfrey, John **532**
Goehring, H.L. **111**
Goldberg, Arthur Abba **452**
Golden, Clint **293**
Goldenson, Rabbi Samuel **276**
Golding, Gary **532**
Goldman, Emma **164, 251, 257**
Goldsmith, Malcolm **234, 243**
Goldstein, George **330**
Goldstein, Ruth Levy **330**
Goldston, Linda Leebov **505**
Goldwater, Barry **477, 484**
Gone With the Wind (novel by Margaret Mitchell) **364**
Google **538**
Gordon & Smith (law firm) **84, 105, 229-237, 240-244, 254, 285, 360, 437**. *see also* Buchanan Ingersoll & Rooney (law firm)
Gordon, Allen Taylor Caperton **231**
Gordon, Benjamin **309**
Gordon, George B. **84, 182, 229-237, 240-244, 360-361, 367, 589 n.159**
Gordon, Smith, Buchanan & Scott (law firm) **437**
Gore, Al **28**
Gould, George Jay **195**
Gourley, Wallace S. **377, 487**
Gow, J. Steele **401**
Grace Steamship Lines **428**

Graham, Billy **408**
Graham, Charles J. **401**
Graham, Louis **198**
Graham, Martha **410**
Granger, Lester **455**
Grant Building (Pittsburgh) **195, 290, 406, 468, 505**
Grant Street (Pittsburgh) **62, 65, 68, 81, 86, 96, 189, 195, 225, 230, 244, 251, 300, 336, 376, 400, 421, 448, 489, 521, 525**
Grant Street Tavern (Pittsburgh) **374**
Grant, Ulysses S. **57**
Grant's Hill (Pittsburgh) **10, 193, 225, 555**
Gratton, Gail **506**
Graubart, Ella **330-334, 347**
Gray, James C. (Pittsburgh lawyer and Standard Chemical president) **249**
Gray, James H. (Pittsburgh lawyer) **346, 373**
Gray, Joseph **157**
Great Depression **195, 269, 279, 285-286, 290, 360, 371-373, 395-396, 397, 418, 448, 551**
Great Fire of Pittsburgh, the (1845) **33-36, 45, 71**
Great Northern Railway **350**
Great Railroad Strike of 1877 **89-96, 110, 133-134, 139, 153-154**
Great Recession of 2008 **540**
Greater Pittsburgh Chamber of Commerce. *see Pittsburgh Chamber of Commerce*
Greb, Harry **275**
Greenbaum, Meyer **234-236, 243**
Greenbelt, Maryland **400**
Greene County, Pennsylvania **112, 163, 198, 327**
Greenfield, Albert M. **268**
Greenlee, Gus **479**
Greensburg, Pennsylvania **6, 80, 163, 181, 246**
Greenspan, Alan **366**
Greer, Morgan **199**
Gregory, Thomas Watt **359**
Grier, Robert Cooper **30, 42**
Griffin, Martin **343**
Griffith, L.B. **198**
Griggs, John W. **351, 353**
Griggs, Moreland, Blair & Douglass (law firm) **432**
Griggs, Thomas N. **432**
Grim, William Simpson, Dr. **163**
Grimes, Martha **336**
Grimes, William D. **332, 336**
Grosso, Tony **489-492**
Grote, Dorothy **334**
Guffey, Joseph **284, 343-344**
Gulf Oil Corporation **76, 400, 529-530**

Gulf Refining Company **270**
Gulf Tower (Pittsburgh) **371**
Gunther, Blair **418-420, 436**
Guthrie, George W. **121, 202, 205-227, 230, 338-339, 554**
  "municipal corporation" **208, 213**
  as mayor of Pittsburgh **215, 225, 227**
Guthrie, John Brandon **205**

H

H.C. Frick Coke Company **84, 142, 152, 172, 177, 181, 185-186**
H.J. Heinz Company **460, 530, 538, 549**
H.K. Porter Building (Pittsburgh) **448**
H.K. Porter Company **470**
Hackney, William P. **529**
Hafer, Barbara **510**
Haines, W.T. **122**
Haldeman, H.R. **490**
Hale, Nelles & Shorr (law firm) **262**
Hale, Swinburne **251, 262**
Hall, Charles Martin **360**
Hall, Gus **427**
Hall, James Parker **242**
Hamilton, Alexander **3, 11-12, 14-17, 25**
Hamilton, Rosanna **109**
Hamilton, Theron B. **345, 347, 458**
Hammond, John Hays **140**
Hampton & Dalzell (law firm) **92, 93, 101**
Hampton & Miller (law firm) **39**
Hampton & Son (law firm) **39, 438**
Hampton Township, Pennsylvania **485, 489**
Hampton, John Henry **37, 39, 52, 64-65, 67, 80-81, 83, 90-96, 101, 120**
Hampton, Moses **39, 53, 65, 80, 120-121, 438**
Hancock, Winfield Scott, General **55-57**
Hand, Augustus **365**
Hand, Learned **365-366**
Handler, Milton **292**
Hanlon, Ned **128**
Hannastown, Pennsylvania **6**
Hanson, Marcella Phelps **505-506, 514**
Hanson, Raymond **505**
Harbison, Francis R. **63, 81, 83, 87, 352, 353**
Harding, Warren G. **203, 295, 359**
Harlem Globetrotters **504**
Harleston, Edwin Nathaniel **339**
Harmarville, Pennsylvania **269, 530**
Harmony Society **43**
Harriman, E.H. **350-353, 549**
Harris, Charlie **462**

Harris, Clara **53**
Harrisburg, Pennsylvania **35, 47, 80, 102, 125, 158, 211, 226, 276, 279-280, 285, 345, 403, 423, 425, 434, 451, 496, 550**
Harrison, Benjamin **69, 149, 161, 168, 171**
Harrison, William Henry **27**
Hart, Edward J. **417**
Hartman, Janice **506**
Hartman, Susan **535**
Hartranft, John W. **91, 94-95**
Harvard University **33, 81, 103, 121, 123, 233, 234, 235, 242, 301, 308, 361, 362, 376, 384, 386, 395, 399, 402, 415, 429, 439-449, 451, 457, 475, 499, 500, 505, 517, 536**
Harvard-Yale-Princeton Club **507**
Harvey, William "Coin" **280**
Hastings, Daniel H. **112-113**
Hawkins, Alexander L., Colonel **163**
Hawkins, Connie **504**
Hawkins, Richard H. **230, 237, 243, 329**
Hawkins, William G. **68, 84, 230**
Hay, Malcolm, Jr. **419**
Hay, Malcom **206**
Hayes, Rutherford B. **90**
Haymaker, John C. **110-111, 212, 336**
Haymaker, Joseph S. **89, 92, 110**
Hays, Arthur Garfield **427**
Hays, William B. **212-213**
Haywood, Big Bill **251-252**
Hazard, Leland Walker **395-396, 398-399, 401, 406-410, 413-414, 416, 539, 554**
Hazelwood (Pittsburgh) **407, 466**
Hazlett, Theodore **403, 406**
Heard, Donald B. **439**
Heard, Drayton **237, 243**
Heard, John J. "Jack" **232, 235, 243, 299, 383, 439-442**
Heidelberg, Louis A. **117**
Heilemann, John **542**
Heinde, Frederick, Captain **158**
Heinitsh, George **443, 447, 449**
Heinz family **527**
Heinz, H. John, III **472**
Hellerstedt, Carl H. **386**
Helwig, Gilbert J. **367, 422, 464, 474**
Henry VI, Part II (play by William Shakespeare) **548**
Herbert, Hilary **172**
Herold, David **55-57**
Heron, James E. **23**
Herriott, Thomas **123**
Herron, Campbell **84**

Hertz, Arnold, Dr. **82-83**
Hibernia No. 2 (steamship) **42**
Hice, Andrew **90**
Hickman, Leon **361-362, 366-367, 398-399, 411-416, 443-448, 484, 539, 554**
  and fiduciary duty to community **410**
Hickton, Jack **496**
Highland Park (Pittsburgh) **68, 459**
Highmark Blue Cross Blue Shield **415, 521**
Hill & Knowlton (PR firm) **392**
Hill District (Pittsburgh) **46, 119, 270, 276, 338, 403, 407-408, 411, 412, 458, 461, 466, 479-482**
Hill, Christopher & Phillips (law firm) **389**
Hill, David G. **382**
Hill, James J. "Empire Builder" **350-352, 549**
Hillman Ventures **534**
Hillman, Elsie **459, 478, 484, 485**
Hillman, Hart **288**
Hines, Earl **337**
Hiss, Alger **417**
Hockenberry, John **489-491**
Hodges, George, Reverend Dr. **207**
Hoffer, Floyd **495**
Hoffstot, Frank N. **223**
Hoffstot, Henry, Jr. **201**
Hogan & Hartson (law firm) **299**
Hogan, Frank **299**
Hoge, Ellen Crayne **327-328**
Hoge, Guy **327**
Holland, William J. **122**
Hollander, Thomas **381, 510**
Holloway, George S. **245**
Holloway, Wilburt **342**
Hollywood Social Club (Pittsburgh) **481**
Hollywood Ten, the **417**
Holmes, J. Welfred **118-120, 125, 335-336**
Holmes, Oliver Wendell, Jr. **273**
Holohan, William V., Major **428-433**
Homestead Grays (baseball) **337**
Homestead Steel Strike (1892) **i, 136, 151-169, 172, 174, 179, 181, 193-194, 245**
  vote to suspend strike **168**
Homestead Steel Works **143, 147-169, 522**
Homestead, Pennsylvania **132, 143, 147-169, 337, 418, 528**
  wage negotiations **147, 148, 152, 154**
Homewood (Pittsburgh) **101, 252, 466**
Hood, James **461**
Hook, William C. **353**
Hoover, Herbert **268, 282-284, 289, 303, 341-342, 359**
Hoover, J. Edgar **255, 258, 427, 432, 486, 487**

Hope, Bob **481**
Hopkins, James Herron **118, 135, 151**
Hornack, Jay **523-529, 539**
Hornblower Miller (law firm). *see Willkie Farr & Gallagher (law firm)*
Hornbostel, Henry **202**
Horne, Lena **337**
Horne's (department store) **403, 455**
Horty, John **470**
Hoss, Stanley B., Jr. **486-488**
Hostetter, David, Dr. **82-83**
Hotel Brighton (Atlantic City) **184**
Hotel Schenley (Pittsburgh) **186, 188**
House Un-American Activities Committee **312, 417-422, 434**
House Ways and Means Committee **149, 194**
House, William H. **110-112**
Houseman, M.H. **92**
Houston Harbaugh (law firm) **543**
Houston, Clara I. **123, 231, 240**
Houston, Cooper, Speer & German (law firm) **504**. *see also Sherrard, German & Kelly (law firm)*
Houston, J. Garfield **421**
Houston, James M. **379, 543**
Howard University **119, 456, 457**
Hoyt, Henry M., Jr. **194**
Hufflings, T.S. **219**
Huffnagle, Michael **9**
Hughes, Charles Evans **216, 293, 304, 306**
Hughes, Howard R. **433**
Hughes, Joseph **478**
Huizenga, Wayne **528**
Humes, E. Lowry **198, 260**
Humphrey, Hubert H. **484**
Humphrey, William E. **360**
Hunsiker, Millard **172, 180**
Hunt, Alfred E. **360-361**
Hunt, William, Dr. **413**
Hunt, Roy **361, 445**
Hunter College **330**
Hunter, Howard A. **344**
Hurd, Seth T. **140**
Hutchinson, Stuart Nye, Jr. **440, 465**
Hutton, Edward F. **295**
Hyatt Legal Services **391**
Hyatt, Joel **391**
Hyatt, Keith **492**

I

I Nostri Tempi (Unione) (newspaper) **272**
I Was a Communist for the FBI (1951) **420**
I Was a Fugitive From a Chain Gang (1932) **283**
Iams, Franklin P. **123, 163**
Iams, Lucy Dorsey **123**
Iams, W.L. **163**
Icardi, Aldo "Ike" **427-436, 555**
Icardi, Dario **436**
Icardi, Eleanor **428**
Icardi, Jeff **436**
Ickes, Harold L. **300, 344**
Immigration Act of 1924 **284**
Imperial, Pennsylvania **274**
In re Agent Orange Products Liability Litigation (1984) **390**
In the Matter of Weirton Steel Company (NLRB 1941) **312**
income tax, federal **69, 196, 259, 266, 480, 490**
Independent Steelworkers Union **385, 525**
Industrial Workers of the World (IWW or Wobblies) **248, 251, 253, 255, 258-259**
Ingersoll Milling Machine Co. **518**
Ingersoll, Frank B. **237, 360-362, 366, 438, 443-448**
Inglis, William O. **77**
Inguito, Galicano, Dr. **495**
Inland Steel Company **385**
Innovation Works **533**
International Brotherhood of Teamsters **385, 418, 469**
International Business Machines Corporation (IBM) **530, 544, 545**
Interstate Commerce Commission **350**
Irene Kaufmann Settlement (Pittsburgh) **250, 270**
Iron City Bank **82**
Iron Mountain (barge) **157-158**
Irons, Harry M. **336-337**
Irvis, K. Leroy **380, 455-461, 465-466, 476**
Irvis, Katharyne **456**
Isaac Newton (steamship) **43**
Israel, Abraham **117**
Israel, Charles **45**
Israel, John **22**
Issoski, George **292-293**

J

J. Painter & Sons Iron Works **84**
J.P. Morgan & Co. **188**
Jackson, Andrew **28-30**
Jackson, Caleb **103**

Jackson, Kenneth G. **309, 505**
Jackson, Jesse, Rev. **528**
Jackson, Robert H. **360-361, 365**
Jackson, Samuel H. **424-425**
Jackson, Shoeless Joe **355**
Jacobsen Manufacturing **518**
James, Arthur **418**
Jefferson County, Pennsylvania **422**
Jefferson, Thomas **18-19, 44**
Jenkinson, Alexander M. **213, 338**
Jewish communities in Pittsburgh **54, 115**
    early Jewish lawyers in Pittsburgh **116-117**
    German American Jews and Eastern European American Jews, divisions between **270, 337, 450**
    Josiah Cohen admitted to bar **116**
    Rodef Shalom **116, 226, 270, 276**
    Tree of Life Congregation **270**
Jobs, Steve **538**
John F. Wilcox v. Semet-Solvay Co. (1905) **231**
Johnson, Andrew **54-55, 57, 199**
Johnson, John G. **106, 351, 355, 358**
    and the "Greatest Lawsuit" **180-185**
Johnson, Johnson & Johnson (law firm) **382**
Johnson, Justin M. **381, 382, 461, 470-476**
Johnson, Livingstone **381, 458, 464, 470-476, 494**
Johnson, Lyndon B. **380**
Johnson, Oliver L. **347, 457, 458**
Johnson, Oliver L., Jr. **458**
Johnson, Philip **521**
Johnson, Reverdy **55**
Johnson, Tom **440-442, 460, 465**
Johnson, William K. **231, 381**
Johnston, Alva **363**
Johnston, Carman C. **288**
Johnston, Joseph E., General **48**
Johnstown Flood (1889) **85, 141-146, 147, 149, 189, 193**
Johnstown, Pennsylvania **146, 279, 391**
Jones & Laughlin Steel **83, 113, 134, 195, 292, 293, 308, 312, 313, 337, 384, 385, 400, 404, 407, 522, 561**
Jones & Laughlin Steel Corp. v. National Labor Relations Board (1937) **300-307**
Jones Day (law firm) **389, 511, 541**
Jones Law Building (Pittsburgh) **267, 503**
Jones, Benjamin Franklin "B.F.," Sr. **83, 84, 85, 113, 133**
Jones, Charles Alvin **203, 237, 243, 432, 435**
Jones, Charlotte **56**
Jones, Cliff **492-493**
Jones, David R. **135-136**
Jones, Edward Purnell **135**

Jones, Herbert **219**
Jones, Mary Milie **510**
Jones, Paul F. **458, 460**
Jones, Richard F. **340-341, 346-347, 459**
Jones, Wesley **257**
Jordan, Angel, Dr. **532**
Jordan, Greg **415, 535, 541, 543, 550**
Jordon, Jim **464**
Joseph, Herbert E. **247**
Jubelirer, Ben Paul **385-386**
Jubelirer, Pass & Intrieri (law firm) **386, 502**
Judicial Code of 1911 **203**
Justus ADR Services (law firm) **546**

K

K&L Gates (law firm) **516, 541, 542, 549.** see also Kirkpatrick & Lockhart (law firm); Kirkpatrick, Lockhart, Johnson & Hutchinson (law firm); and Kirkpatrick, Pomeroy, Lockhart & Johnson (law firm)
Kaiser Aluminum Corporation **366, 411**
Kalis, Peter **516, 541-542**
Kane, John **297, 298**
Kansas City, Missouri **129, 395**
Katarincic, Joseph A. **65-67**
Katz, Henry **479**
Katzenbach, Nicholas **462**
Kaufmann, Edgar **396, 401, 404, 407**
Kaufmann's (department store) **205, 255, 270, 396, 455, 506**
KDKA-TV **409, 496**
Kearney, Kerry **505**
Keaton, Diane **328**
Keck, Charles **283**
Keech, Richmond **434**
Keenan, T.J., Colonel **225**
Keenan, Hugh **36**
Keenan, Thomas Johnston **36-37, 49, 65**
Keevican, Leo A. **451-452**
Kellogg, Paul **215**
Kelly, Clyde **281**
Kelly, Rita **504**
Kelvin, William Thomson, 1st Baron **103**
Kennametal, Inc. **538**
Kennedy, Edward M. **487**
Kennedy, Harry M. **38, 41**
Kennedy, John (Uniontown judge) **23**
Kennedy, John F. (president) **380, 462, 484**
Kennedy, John M. (Pittsburgh judge) **112**
Kennedy, Robert F. **380, 487**
Kennywood Park (Pittsburgh) **252, 459**

Kensel, George **94**
Kenworthey, Charles **406**
Kenyon College **38**
Kenyon, William S. **255**
Kerr & Curtis (law firm) **102**
Kerr, Allen **381**
Kerr, Gregg **443, 447, 449, 525**
Kerr, James W., Colonel **205**
Kerr, Thomas **367**
Kerr, Thomas Bakewell **102-104**
Ketchum Communications **526**
Ketchum, Winthrop W. **69**
Key, Francis Scott **44**
Kiddoo, Joseph B. **50, 52, 99**
Kidwell, Richard P. **546**
Kilday, Paul **433**
Kilgore, Carrie **120, 124**
Kimball, Frank **218**
Kinard, Agnes Dodds **334, 499, 616 n.623**
King, Martin Luther, Jr., Rev. Dr. **462, 464, 466, 470, 476**
    assassination **465**
King, Silver **130**
King, William C. **108**
Kingston, Samuel **34-36**
Kinzer, George **24**
Kirkland & Ellis (law firm) **551**
Kirkpatrick & Lockhart (law firm) **510, 524, 542.** *see also K&L Gates (law firm)*
Kirkpatrick, Abraham, Major **46**
Kirkpatrick, John **95, 116**
Kirkpatrick, Lockhart, Johnson & Hutchinson (law firm) **389, 413, 506, 536.** *see also K&L Gates (law firm)*
Kirkpatrick, Pomeroy, Lockhart & Johnson (law firm) **367, 374, 378, 380, 382, 430, 432, 441, 442, 453, 460, 465, 466, 484, 485, 517.** *see also K&L Gates (law firm)*
Kirkpatrick, Robert **266, 430, 439, 441-442**
Kittanning, Pennsylvania **22, 243**
Kleeb, Robert **300**
Klein, John F. "Smiling Johnnie" **218-219, 222-223**
Kleindienst, Richard **477-490**
Klett Lieber Rooney & Schorling (law firm) **453, 539**
Klett, Edward **452**
Kline, Charles H. **197, 282, 288, 289, 328, 332, 341**
    rackets and corruption trial **282**
Knights of Labor **135-136, 152**
Knights of Pythias **120**
Knox & Reed (law firm) **124, 146, 152, 179, 230, 285, 351.** *see also Reed Smith (law firm)*
    founded **140**

Knox, John C. **366, 367**
Knox, Lillie Smith **140**
Knox, Philander **64, 77, 85, 139-140, 166-168, 172, 174, 179, 183, 188, 194, 196, 229, 231, 236, 243, 357, 366, 438-439, 555, 601 n.683**
    "unknown country lawyer from Pennsylvania" **351, 549**
    and Johnstown Flood **141**
    and the Eighteenth Amendment **196**
    and the Sixteenth Amendment **196**
    as sportsman **139**
    Homestead Steel Strike (1892) **154, 157-159, 161-162, 166**
    Northern Securities case **350-356**
Knudsen, William S. **295**
Konigbserg v. California (1957) **435**
Koninklijke Philips N.V. **538**
Kopechne, Mary Jo **487**
Koppers Building (Pittsburgh) **195**
Koppers Company **76, 367, 400, 503**
Kostman, Leo **503**
Kowall, Carol **510**
Kraft Foods Group **549**
Kramer, Harry **413, 497**
Kramer, Ralph **231**
Kraus, Manuel **332**
Krauthoff, Louis C. **129**
Ku Klux Klan **272, 346**
Kuhn, James Craig, Jr. **432**
Kuhn, Joseph E., Major General **239**
Kunstler, William **469**
Kunzig, Robert L. **424-425, 427**
Kyle, William J., Jr. **361-362, 443-445, 447-448**

L

labor
    municipal corruption as a burden upon **226**
    right to strike **89, 136-137**
    workers' compensation **215-216**
Labor Board v. Friedman-Harry Marks Clothing Co. (1937) **302**
Labor Board v. Fruehauf Trailer Co. (1937) **302**
Lackawanna County, Pennsylvania **145, 199, 211**
Lacock, Hamilton **108**
Laffey, Mary Kate **506**
Lagorio, Frank J.
    first Italian American admitted to Pittsburgh bar **272**
LaGuardia, Fiorello **269**
Lake Chautauqua, New York **478**
Lake Conemaugh, Pennsylvania **141**

Lamont, Nancy **506**
Lamproplos, Milton **446**
Lancaster, Pennsylvania **20, 529**
Landis, Kenesaw Mountain **355**
Landon, Alf **303, 459**
Lang, Edward **222**
Laporte, Ewing **295-296, 312**
LaRussa, Tony **389**
Latham & Watkins (law firm) **551**
Latrobe, Pennsylvania **410, 533**
Latta, James W., Major General **91-95**
Lauder, Dod **174, 176-177, 188**
Laughlin, John E., Jr. **301, 305, 308**
Law & Finance Building (Pittsburgh) **195, 502**
Law and Order League (Pittsburgh) **69**
Law School Admission Test (LSAT) **471**
law schools **33, 121**
Lawrence, David L. **149, 271, 279, 281, 284-285, 312, 332, 344, 402, 405, 408, 412, 420, 423, 425, 427, 456, 478, 480, 481, 497, 520**
Lawrenceville (Pittsburgh) **466**
Lawyer, The (magazine) **516**
Lawyer's Court (Pittsburgh) **202**
Lazard Freres & Company **528**
League for Civic Improvement **459**
Leale, Charles, Dr. **53**
Lee, Henry "Light-Horse Harry", General **16-18**
Lee, Robert E., General **49, 53**
Lee, Lain **463**
Legal Aid Society (Pittsburgh) **381-382**
LegalSifter, Inc. **545**
LegalZoom.com **545**
Legent Corp. **532**
Leishman, J.G. **164-165, 173**
Lend-Lease Administration **334-335, 399**
Leo XIII, Pope **275, 281**
Leonard, Eddie **402**
Levinson, Salmon O. **106**
Levy, Morris **333**
Levy, J. Leonard, Rabbi **226**
Lewis, Captain Samuel **82-83**
Lewis, Loran **422, 459**
Lewistown, Pennsylvania **526**
LexisNexis **544**
Liberty Avenue (Pittsburgh) **148, 195, 217, 279, 401, 521**
Liberty Center (Pittsburgh) **521**
Life (magazine) **308, 504**
Liggio, Carl D. **415**
Ligonier, Pennsylvania **407, 478, 492, 495**
Lincoln, Abraham **i, 22, 40, 44, 47, 55-58, 99, 199, 341, 342, 462, 563**
  assassination **40, 54**
  first meets Stanton **43**
Lincoln, Mary Todd **53**
Lindabury, Richard V. **358-359**
Lindbergh, Anne Morrow **130**
Lindbergh, Charles **130**
Lindsay, Henry D., Rev. **120**
Lipkowitz, Irving **362**
Litman, David **482, 502-504**
Litman, Eugene **527**
Litman, Lennie **503**
Litman, Roslyn Margolis **482, 504-505, 527**
Little Rascals (short subject series) **420**
Little, Nancy W. **144-146**
Little, Norval **242**
Littler Mendelson (law firm) **541**
Llewellyn v. Frick (1925) **242**
Loan, Thomas **249**
Loan, Walter **248-249**
Lobel, Jules **508**
Lochner v. New York (1905) **86**
Lockhart & Frew **82, 83**
Lockhart, Charles **82**
Lockhart, Daniel **46**
Lockhart, George **413, 440-442**
Lockheed Martin Corporation **534**
LoDolce, Carl **429-433**
Loendi Club (Pittsburgh) **119, 335**
Logan, Jim **468-469**
Logan, Lloyd **46**
Logan, Robert **343**
Longenecker, Grace Chambers Humbird **232**
Longenecker, Ralph **123, 230-235, 329**
Long, Haniel **408**
Loomis, Andrew Williams **39, 49, 54**
Loomis, Cyrus O. **50-51**
Loomis, Katharine **334**
Los Angeles Rams (football) **520**
Louik, Maurice **382**
Lovejoy, Francis (Carnegie Steel) **161, 164-165, 178, 185**
Lovejoy, Frank (actor) **420**
Lower Burrell, Pennsylvania **486**
Lowrey, Grosvenor P. **104**
Lowrie, John A. **120**
Lowrie, Walter Hoge **23, 33, 36, 120**
Lowry, James, Jr. **53**
Lubic, Ben **328**
Lucas, John C.B. **19-20**
Lundberg, Ingrid **506**
Lusitania (ocean liner) **235**

Luzerne County, Pennsylvania 69
Lycoming County, Pennsylvania 230
Lynch, Thomas 175-176
Lynchburg, Virginia 340
Lynd, Staughton 522-525, 528
Lyster, Walter J. 275

M

MacConnell, Thomas 23
MacFarlane, James 13
Machinists' and Blacksmiths' Union 135
Macy's (department store) 512
Mad Men (television series) 444
Madden, J. Warren 296-308, 312-313, 334
    and Jones & Laughlin Supreme Court case 303-307
    and Pittsburgh Railways contract dispute 297
    appointed NLRB chairman 298
Madden, Stephen 159
Madison, James 4, 9, 20
Magarac, Joe (legendary steelworker) 283
Magee Women's Hospital (Pittsburgh) 488
Magee, Christopher 58, 110, 153, 206-207, 210-211, 213, 217, 224
    Homestead Steel Strike (1892) 159
Magee, F.N. 83
Magee, William A. 197, 213, 218, 226, 227, 236, 288-289, 329, 336, 340-341
Magee-Flinn machine 58, 110, 207-208, 211-213
Magraw & McKnight (law firm) 100
Magraw, Henry 34
Maheu, Robert 433
Mahone, Andrea 473
Mahone, Glenn R. 473-475
Mahone, Harvey 473, 474
Main & Co. (accounting firm) 243
Majors, Johnny 520
Malone, James F., Jr. 427, 459, 478-480
Malone, James F., Sr. 289, 341-343
Malone, Vivian 461
Maloney, Lawrence 482, 489-490
Mamachtaga 6, 8
Manchester (Pittsburgh) 466
Manderino, Lou 470
Manion Alder & Cohen (law firm)
    see Cohen & Grigsby (law firm)
Mannino, Edward 451
Mansfield, Arabella 115, 120
Mansfield, Jayne 483
Mansfield, William 275-277
Mansmann, Carol Los 482, 511

Mansmann, Cindrich & Titus (law firm) 547.
    see also Cindrich & Titus (law firm)
Mansmann, J. Jerome 374
Manson Family/Tate-LaBianca murders 487
Mao Zedong 436
Marathon Oil Corporation 519
Marcellus and Utica shale plays. see Pittsburgh, Pennsylvania - and natural gas; Pittsburgh, Pennsylvania and the oil industry
March on Washington for Jobs and Freedom (1963) 462-465
Margiotti, Charles J. 422-427, 436
Margolis, Barbara 264
Margolis, Florence Kaminsky 250, 251, 254
Margolis, Jacob 249-252, 264, 269, 270, 338, 384, 421, 431-432
    accused of abetting draft evasion 253
    anarchosyndicalism 250, 256
    Detroit Jewish Chronicle, owner and editor of 263
    disbarment proceedings 261-262
    disbarred 260
    education and background 249
    pacifism 252, 256
    Senate testimony 257
Markel & Markel (law firm) 468
Markel, Gertrude Friedlander and Jacob 330
Marsh, James I. 235-237
Marshall & Brown (law firm) 116
Marshall, Elder W. 238, 243, 338, 439
Marshall, James J. 250, 253, 255, 260-261
Marshall, John 28-30
Marshall, Joseph I. 439
Marshall, Matthew 94
Marshall, Thomas Mercer 7, 39, 54, 68, 75, 93, 95, 116, 150, 155, 168
Marshall, Thurgood 341, 458, 470
Martin, Park 401-404, 409
Martin, Richard W. 264, 289, 341, 398
Martin, William 223
Martino, Leonard 488
Martinsburg, West Virginia 90, 93
Masaryk, Tomas 333
Massachusetts Institute of Technology 530
Mather, Cotton 72
Mather, Robert 106
Matson, Marjorie Hanson 330, 422-423, 424-427
Mattern, Clara 470
Matthews & Wright (investment bank) 452
May, C. Kent 447, 525-527, 531, 539
May, Herbert, Jr. 493
Mayor's Court, Pittsburgh 21

Mayview Hospital (South Fayette Twp., PA) 289
Mazeroski, Bill 526
Mazzei, Joseph 431, 434
McAdoo, Garland H. 471-474
McArdle, James P. 374-375, 377, 390-391
    and the *African Queen* (boat) 377
McArdle, P.J. 226, 373
McBride, Thomas B. 425
McCallum, Pamela 453
McCalmont, Albert 36, 49-50
McCandless & Kinser v. O'Brien (1891) 137
McCandless & McClure (law firm) 39
McCandless, Stephen C. 120
McCandless, Wilson 35, 39, 54, 69, 120
McCargo, David 109
McCarran Act 431
McCarthy, Joseph 420, 431-433, 436
McCarthy, William 90, 92, 95
McCaskey, Donald 444, 449
McClatchy, Kevin 537
McClay, Samuel 231, 438
McCleary, William H. 153, 156-161
McClellan, George B., General 50
McClelland, William 20
McClenahan, David 524
McClintic-Marshall Construction Company 76
McClintock, Oliver 207-210
McCloskey, Eddie 279-280
McClung, Samuel A. 143, 163-164
McClure & Watkins (law firm) 492
McClure, W.B. 30, 39, 75
McConnell, John 527
McCook, George W. 39
McCook, Willis F. 77, 84-86, 178, 218, 222,
    224, 244, 440
McCoy, Jim 462, 463
McCullough, David 142
McCullough, M. Bruce 388
McCullough, Welty 93
McCune, Barron 529
McCune, W.S. 66
McDaniel, Donna Jo 511
McDonagh, Josephine 327, 378
McDonald, Pennsylvania 287
McDougal, Myres 399
McDowell, John 13, 19-20
McGeagh Building (Pittsburgh) 251, 253
McGinnis, Bernard B. 250
McGonigle, John 414
McGough, Thomas 415

McGough, Walter 550
McGovern, Buck, Lt. 328
McGregor, Jack 408
McGregor, James, Major 85
McGuinn, Martin 414
McGuire, John 252
McGuireWoods (law firm) 475, 541
McKay, Marion O'Kellie 297
McKean County, Pennsylvania 248, 277
McKean, Thomas 17, 19, 21, 24, 27
McKee Mitchell & Alter (law firm) 234, 237, 243
McKees Rocks, Pennsylvania 386
McKeesport, Pennsylvania 113, 185, 232, 245, 252,
    275, 337, 522, 528
McKellar, Kenneth 256
McKelvy, James E. 65
McKenna, Charles W. 119
McKenna, Joseph 359
McKennan, John D. 199
McKennan, William 69
McKinley Tariff 149, 161, 168, 182
McKinley, William 119, 149-151, 182, 188, 194, 196,
    209, 349, 351
McKinney, Frank 442
McKnight, Elizabeth O'Hara Denny 34
McKnight, H.D. "Denny" 127
McKnight, Robert 30, 34-35, 100, 127
McLaughlin, James E. 494
McLuckie, John 154, 161-162, 167-168
McMillin, Benton 161
McMillin, Blair 442
McMillin, Edward R., II 442
McNair, William N. 332-333, 478
McNaugher, William 375-376
McQuitty, A.J. 131
McReynolds, James Clark 304, 362
McTernan, John T. 422, 426
McVerry, Terry 482
Meadville, Pennsylvania 25, 198
Meason, Isaac, Jr. 25
Megrew, George 177
Mehard, Churchill B. 237, 333
Mehard, Samuel S. 123, 237
Mehard, Scully & Mehard (law firm) 237
Melaney, William H. 222
Mellon Financial Corporation 414
Mellon National Bank 266, 280, 396, 400, 406, 477,
    499, 521, 524, 527, 550
Mellon Park (Pittsburgh) 400
Mellon Securities Corporation 399
Mellon Square (Pittsburgh) 406

Mellon, Andrew 76, 84-85, 141-143, 166, 196, 229, 233, 280, 360, 396-397, 448
   federal tax prosecution 196
Mellon, James (descendant and biographer) 137
Mellon, James Ross 74, 232
Mellon, John 117
Mellon, Richard B. 76, 166, 213, 233, 266, 288, 396, 397, 399-400
Mellon, Richard King 396, 399-400, 404-408, 414, 460, 520, 530
Mellon, Sarah Jane Negley 72
Mellon, Thomas 23, 34-35, 39, 48, 64, 71-78, 85, 116, 118, 135-136, 139, 141, 232, 244, 387, 563
   admission examination 24
   as city councilman 76
   as Common Pleas judge 75
   as investor 71, 107
   bias against oratorical talent 74-75
   opens T. Mellon & Sons Bank 76
   view of successful lawyer as good businessman 73, 77, 244
Mellon, Thomas, II 232
Mellot, Cloyd "Mel" 447
Melvin, Joan Orie 511
Mencken, H.L. 346
Mercer County, Pennsylvania 38
Mercer, H. Fred, Sr. 383
Merrick, Fred 252
Mervis, Samuel 252
Messenger (steamship) 42
Mesta Machine Company 388
Metcalf & Loomis (law firm) 39
Metcalf, Orlando Williams 39
Metosky, Sandy 506
Metro-Goldwyn-Mayer Pictures 271
Metropolitan Life Insurance Company 402
Metzgar, Henry 92
Meyer, Darragh, Buckler, Bebenek & Eck (law firm) 506, 510
Meyer, John D. 197, 259, 289
Meyer, Unkovic & Scott (law firm) 379, 382, 506
Microsoft Corp. 541
Midland, Pennsylvania 523
Mifflin, Thomas 10, 18
Milburn, John G. 355
Milch, Erhard 419
Milholland, James 237, 243
   and the Milholland Committee 424-427
Miller, Alexander H. 39
Miller, Emma Guffey 342
Miller, Harry I. 237
Miller, J.H. 83

Miller, James R. 234-235
Miller, John S. 354
Miller, Oliver 13
Miller, W. McCook "Cookie" 440
Miller, William 13
Millipore Corporation 534
Mills, Kathleen Merry 505
Minahan, Donald 487
Miners' Association 135-136
minimum fee schedules
   abolition 387
Minneapolis, Minnesota 107, 200
Mister Rogers' Neighborhood (television series) 410
Mitchell, John N. 477-478, 489-490
Molinas, Jack 504
Monaca, Pennsylvania 344
Monahan, Kasper 283
Moncrief, Lawrence 470
Money Honey (1972) 483
Monongahela (barge) 157
Monongahela House Hotel (Pittsburgh) 35, 39, 42, 46, 67, 80
Monongahela Incline (Pittsburgh) 541
Monongahela National Bank 266
Monongahela River 11, 26, 27, 42, 46, 151, 152, 155, 194, 396, 524
Monroe, James 18, 27
Montgomery, Alice Ballard 215
Montgomery, Harry 419
Montooth, Edward A. 51, 168
Moore & Schley (securities firm) 357
Moore, William D., Colonel (Pittsburgh lawyer) 163
Moore, William H. (corporate speculator) 174, 183, 187
Moorhead & Head (law firm) 181
Moorhead & Knox (law firm) 390, 464, 485
Moorhead, James S. 181
Moorhead, Maxwell K. 84
Moorhead, William S., Jr. 485
Morecroft, Gilbert 406
Moreland, Andrew M. 178, 184
Moreland, William C. 94, 109-113, 155, 178, 211
Morgan Lewis & Bockius (law firm) 506, 510, 536, 541
Morgan, J.P. 97, 105, 174, 185-189, 246, 350-360, 549
Morgan, John 447
Morino Inc. 532
Morning Joe (television show) 542
Morris Walker & Allen (law firm) 234, 237, 243
Morris, Edmund 139

Morrow, Dwight **130**
Mortgage Banking Association of America **411**
Morton, James D. "Jim" **448, 481**
Moscatelli, Vincenzo **430, 433**
Moschzisker, Michael von **425**
Moschzisker, Robert von **396**
Motheral, George B. **231, 243**
Motheral, P.K. **243**
Mount Holyoke College **499**
Mount Lebanon, Pennsylvania **330, 417, 499**
Mount Union College **135, 140, 188**
Mount Washington (Pittsburgh) **46, 54, 373, 396, 436, 468, 541, 552**
Mountain, James **7**
Mountain, Sidney **28, 40**
Mrs. Soffel (1982) **328**
Ms. Ogyny, or the Ballad of Barbara Wolvovitz (song by Anne Feeney) **509**
Mudd, Samuel, Dr. **55**
Mulligan, Kathleen **511**
Mulvihill, William H. **239**
Munhall, Pennsylvania **528**
Muni, Paul **283-285**
Municipal Authorities Act of 1945 **528**
Munsch, Martha **505**
Murchison, Clint, Jr. **518-519**
Murphy, David **546**
Murphy, Frank **365**
Murphy, Tom **532-538**
Murray, James W. **67**
Murray, Lawrence O. **220**
Murray, Magnus **40, 205**
Murray, Philip **383**
Murrysville, Pennsylvania **101, 502-503**
Musgrave, John H. **200**
Musmanno, Michael A. **269-279, 282-286, 293, 297, 304, 327, 347, 419-422, 425-426, 432, 434-436, 457, 543**
   and *Black Fury* (1935) **284**
   and Sacco and Vanzetti case **269-274**
   and the fight to abolish the Coal and Iron Police **274-278**
   elected County Court judge **278**
   elected to Common Pleas Court **284**
   New Year's Eve drunk driving court **285**
Myers, Elmer **531**
Myers, Jim **536**
Myers, Marlee **506-510, 536-539, 553**

N

Nabisco **523, 527-528, 538**
Nader, Ralph **228**
Nairn, Regis **502**
Narick, Emil **524**
Nation of Islam **470**
Nation, The (magazine) **262, 299-300**
National Association for the Advancement of Colored People (NAACP) **308, 341, 344, 403, 456-470**
National Bar Association **335, 346**
National Basketball Association **504**
National Civil Liberties Bureau. *see American Civil Liberties Union*
National Gazette **4**, **12**
National Industrial Recovery Act of 1933 **290, 293, 295, 307**
National Labor Board (under NIRA) **291-292**
National Labor Relations Act of 1935 **295-296, 299-312**
National Labor Relations Board **296-298, 301-313, 334, 383, 524.** *see also* National Labor Relations Act of 1935
National Labor Tribune **135, 142, 143, 144, 151**
National Law Journal **536**
National League (baseball) **129, 131**
National Municipal League **217**
National Organization for Women **464**
National Press Club **294**
National Recovery Administration **294**
National Steel Company (Moore) **187-188**
National Steel Corporation (Weir) **290, 312, 385, 472, 505, 519, 527-528**
National Tube Company **185, 252**
National University **271**
Navish, Charles **489-490**
NBC Television **410**
Nebraska Territory **48, 237**
Negley, William B. **51, 65, 67**
Neighborhood Legal Services Association (NLSA) **466-469, 470, 476, 484**
   and abortion rights **467**
   founding of **381-382**
Nelson, Steve **421-425, 431**
Neolinear, Inc. **534**
Nesbit, Charles, Dr. **10**
Nesbit, Harrison **221-222**
Neville, John, General **13, 22, 26**
Neville, Morgan **26**
New Castle, Pennsylvania **117**
New Cumberland, West Virginia **308**
New Deal **195, 203, 266, 267, 282, 284, 285, 287, 290, 294, 295, 296, 302, 307, 335, 345, 398, 399, 562**
New Kensington, Pennsylvania **308, 363, 471**
New Lisbon, Ohio **39**

646 INDEX

New York Central Railroad **82, 185**
New York City bar **64, 66, 103, 115, 119, 129, 194, 215, 267, 517**
    patent lawyers **99**
    rivalry with Pittsburgh bar **103, 351, 550**
New York Stock Exchange **189, 415, 479**
New York Times, The **iii, 100, 111, 112, 161, 180, 181, 184, 193, 209, 213, 224, 254, 330, 407, 460, 507, 509, 528, 552**
New York University **119, 215, 470**
New Yorker (magazine) **363**
Newsweek **407, 457**
Newlin, William R. **392-393, 415, 449, 453, 529, 539, 554**
Newton, Wendelynne **510**
NeXT, Inc. **538**
Nickens, Oswald **464**
Nields, John **293, 301**
Nimick, W.A. **127-132**
Nixon Theatre (Pittsburgh) **283**
Nixon, Clarence B. **459**
Nixon, Richard M. **380, 417, 436, 451, 477-478, 484, 490**
Nock, Albert Jay **222**
Nolin, Samuel G. **242-243**
Noll, Chuck **520**
Norris, Roderick **447**
North Park (Allegheny County, Pennsylvania) **459**
North Shore (Pittsburgh) **538**
North Side (Pittsburgh) **47, 68, 127, 130, 229, 261, 283, 300, 412, 418, 461, 473, 480, 532**
Northern Pacific Railroad **350**
Northern Securities Co. v. U.S. (1904) **353-356, 367**
Northern Securities Company **360**
    and antitrust case. see *Northern Securities Co. v. U.S. (1904)*
Northwestern University **512**
Norton, Lynette **506**
Nott, Charles C., Jr. **247-248**
Novarro, Ramon **271**
Number Six Club **84-85, 128**

O

O'Brien, Charles A. **131, 236, 252**
O'Brien, Frank **528**
O'Brien, Henry X. **372, 435**
O'Donnell, Hugh **168**
O'Donnell, John C. **210**
O'Loughlin, Johanna **505, 510**
O'Neil, J. Palmer **128-130**
O'Toole, James L., Jr. **332**

Oakland (Pittsburgh) **186, 207, 209, 276, 411, 442, 460, 466, 496**
Oakmont, Pennsylvania **379, 502**
Obama, Barack H. **540**
Oberlin College **117**
Obernauer, Harold **424**
Office of Economic Opportunity **380, 465**
Ogburn, Charlton **298**
Ohio Bar Association **378**
Ohio River **6, 7, 9, 18, 41, 44, 46, 292, 396**
Ohio State University **297, 500**
Olbum, David **483**
Old Overholt Whiskey **196, 232**
Old St. Patrick's Church **275**
Oliver Building (Pittsburgh) **195, 234, 240, 244, 442, 448**
Oliver High School **502**
Oliver Iron and Steel Company **83**
Oliver, Henry W. **85**
Olmstead, Frederick Law **212**
Omnibus Crime Control and Safe Streets Act of 1968 **490**
Onda, Andy **422, 425**
One L (book by Scott Turow) **512**
One Mellon Bank Center (Pittsburgh) **521-522**
One Mellon Plaza (Pittsburgh) **374**
One Oliver Plaza (Pittsburgh) **521, 541**
One Oxford Centre (Pittsburgh) **521, 544**
Online Systems, Inc. **532**
Oppenheimer, J. Robert **421**
Order of the Italian Sons and Daughters of America **272, 430**
Organized Crime Control Act of 1970 **488-490**
Orlando, Florida **436**
Orr, Charles P. **200, 203, 255**
Orrick Herrington & Sutcliffe (law firm) **551**
Osmer, James H. **54, 328**
Our American Cousin (play by Tom Taylor) **53**
Over, James. P. (son) **239**
Over, James W. (father) **239**
Oxford Development Corporation **521**
Oxford University **542**

P

Packel, Israel **494**
Packer, Gibson D. **141, 177, 184, 398**
Paige, Satchel **337**
Painter, A.E.W. **84**
Palmer, A. Mitchell **247-248**
Palschak, Clara and Steve **329**
Pan-American Airlines **428**

Pandit, Amy 512-514
Panic of 1873 76, 90, 141
Panic of 1893 103, 169, 279
Panic of 1907 97, 104, 105
Panzar, Joann 506
Papadakos, Nicholas 507, 524
Park, Andrew 289
Parker, Brian 475
Parkinson, Thomas 402, 404
Parks, Timothy 533, 535
Parnell, Charles Stewart 134
Parsons, Albert and Lucy 259
Pashukanis, Evgeny 548
Pass, Joseph J., Jr. 386-387, 502
Passmore, Thomas 21
Patterson, Crawford, Arensberg & Dunn (law firm) 330, 432. see also Tucker Arensberg (law firm)
Patterson, Crawford, Miller & Arensberg (law firm) 234-235, 243, 254, 267, 285. see also Tucker Arensberg (law firm)
Patterson, David F. 111, 161, 165
Patterson, Frank P. 264
Patterson, Hanna 328
Patterson, Simon T. 197
Patterson, Sterrett & Acheson (law firm) 222, 233, 235
Patterson, Thomas 234
Pattison, Robert 158-159, 161
Patton, Benjamin 38
Patton, Robert 531
Pauley, Andrew J., Msgr. 423
Paxson, Edward M. 95, 166-168, 199
Pearson, Alfred L., General 50-52, 91-95, 109, 113
Pease, Robert 412
Peck, Daniel 39
Pei, I.M. 411
Peirce, Robert 483
Pellegrini, Dante 524
Pendergast machine (Kansas City, Missouri) 395
Penn Avenue (Pittsburgh) 48, 207, 220, 279, 405, 521
Penn Cotton Factory Riot (1848) 37
Penn Southwest Association 532
Penn, William 5, 548
Penn-Lincoln Parkway (Interstate 376) 403
Pennington, Captain John D. 197, 289
Pennsylvania Bar Association 199, 229, 304, 392
Pennsylvania Coal Co. v. Sanderson (1886) 144-146
Pennsylvania Coal Company 145
Pennsylvania Constitution of 1790 10

Pennsylvania Constitution of 1838 117
Pennsylvania Constitution of 1874 68
Pennsylvania Constitutional Convention of 1837 45
Pennsylvania Constitutional Convention of 1873 63
Pennsylvania Constitutional Convention of 1967-68 380
Pennsylvania Crimes Act of 1860 166
Pennsylvania Human Relations Commission 461
Pennsylvania Labor Relations Act 346
Pennsylvania Liquor Control Board 197
Pennsylvania Lottery Act of 1971 497
Pennsylvania National Guard 52, 91-95, 163
Pennsylvania Public Utility Commission 403
Pennsylvania Railroad 68, 82-83, 85, 96, 101-102, 109-110, 141, 149, 159, 185, 194, 210, 217, 229, 403, 405
Pennsylvania Sedition Act of 1919 422, 431
Pennsylvania State Board of Law Examiners 200, 330, 428
Pennsylvania State University 20, 128, 471, 560-562
Pennsylvania Supreme Court 7, 15, 17, 19, 20, 23, 36, 37, 72, 74, 76, 80, 86, 109, 130, 135, 142, 144, 145, 166, 200, 203, 230, 233, 262, 263, 277, 330, 334, 354, 396, 402, 405, 406, 420, 421, 422, 425, 426, 432, 434, 435, 436, 474, 484, 510
Pennsylvania v. Wheeling & Belmont Bridge Co. (1855) 41, 43, 55
Pennsylvania Voluntary Trade Tribunal Act (1883) 164
Pennypacker, Samuel W. 213
Pentland, Ephraim 21-24, 27
Peoples First National Bank (Pittsburgh) 398. see also PNC Financial Services Group, Inc.
Peoples National Bank (Pittsburgh) 84
Peoples Natural Gas Company 327, 404
Peppard, S.G. 39
Pepper Hamilton (law firm) 475
Pepper, George Wharton 199
Perkins, Frances 296
Perrin, Douglas 463
Perry, J. Lester 404
Pershing, General John J. 258
Peter Schoenhofen Brewing Company 85
Peters, Richard, Jr. 28-29
Peugeot, Linda and Lori 486-487
Pew, J. Howard 295
Pflaum brothers, Magnus and Maurice 116
Philadelphia Athletics (baseball) 129
Philadelphia Company 398
Philadelphia Phillies (baseball) 129

648 INDEX

Philadelphia, Pennsylvania 4, 5, 6, 8, 11, 13, 14, 16, 21-22, 28, 30, 36, 42, 50, 68, 72, 74, 80, 82, 86, 89-90, 92-93, 95, 102-103, 106, 120, 124, 129-130, 141, 166, 178-179, 181, 185, 199, 206, 209, 215, 268, 271, 280, 284, 285, 297, 333, 345, 351, 389, 395, 405, 420, 424, 425, 451-452, 510, 531, 536, 560-561, 563-565
    bar of 5-6
    first woman admitted to bar 120
Phillips, Harry 298
Phillips, James 290
Phillips, T.W. 440
Phipps Conservatory and Botanical Gardens 397
Phipps. Frank H., Captain 85
Phipps, Henry, Jr. 141, 176-178, 183-186, 397
Picone, Americo 486, 488
Pinchot, Cornelia Bryce 293
Pinchot, Gifford 197, 280, 284-285, 293, 297, 341, 344
Pinkerton Detective Agency 152-153, 163, 165, 172, 179, 194
Pirates of Penzance, The (opera by Gilbert & Sullivan) 129
Pitcairn, Pennsylvania 480
Pitcairn, Raymond 295
Pitcairn, Robert 85, 91, 109, 141, 210
Pittsburgh & Lake Erie Railroad 140, 338
Pittsburgh Alleghenies (baseball) 128
Pittsburgh and West Virginia Railroad 401
Pittsburgh Anti-Conscription League 253
Pittsburgh Association for the Relief of the Poor 90
Pittsburgh Athletic Association 492
Pittsburgh bar 112
    "commodity work" 389, 540, 543, 551
    "delocalization" of law firms 385-86, 542-546
    admission 23, 200-201
    and "court packing" plan of President F. Roosevelt 304
    and Italian Americans 272-273
    and national politics 27, 30, 194, 282, 341, 477
    and the Cravath system 103, 234, 237-238, 244, 389, 453, 512, 514
    and the Great Depression 267
    and World War I 243-244
    and WWII veterans 373, 379, 393, 440, 443, 451, 456, 464
    antitrust law sophistication 367
    arbitration 203
    bankruptcy practice after 1978 388
    collegiality of 30, 375
    company solicitor vs. general counsel 100
    democratization 123, 201-204, 373, 436
    early law partnerships 39
    elite corporate lawyers as peers of industrialists 84, 398
    entry of women and minorities into the bar 115, 198, 327
    first African Americans admitted 118
    first Jew admitted 116
    first members admitted 9
    first woman lawyer admitted 124
    growth 62, 233
    growth of plaintiffs' bar 390
    impact of new technologies on profession 544-545
    increase in number of law graduates after WWII 372
    intellectual property practice, 1980s-90s 388
    law schools begin to replace reading law 122
    lawyers in office buildings 68
    lawyers involved in commerce 72, 398, 414
    marketing and advertising 393
    permanent class of federal lawyers 198
    preceptorship 200
    reading law 22, 33
    rise of law firms 65, 233
    rivalry with New York bar 103, 351, 549-550
    sons following fathers into bar 120
    sophisticated patent bar 99
    specialization 550
    trial lawyers as stage performers 39
    typewriters replace scribes 122
    U.S. Attorneys from outside of Pittsburgh 198
Pittsburgh Bessemer Company 147
Pittsburgh Biomedical Development Corporation 534
Pittsburgh branch of the Federal Reserve Bank of Cleveland (Pittsburgh) 195
Pittsburgh Brewing Company 196
Pittsburgh Burghers 128
Pittsburgh Catholic (newspaper) 281
Pittsburgh Chamber of Commerce 207, 208, 225-226, 478, 524
Pittsburgh Civic Club 381
Pittsburgh Civic Light Opera 407
Pittsburgh Coal Company 76, 231, 274
Pittsburgh Coal Exchange 135
Pittsburgh Colonization Society 45
Pittsburgh Courier (newspaper) 339, 341-342, 345, 412, 455, 461
Pittsburgh Crawfords (baseball) 337, 479
Pittsburgh Cultural Trust 521
Pittsburgh Department of Public Works 208

Pittsburgh Field Club **492**
Pittsburgh Five, the **469**
Pittsburgh Foundry **84**
Pittsburgh Golf Club **331**
Pittsburgh Horse Show **85**
Pittsburgh Housing Authority **402, 457**
Pittsburgh Law Academy **36, 65**
Pittsburgh Leader **184, 210, 218-219, 222**
Pittsburgh Legal Journal **36-37, 49, 57, 65, 67, 137, 225, 378, 448, 565**
Pittsburgh National Bank **398, 494**. *see also* PNC Financial Services Group, Inc.
Pittsburgh Penguins (hockey team) **408**
Pittsburgh Petroleum Company **82**
Pittsburgh Pipers (basketball) **504**
Pittsburgh Pirates (baseball) **127, 129-130, 442, 460, 520, 525, 528, 530, 537, 539**
    sale of team in 1946 **442**
    sale of team in 1986 **528**
    sale of team in 1995 **538**
Pittsburgh Plate Glass Company **83, 247, 295, 395, 398, 404, 407, 409, 414, 508, 521, 522, 527, 537**
Pittsburgh Post **124, 134, 168, 176, 263, 565**
Pittsburgh Post-Gazette **345, 386, 418, 480, 489, 494, 507**
Pittsburgh Press **277, 283, 290, 306, 386, 393, 401, 494**
Pittsburgh Press Co. **386**
Pittsburgh Regional Planning Association **400**
Pittsburgh Rens (basketball) **503**
Pittsburgh Steelers (football) **520, 538**
Pittsburgh Supercomputing Center **530**
Pittsburgh Survey **215-216, 227**
Pittsburgh Technology Council **533**
Pittsburgh Theological Seminary **410**
Pittsburgh Transfer Company **127**
Pittsburgh v. Pennsylvania Railroad (1865) **80**
Pittsburgh, Bessemer & Lake Erie Railroad Company **179**
Pittsburgh, Cincinnati and St. Louis Railway **93**
Pittsburgh, Pennsylvania
    "America's Most Livable City" **394, 521**
    "Pittsburgh Plan" (new city charter), **234**
    "Pittsburgh Renaissance" **401-403, 407-408, 411-416, 451, 461**
    "Renaissance II" **394, 521**
    "Ripper Act" **211-212**
    "typhoid capital of the world," nineteenth century, **209**
    anarchism in **162, 261**
    and "frontier jurisprudence" **31**
    and biotechnology **iii, 382, 530, 533, 534, 538**
    and Native Americans **6-8, 17**
    and natural gas **iii, 101, 551**
    and software **530, 532, 534, 537-538, 545**
    and the numbers racket **479**
    and the oil industry **54, 61, 83, 550-551**
    and the Second American Industrial Revolution **iii, 37, 58, 61, 244, 540**
    and the technology industry **iii, 534, 537, 537-538**
    and the Whiskey Rebellion **14**
    as mecca of Anti-Communism **417**
    as sports town **127, 520**
    City Council bribery scandal **224-225**
    common and select city councils **206**
    corruption in the nineteenth century **107**
    daily life in eighteenth century **5**
    decline of steel industry **382, 522**
    early skyscrapers **195**
    efforts to clean up water supply **210, 217, 227**
    lawyering in **7, 62, 64, 189, 195, 204, 373, 385, 387, 555-558**
    new federal buildings **195**
    Prohibition era **197-198**
    shift of corporate influence from Pittsburgh to New York **189**
    smoke abatement **216, 223, 402-403**
    telephones in **68**
Pittsburgh, Virginia and Charleston Railroad Company **93**
Pittsburghers Against Apartheid **451**
Pius XI, Pope **281**
Planet Hollywood **512**
Players' League (baseball) **128-130**
Plowman, Jack **379**
Plutarch's *Lives* **16, 23**
PNC Financial Services Group, Inc. **415, 510, 527, 538, 550**. *see also Pittsburgh National Bank; Peoples First National Bank (Pittsburgh)*
PNC Park (Pittsburgh) **537**
PNC Ventures **534**
Poffinberger, Judd **374, 389, 441, 465**
Point Breeze (Pittsburgh) **101, 448, 468**
Point Park University **331**
Point State Park (Pittsburgh). *see Point, the (Pittsburgh)*
Point, the (Pittsburgh) **62, 151, 225, 279, 283, 396, 407, 413, 416, 466, 521, 561**
Polier, Isidore "Shad" **308-313**
Polier, Justine Wise **308-309**
Polish Hill (Pittsburgh) **279**
Polk, James K. **30, 35**
Pollock v. Farmers' Loan & Trust Co. (1895) **69**

Pollock, Matthew M., Rev. **108**
Pomeroy, Thomas W., Jr. **367, 378, 440, 484**
Pope & Edgecomb (law firm) **100**
Pope, Franklin Leonard **100, 102**
Porter, H.K. **268**
Porter, Louis Kossuth **259**
Porter, Stephen Geyer **259, 340**
Porter, William D. (Pittsburgh judge) **111**
Porter, William W. (Philadelphia judge) **72**
Posner, Victor **518**
Posvar, Wesley **530**
Potter Title and Trust Company **330**
Potter, John **160**
Pottstown, Pennsylvania **395**
Powell v. Pennsylvania (1888) **86**
Powell, Lewis F., Jr. (Supreme Court justice) **380**
Powell, Lewis (Seward's attacker) **55, 57**
Powers, Leland **247**
PPG Industries, Inc.. *see* Pittsburgh Plate Glass Company
PPG Place **521-522**
Presidential election
   1800 **19**
   1824 **28**
   1828 **28**
   1876 **90, 134**
   1880 **268**
   1888 **129, 149**
   1892 **155, 161, 168**
   1896 **182, 209**
   1912 **227, 339, 357**
   1924 **341**
   1928 **341**
   1932 **282, 303, 342**
   1936 **459**
   1948 **20**
   1964 **477**
   1968 **477, 484**
   1988 **528**
   2000 **28**
   2012 **542**
Pressed Steel Car Company **223**
Preston Gates & Ellis (law firm) **541**
Price, Gwilym **398, 407-409**
Prichard, Charles B. **220, 222, 248, 259, 290**
Prigg v. Pennsylvania (1842) **46**
Princeton University **4, 16, 230, 231, 234, 235, 236, 237, 362, 420, 531, 562**
   "Princeton effect" on enlistment for World War I duty **236**
Prine, Malcolm "Mac" **526-527**
Prohibition Bureau, U.S. **197-198**

Promises, Promises (1965) **483**
Proskauer Rose (law firm) **299**
Proskauer, Joseph **299**
prothonotary, Allegheny County **20-22, 25, 27, 71, 131, 426**
Providence, Rhode Island **437**
Pudlin, Helen **510**
Punxsutawney, Pennsylvania **422**
Purviance, Samuel A. **120**
Purviance, W.S. **120**
Pushinsky, Jon **508-509**

Q

Quay, Matthew **69, 130, 150, 161, 211, 212**
Queenan, Charles J., Jr. **441-442, 517-520, 536, 539-540, 545**
Queenan, Charles J., Sr. **517**
Quinn, Thomas F. **382, 470**

R

Racketeer Influenced and Corrupt Organizations Act (RICO) **486**
Rahauser, William S. **423-425, 427**
Rainey, William J. **172**
Ralston, John M. **254, 267, 438**
Ramsey, JonBenet **496**
Ramsey, William W. **220-223**
Randall, P.J. Clyde **346**
Randolph, Edmund **15**
Randolph, William Maurice **118-120, 125, 335-336, 340**
Ranii, David **393**
Rankin, Pennsylvania **337, 480, 522**
Raskob, John J. **287, 290, 294**
Rathbone, Henry, Major **53**
Rauh, Joseph **399**
Ravages (novel by Eugene Viollet-le-Duc) **483**
RCA Corporation **532**
Reagan, Ronald **451**
Reardon, William **93-94, 168**
Reconstruction **52, 57-58, 474, 561**
Recreation Park (Pittsburgh) **127**
Redevelopment Authority of the City of Philadelphia **405**
Redick, David **9, 15**
Reed Smith (law firm) **85, 140, 141, 415, 475, 535, 541, 549, 550**
Reed Smith Centre (Pittsburgh) **541**
Reed, Anica Barlow Humbird **232**
Reed, David **65, 83, 139-140**

Reed, David Aiken **201, 231, 235-238, 240, 243, 284-285, 299, 438**
    U.S. Steel antitrust case **358-359**
Reed, Earl **287-295, 308, 312-313, 383, 438**
    and "Lawyer's Vigilance Committee" **299-301**
    and Jones & Laughlin Supreme Court case **303-307**
    prosecution of Mayor Kline **288-290**
Reed, Glenn **531**
Reed, James Hay **64, 69, 77, 83, 85, 139-145, 179, 181-188, 244, 188, 201, 218, 231-232, 234, 244, 287, 303, 358-359, 440, 454**
Reed, Katherine Jones Aiken **140, 232**
Reed, Smith, Shaw & Beal (law firm) **188, 234-236, 243, 438**. *see also Reed Smith (law firm)*
Reed, Smith, Shaw & McClay (law firm) **196, 201, 266, 287, 299, 327, 334, 358, 367, 371, 376, 385, 391, 395, 405-406, 408, 430, 438, 443-444, 451, 453, 464, 474, 499, 501, 503, 505, 529**. *see also Reed Smith (law firm)*
Reed, Stanley **303, 305, 346, 365**
Reed, Thomas B. **149**
Regan, Dr. Louis **482**
Reich, Samuel **490-491**
Reid, Whitelaw **161**
Reilly, John **141**
Reiszenstein family **450**
Reliance Insurance Company **483**
Renal Solutions, Inc. **538**
Renzi, Ned **545**
Republic Steel Corp. **309, 385, 523**
Respironics, Inc. **538**
Reynolds Metals Corporation **364, 366**
Rice, Charles Owen, Msgr. **467, 523**
Rice, Walter L. **361-364**
Richards, Layton & Finger (law firm) **292**
Richards, Wallace **400-403**
Richardson, Dr. Andrew **44**
Richardson, H.H. **62, 76, 84**
Richmond, Virginia **49, 50, 119, 213, 338, 340, 475**
Richter, Henry **330**
Ricketson, John H. **84, 85, 93**
Riddle, James **25**
Rigas family **538**
Ringgold, Irwin M. **382**
Rippey, Oliver H. **47-52, 237**
R.K. Mellon Foundation **530**
Roach, Hal, Sr. **295**
Roanoke, Virginia **340**
Robb v. Carnegie Bros. (1891) **145- 146**
Robbins, Edward E. **163**

Robb, John S. **111, 161, 165**
Roberto, Caroline **510**
Roberts, E.J. **120**
Roberts, Owen **304, 307**
Roberts, Richard Biddle **120**
Robertson, David L. **385**
Robertson, S.S. **259-260, 262**
Robespierre, Maximilien de **12**
Robin, Jack **401**
Robinson Venture Partners **534**
Robinson, Joseph **439**
Robinson, William McIlvaine, Sr. **232, 235, 243, 266, 439-440**
Rockwell-Standard Corp. **517**
Rock Island Company **106**
Rock Point Park, Pennsylvania **67, 143**
Rockefeller, John D. **83, 181, 228, 303, 350, 354-356, 440**
Rockefeller, Nelson A. **477, 484**
Roddey, Jim **526**
Rodef Shalom (Pittsburgh) **116, 226, 270, 276**
Roderick, David **519, 524-526**
Rodewald, Paul G. **196, 242, 361, 443-449, 450, 454**
Rodewald, William Y. **450**
Rodgers, Samuel **430, 433, 435**
Rodgers, William B. **211, 222**
Rogers, Fred ("Mister Rogers") **410**
Rogers, Ginger **507**
Rogers, John I., Colonel **129**
Rolling Rock Country Club **492**
Rollins College **410**
Romney, Mitt **542**
Rooney, Art, Sr. **481, 520**
Roosevelt, Franklin D. **195, 203, 247, 266, 281-282, 292, 294, 296, 298, 303, 307, 312, 341-345, 360, 399**
    and "court packing" plan **304**
Roosevelt, Theodore **140, 195, 203, 220-221, 277, 339, 353-354, 358, 560, 562**
    and beginning of Progressive Era **193**
Root, Elihu **358**
Rose, Houston, Cooper & Schmidt (law firm) **379, 504, 543**
Roseman, Jack **532**
Rose Schmidt Hasley and DiSalle (law firm) **450**
Rose, Schmidt & Dixon (law firm) **474, 506**
Rosen, Charles **305**
Rosenbaum's (department store) **455**
Rosencrans, William, General **50**
Rosenzweig, Louis **117**
Ross Township, Pennsylvania **485**
Ross, Eunice **511**

Ross, George H. **380, 382**
Ross, Hugh **165**
Ross, James **9, 15, 28, 40**
Ross, James, Jr. **35**
Rossell, Robert T. **152, 359**
Rostow, Eugene **399**
Roth, Alice **420-421**
Roth, Benjamin **266**
Rowland, Harry H. **418**
Royall, Ann **34**
Rubber Anniversary (1972) **483**
Ruff, Benjamin F. **141**
Ruffner, Susan **510**
Rum Ring cases **197, 289**
Rumsfeld, Donald **531**
Rundle, Robert **434**
Rush, Benjamin, Dr. **410**
Ruslander, Leo **218, 234, 243, 450-451**
Ruslander, Ruslander and Lieber (law firm) **450**
Russ Massacre (1791) **6**
Rutgers University **523**
Rutledge, James **276**
Ryan Homes, Inc. **526-528**
Ryan, T.F. **238**
Rylands v. Fletcher (1868) **145-146**

S

Sable, Robert G. **270, 378, 450-451, 552**
Sacco, Nicola **269, 273-274**
Sachs & Caplan (law firm) **270**
Sadler, Sylvester **262**
Salk, Jonas **382**
Sams, Earl **343**
Sanborn, John B., Jr. **353**
Sanderson, John F. **68**
Sanes, Sidney **422**
Santorum, Rick **542-543**
Sapiro, Aaron **300**
Sarasota, Florida **389**
Sarni, Vincent **537**
Save Nabisco Action Coalition (SNAC) **523, 527**
Scaife, Cordelia **478, 492-494**
Scaife, Marvin **141**
Scaife, Richard Mellon **477-481, 489, 492-494**
Scaife, Sarah Mellon **478, 491**
Scandrett, Agnes Morrow **130**
Scandrett, Alfred K. "Al" **130**
Scandrett, Richard B., Jr. **130**
Scandrett, Richard Brown **130-132**
Scarborough, Joe **542**
Scarface (1932) **283**

Schechter Poultry Corp. v. U.S. (1935) **296, 302**
Scheinholtz, Leonard **385**
Schenck, Albert W. **405**
Schenectady, New York **98**
Schenley Park (Pittsburgh) **155, 156, 186, 193, 349, 397**
Schenley, Mary **397**
Schleifer, Mary Lemon and Elmer **334**
Schlesinger, Hymen **420, 422, 424-426, 432, 434-436, 468, 555**
Schlesinger, Sylvia **420**
Schmidt, Adolph **396, 400**
Schmitt, Joseph **439**
Schnader, Harrison, Segal & Lewis (law firm) **285**
Schnader, William A. **277, 285, 344**
Schneider, Frank J. **527**
Schoonmaker, Frederick P. **203**
Schorling, William **452**
Schoyer, Edward H. **51, 447, 448, 531, 549**
Schoyer, Samuel C. **51, 250**
Schoyer, Solomon, Jr. **85, 128, 130**
Schoyer, William E. **250**
Schriftgiesser, Karl **407**
Schullman, Alexander H. **300**
Schwab, Arthur J. **453**
Schwab, Charles **173-178, 183-188, 245, 303, 306**
Scorzo, John O. **343**
Scott, Anna King **231**
Scott, Hugh **477, 478, 484, 485**
Scott, John **91, 229**
Scott, L. Pearson **234**
Scottsboro Boys **308**
Scott, Thomas A. **90-91, 109**
Scott, William (father) **179, 181-182, 229, 231, 234**
Scott, William R. (son) **234-237, 242**
Scranton, Pennsylvania **198, 211, 219**
Scranton, William **477, 480**
Scully, Arthur M. **259, 262, 264**
Scully, Cornelius **332-333**
Seamans, Frank L. "Zeke" **367, 444-449**
Sears (department store) **412**
Sears, John **451**
Second National Bank of Allegheny **217**
Second National Bank of Pittsburg **217**
Second Presbyterian Church (Pittsburgh) **207**
Security Pacific Venture Capital **534**
Sedgwick, John, General **50**
Seifert, William A., Jr. **439**
Seifert, William A., Sr. **196, 232, 243, 440, 501**
Sell, Edward **63, 122, 382, 529**
Semple, Steele **24-25**

Semple, William 49
Sentencing Reform Act 547
Seven Springs Mountain Resort (Somerset County, Pennsylvania) 377
Severance, Cordenio A. 358-359
Seward, William H. 40, 44, 54
Sewickley, Pennsylvania 144
Seymour, Dan 420
Shadyside (Pittsburgh) 331, 400
Shadyside Presbyterian Church (Pittsburgh) 207
Shafer, John D. 122, 259
Shafer, Noah Webster 51, 124-125
Shafer, Raymond P. 465-466, 477
Shaffer, Theodore J. 246
Shaler, Charles 23, 38-41, 90
Shaler, Stanton and Umbstaetter (law firm) 39
Shallenberger, Oliver 101
Shannon, P.C. 118
Shapira, Meyer 270
Sharon Steel Company 518
Sharon, Joseph 39
Sharon, Len 468
Sharswood, George 390
Shaw, George E. 196, 231
Shepard, Donald 448
Sheppard, Marshall 345
Sheriff, John C. 236
Sherman Antitrust Act of 1890 203, 238, 249, 351-357
Sherman, Harry Alan 418-420, 426
Sherrard, German & Kelly (law firm) 504. see also Houston, Cooper, Speer & German (law firm)
Sherriff, Lindsay, Weis and McGinnis (law firm) 375
Shinn, Thornton 37
Shippen, Edward 21
Shiras, Clara Childs 85
Shiras, George, III 121
Shiras, George, Jr. 64, 70-77, 83, 85, 93, 95, 116, 121, 150, 194, 218, 221, 564
Shiras, Winfield 84-85, 121, 218, 220-224, 564
Shoburt, Fred C. 233, 234
Shoenberger Steel 84
Shouse, Jouett 287, 290, 294, 299
Shriver, R. Sargent 380
Sibray, William W. 247, 254
Sichelstiel, Bertram L. 236
Sickles, Daniel 44
Sign of General Butler (tavern) 24, 44
Sikov, Meyer 265
Sikov, Seymour 265, 375-377, 379

Silverman, Arnold 388
Simmons, Dick 517-520
Simmons, J. Edward 186
Simmons, Paul 474
Simpson, Edward 35
Simpson, Samson 115
Simpson, Stephen 74
Sinatra, Frank 481
Singer, Paul 388
Sister Sledge 520
Skybus 413-414
Slagle, Jacob F. 51, 65, 83, 136
Sloan, Alfred P., Jr. 287
Slone, Victor 253
Smalstig, Linda Shoop 267
Smith Act of 1940 431
Smith, Al (NY governor and presidential candidate) 281, 287
Smith, Albert Y. (Pittsburgh lawyer) 121
Smith, Buchanan & Ingersoll (law firm) 360, 361, 367, 405, 424, 437. see also Buchanan Ingersoll & Rooney (law firm)
Smith, Buchanan, Ingersoll, Rodewald & Eckert (law firm) 432, 437, 439, 448-449, 453. see also Buchanan Ingersoll & Rooney (law firm)
Smith, Buchanan, Scott & Gordon (law firm) 266, 270, 437. see also Buchanan Ingersoll & Rooney (law firm)
Smith, Buchanan, Scott & Ingersoll (law firm) 437. see also Buchanan Ingersoll & Rooney (law firm)
Smith, C.B.M. 121
Smith, Charles Stewart 186
Smith, Edward Grandison (NLRB examiner) 308-312
Smith, Edwin (NLRB board) 298
Smith, Edwin Whittier (Pittsburgh lawyer) 121, 196, 231, 438
Smith, Florence Aiken 232
Smith, George David 362, 366-367
Smith, Henry R., Jr. 457-459, 464, 474
Smith, Jack 501
Smith, James H. (Pittsburgh lawyer) 171-172, 189
Smith, James Ignatius, III "Jim" (ACBA director) 378-380, 382, 392, 432
Smith, Jim (United Steelworkers) 528
Smith, Nellie Fergus 501, 503, 506, 515, 616 n.623
Smith, Templeton "Temp" 499, 503
Smith, Templeton, Jr. "Temp" 503
Smith, Thomas 21
Smith, William L. (Allegheny H.S. principal) 288
Smith, William Watson (Pittsburgh lawyer) 230-235, 240, 266, 443-445, 448-450, 589 n.159

"George Washington's Last Pants" 230
Alcoa case 360-367
Smithfield Street (Pittsburgh) 34, 35, 42, 76, 205, 219, 255, 280, 374, 400, 406
Smith-Ribner, Doris 474, 511
Snee, John V. 479
Snee, Sylvester 329
Snodgrass, Robert 199
Snowden, Edmund 38
Snowden, Felix B. 237, 243
Snowden, George R., Major General 161, 163, 166
Snyder, Edgar 487-488
    and the development of law firm advertising in Pennsylvania 391-392
Snyder, Saundra Gerson 391
Snyder, Simon 24, 26
Soffel, Jacob (court crier) 328
Soffel, Jacob, Jr. (fraud convict) 222
Soffel, Kate Dietrich ("Mrs. Soffel") 328
Soffel, Peter K. 131, 328, 598-9 n.579
Soffel, Sara M. 328-330, 334, 338, 347, 448, 616 n.623
Somerset County, Pennsylvania 377
Sorg, Herbert P. 377
South Fork Fishing and Hunting Club 85, 141-145, 149
South Hills Village (Allegheny County, Pennsylvania) 413
South Park (Allegheny County, Pennsylvania) 413, 459
South Side (Pittsburgh) 35, 79, 130, 133, 134, 139, 151, 153, 154, 158, 165, 217, 412, 522
Southern Christian Leadership Conference 462
Soviet Union iii, 259, 333, 417, 418, 419, 427, 522
Spang, Charles 84
Spartansburg, Pennsylvania 287
Specter, Arlen 525
Speed, James 55, 57
Speer, Edgar (Bureau of Investigation) 259
Spelman College 522
Sprague, Bob 494
Spriggs and Witt (caterers) 336
Sprigle, Ray 346
Springer, Eric W. 382, 470
Sprint Corporation 532
Sproul, William 243, 254
Sprowls, Albert 163
Squirrel Hill (Pittsburgh) 247, 402, 459, 483
St. Andrews Golf Course (Westchester County, NY) 187
St. Clair, David 9
St. Clairsville, Ohio 39
St. John, Vincent 251, 255

St. Louis Browns (baseball) 127, 130-131
St. Louis, Missouri 107, 131, 134, 280, 353, 408
St. Louis Post-Dispatch 131
St. Marys, Pennsylvania 198
St. Nicholas Building 68, 82, 230, 231, 239
St. Patrick's Day Flood of 1936 (Pittsburgh) 396
St. Paul's Cathedral (Pittsburgh) 207, 423, 496
St. Paul's *Letter to the Galatians* 548
St. Vincent College 275, 533
Stack, John 495
Stadtfeld, Joseph 117, 269
Stahl, David W. 382
Staley, Austin 332
Stambaugh, Harry 235
Standard Oil Co. 83, 117, 354-356, 360-361, 440
    and antitrust case. see Standard Oil Co. of New Jersey v. United States (1911)
Standard Oil Co. of New Jersey v. United States (1911) 356, 359, 365, 367
Standard Steel Spring Company 441
Standard-Thomson Corp. 518
Stanford University 298
Stanley, William 100
Stanton Heights (Pittsburgh) 464
Stanton Land Company 464
Stanton, Edward 119, 231
Stanton, Edwin McMasters 35, 38-44, 50-58, 65, 69, 74, 90, 389, 561
    and "inverted pyramid" style 40
    appointed Secretary of War 44
    appointed to U.S. Supreme Court, death 57
    appointed U.S. Attorney General 44
    law partnerships in Ohio 39
Stanton, William Henry 120, 124, 336, 339, 346, 347
Stanton, William Wendell 347, 457
Stargell, Willie 460, 520
Starzl, Thomas 530
Steel Recognition Strike (1901) 245-246
Steel Seizure cases (1952) 384
Steel Strike of 1919 284, 555
Steel Valley Authority (SVA) 528, 539
Steel Workers Organizing Committee (SWOC) 311, 383
Steel, "Squire Thomas" 206
Steffens, Lincoln 107, 206, 209
    "Hell with the lid off" 107
Steingut, Stanley 451
Steps, the ("Amen Corner") 148
Sterling, Thomas 256
Stern, Horace 406, 426
Sterrett & Acheson (law firm) 234, 237, 243
Sterrett, James P. 233

Sterrett, Ross **233**
Stetson, Francis L. **187, 351, 358**
Stetson, Jennings & Russell (law firm) **187**
Stettinus, Edward **399**
Steubenville, Ohio **35, 38, 39, 291, 309, 310**
Stevens, Robert Sproule **399**
Stevenson, Adlai, II (governor of Illinois) **399**
Stevenson, Adlai, I (Vice President) **155**
Stevenson, Arthur D. **458**
Stevenson, William H. **224**
Stewart, Frank R., "Captain" **119, 120, 336**
Stewart, Henry S.A. **85**
Stewart, Thomas **25-27**
Stewart, W. Denning **243, 423, 598 n.546**
Stewart, William Alvah **404**
Stitt, Herbert Lee **120-124**
Stokes, William A. **80**
Stoll, Sheryl Clark **535**
Stone, Colonel William A. **150, 168, 212**
    first Pittsburgher elected governor **212**
    removes Adam Mercer Brown from recorder's office **212**
Stone, Harlan F. **304, 365**
Stone, Stephen **340**
Stoner, James M. **117**
Stonecipher & Cunningham (law firm) **438**
Stonecipher, Cunningham, Beard & Schmitt (law firm) **439**
Stonecipher, Frank W. **438**
Stonecipher & Ralston (law firm) **254, 267, 438**
Stoppel, Nicholas **94**
Story, Joseph **29, 46**
Stout, Mike **523**
Stowe Township, Pennsylvania **271, 273**
Stowe, Edwin H. **52, 118, 124, 182**
Strassburger & McKenna (law firm) **270, 500**
Strassburger, E.J. **500**
Strassburger, Eugene B., III "Gene" **500**
Strassburger, Eugene, Jr. **500**
Strassburger, Eugene, Sr. **270, 500**
Strassburger, Jane Schanfarber **500**
Strauss, Edward K. **452**
Strauss, Samuel **483, 487**
Strayhorn, Billy **337**
Streator, J.B. **163**
strict liability **145-146**
Strip District (Pittsburgh) **89, 133, 210, 217, 275, 279, 360, 478**
Sts. Peter and Paul Church (Duquesne, Pennsylvania) **528**
Student Nonviolent Coordinating Committee **468**

Students for a Democratic Society **468**
Succop, Colonel Bertram L. **289-290**
Sullivan & Cromwell (law firm) **123, 414, 472**
Sunbeam Corporation **519**
Supreme Court, United States **21, 31, 42-43, 69, 86, 194, 273, 293, 302, 312, 346, 352, 353, 384, 385, 391, 431, 444, 458, 470, 484**
Surratt, Mary **54-57**
Susquehanna County, Pennsylvania **118**
Sutherland, George **304, 346**
Sutton, Robert Woods **235**
Swaine, Robert **103, 105**
Swan, Thomas **365**
Swanger, Harry **468-469**
Swearingen, Joseph **259**
Sweeney, Clayton **367, 444, 446, 448-449, 518-519, 531**
Sweeney, Sally **444**
Sweitzer, J. Bowman **49, 51, 237**
Swiss, Irwin A. **333**
Swoope, Henry Bucher **140**
Syndicalist League of North America **251**
Syracuse, New York **118**

T

T. Mellon & Sons Bank **77, 141, 231, 414, 499**. *see also Mellon National Bank*
Tabor, John K. **413, 432, 435**
Taft, William Howard **140, 196, 236, 273, 339, 358**
Taft-Hartley Act **383-385**
Talenfeld, Rebecca Davis and Samuel **330**
Tallant, James C. **502-503**
Tallant, Lucille **502**
Tammany Hall (New York) **67, 206**
Tampa, Florida **389**
Tanner, Chuck **520**
Tanner, Harold B. **437, 610 n.338**
Tarbell, Ida **182, 186, 354**
Tarentum, Pennsylvania **113, 223, 486**
Taylor, Myron H. **383, 398-399**
Taylor, Zachary **27**
Teall, Maynard **243**
Teitelbaum, Hubert **376, 490, 509-510**
Tekulve, Kent **520**
Telford, Thomas **135**
Temple University **505**
Tener, John K. **128, 227, 340**
Tener, Van Kirk, Wolf & Moore (law firm) **387**
Tennessee Coal and Iron Company **357-358**
Tenure of Office Act **57**
Teplitz, Meyer **253**

Terry, Charles A. **100-106**
Tesla, Nikolai **101**
Texas & New Orleans Railroad (1930) **302**
Texas and Pacific Railway **90**
Texas "Black Codes" **52**
Thaw, Benjamin **141**
Thaw, Harry K. **141**
Thayer, Amos Madden **353**
Theophilus, Wayne **382**
Therese & Isabelle (1968) **483**
Thespian Society (Pittsburgh) **40**
Third National Bank **266**
Thomas, J. Parnell **417**
Thomas, Norman **216**
Thompson, A. Marshall **422**
Thompson, George **9**
Thompson, Joseph H. (Pa. lawyer and football coach) **239**
Thompson, Joseph W. (federal judge) **362**
Thompson, Thomas M. "Tom" **447**
Thompson, William G. **273**
Thomson & Bradshaw (law firm) **259**
Thomson, W.H. Seward **247-248, 254, 259**
Thornburgh, Ginny Judson **484**
Thornburgh, Richard L. **382, 466, 478, 484-497, 517, 533, 555**
Thornburgh, Virginia Hooten **484**
Thornton, Bonnie **350**
Thorp & Stewart (law firm) **243**. *see also Thorp, Reed & Armstrong (law firm)*
Thorp, Bostwick, Reed & Armstrong (law firm) **308, 309**. *see also Thorp, Reed & Armstrong (law firm)*
Thorp, Bostwick & Reed (law firm) **300**. *see also Thorp, Reed & Armstrong (law firm)*
Thorp, Bostwick & Stewart (law firm) **254, 288**. *see also Thorp, Reed & Armstrong (law firm)*
Thorp, Bostwick, Stewart & Reed (law firm) **290**. *see also Thorp, Reed & Armstrong (law firm)*
Thorp, Charles M., Jr. **243**
Thorp, Charles M., Sr. **224, 234, 243, 290, 438**
Thorp, Reed & Armstrong (law firm) **312, 367, 383, 384, 386, 389, 390, 438, 471, 472, 505, 506**. *see also Thorp & Stewart (law firm); Thorp, Bostwick & Stewart (law firm); Thorp, Bostwick, Stewart & Reed (law firm); Thorp, Bostwick & Reed (law firm); Thorp, Bostwick, Reed & Armstrong (law firm)*
Three Mile Run (Pittsburgh) **26**
Three Rivers Stadium (Pittsburgh) **412, 416, 520, 527, 537**
Thurman, Allen G. (father) **129**

Thurman, Allen W. (son) **129**
Tichborne Case of 1874 **364**
Tiger, Daniel S. (TV character) **410**
Tilden, Samuel J. **90, 134**
Tillinghast, Collins & Tanner (law firm) **437, 610 n.338**
Time Machine, The (novel by H.G. Wells) **552**
Tioga County, Pennsylvania **212**
Tippins, George **518-519**
Titus, Marcus & Shapira (law firm) **367, 506**
Titus, Paul **367**
Titusville, Pennsylvania **61, 82, 117**
Tocqueville, Alexis de **409, 554**
Tom and Jerry, or High Life in London (play by William Moncrieff) **40**
Torrance State Hospital for the Insane (Westmoreland County, PA) **293**
Trafford, Pennsylvania **383**
Transcontinental Oil **287**
Trans-World Airlines **376**
Transylvania University **33, 56**
Trautman, Leander **254**
Tree of Liberty (newspaper) **26**
Tresca, Carlo **247**
Triangle Shirtwaist Factory Fire (1911) **216**
Tri-State Conference on the Impact of Steel **525, 539**
　　"Save Dorothy" campaign **525, 528**
Trollope, Anthony **61**
True Magazine **428-431**
True Republicans (Friends of the People, Clodhoppers) **24, 26**
True Temper Co. **518**
Truman, Harry S **20, 383-384, 408, 457**
Tucker Arensberg (law firm) **506**. *see also Patterson, Crawford, Miller & Arensberg (law firm); Patterson, Crawford, Arensberg & Dunn (law firm); Tucker, Arensberg, Very & Ferguson (law firm)*
Tucker, Arensberg, Very & Ferguson (law firm) **471, 472, 506**. *see also Tucker Arensberg (law firm)*
Tucker, Richard B., Jr. **432, 434**
Tuesday Music Club (Pittsburgh) **207**
Tufts University **512**
Tugwell, Rexford **400**
Tulane University **468**
Turner, H. Woodruff **442**
Turner, Ralph **296**
Turtle Creek, Pennsylvania **489**
Tuskegee Army Air Field **456**
Tweed, William M. "Boss" **67**
Twitter **i, 24, 544**

Two Oliver Plaza (Pittsburgh) **519**
Tyler, John **27, 30**
Tyler, Mason W. **119**

U

U.S. Freedman's Bureau **52**
U.S. Military Academy, West Point **48, 52**
U.S. Post Office and Courthouse (Pittsburgh) **195, 490**
U.S. Resettlement Administration **400**
U.S. Securities and Exchange Commission **429, 444**
U.S. Steel Building (Pittsburgh) **544**
U.S. v. Booker (2005) **548**
U.S. v. E.C. Knight Co. (1895) **350**
Uber Technologies, Inc. **538**
Ueberroth, Peter **527**
Umbstaetter, Theobald **39**
Underground Railroad **46-47, 54, 117**
Unger, Colonel Elias **142**
Union Depot Hotel (Pittsburgh) **93**
Union National Bank **444**
Union National Bank Building (Pittsburgh) **442**
Union Pacific Railroad **350**
Union Switch & Signal Company **529**
Union Trust Building (Pittsburgh) **195, 243, 250, 251, 253, 258, 361, 437, 501**
Uniontown, Pennsylvania **23, 47, 198, 232, 545**
United Coal Miners' Union **136**
United Electrical, Radio and Machine Workers of America **383, 418**
United Farmworkers **469**
United Mine Workers of America **246, 274-276, 402-403**
United Nations Plaza (Pittsburgh) **411**
United Negro Protest Committee **462-463**
United States Circuit Court of Appeals for the Third Circuit
    designated as appellate court **203**
    established **69**
United States District Court, Western District of Pennsylvania
    and Lincoln assassination **53**
    established **18**
    expansion **203**
United States Law Review **299**
United States Lumber Company **219, 221**
United States Magazine **5, 44**
United States Steel Corporation **85, 189, 194, 238, 245, 252, 262, 350, 351, 360, 385, 396, 398, 399, 403, 406, 414, 415, 519, 525, 527, 528, 538**
    antitrust case. *see United States v. United States Steel Corp.* (1920)

United States v. Alcoa (1945) **360-367, 398, 444-445**
United States v. United States Steel Corp. (1920) **238, 243, 359, 367**
United Steelworkers **246, 385, 524, 528**
University Club (New York City) **186**
University Club (Pittsburgh) **375**
University of Alabama **461**
University of Chicago **231, 242, 522**
University of Iowa **504**
University of Maryland **457, 482**
University of Michigan **121, 123, 124, 140, 268, 531**
University of Missouri **395**
University of Oklahoma **297**
University of Pennsylvania **121, 199, 239, 333, 396, 422, 478, 505, 531, 564**
University of Pittsburgh **8, 27, 33, 123, 139, 198, 205, 230, 231, 232, 233, 236, 239, 240, 243, 249, 265, 272, 288, 295, 298, 308, 327, 329, 330, 332, 338, 340, 372, 373, 379, 382, 385, 398, 406, 408, 418, 428, 438, 440, 456, 465, 467, 468, 469, 470, 471, 481, 482, 484, 499, 500, 501, 503, 505, 506, 508, 509, 532, 536, 538, 543, 547, 551, 560, 561, 562, 563, 564**
    first attempts to establish a law school **33, 122**
    founding of **8**
    law school established **122**
University of Pittsburgh Cancer Institute **530**
University of Pittsburgh Medical Center (UPMC) **530, 546, 547**
University of Pittsburgh Panthers **520**
University of Rome **271**
University of Vienna **269**
University of Virginia **117**
University of Wisconsin **298**
Unkovic, Alexander **379, 382, 383**
Unkovic, Kosto "Constantine" **383**
Unkovic, Nicholas **383-388, 517, 543**
Unverzagt, William **367, 444-445**
Uptegraff, W.D. **106**
Urban Development Act (1945) **405**
Urban League of Pittsburgh **456, 458, 461, 465**
Urban Redevelopment Act (1945) **402, 403, 405**
Urban Redevelopment Authority of Pittsburgh (URA) **404-407, 412, 460, 521, 527, 528**
Utterback, Everett **457**

V

Van Buskirk, Arthur **266, 395-408, 410, 413, 414, 416, 539, 554**
Van der Voort, Robert **405, 425, 487**
Van Devanter, Willis **304, 345, 353**

Vance, Margaret **501**
Vanderbilt, William H. **82, 83, 140**
VanKirk, Thomas L. **367, 415**
Vann, Robert Lee **119, 335-347, 458**
Vanzetti, Bartolommeo **269, 274**
Vashon, George Boyer **117-118**
Vashon, John B. **45, 47, 117**
Veech, James **99**
Velde, Harold **434**
Venango County, Pennsylvania **54, 61**
Verona, Pennsylvania **486, 502**
Vilsack, August A. **222-223**
Vilsack, Stella Brennen **222**
Virginia Union University **338, 340**
Vista International Hotel (Pittsburgh) **521**
Voinchet, Robert G., Jr. **546**
Volk, Charles R. "Dick" **384-385**
Volk, Jane Lewis **506**
Volkanik, Jan (legendary coal miner) **283**
Volpe, Angelo **298**
Volstead Act **197**
Von der Ahe, Chris **128, 130-132**
Voters' Civic League (Pittsburgh) **212**
Voters' League of Pittsburgh **218, 222, 225**

W

Wabash Terminal Building (Pittsburgh) **195, 401**
Wabash Tunnel (Pittsburgh) **413**
Wachtell Lipton Rosen & Katz (law firm) **549**
Wade, Benjamin F. **199**
Wadsworth, James W., Jr. **287**
Wagner, Robert **283, 290, 292, 295-296**
Wagner-Steagall Act
    Ellenbogen as sponsor **283**
Waite, Morrison **122**
Walgren, John A. **272**
Walken, Harvey **527**
Walker, Duncan **40**
Walker, Jonathan Hoge **18**
Wallace, George (Pittsburgh judge) **9**
Wallace, George C. (Alabama governor) **461**
Wallace, George R. (Pittsburgh lawyer) **208, 218, 220, 225-226**
Wallace, Jonathan H. **39**
Wallerstedt, Alvar G. **196**
Walsh, Louis M. **248, 254, 262**
Walter, Charles P. **430, 431**
Walter, George L., Jr. **239, 243, 244**
Walter, Howard K. **243**
War of 1812 **27, 45**
Ward, John Montgomery **128**

Warn, George K. **234**
Warner Brothers **386, 420**
Warren Commission **496**
Wartime Prohibition Act **197**
Warwood, West Virginia **541**
Washington & Jefferson College **33, 249, 288**
Washington Arsenal **55**
Washington County, Pennsylvania **6, 9, 10, 11, 13, 15, 16, 69, 112, 119, 233, 257, 451, 491**
Washington Plaza (Pittsburgh) **411-412, 461**
Washington Redskins **433**
Washington, Bushrod **28**
Washington, D.C. **iv, 28, 44, 49, 50, 52, 53, 55, 56, 58, 102, 119, 140, 151, 172, 173, 205, 220, 240, 243, 247, 282, 285, 294, 301, 361, 389, 399, 420, 433, 440, 442, 448, 450, 451, 452, 464, 472, 475, 489, 490, 525**
Washington, George **3, 6, 7, 11, 14, 15, 16, 19, 21, 28, 205, 295**
Washington, Pennsylvania **163**
Wasson, Joseph C. **220, 222**
Watergate scandal **415, 490, 496**
Watkins, Chuck **492**
Watson & Freeman (law firm) **235, 237, 243**
    use of deceased partner's name on firm **234**
Watson, A.M. **75, 163**
Watson, Agnes Fraser **120-121, 124-125, 328**
    death **125**
Watson, D.T. **51, 64, 77, 81-87, 95, 107, 113, 121, 150, 173, 178-180, 183, 185, 203, 206, 213, 222, 234, 359, 361, 365, 562**
    and "rule of reason" in antitrust jurisprudence **356**
    draftsman of Carnegie's Iron Clad Agreement **173**
    Northern Securities case **351-353**
    Standard Oil antitrust case **354-356**
Watson, John D. **163**
Watt, David **90, 91**
Watts, Harold **274**
Watts, Robert Burnham **300**
Waverly Coal and Coke Company **135**
Waynesburg College **327**
We the People (television show) **420**
Weather Underground **468**
Webb Law Firm **389**
Weber, W.H., Dr. **223**
Webster, Daniel **44**
Wecht, Cyril **481-482, 487-488, 493-496, 496**
Weidlin, Edward **401**
Weihe, William A. **148, 153-159, 583 n.366**
Weil & Thorp (law firm) **181, 220, 234, 235, 236, 243, 248, 270, 450**

Weil Gotshal & Manges (law firm) 512
Weil, A. Leo 117, 181, 189, 218-228, 234, 236, 243, 269, 270, 290, 339, 450, 543, 554-555
   city bribery investigation and prosecutions 223-224
   lawyers as check on municipal correction 218
   reforming Pittsburgh's city charter 225-227
Weil, Andrew 189, 224
Weil, Christy & Weil (law firm) 243
Weil, Ferdinand T. 235, 236, 243
Weir, Ernest T. 287, 292, 294, 296, 299, 302, 308, 309
Weir, Frederick 464
Weirton Independent Union (WIU) 311
Weirton Steel Company 287, 295, 298-299, 301, 312, 385, 525, 528
Weirton, West Virginia 291
Weis, Joseph F., Jr. 377, 420, 432, 435, 469
Weiss, Samuel A. 423-427
Weitzel, Albert 234, 240, 242
Welch, Joseph Nye 431
Wellesley College 329
Wellsburg, West Virginia 551
Wendel, Robert F. 242
Wernecke, Chester 372
West Coast Hotel Co. v. Parrish (1937) 306
West Mifflin, Pennsylvania 486
West Palm Beach, Florida 389
West View High School 531
West View, Pennsylvania 501, 531
West Virginia University 140, 297, 308
Western League (baseball) 129
Western Penitentiary (Pittsburgh) 112, 249, 328, 487
Western Reserve University 99
Westinghouse Air Brake Company 100, 101, 397, 414, 529
Westinghouse Company 248, 367, 396, 398, 400, 404, 409, 471, 526, 527, 532, 538
   reorganization 106
Westinghouse Electric Company 101, 102, 106, 383
   and Skybus 413
Westinghouse, George 64, 85, 97-106, 181, 193, 396, 397, 562, 564
   and natural gas 101, 102
   development of modern corporate legal team 98, 103
   Panic of 1893 103, 105
   Panic of 1907 105
   reliance on counsel 98, 101, 104
Westinghouse, Henry Herman 106

Westlaw 544
Westminster College 308
Westmoreland Country Club 270
Westmoreland County, Pennsylvania 5, 6, 16, 112, 181, 246, 247, 293, 493, 495, 502, 511
Wettick, R. Stanton "Tony" 382, 460, 465-468, 470, 472, 476
Wheeling & Belmont Bridge Company 41-43
Wheeling-Pittsburgh Steel Corporation 84, 388, 522
Wheeling, West Virginia 41, 420, 486, 551
Whiskey excise tax, federal (1791)
   burden on Western Pennsylvanians 11
   enacted 11
   repealed 18
Whiskey Rebellion (1794) 3, 17, 18, 22, 58, 92, 197
   at Braddock's Field 14
   battle at Bower Hill 13
   march on Pittsburgh 14
   Mingo Creek gathering 13, 16
   tarring and feathering 3, 11
White, Edward 359, 365
White, John William Fletcher "J.W.F." 69, 128
White, Tom 466
White, Walter 344
Whitehead, Cortland, Bishop 226
Whitlock & Tait (law firm) 389
Whitman, Walt 52
Wickersham, George 299, 357, 359
Wilkins, Roy 341
Wilkins, William 28, 40, 48
Wilkinsburg, Pennsylvania 248
Wilkinson Sword Company 519
Willard Hotel (Washington, DC) 299
William C. Moreland (steamship) 113
William Jewell College 395
William Penn Hotel (Pittsburgh) 195, 344, 374, 385, 420, 559
Williams & Connolly (law firm) 433
Williams, Edward Bennett 433-434
Williams, Henry Warren 72, 74-75, 121
Williams, Lynn 528
Williams, Mary Lou 337
Williams, Thomas 22-23, 54
Willkie Farr & Gallagher (law firm) 299
Wilmerding, Pennsylvania 397, 425
Wilner, Wilner & Kuhn (law firm) 432
Wilson & Evans (law firm) 300, 305
Wilson, Emily 424, 427
Wilson, I.W. "Chief" 361, 445
Wilson, James 5
Wilson, Robert 220-222

Wilson, Thomas B. **277**
Wilson, Woodrow **203, 227, 237, 247, 295, 333, 357, 358-359, 362, 384**
    and the "Princeton effect" on enlistment for World War I duty **235**
Winchester, Virginia **46**
Winschel, Paul **367**
Winter, Emil **223**
Winternitz, Benjamin **117**
WJAS-AM (Pittsburgh) **275, 283**
Wolf, Robert B. **387**
Wolfe, Jacob **10**
Wolk, A.L. **332**
Wolk, Janice Bowers **505**
Wolvovitz, Barbara
    "maiden name" controversy **508-509**
Women in Pittsburgh legal profession
    and pantsuits **507**
    assumption of leadership roles in the bar **510**
    equal pay among partners **514**
    first woman lawyer admitted to bar **124**
    office workers, wage disparity **124**
    stenographers, change to female workforce **123**
    typewriters as catalyst for women entering legal careers **123**
    women entering downtown firms in 1970s **506**
    women lawyers having no natural base of clients **125**
Women Matter 2: Female Leadership, A Competitive Edge for the Future (study by McKinsey & Co.) **515**
Women's Bar Association of Western Pennsylvania **510**
Women's International League for Peace and Freedom **216**
Wood, Jacques **524**
Woods, George **122**
Woods, John **9**
Woodruff, Clinton R. **217, 227**
Woodside, Robert E. (Dauphin Co. judge) **427**
Woodside, Robert G. (Pittsburgh lawyer) **239**
Woolworth's (department store) **412**
Worker Adjustment and Retraining Notification (WARN) Act (1988) **524**
Workingmen's National Bank of Allegheny **217**
Workingmen's Savings & Trust **223**
Worms, Pamela Lee **56**
Worthington Industries, Inc. **527**
Worthington, Leslie **524**
WQED-TV **409-410**

Wright, Frank Lloyd **396**
Wright, Jonathan Jasper **118**
WTAE-TV **312, 494**
Wycoff, William **367**
Wylie, Andrew **33, 56-58**
Wylie Avenue (Pittsburgh) **71, 335-338, 465**
Wylie, Caroline Bryan **56**
Wynstra, Nancy **511**
Wyzanski, Charles **305**

Y

Yale University **22, 81, 84, 85, 101, 103, 121, 200, 218, 229, 230, 295, 298, 308, 380, 396, 399, 458, 465, 470, 473, 475, 484, 505, 522**
Yard, Molly **464**
Yeates, Jasper **15, 21**
Yoder, Louise **506**
Yost, Gene **534**
Yost, William **111**
Young Progressives of America **458**
Young Republicans **268, 419**
Young, Charles D. **405**
Young, Edwin P. **230**
Young, James S. **203**
Youngstown Sheet and Tube Co. **385, 523**
Youngstown, Ohio **266, 434, 522, 523**
Your Marriage (television show) **410**

Z

Zanella, Joseph P. **486-487**
Zatezalo, Martha **505, 507**
Zatkovich, Gregory **332**
    as governor of Carpathian Ruthenia **333**
Zola, Emile **225**

Made in the USA
Monee, IL
19 September 2019